The Dynamics of Change

Cambridge Studies in the History and Theory of Politics

EDITORS

MAURICE COWLING, G. R. ELTON, E. KEDOURIE,
J. R. POLE, WALTER ULLMANN

THE DYNAMICS OF CHANGE

The crisis of the 1750s and
English party systems

J. C. D. CLARK

CAMBRIDGE UNIVERSITY PRESS

Cambridge
London   New York   New Rochelle
Melbourne   Sydney

Published by the Press Syndicate of the University of Cambridge
The Pitt Building, Trumpington Street, Cambridge CB2 1RP
32 East 57th Street, New York, NY 10022, USA
296 Beaconsfield Parade, Middle Park, Melbourne 3206, Australia

First published 1982

Printed in Great Britain by
Western Printing Services Ltd, Bristol

Library of Congress catalogue card number 81–9999

British Library Cataloguing in Publication Data
Clark, J. C. D.
The dynamics of change. – (Cambridge
studies in the history and theory of
politics)
1. Political parties – Great Britain – History
I. Title
324.24102   JN1118
ISBN 0 521 23830 7

Contents

Preface

I beg to acknowledge the gracious permission of Her Majesty the Queen to make use of papers in the Royal Archives at Windsor.

This book involves an attempt to break through the level of explanatory generalisation about politics established by a number of Edwardian writers and subsequently too often accepted as an undemanding norm. As such, it is based overwhelmingly and in unrepentant detail on the private papers of the individuals involved. For permission to consult, and quote from, their collections of manuscripts I have therefore particularly to thank the Duke of Beaufort; the Duke of Bedford; the Duke of Buccleuch; the Duke of Devonshire and the Trustees of the Chatsworth Settlement; the Duke of Newcastle; the Marquess of Bute; Earl Fitzwilliam and the Wentworth Woodhouse Trustees; the Earl of Harrowby and the Trustees of the Harrowby MSS Trust; the Earl of Lonsdale; the Earl of Mansfield; Earl and Countess Waldegrave; Col Sir John Carew-Pole, Bt; Mr Michael Bond; Mrs D. C. Bruton; Captain J. D. G. Fortescue; Mr R. Money-Kyrle; Mr Victor Montagu; Mr Jasper More; Mr D. W. H. Neilson; Mr F. H. M. FitzRoy Newdegate; Mr D. C. D. Ryder; Mr A. B. Starky; Mr L. G. Stopford-Sackville; and Mr Simon Wingfield-Digby.

For help, advice or criticism of various sorts I am further indebted to Professor Derek Beales; Mr John Brooke; Prof John Cannon; Mr T. R. Clayton; Mr Maurice Cowling; Dr Eveline Cruickshanks; Prof H. T. Dickinson; Dr Declan O'Donovan; Prof G. R. Elton; Dr E. J. S. Fraser; Dr Frank O'Gorman; Dr David Hayton; Mr R. C. Latham; Dr A. P. W. Malcomson; Mr E. L. C. Mullins; Dr A. N. Newman; Dr J. B. Owen; Mr R. D. Ryder; Dr Eric Sams; Prof W. A. Speck; to the staffs of the various libraries and record offices where I worked, especially those of the National Register of Archives; to Miss Catherine Armet at Mount Stuart, the late Mr T. S. Wragg at Chatsworth, Miss Jane Langton at Windsor and Mr S. Bywater at Badminton. Financial support was provided by Corpus Christi College, the British Academy and the Faculty of History. The text was typed, with equal efficiency and patience, by Mrs Hazel Dunn.

Mr W. Rainforth and Dr J. W. Derry provided encouragement at an early stage, and the late Dame Lucy Sutherland at a later stage. Professor Ian R. Christie followed the book with unremitting attention during its writing; to his exemplary care, and to the example of his precise scholarship, much is due. To the late Sir Herbert Butterfield I am indebted for conversations over many years on the nature of politics and the writing of history; in other respects I owe him still more.

Acknowledgement is also due to Corpus Christi College, where I began

PREFACE

my research, and to the Master and Fellows of Peterhouse, who, by electing me into a Fellowship, allowed me to complete it in its present form. But without the support and encouragement of my parents, this project would never have been begun.

June 1980

Note on references

Numerical references in the notes are to the Additional Manuscripts of the British Library (lately the British Museum) unless otherwise specified.

Spelling has been modernised and abbreviations silently expanded in quotations from the original, except where this would interfere with the sense or might be open to dispute.

Folio numbers given are those of the first pages of the documents cited, and not necessarily of the pages on which the quotations occur.

References to documents in published versions are not given unless the original has not been consulted or unless the printed text contains serious errors of omission or commission.

'Walpole' in the notes refers to Horace Walpole (1717–97); the name of Horatio Walpole (1678–1757) is always given in full.

It has not been thought necessary to provide biographical sketches of the individuals mentioned where these are available in the usual works of reference.

Abbreviations

Bedford Corr	Lord John Russell (ed.), *Correspondence of John, Fourth Duke of Bedford* (London, 1842–6)
BIHR	*Bulletin of the Institute of Historical Research*
BL	British Library
Bod	Bodleian Library, Oxford
Chatham Corr	W. S. Taylor and J. H. Pringle (eds.), *The Correspondence of William Pitt, Earl of Chatham* (London, 1838–40)
CJ	*Journals of the House of Commons*
Coxe, *Pelham*	W. Coxe, *Memoirs of the Administration of the Right Honourable Henry Pelham* (London, 1829)
Coxe, *Walpole*	W. Coxe, *Memoirs of the Life and Administration of Sir Robert Walpole* (London, 1798)
CUL	Cambridge University Library
Cust Records	Lionel Cust, *Records of the Cust Family. Series III* (London, 1927)
Dev	Devonshire MSS, Chatsworth
Dickins and Stanton	L. Dickins and M. Stanton (eds.), *An Eighteenth Century Correspondence* (London, 1910)
DNB	*Dictionary of National Biography*
Dobrée	B. Dobrée (ed.), *The Letters of Philip Dormer Stanhope, 4th Earl of Chesterfield* (London, 1932)
Dodington, *Diary*	J. Carswell and L. A. Dralle (eds.), *The Political Journal of George Bubb Dodington* (Oxford, 1965)
Eg	Egerton MSS, British Library
EHR	*The English Historical Review*
Fitzmaurice, *Shelburne*	Lord Fitzmaurice, *Life of William, Earl of Shelburne* (2nd edn London, 1912)
Glover, *Memoirs*	[R. Glover], *Memoirs of a Celebrated Literary and Political Character* (London, 1813)
Grenville Papers	W. J. Smith (ed.), *The Grenville Papers: being the correspondence of R. Grenville, Earl Temple, and the Rt Hon. G. Grenville, their friends and contemporaries* (London, 1852–3)
H	Hardwicke
HJ	*The Historical Journal*
HMC	Historical Manuscripts Commission
HPT	History of Parliament Trust
HW	W. S. Lewis (ed.), *The Yale Edition of Horace Walpole's Correspondence* (New Haven, 1937–)
Ilchester, *Fox*	Lord Ilchester, *Henry Fox, First Lord Holland* (London, 1920)
JBS	*Journal of British Studies*

ABBREVIATIONS

Leinster Corr	B. Fitzgerald (ed.), *Correspondence of Emily, Duchess of Leinster* (Dublin, 1949–57)
LJ	*Journals of the House of Lords*
LWL	Lewis Walpole Library, Farmington, Connecticut
N	Newcastle
Namier, *Crossroads*	Sir Lewis Namier, *Crossroads of Power* (London, 1962)
Namier, *England*	Sir Lewis Namier, *England in the Age of the American Revolution* (2nd edn, London, 1961)
Namier, *Structure*	Sir Lewis Namier, *The Structure of Politics at the Accession of George III* (2nd edn, London, 1957)
Namier and Brooke	Sir Lewis Namier and John Brooke (eds.), *The History of Parliament. The House of Commons, 1754–1790* (London, 1964)
Ne(C)	Newcastle (Clumber) MSS, Nottingham
NLS	National Library of Scotland
NLW	National Library of Wales
Parl Hist	W. Cobbett (ed.), *The Parliamentary History of England, from the earliest period to the Year 1803* (London, 1806–20)
Phillimore, *Lyttelton*	R. J. Phillimore, *Memoirs and Correspondence of George, Lord Lyttelton from 1734 to 1773* (London, 1845)
PRO	Public Record Office
Riker, *Fox*	T. W. Riker, *Henry Fox, First Lord Holland* (Oxford, 1911)
SRO	Scottish Record Office
Sedgwick	R. R. Sedgwick (ed.), *The History of Parliament. The House of Commons, 1715–1754* (London, 1970)
Sedgwick, *Bute*	R. R. Sedgwick (ed.), *Letters from George III to Lord Bute, 1756–1766* (London, 1939)
Sedgwick, 'Pitt'	R. R. Sedgwick (ed.), 'Letters from William Pitt to Lord Bute, 1755–1758', in R. Pares and A. J. P. Taylor (eds.), *Essays Presented to Sir Lewis Namier* (London, 1956)
Toynbee	P. Toynbee (ed.), *The Letters of Horace Walpole* (Oxford, 1903–25)
TRHS	*Transactions of the Royal Historical Society*
Waldegrave, *Memoirs*	James, Earl Waldegrave, *Memoirs from 1754 to 1758* (London, 1821)
Walpole, *George II*	Horace Walpole, *Memoirs of the Reign of King George the Second* (London, 1846)
Walpole, *George III*	Horace Walpole, *Memoirs of the Reign of King George the Third* (London, 1894)
Williams, *Pitt*	B. Williams, *The Life of William Pitt, Earl of Chatham* (London, 1913)
WLC	William L. Clements Library
WWM	Wentworth Woodhouse Muniments, Sheffield
Yorke, *Hardwicke*	P. C. Yorke, *The Life and Correspondence of Philip Yorke, Earl of Hardwicke* (Cambridge, 1913)

I shall endeavour in the first place to establish a truth, of which, you seem, together with a great part of mankind, to have been very little sensible, viz. that his G[race] of N[ewcastle] is (notwithstanding that mark of folly which he wears: Notwithstanding that affected appearance of hurry and confusion, which he assumes, perhaps, as the most easy way of avoiding too pressing solicitations or other private views); is, I say, more deep in device and machination, more versed in ministerial expedients, and more abundant in political resources than any man of this, or perhaps, any other age. You sneer at the proposition, – you have sneered at but it too long (sic). – But if he is that weak man, for whom you take him, let these few questions be answered; How has he foiled the ablest men of this country, undermined S[ir] R[obert] W[alpole]. How defeated those powerful antagonists the Chesterfields and Granvilles, O shame to this country!...How supported himself, according to your mode of thinking, against your own great favourite Minister [Pitt]?...to say nothing of the R[oyal] F[amily] itself, which has been supposed by some in the late reign, to have been subdued and made submissive to his will and pleasure...Has power been acquired, and what is no less difficult, preserved by folly and a dissipation of thought? Or has that appearance of distraction and emptiness been a veil to well digested councils, and schemes properly calculated for the purposes of ambition?...This minister has been the object of both your hatred and contempt; I am afraid he will have his revenge, and set you in a contemptible light to the latest posterity.

An Address to the City of London
(London, 1762) pp. 7–8

Introduction

The true springs and motives of political measures are confined within a very narrow circle, and known to very few; the good reasons alleged are seldom the true ones. The public commonly judges, or rather guesses, wrong...I therefore recommend to you a prudent pyrrhonism in all matters of State, until you become one of the wheels of them yourself, and consequently acquainted with the general motion, at least, of the others; for as to all the minute and secret springs, that contribute more or less to the whole machine, no man living ever knows them all, not even he who has the principal direction of it.

Chesterfield to Stanhope, 15 March 1754:
Dobrée, v, 2098

For my part, I could never perceive such a mighty mystery in politics, as some pretend. I do not know anything else it consists in, but consulting the good of the community, and pursuing short, easy and lawful means, which are always the safest and best, to obtain the end.

The Monitor, 22 January 1757

POLITICAL ACTION AND ITS HISTORICAL EXPLANATION

Eighteenth-century politics have been more often disparaged than understood. Modern writers sketching their general characteristics have held them up for condemnation as shallow, corrupt, incompetently conducted, lacking in principled commitment. Political tactics have been scaled down to cynical manoeuvres in which the issues at stake are presented as seldom more exalted than the distribution of place or pension, peerages or bishoprics, boroughs or military promotion. In reality, similar minutiae bulk large in politicians' business in any age. But for this period especially, political manoeuvre has been used by historians as an index of politicians' moral shortcomings – dismissed as the means of corruption rather than understood in its own right and on its own terms.

Newcastle in particular is supposed to have 'symbolised' such methods, thoroughly and systematically exploiting them. Early-eighteenth-century England has thus been depicted as a 'Venetian oligarchy', its members manning 'the pumps and sluices of the parliamentary system' and enjoying their 'aristocratic perquisites' on a 'spoils system'. Even the Whig–Tory clash at its fiercest, it has been claimed, 'represented not so much a conflict of ideology in a national sense, although that had importance, but personal and factional vendettas at the local level'. In spite of them, there grew up a 'system of government and patronage...developed by

Walpole' into 'the adamantine stability of eighteenth-century oligarchy', 'a self-gratifying oligarchy that held power for its own profit'.

> It was patronage that cemented the political system, held it together, and made it an almost impregnable citadel, impervious to defeat, indifferent to social change ... After 1715, power could not be achieved through party and so the rage of party gave way to the pursuit of place.

Such shallow parodies must rank as historiographical myth, not disinterested analysis. Moreover, they have inhibited analysis, for, in the light of such judgements, political manoeuvres have been held to 'clutter the history of the eighteenth century with trivial detail and obscure the deeper issues which were involved'.

Moralising of this kind about the means of corruption and the rewards of power has almost always absolved historians, in their own minds, from the need to understand what politics in those years was ultimately about and how it worked. The specific consequences have been many. Preoccupations with patronage have given rise to a major misunderstanding about the nature of 'single party government' in early eighteenth-century England: that it was the form of dominance which followed 'the total defeat of the Tory party in 1715 and its obliteration from the serious world of politics'.[1] That misconception has been challenged elsewhere.[2] The ability and industry of statesmen and administrators, too, has been grossly understated. Yet if, at times, historians have tried to redress the balance, to lighten their black picture of the establishment, they have often done so by emphasising and endorsing the propaganda of Whig–Patriot or of Tory oppositions as justified critiques of a corrupt regime. In the process, eighteenth-century rhetoric about corruption in high places has been taken literally instead of being interpreted as part of a political strategy. So too has the eighteenth-century claim that politics itself was a simple pursuit of obvious national interests, unless distorted for reprehensible ends. Here again, moralising has taken the place of explanation; and through a subtle and unnoticed shift of priorities, historians have adopted an anachronistic perspective, properly appropriate only to the early nineteenth century.

More serious still, though less obviously distorting, academic moralising has made eighteenth-century politics seem comfortably familiar: readily accessible to, and easily comprehensible by, the modern observer. The strangeness, the continually developing yet still almost wholly different mental world, of those years has been missed; and the intractability of the problems which arise from the attempt to explain such an alien culture has passed largely unremarked. This book is an attempt to reconstruct the rules of a far distant political game, to trace their development at a period of profound change, and to recapture the particular notion of political action itself as it was then understood. Its object is not to belittle the force of ideas. It is, rather, an example of the ways in which both ideas and tactical manoeuvre mattered, and of the relative weight which ought typically to be attached to either.

Its theme is politics – the political dimension of government's activity. Yet 'politics' was only a minor part of statesmanship as it was then understood. The small numbers and elementary development of the civil service (to borrow a later phrase) meant that by far the larger part of the time of the men who figure here was taken up with the routine business of their offices, whether diplomatic, military, naval, financial, judicial, or that of the Royal Household. These men were often politicians as it were in their spare time. Nevertheless, politics was understood as something different from administration, law, financial policy or war strategy, and is not confused with them in this book. Politics was already both professional and ontological: for these men, politics was an extrapolation of their inner lives.

Despite a modern proliferation of biographies as well as studies of individual ministries, it is still scarcely possible to form from them an authentic idea of what eighteenth-century politics was like to experience or to participate in. Biographies in particular have usually been written on a chronological scale so large as to leave their subjects vulnerable to generalised accounts of individual motive and of the bearing of constitutional conventions on political change. The narrative offered here is consequently highly detailed. It could not have been otherwise. The scale has been deliberately chosen in order that the explanations employed could be fully specific: that is, not of equal standing with any case purportedly established by the presentation of an alternative set of detail.

More sorts of action than high political manoeuvre alone were, in different degrees, talked about by contemporaries in political terms. Yet argument in the press and the activities of the mob are here given little place, not because there was not a great deal of both but because both are shown to be of slight importance by a fully specific account of the ways in which power was actually held and redistributed among the small group of men at St James's and Westminster who really mattered. Through a correct conception of political action, and attention to the appropriate arena, the fight to win and retain power emerges as far more complex, and far less recognisably modern, a process than has been commonly supposed. It is those tactical complexities which are the subject of this study and which reveal other spheres of political action as subordinate. Popular political agitation is demonstrated to be just such a subordinate sphere, even at the moment in 1756 when Newcastle resigned in the midst of the outcry which followed the loss of Minorca. It is remarkable, nevertheless, that politics outside the inner élite was permeated with tactical conceptions derived from its conduct, which, though not accurately understood at large, was seen in terms appropriate to the way it was actually fought out. Public awareness of political issues, too, was widespread. 'We are all politicians in England, from the nature of

3

our constitution', wrote one commentator, announcing his self-evident premise; 'every man thinks he has a right to reason upon all occurrences where the public are concerned'.[3]

There was nothing unusual, in that respect, about the 1760s. Society was equally politicised by the activities of the élite. That process is not the theme of this book, though in order to understand it, it is necessary to relate it to the detailed conduct of affairs at the centre. Attention to the political gestures of mobs, riots, broadsheets and ballads is no short cut; the political situation within which these things were important (when, and in so far as, they were important) was created by the politicians. It was created 'constitutionally'. Eighteenth-century England was not an oriental despotism: the public, its interest, its judgements and its aspirations, mattered intensely. But they mattered practically in so far as, and in the ways in which, they were brought into the political arena by politicians. They had no independent existence there. As de Lolme later described the popular role,

Like those mechanical powers, the greatest efficiency of which exists at the instant which precedes their entering into action, it has an immense force, just because it does not yet exert any; and in this state of stillness, but of attention, consists its true *momentum*.[4]

As such, 'popular opinion' was open to all the vicissitudes which commonly attended political phenomena of that sort. It was open to use, for example, as an excuse and a justification for action the real causes of which were internally-governed high political manoeuvres. Consequently, perspectives on popular politics (as on other sorts) have been manufactured by politicians and historians as part of the same process of interpretation. Often, they have been manufactured falsely; one of the tasks of scholarship is to correct the misconceptions involved in such manufacture, redressing the perspective in which the general features of an age are to be viewed.

Until the Seven Years' War, Hanoverian England lived under the threat (at times immediate, at times distant) of invasion and revolution. The basis of political loyalties was a dynastic commitment. Apart from this, what contemporaries were engaged in was not, chiefly, a 'struggle to defend, amend or radically alter the political and social order'.[5] The minds of leading Whigs, whether in government or opposition, were dominated not by a canon of Whig doctrine drawn from the great seventeenth-century tradition – Harrington, Tyrrell, Moyle, Trenchard, Toland, Sydney and the rest – but by the practical details and daily techniques of their trades as politicians, diplomats, lawyers, financiers or courtiers. So far as is known, the Tories were even less given to political theorising. What mattered to them all was not some clash of radical and conservative ideologies, but (in the absence of revolution) the practice of politics – a practice expressed within and governed by its own terms, evolving its own precedents along its own lines.

The attempt to relate 'what men wrote and said' to 'what they actually did'[6] in politics has been hindered by fundamentally mistaken assumptions about the political realities of Hanoverian England. So, too, historians anxious to establish the existence of an 'alternative structure of politics' from the middle decades of the century in the form of popular political consciousness would have done better first to have discovered what the 'structure' actually was to which the pronouncements of the press and the activities of the mob were allegedly alternative. A new and synoptic view of that basic element in parliamentary politics, the party system, is one outcome of the detailed narrative which follows. But it was not only party structures which diverged widely from modern accounts of them. Eighteenth-century politics cannot be understood on the assumption that it differed from its modern equivalent only in its actors and issues. 'Political action' was itself different; the boundaries of the idea changed through time, just as the reality it described was expanded by the rise of a cadre of professional politicians and propagated by the politicisation of English society. The concept of 'politics' employed by eighteenth-century Englishmen is misconceived, too, if it is treated as no more than an aspect of the changing role of politicians *qua* administrators. The State then undertook few of its modern functions; but where it did, those functions were seldom made political issues. The point is rather that politicians behaved differently *qua* politicians, in attending to any substantive issues, by conceiving differently of political action itself. Any act is incomprehensible without a prior appreciation of the *genre* to which it addresses itself, just as one cannot understand 'Hamlet' without recognising it to have been written as a tragedy. Philosophers are familiar with the need to 'enter into the rationality' of an act in order to explain it. For the historian, this process is partly one of identifying the *genre* of political action, partly of re-thinking conduct in *that* mental language; and it is not here supposed that 'explanation' in this sense depends on establishing a tight chain of causality.

Mid-eighteenth-century assumptions about the sphere of the political, however, were in flux in a way closely linked to the destruction of the Whig–Tory Jacobite polarity. The crucial aspect of political action was thus gradually being transformed from an external assent to principles of party doctrine to an internal search for principles of 'honest', moral, personal action. If contemporaries were confused as to the basis of party-political loyalty, through being seldom called on accurately to discriminate between interested personal attachment, dutiful service to the King, and assent to the tenets of the Whig state, still more have modern observers been unable to conceive of a 'grammar of assent' sufficiently unified to replace the Namierite and anti-Namierite theories of the role of 'corruption'. A greatly exaggerated and *a priori* attention has been paid to both patronage on the one hand and ideology on the other as a result of ignorance about, and misunderstanding of, politics itself.

What was evident in the 1750s was not an articulated clash of clearly held systems of ideas but the misunderstandings, deceits, confusions of mind and cross purposes appropriate to real politicians acting tentatively in a world not yet falsely rationalised by the forward-looking radical perspectives of nineteenth-century Whig historians. Furthermore, political and constitutional conflict is misconceived if seen as a debate between theories of what the constitution *was*. The general outlines of the constitution as then conceived were at once too basic to be open to legitimate challenge by a loyal subject, and too general to incur it. What was at issue was its implementation. The object of contention was thus a disparate collection of precedents existing, not on a high level of generality, but on a middle level as a series of tactical lessons about, for example, how an opposition was to be conducted, how the role of the King could be dealt with, and how a ministry could be made to cohere.

Twentieth-century conceptions of political action differ fundamentally from those current in the eighteenth. They may usefully be contrasted. A modern political scientist has declared that 'The essence of a political situation, as opposed to one of agreement and routine, is that someone is trying to do something about which there is not agreement; and is trying to use some form of government as a means and as protection.'[7] In the 1750s, politics was neither the equivalent nor the inevitable expression of such disagreement; nor did politics come into existence in such situations as the means of solving it. 'Politics' created disagreements in order that they might be resolved by political rules. This semi-autonomous character of political conflict, one essential feature of British politics since 1688 if not earlier, meant that political situations were the expression of men acting politically, not the disease for which political action was the cure. As Dodington argued: 'to people, who by their situation, are thrown into politics, action, in that case, is what life is to the body. We cannot cease to live for a time, and then, take up life again: so in politics we must act, in some way, or another, and we can't cease action, for a time, and then take it up again.'[8]

An uninterrupted current of political activity and consciousness ran on even when there *was* agreement on substantive issues, acting to unsettle the situation and to give occasion for 'political' responses. Similarly, tragedies are not written because of a desire on the part of the public to express pity and terror; those emotions are evoked in audiences which seek to be shown their participation in a wider, a fully generalised human predicament and to have their belief in their participation heightened, not because they are impelled by an overwhelming sense of that participation which demands catharsis. Naturally, this metaphor presupposes the receptivity of men to certain themes; in the same way, political action at any time presupposes conventional motives for conflict, among which is a perpetual process of 'social reconciliation and agreement': 'perpetual disagreements which arise from fundamental differences of condition, status, power, opinion and aim'.[9]

INTRODUCTION

Two false conclusions might be inferred from this general view. The first is that 'Government is routine up to the point where someone questions it and tries to change it; then it ceases to be routine and becomes a political situation.'[10] The reality of mid-eighteenth-century practice was more complicated, for two discontinuous paraphrases of this view then co-existed. According to one of these, 'government' and 'politics' were not discrete in this sense; stable government was merely a political situation with one party securely in control. Yet, further, there existed a notion of political stability unfamiliar to us. Drawn from a view of politics as an art to contain society's tensions by a series of checks and balances, the alignment of their political and institutional expression, the ideal state of public affairs was thought of as tranquil, uncontentious, silent, and static. All disturbances of a system thus defined became, *ipso facto*, illegitimate attempts to engross power. The two views were reconciled, though pessimistically, by the implication of the second: politics in the 1750s was dangerously liable to strike contemporaries as futile, repetitive, and sterile. Even when Pitt and Fox clashed in the Commons on 16 April 1751 over the 'General Naturalisation Bill' (a precursor of the 'Jew Bill' of 1753, a measure much attended to by historians anxious to argue the substantive importance of 'issues'), Walpole recorded that 'people could not help smiling to see Caesar and Pompey squabbling, when they had nothing to say'.[11] Or, as it was expressed elsewhere, a party man

may repeat the same observations and the same wit over and over again at every club; for a party jest is never worn thread-bare, and a party argument never answered, even when it is confuted.[12]

For such reasons, it is wrong to condemn the 1750s by crediting radical activity in that decade with being socially purposive by contrast to 'official' politics: in so far as they were political, they both partook of a common autonomy.

The second false inference which has been drawn is that 'Politics is about policy, first and foremost; and policy is a matter of either the desire for change or the desire to protect something against change.'[13] Politics in the 1750s is not to be condemned as merely factional because it fails to fit some such model. Rather, the decade reveals the validity of an alternative model that registers the concern of politics with the pursuit of power; politics was 'about' policy only in the sense that 'Hamlet' was 'about' a court intrigue in Denmark. Policies were partly contingent upon political action; partly the counters in terms of which political action took place and was registered. But it happened in other terms as well, apart from policy: the arrangement of offices, and personal ambitions for them; votes in elections and in parliamentary divisions; a propaganda war.

If 'policy' is an adequate synonym for 'issues', more may be said on the second point. Ministerial politics have seldom been written about in a way which takes account of Horace Walpole's warning: 'I do not pretend...to assert, that parliamentary determinations are taken in consequence of any arguments the Parliament hears; I only pretend to deliver the arguments that were thought proper to be given, and thought proper to be taken.'[14] Similarly even Bolingbroke, who was atypical in his willingness to express his political stance in general terms, wrote: 'A man who has not seen the inside of parties, nor had the opportunities to examine nearly their secret motives, can hardly conceive how little a share principle of any sort, though principle of some sort or other be always pretended, has in the determination of their conduct.'[15] Nevertheless, his most recent biographer condemns him for not planning a forward strategy and for lacking 'real conviction' in his 'declarations of principle'.[16]

What to modern observers seem failings are in fact among the defining characteristics of a quite different notion of political action prevalent in the eighteenth century. In respect of the content of policies, it has not escaped notice that the 1750s contain no more than premonitions of the great conflicts of succeeding decades: 'The issues of the fifties were... highly personalised as questions of succession to the crown and to high office.'[17] Appropriately, therefore, this is a study of what Horace Walpole called 'the manoeuvre of business';[18] the 'game', as an able Under-Secretary put it, of 'Jeu de Cabinet'.[19] Such a study is not here revealed as an aspect of the history of public administration. Historians still sometimes feel obliged to apologise for presenting the driving force of politics as something other than the rational, disinterested advocacy of policies on their substantive merits.[20] But it is clear from this account that the Whig party in the 1750s was tolerably unanimous in matters of policy until divided by the factious activity of its *frondeurs*; that Newcastle contended less for a set of policies than for the freedom to determine policy consequent on a dominant position in the ministry; that the oppositions of 1754–5 and 1755–6 were launched first and equipped with policies only later; and that the dominant theme in the political activity of the leaders was not an incipient world war but the relations of Court, Ministry and Commons, and the contest for the leadership of the Whig party.

Mid-eighteenth-century politics is not to be dismissed as unprincipled if it fails to seem purposive (in respect of imperial vision or domestic radical zeal) when such an expectation would be premature. It does not follow that politics was not a genuinely national concern; but it does follow that the sort of generalisations about motivation too often employed are discredited by a fully specific account of ministerial and party-political activity *per se*. No individual's career has been more distorted by such misunderstandings than Pitt's. Too often his rise to power in the 1750s has been presented as the apotheosis of a righteous Patriot, winning the confidence of a House of Commons alienated by Newcastle's violation

8

of the constitutional convention that the First Minister must sit in the lower House. But, as is made clear, no such convention is illustrated in the politics of that decade; nor did Pitt's rhetoric win the votes of more than a handful of MPs. Pitt won power – a limited share of power in July 1757 whatever was to happen later within the wartime coalition – through a long succession of behind-the-scenes intrigues in which the traditional arts of manoeuvre counted for almost everything. Exalted expectations of political purity were certainly entertained about Pitt and his allies, and the disillusion of those hopes accounts for the sharp reaction against him after the summer of 1757.[21] But it was not equally true that he owed office to 'overwhelming backing out of doors'.[22] Whether that existed or not, it played a negligible part in the calculations of those with whom Pitt had to deal. Even the Tories, it is now clear, swung round to support him in 1756 after his attacks on them in and before 1754–5 for tactical reasons, in their last manoeuvres as a party: alienated by Newcastle's betrayal of them after the Mitchell affair, they seized the chance of removing an Old Corps ministry and were compelled to support the Pitt–Devonshire administration by their prior commitment against a Fox–Cumberland one. It was undoubtedly necessary to whitewash Pitt's political persona in order to pave the way for tactical co-operation with the Tory party in parliament. But that co-operation was not compelled by Pitt's mass support out-of-doors, nor did any such support carry him to office or sustain him there. It is a detailed narrative of political action alone, like that which follows, which reveals the links between the élite and the populace; it discloses also the content of politics, drawn from the practice of its participants rather than from a view of the ends of their action inferred from a false perspective on its purposiveness. These chapters offer the first narrative of these years able, by adequately explaining one sphere of action, to show how others are subordinate to it.

The language in which 'the constitution' was attended to is a clue to eighteenth-century notions of politics itself. The point, for example, about the vigilance to be exercised over the balance of the constitution is that it prefigured or re-expressed the attention to a national political arena which is necessary if politics in recent centuries was to function as a national drama, the focus of attention, the stage on which issues could be played out in a way which *restricted* the need for involvement rather than *provided* that involvement.[23] Although the claim was often enough made in the 1750s that 'the legislative power is the people's right', it was always vulnerable to the reply that the legislature was the combination of King, Lords and Commons.[24] The theory that English liberties depended on a balance between these three elements was commonly accepted. But, in the light of it, any attempt at democratic or popular action as such could easily appear, or be made to appear, wholly illegitimate. At the same time, the continued vigilance of the people was held to be essential, as a check against the abuse of the other powers. The way in which talk about the constitution was used is a guide to the official view not only of legitimation abstractly considered but also of the proper extent of popular political involvement. In one eighteenth-century view, a popular contract once made surrendered power, which became a trust,[25] just as it surrendered involvement, which was exercised vicariously. Thus the Old Corps found a place for popular opinion as a prop for the Hanoverian succession; and it may be that after the failure of the '45, and reassuring results in the general elections of 1747 and 1754, they came to rely more and more for tactical moral support (as well as for abstract legitimation) on the coincident fact – now becoming apparent – of substantial support at large for the Whig state.[26] 'Whiggism , it was objected against Bute in 1762, 'is a popular principle'.[27]

Nevertheless, eighteenth-century politics was suffused with an aristocratic ethic to an extent which modern academics have usually found difficult either to grasp or to admit. Bagehot correctly wrote:

The London of the eighteenth century was an aristocratic world, which lived to itself, which displayed the virtues and developed the vices of an aristocracy which was under little fear of external control or check; which had emancipated itself from the control of the Crown; which had not fallen under the control of the bourgeoisie; which saw its own life, and saw that, according to its own maxims, it was good...The aristocracy came to town from their remote estates – where they were uncontrolled by any opinion or by any equal society, and where the eccentricities and personalities of each character were fostered and exaggerated – to a London which was like a large county town, in which everybody of rank knew everybody of rank, where the eccentricities of each local potentate came into picturesque collision with the eccentricities of other local potentates, where the most minute allusions to the peculiarities and careers of the principal persons were instantly understood, where squibs were on every table, and where satire was in the air.[28]

Prominent among the political values of such a society were ambition, pride, honour, loyalty, and integrity. It was a society in which it was possible to say, uncontentiously, that man and beast differed not so much as man and man. Neither the public nor the press was admitted by the professional politicans, whether commoners or peers, to be arbiters of what was honourable in their betters' conduct. The newspaper and pamphlet press was not attended to in that way, not because it did not give expression to the 'public mind' (though it did not) but because no such phenomenon had yet been created by professional politicians' appeals to a wider audience. Rather, those men sought for a principle of honourable conduct, in situations where later they were to seek instead for a programme, as a publicly demonstrable guide to action.

If Westminster was as much an hermetic community as in the nineteenth century, the way in which it thought its image was projected differed markedly. The statesmen of the 1750s did not suppose that 'politics was ultimately about the organisation and presentation of the parliamentary community in such a way that the working class could be contained';[29] control of government, rather, was the prize for which they contended in Court, Ministry and Commons. It was the ultimate and most general prize; it was not the means to some other end, least of all to a plan of social manipulation. Hence it was even more the case in the 1750s than in the 1880s that the preoccupations of politicians 'could best be sorted out, not by talking directly to electors, but through the medium of clubs, the lobby, the dinner table, the race meeting, the visit to dine and sleep, the morning call, and the stroll in the park. This was where political work was really done.'[30] For the 1750s, one must add the King's Closet and his mistress', the 'drawing rooms' and levées at Court and Leicester House, and the gatherings at Newcastle's town house which went under the same names. Here power was won and exercised; here was the scene of almost all significant conduct.

This was the most important of the defining characteristics of mid-eighteenth-century politics. Others may be briefly listed. Westminster and St James's was, firstly, a single hermetic world. Beyond it, events at Court were scarcely known. Little more was known outside that world of Parliament's workings; and even within doors, few were aware of the secret history of the ministry. Newcastle himself, when out of office in the 1760s, shared this 'sheer ignorance of fact'.[31] Dodington identified the problem in writing to Fox of

a conversation I assisted at...between a gentleman of much more consequence and understanding than myself, and the late Lord Townshend. The gentleman, with as little reserve as I treat you, entered into a discussion, with his lordship, of public affairs, then a little perplexed. When he was gone, my lord expressed his surprise, as they had differed a little in some points, that a man of his rank and reputation should hold such absurd opinions, which he showed the weakness of, from some facts which the gentleman, probably, could not be apprised of. To which I...replied: 'Really my lord I see no weakness in the gentleman's conversation, but in giving your lordship his opinion how to play a hand of cards, of which he could only see the backs, and your lordship saw the pips.'[32]

If 'Society' was ill informed, the amount of information available to a wider public was still smaller. Political reporting in the newspapers was as yet confined to a bare record of changes of office; occasionally, a curt prediction that such a change was imminent; hardly ever an inquiry into motive, a link drawn between ambition and policy, or a speculation on the reason for ministerial realignments. The 1760s in Ireland were similarly described:

The liberty of the press was, at this period, shackled and restrained with many impediments. The debates in parliament were unreported, and even notes were forbidden, as against the rules of the House; all besides the ministers and members were, not only totally uninformed on the progressive subjects of legislation during the session, but commentaries, indirectly made on the capacity of members, or public functionaries, were punished by arraignment at the bar of the Commons.[33]

The pamphlet press was hardly less ignorant of political tactics. Consequently, the chief obstacle to articulate opposition was a shortage of information with which to attack a ministry's conduct of public affairs. As a result, issues on which an opposition could be successfully launched and sustained day by day were not easy to find. The occasions of opposition were therefore either highly generalised, familiar topics such as militias or the liberties of the subject in relation to measures like the Sheriff Depute Bill of 1755, or topics whose nature was public and, though specific, easily accessible: the Marriage Bill; the Excise; the Jew Bill; Byng; Wilkes. But, for the most part, the process of politics was too private and too complex in the 1750s to admit of accurate popular scrutiny. Political advantage could therefore be drawn from claiming, as was perfectly credible, that

The mechanism of government is too intricate and subtle, in all its various motions, for a common eye to perceive the nice dependencies and the secret springs, that give play to the complex machinery; and, in consequence, the generality of people, while the great political movements are passing before them, are full of undiscerning astonishment, and only gaze on in expectation of the event. Afterward indeed when the historian gives his narrative of facts, when he rejudges the actions of the great, and, from the ends which they had in view, and the means by which they pursued those ends, ascertains the colour of their characters, then the minds of men are opened, and they perceive honour and conquest, or disappointment and disgrace naturally following one another, like necessary effects from their apparent respective causes.[34]

In such a mental world, the very role of the press in promoting public discussion of politics was open to condemnation in virulent terms:

Consider the tendency of these infinite swarms of little books, (which in the view of insinuating and scattering their poison with certainty and celerity, have been rendered both so portable and cheap) under the titles of *Craftsmen*, *Common Sense*, *Cato's Letters*, or, to come lower down, *Tests*, *Contests*, etc. etc. and you will not be surprised at the effect. In their several compositions, the quantity of poison wrought up, is such as no people upon earth ever had constitutions to bear; it catches every sense, insinuates at every pore, and running through the habit, is carried forward by so quick and imperceptible a circulation, that now, at last, the whole mass is so vitiated and spoiled, that it may well be doubted, whether by any political art it may ever be defaecated and wrought off.

In respect of what I am upon, there is no occasion to inquire, in any political controversy, who is right, or who is wrong; it is not the thing in my thoughts, it is not my business; it is the controversy itself that is the SIN.[35]

'Why then', reasoned another pamphleteer, 'should we have recourse to the unnatural unconstitutional method of canvassing parliamentary concerns in newspapers and pamphlets?'[36] Contrary arguments were frequently put and trenchantly argued. But they were neither obviously true, nor the only acceptable attitudes to the role of the people in affairs of state.

Secondly, political leadership issued from a small inner circle, whether of ministry or opposition; mass movements not only had little influence on the self-appointed leaders themselves, but failed to carry independent weight precisely because they were often assumed to be instigated *by* the leaders. They frequently were. Thus in late 1753 Newcastle bought off James Ralph, the able publicist of an incipient Bedford opposition; thus was the 'rain of gold boxes' which followed Pitt's dismissal in April 1757 largely engineered by his supporters;[37] thus did Sackville view the Dublin mob during the Irish unrest of the early 1750s. As it was argued in that capital,

a few men of genius taking hold of lucky occasions may embarrass a government, and by concurrence of circumstances, a multitude may be inflamed... opposition to government is seldom unpleasing to those who are governed; and if appearances be plausible, the arts of fomenting are not difficult, for they have been often practiced... every argument which exalts [the governed] to the level of those whom fortune or dignity intended to place above them, is such incense to vanity as cannot be rejected... [38]

A continuing strand of argument can be found, representing

that the root of popular dissension is to be found in their [i.e. MPs'] own body. Contention within, creates commotion without doors. The disconcerted themselves, or their ready agents, sow the factious seeds of sedition among the people, who are made the blind instruments of vile ambition.[39]

One pamphleteer quoted Dryden to the same effect:

> Observe the mountain billows of the main,
> Blown by the winds into a raging storm:
> Brush off those winds, and the high waves return
> Into their quiet first created calm:
> Such is the rage of busy blustring crowds,
> Tormented by the ambition of the great;
> Cut off the causes, and th' effects will cease
> And all the moving madness fall in peace.[40]

Even Charles Townshend regarded the press as creating 'public opinion' as much as recording it: in the provinces, he wrote in 1763,

if I can trust my judgment, the apprehensions of London are created by the ingenuity of London, and all noise will soon subside in the counties if the daily writers in the prints [i.e. newspapers] could be prevailed upon to withdraw themselves. These gentlemen suppose discontent, to have a pretence for writing; they then exaggerate the consequences, to encrease their own significance, and at last they may realise their own fears, and raise what they pretend to combat. The reader of the news in the country concludes you are upon the eve of a civil war in London; the reader of the news in London is told you are in danger of insurrections in the counties; a furious attack is made, upon this alarm, both by the Court and opposition writers; the whole is a mistake; London mistakes the temper of the country; the counties lay too much stress upon the language and misrepresentations of the prints, and, if you will have a little patience, the stream of government will run as smooth and quiet as ever it did.[41]

These arguments do not, of course, provide a complete account of the generation of popular unrest; but they reveal far more about the assumptions on which politics was conducted at Westminster and St James's. Popular outcries in themselves were not obviously explicable things in the eighteenth century; but their impact on events at the centre can only be traced through a close study of how they were used at the centre.

At a time of instability like that of 1754–7, the character of leadership and the relatively small numbers of the led gave many political phenomena a quixotic air. Ministries, oppositions, parties, seemed to lack momentum or solidity. Newcastle worried continually about sustaining a ministerial 'system' as if its disintegration was always an imminent possibility; he had good grounds for doing so. Group alliances seemed alarmingly unpredictable: Newcastle, Pitt and Fox might all, at different moments, have captured Tory support, and there was a continuing possibility that an opposition might be launched, based on Leicester House. And, in the absence of any other check in the Commons (opposition numbers being so low) the ministry saw its conduct of affairs as subject to an abstract check. The notion of *responsible* administration was of particular importance in the absence of the reality of *accountable* administration. This went some way, Whigs supposed, to justify electoral improprieties in the name of the Whig supremacy and, as their opponents supposed, to give occasion for accusations of arbitrary government.

Furthermore, the existence of an active monarchy gave a substantial parity to the three central institutions of Court, Ministry, and Commons. The greater part of the political activity described in this work concerns the relations not between parties in Parliament or between Parliament and the public but between the three elements in this triad. Yet the scene of important action changed in the middle decades of the century. In c.1742–6 it was undoubtedly the Commons; division lists were compiled, and survive, because the fluctuating balance of groups on the floor of the House was of the first importance. From the establishment of the Pelham regime, the Commons came to matter less. Few division lists survive, because few were drawn up. Politics throve with equal vigour, but in other fields. The struggle for power *between* parties, which was a feature of the 1740s, was largely replaced in the 1750s by a contest for the leadership *of* a party.

What is offered here is an internal view of the evolution of those political events. In its concentration on the leaders, it may seem a traditional exercise. Yet this would be a false impression, for the enterprise entails the disillusion of a number of currently fashionable outlooks and relies upon a new emphasis on the potentialities of narrative technique. It relates also to two trends in scholarship. First, political scientists have cast doubt on whether patron–client relationships can provide a link between accounts of political power on micro and macro levels: that is, in the localities and at the centre. Among them, no consensus has emerged on the problems: 'How does one make the conceptual transition from micro to macro analysis?' and 'At what macro levels is clientism useful as a central, organising concept, and at what stage does the attempt to view society "from the bottom up" lead us into the pitfalls of reductionism?'[42] Among historians, however, there has arisen a greater willingness to treat the (micro) mechanisms of 'patronage' or 'corruption' in any age as part of 'a prudent, necessary and corporate venality'[43] rather than as the central link between two levels of group conduct. Or, as a pamphleteer put it,

The great patronise because they are great, not because they regard the object or need the assistance: and the vulgar cavil at their actions, not because those actions are bad, but because themselves are the vulgar: this is the liberty of English subjects...[44]

At the same time, secondly, historians of eighteenth-century politics at a constituency level have not found in local studies the fresh clues to national politics which some at least of those historians expected them to offer.[45] The conclusions, if drawn at all, have been negative ones. Dr Newman's study of Kent is revealing in this respect. Stressing the importance of local rivalries, he found that although Whig and Tory parties and partisanship existed in the county, 'their differences did not coincide with any in national politics';[46]

It is clear that politics in Kent had little or no connection with national politics, and that elections were largely the result of purely local factors. Despite the intensity of local party politics, they bore little or no relation to what happened elsewhere, and it is in consequence difficult to describe even General Elections in national terms. It was only when national issues penetrated local consciousness that national politics could play much part in the politics of the constituencies.[47]

Dr Newman wished still to argue that the maintenance of a Commons majority could only be explained through a study of the management of the constituencies, that 'the shape of national politics is often dictated by the politics of the constituencies';[48] but his work in fact reveals the absence of a single, national political arena; suggests the importance of Westminster as, rather, the focus of national attention, not the highest tier of a national 'structure of politics'; and implicitly accords both independence and importance to the manoeuvres at the centre, which might otherwise be dismissed as 'merely factional'.

Eighteenth-century politics, then, cannot be explained to sound like politics in the two succeeding centuries not for reasons of style and manner alone but because 'political action' was a different concept; because the exercise of such political action was confined within a far narrower circle (for 'the public', the eighteenth-century historian must usually substitute 'Parliament and Court'); because the politicians of the 1750s only partly anticipated what 'politics' would become (hence the opacity in their correspondence as to motive and intention, though the concept of political action to which they were answerable removed the obligation to be less opaque); and because, as a result of these three considerations, the sorts of evidence which a later age would consider most valuable were often not set down.

The politics of the 1750s, especially, is not to be explained in terms of a series of static states or structures, however conceived. As Richard Pares realised,[49] the period is one in which the familiar guidelines of politics disintegrated. Yet its instability has never been interpreted within a wider pattern or in a longer perspective. Correctly explained, the mid eighteenth century can be seen to be a period of transition in many respects. First, in the transition between party distinctions relying on a Whig–Tory categorisation and the factional groupings which prevailed in the 60s and 70s; between an old and a new generation of politicians; between an age whose central political fact was the Jacobite threat and one in which Jacobitism was a harmless Oxford mannerism; between oppositions purportedly 'Patriot' and oppositions bound by new notions of party cohesion and to issues raised by an incipient radicalism; between an age still debating politics in terms of the language of 1688 and 1714, though an exhausted language, and new preoccupations in the 1760s; and from a world in which politics was conducted behind closed doors to one in which, though the 'manoeuvre of business' was no less of a private and arcane art in reality, the rise of parliamentary reporting brought with it a far greater verbal – if not yet an institutional – accessibility to a wider public.

Such assertions as these depend on the possibility of their demonstration against a precise chronological framework. Yet many eighteenth-century historians have recently turned away from political narrative as traditionally understood, declaring it unprofitable or constricting. The contention here, on the contrary, is that far from having been practised and found unprofitable, it has been found forbiddingly difficult and seldom properly tried. Furthermore, the other things to which political historians have been attracted themselves depend on a version, usually implicit, of the narrative. The history of political argument, for example, can only be reconstituted after taking a view – the correct view – as to the truth of the arguments dealt with, a truth established by reference to a course of events discovered by a narrative.

Political argument must be seen not just as argument *about politics* but as *political* in the sense of being rooted in, and intelligible only in close relation to, the tactical situation which occasioned it. It is as impossible to write the history of attitudes, policies and arguments in isolation from (or with a false understanding of) politics narrowly conceived as is the reverse. Historians of political thought have sufficiently demonstrated the absurdity of setting political philosophers together as if they were attempting answers to the same (ahistorical) questions. Some political historians have failed to draw the lesson, and continue to treat politicians' actions as answers to, or refusals to answer, questions quite inappropriate to their specific location.

It may be supposed that the method advocated in this book is the equivalent of the 'contextual' approach to the history of political thought. This is not so. On the contrary, a correct understanding of political action reveals that the distinction between 'text' and 'context' in the history of either politics or political thought is an arbitrary one, determined by the fiat of modern scholars. Properly, therefore, contextual criticism may equally involve taking the whole of politics as one's text; textual criticism may equally entail treating a text as a context in explaining, for example, the generation of constitutional precedent or the priority of circumstantial evidence in explanations which purport to be motive explanations. In this study, the whole of English politics in the years 1754–7 is legitimately treated as a 'text'. Neither is such an approach to be confused with 'inter-disciplinary' history. Its partisans are usually social historians, unskilled in economics, who seek to annex instead the province of politics. History is not, of course, to be sorted into 'boxes' labelled social, political, economic or religious; but that categorisation is to be transcended (partly, here, by the insight into political dynamics provided by narrative history), not the contents of those boxes merely redistributed between them.

The greatest advances in the understanding of eighteenth-century politics are still to be drawn from pressing further the evolution of narrative technique. Its use in this book involves a claim that men did not perceive political situations in general, but in particular, and in detail on a short time scale. Narrative is the mental language of political action appropriate to men who, in real situations, refrain from basing their actions on a generalised view of their predicament. The historian who supplies a 'general historical situation' where he finds it lacking not only risks mistaking its generality and its features; he is committed to introducing an anachronism. Narrative, by contrast, involves a submission to the partial blindness dictated by events' evolving successively in an order which, if a sequence, is not necessarily a pattern, and to which 'pattern' is ascribed in retrospect in a great variety of ways – the majority of which will enjoy no permanence. Narrative alone attends to this logic of succession, and alone reveals events in the context made appropriate to them by the ways in which men used circumstantial evidence as motive explanations, at the same time as it displays those events in their significant sequence.

Yet narrative does not display (except in the most obvious sense) an order inherent in events themselves. 'Events' are, from the outside, discrete, inexplicable, and arbitrarily defined. Narrative reflects an order given to events by an actor in them in order to take the next step: it displays the coherence, the sequence, the significant selection which the actor adopts as the substitute explanation (no full, ideal explanation being attainable) of his own next action. Ideally, therefore, one historical work ought to combine many narratives – as many as the actors to be traced. Narrative is the only technique which allows actions to be displayed in their significant succession and in the context appropriate to them: that is, in relation to other attendant acts. It is those involved in the action who implicitly designate the significance of the succession and the appropriateness of the context. They have to do so in some way or other to act at all; though in what way is largely at their discretion. And it is only attention to the principles of change in social action – to its dynamics – which makes it intelligible, which allows the historian to reconstruct the conventions. Actions are intelligible only if they can be narrated; for analysis is only an abridgment of narrative.

This is not to say that narrative can make history intelligible as an account of motive. 'Motive' is a term which does no more than identify, with a generalisation, the boundary of what is irreducibly inexplicable in human conduct. Action may nevertheless be made intelligible in some lesser but familiar and useful sense. Narrative substitutes for an explicit (and, therefore, by abstracting, a falsifying) statement of motive an implicit suggestion of motive. That suggestion is drawn from an appreciation of politicians' acts of choice arrived at by close attention to those choices at the same level of generalisation on which politicians moved in order themselves to recognise them as alternatives. It is not by the act of generalising alone that the historian is open to error, but by choosing an inappropriate level of generality; inappropriate because unintelligible as a level of explanation to those whose action it would purport to describe. An adequate narrative thus faces the problem that an 'understanding' of human conduct involves entering into its 'rationality'; but it cannot fully answer that problem, for it is an insoluble one. It provides a satisfactory substitute for an answer in presenting the 'rationality' into which the reader is invited to enter as a reconstruction of political conventions: by displaying events and alleging them to have been the landmarks by which a politician governed his course, that course itself may be tentatively inferred. Such an argument is, of course, a circular one; but since the individual has no less 'circular' an understanding of the priority of motivation and intentionality in his own case,[50] the historian can do no more.

It has not been found useful to use 'character' to explain an action 'irrational' in this sense unless (as is the case occasionally) a display of the choices open to an actor as he saw them still leaves his act 'unintelligible'. That, indeed, is what we mean by 'character' – e.g. impulsiveness, arrogance, timidity – generalisations about the pattern of action to be observed when actors fall short of *their own* standards of rationality. But historians should beware of using (as they have too often done in Newcastle's case) personal characteristics as a blanket cover for political events whose aim and close texture they have failed to comprehend.

There is, therefore, no clear, mutually exclusive difference between the sincere and the insincere assertion of principles. Either may motivate political conduct, and conduct's consistency or lack of it is no sure guide, even to the politician himself, of the purity of his motivation. 'What is human life but a masquerade', quoted *The Test*, approvingly, on 2 April 1757, 'and what is civil society, but a mock alliance between hypocrisy and credulity?' Rather than debate the question of sincerity, which (even if known) does not reveal how political action progresses, the moving force of events in the 1750s has here been explained, procedurally rather than substantively, as the contest for power: the stresses induced in a political system by a number of able and ambitious men competing, often ruthlessly, for primacy. Assertions of policy and principle have their place in a theory of the explanation of conduct only in the more general sincerity of a common ambition.

It seems likely, moreover, not only that this view is a necessary one for the historian to adopt, but also that it is authentic; that it was the theory on which public conduct was dealt with in the eighteenth century. Judges sometimes made this explicit when dealing with the problem of how far the law need take an inner view of motivation, and they answered the question in a different way from their twentieth-century successors. Thus Lord Kenyon declared: 'We must judge of a man's motives from his overt acts.'[51] Mr Justice Willes was even more explicit: 'What passes in the mind of man is not scrutable by any human tribunal; it is only to be collected from his acts.'[52] The comparability of the two spheres of public conduct was noticed by Sir Lewis Namier: 'in the eighteenth century parliamentary politics were transacted, to a disastrous extent, in terms of jurisprudence';[53] but he did not go on to draw a link between such an observation and the opacity of motive, the reticence about intention which is so marked a feature of mid-eighteenth-century politicians' relations with each other, and of their correspondence.

This view of historical *explanation* justifies an assertion of the 'primacy of politics'. The individual's conduct is intelligible only in the sense in which, and in so far as, he invites intelligibility. Social action, similarly, is not immediately comprehensible. It is comprehensible in so far as it is recognised to address itself to a known *genre* of conduct: drama, sport, economic activity, politics. Such *genres* exist not in isolation but in a hierarchy: the sorts of intelligibility of conduct reconstituted in the history of politics are of use in writing the history of cricket, but cricket history sheds little light on the history of politics. Societies may have different arrangements of *genres* of intelligibility – different orders in the hierarchy. Politics is not obviously at its apex: for much of English history, religion occupied that position. But the eighteenth century is recognisably modern in the priority accorded to politics: the cult of the House of Commons, the reverence for the constitution, the sense of party lineage, all the things which are held to have created a self-preoccupied political world in the nineteenth century are to be found prefigured in the eighteenth; less organised, but in many ways more formalised and more hermetic.

Since politics is a *genre* of activity, it has both a methodology and an ontology; the relationship between these two is the central component of 'constitutional history'. It is argued here that that component rests on an implied narrative, and that that implied narrative is false. The eighteenth century is usually seen as 'the classical age of the constitution.'[54] This view is the result of substantial ignorance of the detailed workings of politics, an ignorance dispelled, as here, by a demonstration of how constitutional precedents are generated and used in the business of political manoeuvre. It is not the generalised assertions of political moralising but detailed appreciations of political tactics which show the links between methodology and ontology. Partly for that reason, the historian must not suppose that there was such a thing as 'the constitution' in eighteenth-century England *in an objective sense*. What he observes is a host of assertions about what the constitution was. The aim of his enquiry is to recover the precise tactical context in which these assertions were advanced, and the rules of a complex game, observable only from the outside, which these assertions constituted. It is in these aims that the injunction to attend to the past 'in its own terms' is particularly telling.

Political history, then, involves the reconstruction of the conventions which 'governed' (i.e. made intelligible) certain sorts of action to do with winning and keeping power. It therefore involves the re-thinking of actions within a certain mental world. Yet political action is not to be understood as if it were, in Collingwood's words, a 'logic of propositions': that is, as if politicians assaulted their contemporaries with one political 'act' after another in an attempt to make headway. This is the notion of the function of parliamentary oratory and of political action in general entertained by Basil Williams; many historians have shared his outlook. Yet he gained his experience of the political life of his own day as a Clerk of the Commons. So to see oratory as (a major) part of a 'logic of propositions' betrays an outsider's view of events. Rather, political statements are to be treated as a 'logic of question and answer';[55] each political act then becomes a different form of the question 'will this do, politically?' Or, as Collingwood put it, the historical problem is: what question, what problem, did this person mean this statement or act to be an answer to? Political motivation is therefore to be understood as a series of questions or hypotheses rather than of basic units called motives which, when assembled in a structure, comprise 'character'. Collingwood treated political actions as various forms of answer; it is here argued that they can equally be seen as various sorts of question, posed by politicians when addressing the rest of the political nation. What the political questions of an age *were* is not obvious; but it is the professional politicians who always and inevitably draw up the syllabus of 'issues', and it is to those men that we should look if we would discover the logic which underlay their political conduct.

Political narrative, correctly pursued, involves the recovery of the rules of a political game and the supersession of 'constitutional history'. It does not involve the assertion that politics is itself about ends alone or means alone; a correct view of individual motivation reveals that the relationship is unknown, not just infinitely various. Politics nevertheless has a ritualistic and a purpose aspect. It takes place on a level of generalisation at which each seems describable as the other. Politics entails, therefore, a collective self-deception. It is one to which the historian should permit the reader clear-sightedly to assent, in a common agreement to treat action as rationally comprehensible (based on a use of 'rational' in a special and limited sense) instead of a naive assumption that it is.

History therefore deals properly only with specific, not with general, questions; 'the particular is the only true general'.[56] It is only specific questions of which historical technique can demonstrate the extent to which answers to those questions are inescapably limited and partial. Precise history can therefore be no more than a precise demonstration of its own shortcomings. General questions are properly the province, not of historical explanation, but of religious enquiry. The mode and manner of eighteenth-century political action, too, was ultimately derived from the mode and manner of eighteenth-century religiosity. The next major task is to reconstruct the theological dimension of the public mind in that century.

POLITICAL HISTORY AS PARTY HISTORY

The intellectual history of English public life could largely be written in terms of Englishmen's conceptions of party politics. But it must be written on two levels simultaneously: on the level of historical reality, and on the level of the explanatory devices employed by scholars. This has almost never been done. As a result, the chief influence acting to distort eighteenth-century history in recent years has been the unconscious introduction, to a whole range of its themes, of perspectives drawn from the succeeding century. In that way, historians have often adopted definitions of party properly appropriate only to later periods. Failing to find concrete instances of them in the eighteenth century, they have either denied the existence of parties in that period at all, or conceded that they then existed in only a vague and incoherent sense. Much confused writing about 'Court' and 'Country', and about the 'Whig Oligarchy', has been the result. But a clearer pattern is now emerging. Excellent scholarship concerned with the reigns of William III and Anne has demonstrated beyond doubt the reality and coherence of parliamentary parties in those decades. In 1970, Mr Sedgwick's volumes of the *History of Parliament* performed a similar service for the years 1715–54. But scholars have been reluctant to accept the long continuance of parliamentary parties recognisably similar to those of 1700 or 1710 not least because of the difficulty of reconciling such a theory with the multi-party pattern which, it has been agreed, prevailed in the 1760s.

It is the crisis of the 1750s which is the key to the transition between the two worlds. The political history of that, no less than of other decades, was party history; but in the crises of 1754–7, events were given a special significance as aspects of the history of party. This is not to say that it was the mechanisms of Whig or Tory parties which were of overriding importance. As organisations to marshal MPs in the House, they were elementary; as organisations out of doors, they had a fitful and discrete existence on a local level only. Despite their lack of formal structure, parties nevertheless acted as coherent units in Parliament, and party identities related to such coherent conduct were fully intelligible in the country. 'Party' mattered just as much in other political relations as it did in Commons divisions, and far more than it did in parliamentary elections.

The political activity which made up the triangular relations of Court, Ministry and Commons was saturated with the language, the memories, the preoccupations and the sense of the possible in group conduct of a party world in the process of disintegration. The sheer size of the Old Corps in the Commons made politics there less to do with inter-party activity than politics in the country; nevertheless, for that reason, it became far more an infra-party matter. Oppositions combining party groups had often agonised over the grounds of their collective conduct, though, as in the 1750s, they were seldom successful enough to go on to evolve doctrines of group cohesion separate from the traditional ones of Whig and Tory. And the conduct of the Old Corps in its attitudes to the King, to Cumberland, to Leicester House and to the Tories was still determined in these years by the fact that it *was* a party and by the course of a running contest for its leadership. That contest was profoundly to modify the nature of 'party' itself, though it did not at once affect the Whigs' self-image. Such self-images of party character were attended to far more, from necessity, only in the multi-party situation of the 1760s; nor were the possible distinctions fully apparent until a number of fragments derived from the Whig Old Corps could then be seen side by side.

In the 1750s, men did not choose a party on the basis of their conception of what 'party' was. They fought each other for political leadership; party in its future forms emerged as a result of party fragmentation and of publicists' subsequent theorising on the nature of the fragments, not as a result of prior speculation about the nature of party *per se*. Political parties in England in the reign of George III were the result of the disintegration of the Old Corps and the form which its disintegration took. That process began, not in 1760, but in 1754.

Nor did men fight one another because of their prior commitment to policy. Policies were used as some (among others) of the weapons of that fight. It is now clear that the Seven Years' War, the overriding political issue of the 1750s, was unsuccessful at its outset not because of a poverty of principled leadership (the cohesion and originality of Pitt's wartime strategy have lately been challenged)[57] but for purely military reasons including bad luck and the behaviour of commanders in the field. Newcastle was the victim not of military defeat as the consequence of his alleged preference for quietism and inertia, but of ambitious and aggressive subordinates willing to seize such issues and use them regardless of national danger as levers to force their way into office.

Historians of mid-eighteenth-century party have erred seriously in relying so heavily on the pronouncements of the pamphlet press rather than on what politicians said and did. They have been drawn to that reliance by regarding party as the vehicle of ideology or programme, even if that ideology is held to be chiefly concerned with the nature of the party's own organisation. The account here offered includes no attempt to raise 'party' to a level of coherent abstraction beyond that required to explain the conduct of politicians day by day. They themselves said little about the organisations which provided most of their terms of reference. A chief explanation of this reticence has been that they did not need to; that they could take such generalised descriptions for granted. Though this is true, further points must be made. It seems that politicians were scarcely conscious of generic developments in party, since those long-term developments were not ones which altered the 'texture' of politics day by day. Secondly, men competed for party leadership within a triad of Court, Ministry and Parliament; they did not, in the main, suppose themselves to be contending initially for the control of a party *organisation* as if that would then hold the key to power. It was success in the wider arena which would confer control of the Old Corps. Again, talk about party was what pamphleteers indulged in in the 1750s and 1760s because they knew little in detail about government business or about intrigues between individuals. Such discussions were conducted in general terms to establish the rectitude of individual conduct, not to describe the mechanisms of organisation or allegiance necessary to men acting together as a group. The pamphleteers asked what the strategies were by which groups of men saw themselves as coming to power. They used this question to distinguish between parties, rather than, in the 1750s, to define them. To politicians, party was a particular set of individuals acting together in some form of alliance; what mattered to them was merely whom a party embraced and on what basis those men could assent to act with it.

From the accession of the House of Hanover until the 1750s, public action was dominated by the now-traditional identities of Whig and Tory, and the consequences which might be derived from them. It was a commonplace that the House of Hanover itself had been 'brought' to England 'to try an experiment'.[58] For largely dynastic reasons, party was built around a 'general principle'; and it was recognised that a man could not but adopt a party identity.[59] To profess oneself of no party was the suspected resort of a Jacobite.[60] Whigs believed that they had a stake in the regime – that their property itself depended on the succession.[61] So did much else. The polarity and the party preoccupations laid down in c.1714–17, therefore, proved remarkably durable. Not least was their survival evidenced by the long career of Newcastle himself. As late as 1760, Devonshire could urge on Bute Newcastle's value: that he

had united with him the principal nobility, the moneyed men and that interest which had brought about the revolution, had set this family on the throne and supported them on it, and were not only the most considerable party but the true solid strength that might be depended on for the support of government.[62]

Earlier in the century, men were in no doubt that 'this is a Whig administration'.[63] The periodic co-operation in opposition of Tories and opposition Whigs was recognised as such, being analysed in party terms.[64] Opposition Whigs themselves recognised, in condemning, 'the narrow measure of governing by a party'.[65]

The possibility of Tory infiltration into the Household of the Dowager Princess of Wales, after 1751, was feared precisely as a threat to Whig ideological hegemony. The doctrine 'that a King of England is a King of his people, not of Whigs and Tories' was a 'noble principle', wrote the Archbishop of Canterbury, 'and would to God it took effect truly; but what must be the consequence, when it is only made the vehicle of Jacobitism and tends to overturn a government which began, and can only be supported, on Whig principles?'[66] The Jacobite threat was sustained, in the long run, by the immense economic and military preponderance of France on the continent. It was a predominance which steadily increased.[67] Contemporary Englishmen, with no anticipation of the outcome of the Seven Years' War, looked back to Marlborough's military glories with a sense of imminently fatal national decline. 'We have had our day,' wrote Lord Orrery. 'It ended with Queen Anne'.[68] Towards the end of George II's reign, many members of articulate society were burdened with a sense of national degeneracy and malaise, given special intensity and focus by the military defeats at the start of the Seven Years' War, and finding its most cogent expression in Dr John Brown's *Estimate*.[69]

Although the Tory party was neither unequivocally nor homogeneously Jacobite, the chief alternative to the Hanoverian, Whig regime remained a Stuart, Tory, one. It was presented as both a political and a moral alternative; the Tory critique of Whig England went deep. Whigs were thus indignant at the 'impudent falsehood', inaccurate and polemical as in fact it was, 'that there are no Jacobites in the Kingdom'[70] – a claim soon silenced by the rebellion of 1745. Informed Whigs such as Horace Walpole mocked the assertions of Bolingbroke that party *qua* Whig and Tory had lost its meaning.[71] As late as 1754, one observer wrote of the Jacobites: 'it is obvious that they entertain general and vague expectations of some turn favourable to their cause, founded on the hopes of a war breaking out in Europe'.[72] Just such a war then materialised. It was to be their last chance. Government loyalists predicted that many more would join a Jacobite rising than was imagined if it had any prospect of success.[73] But those possibilities were never tested, for British naval victories in 1759 frustrated the last invasion attempt aimed at overturning, wholly or in part, the Hanoverian succession.

In the 1750s, it was neither obvious nor inevitable that the Tory party would sink into oblivion by the succeeding decade. If its fortunes had been in decline, it was a slow decline, and the party had shown great resilience at the level of over one hundred MPs. Toryism itself was fully intelligible both as an ideology and as a practical identity in which men could still be recognised if they chose; it reminded so until after the winning of the Seven Years' War had removed any danger of a change of dynasty. It was still possible that, short of a revolution, the pattern of group alliances would develop in the 1750s, through the destruction of the Pelhams' hold on the Old Corps, to substitute for it either an Old Corps Whig ministry under new leaders, or very different alternatives. Among the possibilities were a Leicester House–Tory–Whig Patriot alliance under Frederick, Prince of Wales; a professedly non-party Patriot regime built around some other figure (who came eventually to be Pitt); or a Fox–Cumberland regime probably based on control of the Regency and dividing, perhaps, the Whig party. It is the object of this study to discriminate between the elements of a declining Tory Jacobite–Whig ideological alignment and the tactical fragmentation of the Whig Old Corps in such a way as to explain why, in a period of rapid experiment and bitter political conflict, 'party' came to matter less and less rather than more and more.

This outcome was not the result of impersonal or inevitable forces; nor was the weakening of party ties a general tendency in early eighteenth-century politics. On the contrary, party (in the shape of the Whig party) was progressively strengthened by its association with the ministry after the accession of the House of Hanover. In c.1714–17, certain new political conventions were evolved and established which continued thereafter to guide the relations between the central institutions of government. In so far as they affected party, it is possible from that point to distinguish a new party system. In it, 'party' was the basis of ministries but not of oppositions; oppositions were not accorded institutional permanence. They were, rather, periodic campaigns based not on party but, primarily, organised around the reversionary interest, the court of the heir to the throne. Not least because of the dynastic implications was 'formed' opposition long condemned as illegitimate. In 1755 the ideal non-Jacobite Tory was made to declare, as a 'fundamental maxim', that 'No one, but the King's enemy, can censure, oppose and distress ALL the measures of the King's ministry'.[74]

In the later eighteenth century, until the 1830s, that position was largely reversed. Ministries were typically non-party coalitions; oppositions were progressively drawn to a practical and then also to a theoretical reliance on the institution of party.[75] The crucial events which brought about this relatively sudden shift in political conventions were the crises of 1754–7, events during which the Old Corps was fragmented from within in such a way as to establish the future pattern of interest-group politics in the 1760s. This is therefore a study of the decline of party, an account of the manoeuvres and internecine ambitions by which the Whig and Tory parties of Queen Anne's reign were metamorphosed into the factions of the early years of George III's.[76] What broke down in the 1750s was not *the* party system but *a* party system, one among several sets of rules and conventions which have periodically succeeded each other in English politics. Such a transition, like those of the early 1830s, the mid 1860s, the mid 1880s or the mid 1920s, proves a remarkably fertile field of enquiry. As in the natural sciences, there is much that can only be discovered about a subject in the course of its destruction and dissection. So, here, such a process sheds light on the nature of party before and after; re-emphasises the survival of party up to that point in its then traditional sense; and reveals both the priority of political practice and the tenacity of political conventions in the formalised world of eighteenth century high politics.

AN OUTLINE OF HIGH POLITICS 1742–1754

Walpole's ministry was defeated by the co-operation of opposition Whigs and Tories. The latter were under instructions from the Pretender to ally with Whigs in opposition, Chesterfield having obtained a circular letter from James to his supporters to that effect. 'In the light of subsequent developments it is probable that Chesterfield had been authorised by the elements of the Whig opposition headed by the Duke of Argyll to promise that they would restore the Pretender in return for the Jacobite vote, as Sunderland had done in 1722'.[77] This was not how the Whig opposition as a whole was to behave, whether or not Chesterfield, Argyll and Cobham were typical of them. Pulteney, invited to form an administration, reportedly said 'Now, I thank God, we are out of the power of the Tories'.[78]

The resignation of Walpole in February 1742 was followed by the reconstruction of the ministry, a reshuffle of Whigs, but it did not bring about the replacement of a Whig *party* ministry by a non-party or a Tory one. Carteret, Pulteney and their followers were incorporated, and Argyll and Cobham too were given office. Promises of office as soon as vacancies occurred were made to Chesterfield and to the Tory Lords

Bathurst and Gower, but after a reconciliation with the Prince of Wales the King refused in March to admit the Tory Sir John Cotton and the opposition Whig Lord Granard to the Admiralty Board at Argyll's instigation. Argyll, champion of the inclusion of Tories and of the idea of the Broad Bottom ministry, resigned in protest, splitting the Whig opposition.[79] The larger part, including Argyll, Cobham, Pitt, Dodington and Chesterfield, were mobilised against the 'New Whigs', the Patriots who had accepted office with the Prince of Wales, Carteret and Pulteney, and who now voted with the Old Corps to defeat a motion for an enquiry into Walpole's administration. The Tories were also split, Gower and Bathurst retaining their places, the rest returning to opposition. Argyll, whom Sir Watkin Williams Wynn had envisaged as 'the General Monck of a second Stuart restoration'[80] then abandoned the Pretender's service; but after betraying Barrymore to the government in June 1742, Argyll withdrew from politics in terror, and lived in retirement until his death in October 1743.[81]

Jacobite intrigues were not, however, silenced; Barrymore was one of those who (with Beaufort, Orrery, Wynn, Hynde Cotton and Abdy) secretly approached the French government in the spring of 1743 requesting military support for a restoration. That request led to a mission to England that summer by James Butler on behalf of the French government to assess prospects. Bedford and Gower were possibly implicated at this point in favour of a restoration.[82]

The New Whigs meanwhile moved closer to the Pelhams, and were weakened as a force able to make trouble in the Commons when Pulteney accepted a peerage as Earl of Bath in July 1742. It was the Whig opposition in the 1742–3 session which instead advanced Patriot measures (Place and Pension Bills, an attempt to repeal the Septennial Act) – all failed. During the session the ministry performed well, enjoying majorities of about 100, in the face of attack by Pitt and others (in alliance with the Tories) on its Hanoverian involvements. But Carteret (Secretary of State for the Northern Department 1742–4) now came to engross the confidence of the King, though Pelham (Paymaster General 1730–43) led the Commons in succession to Pulteney. Wilmington died in July 1743; Bath then made a bid for the Treasury, with Carteret's backing, despite the King's previous promise of the post to Pelham. His attempt failed, and Pelham succeeded. Yet Carteret's autonomous power was not broken, and resentment at his secret diplomacy grew. In the summer of 1743, the Earl of Orford (as Sir Robert Walpole had become) advised Pelham to drop the New Whigs and take in the opposition.[83]

Throughout the summer of 1743, Cobham and Gower continued negotiations with the Pelhams. Their terms were the dismissal of the New Whigs and the admission of more of their followers to office, especially Tories. But however attractive this was, the Pelhams (with Orford's concurrence) were unwilling to risk the loss of the Prince of Wales's supporters, allied as they were to the New Whigs. Accordingly on 8 December, in protest, Gower resigned the post of Lord Privy Seal and Cobham his regiment.[84] In an ensuing reshuffle of places, it was not Carteret's friends but the Old Corps which strengthened its position; Henry Pelham became Chancellor of the Exchequer in addition to his place of First Lord of the Treasury.[85] The opposition was disunited – Pitt, Lyttelton and others wanted a vigorous campaign against France; Cobham, the Grenvilles and their friends wanted an immediate end to the war. In the autumn of 1743 a committee was formed to co-ordinate the activities of the two opposition groups, composed of three Jacobite Tories – Cotton, Philipps and Wynn, and three Broad Bottoms – Dodington, Pitt and Waller. In 1744 this steering group grew into a Junto of nine – Cotton, Dodington, Pitt and Waller plus another Broad Bottom, George Lyttelton, and four peers: Bedford, Chesterfield, Cobham and Gower.[86]

In the summer and autumn of 1743 James Butler, Louis XV's secret agent, was led to expect widespread support for a Stuart restoration.[87] Plans were made for a French invasion in January 1744, and a suggested list of Charles Edward's Regency Council drawn up in England in December 1743 naming Beaufort, Barrymore, Orrery, Wynn, Cotton, Abdy, Westmorland and Cobham; James added Chesterfield and others.[88] But the French invasion force, delayed until February, was disrupted by a storm as it was about to sail and so seriously damaged as to make the expedition for the moment impossible.

By the end of the 1743–4 session the ministry's majority was dropping; the unpopularity of Carteret and the Hanoverian connection was blamed. In July 1744 Bolingbroke returned to England, cultivating Hardwicke. That summer brought further military problems for the government, and the Tories kept up their requests to the French for an invasion. In August Bolingbroke urged Chesterfield that the Broad Bottoms join with the Old Corps to eject Carteret and the New Whigs by a coup in the Closet. Bolingbroke pursued his contacts with the Old Corps, and from September Newcastle and Hardwicke acted, on the assumption that he would support them, against the New Whigs. This culminated on 1 November 1744 in the Pelhams' refusal to serve with Carteret who, with the death of his mother in October, had become Earl Granville. Granville offered the Tories carte blanche; but they in turn refused to serve with him.[89] George II first tried to detach Harrington from the Pelhams; failing, he offered the opposition a Broad Bottom ministry, excluding Pelham, if Granville could stay. But the Pelhams had already made offers to the opposition for places for themselves and the dismissal of the New Whigs; and this the opposition preferred. On 24 November Granville was forced to resign.

The Prince of Wales's supporters escaped the ensuing purge; but most of the New Whigs were dismissed, and 'New Allies' and Tories included in their place. Bedford became First Lord of the Admiralty, Chesterfield Lord Lieutenant of Ireland, Gower ('the accredited leader of the Tory party')[90] again Lord Privy Seal, Sir John Hynde Cotton Treasurer of the Chamber, and Dodington Treasurer of the Navy. Sandwich and George Grenville were given seats at the Admiralty, Lyttelton at the Treasury, and Tories Sir John Philipps and John Pitt at the Board of Trade. Harrington succeeded to Granville's Secretaryship of State. Thus was formed the 'Broad Bottom' ministry, including Tory peers and MPs, and – on Bolingbroke's advice to Hardwicke – giving Tories greater influence in the localities. George II was persuaded to issue a declaration that JPs would be appointed 'without distinction of parties'. Despite the Pelhams' wishes the King vetoed the appointment of Pitt as Secretary at War, but Pitt was willing to wait. The 'Broad Bottom ministry' proved its viability in the 1744–5 session, despite the doubtful loyalty of the Tories and New Whig intrigues.

Meanwhile, the Pelhams were denied the favour of the Crown, and they continually protested at the constitutional issues this raised. Granville, though out of office, remained 'minister behind the curtain'. During the summer of 1745, furthermore, the Tories reconsidered their position; by the beginning of the 1745–6 session they were all back in opposition. This has been explained as an example of their reverting to their natural stance as opposition back-benchers;[91] but it is properly explicable as a reaction to the rebellion. Even before the rising, after Gower's acceptance of place on terms considered inadequate, the majority of his party realised that his loyalties were to the House of Hanover and transferred their allegiance from him to the Jacobite 4th Duke of Beaufort. Gower retained a following of only six Tory MPs.[92] John Pitt similarly chose to retain his office, which he held until 1755. 'Wynn reverted to opposition, Philipps resigned, but Cotton remained in office, which did not prevent him from joining an appeal [in August 1745] by the Duke of Beaufort, Barrymore, Wynn and other Jacobite leaders to the French government for 10,000 troops, arms and ammunition for 30,000 men, and saddles for a regiment of horse'.[93] They were unaware that Charles Edward had already landed in Scotland in July, on his own initiative and without troops or arms.

At that point the King was abroad, and the ministry divided. Granville's followers on the Regency Board, Bath, Tweeddale and Stair, obstructed decisive action. The conduct of Chesterfield, Lord Lieutenant of Ireland, was equivocal. The loyalty of many of the Whig establishment was suddenly in doubt. In October 1745 it was learned, too, that the French government would send an expedition in support of the rising. On 4 December the Young Pretender reached Derby, his point of furthest advance, but then turned back. 'When news of the retreat reached France the expedition, which was ready to sail under the command of the Duc de Richelieu, on a pre-arranged signal in the form of Cotton's resignation, which never came, was abandoned'.[94] In April 1746 the battle of Culloden ended, for the moment, the military threat; in May, Cotton was dismissed.

By mid 1745, George II was determined to change his ministry as soon as possible. Most of the New Allies favoured the ministry's resignation in protest; but the Old Corps leaders were unwilling to do so during the rebellion. Early in 1746, however, the ministry's tenuous position in the Closet began to undermine their position in the Commons, and Pitt renewed his attacks. The Pelhams failed to come to terms with him in face of the King's veto on his appointment. Then, in February 1746, George II took the initiative by asking Bath and Granville to form a ministry. But they were left with insufficient support to carry on when the Old Corps withdrew *en masse:* Harrington, Hardwicke, Newcastle, Pelham and over forty more of their political associates either resigned or announced their intention to do so. The King was forced to call back the Pelhams. Their terms included the dismissal of the leading New Whigs still in place and an office for Pitt. Even at this moment of defeat, George II was able to deny him the Secretaryship at War; Pitt became instead Joint Vice Treasurer of Ireland in April 1746 and Paymaster General in May.

The ministry rested now on the broad basis of a union between the Old Corps and the New Allies.[95] A Commons division on 11 April 1746 prompted Newcastle to estimate the number of his supporters there as Old Whigs 258, New Allies 31; and 52 New Whigs, whose support was still relied on. As long as it was forthcoming, the ministry's majority was secure.[96] The New Allies' association with the Tories was now at an end: the Gowers and John Pitt turned themselves into Whigs, while the remaining Tories reverted, like Cotton and Philipps, to opposition. 'The "breaking of the old Tory party" by the formation of the Broad Bottom, earnestly desired by Newcastle and confidently prophesied by Chesterfield, had come to nought'.[97]

But the New Whigs, the friends of the Prince of Wales and Bath, then joined the opposition. The ministry was not, henceforth, in an impregnable position. When Harrington resigned as Secretary of State in October 1746, the Pelhams feared a royal initiative to replace him by Granville; but in fact the post went to another New Ally, Chesterfield.[98] Pelham tried to consolidate his position by an early dissolution in June 1747, partly to forestall the preparations of the Prince's party for the elections ordinarily due in 1748. This gambit proved successful;[99] yet a substantial opposition bloc remained.

The Tories were left with a legacy of bitter resentment against opposition Whigs as well as against those who were regarded as traitors to their cause – especially Gower and Bedford. Thus when the Tories reverted to opposition under the leadership of Lord Noel Somerset, who became 4th Duke of Beaufort in February 1745, they were not initially associated with any other group. At the last moment before the 1747 general election Prince Frederick secured a conditional alliance with them on a programme promising 'to abolish...all distinction of party' when he came to the throne. But their combined opposition performed poorly at the polls, and not until the second session, 1748–9, was co-operation between Tories and Opposition Whigs evident in the Commons.

In the new House, in 1747–8, the Prince of Wales's party was the core of the opposition. Its strength steadily grew from about 18 in 1747 to about 60 in 1751.[100] Originally led by Lord Baltimore and Dr Lee, the party was joined in March 1748 by Lord Egmont,[101] who exploited resentment against Cumberland, and by Dodington in March 1749. Its opposition was ineffective until early in 1749 ministerial Whig divisions gave it a prospect of expanding into a majority. Egmont, who with Dodington and Lee drew up plans for Frederick's ministry on his accession,[102] laboured to bring about a closer understanding between the Prince's party and the Tories throughout the winter of 1748–9; by the summer there were signs of success[103] largely as a result of the ministry's intention to act against Jacobite Oxford. The alliance was always a conditional one, for certain specific purposes; it never developed into a full coalition. In September 1749 Sir Watkin Williams Wynn died; Pelham feared that Cotton would then commit the Tories wholly behind the Prince of Wales, which Wynn had not, and would not have done. But the Jacobites proved unwilling to ally firmly with Frederick, though Cotton's leadership was not unchallenged: Walpole recorded that the Tories 'are now governed by one Prowse, a cold plausible fellow, and a great well wisher to Mr Pelham', and that that party had not forgiven Egmont for leaving them and supporting the ministry in 1742.[104] 'In a list drawn up by Frederick and his chief advisers in April 1750, Cotton was put down for his old office of Treasurer of the Chamber. But he does not appear to have made any attempt to integrate the Tory with the Leicester House party, or to have done more than go through the routine motions of an opposition leader, speaking regularly against the Address, the army, and the land tax, till his death' on 4 February 1752.[105]

The unwillingness of the Tories for a closer association may have been a reflection, despite Prowse's influence, of reviving Jacobite hopes. After a year of mounting underground activity, Prince Charles Edward visited London secretly in September 1750. Evidently a plan for a coup was in preparation, involving the abduction or assassination of the Hanoverian Royal Family (though neither Charles Edward nor James would probably have agreed to the second) and co-ordinated with a rising elsewhere in Scotland or England; Prussia gave covert encouragement. The date originally chosen was 10 November 1752, but the enterprise was postponed. After the arrest in March 1753 of Archibald Cameron, who had gone to Scotland the previous September to co-ordinate the rising there, the plan was abandoned, subverted by fears of betrayal and without the Prussian aid which had seemed in prospect.[106] But Cotton's death had already conferred a prominent position in the leadership on younger men with little Stuart allegiance, Northey and Prowse. The latter had been offered place in 1741, 1742 and 1744; 'after the collapse of the Tory alliance with

Leicester House in 1751, Prowse and Northey accepted that the party's interests could only be secured by co-operation with the ministry'.[107]

In 1749 a Whig opposition emerged within the ministry, not dependent on the junior Court. Sandwich, Cumberland, Bedford, Fox and Legge were said to be members, the last two allegedly out of pique at Newcastle's preventing either from becoming Secretary of State on Chesterfield's retirement from politics in 1748 and contriving that Bedford should have the post, George II refusing to countenance Sandwich. Hardwicke was alarmed: the new dissidents were 'effectually doing the business of the Leicester House party for them'.[108] The alliance between the Old Corps and the New Allies, on which the ministry was based, seemed in danger of breaking up. Yet occasions of friction were not easily found. One possible occasion was the Mutiny Bill of February 1750, which controversially subjected half-pay army officers, for the first time, to martial law. Egmont clashed over the issue with Fox, who as Secretary at War was Cumberland's spokesman in the Commons; but the activity of the Leicester House party here served only to align Cumberland's friends with the Pelhams. In the same month a motion was unexpectedly made in the Commons by Egmont, on the orders of the Prince of Wales, for an account of the state of Dunkirk, which was being re-fortified contrary to the treaty of Aix-la-Chapelle. Dodington warned Frederick of the danger of a clash with France, 'in the present condition of this country. – He [Frederick] said the Tories wanted something to be done, and if he did not do something they immediately thought he was negotiating' with the Pelhams.[109]

Hostility between Newcastle and Cumberland grew from 1749 to 1750. Newcastle objected to Cumberland collecting a following of his own within the Whigs. Pelham, on good terms with Fox, tried to repair relations and to stress to Newcastle that the real threat came from the opposition of the Prince of Wales.[110] In April 1750 Pitt, whose 'jealousy is of Lord Sandwich', was reported to have 'detached himself from the Bedfords',[111] presumably as a preliminary to an approach to Leicester House.

Meanwhile, during the summer of 1750, Newcastle, with George II in Hanover, grew increasingly dissatisfied with his brother Secretary Bedford. The choice between the Bedford–Cumberland and the Prince of Wales's blocs gave added importance in the eyes of Pelham and Newcastle to their ally Pitt, and Pelham believed he had Pitt's backing in seeking Bedford's replacement.[112] The ministers may have been encouraged in that desire, even before Frederick's death, by the small success of Leicester House, since 1747, in combining major blocs in opposition. Despite his assurances to the Tories in June 1747, their allegiance was distant and conditional. There were signs of Tory suspicion that only part of his court wished to co-operate with them,[113] though Egmont kept up his negotiations with the Tories, proposing their incorporation in a future government.[114]

INTRODUCTION

The main problem for Leicester House was, rather, to maximise its following of opposition Whigs. As the King aged, there was a steady tendency for the numbers of the rank and file attached to the junior Court to grow; but the more difficult task was to attract politicians of calibre. Pitt himself had been making overtures to the Prince of Wales, at first with Newcastle's encouragement. Egmont supposed that Newcastle had 'been long paying a secret court to the Prince'; that Pitt was urging Newcastle on Frederick, with such success that the Prince was inclined to support 'an administration of Granville and Newcastle'. Egmont continued to warn Frederick against backing either Cumberland or Newcastle: 'I said before him that he was undone if he came into either party.' Egmont was well aware of Pitt's opportunism: in the negotiations with the Prince via Ayscough, as Egmont interpreted it,

Pitt plainly declared his attachment to any King – The father and the son in their turns – magnified Newcastle – gave up Pelham – intimated that Newcastle and/or Harrington would be joint Secretaries of State – Dr Lee Chancellor of the Exchequer and then thinking to speak to the passions of the Prince said jointly we might ruin the Duke of Cumberland for ever.[115]

'In the event the split within the administration came to nothing; neither side called for the assistance of Leicester House; and in the next session Frederick, Egmont and their colleagues continued their attacks on the Administration as before'.[116]

From December 1750, at least, people were expecting Granville to be created Lord President, as a move against Cumberland.[117] Pitt continued to defend Newcastle in debates in the 1750–51 session, and his stand (with Lyttelton, the Grenvilles, Conway and Egmont) against a ministerial move for the reduction in the number of seamen to 8000 was therefore initially excused.[118] Yet Pitt's sudden reversion to opposition on this issue was thought symptomatic of a desire for quick advancement. From identifying himself with Newcastle 'in opposition to Lord Sandwich and the Bedfords', he began perhaps to hope for a Secretaryship of State himself; Walpole imagined this was the case.[119] In fact, Pitt and the Lyttletons were already negotiating, or had contracted, to desert to the Prince of Wales. Pelham expressed a fear that Granville or Pitt might ally with Leicester House out of pique;[120] but it had already come about.

In January 1750 polling had taken place in the Westminster by-election caused by Granville Leveson Gower, Viscount Trentham, one of the sitting members, being made a Lord of the Admiralty. Bedford, his brother-in-law, backed him – despite Tory fury directed against Lord Gower, Trentham's father. Trentham had been declared elected in May 1750 after a scrutiny; there followed a petition against him (despite Cotton's efforts to discourage it) by the 'Independent Electors', led by Lord Elibank and Alexander Murray, both Jacobites, and another presented by Egmont, in January–February 1751. The petitions gave occasion for a clash between Fox and Egmont, who, wrote Walpole, 'used to cry up Fox against Mr Pelham, but since the former has seemed rather attached to the Duke and the Duke of Bedford, the [Leicester House] party affect to heap incense on Pelham and Pitt – and it is returned'.[121] Accusations of sedition were then made against Alexander Murray, who was imprisoned in Newgate until Parliament rose in June 1751, after which he absconded abroad. Both petitions were then withdrawn.

Early in March 1751, the Anstruther affair[122] opened 'the long-smothered rivalship between Fox and Pitt', so that 'Mr Pelham is bruised between both'. Walpole continued:

However this impetuosity of Pitt has almost overset the total engrossment that the Duke of Newcastle had made of all power, and if they do not, as it is suspected, league with the Prince, you will not so soon hear of the fall of the Bedfords as I had made you expect.[123]

By 1751 the Prince of Wales's party was described as divided into three groups, the followers of Egmont, Nugent and Dodington.[124] When Frederick died suddenly on 20 March 1751, most of his followers, led by Lee, abandoned Leicester House for the Pelhams. The Princess immediately adopted a stance of deference and obedience to the King, and Egmont found himself without influence at the junior Court. A group of Tories called on him on 26 March to ask his advice – he recommended inaction for the moment.[125] On 28 March, recorded Dodington, 'Sir Francis Dashwood from the Earl of Westmorland desired to know, if I thought it prudent to make an overture to Mr Pelham, as a party to join him, if he would engage to fix the land tax next year at two shillings in the pound, and reduce the army.'[126] Dodington deterred such an advance, and continued his efforts via the Earl of Shaftesbury to form a union of opposition Whigs and Tories on the basis of a written programme. Despite encouraging signs at first, he was unsuccessful. When the Regency Bill was debated in May 1751 the Tories were silent; Lee, Nugent and all the old Prince's and present Princess's servants joined the court in supporting it.[127]

Meanwhile, in March 1751, it was evident to Fox that Dodington, Egmont and Cobham were 'distracted' – the latter, '*cum suis*', having been 'making court, and with some effect all this winter'.[128] According to Lord Poulett,

Two negotiations were carrying on with the Prince when he died, one by Dodington on the part of the Tories – the other by Lord Cobham on the part of Pitt etc.[129]

– the second of which became known to the ministry when George Lyttelton's letter to his father Sir Thomas, accidentally left unaddressed, was opened in the Post Office in April, the letter announcing that George 'and his friends had just renewed their connexions with the Prince of Wales, by the mediation of Dr Ayscough, which, though not ripe for discovery, was the true secret of their oblique behaviour this session in Parliament'.[130]

The first is confirmed by Dodington: before the Prince of Wales's death, he

had set on foot, by means of the Earl of Shaftesbury, a project for union between the independent Whigs, and Tories, by a writing, renouncing all tincture of Jacobitism, and affirming short, but strong constitutional and revolutional principles...these, so united, were to lay this paper, containing these principles, before the Prince; offering to appear as his party, now, and upon those principles, to undertake the administration when he was King, in the subordination and rank among themselves, that he should please to appoint.[131]

The following day, 22 March, Shaftesbury and William Beckford called on Dodington

to ask directions what to do under this fatal change of situation: I said that it appeared to me that if the Pelham party did not, instantly, drive out the Bedford party, they must be drove out by them, though now the weakest, but would become the strongest, having the King's favourite, and now, only son, at their head, and at the head of the army: that he would, by their party, small as it might be, and the military, force the Regency, and then where are the Pelhams? That this necessity enforced the necessity of the projected union. – That being collected, and publicly purged from Jacobitism, they became a respectable body.[132]

Despite Henry Pelham's continued opposition to the prospect of losing Fox, Newcastle was now able to move against Bedford. In April 1751, recorded Egmont,

Tom Pitt says the Duke of Newcastle is in the Princess's interest, that he wants to rout the Bedfords, Cumberland and Sandwich, to bring in Granville and perhaps the Prince's party with Granville perhaps [Lord] President, Wm. Pitt Secretary of State – which he is pushing for, and Lyttelton to be Cofferer.[133]

It was also more urgent for Newcastle to counter Bedford, for, with Leicester House no longer a viable focus of opposition, the Cumberland group was the only remaining resort for those hostile to the Pelhams. By the end of March, Bedford and Sandwich 'had now got the Duke of Marlborough and Lord Gower on their side' on one issue at least.[134]

Frederick's death had made necessary some provision for a possible future Regency, Prince George being aged 12 and the King 67. The two chief alternatives were to nominate as Regent either Cumberland or the Dowager Princess of Wales, the second 'subject to such safeguards as might prevent the power then placed in her hands from being used against the Pelhams. Contrary to general anticipation they decided in favour of the latter. The cause of their decision was the violent outcry raised by the prospect that the chief power in the state might fall into the hands of the Duke of Cumberland.'[135] To avoid that danger, Princess Augusta agreed to the restrictions on her power in the Pelhams' proposals, and to their nominees in the educational posts around the two Princes.[136]

Cumberland resented the subordinate role assigned to him; according to Walpole 'From this moment he openly declared his resentment to the two [Pelham] brothers, and professed being ready to connect with, nay, to forgive any man, who would oppose them, even Lord Granville, who was not at all unwilling to overset their power, though till that could be done conveniently, he thought it as well to unite with them'.[137]

Bedford was confined with gout while the Regency Bill passed the Lords and was dissuaded by his friends from trying to attend; Sandwich, 'who was not impatient to precipitate his own fall, voted, with the Duke's consent, for every part of the Bill'. Dr Lee spoke approvingly of it; of the Tories, Vyner, Prowse, Lord Harley, Sir John Cotton, Norreys Bertie and Sir Roger Newdigate spoke against. So did Sir Francis Dashwood and Lord Strange, Tory sympathisers among the opposition Whigs. Pitt and Fox clashed in Committee: though Fox supported the Bill, 'he spoke against almost every part of it'.[138] Pitt urged restrictions on Cumberland's power; the Grenvilles joined him in speaking and voting for the Bill, though Lord Cobham spoke and voted against.[139] The crucial division was carried by 258 to 81, 'the greater part of the late Prince's Court' voting for it.[140]

By the end of the 1750–51 session, opposition had almost ceased. Newcastle now moved against the dissidents within the ministry. On 12 June 1751 Sandwich was dismissed as First Lord of the Admiralty; Anson, breaking with Bedford and Sandwich, replaced him. Bedford resigned in protest, refusing the King's personal offer of the post of Lord President. Dorset had become Lord Lieutenant of Ireland in place of Harrington in December 1750, and Granville now replaced Dorset as Lord President; Hartington became Master of the Horse. Yet Newcastle was still dissatisfied that his brother's good relations with Cumberland and Princess Amelia meant that he, Newcastle, was not on an equal footing in the government, despite Holdernesse's appointment to succeed Bedford.[141]

Of the Prince's followers only Egmont continued a low-key opposition in the session 1751–2. Dodington was trying hard to ingratiate himself with the Pelhams. On 4 February 1752 the Jacobite Sir John Hynde Cotton also died, so virtually silencing the Tories. When Parliament adjourned on 19 December 1751, Walpole wrote of:

an era for ever remarkable in English annals! Opposition, which had lasted from the days of Queen Elizabeth, and even the distinctions of parties having in a manner ceased at this period! Popery, which had harassed the reign of that heroine; the spirit of liberty which had struggled against four Stuarts; the spirit of slavery which had wrestled to restore their descendants; all the factions which had distracted King William, possessed Queen Anne, and ridiculed the House of Hanover; and the Babel of parties that had united to demolish Walpole, and separated again to pursue their private interests; all were now sunk into a dull mercenary subjection[142]

to Henry Pelham and the Duke of Newcastle. Bedford was at first disinclined to opposition and was persuaded to engage in it only in January 1752 over the issue of the subsidy treaty with Saxony. But, in the Lords, he found himself alone in attacking it, and incurred the King's displeasure without corresponding gain. The Tory peers conspicuously refrained from supporting him,[143] and when the next day a separate Tory motion was made in the Commons by Harley and seconded by Northey, declaring in general against subsidy treaties in time of peace, it mustered only 52 votes.[144]

It was not clear what course was open to Bedford's group now that it was no longer an enclave within the Old Corps, but was faced with the need to decide whether to become an opposition Whig party or to capitulate. There was still much to play for: Irish politics had taken fire,[145] and Newcastle was aware that if Dorset failed to pacify the crisis, Bedford would be an obvious candidate to succeed as Lord Lieutenant – an office he was to obtain in 1756.[146] Furthermore, a successor was being talked of for Lord Gower as Lord Privy Seal; again, Bedford would be a serious contender.[147]

Having lost the Tories, Bedford and Cumberland now chose to play the Jacobite card against the ministry. With knowledge and suspicions about Jacobite conspiracy still prevalent (the Elibank plot was timed for 10 November 1752), the Commons remained highly susceptible to Whig–Tory polarisation in this ideological field; any lull in the party battle, thus expressed, was only temporary and illusory. As Walpole had written in 1751

Before the Parliament met, there was a dead tranquillity, and no symptoms of party spirit. What is more extraordinary, though the opposition set out vehemently the very first day, there has appeared ten times greater spirit on the Court side, a Whig vehemence that has rushed on heartily.[148]

Now, in March 1752, Cumberland gave the King a list of alleged Jacobites in office in Scotland. 'Mr Pelham said, the attack against him, was for being for the constitution, against military power, or a military government.'[149] Nevertheless, he had to mount an enquiry to check the allegations. And when the Bill regulating forfeited estates came into the Lords, Bedford attacked Argyll, the Pelhams' ally and virtual Viceroy of Scotland, for favouring Jacobites.[150] When the dissensions over the education of the Prince of Wales gathered pace, from May 1752, they did so not least because they found a reception in the situation illuminated by the terms in which Bedford attacked the ministry. Though the attempt of Harcourt and the Bishop of Norwich to oust Stone, Cresset and Scott failed and led to the resignation of the two first in December 1752, the charges they levelled, 'Jacobite connexions' and 'instilling Tory principles'[151] were to be repeated in February 1753 with much greater effect, coming as they did after a 'campaign of vague and anonymous lies which was being conducted against [Pelham's] friends and, through them, against his government'.[152]

In the face of the Bedford–Cumberland threat, men were drawn to analyse the source of the Pelhams' power. According to Horatio Walpole, recorded Dudley Ryder, Newcastle 'courts the Tories, brings them all in from W[estminste]r Hall where they were almost all Jacobites. [Walpole] says as long as Lord Granville is [Lord] President and the Duke of Newcastle courts the King's taste, the King will not change the Duke of Newcastle.'[153] But Pelham himself thought Granville still ambitious; that he simply waited for an opportunity.[154] The Old Corps was vulnerable, thought Newcastle, chiefly to disruption from within; it must therefore be publicly shown that Bedford had no support *at Court*.[155] Pelham was preoccupied with the approaching elections, and with the danger that the Tories would profit from the situation to increase their numbers;[156] yet even Pelham predicted of St James's: 'I fear the divisions in that court will give us more uneasiness than any other public event.'[157] Thus Ralph perceptively wrote that the Court

may be divided, as I humbly conceive, thus. The Princess of Wales, the Lord Chancellor [Hardwicke], the Secretary Duke [Newcastle] (his colleague need not be named), Mr Pelham, Lord Anson, and Lord Hartington, on one side; the Duke [Cumberland], the Princess Amelia, the Lord President [Granville], the Lord Steward [Marlborough], the Groom of the Stole [Albemarle] (though abroad) and Mr Fox (with his great auxiliary, the Duke of Bedford) on the other. The Dukes of Grafton and Dorset I reckon as trimmers that will certainly lean to the strongest; and if Lord Gower is, at present, too much a cypher to be reckoned at all, Lord Winchelsea may, perhaps, in due time be his successor. Thus the two parties, as they stand at Court, stand nearly on equal ground, and from that equality the King may probably find himself in a condition to prefer which he pleases, and, consequently, give the law to both; which was nearly the case of King William in the last year of his life...For a king, so circumstanced, need not yield to either side unless they can talk to him in the name of a majority in Parliament, which also, at present, seems to depend more on himself than anybody else, whether it is understood and acknowledged so to be or not.[158]

Was Granville reliable? Had he joined Cumberland's followers? Who could be trusted? Hillsborough suggested to Dodington that

there must be some disturbance arise from the Pitt party: that though they were so well placed they were uneasy: that they neither were lik'd nor lik'd. I said I could not conceive that they would stir. – He said yes; for that Pitt's passion was ambition, not avarice. That he was at a full stop as things were, and could have no hopes of going farther: he was once popular: if he could again make a disturbance, and get the country of his side, he might have hopes: now, and on this system, he could have none.[159]

Suspicion and apprehension characterised the political climate. On the surface all was strangely quiet. 'There is a dead calm in Parliament', wrote Sir George Lee,[160] Walpole complained that 'it grows past a joke...there is no war, no politics, no parties, no madness and no scandal. In the

memory of England there never was so inanimate an age: it is more
fashionable to go to church than to either House of Parliament.'[161]

That claim was immediately disproved when, in February 1753, Ravens-
worth's accusations of Jacobitism against Stone, Murray and the Bishop
of Gloucester again roused a furore. The Committee appointed to enquire
into the affair reported to the King on 26 February, exploding the lying
allegations of the key witness, Fawcett. Yet on 10 March Bedford gave
notice in the Lords that he would move for papers relating to the charge.
'The political world assumed that this meant that a grand assault on the
government, after long and elaborate preparation, was at last to take
place. It was rumoured that the Fawcett affair was to be combined with
the recent resignations in the heir-apparent's establishment; that Ravens-
worth, Harcourt, and the Bishop of Norwich would repeat their accusations in the House of Lords; that the Duke of Bedford had reason to expect
strong support from normal adherents of the government; and that the
design was to repeal the Regency Act and make the Duke of Cumberland
Regent.' But the debate 'fizzled out without a division' on 22 March;[162]
all the Tory Lords would have voted for Stone and Murray.[163] Pitt intervened to prevent Temple backing Bedford's motion on the issue:[164]
evidently he thought the time not yet ripe. The crisis nevertheless had its
effect. As Chesterfield pointed out, Stone and Murray had protested too
much; they had been whitewashed rather than cleared. It was inconceiv-
able that they had had nothing *whatever* to do with Jacobitism in their
youth:

the affair has affected them both, and they will feel the weight of it as long
as they live. No reasonable man, I believe, thinks them Jacobites now, whatever they may have been formerly. But parties do not reason, and every Whig
party man, which is nine in ten of the Whig party, is fully convinced that they
are at this time determined and dangerous Jacobites.[165]

The arrest in March and execution in June of Dr Cameron must have
seemed, if not more than coincidence, at least a reminder of the continued
potency of the Jacobite alternative. Thus was Murray, Newcastle's protégé
and one of Fox's rivals, gravely handicapped in the race for power which
lay ahead.

A further confrontation came in May 1753 over the Clandestine
Marriage Bill. Bedford, Fox and Nugent all opposed it. Granville did not
attend.[166] And in the same month 'The Protester', an anti-ministerial
paper backed by Bedford, was launched. Judging by the numbers in the
divisions on the Marriage Bill, the Tories did not endorse Bedford. 'The
Protester' may have been a bid for their support. Newcastle was
astonished:

the paper is serious Jacobitism; a comparison in favour of the Tory ministry
in Queen Anne's time, against the Whig ministers at all times; a most severe
reflection upon the King and his family; and a most strong attack and censure

of Sir Robert Walpole and his administration. How this will serve the views of the Duke of Bedford and his great friends I do not see.[167]

And soon its editor, Ralph, was bought off by the government with a pension; his last issue was dated 10 November 1753.

May 1753 had also seen the passage through the Commons of the 'Jew Bill', a private measure enjoying tacit ministerial approval, which provided for the naturalisation of individual Jews by private Act of Parliament. 'It had passed almost without observation,' recorded Walpole, 'Sir John Barnard and Lord Egmont having merely given a languid opposition to it, in order to re-ingratiate themselves with the mobs of London and Westminster.' But during the course of the summer, 'public opinion' took fire, the flames carefully fanned by those who saw in the Bill a classic issue, able to arouse widely-shared xenophobic and Anglican sensitivities. A vigorous pamphlet campaign, conducted in those terms, is strong evidence for the continued currency and potency of such a language of politics. Those who were more aware of the way in which 'issues' were used by politicians were, however, sceptical. The importance of the Bill had been exaggerated out of all proportion: 'Are there not ten thousand insulting Jacobites and favourers of a foreign interest in our land,' asked one pamphleteer, 'to one insulted Jew?' The real explanation, he suggested, had little to do with the merits of the case.

Judaism, in the present cry, is either this, or that, or what you please, to cover a malicious, avaritious, or ambitious design. Judaism is a cant–word to revive, raise and establish an abject and sinking cause. It is a mere Babel of ideas according to the character of the man that uses it...In the mouth of a Jacobite, Judaism is another name for the Revolution in 1688, a limited monarchy, the Hanover legacy, and the royal family; in opposition to an indefeasible, hereditary right, *jure divino*, non-resistance and passive obedience. – In the mouth of a pretended Patriot, and flaming bigot, Judaism is a Whiggish administration and House of Commons, a Protestant bench of Bishops and House of Lords, liberty of conscience, and an equitable toleration; in opposition to High-Church power, implicit faith, damnatory creeds, and a persecution of such as are more righteous than themselves...[168]

With elections impending and all groups sensitive to the consequences for their public images in the constituencies, the ministry quickly gave way. Newcastle moved the Jew Bill's repeal immediately the new session of Parliament began. The House of Lords agreed without difficulty to reverse its previous position. Only Temple, at first, spoke loudly against repeal, seizing with ill-judged enthusiasm an opportunity to denounce the inconsistency of the ministry. Bedford (who had been against the Bill itself) then joined him, though arguing that the repealing Bill as framed did not go far enough and left the Jews in a more favoured position. Temple 'tried to encourage the Tories to continue the clamour', but, according to Walpole, failed. Despite securing the repealing Bill's amendment, Temple kept up his opposition to it, incurring Tory denunciations but not preventing its passage in his House without a division.

Both sides were able to make propaganda use of the issue since Whigs and Tories had been in favour of the original Bill, and a few independently minded men of both parties (like Norbone Berkeley, Tory MP for Gloucestershire) refused to recant their opinions. But in the Commons, the great majority of Tories and ministerial Whigs vied, in an attempt to evade implication with the measure, to introduce and support repeal. Nevertheless, the Tories found opportunities to divide against the government on the form of words used: Newdigate and Northey, in Committee, attempted to replace the words in the preamble declaring that 'occasion has been taken from the said Act to raise discontents' with the alternative 'discontents and disquietudes have from the said Act arisen'. Northey was 'seconded by Prowse, Lord Egmont, and Admiral Vernon. On the other side Nugent, Sir W. Yonge, Sir Richard Lloyd, Mr Pelham, old Horace Walpole, and Mr Pitt, who was just come abroad again after a year of sullen illness, defended the words and the repeal', which passed with the ministry's wording by 113 to 43; the repeal as a whole then passed without opposition.[169] But the Tories succeeded in polarising the ministry on the seemingly unpopular side when on 4 December the Tory Lord Harley moved, and the opposition Whig Sir Francis Dashwood[170] seconded, a motion 'to repeal as much of the Plantation Act, as related to the Jews', namely the section permitting their naturalisation after seven years' residence in America. The ministry refused to be pushed further by popular clamour and secured its defeat by 208 to 88, amid Tory rejoicing at an opportunity to cast themselves in the role of defenders of things English.

Pitt, for the moment, backed Pelham and spoke against the motion. Nevertheless, the threat of factious disruption of the ministry encouraged speculation about possible tactical formulae to restore harmony. Such solutions were difficult to bring about; as Lord Barnard explained to Dodington, 'nobody died to make room, and they [the ministers] could not turn out'.[171] This gave added importance to the English dimension of the Irish crisis. The possibility of Dorset's replacement as Lord Lieutenant led Chesterfield to speculate:

Various successors are talked of, but I believe no-one fixed. Some talked of Lord Holdernesse, who in that case, they say, is to be succeeded in the Secretary's Office by the Solicitor General, Murray. Others talk of Lord Winchelsea, as recommended by Lord Granville; and this I think not improbable; but some, who go deeper, name the Duke of Bedford, and hint that it would be the means of reconciliation between him and another Duke [Newcastle], whose extreme timidity makes him wish for it, and this, I think, by no means impossible.[172]

Yet many men shrank from the clash of ambitions which, they sensed, was impending. Over the Marriage Bill in May–June 1753, Fox had 'seemed wantonly and unnecessarily to have insulted the Chancellor, and had even manifested some fear at having done so'.[173] And in January 1754 he was thought to be 'embarrassed' at the way in which his friendship with Kildare implicated him in Irish disputes and drew down on him the King's disapproval.[174] Pelham therefore wrote: 'I am easy upon that subject, for I am confident [Fox] will act a more honourable part, than *his governors or his followers* wish him to do.'[175] He was right. Fox did not, in early 1754, use Irish unrest as a lever to advance his English ambitions. Yet, in the long term, Pelham was over-optimistic. According to Lord Barnard, lately Henry Vane, MP, Fox 'had asked Mr Pelham for the first vacancy in [the] Treasury for Barrington, but had been absolutely refused'.[176] Fox's ambitions were stifled, not satisfied. Yet despite the conflicts in Dublin intensified by the dismissal of a group of leading Irish dissidents in January, Walpole could still write of England: 'We abound in diversions, which flourish exceedingly on the demise of politics.'[177]

On 7 February Sir John Barnard moved to repeal the Bribery Oath. One observer had written: 'I was surprised to find that most of the Tories are determined to oppose Sir John Barnard's motion; I do not know whether the ministry will support Sir John or give it up for fear the Tories should make use of it as [a] second edition of the Jew Bill.'[178] Now, on 7 February, the ministry evidently did not lend its support. The Bill was rejected without a division,[179] yet only after Fox had spoken for it, breaking his promise to Henry Pelham not to do so. Lord Barnard supposed that Cumberland had commanded Fox to intervene contrary to his undertaking and that Sandwich attended the debate in the Commons to see that Fox did so.[180]

The basic conditions for the survival of ministries had not changed since shortly after the accession of the House of Hanover. From the 1740s, the Pelhams had succeeded in consolidating the Whigs despite divisions introduced into the party by other contestants seeking to win control of it. At one point, those rivals had seemed willing to countenance a Stuart restoration as a route to power, and the Whig opposition had been dangerously implicated in Jacobite schemes. Yet, for military reasons, the danger passed. The Old Corps ultimately resisted attempts to infiltrate the ministry under the rationale of Broad Bottom, and left its Whig opponents seriously weakened by the manoeuvres of 1742–7. The steadily growing power of the reversionary interest was then fortuitously checked by the death of Frederick, Prince of Wales. After that event, and the failure of the Elibank plot, the Tories were left isolated. Leicester House was unable to take political initiatives on behalf of Prince George, aged 12 on his father's death, and what links there were between the junior Court and the Tories quickly disappeared. After 1751, discontented Whigs sought ways of capturing control of the ministry from within by factious manoeuvre, rather than ways of creating a bloc in open opposition under the umbrella of a non-party creed. Part of the strategy of Whig *frondeurs*, therefore, was henceforth to stress the Tories' implication (in fact now fading) with Jacobite intrigue. That strategy was adopted chiefly to serve the ambitions of Whigs within their own party; it was not shared by Whig party leaders. The Tories, therefore, isolated in opposition, found themselves in a tactical situation which encouraged and enabled them to display a greater affinity to the ministry than to its surviving Whig opponents.

From the late 1740s, then, the Pelhams succeeded in neutralising the Tories; not because they were a negligible force (they were not) nor because politics was not polarised ideologically and practically into Tory and Whig (it was) but because the Tory party remained isolated tactically so that its potential, aside from its revolutionary implications, was neither registered nor realised in a political arena. For such reasons, not for the fading of issues expressible in Whig–Tory terms or for the etiolation of the Tory party as a tactical unit, Chesterfield could write of the approaching elections:

The fury of this war is chiefly Whig against Whig, for the Tories are pretty much out of the question; so that, after the new Parliament shall be chosen, the greatest difficulty upon the administration will be, to find pasture enough for the beasts they must feed.[181]

That was not a generally valid account of the working of some eighteenth-century oligarchy but a specific and immediate comment on the tactical outcome of the party-politics of the previous few years.

1

The Accession of Newcastle, March–September 1754

though I see no symptoms at present of foul weather near at hand, yet I know that once in ten or twelve years in this country filthy humours will collect, the whole age turns sour upon a man's hands and the better he has deserved of the public in general the fairer chance he stands of mounting the pilory for his reward.

> Legge to Keene, 9 August 1752: Rylands MSS, 668 no.4.

HENRY PELHAM AND HIS SUCCESSORS

Henry Pelham died at six on the morning of 6 March 1754. Men's immediate reaction of 'confusion and consternation'[1] marked a fear, on the part of both the King and the people, that political tranquillity had died with the man who, pre-eminently, had come to personify it. Historians, too, have not succeeded in distinguishing a Pelhamite political consensus from Pelham's own personal contribution; and Horace Walpole, even without foreknowledge of the intrigues which were to follow, wrote: 'all that calm, that supineness, of which I have lately talked to you so much, is at an end! There is no heir to such luck as his. The whole people of England can never agree a second time upon the same person for the residence of infallibility...'[2] In part, this respect had stemmed from a widespread affection for Pelham's 'most amiable composition' as a man; in part, from the fact of his political blandness and broad acceptability. In part, too, it arose from Whig confidence in his skill as an election manager. In March, a general election was imminent; but there was no widespread expectation of another decisive Whig success. Tory decline and opposition Whig weakness were not pre-ordained facts; hence the general euphoria in the Old Corps at results which government managers were to calculate as only a very slight gain. It was not hyperbole but Whig party self-interest which led Pitt to lament Pelham's loss as 'utterly irreparable, in such circumstances as constitute the present dangerous conjuncture for this country, both at home and abroad';[3] and Pitt's private attitude is fully consistent with the condolences and support he offered Newcastle.[4] The most obvious danger, expressed within the ministry by the Solicitor General, William Murray, and anticipated also at large, was that Pelham's death would 'create great confusion on the elections', both in constituencies where an opposition had already been declared, and in those where 'adventurers' might now take an opportunity to intrude.[5] Newcastle at once had Hardwicke act to secure Pelham's election plans.[6]

Such fears gave an added urgency to the choice of a successor, and the importance of the impending elections reinforced an initially widespread assumption that that successor would inherit Pelham's position intact: First Lord of the Treasury, Chancellor of the Exchequer, First Minister and leader of the Commons. Henry Fox and Sir George Lee both thought they had a claim to be regarded as the ministerial heir-apparent,[7] but Pelham had also spoken in the Commons, at one point, of Lord Egmont as his probable successor,[8] and Egmont had entertained the same opinion.[9] Shelburne later wrote that, by 1754,

Mr Pitt and Mr Fox were just begun to be balanced and played against each other by Mr Pelham, of whom they both agreed to me in one character, and gave several instances of the cunning and duplicity of the two brothers which I cannot recollect. Mr Pitt told me that Mr Pelham used to send for him when they quarrelled, which they perpetually did, to negotiate between them, and went so far as to press him to be Secretary of State, in the room of his brother, without the smallest meaning or sincerity whatever.[10]

Nor was there a shortage of other men whose abilities alone marked them out. The public accordingly speculated on a range of candidates. Lord Cathcart named Fox, Murray, Legge, Sir George Lee and Pitt, with Fox as the favourite at White's.[11] The press generally agreed in favouring Fox,[12] but unexpectedly added Dodington's name.[13] J. F. Pinney listed five candidates: the Speaker, Onslow; Fox; Legge; Lee; and Sir George Lyttelton; reported that Legge and Fox were the chief contestants; and suggested that Lee might be persuaded to act as a stand-in until the elections.[14] Walpole, who had heard the same rumour, commended Lee as sensible, of good character, and 'obnoxious to no set of men; for though he changed ridiculously quick on the Prince's death, yet as everybody changed with him, it offended nobody; and what is a better reason for promoting him now, it would offend nobody to turn him out again'.[15] One newspaper, too, rumoured Lee to succeed;[16] another linked Lee and Fox as candidates for the Exchequer alone.[17] Chesterfield named Fox, on Cumberland's interest, and Legge, Murray and Lee on that of Newcastle and Hardwicke. Any of the last three, he added, would produce no great changes in government; but Fox's promotion would have consequences far from agreeable to Newcastle.[18] Another observer linked Fox, Legge and Lee with Lord Dupplin as the remaining contenders, after suggesting on 9th that Murray had declined.[19] Lord Ilchester's list was the most comprehensive: Fox, Onslow, Dupplin, Sir George Lee, Sir George Lyttelton, George Grenville, Legge and Sir John Barnard;[20] all, still, to succeed to the Exchequer and Treasury together.

Walpole, though more selective in identifying three feasible successors – Fox, Murray and Pitt – emphasised the handicaps which offset the abilities of each:[21]

The Chancellor hates Fox; the Duke of Newcastle does not (I don't say, love him, but to speak in the proper phrase, does not) pretend to love him: the Scotch abominate him, and they and the Jacobites make use of his connection with the Duke [of Cumberland] to represent him as formidable: the Princess [of Wales] cannot approve him for the same reason: the law, as in duty bound to the Chancellor and to Murray, and to themselves, whom he always attacks, must dislike him. He has his parts and the Whigs, and the seeming right of succession. Pitt has no health, no party, and has, what in *this* case is allowed to operate, the King's negative. Murray is a Scotchman, and it has been suspected, of the worst dye; add a little of the Chancellor's jealousy: all three are obnoxious to the probability of the other two being disobliged by a preference.

Historians have been far too willing, by ante-dating and exaggerating Pitt's ambitions,[22] to treat him and Fox as the only practicable candidates in March 1754 and so to falsify a situation in which many men had to be dealt with as contenders for offices the status and possible conjunction of which were themselves in question.

THE INTENTIONS OF FOX AND PITT

Walpole evidently supposed that Pelham's offices were now indissolubly linked. From the outset, however, Pitt employed the opposite assumption in treating the Chancellorship of the Exchequer as the only office available for a member of the Commons. Pitt privately admitted the strength of Fox's claim on the Exchequer alone, for Fox was qualified 'in point of party, seniority in the Corps, and I think ability for Treasury and House of Commons business';[23] but Sir George Lee, too, Pitt considered to be 'papabilis', though he naturally added that George Grenville would be his personal choice. Pitt's remarkable fourth idea was to 'secularise' the Solicitor General – that is, to lure him from the profession of the law by the offer of the Exchequer. Such a move would produce a strong Commons system 'and be perfectly adapted to the main future contingent object, could it be tempered so, as to reconcile the Whigs to it...'[24]

Far from anticipating the attempts of later that summer to blacken Murray with a Jacobite taint, Pitt hoped in March that the Solicitor General might evade such a disqualification. The Exchequer for Murray, too, would not have offered the prospect of his promotion to the Lords; and in Murray as a Commons orator, Pitt recognised his equal.[25] Nor is there evidence that Pitt hoped for a peerage and the Treasury himself. The point to Murray's promotion, from Pitt's point of view, was that it would prevent the ascendancy of Fox. Even if the offices were divided, assumed Pitt, the Treasury could be expected to go to a peer; if that peer were Newcastle, there would be no reason for the vacant Secretaryship of State to be held by a member of the Commons if Murray were intended to lead the House from the Exchequer. Pelham, indeed, reflecting on Bedford's successor in the Secretaryship, had insisted that it should be a peer even though it would dangerously confine the ambitions of a number of able commoners: 'Nature will operate in such a case, and ill humours and discontents, though smothered for a time, will at last burst.'[26] Evidently, in March 1754, Pitt failed to anticipate the plan Newcastle had adopted by 11th: to take the Treasury himself with a minor figure at the Exchequer and promote Fox to a Secretaryship. Pitt was chiefly concerned with Murray not as a rival for that post with himself, but as a counterweight against Fox. Walpole's suggestion[27] that Fox and Pitt would have agreed in Murray's exclusion was an incorrect speculation in retrospect about what he imagined Pitt's motives to have been; perhaps Walpole was misled by the Pitt–Fox alliance in the session of 1754–5.

Sir George Lyttelton made a similar mistake, writing some time later that 'Pitt's opposition at first was the effect of a jealousy, that his Grace's inclination was to make Mr Murray Secretary of State instead of him, which I knew to be false at that time'.[28] This may refer to November 1754, but is then, equally, unsubstantiated. Though a rumour had circulated in January that if Dorset were replaced as Lord Lieutenant of Ireland by Holdernesse, Murray would succeed to the latter's Secretaryship,[29] there is no evidence that Pitt, in March, thought Murray might be destined for any other office than the Exchequer. The tenure of the Lieutenancy was not in question during the English rearrangements of March 1754, and none of the English candidates then acted as if it might be.

Pelham's death found Pitt at Bath, the only one of the contenders out of town, afflicted with a severe attack of gout and unable to travel. Despite Walpole's scepticism,[30] the chronology of Pitt's illness and the handicap it placed on his manoeuvres in March suggest that his physical sufferings, this time at least, were real.[31] In this insecurity, Pitt's reliance on Pelham, 'who had adopted him',[32] seems to have been transferred directly (though temporarily) to Pelham's brother. Whatever the future situation in the Commons, Fox could be halted only if Newcastle took command of the ministry. Far from trying to unsettle the situation, Pitt wrote at once to stiffen Newcastle's resolve to support his King and country, and in terms which admitted of no doubt that that Duke, with whatever combination of offices, *would* succeed to Pelham's role. Then, added Pitt, 'may all good men make it their glory to support your Grace in the generous effort'.[33]

In 1751 the death of Frederick, Prince of Wales, had narrowly averted the already planned desertion to his opposition of Pitt's and the Grenvilles' following. In 1754 that act of disloyalty was suddenly legitimised in Pitt's mind as a desire to protect the junior Court, with which he now had no connections, against Fox and Cumberland. Historians[34] have usually overstated the strength both of Pitt's claims to promotion, and of his position, on Pelham's death. Pitt, however, acted on an assumption of the weakness of both. As a pamphleteer later claimed, Pelham's death raised him only from the third to the second rank of ministers.[35] In a letter meant to be read by Temple to Sir George Lyttelton and the Grenvilles,[36] he outlined his strategy: 'to support the King in quiet, as long as he may have to live; and to strengthen the hands of the Princess of Wales, as much as may be, in order to maintain her power in the Government, in case of the misfortune of the King's demise'. Pitt's interest in Leicester House revived so rapidly only because that Court could now serve to counterbalance Fox. It was no more than a temporary revival, since Pitt chose later that summer to move instead towards the ambiguous alliance with Fox which characterised the session of 1754–5.[37] For the moment, however, Pitt expressed the hope that a reversionary interest might be quietly collected against an inevitable and probably imminent event. Place was not to be pursued by agitation, far less by Patriot opposition. He advised Temple to hold, unostentatiously, dinners for some named friends including those attached to Leicester House; 'in short, *liez commerce* with as many Members of Parliament, who may be open to our purposes, as your lordship can'.[38] Pelham's death, tactically the antithesis of that of the Prince of Wales, offered Pitt a prospect of a major accession of strength; but this was only a speculation about the most favourable outcome he might expect, and for the moment he left indeterminate the degree of activity such a collection of like-minded men would display before George II's death. That calculation would depend, too, on the King's still unknown disposition towards Fox (whom he might be assumed automatically to favour for present promotion) and equally conjectural 'real desire to have his own Act of Regency, as it is called, maintained in the hands of the Princess' of Wales.

The question, then, was the part the brotherhood ought to act in the face of these problems. 'I don't think quitting of offices at all advisable', Pitt wrote, 'for public or private accounts: but as to answering any farther purposes in the House of Commons, that must depend on the King's will and pleasure to enable us so to do'. It was plain that Newcastle and Hardwicke shared his desire to check Fox's advance. He therefore supposed his connection might be courted by the ministers as 'a resource' against the dangers of a Cumberland regency; but for his group to be effective – indeed, for it to maintain 'an existence in the eyes of the public' – they must be distinguished by royal favour: 'one of the connection put into the Cabinet, and called to a real participation of councils and business'. George Grenville was the obvious choice, and ought to accept the Secretaryship at War, if offered it, in succession to Fox. Privately, to Temple, Pitt confessed his expectation that Fox *would* secure the Exchequer, in spite of the ministers' reluctance to surrender it to him. Sir George Lyttelton's news[39] of Fox's opening bids for power, however, found Pitt able to suggest very few tactics with which the Grenvilles might reply. Murray's promotion depended on Newcastle and on Newcastle's success; a Grenville–Leicester House link was a distant speculation. Though Pitt hoped to see Fox gain as little power as possible, he could do nothing himself to stop him: his position was purely dependent on Newcastle. Pitt had failed to prepare his friends for counter-measures against Fox partly from his, Pitt's, refusal to contemplate launching 'a third party, or flying squadron',[40] partly from his weakness without his patrons. Immediately on news of Pelham's death, he wrote: 'The Chancellor is the only resource. His wisdom, temper and authority, joined to the Duke of Newcastle's ability as Secretary of State, are the dependence for government.'[41] Pitt's regard for the ministers, he thought, was too well-known (indeed it was too obviously necessary) for them to need reminding of it. To the Pelhams he owed both his seat and his Paymastership. What Pitt saw as the least unfavourable outcome in the short term, then, was for Hardwicke to reinforce Newcastle and produce a system in which the Grenville bloc would make limited gains, even though Fox, too, would greatly advance his position. If, as Walpole thought, the security of Newcastle and Hardwicke rested on restraining Fox, so much more did the Paymaster's.[42] Within such a system, Pitt could for the moment support the King's ministers; 'and the strongest argument of all to enforce that, is, that Fox is too odious to last for ever, and G. Grenville must be next nomination under any Government'. But even here, Pitt could not call this a conditional commitment: his friends must support disinterestedly, 'from *principles of public good*'.[43]

Pitt's problem was to achieve any advance at all from his initial position of weakness. One anxiety was that Sir George Lyttelton would be manoeuvred into offering assurances without using them to extract concessions. Yet Pitt was disabled from employing 'menace' against the ministers, and it was no part of his intention 'to intimate quitting the King's service; giving trouble, if not satisfied, to government'. To the Grenvilles, then, he announced that he was 'determined not to go into faction'. Short of that, he merely hoped to arouse fears in the ministry by a refusal to renounce 'listing in particular subdivisions' within it and so profit from 'the mutual fears and animosities of different factions in court'. Yet 'this is to be done *negatively* only; by eluding explicit declarations with regard to persons especially; not by *intimations of a possibility of following our resentments*'.[44] Pitt enclosed to Lyttelton a letter to be shown by him to the three Grenville brothers, then to Hardwicke and Newcastle. Pitt stressed that his proposal included no hint

with regard to what consideration I might expect for myself. I think it better that should arise from themselves; at least not come from me. If they are in earnest to avail themselves of me against what they fear, they will call me to the cabinet. Though a cabinet council office may be impracticable at this time, in future it may not, and I may be better able to undertake one. Whether they will do all they can for us, I cannot tell: but their wants are so great, and will infallibly grow so fast upon them, that if God grants us all health, our poor, depressed, betrayed, persecuted band, will have its weight, if we keep our tempers, and hold employments, and act systematically, without haste and fluctuation to the great plain objects of public good: the present security and quiet of government and the maintenance of the future government under the Princess...[45]

Fox's motives and plans at the moment of Pelham's death were simpler but less well documented. His position had long been considered an index of Cumberland's power, and the Secretary at War had openly regarded himself as Pelham's heir-apparent. Fox had been spoken of as the obvious successor to Chesterfield as Secretary of State in 1748; Chesterfield himself had agreed.[46] Even Hardwicke, his enemy, thought of him as 'the first candidate at Court',[47] where he was known, too, to enjoy the favour of Princess Amelia.[48] Dodington recorded that Fox had 'declared that he would have it; that he had served up to it; and it was his due, and was resolved to give way to nobody'.[49] Yet Fox's advantages as a candidate for such a role were offset by his political mistakes in the previous few months. His support for Kildare's petition against Dorset's alleged mis-government in Ireland had not, as Hardwicke and Newcastle knew, endeared him to the King.[50] Pelham had urged Fox to moderation on the issue;[51] Newcastle was unconcerned to repair such errors, and his kinsman and associate Lord Barnard had recently spoken of his own and the ministers' 'detestation' of Fox.[52] Newcastle and Hardwicke must have been aware that Fox was trying to build up an interest in the Treasury; their preference was for Dupplin, rather than for his candidate Barrington, for the next vacant seat at that Board.[53] Lord Barnard recalled two more examples of Fox's 'perfidy' to Henry Pelham: that Fox 'set the King upon him to repeal the Place Bill, which Mr Pelham absolutely refused'; and on the recent attempt to repeal the oath in the Bribery Act, Fox broke his word to Pelham that he would not speak for repeal – on the orders, suggested Barnard, of Cumberland.[54] Thus it was that on Pelham's death the King was believed by some when reported to have declared that he had no favourite of his own,[55] though others still thought it possible that he would insist on Fox.[56]

HARDWICKE VERSUS FOX

There seems little reason to doubt that Newcastle was initially in-capacitated by grief, avoiding company other than that of close friends until he saw the King on 14 March. The initiative, for the moment, was in the hands of Hardwicke and Fox. Fox was known to have called on Hartington before eight on the morning of 6 March.[57] Through him, Fox signified to Hardwicke and Newcastle 'that he was very desirous of living well with them, and that he would act under them and concur in their measures, and desired their friendship'.[58] This must have been the substance of the three 'very humiliating and apologising messages' which Hardwicke claimed to have had from Fox that morning. Hardwicke probably exag-gerated their subservience deliberately,[59] and was later to denigrate Fox with the claim that he 'used, and wrote the most abject submissions, to get the seals'. Fox's version was that he 'only offered, as he really meant, to serve absolutely under the Duke of Newcastle and only required sufficient powers to be able to do it, in the House, without exposing himself'.[60]

The first few days were the most critical. 'It is feared lest the King should insist on Fox succeeding', wrote Dudley Ryder, 'and that the Chancellor will not continue if he does come in.'[61] Yet no such thing happened. George II, who had failed to advance Cumberland to a position of dominance during the Regency Bill affair of 1751, now omitted to promote Cumberland's protégé, Fox. Holdernesse saw the King on 6th, who declared 'that he had come to no resolution upon [Pelham's replacement]; but would previously receive the advice of his servants and take his future determination in consequence of that opinion'.[62] But when Hardwicke had an audience the same day, he reported George II slightly differently: that he had 'no favourite of his own'; asked 'that his servants and friends will take into consideration how to supply his [Pelham's] place in the manner the most satisfactory to the nation, and particularly the Whig Interest'; and ordered him to have Hartington write to call Devonshire to town.[63] This last was almost certainly the King's idea, and was not interpreted by Hardwicke as a move against Fox. Opinion from other quarters, however, was already crystallising against him. Murray was speaking of the possibility of the Chancellor's resigning if Fox were chosen, though by 9th a counter rumour was in circulation that Cumberland had threatened to resign from the army if Fox were not.[64] Lord Bath was said to have written to Hardwicke threatening to organise an opposition if Fox succeeded, and forecasting that Dodington and his following would join him in it. Pitt's letter of 7th was 'leaked' immediately on its arrival in London, and was represented as a threat by the Grenvilles to oppose *en bloc* if Fox had Pelham's place.[65] The Scotch were reported to be 'violent against' Fox; and though his camp thought the Whigs at large were not,[66] important figures were aligned against him.

So also was the whole of another party: 'even the Tories are sorry for [Henry Pelham]', wrote one observer, 'because they despair of getting a Minister of their own choosing, and Mr Pelham was they think the best they could have of another kind'.[67] The reaction of the Tory leaders was immediate. The same day, the Earl of Oxford met the Earl of Shaftesbury to discuss the course their party was to follow. Oxford, though standing well with the Jacobite zealots of his party, had not refused engagements with Whigs. He had been listed as a future Privy Seal in Prince Frederick's plan of April 1750,[68] and was active with Shaftesbury in the negotiations with Dodington aimed at the coalition of the Tories and Leicester House from 1749 until after the death of the Prince of Wales in 1751.[69] Shaftesbury, at least, had been favourably inclined towards the idea of 'separating the Tories from the Jacobites',[70] and on 22 March 1751 had been impressed by Dodington's warning of the potential power of the Bedfords with Cumberland at their head. Dodington had urged Shaftesbury

That being collected, and publicly purged from Jacobitism, they [the Tories] became a respectable body. That if they were applied to for assistance, they might then give it upon such conditions, and for such share of power as they thought safe and honourable for themselves, and their country: secondly, if they were not applied to, and the court took a right turn, they might, like honest and disinterested men, support it without coming into it. . .

Dodington had had no expectation that the Tories would feel attracted to that second option; yet such was to be the case, and his negotiation with them failed. The Earl of Westmorland and Sir Francis Dashwood, associates of Oxford and Shaftesbury, had been inclined, in February 1751, to join Pelham. But, as Dodington then realised, the Tories were not 'united enough, to make overtures as a party' to the ministry,[71] and no formal alliance materialised between 1751 and 1754. Nevertheless, it was known by that date that 'Oxford has long been making court to the Chancellor and if it was he that spoke on the side of the Marriage Bill (and not the Bishop of that name) t'was to get in with him'.[72] Now, Pelham's death greatly accentuated the threat of Fox and Cumberland. As a result of their meeting on 7 March, Shaftesbury and Oxford informed Newcastle via Halifax

That they were determined to support, by themselves and the friends they could have any influence over, his grace of Newcastle in whatever measures he should think proper to take on this unfortunate juncture for supplying the place of his deceased brother.[73]

Newcastle, however, regarded the choice of Pelham's successor as a matter not of discovering the ablest or most widely acceptable candidate but of managing the relations between the candidates' patrons.[74] In such a game, Whig integrity counted for far more than popularity. Less important again were the alliances, achieved or potential, between the contenders. Fox was known to have called at Pitt's town house on the morning of 6th;[75] presumably discovering the Paymaster's whereabouts and ill-health, Fox then ignored him – apparently to Pitt's surprise.[76] Pitt's relations with Fox, like Fox's with Bedford and Devonshire, and Legge's with anyone, were to play no important part in the negotiations of March.

As a temporary expedient, Lord Chief Justice Lee was sworn in as Chancellor, and his brother Sir George as Under Treasurer, of the Exchequer. Fox, after his frenzied and tactless activity on the morning of Pelham's death, 'acted reserve and retirement, and expected to be wooed'.[77] On the basis of his first canvas, he felt certain of Hartington's support, and confident of Grafton's.[78] Walpole claims, too, that Fox received a message from Murray renouncing all competition with him for Pelham's position and emphasising that his career lay in the law.[79] The leadership of the Commons seemed a prize well within Fox's reach.

Evidence for Newcastle's and Hardwicke's speculations on the rearrangement of offices, up to the point of Devonshire's arrival in town on the evening of 9th, is contained in Sir William Yonge's remarks to the Attorney General. He suggested that it had been under consideration to divide the offices of First Commissioner of the Treasury and Chancellor of the Exchequer, giving the first to a peer and the second (if he would accept it) to Fox on the understanding that he 'might probably have it to manage the House'. Yonge doubted whether Fox would accept less than Pelham had held. Hardwicke, Yonge observed, had already acted as if he, the Chancellor, would be First Minister;[80] Walpole confirms that both Hardwicke and Newcastle had been spoken of for Lord Treasurer[81] – a reversion to an earlier practice which would entail a substantial reduction in the status of a Chancellor of the Exchequer, no longer then himself a Commissioner of the Treasury. It seems probable that Yonge inferred from this that Devonshire had been sent for as a possible First Lord; and though the evidence does not bear out such a prior intention, Dupplin later admitted to Ryder[82] that Newcastle and his friends first pressed Hardwicke to accept the Treasury and, when he refused, offered it to Devonshire. Under this plan, the Chancellor of the Exchequer would 'do the business of the House of Commons', and Fox be given some other office. But Devonshire refused in turn.[83]

This scheme, then, rested on the exclusion of Fox from the Treasury. So did another alternative which Yonge reported had been tried and found impracticable before Devonshire's arrival: Sir George Lee, he claimed, had been sounded for the Treasury, if Fox could be prevented from having it. Whether or not the overture to Lee took place, it seems certain that after Devonshire's refusal, Granville called on Newcastle to urge him to take the Treasury himself as First Lord and promote Fox to a Secretaryship of State.[84] With a show of reluctance, Newcastle agreed. Such a plan had several advantages. First, Newcastle would inherit much of the good will felt towards his brother, and at the outset he made great play with being the executor of his brother's methods, principles and intentions. Second, the plan offered the prospect of frustrating Fox, just at the point where even well-informed opinion expected him to obtain the Treasury and Exchequer together.[85] Leicester House, as Dodington recorded,[86] elaborated that speculation:

the plan to disappoint him was, to refuse the Treasury, but to offer him something that was better than the War Office; which they hoped, and believed he would refuse; and then to incense the King against him, and show him, that Fox would take nothing that was compatible with the Duke of Newcastle remaining in power.

Fox's brother disbelieved in the existence of such a design,[87] however, and the actions of Newcastle and Hardwicke can be understood without postulating such a finesse. As Dupplin realised, they were well aware that Fox, through the Treasury, would exercise sufficient influence to command 'the House of Commons and everybody'; 'If he insists on coming in [in] Pelham's room, it can be for no other purpose but to have all power, by which he may remove the Duke of Newcastle and all his friends whenever [he] please[s].'[88] Waldegrave agreed: a man in such a position 'must, in effect, be first minister'.[89] No such expectation attached to a commoner in a Secretaryship of State, and Newcastle displayed no anxiety to exclude Fox from that office. Once he had decided on the move, he even sent Stone to reconcile the Princess of Wales to Fox's promotion, and obtained her civil assent.[90] What Newcastle *was* to do in the following week, as he realised the nature of Fox's ambitions, was to prevent his exercising those powers from the Secretaryship which properly belonged only to a commoner at the head of the Treasury.

On 10 March, Mrs Charlotte Digby had heard of two schemes: one, that Newcastle should head the Treasury and Fox be Secretary of State; the other, to make Fox

Chancellor of the Exchequer, and put some Lord at the head of the Treasury; his acceptance of this last will depend upon whether the power is to be lodged in the 1st Lord of the Treasury or in the Chancellor [of the Exchequer]. These are schemes talked of, but my brother[91] says there is no guessing at which will take place, as the King knows nothing of them yet, the Duke of Newcastle has not yet seen him, and till he does nothing can be proposed.[92]

On 10th, Ilchester heard a rumour that Newcastle was now considering taking the Treasury himself, persuaded by the advice of Argyll and other friends 'that whoever has the Treasury must have the power'. But on 11th, Ilchester found Fox perfectly satisfied: 'he finds there is no disposition to leave him dissatisfied, nothing will probably be settled till the latter end of the week, the Duke of Newcastle is not to see the King till Friday [15th]'.[93] Newcastle, too, had heard by some route that Fox was not initially enthusiastic at the lesser offer of a Secretaryship of State rather than the Treasury,[94] but Hartington, who presumably carried the proposal, reported on the afternoon of 11 March that 'everything goes well',[95] and Newcastle inferred that 'it seemed as if Fox would accept'. It was, indeed, a difficult offer to decline: a great gain in itself, to refuse it would be a blatant bid for absolute mastery.[96] But in the light of Ilchester's observations, it seems likely that Hartington greatly exaggerated Fox's willingness to comply.

It seems likely, too, that Newcastle prompted Murray to disavow any rivalry with Fox after his, Newcastle's, acceptance of the Treasury, and in order not to antagonise Fox, Newcastle's hoped-for subordinate, needlessly. But the Solicitor General had already been effectively ruled out as a competitor by the allegations levelled against him in the crisis over the education of the Prince of Wales in 1752–3. As Winchelsea now realised, Murray had been 'ruined by malice'.[97]

PITT, LYTTELTON AND HARDWICKE

Despite the implications of his letter to Temple of 7th, the Paymaster cannot have been aware of any attempts before that date to sound Sir George Lyttelton; but between then and 10th, Sir George evidently engaged in consultation on Pitt's behalf with Hardwicke.[98] It was these negotiations which Pitt's letter of 10th sought to guide. To reduce the risk of Sir George's error he enclosed a second letter, setting out his position, which was to be shown to Hardwicke.[99] In it, he hinted at the danger of Fox's advance and his reliance on Newcastle and Hardwicke to resist it. Modestly, he demurred to Hardwicke's suggestion that he might play a leading role: even were Pitt's health restored and were he to enjoy the King's favour, he would decline that undertaking. Without the second, he would have no power to support the role:

consideration and weight in the House of Commons arises generally but from one of two causes: the protection and countenance of the Crown, visibly manifested by marks of Royal Favour at Court; or from weight in the country, sometimes arising from opposition to the public measures. This latter sort of consideration it is a great satisfaction to me to reflect I parted with, as soon as I became convinced there might be danger to the [royal] family from pursuing opposition any further, and I need not say I have not had the honour to receive any of the former since I became the King's servant. In this humiliating and not exaggerated view of my situation within the House, of how little weight can I flatter myself to be there? And how vain would it be for me, were I in town, to assume anything like the lead, even though encouraged to it by as animating a consideration as my Lord Chancellor's protection, without the attribution of a weight, which does not belong to myself, and can arise to me only from marks of royal countenance towards me and my friends. Perhaps some of my friends may not labour under all the prejudices that I do. I have reason to believe they do not: in that case should Mr Fox be Chancellor of the Exchequer, Secretary at War is to be filled up.

Without naming Grenville, the meaning was clear. But Pitt did not convey his anger and resentment at what Hardwicke had said in his initial interview with Sir George Lyttelton: 'Nothing can be so glaring, as to say to you in one and the same breath, it was wished I was in town to take the lead, and to lay in a claim to plead the King's alienation of mind against me. Who could his lordship think he was talking to?'[100] Nevertheless, Pitt felt a genuine regard for the Chancellor, whose good offices were, at present, his only hope. Pitt's professions of weakness were at once a pacific gesture to the ministers (a suggestion that he might safely be employed as their tool) and a mark of despair of ever being employed in higher office. Yet, at the same time, Pitt's ambition had been stimulated by Fox's imminent advancement and by what he saw as the ministry's need of Commons figures.

It may be that Sir George Lyttelton's missing letter to Pitt conveyed his impression that Hardwicke earnestly desired the advancement of the Paymaster 'to keep down Fox...as soon as the obstacles in the Closet could be removed; but that was really a work of much more difficulty than Pitt's impatience would believe'.[101] But Pitt's impatience only became important later that year. In March, he consoled himself with the thought that if Fox could be tied down to even moderate gains, his own prospects in the medium term would be much improved. It seems likely, too, that Pitt's dream was for a Secretaryship of State as the unsolicited reward of merit. Although, therefore, he asked only minor offices for his connection, the success of that limited aim was not to shield him from a sense of failure and rejection.

HARDWICKE AND THE CABINET

Sir George Lyttelton, fearful of saying too much, delivered Pitt's letter to Hardwicke without comment.[102] By the afternoon of 11th, Newcastle was evidently willing[103] that George Grenville or Sir George should succeed Fox as Secretary at War; but this was not the result of a negotiation by Lyttelton. Pitt was held ineligible not, apparently, because Fox's post was beneath him but because of the King's aversion and because, in the Paymastership, he already held 'a better thing'. Legge, Newcastle intended, would then be made Chancellor of the Exchequer, not with the lead but 'to manage the money affairs in the House. He will not probably like it in [the] room of as good a thing with less trouble[104] but he must', recorded Ryder, 'be forced to accept it'.[105] George II must first be brought to agree. Here Hardwicke's part was critical. It seems likely that the King's initial intention had been that the Chancellor should merely sound and consult his colleagues on a desirable successor.[106] But on 11th, Newcastle spoke to Ryder as if the matter had been referred to the Cabinet: a step he, Newcastle, regretted. The *Public Advertiser* reported on 14 March that the King had appointed Newcastle First Lord of the Treasury *at* the Cabinet meeting on 12th, and Hardwicke later went further still, writing censoriously: 'to poll in a Cabinet Council for his [the King's] First Minister, which should only be decided in his Closet, I could by no means digest'.[107] It seems that Hardwicke first exaggerated the Cabinet's terms of reference, then used the constitutional impropriety of that task as an excuse for arranging, as far as possible, the outcome of the meeting in advance. In this he was doubly disingenuous, for in the event the Cabinet was presented with a scheme, already agreed to by the King, for its ratification; and Hardwicke later used his initial explanation, as set out in his letter to the Archbishop, to reassure Pitt that he, Hardwicke, had frustrated Fox's bid for office by the finesse of arranging the outcome over the Cabinet's head.[108]

This was the tactic he anticipated in writing to solicit from the Archbishop of Canterbury not his attendance, but a letter (whose precise phrasing Hardwicke suggested) recommending the Chancellor's plan. The King, Hardwicke wrote, had asked him to find the ablest man for the post, though he had hoped no-one would be recommended '"who has flown in his face." The meaning of this is plain, and I have seen Mr Fox through it, though his Majesty has never named him to me.' Fox, that is, had unfairly prejudiced the King against Pitt through Cumberland's weight in the Closet. Hardwicke admitted that he had corrected this and shown the King Fox's unpopularity. If, wrote Hardwicke, Fox

should succeed to the plenitude of power, which Mr Pelham had, there is an end of this administration, and of all that you and I wish well to in that respect. He would also, by his connection in a certain place, have another power added to it, which Mr Pelham had not for several years, the army. So here would be the *Treasury*, the *House of Commons*, and the *Sword* joined together.

Hardwicke claimed it as the opinion of his Cabinet colleagues as well as of himself that there was no MP 'fit to place entirely in Mr Pelham's situation, with safety to this administration and the Whig party'. Accordingly, 'they' had decided to recommend the King to select a Chancellor of the Exchequer from the Commons, and a peer to be head of the Treasury, 'as has been done in many instances'.[109] 'That peer must be somebody of great figure and credit in the nation, in whom the Whigs will have an entire confidence. He must be one, who will carry on the election of the next Parliament upon the same plan, on which Mr Pelham had settled it without deviation. This is at present the immediate fundamental point.' Devonshire having declined, the choice rested on Newcastle. Fox would then expect some promotion; and this was already, secretly, under negotiation. Hardwicke suggested that Holdernesse might take the Secretaryship of State for the Northern Department, and Fox succeed him in the Southern. 'If the power of the Treasury, the secret service and the House of Commons is once settled in safe hands, the office of Secretary of State of the Southern Province will carry very little efficient power along with it.'[110]

Until 12th, it was generally supposed that though a peer would have the Treasury, Fox would take the Exchequer.[111] Dodington records that the King's agreement was obtained on the night of 11th for Newcastle to have the Treasury, Legge the Exchequer and Fox a Secretaryship of State.[112] Though Hardwicke and others spoke as if the Cabinet had made an independent choice, the minute of the meeting[113] is explicit that the scheme was presented to it as the King's idea. Newcastle wrote to Hardwicke on the afternoon before it met to thank the Chancellor for having acted 'to determine the King in an affair of this importance',[114] and it seems that the plan was concerted behind the scenes between Hardwicke and George II. As Murray told Ryder on 14th, the

King, 'instead of taking the recommendation of the Cabinet Council – as he at first referred this to them – he himself ordered the Cabinet Council to give him their sentiments upon that plan and they unanimously approved of it'.[115] And as Bayntun Rolt discovered at Lord Granville's on 12th, the plan was 'ready for the King's fiat'.[116] Fox knew on 12th what had been agreed: that he would be 'at the head of the House of Commons'; and that Legge would rank second at the Treasury Board. Fox looked on his office as settled, and seemed satisfied – especially as it offered a prospect of excluding Egmont, whom he and the Whigs detested.[117] The Archbishop wrote as directed,[118] and the scheme was 'declared', as Dodington put it, to the Cabinet which met at Powis House, the Chancellor's town residence, at 7 p.m. on Tuesday 12 March. The meeting confirmed that the scheme was 'the best adapted to support the system of his affairs upon the same foot, on which they have been carried on for several years with great success'.[119] Hardwicke delivered this minute to the King the next day, 13th;[120] it endorsed the appointment of Newcastle to the Treasury, Legge to the Exchequer, Holdernesse to Newcastle's Secretaryship and Fox as Secretary of State for the Southern Department.

FOX'S REACTIONS, AND THE TERMS OF HIS
APPOINTMENT

Fox had not met Newcastle before the Cabinet meeting on 12th;[121] Hartington had acted as intermediary. On the morning of 13th Dodington heard via Ellis from Fox that he was to have the 'absolute direction' of the Commons, 'but under the Duke of Newcastle and as his man, who was to remain in full power: with the whole confidence, and secret of the King'.[122] Newcastle's account[123] was that he had been pleased to receive 'a very civil message' to himself and Hardwicke from Fox 'signifying that he was very willing to act under them in the Treasury'; another from Cumberland 'something [to the] same effect'; and a message through Hartington which occasioned a negotiation via the Marquis 'in which the Duke thought of nothing but remitting Fox into the Treasury but upon the foot of certain limitations which were to be thought of'. Newcastle was then persuaded to change his plan; to head the Treasury himself and promote Fox to a Secretaryship of State – a position about the powers of which Newcastle was, it seems, silent. But Newcastle named Legge, at the Exchequer, as the man 'to do the business of the Treasury for him in the House of Commons and on whom he should depend as one in whom the Whigs had always the greatest reliance, and one [on] whose capacity he could depend to lay before the House everything necessary'.[124]

By contrast Fox's version[125] was that

my lord Hartington brought Mr Fox word that [Newcastle] relied upon him to manage the King's affairs in the House of Commons, and that whatever was done with the secret service money in that business was to be communicated to him, and that he was to have the disposal of some of the places to put it in his power to manage the House of Commons. Upon these terms Mr Fox sent word that he would accept of, or rather that he acquiesced in the proposal of making him Secretary of State, though he did not much like it.

And on 16th Ryder recorded a rumour that 'the terms are that he [Fox] should have the conduct and management of the House of Commons and be answerable for them; and as a consequence have the disposition of places in the gift of the Treasury in order to enable him to influence the members and also the gentry concerned in the management of the elections for next Parliament. And Fox insists this was the agreement and that Lord Hartington would vouch for it.'[126] Ryder learnt Hartington's version on 23rd: that Fox had asked him to let Newcastle know that he 'had hopes of being admitted to [the] House of Pelham, that he would be willing to act with and under' Newcastle and Hardwicke; and that he was sorry for his stand against the Chancellor's Marriage Act. Newcastle, reported Hartington, had welcomed this advance; especially since Cumberland approved of Fox's playing such a part. By this stage intending Fox for the Secretaryship, Newcastle declared himself willing to entrust him with the 'management' of the Commons; that Fox 'should have all powers necessary for that purpose, and mentioned his participating [in] the secret service money for that purpose, as well as have his recommendations as to places and participate also in settling the boroughs'.[127] So, at least, Hartington was saying by 23rd; but his recollection is in doubt, for by then the crisis of Fox's withdrawal and the stark alternative between Newcastle's and Hartington's version of events had led the Marquis to give Newcastle's suggestions a clarity and cohesion which they had not possessed at the time. Exactly what terms Fox supposed were agreed on, before the Cabinet meeting on 12 March, is not certain. Probably Hartington's friendship and ambitions led him to overstate the concessions to Fox; and it was Hartington's accuracy as an intermediary as much as Newcastle's good faith which was in question. Evidence does not exist with which to evaluate the Marquis's role, but there are indications that it was *Fox* who exaggerated the advantages of an indistinctly outlined position, whether from fear or ambition; and that his subsequent talk of Newcastle's duplicity is intelligible as an excuse, not a motive, for a step which he, Fox, later came to look on as a mistake.

Fox was, seemingly, initially satisfied with the result of the Cabinet meeting on 12th; his slight apprehension was only at his capacity for a Secretaryship of State, for he had no experience of the predominantly diplomatic business of that office.[128] That it was Fox who developed unfounded doubts about the genuineness of the terms on offer rather than Newcastle who modified them is suggested by two letters which

Fox then received. One, from Horace Walpole,[129] stressed the duplicity of Newcastle's character; predicted that Newcastle sought to betray Fox as soon as he had detached him from his connections; and advised him to decline the Secretaryship. But of crucial importance was a reply by Hanbury Williams to Fox's message via Henry Digby on the result of the Cabinet meeting.[130] Arriving at midnight on 12th, the letter destroyed Fox's composure and left him, in his wife's words, 'perplexed and disturbed'.[131] Hanbury Williams argued that the scheme, *contrary to Fox's expectations*, involved someone else's being put over his head in the Commons. As Secretary of State, Fox would seldom speak there, and would have nothing to do with financial matters. 'The connection of the manager of the House of Commons is so interwoven with all Treasury and Revenue business, that I don't comprehend how they can be separated.' Newcastle could not deal with MPs; moreover, he was incapable of doing the technical business of the Treasury. Someone else must: 'whoever is known to do the business, will directly or indirectly have a great share of that power that 'tis necessary to have to govern and oblige the House of Commons with'. Such power would not, Hanbury Williams implied, be put into Fox's hands. 'Is Mr Legge to manage the whole revenue and money affairs in the House of Commons? If he is, he is the head of the House of Commons, and you are not. If he is not, he is a fool for changing his present employment.' Men would be found for Secretary at War and Treasurer of the Navy, he warned, in no connection with Fox; 'so that neither your support in the House nor out of the House will be such as the *Leader of it* can depend upon for assistance and protection'. Fox should, at least, thrash out with Newcastle the exact terms of his position; should 'settle the meaning of the words, *First Person in and leader of* the House of Commons'; and, if Secretary of State, should insist on the Northern Province (the senior post) as 'a kind of touch stone as to the confidence they profess reposing in you'.[132] That suspicion, at least, had already been justified.

The following morning, 13th, Hartington took Fox to a meeting of reconciliation with Hardwicke, which passed civilly enough, and then on to Newcastle. Sir George Lyttelton was rumoured to be destined for Treasurer of the Navy and George Grenville for Secretary at War;[133] but the ministers were already aware of 'some demur' through Cumberland's objecting to the latter appointment,[134] and it may have been this that gave rise to a speculation that the diplomat Joseph Yorke would take that office and Grenville, the Treasurership of the Navy.[135] Now, on the morning of 13th, Newcastle found (as he told Ryder and Legge on 15th) that Fox, as Hanbury Williams had suggested, insisted on spelling out the terms in three respects:[136]

that as it was declared to Lord Hartington that Fox was to be Secretary of State and have the management of affairs in the House of Commons he must have that power without which he could not answer for the House, viz. the care of the Secret Service money, the disposition of places in grant of the Treasury, the settlement of the Members of Parliament for the next general election.

As to the first, he soon gave up that when the Duke told him it was impossible that more than one should have that confidence.

As to the second, the Duke said he never meant to give up that power which properly belonged to his office, nor was it necessary to any service Fox was to do in the House, which was to represent all affairs within his competence to the House, which would naturally lead him to be the head of the House of Commons. That he should always receive his recommendations with great regard and superior to any other, but could be under no obligations of that kind beforehand. To this Fox seemed to acquiesce.

As to [the] third, the Duke represented that there had been a plan settled by his brother which appeared in his own hand and which he desired and intended should be pursued. To which Fox said that might be proper but there must be some places not quite fixed, others might want varying, and he thought it reasonable he should be privy to the filling them up. This however he in some degree yielded.

Fox's account of the interview[137] confirms Ryder's; but, as well as being more derogatory in tone to Newcastle, it passes over the extent to which Fox apparently agreed to Newcastle's interpretation. Only afterwards, it seems, and in consultation with Hartington, did Fox turn his fears that Newcastle *would* behave treacherously into a claim that he *had* so behaved. Thereby, Fox's error in refusing promotion could be explained away. Ministerialists, however, imagined that a negotiation was still in progress, not that a definite offer had been made and accepted, and that it failed because Newcastle and Fox could never *reach* agreement on terms.[138] Dodington wrote that 'they parted dissatisfied', but, significantly, left the reason ambiguous: whether because it 'was not meant' that Fox should have the 'absolute direction' of the House, or because he 'was not to be trusted with sufficient powers to execute it properly'.[139] Hardwicke always spoke as if the ministry had been willing to offer Fox a viable role, 'but he threw it away';[140] though the stage which the negotiation with Fox had reached by 13 March is in doubt, there is no evidence for the ministers' having set a 'trap' for him.[141] Horace Walpole's less than adequate explanation was that 'Fox felt he was bubbled[142] – yet was irresolute. He seemed unaccountably to have lost the spirit which the Duke seemed as unaccountably to have acquired.'[143] Yet others, on Fox's behalf, were less uncertain. Though there is no record of his saying so at their meeting on the morning of 13th, Hartington was later convinced that Newcastle had altered the terms of the bargain and supposed that others – he named Stone and Murray – had persuaded Newcastle to retract what he had said out of apprehension for their own power.[144] Hartington put this to the Chancellor later on 13th, who promised to see Newcastle the next day. But Newcastle sent for Hartington later that night; Walpole, repeating the Hartington–Fox account, described Newcastle as 'not repentant;

he was not apt to repent of advantageous treachery. He would not deny the breach of his engagements, but honestly declared he would not stand to them. Lord Hartington, as if avowal of treachery repaired it, expressed no resentment. His impartiality was ludicrous...'[145] More probably, however, it suggests that Hartington was not then aware (and only later was persuaded) that a firm commitment existed on Newcastle's side, to abandon which would be an issue of honour. In any case, Cumberland, by chance detained in town due to Princess Amelia's illness, advised Fox against accepting on terms thus defined.[146] Ilchester suggested he was motivated by personal resentment that Newcastle treated coldly his offers of rapprochement.[47] Hartington called on Fox that evening, after seeing Newcastle, as Ilchester put it: 'not to explain off the morning conversation but rather to confirm it'.[148] A sense that all was not well was felt in political circles; Fox was still thought willing to succeed to Pelham's role, but the odds at White's were no longer so heavily in his favour.[149]

Fox, late on 13th, was at a loss what to do. A group of his friends at supper that night failed to give a clear lead.[150] To Walpole he wrote promising that 'you will not see me united' with Newcastle, but inconsistently excusing himself – 'I do not know how I could avoid accepting...'[151] By the following day, however, his mind was made up. Just before his first audience since Pelham's death,[152] Newcastle received a letter in which Fox asked that the King should not be told that he had accepted the Secretaryship. Such a promotion, Fox insisted, must mean that the King intended 'that I should with and under your Grace have the management of his affairs in the House of Commons. This was the whole tenor of your Grace's messages by Lord Hartington, which your Grace's conference with Lord Hartington and me yesterday morning and with Lord Hartington last night have totally contradicted.' Unable therefore to answer for the King's affairs in the House, Fox promised his loyal support from the Secretaryship at War.[153] Newcastle interpreted this, probably correctly, as a bid for the management of the Commons and the disposition of the secret service money;[154] one MP, in the House on 14th, formed the same impression.[155] Chesterfield, too, assumed at once that Fox, 'animated with revenge', had designs on the Exchequer, the Treasury, the management of the elections and of the House.[156] And Fox was wrong in claiming, even if he believed, that the position of a subordinate Commons manager (without the disposition of places or secret service money) was untenable, for both he and Robinson later filled it with success. Nor did Pitt suppose that patronage was a key consideration; rather, he drew Newcastle's attention to the other elements which made up 'leadership' in the Commons. Once numbers had been assured in the elections of April, place, profit and the prospect of either were not – it will be shown below – crucial determinants of individual allegiance in the ongoing life of the House. It was other assets – in particular, ministerial and party unity – the lack of which Newcastle was to feel most.

Fox, therefore, had to cast about to justify his action. That justification was far from obvious, even to his closest associates. On 14 March, Harry Digby wrote his brother a letter explaining Fox's conduct;[157] Fox, then entering the room, corrected his friend's text. Digby wrote:

The Duke of Newcastle has since seen my Lord Hartington, and [flatly denies every] (without denying one) word of the messages he sent by his lordship to Mr Fox [, and his](. His) Grace (however) declares that he does not intend Mr Fox should have any power whatever out of his own office. My lord Hartington is, as you may imagine, extremely angry at the Duke of Newcastle for [denying] (going contrary to) all he had before said to him, and declares that he never will have anything more to say to his Grace.

Mr Fox has this morning wrote to the Duke of Newcastle to tell him that he accepted the post of Secretary of State upon the terms that his Grace at first proposed through my lord Hartington. But since his Grace denies the [having offered any such terms] (very terms he owns he offered), he begs if his Grace has not yet told His Majesty that he accepted of that post, that he would not tell him so . . .

On one hand, then, Fox argued that Newcastle, despite his offer to Hartington to the contrary, now intended that he, Fox, should have no power whatever 'out of his own office', the Secretaryship. It would be foolish, therefore, to accept on terms so limited: 'no direction or lead in the House of Commons, nor . . . any hopes of confidence or favour from [Newcastle] (for I never desired to go to the King or to anybody but to his Grace) sufficient to do his business'.[158] It was, presumably, such arguments that he urged on Lady Yarmouth on 14th.[159] Yet secondly, to others, Fox admitted to a political error but excused it on grounds of honour. To the suggestion that he ought to have accepted the Secretaryship on the terms offered, waiting for further opportunities and using the position gained to advance his power,[160] Fox objected that it amounted to a betrayal of trust – 'making use of the favour you receive against those who confer it. *What can't be done with honour can't be done at all.*' Still less would he go into opposition, which was 'unjustifiable' on grounds of 'private anger'.[161] Thirdly, he began to sow suspicions of the influence of Stone and Murray, resentful as he claimed they were at Newcastle's rapprochement with Cumberland.[162] Newcastle was at particular pains to deny this. He never, he claimed, intended to remove Murray from his profession into a Secretaryship; even when Hardwicke had been intended for the Treasury, Newcastle spoke of Murray as the next Chancellor.[163] Lord Barnard, too, had dismissed the idea when it had been raised on 7 March.[164] In general, Fox's campaign of self-justification seems to have been successful. 'He is commended by many', wrote Ilchester, 'but none of those many are persons who understand politics or the present situation of the court.'[165]

Fox's letter was officially delivered to the King by Hardwicke at mid-day on 14th.[166] As Newcastle told Ryder and Legge on 15th, George II objected that Fox

complains he cannot be answerable for the House of Commons, but he the King never meant he should but to be on the same foot with Craggs and other Secretaries of State in the House of Commons when the principal had been a peer, and if he did not like it he had another to put in his place. And spoke with great kindness and affection to [the] Duke of Newcastle for old and faithful services, his confidence in him which he intended to continue in him and not in Fox. And as to the Secret Service money that must be between him and the Duke of Newcastle and could not nor ought to be communicated to more. And as to places he thought there was no ground for the Duke to quit that power, and particularly advised the Duke never to make promises before-hand.[167]

The King's own idea (as Hardwicke emphasised) was that Sir Thomas Robinson should have the Secretaryship if Fox continued to refuse it.[168] The dispute now became overtly one on the constitutional precedents for that role. Ellis was spreading Fox's account of the offer as he under-stood it,

adding that as a proof of what Mr Fox meant, he instanced Mr Craggs being Lord Sunderland's man, when he had the Treasury, and was in full power, with the late King. And also that he [Fox] had declared to the Duke of Newcastle that he never desired to touch a penny of the Secret Service money, or know the disposition of it, farther than as it was necessary to enable him to speak to the Members without appearing ridiculous.[169]

The political problems raised by Pelham's death were acute not least because constitutional precedents offered no clear guide to their solution. As Mann wrote from Florence, 'I don't understand how the Duke of Newcastle can be at the head of the Treasury without being alone and with the title of Lord Treasurer. We here suppose this will be the case soon – but...I perceive that there is no rule to guide one's suppositions by...'[170] It was generally thought that only a peer would command sufficient status to inherit the vacated Secretaryship of State,[171] and rumours were current in the press that Newcastle's standing would further entail his holding the office of Lord Treasurer.[172] Even after the settlement of a Commission, it was thought possible that Newcastle would go on to supersede it and take the Lord Treasurer's staff, since 'the title of First Commissioner is not equal to his importance'.[173] Mann, like most others, assumed at first that one individual would take over Pelham's position entire, and that the problem was the absence of candi-dates 'in whom the necessary qualifications unite'.[174] Walpole, similarly, spoke as if the long tenure of Sir Robert Walpole and Henry Pelham, and the consequent pre-eminence of the Commons (rather than a constitutional principle or the current abilities of its leading members) led men to expect Pelham's successor to be chosen from that House.[175] If no single man were held able enough to combine the Exchequer and the Treasury, the situation was fluid. Walpole, Pitt, Chesterfield and (one suspects) many others did not expect Newcastle to emerge as the victor;[176] but it does not seem that men supposed it to be a constitutional maxim that the leader of the Commons had to be Prime Minister and hold the offices of First Lord of the Treasury and Chancellor of the Exchequer. No objections were raised to Newcastle's promotion on those grounds either by the public in March or by the House itself in November; Pitt was soon to endorse systems in which, firstly, Devonshire's tenure of the Treasury implied only nominal leadership of the Ministry; and, secondly, in which he, Pitt, would be supposed to lead the wartime ministry from a Secretaryship of State. If, then, Pelham's offices were to be divided, Fox's standing allowed two alternatives: for him to take either the Exchequer or a Secretaryship of State under a peer at the Treasury.[177]

Devonshire, Newcastle and Grafton stood first in status among the politically active Whig peers.[178] But since each was capable of being a real, not merely a nominal, leader of the ministry, the position of a commoner in partnership with one of them was problematic. The status of the Chancellor of the Exchequer, too, was undefined. The Treasury had been in commission for only just over half the period between the Restoration and the Hanoverian accession; from 1702 to 1714, the ministry had been dominated by Lord Treasurers – Godolphin, Oxford, Shrewsbury – whose Chancellors of the Exchequer had carried little weight (except when Harley held the office, and the Treasury was in commission, for a few months in 1710–11). Since 1714 the Treasury had been permanently in commission and the post of First Commissioner usually held by a commoner;[179] but Walpole had dominated it, in his two periods of office (1715–17 and 1721–42), occupying also the Chancellorship of the Exchequer. Indeed, since 1721 the First Commissioner had always held the Exchequer with the exception of Sandys' brief tenure of the second post from February 1742 to December 1743. It might credibly have been regarded as an incidental office, contingent on the First Lord's dominance in the same way that the post of Under Treasurer of the Exchequer had come to be held automatically by the Chancellor of the Exchequer himself.[180] Thus, similarly, among the most recent plans for Pelham's replacement – those for the accession of Prince Frederick – Lord Egmont (as an Irish peer able to sit in the Commons) was to be both First Lord of the Treasury and Chancellor of the Exchequer.[181] A recent scholar was inferring a precedent rather than observing one in arguing that from 1710 'it was the custom for the Chancellor to occupy the second place in the Treasury commission when the First Lord was in the House of Lords',[182] for in 1754 that situation had arisen only once since 1721. Any such expectation was probably, in large part, a reflection of the personal standing of the men who had held the Exchequer. This need not have lessened Legge's chagrin when in 1754–5 he found himself ranking third in the Treasury commission behind Darlington, the first peer since the Revolution to take a minor seat at the Board when the First Lord also sat in the upper House.

The position of Fox as a Secretary of State was even more open to doubt. The structure of central government itself was not static, but reflected both the reassignment of business among the departments and the actions of politicians willing to debauch forms and institutions in the pursuit of ambition. The different Secretaryships of State were, strictly, fragments of a single office: 'all Secretaries are competent to discharge the same functions...The division of duties between the Secretaries is purely a matter of convenience and is regulated by the King's pleasure, which need not be expressed in any formal manner'.[183] In the eighteenth century, this flexibility was a practical fact as well as a constitutional tenet. Fox was later to demand that the Secretaryship at War be advanced to rank as a third Secretaryship of State, and Halifax to make the same claim for the Presidency of the Board of Trade. A Secretary of State for Scotland had existed at various times from 1709 until its business was merged with that of Newcastle's office in 1746; from 1768 to 1782 there was to be a Secretary of State for the Colonies; and a third Secretaryship for War and the Colonies was to be created in 1794. In 1782, the business of the two Secretaries was divided between them on a domestic/foreign basis. Before that, their sharing of responsibility, amounting to a partnership, has given rise to the claim that it was 'a well established custom that when one of the Secretaries was exceptionally prominent, his colleague should be an administrator rather than a politician'.[184] But the Northern Department was generally regarded as of higher status, and the Pelhams' exclusion of Bedford from the ministry in 1751 was interpreted, further, as a 'design to curtail the Southern Province'.[185]

No commoner had held a Secretaryship of State, and never had the Commons been led by a man in that office,[186] since Craggs (from March 1718 to March 1721); and George II was fully aware of the great honour which the offer of it in 1754 conferred on Fox.[187] The Exchequer had been held in 1718–21 by John Aislabie; neither he nor Craggs apparently carried much weight against the First Lord of the Treasury, the Earl of Sunderland. Now, however, memories were dim enough for both the King and Fox to point to this same example in support of their contrary views. But although an argument from precedent carried some weight, it seemed clear that personal standing would determine precedence among the two Secretaries and the First Commissioner of the Treasury. Indeed, the Exchequer might be added to that list, for in the majority of the ministerial plans of Prince

Frederick's opposition, Sir George Lee is assigned the Exchequer and Egmont a Secretaryship of State in what is obviously a shared leadership, under the nominal authority of the Earl of Carlisle at the Treasury.[188]

NEWCASTLE'S ALTERNATIVE SYSTEM

Fox was not due to have an audience until the morning of Saturday, 16 March; before then, the final outcome could not be known.[189] Newcastle meanwhile made every effort to reach agreement. A meeting was arranged on 15th between Fox, Hartington, Holdernesse and Hardwicke. According to the last, Fox finally insisted on having the conduct of the Commons, being answerable for affairs there, and having the disposition of places in the Treasury's gift in order to manage the coming elections. As Hardwicke told Ryder on 16th, Hartington 'in part vouches for this intent and what the Duke of Newcastle told him'.[190] Ilchester admitted that Hardwicke had civilly and sincerely tried to persuade Fox to accept, and treated this interview as his brother's last chance to do so. Newcastle's claims, Ilchester thought, were 'in words endeavoured to be softened to [Fox], and the word management explained but never explained so as to mean the management of the House of Commons'.[191] Newcastle professed himself willing to do much to conciliate Fox; but the obstacle was the King.[192] Fox discovered the truth of this only in his audience on 16th. George II, he wrote,[193]

was possessed of two things: the first, that I had insisted on the government and secret service money of the House of Commons, independent of the Duke of Newcastle. 'You would be above everybody, above the whole Council', says he. Stop here, my dear Lord, and think of the shameless want of veracity in the man we have to deal with.

I endeavoured, appealing to your lordship, to undeceive H.M.

The other thing was, that I ought to be responsible for nobody. Lord Sunderland, he said, placed little or no confidence in Craggs; and in short avowed in the most restrained sense, what he proved to be the Duke of Newcastle's intention, contrary to his promise.

I showed him, in this way, how dangerous a man I must be if Secretary of State, and begged him to judge of my intention to act like an honest man and do no mischief, by not taking into my hands so great an engine to do mischief with, as taking, with my weight (for I spoke freely and not modestly) in the House of Commons, the office of Secretary of State without being responsible to the Minister...My declining was accepted, and I was dismissed rather graciously than otherwise, still Secretary at War.

Fox, coming out of the Closet, appeared 'extremely confounded' and pretended to the Chancellor that the King had not mentioned the matter. But George II left Newcastle and Hardwicke in no doubt about the principles on which he supported their system, telling them 'that he never understood or meant that Fox should have any of the power of the Treasury or be concerned in the election, and that he meant nothing but that he should be Secretary of State in the House of Commons as other Secretaries of State commoner have been and acted where the Treasurer or First Commissioner was a peer'.[194] The same day, it was known that Legge was destined for the Exchequer,[195] and Newcastle plainly saw him standing in the same subservient relation to himself as had Dupplin to Henry Pelham.[196] Legge had not risen by ruthless ambition; describing himself as 'the most errant *fortunae filius* that ever lived', and claiming that 'the death of Mr Pelham has sucked me into this whirlpool', he wrote: 'All I have now to do is to look out for the first favourable opportunity of making my retreat'.[197]

Without holding the Lord Treasurership, therefore, Newcastle was in almost as strong a position as if he had. Horace Walpole wrote flippantly that Newcastle, freed from the 'clog' of his brother's timidity, 'has declared himself sole Minister, and the K[ing] has kissed his hand upon it'.[198] Already, it was to Newcastle, not to Hardwicke, that application for place was made by such men as Charles Townshend, Barrington and Bath.[199] On 13th, Newcastle had Dupplin obtain from West a list of Henry Pelham's election arrangements,[200] and on 15th, Newcastle, Dupplin and Roberts worked through a similar list of constituencies and candidates.[201] The following day began Newcastle's long series of daily memoranda on election business, in which the state of the campaign was set out in the fullest detail.[202] From 15th, it seems, Newcastle assumed the mantle of leadership. His doing so, from the start, embraced a paradox. Hugely successful in the pursuit of power, eager for public business, he nevertheless came to office in a mood of modesty and diffidence. In the technical manoeuvres of his succession, he was aware of his debt to Hardwicke – who, he supposed, had 'placed' him in the Treasury.[203] Moreover, Newcastle realised his inexperience in the technical business of his new office; his career, long and creditable as he knew it to be, had been taken up with the largely diplomatic concerns of a Secretaryship of State.[204] He accepted office now only reluctantly; not until pressed to do so by personal friends (Granville, Hardwicke, Lincoln, Argyll); and from a sense of duty, a determination to preserve his brother's system. Not least did this involve an attitude towards Europe: a dependence on the Austrian alliance, the Barrier, and treaties with minor German states as the only counterpoise to French power.[205] The appointment of Sir Thomas Robinson and Holdernesse as Secretaries of State confirmed this, and revealed 'the King's intention of leaving the greatest share of his confidence in the Old Channel, and by this means the foreign system will be supported upon right principles with consistency and dignity'.[206] Others shared Newcastle's wishes, and looked to him for a similar reassurance. The Archbishop of Canterbury advised that the best way of securing the plans for the elections 'will be to let the world see, that His Majesty will as much as possible keep steadily to his old administration'.[207] Hardwicke wrote that, during the negotiation, 'My great objects were to support the system, of which Mr Pelham had been, in a great measure, at the head; by that means to preserve and cement the Whig Party; and to secure the election of a new Parliament upon the plan he had left...'[208] Joseph Yorke recommended the transfer of Newcastle to the Treasury, since 'I see nothing else that can keep the Old Corps together, or prevent the arts of faction from undermining the present system of government'.[209] The satisfaction of such men was increased by the reflection that Fox's camp had shown its hand by 'an ill judged demand of extraordinary powers'[210] – 'to be Prime Minister' as Joseph Yorke put it[211] – and had been frustrated.[212]

It was, therefore, not surprising that a final overture from Fox's quarter was rebuffed. On 19th, Newcastle had a visit from Legge bearing Hartington's suggestion that Newcastle had spoken so 'reasonably' to the Marquis on 16th that he, Hartington, thought Fox should accept without conditions. Newcastle was delighted at this mark of victory but determined to stonewall by professing obedience to the King's commands. George II had already spoken to him of his decision to give the vacant Secretaryship to Sir Thomas Robinson,[213] and Newcastle (who thoroughly approved) told Legge.[214] Though mildly apprehensive that Devonshire lay behind this new initiative, Newcastle was aware that the matter would be closed if Holdernesse saw the King first the following day and formally concluded Robinson's promotion.[215] That autumn, the King was to surprise Newcastle by claiming that Robinson had been first proposed by Hardwicke and agreed to by him as the man *he* had already thought of.[216] Hardwicke did not directly challenge this, but added:[217]

There are some, who will say that I threw out to the King a person, to whom I knew he had an inclination, on purpose to defeat Mr Fox; your Grace knows that was not the case, and that no hint was given of Sir Thomas Robinson until after Mr Fox had refused, and the King had put a negative upon Mr Pitt.

The implication is that some hint *was* given, and that Robinson was installed by a ministerial finesse; but this was far short of a conspiracy to subordinate the Commons to the Lords. Nor could a final offer from Fox have been foreseen before 19th. Yet the effect of Robinson's installation was to be exactly such a frustration of Fox's last overture. Even this, however, was seen as a real and vital battle, not as a foregone conclusion; and it was only after Legge's visit on 19th that Newcastle felt able to move on to consolidate his position. A Treasury Board had been gazetted on 18th, obviously a holding measure, which omitted Lord Chief Justice Lee (the temporary Chancellor of the Exchequer) and retained the four former members: Sir George Lyttelton, John Campbell, George Grenville and Lord Barnard, with Newcastle as First Lord. Once Fox's defeat became plain, Newcastle was to remake the Board in his own image. The final version was gazetted on 6 April. John Campbell, a close friend of

Fox, was bought off and his place given to Lord Dupplin. Sir George Lyttelton and George Grenville were removed to the offices of Treasurer of the Navy and Cofferer respectively. Nugent and Legge replaced them on the Board – the one loudly adulatory of Newcastle, the other still apparently reliable.[218] Legge, indeed, was one of few of Fox's friends who judged him to have acted unwisely.[219] George Grenville recorded that his promotion and Lyttelton's were 'notified to us' only a day or two before they were carried out, and were not the subject of negotiation with the ministry.[220] Murray's promotion came unexpectedly: on the sudden death of Lord Chief Justice Lee, Sir Dudley Ryder was advanced to that post and Murray succeeded as Attorney General.[221] Sir Richard Lloyd was made Solicitor General later in April.[222]

Legge was not optimistic of the result of his final overture;[223] sent to see Hardwicke, he found him (having been briefed) advancing the same line as Newcastle. After the King had approved a scheme so laboriously arrived at, the Chancellor maintained, it would not be 'dutiful or decent' to throw it open once more to negotiation. Hardwicke, too, was delighted: Fox had put himself in the wrong in the eyes both of the public and – more important – of the King. 'It is not our business', he told Newcastle, 'to help them out of this difficulty.' Fox had chosen his course of action with deliberation, and had deliberately misrepresented Newcastle's position to George II. As it was, Newcastle had captured the sympathy of 'all those who are *not strictly our friends*, but wish better to us than they do to Mr F's clique': those sympathisers, and the Princess of Wales, would resent any weakening towards the Secretary at War. Later, of course, the King might 'do what he pleases upon a proper submission'.[224] 'So has this great affair', wrote Ilchester, 'passed away as a dream.'[225]

By late March, it was clear that the favourite had not only been 'dished', but left in a position little stronger than Pitt's. Fox had committed 'the greatest act of folly in the world';[226] as he realised, 'as great a mistake as ever was made by man'.[227] Moreover, with the choosing of a new parliament in their hands, Fox thought the new ministers fully able to sustain themselves: 'to let you know what I think of it, I think they may go on very well, I never imagined otherwise: opposition does not arise from one man however great, and were an opposition ever so powerful to arise, I would not join it, no not in points where I might in opinion agree with it'.[228] Fox was bitterly unhappy, crushed by his defeat; and, to his wife's dismay, began to drink heavily. Once the immediate prospect of negotiation had passed, self-pity became his dominant emotion: he excused Newcastle for the mishap – a 'little difficulty which might have been got over with a small degree of temper and dexterity' – and blamed himself and his friends.[229] Even after two years of (for Fox) political advance, Lady Caroline could remark that her husband had not recovered that good humour and equanimity which he enjoyed before Henry Pelham's death.[230] In the summer of 1754, however, pity qualified the resentment which his family might otherwise have felt. His brother thought no point of honour would have been raised by Fox's acceptance, and that he had, strangely, allowed a prize to 'slip through his fingers merely upon punctilio'.[231] Cumberland and Lady Yarmouth, more tough mindedly but less accurately, supported Fox's refusal of office;[232] but Fox merely blamed those, especially Hanbury Williams, Ilchester and Cumberland, who had influenced him to refuse.[233] Ilchester wrote: 'I begin to perceive that [Fox] has been misled in this affair by His Royal Highness the Duke [of Cumberland] who finding his offer of reconciliation to the Duke of Newcastle but coldly received was a good deal heated and being so encouraged my brother in that unhappy way of resolving.'[234] Without grounds of hope, Fox remained politically quiescent until the ministry again chose to sound his disposition in July.

Pitt waited at Bath in a mood of dutiful expectancy, impatient for news which was not to come.[235] Sir George Lyttelton asked both Newcastle and Hardwicke to write to the Paymaster with an explanation of the situation. To the Chancellor he was weakly deferential: 'I hear from good hands that Mr Fox says he wishes to serve with, and *under*, Mr Pitt. I wish to have Mr Pitt serve with, and under, your lordship.'[236] Yet, in fact, neither Pitt nor Lyttelton saw how to derive advantage from Fox's defeat, and it is not clear that Sir George ever treated with the ministers for Pitt's promotion in office. Newcastle's exchanges with the Paymaster explore, rather, the issues of Pitt's disappointment and its consolation. If, as Horace Walpole claims, Lyttelton 'undertook to be factor for his friends' and, unauthorised, gave Pitt's assent to the new system,[237] he can have done so only in general terms, quickly drowned by Pitt's own loyal effusions. Not only did Pitt stand forth as a reliable subordinate; he encouraged Newcastle in exactly that element in his position which was central to his victory over Fox. To hold the powers of the Treasury during a general election might allow Newcastle to 'lay the foundation of the future political system so fast as not to be shaken hereafter'. Pitt, instead, appealed to Newcastle's soft-heartedness, representing in affecting terms the growing load of his public humiliation at the sight of others being so often offered office over his head: Fox, then Legge for the Exchequer; Fox, then Robinson for a Secretaryship. Pitt admitted the ability of both the successful men, but pointed to his own claims: his experience of Parliament; his zealous defence of the Pelhams' measures, especially 'on the points that laboured the most, those of military discipline and of foreign affairs; nor have I differed on any whatever, but the too small number of seamen one year, which was admitted to be such the next. And on a crying complaint against General Anstruther'. But such merits could do nothing in face of an 'indelible negative', the King's personal aversion. Though Pitt professed an 'unshaken purpose, to do nothing on any provocations, to disturb the quiet of the King, and the ease and stability of present and future government', he warned that he could not take an active part in the Commons 'in my degraded situation', and doubted his ability to retain the Paymastership 'without losing myself in the opinion of the world...If anything can colour with any air of decency such an acquiescence, it can only be the consideration given to my friends, and some degree of softening obtained in His Majesty's mind towards me.' Pelham, Pitt reminded Newcastle, had intended Sir George Lyttelton to be Cofferer when that office fell vacant. George Grenville, Pitt suggested, might be Treasurer of the Navy. 'Weighed in the fair scale of usefulness to the King's business in Parliament, there can be no competitors that deserve to stand in their way.'[238]

Pitt's reactions offer a good guide to his political talents. An orator and a parliamentarian rather than a politician, he appealed as the first to be taken seriously as the second without, in the spring and summer of 1754, establishing his claims to be respected as the third. But the tactical superiority of Newcastle, as able a politician as was consistent with the lack of oratorical gifts, was apparent. He had needed to do almost nothing to frustrate Pitt's ambition; even Fox had left Pitt out of account, whether as a potential ally, rival, counterpoise or common threat, when urging on the ministry his own claims to office. Devonshire had favoured Pitt's inclusion in the ministry; his later opinion of its impracticability[239] is probably a reflection of the plausibility in hindsight of Newcastle's reasons for not doing so. But in March 1754 Devonshire was left unconsulted, and Sir George Lyttelton apparently neglected those few possibilities of a negotiated advance which did exist. As George Grenville recorded,

Sir George Lyttelton had pressed Lord Temple, with whom he then lived in friendship, to know what he desired; but Lord Temple declining to give any answer, Sir George Lyttelton informed the Duke of Newcastle that he was satisfied his view was the Garter, and therefore no offer was made to him.[240]

Pitt was unaware of Newcastle's prior decision to give office to just those of his following whom he, Pitt, recommended. In any event, it hardly mattered. He remained convinced, as his friends knew, of the necessity of retaining office in the prevailing uncertainty – a conviction which was to sustain them until their dismissal in November 1755. Pitt's intention was later to seem similar to the plan which Fox (disingenuously, and in retrospect) had disavowed: to stay in, holding the highest office available, in order to profit from the best chance that arose. But the Paymaster was led to it, in contrast, through an appreciation of the unacceptability of the alternative:[241]

merely quitting is annihilation: quitting to disturb government, and make ourselves be felt, must at this time, be faction: and faction for others' benefit, not our own. It must increase the present confusion, and produce a system I never think right for this country. Were this conduct sure to turn to our own benefit in the scramble, I can never bring my mind to engage in faction, in so dangerous a public conjuncture...[242]

With such a show of propriety was weakness rationalised.

Dodington and the Princess of Wales found themselves in positions similar to those of Pitt and Fox. Dodington first explored the possibility of urging on the Princess that his 'first engagements were to her, and her House'; but she expected Fox to emerge as the victorious candidate, and was unwilling herself to take any active part to secure a greater influence in the administration. 'She replied, "What could she do? To get things in the hands of certain people, was as impossible as to move St James's House, and for anything else, what did it signify? Besides, she supposed they knew where Leicester House stood: it was open." '[243] Dodington then directed his efforts, instead, at Newcastle; but here he was at a disadvantage. Electoral arrangements had already been made with Henry Pelham, in return for which the latter was, Dodington claimed, to 'remove the personal misrepresentations that I lay under with the King, at a proper time, and to bring me into the service, in a proper manner'. Dodington stressed that he meant to perform his undertakings, whatever the return; without insisting on a particular office, he drew Newcastle on to talk of the state of vacancies and applications and hinted at what would be agreeable: Robinson's old place, or the Treasurership of the Navy.[244] But, unable with honour and propriety to name an office specifically or to make his exercise of electoral patronage on behalf of the government a quid pro quo, Dodington had no other course when he discovered that all eligible employments had been filled than to continue to remind Newcastle of his claims on office and to insist, with an ineffectual menace, that he was 'determined to make some sort of figure in life'.[245]

Sir George Lyttelton called to present Newcastle with Pitt's letter on 26 March;[246] not until 2 April did Newcastle reply. He insisted, above all, on his regard and affection for the Paymaster. Though sympathising, he pointed out that Pitt's situation was not as bad as it might have been; that of his friends, better than could have been expected. Newcastle had obtained the posts of Treasurer of the Navy and Cofferer for George Grenville and Sir George Lyttelton, to their complete satisfaction,[247] as a mark (Newcastle claimed) of regard for Pitt. Legge, too, was known to enjoy the friendship of Pitt's connection as well as the good opinion of the Old Corps; but Pitt's stature made it unthinkable for him to hold the Exchequer alone with another man at the Treasury. Fox's promotion to a Secretaryship, wrote Newcastle, was 'a plan...made with a view to make my going to the head of the Treasury the more palatable to those, who might be supposed to be the least pleased with it'; that having failed, the King himself named Robinson. This, Newcastle represented as a choice inoffensive to Pitt: Robinson was honourable, able, and loyal; but lacked 'those parliamentary talents, which could give jealousy, or in that light set him above the rest of the King's servants' in the Commons. Newcastle hinted at a long-standing desire to promote Pitt to that office, as having 'all the necessary qualifications both within and out of the House', and claimed to have equally long regretted that the King's aversion prevented it. That aversion could not be surmounted, but its consequences had been softened by the promotion of Pitt's friends. Newcastle promised his efforts to obtain 'an alteration of manner, and behaviour' in the King, and thought events had given a good prospect of it: 'I hope some prejudices, which I have long lamented, will be got over, when the King sees, and feels the good effects of his having got them over to a certain degree.' But more could not have been attempted now without the risk of throwing everything into the hands of 'those who wish us ill'.[248] Sir George Lyttelton had been persuaded of the truth of this by Charles Yorke:[249] that an attempt to force Pitt on the King would only have driven George II into the arms of Fox – 'who, with a very considerable number of the Whigs, was ready to support him against such a compulsion, and might probably have made his party good: Mr Pitt's popularity not being yet acquired'. Hardwicke was sure, and Lyttelton had been convinced, that the King could have been brought to give Pitt a Secretaryship by the end of the year, had the Paymaster acted in a proper manner in the meanwhile.[250]

It is not clear, however, that any such specific promise was ever made to Pitt. Hardwicke wrote, by the same post as Newcastle, rather to congratulate him that things were no worse. Fox's triumph had been only narrowly averted, but Hardwicke had persuaded the King of the necessity of able spokesmen in the Commons and disposed him in favour of Grenville's and Lyttelton's appointments. Pitt had not been neglected; Newcastle and the Chancellor had done everything possible to make an impression on George II. The two offices proved that a limited success had been gained. 'I agree that this falls short of the mark,' continued Hardwicke, 'but it gives encouragement. It is more than *a colour for acquiescence* in the eyes of the world; it is a demonstration of fact', and a warrant for Pitt's taking an active part in the Commons. Most significant was Hardwicke's practical advice, for since it rested on an assumption of Pitt's future loyalty, Hardwicke was unknowingly pointing out a strategy for undermining Newcastle: 'there are certain things, which ministers cannot do directly...in political arrangements, prudence often dictates to submit to the *minus malum*, and to leave it to time and incidents, and perhaps to ill-judging opponents, to help forward the rest'. One such incident had already happened, in Fox's refusal of the Seals; Pitt might reasonably wait, trusting to the friendship of Hardwicke and Newcastle.[251]

For one reason, Pitt could do little else until the election, since he relied on Newcastle for a seat at Aldborough.[252] He took Newcastle's letter as sufficiently sincere,[253] however, to cast his reply[254] in a tone of injured reproach. Had Fox been placed at the head of the Commons, or if Murray could have been, it would have been justified by their ability and he, Pitt claimed, would willingly have served under them. Nor was he too proud to accept the Exchequer if Newcastle held the Treasury: Pitt's health prevented his holding the post, but his honour would have been saved if the King could have been brought to agree to its being offered, and he would then have yielded place to Legge. But his health, he argued, did not disqualify him from a Secretaryship; he was barred from promotion by 'the suffrage of the Party' and by the King's apparently irremovable personal negative. Though resolved to defend government, he was therefore disabled from being of use to it. Nothing remained but 'a retreat'; and he asked Newcastle to find him such an office. Least hopeful of all was Pitt's reaction to George Grenville's and Sir George Lyttelton's new offices, which he treated as a valuable reinforcement for Newcastle rather than an obligation on himself or a mark of a softening of George II's attitude. Nor did Pitt treat it as such in his franker, more personal reply to Hardwicke.[255] There, what he wished to be thought his private motives were more clearly revealed, for Pitt's regard for the Chancellor, Fox's enemy, was warm.[256] Pitt did not reproach Hardwicke that more might have been done; instead, he took George II's refusal, despite 'such an urgent want of subjects to carry on the King's business in Parliament' as evidence that his objection was irremovable and probably reinforced by Pitt's present failure. Only the King's death could break such a stalemate: there was no point in hoping to draw advantage from any more minor political accident. Pitt had served for ten years on the basis of such a hope; it was now exhausted.

I am come finally to feel all ardour for public business extinguished, as well as to find myself deprived of all consideration by which alone I could have been of any use. For indeed my lord I am persuaded, I can be of no material use under such circumstances, nor have I the heat or the presumption to attempt an active, much less a leading part in Parliament. The weight of irremovable royal displeasure is a load too great to move under: it must crush any man who is firmly resolved never to move to the disturbance of Government; it has sunk and exanimated me. I succumb under it...

Both publicly and privately, Pitt repeated his desire for 'a retreat', an office of honour rather than of business, in return for a passive support of government. 'I am willing to sit there', he wrote, 'and ready to be called out, into action, when the Duke of Newcastle's personal interests might require it; or Government should deign to employ me, as an instrument.'[257] Though still ambitious for George Grenville when, at some future date, men's standing in the Commons would again command promotion,[258] Pitt himself was sunk in despondency and inertia, seeing no way to break out of a hopeless position.[259] 'I consider my political life', he wrote to Newcastle, 'as some way or other drawing to a conclusion, or rather as arrived at its period.' He lingered in Bath, 'not in a haste to see London, as a scene that administers no kind of satisfaction'.[260] How far Newcastle and Hardwicke took Pitt at his word is unknown. They may have agreed with his estimate of the end of his political career; they may, as is most likely, have looked on the royal negative as a valid exercise of a prerogative which they could not challenge even had they wished. If any of Pitt's professions were to be believed, that of offering no opposition to government was most welcome; and, until the un- certainties of the session began to approach in the autumn, there is no indication that the ministers took the trouble either to sound Pitt's future intentions in detail, or to seek to find for him that 'retreat' which – it is just possible – really would have been the price of his withdrawal from active politics. Newcastle's victory in March made it far less necessary for him to look to the Grenvilles as allies against Cumberland. Indeed, it was Fox himself whom Newcastle was later to feel able to recruit, on strictly limited terms.

FURTHER DEVELOPMENTS AND THE ELECTIONS

Within a month of Newcastle's promotion, it is possible to trace the first occurrence of those accusations, made in and about the particular events of March and April, which were later to be held to discredit his conduct of affairs as a whole: treacherous manoeuvre, arrogant high- handedness, and a design to manage the Commons from the Lords. But these charges took their rise from a more prosaic, and more fortuitous, combination of the immediate circumstances: in chronological order, Fox's ill-advised refusal of promotion and the excuses which followed; an unpleasant episode concerning the disposition of the Privy Seal; and the equivocal relationship between Dupplin and Legge in the face of an imminent general election.

The Privy Seal fell vacant when, as Newcastle supposed, Lord Gower asked to resign it from ill health. Newcastle quickly obtained the King's consent for Marlborough to succeed, and Rutland to follow Marlborough as Lord Steward; and told both Dukes of their promotion.[261] Newcastle was allegedly under pressure from the Manners family to prefer Rutland on pain of their opposition, and Walpole thought Gower had been pushed into a resignation, 'the first sacrifice to the spirit of the new administra- tion'.[262] But Gower then denied he *had* resigned; his wife was reported 'ready to tear out anybody's eyes that says he has',[263] and exchanged accusations of lying with the Chancellor.[264] Newcastle was upset by such acrimony, but worried mostly by the possibility that it would damage his standing with the King.[265] Gower appealed to George II,[266] and although the King's confidence was fully with his ministers, Gower remained in office until his death on 25 December that year.

Thomas Hay, Viscount Dupplin, owed his immediate importance not to his seat at the Treasury Board, but to his being the man best informed on Henry Pelham's detailed intentions for the general election. He and John Roberts, Pelham's secretary, were involved in consultations from the outset, and Dupplin had acted as Newcastle's aide-de-camp in the days immediately after 6 March.[267] To Henry Digby, it seemed as if Dupplin and Newcastle were managing the elections between them.[268] But Newcastle had always looked on Dupplin as an able and loyal subordinate, not as a politician of independent standing;[269] it was the immediate prominence of election business which gave his position a different appearance at large. 'Henry Legge is to be Chancellor of the Exchequer,' wrote Walpole, 'but the declared favour rests on Lord Dupplin.'[270] Others agreed: 'By all accounts Lord Dupplin is a man of great consideration on this occasion; Mr Pelham it appears paid a great regard to his judgement, and the Duke of Newcastle now no less.'[271] Lord Cathcart saw the importance of the prominence of election business in writing: 'I don't exactly know what business goes properly through the hands of Mr Legge as Chancellor of the Exchequer, but the acting man in the Treasury and person upon whom the election plan and every-thing relating to it seems to turn is Lord Dupplin.'[272] Legge could hardly be expected to accept with equanimity the transfer of the political function of the Exchequer, and had no reason to think it only a temporary expedient. Waldegrave recorded that Newcastle chose Legge 'thinking him a quiet man who understood the business of his office, and having been accustomed to act in a subordinate station, would do whatever he was directed'.[273] Moreover, the new Commission of the Treasury, dated 6 April, ranked him third behind the newly created Earl of Darlington.[274] Fox's camp already knew that it was not affection for Newcastle which drew Legge to accept and hold office, but a belief that Fox had acted wrongly;[275] Walpole added that Legge had accepted unwillingly.[276] Although Newcastle was correct in his estimate of Legge's political weight – Legge failed, in the next three years, to establish his independence or stature as a figure of the first rank – his inferior status at the outset focussed dissatisfaction by highlighting the constitutional issues raised by a ministry led actively as well as nominally from the House of Lords.[277] Here, too, the existing precedents offered little guide to the extent of Newcastle's legitimate interference. But he supposed, correctly, that the constitutional issues would be overlaid by, and made to serve, the political purposes of those who might seek to topple his government next session. To Dodington, Newcastle remarked 'that by a strange fatality the direction of the House of Commons was fallen upon him, who had never thought of it; and he must expect that the great attempt would be, to show that he could not do it'. This, he claimed, must govern his choice of ministers there;[278] but he apparently gave little thought to the problem of the nature of their leadership beyond expecting them to do the business of their offices and present the House with any necessary information.[279] No provision was made, in the spring of 1754, for an Old Corps group leader on the floor of the House. Such circumstances gave all too much credibility to a contemporary myth established also in the historiography of the period and summarised by the editor of Waldegrave's *Memoirs*:[280] that Newcastle, at or soon after Pelham's death,

seems to have entertained the project of engrossing all ministerial power entirely to himself. With this view, he intended to admit no leading member of the House of Commons into the cabinet, or at least to entrust none there with the secrets of his government. He thought to elude all opposition by keeping the two most formidable men in that House, Mr Pitt and Mr Fox, in subordinate offices, and inspiring each other with jealousy and apprehensions of the other's approaching advancement. But they were too sagacious to become the dupes of such an artifice; and partly from resentment, partly from a principle of attachment to that assembly to which they owed their importance,

joined in the 'imperfect concert' of their parliamentary opposition of that autumn. This was to be the fiction elaborated to excuse the action of Legge, Pitt and Fox in seeking, that summer, for a way to oppose Newcastle; and, in time, the myth that Newcastle sought to subordinate the Commons to the Lords[281] became in Fox's hands the key claim identifying 'the system begun at Mr Pelham's death' and accounting for its impracticability.[282]

This was not obviously the case in early 1754. Then, two things pointed the way in the search for such a justification: predictions that the system of March–April 1754 was only a temporary one, designed to conduct and survive the elections; and speculation on the nature of the opposition that might be encountered in the next session of Parliament. Such forecasts were linked by a common uncertainty about some of the basic guidelines in politics. People's anticipations of the form which opposition might take were some guide to their notions of the nature of 'party', for the previous three years at Westminster had been held to be marked by its conspicuous quiescence.[283] Although traditional party identities were often vivid at a local level, their existence did not of itself fuel a party contest in most constituencies; Horace Walpole even wrote of the famous Oxfordshire contest as 'a *revival* of downright Whiggism and Jacobitism; two liveries that have been lately worn indiscriminately by all factions'.[284] Although it was clear also what was meant by the two party labels in Parliament, it was not obvious that ideological differences there were of a kind which could be expected automatically to give rise to a 'formed' Tory campaign of opposition in the ensuing session, or to inhibit the emergence of a Whig opposition. Yet, though the future conduct of Whigs and Tories was in doubt, and the relevance and accuracy of their party identities therefore vulnerable in the vicissitudes of manoeuvre, those parties were intact, not fragmented. It was not apparent that, in Pitt's phrase, there existed 'particular subdivisions' within the Whigs in which he might enlist. Newcastle, like Pitt,[285] still saw political identities in Whig–Tory terms alone and – though he considered that problems of ministerial stability could be expected to arise *within* the Whig party – he did not hypothesise on how this might come about. 'The great point will be to keep our friends together, and that they should do right, when they are chose; for from the enemy we have nothing to fear.'[286] Though Fox was publicly known to have 'no exception' to Newcastle, his antagonism towards the Chancellor was public and bitter. This, rather than accurate knowledge of the existence of a Cumberland faction, gave rise to another forecast:[287] the

elections...go so much in favour of the Court that there will probably be a very strong opposition in the House of Commons...never was there a time when such immense sums were expended to get into Parliament as the present, and there are not in the kingdom ten oppositions upon the old principles of Court and Country.[288] All oppositions almost now arise between those of the same party who will expect to be indemnified by places, but where those places are to be had that will satisfy all is to me a mystery. Thus the disappointed will certainly list under the Duke of Cumberland's banner, who, it is plain, by Mr Fox refusing to be Secretary of State, intends to oppose the present administration.

Hanbury Williams predicted that an opposition would be provoked by Newcastle's personality: 'his disagreeable manner, his affronting vivacity, his captiousness, his jealousy, his intriguing genius, and the very little knowledge he has of the world and mankind';[289] but was not a dispassionate estimate. Chesterfield, on the contrary, thought the problems would arise from Fox's spirit of revenge.[290] Pitt, unconsciously anticipating the line he was later to pursue, hinted to Newcastle at the prime importance of the arrangements to be made between Commons leaders: 'Indeed my lord the inside of the House must be considered in other respects beside merely numbers, or the reins of government will soon slip or be wrested out of any minister's hands.'[291] Newcastle imagined, however, that this was precisely the problem he had dealt with by the distribution of office among 'the most efficient men' in that House.[292]

The Princess of Wales, Cresset and Dodington shared this estimate of Newcastle's aims, but condemned their application. Dodington claimed that Newcastle 'had the ball at his foot when his brother died, and might have made a lasting and advantageous settlement for himself, and the country, but had not endeavoured to oblige one efficient man, besides his known enemies'. Cresset agreed: such a use of favours was wasted.[293] But an assessment of the efficacy of Newcastle's new system was delayed both by the immediate business of the elections and by an expectation of rearrangements after them. Chesterfield had looked on the ministerial scheme including Fox as Secretary of State more as a temporary expedient with a view to managing the elections than as a permanent administration.[294] The second scheme carried no greater air of permanence, not least because Sir Thomas Robinson was rumoured to have accepted office unwillingly and with a promise that he might soon stand down.[295] On his kissing hands, one observer recorded: 'they say it will be only *pro tempore* – Everybody says things will be overhauled before [the] next Parliament meets. . .'[296]

Walpole predicted, on the basis of most of the election results, that 'the new Parliament. . .will not probably degenerate from the complaisance of its predecessor'.[297] How widely this confidence was shared is difficult to know. Whatever the expectation at large, in one way the elections made a reshuffle of posts less likely, for the ministry scored what was regarded as a major success. Newcastle reckoned his losses at 29, his gains at 33.[298] One list [299] gives the figures Pro 366, Con 164, Doubtful 26: a majority of 202 over Cons, and of 176 over Cons and Doubtfuls combined. A full list exists of the 26;[300] of the 164, 106 are identified as Tories,[301] but only 42 of the remaining opposition Whigs are named (including ten followers of Bedford, three of Lord Gower, and three of Sandwich; Lord Egmont; but not Sir George Lee). Another list[302] gives For 365, Against 152, Doubtful 35; and a few seats still remained in doubt through petitions and double returns. But the scale of the Whig preponderance was not in question: 'Mr Stone's and Mr Roberts' calculation. Majority 189. In all events 140'.[303] Previously, Newcastle had imputed 'a great part' of the King's kindness to him 'to the exigencies of the times';[304] Hardwicke had thought George II's support cautious and provisional, waiting for some evidence of the ministers' success.[305] Now, the Chancellor found the King 'in the highest glee and satisfaction about the elections'. Hardwicke persuaded him both of the importance of Newcastle's labours and that the success was a mark of national confidence in the administration as settled.[306] From this point, the ministers assumed they were in possession of the King's confidence;[307] if others, later, were thought to be making ground in the Closet, it was to be resented as a threat to a security there which the ministers had already won. And on 2 July, the King on his own initiative granted Newcastle a supplementary salary of £4200 p.a. out of the secret service fund, so making the Treasury almost equal in value to a Secretaryship of State.[308]

THE FIRST DISTURBANCES, AND LAST OVERTURES TO FOX, MAY–AUGUST 1754

The first hint of disturbance was given by Legge. From 31 May to 5 June, the new Parliament met to insure against the provision of the Regency Act that the last Parliament to sit in George II's lifetime should be recalled on his death. Legge presided at the Cockpit meeting at which the King's speech was read to the ministerialists. Walpole records that, by it, 'The little man lost his temperance of spirit, and began to deceive himself into an opinion of being a Minister: the Duke of Newcastle, as severe a monitor to Ministers of their nothingness as the most moral preacher, and more efficacious, soon shuffled him out of his dream of grandeur...'[309] But Walpole confused this with the issue of Legge's rank at the Treasury Board. There, he recorded, Newcastle gave papers across Legge for Dupplin to read, and sent Dupplin to conduct financial business for the government in the City. Neither of those things need have been remarkable in itself, and it is difficult to establish whether Legge's resentment did not spring rather from his ambition or his groundless assumption of provocation; it would, however, be wrong to see him as the innocent victim of Newcastle's mistreatment. Legge's inordinate ambition and persistent insubordination were to become clear only later, but Winchelsea was to pronounce in retrospect: 'He had more masters than any man in England and never left one with a character'.[310] From the beginning, he incurred the King's distrust.[311] The circumstances of his undertaking the task of addressing the Cockpit meeting are unclear, but suggest that he was not offered it without some misgivings on Newcastle's part.[312] It may not therefore be coincidental that Legge had just received financial independence (to Pitt's satisfaction[313]) through a legacy of over £40,000 on 25 March,[314] nor that he employed a well-worn excuse: 'Legge gave an artful turn to his disgust, and vaunted to the Whigs that his want of favour was owing to his refusal of acting in concert with Stone and Murray'[315] – precisely the same malign but secret influence that Pitt was hinting at rather than accuse Newcastle of 'insincerity intentionable'.[316]

The reversal of Pitt's favourable disposition towards Murray of March suggests his new opinion as a tactic. Other circumstances support this view. It became known, perhaps by the Paymaster's telling Fox, that 'the Chancellor, ever since Pitt's return [to town] had falsely boasted to him of having proposed him [Pitt] for Secretary of State'.[317] This too was a tactic, for though the evidence that Newcastle or Hardwicke had *openly* urged the King to accept him in that office is slight,[318] Pitt had also professed himself genuinely convinced of their disposition to help him and cannot have failed to see in their letters and conversation a suggestion that a Secretaryship of State might eventually be open. Then, too, Pitt was reported to have told Newcastle (what he had before written, though with a different intention) that Fox should have been at the head of the Commons. Now, that remark was an indication not of Pitt's private despondency about Fox's prospects, for those prospects had disintegrated, but was instead an early move in an incipient alliance between the Paymaster and the Secretary at War which the second could now be expected not to dominate. Consequently, 'Their mutual discontents soon led Pitt and Fox to an explanation on their situation, and on all who had endeavoured to inspire them with jealousy. Pitt complained most of Mr Pelham, who, he said, he had always deprecated, but always fomented their variance.'[319]

The date of any such understanding is unknown. It seems likely that, at the outset, it was a gradual establishing of sympathy rather than a specific agreement on a future course of action. Dodington was aware, as he told Newcastle in late June, only that 'those in considerable places differed amongst themselves and almost all disowned immediate dependence, obligation, and allegiance to the Duke – and they might, on such an occasion, perplex, and form followings, without being seen to do it, etc.'. The Grenvilles had already offered to support Dodington in a petition at Bridgwater, and he believed Fox would not back Egmont there against him.[320] Dodington's source on the leaders' dispositions had been Hillsborough, a friend of both Pitt and Fox. 'Everybody of consequence was dissatisfied', he had reported. Dodington (who, still without a place, like all 'outs' would have it thought that office bought loyalty) replied: 'I said I could not conceive that, as they had just had everything divided amongst them'. Hillsborough pointed out that Pitt's 'passion' was not money – 'it was ambition, power, of which he had no share; this made him very uneasy, which was highly increased by the late promotions', especially of Fox, 'his most inveterate enemy'. Both Pitt and Fox had, therefore, much to dissimulate before a rapprochement could seem credible. For the rest, Pitt was evidently making public his arguments to Newcastle and Hardwicke of 4 April. Legge, Hillsborough reported, had accepted the Exchequer unwillingly, though

when he was put there, he thought that he should be supported: he expected to be at least as well with the Duke of Newcastle as anybody, though he was to act an under part; but he found himself, instead of better, not so well with him as the rest of his colleagues; that he knew nothing of what was doing, or to be done, and was not considered at all, in anything. That George Grenville was in the same way of thinking, and expected very different treatment, consideration, and communication, from his rank in the House of Commons. Besides if he had less reason to be displeased, nothing would make him easy while his great friend Pitt was dissatisfied.

Fox continued to complain of Newcastle's withdrawal of his offer of a Secretaryship together with 'proper powers to be at the head of the House of Commons'; but despite Newcastle's distrust, Hillsborough believed, Fox would 'meddle very little' and by giving no offence, offer Newcastle no opportunity to turn him out.[321]

Such was not, however, Newcastle's intention. On 5 June, the day Parliament broke up, Hardwicke had a conversation with Devonshire. On 29 August, Fox told Stone what he understood to have been said:

Mr Fox asserts, that my lord Chancellor said to the Duke of Devonshire, 'Does your Grace know Mr Fox's way of thinking or his disposition?' [Devonshire:] 'No, my lord, I have not seen Mr Fox some time; but my lord Hartington would be the proper person to know it by.' Which enquiry my Lord Chancellor seemed to encourage. The Duke of Devonshire then suggested the idea of the Cabinet Council (without Mr Fox's knowledge as he says). To which my Lord Chancellor replied, that he should have no objection to it, though at the same time stated objections which might arise, but promised to have it in his thoughts, whilst he was at Wimple, where he was going the next day, and would communicate it to the Duke of Newcastle. And then my Lord Chancellor said that, if there was the same disposition on all sides, *he* should hope that, in the course of the summer, something might be struck out to make Mr Fox easy, or to make things easy.[322]

Fox was convinced that this was a positive overture on Hardwicke's part; the ministers were not. Hardwicke's fourth son, John, wrote: 'It seems by his present behaviour as if [Fox] hoped to bring about, by soothing and flattery, what he has found impracticable, by intrigue and violence.'[323] Not until 9 July was the exchange followed up. On that day, Stone (on whose initiative is uncertain) had a three-hour conversation with Fox about the events of March. Stone claimed that he urged Newcastle to a reconciliation; succeeded in persuading Fox that he, Stone, was at least 'neither friend nor foe'; but left Fox with the impression that his ill fortune in March was owing to the influence of Newcastle's confidant Lord Lincoln. Referring to the Hardwicke–Devonshire interview, Fox wrote: 'As to what has passed lately, if he knows it, as I suppose he must, he did not however touch upon it, and I dare say he does not think I am even privy to it'.[324] Accordingly, he gave nothing away which might suggest to Stone that he was; but, instead, waited in expectation of some overture from Newcastle. Already, the latter had noted, in a memorandum of 'Business with the Attorney General', 'Mr Fox to be called to the Cabinet Council'.[325] Stone, too, in his interview with Fox, had carried professions of friendship from Murray. It is not unlikely that Newcastle was prompted by concern for the Attorney General's newly apparent low morale and his exposed position in the Commons; but it is clear that Newcastle already sought the active support in that House of one of the major alienated figures. His anxiety must have been increased by the disposition of Dodington, who was still receiving with scepticism Dupplin's assurances of Newcastle's intention to include him in 'his connection' and remove the royal proscription. Then, Dupplin promised, he 'could have the pleasure of communicating everything he knew and heard, with me confidentially, and should look upon me, and himself, and the Attorney and Stone (*who was by* when he talked to the Duke) as one person'.[326] But on 18 July, Newcastle was forced to admit that he had made no impression on the King, and that despite Dodington's efforts and financial sacrifices in the elections, George II 'would not receive me to any mark of his favour'. The following day, Dodington declared – significantly, to Murray – 'that I looked upon myself as free of all engagements, after such a return, and expected to have no hints thrown out of breach of faith, etc., whatsoever party I might take'.[327] More important than his disaffection, however, was the implication that there now *was* some other group for him to associate with.

Dodington's attitude was apparently unconcerted with Legge's. But Newcastle was soon given reason to fear that Legge's was linked to Fox's – dangerously, and in a way that might close to the ministry one avenue of advance. Newcastle had a visit from Legge on the morning of 18 July; they spoke of the Commons, of Pitt and Fox. 'As to the first he talked plainly enough, and well', Newcastle thought; 'as to the *latter* very dryly, and not very intelligibly'. But Legge had taken to speaking of Whiggery in general terms – 'that is, he dropped, that the Whigs had no reason to be displeased with *Pitt*'. Only after Legge's departure did Newcastle learn that someone had been using the most serious of all slurs in talking of the 'absurdity' of a Tory head (meaning Murray) to a Whig body (the ministerial party in the Commons). This was a serious danger. As Pitt had realised much earlier, Pelham's death left Murray, even without the lead, as 'in effect, the great strength of [the ministerial system] in Parliament'.[328] Angrily, Newcastle asked Hardwicke, whom Legge was to see that evening, to demand an explanation, 'for if Mr Legge does not satisfy me upon this most infamous calumny upon me, I will join Mr Fox, rather than have anything to do with Mr Legge'[329] – whose conduct he threatened to lay before the King.[330] Reflection must have shown Newcastle that though Legge had set out to create trouble before his interview on 18th, he had done so, too, before Dodington's new disposition was known and, probably, without the state of Fox's negotiation being public. But the following year was to be characterised not by Patriot opposition in the 1730s sense among the Whig *frondeurs*, but rather by their attempts to reassert a language of Whig and Tory and by the ministry's denials, for tactical reasons, of the continued significance of party labels. Those attempts were not generated by the course of business in the Commons in the session of 1754–5, despite the *causes célèbres* which occurred there; their significance was that they offered a prospect of co-operation in opposition of Pitt, the Grenvilles, Fox, and Legge. Newcastle's problem, which it was not yet possible to anticipate, would be not merely one of selecting a recruit from among the disaffected, but of detaching men from an alliance aimed at his, Newcastle's, removal.

Although Newcastle had not yet formed a view of affairs in which Legge and Fox were mutually exclusive choices, a sounding of the second had already been taken. Stone had another three-hour meeting with Fox on 17 July and for the first time Newcastle's adviser raised the subject of the Chancellor's interview with Devonshire on 5 June. But Stone argued that little could be inferred from it: Newcastle had not known in advance, for the initiative had been taken by Devonshire, not Hardwicke. Nevertheless, Stone urged, the ministry would be happy to *receive* an overture: 'That is,' inferred Fox, 'the Duke of Newcastle and he etc. wish it, but the Lord Chancellor and H.M. will only wish it, or perhaps only consent to it, on its coming to them prepared by, and as from, the Duke of Devonshire'. Furthermore, Fox thought that Stone hoped that Hartington would be invited by Hardwicke to submit some such proposal,[331] and a visit by the Marquis to the Chancellor was soon arranged. Hartington thought, though he knew Fox doubted, that Stone genuinely sought to make up the quarrel.[332] This offered some hope of a negotiated settlement, for both Fox and the King felt that a gesture of submission must come first from the other side. Fox therefore advised Hartington what to say:

As HRHss [Cumberland], your father and your lordship all agree that some apprehension brought it on, it may not be amiss to say you wish it to keep me from opposition, which, let me intend what I will, my temper, out of humour with persons as I must be, will, you may say you know, carry me into. And when once in, I own I cannot stop. I think there can be no harm in saying, that this, if nothing is done, will have made it worse...

If Hartington were asked to enter into terms, he should say no more than that he would acquaint Devonshire and Fox; that Fox would insist on nothing more than Devonshire and Hartington thought reasonable; 'and that you will not be unreasonable, or aim at anything for me that can create any future discourse about confidence and power'.[333] This was precisely what Fox was eventually to receive: a position about the status of which there *could* be continuing disagreement. His briefing of Hartington, too, highlights the reason for the long delay of any ministerial offer. Though Fox relied on the weight the Devonshires' advice would carry, he was quite unable to use the existence of any personal alliance as a threat. Newcastle's fears, awakened by Legge's visit on 18 July, were probably therefore allayed (though temporarily) by Hartington's innocuous interview with Hardwicke,[334] and Hardwicke's reproof of Legge;[335] for there is no evidence that Newcastle, despite the King's excellent disposition[336] towards him, protested to George II about Legge's behaviour, and by 3 August Legge was a guest at Claremont. Newcastle, too, could still write: 'Our Court affairs go better and better. The great negotiation with Mr P[itt] is still on foot...'[337]

Fox evidently gave an account of the Hartington–Hardwicke interview to Cumberland, who approved of what Hartington had said.[338] Nothing is known directly of what passed between Hardwicke and Hartington; but Fox was left deeply dissatisfied, and made his resentment of the Chancellor plain when Stone visited him on 29 August. Hardwicke had apparently emphasised that he had 'meant nothing' in his conversation with Devonshire on 5 June, 'nor does anybody mean anything now'. Fox thought this treatment 'contemptuous', [339] and for the first time gave Stone an account of the Devonshire–Hardwicke interview as he understood it.[340] Stone, who had seen Newcastle and Hardwicke, offered their interpretation of what happened on 5 June. This is the version of their conversation which Fox prepared for Devonshire:[341]

Mr Stone, on Thursday August 29 (being with Mr Fox in consequence of former visits on the subject) told him that he had seen the Duke of Newcastle, and afterwards the Lord Chancellor at his lordship's own desire to hear what had passed between the Duke of Devonshire and his lordship.

Lord Chancellor told him that he went to Devonshire House the day the Parliament broke up to pay his respects, and give his Grace an account of what had passed in the short sessions, and the King's motives etc.

That then his lordship did say that Mr Fox's not appearing caused speculation, that he had been sworn without, but had not been sworn within doors, people were at a stand, and thought it strange, but went no farther. That then the Duke of Devonshire said he was sorry the arrangement proposed at Mr Pelham's death had not taken place, and 'He believed Mr Fox was very sorry for it too', that his Grace wished it could be set right again and 'believed there was a disposition in Mr Fox' but then he must have rank equal to any body in the House of Commons, and be a Cabinet Councillor. To this, Lord Chancellor said he saw at that time those objections, which are not since vanished, but did not think 'He ought single' to give a negative 'to a proposition of the Duke of Devonshire's'.

Mr Fox said this state of the case totally altered it; for certainly Lord Chancellor might take a proposal of the Duke of Devonshire's into consideration, and decline it civilly. But if without meaning anything ('He certainly meant nothing', says Mr Stone) if without meaning anything (continued Mr Fox) he *first* enquired of the Duke of Devonshire into my disposition – 'My lord sees the inference', says Mr Stone, and says he first mentioned your name, as to your not being sworn in Parliament, but the rest his lordship says (I think he said, 'insists') sprung from the Duke of Devonshire. Mr Stone several times said Lord Chancellor meant nothing; particularly when I asked Mr Stone how his lordship would construe his telling Lord Hartington to tell the Duke of Devonshire that he would turn it in his thoughts at Wimpole and did not doubt if there was the same disposition in others as in him, that in the course of the summer something might be found out. 'That was too much', says Mr Stone. 'Ay', says Mr Fox, 'if he meant nothing'. 'He certainly meant nothing', says Mr Stone.

As in March, Fox appeared neurotically over-eager to see a deliberate act of betrayal in the form of a retraction of a suggestion once advanced.

FROM DISAFFECTION TO OPPOSITION, SEPTEMBER 1754

By his interview, Stone put himself and Hardwicke needlessly in the wrong; but there is no evidence that the Chancellor ever discovered the misconception that was the occasion or excuse for Fox's new resentment. Fox, too, was presenting at this stage very different faces to the ministers and the King. Though aware that Fox's reception at Court had lately improved, Newcastle in early September was still sure of his own standing in the Closet. Fox, he supposed, had achieved good (formal) relations with George II by abandoning his former conduct, and had discontinued his recent negotiations for fear of royal offence. The King was more than formally kind to Newcastle, however, and he was delighted at the similar reception given to others of his team. 'Sir Thomas Robinson',

George II had told him, 'is the best Secretary of State except yourself that I ever had.'[342] Nevertheless, in respect of Fox's standing with the King, Newcastle was aware that the Secretary at War had made substantial gains in the public favour of Lady Yarmouth. To her, according to Münchausen, Fox had related his own version of the negotiations of March, including his excuse for refusing: that the Secretaryship had been offered him, not from the King, but from Newcastle. Münchausen had pertinently replied that, if so, Fox might still properly have accepted the office during his audience (on 16 March). Newcastle expected Lady Yarmouth to be told Fox's full story, including the course of the 'late pretty negotiations' through Devonshire, Hartington and Stone. He consoled himself that George II must have heard most of it already, without apparent effect, and felt confident that the King 'will see through the whole, and adhere to what he has done';[343] the ministry, then, would be able to face the Commons with success. Newcastle judged Fox's intentions correctly. Until the middle of September, Fox continued to pursue the possibility of a negotiation through Lady Yarmouth's channel, and laboured through her to modify what she reported as George II's opinion: that Fox was '*un ambitieux qui demandoit des conditions bien fortes*'.

Newcastle was struck by what Stone reported of Fox's hostile manner: that he 'looked upon the thing as over, that it had better not have been begun'; that Newcastle might have taken the opportunity of the Devonshire–Hardwicke meeting, and his not doing so proved a desire to keep things as they were. Accordingly, Newcastle enclosed an exact minute of what Stone had said.[344] Still more was Newcastle apprehensive that Fox would represent him to Lady Yarmouth as having intended all along to deceive Fox and to 'amuse' Devonshire.[345] It seems likely, too, that Newcastle and Hardwicke were already beginning to draw inferences from two different sets of events. The negotiations for the possible dismissal of Clements from the Irish government were at a critical stage; the Primate wrote repeatedly, stressing both the danger of irresolution and the involvement of English malcontents in instigating and promoting Irish disorders.[346] Secondly, Fox had taken offence at not being informed (as was proper) of orders relating to military dispositions in North America, complaining directly to the King. Holdernesse defended himself in the Closet with acrimony,[347] but Fox apparently carried his point.[348]

The Chancellor was not surprised at seeing good humour in 'one part of the Court': 'I never laid much weight upon it, but always thought it arose from a mixed motive, partly personal and interested as to complaisances in the Treasury, and partly political to smooth the way a little for the late advances.' He challenged, too, Fox's version (in Stone's minute) of the meeting on 5 June; Fox, he claimed, had omitted mention of the first part of the conversation (which showed the initiative to have been Devonshire's).[349] For Hardwicke, the negotiation was over: he would have no more to do with the Secretary at War. What mattered henceforth was Fox's ability to devise an adequate public justification for his discontent, and his success within the Cabinet over a matter which Newcastle could hardly deny fell within the province of his department: military dispositions in North America. Newcastle thought deeply in an attempt to explain Fox's behaviour in terms of the plot he suspected it to be. The paradox, as he saw it, was Fox's apparent desire for a reconciliation with the ministry rather than an understanding with potential *frondeurs*. Pitt's 'dissatisfaction', Temple's 'open opposition' and Legge's 'pragmatical discontent', Newcastle thought, must be known to Fox's camp; they must see, too, that Murray was the only major figure in the Commons on whom the ministry could rely:

from thence they conclude, (and with reason) that if they can blacken him, with the Whigs, we shall neither be able to employ him with success, nor, *he* be willing to be employed, and in this, they are in the right ... In order to this, they are now to make this little *Legge* declare himself a Whig, that he owed his situation to the Whigs, and that he was so good as to declare to everybody, *that I was a Whig.* They imagined, that I should not bear this behaviour, that I should grow cold to Mr Legge, that he would (as we know, he has done), complain of want of confidence, and then the reason was obvious, the Duke of Newcastle will have no confidence, in anybody in the House of Commons, but the Attorney General. The absurdity, of having a Tory head, to a Whig body, we know, was the constant topic. During this time, Mr Fox was to cajole, in order to get in, he was to blame this false accusation of the Attorney General, and to declare, that he, Mr Fox himself, (the hero of these Whigs) had no more right to be called a Whig, than the Attorney General had.[350]

That is, he would appear to stand forward in Murray's defence. This was an ingenious explanation. It took a realistic view of Fox's disingenuousness and so revealed how two charges, those of a Tory taint and of the domination of Lords over Commons, might be tactics working in his favour. But as an account of an incipient opposition it was too subtle to be realistic, and depended on Legge's having acted in conjunction with Fox – something of which Newcastle apparently had no firm evidence. Nor is it clear that Fox actually was defending Murray in August and September, though Newcastle presumably had grounds for this view. What mattered, therefore, was not the possibility that an opposition might succeed on such a plan, but Newcastle's reactions on the basis of his misapprehension. If, he supposed, the charges against Murray and about his own system for the management of the Commons were believed, the ministry could only survive in the House through Fox's promotion. Thus it was that Newcastle's misconceptions of Fox's strategies were transformed into an opinion of the weakness of his own position.

Newcastle's reply was to seek a propaganda victory; correctly identifying the opposers' motives to the public became 'the first and principal part of our present system'. Hardwicke and the Archbishop of Canterbury were asked to make it clear to the Devonshires, at least, that Legge's charges were no more than self-interested stratagems: 'if it was once thought, that we three, thought alike upon this subject as we do upon all others', wrote Newcastle, 'though late, I am persuaded, we should soon see an end of these attempts'. Legge, too, should be treated with 'authority, and contempt'. If such a response were effective, the ministers might go on with their intention of including Fox; the Princess of Wales, though personally hostile to him, would acquiesce. So would Hardwicke. Though the King had apparently not been told of the difficulties in Parliament, Newcastle saw the elements of strength in the ministry's position:

I know, we have as good a body of friends in the House of Commons, as ever men had, we have the King, we have the nation at present, and we have, and shall have, the House of Lords. I will hope that we shall not suffer three ambitious men in the House of Commons (of which, two, are at this time, guilty of the highest ingratitude to us), to defeat all our good designs for the public, and to convince the King, that we can't serve him, without their being our masters.[351]

Accordingly, Newcastle continued to consult Murray in detail about national finance and American affairs, and in such a way (though this was never made explicit) as to imply that the Attorney General would take a very prominent part in giving a lead in the House.[352] Formally, however, a decision on Murray's role had not been reached. He and Charles Yorke, Newcastle noted, would 'take any part, that may be proper for them'.[353] Hartington reported: 'it seems to be almost an universal opinion' that affairs in the Commons 'cannot go on quietly upon the footing they are at present for nobody seems satisfied, nobody seems to think that it can hold even those that have been provided for'.[354] But if there was an expectation of a rearrangement, there was not an equal expectation of a ministerial collapse. Momentarily, Newcastle's freedom of action was considerable, although in one way he stood alone: 'If we can go on, with success, all will be right in the Closet, if we cannot, nothing would make it so.'[355] It was still to be determined whether, and how far, Pitt, Fox or Legge were to be informed of the business of the session, or George II of their discontent. The King's advice, Newcastle thought, might be taken on how they should be negotiated with, and Newcastle was inclined that they should be – but if they were not to be employed, Newcastle minuted for consideration 'how far it may be prudent to inform my lord Hillsborough, Lord Barrington, Mr Nugent, Mr Charles Townshend and Lord Dupplin, with the plan of business for the session; and with the dissatisfaction of Mr Pitt, Mr Fox and Mr Legge; and to empower them to act; and Sir George Lee'. It might be possible, Newcastle thought, to proceed on the basis of unanimity, rather than alliances within the Whigs, if the King could be brought to insist on his servants acting together. Newcastle's preference was that Legge's agitation be restrained by frank reproof, and that Stone tell Fox that the ministers 'were very ready to enter into a proper communication with him upon general business, and the plan of the next session'.[356]

Moves were made in that direction. Legge was spoken to by Hardwicke, and invited to Claremont, with a view to a reconciliation.[357] It must have been the ministry's increasing inclination to a rapprochement with Fox which lay behind the Princess of Wales's acute anxiety that they would succeed: she would, Newcastle had heard, 'do anything rather than that'. This 'much strengthens our own opinion and resolution', but it scarcely surprised Hardwicke: 'I always was convinced that was her real opinion at bottom'.[358] Newcastle had travelled to Wimpole to arrange the plan of the session with Hardwicke; but at an audience on his return, George II anticipated his explanation, asking

'Who is to take the lead in the House of Commons[?] I know it is Sir Thomas Robinson's place, and rank, but he does not care for it.' To which I replied, 'Sir Thos. Robinson, Sir, will always be ready to give the House, the necessary informations, but as to the rest I believe it must be divided, the Chancellor of the Exchequer by his office must lay everything before the House that relates to the revenue, and there is the Secretary at War, and the Paymaster.'[359]

If Fox were ever to be promoted, then, it must be to an office whose scope was strictly limited to its formal sphere. Robinson's leadership of the Commons was to be treated as a matter of expounding ministerial policy and securing assent by persuasion. This was not an unreasonable idea, and was faithful to one aspect of the role of spokesmen in that House. Departmental individualism was to fall short, rather, as a plan for governing the relations of the major figures, the sum of which is what is meant by that abstract term, 'the ministry'. With this disadvantage, such a policy accommodated Sir Thomas Robinson, innocuously, in the position of 'professed minister' – a role which, though scarcely defined, might be merely formal in so far as it went beyond the departmental duties of the Secretaryship. At the same time, this empty identification of Robinson's primacy could appear as an alternative to, though it might have been a disguise for, Newcastle's evident preference for Murray. Robinson would 'inform the House of facts'; the Attorney General and others would 'do the business of the King and the public'.[360] Naturally, too, it was only a response to the dissatisfaction of Fox, Legge and Pitt: as the King realised, the success of the doctrine depended on their submission to it. Newcastle promised to talk 'strongly' to Legge, but George II tartly observed that Pitt had been placed in a position from which he could now challenge the system on the insistence of the Pelhams themselves. Newcastle pleaded necessity: 'the circumstances of the times, and Mr Pitt's abilities'. Nevertheless, despite the doubts surrounding Robinson's leadership, another set of inhibitions acted to discourage the emergence of opposition.

The King said, 'I don't suppose, *Fox*, is in good humour but after the strong assurances, *he gave me*, I don't believe he will enter into opposition'; I said we had nothing to do, but to pursue the plan of measures, that His Majesty should approve, and *then*, I hoped, they would not oppose them. H.M. said, if Pitt acts ill, Fox may have his place. And I am persuaded H.M. thinks, that would set all right. I told him we were ready to communicate to Mr Fox the plan of the session, *not to give him a handle to say that he was not informed*. That, the King liked, and upon the whole, things ended, tolerably well, though it is plain His Majesty had been talked to, favourably for Mr Fox, and particularly, that somebody should take the lead.

Hence George II's opening question. The next step, Newcastle supposed, was to make it clear to MPs that the King insisted on their supporting his measures. To dissociate the news from the recent negotiations via Andrew Stone, which had been concerned with the possibility of a new *office* for Fox rather than (as was now the issue) a new *role*, Hartington might tell Fox of the ministry's willingness to talk to him 'upon *general business*, and the plan of the session, if he is disposed to it'.[361] Departmental individualism did not entail that subordinate ministers in the Commons be ignorant of the administration's programme, nor that they lose their voices in the Cabinet; merely that no single man seize and exercise the independent leadership on the floor of the House that Sir Robert Walpole and Henry Pelham had held.

But before Fox could be spoken to, Newcastle had 'a most extraordinary conference'[362] with Legge on 26 September. Newcastle began by telling him

very sincerely the reasons of my reservedness to him: his discourses about the Whigs, though he allowed me to be a Whig; his declarations about taking in Mr Fox, satisfying the Duke [Cumberland], giving Lord Sandwich a pension, etc. to which I had no objection, but looked upon these discourses as indications of dissatisfaction *with what was*; and lastly his complaint of want of confidence from me; to all of which he did not say one single word, either negatively, affirmatively, or by way of excuse for what had passed, or promise for the future. But in a most extraordinary manner said that his opinion was that this Parliament (or House of Commons) would not go on without a minister in it (a Cabinet Councillor if you will), who shall go to the King *himself*, speak from *himself*. – And then I added, *independently of any other minister?* He said, that as you will, *subordinately*. I said, *those were only words*; I observed to him that this was directly contrary to the King's present *system*. He said, you will see. And then I told him, *if that was the case*, the King must then find out the person, and I think (though I will not be positive) he then said, the cards then must be new shuffled; he disclaimed meaning himself, said he would do the part of his office as well as he could, but he would not act the *mock minister*. I told him Sir T. Robinson would inform the House of facts, and I supposed he would take his part in defending them, and in the other branches of business. He said, when he was informed, he would do as well as he could, but that only very coolly and very slightly.[363]

The dispute was now, on the surface, a semantic one on the degree of 'independence' or 'subordination' of the Commons leader; but the point at issue was real. Newcastle adhered to his plan so far as to tell Legge what the business of the session was to be. This left him no adequate excuse for not supporting – as he admitted, in effect, to Anson. The issue, then, was reduced to whether the Commons would infringe the King's prerogative, at that date unchallenged in theory, freely to choose his own ministers. But for Newcastle, the interview on 26th was momentous for the inference he drew from it:

the grand secret is out; the three great men, Fox, Pitt and Legge, have agreed upon this principle, that there must be a minister in the House of Commons; and the first two, or perhaps all three, think they have a chance for it. L[ady] Y[armouth] has had a general account of this conversation, and by that I find that this doctrine has been preached to her; the success of it at Court will depend upon the success of it in the House of Commons. I really think it is a cant word given out by these gentlemen, which will affect few or none but those, who, for private views, or private connections, think and act with them.[364]

It is not clear that Legge had given any other reason for Newcastle's inference of a triple alliance than the implication that Fox was the obvious choice for Commons minister. But it could only have been Fox who expounded this to Lady Yarmouth as a doctrine, and Legge's earlier advocacy of Fox's inclusion made the case convincing. Pitt seems to have been included by association, but the prediction was to prove justified. Newcastle did not expect open opposition; merely that the malcontents would 'sit silent'. But any prospect of Fox's inclusion on terms was for the moment at an end. Here was the central issue. New-castle may have exaggerated the coherence of the opposition which the evidence then available revealed; he did not exaggerate the threat it came to pose to his system. By overstating the challenge now, therefore, Newcastle was able effectively to meet it. Lady Yarmouth had argued that Fox 'would be contented with *little*, but every day', Newcastle claimed, 'produces some proof, that that *little* means a good deal; and if granted, may end in the whole, or an attempt for it'. 'Who can share the ministry with Mr Fox', he added, 'or with anyone, who has the House of Commons, and is minister in the Closet, for the House of Commons. There, it all centres, there, Mr Pitt may bring it, and there poor, idle Legge is driving it. If ever I could have entered into any notion, of admitting Mr Fox upon terms, this conversation with Legge would determine me against it'. As Lady Yarmouth explained,

they all applaud my conduct in the Treasury, and in the choice of the Parliament, *But that somebody must take the lead in the House of Commons*; that once granted, that *somebody* must be Mr Fox, and that leader must be Minister, or will make it impracticable for anybody else to be so.[365]

Hardwicke agreed with this estimate of Legge's intention: 'It all tends to one point, to prove the necessity of a single leader in the House of Commons, and they know that, as the King is prejudiced against others, that must centre in Mr Fox. When that is attained, in the degree they mean it, there will, in my apprehension, be an end of your Grace's chief power as Minister of this country'. Hardwicke advised that the doctrine should be mentioned to as few people as possible, and spoke as if its significance should be minimised with the King. Though silent on the subject of Pitt, the Chancellor still spoke as if the ministerial overture to Fox via Hartington would go forward;[366] it was Newcastle who had already decided, alone, to break it off. Furthermore, he was making plans for the coming session without Fox's promotion. 'We have a good second rank', he reminded Murray: Hillsborough, Barrington, Dupplin, Nugent, Charles Yorke, and – included without hesitation, now that the Princess of Wales had taken strong alarm at Fox – Sir George Lee. Although Egmont was still ill-disposed as a result of the hostilities of the general election, Lee represented the prospect of substantial official support from Leicester House. Newcastle might have added Charles Townshend, and H. S. Conway, who was to second the Address. All were committed ministerialists.[367] Hume Campbell, he thought, might be involved; Newcastle suggested two of Temple's followers who might be won over; and promised, though unenthusiastically, to find a seat for Sir Richard Lloyd, the inadequate Solicitor General.[368]

Despite the warnings of Richard Pares and Mark Thomson,[369] it is still often supposed that 'Walpole's premiership inaugurated a new type of prime minister, seated in the House of Commons, as first lord of the Treasury and chancellor of the Exchequer, with the dual function of "minister with the king in the House of Commons" and "minister for the House of Commons in the Closet"'; and that Newcastle's 'appointment in 1754 represented an attempt to revert to the pre-Walpole type of prime minister'[370] – an attempt which failed since it defied a constitutional convention which Walpole had established and which accurately identified political realities. From the early eighteenth century, it is supposed, the growing power of the Commons inescapably dictated that the Prime Minister should sit in that House as First Lord of the Treasury. Yet the story of Newcastle's assumption of the leadership shows these theories to be no more than historians' fictions, concealing ignorance of the political complexities within which constitutional assertions had meaning by accepting opposition apologetics taken out of context. The slightly different accusation was made that Newcastle's regime represented an attempt to dominate the Commons from the

Lords, but the groundlessness and the tactical location of that charge has been revealed above. Similarly, the claim that the Commons must be led by a minister in it was not widely accepted and was effectively countered by the ministerial defence that this would confer on that individual the leadership of the ministry itself: this further claim was not even explicitly voiced. Nor was it the case that contemporaries' speculation about Fox, Pitt or Murray as Henry Pelham's possible successor revealed a sense of such a precedent: those anxieties marked, instead, uncertainty about how Pelham's combination of offices might be shared and an appreciation of the threat of disruption posed by these Commons orators.

The 'constitutional' conceptions held by the orators themselves were not a fixed framework but a set of rules in a social etiquette, of varying degrees of explicit articulation, which could be changed as well as broken in the activity of politics. Yet it is not the case that the rule of constitutional law emerged, to flower as a stable Victorian polity, out of a fertile ground of contradiction and inconsistency in eighteenth-century faction-fights. Constitutional assertions can be explained in that century, but only in relation to a tactical context precise and detailed enough to be appropriate to them, and to reveal – for example – the intentions which lay behind Pitt's reversal of position by the time of his interview with Newcastle on 2 September 1755 when he claimed that 'He liked a lord, First Commissioner [of the Treasury] very well.'[371] Despite what he then said, statements of principle were indeed made near that time which seem to be accurate expressions of the modern convention. Yet far from being explanations, it is explanation which those remarks stand in need of. Thus in 1803 Pitt's son stated as an 'abstract truth' the 'general principle' of 'the absolute necessity there is, in the conduct of the affairs of this country, that there should be an avowed and real minister possessing the chief weight in council and the principal place in the confidence of the King...That power must rest in the person generally called the First Minister; and that minister ought...to be the person at the head of the finances'.[372] But he advanced that doctrine only when it became tactically relevant in his contest for primacy with Addington; and it was even then no part of his argument that the First Minister must necessarily sit in the Commons. Similarly, in 1809 Canning's claim that 'a *Minister* – and that Minister in the *House of Commons* – is indispensable to the well-carrying-on of the King's Government in these times'[373] was politically grammatical only as part of his rivalry with Perceval and Castlereagh and contest for the leadership with several other almost equally eligible figures, not as a reaction to some attempt to domineer by the aged and by then epileptic First Lord of the Treasury, the Duke of Portland. And once Canning's disruption had brought down the ministry, Portland was replaced by a commoner, Spencer Perceval, only because the two sections of the opposition, led by 1st Baron Grenville and 2nd

Earl Grey, failed to agree. Nevertheless, the same doctrine has been repeated as an explanation of the crises of 1754–7:

by the end of the reign of George II oppositions on the lines of that originated by Walpole in 1717–20 had in practice become a part of the working machinery of the constitution. So had Walpole's other innovation, that of a leader of the House of Commons combining the offices of first lord of the Treasury, chancellor of the Exchequer, and prime minister. When Newcastle in 1754 tried to revert to the pre-Walpole practice of appointing a peer to the Treasury with a subordinate minister under him in the Commons he was told by Pitt that 'there must be a minister *with the King* in the House of Commons'. After the collapse of this attempt Hardwicke drew the moral:

> It cannot be disguised that the avowal and appearance of the same sole power in your Grace, in the House of Commons, is not to be expected. All sorts of persons there have concurred in battering down that notion, and the precedents of my lord Godolphin's and my lord Sunderland's time have been overruled by the long habits of seeing Sir Robert Walpole and Mr Pelham there, which go back as far as the memory of most people now sitting there, or indeed in business, now reaches.

Similar experiments made by Bute and Chatham in the next reign were equally unsuccessful. It was not till George III found in North a minister with the qualities required for working Walpole's system that he was able to form a stable ministry.[374]

In fact, Hardwicke was (as has so often been done in English politics) excusing a failure to prevent a dangerous and unpleasant phenomenon, Pitt's tactical success, by explaining it as an unavoidable realisation of a constitutional precedent. Yet before that time, no such precedent had taken root; and, as is shown below, the attempt to argue in the Commons in November 1754 as if it *had*, was a complete failure. Nor, despite the way in which Hardwicke apparently drew a lesson from events, did *force majeure* in 1756–7 *establish* such a precedent as an accurate comment on political realities. Miss Kemp has argued, even of a later period, that the younger Pitt, like Lord North, 'was concerned principally with the relation of a prime minister to the other ministers, and not with his relation either to the King – whose confidence was the essential basis of the prime minister's position – or to the Commons'.[375] There was undoubtedly a tendency for the First Minister to seek to hold the most important office, that of First Commissioner of the Treasury; it was not equally true that he was drawn to sit in the lower House. Even if Walpole's success in curing political disorder did derive (as some have argued)[376] from his combining the positions of Prime Minister and leader of the Commons, the lesson was lost on contemporaries. Ministries therefore continued to be launched in the 1750s, 1760s, and indeed until Lord Curzon was passed over in 1923, under a peer as Premier and while political circles displayed – if any – only disconnected and occasional apprehensions that such a system would have a shorter life expectancy than one led by a commoner. For that failure to anticipate later doctrine there was ample justification. Of the eleven First Lords of the Treasury between Henry Pelham's death and the younger Pitt's appointment in December 1783, only two sat in the lower House; of those two, only one enjoyed a long tenure. Moreover, of the nine peers, it could be argued that only one was a figurehead (Portland, April–December 1783). Whatever may have been the case later, it was clear in the years 1742–83[377] that the *creation* of a ministry usually depended not directly or initially on the leadership of a majority in the Commons, but rather on the negotiation of terms which would combine together in a working relationship a relatively small number of political heavyweights. A tendency to view opposition from within or without the ministry as equally and merely factious meant that the means of *sustaining* ministries were often seen, with good reason, in the same way: as a succession of renegotiations or recastings of the 'system'. In this lay Newcastle's chief skill; his success is a measure of its importance, and the primacy of 'manoeuvre' (in the Court and the ministry) over 'leadership' (in the Commons) explains the paradox of the continuing dominance of the aristocracy and the simultaneous insignificance of the House of Lords *per se* during the same period. Politics was a matter of the triangular relations of Court, ministry and Commons; and the ministry was the virtual preserve of the peerage.

As the account offered above suggests, the conventions which governed political conflict in the mid eighteenth century were both far more complex and far less modern than has been supposed. They were also in flux, and men's distant memories of the practices employed in the party battles of Queen Anne's reign counted for little in deciding their future pattern in comparison with the course of the bitter conflict for supremacy in which Newcastle, Hardwicke, Fox, Pitt and others were engaged. By late September 1754, however, Newcastle supposed he knew the terms in which the dissatisfied laid claim to power, and imagined he had dictated the form of the debate in such a way as to inhibit their success by devising an alternative explanation of how authority might be distributed in a ministry whose leader both held the Treasury and sat in the Lords, though a demand had not yet been openly voiced to have a single leader *of* the ministry *in* the Commons. Nevertheless, it was a measure of Newcastle's success since March that his leadership of the Old Corps was still unquestioned. So was his position at Court, where he had survived an initial reluctance on the part of George II to grant him 'the favour of the Closet' – the lack of which had seriously weakened the Pelham administration at its outset in 1744–6.[378] As a result of events in the lower House, Newcastle was later to obstruct Fox's ambitions by claiming in November that Sir Thomas Robinson, the senior in rank there, already exercised the leadership in the degree which Fox sought. In September, a less extensive role was supposed to attach to Robinson's position. But by this language of departmental individualism, which was seemingly only an insistence on strict propriety,[379] Pitt could be silenced, Fox restrained to the necessary compass of Cumberland's military authority, and the way left open for a symbolic union with Leicester House which would entail inclusions in the ministry's personnel on an individual basis alone.

2

The Defeat of the Pitt–Fox Alliance, October 1754–March 1755

The offenders and the offended have too often shown their disposition to soothe, or to be soothed, by preferments, for one to build much on the duration or implacability of their aversions.

> Horace Walpole to Mann, 1 Dec 1754
> HW 20, p.453.

The last opposition was a coalition of disappointed Patriots with disaffected Tories: the views and objects of the first ceased with the death of the late Prince of Wales, and they are become reasonable and practicable mortals reunited to the Old Corps; the Tories are not inconsiderable in numbers, but, for want of heads and hearts, and the plausible pretext of patriotism, they are loose, disconcerted, and a band incapable of acting, and will continue so as long as the ministry has no other demands to make but what is necessary for the current service of the year in time of peace...

> Horatio Walpole to Joseph Yorke,
> 23 July 1753: W. Coxe, *Memoirs of Horatio, Lord Walpole* (London, 1802) p.431.

The central theme of the 1754–5 session was not the defeat by Fox, Pitt and Legge of an unconstitutional attempt by Newcastle to subordinate the Commons to ministerial direction from the Lords, or their compelling him to share his sole power through the informal opposition which they offered to his measures from the Treasury bench.[1] It is on the contrary the story of Newcastle's successful efforts to prevent their ambitions from destroying his ascendancy. He had long been ready to recruit or accommodate Fox or Pitt on his own terms, and the session was remarkable for the success with which he resisted their incipient conspiracy – a success witnessed by his willingness, even in March 1755, to give Pitt cabinet rank. Newcastle was able, too, to preserve his position in the Closet and simultaneously make use of Cumberland's talents while restraining the parliamentary consequences of the captain-general's close involvement with the formation of war policy. Newcastle could therefore devote great efforts to broadening his political base by bringing about an alliance with Leicester House and achieved a valuable working relationship which lasted into the summer of 1755, though without finally succeeding in contriving a solid and stable parliamentary bloc by installing both Lee and Egmont in office. More significant in the long run, the widening tactical possibilities entailed by the impending realignment of parties were initiated by the Tories' attempts to profit from divisions within the Whig bloc. The relation between possible Tory allegiance and a scheme of ministerial reinforcement involving either Egmont and Lee or Fox was a complex one. It was Newcastle, nevertheless, who displayed skill in his management of that relationship and originality in his realisation that an understanding with the Tories was feasible, useful in itself, and an inhibition on the activities of Whig *frondeurs*. The surviving evidence for these possibilities is imperfect; the course of events is here traced through the stages of the negotiations in which Newcastle met, played off, and finally frustrated the disruptive initiatives of Fox and Pitt. Those negotiations reveal that Fox's inclusion in the Cabinet in early December 1754 did not mark the establishment, in his alleged domination, of a system which excluded Leicester House; much less was it a transfer of substantial power from Newcastle's hand to Fox's. This chapter offers a reconsideration of the nature of Newcastle's ministerial systems in the autumn of 1754 and the spring of 1755 through a new examination of the evidence for the manoeuvres during which the first was replaced by the second.

AMERICA, SEPTEMBER–OCTOBER 1754

The rejection of Fox's last overtures of the summer left his friends indignant. Marlborough wrote:

nothing is left but to oppose [Newcastle's and Hardwicke's] destructive measures and try to prevent the Whigs from being undone...I really think if we should be drove to it, such an opposition may be formed, as to make the D[uke] of N[ewcastle's] situation much too tottering for his giddy head.[2]

Fox's 'attack upon my lord Holdernesse, for not informing him of the orders sent to the troops in North America',[3] may have been an opening move in such a campaign. If so, at its outset, American affairs hardly figured in it.[4] On 3 September, news reached England of the capitulation on 4 July of Washington's force on the River Monongahela, a tributary of the Ohio.[5] The defeat gave, wrote Walpole, 'a reverberation to the stagnated politics of the Ministry'; the ministers were thrown into a frenzy of activity over military dispositions, he claimed, though Fox, Legge and Pitt were excluded from their deliberations.[6] In reality, the ministers' anxiety did not begin until three weeks after the defeat became known. Their disquiet was occasioned by Fox's conduct, once Newcastle had decided (on the basis of his interview with Legge on 26 September) to abandon his plans for the Secretary at War's negotiated promotion on terms. It was only then that Fox took up American policy for domestic purposes and that the division of blocs within the Cabinet came to be defined, and personal challenges to Newcastle's primacy expressed, in terms of the content and control of North American policy.

The rivalry thus engendered was to see Pitt attempting and failing to outbid Fox, and Cumberland inheriting the lead on those issues by default. But this rivalry, far from inducing fragmentation, was the effect of events in the summer of 1754 which had either produced agreement between Pitt, Fox and Legge on the grounds on which Newcastle's regime was to be challenged or opened the way for such agreement. To outside observers, no clear alliance was apparently signalled by their doctrine on the leadership of the Commons. Some predicted that either Pitt *or* Fox would soon be in opposition,[7] a view which was echoed by Newcastle's attitude to group alliances. Legge's personal demerits, too, gave him something of the air of a Foxite agent when, in reality, Fox was at times sarcastic and dismissive towards him; Legge tried to cultivate the favour of both Fox and Pitt,[8] but succeeded with neither. Pitt was thought to resent Legge's tenure of the Exchequer, and to have preferred George Grenville for that office.[9] Yet Hardwicke was warning that Fox was both implicated in the Irish crisis and was the only man the Cabal could intend for leader of the English Commons.[10] If, then, some form of combination to further the slighted interests of the Secretary at War did not yet exist, it appeared only too easy to create one.

The plan of the session, Ireland, and the rationale behind a Pitt–Fox–Legge alliance continued to preoccupy Newcastle in September even after news of Washington's defeat;[11] nor did observers suppose that military events in America had any bearing on Newcastle's position within the ministry.[12] Not until 21 September did he write that 'the opposers I hear will endeavour to make some attack' on that issue; but he showed no insight into the form it might take, and read no significance into the concurrent rumour of the Princess of Wales's apprehension of a ministerial rapprochement with Fox.[13] Nothing was heard from Pitt, who remained absent in the country. At meetings held in late September to discuss the reinforcement to be sent to America, no deep divisions were apparent: 'everything passed extremely well, and civilly,' wrote Newcastle, 'and the business very unanimously and properly agreed and settled'.[14] Halifax and George II, too, were satisfied; only the Chancellor showed concern, and that only at the expense.[15]

On 26 September, Newcastle had his decisive interview with Legge. At the same point, however, harmony still prevailed on American affairs. That day the Cabinet decided, as Cumberland had proposed to Robinson on 22nd,[16] 'to send, *forthwith*, two Irish regiments to Virginia, there to be filled up, to the English complement, to begin early in the spring, to drive the French from the footing gained on the Ohio, attempt then, the demolishing the French fort, at Crown Point, and afterwards proceed to the isthmus on the Bay of Fundy'. This scheme was preferred to Granville's who, as Newcastle wrote,

was for sending no regiments at present, for raising a strong American army to consist of 5 or 6000 men, and to begin in the spring, or early in the summer, with an attempt upon the French forts, on the River St Johns, when perhaps the French, by the notice they must have, would be too strong for us, and I am firmly of opinion, that if my lord Granville's scheme had taken place... we should either have risked a general war, or (which is more likely) have done nothing at all, and I have been reproached the whole winter for doing nothing.[17]

Fox and Cumberland were closely consulted and approved the arrangements;[18] but the latter soon intervened to extend the agreed plan to include also the raising of two colonial regiments, to be commanded by Governors Shirley and Pepperell. Newcastle's reaction was cautious: he feared that more extensive operations in America might trigger the outbreak of war in Europe, and was anyway reluctant to allow the expense of American preparations to interfere with his plans for the reduction of interest on the national debt in the coming parliamentary session.[19] He described his hesitation to Hardwicke:

I wrote immediately to Sir Thomas Robinson, and afterwards spoke to the King, that nothing might be done at present, but what was necessary for the sending the two regiments to Virginia. I own, I did think, that our present operations should be confined to the Ohio, and Crown Point. And, as the great, and most expensive one, was that, which related to the forts on the River St John, I did apprehend, that we had time enough to deliberate upon that, and to make the necessary preparations for it. Sir Thomas Robinson did accordingly defer his letters to Governor Shirley and Sir William Pepperell; as well as the orders to the Ordnance, for arms, stores etc. for that service.

But on 2 October Newcastle met Pitt, briefly in town, and Anson.

I find, they are both of opinion, that directions should be immediately given for the sending away the two regiments, with arms, ammunition etc.; and for raising the other regiments [in America] for the service to be performed on the River St John. Lord Anson is clear, that those regiments will be wanted, even for the reduction of Crown Point; and he thinks most strongly, that no time should be lost, in giving orders for raising them.

Newcastle had told Pitt for the first time

what was designed for North America, and also...my lord Granville's notions, which had not been followed. [Pitt] talked upon the affair of North America very highly; that it must be supported in all events, and at all risks – that the Duke's scheme was a very good one, as far as it went; – that it might do something; – that it did not go near far enough; that he could not help agreeing with my lord Granville; – that he was for doing both, sending the regiments, and raising some thousand men in America: – that we should do it once *for all*...

It was Pitt, then, not Fox, who first seized the possibilities which the fluidity of North American policy created. But Newcastle did not make a stand on the point:

This discourse, joined with Lord Anson's opinion, has made me suspend at least the stopping the orders for the raising the two regiments, etc. and for providing all the artillery, proposed by the Duke [of Cumberland]. Lord Anson is gone to Newmarket. He will acquaint the Duke, that it is his opinion, and also the opinion of those who are best acquainted with that country, that these two regiments cannot be completed in North America; and to propose, that they should be made up to the English establishment, before they embarked. I must beg your lordship's opinion upon the whole. I cannot take upon me, to determine finally without it.[20]

Hardwicke, equally, chose not to make an issue of it: he had, he wrote, objected to the expense 'in a general view, and without any imagination that what had been resolved upon would, in any degree, be altered'. Seeing the chance of domestic political advantage, he was evidently encouraged by Pitt's disposition. Though 'the possibility or probability of lighting up a general war in Europe' as a result of North American campaigns had to be taken seriously, his conclusion now was that 'the consequences as to Europe will probably depend upon other circumstances and events'. Since, wrote Hardwicke, Pitt had 'expressed himself so zealously and sanguinely for [these measures], I hope he will support them in Parliament, and dare say your Grace did not omit the opportunity of pressing that upon him. There is something remarkable in that gentleman's taking a measure of the Duke's [Cumberland's] so strongly to heart, and arguing even to carry it farther.'[21] Hardwicke offered no further suggestions, but he did not try to persuade Newcastle that Pitt's attitude indicated an enthusiasm for American measures irrespective of domestic tactical calculation. Within a week, too, it came to be reported (almost certainly falsely and on Pitt's authority, in the light of the lack of corroboratory evidence) that when on 2 October Newcastle had begun to explain the Ohio expedition to Pitt, the Paymaster had replied ' "Your Grace, I suppose, knows I have no capacity for these things," (being dissatisfied that he was not made Secretary of State) "and therefore I do not desire to be informed about them." '[22] Meanwhile, before Anson could return from Newmarket, Fox, as if to outbid Pitt, acted independently to advance preparations for both expeditions at once: one to Virginia for the Ohio campaign, the other for Nova Scotia. The Board of Ordnance was to advertise for transports; Fox obtained the King's signature, on 7th, on warrants to raise two colonial regiments and on commissions for their officers. On 8th, to Newcastle's astonishment, the Secretary at War published a notice in the *Gazette* ordering those officers to report for embarkation: a provocative violation of the Cabinet's agreement on secrecy.[23] These events conflicted inconveniently, for Murray, with his last attempt to avoid a prominent role in Parliament. On 6th he wrote to Newcastle from Bath:

As to the H[ouse] of C[ommons]. I am very sorry for the part the 3 take. In one it is able, and in him perhaps everything is bonne guerre. How closely it is concerted, how deep it is laid, or to what length it may be carried perhaps nobody can tell. Till the cards can be new-shuffled, to use the phrase your Grace mentions, it is absolutely necessary that there should be one to take the lead; it is necessary because the word is given out; it is necessary, where different colours may fly by surprise, that there should be a standard which may be followed by the eye; a short signal will catch willing ears. That person, for 10,000 reasons, can only be the man your Grace mentions [Sir Thomas Robinson]. Against any opposition yet declared there will be no difficulty. If a new one is made, that will be a new scene.

There is another person [Murray himself] who must do as much to avoid the appearance of taking the lead or being intended to lead, as the reality. It imports you greatly to divert all appearances of it. His zeal for the King's service and your Grace's administration won't be doubted. But if ever he is mentioned I think you should affect to put him after the 2nd line, from this circumstance, that he can only attend occasionally, which is true, upon great days and debates, whereas the others are always in their ranks.

Sir Thomas Robinson, therefore, should write the circular letters.[24]

By the time this letter arrived, however, Newcastle had acted decisively against Murray's rival. 'I have this day gained a most complete victory in the Closet over Mr Fox', he wrote on 8th;[25] all Fox's orders were suspended pending a meeting of the inner Cabinet with the Secretary at War the following night. What then took place is not exactly known, but Anson soon reported George II's consent to the two regiments' being made up to strength before leaving for America, a step evidently approved of by Cumberland. In order to consult him,[26] Fox then asked for a postponement until 16th of the meeting which would decide a date for despatching the officers, and Robinson observed: 'I should think that Mr Fox is stopped in his speed.'[27]

Newcastle was less sure: Pitt and Fox, he knew, had had a three-hour conference alone. Royston later noted on Newcastle's letter of 12 October: 'The Duke [Cumberland] and Fox were at this time pushing things towards *war*; Pitt without doubt [in] concert and co-operating with them – because he knew the Duke of Newcastle would be distressed by such active operations in the then state of the House of Commons – where with a very great party and the real power at Court his Grace had nobody to take the lead.'[28] At the same time that he was seeking careful analyses of the state of parties in Ireland,[29] Newcastle was predisposed to see a similar conspiracy at home. 'We have our intrigues and cabals here, as well as you', he wrote to the Irish Primate; 'They, I am sensible, are not altogether unconnected with yours.'[30] Yet the seeming failure of the first round of dismissals of Irish dissidents emphasised to Newcastle the wisdom of the familiar Pelhamite reluctance to provoke the formation of a Whig opposition bloc, if malcontents could be accommodated in office. Dissatisfaction of such an order was now publicly evident within the English ministry. To Dodington, Hillsborough summarised one observer's impression: 'nobody in office, satisfied, or would act, beyond their particular department. Nobody impowered, or would take the lead.' Pitt, Hillsborough therefore predicted,[31]

is likely to resign, but not go into opposition. – Fox and Pitt, are willing to see the first, at the head of the Treasury; the other, Secretary; but neither would assist the other. [Dodington] Asked if that was not a virtual union. [Hillsborough] Near it: Mr Pelham had the address to play the one against the other: the Duke had not. He [Hillsborough] had talked to the Duke of Newcastle about this, who told him all would go well: let them do the duty of their offices.

It was this limit that the Secretary at War continued to overstep in his conduct of American business. Unauthorised, on 12th he sent orders to the Admiralty to have the Navy Board contract for shipping both for the two Irish regiments destined for Virginia on the Ohio campaign and for the officers to staff the two regiments of Shirley and Pepperell. 'Thus your Grace sees', Robinson wrote, 'that *so great a stop is not put to their speed.*' Again Sir Thomas intervened to delay the conclusion of any such contract.[32] But there was little doubt in Hardwicke's mind that military dispositions were now wholly in Cumberland's hands;[33] even Henry Pelham, he wrote, was able to do little once the King and Cumberland had agreed on points of strategy.[34]

Newcastle apparently agreed; indeed, the point was not the timing of preparations for the expeditions but the political potential that Fox might draw from it. It is remarkable that, from mid October, American issues suddenly ceased to matter in the struggle for the leadership; at that point, 'the Parliamentary campaign opening so warmly', as Walpole wrote, 'has quite put the Ohio upon an obsolete foot'.[35] On one hand, the chosen policy was obviously Cumberland's;[36] but Newcastle and Robinson had fully demonstrated their ability to use their influence in the Closet to halt any independent initiative by Fox,[37] and Pitt had not pursued the matter. On the other, as the approaching session offered the malcontents a wider political arena than that created by their departmental business, the issue of Fox's disloyalty widened also. Hardwicke had already observed, though without implying that his remarks covered Pitt or Legge: 'I think there is an affectation in some persons to make a parade with this affair, and a design to make use of it to let themselves again into business...' Yet the Chancellor sought, not wholly consistently, to draw reassurance from the conferences between Pitt and Fox. 'I suppose in time,' he wrote, 'fire and water may agree'; but he did not predict that this was very near. Rather, he suggested again, as he had done on 3rd, that Pitt might now be expected to support the Cumberland strategy. The Paymaster's responsiveness to Fox's and Cumberland's concern to improve the lot of the Chelsea out-pensioners, too, suggested that 'it looked as if [Pitt] was determined to have no demerit with the Duke [Cumberland]'.[38] Newcastle does not seem to have shared this view; with reason, for Pitt, though formally professing himself 'attached to the Duke of Newcastle's power, and to him himself', was reserving his freedom of action on election petitions in a way which, if it argued no immediate desire to co-operate with Fox, suggested a much more immediate source of difficulty with the ministry.[39]

Pitt was, indeed, about to bind himself to the Grenvilles by his forth-coming marriage; but there is no evidence that this automatically created a Grenville bloc in Parliament in the 1754–5 session. Newcastle did not anticipate that it would, nor in retrospect did he suppose that it had done so. On the contrary, the experience of the session proved (as Horatio Walpole predicted) that there were neither occasions nor plat-forms for launching a formed opposition. Moreover, the Grenvilles were not without their internal divisions: Sir George Lyttelton, in particular, was drawn to the ministry by his ambition for a peerage.[40]

OCTOBER: THE PRELIMINARIES

In October, Newcastle was predisposed (though Hardwicke had given him some cause) to see Pitt's and Fox's attitude to North America as a consequence of a collective conspiracy when, probably, it was the out-come of their individual ambition. Already, Newcastle was widely known to have spoken of the unreliability of his 'first rank' in the Commons (Fox, Legge, Pitt and Grenville) and of the strength of his second (Hillsborough, Barrington, Dupplin, Nugent, Charles Townshend).[41] Though Newcastle sought to frustrate a hostile conspiracy, he had no need, as yet, to court Pitt or Fox: he could choose as between two relatively minor supporters. *Their* performance of their departmental duties would be sufficient; Murray's or Robinson's, like Newcastle's, would not. More-over, Fox, Pitt and Legge had not gone so far as to eliminate the possibility of their being brought into line by firm and frank treatment, just as it was thought that Clements, the last major Irish dissident still in office, might be also.[42]

Newcastle's response to the anticipated alliance of Pitt, Fox and Legge was therefore twofold. Departmentally, he had already advanced a theory of confining ministers to their offices' formal spheres of responsibility, with Robinson to 'inform the House of facts'.[43] Secondly, Newcastle now sought to break the personal ties of the connection which he imagined was formed against him by the manipulation of group alliances. Later, he was widely believed to have attempted to establish a regime of sub-ordinate Commons managers, and fears of a major shift in the balance of the constitution in favour of the House of Lords were retrospectively magnified in the different constitutional perspective of the 1760s.[44] Those appearances were largely the reflection of his reliance on a talented but underestimated second rank of Commons spokesmen which was com-pelled by the unpredictable behaviour of the more familiar figures. Partly, too, it was the consequence of the inhibiting effect on other ministers of the very idea of purely departmental responsibility Newcastle used to restrain his disloyal subordinates; but this in turn meant that he was faced with the problem of inducing the members of the administration to act in a collective ministerial manner at all. This also implies that

Newcastle's decision to re-make the leadership pre-dated (and does not therefore prove) the alleged failure of Sir Thomas Robinson in the face of the showy rhetoric of the opposition in the Commons which was so to impress Horace Walpole. Newcastle's conduct of the realignment was based on a more realistic estimate of the importance of the challengers, for he was far from intimidated by their oratory. At the most critical point, Waldegrave told Fox 'what I always thought, that they [Newcastle and Hardwicke] considered themselves on such ground, and so sure of a majority, that the terror which his lordship [Waldegrave] owned in their situation would influence him, of our [Fox's and Pitt's] junction, etc. had no effect, nor would have till it was too late'.[45] Walpole confirmed that 'the Duke of Newcastle, who used to tremble at shadows, appears un-terrified at Gorgons!'[46] Even after the autumn session, the Duke claimed: 'I think I can answer for the House of Commons, in the present con-juncture – I might almost say, for the King, the Parliament and the nation', backed as he was by 'the determined zeal and resolution of a greater majority than ever was known in the House of Commons'.[47]

In October, West was speaking of his fears that a lack of enthusiasm in City financial circles would make the ministry's position impossible;[48] but to Newcastle, who had recently predicted that his American policy would make no new tax necessary and who hoped to apply much of the produce of the Sinking Fund to the discharge of the national debt,[49] such fears seemed greatly exaggerated. One cause for encouragement was the failure of any link to emerge between Whig dissidents and City Toryism. Sir John Barnard was fully consulted by the ministry on the supply for the coming year, and was persuaded to consent to Newcastle's estimate of expenses for the North American campaign.[50] Though personal friends, Pitt and Beckford were to find themselves at odds in the coming session over major issues,[51] and no convergence was apparent until after Pitt's repudiation of his links with Fox and his and Bute's assumption of the lead at Leicester House in late 1755. Divided loyalties in election con-tests had been, since April, major obstacles to a rapprochement between Fox and the Grenvilles,[52] and though Pitt's manner may have led some of the public to expect him rather than Fox to head an opposition, this did not imply Newcastle's weakness. Rather, declared Joseph Yorke, 'nobody seems to doubt your Grace's strength, for the support of your own administration'.[53]

What underpinned Newcastle's position was the increasingly obvious dependance of American policy on the ministry's success in the conduct of its alliance system in Europe. This solidified royal support behind him at the same time as it both placed temptation in the way of Pitt not to co-operate with the ministry, and made the eventual assent of Fox ever more likely. European diplomacy was the area in which Newcastle, Holdernesse and Robinson were pre-eminent and indispensable: until the uncertainties with which they contended had been resolved (as contemporaries supposed) by the Convention of Westminister with Prussia in January 1756, the King could entrust no other set of men with this responsibility. They, equally, were unable to enter into domestic connections which were inconsistent with their basic European commitment, although negotiation was possible about its form. It was this which was finally to destroy the chance of a lasting pact, not directly with Egmont or Leicester House but with the Tories, at the beginning of the 1755–6 session; but meanwhile, unwilling to go to the lengths of a formed opposition, the junior Court could only acquiesce with passive apprehension in Fox's growing importance in the conduct of American policy, and neither Lee nor Egmont could offer a challenge to the role of Commons leader which it was (wrongly) feared that Newcastle, in December, enlisted Fox to fill.

Newcastle saw that the weakness of the malcontents lay in the lack of a convincing issue: 'I don't find that *measures* are blamed; the only point of difference is personal'.[54] European entanglements had not yet been made a pretext on which an attack on the ministry could seem other than factious. Concerting the King's speech between themselves, Newcastle and Hardwicke designed it to signify a general support of 'the Concert with Russia, or any other scheme of not leaving ourselves at the mercy of France',[55] and interpreted its favourable reception as such a general support. Even as late as 11 November, Gilbert Elliot could discover nothing more specific than 'general expectations, that there are likely to be divisions, when business begins...'[56] Newcastle's basic outlook was widely shared. Horatio Walpole privately admitted[57] himself unable to see why things should not go on in the House on their current footing,

if the King pleases, for I can't see from what quarter, nor upon what foundation, trouble or opposition can arise (as long as the peace abroad is maintained); the Tories are few in numbers and those few are scanty in knowledge, and in abilities of speaking; they can undertake nothing from their own strength, they would readily [?join] as they have ever done with ambitious and discontented Patriots in opposition, to perplex the government or administration; but where are those Patriots to be found, since the Prince of Wales's death; most and indeed I think all those that have any talents, or are of any weight, that were formerly so, have now employments...if nothing is proposed in Parliament but what is a public concern, and as such is made a measure of the Court, and if the managers that are to open, and support the proposal, are men of capacity and do it ably, I think the body of the Whigs (laying aside their private partiality for one man in preference to another) will concur with the ministry in doing the business of the nation, upon that honest principle which your lordship mentions for your own conduct, and will always govern me, which is in wishing well to the whole to keep things quiet, and to the satisfaction of his Majesty...

Fox and Legge should therefore cheerfully support the ministry's measures, even beyond their departmental responsibilities, and suppress any sense of grievance:

Should a few of the Whigs, even men of parts and capacity try to clog or interrupt the business; instead of having any followers, they would be deserted by the friends they have. The spirit of opposition died...[in 1751] with the Prince of Wales, the object in Parliament is Court preferment, the men of business and eloquence are more numerous than ever I knew. The King is absolute master to choose whom he will employ, and his choice will be submitted to, and this will continue to be the case unless some unforseen extraordinary event shall happen, and until a difference shall arise between the Court of St James's and Leicester Fields, which as persons and things are circumstanced in both seem[s] to me at a great distance.

But this did not conclude the matter; Elliot thought that despite the 'discordant principles' on which the administration was based, it was equally likely to establish itself strongly as to disintegrate.[58] Ways of exerting pressure still remained open to the discontented. To Argyll, Newcastle explained his view of the coming threat:

Open opposition, perhaps, we may not *yet* have. But I have no reason to think, that all endeavours, steering clear of open opposition, will not be used, to distress, and embarrass. The great point, which is now professedly avowed, is, the necessity of having *a Minister*, or *the Minister* (and these are synonymous terms) in the House of Commons. They [the Commons] have a Secretary of State; a Chancellor of the Exchequer; a Paymaster General; and a Secretary at War – But will they dictate to the King, where he shall place his confidence; or a certain degree of it? This doctrine, however, will make the attendance of all our friends necessary.[59]

What alarmed Newcastle most was not the potential appeal of that doctrine at large but its relation to the temper of the Closet; for he was hypersensitive to the gradations there of confidence and regard, indispensable supports of government but ones which varied with each alteration in the King's mood.[60] In mid October, Newcastle wrote: 'I think I see, a coldness and reservedness in the Closet, almost ever since the North American affair came on, except that one day that Mr Fox's orders were suspended'. An application from H. S. Conway to be a Groom of the Bedchamber scarcely improved the royal mood.[61] At home, Newcastle predicted, 'I believe, the plan of the Closet is, to stand by; look on; and, if we can support ourselves, to be pleased with it. But to avoid, as much as possible, to make our cause their own; and to do anything, previously, to assist us.' Drawing on an Irish analogy, he speculated whether the ministers should not 'talk a little in the *Bessborough strain*' to convince the King of the need an administration had of overt royal favour.[62] Hardwicke, however, disagreed with Newcastle on the relation between English and Irish unrest. Such a charge of disloyalty, too, could be used by Dublin Castle against the English ministry, but not with the propriety by the latter against the King. But the Chancellor saw that 'if the condition *of making ourselves answerable for the success* should be pinned upon us, it might puzzle us what to say, especially as one great measure of government [North America] is now entirely under another direction [Cumberland's]'.[63] In the long term, Cabinet unanimity in responsible commitment to a line of policy was inconsistent with the close involvement of the monarch or another member of his family in the formation of that policy; what is seldom appreciated is the way in which George II, like George III, at times took the lead in promoting responsibility and therefore, incidentally, unanimity of commitment among ministers often too reliant for their resolution on Court favour. But there was a practical aspect to Newcastle's present insecurity, as his genuine fears of the parliamentary effect of his loss of command over military patronage shows.[64]

In these circumstances, Newcastle was able to effect significant improvements, before the opening of the session, in the attitudes of Legge, Lee and Conway. The first was perhaps flattered by being chosen to write the circular letters despite Murray's advice that Robinson should do so;[65] there is no evidence to suggest a tactic on Legge's part behind Newcastle's observation of 'the turn which Mr Legge seems to have taken. The humour is quite cleared up, I have given him strong assurances, with which, he seemed very well pleased.' But Legge then professed to Robinson a fear of standing up to Fox, if the latter were hostile in the Commons; and a desire to see Fox in the Treasury, presumably as Chancellor of the Exchequer, and Pitt as Secretary of State. Newcastle inferred that this was the outcome of Legge's weakness, and expected to go on with him by indulging his vanity and stiffening his resolution in defence of the Budget.[66] Here Legge deceived Newcastle, but it was to be Newcastle's misapprehension which most accurately described Legge's conduct until his refusal to sign the Hessian warrant in July 1755. No dramatic assault was to be launched on the ministry from Legge's or Fox's quarters in 1754: and an indication of Cumberland's broad assent was Conway's availability, apparently at the price of Groom of the Bedchamber.[67] 'He is a great acquisition, if *we* can get him', wrote Newcastle. He spoke, too, as if Leicester House could be set in motion on request: for, as yet, Pitt had no links there. Through Stone, Newcastle approached the Princess of Wales to ask that she 'would immediately speak to Sir George Lee, and her principal servants, to be active this session'.[68] Lee proved well disposed, and moved the Address in the Commons on 15 November. There seems to have been a prospect of securing George Hay,[69] an able speaker and a friend of Potter, though counted as a ministerialist; Grafton, who may have favoured Fox's promotion in March, was now well disposed; and a confidential overture had been received from the Bedford quarter.[70] 'They say, we shall have great warmth this session', Newcastle wrote, 'but I scarce believe it'.[71]

As a defence against responsibility for the instability which would attend on inadequate royal confidence, Newcastle now raised the question of the authorship of the ministerial system of March 1754. To Hardwicke, he repeated, fell the duty of talking to the King 'in the *Bessborough way*' since

you had the *sole hand* with the King, in the present arrangement; and in all, that passed originally upon it. I have nothing to answer for, but as far as depended upon me, the conducting the King's affairs, in the several branches, belonging to me, in a proper, unexceptionable, and, I may add, successful manner...I do not hear (perhaps, I may flatter myself) one single word pretended to the contrary. The whole point is, the Minister, or a Minister, with the King, must be in the House of Commons. That Minister can be nobody, but Mr Fox, ergo.[72]

While Hardwicke acknowledged this, he resented the association of the present conduct of the ministry with the responsibility for its establishment: Newcastle, he maintained, was confusing a doctrine covering the internal relations of the ministers with an account of the relations between the ministry and the Crown:

I think you state your case imperfectly when you say – 'That you have nothing to answer for, but, as far as depends upon you, the conducting the King's affairs in the several branches belonging to you in a proper, unexceptionable, and successful manner'. I apprehend your Grace means by this, *in the Treasury*. That you have so conducted them there is undoubtedly true...But...the world will not think that enough. Hitherto nothing of very great public consequence has come within that Department. It was *enough* for a Lord Wilmington at the head of the Treasury, but not for the Duke of Newcastle. You are the King's Minister, or he has no Minister; and you must be so, and the world will look upon you in that light, or else this whole system must sink into nothing.[73]

But Newcastle could reply that Hardwicke had mistaken departmental individualism for a theory of the leadership of the ministry as a whole:

your lordship extremely misunderstood my letter, if you imagine I intended to confine by it, my situation to the Treasury *only*. By 'the several branches belonging to me', I could not mean one branch, only: I meant as much as I ought to mean, with truth, propriety and decency.

Newcastle had been caught in an attempt at evasion, but his claim to constitutional rectitude left the issue open. His formula could not be more than a profession of propriety not least because at that moment he saw in the Irish crisis a growing threat to his conduct of the session at Westminster. 'I differ from your lordship', he wrote to Chancellor, 'in thinking that there is so much difference in the cases; the views are the same to both, viz. to defeat the present administration, and the persons who must do it, and propose to advantage themselves by it, are also the very same: to speak plain, the Duke [of Cumberland] and Mr Fox.'[74]

Newcastle's English response, to resist the attribution of greater status to his Commons ministers, appealed to perfect constitutional propriety. Thus Horatio Walpole condemned the new doctrine: 'so to add new dignity or power to employments that have never yet had them, (let the persons enjoying those employments be never so able) in order to encrease their authority in Parliament, may be a precedent of ill consequence...'[75] To combat it, at least two ministerial arguments were circulated. Privately, Fox's troublemaking over the dispatch of troops to America was *now* interpreted as a challenge to Robinson.[76] Publicly, scepticism was expressed about the current fears for the constitutional position of the Commons. The Secretary at War had launched his agitation on precisely those military issues most likely to alarm Leicester House, align Egmont behind Lee, and discredit the theory he, Fox, was propounding. Hardwicke reported that Lee 'despises very much the doctrine lately propagated of a *Minister with the King* actually sitting in the House of Commons, and sees the design of it just in the light we do':[77] that is, of Fox's pursuit of power.

There is evidence that Legge was beginning, at this point, to abandon his previous restraint. At a pre-session dinner on 5 November, his conduct was 'dry' and 'as disagreeable as possible';[78] in private, he began to criticise Newcastle's arrangements for the election petitions as an infringement of the Commons' liberty of decision. Newcastle commented: 'I am weary of negotiation with Mr Legge, who is watching to expose me... An open opposition, in Court or Parliament, I understand, and can avoid. But a gentleman at the Board with me, and brought thither by me, I cannot suffer to act in the manner he does. I shall be obliged, whatever is the consequence, to lay this behaviour before the King'.[79] Legge seems to have been ignorant of this growing dissatisfaction with his conduct, and was closely involved with the ministry in arranging speakers on the Address.[80] Fox, however, must have been aware of the coolness with which he was himself regarded. Newcastle initially did not invite him to a pre-session dinner on 11th, and Fox did not intend to be present at the usual meeting of 'a select number of members' on 12th to hear the King's speech.[81]

The Duke of Beaufort, nominally one of the leaders of the Tory party, had earlier inquired: 'Is there not to be a change in the direction of the lower H[ouse] before the Parliament meets [?]'[82] By November, Newcastle was aware, too, that speculation was rife of changes in the ministry involving Fox's promotion to the Exchequer, and that Legge was talking of the impossibility of the Commons' system going on as it was.[83] His intelligence suggested two unknown quantities: 'a sort of flying squadron under my Lord Egmont and a union of the Beckfords and Sir John Phillips led by (the as yet undeclared) Barnard.[84] Unknown to Newcastle, others were indeed making overtures to Egmont, currently by far the most important figure of the last Leicester House opposition to remain unreconciled to the ministry since 1751. That prominence and isolation alone had prompted speculation that the ministry would find a way to accommodate him, though there seems to be no foundation for the rumour in March 1754 that he would have a seat at the Board of Trade.[85] Now, through Potter, an offer was made 'a few days' before Parliament met to incorporate Egmont's appointment as Secretary of State in the Lords in a scheme to instal Fox as First Lord of the Treasury and Chancellor of the Exchequer, and Pitt as Secretary of State, in the Commons.[86]

Though the author of this offer is not recorded, the probability is that it was Pitt's plan, unconcerted with Fox. Egmont's answer has not survived; but there are no grounds to think it other than negative, for it was Sir George Lee, if anyone, who dictated the prospects of parliamentary oppositions through the political orientation he could give to Leicester House. Yet Egmont's record of the overture may be the only evidence for Pitt's intentions in bringing about a tentative alliance with Fox in November. At this stage, moreover, the situation was fluid to a degree which was later forgotten. Similar evidence for the second possibility, that of a Beckford–Philipps–Barnard alliance, is lacking; and it seems more likely that the Tory opposition hinted at since the summer of 1754 was never a reality than that it was averted by Newcastle's rapprochement with that party. In the 1754–5 session, Pitt and Legge were to attack Jacobitism for tactical reasons; not until late in 1756 did Pitt's Patriotism have a Tory appeal. Newcastle's efforts could therefore be directed both at a lasting union with Sir George Lee and Leicester House, and at the acquisition of Egmont. Joseph Yorke saw that, if successful, the move 'certainly widens the Whig Bottom in case of any unfortunate event [George II's death] which every prudent man ought to have constantly before his eyes'.[87]

PARLIAMENT, NOVEMBER–DECEMBER 1754

The session opened on 14 November. On the second day, before the debate on the Address, Egmont was approached by Daniel Boone, a Leicester House MP, who

told me the *Duke of Newcastle* was greatly frightened – and that lord Egremont had told him to tell me so – and that the Duke was in the utmost degree desirous of making friendship with me – and would do anything to compass it only wished to know what would content me – That he had already prepared the way with the King – and that the King had never expressed himself so favourably of any man so much in opposition as I had been.[88]

It seems likely that Egremont misread Newcastle's manner and exaggerated his apprehension of opposition: an exaggeration which Egremont's account very probably added to. But it is unlikely that Egremont was acting entirely on his own initiative. There are no indications that Newcastle was aware of any other overtures to Egmont; though, therefore, Newcastle did not record his intentions with regard to the Tories, the circumstantial evidence remains that Egmont had lately been the chief agent for an attempted reconciliation between that party and

Leicester House, and that Egremont, the son of the late Sir William Wyndham, had himself sat as a Tory MP before going over to the government after Walpole's fall.[89] According to Egmont, he replied to Boone

that the Duke [Newcastle] was in great danger – that I was free to own I did not like the faction forming against him which would end in passing the Regency in case of minority into the hands of the Duke of Cumberland – that I wished to prevent it. But I believed the measures pursued by the administration would render it inevitable – as to myself, my sole object was a retreat with honour – *otium cum dignitate*. . . Upon the Address immediately after I spoke moderately – showed the danger of our affairs in all parts – declared I would strengthen the King and support all reasonable measures for that purpose – but admonished ministers not to make such pitiful speeches about our [?false] tranquility, for the King or Parliament to make such absurd advances to countenance such false representations of our state. From this 14th November for a week or ten days frequent hints from Boone about the Duke of Newcastle's desire to be well with me. . . Boone said some negotiation would be carried on with me through Lord Egremont.[90]

The start of the session was encouraging. Dupplin, an unquestioned personal friend of Newcastle, became Chairman of the Committee of Elections; Sir George Lee moved the Address, as a sign of the disposition of Leicester House, and no division was forced. This unanimity was the first public sign of the Tories' new attitude: having, as Almon later expressed it, 'made themselves ridiculous by their opposition. . . they came over to the ministry, in order to get something, as they termed it; and some of them were gratified'. But, as he recognised, 'By this means the ministry became such a jumble, that it laid the foundations of the most grievous disturbances.'[91] Evidence of the distribution of place or pension to the Tories is lacking; but the failure of Pitt's and Fox's agitation in the Commons before Christmas was closely related to the accommodating attitude of the Tories towards Newcastle's administration, an attitude which became fully apparent with the Mitchell election petition in early 1755. Just as in 1742, when the Tories were brought to quiescence vis-à-vis the Court, and even to hold office, following a reconciliation between the Prince of Wales and George II,[92] so now the good relations between Leicester House and St James's allowed many of them to show sympathy with Newcastle's designs. This did not entail that party identities lost their meaning: as early as 18 November, the Oxfordshire petition generated a clear-cut division of 267 Whigs to 97 Tories.[93] Yet the decline of Jacobite activity, and the absence of independent tactical opportunity open to the Tories, seemed at last to have released the government from the fear of that party's doctrine. Both Newcastle's negotiations with major figures and the events of November and December in the Commons were, in an important sense, episodes in the history of party: they are intelligible only in relation to ambitions to seize the leadership of the Old Corps; to the tactics of Newcastle's resistance; and to the way in which the Whig–Tory polarity (intelligible though it still was in its traditional ideological terms) was ceasing inescapably to dictate the pattern of party alignments.

Newcastle's view of the root of the disturbances was easily expounded:

Some Great Persons in the House of Commons don't think their merit rewarded; and therefore endeavour to have it thought that there is a necessity of having a Minister, or the Minister, in the House of Commons; concluding, I suppose, that, that principle once established, everybody has his chance. As this affects the King's system and present arrangements only, and not the conduct and behaviour of any particular person in his employment, I am persuaded, much the majority of the House of Commons will not enter into any scheme of this kind

which he slighted as 'this principle *or trap*'.[94] Here he judged the mood of the House more correctly than did his opponents: there was widespread support for such an approach, since, as these events reminded observers, 'It hath often been said in a parliamentary way that the alteration of Men without Measures would do no service to the Constitution'.[95] The Commons proved unsympathetic to merely personal attacks, especially at the beginning of a new ministry. Sir George Lyttelton wrote in retrospect: 'It was quite impossible for me, as a man of honour or integrity, to join in an opposition, which, at the beginning of it, in the year 1754, and through the ensuing session of 1755, had not even the pretence of any public cause, but was purely personal against the Duke of Newcastle...'[96] Waldegrave evidently repeated Fox's view in writing of 'a kind of parliamentary opposition' which, being in place, 'could not decently obstruct the public business, or censure those measures which they themselves had already approved of. But still they might attack persons, though not things; or might oppose in questions of an indifferent nature, where the affairs of government did not appear to be immediately concerned.'[97] Pitt, though professing his loyalty to Newcastle, had claimed that he was still fully at liberty to follow his conscience over election petitions in the House.[98] Thus strictly defined, opposition might indeed have been consistent with a place on the Treasury Bench; but the vague conception of their activity which Waldegrave recorded allowed them to go much further. Yet, at the outset, Pitt was silent: those who saw a conspiracy at work had to infer that he had 'tutored the others'.[99] On the second day of the session, Potter, a follower of Pitt, began the debate on the Address with the argument that 'they had been used to see a Minister sitting in that House'; but he drew no response, and did not pursue the point.[100] The issue obviously had no parliamentary potential; it was not revived that session. Egmont was 'very moderate and mild, and as complacent as an opposer can be imagined to be'. 'I was told', wrote Hardwicke, 'that, though Mr Legge stopped short, he spoke with spirit; and your Grace judges right that he ought to be encouraged and kept up.'[101]

Others saw things differently from the dissidents. Samuel Martin, Legge's secretary, interpreted Conway's appeal for personal ambitions to be sacrificed in the national interest as an obvious reference to

the dissatisfactions of Mr Fox and Mr Pitt. For Col. Conway had before this speech lamented their discontents in a private conversation with Mr Legge. The House took no particular notice of this passage by any expression of applause whether through ignorance of the meaning, or as not disapproving the resentments of these two gentlemen. Mem. and I did inquire and found some people understood the matter in this light and others not.[102]

In the House, although those ill-disposed to the ministry claimed that there was 'no Minister, nor indeed any declared Leader' there,[103] a deliberate order of precedence was seen to exist. Newcastle resented Legge's implication that Robinson was 'set up purely for a show in the House of Commons',[104] though Sir Thomas was evidently preserving a low profile. Robinson took Henry Pelham's seat, with Murray on his right. Fox and Pitt sat to his left, with Legge on Pitt's left: 'So that he [Legge] placed himself at a distance from the Attorney General whom he does not love, and near Pitt and Fox whom he desires to cultivate, his proper seat being next to Sir Thomas Robinson as his office of Chancellor of Exchequer is next in rank'.[105]

Clearly, Legge had not yet achieved a formal commitment to Fox or Pitt; and his speech satisfied Newcastle and George II to an extent which embarrassed him with their praise.[106] He was accordingly asked to draft the King's reply to the Address,[107] and Newcastle called on him on 16th to congratulate him on his performance in the House. His answer was astonishing. Legge, Newcastle wrote, 'still insists upon bringing in *His Two Friends*, as he calls them, *Pitt and Legge* [sc. Fox], Mr Pitt is to be entreated with civilties and confidence, which I think everybody would be ready to show him, but...Mr Fox *must* be Secretary of State, not in the room of Sir T. Robinson, who should be made a peer, but of my Lord Holdernesse. This is a most impudent scheme to get the whole into their hands.'[108] The two Secretaries would thus be Robinson in the Lords and Fox in the Commons; if this demand was sanctioned by Pitt and Fox, it represented a significant retreat from what was apparently Pitt's plan in early October. The satisfaction of these two, Newcastle thought of as Legge's 'old point'; the new element was Pitt's willingness, as Legge now believed, to desist from his, Pitt's, ambition for the Secretaryship in the face of royal antipathy, and to support the ministry at the price of the King's personal countenance and regard alone. What struck Newcastle was Legge's strong insistence on Fox's Secretaryship; his surprise suggests ignorance of the previous plan, disclosed to Egmont, for Fox to take both the Treasury and the Exchequer. Newcastle was sceptical about Pitt; 'when *I* flung out that very thing to him, he treated it as *words* and *mere amusement;* but...if he would be satisfied with that, one might endeavour to bring that about'. But he treated

Robinson's peerage and Holdernesse's removal as 'too great and too difficult a thing for me to say anything upon'. Legge 'said remarkably, "he left it with me to consider" and repeated his nonsense of uniting by that means *the Whigs*'; but Newcastle drew a different inference. 'It is plain to me that this proceeds, first from their seeing that they are *beat*, then from a most thorough combination in the *three* to get at once the House of Commons and consequently the whole administration, into their hands.'[109]

Newcastle regarded this as proof that Legge 'is, and has been, linked against us'. Hardwicke was sceptical: the scheme was 'absurd' and 'chimerical'. The King was to be encouraged to adhere to the vigorous spirit and language he had shown in praising Legge's performance – that would 'do good, and, to a certain degree give strength'.[110] The Chancellor was certainly right to fear a reversion in the King to 'his former doubts and diffidence' more than any plot on Legge's part. Newcastle's estimate that the conspiracy was beaten went further: it was a judgement based, as yet, only on the failure of the Commons to respond to opposition talk about the place of a minister, and on steadily improving relations with Egmont. Advances to him continued through Egremont and Boone,[111] culminating in a meeting with Egremont on 27 November. Meanwhile, until the Reading petition clash on 25th, widespread satisfaction was expressed at Newcastle's possession of a solid and unprecedentedly large Whig majority. Joseph Yorke was delighted with the good signs at the opening of the session, and the prospects for 'the maintenance of the old system, of which your Grace has for so many years been the unwearied champion'.[112]

In the Commons on 18th, Sir Francis Dashwood

moved, that the Sheriff of Oxfordshire should be ordered to the Bar of the House to be examined as a criminal for malpractices [i.e. for making a double return], the New Interest [Hillsborough and Conway] insisted that the examination of the Sheriff and the merits of the election should go together...

The Whigs carried their point in a division by 206 to 97.[113] But on 20 November the Tories unexpectedly repeated their procedural motion in an attempt to have the return considered separately from the merits of the election. Fox, coming in before the question was put, spoke against; so did Pitt, 'very emphatically'. Prowse answered him; but 'at last the Tories in a manner gave up the question, Colonel Townshend having spoke against it upon the foot of its being in effect the same as what had been rejected before...'

On 21st, the motion to fix a day for hearing a petition against the Mitchell return was carried, against the sitting members, by 154 to 127.[114] Fox and Charles Yorke spoke against the motion; 'Pitt went away and the Grenvilles were absent'; Legge 'and others of the placemen spoke for it' on the side of Newcastle's candidates, the petitioners.[115] Nevertheless, Newcastle's calculations assumed Legge's disloyalty. When, on the morning of 25 November, Pitt descended from the gallery to deliver a tirade against the electoral corruption revealed by a petition at Berwick, Legge's only defence of the ministry was to give 'his *assent* and *consent* to the maintenance of the dignity of the House of Commons, which, he hoped, they would think best maintained by a steady adherence to Whig principles, *on which, whether sooner or later, whatever is to be my fate,* I am determined to stand or fall'.[116] Thus phrased, Legge's remarks revealed his sympathy with the extreme Whigs who sought both to frustrate ministerial co-operation with the Tories, and to recommend themselves to the Old Corps, by stressing the value and continued relevance of party distinctions. What was most important in Pitt's and Legge's speeches was thus their tactical context. On the merits of the Berwick return, Pitt was wide of the mark, and neither Legge nor any other minister had a case to answer; for Wilkes, the petitioner, though later enlisting the Grenvilles' support, remained Newcastle's candidate.[117] Moreover, Wilkes had spent £3–4000 in bribery during the election;[118] was unaware of Pitt's intention to intervene; and sat in terror while he spoke, fearing that Pitt's wrath would eventually fall on him rather than on Delaval, the other candidate.[119] But the Paymaster had resurrected the language of Commons independence in a newly explosive context: if they did not assume a sense of their own importance, he challenged, the House would 'degenerate into a little assembly, serving no other purpose than to register the arbitrary edicts of one, too powerful, subject',[120] and would become 'the contemptible appendix of he knew not what'.[121]

Fox supposed the attack to be levelled against the Tory taint carried by Murray, who sat silent while it was delivered, and Horace Walpole repeated this view. But the target was not self-evident. Pitt's tactics were not apparent, and his rhetoric was therefore open to interpretation. Calcraft, despite seemingly being given the Foxite account of the speeches' meaning, observed that 'The House in general looked all confusion';[122] Martin thought these passages

clearly referred to the Duke of Newcastle. Upon enquiry I did not find that everybody understood them as I did to insinuate that the House ought not to submit to be governed by the Duke. And what he [Pitt] said of Whiggism alluded to a scheme of the Duke's to erect a kind of aristocracy, to carry on the administration in the hands of nobility alone, and to expect compliance from the House of Commons without any minister placed among them. This I have private reasons to know.

Mr Legge's speech was meant to hint his concurrence with Mr Pitt's sentiments, suggesting withal that the Duke of Newcastle entertained favourites about him disposed to toryism with whom he could never think of entering into a connection. This was very darkly insinuated, but was perfectly understood by Mr Fox as I perceived by a subsequent conversation with him in the House.[123]

Hence Fox's observation about Murray, who may well have felt reluctant to cast himself as the chief opponent of a combined Commons force of Pitt, Fox and Legge; especially since Murray's natural talents had led several to remark that in the debate on 15th, he had 'taken upon him the air and appearance of the minister who was to lead the House'.[124] Presumably it was Legge who interpreted Pitt's speech to Martin; but if he would not have known without a private briefing, Pitt's display must have been less than fully effective. Thus Horatio Walpole, who thought Pitt's Berwick oration and its 'strongest expressions of true Whiggism... were plainly calculated to ingratiate himself with the *Old Corps*' in preference to the slighted Newcastle and Murray, knew that many Whigs had understood it otherwise, 'as an intimation of his returning again to be an Old Whig and Patriot, on the other side of the House', so that Pitt's 'Whig principles...are interpreted...in a very different sense from what he intended'.[125] Horatio Walpole's guess was correct. Pitt's performances in Parliament throughout the winter were those not of an incipient Patriot in its earlier sense, as a strategy for constructing a Tory–opposition Whig alliance, but in a new sense: as an assault on such tactics pursued by the ministry itself. This realignment of arguments was not at once obvious. But in late December, John Sharpe reported to Sir Dudley Ryder that

one of the principal Tories told him they disliked Pitt so much that if he was to be out of place and should come over to their side of the House, they would to a man leave it and go to the Ministry to show their aversion, though they would not join with the Ministry.[126]

In the Commons the same evening, Pitt pursued similar themes in condemning Robinson's cavalier description of the sitting member's defence against a ministerialist's petition at Reading as a 'poor cause'. Robinson was provoked to an assertion of his own Whiggism. Ellis thought the defence unnecessary, and that his hearers were surprised by it.[127] But Robinson was correct in thinking that Pitt was attempting to slight him, for the Paymaster not only ignored the merits of the Reading petition,[128] but went so far as to insult – quite unjustly – Robinson's ambition for the post of Secretary of State. The miscalculation may have been immediately clear, for after Robinson's spirited reply,[129] 'Mr Pitt standing up again and beginning with much flattery to Sir Thomas the House gave him a deep groan; as a mark of disapproving such gross dissimulation so inconsistent with his former invective'. Fox undertook a defence of Robinson, but in satirical terms evidently calculated to discredit him. Legge made no defence; 'a great number of people have concluded from thence that he wishes [Pitt and Fox] success'.[130] Nevertheless, their indulgence in personal hostilities had lost the sympathy of the House. 'I have found since', wrote Legge's secretary, 'that a great many people disapproved of the violent manner in which Mr Pitt attacked Sir Thomas Robinson.'[131] Hartington, in retrospect, thought Pitt had opened the attack on Robinson 'prematurely', led into it by 'impetuosity of temper (worked up by his ambition)'.[132] Horatio Walpole observed that 'the whole cry at this end of the town, as well as in the City' was against the 'insatible ambition' of the orators.[133] George Grenville admitted he had tried to dissuade Pitt from 'pushing things to extremities. I did this from opinion, as there was then no measure on foot to oppose, and from a consideration of Mr Pitt's circumstances...'[134] – that is, his need of the income of his office after his marriage to Grenville's sister on 16 November. The Paymaster's philippics on corruption, though compelling in their rhetoric and unexceptionable in their principles, made no difference to the outcome either of the Reading or of the Berwick petitions.[135] As Horatio Walpole realised,

the body of the *Old Corps*, that attended the Committee, showed an approbation to Sir Thomas Robinson's behaviour and great resentment towards that of Mr Pitt, and even of Mr Fox, and as to Watson's election at Berwick, they are universally for him and Mr Pitt never could have taken so ill a time to declare his Whig principles...[136]

It is more difficult to discover what else his speeches were intended to do. Wilkes was an unprincipled careerist,[137] a client of Newcastle, and apparently unknown to Pitt; his petition, once the facts became clear, could not credibly be used as an occasion for displays of Patriot rhetoric, and Pitt did not repeat his early gesture of support. Delaval, Wilkes's opponent, was returned on the interest of Fox's ally the Earl of Northumberland: if this was known to Pitt, his restraint may have marked a desire for an alliance with Fox. But the prior existence of such an alliance is disproved by the course of the Reading petition. Pitt was involved on behalf of the sitting member, Fane, through a chance meeting with him in October, but though the Paymaster was initially enthusiastic and spoke at that date of his pleasure at being able to serve Bedford, Fane noticed that Pitt's 'zeal did seem to me very much to cool' when he told him that Fox had already 'expressed himself zealous in my support'. Fane nevertheless exhorted Bedford to consider 'whether any man in this country has half the chance of uniting these two opposite factions [Pitt and Fox] as the Duke of Bedford has, and if they were united what the consequence must be...' Pitt's objects, Fane suggested, were the Chancellorship of the Exchequer for George Grenville and a seat at the Treasury Board for Potter: Fox could be expected to find such terms acceptable.[138] That this was almost certainly a considerable underestimate of Pitt's long-term ambitions was probably not apparent in 1754, and there is evidence of Fox's co-operation at this time with the Grenvilles over another petition, that against the Oxfordshire return.[139] Bedford's reactions to Fane's suggestion are, however, unknown.[140] Fox was seemingly unaware that Pitt would speak in support of Wilkes; though Bedford and Rigby had been loudly and vigorously canvassing support, with Fox's full sympathy, for the sitting member at Reading,[141] Fox himself wrote as if Pitt's 'sole motive' in speaking that evening had been a personal one; to make 'a panegyric' on Fane.[142] When the

Committee rose, added Fox, the Members gathered 'at once into knots of two, or three, or four whisperers, who, I suppose, did (what I cannot yet do), make some conclusion'. His only suggestion was that Newcastle had provoked Pitt's outburst.[143] It does not seem that Bedford told Fox of Fane's suggestions, much less that he acted as the agent of a Pitt–Fox rapprochement. Bedford perhaps doubting the prospects of any opposition in the coming session, had already put out private feelers to the ministry,[144] and there is no evidence that Pitt took the lead in seeking closer relations with him. Indeed, no co-ordination was apparent until Pitt's conference with Fox on 27 November.

Fox claimed that he attempted a defence of Robinson on 25th,[145] while avoiding the sore question of the latter's appointment as Secretary of State. But Walpole supposed[146] that Fox had damned his colleague by faint praise, and Martin agreed: 'here Mr Pitt and Mr Fox were both universally understood to have fallen upon Sir Thomas as the immediate representative of the Duke of Newcastle, and sent to declare his sentiments to the House with regard to the Reading election': an opportunity to resent an apparent attempt to dictate to the Commons which Fox also took, though only in private.[147] Lord Trentham, presumably on intelligence from Rigby or Bedford, interpreted events in the Commons during these days as evidence of a 'union and alliance of abilities'.[148] This was largely inference. As Dudley Ryder wrote:

I find it is the general sense that Legge will not be able to support [himself] as the [principal] speaker and Prime Minister to inform and communicate to the House, to guide its motion. That Fox and Pitt and the Grenvilles and Lytteltons are united. That people say there is nothing but a Scotsman and two Irishmen to defend ministerial measures – meaning, I suppose, Murray and Lord Hillsborough and Nugent – and in truth it seems to me very difficult to support the Duke of Newcastle without taking them in.[149]

Ellis, as a close associate of Fox, was probably more accurate in writing of these events as 'foundations which have been laid of disposition and goodwill between our friend [Fox] and those whom we have formerly considered in a more distant manner though adopted into and made part of a former system'; a 'great man' in the ministers' confidence, he added, was saying that things could not go on as they were, and Ellis suspected negotiations impending.[150] It seems that Hartington had already heard of, and mentioned to Fox, a probability that Pitt and his associates would be turned out and he, Fox, offered the Paymastership: 'a more disagreeable, delicate, embarrassing, and if accepted, perhaps a more disgraceful affair', wrote the Secretary at War, 'could not happen',[151] especially since he feared that he might be dismissed if he refused. Cumberland had heard the same story via Hartington, and added that Fox would be given Cabinet rank and the lead in the House.[152] He advised Fox to wait quietly for Newcastle's overture: if it proved 'improper', 'I hope you'll desire to give your answer to the King yourself, and, without mentioning what is passed, repeat your promises of not opposing and declining the offers, as they would not enable you to remedy the disorders now risen in the House of Commons'.[153]

Hartington's intelligence was presumably known to Fox before the clash over Berwick; there is no evidence that Pitt knew the uncertainty of his tenure. Fox's part in the debate should, then, be read primarily as an attempt to recommend himself as one able to remedy the disorders, and present Robinson as one unable to do so. Fox's was not so much a gesture of opposition to Newcastle's ministry as a bid for place within it. Although the example of Pitt had carried him too far, he now fell silent, on Cumberland's instructions.[154] Pitt did not. In his speech on Berwick, he had delivered an 'eloquent exhortation to Whigs of all conditions, to defend their attacked and expiring liberty, etc'.[155] A similar opportunity presented itself in the debate on the army on 27th. Richard Beckford opposed, moving for a reduction of numbers to 15,000 and suggesting 'that the Opposition were Whigs and the Ministry Tories'. Fox replied briefly, confining himself to the subject. Barrington and Nugent then 'made unnecessary, and fulsome, speeches; both declaring, the extreme popularity not only of His Majesty but of his Ministers, and *that there were no Jacobites in England*'.[156]

Mr Nugent observed that he thought there were but few Jacobites in the kingdom, that many had formerly thought themselves Jacobites who when the occasion came [in 1745] were surprised to find they were not so,...This doctrine of Jacobites brought up Mr William Pitt who said he could not sit still and hear it asserted that there was no Jacobite faction in the kingdom and that when any gentleman said there was not he did not think he meant what he said...[157]

Pitt's speech turned on Jacobitism, wrote Fox: 'the tendency of too great security on that head; and...that seminary of disaffection, Oxford'.[158] Martin, too, was impressed by Pitt's tirade 'on the subject of Jacobitism, which he said was by no means extinct in this kingdom; and that no position could be more dangerous and fatal, than the soothing doctrine which holds Jacobitism to be at an end'.[159] That that doctrine should be advanced by ministerialist spokesmen was remarkable, and Pitt's reaction may well have been provoked by astonishment rather than a premeditated campaign of opposition. Newcastle's conciliatory attitude to the Tories could be expected, by lowering the ideological temperature, to shield Murray and, at the same time, to offer the prospect of a *modus vivendi* with that party and with Leicester House. It was such possibilities that Pitt sought to resist. As Martin recorded, his

encomiums of Whiggism in his former speech, and invectives against Jacobitism in the latter appear to be both calculated to the same end – to court the Whigs and to prepare them for jealousies of the Attorney General and Mr Stone, whom the Duke of Newcastle places the highest confidence in, and whom Mr Pitt and his friends heartily hate.

I am confirmed in my notion of these his views, by Mr James Grenville his friend and favourite who spoke in the same debate to the same purpose, and owned to me the design which I have mentioned.[160]

Pitt's attack on the Tories in late 1754 was as new a departure as the ministerial attitude to Toryism, and circumstantial evidence suggests it was a last-minute response to ministerial policy in the Commons. Earlier, no such aversion to the Tories had been apparent. He must have been aware of Prince Frederick's desire for an accommodation with that party, yet this did not deter Pitt from plans to join Leicester House – plans frustrated by the death of the Prince of Wales in 1751. For the Paymaster's attitude to the Tories between 1751 and 1754 there is little evidence. It is not clear that he took any part in the outcry over Stone and Murray, or in agitating for the repeal of the Jew Bill; and in 1754, while taking the waters at Bath, he accepted without evident misgivings or aversion an invitation to dine on 25 October at Badminton,[161] the nearby seat of the Duke of Beaufort. Moreover, he had announced his visit in a way which he can hardly have expected to remain a secret from the Grenvilles.

Now, on 27 November, Fox (showing a remarkable ignorance of Pitt's tactical intentions) supposed him provoked by Nugent's praise of Newcastle, but recognised the real damage the Paymaster did to Murray's political standing. Some of the terror usually attributed to Murray is, however, a retrospective prejudice on Horace Walpole's part. At the time, he recorded that the Attorney General 'seems cowed', but that it was Legge who 'crouches under the storm'.[162] Nor is there evidence to confirm Elliot's claim[163] that Murray's plan was to defend public measures with ability and firmness, but to act with 'reserve and feebleness on every personal attack' in order to reveal the weakness of other Commons ministers. While not believing Pitt's rhetoric, Fox professed similar grounds for opposition:

Old Horace advises Pitt, Legge, and me, not only to be easy, but to be cheerfully active, and says the Old Whigs will hate us if we are not. In short, *advises* more than the Duke of Newcastle can even presume to *wish*. I see no Whiggism in this. And, as it is clear now, that the House of Commons are to have no share, and that Lord Chancellor, Lord Granville, and the Duke of Newcastle are determined to depress them, not to resist seems too much to be expected.[164]

But Horatio Walpole was better informed about the feelings of the Commons at large:

Upon the whole Pitt's speech was a masterly and incomparable performance, and pleased the whole body of the Whigs and would have pleased them more had it not been evident, that what he said to Lord Barrington and Nugent, proceded purely from their having spoken in praise of the administration, and this notion of his and Mr Fox's design to distress the ministry, by all possible means, without opposing the public measures is so prevalent; that all their eloquence and abilities in support of true Whiggism, will not overcome the prejudice that day by day increases against them; of their having agreed (though once rivals) to lay hold of all occasions to perplex and expose the administration; and the means they have hitherto taken for that purpose far from answering the ends they proposed, have had a very different effect, and recoiled upon themselves...[165]

NEWCASTLE'S OVERTURES: EGMONT AND THE TORIES

On 29 November, Charles Yorke reported: 'the Whigs...suspect that Pitt is connecting with Fox and that the Grenvilles may be so likewise, but Lyttelton is not'.[166] The Commons' suspicions were correct. Despite others' opinions of Pitt's miscalculation in the House, Fox expected to receive ministerial offers; in preparation for them, he had a two-hour conference with Pitt on the morning of 27 November. In this context, it seems probable that Pitt's attacks on Jacobitism later that day were intended to prevent Fox's participation without him in an Old Corps scheme incorporating Lee, Egmont and the Tories. If so, it would explain Horace Walpole's observation that it was only now that Pitt 'sought heartily and sincerely to league with Fox' and 'set...at defiance' the ministers, who, he saw, were trying to divide him from his ally.[167] Embarrassed and uneasy, Fox was agonising in advance about the offer he was drawn to accept, and the barrier his honour posed to his sacrifice of Pitt. As yet, however, Newcastle's partly understood manoeuvres alarmed him:

There are symptoms of Lord Egmont's having been talked to, and certain verified tokens of union between Murray, Sir G. Lee, and some Tories. Pitt assures me, it is the *Testament politique* of Lord Bolingbroke, lodged in great hands, and really brings more circumstances than your Lordship would imagine to warrant this assertion. If so, Horace [Horatio Walpole] is not only working hard, to fix the sole power of the Duke of Newcastle *now*; but in the end to accomplish a scheme of Lord Bolingbroke's. They are not [mss. torn] two men in the world he is most obliged to. So that is strange; but that he should call it old and true Whiggism is more than strange, it is absurd, and indeed provoking.[168]

Nothing had evidently yet been said to Fox. His fears were more unjustifiably exaggerated than Newcastle's, for Murray's Tory associations were a fiction which had been deliberately revived that summer. Yet Fox's apprehensions, too, had a basis in fact. Newcastle had deliberately sought to conciliate Egmont and the Tory party. In October he was accused of preferring the pockets of the country gentry to the reduction of the national debt.[169] Despite the quiescence of Leicester House, too, Newcastle's aim appeared to be to broaden the bottom of the administration and weaken 'faction...by taking off able leaders';[170]

he was merely delaying removals until arrangements could be made, and the King's approval gained, for an alternative system. Newcastle still adhered, on 28th, to his preference for the dismissal of Pitt and the removal of Legge[171] to another office; he looked to Sir George Lee as the fittest replacement for the latter, 'if he will accept it'. Egmont was to be brought in immediately; meanwhile, 'it should be known to all our friends, that Sir Thomas Robinson is to be the person at the head of the House of Commons, for which he has shewed himself more capable, than was imagined before'. This public confirmation was recommended at once, to gain time for sounding opinion, and to avoid the 'immediate opposition to all our present measures' which Newcastle feared would follow one dismissal alone.[172] Nevertheless, some such move was widely expected: Pitt could hardly be continued in office, it was thought, after his attack on Robinson.[173]

Much turned on the reaction of Egmont. He met Egremont at White's on 27 November, probably after Pitt's Commons speech but apparently without the interview being related to Fox's meeting with Pitt the same day. Ominously, Egmont professed indifference for place, employment or power at the same time as he warned the ministers 'that I knew the administration was undone without me...That the D[uke] of C[umberland] and his party with Fox and Pitt would extinguish them – would engross both civil and military power – ruin the Princess – possess the Regency and the young Royal Family and carry things in the highest mode of government':[174] that is, in an arbitrary manner. Egmont offered to stand against them (if 'enabled' to do so) only on condition that the ministry 'absolutely...give up those two dreadful measures which they still obstinately pushed in all this danger and distress – viz. 1. absolute power by the instructions over the Colonies principally in America[175] – 2. infamous attempt to make the revenue in Ireland a Civil List'.[176] Without this, Egmont claimed he would lose the influence he exercised over 'the parties in Parliament'.[177] His antipathy to the Fox–Cumberland group, and his hatred of Pitt, dated back at least to his position as chief adviser to the Prince of Wales in 1749–51. But now he evidently underestimated the loyal bloc of the Old Corps and the strength accruing to Newcastle from the main wing of Leicester House and Sir George Lee; Egmont's reluctance to take office thus paradoxically worked to allow Newcastle to defeat Pitt and Fox through reconciling Egmont to the ministry without a Cabinet place, presenting Fox with a *fait accompli* forcing him to break with Pitt, and incorporating Fox on terms similar to those he rejected the previous March.

The evidence fails to bear out Walpole's assertion[178] that Newcastle 'saw his mighty power totter' and sent for Fox to rescue him. Waldegrave claimed[179] that he terrified Newcastle with forecasts of the consequences if Fox and Pitt were to join in open opposition; but he tacitly admitted that that situation had not yet arrived. There is no evidence of terror in inner ministerial circles, only of long-pending plans for a reshuffle. Egmont's declarations on 27th were duly reported to New-castle: 'No ministerial office. Any [other] that the King shall think proper. Attached to the King and his ministers'. Pitt's removal was then determined on; Newcastle hoped to be able to transfer Fox to the Pay-mastership, drop Legge, and replace him with Horatio Walpole.[180] These aims are recorded also in an undated memorandum[181] which points to Newcastle's desire 'to get through the public business before the removals'. Then, Fox was to be treated with first, after a sharp warning from the King on the unacceptability of his 'behaviour and connection'. The object was to 'break the connection with Pitt', but Newcastle reproached himself: 'Fool to give Mr Fox the advantage of knowing the King's intentions as to Mr Pitt'. As Newcastle expected, Fox told Pitt, but the alarm was a false one: once Newcastle had out-manoeuvred Fox, he found he had outmanoeuvred Pitt, too.

Newcastle met Egmont for four hours on the night of 1 December.[182] The terms of the discussion are nowhere recorded, but it seems unlikely that Egmont departed from the position he had already explained at length. Granville understood that Egmont, impracticably, insisted on a Secretaryship of State,[183] and presumably an English peerage. Never-theless, the Duke of Beaufort was encouraged by the news of Pitt's and Fox's disruption, particularly with respect to the Oxfordshire election petition: 'For if Fox is turned out how can his associates and allies stay in, and then surely those who remain in power will out of resent-ment to them put a stop to violent measures' against the Tories.[184] It is probable, therefore, that that party was induced to come to an under-standing with Newcastle both by the danger of a Pitt–Fox entente and by hopes of profiting from its destruction. They thus met half way the ministry's willingness for a rapprochement.

Moreover, an urgent cause for action existed. On 3 December they lost a division on that test-case, the Oxfordshire petition, by the decisive margin of 272 to 117.[185] On 4th, Martin recorded a rumour 'that some of the Tories are to be taken into office' and that Eliab Harvey '(who converses much with that body)' had offered a bet on the date. Two days later, Martin heard from Lord Temple 'that he had heard and believed the Tories had sent the D[uke] of N[ewcastle] a deputation by Lord Egmont, Prowse, Sir Ja[mes] Dashwood and a 4th person, to let him know that the body of Tories would assist him in all points not directly inconsistent with their political creed'.[186] Unless the meeting of 1 December was referred to, confirmation of such a visit from min-isterial sources is absent; it may be that the fact of negotiations with Egmont was inflated into an exaggerated alarm by Pitt's camp in an effort to frustrate any such alliance by emphasising its ideological aspect. Nevertheless, Newcastle's main asset for the moment was that there was 'no-one to the right of him'. Evidence is lacking of any precise agreement with the Tory leaders, and the rank and file of that party did not display a purposiveness in their voting in the coming months which would suggest a shared knowledge of such an undertaking. Nevertheless, other and familiar reasons acted to inhibit their cohesion. Henry Shiffner complained of the promised Tory support for his petition against Daniel Boone (backed by Egremont) at Minehead:

Can any set of men ever think to be of any consequence in the politick scales unless they will support their measures by numbers and attendance? At the Cocoa Tree numbers are counted, strength is computed, and it is agreed that they consist of a number not to be despised and that 90 may carry some weight with them; well what is the consequence of this in the House? Why a motion is made, attendance, close. Attendance is promised, notice is given of the day, and all goes swimmingly till the critical minute; then one is out of town, another at home, a great many at the bottle, and hardly any at the place of action, except the opera, play or burletta is mistaken for it...[187]

Yet Shiffner was an outsider, a newcomer to parliamentary politics, and a stranger to the party to which he appealed. Despite a few spectacular incidents, the session before Christmas showed that no formal opposition to the ministry existed on the part of the Tories. As Gilbert Elliot wrote, 'We have sometimes heats in the House, but few or no debates, as there has scarce been any opposition to measures.'[188] And after Christmas, events in the Commons were to demonstrate even more clearly a Tory willingness to countenance the Old Corps in the face of a Pitt–Fox–Cumberland threat, just as once they had preferred Walpole to his opposition Whig rivals on some issues.

THE UNDERSTANDING WITH FOX, DECEMBER 1754

Fox was to have an audience of the King on 2 December, 'where the Duke [Cumberland] thinks I am to be offered Paymaster in Pitt's room with Cabinet Counsellor and the direction of the House of Commons'.[189] Even before that, Legge had spoken on 1 December of Newcastle's decision on Granville's advice to turn out Pitt, replace him with Legge, and install (not Horatio Walpole, but, far more credibly) Egmont at the Exchequer. Fox may have been Legge's source, as he was Pitt's. Martin checked this with Hume Campbell, who told him, presumably from ministerial sources, a slightly different story: of Pitt's intended dismissal and Egmont's being destined for office, though he did not know which office; that no resolution had been taken on turning out Fox; and that Newcastle had had 'a discourse' with Hume Campbell on the need for Legge to 'exert himself with more spirit' than he had shown on the Mitchell petition and other issues, not mentioning another post for him, but hinting instead at his removal.[190] During the audience, George II put similar pressure on Fox, who was obliged to deny any political connection with Pitt. It seems that Fox was unable, before the

King, either to ask openly for the office of Secretary of State or to avow links with Pitt without violating constitutional propriety. Fox was evasive when George II demanded that he support his business: he 'seemed to imply he would do it, provided he was so far enabled that he could do it effectually and with credit to himself, and that he did not mean to be unreasonable in his demands': that is, that the War Office be advanced to rank as a third Secretaryship of State. That would allow him to stand up to Pitt. Fox's offer, as Waldegrave interpreted it, was that

he was ready and willing to act, not only in concert with the Duke of Newcastle but to be entirely under his direction; that he did not desire to have anything to do with the secret service money, or to have the disposal of any places, or to have any real power, only that the appearance of it was necessary.

He warned against Pitt's expulsion; and that if he, Fox, were put 'in some degree at the head of the House of Commons, Mr Pitt would either resign his employment or lose his credit by acting an under part, or else would oppose in place, which would be a justifiable reason for turning him out'. A similar objection held against Fox's taking the Paymastership, a move which would fail to make him 'a minister': that is, confer Cabinet rank.[191] Fox was taken, therefore, to be declining the lead from the consequences his promotion threatened to the ministry (a position consistent with the preservation of his private alliance with Pitt).

But it is evident that the King offered Fox nothing during their meeting, and no terms were settled.[192] Fox then saw Pitt, and, intercepting Waldegrave before the latter could call as arranged at Newcastle House,[193] it seems that Fox turned his suggestions to the King into a treacherous manoeuvre without Pitt's knowledge. For Fox's terms, with which Newcastle was presented by Waldegrave on 3 December, though more assertive than the lukewarm assurances George II had drawn from the Secretary at War,[194] now entailed Fox's sacrifice of the Paymaster. If, therefore, there was a Tory offer via Egmont between 4 and 6 December, it would have come too late to have its maximum effect; and Newcastle is not open to the accusation of having fatally delayed an accommodation with Leicester House in the hope of contriving an alternative alliance with the Tories. Waldegrave claimed Fox had been asked to 'take the lead in the House of Commons, by what his Majesty was pleased to say to him, of supporting his measures and ministers against any attack'; and that Fox was willing to work 'with' and 'under' Newcastle from (though here Waldegrave was tentative) the War Office elevated to a third Secretaryship. Fox had not said that he would insist on this, however, and Newcastle jibbed at what the orators' earlier talk about the control of the Commons made appear too high a price; he could now afford to revert to the offer of the Paymastership plus 'respect and confidence', under Robinson's primacy. Waldegrave doubted whether Fox would agree, but reconciled the two views by interpreting Fox's claim to the leadership of the Commons narrowly, as excluding a voice in appointments to offices or the disposition of secret service money, 'if any such was', and as no more than the consequence of the other marks of status to be given him. Fox had thus in effect offered to undertake the dangerous and equivocal role he had declined that spring; and now, the rhetoric in which Pitt, Legge, Potter and others had since indulged was to deprive him of the formal definitions of his status which he might then have enjoyed.

Fox waited for Newcastle's reply in a mood of uncertainty and a state of dependence.[195] Waldegrave told him, presumably on 4th, that the King was even less inclined to make him a minister than was Newcastle.[196] To Pitt he wrote[197] that Newcastle, on 3rd, had interrupted Waldegrave's report of Fox's audience to assert that the King could not have meant to offer the lead of the Commons – Fox implying, the lead extensively conceived, as a threat to Newcastle's power. He was deceiving Pitt, for he had abandoned any such claim and had left Newcastle with what he hoped was a far more acceptable scheme. Instead, he played on Pitt's other fears of a plan for the subordination of the Commons. When Waldegrave returned to the King on 3rd, George II had evidently been briefed on Newcastle's view of Robinson's status,[198] for he 'gave a negative to the lead of the House of Commons. He will have no Leader there. What he expects and requires is that his servants should act in concert and with spirit in their respective departments etc., and not quarrel among themselves'.[199] Fox would then be treated with 'regard, and confidence from the King's servants, and with grace and favour from his Majesty'.[200] Fox told Pitt that the King's intention had been to offer him Pitt's employment: his refusal made him feel sure of Pitt's loyalty,[201] and he closely consulted the Paymaster on the text of the written reply the King demanded to set out Fox's terms. He suggested to Pitt two possible answers: one, to agree with the King's view of the lead, while warning that Fox could do no more in his present situation; the other, which arose in conversation with Waldegrave and Newcastle, was that if Fox got 'this nothing' (Cabinet rank) he must pretend it was 'nothing' to Newcastle and the King, but 'must talk in the House as if it was the lead, and if no good comes (and I believe no good will come) of that', Fox might 'at all times take to sitting still, or quitting'. This last was a close approximation to what was to be the situation that spring; but it plainly offered nothing, immediately, to Pitt.

Fox and Pitt apparently met on the evening of 4 December. 'Fox irresolute, affecting content, borne down by the Duke [? Cumberland] from opposition, and aspiring at sole power...would not enter into real measures.'[202] On 5th, Fox wrote: 'it has been said, I had better not name the Cabinet Council': that is, demand Cabinet rank for himself as the public mark of favour which would enable him to undertake business effectively. Fox had therefore 'curtailed, with design, the particulars of what I am to undertake',[203] though Pitt suspected that some phrases in Fox's draft letter to the King carried 'the air of a sort of capitulation; (if taken in one sense)'.[204] To Pitt, then, Fox pleaded the necessity of accepting a less than ideal scheme; to Newcastle, he pleaded submission and sacrificed Pitt's ambitions in order to secure whatever *was* available. Already, it began to be said that Fox was about to be promoted, but Pitt and 'some of his friends' dismissed;[205] and that Fox had vehemently denied to the King any connection with the Paymaster.[206] Fox's loyalty to Cumberland could now scarcely be concealed from Pitt, for the Duke insisted on Fox's inserting the qualification 'in the present state of the House of Commons' – 'that I might not be supposed absolutely engaged, and have no words to show that guarded against a certain event [George II's death], which he [Cumberland] agrees with me, though you don't, must and should put an end to this scheme, not too promising as it is'.[207] Fox now saw that his only hope of the highest power lay with a Cumberland regency: and for that reason, Pitt was ultimately impelled in a direction which eventually led to another quarter of the Court. The final version of Fox's letter to the King included this caveat and omitted, as Cumberland asked, the explicit reference to a Cabinet seat.[208] To Pitt, Fox excused himself that this demand could be taken as read. Pitt appeared anxious to push Fox to demand a Cabinet place *tout court*, as if in search of a decisive victory or a shared defeat; he amended Fox's phrase claiming a wish for 'neither money nor power' so as to accommodate an implied bid for rank. Fox consented. Though he told the King that he was in no conjunction with Pitt, and even brought Pitt to deny (in a private letter) the existence of such a formal undertaking, Fox was still assuring his ally that 'on no consideration, will I venture on this weak scheme, unless strengthened by your acquiescence in it'.[209] Despite what might almost have seemed an abandonment of the Paymaster in December 1754, Fox's co-operation with the ministry rested until May 1755 on his uneasy assumption that Pitt *did* acquiesce.

On 10th, Newcastle, Hardwicke and Granville met to consider, on the basis of Fox's written answer to the King, 'whether anything less than the Cabinet Council can be suggested in order to comply with Mr Fox's request'.[210] In the light of the surrender which lay behind Fox's offer, Newcastle and Hardwicke[211] supposed it might be sufficient if Fox were assured that he would be 'constantly and early informed of all advices that may come from abroad, and all other matters, that may any way relate to the business of the House of Commons...' The first draft of their memorandum proceeded on the assumption that the King might decide to call Fox to the Cabinet; the second arranged for Waldegrave to tell Fox that the King would do so: a promotion

not intended [by the King] in the least to interfere with or derogate from the priority, belonging to His Majesty's Secretary of State in the House of

Commons; and that it is not His Majesty's intention to confer any power or confidence, independent of such ministers, as His Majesty shall think fit to entrust with the conduct of his affairs. That, with regard to Mr Pitt ... it may be most advisable to suspend coming to any resolution upon Mr Pitt's subject for the present; but to leave him under the uncertainty, under which he now is.[212]

Fox was unlikely to object to the last condition. Already he had told Waldegrave that if anything short of Cabinet rank would be an excuse 'for my altering my conduct with regard to the ministers, let it be proposed. I do not desire to know, much less to determine, what Mr Pitt is to do or be'. In his letter to the King on 10th Fox waived the lead, and his only specific request was carried verbally by Waldegrave: to be excused from taking Pitt's place.[213] Thus although Fox was happy to accept Cabinet rank, Walpole's implication[214] that it was a demand communicated informally by Waldegrave is an overstatement. Fox's indifference to Pitt, too, is fully substantiated.[215] Once Fox had spelled out, in an interview with West on 11 December, his consent for 'Sir Thomas Robinson to be at the head of everything. To have all the meetings at his house' even in spite of Pitt, who 'would certainly fly out',[216] Newcastle and Hardwicke made their memorandum of 10 December the basis of the King's written reply via Waldegrave on 12th.[217]

Fox, granted the Cabinet but formally denied both the lead and the elevation of the Secretaryship at War, was acceptable to the ministry on condition of the King's willingness to talk sharply to him if he stepped out of line.[218] Evasively, he professed ignorance to Pitt of what was to be done about the Paymaster, and added: 'I find nothing is so terrible, as what, if they knew us, they ought to wish, our being in conjunction with them and in their service'.[219] This was absurd; but, luckily for Fox, Pitt could not know enough of the terms of the arrangement to see it as treachery. Rather, he supposed simply that Fox had failed, though reprehensibly, to take advantage of his position; he continued to suppose so until September 1755 when he declared privately to Dodington that 'He Pitt was ready last session, to go any lengths, against the Duke of Newcastle – when it came to the push, Mr Fox owned he could not; and went on, through the whole session, compromising everything when it began to pinch...'[220] Horace Walpole, however, made the plausible claim that Fox, on his promotion, 'privately foreswore all connection with Pitt' and that Newcastle 'leaked' this information to the Paymaster.[221] Such actions may have been in character, but it seems likely that the claim was Walpole's hypothesis to explain, at Newcastle's expense, Pitt's breach with Fox on 9 May; it is not elsewhere corroborated. It seems that it was Hardwicke's advice, too, which induced the King not to dismiss Pitt;[222] Fox did nothing to persuade George II to tolerate the Paymaster. In any event, it was immediately clear to the public that, as a result of the deal with Fox, 'all is quiet again',[223] and that in the ministry's conduct of affairs, 'all will go right now'.[224]

THE CONSEQUENCES: BEDFORD AND LEICESTER HOUSE

On 11 December, Newcastle summarised the situation to Sir Dudley Ryder:

The Duke of Newcastle says that none of all the Whigs in the House, which is a very good one and well affected, have said they desired that both Pitt and Fox should be removed, but principally aim at Pitt. That Sir G. Lyttelton in particular has expressed his great dissatisfaction with the conduct of Pitt. That however the Grenvilles are so connected that they will stand by Pitt. That at present nothing is determined with respect to Pitt, though I perceive it is meant to turn him out. That Lord Egmont is to come in, but I do not know into what post. Nothing said about Legge, the Chancellor of the Exchequer. The King says he will not have anyone Prime Minister in the House of Commons.[225]

Meanwhile, two developments had in the main offset each other. Two days after the army debate on 27 November, Sir George Lyttelton carried an offer of carte blanche to Bedford in return for his support. Bedford proved hostile, informed Pitt, and claimed that the overture was commissioned by Newcastle.[226] Lyttelton maintained the initiative was his own. Temple remarked to Legge on 6 December: 'In either case he was endeavouring to collect a strength to resist his old friend Mr W. Pitt: from whence it is clear that he prefers his office to his old friendship, and old obligations'.[227] Pitt duly broke with Lyttelton, who was destined to succeed Legge at the Exchequer in November 1755. Murray thought Lyttelton's mission was justified because Bedford 'had in fact talked that he was willing to come into the ministry not finding that an opposition could have been formed, but now finding one beginning to start had certainly made him to change his mind'.[228] Presumably Newcastle agreed.

Egmont, simultaneously with Fox's promotion, was rumoured to be destined for the place of Comptroller of the Household, defending himself from his friends' suspicion of office by claiming that it was at the Princess's 'special command'.[229] Walpole claims further that Fox then gave Egmont a prior sight of the Mutiny Bill, one of the clauses in which extended its operation to America, and that, 'struck with the old sounds, and forgetting his new engagements, [he] could not resist the impulse of haranguing' against it in the Commons on 11 December. On that occasion, Charles Townshend, 'hurt at a new promotion over his head', attacked first Egmont's arguments and then his acceptance of place. 'Lord Egmont was abashed, replied with confusion...He was overpowered by the attack, and excused himself from accepting the promised employment.'[230] That is: Fox, admitted after being defeated by a Newcastle–Egmont–Tory understanding, turned the tables on Egmont by a finesse.

The evidence does not bear out this interpretation, and an alternative account exists of events in the Commons:

Lord Egmont is certainly in treaty and Charles Townshend seems to regard him as a rival for a seat at the Treasury Board, for last night he upbraided him for his present coolness upon some topics, which at the opening of the sessions, he threatened to lay before the Parliament as public grievances, such as the causes of the present discontents in Ireland, and the Plantations, and to which his lordship gave a very confused answer, declaring he had never yet deceived the public. This occasioned a very hoarse laugh, for when brought in by the opposition in 1742 he joined Lord Granville's administration and when brought in by Mr Pelham, he declared against him...[231]

Evidently, then, Townshend did not assume that Egmont had already agreed to take office, and a rumour of Egmont's promotion to the Treasurership of the Household spread only after Townshend's speech.[232] It seems that a precise offer of office was never accepted by Egmont, not that he retreated from an agreement once made. Such an offer by Newcastle, too, would have been in spite of Horatio Walpole's advice against Egmont's inclusion as a man unpopular with 'the body of the Whigs' and as a reinforcement, 'that the chasm of debate might be filled up on the ministerial side', made unnecessary, as well as difficult in the Closet, by Pitt's not being dismissed. Treating them as Commons debaters only, Walpole warned that Egmont's gain would not outweigh the opposition of Pitt, Potter and George Grenville which it would in time entail through the scope it would give to the King to insist on the latter's removal.[233]

These or similar calculations may have prompted Newcastle's interview with Sir George Lee on 21 December. He found that Sir George preferred to retain his place in the Princess's household even if he took a ministerial post, since his health – he said – would not permit him to hold office long. Evidently Newcastle was considering him for the Exchequer. Egmont, too, was still a possible recruit whom Leicester House would be happy to see in alliance with the ministry. Newcastle wrote:

I have explained the whole, very fully to him [Lee]. I find, he apprehends, that the Princess of Wales has great fears, and alarms, from what has lately happened relating to Mr Fox. But he has no notion of her being the least uneasy, or thinking herself slighted, in the affair of Lord Egmont. He has promised to explain both, to her, in the course of this day; and thinks (if I can judge by his whole discourse) those explanations will greatly soften the other one; and entirely remove any blame from us, with regard to the other...But that, which gives me the greatest comfort, is that Sir G. Lee seemed firmly of opinion, from a conversation which he had with Lord Egmont, on Thursday last [19th], that he will take the Comptroller's staff: which will be the greatest disappointment to all those, who may have been endeavouring, and intriguing, to keep him out

– that is, Fox and Pitt. The disposition of Leicester House was confirmed by a message from Stone via Waldegrave, and a letter from Egremont.[234] Yet Newcastle wrote on 23rd of his 'most unfortunate interview' about to take place that day with Egmont, as if the latter would have to be disappointed of an expected place.[235] In fact, Egmont obtained a lesser mark of favour, a Privy Councillorship,[236] though Newcastle was at pains to inflate its importance and spoke as if it, too, might cement Egmont into the ministerial system.[237] The reason for the latter's disappointment is not clear. It seems probable that the King had obstructed the promotion of a man personally uncongenial to him; Egremont looked to the Comptrollership as an ideal way of softening these royal dislikes by frequent contact.[238] Yet in his audience on 26 December, Newcastle discovered 'a kind of new disposition' in George II towards Egmont, for the King readily agreed to the Privy Council and seemed well disposed to Egmont's having the Comptrollership, too, in Hillsborough's place. An important element in the King's change of heart was probably what Newcastle told him of Egmont's condemnation of Pitt's and Fox's conduct. George II was more apprehensive than Newcastle about the course of events during the coming session, but imagined that, after the deal, Fox would now have 'no pretence'. 'I mentioned Sir George Lee, and Legge', wrote Newcastle, 'as the only necessary measure remaining, to make everything easy, and quiet. The King did not object, and I have a sort of tacit consent to find out something for Legge, but I did not see the *glee* upon this subject, which I observed before. I fancy somebody has been throwing out *things* against Sir G. Lee.'[239] Nevertheless, Newcastle was able to secure George II's consent[240] that Lee should have the Exchequer, and continued until the summer to assume that the step was possible. To others, it later seemed that Legge 'would have been turned out long ago if Sir George Lee would have accepted the post',[241] and Fox reported that Lee had refused the Exchequer with the Princess's 'privity'.[242] But to the inner circle of the ministry, it seems probable that Lee's continued friendliness confirmed the impression he gave Newcastle on 21 December, that his demurral was not a final refusal.[243] Even by mid January, however, Newcastle was no closer to finding an office which Egmont wished to take;[244] Horatio Walpole was surprised that Egmont had not taken the Comptroller's staff from Hillsborough,[245] but evidently knew nothing of the cause.

Horace Walpole imagined that Fox's inclusion left Newcastle 'affronted – and omnipotent',[246] and Hardwicke thought things were settled on a 'clear and limited foot'.[247] Even a month later, Bedford wrote: 'everything is, I believe, likely to jog on quietly during the remainder of the sessions'.[248] A principal asset of the new system, however, was that it was open to representation in several different ways. In general, the Whigs were happy with it;[249] but Granville spoke[250] of Fox's substantial power, and Chesterfield wrote:[251] 'I think I see everything gravitating to Fox's centre, and I am persuaded that in six months' time, he will be the

Minister'. Leicester House, and independent sentiment, were thus secured even more firmly to Newcastle's side, as were the other dissidents, by mutual antipathies. Newcastle noted: 'Lord Egmont and Sir G. Lee will keep Mr Fox to his word. May prevent Pitt flying out or render it of less importance.'[252]

Legge's position was completely undermined by the deal: he was retained in office, but powerless and without credit. Neither Pitt nor Fox had sought to make conditions on his behalf or to work with him as an ally. Two months later, despite his successful defence of the Budget in the Commons, the Chancellor of the Exchequer described his position to Sir Dudley Ryder:

He says he is himself not upon a good foot with the King or Duke of New-castle, that till the sitting of Parliament [in November] the King never spoke to him, and he having by desire prepared the draft of an address, the Duke of Newcastle expressed great compliment to him upon it, and equally when he prepared the draft of a few words for the King to answer: and then the King received him very graciously and spoke mighty kindly to him. But the affair of Pitt's abuse of Sir Thomas Robinson coming on, and he Legge saying nothing to defend him, was taken so heinously that the King has never spoke to him since. That he himself told the Duke [of Newcastle] when he first accepted the place of Chancellor of the Exchequer that he declined absolutely being concerned in any politics, that he desired the disposition of no place, that he wanted to be left singly to the business of the Exchequer, and he would become master of that to improve and support the revenue, and only desired he might have the liberty of acquainting the King with the debates in the House of Commons, but Sir Thomas Robinson was applied to by the King upon it, and however afterwards told Legge he was to do it for the future. But yet that was denied him, which has occasioned some misunderstanding, that he looks on himself as very ill at court.

'I find he rather favours Pitt', concluded Ryder, 'but thinks the Duke [of Newcastle] is afraid of trusting too far a man of parts.'[253] Joseph Yorke reflected ministerial opinion more accurately in writing of Legge as 'a sneaking fellow' who had 'deserted and run away in the middle of the action'. He added: 'I am sorry Pitt has thrown away so fine a game into the hands of Mr Fox'[254] – as indeed he had, for Fox was professing himself 'reconciled to those whom I with reason hated'.[255]

George II was even putting pressure on Hardwicke to pursue con-sistency by dismissing the Paymaster. The Chancellor agreed with the King's reflections on Pitt's character, but persuaded George II not to remove him on pragmatic grounds which included Fox's professed un-willingness to take an active part against Pitt if he, Pitt, were turned out.[256] It seems probable that Hardwicke, to secure by any means the King's agreement that nothing should be done about Pitt, was exag-gerating Fox's resolve. Events were soon to prove him far less enthusiastic a supporter of Pitt than had been feared. Newcastle had earlier been willing to postpone Pitt's dismissal when it would have endangered relations with Fox, and when the latter was anxious not to be offered Pitt's place; now, he commented: 'Mr Fox the King's reason [for] keeping Mr Pitt in, not mine'.[257] Pitt's retention once secured, Hardwicke persuaded Devonshire to agree to the new scheme.[258] Hartington's subsequent appointment as Lord Lieutenant of Ireland both removed him from the Cabinet and confirmed his father's broad adherence to the ministry. Newcastle thus contrived in three months to confine Fox's immediate support to Bedford and Cumberland alone. Bentinck provided the best appreciation of the outcome:

> The key of the whole is this in my opinion. Fox has had art enough to set Pitt a-going to serve his own private views. Pitt has lent his paws to draw the chestnuts out of the fire. Fox is made a Cabinet Councillor, but with very limited clauses writ with the King's own hand. Pitt remains what he is provisionally. This is only patchwork to gain the end of the sessions. And then I doubt whether the *Orators* will be the gainers. The King sticks firm to his old servants. And the Duke of Newcastle and the Chancellor will stand their ground, and maintain themselves contra quoscunque... Whatever changes may happen in the subordinate posts, the great point is and always will be, who remains in credit in the Closet.[259]

Joseph Yorke agreed, but went even further in his estimate of Fox's aims: '*P*'s not going out will I suppose be a great disappointment to *F*; as it will render his scheme abortive, at least that part of it which was founded on the strange conduct of the former; I hope now we shall rub on quietly through the rest of the session at least...'[260] Newcastle had evidently achieved his long-standing plans for Fox without admitting Pitt, and while at the same time bringing Leicester House as close to office as their diffidence of it would admit. Despite Fox's denials to the King of connections with Pitt – denials which were soon public[261] – Pitt had no basis for independent action against him or Newcastle until he and Bute began to appropriate Leicester House from Egmont and Lee in late 1755; without such a basis, the Pitt–Fox alliance was no more than a fiction working in Fox's favour. But Pitt could as yet gain nothing by forcing Fox to define their relations more clearly, and in spite of Fox's veiled duplicity the breach between them did not take place until their interview on 9 May that year.[262]

LATER CONSEQUENCES: THE COURT

Meanwhile, the rearrangement of offices in the wake of the deal was disturbed by the deaths of Gower on 25 December (Lord Privy Seal and Master of the Harriers) and Albemarle on 22 December (Ambassador in Paris, Groom of the Stole, Governor of Virginia, Knight of the Garter and Colonel of the Coldstream Guards). Hardwicke assumed Marlborough would succeed Gower as Privy Seal and Rutland have Marlborough's place of Lord Steward; the vacancies of the Stole and Virginia might be managed to deal with the problem of Egmont and Legge: 'I don't pretend to know how, but your Grace, who has great dexterity in turning and shaping these things, may be able to chalk it out'.[263] Newcastle at once offered the Privy Seal to Marlborough, to be received at Court on 6 January, and told him that Rutland, a relative of Gower's, would succeed him.[264] Among the remaining vacancies, Newcastle hoped to find something for Legge in order to replace him by Sir George Lee at the Exchequer, and to find an alternative for Hillsborough, then Comptroller, so that Egmont might have his place.[265] Newcastle listed Poulett (an associate of Egmont's, with whom he had co-operated over the Bridgwater election of 1754) for Virginia, but remarked on the difficulty of satisfying both, 'viz. the doing something for Mr Legge, and my Lord Egmont'.[266]

To Newcastle's consternation, the King then advanced Rochford as his preferred candidate for the Stole: a choice Newcastle and Hardwicke thought thoroughly unsuitable, partly because it would close a vacancy into which they might fit Dorset,[267] soon to be deposed from the Lord Lieutenancy of Ireland. Hardwicke speculated on the changes this would force in their plans; Newcastle had 'more than once' spoken of Bedford for the Lieutenancy, and, thought the Chancellor, 'if he was taken in, I don't see from what quarter an opposition could possibly arise'. As things were, Egmont's prospects shrank to the Parks and the Privy Council; Legge might be 'contented with a peerage in remainder alone'.[268] But the difficulties soured the atmosphere in the Closet, and Newcastle complained of his lacking 'spirits for the support of an administration, which the King will not do the most common things to countenance'.[269] These symptoms soon culminated in an astonishing royal outburst and in a revival of George II's former language. Newcastle appealed[270] for Hardwicke's intervention in the Closet against

His Majesty's direction to me, 'to confine myself to my Treasury, you will have enough to do to set that right. You have been attacked, or objected to, for meddling with everything'. Your lordship will show, if you think proper, how contrary this is, to what we apprehended to be His Majesty's first intention; when the King told me himself, 'I have made you as it were First Minister, you will be informed of everything'. And Mr Fox at that time told my Lord Granville, that the King had said so to him in still stronger terms.

Newcastle jumped to the obvious conclusion about the origin of such an alteration: it arose, he thought, from Fox's suggestions to the King about Newcastle's ambitions, 'and from the King's thinking that now Mr Fox being in good humour, he may safely confine me to the Treasury, and perhaps by that means throw the power wherever he pleases'. Earlier George II had defended himself against Fox's complaints of Newcastle's primacy by claiming

I have particular persons, or ministers, for particular branches, the Secretaries of State for theirs, the Chancellor, the Treasury etc., and what was his Majesty's, *then*, kind remark to me upon it, 'you know there is no such thing as First Minister in England, and therefore you should not *seem* to be so'. So that what His Majesty then meant, *seemingly*, kindly, he now avows, as his principle, his design, his order, his measure.

Grafton confirmed these suspicions that Fox was behind the new attitude; and Newcastle agonised over its parliamentary repercussions. He could scarcely disobey a direct royal order, if it were to be given, thus to confine himself: but in that case, 'applications' could only find their way to Fox. Rochford's appointment as Groom of the Stole would mark just such a public success for the Cumberland interest; moreover, Rochford might be succeeded in the Bedchamber by Lord Essex, Bedford's nephew and Fox's friend.[271] The King appeared to have called the bluff of the official interpretation of Robinson's role – the version designed to thwart Fox. Newcastle could not but see this as deliberate; he contemplated resignation, but asked Hardwicke to discover 'how far the principle is rooted, I am afraid you will see it has been growing some time, the effect of different Cabals, and has now taken root' as an independent royal attitude. Meanwhile, it should be kept secret.[272]

The King's motives were, however, more restricted than the implications of his doctrine. This became clearer to Hardwicke[273] during his audience on 3 January, for George II's first concern was to reproach Newcastle with meddling 'in things he has nothing to do with. He would dispose of my Bedchamber, which is a personal service about myself...' Hardwicke argued that something would have to be found for Dorset, implying Groom of the Stole, if he were to be dismissed from the Lieutenancy; but the King was hostile. The Chancellor then changed the ground, and argued that the Treasury's responsibilities, of necessity, went far beyond financial management alone; that its business

extended through both Houses of Parliament, the members of which were naturally to look thither. That there must be some principal person to receive applications; to hear the wants and the wishes and the requests of mankind, with the reasons of them, in order to lay them before His Majesty for his determination. That it was impossible for the King to be troubled with all this himself. This he in part admitted, but there were some things nobody should meddle in, etc. I said it was only a method of laying things before him, and the absolute final decision was in *him*. That it had always been the usage in this country, and I supposed was so in others. That without it no administration could be enabled to serve him; that ministers bore all the blame and resentment of disappointed persons, and they could never carry on his affairs without having some weight in the disposition of favours. The King said, he had seen too much of that in this country already, and it was time to change it in some degree...I let him know that such things would naturally create appearances and interpretations in the world that, by weakening his administration, might give rise to disturbance in Parliament, and alter that state of ease and quiet, which His Majesty, and his servants under him, had been endeavouring to bring about. That people would be looking different ways; and every question upon an election might become a contest between different sides of the Court. But the King seemed to despise such fears at present.

The King's remarks to Newcastle amounted (to borrow a phrase recently given currency) to a 'new Toryism', here paradoxically employed as one sort of anti-party doctrine against ministers who themselves, in another way, were asserting the death of party. George II was adopting, from Whig dissidents, a theory which in his hands articulated the executive's perennial urge to minimise the restraints of political organisations. The ministers, claiming that ideology was dead as part of the drive to widen their bottom, maintained that it was they who truly faced up to the political realities and obligations imposed by the responsibility of governing. But the resolution of the immediate crisis did not clearly solve these questions, for the King's was a language which, though adopted by Fox, did not reveal the distribution of power within the ministry between the latter and Newcastle. Neither Hardwicke nor Münchausen thought Fox personally concerned in the King's outburst, nor did Hardwicke suppose that the difficulties over the vacancies of the Groom of the Stole, Colonel of the Guards or Lord of the Bedchamber arose from Fox's advocacy of candidates for them.[274] Newcastle admitted: 'whether any direct application may have been made to [George II] or not, either from the Lady, the Duke, or Mr Fox, I know not'.[275] He nevertheless supposed the King to be taking advantage of the opportunity created by Fox's advancement to assert a 'principle of *confining me to the Treasury* and, I suppose, all of us to our respective offices'.

The problem was to prevent George II from employing a form of words which penetrated vulnerable points in Newcastle's view of correct conduct. Hardwicke's attempt at dissuasion had failed. Newcastle resorted to coercion:

Humility, submission, obeying and feeding we have seen (though attended with all imaginable success), will not do; there must be a mixture of something else which may *donne à penser*, strike some fear. The branch of foreign affairs has the greatest weight with us. We [i.e. George II] have at present *the Hessian Convention for troops*, much at heart, Lord Granville is against it. I promised the King, to alter M. Münchausen's draft of it, in the holidays. Nothing seems to me so natural as for me to tell Münchausen that, as His Majesty is pleased to confine me to the Treasury, I could not meddle in any foreign affair. It would be contrary to His Majesty's intention, and dangerous for me to attempt, and return him the draft unaltered, and at once wash my hands of the Hessian Convention, Russian Treaty and Saxon and Bavarian subsidies which will soon come under consideration. This would have an effect.[276]

Its effect was to silence the King completely. No more was heard of his doctrine, and there is no evidence that Fox even knew of Newcastle's alarm. A partial victory over the distribution of offices had however been won not by the Cumberland faction, to whom some of them went, but by the King. For that reason, Fox drew no accession of strength from the rearrangement. Lord Tyrawley secured the Coldstream Guards, not Lady Caroline Fox's uncle Lord Cadogan; Joseph Yorke was given the Colonelcy of the 9th Regiment of Foot.[277] Rochford, on the King's insistence, was appointed Groom of the Stole; when Lord Poulett resigned the Bedchamber in protest, Lords Orford and Essex[278] were appointed there, thus dividing the two vacancies. In February, the Earl of Hertford was nominated to the Paris embassy, and the Earl of Loudoun (not Lord Delawar as Newcastle feared) to Virginia. Neither was an opponent of Newcastle; neither subsequently mattered. The Foxhounds went for the moment to Lord Robert Sutton, a dim figure but a loyal member of the Rutland clan, whose articulate and able leader in the Commons – John, Marquis of Granby – was to render valuable service. Finally, Newcastle left the Garter unfilled, thus holding seven candidates in suspense at the prospect of three vacant titles.[279]

Forbearance on employments about the King's person also gave a certain strength. 'The doctrine of counterbalancing, I have always liked. Since we are not to meddle with the Bedchamber, with the Garters, or indeed almost with anything', wrote Newcastle, 'may not we insist upon our parliamentary arrangements [?] Sir George Lee, and Lord Egmont immediately, and such others as we may judge proper, and necessary'.[280] But as the price of victory in the realm of theory, the immediate vacancies for Legge and Egmont had been lost; Newcastle was compelled to wait for others to occur, and at the end of January he was still awaiting, for the same reasons, an opportunity to enlist two crucial figures: 'We only want to complete our system, and our security, by making Sir George Lee Chancellor of the Exchequer, and giving some considerable employment to my lord Egmont'.[281]

THE SYSTEM IN ACTION: PARLIAMENT, JANUARY–MARCH 1755

The Parliament Newcastle faced after Christmas was widely expected to be quiescent, and fulfilled its promise. Chesterfield linked it with Fox's having the lead. Pitt, 'though very angry, rather hints than declares opposition, unwilling to lose his employment, and, at the same time, unable to stifle his resentment'.[282] Only later did Andrew Mitchell describe the Commons as 'a rope of sand, without connection, and without a leader, this gives encouragement to faction and cabal'.[283] The long-term weakness was the absence of any new definition of the relative positions of Fox and Robinson: the situation accordingly reverted to what it had been before Newcastle misleadingly claimed that Robinson already occupied the position Fox sought.

The general opinion was that business in the Commons (especially the Oxfordshire petition, which occupied much time) was merely dull.[284]

William Guthrie was more perceptive in writing: 'Never was there so poor, so shabby, so insignificant a session of Parliament, as the present is...Patriots we have none: all is election jobbing'.[285] Even the Oxfordshire petition was not conducted in the Commons in the language of patriot or party polemics, but was argued as a technical electoral dispute. Boredom probably explains the very thin House on Saturday 11 January, when the Tories achieved a remarkable success in defeating Legge's motion to adjourn discussion of it.[286] The defeat 'has occasioned such an alarm', wrote Horatio Walpole, 'that it is thought the sitting in a Saturday will be dropped'.[287] Other temptations were placed in the way of the Whigs. On 5 February the House considered a Tory petition against the sitting Whig member for Carmarthen. Egmont found himself speaking with Northey, Prowse, Fazackerley, Morton and Richard Beckford against Fox, Nugent and Hillsborough; again the Tories won in two divisions, 73 to 71 and 73 to 72. 'This success (immaterial as it is)' wrote one observer, 'was I believe wholly owing to the Masquerade, to which *very few* Country Gentlemen were invited.'[288] When Whig organisation faltered or was divided, the Tories were still capable of profiting from their opponents' mistakes.

Pitt's brief anticipation in early 1754 of a flirtation with Leicester House had come to nothing; if his attempts to gain power within the Old Corps had for the moment failed, it was not apparent that any other course was open to him. The major option still seemed, for him as for Fox, to fight his way to the top of the Whig party. In the session before Christmas, the House had shown itself willing to listen to Patriot rhetoric but quite unwilling to realign itself in response to it. Partly owing to the disposition of the Tories, 'Patriot' issues were temporarily unavailable; even Pitt was compelled to stifle his resentment, and Fox remarked at the end of January on the irrelevance of political oratory: 'Tickling the palm, not the ear, is the business now, and he that can do the first is the best orator let him speak ever so ill.' There, thought Fox, lay his supremacy over the Paymaster.[289]

On 15 January, Sir John Philipps and the Beckfords laboriously attempted to oppose the unlikely object of the Bristol Nightly Watch Bill on grounds of high principle. But Barrington mocked the attempt and made William Beckford appear to be seeking its rejection for reasons of local electioneering advantage alone. Pitt gave his assent to the Bill, stressing the importance for English liberties of the independence of the executive from the electorate; spoke with contempt of a populace blinded with the passion of their passing loves and hates; and warned of the danger of executive power passing into their hands. Although Northey, in speaking against the Bill, avoided a direct clash with Pitt[290] the prospects for patriot invective looked slim. According to Robert Ord, MP, the Paymaster 'still continues to abuse [the] Attorney General' who 'plainly appears afraid of entering the lists with Pitt',[291] but this no longer caught the imagination of the House as it had before Christmas. On 27 January the Bristol Nightly Watch Bill passed its second reading, arousing no interest, by 113 to 74.[292] As late as 28th, Bedford wrote that 'everything is I believe likely to jog on quietly during the remainder of the sessions' and suggested that election petitions were of no political importance.[293]

This was not to prove to be the case. On 27 January, Fox clashed with Sir John Philipps in the Committee on the Colchester petition,[294] and clashed again, more bitterly, with Sir George Lee 'and his friends' on 28th in trying to bring forward the Appleby petition by persuading the House to sit on 30 January, a public holiday on the anniversary of Charles I's martyrdom. Others besides the Tories were offended in 'the fullest House of Commons that has been this year', and Fox was obliged to withdraw his motion.[295] The course of business in early February raised Tory hopes on several occasions. On 5 February they won two divisions on the Carmarthen petition by 73 to 71 and 73 to 72.[296] On 8th they lost an unequal division over the Radnor by-election by 48 to 5, though pushing the Whigs close over Oxfordshire, losing by 49 to 38.[297] But on a motion to agree with the Committee on the Bristol Nightly Watch Bill the Tories lost by 153 to 71 on 14 February,[298] and on the third reading on 19th the Whigs defeated an amendment by 185 to 55.[299] Philipps, Northey and Richard Beckford continued to take part against it, and Prowse and Sir John Cotton joined Richard Beckford over Carmarthen. But despite Tory efforts, it was only Whig apathy which granted them such successes as they could record.

On 12 February, Legge opened the Budget 'in a very clear and masterly manner above what many expected, who were convinced of his abilities for the discharge of his great post, but did not think he would be able to set them out so well in public'. Legge won approval from independent sentiment by his care for the health of the Sinking Fund, which would allow him to liquidate £700,000 of the Navy Debt, declaring that 'was it left to operate, [it] would enable us in two years to pay off two millions of the national debt, and would always be a constant and sufficient support against any war in which this nation *ought* to engage': an emphasis approved by the whole House.[300] Legge had been prematurely dismissed by Chesterfield as 'nobody, and consequently discontented, but silently so, in the hope of being Mr Pitt's successor next session'.[301] Now, he had boosted his value to the ministry by improving his standing among the independents. Their disposition explains the relative silence in which two subsidies were voted in the Committee of Supply: £32,000 for Saxony, £20,000 for Bavaria.

The situation in February was complicated by the overlapping of three elements: the Sheriff Depute Bill, artificially elevated to an issue of principle; the petition on the Oxfordshire election, a straight Whig–Tory fight; and the climax of the Mitchell petition, 'a most absurd jumble of interests'.[302] Newcastle's settlement of the ministry had in fact placed a major barrier in the way of any attempt to use those disturbances for private advantage, and their tactical implications for Pitt, Fox and Legge appear disjointed as a result; one measure of this is the fact that almost all the leading politicians in the Commons – George Grenville, William Pitt, Sir George Lyttelton, H. S. Conway, Granby, Dodington, Sir John Barnard, Sir Thomas Robinson, William Murray, Sir Francis Dashwood as well as Lord Granville, and others – could remain carefully neutral in the Newcastle–Fox contest on the Mitchell petition.[303] One theme common to these three issues, nevertheless, was Newcastle's concern to limit their implications. As he wrote of the first: 'if we recede now, our opposers will take great advantage of us in the Closet...'[304] Conversely, the appearance of victory on issues susceptible to royal influence was essential as the public index of the favour enjoyed at Court. Mitchell, too, reflected primarily a split in the Whig bloc between Newcastle and Fox. The Tories' role was important only because it was generally supposed, by late February, that the Court members were divided almost equally on that question, and that 'the minority' held the balance.[305] But Newcastle's good relations with them meant that they co-operated in playing down the importance of party identities in terms of commitments to principle.

The Sheriff Depute Bill provoked a Patriot outburst unexpectedly, for it was a young Scotch member, Elliot,[306] who on 20 February struck a dramatic note in attacking 'upon Revolution principles'[307] a measure which perpetuated the emergency expedient of continuing the tenure of the Sheriffs Depute during pleasure. Newcastle had had advance warning of opposition and was determined to oppose what he regarded as a 'Scotch Cabal'. Andrew Mitchell expected the Bill to pass, 'though great pains has been taken to give very unfair impressions of it'.[308] Yet whether from ministerial management or the implausibility of the attack, only five Scots voted in the minority of eighty against the Bill, the rest dividing for it. Murray had predicted that 'Fox will avoid appearing in it, when he has made it impossible [for the ministerialists] to recede'. On the first day, several Tories were drawn to speak with Elliot, who nevertheless lost the division by 189 to 80. Murray, though present, remained silent.[309] But before the second reading on 26th, Newcastle was alarmed by the report of Andrew Mitchell, a Teller on 20 February, that sixteen Scots would change sides:[310]

it is whispered that both Mr Pitt and Mr Legge will take the other side of the question, and in short all those, who don't wish well to your lordship, and your humble servant. What part another considerable man in the House of Commons [? Fox] will *really* act, nobody can tell. I have seen Sir T. Robinson this morning, by whom I find, that the D [Cumberland] was far from being in such good humour, as he had been the former time.[311] Mr Fox has been long with Mr Pitt, and with Lord Sandwich. The latter visit was to be sure of the

142

Mitchell election. But considering all these circumstances together, whether we should [? adhere], and what steps should in that case be taken; and what should be said to the King upon it [?]

Hardwicke, fortuitously on the other side to Newcastle in the Mitchell dispute, was hindered also by the Scots Bill's having identified the basic divide as that between arbitrary lawyers and their opponents. On 26th, the opposition to the Sheriffs Bill, 'the only point that has been brought to a head this session', was taken out of the hands of its initiators by Pitt, Grenville and Charles Townshend.[312] But Murray mocked the idea that Revolution principles were impaired, and Egmont had difficulty in challenging him on points of law. Pitt and Fox spoke equivocally. Pitt produced a declamation on liberty, without directly opposing, and sought to amend the Bill in Committee; Fox reserved his position wholly for that stage, and no division was forced.[313]

Before the Committee on the Scots Bill, due on 4 March, the alignments to which it gave rise were reflected in the division of 28 February in the Committee on the Mitchell petition. Lord Falmouth reported to Newcastle that 'the Scotch, the Duke's household and Army influence have carried this point against us' by 188 to 162.[314] This was the division, wrote Walpole, 'when Mr Fox, attacking and attacked by the law, of which body was Hussey, one of the petitioners, beat four lawyers and Nugent...' in Newcastle's camp: that is, the Solicitor General, Lloyd; Hume Campbell; Henley; and the Tory lawyer, Morton. Mitchell had become a veiled issue of confrontation: Fox adhered to the cause of Sandwich, a follower of Cumberland; Newcastle supported the Edgcumbes, Boscawens and the petitioners through the thin disguise of Lord Lincoln's agency.[315]

The outcome was to be decided by the way in which the Tories were brought finally to commit their support behind Newcastle. But, at the outset, the opposite choice seemed possible. According to Newdigate, in the face of a string of speakers for the petitioners (Lloyd, Hume Campbell, Henley, Morton, Legge, Nugent and Northey) including some Tories, Fox 'seemed going to give it up when Sir J. Philipps rose and spoke for the question, upon which Fox immediately divided'. His was, evidently, a sudden, opportunist attempt to split 'the minority'. It succeeded: 'about 20' voted with him.[316] Clearly some effective response was called for among the pro-Pelhamites of that party. Walpole records that, after this vote, Northey offered Newcastle Tory co-operation in return for the dismissal of Fox and Pitt, who incurred Tory hatred 'the one for always attacking, the other for having deserted them', and for the surrender of the Oxfordshire election.[317] If so, Northey was offering what his party had just shown itself unable to provide: a united and directable voting force. Moreover, it was a demand of a very major concession in return for what (since the Egmont overture of early December) Newcastle already enjoyed on major issues: general Tory co-operation. Clearly, such an exchange would be very unequal: Pitt and Fox, even if their loyalty was for the moment in doubt, were far more useful politically than an inarticulate Tory bloc. Once again, no public and precise treaty was apparently concluded.

On 4 March, the Lords sat in Committee on the Bristol Nightly Watch Bill. Bedford and Sandwich opposed it, 'but with no effect', and it passed without amendment.[318] The Sheriffs' Bill had come on in Committee in the Commons the day before. In anticipation, Boscawen (returning Newcastle's help at Mitchell) took part in organising Scots votes;[319] through West, Newcastle arranged a compromise which satisfied the speaker and Sir George Lee, and drew from the latter an unusually emphatic profession of his desire to support Newcastle's administration.[320] In face of the ministry's willingness to give ground over the length of the final term for which the Sheriffs were to hold their offices at pleasure, both Pitt and Fox were betrayed into tactical errors. Pitt spoke unremarkably in favour of liberty, but agreed to the compromise and commended 'the universal zeal to strengthen the King's hands': hardly a step to allay fears of arbitrary power in the hands of the law officers. Fox, taking precisely the same line in accepting the compromise, mocked one of Onslow's 'pompous polemics' on liberty – 'this was the truest triumph of Revolution principles, for it was the sound that triumphed, not the sense'.[321]

Why Fox, in particular, should neglect such an opportunity is unclear. But it may not be coincidental that he was heavily engaged in the Haslemere contest on behalf of one of the petitioners, Oglethorpe. Onslow, the Speaker, was 'solemnly and eagerly set'[322] on the side of the sitting members, Molyneux and Webb. On 13 March, Fox was forced to surrender on behalf of Oglethorpe;[323] Fox's attack on Onslow on 3rd may have been an impolite outburst of the rancour generated in a losing cause. Rigby, too, had been attempting to defend one of the sitting Members for Colchester, Charles Gray, a Tory, against the petition of the ministerial candidate Isaac Rebow.[324] On 19 February, Sir Roger Newdigate recorded Gray's surrender;[325] it was publicly registered on 13 March when the House agreed to the report from the Committee unseating Gray and declaring Rebow elected.[326] The Patriot sentiments evoked by Onslow and the Scots failed to align the Tories decisively against Newcastle, and it must have been apparent also from the Bristol Nightly Watch Bill and the fate of these petitions[327] that a Fox–Bedford connection could offer them nothing.

At the Horn Tavern on 4 March, 53 of 'the minority' met 'to consider what measures to follow in regard to the two contending parties for power'.[328] Walpole suggested, wrongly, that the Tories were aware that Newcastle had rejected Northey's offer; now,

Fazackerley informed them that they were to take measures for acting in a body on the Mitchell election: he understood that it was not to be decided by the merits, but was a contest for power between Newcastle and Fox: whoever carried it, would be Minister: that he for every reason should be for the former. Beckford told him, he did not understand there was any such contest: that he did not love to nominate Ministers: were he obliged to name, he would prefer Mr Fox. The meeting, equally unready at speeches and expedients, broke up in confusion.[329]

Newdigate recorded a meeting of 'about 40 Members – agreed as Michael [i.e. Mitchell] election not advanced far enough to judge of the merits to meet again on Friday [7th]'.[330] On 5th, Northey told Bayntun Rolt 'of the resolution of the Tories at their meeting to keep together on the merits – if incline at all, against Mr Fox'.[331] On 7 March

Sixty-Two Tories met again at the Horn, where they agreed to secrecy, though they observed it not; and determined to vote, according to their several engagements, on previous questions, but not on the conclusive question in the Committee.[332]

According to Newdigate the decision was 'not to vote in the decisive question in the Committee of Michael election but to stay for the Report'.[333] According to Ryder, the Tories' next arranged meeting (presumably on 7 March) had been 'to determine which side they shall take [on Mitchell], and also which side they shall take in the whole of their conduct in the House as between [the] Duke of Newcastle and Fox'.[334] And on 10th, Bayntun Rolt recorded: 'to the House – the Duke of Newcastle told me that the Tories were to make the Oxford election the condition of their supporting him in the St Michael's etc. – my opinion he should reject it with indignation'.[335]

Of Newcastle's response to Northey's offer there is no direct evidence, but it seems almost certain that he had not yet rejected it, and the Horn Tavern meeting on 4 March cannot have been under the impression that he had. Fazackerley's remarks there must therefore have been a bid for Newcastle's co-operation, not a capitulation to him. It is unlikely, too, that Newcastle had replied by 12 March, on which day another Tory meeting took place at the Horn. 'Forty of them', wrote Walpole, 'having omitted to summon twenty nine...met again to consider if they should adhere to their last resolution'.[336] Newdigate, too, wrote of a meeting of 'above 40' who 'determined to remain by [their] former resolution'. Accordingly 'All the minority except a few came away before the division' at the end of the Committee stage, which was won by the sitting members (i.e. Fox) by 158 to 141.[337] Only eight Tories voted, four on each side.[338] The position of the party as a whole was well known: 'Most of the gentlemen in the minority went out of the House when the question was going to be put, so that they have reserved to themselves which side of the question they shall be of when the Report is made to the House'.[339] Again, the implication is that the Tories were trying to put pressure on Newcastle to agree to their offer of co-operation.

Mitchell had been 'made at last so much a party affair', wrote Gilbert Elliot, 'that no-one could go off without the imputation of having yielded to an undue influence...the Tories are divided, if they continue so, the sitting members are likely to prevail, if they agree, which is rumoured, the petitioners are likely to prevail'.[340] It is not certain that this was Newcastle's opinion, however. Boscawen reported many Whigs of the opinion that he and Newcastle would succeed, even 'without the assistance of the gentlemen that assemble at the Horn'.[341] Whatever the numbers in prospect, Newcastle's response to Northey's offer was neither to accept it nor reject it: he played, instead, a waiting game.

Meanwhile, the Oxfordshire petition, overshadowed for the moment by Mitchell, ground slowly on in Committee in an atmosphere of increasing boredom. On 22 February, only two days after the important vote on the Sheriff Depute Bill, the Whigs mustered only 44 votes in a division on the Oxfordshire petition against the Tories' 36.[342] On 13 March only 25 Members were present and the House was counted out. The same almost happened a second time on 18th.[343] On Saturday 22 March Fox intervened to adjourn proceedings until Monday 7 April, leaving the House free to deal with Mitchell.[344] The King, planning a summer visit to Hanover, was anxious that proceedings should be over by 15 April;[345] it cannot have been obvious that they would be.

Fox seems not to have slackened his efforts in the Mitchell Committee,[346] but was hampered by being unable to represent the issue as a decisive vote in his rivalry with Newcastle.[347] Election petitions were not an obvious issue of confidence, and the indications are that major figures were anxious not to interpret them otherwise in an effort not to become involved in Fox's personal ambitions. It is remarkable that Pitt and the Grenvilles, from the outset, took no part in the Mitchell dispute;[348] to have engaged on Fox's side would presumably have been to surrender any prospect of promotion within the Old Corps induced by their activities as *frondeurs* on the floor of the Commons, and it must have been plain from the House's reception of such agitation before Christmas that there was no possibility of storming the Closet by such means.

The Report from the Mitchell Committee, taking the side of Fox's candidates, was presented in the Commons on 24 March. Earlier that day, 68 Tories met at the Horn Tavern. Newdigate wrote:

Sir J. Philipps proposed to disappoint both parties by voting against both and making it a void election. Sir Charles Mordaunt, Mr Northey, Mr Crowle, R.N. [Newdigate], Mr Bertie against it. Nothing in the evidence to warrant it. Mr Beckford for it. Came away without any joint resolution. House. Report read. Mr Henley moved to disagree with the Report, Mr Potter for it, and Ellis, Fox etc. For disagreeing Nugent, Sir W. Yonge, Thornhagh, Northey. Question to agree [with the Committee] upon Mr Clive. Ayes 183 Noes 207. No division upon Stephenson. Question for Lutterell. Sir J. Philipps moved to make it a void election by rejecting the petitioners to[o]. Opposed by Northey, R.N. and Sir Robert Long. Question Ayes 201 Noes 178. These questions were carried by the bulk of the minority who were clear from engagements to either side and determined only upon the merits which were strong with the petitioners.[349]

In the first of the two divisions, 17 Tories opposed Newcastle; 55 voted for his candidates, including Sir John Philipps. In the second, Northey, Long, Newdigate 'and the whole party deserted [Philipps] but about five or six', according to Rigby; 'two or three' according to Lord Digby. Philipps, voting against both sets of candidates in turn as he had proposed, found himself aligned with Fox in the second division; but this was an eccentricity. What counted was his vote for Newcastle. In the first division, too, Fox's other Tory champion William Beckford, though present at the Horn Tavern meeting earlier, now absented himself. Sir George Lee and his brother John, who voted with Fox's friends in the first division, changed sides to vote with Newcastle's in the second.[350] Sir George thereby confirmed the adherence of most of the Tories to Newcastle, for there could now be no alternative route to a liaison between that party and Leicester House.

Fox berated him but was then compelled to pass the defeat off lightly as if no challenge to the minister had been made. But his alienation of the Tories was decisive. 'All that is to be gathered from this', wrote Lord Digby, 'is that it is a measure among the Tories (whether by private negotiation or not I cannot tell) to show their inclination to the Duke of Newcastle rather than Mr Fox'. But it was not such a trivial matter; as Lord Digby realised, 'if there had been no Tory in the House we should have carried it by 14',[351] and the consequences for Fox's rivalry with Newcastle would have been profound. Rigby appreciated the significance of the reverse better in writing to Bedford: 'I hope your Grace nor none of your friends, will ever have mercy upon these rascally Tories any more'.[352] On 29 March, he wrote again:

A report prevails strongly that the Tories are to have another election given up to them, and Leicester and Carmarthen are each thought likely to be the sacrifice. Sir William Meredith, as determined a Jacobite reckoned as any in the House of Commons, has been at Newcastle House since the Mitchell division: and the credit of that whole transaction on the part of the Tories is now given to Sir Walter Bagot, who came to town on Sunday night [? 23rd], and supped at the Cocoa Tree: and to confirm that idea a little, and in some measure to account for it, Mr Legge is certainly upon much better terms with the head of his Board than he has been for some weeks past.[353]

Bagot was Legge's brother-in-law. Meanwhile Meredith, Tory MP for Wigan, wrote to Lady Luxborough, Bolingbroke's half-sister, with an account of the situation. William Shenstone summarised the letter:

It seems, F[ox] in his opposition to the Duke of Newcastle, is supported by the Duke of Cumberland, his army, and the Scotch: that the ministry (or the Duke of N[ewcastle]'s party) seem not displeased with a prospect of uniting with the Tories, who now hold the balance; and it seems the Tories, by Sir William's letter, are as little displeased to unite with the ministry.[354]

But the negotiations of the succeeding months were plainly to show that the Tories, if they had held the balance for a brief moment, did so no longer. Lord Digby complained that Fox and Sandwich had been beaten by 'a confederacy of Tories' who merely pretended to vote on the merits,[355] and Walpole suggested that at the meeting that morning they 'took the shameless resolution of cancelling all their engagements, in order to defeat Fox'.[356] But it seems that no offer had been received from Newcastle, and Newdigate's account is probably accurate in suggesting that his party was unable to agree, at their meeting on 24 March, on an official course of action. That, indeed, was their official defence. The *Evening Advertiser* denounced their conduct:

On the ever memorable Mitchel affair, these pretended Catos met at the Horn Tavern, and, without waiting to hear the merits of the cause, fairly put it to the vote amongst themselves, what side they should, one and all, unite for: And to the everlasting shame of all their pretences to honour, honesty, and public virtue, they gave their votes in a body, agreeable to this predetermination, and contrary to what a great part of them had declared to be their sentiments on the merits of the cause...O Mitchel! sound of shame, ever to be echoed to the confusion of Old Interest pretenders to integrity! Let the Horn Tavern never be forgot; and whenever corruption, venality or any cant of the London Evening Post's is named by a True Blue, bellow Mitchel in his ears: Mitchel! Mitchel and the Horn Tavern!

The *London Evening Post* replied, correctly though inadequately, that at the meetings on 4 and 7 March the Tories had voted not to commit themselves on the merits of the case until all the evidence had been heard; but concluded limply:

At the third and last meeting, which was many days after the Committee had come to a resolution, and was on the day the Report was made, the merits only were then taken into consideration. The consequence was a variety of opinions, and the event showed a disunion in consequence thereof.[357]

By that indecision, the Tories' strategic advantage was surrendered in return for little more than Newcastle's good will. Their failure was not immediately apparent: Joseph Yorke, for example, who overestimated Tory cohesion, thought them dangerous recruits, as a bloc, to any party.[358] Speaking of the Hardwicke–Fox alliance over the Mitchell petition, he added: 'the strength lost on our side will perhaps turn out hereafter a defeat for the other, and we are unfortunately mixed with both'.[359] But Lord Digby, likewise lamenting his side's defeat over Mitchell, ended on a note of modest satisfaction: 'I don't apprehend any bad consequences from this as it has turned out nor did I hope for very good ones had it ended otherwise. Mr Fox does not seem vexed at it at all'.[360] A contest on an election petition, with no further moral drawn, was the ideal cloak for activities against Newcastle. Later, Fox could pretend surprise that he had incurred unpopularity among the Whigs, and claim that 'I opposed no one nay supported every public measure last sessions, and it was particularly unfortunate if the Whigs disliked my behaviour in a session in which I entered with them in every point; at the end of which the Tories for my behaviour in that sessions declared themselves my enemies in contradiction to the Minister...'[361]

But in March 1755, the failure of the Mitchell petition restored their positions to where they had been in December: Fox had not been compromised, nor Newcastle weakened. Partly for this reason, partly from the unique divisions within the Old Corps, Mitchell offered no guide to the future constellation of forces. As Horatio Walpole had written of an early vote on 21 November, 'There is no measure to be taken relating to the disposition of members from this division'.[362] Newcastle's task was now to return to the problem of rearrangement which had been shelved for three months. His distrust of Legge was as strong as ever; yet Legge, whether or not an agent for Tory support, had voted with Newcastle over Mitchell, had retreated from a proffered commitment to Pitt and Fox, and was earning a growing reputation for financial ability. Following up his Budget, he performed well in the debate on 26 March in the Committee of Supply when the Commons granted an extra £1 million for armaments, and incurred only minimal Tory opposition. Northey even spoke for the motion.[363] 'Mr Fox and his land-war party sat mute, whilst Mr Legge with great openness and perspicuity explained the present schemes; as they were calculated, to exert our whole strength at sea, and, if possible, nowhere else.'[364] Not until very late that summer did a suspicion gain currency that the ministry's intended strategy was other than that which Legge had outlined. Back bench sentiment was satisfied. So was the City. The £1 million loan opened on 9 April; the books closed on 14th, with £3,883,310 subscribed. 'The credit is higher than ever', wrote Newcastle.[365] In March he had noted: 'Mr Legge. Whether to be continued, and in that case, what explanations, and by whom. If to be removed, what to be done for him, and who [is] to be his successor.[366] Hardwicke replied: 'Mr Pitt. In the present circumstances of public affairs, it might be thought undesirable to remove him...To sound Sir George Lee, as to the measure of removing Mr Legge at present, and particularly with regard to Mr Pitt, and not to determine, till both Sir George Lee's, and the Princess's opinions are known.'[367] The possibility of Lee's inclusion in Legge's place had declined. Evidently his long hostility over Mitchell was not effaced by his late conversion, for the coolness did not apply to Leicester House as a whole: Newcastle still hoped to find 'some considerable employment' for Egmont,[368] who had voted against Fox over Mitchell and of whose impatient dissatisfaction he was only later apprehensive.[369] Hardwicke suggested: 'Lord Egmont. To try to get him Sir William Yonge's place.'[370] Legge's demotion, however, was a major step, and one which Newcastle was not willing to undertake lightly; in the event, Legge remained until his rebellion in August made his retention impossible.

The Oxfordshire petition dragged on in the Commons during April, though robbed of its interest after the Tory failure to tie Newcastle down to concessions over Mitchell. Tory numbers in divisions on Oxfordshire now showed a marked falling off. They lost by 37 to 90 on 8 April, by 30 to 60 and 30 to 62 on 12th, and 49 to 91 on 15th.[371] But they revived for the final divisions, which took place on 23 April. Sir Francis Dashwood moved to admit the legality of the copyholders' votes, seconded by Peniston Powney. Ellis moved the previous question, seconded by George Grenville, and won by 242 to 107.[372] The evidence was next summarised for each side by Lord Hillsborough and Sir Charles Mordaunt. Sir John Barnard then 'moved the Previous Question in order to put a question upon the illegality of the return first', but was defeated by 231 to 103.[373] The main question to declare Lord Wenman elected was then put and lost by 98 to 228. The defeat was final and crushing; Sir James Dashwood was rejected, and Parker and Turner declared elected, without further divisions. Fox's friends took the opportunity to revenge themselves for the Tories' behaviour over Mitchell,[374] and Newcastle did not choose to intervene in an issue which classically polarised Whig and Tory. Partly because it did so, the Tories' defeat was a foregone conclusion, and passed almost unremarked. The focus of political attention had already moved on.

Hardwicke continued to advise Newcastle against Pitt's removal, and proposed using Horatio Walpole to take a sounding of his attitude.[375] Newcastle was well disposed to this and was even prepared to consider 'Whether [Pitt] might not be in the Cabinet Council before the King goes abroad, or have a promise of it afterwards'.[376] To that end, he wanted the King's approval to begin sounding major figures so that some 'settled consistent plan' could be drawn up during the summer, 'in order to propose to His Majesty, the means of getting the assistance of those who may be willing to support thoroughly His Majesty's measures' – not, by implication, the disaffected Whigs.[377] Newcastle could well afford delay. Both Fox and Pitt[378] were left in divided and dependent positions; as Royston later wrote, Pitt had 'withdrawn himself from the House and had entered into no engagement with the P[rince] of W[ales], but was open to treaty and had neither declared *for* or *against* measures.'[379] Egmont's general adherence, too, was assured. Newcastle had survived the session and arrived almost at its end with his options intact. Events had served only to deepen the distrust between rivals who were in fact competing, as had become evident, for the favour of a ministerial offer of alliance on terms of limited power. Walpole had shown a sense of this in writing: 'The Junto, who had laboured to keep Pitt and Fox disunited, more than to secure either of them, were reduced to take the one or the other' at the end of 1754.[380] Taken literally, this was a misconception; Fox had not compelled his promotion, and events were to show that he had accepted a mark of honour which, while itself conferring no more real power, was sufficient to identify him with the ministry closely enough to act as a deterrent to a still closer identification in the form of a leading part in the conduct of business in the House. Nevertheless, that business had proceeded sufficiently smoothly, it seemed, to permit George II's early departure on his summer visit to Hanover – which, it had been predicted, the ministry could not arrange.[381]

Historians have thought it obviously the case that a ministerial system was unworkable without a First Minister in the Commons. They therefore attributed Newcastle's difficulties to the absence of such a Minister, and (guided by their preconceptions) singled out certain dramatic features of what was taken to be a parliamentary opposition in order to argue that its attacks revealed the weakness of the ministerial system in the Commons. As has been shown, both the preconceptions and the inferences were false. In reality, the system was viable; in both its variants (in late 1754 and early 1755) it defeated its disconcerted opponents in the lower House. Newcastle averted the danger he had foreseen in September, that Fox would become 'Minister in the Closet for the House of Commons'; he was able to do so partly because it was neither necessary nor inevitable that anyone should fill such a post. In March 1754 Newcastle had assumed the position of First Minister without any apprehension among the public at large that such a position could not legitimately be filled by a peer. As has been shown, such allegations at the time were closely related to Fox's ambitions and tactical failures during the spring. In November, equally, the Commons had not taken the claims of Potter and others as valid comments on the way in which governments must work, but as episodes in a disruptive campaign. The alleged subordination and dependence of the Commons, indeed, was a familiar 'Country' point.[382] No more original had been Pitt's tirade against corruption at Berwick, for he had replied to a petition against his own return for Seaford in 1747 in terms as cynical and dismissive as those he condemned when used by Delaval. On this question, as with opposition claims on a Commons minister, Newcastle had shown himself fully aware of the tactical implications of principled rhetoric. In the ordinary course of events he would have proceeded, before the autumn, to the choice of allies. It is generally supposed that he was overtaken by circumstances: that the formation of the Regency, made necessary by George II's departure for Hanover, and Bute's detonation of a Leicester House opposition in April 1755, launched a train of events, including an outcry against the subsidy treaties of that summer, which was wholly out of Newcastle's control and which forced him to capitulate by agreeing to Fox's inclusion as Secretary of State in November. In the next chapter it will be argued that Newcastle held throughout the summer the initiative he had preserved in the winter of 1754–5; that he spent considerable effort in exploring the alternatives which his manoeuvres had made practicable, though those alternatives were eventually ruled out by a royal veto; but that in the end the Leicester House opposition of Pitt and Bute was organised only *after* Newcastle had secured a bargain with Fox, and one which conceded to his subordinate a power far more closely circumscribed than has been thought to be the case.

3

The Reconstruction of the Ministry, April–September 1755: Leicester House and the Recruitment of Fox

...the Duke of Newcastle was absolute. He had all the advice from wise heads that could make him get the better of rivals, and all the childishness in himself that could make them ashamed of his having got the better. If his fickleness could have been tied down to any stability, his power had been endless. Yet, as it often happens, the puny can shake, where the mighty have been foiled – nor Pitt, nor Fox, were the engines that made the Duke of Newcastle's power totter.

Walpole, *George II*, ii, 35.

Pitt 'told me himself in 1767, that the world were much mistaken in thinking that he did not like patronage, for he was but a little man in 1755, and was obliged to act the part he did...'

Shelburne in Fitzmaurice, *Shelburne*, 1, 59.

There are so many wheels within wheels that no eye can see the whole, and such unsteadiness in people's conduct (to give it the gentlest name) that from knowing what a man's connections are today you can scarce guess what they will be tomorrow.

Stormont to Huntingdon, 20 Oct 1755: HMC *Hastings*, iii, 106.

THE KING'S DEPARTURE, APRIL 1755

Early in April, Newcastle learned from Fox through West of the speech and motion which Lord Poulett intended to make against George II's leaving for Hanover.

The speech is personal upon me, *my weakness*, in placing my confidence in *two men*, notorious enemies. To the *Revolution*, the *Succession*, and Whig Cause; if the Minister wanted the power to stop the K[ing], he should be assisted by Parliament, if not, it is worse. That their comfort is, that we have a Prince of the Blood, able to give counsel, and to command our armies, where he is properly at the head, and to give counsel, if *the Minister* will call him to it.[1]

Poulett, having just resigned from the Bedchamber in protest at a promotion over his head, cannot have been better inclined to Fox for the latter's having joined in filling his place. There is no sign that

Newcastle suspected Fox's complicity in, or approbation of, Poulett's *démarche*, and Newcastle was pleased to learn that Granville had chosen to intervene, apparently on his own initiative, to warn the Lord Mayor of London against 'promoting an address to his Majesty on the subject of his going abroad'.[2] Nevertheless, the First Lord saw Bedford's return to town as a move 'to join Lord P[oulett]',[3] and reacted as if to an extension of Bedford's attack in opposing the Address on the augmentation of forces in March.[4]

On the evening of 12 April, Newcastle arranged a meeting of the leading ministerialists: himself, Hardwicke, Devonshire, Hartington, Grafton, Waldegrave and Horatio Walpole. With the alienation of Leicester House still in the future, it must have seemed that a bid for power within the Whig party was being made by the strongest and most ambitious rival sector of the Court, the Duke of Cumberland's: a bid timed to coincide with the sudden removal of the personal royal prop to the position of Newcastle and Hardwicke. In March and April, fears of Cumberland's potential power were widespread and seem to have reached a peak.[5] Yet there is no evidence for such an initiative, or for Bedford's involvement in it. Nor was backing for Cumberland or Bedford forthcoming from another quarter. Sir John Philipps and William Beckford had been alone in opposing the Vote of Credit of £1 million,[6] and Rigby imagined the ministry still enjoyed the effects of that Tory co-operation which was seen during the Mitchell petition.[7] Poulett's motion was made on his own initiative. Though it touched on a sensitive issue, he laboured under the disadvantage of not being taken seriously. Bayntun Rolt had earlier 'found him exasperated against news writers for not publishing his politics'.[8] During March, Poulett had continued to urge his objections to the King's journey on leading politicians, including Egremont and Bedford, but found them unresponsive: not surprisingly, in view of the 'strong absurdity in not seeing that it touched only [George II] and not the ministers'.[9] By the end of that month it was clear that his 'politics' were 'both ridiculous and dangerous',[10] widely derided as taking seriously a homily about royal government which was seldom meant literally;[11] and the manner and language of the motion was offset in any possible appeal to Tory sentiment by its promotion of Cumberland. The 'extraordinary confidence'[12] which Hardwicke feared Poulett placed in Fox was exaggerated or misplaced, for Fox sought to restrain his supposed ally; the contrast between the wording of the motion as put on 24 April and Newcastle's apprehensions suggests that an element of personal invective against the Minister may have been omitted, probably in the speech which Poulett was reported as having prepared, but which he then refrained from making.[13]

Poulett's motion was explosive not in its own right but because of its bearing on the issues raised in the establishment of a Regency. Hardwicke speculated that 'the latter part looks as if it aimed at the Duke's being Regent, and yet it may import only the taking him into the *consultation* and *secret* of affairs': that is, into a degree of confidence he did not yet enjoy. The Chancellor warned against any such concession to buy Poulett's silence, and recommended that Fox should speak to the King about his relations with the Earl.[14] At this point, what was at issue was the responsibility for the Regency's composition. It may be that the Chancellor wished to present Fox as the advocate of Cumberland's inclusion: a move which would inevitably act further to alienate Pitt from the Secretary at War. Nothing compelled Newcastle and Hardwicke to shoulder the responsibility for this necessary but unpopular measure. Their success in avoiding it has led historians to assume that, in the face of Newcastle's disapproval, the King secured Cumberland's seat on the Regency Board and that he would have preferred his son to be sole Regent. This was not the case. Waldegrave recognised that Newcastle could have prevented both Cumberland's and Fox's inclusion.[15] Dodington perceptively observed 'that the Duke is full as much indisposed to the Duke of Newcastle as the Princess'. He knew of, but took out of context the fact that Devonshire had pressed Cumberland's claims to a sole Regency, and supposed that he, Devonshire, 'was the cause of the Duke being in the Regency this time'.[16]

Dodington apparently spoke of the opinions canvassed at the meeting on 12 April, where the issues of the Regency and Poulett's motion intermingled. Horatio Walpole, who had been invited by Newcastle, had drawn up a minute[17] which formed the basis for part of the discussion. Hardwicke had read Walpole's document in a previous interview with him and had voiced fears of Cumberland's unpopularity; his being made a Regent, too, suggested the Chancellor, 'might fling the administration wholly into HRHs's hands, jointly with others that are now in his immediate confidence, and are no friends to the principal ministers'.[18] In the version of his minute which Walpole apparently read at the meeting,[19] he urged the danger in face of impending war of the administrative difficulties and delays which would result from the King's absence and Parliament's prorogation, as well as the outcry 'both from the well affected and disaffected, against his Majesty's ministers'. His argument contained a veiled threat: 'As the Duke of Cumberland is not one of the Regency, he will not, it may perhaps be apprehended, look upon himself to be so absolutely under the direction and orders of the Regency, as to obey implicitly, without knowing the King's pleasure, their plans or orders'; and that his poor relations with Newcastle would hamper Cumberland's activity in his military role. The occurrence of 'general distress or alarm' might then compel his elevation to sole power. Walpole recommended the ministers either to represent to the King the impossibility of their conducting the government in his absence and to urge him to remain, or to ask him to appoint Cumberland as Regent with the assurance of their support. The expected objections of Leicester House might then be allayed by prior arrangement and full consultation; if they could not be pacified, the Princess must prevail on the King to stay in England. If none of this could be brought about, 'it is to be apprehended that persons of great weight and consideration, and who will by no means go into a peevish motion of a disgraced Lord of the Bedchamber, may, when that is over, take some step of the same nature afterwards, if the King perseveres in his resolution of leaving these kingdoms at this juncture'.[20]

Walpole's was a personal initiative unconnected with Poulett or Bedford. In his private memorandum to Devonshire, he even recommended killing Poulett's motion by moving the previous question. But calculation entered into Walpole's public role, for in private his advice was based on the assumption of the King's departure. Poulett genuinely did, as Walpole did not, wish to prevent this: but the ministers were not at liberty to make their disquiet public. Waldegrave's account of this meeting, prepared for Fox, sets the Regency affair in a different light:

the Duke of Newcastle first mentioned the affair to L[ady] Y[armouth]. The article of sole Regent was mentioned, not as a measure to be executed, but as what had been talked of and it was her opinion the King would never come into it: it was even said that as to making the Duke one of the Regency would be attended with difficulties. That the King was not at present over fond of the Duke;[21] that there might be jealousies in the King, concerning him. And that there must be jealousies in the Princess of Wales's family. Yet on the other hand that the King was so intent on going that he would come into anything to get away in quiet. She advised the Duke of Newcastle to lay everything before the King just as it was, but not to offer his own opinion.

Waldegrave claimed Newcastle did so, and secured the King's promise to return at once if necessary; 'He seemed to agree to the D[uke of Cumberland] being one of the Regency, if it was insisted on, and added in case he does not agree with you I am certain there is none of my servants but Mr Fox who will agree with him.'[22] This was evidently made known on 12 April; Newcastle was thus able to present the meeting, not with a fait accompli, but with the plan of a compromise for which others stood forward unwittingly to take the discredit. Cumberland's limited advancement was a check, not a licence, to Fox. Devonshire, on Horatio Walpole's prior prompting, stressed the need for the King to leave full powers and hinted at a motion similar to Poulett's unless the King 'gave us that security which we had a right to expect'. The general sense of the meeting then expressed itself in favour of Cumberland as one of a Regency Council in deference to his standing and offices.

It was also hinted that if as Prince of the Blood he could not be joined in a Commission of the Regency whether the necessity of the times did not require that he should be sole Regent. This both the Chancellor and Duke of Newcastle seemed to disapprove of, not directly by objecting, but by expressing their desire of having nothing to do with affairs, any farther than related to their respective offices. Indeed nobody seemed to wish it, any farther than as a remedy in case no other could be found.[23]

As Horatio Walpole put it:

Your Grace was pleased to say at the meeting, that HRHss, had been acquainted by the proper officers in their respective stations with everything that had been done, since the first appearance of troubles, and that his Majesty was apprised of it, and satisfied with it. But your Grace will pardon me for asking and appealing to yourself, whether such a communication to the Duke of Cumberland by the officers in their several departments though very respectable persons, of what has been projected, can be looked upon by his Royal Highness without any previous conference with him, by Lord Chancellor or your Grace, as such marks of confidence for his sentiments and advice, as can satisfy one of his dignity in matters, where he may be principally useful and necessary. He without doubt considers it as a communication *après coup* and to save appearances only...[24]

Instead, much of the discussion turned on the possibility of vesting a concentration of power in a Regency Council 'beyond what had ever beeen granted, in the absence of the sovereign', and Horatio Walpole was compelled to conceal the extent of his dissatisfaction.[25] The grounds of George II's diffidence over Cumberland are nowhere made explicit. Perhaps he resented the backing his son gave to Fox's disruption during the previous session. Despite Newcastle's claim that the King had been satisfied with the extent of his son's involvement in military preparations, George II took part, in April as in January, in framing the limits to the power of the Cumberland interest. By contrast, it is apparent that Newcastle undertook the major part behind the scenes in securing even this confined position for the Duke, as he had previously done for Fox.

Poulett's initiative remained to be checked. Horatio Walpole, defeated over Cumberland's standing, now stressed again what was little attended to at the meeting on 12th, the potential popularity of such a motion and the threat of a parliamentary opposition based on it: 'nobody knows who may take a part in it when once started'.[26] Newcastle evidently warned his allies to be present to resist the motion.[27] But Poulett, once in the Lords on 17th, engaged in a whispered round of discussions and was eventually dissuaded from speaking by Fox,[28] who in an audience on 16th had urged Bedford's opposition to the motion while, wrote Rigby, 'expressing himself as eagerly as if he [the King] could distinguish between their attacks upon his ministry and himself whenever he chooses to do it, and at the same time with the greatest satisfaction that your [Bedford's] opinion was on his side'.[29]

Poulett, repentant, sought the King's pardon through Fox and Lady Yarmouth; but an unfriendly reception provoked him to renew his motion. The reported intention of Tories Sir Cordell Firebrace and Sir Francis Dashwood to move the same motion in the Commons on 24th was frustrated by a motion to adjourn the House; but the same day,

Poulett brought it forward in the Lords.[30] Chesterfield, 'who of all men living seemed to have no business to defend the Duke of Newcastle after much the same sort of ill usage'[31] appears to have seen it, on its merits alone, as 'an indecent, ungenerous, and malignant question'[32] for he moved and secured the adjournment. Poulett, his motion not even discussed, was left as an object of ridicule: a more just verdict than the suspicion of Joseph Yorke that 'The whole history of Lord Poulett is a curious one, and seems to be a game played by some particular persons, to serve a purpose, for sure nothing can be so unjust as scolding the *Duke of Newcastle* with Lord R[ochford]'s being put over his [Poulett's] head...'[33] It was Newcastle, if anyone, who drew advantage from the episode, for it acted only to discredit the case for a sole Regent which – as Horatio Walpole showed – could be argued forcefully on other grounds.

THE REGENCY AND THE SOURCES OF OPPOSITION

Parliament was prorogued on 25 April. Cumberland, from the King's embarkation on 28th, acted as President of a Regency Council of sixteen. Among them, he, Marlborough, Fox and Granville have been identified as forming a war party.[34] It is not intended here to examine the work of the Regency in the conduct of military and diplomatic policy during the summer of 1755; but three points must be made in general. First, as Waldegrave recorded, 'The Lords Justices, I mean the leaders only, who in their private meetings determined all affairs of consequence, were the Duke, the Chancellor, Lord Granville, the Duke of Newcastle, Lord Anson, Sir Thomas Robinson, and Mr Fox':[35] a majority of 4 to 3 at least for Newcastle. Neither Waldegrave nor Horace Walpole anywhere wrote of Cumberland's position in the Regency as a victory for, or as reflecting the favour enjoyed in the Closet by, the Fox camp. Walpole recorded Pitt telling Fox in their conversation of 12 May: ' "Here...is the Duke King, and you are his Minister!" "Whatever you may think," replied Fox, "the Duke does not think himself aggrandised by being of the Regency, where he has no more power than I have." ' Walpole claimed, too, that Newcastle had the Duke named for the Regency 'without acquainting him or asking his consent'.[36] Secondly, Waldegrave observed a reversal of the hawkishness which characterised the autumn of 1754 (when Fox and Cumberland were making the running in military policy) and the caution, even the hesitancy with which the Regency brought itself to give orders to Hawke's fleet.[37]

Thirdly, the Regency was important in this context chiefly in relation to the re-emergence of formed opposition led from Leicester House, and to Pitt's abandonment of the Old Corps in favour of the junior Court. By the end of March, Newcastle was undecided between Pitt's removal and his immediate or eventual promotion to Cabinet office.[38] The tenor of Newcastle's approach was personally neutral, one of willingness to decide on pragmatic grounds. The Chancellor had advised against Pitt's dismissal and recognised that Legge's demotion, which would have implications for Pitt's position, must await the sounding of Sir George Lee and the Princess.[39] Meanwhile, just before the King's departure, Hardwicke prompted Horatio Walpole to undertake an unofficial mission to Pitt.[40] Its result is not directly known. Only weeks later did Newcastle decide to seek the King's consent to treat with 'the principal persons' with a view to framing a system to support the King's measures in the autumn, adding: 'it is by no means proposed to engage His Majesty in anything, but only to learn upon what terms His Majesty may have the assistance of those, who may be of use to his service'. Though there is no evidence that Newcastle wrote in the knowledge that Pitt would welcome an overture, it seems unlikely that the Paymaster had yet done anything to deter one.[41] The names Newcastle listed were, accordingly, Pitt, Fox, Legge, Egmont and Dodington; Bute was not mentioned.[42] But the measures to be promoted are not set out, and in April Newcastle showed little more insight into what the issues were later to be than did any of the candidates.

Pitt himself, probably after Walpole's overture, was half in hopes that Fox would treat for him and the Grenvilles when approached by Newcastle, but saw Fox's strength: 'possessed as he is of the Duke, pushed and supported by Lord Granville, reconciled with and assisted by Stone, favoured by Lady Yarmouth, and liked and trusted by the King, we shall be left without a remedy'. But to accept Fox's help would be to be 'embarked in his bottom, in all appearance, for times to come'. To forestall such a choice, Pitt suggested his friends 'resolve to talk for ourselves, and endeavour to bring things to some explanation, before the above mentioned conjuncture is actually come upon us' – to pursue the opportunity Walpole's approach had indicated, and discover whether the favourable dispositions there conveyed offered the abrogation of 'His Majesty's irremovable displeasure'. Pitt's services might be rejected constitutionally if the King thought them 'useless', but Pitt would blame on others any royal opinion which saw him as 'not *worthy to be trusted*' in the Closet. Pitt seems to have brought himself to the point of decision, determined not to 'waste my life under a delusion...' and seeking a categorical decision, so that 'I may no longer look towards impossible things'.[43]

But in raising Pitt's hopes for both an immediate settlement and a substantial gain, Walpole had made a tactical error. Hartington learned that Newcastle 'flew out violently with Horatio Walpole for having gone so much farther in his negotiation with Pitt than he was authorised and that he either *would* or *could* make good'. Both Hartington and Ellis felt Walpole 'had done it with perhaps a view to make him more open to treaty if it should be thought advisable or to get more the possession and direction of him or to sow the seeds of separation between'

Pitt and Fox.[44] It is not known whether any positive terms were advanced to Pitt; apparently, according to Newcastle's version (relayed to Dodington via Halifax) Pitt was moved to reply, consistently with the spirit of his letter,[45] that he did not insist upon a Secretaryship of State immediately, but only when a vacancy next arose; rather, that 'as a proof of the D[uke of Newcastle]'s sincerity', he should 'take off all marks of proscription' and that the King should in future treat him, Pitt, with public signs of favour. According to Horatio Walpole, his apparent consent to this was what aroused Newcastle's anger.[46] Nor is it known whether Pitt heard of Newcastle's reaction to Walpole's news; more probably, he drew inferences from the silence which followed from Newcastle's quarter in May.

Meanwhile, apparently ignorant of Newcastle's relations with Pitt, Bute speculated on the effect of a reversionary interest *per se*:

Next session brings the Prince to age; I think 'tis likely a strong party will be formed; that will set both Fox and the Cardinal [Newcastle] at defiance; if Pitt can be induced to join, a point I have much at heart; the prospect will be pleasing though I cannot say in the midst of such corruption, my hopes can be ever sanguine.[47]

It has hitherto been assumed that Bute's letter represented the junior Court's official position; and that, from April, 'Leicester House had come to the conclusion that the only remedy was that a strong party should be formed to set a Fox–Newcastle administration at defiance' in reaction against the power conferred on Cumberland by his inclusion in the Regency.[48] In fact, as has been shown, the arrangement of December 1754 did not constitute a Fox–Newcastle ministry; nor is there good evidence for the other elements in this argument. Bute's letter was probably only an exercise in thinking aloud; what is most remarkable about it is his faith in the efficacy of a rival royal focus of opposition despite the dearth of 'issues' and the absence of its future leader. Gilbert Elliot, presumably on hearsay evidence recorded at a later date,[49] supposed that the subsidy treaties formed one ground of Pitt's alliance with Leicester House; George Grenville, whose account[50] confirms Elliot's in most other respects, fails to mention any issue on which a coincidence of policy was discovered or contrived. Elliot was led to suppose Bute's interview with Pitt at Sir Richard Lyttelton's was accidental; Grenville reveals that Bute arranged it, after a message carried by Lyttelton 'desiring to know the state of our [the Grenvilles'] connection with the Duke of Cumberland and Mr Fox, and whether we were at liberty to enter into the closest engagement with Leicester House'. Evidently, nothing in Pitt's conduct had yet marked him off from cordial relations with the quarter of the Court from which Bute, like Newcastle, expected any serious political initiative to come. Pitt's disclaimer of allegiance to Cumberland allowed the negotiations to proceed to the point where Pitt, according to Grenville (whose source must have been Pitt), received the Princess's personal assurance of her 'protection and support'. Grenville remarked:

That Court had been unkindly and harshly treated by the King, and conceived great umbrage at the power and authority of the Duke of Cumberland: these dispositions, which bore so great a resemblance to those we were in, soon formed our union with Lord Bute, and that part of the Royal Family.[51]

The elements supplied by retrospect should be eliminated from Grenville's account. It is not true that the Princess's 'marks of favour were given in the most public manner, and our attachment as publicly avowed'. Both were conceded privately, if at all; more probably, they were not given in any form specific enough to bear revelation until just before the opening of the next sessions. Secondly, Grenville supposed, as Ilchester later claimed,[52] that Cumberland's growing power alarmed the Princess and that she looked about for followers as a consequence. In fact, as has been suggested, neither Fox nor Cumberland enjoyed or claimed the power which it was an article of Pitt's creed by 9 May to credit him with; Pitt's arguing thus was part of an attempt to profit from the Fox–Newcastle rivalry within the Old Corps. Nor is there any evidence that the Princess was so motivated, for she began to voice this disquiet only later in the summer, *after* Pitt's break with Fox, on the occasion of the Wolfenbüttel marriage alarm and the Portsmouth visit. The issues of the Regency and the Hanover connection were both developed later to give expression to an opposition initiated by Bute and Pitt for their own ends, and at the outset classically and solely based on the reversionary interest's appeal to the politically malcontent. It was not immediately endorsed by the Princess. Her personal hostility was largely focused on Newcastle, was effectively veiled from him until the autumn, and was only distantly related to Bute's aims. What then passed gives the impression that two factions existed within Leicester House, the Bute–Pitt and the Egmont–Lee interests; not until late October did the Princess choose between them or authorise either to commence an overt opposition to the ministry. Even then, it was not unequivocally sanctioned by her.

PITT'S BREACH WITH FOX, AND THE LAUNCHING
OF A LEICESTER HOUSE OPPOSITION, MAY 1755

Horace Walpole offered three explanations of the inception of a Leicester House opposition, seemingly unaware of their inconsistency. First, that Pitt had sent Horatio Walpole to Newcastle 'the day before the King went abroad' with a demand for the Secretaryship of State; and not getting a favourable answer, 'From that moment, it is supposed, Pitt cast his eyes towards the successor'.[53] Although, as has been shown, the suggestion of the Secretaryship came from Walpole, Newcastle's response may have broken Pitt's patience. Horace Walpole, however, did not know this: he only supposed it. Secondly, he suggested 'the truth seemed to be' that Pitt, 'being united with the Princess', learned of 'Fox's having disclaimed him'[54] – that is, in the negotiations of December 1754. This would certainly have given Pitt cause to break with Fox, but there is no evidence that he or the Princess discovered anything new in these weeks about Fox's conduct the previous winter. And, thirdly, that a break with Fox was the already-agreed price of the Princess's alliance, and that Pitt had had a private audience with her the day before his meeting with Fox at Holland House (on 12th).[55] But this third theory fails to explain the fact that at his second meeting with Fox, Pitt tried to palliate what he had said at the first. Dodington recorded Fox's better guess: '*I know Mr Fox* imputes it to a design of [Pitt's] fixing himself with the Princess, and that in order to do that, it became necessary to declare off with him, Fox, as the Duke of Cumberland's man: I do not think so, it is too refined for me; I think nobody but Cresset (if he) is in a settled confidence of measures (if there be any) with the Princess, and so I told him [Fox].'[56] In fact, Dodington's account of the junior Court was consistent with Fox's suggestion. Far from being the price of the Princess's alliance, Pitt's outburst at Fox was either an attempt to force her to support Pitt in a Leicester House opposition which he and Bute had sought to launch in advance of her approval, or an accidental revelation that that was indeed his strategy.

This explanation is established by a memorandum of Sir George Lee:[57]

On Monday 5 May, 1755, the Princess of Wales gave Mr. Pitt (pursuant to his desire) an audience at the Earl of Bute's house in South Audley Street, in consequence of a conversation which had past between the said Earl and him a few days before. At that audience, as the Princess told me, Mr. Pitt declared the great duty of himself and his friends to her and their desire to support her and preserve the independence of the Prince whenever he should come to the Crown; that great numbers were in the same opinion, but were deterred from declaring themselves from an apprehension that she and the Prince were under influence from Mr. Stone, and that she was quite connected with and was the support of the Duke of Newcastle, that this gave the true constitutional Whigs who acted upon Revolution principles great alarm, for as to the Duke of Newcastle he had deceived all mankind, and it was impossible to act with him if he was to be continued minister in a future reign. Her R.H. replied that she was not in any sort influenced by Mr. Stone, and she was sure he had never attempted to inculcate any Tory principles into the Prince; and as to the Duke of Newcastle she had no other connection with him than as the King's minister; that she should always countenance those the King employed, and should never oppose the King's measures; in the conversation she was pleased to say she confided in me, whereupon Mr. Pitt desired he might have a conference with me the next night, and concluded with assurances of his duty, and that he would endeavour to bring as many persons to her interest as he could.

Accordingly, by Her R.H.'s command, on Tuesday evening 6 May, I met Mr. Pitt at the Earl of Bute's, where, after mutual compliments, we declared a desire of cementing friendship; he declared his attachment and his friendship to the Princess and her family, and that upon her honouring him with her countenance he would do all he could to connect people to her, that she might have a strong party if any thing should happen; talked of the apprehensions of Mr. Stone's influence, for which I assured him there was not the least foundation; said he had had great offers from the Duke of Newcastle, but he would have nothing to do with him; commended me for refusing the office of Chancellor of the Exchequer, declared against the Duke of Newcastle and Lord Granville as ministers; spoke much in honour of Lord Chancellor, and wished him to be the minister; pressed much to know whether Her R.H. had any connection with the Duke of Newcastle, for unless he could be authorised to assure people she had not he could not do her any service, though as to himself he was satisfied from what she had been pleased to say to him, which I had confirmed; I ventured to assure him she had no other connection with him than as the King's minister, and one whose interest appeared to be the same with her, though this winter he had done every thing in contradiction to her interest, for he had thrown the game into Mr. Fox's hand, who was in a plan opposite to the Princess's; he would make no explicit declaration about Fox, further than that he would never do any thing for or consent to putting the House of Commons into Fox's hands; he pressed again to be empowered to declare that the Princess would not recommend the Duke of Newcastle to the Prince for his minister, and said it was too much to expect from me a declaration in the Princess's name without her authority; upon which he begged I would see the Princess and know her sentiments, for such a declaration would be of great use, which I promised; we both declared this was a defensive treaty only to connect people together, but did not bind us to hostilitys against any person, or to opposition to the King's measures.

On Wednesday, 7 May, I waited on the Princess, acquainted her with the substance of our conference, and by her command the same day made the following declaration to Lord Bute, to be by him delivered to Mr. Pitt: viz. that Her R.H. had no partiality for the Duke of Newcastle, that she had no private or particular connection with him otherwise than as the King's minister, and that she had no thoughts of recommending him to the Prince as his minister, but she did not think it proper for her to declare against having to do with any body, and as to Lord Chancellor, she had a great esteem and regard for him.

Lord Bute asked me how far I thought Mr. Pitt and I were engaged by what had passed between us. I replied that I thought we were bound to enter into no concert with the Duke of Newcastle without communicating to each other, and he said he was of the same opinion; it was agreed that Lord Temple, Lord Egmont and Mr. Geo. Grenville should be informed of what had passed.

Pitt's talk on 5th of Stone's influence had been recognised as the red herring it was; his preoccupation was evidently the extent of the Princess's links with Newcastle. But her disclaimers that day did not go far, and Pitt's professions of support begged the question. Sir George Lee, on 6th, proved equally sceptical at Pitt's alarms over Stone's influence and cannot have welcomed unequivocally Pitt's congratulations that he, Lee, was not at that moment Chancellor of the Exchequer. Lee evidently did not give Pitt authority to deny Leicester House's allegiance to the ministry in any usable form: that the Princess had 'no other connection' with Newcastle 'than as the King's minister' could mean nothing or everything. Yet, on his side, Pitt was reluctant to announce his hostility to Fox; Lee does not seem to have seen these conversations as an opportunity to create an anti-Fox alliance or to bargain about its terms. The 'declaration' which Lee conveyed to Bute on 7th was accordingly as enigmatic as what the Princess had said to Pitt on 5th. No wonder Bute asked for an explanation of what had been agreed; but Lee's account of it on 7th hardly went beyond what had been understood on 6th. A defensive treaty against Newcastle was of no use to Pitt and Bute: it was they who sought for a way to attack the Minister, not vice versa. It was Lee's antipathy to Fox which allowed Pitt to represent good relations with Leicester House as more purposive than they were. Pitt's only tangible gain was that the way was now open for him to force the hand of the junior Court by worsening relations with Fox and Newcastle in a way which would both make an opposition to them less avoidable, and place Lee and Egmont in a far weaker position in relation to Pitt and Bute at Leicester House. As yet, however, these were speculative possibilities only;[58] Sir George Lee's time was still 'wholly spent between the Commons and Kew'.[59]

On 7 May, Dodington recorded:[60]

Passed the evening at Leicester House. The Princess was clear the Duke of Newcastle could not stand as things were. Desired that it should be understood that Leicester House had no communication with Newcastle House; but not that she said so, because it would be told at St. James's House, where she desired to avoid all disputes.

From Sir George Lee's account of the negotiations of 5–7 May, it is clear that Dodington's observations should not be interpreted as evidence of an opposition already formed. Pitt was not therefore fulfilling the terms of a bargain when, on 9 May,

Mr Pitt came to Lord Hillsborough['s house] where Mr Fox was; who stepping aside, Mr Pitt thinking he was gone, declared to Lord Hillsborough that all connection between him and Mr Fox was over, that the *ground was altered*, that Mr Fox was of the Cabinet, and regent, and he left exposed etc. – That he would be *second* to *nobody*, etc. – Mr Fox rejoining the company, Mr Pitt, heated, said the same, and more to him: that if succeeded, and so made way for him [Pitt] he would not accept the seals of Secretary from him. That would be owning an obligation, and superiority, which he would not own. He would owe nothing but to himself: – and much more very high and very strange conversation. – Fox asked him what would put them on the same ground: he said, a winter in the Cabinet and a summer's Regency.

He talked the same over again to Lord Hillsborough who endeavoured to soften matters; but he was unalterable; and desired Lord Hillsborough as a friend to take an opportunity to tell Mr Fox that he wished there might be no farther conversation between him [Pitt] and Fox about it; that he esteemed him, but that all connection was over between them.[61]

Fox's version of the episode was recorded by his sister-in-law, then staying at Holland House:

I am afraid Mr Fox and Mr Pitt have had some difference; the former says that the latter is angry and jealous at his being Privy Councillor and Regent; for he has in a manner told Mr Fox so, and also hinted to him that he suspected the Duke [of Cumberland] and he had made terms with the Duke of Newcastle in order to get the Duke made Regent. His expression was that in fact the Duke was now King of England and Mr Fox his First Minister; and, in short, seemed to declare off and to tell Mr Fox that they must each act for themselves separately...Mr Fox seemed not to know what to make of it. But by what he told my sister and I, it was, I think, very plain Mr Fox is uneasy about it and very angry with Pitt. My sister is very sorry, because she thinks it of great consequence to Mr Fox to keep well with Pitt; I own I think so too. He says not; for that as the Tories are with the ministry no opposition would be strong enough to do any good. He seems in vast doubts how to act, and always says he has committed one fault never to be retrieved; and that thought I believe is what prevents his acting with as much spirit as he would have done once.[62]

Evidently she spoke of Fox's refusal of a Secretaryship of State after Henry Pelham's death. But, as Fox now correctly realised, the alignment of forces in the Commons meant that his alliance of that winter with Pitt was worth little.

To Pitt, however, it had been more valuable. His outburst was emotional and ill-considered. At the least, it can only have been an untimely disclosure of his future position. Accordingly he sought[63] another interview with Fox; they met at Holland House on 12th. Fox, who had just consulted Cumberland,[64] received from Pitt

the utmost civility, professions of friendship to me, and enmity to the Duke of Newcastle, and to Stone, and to Murray. He blamed me for nothing, but we were upon different lines, not opposite, but converging; (a word I do not quite understand). However we are to act separately as shall seem best to us, and wish one another perfectly well.

I do believe he [Pitt] has no treaty nor views of treaty with the Duke of Newcastle. Nor can I guess what he can have in view at Leicester House, where however I am informed, (how truly I do not know) that he is better; and where, I have *good* information that my friend Stone is extremely out of favour. Upon the whole, I cannot understand what his view is, nor do I indeed comprehend what he *says* on the subject. It...points to nothing yet decided even in his own mind. His Royal Highness *the Duke* wishes it may not be known, which your lordship will I hope approve of; and thinks it may be better for me and is by no means worse in any view.

At all events, I am in Pitt's own opinion, given me upon his honour, blameless.[65]

Fox's main danger had been that Pitt would independently conclude an alliance, excluding him, with Newcastle. Now this possibility was at an end; but, as Cumberland realised, Pitt's stance narrowed Fox's options. His future lay within the Old Corps. Without Fox or the Tories, it was not clear that Pitt had any future out of it. Even at the end of May, Temple wrote to George Grenville in terms suggesting the stagnation of their political fortunes, not the promise of an incipient opposition.[66] The same day, he attempted to persuade Dodington of their satisfaction with Fox: 'they had no suspicions, and were willing he should try the same conduct for 2, 3, 4, months; but thought something must be settled before the opening of the session. They are desperate with the King, and have not been able to get possession either of Leicester House or of the Duke of Cumberland'.[67] Horatio Walpole admitted to Fox his impression that Pitt was 'embarrassed, and come to no resolution what to do' next sessions.[68] Hartington and Cumberland agreed that Pitt's motives were merely personal, 'the same impetuosity of temper (worked up by his ambition) that made him prematurely begin the attack upon Sir Thomas Robinson last winter'; at the same time, Hartington thought Fox 'should keep well with [Pitt] if you can, or at least have the appearance of it', and that Pitt's outburst did not prevent this. His friendship would be valuable to Fox both through his ability and integrity, and since 'it enables you to treat better with his Grace of Newcastle'. That duke, thought Hartington, had dropped his plans for a 'treaty' with Pitt; 'by the last conversation I had with the Duke of Newcastle I thought his intention was to cultivate you in order to try to get well with His Royal Highness, and I hope he will continue in that resolution, for there is no sense or safety for him in anything else and the best service he can do the King and his country'.[69] Fox agreed with the advice he was given. Pitt, far from being 'in treaty' with Newcastle, obviously meant his

frank and voluntary declarations...of contempt for his Grace, of indignation that such a genius should conceive, much more succeed in, an attempt to make fools of all mankind, [and] of resolution to take every opportunity of destroying, or at least bringing within narrow bounds, his power...besides, I am pretty sure the Duke of Newcastle does not at present intend to treat with any body. His treatment of the Duke [of Cumberland], whom he makes use of as he does of everybody else, as far as is absolutely necessary and no more, convinces me, that as yet at least he intends to make next winter pass as the last did. I think Pitt has his managements at Leicester House; but by what channel, to what view directed, or with what success, I do not know.[70]

It is not certain what contacts Pitt had with Lee or the Princess between 9 and 12 May.[71] But Pitt's partial retraction at his second meeting with Fox; the conspiracy of both sides[72] to suppress the story of events in Hillsborough's garden; Pitt's conduct for the rest of the summer; the verdicts of contemporaries already cited; and Temple's letter to Grenville of 29 May[73] all suggest that Pitt's démarche was disavowed, and Pitt himself silenced. Lee and Egmont evidently remained, for the moment, in control. Whatever had been said to Fox, Pitt gave the ministry no reason yet to anticipate an opposition à l'outrance; and Cumberland's desire that the terms of the exchanges with Fox should not be known was, remarkably, observed until the autumn despite Hillsborough's presence and Dodington's having learned what passed on 9 May.[74] Ellis, only partly in the secret, ascribed Pitt's outburst to Walpole's artful contrivance, not to an incipient opposition by Pitt.[75] Even at the end of May, the Princess of Wales, lamenting 'the melancholy prospect of hers and her son's affairs', saw no political option to remedy them: 'if she was to stir, it would make things worse; she saw no way to extricate herself'.[76]

From Dodington's thorough account of what was being said at Leicester House in the spring, it seems that the themes were, rather, 'the weakness, meanness, cowardice and baseness of the Duke of Newcastle'; the need to arrange a new system with the Princess's co-operation, the ministry's being no longer viable through Newcastle's incapacity; an unspecific sense of national degeneration – 'there was no violence, no oppression, no particular complaint; but the nation was sinking by degrees'; and the complicity in the (establishment Whig) 'consuming system' of the suspected Jacobites, Stone and Murray.[77] As yet, then, Leicester House was confined to an old and tenuous rhetoric familiar to opposition Whigs: corruption and ministerial flirtation with Jacobitism. Even in late September, an opposition was expected 'chiefly on account of the influence which Mr Stone and the Attorney General are supposed to have over [Newcastle], and which the Whigs and Dissenters are greatly averse to'.[78] Pitt made an almost identical objection to co-operation with Fox, who 'lived with his greatest enemies: Lord Granville, Messrs Stone and Murray...But he (Pitt) would always act upon plain Whig principles, and would never have anything to do with Stone, or Murray'.[79] Discounting one entire theme of Leicester House's later appeal, Dodington imagined that only 'private dislikes (trifling ones, I believe)' prevented the Princess from joining Cumberland and others of the King's servants (inhibited by the threat of loss of place) to bring down the contemptible Newcastle.[80]

THE RESPONSE OF FOX AND NEWCASTLE, MAY–JUNE 1755

These qualifications to the received account of the history of Leicester House in the spring of 1755 go far to justify Newcastle's conduct during the rest of the summer. From his viewpoint, too, the linked problems of Egmont, Lee and Legge were temporarily 'on ice'. Legge, though he knew Newcastle was 'beating up for volunteers to fill my office without saying a syllable to me upon the subject' refused to be the first to begin hostilities.[81] There was, indeed, little else he could do and nowhere else to go: his behaviour the previous session had made him neither a necessary nor a congenial ally to any of Newcastle's rivals. Halifax, too, voiced articulate discontent, at Dodington's prompting: again accusations of 'The insufficiency, falseness, and meanness of the Duke of Newcastle's administration'; again a sense of helpless personal frustration; again vague talk of national degeneration. 'The remedy we could not find, though we agreed, that neither the Duke nor the country could go on, without other management, or other hands.' Evidently, no saviour existed who could draw on all these moralising aspirations: certainly not Pitt. But Halifax, though guided, was drawn presciently towards independent and Tory sentiment: 'he saw nothing to help [Newcastle], but my friends, Talbot, Dashwood and me'. Dodington saw briefly in Halifax the agent for a ministerial reconstruction on a basis of national regeneration, and played on the Earl's resentment at the preference shown to Holdernesse, Robinson and Fox. But Halifax let slip his alienation from Pitt, Fox and the Grenvilles, and his particular suspicion of the second; 'He said that unless the Duke of Newcastle made a new system, he was sure he could not go on; but if those should succeed, it would be a very flimsy, and short administration; for neither the nation, or the people of quality would confide, or acquiesce in either of them'.[82] Halifax was in a genuine dilemma: but one not open to exploitation by potential opposition, for he had told Newcastle that it would be resolved by a mark of distinction: the Garter. 'I said I wished he had put his weight rather upon a share in government', wrote Dodington, 'and a power to serve his country, at this exigence'.[83] But Halifax did not rise to Dodington's suggestion that he might take the seals of Secretary of State as part of a deal; and while a Garter remained vacant, he was willing neither to resign nor to oppose.

Newcastle, meanwhile, was pursuing his interest in Dodington, Pitt and Fox in relation to what he knew of the disposition of the Princess. Dodington had spoken strongly for the Vote of Credit of £1 million in March,[84] commending the vigour of the ministry and the ability of the Admiralty; now, Newcastle sought, though without satisfaction, clarification of his slightly suspect reference to the 'insidious' treaty of Aix-la-Chapelle and his implication that the ministry might have applied to Parliament sooner for present aid.[85] Hardwicke had a satisfactory discussion with the Princess on 16 May which raised, without resolving, the questions of Egmont and Lee; and found her well disposed over the issues of the disposition of power created by Cumberland's position in the Regency. 'She owned herself convinced of the necessity of it', wrote the Chancellor, 'and I showed her, in a proper manner, that it would not alter the state of things after the K[ing]'s return'. 'She, on her part, expressed herself extremely well satisfied with us and our intentions towards her and her family'; Hardwicke was struck only by her praise of Pitt's abilities and by her commending nobody but the Bishop of Peterborough among Prince George's governors. The Chancellor responded to the desire she expressed that a system be formed for the next Commons session by explaining the ministry's intentions and its reflections on how 'the system' had failed in the last.[86] He can have had no intimation of a formed opposition's being either designed or arranged; but little use was apparently made of the information he let slip. The Princess must have been already aware of the ministry's desire to recruit Egmont and Lee; if she were not dissembling the nature of a prior deal with Pitt, she may have hoped to include him with these two in a peacefully negotiated addition to the ministry; otherwise, her praise of Pitt and veiled slight on Stone would have been pointless. It is possible that she failed to learn from Hardwicke, through the Chancellor's personal distaste for the Secretary at War, of Newcastle's preference for Fox; but she revealed no fear that Newcastle's relations with Fox were about to become closer and more exclusive rather than the reverse.

Fox's course was, meanwhile, clear; for co-operation with Cumberland and the ministry were pointing in the same direction. His interviews with Pitt, concealed as he thought from Newcastle, and his knowledge of Horatio Walpole's advance, gave him good grounds to discount a Pitt–Newcastle rapprochement. But Fox had ceased since January to rely to any degree on Pitt's analogous position as a source of strength, and the failure of the Pitt–Fox alliance to amount to more than a bargaining counter meant that Fox was compelled to hope for, but could not command, a closer involvement with the ministry. Hartington imagined Newcastle was disposed, even impatient, to treat with Fox as part of a consolidation of good relations with Cumberland.[87] Ellis added:

I am persuaded that you now think it may be advisable to treat if any reasonable terms may be obtained. That fashion it as you may, the D's [Newcastle's] meaning and intent will be not to part with any essential power. But as things now stand I see nothing left but to make the best terms and that you should afterwards make the most of the means which that situation may afford towards the obtaining essential power to which I think very possibly good management and conjunctures co-operating may lead you.[88]

The assurance of his blamelessness in Pitt's eyes was a welcome release from the moral hangover of Fox's conduct in the past winter. Now, his prospects of office were enhanced not by the impact either of his late disaffection or of a Pitt–Leicester House opposition but by his standing in the Whig majority and Newcastle's reliance for advice and assent in the reshaping of the system on Fox's close acquaintance, Hartington.[89] The Devonshires were of particular importance at this point to Newcastle: not only was their ministerial stature considerable and their borough patronage significant (their immediate following in the Commons numbered about six)[90] but they cultivated a special sense of their Whig integrity and represented the largest floating vote on the Regency Board. Devonshire was on close terms even with Legge;[91] Cumberland could write of 'my friend Harty'.[92] Fox's value for Newcastle at times lay less in his links with Cumberland, whose reticence had now been demonstrated past Newcastle's surprise, than in his relationship with the indispensable Lord Lieutenant. 'We must get my lord Hartington and the Devonshire family with us, if we can', he wrote; 'I foresee our *future plan*, may not be exactly, what his lordship would wish'. Nevertheless, Hardwicke's interview with the Princess persuaded Newcastle that the initiative was his: 'the whole will depend upon the system for next winter'.[93]

Newcastle's hopes of Hartington did not extend to a full communication of Irish business to Devonshire, but Fox was anxious to follow the advice of both Cumberland and Hartington in preserving as far as possible the appearance of a *détente* with Pitt. This was possible, as Fox recognised, since although Pitt 'has managements I do think at Leicester House, which, like everything at that Court, are inscrutable. He has none with the Duke of Newcastle'.[94] As Fox suspected, Newcastle was 'trying to be better' with the Princess; we know of audiences at Kew in mid May[95] and on 7 June.[96] One of Newcastle's aims had been 'To know what correspondence she may have had with Mr Pitt; and what his views are'.[97] But his reception at the second audience was 'extremely cold', and the Princess made 'no professions of her regard, or support of us'.

I talked with the utmost freedom, and sincerity, both as to persons, and things... I entered truly into all that was passed, and into the measures that might be proper to be taken in the House of Commons. Fox, Pitt, Legge, Lord Egmont and Sir G. Lee, were fully talked over by me. She admitted we never could, or can do now without either Pitt, or Fox; she was much inclined, as we all are, for the former; but said she knew the King would not make him Secretary of State, but fancied his vanity might be satisfied with regard, and confidence; she did not blame, but showed a concern, that nothing had been done for Egmont, whom she has lately greatly distinguished by passing a day with him at his house at Charlton, and insisting with Lord Waldegrave to bring the Prince of Wales *thither* in the afternoon. I think she at last agreed, that we should endeavour to keep Pitt in good humour, leave Fox where he is and take in Egmont, and Sir G. Lee. I have talked this very fully over, with my Lord Chancellor, my lord Waldegrave, my lord Ashburnham and Mr Stone. We all agree, that this behaviour is occasioned by Cresset's peevishness, and Egmont's and perhaps Sir G. Lee's disappointment, [? who] they all imagine by it, that they shall force us into their measures, viz. to take in Sir G. Lee and Egmont and be more alienated from the D[uke of Cumberland] and Fox. But indeed, I don't well see, how the latter is possible. There is nothing with the *Duke* but proper and necessary civility, and concurrence in business. In that His Royal Hss. does his part, and we should be too much to blame, if we did not do ours. And it is now plain, that neither side, are in the least disposed to go farther, and that is very happy for us. We all think, that this ill humour, which is certainly a part acted, must go off. For they can go nowhere else, and by attempting it might hurt themselves more than us.

Charles Yorke is to try his friend Pitt, and if anything is to be made of him, my lord Chancellor and I are to have a conference with him. Nothing at all passes good or bad between Fox and us, but that is certainly wrong, and must to a degree be altered.[98]

Newcastle seemingly had not revised his opinions in the light of an alarm which spread just after his audience: 'it was related all over London that several barrells of gunpowder had been discovered under Kew House and the Prince's House, that the Swan was likewise loaded with gunpowder and that the Prince of Wales had been shot at and narrowly escaped the ball. We had yesterday morning several messengers from town to know whether we were not blown up', wrote the Bishop of Oxford, then at Kew.[99] Whether this baseless story was generated spontaneously or was initiated by either Bute's or Egmont's and Lee's camps within Leicester House is not known. Newcastle would evidently still have been inclined to suppose the third. Nevertheless, his happiness with the conduct of the Regency prompted Ellis to remark on his apparent confidence that he could use everyone for his own purposes, and survive the summer and the next sessions through divisions among the malcontents.[100] But 'extraordinary appearances' at Kew on 22 June revised Newcastle's earlier information[101] that Cresset was the instigator of the Princess's unfriendliness. Now, he thought he detected there a union between 'Mr P[itt] and Lord E[gmon]t' although Waldegrave and Andrew Stone differed from the 'disagreeable condition, your Grace apprehends':[102] presumably, that their union was part of a formed opposition. Newcastle's experience probably led him to suppose that Egmont exercised the same influence at Leicester House that year as the last; Stone, that Egmont's close links with the ministry would draw Pitt in, too.

Newcastle's fears were not, as has been supposed, confirmed by the affairs of the Portsmouth visit. On 22 June, Cumberland proposed to the Princess that Prince George accompany him to review the fleet. Such an expedition had once before passed off successfully when they travelled to watch the launching of ships at Woolwich.[103] Now, the Princess conferred with Waldegrave and at first approved;[104] but by 24th had changed her mind.[105] Hardwicke, however, was reluctant to meddle in what he called a 'family-affair',[106] drawing no further moral; and Newcastle's chief sentiment was regret that Prince George had lost an opportunity to appear publicly to advantage 'in countenancing with his presence, the favourite object of this nation, viz. our naval force', not apprehension that Cumberland's image might have been damaged or opposition provided with a justification.[107] Cumberland, indeed, passed the affair off, 'and says it is only from a resolution she had taken not to be accountable for anything with the King. But Fox is very uneasy, and very solicitous to unite the Duke and the Princess and it is the only sound ground. But I think', concluded Dodington, 'it will be exceeding difficult, if possible, to effect'.[108] Newcastle as yet made no such attempt. Instead, he awaited the outcome of a sounding of Pitt by Charles Yorke: 'till we know his final resolution, we can't go to work anywhere, and it is high time, that something was put in motion. Intrigues are certainly *on foot*, and parties will be taken, which perhaps might have been prevented, before engagements were made'.[109]

With this single exception, Newcastle still held the initiative. Dodington recorded on 29th: 'Mr Fox passed the morning here. Very much talk to no purpose. None of them dare come to any resolution'; the same day, Legge wrote to Hartington of his ignorance of, and anxiety over, the form which the impending 'revolution' might take.[110] Fox himself wrote:

What E[gmont] or P[itt] will do nobody can tell, nor should I care if it were not in concert with Leicester House. As for what they can do after what they have declared – they are capable of the shortest turns, and Pitt already says that it is right to defend Hanover, but to what degree we should contribute to it is the question? Which is keeping himself for sale, but I own I do not see how they will buy him. I am in the dark, but see anything likelier than my junction with the Duke of Newcastle, because I am persuaded he, above all things, is afraid of being thought friends with the Duke, and determined not to be so...I don't see what Pitt can do with the Court, but had he meant opposition, he could not have thought it necessary to break so abruptly with me.[111]

Fox still imagined himself an essential actor in any opposition, and could not conceive of Leicester House staging such a performance without its familiar cast. In July, there *were* good grounds for only expecting it to occur if Pitt and Egmont found a basis of co-operation. Newcastle was now in touch with the first through Nugent and judged him to be, though arrogant, not 'desperate':[112] Egmont made a virtue of the help he had given Newcastle behind the scenes in the past, and contented himself now with hinting in ominous but enigmatic terms at some great change of heart as the condition of Newcastle's continuance in power.[113] Such talk indicated only a poverty of contrivance on the part of potential opponents, and probably suggested to Newcastle that closer links with Fox would not of themselves produce a Leicester House opposition in reaction against Cumberland. Hardwicke interpreted Egmont's remarks as revealing a tacit desire for office; his only anxiety was lest Dodington stand in the way of Egmont's satisfaction.[114]

NEWCASTLE'S OVERTURES TO PITT, JULY 1755

At the same time, Newcastle was forced to make overtures to Pitt from a constricted position, for the implication of trends in foreign policy now became clear: at least to Newcastle. Although Cumberland 'gives up the Continent for this year' – that is, an army in Germany – the issue would recur the next year and would demand some provision from Parliament. Newcastle saw with alarm both the political and military implications of flatly opposing a belligerent measure of the Duke's,[115] and the alternative – presenting an opportunity for the repetition of Pitt's anti-Hanoverian rhetoric of the 1740s. Fortunately, Pitt never raised the issue of subsidies, nor did he demand an office which would in effect have been a challenge to the ministry's European policy. James Grenville met Halifax on 2 July and disclaimed on Pitt's behalf any ambition of being Secretary of State; all he required was 'confidence, and regard.' Halifax gave every hope that both would be forthcoming.[116] Hardwicke, however, doubted whether these familiar words carried their old meaning. 'He has had confidence and regard, and thrown it away. It has been assured to him over and over again, and yet declined. Does it not therefore mean some other kind of confidence and regard arising from employment?' If so, and if Pitt really waived a Secretaryship of State, he might be satisfied as Fox had been by Cabinet rank: a cheap bargain, if the King would agree.[117]

These thoughts were confirmed by the meetings Pitt had with Hardwicke and Charles Yorke in turn on 6 July. Pitt claimed that he had waived the Secretaryship in his April interview with Horatio Walpole; now, as then, he sought 'a pledge of security, which might be the beginning of confidence': that Newcastle should speak to the King in favour of Pitt as the necessary person 'to be trusted with the debate of' the House of Commons, and try too to improve the disposition of Lady Yarmouth towards him.[118] These points were accepted by Newcastle and formed the basis of the plan he forwarded to Hanover for approval on 11 July.[119] Every pressure was used to enforce the advice. Its acceptance was held to decide the fate of the administration. Impracticable measures (an excessive continental commitment) or inadequate support would, it was urged, equally destroy the ministry in the Commons. Pitt and Egmont were essential there; and to buy the first with Cabinet rank only, the second with a Vice Treasurership of Ireland in the room of Yonge or Cholmondeley, would be a small price. Egmont had been disappointed the previous session; 'if nothing is done for him now, we must expect the warmest opposition from him'. That accomplished, Sir George Lee would be an able Chancellor of the Exchequer and a useful acquisition in the Commons; Fox could have no objection, having been 'gratified in the manner he desired'. Two ends would thus be gained. First, and primarily, the internal dissensions which marked the previous session would be eliminated – where, despite a great majority, 'persons in the first station there, in His Majesty's service, have not supported the King's measures in the manner they ought to have done'. Secondly, an anticipated difficulty would be forestalled: 'whatever party His Majesty shall think proper to take, with regard to the Continent, such opposition may arise to it, in the House of Commons, as may give great disturbance, and obstruction to public business; if that opposition should be headed, by persons of weight and ability there'. No names were suggested as participants in an opposition which had not yet emerged, but it was claimed of 'great men' in the Commons that 'their significance will always rise, in proportion, as the difficulties and distresses of the public advance'. That stage had not been reached; and, with these promotions achieved, Newcastle and Hardwicke declared they could be answerable for the success of business in the House.

Newcastle's scheme was almost identical to that which had been on the brink of completion for six months. The difference was that Pitt had succeeded in joining it. He did so not as a consequence of his oratory the previous session, nor in order to restrain his objections to Hanoverian involvements (on which, as yet, he held silence) but, seemingly, through having linked himself (not to Bute, but) to Lee and Egmont. Fox, closely in touch with events at Leicester House through Waldegrave, wrote that Pitt 'has made his way there a little', but that 'Cresset and Egmont alone have interest' with the Princess, and that Egmont 'is better than anybody with the Prince'. In April, Pitt, 'finding himself desperate at St James's, endeavoured at the reversion, and found that incompatible with any *liaison* with the Duke'; but had achieved only a limited success '(through Lord Egmont it is supposed)'. Fox guessed that Newcastle was using the understanding apparently emerging between Pitt and the Lee–Egmont team to secure the alliance of all three – to Fox's immense disadvantage.[120]

Holdernesse wrote back with the King's reluctant but definite consent on 20 July; the letter arrived on 25th.[121] It was a remarkable achievement for Newcastle to have overcome such a long-standing personal antipathy on the part of George II.[122] Pitt's Cabinet rank and Egmont's Vice Treasurership were acceptable, if a vacancy arose naturally for the latter; and though Lee was not explicitly sanctioned, Newcastle expected no difficulty on his score,[123] since he imagined he already had the King's consent to promote him in Legge's place. Now, Newcastle promised that he and Hardwicke 'will immediately go about putting [the scheme] in execution'.[124]

Yet in the two weeks since 11 July, one thing had changed – and was to seem the catalyst of what followed. At the King's invitation, the Duchess of Brunswick-Wolfenbüttel arrived at Hanover with her two daughters, the elder of whom, Sophia, herself the niece of the King of Prussia, George II had in mind as a bride for his grandson. Walpole wrote that the suddenness and imminence of the match 'at once unhinged all the circumspection and prudence of the Princess'.[125] Waldegrave claimed (and Walpole endorsed his opinion) that the Princess feared for her influence over her son, and 'did everything in her power to prevent the match. The Prince of Wales was taught to believe that he was to be made a sacrifice, merely to gratify the King's private interest in the Electorate of Hanover'. 'From this time, all duty and obedience to the grandfather entirely ceased...'[126] Yet, if so, it was not at once apparent to Newcastle; signs of a changed attitude accumulated piecemeal. Even as late as 6 August, Dodington was convinced by the Princess that she had 'no fixed digested political plan at all: or regular communication in politics, with anybody, but Mr Cresset'. Dodington

said that the general diffidence she described, was cause of the infinite speculation, and refinement that now reigned; for as nobody knew, so everybody was guessing each other; in which, HRH had a principal part. She said sure nobody could stand clearer than she; that everyone must know everybody that she saw, and when.[127]

On 16 July, Fox wrote of Stone's being out of favour with the Princess, owing, as Waldegrave supposed, to Stone's approval of moves to bring Fox into the heart of the ministry against a background of increasing jealousy of Cumberland.[128] But what the Duke had done to incur this fear is not apparent: and it seems likely that Waldegrave, before he had time to reflect, attributed to Cumberland the defensive jealousy actually evoked by the rumours of a Brunswick marriage. The Princess's coldness to Newcastle, Waldegrave imagined to be 'political and not unalterable, but perhaps rather put on in order to draw more court from the Minister, or let me add perhaps to frighten him from any conjunction with the Duke'.[129] Then, by mid July, James Grenville on Pitt's behalf was misrepresenting the nature of the exchanges he carried between Newcastle and Pitt on 2nd, claiming that Newcastle had offered friendship and affection, and that Pitt had contemptuously rejected them.[130] Further, at the Treasury Board on 24 July, Legge silently omitted to sign the warrant for the levy money payable under the subsidy treaty with Hesse Cassel; and began in private to claim exaggerated credit for not doing so.[131] Newcastle asked that no notice be taken of it (he still hoped to buy off Legge with a peerage, just credibly a reward for his services at the Exchequer) and, in fact, the news was not immediately spread outside Leicester House even by Legge.[132] But, in the light of what Newcastle only now identified as a growing feeling against subsidy treaties as a snare to involve Britain in a land war, he wrote of Legge's action: 'The worst is, it looks as if it was in concert with somebody; and certainly whoever breaks with us the next session, will put their quarrel upon that popular point; and that, I dare say, is Legge's chief reason'.[133] Horace Walpole developed this explanation thus: the Princess was faced with the problem of resisting the marriage without seeming to defy the King; 'Here Legge's art stepped in to her assistance; and weaving Pitt's disgusts into the toils that they were spreading for the Duke of Newcastle, they had the finesse to sink all mention of the Brunswick union, while they hoisted the standard against subsidiary treaties'.[134] The only confirmation from sources internal to Leicester House is circumstantial: it was apparently only in early August that Hanoverian connections began to be spoken of and urgently attacked there,[135] and only from mid September that the pamphleteers began their attacks on the subsidy treaties.[136] In any event, what attracted Newcastle's attention was not reaction to the subsidy treaties at large, but the role that issue might play in an older game: the contest for the leadership which had begun on Henry Pelham's death. Walpole was equally realistic about Legge's gesture:

It will not make *him* popular; there is not a mob in England now capable of being the dupe of patriotism; the late body of that denomination have really so discredited it [in the 1740s], that a minister must go great lengths indeed before the people would dread him half so much as a patriot! On the contrary, I believe nothing would make any man so popular or conciliate so much affection to his ministry, as to assure the people that he never had nor ever would pretend to love his country.[137]

Despite Hardwicke's uncertainties[138] about the King's disposition towards the Paymaster, Newcastle was resolved that the approach to the Princess, and the offers to Pitt and Egmont through her, were to go ahead. Stone was to be used to carry the news to Kew; Charles Yorke was to write to Pitt, who at that moment was out of town.[139] Newcastle spoke to Halifax of his desire to secure Dodington, and the news was duly passed on.[140] Sir Thomas Robinson was sent to Lee; despite an aversion to subsidies, he found him 'extremely well-intentioned', and imagined Pitt and Egmont would fall into line. Lee spoke of 'all his reasons for not engaging last year, and that which would be his most prevalent one for engaging now, viz. the too-great influence of an uncle over a young King, if invested with all the civil as well as military power'.[141] Evidently, he was talking the language of Leicester House without being privy to its tactical context. But it is not proven who else *was*, by late July. Fox considered that Egmont 'was thought to have the chief management' at the junior court, and 'that the Prince was much fonder of *him*, than of any man living'. Yet Dodington, on the evidence of Fox and Walpole, supposed that neither Pitt nor Egmont but only Cresset was in the secret.[142]

THE LEICESTER HOUSE RESPONSE, AND HARDWICKE'S MEETING WITH PITT IN AUGUST 1755

It seems likely that Leicester House's plans took on shape and direction only after Legge's act on 24 July and its unexpected notoriety which later followed. As a result, Pitt 'introduced him to Lord Bute, and recommended him in the strongest terms to Leicester House, as the person fittest to put at the head of the revenue, as Chancellor of the Exchequer, in the future reign'.[143] Grenville's comment reveals the prominence which the reversionary interest still held in the minds of his circle: Legge was apparently not led to expect the office on Newcastle's fall at the hands of a parliamentary opposition.

Legge had been encouraged in his refusal to sign by Devonshire's principled and disinterested approval of the move the same morning,[144]

and Newcastle saw that, though Legge 'must be got out of the Treasury
...the point is too popular to let him go out upon it'.[145] Horatio Walpole
thought Legge was deliberately giving an occasion for his dismissal,
though this was denied.[146] Newcastle anticipated two popular cries: one
in favour of Cumberland and belligerence,[147] the other in favour of 'sea
war, no continent, no subsidy',[148] the latter as yet without a more important proponent than Legge. Had there been, Fox might have had a
clearer idea of the form the ministry's response might take.[149] Newcastle
nevertheless imagined his powers in relation to Pitt 'ought *amply* to
satisfy him',[150] and arranged through Peregrine Fury that Pitt call on
Hardwicke when he came to town.[151]

The interview took place on 9 August, after Pitt had had a satisfactory
talk with Sir George Lee but before he had been able to see Bute.[152]
Hardwicke stressed his services to Pitt the previous winter and emphasised
that Pitt's own conduct had then prevented progress in the Closet. Now,
Newcastle had achieved there the success impossible at the time of
Walpole's overture in April, short of the Secretaryship which Pitt himself
had disclaimed. He disclaimed it again, unless it were by the King's own
choice, and placed his ambition on 'His Majesty's gracious reception and
countenance' for himself and his friends; but visibly refrained from
making any comment on the possibility of promotion to Cabinet rank.
This was Hardwicke's version, written on the day of the meeting. Pitt,
however, just before his interview with Newcastle on 2 September, claimed
to Dodington[153] that Hardwicke had suggested that if Pitt support cordially now, it might be possible to overcome the King's aversion to him 'if
any accident should happen' to Robinson or Holdernesse, and secure him
one of their posts; and that Pitt then protested that he had never specifically applied for the seals and would never accept them against the King's
and the ministers' aversion. It may be that Hardwicke allowed himself to
be corrected by Pitt, or that he suppressed the full extent of Pitt's ambitions in order to bring Newcastle round by degrees. On 9 August, however,
Hardwicke apparently failed to notice the element of opportunism in
Pitt's remark that, 'in the present situation of affairs', the Secretaryship
was not 'a desirable pillow to sleep upon'; and laid open the whole of
Newcastle's proposals. Pitt insisted on prior consultation about the
measures he was to join in defending in the Commons, and Hardwicke
agreed, summarising them:

'twas all open and above board, the support of the maritime and American war,
in which we were going to be engaged, and the defence of the King's German
dominions, if attacked on account of that English cause. The maritime and
American war he came roundly into, though very onerous, and allowed the
principle, and the obligation of honour and justice as to the other, but argued
strongly against the practicability of it; that subsidiary treaties would not go
down, the nation would not bear them; that they were a chain and connection,
and would end in a general plan for the Continent, which this coutry could not

possibly support;...that above all he could never give his consent to the mortgaging or funding upon the sinking fund, but, whether in place or out of place, was bound in conscience to oppose it...

– and that he had rather pay the King five millions in damages at the end of the war if Hanover were overrun than defend it by subsidies. This took Hardwicke aback; he urged the absurdity of the idea, explained the reasons behind the existing subsidy treaties, and professed that he 'knew of no intention to go further': but he had no authority to produce the evidence to refute Pitt's claims that the ministry's admitted treaties were made as parts of a general continental plan. In fact, the administration had throughout the summer fought a private battle with the King to avert such an interpretation being placed on their German commitment. Now, Pitt appeared to object most strongly to the Hessian treaty and almost to acquiesce in the Russian; then, probing further, he asked the opinions on the subject of others of the King's servants, naming Legge, Fox and Lee. It may be that Pitt was feeling for the consequences of a revived report that Lee would soon have the Exchequer, and Egmont the Vice Treasurership of Ireland vacated by Yonge's death on 10th.[154] Hardwicke stalled, claiming to presume their support. It seems possible that Pitt himself was both undecided on the subsidy issues and uncertain of the attitude on the matter of Leicester House personnel who had long been on the verge of office; for at last he declared he needed to consult his friends before declaring his opinion. The Chancellor suggested a meeting with Newcastle, which Pitt received well, and which, Hardwicke hoped, would suggest an answer to his chief uncertainty: 'My own opinion is, that he will appear to close with, or at least not to reject, the proposition, so far as it regards himself *personally*; that he will still go on to make difficulties upon measures. Those difficulties may be real, or they may be made use of colourably to raise the terms for himself, as being the more honourable shape to turn it in.'[155]

Newcastle's problems were both tactical and substantive. The great majority of people were open to promptings against subsidy treaties, from memories of their burden in the war of 1739–48,[156] from feelings of insular self-sufficiency, and from a failure to discriminate between the type and scope of obligation included under one title. Devonshire was opposed, on grounds of high principle;[157] Fox, as yet, was inclined against: 'most people, I find, being in their own minds of the same opinion', and from apprehensions about raising the finance to support the treaties and the majorities to vote them. He admitted: 'Legge...I believe, makes no scruple of declaring his opinion; I have been more cautious in giving, I may say, in *forming*, mine, but have by not signing it at the Cockpit, kept myself at liberty. Pitt's and Egmont's opinions in this regard I don't know.' With the possibility of a civil war within the Court still unresolved,[158] it was prudent to avoid a clear commitment on policy issues of such extreme contentiousness.

Newcastle, similarly, thought Pitt would temporise, would not reject the proposals, 'but will make use, both of measures and persons, to avoid closing thoroughly with us, and in order to raise his own demands'. The Secretaryship seemed to Newcastle the next of these – a step at odds with his own advice and with the King's feelings. At this point, Newcastle's long-standing distrust of Pitt's integrity worked not directly to exclude him from office (which Newcastle sought with honest persistence) but to inflate Pitt's claims in Newcastle's mind to what the Duke felt were realistic proportions: and thus eventually to prevent Newcastle closing with him at all. Meanwhile, as part of the shadow-boxing over 'issues', Hardwicke was asked whether they should show Pitt the critical minute of 30 July in which the ministry had made its stand, as it thought, against the trends in the King's intentions which Pitt was condemning as the ministers' own. Inconveniently, Yonge's death then revised the time-table of promotions; and Newcastle at once wrote to Egmont with an implied offer of the Irish vacancy.[159] Only the latter's absence in the country[160] prevented a meeting at which Newcastle would have discovered the Earl's position on subsidies and acquainted him in general with the overtures to Pitt and the ministry's scheme for the Commons. That Egmont would succeed Yonge was 'generally taken for granted'.[161] And it was the still unsolved problem of the Paymaster alone which inhibited Newcastle from exploring the new situation by dealings with Lee, Legge or Fox: 'of all whom possibly, *he* may know as much, or more than *we* do'.[162] Hardwicke shared this fear: as to Fox and Legge, 'I verily believe he knows more than we do, and I am credibly informed that the doctrine against subsidiary treaties has gone a great way and taken deep root, and that they are forming a House of Commons cabal against these measures. I am told that Mr Fox is secretly in it, but this I do not affirm.'[163]

FOX

Fox's participation would have been consistent with his links with the Devonshires and with a desire for a lever against Newcastle, but inconsistent with a deeper loyalty to Cumberland. Hence the equivocation, though worrying, was not a real threat to Newcastle and Hardwicke. In fact, Fox's main hopes were already pinned on the 'reversionary interest' *within* the Devonshire family: on the hope that Hartington might contrive his removal, by implication to a better office or a quieter one.[164] The Marquis, however, advised Fox to 'keep cool and as quiet as you can'; his enemies would then be unable to eject him. Opposition would involve Fox with 'people whose principles you detest'; and the notion of opposition itself, pursued with integrity, would bind Fox – as Hartington reminded him – to his earlier declaration: 'If ever I go into opposition, I will never come back but with the whole.'[165]

Thus the Chancellor advised Newcastle not to mention Fox in his interview with Pitt; nor, for similar reasons, Legge, Lee or Egmont. The timing of Legge's dismissal was in the ministry's hands; Lee and Egmont were being courted separately. If, as Hardwicke imagined, Pitt were really prepared to stop short of the Secretaryship, Newcastle need not do more than talk in general terms of the policy which had inspired the minute of 30 July. If more were necessary, a promise to *recommend* Pitt to the King for the Secretaryship would be harmless because hopeless of result. On second thoughts, Hardwicke's confidence in the success of another part of the manoeuvres made him suggest that Newcastle talk of Egmont as if his succession to Yonge were already assured, though Egmont himself was not to be closed with until the return of the messenger from Hanover; meanwhile, he was to be sounded on subsidies, in which his past declarations in the Commons[166] in favour of the Russian treaty and the reported tenor of his present conversation gave great cause for hope.[167] The sounding was taken by Stone, and though Egmont's manner was not as agreeable as expected, expectations were maintained.[168] Stone had found the Princess well disposed, 'particularly, [with] what related to Lord Egmont', and formed the impression that it was Lee who was leading Leicester House opinion against subsidies; the Princess's apparent ignorance of Pitt's 'disposition, or intention' lent support to hopes that almost everything was still negotiable.[169]

Newcastle arranged to meet Egmont on Tuesday 26 August, and Pitt on 2 September. He and Hardwicke imagined[170] he had secured the wholehearted approval of the Princess and Cresset in the attempt to prevent a breach in the Royal Family by 'our present scheme...viz. Mr Pitt and Lord Egmont'; and that the Princess would, as Newcastle suggested was essential, 'do all in her power to promote our success with *both*'. He was confident, and Hardwicke again agreed, that the communication[171] to Leicester House of Holdernesse's instructions in relation to the Brunswick marriage, and how far it was from completion, would alleviate their major anxiety. But on 20th Newcastle heard from Granville[172] his first hard news that Pitt and Legge were committed to oppose the subsidies from the first day of the session, and that Egmont and Lee 'would probably concur'.[173] Lee had spoken strongly to the Lord President against both Hessian and Russian treaties, who had however defended them, not quite correctly, 'as if subsidiary treaties and continent measures, were our present system...All this was to magnify the danger in order to introduce the remedy'. Granville spoke of Fox's claiming to be uncommitted on the issue and likely to join the opposition unless satisfied; that Newcastle must have a lieutenant and that he, Fox, was willing to undertake the task. To Granville, Newcastle 'ridiculed a little the notion of *a lieutenant*, who was to be general over me' and stressed that Fox's links with Cumberland made him unacceptable in such a role. Granville had made what sounded like an offer on Fox's behalf: to come in alone and 'give up *everybody*' for Newcastle.

But the Minister still had hopes of Pitt and Egmont. Fox expected the latter to decline Yonge's place; Newcastle disagreed, and so did Hardwicke.[174] Granville urged that Pitt would not make up with the ministry, was inseparable from Legge, and that the latter had drawn great popularity from his refusal to sign the Hessian warrant; that Fox had omitted to sign the ratification for the same reason. Newcastle insisted that he expected a parliamentary majority for both treaties; Granville, that the Commons would force Newcastle to take a lieutenant, talking remarkably of Legge's 'consequence' and the possibility that Argyll might be backing him. Newcastle inferred from this that Fox was aware of the negotiations with Pitt and Egmont; that he was afraid of their success; and that, therefore, he was attempting to secure the best bargain he could at the price he pretended the others would not give: unconditional support for the King's measures. Newcastle was unimpressed, resolved to pursue his existing plans, and 'endeavour to bring that system to bear': otherwise, Granville's proffered reinforcement 'can never take place'. Fox, implausibly, denied that Granville's remarks were an overture from him; but it seems that Fox drew lessons from Newcastle's remarks to a third party about Granville's suggestions: the Minister's smug confidence that Cumberland would keep Fox in check, and reliance on the prospects at Leicester House opened up through Egmont's agency, sickened Fox, reinforced his conviction of Newcastle's insincerity, and strengthened his resolve to 'remain out of the question, nor will ever again I think verily come into it till the question is the ruin of his Grace...'[175]

One idea Newcastle did remember from Granville's proposals: that Sir Thomas Robinson should be removed to the Lords; 'that by that we should take away the priority of office, the cause of envy. Though I see with what view, he proposes it, I am not sure, that such a step may not facilitate our affairs with Mr Pitt.'[176] The Chancellor doubted it. It was, after all, only part of the plan once advanced so inconveniently by Legge, and resisted the previous autumn. 'If it were practicable, and could be made part of the terms of a solid connection with Mr Pitt, in such a shape that he may [be] depended upon, it may be of real utility; otherwise it may do more hurt than good.' As it was, the extent of Pitt's contacts at Leicester House were not apparent; a quick approach to him was essential, for an extensive opposition to subsidies *was* planned as Granville forecast. Hardwicke knew already that Lee had spoken against the treaties but could not believe that any of the King's servants would oppose them in the present national emergency. Nevertheless, Fox's overtures might usefully be kept alive by a civil reception, if only as a stimulus to Egmont and Pitt. Hardwicke was firmly convinced that Fox would not oppose the treaties in the House: 'He cannot do it without destroying himself. May there not be more danger of his running races of merit on the other side? If there is, that may on the other hand operate well as to Pitt.'[177]

Newcastle gave no particular answer to Granville's proposal.[178] The Lord President called Newcastle's 'no scheme at all' when recounting it to Fox: to gain Egmont with Yonge's place, to gain Pitt through Hardwicke's mediation, to assume Fox's acquiescence as a consequence of Cumberland's influence, and 'to carry things through without parting (as Lord Granville expresses it) with the least emanation of his power to anybody'. Fox was checked; he admitted his preparedness to 'be quiet... if H.M. will let me be so' and again claimed to aim only at a quiet place. Newcastle's scheme,

as far as it regards Egmont and the Princess I believe it will succeed. I have less reason to think than I had, that Pitt is well, or that Egmont intends he shall be well, at that Court; and I do not imagine anything will be found to engage Pitt. The Duke of Newcastle dropped to Lord Granville making him Chancellor of the Exchequer, but I fear he will be too well advised to give it, and Pitt not well advised enough to take it.[179]

NEWCASTLE'S INTERVIEWS WITH EGMONT AND PITT, AUGUST—SEPTEMBER 1755

The letters[180] from Hanover indicating the King's approval of an offer to Egmont arrived on the day of Newcastle's interview with him, 26 August. Ominously, Holdernesse had had no reply from the King to his representations in favour of Pitt. But Newcastle was encouraged by a full and frank discussion with Egmont in which he explained the purpose of the Hessian and Russian treaties and the ministry's stand against continent measures. Egmont, remarkably, made no objection to ministerial policy, 'but I think he apprehends, we shall want strength in the House of Commons, that is, speakers, and in that sense getting *Pitt* does everything'.[181] The exaggerated importance attached to Pitt by men such as Egmont who were themselves essentially Commons orators was not shared by Newcastle. But Egmont, eager for place and hopeful of an English peerage for his son,

showed a real inclination, to support, and be well with us. He often said, he could be of no stature alone, and I soon found, that he wanted Mr Pitt to come in heartily with him, and that there was a pretty strong connection between them, but he must not know, that I made that observation. He said he desired not to stand in Mr Pitt's way, or to create any difficulty with him.[182]

Newcastle declared the impossibility of making Pitt Secretary of State, apparently to Egmont's surprise; but the latter nevertheless discounted the rumour that Pitt would not make up with Newcastle. 'He said, there might be some foundation for such a report, but not much.'[183] It had been arranged for Cresset to sweeten Egmont before the meeting;[184] after it, the latter was due again at Kew, 'and I hope' added Newcastle 'the Princess will fix him so that I may write word that the thing is done'.

Newcastle openly refused Darlington the Vice Treasurership, claiming it had been long destined for Egmont and delighting in the prospect of such an accession of strength in the Commons.[185] As Fox understood it, Newcastle, in his interview on 26th,

asked if he might write to Hanover, Lord Egmont said he could not quite authorise his Grace to go so far yet, but desired a few days; which the Duke of Newcastle interprets to be to consult Pitt. His Grace is to see Pitt, but Legge says Pitt is in no disposition to be paid with such counters as his Grace has to give him ... The Duke of Newcastle told a friend of mine he had had an overture from me by Lord Granville, which is not true, but his Grace might perhaps from what Lord Granville said conclude it came from me. My friend asked him why he did not close with me then?

The answer was that Newcastle supposed him, Fox, to be controlled by Cumberland, and that the ministry had 'expectations through Egmont, etc. at Leicester House'. Directly or indirectly, therefore, Newcastle let Fox know that the ministry was on the point of closing with Egmont,[186] and what must have contributed most to Newcastle's optimism was Egmont's ill-informed admission that he thought Pitt and Lee 'tolerably well together'.[187] It began to seem as if, as Newcastle had hoped ever since the dissolution of the Pitt–Fox and Egmont–Lee alignments of late 1754 had become evident, that Egmont and Pitt could be dealt with in succession, and Lee isolated and treated with separately. Legge was doomed, so that a Fox–Legge scheme, which Hartington hoped for[188] on the model of the previous autumn, was out of the question; but filling the latter's office, Newcastle imagined, was still his major difficulty unless Pitt insisted on an unobtainable Secretaryship of State. 'Nothing is determined about the Chancellor of the Exchequer...I think, there is nobody but Sir G. Lee. I have thought of everybody; and the objections to all the rest, are insurmountable':[189] including, presumably, to Pitt.

Newcastle's predictions were very nearly correct. Egmont asked for a meeting with Pitt.[190] Bute imagined Legge was deliberately avoiding him and was uneasy that Pitt should arrange to see Newcastle without meeting him first:[191] there was something inexplicable in the appearance of events. But Pitt then agreed to see Bute and to postpone Egmont's meeting until after he, Pitt, called on Newcastle on 2 September.[192] This meeting apparently also took place without Pitt's having met Legge since his return from the country: if so, Legge's absence would add credibility to Walpole's story[193] that Fox, hearing (presumably via Granville) a rumour that Pitt was to have the Exchequer, asked Legge to advise Pitt to take it, hoping thereby to save the Paymastership for himself. Walpole adds that 'Legge was suspected of not having reported the message, to which he affirmed that Pitt had not listened'.[194] It seems possible that Legge was manoeuvring independently of Bute to provoke Pitt to a confrontation with Newcastle, and by 1 September was claiming to be confident of the result.[195]

Newcastle's two-and-a-half hour meeting with Pitt took place on the evening of 2 September.[196] Pitt's civility hardly softened the shock of his bid for a position which, Newcastle saw, entailed the complete overthrow of the current system. Pitt dismissed his meeting with Hardwicke as a 'preparatory conversation' only. Newcastle nevertheless outlined the plan to which the King had consented: Cabinet rank, and the King's public favour. Pitt replied that the rank alone would give him no more power to take an active part in support of measures:

That the House of Commons was now an assembly of atoms; that the great wheels of the machine were stopped; that *this* could not be thought sufficient to put them in motion...He then repeated word for word, the same plan and system, which Mr Legge proposed to me the last year; viz. that the business of the House of Commons could not go on, without there was a minister (a subordinate one, perhaps) which should go directly between the King and them

– if not Pitt, then another. But Pitt's own active support of measures was only possible from 'an *office of advice*, as well as of *execution*', the distinction on which the whole interview was to turn. For, in a real sense, Cabinet rank alone conferred the privilege of advice; the posts in which immediate and unreserved access to information gave a further advantage still were those few at the very heart of the administration. Newcastle thought Pitt spoke as if only the Secretaryship of State would fit his meaning, and that his serving there would mean '*voix en chapitre*, both as to the recommendation to employments, and the determination of measures'. But, as if to interpret the practical extent of his claims, Pitt denied any ambition to succeed Sir Robert Walpole or Henry Pelham and demanded only that the Commons be put into commission. Newcastle suggested that the role he proposed for Pitt amounted to First Commissioner of that House. Of course, he denied Pitt's charge of exercising 'sole power': his position was 'not my choice, but the King's command'; he would retire if he were 'disagreeable' to the Commons; the King could then appoint a commoner as First Lord of the Treasury. Pitt 'said *that* was not at all necessary. He liked a Lord First Commissioner very well; but then, there must be a Secretary of State, a man of ability in the House of Commons, and a Chancellor of the Exchequer, well supported': the cue for an eulogy which finally damned Legge in Newcastle's eyes – as, perhaps, Pitt intended. Though in strict propriety it was illegitimate to demand an office by name, Pitt's own ambitions were obviously directed at a Secretaryship of State, and he tried to lead Newcastle to some definite pronouncement; but the latter was not to be drawn to say more than was contained in the formula 'confidence and regard'. Pitt then bluntly, probably undesignedly, said that everything was at the end if Holdernesse or Sir Thomas Robinson were not otherwise provided for. Later, he claimed that Newcastle had repeated Hardwicke's hints of a Secretaryship 'if any accident should make a vacancy'.[197] Newcastle was unwilling to make empty promises to Pitt; if he did use the phrase, in a fluster (though it is unlikely that he did so), it was unfortunate, for it distracted Pitt from the real concessions which he had to offer; and he did not record it afterwards. But as if to admit that his was not an ultimatum, Pitt allowed himself to be steered into a discussion of foreign policy. He pursued a familiar line: 'he urged the want of a House of Commons minister in the administration, to be the occasion of the subsidiary treaties, now supposed to be entered into; for that such a minister, by his representations, would have prevented them'. Pitt objected chiefly to the Russian treaty as establishing that subsidy system, which, Newcastle told him, the ministry had worked throughout the summer to avoid; warned that Devonshire would attack it in the Lords; and threatened to echo him in the Commons. But even here the position was uncertain, for Pitt suggested that he might, and once that he *would*, acquiesce in the Hessian treaty if it were the only one. Waldegrave later wrote: 'He also declared against continental measures, and against all treaties of subsidy; but as this declaration was reserved to the last, it seems possible it might have been totally forgot, if the answer to the preceding articles had been satisfactory.'[198] Newcastle concluded:

There are, in my opinion, but three measures to take – the first I most incline to:

First, as the present difficulty arises from a combination in the House of Commons, thus circumstanced, originally confined to Fox, Pitt and Legge; to which my Lord Egmont, and Sir George Lee, have, in some measure, since acceded, and from which Mr Fox has, in some measure, of late receded; this combination is against me; that is, against anyone in my station, not in the House of Commons. The most natural remedy, the most easy way, would be for me to retire; and the King to put Mr Fox at the head of the Treasury. Business would go on so, for this session; for Mr Pitt could not object to a measure, which he, himself, had brought about; and was founded upon his principles. I am serious in thinking this rightest measure of all; the best, at present, for the King's measures; possibly, the most agreeable to himself; and, I am sure, the most honourable, the most easy, and the most agreeable to me, in the present circumstances.

The next way, for me to continue where I am, Mr Pitt Secretary of State, Mr Legge, Chancellor of the Exchequer. Whether this is, in any shape, practicable, I leave to your Lordship, and all, who know the King, to determine.

The third and last, then is to accept Mr Fox's proposal, made by my Lord Granville, viz: to take Mr Fox in, to do the business of the House of Commons. In this case, there must be an entire confidence in him. His great Protector [the Duke of Cumberland] must say, what part he *would* act; and the great Protectors of the others, must be told, what part they *must* act. The Duke of Devonshire must explain himself; and my Lord Hartington also. Mr Fox must engage to act with whatever Chancellor of the Exchequer the King would appoint; for a new one, upon this system, there must be. Dodington perhaps, should be taken in; the Attorney General [Murray] should be brought, to take an active part; and all our friends of the law. In short, a system should be formed, in which, every one in both Houses, and every member of the

Cabinet council, should previously engage to take their share; and every person in employment, should be required to assist.

Hardwicke could only guess at the reasons for Pitt's more uncompromising stand: the advice of his friends, or perhaps the news of Braddock's defeat.[199] But the Chancellor reminded Newcastle that nothing essentially new had been advanced by Pitt, and that some of his menaces were unreasonable speculations: Devonshire was not likely to attack the treaties openly, and Pitt could hardly think so highly of Legge, of whom he had previously spoken 'rather in a light of contempt'. It must indeed have seemed that Pitt's advocacy of Legge was only a consequence of the resuscitation of a principle moribund since December 1754. Hardwicke failed to draw the inference that they were united in the service of Leicester House, though it is striking that Pitt completely omitted any reference to the junior Court in his catalogue of threats or in the very full account which he gave to Dodington on 3 September of his interview with Newcastle and hopes of the co-operation of others – Legge, Egmont, Hillsborough, Dashwood, Oswald. Even more remarkable, if Pitt were already cemented by Bute into a concerted plan, was his ignorance of the intentions of all these figures except Legge:

He said that Mr Legge was firm as a rock. He was shy about Lord Egmont but said he had seen him, receiv'd very kindly, seemed to enter into the thing, but what might happen when offers were made, he (Pitt) could not tell. Desired me to apply to Lord Hillsborough, and Sir Francis Dashwood: I mentioned Oswald: he said, he thought he was in it. (If so, it must be by Legge). I asked him if he had communicated it to Mr Fox: He said, No, nor did not design to do it. He would tell me the whole of his thoughts of that matter:

That he wished Mr Fox very well, and had nothing to complain of; but that they could not act together; because they were not upon the same ground. . .

Besides, Mr Fox lived with his greatest enemies: Lord Granville, Messrs Stone and Murray: 'twas true he owned it. But he (Pitt) would always act upon plain Whig principles, and would never have anything to do with Stone, or Murray. – That the Duke of Newcastle had told a great person that Mr Fox, very lately, had offered himself to him. – I said, I was confident it was false. – He said that he knew the Duke of Newcastle was a very great liar, and therefore, if Mr Fox denied it, he should not hesitate a moment, which he should believe. – I, then, said, that those who united in this attack, were to part no more, and therefore it would be proper to think what was to be held out to them, if we succeeded. – He declined that, and said that it would look to[o] much like a faction: there was nothing 'country' in that: – If we succeeded, to be sure those who contributed must and would be considered, when, first, opportunity offered, but to engage for specifical things, and times, he thought no one man had any title, except myself; that for me, anything, everything that I liked, ought to be the common cause, and with me he was ready to enter into any engagements.[200]

Pitt's hidden design, Hardwicke thought, was to represent his alliance with Legge as more solid than it was, and to annoy Newcastle with praise of a personal enemy. Dodington, too, thought Pitt overstated the strength of their connection. Hardwicke failed immediately to perceive that it was Legge's discovery of the subsidy treaty issue's appeal at large which made inevitable for Pitt his commitment to Leicester House on that basis and made Legge a desirable asset.

The two elements from Pitt's position which Hardwicke chose to single out were those most reminiscent of past battles. He was surprised that Pitt should revive the issue of a minister with the King in the House of Commons: an issue which

we heard much of, even before this Parliament set down, but, notwithstanding all the awkwardnesses of the last session, none of us thought that the principle made much way in general. 'Tis espoused by a few, who are, or would be, leading men there, and they sound it high in order to make it popular. When they say *a subordinate minister*, 'tis what they don't mean...their meaning is to be in the place of Sir Robert Walpole, or Mr Pelham. If the King would give sufficient confidence and authority to his first minister to confine it to this *subordinate* character, possibly there might be no great hurt in it; for I have long been convinced that, whoever your Grace shall make use of as your first man, and man of confidence in the House of Commons, you will find it necessary, if he be a man of reputation, and ability, accompanied with the ambition naturally incident to such a character...to invest him with more power, than, from the beginning, you thought fit to impart either to Mr Legge or Sir Thomas Robinson.

Had Newcastle needed reminding, the dangers of such a deal with Pitt were now vividly before him. But this was not Hardwicke's intention in discussing, secondly, Pitt's personal ambition for the Secretaryship. If Newcastle would declare his wish to see Pitt in that office, the Chancellor felt sure the Paymaster 'would close and take *his active part* immediately, even without any present promise or declaration from His Majesty'. Without that, Hardwicke saw no prospect in further discussions with Pitt. He passed on to consider what Newcastle identified as his three options. First, to resign and be succeeded of necessity by Fox. This would be 'the most easy, quiet, and safe' but was open to Newcastle's objection against 'quitting the King in a second rebellion',[201] to forcing George II's hand by a co-ordinated resignation as in 1746. Pitt himself now spoke against the tactic (with a false innocence, for to it he had owed his Paymastership) and Newcastle was sincerely unwilling to repeat a disagreeable device without the excuse of necessity.

Next, Hardwicke turned to Newcastle's suggestion that he might remain at the Treasury with Pitt as Secretary of State and Legge as Chancellor of the Exchequer. The problem lay in gaining the King's assent, which Hardwicke thought only necessity would extract from him. In mitigation, the Chancellor suggested that Newcastle's own position in that case would be 'the same, in my apprehension, as you would find it with any other man of ability and ambition in the House of Commons.

Pitt has it to say that we originally agreed to it in the case of Mr Fox, and he himself threw it away.' But it may be plausibly argued that Newcastle had indeed intended, in March 1754, that Fox should exercise only the semblance of the power which the Secretaryship of State promised: and that he continued to act as if the problem were to find a successor to a post thus limited in practice.

Thirdly, Newcastle might accept what was taken to be Fox's suggestion via Granville, and which Hardwicke promised not to obstruct if Newcastle thought it right:

I will only state the difference between Mr Fox and Mr Pitt in respect of yourself. Mr Fox has a party in the House of Commons, and a great protector and support at Court, besides the personal inclination of the King. Mr Pitt has no party of his own there; no support at Court; and the personal disinclination of the King. He must therefore probably depend, at least for a good while, upon those who bring him thither. Your Grace knows also how disagreeable the uniting with Mr Fox will be to one branch of the royal family; and upon these two points I leave it.

Hardwicke showed no appreciation of Pitt's Leicester House links, or of his value except as a hired Commons orator: his very appeal lay in what was claimed to be his lack of political allies. In thus outlining the situation to Newcastle, the Chancellor was not simply summarising the obvious: he was, through his omissions and admissions, bowing to Newcastle's discretion. For in suggesting that the Paymaster would not make Legge's tenure of the Exchequer a *sine qua non*, he prompted Newcastle's desire to persist in his attempt at a satisfactory arrangement of Pitt and Egmont;[202] and in missing the significance of Leicester House, he missed also what in retrospect has appeared the approaching imperative of a closer liaison with Fox.

Newcastle travelled to Wimpole to meet Hardwicke on 9th; armed with Holdernesse's opinion,[203] he persuaded the Chancellor of the improbability of the King's agreeing to Pitt as Secretary of State; and then, though with difficulty, dissuaded him from his intention of nevertheless giving Pitt an empty promise of their willingness to urge that promotion on the King – in the knowledge, to be kept from Pitt, that it would never be granted.[204] Newcastle took with him to the country some unrecorded intelligence about Leicester House and 'some scheme to suggest to your lordship, which I would keep an absolute secret from either of the parties, till I know your thoughts upon it. . .'[205] This scheme may be reconstructed from one of Newcastle's memoranda.[206] Egmont was to have the Exchequer and Legge to be removed to the consolation of a Vice Treasurership of Ireland. Hillsborough would become Treasurer of the Household *vice* Sir Conyers D'Arcy and Dodington, Comptroller, *vice* Earl Fitzwalter. Barrington was listed for Secretary at War, the young Charles Townshend would replace Darlington at the Treasury Board, who would oust Barrington as Master of the Wardrobe; Sir George Lee would become

Treasurer of the Navy *vice* George Grenville, and James Grenville would be dismissed from the Board of Trade. If Pitt then resigned, Fox would simply replace him in the Paymastership. It is evident that Newcastle did not imagine there to be a Leicester House opposition united against him: he was happy to treat with Egmont and Lee as if either could be accommodated irrespective of Pitt's plans, and was nonchalant at the prospect of hostile orators in the Commons. In framing a system, oratory was not the first consideration. An Egmont–Fox–Lee alignment counted for more of solid worth than did Pitt and Grenville in the other scale.

Only now did Bute's activity begin to bear fruit, for the first stage in his assumption of control at Leicester House was apparently to persuade its two established leaders against a separate deal with the ministry. Pitt met Newcastle and Hardwicke again on 12 September having been briefed by Bute: 'You have been painted here as one determined to opposition, unless gagged by the Seals; in other things, your conversation has been tolerably represented; there are still hopes of you; which is one reason for this 2nd conference.' But, on their side: 'S[ir] G. L[ee] nailed, and steady, E[gmont] has been here and still doubts, but there is little to be feared from that quarter; on the contrary, 'twill do at last.'[207] He was right about both men, who had still been wavering as late as the beginning of that month. The meeting on 12th silenced any residual anxiety Bute may have had about his colleague, for the Paymaster was 'as negative as ever'. Newcastle, however, was delighted by Hardwicke's conversion in the face of Pitt's resistance: privately, 'he said to me, there is nothing to be done with *this man*, we must therefore make the best terms we can, with the other'.[208]

The evidence at this point fails to establish conclusively who 'the other' was: Egmont or Lee. On 15th, Newcastle was to see the first and Hardwicke, the second.[209] Newcastle's memorandum[210] suggests the Chancellor had spoken of Lee, for Sir George was there treated as a straight alternative to Pitt, to whose loss Hardwicke was now resigned. But, on 15th, Lee refused the offered terms on two grounds: '1. His objections to the two treaties of subsidy...2. His other objection arose from *Mr F*[ox], with whom he declared he could not act; that he could never rely upon such support; and could never be connected there.' Consequently, Hardwicke suggested Newcastle pursue the offer of the Exchequer to Egmont.[211] But it was refused, and within a day the news was public.[212] Although Newcastle continued to receive good reports of Cresset's disposition, of the Princess's growing alarm and desire to avoid 'confusion', and of Egmont's dissociation from and disapproval of 'the intrigues that have been carrying on' at his Court,[213] the possibility of an arrangement with Egmont and Lee, which had occupied Newcastle for over a year, was now at an end. Its termination was marked not by Newcastle's realisation of its impossibility, but rather by his desire to combine it with a closer alliance with Fox: 'If the Princess of Wales can be brought off so far, as to make Lord Egmont accept Chancellor of the Exchequer, and Sir George Lee, concur in our measures, things may go very well yet.' But there was a new urgency: the King, on his return, 'said Legge must be turned out' and did not rescind the 'full power' he had given Newcastle to deal with Pitt.[214]

THE DEAL WITH FOX, SEPTEMBER–OCTOBER 1755

The second Earl of Hardwicke later remarked on a gap in his father's correspondence with Newcastle 'about the reconciliation with *Fox*, when my father's opinion though indirectly given was for Pitt. The K[ing] came over in ill humour, and the Duke [of Cumberland] got about him; and Murray with other friends of the Duke of Newcastle's were for Fox.'[215] What moulded Newcastle's opinion was not Hardwicke's advice of 4 September but a dinner party of intimate friends on 17th: Waldegrave, Murray, Lincoln and Ashburnham.[216] Two choices remained, thought Newcastle: to stand down, or make up with Fox. Lincoln and Ashburnham (and, until 17th, Murray) favoured the first alternative, but recommended it in such a way that Newcastle recoiled from placing his own ease and honour before the King's service. He agreed with Granville's blunt reminder that it would be 'deserting the King, and running away', and wrote: 'I conclude this will end in making up with Fox, and I hope in a reasonable way, for I will do nothing, that must necessarily make him independent, or my master.' Waldegrave, the best informed among them of Fox's intentions, thought it practicable;[217] but the catalyst was Münchausen, who, sharing Granville's feelings, reported to the King that Newcastle would quit. George II, already disturbed by the First Lord's spontaneous and humble offer to exchange offices with Granville, saw Newcastle in an audience charged with high emotion. The latter 'melted; and told him I was ready to go into any breach for his service'; and, in return, secured the King's promise of support and consent to his treating with Fox to form a system for the Commons.[218]

Newcastle arranged for a meeting with Fox on 20th, in the presence of Waldegrave. Fox was warned that everything was agreed with the King and the Chancellor, and that he could emphatically not expect the Exchequer.[219] But Fox had never bid for it; Walpole recorded that he never even expected to be applied to.[220] Though preserving a convenient silence over subsidy treaties, Fox had declared himself 'no longer a candidate for power under the conduct of such a minister' as Newcastle:[221] who, as has been shown, knew of his ambition for the Paymastership. The terms now devised for Fox's contract took advantage of this reticence: in return for an active role in support of measures, 'he should have all the necessary assistance given him, by his Majesty's servants, to enable him to do it, with credit and success'; they were to act in the strictest concert; he would be called to the private meetings of the King's servants to assist in the formation of measures; he should inform MPs at the pre-session meetings of forthcoming business; 'that he as well as Sir T[homas] R[obinson], should report to the King (if His Majesty thinks proper) what shall pass' in the Commons.[222] But the last point carried the overwhelming implication that Fox was not to succeed to Robinson's Secretaryship. The need for such a step became apparent only during the meeting.[223] Newcastle then claimed Granville had demanded the Exchequer for Fox, and Newcastle refused it 'as it must, in the hands of him who had the conduct of the House of Commons, destroy his [Newcastle's] power entirely. I, very artfully', wrote Fox, 'because directly contrary to my opinion, agreed that it would, so it now stands that he won't let me be Chancellor of the Exchequer, not that I refused it.' Fox was aware of Ellis's opinion that the limited access to the King which the Exchequer gave under a peer First Lord of the Treasury would render the post insignificant; and apparently agreed. But this left a Secretaryship as the only acceptable alternative office. Fox listened to what he took to be Newcastle's meaningless promises on consultation: 'upon the whole, it is plain he does not intend to part with any power more than in March was twelvemonth; though he endeavours to varnish the design over, which he thought could not appear too bad to me then': that is, the offer of March 1754 as Fox imagined it to be, a snare and a delusion. Newcastle, in contrast, thought himself to have offered 'the conduct of the House of Commons', a task not dependent on, and dangerously combined with, high office. He imagined, nevertheless, that 'Mr Fox was well inclined; but his friends think it necessary, that he should have some public mark of confidence, and distinction. That of the Secretary of State, has been mentioned by Mr Fox.' The latter's account suggests that Marlborough put him up to the request, imagining it to be attainable through Newcastle's fright, and that the ministry needed Fox to 'stem a torrent'.

In fact, it was only Fox who claimed to think Newcastle frightened, and even he knew that the First Lord saw that he, Fox, had no intention of joining opposition: 'I could not disguise that, without saying, "If I am satisfied, this measure [subsidies] is right; if not, most destructive", which is a profligacy I could not put on for half an hour.' Once his course was plain, Newcastle moved with speed. He met Fox on 20th, and received his modest requests for his friends: the restoration of Hillsborough to the King's favour, and places for Ellis, Lord Bateman, W. G. Hamilton, Sir John Wynn and George Selwyn.[224] On 25th, it was agreed that Fox was to succeed Robinson as Secretary of State, that the latter was to be bought off with his old post of Master of the Wardrobe and a pension of £2000 p.a. on Ireland for thirty years; and that Barrington would succeed Fox.[225] By 25th, Newcastle was willing to speak publicly of his reasons:

He said W. Pitt had absolutely refused to support the treaty with Russia, and so has Dr Lee and Lord Egmont, though the opposition [? from the] first has been offered to be admitted to Cabinet Council. He looks on it as a combination in which the Grenvilles and that clan are connected. He says Fox says that his continuing in is owing to Pitt's refusal...Says he is afraid the Princess of Wales is in the cabal and Cresset was now sent for by the Duke of Newcastle by the King's order to speak to her. And the reason of his judging of the Princess's inclination is from Dr Lee and Lord Egmont, who he says are her greatest advisers.[226]

Evidently, Newcastle did not identify people's choice of position on the question of subsidies and a 'continent war' as the consequence of a formed opposition at Leicester House led by Pitt and Bute. No such opposition yet existed, and, in its absence, even Fox was still at a loss to explain Pitt's attack on him of 9 May. It could only, Fox thought, have been a personal reaction against Cumberland's power; 'and yet that does not quite solve it'.[227] Even at the end of August, Fox had 'less reason to think than I had, that Pitt is well, or that Egmont intends he shall be well, at that court'.[228]

A necessary condition of Fox's promotion was the loyal and self-effacing willingness of Robinson to step down. Then, with Hardwicke having given up Pitt, the Cabinet was, in general, in favour: Granville had always backed Fox, and Fox himself spoke of accepting office on the advice of Marlborough, Granville and Waldegrave as well as of Cumberland.[229] Less widely apparent, but evident certainly to Newcastle, was Cumberland's willingness to encourage complacency and moderation in Fox's conduct.[230] This lay behind Newcastle's confidence that Fox wished to behave well; more importantly, Newcastle saw that the Secretaryship would bind Fox to defend the administration's measures in a way no minor post could do.[231] Above all, Newcastle had been able to rely on the King's assent to every item in his programme except the Secretaryship for Pitt. As he had written:

I think both the King and my lord Holdernesse very properly combine our *home situation*, with the foreign one, and in order to support the one, His Majesty possibly might be brought to consent to whatever your Lordship and I should propose with regard to the other.[232]

Fox boasted that the ministers had at last told the King 'that hated truth "that the business could not do itself any longer in the House of Commons without any other conductor than a Minister not there"'.[233] In reality, Newcastle's tactical calculations had been concerned with denying Fox and others primacy within the ministry as such, not of the Commons. Newcastle was pleased that the appointment of Fox, by appealing to the very doctrine about the leadership of the lower House which had earlier been propagated, would silence Pitt;[234] but the reasons for Newcastle's move had been very different and far more complex. Fox's gains from the new scheme have, accordingly, been exaggerated. He had earlier declined taking office 'until the question is the ruin of his Grace',[235] and Almon called the new arrangement 'The Duke's [Cumberland's] Ministry',[236] but Fox admitted that his patron took no part in the negotiations,[237] and though Cumberland himself described Fox's success as 'a thorough vindication both of the judgement and honesty of the part you have acted ever since Mr Pelham's death', he called the position gained the leadership of the Commons, not the ministry, and added: 'How far the Duke of Newcastle can bring himself to give you power I still doubt.'[238] Speaking of Pitt, Waldegrave said that Newcastle was 'not sufficiently intimidated to make any man a minister who had frankly told him he would not be directed';[239] the remark applies equally to Fox. And the only occasion on which Newcastle is known to have said of Sir Thomas Robinson that 'the House of Commons has tore him from us' was when writing to Robinson himself to soothe the feelings of his old and respected friend.[240] In fact, Newcastle had caught Fox by giving him an opportunity to play what he considered his trump card in another emotional audience on 23rd. Fox wrote:

I have never declared my opinion of the subsidies till this morning to the King. H.M. is in great distress. They have been obliged to tell him that the House of Commons could not go on without some authority within it; that almost every principal person there had declared against subsidies; and they could not name one such who had declared for them. They had tried Pitt, Sir George Lee, and Egmont, that the two first and Legge had declared against them, that Egmont doubted and declined accepting the place, that in this situation they had spoken to me. Lord Granville had before spoke of me to him, but could not tell him my opinion.

But then, linked as he was to Cumberland, Fox could scarcely in the end adopt any other attitude toward the treaties. Even now, the King mentioned no specific office: that was fixed by Newcastle, later the same day.[241] After he had revealed his assent to the subsidies, Fox's position was considerably weakened, for he was forced to admit that he would be for them in or out of place. If out, he could only threaten that he would, 'in the act of vindicating the measure declare war with the Minister': hardly a credible menace.[242]

Newcastle had been convinced that if Fox were to be enlisted, it must appear as his and Hardwicke's act, not as a storming of the Closet or a capitulation from necessity. This had been achieved, for conflicting rumours were current until the last moment.[243] Joseph Yorke wrote:

It was very clear that Mr F[ox] was the last resource, and though he may value himself upon his success, and think it owing to the superiority of his conduct, yet it appears clearly that he is much more indebted to the absurdity and factious spirit of his rivals.[244]

That the imagined alternative was Newcastle's fall from office only highlights the importance of his success. Secondly, it had been made Fox's interest to support measures; and thirdly, Newcastle had checked that there was no possibility of Fox's 'gaining any separate credit with the King'. Argyll compared Newcastle's and Fox's accounts of the deal, found an 'almost total' disagreement, and predicted that the system would soon disintegrate.[245] In fact, Argyll was only identifying the tactical errors which marked Fox's defeat. There is overwhelming evidence that Newcastle was delighted with Fox's co-operation and compliance in the weeks after the bargain.[246] The King had assured Newcastle on 3 October 'that Fox is to be subordinate to you – I [George II] told Fox, that the ministers had brought him in, that if he did not behave well (or to that purpose) they would quarrel with him, and so should I too. Fox is not popular.'[247] Waldegrave probably reported Fox's own impression that the private conduct of the King towards him conformed to these principles.[248] Newcastle wrote:

I am firmly convinced, that the King is sorry for the necessity of doing what is done; that he is resolved to support my lord Chancellor, and me, at the head of his affairs. That any attempt from Mr Fox, for altering that resolution, would ruin Fox at once; and that the King will not suffer Mr Fox to do anything, *even in the House of Commons*, without previously consulting me. And I am persuaded, Fox sees it in this light. I told the King, Fox said, we must *stand, and fall, together*. The King said, he (Fox) may very well *fall, without you*. This being the state of the case; the making Fox, *thus*, Secretary of State, was the best thing for me. He has an office which, the King told me, he would *do ill* in. He can seldom see the King, without Lord Holderness. He is removed from Secretary of War and so far removed from *the Duke*. But, above all, it has given me an opportunity to show the world, that the King would put into that office (as he has done) the man, the most declared friend of mine, *my Lord Barrington, without consulting the Duke.*[249]

And, unknown to Fox, it was Newcastle and Hardwicke who continued, in private, to arrange the terms of the Speech from the Throne and the Commons Address in reply.[250]

In April 1755, the main threat to Newcastle's position had seemed to come from Cumberland; but his installation in the Regency finally alienated Pitt from Fox. It was not a move designed to shut the door on Pitt's promotion within the ministry: Hardwicke was still a warm advocate of such a step, to which Newcastle was well inclined. At that point, his options were still open, and the tactical schemes which he considered for the ministry's reinforcement explored a number of possibilities involving Pitt, Fox, Legge, Egmont, Lee and others.

It was Bute who first made an overture to Pitt, but when Pitt followed it up in an audience with the Princess, he was unable to pin her or Lee down to a treaty; later, therefore, he tried to repair his probably accidental outburst of resentment against Fox in Hillsborough's garden. He and Bute were henceforth committed to launching a Leicester House opposition; but they had great difficulty in doing so. Only in mid

September did Bute secure Egmont and Lee to prevent them treating separately from Bute and Pitt. The rise of the subsidies issue thus eliminated one of Newcastle's options; it did not prevent him from closing with another. Fox was incorporated into the ministerial system, on terms which were freely negotiated, in a manner which reveals Newcastle's continuing control. It was not a capitulation in the face of a menacing formed opposition; none such yet existed. Rather it was the final rejection of Pitt, as he saw it, which gave a major impetus to the attempt to launch such an opposition in the autumn of 1755.

4

'That Exploded Trick': Newcastle, Fox and the Defeat of Leicester House Patriotism, October 1755–March 1756

as the Duke of Newcastle has so often turned in and out all men in England, he *must* employ some of the same dupes over again.

> Horace Walpole to Mann,
> 21 Dec 1755: HW 20, p.516

Places, as you will see by the newspapers, are emptying and filling up every day. The Patriot of Monday is the Courtier of Tuesday; and the Courtier of Wednesday is the Patriot of Thursday. This, indeed, has more or less been long the case, but I really think never so impudently and so profligately as now.

> Chesterfield to Dayrolles,
> 19 Dec 1755: Dobrée, v, 2169

As to Mr Pitt I always have been greatly prejudiced in his favour, but I know his ambition to be unbounded and if he sees his way at Leicester House, the warmth of his temper and his passions will carry him any lengths, his former oppositions sufficiently prove it.

> Hartington to Devonshire,
> 8 Nov 1755: Dev 260/181.

THE COMPLETION OF THE SYSTEM

Fox's promotion became public on 26 September;[1] a rumour of Pitt's resignation soon followed it.[2] The junior Court, in its earlier preliminary moves against subsidies, had taken pains to enlist the assent of several senior figures. Now, they tried to take advantage of that prestige at once. Devonshire, in particular, was approached by both sides and looked on as the final arbiter of conscience;[3] Fox had expected him to 'come to town to the meeting of the Parliament on purpose to get [the Russian subsidy] condemned, which he can go farther towards effecting than any twenty lords in England'.[4] But Devonshire was offended that it was said, prematurely, that he had *declared* open opposition to the treaties and that Newcastle had described him as more closely attached to Pitt than to Fox. Angrily, he asserted that he was under no engagement.[5] Horatio Walpole, though he approved the Hessian, jibbed at the Russian treaty, against which he claimed to have been advised on grounds of policy and its unpopularity by Sir Thomas Robinson himself.[6] Not even a discussion with the quixotic Hanbury Williams, the negotiator of the Russian agreement, could move him from an opinion thus reinforced. Walpole, however, feared 'a triumvirate that are determined enemies to the Duke of Newcastle': Fox, Pitt and Legge, joined 'not altogether in a concert', but in the act of attacking Newcastle through the subsidy issue.[7] He added: 'Some orators will be for or against the Russians, if we must have them, as they shall be satisfied or dissatisfied in their aspiring views'. This was immediately justified by the arrival of the news of Fox's promotion; amused, he commented: 'the consequence of the rupture of a triumvirate among the Romans usually ended in a civil war between the contending parties for power'.[8]

Horace Walpole neatly characterised some reactions to the treaties: 'Mr Legge grew *conscientious* about them; the Speaker, constitutional; Mr Pitt, patriot; Sir George Lee, scrupulous; Lord Egmont, uncertain; the Duke of Devonshire, something that he meant for some of these; and my uncle, I suppose, *frugal*...'[9] Legge and Pitt had been spreading 'hints' of an attack 'in some shape or other' on Newcastle since at least early September. Even then, Horatio Walpole, who claimed to have 'no great reason, but quite the contrary to defend' Newcastle, observed: 'as I apprehend that *more power and not better measures*, is the chief aim, of some of those discontented patriots, I can't see for what purpose I should join in an offensive part...'[10] In his unwillingness to take the issue of principle at face value, he went as far as Newcastle's identification of the dissent as 'Ambition in some, and vanity, pride and conceitedness in others...;[11] an impression supported by the fact that news of Pitt's declaring against the Russian treaty apparently became public only just before his second meeting with Newcastle on 12th.[12]

In the weeks between the recruitment of Fox and the opening of the parliamentary session, the opposition took on a form dictated not by Pitt and Bute, around the axis of Leicester House, but by the manoeuvres of the ministers to complete their new system. The immediate reactions of the disaffected to the events of 20–23 September had been too slow to forestall Newcastle. Potter heard of Pitt's conversations with Hardwicke and Newcastle from James Grenville in London only on 19 September;[13] Pitt was then in Bath having apparently been steeled by Bute to do nothing more constructive than refuse the ministry's advances. Not until 4 October did Pitt arrive in London.[14] It was Charles Townshend who approached the proto-opposition through Bute's brother, not vice versa, and only after having received an offer from Newcastle of a seat at the Treasury.[15] Dodington was playing a double game: encouraging Pitt's confidence on 3 September, warning Halifax on 6th not to reveal his opinion of the treaties; and though at first inclined against, and anxious to reconcile the leaders of the junior Court with the ministry, increasingly enthusiastic about Fox's accommodation with Newcastle which implied the contrary effect.[16]

Bedford and George Grenville were also in the country; it was Potter who acted on news which included, from some source, a distorted account of Newcastle's audience on the King's return and offer to exchange posts with Granville. Potter hoped to arrange 'that Lord Gr[anville] and his Lieut[enant] Mr Fox should find themselves disabled to undertake what the Duke of Newcastle refuses'; he accordingly approached and secured Dr Hay, from whom the administration expected able support in the House, and travelled at once on 20th to Woburn to confront Bedford with the momentous news of Pitt's meeting with Newcastle. He evidently concealed both his knowledge of the King's supposed indifference to the opposition of six or seven men to the treaties and smug confidence in the popularity of those measures in England, and also Newcastle's 'earnest request', as he had heard it, that Granville might replace him as Minister so that the treaties would pass without attracting opposition from hostility merely personal and directed at Newcastle alone. Potter rephrased this into an unattributed rumour that Newcastle would resign if the Russian treaty were not carried, but laid most stress on a selective account of Pitt's interview with the First Lord. Bedford 'took the whole exactly as I wished, fell into the strongest panegyrics on Mr Pitt's virtue and abilities, saw the immediate destruction of the Duke of Newcastle if nobody was weak enough to interfere, hoped in God no one of his friends, particularly Mr Fox, would attempt it'. Potter secured a message of wildly enthusiastic support for Pitt and whatever action he chose to take, and hastened with it to Bath, imagining Bedford perfectly immune to Fox's and Cumberland's persuasion[17] — a revealing attitude, for he cannot with certainty have known of, and did not mention, Fox's deal.

Pitt was grateful for Bedford's confidence, and Temple called at Woburn to convey his thanks. Potter had an interview[18] with Bedford early in October to repeat Pitt's regard. But Potter was alarmed to discover that Rigby had called at Woburn the day after Potter's last visit; and spoken to very good effect in Fox's interest. Potter told Bedford that their hopes in late September of Newcastle's impending fall had been 'blasted in the very manner he [Bedford] himself had suggested by Fox's eagerness for place and power, as he had now most effectually secured him in his office, perhaps for life'. Bedford slightly changed the emphasis: Fox had accepted unwarily, not as Potter put it from a thirst for power and money. Bedford's crucial refusal to take so favourable a view of Pitt's motives as he had previously done was the result of Rigby's disclosure of the encounter in which Pitt broke with Fox in Hillsborough's garden on 9 May. The general ignorance of this made it still believed that a Pitt–Fox union in opposition to the treaties existed until Fox was bought off from it by the ministry.[19] Fox had apparently told Rigby

198

that the reason for his accepting the ministry's offer was Pitt's telling him, as Bedford disapprovingly put it, 'bluntly and without provocation ...that he would neither go with him into Court or Opposition...' This pro-Fox interpretation was probably that which Newcastle also gave to the interview of 9 May when he heard of it from Granville early in October.[20] Potter, in now admitting his knowledge of the conversation to Bedford, implicitly admitted also that he had kept the secret in order to present Fox as deserting Pitt; but defended Pitt's conduct during his 'union' with Fox of 1754–5 as quite lacking 'all ideas of rivalship or of private animosity'. *Fox* had betrayed *Pitt*, claimed Potter, and, far from approving the former's conduct, Pitt condemned him for it in the interview of 9 May which did no more than mark the resulting breach. Bedford was a little appeased, but still insisted on hearing both sides of the case when in London at the end of the month:

That Fox had sent to him the strongest assurances that he came in with a view to strengthen himself in the Closet and to undermine the Duke of Newcastle, that he had come in against all the efforts both of the Duke of Newcastle and Lord Chancellor by the influence of the Duke of Cumberland.

I [Potter] told him this was very inconsistent with all the declarations both of the Duke of Newcastle and Lord Chancellor who expressed to everyone who would hear them their high satisfaction not only in the assurances Mr Fox had given them but in the candour of his conduct since. That one way or other Mr Fox's conduct was unjustifiable for if he really meant to support the Duke of Newcastle he betrayed his friends who wished to oppose him, and if he really meant to undermine him he was the villain who smiles in your face and stabs you to the heart. Yes but says he Fox insists he has made no promise except that he will do the King's business. However, I think on the whole as you do, that Fox's acceptance has been precipitate and ill-judged. That he has saved the Duke of Newcastle who without his acceptance was absolutely undone. That Fox could have run no risk in standing out as Mr Pitt had refused first and as if the Duke of Newcastle fell, he stood first in the graces of the Closet. That he might have refused now with much more safety than he did a year and a half since, and as he lost no favour then he could have lost none now.

Potter urged his second argument: that Fox was doomed in the public eye, for 'the idea of a continent war and subsidies was in the minds of mankind the same and though he might get a majority for a day he would feel the weight of that day while he lived'. Bedford was impressed most by Potter's assurance of Devonshire's aversion to subsidy treaties, which harmonised with his own aversion to any continental presence, but had seen no-one since Temple's visit to Woburn and was determined to wait until returning to town before 'I resolve on the part I shall take'.[21]

It is evident that Fox immediately threw himself into the party battle on Newcastle's behalf, on the assumption that Legge and Pitt were in alliance and would soon be out of office if they opposed.[22] Newcastle realised that his ally 'comes in, the declared, avowed opposer of the

Duke of Devonshire's, and Mr Legge's, measures, and combination; and that must turn out to the service of him, (I mean myself) against whom, personally, both the Duke of Devonshire, and Legge, direct all their malice'.[23]

But in late September and early October, Fox's support of the ministry was subject to two interpretations. The first was the approach he demonstrated to Newcastle, one of wholehearted willingness to support the treaties: Pitt's conduct had forced him to take the Secretaryship. The second was that spoken of by those who set a higher estimate on Fox's ambition, or sought to justify what was called his desertion of Pitt. Horace Walpole, who like Chesterfield and probably Granville, imagined Fox soon to be 'First Minister – or what one has known to happen to some who of very late years have joined to support a tottering adminis-tration, is to be ruined', wrote that Fox 'seems sensible of the alternative, profess no cordiality to Duke Trinculo, who is viceroy over him, but is listing Bedfords, and whoever will list with him as fast as he can';[24] that he was 'endeavouring to bring the Bedfords to court; and if any other person in the world hates King Thomas [Newcastle], why Mr Fox is very willing to bring them to court too'.[25] Walpole claimed[26] that Fox's initiative through Rigby came when Stone told Fox, after the latter's acceptance of office, that Newcastle would have resigned had he not done so; that Fox then suddenly realised his mistake, and set about working to undermine Newcastle. But it seems unlikely, in view of Fox's earlier pronouncements, that he had not entertained contradictory motives throughout the negotiation. Rigby used the same excuse to Bedford's friend Earl Gower, urging the necessity Fox was under through his desertion by Pitt (though not mentioning that this took place as long ago as May), and adding the damning intelligence, which Bedford now heard for the first time, that Pitt's conduct then was 'the terms of favour at Leicester House'.[27] Again he stressed that Newcastle's 'fall' had not been 'broken', and that real power had been conceded. Although Newcastle was 'this very day in all probability treating with every man that can pretend to take the lead in the House of Commons', Rigby claimed that this was beyond the Minister's power as a result of his deal with Fox, and admitted acting himself as the organiser of those willing to support Fox as 'first man in the House of Commons'. Fox was, claimed Rigby, determined to act 'not as agent or tool, or *Legge* to the Duke of Newcastle; but looking upon that measure, as a mode of his destruction, which inevitably must follow...' Surely, Gower could not welcome a link with Leicester House, 'who as far as they dare under-hand are to oppose the treaties'?[28] But Gower kept Rigby waiting for an answer,[29] until Fox himself was driven to use him for an overture to Bedford in mid October. Although Newcastle was to contain Fox's ambitions in the session of 1755–6, therefore, they remained a latent threat. In December John Morton received from Hume Campbell, in a bundle of other papers and apparently by accident, a hypothetical ministerial scheme in which Fox's friends were given promotion, among them Marlborough and Sandwich, and Bedford included as Secretary of State in place of Holdernesse. Fox, recorded Ryder on 7 December, 'has lately said that the Duke of Newcastle would not be a minister six months longer'.[30]

LEICESTER HOUSE: THE AFTERMATH

Meanwhile, Newcastle had been trying to cope with the reaction of Leicester House to the deal with Fox. It was no part of Newcastle's expectation that a Secretaryship for the latter ruled out links with Egmont and Lee; although the first declined the Exchequer (Newcastle's original plan), rumours were long current of his inclusion in some other office.[31] The Princess's 'violent rage' at the news of Fox's incorporation, directed at Cresset on the night of 25 September, may have been in part a recognition that a link with Egmont and Lee was now impossible; but it was also an expression of frustration in the face of a dilemma. Openly to oppose the treaties would be to defy the King. Rather than that, she professed 'she would *never* oppose the King, but she would be *tranquille*, would do nothing, nor speak to anybody, nor influence any of her servants one way, or other'. Then, in self-contradiction, she pointed in silent menace to Sir George Lee's known thoughts. But after this angry scene, Newcastle discovered an interesting secret from Cresset. In March 1754, Newcastle had sent Stone to the Princess with news of his intention to make Fox Secretary of State, and received back a very civil assent. 'Mr C[resset] *now* tells Stone, that the Princess then said to him upon it, "I had obligations to the Duke of Newcastle, but now, *nous sommes quittes*." And this has certainly been boiling ever since'.[32] This was probably no more than an excuse, a rationalisation of her present position. Nevertheless, it harmonised with Newcastle's interpretation of events. It was becoming apparent to him, if only in retrospect, that aversion to himself and Fox had governed the Princess's conduct;[33] Bute was never considered as a leader at that court since in reality he was still only a minor figure. Hardwicke first mentioned him in an aside: why not try to buy off Bute,[34] 'who has credit there, and undoubtedly would be glad of something for himself'? Lord Royston noted later: 'NB How comes no notice to be taken of Lord Bute in these letters[?] He had then the influence at Leicester House, and when I came to town in November, I was told it by my brother John, who had it from Fox's friend Hamilton'.[35] But this was still weeks away: weeks in which the real power of Egmont and Lee was destroyed (after the end of the tactical option which had sustained it) and that of Bute and Pitt rose. Even then, appearances outlasted the reality. Walpole recorded that Sir George Lee contributed to the debate on the Address 'as representative of the Princess's sentiments'.[36] Almon pointed out that Pitt was 'generally supposed to belong' to Leicester House; 'but it was not true: he was their friend, but not their coadjutor'.[37]

In September, when he still hoped to use Münchausen to conciliate the Princess, Newcastle was explicit that the 'remonstrances should be founded on *Egmont* and *Lee*, and not on suspicion'.[38] But Hardwicke reminded him of the Princess's responsibility for the necessity of giving Fox office: she had been told last summer of the ministry's intention to bring in Egmont, Pitt and Lee; 'she has at least acquiesced in *their negative* to that arrangement, and to (what makes it still more impracticable) to public measures'. Hardwicke hopefully but vaguely suggested that Granville, an advocate of Fox's inclusion, and 'as much concerned to reconcile this step with the principle of the Regency Bill as anybody' should be sent to see the Princess, after Waldegrave had raised the question of an increased allowance for the children. 'Your Grace is certainly right', added the Chancellor, 'that, whoever goes, should found themselves on the appearances from *Egmont* and *Lee*'. Best of all, the King should see her.[39] In the event, Münchausen was sent.[40] Newcastle's optimism about his mission probably rested on the common assumption that although Pitt had applied to the Princess for her interest, 'and indeed all parties have applied to her, she has acted, as she always does, with the greatest prudence and does not interfere'.[41] Similarly Archbishop Herring, an intimate of Sir George Lee's, felt sure after a conversation with him on 8th that he would not speak against the Hessian subsidy or join in fomenting a division within the royal family, and that though he had refused the Exchequer he did so from honest principle. Lee protested he was 'listed into no particular services' but spoke against a subsidy policy and echoed Pitt's declamation of the previous autumn – for MPs automatically to sanction a government's treaties would be 'telling in the House, only to register the acts of a minister'. Nor could Lee – reported Herring – pretend to lead the Commons without such a share of power as Newcastle would not, in his jealousy, grant.[42]

The Princess, according to the Archbishop, was well disposed;[43] a consequence, as Cresset's report to Newcastle via Stone on 30 September gave the impression, of her fears of a message from the King reproving 'the behaviour of her servants'. Cresset, pacifying, advised that she would not 'meddle' and that any message would itself open a breach in the royal family. Münchausen had an audience of the Princess the same day and thought the prospects good. Newcastle was sceptical. Lady Yarmouth only raised his fears by implicity endorsing the dark rumours Newcastle had apparently just heard of a scandalous relationship between the Princess and Bute.[44] Hardwicke was appalled, and looked on the ill prospects rather as a reason for a formal warning than for refraining from one: once overt hostile acts had occurred, the situation would be irretrievably lost.[45] Newcastle apparently knew nothing of

Hardwicke's information about Lee when he met Egmont at Kew, probably on 11 October,[46] full of an astonishingly revived confidence[47] that the Earl would accept office. Egmont strengthened this confidence by approving the ministry's measures and condemning the opposition to them. He ridiculed Lee and his weakness in repeating Pitt's opinion on subsidies 'in a way not to be able to depart from it', but admitted at the same time that Lee and Pitt had been closely allied since Fox's promotion to the Cabinet. This both confirmed Newcastle's most recent estimate of Lee and called in doubt his truthfulness, since – as Newcastle told Egmont – Lee had earlier given Pitt's continuance in office as a reason for not accepting the Exchequer. Hardwicke corrected this: 'What he said was "that it was impossible for anyone to go on in that station in the House of Commons, with the principal places filled by the enemies of the administration"; wherein he then included Mr Fox, as well as anybody else'. But the Chancellor went further than Newcastle in claiming that Lee's attitude indicated official policy at Kew. Egmont, seemingly ignorant of Newcastle's new view of Lee, announced that he had suggested to Sir George that he and 'the rest' (among whom Egmont seemingly included Pitt) would be forgiven and negotiated with if they made only a token opposition to the Russian treaty, 'as it were pro forma'. Lee was well disposed to the idea and seemed to Egmont in that case to be again inclined to accept the Exchequer. But Newcastle ridiculed the plan and refused Egmont's offer to make the same suggestion to Pitt: everyone would then expect that liberty, and the subsidies would be lost in the Commons. The principle later to emerge as 'collective responsibility' had of necessity evolved thus far: as Hume Campbell put it to Newcastle on 15 October, 'whatever might be last winter yet if people may oppose and be paid everybody that desires pay will oppose'.[48] Hardwicke agreed that Egmont's proposal was absurd, though it might be reasonable to break a formed opposition by taking in one or two of its leaders after their faction had been beaten; and, while they both expected difficulties, the possibility of defeat seems never to have occurred to either Newcastle or Hardwicke. The lesson the Chancellor drew was that 'The weak part, taken by Sir George Lee, is one of the strongest proofs of the resolution *there* [Kew] being fixed'. Newcastle was far less willing, in the rearrangement of 1755–6, to countenance dissent within the ministry than he had been in 1754–5; especially if it signified allegiance to a formed opposition. The limited freedom later allowed to Dodington was not an exception to this principle, for it was a concession from a position of strength to a man whose apostasy had already been bought.

Though claiming to Newcastle to be at liberty, Egmont declared himself reluctant to come in alone. Lee had disclaimed, to Egmont, wanting a new administration, but now also refused to act with Fox. No such aversion hindered Egmont, but rather his personal loyalty to the Princess. She, he thought, might be won over by indulgence in 'little things', the promotion of her servants (Egmont mentioned Sir John Cust and Sir Edmund Thomas), and an increase in her allowance. Newcastle duly made the suggestion to the King, adding a measured warning: 'Sire...it is my duty, to tell you, that I find more difficulty from the notion of opposition from that quarter, which affects particularly all the young men, than from all other causes whatsoever.' But George II refused. Already, the Princess's ingratitude (as he saw it) was making him intransigent. Newcastle observed: 'what is worst of all, this behaviour of the Princess will make the King repent [of] what he did in the affair of the Regency, and recommend those to him who opposed it, and were of a contrary opinion; and thus Her Royal Highness absolutely does Mr Fox's business, as much as Mr Pitt has done'. Newcastle, left dizzy at these fast changing alternatives, was now briefly unsure whether, since 'Mr Legge cannot stay', Egmont would accept the Exchequer or whether it should even be offered him: if not, might not Granville bring Fox to believe that *he* might have had the post but for Newcastle's jealousy? Dodington was out of the question, and Barrington could not be taken from the War Office: Dupplin might, he hazarded, fill the gap temporarily, or even – looking further afield – John Campbell.[49] Hardwicke urged the unsuitability of their much loved but unfortunate friend, Dupplin: Fox favoured him with an obvious design to have a weak colleague. Evidently there were growing attractions in a Chancellor of the Exchequer coolly disposed towards Fox, and Hardwicke favoured Egmont's installation before the session opened.

Newcastle launched a final overture to Egmont via Lord Chief Justice Willes; but the latter reported back that 'I could get no other answer, but that he had given your Grace an answer several times before': a negative. Nor could Willes draw a favourable response from Hay,[50] whom Potter had engaged. Newcastle sanctioned, too, the chance Hume Campbell offered of a last approach to Lee, with a hint of the Exchequer; but the result was as before. 'He is determined', discovered Hume Campbell the same day, 15 October, 'would do nothing with Fox, and I find that is the *ground* to oppose and the subsidy treaties the *pretence*'.[51] Lee, as the King imagined, merely replaced Fox in the Pitt–Legge–Fox alignment which was generally thought to be still waiting for power.[52] Hume Campbell, however, suggested that if the difficulty about persons could be got over, measures would not be an obstacle. That difficulty was, nevertheless, formidable. Lee refused absolutely to serve in a ministry with Fox, and spoke to Hume Campbell as if Egmont were securely theirs. More obstacles were being advanced to a reconciliation: Fox's presumptuous claim, in his circular letters, to manage the Commons; the King being forced to give an exorbitant price to remove an able Secretary of State; 'That this had been a scheme of my Lord Chancellor's, and the Duke of Newcastle's, for one year and half (I aver Sir George Lee knows the contrary). But, or and, there was a strong party, who would *stand* by, *support* or *protect* (I can't say which) the Princess of Wales, and her son. This is talking high indeed'[53] – and Newcastle dared not report it in the Closet. Waldegrave was wrong in supposing that George II had 'received thorough information' about the Leicester House opposition within a week of landing in England.[54] His ministers were not fully informed of, and withheld information about, a phenomenon as yet only moving towards what they all feared. But George II gave the ministry every support: Fox could not fairly be attacked for his conduct before starting in office, the King told Newcastle; 'this of Fox, *was only a pretence*. That the measure of opposition from Leicester House, was taken before anything of that kind happened etc.' But George II, knowing less than his ministers of the seriousness of the situation, was determined not to show resentment and to attempt a reconciliation through Waldegrave, Stone and Lady Yarmouth.[55]

FOX'S FRIENDS

Meanwhile, since the promise of Fox's Secretaryship had been made, the struggle had been going on for the inclusion or the allegiance of less central figures. Legge, rather than resign,[56] still waited passively to draw credit from his dismissal. Fox had taken over from him the task of writing the circular letters[57] and was gathering the administration's supporters for the Cockpit meeting. But Fox's main contribution lay in the ministry's relations with Bedford, Devonshire, Argyll and Dodington. Argyll promised the support of his Scottish bloc in the coming sessions,[58] and Devonshire professed his personal attachment despite the use made of his name against the treaties.[59] On 2 October, Fox reported a good prospect of accommodation with Dodington; sensing a desire in him to take part in a political scheme involving himself, Murray, and Hillsborough, Fox suggested that Halifax was the agent most likely to bring Dodington's agreement, and added the further recommendation that Dodington wished to bring with him Sir Francis Dashwood.[60] Fox secured Newcastle's approval both for this and for Dodington's unspecified 'proposed measure with Legge':[61] possibly an echo of Newcastle's plan of 5 September which linked Legge's transfer to a Vice Treasurership of Ireland with Dodington's installation as Comptroller and Hillsborough's as Treasurer of the Household. Newcastle had a long interview with Charles Townshend, between 2 and 4 October, and offered him a seat at the Treasury. He deferred an answer and wrote to consult his brother George, then in the country, with 'a full account, as far as he knew, of the present situation of things; which', wrote Bute's brother, 'by what he told me, he did not make better than they really are'.[62] Newcastle wrote too, promising to 'set things in a different light, from what perhaps they may appear to you at present'.[63] But George Townshend, Fox's 'personal enemy',[64] was evidently disinclined to co-operate. By 7th, Bute had discovered George Townshend's answer: personal regard for Newcastle but a refusal formally to support measures.[65] With Charles Townshend unavailable, Darlington and Dupplin were replaced at the Treasury Board by Wyndham O'Brien, a government supporter in Egremont's interest, and Henry Furnese, brought in as part of the price of Dodington's accession. The First Lord wrote to Halifax, offended at Fox's promotion, to ask that he negotiate also for Dodington. Newcastle represented his desire to recruit Dodington as a long standing one[66] and let Halifax into the secret: the intended office was the Comptrollership. 'Your friend Hillsborough will then be pleased with the other staff' – that of Treasurer of the Household.[67] Fox enforced this, urging the King's willingness to drop the proscription of Dodington, and the latter's inclination 'to make one in a political system with your lordship, Lord Hillsborough, and your humble servant'.[68]

At this point a difficulty intervened. Fox had suggested to Newcastle that an employment for Sandwich, without the latter's solicitation, would secure him;[69] and, at Newmarket, Cumberland prompted the Earl to ask for the Vice Treasurership of Ireland, a profitable sinecure.[70] But Hardwicke objected to giving away too much too soon,[71] and to add a further difficulty, coinciding with Newcastle's final interview with Egmont and apparently after Halifax had revealed to Dodington the secret of his intended office, the latter refused it (implying that it was inadequate) at a meeting with Newcastle on 10th, and with Halifax suddenly displayed a 'wild' aversion to the Russian treaty.[72] Sackville, too, resenting his and Dorset's removal from the Irish government and the promotion of Fox, the supposed patron of the Irish opposition, refused his support in the Commons: he was, he claimed, too much in disgrace to act there without a mark of favour. In November, Sackville refused Newcastle's offer that he should move or second the Commons' Address; it is not clear how Newcastle won him over to support the ministry, and speak effectively in its favour, by early December.[73]

Fox was of value, too, from the men in place he could count on to co-operate in the rearrangement. On 14th, he wrote to Gower with an informal but definite offer of the Privy Seal for Bedford.[74] Horace Walpole claims Fox secured Marlborough's prior consent to part with the office;[75] even when Bedford refused to be associated with Newcastle in an administration or to support the subsidy treaties,[76] and when the Privy Seal went to Gower himself, Marlborough made no audible protest. Bedford, however, after Rigby's revelations, was not completely lost; to Granville, he spoke as if indisposed to act with hostility or 'to be in any connection of opposition'; Granville believed 'that the person, you may guess whom I mean [Cumberland] can secure his assistance

in the King's measures'.[77] The frigid reception Bedford gave to Temple
and Egmont at Woburn seemed to bear this out.[78] But Bedford's followers were far more eager to support the ministry by co-operating with
Fox than was the Duke himself.[79]

Fox shared with Newcastle in the blandishments being offered to
Horatio Walpole,[80] and even took pains over John Campbell, Newcastle's distant guess for the Exchequer.[81] Newcastle himself undertook
the advances to Gilbert Elliot[82] and Hume Campbell. The latter was
obdurate, claiming to confine his ambition to the law, aiming in particular at a Chief Justiceship, and stressing that any post, to be attractive,
must be permanent. A further difficulty was the overlap of this negotiation with Fox's relations with Argyll, the local rival of the Marchmonts
in Scotland. Sir George Lee, whom Hume Campbell saw on Newcastle's
behalf, played on the possibility of Argyll's hostility to the treaties;
Hume Campbell thought there was an opportunity to score against
Argyll; but, failing to see it, offered Newcastle his support for measures
in return for the Chancellorship of the Duchy of Lancaster for life with
its salary of £500–600 p.a. made up to £2000 p.a. during pleasure,
as a compensation for devoting his time to the Commons rather than
the law.[83] He hoped, in that case, 'that John Morton,[84] member for
Abingdon, is to have my silk gown if he will act', and that William Noel
would do likewise for the promise of a Chief Justiceship;[85] Newcastle
was enthusiastic, and confident that he could secure Argyll's adherence,
through Fox, by appointing Argyll's nominee a Baron of the Exchequer
in Scotland. Horatio Walpole's loyalty would be ultimately determined
by the promise of a peerage, which Newcastle felt could now be obtained
for him. Thus, in mid October, Newcastle summarised the position: 'Our
line of battle in the House of Commons is not so weak a one, as may
have been imagined'. 'For', he included Fox, Murray, Hume Campbell,
Charles Yorke, Horatio Walpole, Hillsborough, Barrington, Sir Thomas
Robinson, Lord Dupplin, Oswald, 'Moreton the lawyer for whom H.
Campbell answers', Nugent, and Alderman Baker. 'Doubtful' were
George and Charles Townshend, Noel, Henley, 'and I hope not Dr
Hay'. 'Against' comprised Pitt, Dodington, Legge, George Grenville,
Potter, James Grenville, the Beckfords, 'and, I hope not', Egmont and
Lord Strange.[86]

The Exchequer was the major gap in the system. Newcastle accurately
interpreted Dodington's conversation of 10 October: though he would
have been an acceptable colleague at the Board, he had now ruled
himself out. Indeed, his latest terms included cabinet rank for Halifax;
provision for Furnese, Talbot and Tucker; the Comptroller's staff for
Dashwood; and liberty to oppose the treaties, though 'with all the
decency that is consistent with truth'.[87] These men might willingly have
been recruited as individuals, but Newcastle resisted their inclusion en
bloc. He turned instead to consider Barrington for the Exchequer – a

dizzying rise – but saw this entailing an exchange with Dupplin, and refused to part with the latter from the Treasury.[88] It is unknown how well informed Newcastle was of Egmont, but the possibility of his inclusion had evaporated since their meeting on 12th; his answer through Lord Chief Justice Willes was evidently taken as final. He appears to have become trapped in a complex, debilitating introspection about the propriety of his conduct and the motives of those with whom he negotiated: though he could not in conscience oppose the subsidies, he looked to his refusal of office as the public proof that he supported them from opinion, not self-interest; and, recalling the alignments of the previous winter, he pointed to the inclusion of Fox as a new departure totally irreconcilable with his principles and connections. From caution as well as personal loyalties, he would not come in alone.[89] He needed not have been so scrupulous: as the Princess began to cast off her accustomed prudence,[90] Pitt and Legge rose in esteem at Leicester House,[91] and first Egmont, then Lee, found themselves cyphers there.

Horatio Walpole, five years older than the King, preferred to hold out for a peerage in the present reign;[92] at last, Newcastle secured him a promise of one at the end of the sessions,[93] 'if he is a good boy in the meantime'.[94] On his arrival in town, Newcastle gave him a mass of confidential diplomatic papers which completely satisfied him on the subsidies policy.[95] Others' motives were less easily handled. The evidence at this point is fragmentary, for the events were confused. On 20 October, Newcastle was apparently considering Edgcumbe for the Vice Treasurership of Ireland, and Lord Powis or Sir John Ligonier as Treasurer of the Household.[96] On 23rd, after the final refusals of Egmont and Lee, Newcastle offered Hume Campbell the Exchequer, 'which I refused,' he wrote, 'as not possible for life. The affair I wrote of is to be settled and Edgcumbe wrote to on it, (perhaps he won't quit it). That is possible. I was asked if in that event I would take Vice Chancellor [sc. Treasurer] of Ireland. That is liable to the same objection of duration'.[97] Apparently Hume Campbell had then been conditionally offered Edgcumbe's seat at the Board of Trade, and had refused; only the Duchy of Lancaster plus a pension of £1000 a year was acceptable; and Morton's co-operation, he urged, depended on his.[98] Yet his desire for an accommodation on a secure basis remained strong, and he was genuinely alarmed at Gilbert Elliot's tactical error in answering Fox's circular letter, not Newcastle's.[99] Hume Campbell was the victim of a common dilemma, torn between a desire to use this chance to ingratiate himself with the King and repair the effects of his association with Leicester House,[100] and apprehension that a place at pleasure would be precarious with the prospect of the approaching death of a whole generation of senior politicians including the King.[101] He could not, he wrote, accept the Exchequer now that Lee had refused it without offending Sir George. 'Many other reasons now the Princess of Wales has taken part against the ministry will occur why I should not jump out of the law line to be the butt of the House of Commons in money matters'. He objected to Newcastle's alternative offer of the Scottish place of Lord Clerk Register with a salary made up to £2000 per annum,[102] but when he later returned to the possibility of the Exchequer plus a pension, Newcastle's reaction suggested it was secretly disposed of.[103] The difficulty was the King's antipathy to a man who had been Solicitor General to Prince Frederick until his death.[104] With matters in suspense, Hume Campbell absented himself from Fox's meeting at the Cockpit[105] and remained silent in the debate on the Address the following day.[106] Newcastle again inclined to agree to Hume Campbell's demand of the Duchy of Lancaster,[107] but this proved impossible to bring about. To avoid disobliging Argyll, and after a brush with Hardwicke on the etiquette of nominating to legal offices, Newcastle finally agreed with Hume Campbell on the post of Clerk Register with an augmented salary on 9 December;[108] and the lawyer intervened in the Commons to great effect and in what was obviously the winning cause on the following day.

Sir George Lyttelton's attitude throughout the summer had been favourable but non-committal, sustained by Newcastle's help for his family interest at Bewdley against Fox and Winnington.[109] Newcastle took pains to persuade him to assent to the ministry's foreign policy, and Lyttelton wrote as if he had lost the friendship of his former allies before closing with the ministry, through having stood out against 'the unhappy mistakes of my friends in their political conduct'.[110] His availability once known, and in the absence of other candidates, Newcastle evidently had no difficulty in obtaining a favourable reply: 'The King will make Sir George Lyttelton Chancellor of the Exchequer, who upon the whole is the best man':[111] a promise given in time for Lyttelton to speak for the ministry in the debate on the Address. Dupplin remarked: 'That promotion seems to be a good deal talked of, and I have heard no disapprobation';[112] Lyttelton received the Seals on 21st, wrote Newcastle 'to the general joy and approbation of *King* and people which pleases me'.[113]

Even Bedford, whose loyalty had been finally secured, offered an assurance not to obstruct Sir George's re-election.[114] Earlier, Fox had found that Duke firmly against the idea of joining Newcastle's administration and even undecided whether to oppose the treaties in Parliament;[115] John Yorke's information was that 'the orators' regarded Bedford's enthusiasm for their cause as stronger even than Devonshire's.[116] At Fox's suggestion, Newcastle asked Hardwicke to meet Bedford on 2nd and expound in detail the ministry's foreign policy, its resistance to the King's designs, and its plans for a domestic system. He did so not without apprehensions of Fox's role. 'Mr Fox is not sorry to allege my lord Duke's resolution, *not to be one in the administration with me*; I could return the compliment to Mr Fox, but that is nothing.'[117] Bedford was carefully comparing each side's case, and arranged to see Pitt after meeting Hardwicke, actually on 3 November. Pitt was pessimistic – 'I go without the least expectation of any effect';[118] his estimate was correct. Bedford had heard the Chancellor with sympathy, especially his declaration against a 'continent war'; Hardwicke reported an apparent unwillingness to join in fomenting division, convinced the Duke of the rightness of the Hessian treaty and of the strength of many of the arguments in favour of the Russian. Bedford agreed not to offer an opposition to them in return for Hardwicke's assurance that no more were to follow. What motivated Bedford perhaps most deeply, and was evident to the Chancellor, was disapproval of a division in the Royal Family; beside this, the memory of Newcastle's ill-treatment of him scarcely mattered. Although Bedford was satisfied at the prospect of Fox's office, he expressed regard, too, for Pitt: and it is by no means apparent that it was Fox's friendship rather than Hardwicke's advocacy and arguments which persuaded him.[119] Nor did Fox believe this, reporting rather of Bedford: 'He is much struck with seeing Pitt's government established in another court, and however he may dislike ministers or measures, he will never he says, give in to another Leicester House opposition'.[120] Bedford then left town without seeing Pitt. The Paymaster was disappointed: 'This softness to measures and firmness against persons shows him more of one faction than I thought him'.[121] Bedford was kept informed of the texts of the Speech from the Throne[122] and the Addresses in reply, the Lords' Address being altered at his instance; in return, all Bedford's friends were ordered to attend the pre-session meeting at the Cockpit.[123] On the motion for the Address on the first day in the Lords, Bedford spoke 'short, well, and for us, and with decency'.[124]

THE SUBSIDY TREATIES AS AN ISSUE OF OPPOSITION

The considerations which decided Bedford's allegiance were also those which determined the prospects of the opposition at large. In September, the issue at stake had still seemed to be the treaties *tout court*, and it was against them that a great deal of respected Whig opinion at first inclined. Pitt's opposition was initially declared 'against the Russian subsidy, which, I am told', Fox wrote, 'is growing as unpopular as the Excise'.[125] Not only Horatio Walpole,[126] but Sir Thomas Robinson himself was regretfully and sincerely if quietiy inclined against it;[127] though it is not clear whether Newcastle knew of his opinion, the exchange of Fox for Robinson was of far more direct advantage than Fox's protagonists, including Horace Walpole, were ever aware. At this point, Newcastle's sources were telling him that the Russian and other subsidies gave 'general disgust though not so far as to occasion any great clamour',[128] and it was only during September that the disaffected could begin to organise an opposition on that basis. At first it was pretended that the personnel of Leicester House would adopt a disinterested opinion towards subsidies according to their conscience;[129] but it was soon reported that 'it seems to be in everybody's mouth that Leicester House is taking some turn that was not expected'[130] and adopting a line of conduct plainly at odds with the Princess's privately expressed desire to avoid a breach in the Royal Family.[131] By mid October, Horace Walpole wrote of 'A strong faction, professedly against the treaties, openly against Mr Fox, and covertly under the banners of...Lady Prudence'.[132]

Yet by the opening of the session, she had not made her opinion of the treaties publicly known.[133] Even stock issues like those of subsidy treaties and the threat of invasion, which both concerned MPs and could be used to stir passions without doors, had no necessary impact on parliamentary politics independent of the tactical context within which, and the party vehicles by which, they were given political significance. As Walpole wrote, ironically but with truth, 'we have got two new parties created, and if you imagine that the invasion is attended to, any more than as it is played off by both these parties, you know little of England'.[134] The scale of Leicester House's ambitions therefore became a matter of public speculation. Wilmot wrote as late as 24 October: 'I hear people conjecture differently about the views of Mr Pitt, who, 'tis said, has taken the lead at Leicester House; some think they extend no further than to defeat the foreign subsidies; others, that he is endeavouring to work up an opposition from Leicester House, as in the late Prince of Wales' time.[135] But this became apparent only relatively late. Not until 21 October did Fox observe that Pitt and Legge were in alliance, and Wilmot reported to Devonshire

that though Mr Legge's connection with Mr Pitt, with respect to the subsidies, is such as determines him to resign, in case Mr Pitt should be turned out, and he not, he has declared to me that he will not enter into a general opposition to the King's measures, if they are such as your Grace approves...[136]

Shortly afterwards, Fox recorded his new impressions of the junior Court:

Leicester House is as much in opposition as ever it was formerly. On Sunday I was there, and at no time did the late Prince of Wales lay his designs before his drawing room or mark them more strongly than she and her children did hers. Pitt is quite master, Egmont does not like it. Pitt acted, and was treated as the Minister there, as much as Sir R. Walpole in Q. Caroline's drawing room. I am sorry to say Legge had a prodigious share of distinction too, because it shows he is deeply engaged, and engaged in what your father will no more approve than you will. He was here this morning and did not deny that the opposition could not stop at the subsidies. I think he wonders at, and regrets his situation, but he will not know where to stop nor stop I think. It is a pretty time for the Royal Family to divide. And it is a pretty point too for any of them to hold out for discussion to the people, and yet there is as much industry used as in the Excise time or in 1744, to show the clog Hanover is upon England.[137]

As soon then became generally evident, the opposition was not levelled against the treaties alone. It was an opposition on the classic model which, as Hartington saw, 'considering the King's age will soon become very formidable'.[138] As a result, it seems that the consequent prospect of a civil war at court, 'where I should think true friends to their country and Prince should least wish it',[139] acted as a strong inducement to many to accommodate their opinions to those of the ministry at a time of national crisis. As Hartington urged his father, 'I am persuaded whatever you may think about subsidies, that you will not approve of that sort of work...'[140] Although the implications of Leicester House's activity were now plainly more far-reaching, the subsidies were of necessity the theme of their activities. Already Pitt was reported to be working to stir up a clamour in the City against them through his old associate, Glover.[141] It has often been assumed that the prospects for such a platform were excellent, and although there existed a residual and un-discriminating English antipathy, which could be exploited, to any form of continental involvement, two qualifications must be stressed. First, the Hessian and Russian treaties were consistent with the policy set out in the ministry's minute of 30 July: that is, to decline to participate on land in a general European war.[142] Second, whatever the susceptibilities of the mob, the sceptical resistance of the political class to issues of patriot rhetoric was at a high point. Horatio Walpole's first reaction to the Hessian treaty alone was a dispassionate and calculating approval.[143] Horace Walpole wrote in the same month that the King's negotiations proceeding in Germany were not likely to be so well received by Parliament 'as our French triumphs [by] the City, where nothing is so popular as the Duke of Newcastle'; Edward Walpole, announcing to Fox his reluctant decision to oppose the treaties from opinion, excused himself: 'I am...far from seeking an occasion to distinguish myself by a factious levelling spirit or from putting on the guise of virtue by that exploded trick of popular opposition to the government when embarrassed and under difficulties...'[144] Fox himself drew attention to past subsidies which the present malcontents had acquiesced in: the Hessians hired by Sir Robert Walpole 'on account of Ripperda's treaty with Vienna'; Granville's prodigality towards the continent, continued after his dismissal; the subsidies to Electors just granted in an attempt to secure the election of a King of the Romans.[145] He demanded rhetorically: 'can one, dear Sir, after all this, imagine that mere conscience dictates violent, and they say national opposition to subsidiary treaties entered into merely (and exclusively of all other German considerations) to prevent or resist any attack on HM's Electoral Dominions, if invaded, certainly invaded in a

British quarrel only[?]'[146] The obligation Fox pointed out was to prove at least as effective in its appeal as the opposition's stress on English self-interest narrowly conceived; and George Grenville, writing in August from a wet and wintry country retreat, was filled with equally gloomy anticipations of the opposition's prospects in town when the session came on.[147] Even Pitt apparently sold Legge to Leicester House as the most suitable Chancellor of the Exchequer in the *next* reign, implying that no parliamentary success was likely to depose Newcastle in George II's.[148] This pessimism probably lay behind the reported willingness of Pitt and Grenville not to oppose the Hessian treaty if the Russian were not brought before Parliament,[149] but the ministry did not respond to the overture. Coinciding with Lee's offer to make only a token, conscience-saving opposition to the Russian treaty, 'as it were pro forma', Newcastle was being promised, from a City source, that patriot rhetoric would count for little in the Commons:

Alderman Baker told me yesterday, that if Fox acted sincerely, he would risk his head, that we carried everything in the House of Commons, *two to one*. We are not (says Baker) now to be governed by speeches, that is over; 'All we want, is a man to lead us, and depend upon it we will follow'.[150]

Despite what in retrospect has seemed the predictable hostility of the Tories to subsidy treaties and continental military involvement, their course was not self-evident to the government before Parliament reassembled.[151] As in the previous session, the Tories were capable at the outset of showing a residual support for Newcastle's ministry: on 2 December, for example, when 'several of the old interest divided with the co[ur]t' over a prize bill.[152] Coming after the moves for Tory rapprochement with the Old Corps between the death of the Prince of Wales in 1751 and the spring of 1755, the autumn of that year saw no immediate co-operation between that party and opposition Whigs. As late as September, Pitt showed signs of being still a sardonic critic of the Tories;[153] the first distant contact between them seems to have come only at the end of that month, and initiated from the Tory side, not Pitt's.[154] Evidence of any subsequent liaison is not extant; and it is unlikely that any close co-operation between Tories and opposition Whigs took place in the session of 1755–6, even on an informal level. One problem in the way of an understanding of that kind was that although the orators – the Tories' 'new, or rather old (I know not what to call them) allies', as Blackstone put it – showed by their conduct in the Commons 'that continent measures may be thoroughly disliked, without any tincture of Jacobitism',[155] the invasion threat resurrected for the penultimate time the menace of a French landing aimed at overturning the Hanoverian succession. Sir Dudley Ryder recorded an opinion of Horace Walpole's which he omitted to include in his letters and memoirs:

Thinks if the French should conquer they would not make us a province of France for fear of the rest of Europe, which however would make them less solicitous about the rest of Europe. Thinks they will certainly proclaim the Pretender King of Scotland and continue King George King of England.[156]

Yet the political implications of the threat were no longer immediate and obvious. As the King joked to Lord Barrington, 'he was sure the Tories must like him better than the Pretender who if they used as they did him he would certainly hang them'.[157]

THE PARLIAMENTARY SESSION, NOVEMBER–DECEMBER 1755

In the weeks before the opening of the session on 13 November, the opposition was not greatly successful in collecting numbers from the back benches. 'I do not hear of more defections than of those consequential of those we know', wrote Ellis.[158] With Devonshire intending to remain in the country until 7 November,[159] there was lacking a disinterested figure of stature sufficient to give to the opposition the sort of *imprimatur* which Devonshire's son was to confer on Pitt's ministry of 1756–7. Fox was confident from an early stage of a decisive majority,[160] especially if Argyll played his expected part.[161] There attended at the pre-session gatherings 63 Lords and 289 Commons, which latter 'is by near 30, a greater number than ever met there before'. It included all Bedford's followers and Hartington's two brothers, 'the Duke of Devonshire disclaiming greatly using any influence over *their* opinions'. Devonshire himself was too ill to come to town. Fox presided at the Cockpit meeting; among those Whigs absenting themselves were Legge, Pitt and the Grenvilles.[162] In the Commons debate on 13th, in two divisions on leaving out of the Address expressions of a resolve to support the King's German dominions, the opposition were defeated by 311 to 105 and (some members then leaving) by 290 to 89. According to an initial report, among the 105 were some 76 Tories, 'so that the great men could avail themselves of no more than 30' Whigs.[163] A more careful count raised this to 37, but revealed the flaws in the opposition Whig front. As with the Irish 'Money Bill' of December 1753, the vast majority of the country gentlemen had remained loyal; opposition came from among the ministers.[164] Of the 37 only four were Scots,[165] and none adherents of Bedford and Devonshire.[166] Of the five earlier identified as Pitt's group, one declined to vote with the minority; so did one of Legge's party of four; and of twelve previously ascribed to the Prince of Wales, six were recorded as 'not against'.[167] Equally important was the corollary that only 68 Tories voted on the first day. Newdigate's observation confirms this: 'Many of the Country int[erest] are absent...'[168] Dudley Ryder added:

The Whigs were so great a majority the first day's debate that the present minority opposition from Pitt, the three Grenvilles, Dr Lee and Dr Hay, who are the principal opponents, cannot make of themselves 10 members exclusive of the Tories who don't love them.[169]

Although Northey and Dashwood spoke on the same side as Pitt's opposition,[170] this did not disguise the deep divisions between them which the greater part of a session of such coincidence was to do nothing to eliminate. Nor was Pitt's inner circle perfectly amicable, for his designation of Legge as his future Chancellor of the Exchequer without having consulted Grenville was, wrote the latter, 'so contrary to those repeated professions of his [Pitt's] wishes to see me at the head of the House of Commons, that it gave me a proof how little reason I had to depend upon them'.[171] Horace Walpole concluded:

The Duke of Newcastle thought himself undone, beat up all quarters for support, and finds himself stronger than ever. Mr Fox was thought so unpopular, that his support was thought as dangerous as want of defence; everything bows to him. The Tories hate both him and Pitt so much, that they sit still to see them worry one another: they don't seem to have yet found out that while there are parts and ambition, they will be obliged to follow and to hate by turns every man who has both.[172]

Although the subsidy issue deprived Newcastle of the support of such Tories as attended, it proved insufficient to ensure their attendance en bloc. What remained to be seen was whether Pitt or Bute would succeed in welding the disparate groups potentially sympathetic to them into an effective force.

The opposition's strength lay in the quality of its oratory: Pitt's and Grenville's performances were universally applauded. Yet the ministry showed its ability to rise to the occasion with an adequate response, often from unexpected sources. West ranked Murray's speech with the two others (Horace Walpole thought him better than Grenville)[173] and W. G. ('Single Speech') Hamilton chose this occasion for 'the very best performance I ever heard'.[174] Nor was Pitt's an unanswerable speech: Ellis called it 'an unequal performance, some parts very fine, others languid'.[175] The opposition, too, suffered a 'schism' over the arguments it deployed. Grenville admitted they spoke 'upon plans a little different'.[176] 'Lord Egmont spoke for the subsidies but against inserting the words in the Address for assisting His Majesty's dominions because he thought the measure would be looked upon by the people to be only for the sake of Hanover. Mr Dodington and Sir Francis Dashwood spoke against subsidies but for the words promising to assist Hanover.'[177] The weakness of Dodington's arguments patently 'betrayed his willingness to turn defendant'.[178]

In the Lords, Newcastle's victory was crushing. Temple launched an able tirade against the treaties[179] and Halifax, whom Cumberland had failed to persuade, also spoke against; but 'There was no division, and not above two or three negatives.'[180] Although Bedford reserved his position on the treaties, he spoke for the Address. Newcastle exulted in the majorities and looked on them as a vindication of his system. 'We must expect long days, but I think with these majorities we have nothing to fear. There were scarce ever fewer Whigs in the minority than in this last. Though there never were points more laboured than these were, and supported by very fine speeches.'[181]

On 14th, Fox received the Seals of Secretary of State, and was re-elected without opposition at New Windsor on 19th.[182] Newcastle then acted quickly and without consulting his new ally[183] to remove Pitt, Legge and George Grenville on 20th; they received their letters of dismissal the next day, 21st, and Sir George Lyttelton was given the Exchequer Seals at once. This was a daring move; and it had been far from clear what could be done with the malcontents. 'You will want to know,' Walpole had written, 'what is to be the fate of the ministry in opposition: but that I can't tell you. I don't believe they have determined what to do, more than oppose, nor that it is determined what to do with them.'[184] Until just before the event, Fox had known only of Newcastle's long-standing intention to dismiss Legge; Conway had hoped that even he might remain.[185] The example of the session of 1754-5 may have created a general assumption that Newcastle would rather tolerate a dissident than provoke him to irretrievable opposition by dismissing him from office.[186] But this had been an exceptional session, in which Newcastle had avoided disturbing a system held in balance by opposing tensions while he sought to frustrate the Pitt-Fox alliance without driving them into opposition together. Now that a choice between alternatives had been made, Newcastle reverted to the pattern of dismissals last demonstrated in Ireland in early 1754.

The immediate reaction of the dismissed supports the view that Newcastle was acting from strength. 'The Outs seem crestfallen and not to like their situation', wrote Hume Campbell.[187] Viscount Stormont observed that the opposition in the Commons

will not be near so considerable as was apprehended: it may and will be clamorous and virulent but cannot be formidable as it has neither numbers nor popularity to support it. The majority is greater than ever was known, and the popular cry strong in favour of the Ministry and against the leaders of the opposition, whose being turned out seems to have given general satisfaction.[188]

After their effort on the first day the opposition fell silent in face of the ministry's evident success in raising the supplies. The four shilling Land Tax passed 'without a single objection'.[189] With one exception, all now was to turn on the debate on the treaties in December. The exception was the personal aspect of the antagonism, which Newdigate characterised: 'W. Pitt and H. Fox single combat.'[190] On 21 November George Townshend challenged the expression in Fox's circular letters 'to have the conduct of the House of Commons', which Newcastle had thought merely tactless and high-handed,[191] as an affront to the constitution and the Commons.

But it must have been obvious that the opposition was attacking Fox's ambition to play the role which Legge, during the whole previous year, had demanded should be played in the Commons, and Fox escaped now with an excuse and an apology.

From being the ministry's hired orator, Pitt immediately became the opposition's. On 20 November his brother-in-law Temple offered him £1000 p.a. 'till better times'. He accepted at once,[192] and on 21st launched a full dress attack on 'the whole conduct of the administration during the whole summer, and the long neglect of our colonies preceeding that time which had bred this war...';[193] that the state was 'delivered up to His Majesty [on his return] more like the wreck of a state, than a great mighty kingdom, that this must come under a judicial consideration':[194] the first rehearsal of Pitt's later preoccupation. This time, it failed in its appeal. Fox, denying Pitt's charge that he had seized his present office, rightly reminded the House that he had remained quiet that summer until called for; and why, he retorted, if Pitt had been aware of the nation's decay since the peace of Aix-la-Chapelle, had he not protested against the neglect on the part of the ministry of which he had been a member? Pitt claimed to have been 'assassinated by the strokes of Court stilettos', misrepresented by an inner circle and excluded from the King's confidence. But the coincidence of this outlook with his dismissal the previous day robbed it of all credibility.[195] No division was forced.[196]

Fox and Murray did well. Murray made Pitt explain that he had not been offered to be Secretary of State which he would have insinuated and without explanation would have been believed. Murray also insisted that you had endeavoured to procure the assistance and support of everyone who supported your brother[197]

– that is, that the ministry represented the true Whig consensus. Fox, who 'cries up *Murray* to the stars',[198] was as satisfied as Newcastle with these first clashes,[199] of which the latter wrote: 'on the debate upon the fleet, Mr Fox and the Attorney General got a complete victory over Mr Pitt': Fox getting the better of the personal exchanges, and Murray answering 'with great spirit...pleased all our friends'.[200]

Although Pitt, Legge, Grenville and Elliot joined with the Tories in backing a 'bill for the encouragement of seamen' on 2 December, they mustered only 81 against the ministry's 211.[201] On 8 December, Fox wrote: 'We sit late every day and hear fine speeches, but seldom divide... Everything goes well in Parliament between [the] Duke of Newcastle and me.'[202] The crisis came two days later when Barrington moved to refer the treaties to the Committee of Supply. The same day, Temple moved a motion of censure on the treaties in the Lords with predictable results. Devonshire, from whom or from whose example something might have been hoped, had died on 5 December; and Bedford had been won over by the ministry. Horatio Walpole wrote of the second:

what has certainly contributed (as mankind is made) to the majority, is the most masterly stroke in domestic policy I ever knew, which is that the pride, disgust, and unrelenting animosity, as it was thought, of a great man who your poor father called Totty, against the chief minister, has been so far allayed and vanquished, by the admission of his friends into employment (himself as it were represented by my Lord G[ower] being made Privy Seal) that, he himself supported the treaties in the upper House, and all his friends and relatives have voted with the ministry in the lower...[203]

Chesterfield, too, supported the Russian 'as a prudent eventual measure at the beginning of a war, and probably preventive even of a war, in that part of the world; but I could not help exposing, though without opposing, the Hessian treaty...'[204] His was described as 'the finest speech that ever was made'.[205] One observer noted: 'The argument there was entirely on your side; and demonstration finds its way much sooner to that House than to the other.'[206] Hardwicke agreed. 'We had as great a day as ever I saw in the House of Lords...Our superiority in argument was as great as in numbers.'[207] Temple's motion of censure was rejected by 85 to 12; Egremont then tabled a motion approving of the treaties which passed without a division.

In the Commons, the debate turned on Potter's objection that the treaties were contrary to the Act of Settlement. Fox tried to avoid the debate and go straight into the Committee, though in vain. But he admitted that Hume Campbell '(gained, (between your Grace and me,) at much too dear a rate) signalised himself in an exceeding good speech',[208] only committing himself to the rash assertion 'that his ears and those of the House had been wearied and their attentions diverted from the great matters before them by perpetual invectives; that it was more becoming *men* to stand forth as accusers and to prove, if they failed they should be *punished* as calumniators, and that instances of this sort might be shown on the Journals'.[209] Then, recorded Fox,

Murray spoke admirably keeping closely to the point and unanswerably. Pitt fell on both, but used the latter with great respect. As to Hume Campbell's doctrine he treated it as tending to destroy all liberty of speech, privilege of the House, and fundamental security of the Constitution...[Pitt] lashed him ...with the most scurrilous as well as fine language I ever heard...believe me this went many bars' length beyond any abuse you ever heard. Hume Campbell hung down his head, did not even offer to get up, and left me to answer for him.[210] I then found the advantage of not having ever been in opposition[211]... I am told, I spoke as well as ever I did in my life, and, without any scurrility, hurt Mr Pitt I believe, exceedingly. I desired abuse might go on with impunity, after it had gone on for so many years together with impunity against the great Sir R. Walpole, and since that, against another great man. I neither saw nor foresaw a minister who could say, Sir R. Walpole might, but I must *not* be slandered with impunity...But the eyes of the people were opened by the repeated instances by which declaimers had shown them the real views and designs for which they made their declamation. I therefore wished him to go on, and assured him I heard his invectives with admiration and that they were an amusement, and in the present disposition of the people and their representatives, it must be the ministers' own faults if they felt any uneasiness from them. In the argument (which he is not good at) we had much the better of it.[212]

In some ways, Fox was the better House of Commons man; Pitt's strength was in harangue and the set oration, not in debating skill. West recorded Fox's closing remarks: 'that the House had been so much used to them from that quarter, that they had lost all force within those walls and even without and that the ministry had *sense* and *virtue* enough to look on them only as amusements for the day'.[213]

As before, Pitt's tendency to indulge in bitter personal attacks distracted attention from the main theme of his argument and rallied support to its victims. West noticed four men won over to the Ministry during the debate, including Oswald; Andrew Stone noticed two others, and observed that, as if at Pitt's virulence, the next two opposition speakers seemed abashed: 'It was observed, that Sir George Lee was much cooler in his manner, than he seemed on the first day of the sessions. Mr Legge spoke also, with moderation.'[214] Pitt's attack on Hume Campbell seemingly turned on accurate intelligence about the financial terms of the lawyer's deal with the ministry,[215] obviously an embarrassing disclosure, rather than on the terms of the subsidy treaties. Horace Walpole is, almost singly, responsible for the claim that Hume Campbell was 'annihilated';[216] Fox's smug account of how he rescued the ministry single handed does less than justice to the new recruit and gives more than due praise to his opponent. As late as 8th, Hume Campbell was boasting at dinner that Pitt was 'nothing but impudence and insolence'.[217] Neither West nor Stone, reporting privately to Newcastle, made anything of the lawyer's reaction to Pitt's attack on 10th; both praised the ability of Hume Campbell's speech, and Newcastle seems to have taken no notice of the episode in the negotiations surrounding the former's acceptance of the place of Lord Clerk Register. Stone concluded: 'Upon the whole it was a day of great success, and as great a superiority in argument, as numbers.'[218] The treaties were referred to the Committee of Supply by 318 to 126, Egmont and Sir John Cust from the junior Court voting with the majority. The opposition, as Fox's self-styled *commis* described it, 'consists of little more than [Pitt's] own family, the Grenvilles, 2 Townshends and the Tories'.[219]

The ministry's total was the highest it was to muster in that Parliament, and remarkable by the standards of the time. The Committee met on 12 December, and sat until 3 am the following morning.[220] The issue of the legality of the treaties had been decided; the debate proceeded on the expediency of them. It was 'tedious and bad', wrote Fox, with some abuse of Newcastle by the Townshends and of Fox himself by Pitt.[221] Charles Yorke thought that 'Mr Pitt spoke in a much lower tone last night, complained he was not well; made apology for invectives';[222] and lost the division by 289 to 121.[223] The Report from the Committee was debated in another late sitting of the House on Monday 15th. Horatio Walpole commented on two performances, the first, Murray's:

I am persuaded it carried conviction to the minds of all parties in the House, and Mr Pitt in answer to him, without the least invective (which has generally been the *forte* of his harangues) laid hold of every topic and with strength of imagination illustrated the various shapes by a flow of more than Ciceronian eloquence, gave such surprising and agreeable turns to what the Attorney had said, that although he did not make any real breach into the solidity of his argument, the great ingenuity, and art employed to efface the impression made by Mr Attorney, was entertained with great pleasure and applause by the whole audience; and indeed I believe they were the two most masterly performances in different kinds, that were ever heard or read before.[224]

Nevertheless, at the culmination of the opposition's efforts, the administration secured its defeat by 259 to 72.[225] The ministry's crushing majorities, and the falling off in the opposition's total, were widely regarded as final. Lord George Cavendish expected no more business of importance before Christmas.[226] Digby later confirmed this: 'We have had nothing in Parliament since worth speaking of and now we hear of nothing but the disposal of places.'[227] Attention has been distracted from the numerical success of the Newcastle–Fox system by the brilliance of the oratory deployed in opposition to it. Nevertheless, during these years, Pitt's rhetoric never won a single division in the Commons he is supposed to have dominated. Why did he fail so badly?

Several answers may be suggested. As has been noticed, the merits of the argument as well as an equal share of debating skill were held to lie with the ministry. Pitt's appeal, too, was often in acting as the conscience of the House, giving expression to what all had thought but could ne'er so well express. What mattered was that these aspirations about the constitution and the purity of public conduct should be loudly asserted, not that they should be acted upon, in order for them to be venerated. Horatio Walpole wrote:

although great parts, and power of words prevail more in the opposition, than I ever yet remember...the majority in the House, and I think a steady and willing majority has been in all questions relating to the measures greater than ever, and the boldest, and most musical eloquence, of the principal opposer, is heard with pleasure like *Mingotti's*[228] upon the stage, but after the opera is over, make no impression, and what has been said is entirely forgot; and indeed the opposition among the well-affected without doors is far from being popular, or the measures unpopular, a truly British cause being the foundation of them, under the government of a King who is personally adored...[229]

'All the methods possible are studied by the opposition to give trouble', wrote the Solicitor General. 'I find neither the House nor the people are at all moved by their abusive speeches in Parliament.'[230] This was not unusual: as Mann had predicted,

I see, and am glad of it too, that all is to be quiet, or what is almost the same thing, that the opposition in the House will probably have no effect out of it...[231]

Waldegrave noticed that the ill-humour of Leicester House did more good than harm to the ministerial majority; that 'the sober and conscientious part of the world' disapproved the fomenting of a schism in the Royal Family, and that others were deterred from action by the rumours concerning the Princess of Wales and Lord Bute.[232] In the face of these difficulties, it seems clear that a full-scale 'formed opposition' failed in fact to emerge under the auspices of Leicester House. There is evidence that the Princess regretted, by Christmas, the extent to which she had been associated with the disruption to date.[233] Ryder heard via one of his fellow judges, Henry Bathurst, from his father Lord Bathurst, a courtier at Leicester House, that 'the Princess of Wales stands neuter in these disputes, leaving her servants to do as they please'.[234] The prospects of those who had been dismissed from office were therefore poor, and were initially recognised, by informed observers, to be so. It was not a cause which large numbers of MPs were likely to join from a calculation of its probable success. William Warburton dined with Pitt and found that he 'appears very gay, very disengaged; yet, through all this, I think I can see the marks of a restless disappointed ambition'. Warburton added: 'I am much deceived in him if he had ever the least notion of friendship, but as the foundation of a political connexion.'[235] Nor was the leadership of the junior Court united. In January, Ryder observed that Sir George Lee, 'who finds himself much deceived in thinking he has the influence [? at Leicester House] and that he is the dupe of others, seems sick of his own conduct. (Has given one vote against the opposition, has stood away in some others.)'[236] Rather, the wrath of the malcontents was too obviously linked to their personal fortunes. George Townshend was thought to have joined the opposition, from an aversion to Cumberland, on Fox's promotion; in 1750 he had resigned his lieutenant-colonelcy after an electoral clash with the Duke and his Secretary at War. Charles Townshend was supposed to take the same side out of pique at not being made aide-de-camp to Ligonier. Pitt was known to have been offered cabinet rank that summer, and his refusal could only seem a bid for still greater power. Horatio Walpole recognised that 'opposition from resentment, or insatiable, and disappointed ambition, in doubtful times is not new, for that is the season to sow seeds, of false patriotism';[237] but those seeds made very little progress that autumn. The resolve of the ministry's waverers was, instead, stiffened by its successes in November and December. Nevertheless, critics of the Old Corps both among contemporaries and later historians have argued that place, and the prospect of place, was the cement of the bloc of 318.[238] Even Joseph Yorke imagined the opposition's numbers would rise 'when all the employments are filled up'.[239] The myth that the House of Commons could be 'bought' by cash payments from the secret service fund or that its behaviour was fully explained by the structure of borough patronage have long since been exploded.[240] More persistent has been the same myth in a slightly different form: that, in the absence of party cohesion, majorities could be cemented among MPs once elected by the distribution of places or pensions. The promotions organised in late December 1755 and January 1756 offer a test of this theory.

FURTHER PROMOTIONS, DECEMBER 1755 – JANUARY 1756

Newcastle was certain of Bedford's support, at the price of an employment for his brother-in-law Lord Gower, on 6 December.[241] The disposition of the other posts, though an intricate negotiation, was not fought over by Newcastle and Fox. Court offices were resolved peacefully. Arundell was bought off with an Irish pension,[242] freeing the post of Treasurer of the Chambers, eventually filled by Fox's friend, Lord Hillsborough; the latter's place of Comptroller of the Household went to Newcastle's nominee, Lord Hobart. Fox had offered his follower Ellis a choice of the Treasury or the Comptrollership;[243] and when the second place was out of the question (whether through Newcastle's action or Ellis's refusal is unclear) pressed hard for the first: 'Your being in the Treasury will justify me to the world.'[244] But Ellis firmly resisted the prospect of an office of business,[245] and Fox agreed to Newcastle's suggestion that Ellis take a third share in the Vice Treasurership of Ireland with a former incumbent, Cholmondeley, and one other. This eased the demands on the Treasury Board, so that Newcastle was able to secure a seat there for his follower O'Brien in place of Ellis.[246] Newcastle had apparently been willing to go so far as to have Dashwood at that Board, and although it seems that this was not made clear to Sir Francis[247] (Newcastle used Fox to offer him the Comptrollership or another important but unnamed post),[248] he refused any office from personal loyalty to the ex-Jacobite Earl of Westmorland. In place of Ellis and Charles Townshend at the Admiralty, therefore, were installed Lord Bateman and Richard Edgcumbe, both Foxites.

Newcastle's ingenuity was the key to another small round of removals. With the post of Cofferer still open, he suggested that a share in the Vice Treasurership of Ireland or the Treasurership of the Navy go to Dodington – in the face, as he knew, of the King's likely disapproval. But Dodington's acceptance of the latter place[249] in the room of George Grenville meant that the Duke of Leeds,[250] a Newcastle sympathiser, could then replace Sir George Lyttelton (the new Chancellor of the

Exchequer) as Cofferer, and Lord Sandys, a friend of Hardwicke's,[251] later replaced Leeds as Chief Justice in Eyre.[252] This succession, like the first, depended on Egmont's reaction to the place Newcastle felt obliged to offer him, the Irish Vice Treasurership; he 'absolutely refused, with some resentment at being so often asked'.[253]

Newcastle had already thought of Rigby for the Board of Trade before Fox suggested him,[254] for Newcastle was determined to confirm Bedford's good disposition. Gower, to that end, became Privy Seal; Marlborough, a Foxite, taking the vacant post of Master of the Ordnance.[255] It seems likely that it was a seat at the Board of Trade which William Sloper, one of Fox's five specified friends, refused for unknown reasons.[256] Newcastle then inserted his adherents Soame Jenyns and John Talbot, 'to your amazement and mine'.[257] Fox's follower W. G. Hamilton secured a seat there in January not through Fox's standing but after threats to join Pitt.[258] The third new man at the Treasury Board, after Dashwood's refusal, was Fox's: Henry Furnese, of whom Walpole spoke contemptuously as 'that old rag of a dishclout ministry';[259] 'Lord Sandys and Harry Furnese, two of the most ridiculous objects in the succession to my father's ministry, again dragged out upon the stage...'[260] Furnese and O'Brien replaced Lords Darlington and Dupplin (Newcastle's friends), who now shared Pitt's office: 'George Selwyn says, that no act ever showed so much the Duke of Newcastle's absolute power as his being able to make Lord Darlington *a Paymaster*.'[261]

Egmont's refusal allowed the conclusion of two circles of removals which depended on him.[262] Newcastle presented the final scheme in the Closet on 18 December.[263] There was one difficulty: Sandys objected to taking a third share of the Irish Vice Treasurership and was afterwards given the office surrendered by Leeds. Sandwich's inclusion with Ellis and Cholmondeley was, then, a last-minute concession by Newcastle, not a premeditated Fox victory.[264] There Fox's gains stopped, for he was unable to secure another place at the Admiralty Board for a Commons spokesman.[265] It seems that Dodington and Furnese were acting together, but Dodington's failure also to involve Dashwood[266] meant that Fox's recruits lacked something in prestige. Walpole spoke of 'that so often *repatrioted* and *reprostituted* prostitute Dodington'[267] and summed up the whole: 'many of the new recruits, old deserters, old cashiered, old faggots, add very little credit to the new coalition!'[268]

It was recognised that the promotions were of 'silent voters', as well as speakers in Parliament;[269] and if the mediocrity of the recruits weakened Fox's hand against Newcastle, the latter gained two things. The first was inclusiveness, the air of authority and solidity lent to a ministry by the assent of a range of different groups. As Devonshire put it, 'the bottom seems so wide that for the present there can be no apprehensions and the majority must continue very large'.[270] Second, the opposition was denied a chance to procure a base that would confer this credibility on a patriot stance which had so obviously lacked it. There were signs that Leicester House was less willing for its name to be used to sanction acts of opposition (although relations between the two courts were frigid, they were still formally correct); and with the opposition's totals in divisions falling, Chesterfield admitted himself unable to account for the junior Court's conduct or to explain how it could be in their interest to quarrel with St James's.[271]

Fox recognised that both his and Newcastle's friends were dissatisfied with the result, and reasoned that the distribution of offices therefore represented a fair compromise.[272] The extent to which the balance was changed in Fox's favour can be exaggerated. Chesterfield predicted that power was about to fall into Fox's hands,[273] but had been repeating this prediction at least since the spring of 1754. Of those now coming into, rather than simply exchanging office, nine might be counted sympathetic to Fox and seven to Newcastle.[274] But in many respects the distribution of power within the ministry was unaltered. Fox scarcely treated Dodington as an ally; thought the Attorney General had played a bigger part in his recruitment; and recognised that Dodington had made no friends to protect him from dismissal on 'the least inclination to false play'.[275] The arrival of Furnese at the Treasury Board did not outweigh Legge's deparure. The transfer of Edgcumbe offset Rigby's seat at the Board of Trade, and Fox's net gain of one on Hamilton's arrival did not upset the balance in Newcastle's favour. Fox gained one, also, on the Admiralty Board: but there matters were settled not by majority vote but at the discretion of the First Lord, Anson.

If the arrangement did not represent Fox's success in storming the Closet, neither was it an attempt to buy back the waverers of the Old Corps. The list of those Whigs who voted against the Address on 13 November[276] contains the names of nine men elected with the ministry's or Newcastle's personal backing and whose support had been expected.[277] None now received office or pension. Of four opposition Whigs, apparently unconnected with the major blocs,[278] only one – Dashwood – was approached, and he only as a result of the ministry's overtures to Dodington. Furnese, and Dodington himself, were bought from an opposition already overt, and W. G. Hamilton from an opposition which he threatened. George Colebrooke was in the process of joining his brothers Robert and James in their support of Newcastle and was not given an office in order to encourage him to do so. With the exception of Dodington and his ally, no other places were on offer to the blocs (identified as the Prince of Wales's, Pitt's, Legge's and Dodington's) in the list of 13 November; and with the exceptions of these two, few men's votes were given in the Commons for the rest of the session otherwise than as they had been given until the Christmas recess. In the absence of division lists, the small numbers voting for the opposition in the spring of 1756 suggest that the nine erring members of the Old Corps returned to their allegiance. The lack of comment on Whig disloyalty by Andrew Stone, West or Dupplin lends support to this view; and Newcastle saw no likelihood of his majority decreasing.[279] Just as the Tory vote this session was apt to divide on each side of a motion according to the dictates of conscience, but with an underlying tendency to vote against the court; so any members of the Old Corps voting against the ministry were indulging a temporary, local inclination on particular issues. No pattern of disloyalty is apparent.

THE PARLIAMENTARY SESSION, JANUARY–MARCH 1756

The session from Christmas until the end of March is of interest for Newcastle's handling of the implications of Fox's new prominence, and for the confrontation between the opposition and the new ministerial team in the Commons. Fox's success in the Commons before Christmas had strengthened anticipations that he would win the current round with Newcastle, and, ingratiating himself with the King, 'probably fix his ministry for the remainder of the reign'.[280] As yet, however, relations between Newcastle and Fox were idyllic,[281] and an unnatural calm prevailed in the political world:

the opposition, like schoolboys, don't know how to settle [to] their books again after the holidays. We have not had a division; nay, not a debate. Those that like it, are amusing themselves with the Appleby election. Now and then we draggle on a little militia. The recess has not produced even a pamphlet. In short, there are none but great outlines of politics...[282]

Even Legge predicted that the session would be a short one once the Appleby election was compromised: 'The supplies I hear will be closed in a few days and the Ways and Means communicated to the House. When that is over I don't see any public business that is likely to detain us long and I don't imagine we shall be kept together longer than is necessary for the mere love of our pretty company.'[283] Evidently, the opposition had difficulty in discovering an issue to serve as a focus. The opportunity of Appleby was missed, despite Fox's awareness that his personal influence could not carry it in the Commons for the Lowther interest and despite also the concurrence of the Tories and Scotch against him.[284] The indifference with which the ministry regarded the early stages of George Townshend's Militia Bill (backed though it was on 21 January by Pitt) indicates that it was not promoted, or regarded, as a party point.[285] The question of the treaties was no longer available: the conclusion of the Russian treaty, far from throwing Prussia into the arms of France as had been warned in the debates before Christmas,[286] swiftly induced Prussia to conclude an alliance with Britain. The ministry's policy was triumphantly vindicated, and they exulted accordingly.[287]

Horatio Walpole even claimed that 'the subsidiary treaties as they have now been contracted are extremely popular in the nation, and the opponents unpopular',[288] while Fox wrote privately of the Prussian treaty as preventive of more subsidy demands from Germany.[289]

The occasions of opposition seem rather to have been those on which Pitt had an opportunity for a personal contest with Fox. The first arose on 23 January when Fox defended Admiral Knowles from Beckford's charges of maladministration in Jamaica (of which an enquiry later cleared him).[290] The same day, Sir George Lyttelton opened the Budget in the Committee of Ways and Means. Few men's ability has been so belittled by an aside as Lyttelton's by Horace Walpole's that he was 'strangely bewildered in the figures; he stumbled over millions, and dwelt pompously upon farthings'.[291] In fact, the honours lay rather more with the ministry. Newcastle and Dupplin were wildly enthusiastic about Sir George's able and creditable performance;[292] even Walpole, at the time, allowed that the new Chancellor performed 'well enough in general' and, in reply to Pitt, 'kept up his spirit, and returned the attack on [his] eloquence'.[293] Lord George Cavendish thought the Budget debate simply dull (nothing at all was said on the Report from the Committee):[294]

P[itt] less fine I think than ever I heard him and in my judgment...he quite mistakes his own game. Mr Chancellor of [the] Exchequer did not make a shining figure and to say the truth he had not the part quite perfect, though I heard several people say and compliment him upon it as the finest performance that ever was made upon such an occasion but though he did not make so good an opening as was generally expected, where it was least expected he did well in answer to Mr Pitt but destroyed it all immediately by complimenting that gentleman in return for very rough handling that he gave him in reply and saying how well he knew and [illegible] the virtuous pride of his heart and how great concern he was under that he was not in employment and so forth and was to the full as lavish in that way as t'other had been in the contrary nor was it made less strong by Mr Fox's getting up to say how glad he was that it had ended so amicably...[295]

It was widely acknowledged that the government had secured far more favourable terms for its loans than could have been expected at a time of crisis; and necessity must have reconciled many to the expedient of using the Sinking Fund as collateral for those loans until the taxes which were to yield the interest charges had been voted.[296] The opposition's showing in the division on 30 January was remarkably poor: 56 to the ministry's 231.[297] Those numbers scarcely revived in the following month. Walpole observed that 'the opposition cavil, but are not strong enough to be said to oppose',[298] and concluded from the Budget that the opposition 'is nibbling, but is not popular, nor have yet got hold of any clue of consequence. There is not the vivacity that broke forth before the holidays.'[299]

The opposition's second attempt to find a 'clue' was George Grenville's motion of 26 January condemning as unconstitutional the warrant to share among three men the office of Vice Treasurer of Ireland. Newcastle apprehended 'as great a point of opposition, as they will bring before us this session';[300] he thought it was aimed at the late rearrangement of offices in general and, personally, at the Treasury.[301] In the House, Murray stressed in reply the dangerous precedent of the Commons' assuming a right to determine the legal interpretation of an Act of Parliament: the clause in the Act of Settlement under which the division of the office was challenged. 'Mr Pitt took a world of pains with his overflowing and overbearing eloquence, to animate the House in support of their rights and privileges' and inveighed, as Grenville had done, against what he condemned as the attempts made that session to erode other provisions of that Act. Fox replied, defending Murray's position and rebutting Pitt's charges 'with a manliness of spirit, and force of argument, in justification of the majority of the House that I scarce ever heard before'. The Commons, obviously alienated by Pitt's diatribe, agreed without a division to Ellis's suggestion to call for more information from the Irish records. Another exchange between Fox and Pitt the same day on the use of foreign Protestants as officers in America drew down a rebuke on Pitt from Speaker Onslow.[302]

On 28th, in the Committee of Supply on a grant of £115,000 for America, Pitt launched a still more wild and inflammatory attack on Fox:

he said I talked gibberish, had moved the money perhaps in order to get sham receipts from the Colonies, and let the money be sunk in some corrupt, avaricious etc., corner of the court, and he believed there was such an intention; then he arraigned all that had been done this session, defied *the gentleman and his House of Commons*, and said the ministers clashed in everything else, and hated one another, but united only in a formed design to subvert the constitution, etc., etc., etc.[303]

Pitt had gone too far, for the allegation was groundless and the insult general to all MPs; his speech was not well received. Fox answered

in support of the majority of the House, and [was] heard with great applause and satisfaction, excepting a few, a very few indeed, by the whole House, and he gained as much, as Pitt lost, reputation and credit, by this altercation between them; and that is saying a great deal. The debate was almost entirely between these two only; and indeed as it was in a Committee where anybody may speak as often as they please, there was not room, as they immediately rose upon another like two game cocks, where I believe everybody acknowledges that Pitt gave the most strokes, and that Fox carried the best heels.[304]

Fox taunted the opposition that Pitt's attacks were conferring credit on him, Fox, and casting an aspersion not on the ministry but on the Commons as a whole – on the actions of 'a more memorable majority in the first instance than had ever appeared on their Journals'.[305] Pitt lost his self-control: 'He and Grenville were like men beside themselves, lost in passion'; only Dupplin's calling them to order prevented still fiercer exchanges. Fox wrote that Pitt

has, the four last times he has spoke, made such violent speeches (not good ones in their kind) upon such trifling matter, which I have been obliged to take such advantage of, that he is lowered and I am raised by it beyond what his enemies or my warmest friends could have wished...the Speaker (not apt to be explicit) says I had a complete conquest, and that if Mr Pitt goes on as he has done these three last days, and does not provide better matter to make his fine speeches upon, he will soon grow as insignificant as any man who ever sat in that House.[306]

During February the opposition contested, time after time, the bill to allow foreign Protestants to serve as army officers in America; but their showing was poor.[307] Though the exercise may have been intended to cement the Tories to Pitt and the Grenvilles, the small turnouts are evidence of the lukewarmness with which the Tory party greeted the issue. Little public interest was aroused. Attention focused, for the moment, on the menacing aspect of foreign affairs.[308] The opposition appeared depressed by their desperately small following in divisions,[309] and Pitt, whose ill health may have been psychosomatically as well as tactically and disingenuously related to his political fortunes, was reported to be unwell and about to leave for Bath.[310] After clashes with Fox on 10 February on the Foreign Protestants Bill, and again on 23rd on its second reading,[311] Pitt partly withdrew from the Commons, and his few appearances in the House during the rest of the session were ineffective.[312] The exposure of Pitt's inconsistencies, argued one pamphleteer, was the reason for his silence there.[313]

But the Commons' business was unexpectedly prolonged. The House did not rise till 27 May, and the course of events was not altogether smooth. Of Lyttelton's proposed new taxes on cards, bricks and plate, put forward on 25 February, the first passed uncontentiously; the second met with widespread, reasoned opposition and was dropped after the committee stage.[314] The third was persisted in by the ministry and after a display of financial ignorance in the House to which Legge was the only exception,[315] the tide of back bench sentiment swung against the Bill so that, on an accidental division[316] on 17 March, the motion to proceed to the second reading was carried by only 129 to 120.[317] Fox blamed it on Lyttelton's irresolution[318] and set about to reassert Old Corps discipline. Newcastle blamed it on Legge's example.[319] But it is noticeable that although City moneyed men were among the ministry's deserters in this division,[320] and although the Common Council petitioned the Commons against an extension of the excise laws such as would be used to collect the new tax, the opposition made no particular effort to harness this new source of possible support; and it immediately evaporated. An attempt to interpret the Act of 10. Will. III c.1 limiting the numbers of the standing army as an Act still in force rather than applying to a single situation only came to nothing on 12th.[321] Nor was the alignment generated by the Linnen Bill exploited, for it passed its third reading by 154 to 71 on 16 March with 'the Members in the City, some of the Yorkshire gentlemen and most of the Tories'[322] in the minority; and Pitt in the majority, vocal in his support of Scottish commerce. In return for Newcastle's help, Argyll canvassed against the 'very unaccountable' opposition to the Plate Bill,[323] and with the Bedfords' backing[324] secured its second reading, shorn of its most unpopular features, by 245 to 142 on 22 March. Despite what West called 'A great attendance of the Tories', Pitt was not present.[325]

In the aftermath of Fox's recruitment it had been the ministry which had succeeded in capturing, or denying to Pitt, Fox's powerful friends – Bedford, Devonshire and Argyll especially. The opposition was thereby much weakened. Newcastle had persisted in his approaches to Egmont and Lee, but without effect: the subsidies issue and Fox's promotion prevented them from accepting office. Their power within Leicester House now crumbled with the end of that tactical option, not because Pitt and Bute were able to offer an immediate alliance with the Tories. By late October, it seemed clear that the junior Court had embarked on a full-scale opposition; but Bute's interest within Leicester House was not markedly successful in collecting recruits. The ministry's victories over the subsidy treaties were crushing in both Houses. The dismissal of Pitt, Legge and the Grenvilles left them in a weak position; Fox and Murray, too, showed considerable ability in dealing with the orators' assaults in the Commons. The opposition's conduct, after Fox's promotion, highlighted Fox's role as Pitt's antagonist; the possibility that Fox would use his position within the ministry as a springboard for a further campaign against Newcastle was, for the moment, postponed.

Apart from a miscalculation of feeling over the Plate Bill, the ministry had never been seriously imperilled. Leicester House patriotism had failed not only in divisions but in the discrediting (as contemporaries supposed) of its strictures on the Hesse Cassel and Russian treaties by the conclusion of the alliance with Prussia. Consequently, the ministry had not been given any incentive for a deal with the leaders of the opposition either individually or *en bloc*. By the end of March, Legge supposed that the situation into which 'the contrivance of enemies, the acquiescence of friends, and the universal appetite of mankind to seize for themselves, have thrust me' was 'probably...a desperate one' if his ambition were ever again to hold office. Neither he nor Pitt could now profess more than they did: a responsible contribution to constructive opposition, eschewing anything virulent, personal, factious, frivolous or vexatious.[326] Leicester House in 1755–6 is thus the only example in England or Ireland during the 1740s or 1750s of a patriot opposition

silenced not only by the tactical successes of ministerial manoeuvres but
also by the bankruptcy and exhaustion, as it seemed to its participants,
of the classic cries of patriot rhetoric. Horace Walpole had noticed the
same emptiness and sterility in the arguments deployed in the debate
on the army on 27 November 1754;[327] the opposition's failure in early
1756 is analogous. J. R. Western's observation[328] on the 'infuriatingly
repetitive and backward looking character' of the militia debates is
particularly appropriate to Townshend's bill of 1755–6, the early stages
of which evoked massive and almost unanimous indifference at Westminister. One Foxite pamphleteer confessed that autumn:

I can hardly account for that feebleness of spirit, with which our present Patriot
forms his opposition to the measures of the court. All the *technical terms* of
bribery and corruption, subsidies, national debts, places, pensions and standing
armies, are still remaining in our language. Have they lost their original meaning?
or are they fairly worn out, (the common fate of other words) by being used
upon every too light and trivial occasion? Or have they lost their importance and
dignity, by being prostituted to serve bad purposes of personal resentment, envy,
or ambition? Why does our orator [Pitt] in vain pronounce them with his usual
declamatory tone? Why is the solemn asservation no longer believed? Why the
vehemence of his action no longer alarming...[?][329]

The answer, he suggested, was that Pitt had forfeited credibility by his
conversion to support those measures, including Hanoverian measures,
which he had opposed as a member of the opposition until bought off
from it by the Paymastership in 1746. Other writers drew the same lesson;
one declared:

...were I to see another gentleman an advocate for every connection with the
continent, that can engage us as principals in a war there; should the same
gentleman, after a long series of inconsistent conduct, which was visibly
influenced, not by any conjuncture of affairs abroad, but by the situation of the
Ministry at home, all at once adopt the principle, that our connection with the
continent, even in the smallest degree, is ruinous to Great Britain, I own I
should be uncharitable enough, to put a very indifferent construction upon the
motives of such a gentleman's opposition.[330]

More damning still was a contrast and analogy with Ireland: January
1756 saw the apostasy of the Irish leaders,[331] when tactical defeat followed by the acceptance of place, pension and peerage silenced the most
prestigious and vocal patriot opposition England or Ireland had seen
since that which had secured the fall of Sir Robert Walpole, and when
the Lord Lieutenant was able to report that 'all the Country Gentlemen
declare they have done with Parties and will belong to Government for
the future'[332] – a 'complete victory and triumph' which Newcastle
imagined Devonshire had won, not merely over the Patriot party in the
Dublin Commons, but over 'patriotism' itself.[333]

5

The Resignation of Newcastle, April–October 1756

Every man who pretends to be Minister in this country, *is a fool*, if he acts a day without the House of Commons; and a greater fool, if he depends upon any, of whom he cannot be sure...

> Newcastle to Murray, 30 May 1756:
> 32865, f.143.

...though nothing can be done without it, the word majority alone will not always settle the tranquillity of the nation.

> Herring to Hardwicke, 23 October 1756:
> 35599, f.334.

One of the chief causes of this unfortunate situation is, that we have now in truth no Minister; but the administration is a mere Republic, and carried on by the Cabinet Council, the individuals of which think only how to get the better of each other.

> Chesterfield to Dayrolles, 17 June 1756:
> Dobrée, v, 2191.

What will come out of all this, I am at a loss to know. The King and the public will suffer in parliamentary confusion, from causes, which I have never thoroughly understood...It is the wicked nonsense of faction for power, and lucrative employments, which will disable government from acting, according to the true sense and for the true ends of government... [will] destroy or intimidate the best administrations in this perverse or corrupt country.

> Charles Yorke to Royston, 17 October 1756:
> 35360, f.254.

Rear-Admiral Byng sailed on 6 April with a squadron of ten ships of the line for the defence of Minorca. A French invasion force landed there on 18 April and besieged the garrison in Fort St Philip. Byng made a slow passage, reaching Gibraltar only on 2 May; on 20th, he engaged the French fleet off Minorca and after an indecisive action returned to Gibraltar. The garrison of St Philip's surrendered on 28 June. Hawke had already been sent to supersede Byng, who arrived back at Spithead under arrest on 26 July. His court martial met on 28 December, and delivered its verdict on 27 January 1757. After the failure of moves on his behalf, he was shot on 14 March. The political expedients of these months therefore took place against the background of a public outcry, a continuing debate about the merits of the government's naval strategy, and a contest over the division of responsibility for it among the ministers themselves.

It has been assumed that the events which led Newcastle to resign in October 1756 illustrate the power of an opposition based on Leicester House; that 'Pitt, with the support of the heir apparent, overturned the Newcastle government'.[1] That assumption once established, historians cast about to discover the means by which the opposition must have produced so dramatic an effect. That misconception had two main results. First, the weakness of the parliamentary oppositions of 1754–5 and 1755–6 was overlooked, and the ministerial events of those years explained, on the contrary, as agitated concessions to parliamentary attacks. Second, Newcastle's fall was described in the light of his alleged character and of the presumed pressure of public opinion: the scale of popular unrest, comparable in the mid eighteenth century only with the Excise crisis and the affair of Wilkes, has seemed fully sufficient to explain a failure of nerve in a man whose personality is commonly held up to ridicule. A typical claim was voiced by C. S. Emden: 'In 1756 Newcastle, and in 1763 Bute, resigned, chiefly it may be presumed, because they were unable to face the clamour of the people' both directly and, in Newcastle's case, through the prospect of desertion in the Commons of MPs moved by similar motives and by Pitt's patriot oratory.[2] Among more recent scholars, Dr Langford cast doubt on the genuineness and spontaneity of the 'rain of gold boxes' which followed Pitt's dismissal in April 1757 and preceded his return to office in July, and wrote of his 'strong suspicion' that many of the addresses and instructions of 1756, too, were rigged by Pitt's followers and the Tories. Yet he maintained that, however fraudulent, 'these pressures... transformed the political situation', played 'a critical part' in Pitt's return to office in July 1757, and 'an important part in the destruction of the Newcastle Administration' in November 1756.[3] Dame Lucy Sutherland wrote similarly that Newcastle's government 'fell before an upsurge of public indignation', though arguing also that 'it is necessary neither to antedate Pitt's reputation nor to exaggerate its importance. It was only in the five months leading up to his entry into power on the crest of a wave of popular support that the influence of this public opinion became a decisive factor in determining the conduct of politicians...'[4] While the qualification is a wise and necessary one, the account offered here does not establish the importance of that influence even for the five months up to November.

Yet knowledge of the way in which fear of public opinion or of mob violence played its part in Newcastle's plans and motives has progressed little beyond Emden's vague and slipshod assumptions about what must have been the case.[5] No solution has hitherto been found to the problem of how such extra-parliamentary phenomena were viewed and dealt with by the small circle of politicians whose co-operation was the first condition of a ministry's success. It will here be shown that while public unrest explains much of Newcastle's anxiety during the summer of 1756, it was far less important in Newcastle's mind by October; that it was not a principal cause of his resignation, but was deployed politically by others in such a way as not to realise its potential tactical effectiveness against the ministers; and that it was a reflection of the circumstances which led Newcastle to resign rather than the form taken by those circumstances themselves. Waldegrave recorded indecisively that it was the loss of Minorca which was 'the principal cause of that popular discontent and clamour which overturned the administration; or rather occasioned the panic, which obliged our ministers to abdicate'.[6] This chapter resolves the confusions about the role of 'popular politics' which underlay Waldegrave's uncertainty by an account of the negotiations, largely unknown to the public, which in fact determined the relations of the rival forces. Although his principal assertion that 'The summer of 1756 was the triumph of faction and of party violence'[7] should be preferred, it, too, must be modified in the light of a correct appreciation of the party-political courses open to Newcastle, Fox, Pitt, Bute and others during a parliamentary vacation in which most of the tactical possibilities were attempted and found unattainable.

THE COMMONS, APRIL–MAY 1756

Quite absent from the political world in April was that mood of enthusiastic participation in national regeneration often associated with Pitt's later periods in office. Egmont confessed:

In this sad state of things and men – whom with respect to the first all our interests seem to be irrevocably shattered, and with respect to the latter I am unable perfectly to understand what any of them mean, and less able in my judgement to act with any of them in these things that I know they do mean – I have for the present set up my rest in the innocent satisfaction of a private life...[8]

Pitt might have said as much; his attacks on the ministry's conduct of the war did not begin in earnest until 7 May. Even the Militia Bill enjoyed, as yet, an uncontentious passage through what Horace Walpole called 'that solitude',[9] the Commons. It owed its smooth progress not least to being 'a very popular, and plausible object among those who are best affected to this government.'[10] Support for a militia was still widely interpreted, Newcastle realised, as zeal for the administration.[11] Yet in private, he, Chesterfield and Devonshire shared the same principled objections: that it was as dangerous to constitutional liberties as a standing army;[12] that it was expensive, would increase the power of the crown, would distract the attention of the people from industry and agriculture, and 'would breed up our people to a love of arms, and military government...would tend more to make this a military country, and government, than any scheme I have yet heard of'.[13] Those fears were not made public: Newcastle allowed the Bill to pass the Commons (with the intention of killing it in the Lords)[14] in order to persuade the lower House to approve the employment in England of German mercenaries. The Whigs[15] chosen to speak for them, on the other hand, recommended German troops as a temporary expedient only until 'a more natural, and national defence', the militia, was ready.[16] Yet the approval of that expedient was the occasion for some self-satisfaction in ministerial circles, where it was supposed that French invasion plans had relied on the impossibility of carrying the Hessians and Hanoverians in Parliament.[17]

This plan was successful not least because the Tories did not regard the Militia Bill as a simple alternative to the use of mercenaries. Although a few of that party were engaged in the conduct of the Bill, wrote Horatio Walpole, in general they 'do not approve it extremely':[18] a Militia Bill still seemed (as it was later still more strongly to seem in the localities) almost a ministerial measure, and the Tories were disposed to share fears of military government. Only later did the Bill's rejection give scope for the contrary accusations against the ministry of arbitrary designs on the constitution through an inflated standing army and by preventing the emergence of a popular, constitutional force which could be a check on it.[19] But as late as 5 May, Bayntun Rolt discovered in the Commons that the Tories were 'not inclined to the Militia Bill though obliged to support it': an observation which Tory MP Edward Kynaston confirmed.[20] That so few of either party were present in the Commons during the militia debates suggests that the Tories were as willing as the ministry that the Bill should be killed in the Lords.

Parliament had been notified on 23 March that a requisition of troops had been made under the terms of the subsidy treaty with Hesse. Then, Fox and Murray had spoken for the measure; Bedford and Cumberland had lent their support,[21] and an Address of Thanks was returned by the Commons *nem. con.*[22] On 29 March, Lord George Sackville moved an Address to the King to send for Hanoverian troops.[23] Despite opposition Whig weakness, such issues could be relied on to incur Tory dissent. The question was its organisation and strength. Pitt had been

in the country with a swelled face, which it was thought he would gladly avail himself of to avoid that debate: but Lord Temple went down and hauled him to the House with blisters behind his ears and flannel over his cheeks. The Tories, his Lordship told him, were all to be gained by it. Sir Richard [Lyttelton] had made a great dinner for them, and this would confirm the treaty of alliance. But he was scarce seconded by any of them in the House of Commons;[24] and when the question came into the House of Peers every Tory Lord, to a man, stayed away. Lord Temple maintained the debate almost single.[25]

No clearer gesture of the Tories' deep suspicion of, and hostility towards, opposition Whig Patriots could have been offered. Pitt could only continue to claim, as opposition Whigs had done since the 1730s at least, that party was dead;[26] but this was neither obviously true nor an invariably successful formula for the co-operation of opposition groups.

Pitt made a two-hour speech but was reported 'quite cut down' by Sackville's reply.[27] 'The administration all sat still and would say nothing, pretending it the motion of a private member, not their motion'.[28] In the Commons, the Address was voted *nem. con.* after Northey's motion for the Orders of the Day was lost by 259 to 92. A motion to adjourn at 10.30 p.m. was lost by 88 to 187. The third reading of the Plate Bill was then taken, whereupon 'all the minority left the House'.[29] In the Lords, Temple's patriot pretensions were treated, too, with unexpected roughness by Winchelsea. National security was full justification for an emergency measure taken under threat of invasion; the situation offered no scope for Tory action, and Sir George Lyttelton predicted that even the Prince of Wales would soon be alienated by the Grenvilles' irresponsibility: 'all their politics are of a piece, taken up in a heat, or founded on false and groundless presumptions...'[30] Even Pitt admitted that the King could have sent for the Hanoverians without a parliamentary address for that purpose.

The future success of opposition was unsuspected in April, for reasons already outlined. Pitt spent most of his time at Wickham, 'except on busy Parliament days'.[31] He and the Grenvilles were not involved in the preoccupation of the moment, Bedford's Road Bill, a trivial issue which occupied an inordinate amount of Commons time and in which purely personal rivalries aligned Fox, Rigby and Bedford with much of the Cabinet against Grafton, Newcastle, Argyll, the Scotch, and the Bishops.[32] Horace Walpole hinted at Fox's ambition as 'the engine behind the curtain'; but with Newcastle inclining to the loyal Grafton, Bedford's defeat was not long in doubt,[33] and the possible implications of such an alignment of forces were never worked out.

The estimate for the Hanoverians was voted in the Commons on 7 May, after 'the ministry' had carefully absented themselves from the Report stage of the Militia Bill on the night of 5th[34] – partly, perhaps, in apprehension after news of the French landing on Minorca.[35] As fears for Port Mahon grew, apprehensions at Westminster that the real French objective was an invasion of England came from mid May to seem illusory.[36] Nevertheless, that danger and the alarm without doors were still presumably sufficient to induce Pitt to speak *for* the Hanoverian troops in the Committee of Supply on 7th and 12th.[37] This he compounded for by an attack on Newcastle, on the ministry's naval strategy, and on its alleged desire to launch a continental war. Fox excused himself for an inadequate reply – '*the loss of Minorca is a weight that it is not easy to debate under*'.[38] But the Commons was not impressed by

Pitt's onslaught, the timing of which, at least, was probably dictated by opportunist considerations. On the following day, there was 'not a good word said' when the Committee's Report was received;[39] less than fifty members were in the House, and West reassured Newcastle that 'People in general think Mr Pitt took a very improper opportunity for making his harangue and the City are very sanguine about Minorca...'[40] Hardwicke agreed: Pitt's charge that the ministry deliberately intended to lose the island, that Minorca had been sold to the French, was wild and absurd: 'It was scouted and ridiculed by everybody'.[41] It was not this or the City's attitude which worried Newcastle, therefore, but the personal nature of Pitt's attack on him in the light of the evidence of Fox's self-seeking: 'I see plainly where Mr Fox would lay all the blame, viz. the not augmenting our force at home, when he, in *opposition* and conjunction with Mr Pitt, pretended it should have been done'.[42] Newcastle's feelings were ones of anger and impatience. No fears were yet apparent of the collapse of his system: rather, Newcastle contemplated (without finding) some form of disciplinary action against the erring Sackville and Fox. It was no coincidence that rumours began to circulate of Fox's expulsion from the ministry,[43] and it was from early summer, antedating the public outcry over Minorca, that Newcastle's sympathisers, too, first and principally feared the ruin of his system from rivalries within it.[44]

Whatever the intentions of its sponsors, it seems likely that although the Militia Bill itself was uncontentious in party terms, the ministry's rejection of it would have been. Sir George Lyttelton therefore smoothed its path once again in order to secure the application of the produce of the Sinking Fund to the supply of the year.[45] Then, on 12th, he 'bore the brunt of the day'[46] in moving for £1 million on account for war supplies. In the absence of news from Minorca, however, the opposition lacked specific grounds for criticism. Northey hinted at an enquiry into the misapplication of funds but admitted his reluctance to disturb the unanimity of the last two years in the granting of supply. Beckford dwelt in general on the ministers' neglect and incapacity; Pitt echoed this, though formally approving the vote of credit, and attacking in largely personal terms: 'He compared the Duke of Newcastle to a child in a go-cart upon the brink of a precipice, and that it was but common humanity to stop it, or admonish the child's nurse of its danger (especially if it was a good *shrewd* nurse, and then turned to Fox)'. But again the debate ended, without a division, as a personal contest between Pitt and Sir George Lyttelton, in which the Chancellor made a fully adequate defence; and on 14th the Committee of Supply voted by 210 to 55 the funds to fulfil the terms of the treaty with Prussia. Apart from Sir George Lyttelton's error on 20th, when he unexpectedly provoked a division and won it by only 37 to 36,[47] the session in the Commons closed uneventfully. In the Lords, the ministry's intentions were concealed until the last moment. A faint opposition was offered to the second reading of the Militia Bill on 18th; but once the financial business of the Commons was over, Newcastle, Hardwicke and Granville took part for the first time to secure its rejection by 59 to 23, at a moment of public optimism about Byng, on the third reading.[48] Unhappily, its sudden failure found Bedford, Halifax, Stanhope, Temple and Bath among those left isolated in its support.[49] Although this move had been anticipated, it still came as a surprise to most;[50] but the ministry's troubles were postponed by the swift prorogation of parliament on 27 May, in a haste which Waldegrave thought designed to avoid a motion for an enquiry which would follow if Minorca were lost. Even so, he thought this would produce only a torrent of abuse, not the ministry's defeat, 'for Pitt and his party were become quite desperate...'[51] In contrast, the ministry's Commons managers were thoroughly satisfied with the session. Sir George Lyttelton was proud almost to excess of his showing against Pitt in the House, and imagined the King, the public and the ministry agreed with his estimate of his victory.[52] Fox, too, looked back on 'a sessions wherein everything has gone surprisingly well'.[53] The ministry was intact, and the loyalty of its back-bench supporters was unquestioned. Opposition Whiggery had been proved weak; its doctrine discredited, it had been spurned by the Tories and the support it enjoyed at Leicester House had grown more, not less equivocal as its tactical failures revealed themselves in the Commons.

ACCOUNTABILITY AND DEPARTMENTAL INDIVIDUALISM

The growing danger to Minorca raised, in an insistent form from May, the question of the division of responsibility among the ministers for the government's actions. But the inner circle of the ministry imagined its naval dispositions to be defensible, and the evasions with which it responded were a measure, rather, of the tensions suffered within its hierarchy. Officially, the prospects of Minorca's survival were held to be good;[54] yet Fox anticipated its loss from the first news of the French landing, and was inhibited from a full and open defence of Newcastle in the Commons on 7 May. Sackville at the same time held that 'the danger Minorca was in was a proof of our not being sufficiently or early enough armed at home, (which he was not to answer for) and a justification of his motion for the Address to bring Electoral troops here'.[55]

Newcastle reprimanded him, but did not use the notion of collective responsibility to disclaim *any* share of responsibility. Rather, his view of ministerial unity had two consequences. First, it was a defence against the charge that, as First Minister, he bore *more* responsibility than anyone else. It was a claim that Pitt continued to make, and repeated in his interviews with Hardwicke in October. Pitt did not argue (as would have been unprecedented) that *all* the ministers were accountable for the ministry's decisions; not until the nineteenth century was 'account-ability' linked in that way with a convention of the replacement of the ministerial team as a whole by its rival in opposition. Nor did Pitt assert that Newcastle had had the direction of the war, but rather that the errors occurred '*during my administration*. And, I hear, he has since said, that as *First Minister*, I ought to have observed *others*; a pretty great, and difficult task'.[56] In Newcastle's view, Anson was left with the departmental responsibility for proposing the disposition of forces, to which his colleagues had, without challenging his technical knowledge, assented. 'I don't remember', wrote Newcastle to Fox, 'that I ever differed in opinion from the rest of the King's servants in relation to Minorca. I don't think the defence of what was done difficult, though I am not more concerned to defend it than others'.[57] Yet Fox, from his eminence in the Commons (even if it were not defined as pre-eminence) *had* such a concern which Newcastle rightly felt was being shirked for tactical reasons.

Second, every minister might employ a good explanation for the dis-position of forces: the threat of invasion which, when it lifted in May, was too soon dismissed as illusory. Newcastle protested that one could not 'make civil ministers responsible for not acting contrary to plain facts' – that is, for not sending away more ships in face of an invasion threat – 'and the opinion of military men, at sea, and land, who are the best or the only judges'.[58] He realised nevertheless that public indig-nation would be imprecise and inconsistent in its choice of targets: he and Hardwicke, he wrote, were 'the chief persons; and *officially* I am the most aimed at, and made the more responsible, but you will come in for your share'.[59] As this remark suggests, Newcastle's notion of departmental government left room in one sense for the primacy of *a* Minister, himself; Newcastle defended such a scheme as the only guarantee of the resolute conduct of policy against the inaction threat-ened, not by his own system, but by the conduct of opposition. As he told Granville, 'the government must not stand still; or be governed by a Committee of the House of Commons'.[60]

Pitt, however, in parodying Newcastle's principle of departmental in-dividualism, denied on 7 May that this permitted effective leadership at all:

I don't call this an administration, it is so unsteady. One is at the head of the Treasury; one, Chancellor; one, head of the Navy; one great person, of the Army – yet, is that an Administration? They sift and shuffle the charge from one to another: says one, I am not General; the Treasury says, I am not Admiral; the Admiralty says, I am not Minister. From such an unaccording assemblage of separate and distinct powers with no system, a nullity results. One, two, three, four, five Lords meet; – if they cannot agree, oh! we will meet again on Saturday; – oh! but says one of them, I am to go out of town, – alas! said he, when no parties remain, what aggravation of the crimes of the ministry that no good comes from such unanimity.

Fox challenged him to declare whether he wished to see a ministry clearly led by a single man; Pitt replied, playing on evident rivalries, that 'he did not wish to see a single Minister, but a system and decision ...were Mr Fox sole Minister, there would be decision enough'.[61]

Newcastle was unmoved by this analysis, possibly because, although a telling parody of his ministry, it was inconsistent with the main theme of the opposition's attack: 'to fling it *singly* upon me, or if that can't be done, to make me answerable for other people's neglects, or weaknesses'.[62] Newcastle firmly rejected responsibility 'for measures, where *others* have the principal, if not the *sole*, direction',[63] and in which he had had no more share than any other member of the Cabinet. This doctrine was not without justification, for Newcastle did receive reports (among others to the contrary) that City opinion did not blame him more than Anson or Fox.[64] But in private, he was resentful of the conduct of naval affairs and, without actually naming Anson, implied a severe censure of him.[65] Fox, too, began to talk of the naval measures he *would* have taken but for the opposition of the Cabinet;[66] long pessimistic about the success of a Commons system without Pitt, he insisted in that case 'that he should not be answerable for the miscarriage, or have it any way imputed to him'.[67]

Pitt, though his arguments on 7 May were contradictory, said enough to make Newcastle believe the attack levelled solely against him; more dangerously, Pitt plainly tried to drive a wedge into the ministry, first by a compliment to Fox, then by praising and exonerating Anson and the Admiralty.[68] Hardwicke thought Newcastle's fears exaggerated and that he was wrong to draw such a conclusion: 'Opposers in Mr Pitt's situation will always principally strike at the first. There is in that a mixture both of malice and of politics'.[69] Those who singled out Newcastle for heaviest attack, Hardwicke assured him, 'don't believe themselves'.[70] But the opposition had found a powerful lever: again on 12 May, while apparently remaining silent as to Fox's involvement, George Grenville 'extolled Lord Anson and cleared the Admiralty as to Minorca'; Legge joined in praise of Anson and 'insinuated as if he knew Lord Anson was of a different opinion with regard to that measure; which Mr Fox (who spoke after him) in his sly way said he wished had not been said...whether he meant to insinuate commendation or blame on Lord Anson I cannot tell'.[71] Moreover, Fox was not compelled to retract, for the ambiguity of his own position was preserved in the statement he made in the Commons on 14 May:[72]

that Lord Anson had given him leave to declare that the reports concerning his differing with the Ministry as to sending ships to Minorca are absolutely false, particularly that he never did desire more ships for it than the ministry were willing he should have, that he never differed with them about it, that he never declared so, that he never could have more than he had consistent with the safety of this country, and that he never said otherwise.

In short, that Newcastle had not obstructed the despatch of ships sooner. Newcastle nevertheless supposed that, after this declaration, the Commons were satisfied with him. At dinner on 17th, he admitted to Fox that from this public affirmation of ministerial unity, 'nobody blamed him, that the City imputed nothing to him, as it was not his province'. Yet he may have relied too heavily on the over-optimistic West as his source: Fox challenged this estimate of City opinion and added 'it would be ever true, that those who had the chief direction, in an administration, would bear the greatest share of blame, and that those deceived him, who told him it was otherwise, now'. Fox struck here at that innermost circle of the ministry, from which he had been consistently excluded even since his promotion to the Cabinet in September 1755. To Newcastle in person, Fox deferred, claiming to have defended him on 12 May with his own doctrine – that he was 'answerable but in an equal degree with others'; but observed also that 'all friends hung their heads, and that not a man could be, or even seemed, persuaded, that a squadron could not be sent sooner, or that all was done that could be done'.[73] By October, even Anson had come to use Newcastle's doctrine to defend himself from sole blame for the conduct of affairs in the Mediterranean, 'in which he had no share but in conjunction with the rest of the Council'.[74]

To Dodington, Fox claimed to have fully discharged the obligations to Newcastle which he undertook at his promotion, despite Newcastle's patent dissatisfaction; it was apparently Dodington who then sowed in Fox's mind the fear of being made the ministry's scapegoat – a possibility which Fox had not considered. After all, he had 'always hinted at sending a squadron to Minorca sooner...the Duke of Cumberland pressed it, strongly, so long ago as last Christmas'.[75] Yet if Newcastle and Pitt did not grasp the modern doctrine of collective Cabinet responsibility, neither did Fox. He sought to exonerate himself throughout merely by claiming, like Newcastle, to have given the correct advice early enough; in so doing he fell short of Newcastle's requirements without adequately meeting Pitt's challenge. But this was to become apparent only in September.

LEICESTER HOUSE AND THE LORD CHIEF JUSTICE,
MAY–JUNE 1756

Two events acted further to unsettle a situation already unstable after Fox's attempt at dissociation from responsibility over Minorca. On 25 May Sir Dudley Ryder, the Lord Chief Justice, died unexpectedly; and it became clear that Murray's ambition led to that office. On 4 June

Prince George came of age, and the problem of his Establishment became even more pressing. Despite the events of the 1755-6 session, Leicester House had always kept Pitt and the opposition in the Commons at a certain distance – one which was increased with their poor showing in Parliament. There had never been a formal breach between the two Courts of the sort which had existed until 1751; it was the consequences of just such a breach which were now feared,[76] and which the ministry sought to avoid.

On 15 April, George II was presented with, and approved, Newcastle's proposal for the junior Court to be given an allowance of £40,000 and Prince George to be installed in appartments at St James's and Kensington, so removing him from the influence of his mother and of Bute.[77] Considerations about Minorca aside, the speedy adjournment of Parliament may have been encouraged by the threat of a motion to settle a provision on the Prince if the House sat after his birthday.[78] At first it was given out that no establishment would be fixed that year owing to the bad relations between the two Courts;[79] this was probably a screen, for Newcastle and Hardwicke were soon arranging matters in private conferences from which Fox was excluded.[80] Fox asked a place in the Prince's household for Lord Digby, but – probably as a result of Fox's equivocal behaviour in the Commons – Newcastle refused even to admit that the matter was under consideration.[81] When the news became public, however, applications flooded in. Chesterfield advanced Huntingdon as a Lord of the Bedchamber. Newcastle intended Rockingham to be Master of the Horse, and (with the King's approval, as he claimed) Waldegrave to be Groom of the Stole.[82] Fox, resentful at having (as it seemed to him) incurred the King's anger as a consequence of Newcastle's distrust,[83] enlisted Murray to urge on Granville (and implicitly on Newcastle) the services he, Fox, had performed throughout the session. Murray added his private advice that a place for Digby would avoid a breach with Fox: 'Indeed we have too many ruptures upon our hands already'.[84]

This was Murray's last intervention on Fox's behalf. On Ryder's death the following day, all his efforts were directed to securing both Newcastle's consent to his succeeding to the Chief Justiceship and support for the simultaneous grant of a peerage. Although it was thought that he 'could have no competitor', Murray was equally regarded as essential to Newcastle's system in the Commons.[85] If he were to be spared, he could scarcely encourage Fox's discontent or dwell on his possible disloyalty. Fox was confident of Murray's success, but while admitting his value he did not suppose that his loss destroyed the system. Indeed, Fox was piqued at Newcastle's despondency: he 'sees it in the light of the greatest loss to him', wrote Fox, 'and has said that there is nobody now but *me* there'. That attitude was only redeemed by what he saw as Newcastle's willingness, as a result, to 'unite firmly and thoroughly with me'; proof, he added, 'that he had not meant to do so yet'. Oblivious to his conduct in May, Fox suggested that an Earldom for his brother Ilchester would be an acceptable 'public mark of the favour, which I am not in', but which, if offered, might effect a union.[86]

Although Newcastle admitted Murray's professional claims to legal promotion, he insisted on drawing unforgiving conclusions from Fox's conduct. He, Newcastle, was to be made to 'answer for everything'. Fox could not be trusted; perhaps by 'mistaken interest', he still entertained 'other views', and sought to be alone in the Commons in order to dominate the ministry. Newcastle had, as yet, no solution to this threat. As Horace Walpole saw, Murray was 'equally the buckler of Newcastle against his ally, Fox, and his antagonist, Pitt':[87] henceforth, a challenge was to come from both those quarters.

Our friend Stone said most wisely to me – The Attorney General out of the House of Commons – Fox disobliged – the possibility (I wish I could not say, the probability) of a breach in the Royal Family – an alliance between the House of Austria and France – four terrible events – and what is worse, not in my power to prevent any one of them.

To Murray, Newcastle complained: 'nobody but yourself will or can support me; and I will add farther, will or can in the House of Commons support the King and his ministers, against such a formed opposition, and in such a critical conjuncture'. Since Newcastle could not resign with 'honour and credit', he still hoped that motives of duty to the King would induce Murray to waive or at least postpone his departure, urging the Attorney General:

Your case is Sir Robert Walpole's, though in a higher degree. Sir Robert might have had a *Deputy* in the House of Commons, who would, who could, have done his business; if his own jealousy would have permitted him to have had one. The King can have no other Deputy but yourself; and after that, I will not repeat any other motive.[88]

Newcastle was nothing if not resourceful in misrepresenting the relative position of the ministerial spokesmen in the Commons. Murray reminded him of what had been the agreed rationale of the system:

I should not be able to stand the shame nor you the reproach of such a measure, especially in our present situation. If I would have taken it, could you have supported me in the place of Sir Thos. Robinson? If I would have taken it, could you have supported me in the place of Mr Fox? I have, with your judgement and approbation carefully avoided the appearance of being the Minister in, or having the lead of the House of Commons. If I should be now marked as such your enemies will run at you through me, and those who are politically connected with you will grow jealous.[89]

This was true: Fox would dangerously resent the loss of the improved position which he would otherwise inherit on Murray's promotion. But Newcastle was honest in his account of the party situation. As the

Speaker suggested, Newcastle saw that Murray's place could only be filled from the opposition or by Fox. The first alternative carried the threat of a substantial access of power to Leicester House. The second would mean Newcastle's 'sole dependence' on Fox; but Newcastle had no confidence that Fox could stand up to Pitt alone, and explained to Murray the grounds of Fox's inferiority. Pitt would bear him down in debates on foreign affairs, where Fox was 'totally ignorant'; on other matters, Fox would be superficial, 'endeavour to skim it over, and naturally to let it light upon himself as little as possible'. The lead had, indeed, always been taken by others: Murray, Sir Thomas Robinson, Sir George Lyttelton in turn. The outcome of Fox's failure would now be 'a coalition between Fox and Pitt, by sacrificing me': a possibility which Fox was to pursue later that summer with every hope of its practicability, and which Newcastle had frustrated with such difficulty in the winter of 1754–5. And last, to insist that the undesirable was also impracticable, Newcastle argued that his friends suspected Fox too deeply to be persuaded to act with him with sufficient confidence.[90]

Once the session was safely over, Waldegrave was sent to Leicester House on 30 May with the offers first set down in the minute of 4 April. In replies rumoured to be drafted by Legge,[91] the allowance was accepted but the offer of a move to St James's left unmentioned[92] and effectively refused. Informally, the Prince now asked Waldegrave to ask the King not to appoint him to the new Household, where Newcastle intended that he be Groom of the Stole. Waldegrave agreed to delay his decision, but warned Prince George that if he were not to change his residence, the King would expect compliance in his choice of the new Establishment.[93] That an announcement of the Household had been imminent is suggested by the accurate reports which circulated of the distribution of offices on the lines of Newcastle's first intentions.[94] Through Stone, too, Prince George expressed his wish that Bute have 'one of the principal posts' in the new establishment, and Murray and Devonshire joined with Stone in support of the Prince's request that no appointment be yet made which would exclude Bute;[95] a decision was accordingly postponed.

This balance of force was not altered in its essentials by the arrival on 2 June of news of Byng's action on 20 May and his later withdrawal.[96] Although it came from French sources it was credited sufficiently for the Cabinet to decide at once on Byng's replacement by Hawke.[97] Public discontent, which had till then been simmering, was raised to fever pitch and kept there in anticipation of the news, which came on 14 July, of Minorca's fall.[98] Although there were some at first within the ministerial camp disposed to think Byng's withdrawal prudent,[99] the initial outcry was directed almost unanimously against the Admiral's cowardice; even George Grenville thought Byng's slight inferiority in strength no excuse for a retreat after such a faint attempt.[100] Yet far from smug confidence that power would fall into his and his friends' hands,[101] Grenville's reaction was one of despondency in the face of impending national disaster which he no more than Fox or Newcastle saw how to avert.[102] Though Charles Townshend had a vague sense of the possibility of exploiting the unrest, Pitt showed no more constructive foresight than did Grenville. Potter indeed advised Pitt

That the fright of the Duke of Newcastle, like the rest of his frights proceeds from his ignorance: such is the temper of the House of Commons that if the whole business rested on Sir George Lyttelton and Lord Dupplin, the debates on the Court side would be shorter, but there would not be a single vote less... whatever sacrifices have been made to opinion [by the opposition], the reputation of those who made them is increased in the minds only of a few. Hanover treaties and Hanover troops are popular throughout every country [i.e. county]. The almost universal language is, opposition must be wrong, when we are ready to be eat up by the French.[103]

The news of Byng and Minorca did nothing in May, June or July to strengthen the hands of Pitt or Fox. It increased Newcastle's agitation; but, since he was conscious of the King's consistent loyalty,[104] he was worried by the parliamentary consequences not of public discontent or its manipulation by the opposition but of the crisis in relations between St James's and Leicester House, 'where there will be room for great Court play on both sides'.[105] It was such fears, Newcastle thought, which inclined the King temporarily to humour Fox.[106] Yet in dealing with Leicester House, Newcastle was helped by Pitt's reticence during these weeks. This may have been the result of Potter's intelligence that George Stone had been hinting the ministry's desire for a rapprochement with Pitt. If Murray were promoted, reported Potter, Pitt would of necessity be invited in; Sir George Lyttelton, Holdernesse and Charles Yorke would then leave their offices to be filled, by implication, from the opposition.[107] It seems likely that Pitt as yet preferred quiescence and the prospect of an accommodation with the ministry to a vigorous marshalling of public opinion.[108] There is no evidence that he took any action during the summer to forward Leicester House's desire for Bute's appointment as Groom of the Stole,[109] or that he was in any way concerned in the negotiations between the two Courts over the Prince of Wales's future Household. Those matters were outside the proper sphere of a commoner; for Pitt to have been involved would only have incensed the King further. Such things were not, therefore, open to exploitation for political advantage.

If Pitt was inactive, Fox was positively subservient. On 4th, Newcastle learnt that he had assured the King that he, Fox, would do 'whatever your Majesty would have me' in the affair of the Prince of Wales, and told Lady Yarmouth 'that when he came into the King's service, he was always determined to serve the King, against the Prince of Wales as well as against anybody else'. 'Mr Fox is in high spirits', concluded

Newcastle.[110] In return, George II treated favourably Fox's request for Lord Digby. Newcastle was content to do nothing about these developments. After the difficulties of Fox's enlistment, it never occurred to him that Fox should be exchanged for Pitt and no preparations were made for his dismissal; nor did Newcastle ever pursue the King's suggestion that Devonshire be won from his loyalty to Fox.[111] After 4 June, when Prince George came of age, the prospect of a Fox ministry built around a Cumberland Regency (a distant echo of the potential power of which was heard in 1765), which had long been fading, was finally extinguished. Fox was, even more evidently, left in a quandary. Newcastle was convinced, from 12 June at the latest, that Murray would not stay;[112] and Fox was anxious to profit from his going. Yet the international situation (until the Prussian invasion of Saxony on 29 August it was supposed that Britain was engaged without an ally against France and Austria) and the public outcry led Fox to doubt, and to continue to doubt where Newcastle ceased to do so, the ministry's ability to guarantee him his new position.

It was not least Newcastle's perpetual desire to reconstruct and strengthen his system in the face of threats to it which led him to seek to accommodate the Prince; and that Court's reticence early in the year on all subjects except office for Bute had given more cause for hope than had long existed.[113] Such a possibility, if real, might have been threatened by the King, who on 5 June returned a strict warning via Waldegrave, as Newcastle recorded it:

That my lord Waldegrave would speak plainly to him, that the way HRHss was in, *would not do*, that the P[rince of] W[ales] and the Princess his mother, were upon the brink of a precipice...that the King had the absolute power over His Royal Highness. That he could place, and displace his servants. That the King was determined to make use of his power; that His Majesty (from not knowing my lord Bute) had not the same opinion of him, that His Royal Highness had; that the King looked upon my lord Bute, as closely connected with Mr Pitt, and the opposition, and that therefore his Majesty did not think him, a proper person to be put about His Royal Highness.

Bute's promotion was refused, and a change in residence insisted on. Yet, in a second interview on 6 June, Prince George explained away his earlier objections to a household appointment for Waldegrave, and offered him the post of Master of the Horse rather than Groom of the Stole. He asked only that Bute have an office and that he should not be forced to live away from his mother. The Princess herself added

That the King was mistaken in my lord Bute's character, or *behaviour*; that so far from encouraging the Prince of Wales to support the opposition, he had consistently told him, that he should have no *politics*, but the King's, and in everything act according to the King's will.

Waldegrave repeated this reply to the King on 9 June; told Newcastle of the Princess's desire to receive one last overture;[114] but repeated to Newcastle his request to resign.[115]

ALTERNATIVES TO MURRAY, JUNE–AUGUST 1756

Newcastle's immediate problem was to take advantage of the opportunity for an approach to Leicester House in a way which would not provoke them to the alliance with Fox and Pitt which he, Newcastle, feared would form before the next session began. Although Ilchester would obtain his earldom, Fox was not happy and would be still more dissatisfied when he found that Lord Digby would not receive the coveted post of Lord of the Bedchamber to the Prince of Wales.

For my own part, I really think, as I said in my letter to the Attorney General, that before six months are over, we shall hear of some negotiation between Mr Fox and Mr Pitt, and Leicester House.

To frustrate it, he was willing to countenance a secondary arrangement: a treaty with Pitt; some 'further security' for Fox's behaviour which would allow him to be given a greater part to play; or leading roles for younger men like Hume Campbell, Henley and Charles Yorke.[116] But with the arrival of Byng's own account of his action on 20 May, Murray demanded that his promotion occur that term.[117] This finally ruled out a scheme which Newcastle hoped against hope might be an acceptable inducement for Murray to stay;[118] so, on 28 June, Hardwicke laid the matter of Murray's promotion before the King, and gave it his support.[119] George II agreed to the promotion but refused for the moment the peerage which Murray had demanded as a *sine qua non*.[120] This royal obstruction was convenient: Murray had rejected Newcastle's plea for a delay in which to discover a system for the Commons,[121] but could do nothing in face of the King's wishes. Now, he agreed to delay his promotion until the beginning of Michaelmas Term in the hope that the King might then be willing to grant a peerage also.[122] Fox knew of the delay, inferred that Newcastle was responsible, and was furious.[123] Already, it seems, Fox had come to see his interest to lie in the disruption of Newcastle's system rather than in fighting his way to a more commanding position within it.

Newcastle was under exceptional stress at a time when his morale was low. Depressed by the death of a sister, Lady Castlecomer, on 27 June, he was burdened already with a sense of the emptiness of his personal relationships: 'Every day convinces me, that it is impossible for *me*, almost to oblige anybody; or to avoid being suspected of falsity, and duplicity, even to those, for whom I have, and have always professed, the greatest friendship.'[124] It was this especially which made Newcastle repeat his hopes of a retreat with honour;[125] but, as so often, those hopes were an index of the tension he endured rather than plans or excuses for seriously-contemplated resignation. These anxieties may explain the strain which suddenly and needlessly soured Newcastle's relations with Hume Campbell, whom he apparently disappointed over a job. When they met, Newcastle

desired I would take an active part. I told him as far as he would let me. I had no difficulty and was still ready to do all I could but that without being informed of what they meant to do beforehand I really could not...He did not seem to understand that there was any occasion to tell his friends anything of his intentions at all.

Hume Campbell was, however, induced to say something in reply to Newcastle's question – how they should go on in the Commons without Murray – and was persuaded to agree to meet Fox, presumably for a technical discussion of Commons management.[126] The lawyer's limited and cautious commitment to a political career, expounded at length to Marchmont, made him unusually tolerant of Newcastle's view of his Commons subordinates at the same time as it made him unwilling to play the more prominent part to which his abilities entitled him. Nevertheless, Newcastle knew that Hume Campbell was safe.

The unreliability of Fox and the calculated lukewarmness of Hume Campbell, therefore, focused attention on the other alternative, Leicester House. The Cabinet on 7 July was united behind a policy of settling no Establishment until it was known whether the Prince held out for Bute and against the move to St James's,[127] and it was generally understood that the conduct of the junior Court was responsible for the suspension of a decision.[128] A prospect of its division was suddenly opened up by the King's unexpected[129] agreement that Bute be offered any proper mark of regard, including a pension but excluding office about the Prince, if he renounced Pitt and opposition. Bute was therefore under pressure, and Newcastle had Murray ask Argyll to approach him.[130] Argyll, however, proved less useful than Newcastle expected, for he was unaware that the Prince had insisted on Bute; and though he confessed to having hoped for years to link Bute to the administration, Argyll knew too little of Leicester House to judge the consequences of an overture.[131] Nor was Argyll well disposed to Newcastle, for a typical example of the latter's inconsiderateness left Argyll publicly angry, at Newcastle's levée, at the disposal of a living against his recommendation.[132] In any event, Argyll's mission was hopeless: before it took place, Prince George's reply formally set out his insistence on remaining with his mother and on 'some principal situation about my person' for Bute.[133] The result was deadlock; in mid August, Bute boasted 'that till now they [the ministry] can meet with no man rash enough, to bid defiance to the P[rince] by coming into those offices he insisted upon naming...'[134]

Fox's behaviour meanwhile gave great cause for alarm. This had not openly been the case as recently as the beginning of July, when Fox implied that he expected to face Parliament that autumn in trying to

247

persuade Ellis to collect information on naval affairs in order to become (what Fox claimed to lack the specialist knowledge for) 'a champion to stand in this Minorca breach'.[135] Fox professed ignorance of how to retrieve the nation's fortunes and, therefore, that he was not ambitious of power. But by the middle of that month, in an obvious hint at Pitt, he added: 'If there is in this island a man who could give me a hope of success in war, or security by peace, I wish him minister.'[136] Fox was far, however, from being a passive observer of the ministry's policy. Newcastle had already discovered that Fox had made an unauthorised suggestion to Viry, the Sardinian ambassador, that Gibraltar might be given up to Spain in return for her aid in recapturing Minorca, and was furious at such 'imprudence, folly, ambition and double dealing with us all'.[137] Soon, another example came to light: Fox's private criticism of Newcastle's and Hardwicke's attitude to Prince George.[138] Then, on 19th, Fox clashed with the King himself in a sudden and heated exchange in the Closet.[139] As late as 4 June, George II had been well disposed towards Fox; but by early July, his disloyalty had brought the King to an attitude of deep distrust. 'He is black,' Newcastle was told in one audience; 'I know him, tho' I don't show it.'[140]

It seems likely that Fox's growing intransigence lay behind the changed attitudes apparent in Newcastle's and Hardwicke's minute of 22 July.[141] Either Fox or Pitt, it was stated, must be allied with; but now, that alliance was admitted to mean the granting to one of them of 'the chief, though not the whole, conduct of the House of Commons'. Pitt 'seems, at present, out of the question' through his past conduct, his connections, and George II's personal antipathy. The King's permission was therefore to be sought to treat with Fox; and, as a safeguard against his possible indiscipline if thus advanced, subordinates were to be accorded greater prominence as a counterpoise. Sackville and Conway were named for this role. Each was the King's own choice.[142] Hardwicke had already spoken to Dorset about his son's allegiance and had been reassured that the family was still disposed towards its old friends: Sackville would be 'ready to take on, and to act a clear and strong part in support, on being properly distinguished'.[143]

The secret that Argyll was authorised to treat with Bute was apparently kept from Fox until 30 or 31 July,[144] and it is not evident that he knew anything of the ministry's new determination to reach an understanding with Leicester House before his meeting with Newcastle on 29th. After that policy had been adopted, West had met Fox and had found him cordial: he 'talked much of the meeting the Parliament, and thought it was absolutely necessary to get either the Earl of Bute or Mr Pitt and that family. He said he was astonished at your Grace's firmness and intrepidity...'[145] This unexpected eagerness gave away Fox's game and revealed his appetite for power. Here, blandly advanced, Newcastle thought he saw the conspiracy he had feared. There is no evidence that

Fox can have been led to this disclosure in a calculated attempt to forestall the ministerial overture to Bute behind his, Fox's, back. More probably, it stemmed from Fox's realisation, as the public clamour reached a crescendo, that his earlier attempts within the Cabinet and at large to dissociate himself from responsibility would count for nothing: he would share, and was sharing, in the general obloquy.[146] Moreover, Newcastle bore up better under the torrent of public abuse, thought Fox, than he did himself; and as 'the only figure of a minister' in the Commons, he expected the attack there to fall principally on him.[147] Newcastle knew that Fox hoped for a strengthening of the system with Pitt as Secretary of State and himself in 'some lucrative employment', but Newcastle now thought that the conduct of Cresset and Lady Yarmouth gave him reason to suspect that George II might be willing to accept Pitt.[148]

This suspicion reinforced what Newcastle knew of Fox's desire to favour Prince George. It proved, he thought, Fox's determination to buy his way into an alliance with Leicester House, even though Newcastle was ignorant of how far the alliance had been arranged. He therefore decided to show Lady Yarmouth the minute of 22 July in the hope of discovering her and the King's real intentions towards Pitt. He asked Hardwicke whether he should also tell her of Fox's recent plea for a reconciliation with Leicester House: 'It might certainly contribute to the measure about *Pitt*; but it would as certainly still more alienate the King and her against Fox, and make them conclude, what they now suspect, that Fox has a management both for Lord B[ute] and Pitt.'[149] But though Newcastle's fears were to prove true to Fox's intentions, Hardwicke correctly saw that Fox's game had not reached so advanced a stage. Fox's disclosure, he thought, was meant only to 'sift and sound a little': Lady Yarmouth should not therefore be told this news, at least until Newcastle's interview with Fox on 29th. It would only rouse the King's aversion to Fox, and do harm if the ministry were finally compelled to go on with him on the lines of the minute of 22 July.[150]

When Newcastle met Fox on 29 July, their conversation had a familar ring. Newcastle spoke of Hardwicke's and the King's consent that Fox be offered 'all the confidence, share of power, favour etc. which was absolutely requisite to carry on the next difficult and most irksome sessions'. Fox placed little value on such offers. Though more sincerely meant than before, he thought, their outcome would be the same. To Devonshire, Fox claimed to see no other course than that which Cumberland recommended: 'to take his [Newcastle's] promises and not depend upon them'. This was far from true. Fox did see another choice open to him, and his anxiety at the discovery that Argyll had been secretly authorised to negotiate with Bute is a measure of how seriously he expected his own future to lie within a Pitt ministry.[151]

Fox, caught out and upstaged by Newcastle, was forced to explain himself on 29th by misrepresenting his preference: it had, he claimed, been for the ministry as a whole to reconcile itself to Leicester House through agreeing to Bute's having some office about Prince George; or, if that were impossible, by making Pitt Secretary of State. To a degree, Fox professed himself despondent: he could not *leave* the ministers (they had got to Bute first); nor could he *save* them, in the current desperate state of the war.[152] Newcastle's present problem, as Fox foresaw in his conversation with Stone,[153] was to obtain Pitt's assent to a system in which the old figures were still involved; it may be that it was the patent feasibility of this, in Fox's judgement, which led him to make the proposal in order to profit from it equally with Newcastle. Fox, Walpole recorded,[154]

saw Newcastle flinging up works all round himself; and suspected that Pitt would be invited to defend them. He saw how little power he had obtained by his last treaty with the Duke. He saw himself involved in the bad success of measures on which he had not been consulted, scarce suffered to give an opinion; and he knew that if Newcastle and Pitt united, he must be sacrificed as the cement of their union.

But the nature of Fox's prior duplicity reveals the deceptions embodied in Walpole's apologia, and disproves the generally accepted thesis that it was Newcastle who was disloyal first. At once, Fox sought 'a great deal of discourse upon the times' with Rigby, as Bedford's agent, and continued his advances during that month.[155]

On 4 August Fox admitted to Hardwicke that he now knew of the overtures to Bute; desired that they might go on; recommended an alliance with Pitt, but urged that Bute, whom he supposed to be the key figure at Leicester House, be had on *any* terms. Hardwicke objected, evasively, that such a deal was the King's personal and private responsibility. As to Pitt, the Chancellor pointed out that George II would probably not accept him; that he was unlikely to come; and that his ambition was the Secretaryship, from which the ministry had no desire to displace Fox. What Hardwicke did not reveal to Fox was the ministry's hope of a deal with Bute alone. Yet with strange alacrity, Fox then expressed himself willing to leave his office for a post not of the Cabinet, and pointed – almost, it seems, with satisfaction – to the King's dislike of *him* as an inducement which he hoped sufficient to make Pitt acceptable.[156] To his immediate circle, the sincerity of Fox's offer, when it was known, looked highly dubious.[157] Yet on 6 August, when Fox met Newcastle, their conversation followed a similar path – to Newcastle's mild satisfaction.[158] Reassuring, too, were the signs that the junior Court was showing a strong tendency to accommodation.[159] Fox, having chosen his new role, committed himself to it wholeheartedly and expressed regret that Newcastle had not taken the opportunity for a still closer friendship when it had been offered by Leicester House at the price of Bute's installation as Groom of the Stole.[160] Walpole accepted this at face value and recorded his belief[161] that Newcastle might have been reconciled to

Leicester House by the early concession of that office. McKelvey[162] follows Walpole's interpretation; but its improbability should have been suggested by the moral fervour of Bute's ambition alone even without Waldegrave's testimony to the patent insincerity of the junior Court's gestures of submission in the hope of Bute's acceptability.[163]

An opportunity to test the King's reaction to the prospect of a Pitt–Fox administration without Newcastle came after a letter in the *Public Advertiser* on 18 August praised Pitt and Fox and proposed making them *'Joint Ministers'*. Newcastle seized on it at once, partly because the letter sought to dissociate Fox from all blame for Minorca and partly because it heightened Newcastle's already acute fears of a conspiracy.[164] Hardwicke showed it to the King on 20th. George II was struck by its similarity with Fox's scheme, and his reaction reassured the Chancellor that no such plan had been proposed in the Closet secretly. Rather, George II realised its impracticability before Fox did. 'The King, putting on an air of contempt, said "That will never do. Nobody will submit to that, I am sure the House of Lords never will; and I believe the House of Commons would not." ' To Newcastle, Hardwicke reinforced the moral: something should be said to Pitt, he urged, in order to forestall a connection of the sort which threatened.[165]

The result of Argyll's overture to Bute then became known. Murray saw Argyll on 22 August, only to discover that Bute had replied in platitudes. The Prince's request, that Bute be Groom of the Stole, remained. Argyll had never proceeded on any assumption except that Bute was excluded, though he regretted it as a policy which 'necessarily threw them into other hands and connections'. Moreover, Bute would leave for Scotland in a few days, as if to emphasise the impossibility of further negotiations[166] without a major concession. But that, Newcastle was not authorised to offer.

PITT WITHOUT BUTE, AUGUST 1756

Some new line of advance was essential. Pitt might be tried as Hardwicke suggested, though Newcastle had no expectation of success.[167] Egmont, too, apparently offered the prospect of an accommodation, and Nugent worked to promote it;[168] Oswald's promotion would give the Admiralty 'an efficient man in the House of Commons'.[169] Hardwicke, meanwhile, unaware of the end of the negotiations through Argyll, sought better to dispose Newcastle in favour of Pitt. Through Dr Squire,[170] who was sensitive to such fears, he warned that the King, despite his apparent support, might prefer some other ministry which could guarantee to conduct his business in tranquillity; and that Fox, as the chief agent of a Cumberland system, might offer such a combination. Hardwicke himself claimed to think that it would command a majority, once in possession of the Treasury; and that Fox already had 'the greatest interest in the

House of Commons'.[171] All this, and Hardwicke's disquiet about military dictatorship, was speculation; though probably sincere, the expression of such fears now also served a purpose. There is no evidence that the Chancellor knew anything in detail about the allegiance of MPs or about secret negotiations in the Closet. Moreover, such fears seemed inconsistent with Fox's recent effusive submissions.

Newcastle was, therefore, unmoved. Admittedly, Fox was unreliable; yet Hardwicke was no more accurate in pointing to the long interval between him and Newcastle's next spokesman in the Commons, Nugent. This was unfair to Sir George Lyttelton, Hume Campbell, Barrington, Sackville, Dodington,[172] Conway, Dupplin and Charles Yorke, each of whom might still be counted on. Hardwicke thus added little to the force of his argument that Newcastle should gain Leicester House at all costs, for he was ill-informed on what the cost would be. The Princess might be persuaded of her true interest, he suggested, without conceding the Stole to Bute. Egmont's good disposition, he added, offered the prospect of obliging her through advancing him, as one of her servants, to the Chancellorship of the Exchequer. Again, Hardwicke spoke in ignorance of the state of Egmont's interest at the junior Court; and it seems likely that the inference he drew from his denial of the possibility of a Pitt–Fox alliance was equally misconceived. It was impossible, he told Squire, because 'Mr Pitt will never submit to act a subordinate part to Mr Fox and to support him in the first place; and because Mr Pitt is fully satisfied that his M[ajesty] is irremovably fixed never to admit him into his Closet'. That being the case, the Chancellor hinted that Newcastle channel more nominations to preferments through his own hands rather than Fox's. But the only possibility really was, as Hardwicke and Fox equally failed to realise, Fox's serving in a subordinate station in a Pitt ministry. Fox thus miscalculated his own prospects; Hardwicke, who estimated them more accurately, thereby (ironically) misjudged Fox's intentions.

More important than Hardwicke's advice was Dr Squire's news. Sir George Lee's relations with the Princess, he reported, were now merely formal. Bute monopolised her favour, and she professed to be 'free from all political connection which may be detrimental to his M[ajesty's] measures; she talks of Mr Pitt in terms of her ancient resentment, and is extremely displeased with the Duke of Cumberland for some little slight lately shown by him to some of her servants'.[173] This news made it seem possible to Newcastle that Pitt might be treated with separately from Bute. Yet Newcastle did not propose, even now, to concede a number of offices to the Grenvilles *en bloc*; he was considering only Oswald for promotion to fill the dying Furnese's place at the Admiralty, and Stanley as his replacement at the Board of Trade.[174] The failure of the overture through Argyll, of which Hardwicke was told on 28th, left Newcastle preoccupied with Fox's threat. On the evening of 26th, after the arrival of Squire's letter, Newcastle traced the rumour to its source and discovered that Chesterfield had only guessed that Cumberland had advised the King to put Fox at the head of the Treasury. But this probably discredited Chesterfield's further observation that Pitt and Fox could not agree, and that Fox would never act in a subordinate place to Pitt. At this point Newcastle was once again made aware that the pamphlet press was ignoring Fox's share in the ministry's responsibility, and one Foxite writer (Alderman Beckford, thought Newcastle) arguing that he, Fox, should undertake the administration with Pitt. Newcastle knew also that Fox was speaking in private in a way inconsistent with his defending the ministry's record in public. 'Everybody will not agree, as to Mr Fox's inclinations', he wrote, 'but everybody must agree, that were they never so good, it would not be in his power to do it. He says so, in effect, himself, *at present*.' It followed that a parliamentary opposition could emerge, based on the most dangerous constellation of forces: 'if Leicester House is publicly, or even privately, *known* to be at the head of the opposition, though ruin and destruction may attend them, it will not the less affect others; the King's quiet must be immediately disturbed, and perhaps confusion, and even insurrection in parts of the Kingdom to encourage a foreign enemy to invade us...'

Caught between the inability of Fox and the unattainability of Pitt, Newcastle could profess himself inclined to resignation; and if Leicester House were to pursue the course he most feared, he thought 'to some degree' that resignation was tactically the correct step also.

If I may be permitted to go, Mr Pitt, Mr Fox, the D[uke] of B[edford] and perhaps some still more considerable person [Cumberland] must be at the head of affairs. If I am to stay – with whom? Mr Pitt, I am told, will not act with me; I fear, he will on no account support the King's measures. The Princess of Wales will certainly not support the King's measures and administration, if my Lord Bute is not gratified in being put about the Prince of Wales, and I have my doubts, whether she would do it *thoroughly* if he was. But means may be found to know that beforehand. The great question is, should the King be advised to comply – should the Council be again consulted upon that question? ...Can anything be set on foot with Mr Pitt exclusively of Leicester House?[175]

The present crisis might even force the King to agree from necessity to a proposal of this sort:[176] Newcastle and Hardwicke should consider now whether they could accept 'Mr Pitt coming in conquest over us'.[177] Hardwicke was predisposed to Pitt's inclusion on terms, and argued that his reported unwillingness to act a second part to Fox was no objection to his, Pitt's, recruitment to the ministry. Again he warned that George II might act on Newcastle's implied offer to step down, and urged Newcastle to pursue a solution which linked an accommodation with Pitt to an answer to the problem of Bute. He was willing to acquiesce in Bute's having the Stole, he said, if the rest of the Cabinet insisted on it: such a move was the most like an alliance as the natural result of the reconciliation of the two courts, the least like a forcing of the Closet by opposition.

It would also be a step sufficiently important to remove the odium which would attend another Pelhamite resignation in wartime of the sort which had so unpleasantly 'forced' the King in 1746, and which would avoid, too, the consequence of a resignation now: the supremacy of Cumberland. Hardwicke claimed to be optimistic on the prospects for such an arrangement:

You have been told that Mr Pitt would not act with you. I was told that Mr Legge talked another language not long ago, but will not answer how far it is to be depended upon. One thing I am persuaded of, that, if his ambition was gratified in the point on which he has set his heart, *that* would not stand in his way; and measures are always capable of being distinguished by some new turn to be given to them. A small turn did the last time with the same gentleman[178]

– that is, in 1746, when Pitt was bought off from a patriot opposition less virulent only than that of 1756.

Yet Hardwicke offered no specific proposal for uniting Commons leaders; nor, to Newcastle, did the King on 2 September. But George II checked himself when about to make a suggestion; and, from Lady Yarmouth, Newcastle inferred that it would have been a proposal to replace Fox with Pitt as Secretary of State without yielding to the demands of Bute (on whom the Stole, she claimed with Waldegrave's backing, would not confer a political obligation). 'Everybody (and my Lady Yarmouth amongst them) is full of the coolness, with which Mr Pitt was received at Leicester House; and the more particular coolness, between him and my Lord Bute.' Newcastle was sceptical of this and of Fox's remarks about Bute and Pitt. On the basis of a conversation on 2nd, Newcastle thought Fox would not insist on the pursuit of alliance with either of those men; it was not his real inclination to be replaced by Pitt *tout court*. In this, Newcastle was certainly correct. But there may have been some truth in Fox's warning that, if no overtures were now made to either, Pitt and Bute would be reconciled in opposition:

That he took it for certain, that my Lord Bute, and Mr Pitt, were not now well together...That if we took neither of them, they would, they must, unite, though *he believed*, they would wait to the last, before they did it. That Mr Pitt (he supposed) knew what we knew; that my Lord Bute had been negotiating with us, to come in without him; which Pitt would never forgive, except *we took them together*.

Bute's promotion to the Stole, declared Fox, was immaterial; but it would be damaging if he were able to compel it. Yet Pitt would not come on terms less than ones which would make him 'a conqueror', and to make him an offer only to have it refused would be disastrous. This, as Newcastle saw, was a very different position. He supposed Fox now feared that his, Fox's, offer to step down in Pitt's favour might be acted upon. It seems probable that Fox's response was to attempt to persuade Newcastle of an imminent link between Bute and Pitt while arguing that only together would they be an adequate reinforcement, in the knowledge that, if together, they would never come; and, if thought to be allied, they would never be invited. This last was an accurate forecast. Explaining Fox's conversation to the King on 3 September, Newcastle discovered that George II 'wishes to avoid both my Lord Bute, and Mr Pitt; and seems to think it practicable. That is the question.'[179]

To Hardwicke, however, the question was still what the King's real preference was – whether he was willing to dispense with Newcastle for a Fox–Cumberland ministry, or whether he would at last accept Pitt. Lady Yarmouth had apparently spoken as if the King's aversion to Bute had brought him to do so; but Granville thought George II remained set against both, and the King's remarks to Newcastle on 3 September were further evidence that George II preferred such a course. Granville, recorded Newcastle,

is very angry with Mr Fox, and me. He calls us cowards, that we are frightened with nothing, that this clamour must blow over, as being entirely without foundation. That we want neither my Lord Bute, nor Pitt. That the latter won't come, and would not remove the national clamour, if it was founded; that the former should not be gratified, so contrary to the King's inclination and declaration; and that his Majesty would never forgive *anyone* who forced him, or gave him that advice. This he has talked with full force to Mr Fox...[180]

There only remained the possibility of an increased reliance on more minor figures. Here, too, problems had arisen since the end of the session in May. Sackville had quarrelled with Anson, and Hardwicke feared the issue was not merely personal: 'If his lordship goes into opposition, or half opposition, it will be from motives more deeply rooted, and of a higher nature.'[181] Fox reported to Newcastle his conviction that neither Sackville nor Bedford would be brought to say that a fleet could not have been sent sooner to the Mediterranean.[182]

BUTE WITHOUT PITT, SEPTEMBER–OCTOBER 1756

Newcastle summarised the underlying problems to be dealt with by a meeting of the Cabinet on 9 September:

The present great consideration is reduced to the following questions: Can we go out? Can we go on in the House of Commons, with Mr Fox in the temper he is, and in the circumstances we are, without either Leicester House or Mr Pitt? Can we get either or both? By what means can we get either? Should those means be tried or not with either, with both, or with which of them?[183]

Fox saw things differently:

I believe we are to have a meeting on Thursday [9th], in which I suppose I shall be alone for advising HM to give Lord Bute the employment, desired for him by the Prince and Princess of Wales. I will give it, and must insist on HM's knowing I give it. I suspect HM has been told that I have been making court

255

there, which is very false. He shall know my opinion and the honest reasons of it, I have no underhand, indirect ones.[184]

But at the meeting on 9th, he was given no opportunity to demonstrate his position. To his surprise, the Prince's household was left unmentioned: that issue, he realised, was to be settled by George II, Newcastle and Hardwicke alone. Fox was outraged to discover the same day (by what means is unclear) that he had long been quoted to the King as being in favour of Bute's having the Stole: 'in fact, till I knew all, which was not very long ago, I gave no opinion' – *formally*.[185] This added greatly to Fox's fears that he was being misrepresented in the Closet as treating with Leicester House – a course of action which was still, for him, a dangerous and unexplored ambition. But there were advantages in being excluded from consultation, and Fox accepted his position as yet without complaint. As Murray observed, not to be previously consulted on a measure generally but unofficially known, allowed some ministers to claim later (as with the Prussian treaty in the summer of 1755) that they had had no hand in it.[186] In 1756, it was only in October that Fox interpreted this convenient anonymity, which he had until then even boasted of,[187] as an affront. For the moment, Fox appeared to Newcastle 'grave, and rather down' – alarmed, as Newcastle thought, 'about the treaties the King is entering into, as Elector, for troops, the expense of which, I owned to him, I thought must be made good by us'. In reality Fox's unease related just as cogently to his fears of the results of an accommodation with Bute, and of the King's having been told, with truth, that Fox had advised it.[188] But, for the moment, this was disguised. Newcastle had a two-hour interview with him on 24 September, covering all aspects of business. 'Upon the subject of Leicester House, Mr Fox indeed talked plainly, and properly', wrote Newcastle, 'and in that we entirely agreed.'[189]

Newcastle was at Kensington on 9th, probably after the Cabinet, and observed: 'things go very well at Court, it looks nearer an accommodation with Leicester House, than I have yet seen it'.[190] Evidently George II was relaxing his previous exclusion. On 11th, the King told Waldegrave of his intentions with respect to Bute,

which his Majesty said, 'His servants in the House of Commons, Mr Fox and my lord Barrington, had thought necessary for the success of his affairs there.' My lord Waldegrave approved the King's resolution, in *the present circumstances*.[191]

Hardwicke thought 'a little extraordinary' the King's claim that Bute's proposed promotion was at the suggestion of the ministry's Commons spokesmen.[192] As Fox suspected, it must have been Newcastle who planted that suggestion in order to damage Fox's standing in the Closet. Newcastle's confidence and resolution at this point were growing,[193] and the prospect of an arrangement with Leicester House can only have led him to envisage a reduction in his reliance on Fox. That prospect was encouraged by Waldegrave's news that 'for this last month, neither the Princess, nor Lord Bute, have talked against measures, and the administration, as they used to do'.[194] Nevertheless, a problem arose over the man to undertake the final negotiation. Newcastle was to see the King on 13th,[195] and probably heard then of Waldegrave's reluctance to undertake the role. His objections were relayed to the King,[196] who agreed that the overture should be delayed until Hardwicke's return to town. The Chancellor meanwhile wrote to urge that Waldegrave should be chosen: 'the éclat will be less, and the appearance of submission on his Majesty's part less, than if either his Treasurer, the President of his Council, or his Chancellor, should be sent in form to declare such an acquiescence on his Majesty's part to his grandson'. Yet there should be no delay;

There is nothing further to be deliberated upon about it. It is impossible to take any persons to stand by in the light of witnesses; it seems also as impossible to have any specific assurances drawn up in writing. The only thing of that kind would be a letter from the Prince of Wales to the King full of duty and gratitude (which I think your Grace once hinted) in which assurances may properly be given, but they can be only general.[197]

The previous day, however, the junior Court seems to have sent exactly such letters on its own initiative. They were presented in the Closet by Waldegrave, who was encouraged by the reaction despite the King's suspicion.[198] Newcastle was to see Hardwicke on his arrival in London on 27 September,[199] and that day the Chancellor drew up a minute suggesting the course to be pursued: acquiescence in the Prince's two requests.[200] Problems still remained about the wording of the King's message and about the filling of minor household posts, which were the subject of changes of plan. Particularly intractable was the problem of the offer of a place at Leicester House to Rockingham, who was torn between ambition and reluctance to leave the King's service against his, George II's, personal inclination.[201] The final list of the new household was still not complete when Waldegrave delivered the King's verbal message on 4 October, consenting to the Prince's remaining with his mother and to Bute's promotion to the Stole. Prince George 'showed all the satisfaction, and gratitude, that was possible', thought Newcastle; and the King was 'very well pleased' with the Prince's and Princess's written replies, brought by Waldegrave on 5th.[202]

From September, the substance of the ministry's business changed as the pace of the war accelerated. The Prussian invasion of Saxony, launched unexpectedly on 29 August and pursued with speed and success, revealed Frederick as the militarily efficient continental ally England had so long lacked. His pre-emptive attack transformed the European scene: it was that, not the Prince of Wales's new Establishment, which preoccupied Newcastle and his colleagues in September. More and more attention, too, came to centre on the subsidy treaties George II was entering into as Elector and on the dispute with Spain over the principle of 'free ships free goods.' Finally, there was a lull in domestic activity of the sort which was usual in the weeks before the opening of the session. Walpole wrote: 'The rage of addresses did not go far: at present everything is quiet. Whatever ministerial politics there are, are in suspense.'[203] Hume Campbell added: 'People here are more quiet, less active or thinking of any sort of politics than at a distance can be imagined.'[204] The approaching reconciliation of the two Courts was publicly anticipated, 'as there have been ways found of securing the assistance of one who has the greatest influence there'.[205] It contributed to an expectation of growing stability, and, as Rigby predicted, of the fragmentation of the opposition. Pitt, and perhaps Legge too, would be 'left in the lurch', and Bute set against Pitt.[206] Sir George Lyttelton wrote:

Whether in consequence of this [reconciliation] Mr Pitt and his brothers will accede to the Government I cannot tell, nor even whether the government will offer such terms to them as they can accept, or any terms at all. But the difficulty of the times and the temper of the ministry incline me to think that they would be treated with now, if they were in treatable dispositions. Their dispositions I suppose will be sounded. Much will depend on the credit they think they shall preserve at Leicester House, after the accommodation. Legge it is thought has the chief credit there; perhaps he may be treated with easier than they. If they remain still in opposition it may be possibly be opposition for life.[207]

After the exchange of conciliatory messages between Prince George and the King, confidence in a political alliance based on a settlement of the Royal Family increased: one less informed observer reported that talk of the inclusion of Pitt and his friends was general in early October, though he could not predict in which offices: 'Upon the whole, matters seem to tend to an accommodation among our great men.'[208]

Rigby's reaction was premature. The pattern of forces in prospect did nothing to encourage Fox to a more vigorous approval of the ministry's measures, as Newcastle discovered in an interview on 24 September: on every subject except that of Leicester House,

I saw a shyness, and reservedness, and plain dissatisfaction, but however we must go on, as well as we can. This conference ended, as all others have done, with demands of *jobs*, etc., which puts me quite out of patience.[209]

Whether or not these feelings were apparent to Fox, such demands were to become ever more frequent. Within days, he applied for a newly-vacant Prebend's stall at Windsor.[210] It may have been that Fox was genuine in seeing Newcastle's attitude over patronage as indicative of a determination to edge him away from ministerial power, and that Newcastle genuinely failed to see that his actions might appear in that light. It seems more likely, however, that Fox's use of such issues reflects the hesitant stages of his final resolution to bring down Newcastle's ministry by resigning from it.

There were four main elements in Newcastle's plan for the approaching session. The Cabinet, including Fox, were resolved to recommend that Parliament should finance the treaties for troops entered into by the King as Elector for the defence of Hanover, attacked *en haine* in an English quarrel.[211] Then, to offset this and make good Hardwicke's argument that a militia was acceptable on principles other than those on which Townshend's Bill had been based, Newcastle instructed Barrington to draw up a revised scheme.[212] Thirdly, a round of promotions was envisaged: Oswald to the Treasury; Stanley to the Admiralty; and either Charlton, Frederick or Elliot for two vacancies in the Board of Trade. Lord Strange was to have the Comptroller's staff, if it fell vacant. The Princess, too, once accommodated, might be used to break into the opposition – perhaps even to gain Legge.[213] Finally, the Princess herself was to be conciliated by the indulgence of the junior Court's requests over the new household. An inviting prospect was temporarily opened up; Newcastle speculated 'Whether this is to be carried further, with regard to *any*, or *all* the opposition?' – and pursued his plans for the rearrangement of legal offices, which would follow Murray's promotion, in a mood of quiet confidence.[214]

It was in this apparently losing position that Fox resorted to desperate measures. On 5 October, he heard (though Newcastle, apparently, did not) news which cast doubt on Pitt's being out of favour at Leicester House.[215] Suddenly, Fox insisted that Newcastle's intention to make Lord Digby a Lord of the Bedchamber to the Prince had been a firm promise, and one which, if broken, 'is a greater disgrace to me, than ever was yet undeservedly put on any man'.[216] Fox could not be certain of defeat on this issue, but now linked his ability to stay with honour to the disposition of an appointment which Newcastle knew to be a matter for the King's personal prerogative. Newcastle thought he had made it clear to Fox that the offer of the post to Digby had been conditional, based on the King's assumption that Rockingham would refuse the transfer and prefer to serve in the King's Household; Huntingdon would then be Master of the Horse to the Prince, so creating a vacancy for Digby in the Prince's Bedchamber. Fox claimed to have understood that if Rockingham went to Leicester House, Huntingdon would succeed him as a Lord of the Bedchamber to the King and an office about the Prince, therefore, be opened for Digby.[217] George II had, Newcastle admitted, suggested that alternative; but Newcastle had also warned Fox of his impression that if, contrary to expectation, Rockingham chose to go to Leicester House, George II might decide not to change his long-standing intention that Huntingdon should be Lord of the Bedchamber to the Prince. Newcastle urged that a private royal decision of this sort could not imply a ministerial disgrace;[218] but it was not Fox's purpose to allow himself to be conciliated. 'I believe if he was as well in the Closet as he could wish', observed Murray, 'he would be embarrassed with the situation.'[219] Angrily, Fox withdrew his offer to resign in Pitt's favour. If he were now to go, it could only be by his dismissal; and if he were to leave the ministry thus, the implication was already strong that it would incur his enmity.[220]

By this step, Fox at once ensured that Newcastle would have to be far more certain of the loyalty of Leicester House before trusting to their alliance; and, as Hardwicke warned, the Prince's personal assurances of loyalty might be interpreted as confined to the person of the King without any further political consequences. A visit by Granville was expected to gather more intelligence of the junior Court's disposition; Newcastle hoped it might also persuade the Princess to begin moves to recruit other individuals from the opposition. Hardwicke urged haste, before the opposition could recover from the shock,

fall into some new arrangements among themselves; and perhaps make some new tentatives, or enter into some new intrigues, though more concealed, with Leicester House. Mr Pitt is undoubtedly the material man. As to Mr Legge, I should think this may bring him without great difficulty.[221]

Hardwicke was misinformed. With Lady Yarmouth's communications with Leicester House deteriorating through Cresset being 'out of favour' there,[222] the extent to which Legge had risen to prominence was disguised from the ministry. But Hardwicke's forebodings of the Princess's continued frigidity towards the ministers were not yet to be confirmed.[223] Newcastle was convinced that he had lured Leicester House into a position to depart from which would entail a public breach of its undertakings, and that the reconciliation of the two Courts had removed the main support of opposition. The problem as Newcastle, Sir George Lyttleton, Nugent, Barrington, Oswald and Stone all saw it was now – as a consequence of the understanding with Leicester House – to divide and accommodate the leaders of the parliamentary opposition. There were two obstacles to the success of such a course. The first was Fox, whose 'late behaviour. . . shows pretty plainly that he is always upon the *catch*; and that *we* can do nothing to satisfy him; and therefore how unsafe it must be, to have our single dependence *there*. His two great friends, the Attorney General, and Mr Stone, give him up entirely in this transaction; and have not one word to say for him.' Oswald spoke to Newcastle of the parliamentary implications of unity in the royal family;

That if those in employment were cordially together, (meaning Mr Fox) that was a great point; of which however he seemed much to doubt; and very shrewdly said, that the Attorney General was, last session, the *cement* between *Fox and us*; that when he was absent, it plainly appeared, there was neither union, nor concert, amongst us; that the Attorney was gone.[224]

Oswald here echoed the outlook of Murray himself, who admitted to Newcastle:

Till you could find a better system, I wished to be a kind of cement between you [and Fox], I wished to spread the connection and cover heats. Good effects were sometimes found from it the last session. He [Fox] bore me good will because he knew I was no competitor, and that I meant to keep all together.[225]

Oswald's remark described the conduct of business on the floor of the Commons; Murray's was meant in a more general sense. On neither level did Newcastle dispute their accuracy.

The second difficulty was the King's probable unwillingness to suppress his resentment further by accepting Pitt in addition to Bute, though Newcastle hoped George II's dissatisfaction with Fox might bring him to it. The uncertainty surrounding the future was a hindrance, too, in consolidating the support of ministerial figures of the second rank. Oswald had refused offers from Bute the year before, and was now interviewed by Newcastle for a seat at the Treasury Board in return for his whole-hearted loyalty; he declared himself willing to support in any event, but insisted that 'if he came into the Treasury, it was to take a more considerable part'. Oswald thought it possible to blunt the edge of the opposition as a consequence of the reconciliation of the two Courts, by taking in at least some of its key members. Newcastle listed them as Pitt, Grenville, Legge, and the Townshends;[226] Oswald inclined to think Legge and the Townshends 'the most easily gained'.[227] There were signs that Granville's visit had been too long delayed, and Hardwicke favoured an immediate approach to the individuals Newcastle had mentioned without waiting to act via Leicester House.[228] At the same time Rockingham, apparently oblivious of the ministerial schemes which depended on his choice, decided to keep his place as Lord of the Bedchamber to the King.[229] The way was now open for Digby's promotion, and Newcastle told Fox of it on 12th.[230]

FOX'S TACTICS

The day before, however, Fox had decided privately to resign, intending to break the news to the King on 13th. He prepared Newcastle to take his resolution seriously by an interview with Stone on 11th, and the same day set out his reasons in a long letter of self-justification to Devonshire. In both, he evaded the implications of Digby's impending promotion by denying that that affair was the cause of his going. Instead, Fox repeated to Stone his complaints of the royal displeasure which, though he did not accuse Newcastle and Hardwicke of promoting, he maintained they could have effaced. Fox claimed to be Newcastle's 'substitute (and I had never pretended to be more)' in the Commons; that he[231]

found himself in the most disagreeable situation imaginable: hated by the King, and by the Princess of Wales, on account of his attachment to the Duke [of Cumberland]; exposed to the resentment of the nation more than anybody, on account of his being the principal person in the House of Commons. Responsible for the House of Commons, without any credit to support it...

– a circumstance proved, as Fox wrote to Devonshire, by Newcastle's showing him on 7th a list of the Prince's Establishment which contained the names of eight MPs whom Fox never knew were intended for places there. It proved Newcastle's opinion of Fox's 'total insignificancy'.

After seeing Stone, Fox met Cumberland and persuaded him of the impossibility of his going on longer. Fox proposed to tell Lady Yarmouth that his relations with Newcastle had led him to withdraw his offer of co-operation in the treaty 'intended or begun' with Pitt; but to recommend that the treaty be concluded, for he, Fox, could no longer act as Secretary of State. He would then add an empty promise to do all he could for the King's service in any office 'not of the Cabinet or Court'. If a treaty with Pitt were concluded, Fox would then in fact find himself of no political consequence and without a basis for opposition. If, as Fox thought more likely, Pitt refused, Fox would be open to charges on the point of honour; of deserting the King's service, from cowardice, resentment or self interest. These he would meet by offering to carry on the King's affairs if he were given an understanding that he might quit at the end of the session 'with some mark of his favour'. Cumberland approved this course. Fox asked for Devonshire's advice: 'Your Grace will take into your consideration, that I not only would not, but could not carry on the King's affairs without the Duke of Newcastle. It is absolutely impossible to go on with him. I therefore must get out of Court.'[232] Devonshire, too, was persuaded to approve Fox's conduct.[233] It seems, however, that Stone was not told, as Cumberland and Devonshire were, of Fox's willingness to hold office for one more session. To Newcastle, therefore, Fox presented a much starker threat: his resignation patently did not mean that he thought Newcastle *would* succeed in an approach to Pitt, or that he, Fox, would *not*. To Bedford and Digby, Fox could misrepresent Newcastle as 'in treaty, or rather intending to try to treat' with Pitt[234] and that, foolishly as ever, Newcastle would seek to replace Fox by Pitt. Again Fox omitted all reference to the offer he had already made, impracticable and merely cosmetic as in fact it was, to go on for one more session; he would, he now said, make that offer to the King if a deal with Pitt were impossible in the wake of Fox's resignation. He added that Digby should say nothing to Bedford of 'any fixed intention':[235] Fox must always seem the passive victim of Newcastle's overbearing methods, not the active subverter of his ministry. Bedford, from Woburn, gave exactly the required reaction: Newcastle's secret negotiations with Pitt excused Fox's conduct in seeking to step down, and Bedford 'saw no salvation for this country but in a junction between you and P[itt].'[236] Thus it was, when Fox resigned on 13th, he did so professing to be both without complaint and innocent.[237]

Newcastle heard on 12 October of Stone's deeply ominous interview with Fox. What struck Newcastle most was that Fox had not mentioned his earlier offers to support from an inferior station: 'which shows to me very clearly, that that proposal proceeded more from discontent, than real concern for the success of affairs'. Newcastle repeated this observation to Lady Yarmouth, but instead of further advocacy of a union with Pitt, he was astonished to discover that she had reversed her position, now saying

that we must do the best we could with Mr Fox; for *that we could not change him*. And I own I fear that the turn will now be, to be more complaisant to Fox, in order to keep out the other; and to make it more practicable, to go on as we are. This (if so) at once destroys all thoughts of our breaking into the opposition.

Nothing had happened to alter Lady Yarmouth's opinion of the opposition's willingness to accept office; it seems likely that her reversal was the result of a meeting with Fox on 11th or 12th, or reliable news of his current disposition. Her implication that it was Newcastle who was seeking to edge Fox away from real power is strong evidence that it was Fox or one of his friends who had been her source, and that what had been told her amounted to a threat by Fox to resign if his position were weakened by the inclusion of others. It was this, now, which made it impossible for Fox to be changed; and if Lady Yarmouth's attitude is a good guide to the King's, George II became fully committed to Fox's retention only a day before he resigned.

Newcastle was temporarily at a loss. With Fox insisting (as it seemed) on staying, the King would certainly refuse a proposal in favour of Pitt, acceptable to George II, if at all, only as an alternative. The Townshends would never come, Newcastle thought, as things were; nor would the King have them. Legge might perhaps be won over, but only at the price of a peerage – which would remove him from the scene of action.[238] Hardwicke's advice was out of touch, for he imagined that Fox might still be retained by the offer of the Paymastership; that the prospect of breaking into the opposition remained good; and that the King might be brought to agree, if Pitt were not proposed to him first. Hardwicke wrote:

One word more as to the taking in any of the opposition. Your Grace may perhaps not dislike the present situation at Court for the indisposition of the King to Mr Fox, and to go on with him, in his present state of humiliation there. If that be so, you are in my opinion in the right *as to Court*; but, at this juncture, that is not the only, nor perhaps the most essential part. The present state of affairs makes it necessary to have the first attention to *the House of Commons*, without which the power in *the former* cannot be maintained.[239]

This, too, was unfair to Newcastle, who had pursued no move for Fox's dismissal and whose whole policy had shown a just appreciation not only of the importance of the Commons but also of the implications there of relations between St James's and Leicester House. Yet the one thing which neither Newcastle, Hardwicke, Pitt or Fox apparently mentioned was the prospect of improving their position in the Commons, at

Court or in the ministry by extracting advantage from that nebulous generalisation, 'public opinion'.

THE RESIGNATION OF FOX AND ITS CONSEQUENCES, OCTOBER 1756

Newcastle was relieved from his dilemma by Fox's letter of resignation on 13th. As in March 1754, Fox's action had an air of impetuosity, even caprice; and the decision was apparently concerted with no-one but Cumberland. Bedford did not know in advance;[240] and the circumstances of Fox's going made Rigby fear for him 'that mankind will attribute to his ambition what really proceeds from ill usage...'[241] Fox excused himself implausibly to Hardwicke by arguing that he, Fox, should resign at once so that it should not look like 'a struggle for power'.[242] Plainly, however, it did; though Devonshire, still warning Fox against the next, dishonourable, step of joining opposition, apparently thought ill treatment by Newcastle had provoked him to act rashly.[243] Bedford, however, weighing affairs from a distance, wrote a justification of Fox which entailed Newcastle's resignation: just the course of action which Fox would compel him to. But Bedford's analysis clearly showed, too, the dangers of resigning before Newcastle. Fox could hardly then support measures if Newcastle were rash enough to go on; but if Fox could not condemn past policies while remaining Secretary of State, how could he condemn them out of office in the light of his recent attitude and his assurances to Newcastle and the King? When Fox's decision was known to Bedford, the future course was plain. If Newcastle still refused to negotiate, Fox should bring down the ministry by allying with Pitt, each taking the most appropriate department: Fox the Treasury, Pitt a Secretaryship of State. This was an optimistic view of the outcome, however: 'You may possibly think the Bath waters have turned my head when I chalk out such Utopian schemes...'[244]

If Fox condemned Newcastle for planning (as he supposed) to dismiss him without first securing Pitt, Fox was infinitely more rash in actually resigning without taking a single sounding of the opposition. Nevertheless, it has been suggested above that what Newcastle called 'a kind of resignation'[245] was a real resignation, and that Fox therefore misrepresented his own motives in his letter to the King.[246] There, he laid most stress on Newcastle's request through Barrington that he, Fox, step down in favour of Pitt, which Fox claimed still to be willing to do. He offered, next, to support the King's measures from any office not of the Cabinet. Thirdly, he complained of his declining credit in the Commons through 'want of support' from Newcastle, determined as he was to edge him away from power. Elsewhere, for the ministry's ears, he gave priority to this reason: '(the old story)' as Newcastle called it.[247] Yet it has been shown above, first, that Fox was unwilling to be replaced by Pitt and had only offered so to be replaced when he knew it to be an impossibility and when the offer served to screen his own motives. Secondly, that Fox was aware of the vacuousness of an offer to support a Newcastle ministry's measures when his own withdrawal from the Cabinet would, and was intended to, secure its collapse. Thirdly, it has not proved possible to discover a decline in Fox's credit in the Commons in the spring of 1756, and his demands for jobs in the autumn have been shown to be tactically inspired moves in his campaign.

Newcastle had not expected Fox to commit political suicide, imagining rather that he would take advantage within the ministry of Murray's promotion. Newcastle's initial belief, therefore, based on a conversation with Granville (who had tried unsuccessfully to dissuade the Secretary of State) was that Fox 'makes use of this opportunity of distress, to put his knife to our throats, to get his own terms; and all the power, he wants; which, he thinks, *we* cannot now refuse him'. Horace Walpole's opinion, too, was that Fox 'hoped to terrify, and to obtain an increase of sway'.[248] Newcastle continued:

He talked the old language – that *I* thought, *I* could govern the House of Commons, without giving power to the person at the head of it; and such stuff, as that. Have not Mr Fox's friends been sufficiently considered, in the House of Commons? Have I failed to support any one single recommendation of his to the King? His Majesty knows the truth of this; and has often blamed me for it. But I showed him [Fox] the list of the persons, proposed for the Prince of Wales's family – I aver, before the King had seen it; before I had spoke to any one man there named, except the Lords of the Bedchamber; and acquainted him with all, that had passed. I took the only friend, he recommended, down immediately; and recommended him to the King. In short, more attention I could not show, *even to your lordship*.[249]

To Newcastle and George II, the charge of starving Fox of his proper share of recommendations was as plainly false[250] as the story that Newcastle was negotiating with Pitt and had sent Barrington with a request that Fox resign:

I never sent Barrington – he went sillily, of his own head. He had teased me about Pitt; and I told him, I did not know, whether his friend, Fox, was in earnest; I might disoblige the King, by proposing Mr Pitt; be rejected, (as I concluded, I should), by Mr Pitt. And be thought, by Mr Fox, to be turning him out. This is my real crime to Fox. In short, he will go, or insist upon more power, than can be given him, except he had the Treasury; which, I heartily wish, he had.[251]

After Pitt's refusal to treat and before approaching Granville, Newcastle invited Egmont to be Secretary of State; but he refused on 19th, his ambition being for an English peerage alone.[252] Glover claims that in October Newcastle offered the seals first to Halifax, then to Egmont.[253] If Halifax too was approached, it seems likely that both occurred before Newcastle made a final, self-deprecating offer to Granville that he should take the Treasury with Fox at the Exchequer. Again the Lord President refused, reminding Newcastle of the real choice: to give Fox what he demanded or to bring in Pitt – 'who certainly', Newcastle now thought, 'will not come'. Newcastle's misapprehension – that Fox still acted in pursuit of a larger share of power within his, Newcastle's, ministry, and that he might be dealt with, as in the past, on the basis of a sharing of power – was soon corrected by the reflection that if Fox seriously intended to resign, he must either be in, or soon form, an alliance with Pitt. 'Mr Fox had better say at once, [that] nothing will satisfy him, but being at the head of the Treasury. You see, all his complaints tend, to throw envy, and odium, upon me; and to flatter the principles of Pitt, and Legge, about the House of Commons.'[254]

In the immediate aftermath of his action, Fox was at pains to deny any links of his own with Pitt and to urge that the ministry pursue theirs,[255] for it was the existence of ministerial overtures alone which could justify his conduct. This did not convince Hardwicke, who thought that Fox depended on the King's not wholeheartedly agreeing to a scheme for a reconciliation with Pitt; that George II may have been freshly prejudiced against Pitt, perhaps by Lady Yarmouth; and that neither Cumberland nor Fox intended that he, Fox, should really resign. Yet what Barrington's mission suggested about an impending deal with Pitt might, Hardwicke wrote, have made Fox

apprehend the resolution might soon be taken, and therefore determine to be beforehand. I should also conjecture that, seeing a kind of reconciliation made with Leic[ester] House, he may think that measure may have an effect upon the opposition, to make them, in a little time, the more inclined to approach nearer to the administration, and therefore he may intend to bring on a difficulty before you are ripe for it; and choose to appear to quit rather than be dropped.[256]

Newcastle, too, vehemently urged George II to believe that he would not, on his own initiative, offer the Secretaryship of State to Pitt. Walpole records that Fox was 'casting about for means of union with Pitt'; that Fox had asked him to tell Pitt that he, Fox, would be willing to join him as soon as he was ready to break with Newcastle, and that Walpole had refused to participate in what he saw as a dishonourable manoeuvre.[257] Fox was still inhibited from pursuing such a design openly; but the chief reason for Fox's inability to exploit the situation was Newcastle's success in persuading the King, not just that *he* was not treating secretly with the ex-Paymaster, but that Fox had resigned for tactical reasons and that his excuses were 'pretences to get more power. To cover the true reason of his quitting, if he quits.' And, in that case, Fox's reiteration of the old talk about the power of the minister in the Commons made him seem, to the King, to be courting once more the support of Pitt and Legge, 'who both went into opposition upon that principle'. Newcastle was convinced that Fox's promotion to the Treasury would mean total surrender;[258] but as soon as the shock of Fox's message of 13th had subsided, he became quickly less inclined to believe that Fox could really intend to quit *tout court*. Again, he saw the influence of Cumberland behind Fox's intransigence; but reasoned that the Duke wanted to provoke Fox to violent gestures which could then be moderated. Newcastle even suspected Fox of reverting to his designs on the Paymastership.

Granville's suggestion that Fox was 'inflexible' was at odds with Newcastle's judgement. He consciously doubted the Lord President's sincerity, and apparently suspected him of preferring Fox's departure in the hope of its entailing Newcastle's own fall.[259] But Granville's opinion that Pitt would not come harmonised with Newcastle's growing fear that that and the King's aversion to Pitt had been the basis of the deliberately concerted conduct of Cumberland and Fox; and that they supposed they would force the King to take Fox on his, Fox's, own terms. This, Newcastle was determined to resist. He had no cause to regret his treatment of Fox, whose grievances he saw as 'trumped up' to transfer the blame to him, when in fact Fox quit from dissatisfaction with the King's treatment or fear in face of the current state of affairs. Now, too, Fox's complaints over appointments were aimed at winning the sympathy of the Princess, and his language about sole power was meant for Pitt, Legge and the others: 'the old, stale charge, of my assuming too much power in the House of Commons, in order to recommend himself to the opposition'.

Hardwicke was still in the country. By letter, he received an account of Newcastle's audience on 14th:

'But,' said the King, 'what is to be done?' I said, 'Sir, my Lord President said, there was but one of two things to do; – either to gratify Fox, in what he wanted, (which, said I, would, perhaps, be giving Mr Fox more power, than your Majesty would think proper); Or, to take in Mr Pitt.' 'But,' replied the King *peevishly*, 'Mr Pitt won't come.' 'If *that* was done,' I said, 'we should have a quiet session.' '*But Mr Pitt won't do my German business.*' 'If he comes into your service, Sir, he must be told, he must do your Majesty's business. I have wrote, Sir, to my Lord Chancellor.' 'Well, what says the Chancellor?' 'I have not his answer; but I know, what he will say. – If this gentleman won't continue, we must go into the opposition.' 'But I don't like *Pitt. He won't do my business.*' 'But, unfortunately, Sir, he is the only one, (in the opposition) who has ability to do the business.' 'Something must be done, my lord. You must consider. – I will talk to Fox; and see, what I can do.' 'He will not talk to you, Sir (as I understand by my Lord President)', – 'I will begin with him'. 'Sir Thomas Robinson told me, Sir, that, if it was now made up, it would break out again, in a month, or six weeks.' 'We shall, however,' says the King, 'gain time, if *he* would stay, this session only.'

Plainly, George II wished to avoid Pitt and, thought Newcastle, would be willing to do much to conciliate Fox (if only for one session) despite his bitter resentment of Fox's conduct. Lady Yarmouth was equally committed to the same course, but less hopeful that Fox might be induced to stay. It seems likely that the King had known of Fox's offer to do so, probably through Cumberland, for some time. If so, it may well have disposed him better towards Fox than Newcastle had reason to think. Newcastle was not inclined to solicit Fox's aid; his subordinate was treacherous, a deserter, and anyway incapable of doing the King's business. Pitt was preferable, even if he came 'as a *conqueror*', an outcome which Newcastle 'always dreaded'. Since he *could* conduct business in the Commons, the King might now be persuaded to accept him. On such generous terms, 'I think, Pitt must come; and, if Leicester House are not in the combination with the Duke of Cumberland, and Fox, their eyes must now be opened. They must make *Pitt* come'.[260]

Newcastle, from his antipathy to Fox, thus reached the same position as did Hardwicke from his preference for Pitt. Naturally, Hardwicke played on Newcastle's aversion; and without mentioning the possibility of the ministry's resignation, urged that Pitt and Fox were two mutually exclusive alternatives.[261] The same suspicion was slowly dawning on Fox from Lady Yarmouth's conversation and from the King's reaction to Fox's letter, officially delivered by Granville on 15th. As yet, however, he remained inflexible, despite George II's appeal to his honour and conscience to stay.[262] The King rejected Fox's allegations about places; 'neither he nor the Duke of Newcastle', wrote Fox, 'yet give up their system of governing without communicating any power to a commoner'.[263] Fox expected even Cumberland to press him to stay another session (an impossibility when it must be known that Fox would eventually go); how then could Newcastle remain in the face of 'Mr Pitt opposing both, on strong and popular points? How many will choose to oblige him? How very many more will choose at least not to disoblige him and their constituents too, to oblige an expiring administration?' Fox did not know the answer to these questions, for he had not been calculating the allegiance of MPs and did not act on the basis of an estimate of numbers. During the summer he had even predicted, to Ilchester, that 'there would be no great difference between the number of votes this sessions and last'.[264] Now, Fox worked hard to persuade his friends that, on reflection, he found the plan of continuing for a session less and less practicable;[265] but this was disingenuous. Its impossibility must have been apparent from the first, and (as has been argued) Fox never intended to be held to the promise. Now too, while admitting that no overture had been made to Pitt, Fox felt sure the ministry would make such an offer; but if Pitt refused, 'Dear Brother, tell me what I can do'.[266] Not only a profitable lesser office, but an honourable resignation itself, now depended on Pitt's willingness to negotiate: the very thing Granville reported the King as least willing to contemplate.

Newcastle found the mood of the Closet altered on 15th; George II, perhaps under the impression that Pitt could be treated with separately from Leicester House, authorised an overture to him. Newcastle secured authority to offer Pitt a good reception from the King, and, if necessary, the Secretaryship of State in return for his support of measures. This was not disclosed to the Lord President, who carried in Fox's message immediately after Newcastle; 'Lord Granville told me, that he found, the King was so angry with Fox, that he had rather have anybody, than him'. Newcastle therefore imagined Fox to be immobilised in an impossible situation: even if he discovered that an overture had been made to Pitt, his message to the King had condoned it in advance. This was the first Newcastle had heard of the King's reaction to Fox's most recent behaviour. With Granville also licensed to try to make Fox change his mind, the approach to Pitt became all the more urgent. Newcastle and Hardwicke would be in difficulties if Granville persuaded Fox to withdraw that part of his letter which the King had found objectionable (that is, Fox's complaint of lack of sufficient confidence for the conduct of Commons business). Newcastle recorded: 'The King asked me, "Suppose Pitt will not serve with you." "Then Sir I must go...If, Sir, there is a concert between *Fox and Pitt*; they must make the administration."' It was to prevent such a possibility that Newcastle asked Hardwicke to arrange to meet Pitt in town on 19 October; and Newcastle attached great importance to Hardwicke's taking the irreversible step of writing to Pitt quickly, before Granville could see Fox.[267] This haste was justified, for though the King had not revealed the overture Newcastle launched, he had asked Granville's opinion in such a way that the Fox camp at once inferred that Newcastle was treating with both the Princess and Pitt.[268]

Hardwicke wrote as requested;[269] but with misgivings, for he saw hazards in approaching Pitt before the results of Granville's and Cumberland's audiences were known. If Granville were successful in reconciling Fox, the King would not accept Pitt, and permanent damage might be done to the latter's disposition. Moreover, Cumberland

cannot be in earnest that Mr Fox should quit, and therefore there must be some underplot which don't yet appear; at least there is room to suspect it. Mr Fox, by the preamble of his paper, will have the merit of proposing Mr Pitt to be Secretary of State, and quitting in his favour; and this directly to the King himself, which he will say nobody else would do. It gives room also to suspect (as your Grace has done) that there may be some concert between him and Mr Pitt, and if so, what can the terms be, except that Mr Pitt shall absolutely refuse to come in, unless the administration is changed? I am told, that Mr Pitt's little place in the country, is very near Mr Calcraft's, where Mr Fox uses frequently to go down on a Saturday...[270]

Thus Newcastle was predisposed to interpret a refusal by Pitt as evidence of what Fox had covertly sought but had not brought about, a Fox–Pitt alliance. The ministry was in no position to dispel such fears; Hardwicke confessed to having had no 'channel' to Pitt since September 1755. Fox was at this moment professing a wish that Pitt would be reconciled with the Old Corps;[271] but by delaying the final step of bringing the seals to Court, he convinced his friends (Granville in particular) that he intended to offer terms in his audience, arranged for Monday 18 October.[272] Granville approved, and after Newcastle's unsolicited offers to him of the Treasury, may have seen in Fox's advancement an alternative to Newcastle's dominance.

Bedford, more deeply hostile to Newcastle, disagreed. Evidently taking Fox's offer to go on another session as sincerely meant (when in fact it had only just become a dangerous possibility), Bedford warned against what he feared to be Cumberland's advocacy of that step. Lord Digby seconded Bedford: experience showed that nobody could act with Newcastle, and only an extreme crisis would force George II from his policy of governing through that minister alone. Without Fox, Digby argued, Newcastle must resign when Parliament met; Fox could then choose his office without facing the problems of the defence of past measures in the House. Ilchester was more inclined to think it feasible for Fox to go on, but reminded him that no honourable terms of retreat had been offered; 'To tell the King you will serve this session and run all risks or to resign without going into opposition are the only methods I can think on both vastly unpleasant'.

Bedford's, Digby's and Ilchester's advice arrived only after Fox's audience,[273] which was apparently calm but inconclusive.[274] Yet in fact it allowed Fox to claim that his resolution not to remain in the Cabinet was powerfully and justifiably reinforced. To Devonshire, he explained that the King's personal hostility was the result of his, Fox's advice that Bute should have the Stole: advice which Fox had never, he claimed, given in Cabinet or to George II, and only at a late stage, in private, to Newcastle. Then, too, his proposed resignation had been made public by the ministry; this, and the fact that overtures had been made to others, Fox advanced as excuses against his going on for another session. He added that he knew nothing of Pitt's disposition; he merely hoped that, if his resignation brought down Newcastle, it would throw the conduct of the war into Pitt's hands.[275] To Bedford, Fox explained the audience differently, and in a way to stimulate the Duke's desire to oppose Newcastle. The King, he reasoned, was trying to keep the ministry's options open until Hardwicke could invite Pitt; but Fox expected Cumberland on 20th to approve his resignation and so bring to an end 'the Duke of Newcastle's reign'.[276] Yet Fox could not legitimately declare open hostility to both Newcastle and Pitt. Apparently before his audience on 18th, he had made a last offer to Hardwicke. Professing a lack of resentment or ambition, he urged his willingness to support the ministry in an inferior employment if Pitt could thereby be recruited. In this form, his offer was not made 'in hopes of more power' – 'my aim is to get out of Court, and my justification in so doing, the impossibility of my carrying on the King's affairs now as a minister, even if I had more power given me'.[277] It was to be the failure of Hardwicke's offers to Pitt which re-activated Fox's ambitions, partly now from necessity, turning them into a direct bid for power.

Though it was unknown in Fox's camp,[278] it was already correctly suspected in Hardwicke's[279] that Pitt was determined to reject any ministerial scheme with Newcastle at its head (perhaps because of the danger of a Newcastle–Bute deal which it would perpetuate) or any proposal to screen Newcastle's retreat if he stood down; but Pitt's position had been taken up without knowing how far George II would be willing to comply.[280] His friends encouraged him to believe that the King would take anyone able to promise the quiet conduct of his affairs, but that Fox lacked general popularity:

That his close connection with the D[uke] of C[umberland] represents him as an object of jealousy; and that to make such a man Minister, would be for the King to be governed by his son. That the only fear of you is your connection with L[eicester] H[ouse], but that this is an evil the least feared at present; that the first offices should be at your disposal and real power put into your hands. That you should take the Treasury yourself.[281]

Hardwicke saw Pitt for three-and-a-half hours on 19 October. 'His answer is an absolute *final negative* without any reserve for further deliberation.'[282] Hardwicke offered,[283] baldly, the Secretaryship of State *vice* Fox, plus a good reception from the King. Pitt again professed to seek no office; but he would support measures on certain conditions. Foreign troops must be dismissed and a militia agreed to. 'Reparation' must be made for Holdernesse's breach of the constitution in ordering the release of a Hanoverian soldier, arrested on suspicion of a minor offence, from the custody of the civil magistrates at Maidstone: a step which Pitt described as 'the most atrocious act of power and the grossest attempt to dispense with the laws of England that had been committed since the days of Lord Strafford'. An enquiry must be permitted into the loss of Minorca and military failures in North America. A scheme of measures must be adopted, and previously explained to Pitt, of which he could approve. Finally, Newcastle must go; his position as First Minister made him responsible for the mistakes in the conduct of the war, and the national outcry against him made it impossible for him to sustain the government either alone or in alliance with anyone else. Once prompted, Hardwicke extended his offer of office to include Pitt's 'particular friends'. Pitt, according to his own account, replied: 'I take for granted...you cannot possibly mean the little knot of my own relations...I consider every man as my particular friend whose service the public stands in need of at this particular juncture. Thereupon the Chancellor said, "I now begin to perceive that your intentions aim at no less than an entire change of Administration."' Hardwicke need not have been expected to have recognised this from the outset, since, most importantly, he disagreed with Pitt's allocation of responsibility: Newcastle 'has had no more direction in the measures of the war than any one of the seven of us' – that is, the inner Cabinet of Newcastle, Hardwicke, Holdernesse, Sir George Lyttelton, Granville, Anson and Fox. This was strictly true. As Newcastle continued to emphasise, he had had no share in the direction of the army; in naval matters, 'no other share but concurring in what was the unanimous opinion of every person present'; had had no part in appointing commanding officers to either service; and had never given any of them an order, 'except what immediately related to the Treasury'.[284] Martin critically rationalised the ministerial offer: Newcastle and Hardwicke 'appear to have laid it down as a maxim, that all men were eager and ready to accept great offices without standing upon any conditions regarding the public'. Among other things, 'the late negotiations for power, or dignities, concluded by Lord Bath and other formidable patriots, who had altogether dropped the public in their interested treaties [in 1746], might very plainly countenance these notions of the profligacy of Englishmen'.[285] It is evident that Newcastle and Hardwicke were still behaving as if – as was true as recently as the early spring of 1756 – Patriot ideology were dead.

Pitt declared that his demands were not negotiable. Newcastle was shocked and saw no immediate course of action. 'God knows, what will become of the King and the public; for that is our concern. I cannot conceive what is to be done next, except my retiring from business, and then those gentlemen must carry it on.'[286] Yet this state of mind was only temporary. On reflection, his qualified resolution to go on was still qualified only by a willingness to retire if the King wished it as a necessary condition of others' accepting office. But this made it an offer to go only if the King submitted to being forced, which he would do only in the last resort. To make him even more unwilling, Newcastle urged that George II be shown that the accusations against Newcastle's conduct of the war were based on false claims about the constitution, and that, as Newcastle believed, events revealed a conspiracy between Pitt and Fox 'to make themselves necessary and masters of the King'. 'They deny any concert', wrote Hardwicke, 'but I am convinced that I see symptoms of it'.[287]

Hardwicke reported the terms of his interview with Pitt to George II on the following day. The King disapproved of Pitt's suggestions.[288] Newcastle was faced with conflicting advice about his next step. The situation was unprecedented. Some of his friends advised resignation; others urged resolution.[289] Observers drew different lessons from these attitudes. Rigby, on the eve of a journey with Fox to consult Bedford at Bath, believed Newcastle intended to face Parliament without the support of either Pitt or Fox.[290] Granville, indeed, had strongly urged that the ministry needed neither Bute nor Pitt;[291] but this idea went much further. Fox, however, took his cue from what he guessed had been Pitt's reply to Hardwicke: not an 'absolute negative' but an insistence that Newcastle, who had monopolised the King's confidence, must go. Fox thought it just possible that, if this occurred, Pitt might accept office with a few other changes.[292] If not, the obvious alternative was an arrangement with Pitt. By now Fox realised that, if public knowledge of his resignation really had made his continuance impossible, neither had he been asked to do so, except once by Lady Yarmouth.[293] This was a blow to his pride. Already, Fox was marshalling and preparing his followers: Bedford, Hillsborough, W. G. Hamilton, Oswald, Dodington (and, through him, Halifax).[294]

Lacking detailed information, Fox interpreted Pitt's first-ever visit to Lady Yarmouth on 21 October in the same way, as an attempt to persuade George II to part with Newcastle.[295] That once achieved, wrote Fox, 'I think it can hardly end worse for me than in the offer of a good place' in a Pitt ministry.[296] He did not know that Pitt, in supreme self-confidence, had submitted via Lady Yarmouth a plan for a ministry complete except for a Lord Chancellor and a First Lord of the Admiralty.[297] Unknown, too, to Fox, Bedford or Devonshire, the last was named as its nominal head. No office was left vacant to which Fox could reasonably aspire. Hardwicke heard a rumour the same day that Fox was not mentioned in Pitt's scheme, and inferred that it 'looks a little like concert with Leicester House'. This was the first real evidence the ministry had of such a reconciliation, and Hardwicke did not at once attach great weight to it. Despite the King's disposition, the Chancellor had predicted, before hearing of Pitt's proposal, that George II would offer Fox some lesser office not of the Cabinet.[298] If no understanding between Pitt and Leicester House existed, the chances of Fox's acceptance, despite the feared alliance with Pitt, would be substantially increased.

Devonshire only heard of Pitt's plans by chance, after Legge approached Sir Robert Wilmot on 22nd for advice on a problem of honour: whether he could accept the Exchequer without being also First Lord of the Treasury. Apparently, Legge had not been previously consulted and was not on good terms with Pitt. The latter's scheme may well have been drawn up, as a basis for discussion, only after the news of Fox's resignation became public in London on 19th.[299] Legge was eventually brought to agree by the realisation that to enjoy both offices would make *him* Minister. But he refused to consider accepting the Exchequer if Devonshire were not at the head of the Treasury: rather than that, he should prefer a peerage and the Treasurership of the Navy.[300] Over a week later, Charles Townshend truly wrote of there being, 'among those expected to form the new ministry, still more irreconcilable opinions and interests than subsisted under the former'.[301] Devonshire thus eventually found himself at the head of a ministry not so much from his acceptability to the Old Corps as from his utility in uniting an opposition divided by personal rivalries between Pitt, Legge, and Bute's Leicester House.

The danger of Pitt's advancing Devonshire as a neutral conciliator to head a ministry was that (as Wilmot realised) it paved the way for either Legge *or* Fox at the Treasury, 'and in reality most effectually' for the second.[302] Suspicions had not been entirely allayed that Fox sought the chief power in the next administration. Through West, Barnard warned of such a threat.[303] It was brought marginally nearer by the King's rejection of Pitt's proposals, of which Hardwicke told him in a second interview on 24 October. The Chancellor added, in extenuation, that the ministry would accept both an enquiry and a militia bill in some form; but Pitt again rejected anything less than full compliance.[304] By the following day, 25th, Fox had discovered this and that Pitt had submitted a list of his administration; he thought, too, that Newcastle's friends took care that he, Fox, should know of his exclusion. This was his first news that the opposition would reject a possibility on which he had relied for so long. His meeting with Pitt three days later confirmed it, but meanwhile he still thought 'very silly' any such attempt by Pitt to name places before knowing whether he could bring about Newcastle's fall. The information, he realised, had escaped through 'an oath of secrecy' and could not be relied on. It might easily be part of a design by Newcastle to prevent Fox from having any other recourse.[305] Almost certainly by speculation rather than knowledge, Fox expected by 25th that Newcastle would offer him the Paymastership in return for his promise to support measures; and, if Fox refused, face Parliament without reinforcement. 'This looks too much', he added, 'as if I should be drove, whether I will or no, into opposition.'[306] Though both courses were unpleasant, Fox now wanted to be driven there rather less. The Paymastership under Newcastle looked decidedly more attractive. But things had gone too far, and Newcastle's ministry was now too unstable, for him to accept. Sir George Lyttelton, whom Fox thought was offering Newcastle to undertake everything in the Commons,[307] could hardly stand against Pitt: Dupplin and Barrington did not expect him to succeed.

And yet I am at this instant uncertain whether it is not Lord Chancellor and the Duke of Newcastle's determination to go on without either of us. In this case, my dear lord, am I not to join with Pitt[?] If a man incapable will be absolute, is it distress to HM's affairs if you turn him out? Consider how far that argument will go? Let him take Pitt, I'll trust to his sharing at least the power, and I would in that case take a place not responsible and support, it is what I shall like best. But if Lord Egmont to whom they have offered the seals should accept, would your Grace think it dishonest opposition that should wrest out of the Duke of Newcastle['s] and Lord Chancellor['s] hands, the power? But suppose, that, on the other hand, they should try to regain me. I this morning thought the first was their scheme, I this evening think the last is. I have heard, too, that they hope some assurances from the King may do. Such an attempt would not much embarrass me, but if they go farther it will. With the Treasury and the King, he is absolute. Suppose he gives up the former, or gives it up in some shape or degree. I fear offers of this kind knowing their perfidy more even than I feared opposition. And besides, though I long, for the sake of this country, to see Lord Chancellor and the Duke of Newcastle out of government, I have not wisdom to see so clearly what would help us, as to make me wish to have any share in it myself.[308]

Fox was cut off from Cumberland, who had left for Windsor on 13 October and remained there; Fox did not see him until 28th.[309] No correspondence between the two survives for these days, and Fox certainly behaved as if in confusion and unadvised. On 24th, he and the rest of his camp[310] believed that Newcastle was probably determined to go on alone. This would have entailed Fox's open opposition.[311] He then swung, late on 25th, to an expectation that Newcastle would try to win him back. Fox was baffled at the prospect, for he had relied on Newcastle's having determined not to try such a course. But with both the Treasury and the King's confidence, Newcastle would still be Minister. Nor would Newcastle's sole power be ended by simply placing another man in the Secretaryship of State: that would require the new man to have real power and credit from the King.[312] Fox, however, still professed to Devonshire not to wish to inherit sole power, for he did not see how to use it to rescue the country. 'I want to turn them out, and be in no responsible place myself.' These were difficult elements to combine, and (save the visionary idea of Newcastle recruiting Pitt and then stepping down into an honorary office) Fox never clearly imagined an arrangement which could successfully combine them. Henry Digby, speculating before hearing the news of Newcastle's resignation, thought it would end in Fox's going into opposition and joining Pitt.[313] Bedford, whom Fox and Rigby travelled to consult at Bath on 23rd, was ready for vigorous opposition to displace Newcastle and Hardwicke alone; but showed Fox no signs of links with Pitt.[314] Fox weakly suggested that Bedford and Devonshire might be brought together, but nothing came of it. What Fox wanted most was Devonshire's sanction for the course he was inclined to: 'if they go on without either [Pitt or Fox], may I not join with Pitt?'[315]

Fox's anticipation proved wrong. Newcastle, like George II, Lady Yarmouth and Hardwicke (as Horace Walpole told Fox)[316] felt sure Fox was irreconcilable; his plans, briefly, were to find a Commons leader other than Fox or Pitt.[317] Failing in this,[318] Newcastle told the King on 26th that he could not undertake to conduct business in the Commons, and asked leave to resign. George II agreed,[319] and the news was public the next day.[320] Devonshire was sent for to town.[321] Pitt and the Grenvilles had meanwhile retreated to Stowe as a mark of dissociation from Newcastle, leaving Hillsborough to deny accurate rumours of the ministry Pitt had proposed to Lady Yarmouth: that is, of 'a family administration'.[322] But these rumours confirmed what Fox had heard: his place had been offered Pitt, who had demanded, in addition, jobs for his friends and the removal of Newcastle. It was clear, too, from the levée at Leicester House on Sunday 24th that Pitt had acted in concert with that Court. 'All treaty with him', inferred Fox, 'is over.'[323]

PITT, BUTE AND LEICESTER HOUSE:
APRIL–OCTOBER 1756

Pitt's subsequent success has led those who wrote after his lifetime to misrepresent his political conduct throughout the 1750s as more principled, more purposive, more consistent, and more in tune with political possibility than he, his allies or contemporaries saw or could foresee. At no time is this false perspective more distorting than in mid 1756 – months in which Pitt's best course, his 'platform', and the alliances open to him were uncertain because they were both more various and more difficult of attainment than those which confronted Newcastle or Fox.

Pitt, long absent from the Commons early in the year, had been unable to command Tory support there or in the Lords at the end of April on the issue of the Address to send for Hanoverian troops. In the face of the threat of invasion, he then quickly reversed his attitude to the use of German mercenaries in England. The possibility of a Tory *démarche* was foreseen by Horatio Walpole if the Militia Bill were rejected: it would, he wrote, allow raising a clamour 'not only by the pretended Patriots in opposition, but even by the Tories, who do not approve the present plan'[324] – but, by implication, they were the group otherwise *least* likely to join in a successful opposition. In such circumstances, recruits to the opposition were merely men whom the ministry had alienated. Gilbert Elliot, for example, was bound closer to the Grenvilles by the rejection of the Militia Bill in the Lords; as a man of principle, he rejected Granville's description of it as 'a shoeing-horn to faction'.[325] But although there is evidence that Charles Townshend, George Grenville and Temple were following closely the fate of Minorca in June,[326] it is not clear that Pitt shared their involvement or that he saw how *party* advantage might be extracted from military reverses. Nor is it evident during the summer that it was not Temple (as in April and May) rather than Pitt, who for the moment was taking the initiative. It may or may not be true that Pitt had 'steadily been increasing his hold on popular sympathies'.[327] But, if so, it is remarkable that there is no evidence that he was aware of it. His conduct, rather, bears out his later remark to Shelburne: 'Lord Chatham told me that he could never be sure of the public passions, that all he could do was to watch, and be the first to follow them.'[328] Potter's advice pointed rather to Pitt's rallying to the government in a time of extreme national emergency, as any loyal Englishman should do; and Potter's fear was that the Grenvilles, far even from

levying violent opposition on the ministry, would remain completely inactive in the face of an impending national disaster which they had no
plan to avert.[329] As if to confirm their lack of political resource, the
opposition failed to make the anticipated motion for an enquiry at the
adjournment on 18 June.[330]

A measure of the complexity of the situation was the distance and
distrust which grew up between Pitt and Bute. No sign of it was apparent
in mid June, when Legge discussed with both men the possibility of
promoting Morton to be Solicitor General to the Prince of Wales.[331] But
it was Legge who warned Pitt against the tactical consequences of a
reconciliation of the two Courts: 'I fancy it will not be long before you will
receive proposals in the spirit of those made by the drunken man to his
friend to come and roll in the kennel with those whom no man living,
not even yourself were you so disposed, would be able to lift out again.'[332]
By late August, there were signs that the Princess was giving voice to her
old suspicions of Pitt as the developing rapprochement between Leicester
House and St James's made it politic to do so and removed a reason for
not doing so.[333] Evidence is lacking to support the view that Leicester
House grew 'daily closer to Pitt as affairs grew blacker', or that 'Pitt
called the tune' during the summer.[334] Although little is definitely known
of Pitt's intentions until October, it seems likely that his relations with
Bute grew distant in early September because of his justified suspicion
that the reconciliation of the two Courts had been achieved by sacrificing
his, Pitt's, ambitions. Fox thought this certainly the case.[335] Waldegrave,
too, recorded that the concession of the Stole to Bute produced a 'general
opinion, that Leicester House would enjoy the fruits of the victory, and
cause no future disturbance...'[336] Though there were indications that
(as one might expect) Bute tried to keep in touch with Pitt,[337] evidence is
lacking that Pitt was cordial in return.

Pitt undoubtedly remained on good terms with George Grenville and
Temple, and told them of his decision to meet Hardwicke on 19 October
without first seeing Bute.[338] His determination was probably reinforced
by Potter's (erroneous) intelligence which implied that Leicester House
was organising behind his back a cabal including Legge but excluding
Pitt.[339] Pitt had, indeed, no reason for an unquestioning faith in his allies'
loyalty. In January, he had given every sign of believing Fox's broad
hints that George and Charles Townshend had offered Newcastle to give
up Pitt and loyally to support the ministry if Newcastle would drop
Fox.[340] As late as 1 October, it was reported that Charles Townshend
had accepted a seat at the Treasury.[341] In October, Pitt summoned to
town George Grenville, Temple, Sir Richard Lyttelton and James
Grenville to hear a report of his interview with Hardwicke on 19th; but
afterwards, they returned to the country.[342] The negotiations of October
were conducted by Pitt without inviting the participation of his subordinates.

At the same time, it is not clear that Pitt or Bute made any further efforts to court the Tories during the summer or exploit by an articulate alliance the massive and widespread public indignation at the conduct of the war. Such Tory recruits as were won over seem to have been collected by others.[343] Dame Lucy Sutherland correctly pointed to the failure of Pitt's oratory at once to create, or to mark him out as the leader of, a strong opposition during the summer. Even the Tories, she observed, were not unanimous in seeing him rather than Fox as their natural focus of loyalty; William Beckford, for example, did not transfer his allegiance from Fox to Pitt until early November.[344] What produced an opposition was not Tory or public opinion but the tactical possibilities which Pitt imagined to be opened up by Fox's resignation, coming as it did after the manoeuvres of the summer. In the absence of opposition direction of it, Newcastle received evidence that 'independent' sentiment was as fickle as he imagined it to be. The Prussian invasion of Saxony and the victory of Lobowitz, news of which arrived on 11 October,[345] were greeted with enthusiasm even by Tories Sir Robert Long and Peniston Powney.[346] Lord Ilchester reasoned that this would encourage Pitt to a deal with the ministry: 'There is so much joy at the Prussian victory that makes meddling with German affairs in Parliament less unpopular, and perhaps Mr Pitt less scrupulous to meddle with them.'[347] Horace Walpole agreed, regarding George II's supposition that Pitt would not do his German business as too great a compliment to Pitt's integrity. His unprecedented visit to Lady Yarmouth on 21 October, Walpole added, contained hints of a good disposition towards Hanover.[348]

Such possibilities were ended by the stringency of Pitt's terms, conveyed to Hardwicke in his interviews of 19 and 24 October. It seems likely that the experiences of the previous three years had made Pitt cautious about the dangers of an accommodation on terms 'by which we should all have been at once high in office, if we would have consented to have made ourselves low in our own and the public opinion'.[349] But such was the basis for the reconciliation which had almost been achieved that summer between the ministry and Bute. The rejection of Pitt's initial demands in October transformed this situation. On 25th, Fox noted: 'This transaction has made Pitt and Lord Bute friends again',[350] though he imagined falsely that Pitt's proposals had been previously concerted with Leicester House.[351]

NEWCASTLE'S ATTITUDES TO RESIGNATION, APRIL–OCTOBER 1756

Historians, on Fox's own evidence, have refused to take seriously his factious disruption of Newcastle's ministry and have emphasised only one side of the question: Newcastle's distrust of him. This chapter has demonstrated the threat which Fox posed to Newcastle throughout the summer;

that it was Fox's resignation which led Newcastle in turn to resign; and that Fox's actions were based on a miscalculation about the possibility of an alliance, instead, with Pitt. All this is very far from a simple failure of nerve on Newcastle's part. In April he intended, as in the past, to discipline erring members of his government. His confidence in the strength of his position was undermined first, and chiefly, by reflection on the international scene. England had engaged in a war against France and Austria together, and apparently without an ally. Misfortune aside, England alone was not a match for the greatest power in Europe.[352] Until Prussia's victories in Saxony, events in England were played out in the face of an impending national disaster of which the loss of Minorca seemed only the first instalment. But, from September onwards, England's strategic prospects markedly improved; and, with them, Newcastle's morale.

In mid May, before the reconciliation with the junior Court, Newcastle had been led to pessimism, too, by his view of the domestic alternatives: Fox's dominance or a deal with Leicester House which would elevate Bute. Murray's desire for promotion, and the conclusion of an alliance between France and Austria on 1 May, made this tension critical. For the first time, Newcastle began to speak, though as of a distant hope, of his desire to step down if he could do so with 'honour and credit', and consistently with his duty to the King.[353] This, as yet, he saw no way of doing; hence he argued against Murray's promotion, at first, as if that step would entail the (dishonourable) fall of his administration. In mid June, Newcastle was still pessimistic about the possibility of forming a system able to survive in the Commons,[354] and his yearning for a release from tension remained.[355] But by August, this note of despondency was muted; Newcastle was interested now in the possibility of an accommodation with Pitt or Bute.[356]

It is remarkable that Newcastle's qualified optimism revived from consideration of the balance of forces between Westminster, St James's and Leicester House just as the first wave of Addresses and Instructions from the country was at its height.[357] Yet these Addresses were phenomena about the results of which Bute was not enthusiastic[358] and about which Pitt, apparently, was silent. 'Surely, my lord,' West advised Newcastle in August, 'it is well the crisis of the distemper appears so long before the meeting of Parliament...I think it very happy the [City's] Address is worded in the violent way it is, for it now begins, and every day will, more and more, open the eyes of the people, to penetrate into the views of the Jacobites that began, of the discontented out that improved, and of the party in, that hopes to avail themselves of it.'[359] Newcastle was similarly angry and indignant in the face of the press campaign, not intimidated by it. Rather, he attended to it as an aspect of internal, 'high political' tactics – in particular, to single out and exonerate Fox,[360] or to shift the blame from Byng to the ministry; in general, he agreed with Barnard that 'it was condemning without hearing, and being the tools and instruments to get people into employments who wanted them'.[361] Newcastle was aware that Addresses and Instructions were seldom spontaneous on either side. Edmund Law, Vice Chancellor of Cambridge and Master of Peterhouse, had written in April to ask whether the University should offer a loyal address;[362] at Bristol, an offer was made to organise a counter-address sympathetic to government.[363] A little well-directed influence, if applied in time, could prevent even Grand Juries from addressing.[364] The opposition was not more backward. Newcastle was sent George Townshend's letter to the Mayor of Southampton recommending a petition to the Commons in favour of a Militia Bill,[365] and knew of Charles Townshend's outrageous and unprecedented step in writing circular letters to corporations soliciting Addresses to the Crown or Instructions to MPs.[366] But if the City of London's Address made little impression on George II, those of less self-willed corporations were hardly likely to do so.[367]

Although Newcastle still, in August, expressed a wish to resign, he did so less frequently. He fully expected that 'the violence without doors, will soon come within';[368] but he anticipated this only until the reconciliation with Leicester House had been concluded, and after August his reviving resolution extinguished his expectation that the approaching clamour at Westminister would *force* him from office, however much he might still prefer the prospect of tranquillity from personal motives. By early September Fox, too, was declaring that 'he thought our opposers had hurt themselves by their early addresses'.[369] Sir John Barnard and Lord Walpole were loudly indignant at the constitutional impropriety of addressing,[370] and the ministry had intelligence that many others, even among the Tories, shared this view.[371] Like Barnard, who declared he 'could see no motive in the discontent they wanted to raise than to get some people in power and others out',[372] Newcastle and Hardwicke looked on the political implications of articulate discontent as no more than an indication of the intentions of its organisers, and on the internal motivations of public clamour as fickle and easily reversible by military success.[373] Thus it was that by mid September Calcraft reported that Newcastle and Anson 'both think themselves quite secure and are mighty easy'.[374] The news of the King of Prussia's brilliantly successful invasion of Saxony provided just such a hope of a reversal: the Prussian victory at Lobowitz was greeted with inordinate rejoicing, for it signified the accession of a militarily efficient ally and transformed the prospects of the war in Germany at the same time as it justified the Convention of Westminster which the ministry had concluded in January. Newcastle was assured by Grafton and others that the administration's prospects in the Commons were significantly improved by Frederick's victory.[375] These more favourable prospects have been obscured in retrospect by Fox's resignation, which followed soon afterwards. Together with the assumption that

George II still placed firm confidence in Newcastle, however, they explain the persistent apprehensions in Fox's camp that Newcastle would nevertheless face Parliament without him.[376]

From the time of Fox's resignation until his own, Newcastle was noticeably unconcerned to weigh the parliamentary prospects of ministerial permutations by estimating the number of MPs whose loyalty they might command. His whole energy was devoted to bringing about a system on one of a limited number of patterns which successive experiments had made him regard as viable. Since Henry Pelham's death, Newcastle had so come to look on the business of political leadership as the art of devising and sustaining compatible ministerial combinations that the extent to which a massive Old Corps majority might survive ministerial schism was virtually ignored. What the public outcry of the summer had done was not to force Newcastle to resign but to incline him to believe that resignation was the only honourable alternative if his ministerial schemes proved unattainable. It was this conditional belief which came to the fore in the days after Fox's resignation, and which explains why Newcastle did not share Granville's and Grafton's confidence, expressed also by Potter among the opposition, that the ministry was sufficiently strong in numbers to face the Commons. It was not that Newcastle calculated otherwise; rather that he had given the matter no thought. Even Fox, in October, could not represent 'the impossibility of my carrying on the King's affairs now as a minister, even if I had more power given me' as a question of numbers.[377] Fox's closest friends wrote in quite different terms: that Newcastle

took a great deal of pains, I believe, to set the King against Mr Fox, and kept him in a total ignorance with regard to measures of the greatest consequence. This was usage hardly to be born by a man of honour...He seemed to think that as his Grace did not trust him, and showed no favour to his friends in the House of Commons, his credit must sink there; that the clamour of the people in the country was very violent; that it was hard to bear the blame of measures concerted by other people; that it was disagreeable to support unpopular measures for a King who had shown so great a dislike to him. These considerations made him determine to resign.[378]

It has been argued above that Fox's assertions of the impossibility of his carrying on were tactically inspired; if there is no evidence that Newcastle or Pitt were counting heads in the autumn of 1756, there is equally no evidence that Fox was doing so. Walpole's fall in 1742 had been preceded by a long process of closely-observed attrition as his back-bench following had been eroded by abstentions and desertions to the opposition; no such process was in evidence in the spring, summer or autumn of 1756. On the contrary, the five months after Christmas had seen a significant parliamentary victory over Pitt.

In May, Newcastle feared that the result of Murray's promotion would be Fox's dominance of the ministry. Fox, at the same time, may have been encouraged by Pitt to think a Pitt–Fox ministry possible, and even Newcastle took that threat seriously. His first preference was to remove the chief prop of opposition by taking Prince George from the custody of his mother and Bute. But this attempt ended in failure, and at the end of July Newcastle sounded Fox. Fox was only provoked, however, to an increased attention to tactical devices to destroy the ministry. Early in August, he professed a willingness to step down to a place below Cabinet rank, and – for tactical reasons – pressed the ministry to make an accommodation with Leicester House. Yet by the end of that month, it seemed possible that Pitt might indeed be treated with separately from Bute, recalcitrant as the latter still was over the Stole. But from mid September, the King relaxed his exclusion on Bute, and an alliance between the Courts stemming from his appointment seemed a possibility; Pitt might then be left isolated in opposition.

Fox's resignation destroyed the possibility of separate deals with either Bute or Pitt. This was not immediately obvious: once Newcastle had realised the improbability of Fox's being brought to retract his resignation, an advance to Pitt through Hardwicke was launched with a degree of confidence[379] which reflected the reconcilation within the Royal Family rather than detailed knowledge of Pitt's disposition. Fox's resignation, like Murray's, undoubtedly added to the burden of Newcastle's cares; but he had often before survived in a state of tension and agitation. It was Fox's desertion itself, not Newcastle's state of mind, which was the new element in the autumn of 1756; nor did those closest to Newcastle predict that that tension and agitation would result in his resignation. Sir George Lyttelton, for example, did not know as late as 23 October whether Newcastle would resolve to go on;[380] Fox did not know on 26 October,[381] and Rigby thought on that day that Newcastle *would* do so.[382] Nor was it generally realised until after Hardwicke's second meeting with Pitt on 24th that the latter would insist on Newcastle's departure.

It is an absurd exaggeration to claim that Newcastle was at any point 'distracted', 'frightened nearly into hysteria',[383] or 'consumed' with 'personal terror'.[384] His conduct of affairs has been shown to be very far from the explanation that he 'simply lost his nerve' and had come over three years to look on the parliamentary opposition as 'irresistible'. In fact, Newcastle was acting from a realistic and comprehensible view of the tactical alternatives, the last of which was cut off by Fox's resignation and Pitt's refusal, and from a set of personal motives which had nothing to do with cowardice but a great deal to do with honour and duty. Had he not resigned, he told Hume Campbell, 'the world would have said that he was hanging on every twig only for the place. I said he judged very right.'[385]

6

The Pitt–Devonshire Ministry,
October 1756–March 1757

He [Pitt] passed his time studying words and expressions, always with a
view to throw the responsibility of every measure upon some other, while
he held a high pompous unmeaning language. Yet good as his parts were,
he was afraid to trust to them, and was a complete artificial character.
It gave him great advantages to serve a turn, by enabling him to change
like lightning from one set of principles to another, for which to do him
justice, he had an extraordinary quick eye, which enabled him to judge
mankind *en masse*, what would do and not do: by nature insolent and
overbearing, at the same time so versatile that he could bend to anything.

> Shelburne, in Fitzmaurice, *Shelburne*,
> i, 60.

FOX'S ATTEMPT TO LAUNCH A MINISTRY,
27–31 OCTOBER 1756

With his summons to London, Devonshire probably received Wilmot's
news that Legge, briefly in town, was hostile towards Pitt and the
Grenvilles and inclined to be connected again with the Old Corps,
particularly Devonshire. Legge's move was not 'convertible', thought
Wilmot, to backing for Newcastle; but he might be brought by Devonshire
to take a part in a ministry without Newcastle or Pitt if he were not
expected to defend the measures he had spent the summer in attacking.
Legge, predicted Wilmot, would join the ministry if Fox took the Treasury
and Exchequer under Devonshire's patronage, or would accept the
Exchequer or a Secretaryship of State if Devonshire had the Treasury;
but if Bedford had it, Legge would support measures while refusing place.
On 24th, Legge intended to write to tell Pitt that he would accept the
Exchequer under no-one but Devonshire; Wilmot stopped him, lest Pitt
take advantage of such a letter.[1]

Thus, by chance, Legge's potential disloyalty was never revealed to
his allies before the course of events silenced it. Nor was Fox probably
aware of it until after Devonshire arrived in town on 29th. But on 27th
the King had sent for Fox, told him of Newcastle's decision, and com-
misioned him to form an administration. Moreover, he gave him reason
to hope that a Fox–Pitt combination would be acceptable. Fox avoided
naming a place for himself, but undertook the government and agreed to
sound Pitt at once. Meanwhile he wrote to Legge in the country that he,

Fox, 'would submit *to tug at any oar* and lend his assistance in any situation wherein he did not expect to be a minister, but begged still to have a lucrative office. But notwithstanding such pretended resignation of all views to ministerial power,' Martin saw, 'there is no doubt but he harboured a secret flattering hope to bring Mr Pitt into an union' and joint administration.[2] Probably, therefore, Legge was suspicious. Hardwicke, too, recognised that the King's commission had re-awakened Fox's ambitions, so that he fancied Pitt would join him and he, Fox, be at the head of the Treasury, 'which is the ambition of his heart'.[3] Such ideas came as no surprise to many of the Old Corps. Grafton, whose opinion Newcastle respected, thought Fox 'will do *anything*', even withdraw his resignation, if the terms were right.[4]

The key to success was obviously a union between Fox and Pitt, and Marlborough looked to Bedford to forward it.[5] It was viable because, as was widely anticipated, Newcastle would expect his friends and followers to stay in office and support the King's government.[6] The Chancellor was not expected to resign, and Newcastle's refusal of place or pension avoided the division of his party by charges of public duty betrayed.[7] Bedford was persuaded; he urged Rigby that Fox should take the Treasury and the Exchequer, 'with the splendour he called it of Sir Robert Walpole or Mr Pelham': a position, Rigby thought, which would guarantee the allegiance of 'the understrappers chose upon the Pelham bottom'.[8] Others among his sympathisers were sufficiently optimistic to believe momentarily in the possibility of a Fox ministry with Bedford and Halifax as Secretaries of State[9] – and, by implication, without Pitt.

By the most perceptive of his advisers Fox was urged to an accommodation with Pitt, which was his preferred solution; and reminded that, just as Newcastle could not survive without one of his two chief rivals, so Pitt could not go on without either Newcastle or Fox himself. Stone therefore advised Fox to keep secret the 'restriction' on Pitt in the message (presumably from the King) which Granville brought Fox on 27th.[10] Fox saw Granville again for an hour at 10 a.m. on 28th,[11] probably in an attempt to relax this 'restriction'. Arriving late for the Prince of Wales's first levée, he met Pitt by chance on the stairs of Savile House. But instead of a willingness to share power or to accept Fox in a subordinate situation not of the Cabinet, Pitt pointed to the terms of his conversation with Hardwicke and insisted that Fox would have no office whatever in the new administration.[12] This was a shock. Pitt's demands seemed absurdly inflated, but he agreed to meet Devonshire or Bedford, and Fox preferred to look to what he would say then as his final answer. Bedford, however, left London for Woburn the same day, surrendering by implication any claim to a leading role in the new ministry or its establishment. Whether he saw Fox before his departure is not known. That evening, Fox went to Windsor to consult Cumberland.

At the same time, Fox could not bring himself to believe that Pitt was, even now, firmly united with Leicester House. Inheriting Newcastle's assumption that he was not, Fox looked to Bute and Legge as possible allies in a system which, he thought, could already rely on Bedford, Marlborough, and Devonshire in the Lords. Moreover, Fox had promised George II to approach 'all the considerable people who supported the ministry last year'.[13] It was this prospect which Fox held out to Argyll on 28th.[14] Rigby, too, thought Pitt's refusal would force Fox to go on alone.[15] Henry Digby agreed, and thought such a system could survive if enough men, Legge in particular, were detached from Pitt to make his merely 'a family opposition'.[16] Fox, too, believed after his meeting with Granville on 28th that he had been commanded to form an administration either with or without Pitt;[17] and, disclaiming all insistence on the lead in the first case, declared himself happy to avoid the position of First Minister – 'the station I shall be forced into if we do not join'.[18]

So far, Pitt's terms had not been the subject of negotiation with the Old Corps. Yet neither had the scheme been carefully concerted among Pitt's followers. To do so would only have emphasised their divisions. Leicester House, in the person of Bute, seems to have been wholly excluded from Pitt's calculations; nor is there evidence for prior arrangements with the Tories. Pitt's manner, rather, was dictatorial. He did not manoeuvre against Newcastle or Fox. To his own following he was equally summary. Potter encouraged offers being made Pitt of the Treasury with the lead in the Commons; 'the only fear of you is your connection with L[eicester] H[ouse]'. He added a hint that an overture had been launched to Legge from the junior Court, 'and that a cabal is publicly talked of in which you are no party'.[19] Legge was widely regarded as being, as yet, in better favour at Leicester House than Pitt, and there is no evidence that this opinion was mistaken. Legge was far from reliable as an associate: later, it was even suggested that he held Anson in such regard as perhaps to be unwilling to join in an attack on him,[20] and Legge certainly intervened to protect Cleveland,[21] who as Secretary to the Admiralty was closely associated with Anson's record as First Lord. For either reason Pitt let the Grenvilles know that he met Hardwicke on 19 October both without first seeing Bute and resolved to refuse to accept a part in a Newcastle ministry.[22] Pitt summoned George Grenville and Temple to town, and they met at Sir Richard Lyttelton's to hear a report on Pitt's interviews with Hardwicke and Lady Yarmouth.[23] It seems that Pitt only then disclosed to his followers the offices he had demanded for them. Later accounts of Pitt's interview with Hardwicke on 19th dwell on Pitt's demands about measures and his exclusion of Newcastle; but it is not certain that he did not also discuss specific offices for his followers, and meet with a degree of encouragement.[24] George Grenville (though at this point doubtfully reliable) claims Pitt reported that his demand of the Paymastership for Grenville 'was consented to without any difficulty'.[25] It may well have been such agreement on minor offices which encouraged Pitt to visit Lady Yarmouth with a complete ministerial list on 21st.

Glover met Temple, George Townshend, George Grenville, Sir Richard Lyttelton, Elliot and others at dinner, probably on 23rd. Pitt's list of 21st had included himself and Sir Thomas Robinson, in place of Fox and Holdernesse, as the two Secretaries of State. Glover now reported George Grenville as embarrassed by what he thought to be the King's refusal to give up Holdernesse, and George Townshend allegedly wrote to Temple that night declining office if Holdernesse were not dismissed. The Grenvilles were in possession of a written list, but one which differed from Pitt's of 21st for reasons which are not clear. Glover drew up a statement of the principles which should animate the new administration; George Townshend delivered it to Pitt the following Monday (? 25 October), but seemingly without discussion of his stand against Holdernesse. Nor was Townshend's objection to prevent him from playing a leading part in marshalling the Tories in the Commons during the coming session.[26]

Legge, too, came to town on 21 October,[27] by which time Pitt had already proposed him for the Exchequer. When Legge met Wilmot the following day, he disclosed his extreme unease (of which there is no sign that Pitt was aware) at the proposals Pitt had made him, in confidence, with Temple and George Grenville. 'Pitt has an ascendency that hurts the other and I think Legge *feels* that he talks ministerially to him already'. At Wilmot's suggestion, Legge was satisfied with some concession to 'two or three of his friends', to which Pitt agreed the same day; but Legge had not considered, since Pitt had not, the possibility that Devonshire would refuse the Treasury. In that case, Legge told Wilmot, he would refuse to sit on the Treasury Board in second place to another.[28] By the next day, 23rd, Legge was clear about the alternative schemes in which he would support or join ministries of Fox, Devonshire or Bedford. His resentment against Pitt and the Grenvilles was more bitter; but he 'found himself so hampered with them that he could not tell how to oppose them *at present* without appearing as changeable as the wind'. In that impasse, Legge went out of town on 24th.[29]

But on that day, Pitt learnt from Hardwicke of the King's refusal of the suggestions he put forward on 19th, and informally on 21st. 'This transaction', observed Fox, 'has made Pitt and Bute friends again.'[30] To Bute (as to Legge) the King's answer must have proved Pitt's refusal to compromise at the expense of a Leicester House which, in the past three months, had done all too little to deserve his continued loyalty. Thus the real difference between October 1756 and December 1754 or September 1755 was not that there was a public outcry (there was; but it was already effectively over, and played little part in the leaders' calculations) nor that there was a prospect of difficulties in the Commons (as there was on both earlier occasions) but that in 1754 and 1755 Newcastle succeeded in persuading a section of the opposition to betray the rest. In 1756 this did not come about. In part that was the result of the antagonism, now open and intransigent, of Pitt's and Fox's camps; in part of Newcastle's and Fox's ignorance of weaknesses within Pitt's following; in part, because of Newcastle's decision to stand down from the ministry; in part, because of the skill with which, at the end of October, Pitt compromised his Patriot stance sufficiently to comply with tactical realities, but discreetly enough for his faction still to be held to him in uncritical doctrinal subordination.

On 26th, Wilmot reported that 'the Pitts and Grenvilles are gone out of town determined not to take any share in concert with the Duke of Newcastle'.[31] Those departing are unlikely to have included Pitt himself, who met Fox on 28th and Devonshire on 30th. Pitt and Bute, therefore, were the only two leaders of their connection in town in the days between the rejection of Pitt's demands and his modification of his stipulations about measures in his first meeting with Devonshire; but whether Pitt consulted or deceived Bute is not revealed. The opinions of all the major figures on the likely outcome were, however, in a state of flux. Legge returned to town on 30th having cooled in his resentment of Pitt; willing, for the sake of Patriot measures (as he put it), to accept the Exchequer under a compatible First Lord – preferably Devonshire himself; and dismissive of the suggestion that Pitt might not co-operate in such a scheme.[32] Walpole wrote that Fox

had writ a confidential letter to Legge, begging him to come to town, and concert measures with him on the deplorable situation of affairs. Legge made no answer. Fox in wrath sent for his letter back; Legge returned it at once without a word; and depending on his favour with Lord Bute, now thought himself so considerable a part of the new accession, that he hoped to engross the Treasury himself; and actually proposed Lord Hertford for First Lord.[33]

Devonshire, the 'great engine, on whom the whole turns at present',[34] arrived in town on 29th, saw the King on 30 October and, as already arranged, met Pitt the same day to try to persuade him to join an administration with Fox. Pitt claimed to adhere to the conditions he had explained to Hardwicke; otherwise, he and his friends would forfeit the regard of the public and could be of no service to the King. But he went on to interpret his earlier demands in a remarkable way. The enquiry into the conduct of the war, he assured Devonshire, could not end in the punishment of the ministers, for they had never been suspected of treachery.[35] They were guilty not in the legal sense, deserving loss of life or property, but guilty of neglect or incapacity, warranting only removal from office. Since this had been brought about, the enquiry could only produce evidence which would justify their exclusion. In the matter of the Hanoverian soldier at Maidstone, Holdernesse could incur no penalty for an error in law, made in any case on the advice of the

Attorney General. At worst, the Commons would vote a resolution vindicating the law on that point. It was obvious to those who knew of his official demands that Pitt had stifled his Patriot zeal. The idea that he genuinely changed his mind, wrote Martin, 'requires some particularly strong evidence to gain belief with men acquainted with the ways of the world, and prepossessed with a notion that interest and ambition are the ruling principles of all candidates for power'.[36] But it was this alone which made possible a Devonshire–Pitt ministry on the basis of the continuance of many of Newcastle's junior ministers (and Holdernesse) and the absence of a complete repudiation of the late ministry's measures which would alienate the majority of its supporters in the Commons.

Pitt, then, refused to act if Fox held ministerial office. But although critical of Anson, he had not, to Devonshire, named a replacement, and had not specified a First Lord of the Treasury.[37] Fox knew the same day in general terms that Pitt had been more moderate, but not sufficiently so to revise the exclusion put upon him in their chance meeting.[38] Between Newcastle's resignation and Pitt's interview with Devonshire, it was known that Fox's camp had dismissed Pitt's demands as arrogant, excessive, and impossible for the King to consent to. To some, including Halifax, Fox had threatened to undertake the ministry alone; and his efforts had been apparently directed to that end.[39] Had Pitt continued unreasonable, Fox would have had no other course; but two things had changed. First, Pitt had compromised the views which stood in the way of his co-operation with Devonshire. Second, Pitt's opposition bloc had stood firm against efforts to split it; or (what had the same effect) its inner strains passed unnoticed.[40] The key man was Legge, whom Devonshire knew to have dropped his demand for the Treasury in addition to the Exchequer; nor was he open to Devonshire's suggestion that he should act reasonably if Pitt would not: Pitt, Legge assured Wilmot, would 'hearken to reason'. Legge was, Wilmot reported, willing to take the Exchequer alone under a proper First Lord, and had suggested Devonshire himself.[41] Thus though Devonshire knew via Wilmot about Legge's doubts, he had no interest in spreading knowledge of them. Newcastle and Hardwicke were apparently unaware of Legge's disclosures, but knew (what Devonshire seemingly did not know) the contents of the ministerial scheme Pitt submitted secretly to Lady Yarmouth on 21 October.

Fox's bid for the Treasury in a joint ministry now collapsed. Pitt plainly spoke in concert with Legge and Leicester House, and was determined that Fox should not have that office. Fox could hardly blame him: 'he sees, in that case, that the moment the enquiry is over I am as much master as if he was at the Board of Trade instead of Secretary of State'; 'what would he be but Paymaster again under another Pelham, with an employment of a higher rank?' But Fox's ambition to seize the lead alone, which was so often a powerful spur to his disruption and intrigue, again wilted just as his goal seemed within reach. National duty and avarice, too, both pointed in another direction: for Fox to accept the Paymastership in submission to Pitt as Secretary of State and Legge as Chancellor of the Exchequer. Fox's friends might object, but

what is my choice? This, or being Prime Minister (which I may be) with Leicester House, Pitt etc. opposing, the clamour of all England directed at me in my first year as much as at Sir Robert Walpole in his last or more; and the Duke of Newcastle and Lord Chancellor, withdrawing from under me all the strength they furnish. Then the times, and fresh calamities happening every day.[42]

He would, therefore, as he assured Stone, 'consent to act in the House of Commons under Mr Pitt'.[43] But Fox abandoned his bid for the leadership at a moment when to do so left him with no lever to induce Pitt to comply with his lesser aim.

THE PITT–DEVONSHIRE MINISTRY, 31 OCTOBER–12 NOVEMBER 1756

On 31 October, Devonshire reported to George II his conversation with Pitt; and on the following day told Pitt that the King 'was disposed to comply with all the conditions of a public nature demanded: and desired to see Mr Pitt's list of the alterations he would propose to make in offices and employments'.[44] Pitt had not yet been openly more specific on this than exclusions on Newcastle and Fox and dark hints about the ultimate control of both navy and army.[45] Now, however, he submitted Devonshire a list.[46] Calling his followers again to town, Pitt justified what was evidently a revision of the list which Glover records the Grenvilles discussing (possibly on 25 October) by claiming that he, Pitt, had with difficulty persuaded Devonshire to accept the Treasury.[47] The latter was, at the same time, in possession of a list submitted on the same day by Fox,[48] part at least of the contents of which was the subject of negotiation between Devonshire and Pitt. Both schemes agreed on putting the Great Seal into commission, or into the care of a Lord Keeper, with Lord Sandys as Speaker of the House of Lords; Pitt as Secretary of State; Legge as Chancellor of the Exchequer; a peerage for Hillsborough; and George Grenville as Treasurer of the Navy. Thereafter they differed widely. Fox, however, was willing to provide for all Pitt's friends, though in different offices from those Pitt listed, under the figurehead Lord Berkeley of Stratton at the Treasury; Fox put himself down for the Paymastership. To George Grenville, Pitt blamed Devonshire's insistence for Grenville's being listed for Treasurer of the Navy, not Paymaster, in Pitt's scheme. Grenville's dissatisfaction was heightened when his brothers gave him the (misleading) impression, a few days later, that Pitt had agreed to Fox as Paymaster.

Pitt, meanwhile, had retired to Hayes, suffering (or pretending to suffer) from gout.[49] His success was by no means assured. Fox, who had made only three minor points in his own plan *sine qua non*, was still optimistic, especially on the reflection that Legge[50] had himself suggested Lord Berkeley of Stratton for the Treasury. On the evening of 2 November, Fox dined at the King's Head[51] with his backers Bedford, Marlborough and Devonshire, and urged the danger of Pitt's domineering ambition:

However, as they had not presumption enough to name the First Lord of the Treasury, of which Mr Legge was to be a Commissioner and Chancellor of the Exchequer, it was hoped by us then present, that the King by nominating the Duke of Devonshire First Lord, such a control would be laid on Mr Pitt and his friends, by the Treasury continuing in the King's power, that Mr Fox, though not in a Cabinet Councillor's place, would still keep such a weight in the House of Commons as would hinder Pitt and his party from getting the absolute ascendancy over the King himself, and confine them to that proper degree of power they had a right to expect, and in which they might have been useful to the public.

This effectively stiffened the resolve of Devonshire, who had inclined to agree with Pitt's terms; but he refused to accept the Treasury with Legge at the Exchequer. Newcastle soon knew, via Holdernesse, that Devonshire had changed his mind about Pitt; though not for what reason.[52] The plan to which Devonshire had in fact agreed was to give Fox the Exchequer, take the Treasury himself, and nominate its other members; but agree to Pitt's proposals in most other respects. Legge, however, was to be excluded. If Pitt were to insist that Fox should not be Chancellor of the Exchequer, Dupplin or another insignificant figure would be named, and Fox be Minister for the House of Commons with the office of Paymaster. Fox wanted Devonshire to remain Lord Lieutenant of Ireland in addition, wrote Walpole; 'that so, if they could weather the approaching session, the Duke might be ready to resign the Treasury into his hands, which seemed to be the drift of his intrigues: – if Devonshire could not keep Ireland, then Bedford was designed to it'.[53] A meeting of the Cabinet and others was to be held at Devonshire House on the night of 3rd to rally the support of major figures behind the scheme and set a limit to the subsequent concessions to be made to Pitt.[54] The King commanded Bedford to attend;[55] Fox invited Egremont, still evading involvement with politics by remaining at Petworth.[56] In defiance of these appearances, Pitt continued to increase his demands; it was quickly known in Fox's camp that he had asked the Admiralty for Temple;[57] and, prompted by Charles Townshend,[58] was increasingly reluctant that Holdernesse should continue as Secretary of State. Pitt lodged a claim for the Northern Department, and suggested to Devonshire that Sir Thomas Robinson should be given a peerage and the Southern. Not until 2nd, however, could Pitt tell Devonshire that he had persuaded Temple, despite his misgivings, to accept.[59]

Granville, Fox and Devonshire followed Bedford into the Closet in turn on the morning of 2 November. Granville carried in a plan, drawn up by himself, which closely echoed that put forward at the King's Head meeting on 1st: Devonshire First Lord of the Treasury, Fox Chancellor of the Exchequer, Pitt Secretary of State, a peerage for Legge, and further consideration of Pitt's other proposals.[60] Bedford was encouraged both by the King's and Cumberland's reception and the reflection that for Pitt to refuse would put him beyond the sympathy of reasonable men. Charles Townshend reported Waldegrave saying that 'the appearance today was, that old faces were growing again into more favour than new'.[61] Granville's proposal was referred to the meeting on 3rd.[62] Suddenly this plan was shattered. Walpole and Conway had heard of the scheme at dinner on 2nd via Grafton and Hertford, and were horrified: they 'saw plainly', claimed Walpole, 'that Fox was precipitating the King and the chief persons in England upon a measure, from which it would be impossible for them to recede, to which it was impossible Pitt should submit, and that in consequence of such a rupture at such a crisis, heated as the passions of men were, even a civil war might ensue'. Walpole claimed that he persuaded Conway to go at once to Devonshire to explain things in this light, and that Devonshire was persuaded.[63] Fox and Granville saw Devonshire on the night of 2nd and met an absolute refusal to take the Treasury with Fox. The united front, which the Cabinet meeting on 3rd was to have cemented, was at an end. It was boasted that Fox, on Devonshire's refusal, had the option of being either First Minister or in no office;[64] in fact no such possibility was ever open, for, in an audience on the following morning, 3rd, Devonshire accepted the Treasury with Legge, though without agreeing to Pitt's demand to succeed Holdernesse.[65] Devonshire, wrote Waldegrave, 'did not accept until His Majesty had given his word, that in case he disliked his employment, he should be at full liberty to resign at the approaching session of Parliament'.[66] This assurance the King presumably now gave. Devonshire's promotion was not anticipated by Legge, who, about to leave town, had written to Pitt demurring his claims to cabinet place if it obstructed a settlement.[67] Charles Townshend, too, was due to leave town, apparently believing that Fox was about to undertake a ministry which would collapse in a few weeks.[68] But, at the news, Fox himself was bitter at what he saw as Devonshire's betrayal, suspected the intervention of Leicester House, but had no accurate knowledge and was unaware of Pitt's news of Temple's decision on the Admiralty. He realised that Devonshire was 'the only man that could make the late administration, and that part of the Court that hates me, behave tolerably'.[69] Offered the Paymastership by Devonshire after his audience on 3rd, Fox refused any office; 'by a combination of circumstances obvious to your Grace', he explained to Bedford, 'I cannot be a minister (without the Duke of Newcastle, etc. and against Pitt, etc.) without being the *Prime*

Minister...there is in this foolish and arrogant scheme, peace in the House of Commons, and therefore I am for it'.[70] Yet Devonshire might reasonably have been surprised at Fox's refusal of an offer which met the lesser of his ambitions: a lucrative minor office, without responsibility, in a Pitt ministry. It seems likely that the unexpected frustration of Fox's ambition for the chief power provoked him, as in March 1754, to reject a lesser role which on calm reflection he considered feasible. Only a small circle knew of the tactical complexities in which Fox's ambitions foundered. Yet, since his drive for power had long been obvious, generalised explanations were, instead, put forward for his failure. He and his party, it was suggested, 'could not stand the torrent of the P[itt]s and the G[renville]s against them in the H. of C[ommo]ns'.[71]

Devonshire asked to meet Pitt on 4 November. Ill of the gout, he declined. Devonshire therefore called on him at Hayes. Pitt was unwilling to accept if Holdernesse remained, and deferred his answer.[72] Meanwhile he summoned the Grenvilles 'to consider whether Mr Pitt should, at the hazard of breaking the whole, not insist upon being appointed Secretary to the Northern Department instead of the Southern, which the King had refused his consent to'.[73] No royal objection had evidently been made to places for Pitt's other friends, including Temple and four or five men on the Admiralty Board. Fox seemingly reported Devonshire on his return from Hayes: 'I might be Paymaster, though Mr Pitt thinks that would be too like Mr Pelham in the year 1742, and that I had better let G. Grenville have it, and be Tr[easurer] of the Navy'. Again Fox declined.[74] Nothing now remained but to secure as many places as possible for his own followers and allies in an administration which Pitt's party was too few to man fully. Above all, he sought to persuade Bedford to accept the Lord Lieutenancy of Ireland in succession to Devonshire,[75] possibly not least to close a vacancy into which Holdernesse might conveniently be moved.[76] Concealing his resentment, however, Fox professed to Devonshire and the King his sincere desire for a quiet session and the scheme's survival: 'I would even give up the Northern Province to make it go'.[77] Bedford refused to co-operate with a ministry he held to be factious, but via Gower assured the King that he would not obstruct his service. Devonshire welcomed this offer, reported Gower; 'I think you may keep him out of Legge's hands'.[78] Fox had similar hopes. Again he wrote to urge Devonshire 'to take the more upon you, and to convince the world, that you are *in fact the Minister*'.[79] Devonshire should refuse to discuss a ministry until the King had ceased to accept Newcastle's advice; then, Devonshire should make final his scheme, 'carry your paper as it shall then stand to the King, and tell him it must be complied with or you must decline, what you cannot be understood to have undertaken but in confidence that HM would give you the means of going through with it'.[80]

Pitt and Fox were thus not distinguished by principled views on the relative claims of Crown and First Minister; for both, constitutional assertions waited on tactical necessities. Yet Fox was not hopeful that Devonshire would effectively stand as the barrier against Pitt. Devonshire, Fox thought, had been duped by Legge; and, on his own account, Legge at once began to make conditions – Oswald as an assistant, and Lord Duncannon, not O'Brien, on the Treasury Board.[81] Horace Walpole thought this proceeded from Legge's opinion that his, not Pitt's, was the chief influence at Leicester House,[82] and not until Argyll arrived in town did Fox learn on 17 November that 'Pitt is full as well with Lord Bute as Legge'.[83] Nevertheless, it was with reason reported that Legge 'is not looked upon at present to be a man entirely at Mr Pitt's disposal'.[84] It seems more likely that Legge's stipulations proceeded from genuine disinclination to take office: 'The state of the country is deplorable, the state of parties very unpleasant and I am pitched upon to stand almost in the breach and that in such a manner that with all my hatred to business and love of private life I cannot escape without shamefully running away';[85] but these fears were not widely known.

Having evidently persuaded the Grenvilles to waive their objections to Holdernesse continuing in the Northern Department, Pitt accepted on 6 November. His problem in forming an administration was that his following included too few figures of the first rank to occupy its commanding heights, but too many minor figures to be easily accommodated in lesser office. Horace Walpole wrote that 'Remnants of both administrations must be preserved, as Mr Pitt has not wherewithal to fill a quarter of their employments';[86] but Legge apologised for Lord North's not being included 'in the first cargo for the vessel is small and the passengers many',[87] and Henry Digby recognised that since Devonshire 'goes upon a system of keeping things quiet...he cannot well begin by turning out people without satisfying them'.[88] Thus it was reported that Temple had (unsuccessfully) pressed Lord George Sackville to take a place;[89] Pitt seems never to have attempted to reverse George Townshend's disinclination to office; and, committed as the latter already thought himself 'to undertake the whole burthen of the inquiries and Militia Bill',[90] his independence could be turned to positive tactical advantage. The Townshends nevertheless made a *sine qua non* the place of Cofferer for Charles Townshend *vice* the Duke of Leeds, a non-political figure whose seemingly unjust sacrifice, impending since its inclusion in Fox's scheme of 1 November, Newcastle had particularly resented.[91] Devonshire immediately ran into difficulties over other appointments on his list. The King, his resolution perhaps stiffened by a long visit by Newcastle on the morning of 9th, brusquely insisted on retaining Barrington as Secretary at War rather than accept Ellis: Potter therefore could not succeed Ellis as Joint Paymaster General for Ireland (a position he achieved only in July 1757). The post of Treasurer of the Chamber was a possible alternative for him, though the King refused to remove its holder Hillsborough at the cost of an English peerage. Darlington, who shared the Pay Office with Dupplin, was dismissable; if Dupplin could be provided for, the Paymastership lay open for George Grenville, which office Pitt had promised him; and Grenville would not then require the Treasurership of the Navy, Dodington's office, which Temple thought might satisfy Charles Townshend. But if Potter were Treasurer of the Chamber, or the King's refusal over Hillsborough stood, it was not clear where Dupplin would go. Sir Richard Lyttelton also raised a problem by refusing both the vacant Jewel Office and the Household post of Comptroller.[92]

The only solution seemed for Devonshire to insist to the King on terms. Before he could do so, the hostile reception the new ministers met at Court on 10 November, the King's birthday, provoked Temple to action independent of Pitt.[93] A meeting of his following in town that evening agreed that Temple should call on Devonshire on 11th, the day on which Newcastle was due to resign, 'to acquaint him that our situation was now grown so very delicate and so very unpromising that I no longer found myself at liberty to proceed a step further'. Bute accompanied Temple and emphasised the support he enjoyed from Leicester House. Legge added his weight. Devonshire 'seemed to feel and admit the force of all we said, hoped however that he should be able to improve for us our Court situation and begged that we would not refuse ourselves to government at this conjuncture'. Devonshire had drawn up a ministerial list, a revision of that which George II had summarily rejected on 9th. Temple at first refused to modify Pitt's latest demands,[94] but it seems to have become more and more clear to him that Devonshire had been and would be firm with the King, and obtain the best terms. So, point by point, Temple found himself agreeing with Devonshire's arrangements. Bute undertook to try to persuade Charles Townshend to waive his demand for the place of Cofferer and accept the equal one of Treasurer of the Chamber. Charles had left town; Bute however found George Townshend and put sufficient pressure on him, by taking the name of the Prince of Wales, to make it almost certain that his brother would have to agree.[95] Sir Richard Lyttelton had been brought reluctantly to accept the Jewel Office; Temple unwillingly swallowed the dizzying promotion of Potter to share the Pay Office with Dupplin, leaving George Grenville disgruntled in the office of Treasurer of the Navy.[96] Lord Pulteney could not be given office, but in a memorandum of 11th waived his claims to it. For the rest, Devonshire successfully stood out for a number of Fox's friends: a peerage for Hillsborough; William Sloper for the seat at the Board of Trade vacated by John Talbot's death on 26 September,[97] the rest of the Board remaining unchanged; the Band of Pensioners for Lord Berkeley of Stratton; Lord Bateman for Treasurer of the Household, and Richard Edgcumbe for Comptroller, the last two freeing seats at the Admiralty Board. Henley, a friend of

Fox, became Attorney General. But nothing was done about Cumberland's power in the army. The Secretaryship at War, coveted by Charles Townshend, and for which Ellis had been proposed to the King, remained with Barrington. Holdernesse was continued; and, to almost equal surprise, Nugent kept his seat at the Treasury. Temple explained 'that Lord Granville insisted upon it, and there was no contending with that new and potent ally, who had so much personal weight in the Cabinet'.[98] Murray declined the Lord Chancellorship,[99] and the Great Seal was put into commission. Halifax, who remained at the Board of Trade, was reported 'not of the present ministry, but better than ever with the Duke of Newcastle'.[100]

THE NEW MINISTRY: PROSPECTS AND PARTY COMPOSITION

Temple appealed to Pitt for a final decision; Devonshire and Legge went to Hayes to obtain it.[101] Pitt agreed, and Devonshire explained a near-complete scheme to Hardwicke on the night of 12 November.[102] It was a scheme which, through the coincidence of Pitt's dictatorial manner and Devonshire's regard for tactical realities, had obviously been drawn up 'without the consent of some of the parties'.[103] From the outset its prospects were dubious. Walpole predicted that, without either Newcastle or Fox, Pitt would not last six months.[104] Newcastle, though not estimating a life-span, agreed: Pitt would have difficulty in surviving,[105] and Devonshire in trimming between Pitt and Fox.[106] Old Corps Whigs looked on the whole affair since mid October as a factious contest over places in which Pitt and Fox had entirely omitted a responsible co-ordination of policies: 'We are not squabbling about measures but about men'.[107] Even so, that nice arrangement had only produced what Walpole called 'the most perplexed and complicate situation that ever was'. Pitt had brought about 'as extraordinary a revolution as this country has ever seen in its administration';[108] but at the price of its precarious instability. 'The only discontented', wrote Glover, 'were the King and both Houses of Parliament'.[109] So improbable did the retirement of Newcastle and Fox seem that Chesterfield speculated: 'There must be, to be sure, a *dessous des cartes* which, when one does not know, one can only think at random and talk absurdly upon those matters...'[110] In one light, it seemed 'one single family against the united force of the principal nobility',[111] a ministry which had obviously stormed the Closet, and by methods more than ordinarily objectionable:

It is become the curse of this nation with our mock-Patriots, first to push the nation into a war right or wrong, upon any motive, or no motive; and then to make use of the distresses and difficulties which a war will necessarily bring on a trading nation, in order to raise a clamour against the ministry, and place themselves in their stead.[112]

Equally, the ministry was credited with a wide range of Patriot pro-grammes, the frustration of which would do it positive damage; it had generated such enormous expectations as to be, *de facto*, a ministry with a mandate. Pitt was looked to as 'the instrument of our deliver-ance',[113] the agent of national regeneration. But, in an eighteenth-century context, this was a source of weakness rather than of strength. 'Some people imagine', wrote one MP, 'there will be a new [Parliament] called'.[114] But there is no evidence that Pitt even contemplated asking the King for a dissolution. Such a request would probably have been refused, and the dismissal of the new ministers, which always threatened, thereby precipitated. But in the absence of that Patriot millennium, a Parliament elected freely and without the intervention of ministerial in-fluence, a greater moral responsibility devolved on the ministers them-selves. 'One thing seems certain', wrote an anonymous correspondent, 'that it is next to impossible, that the new ministry can keep their ground, without doing some great and popular things'.[115] Lord Lyttelton, too, realised that its problem was

how to lay or how to direct the storm they have raised. Enquiries are promised; the nation demands them; the late ministers desire them; but the conduct of them in parliament is no easy matter. In the addresses for enquiries a Jacobite spirit has mixed itself very strongly with the discontent infused or encouraged by the late opposition. How is that spirit to be satisfied or suppressed? A new parliament is demanded, a parliament chosen without any corruption, a law for triennial parliaments, and such other propositions. Mr Pitt is said to have promised these things, particularly the first. The foreign troops are to be also sent away and eight thousand men to be sent to America. What will remain for the defence of this kingdom? The Militia Bill is to pass; but will the Bill be an army? Will it supply the void of these regular troops before a man is disciplined by it, or even raised? Another declaration is, that we are to pay no subsidies to any foreign Prince. What will become of the King of Prussia next year, what will become of Hanover?[116]

Walpole was more specific:

Mr Pitt accedes with so little strength, that his success seems very precarious. If he Hanoverises, or checks any enquiries, he loses his popularity, and falls that way; if he humours the present rage of the people, he provokes two powerful factions. His only chance seems to depend on joining with the Duke of Newcastle who is most offended with Fox; but after Pitt's personal exclusion of his Grace, and considering Pitt's small force, it may not be easy for him to be accepted there. I foresee nothing but confusion; the new system is composed of such discordant parts, that it can produce no harmony. Though the Duke of Newcastle, the Chancellor, Lord Anson and Fox quit, yet scarce one of their friends is discarded. The very cement seems disjunctive: I mean the Duke of Devonshire ...If he acts cordially, he disobliges his intimate friend Mr Fox; if he does not, he offends Pitt.[117]

A measure of Devonshire's success as a mediator was that Fox had been disobliged, and Pitt offended, already. The ministry's numerical weakness, disfavour in the Closet, and uncertain leadership were all widely appreciated. To Lord Lyttelton, both Devonshire and Pitt could credibly be presented as First Minister,[118] and though once Pitt was ordered to prepare the Speech from the Throne the order of precedence was apparent to Newcastle,[119] others were not equally sure. The ministry's fall was widely thought to be imminent; that and Pitt's absence led Barrington to write after Christmas: 'The Duke of Devonshire though at the head of the Treasury is not *yet* considered as the First Minister; but I cannot tell you who is considered in the light of being a minister in any sense of the word'. Pitt's arrogance and aloofness have led many historians to suppose that his political position within the ministry was one of personal dominance. On the contrary; circumstances forced him to be far more evasive than Newcastle about the ministerial standing to which he laid claim. 'Though I use the word ministry', continued Barrington, 'I can scarce explain what I mean by it; for how can the word be understood in the common acceptation, when they who have the ministerial places have neither the confidence of their master or the support of the parliament. I think there are visible signs of disunion and discontent among themselves.'[120] More important, the centrality of Devonshire's contribution meant that the ministry was launched on the basis of no calculation by Pitt about the prospects of winning the support of enough of the Old Corps in the Commons to carry on with their backing and that of Leicester House and the Tories. The reversionary interest, once established, might have been expected progressively to erode an Old Corps remaining in equivocal and inhibited opposition, just as the younger Pitt's ministry gathered strength in 1784. Yet no such thing happened during the Pitt–Devonshire administration, and no such calculation was made at its outset. Not for half a century had a ministry lacked an obvious party basis, and the absence of precedents in the mind of the political public as well as the insecurity of tenure of the ministry helped to disguise its originality in that respect.

Yet if its party composition was not made explicit, the fall of Newcastle was widely regarded as having had a major impact on the Whigs. 'Ever since I have known the world', wrote Fox's henchman Calcraft, 'I have honoured *that Old Corps*, which I am sorry to see totally gone'.[121] Chesterfield congratulated himself at having, long before, 'got out of that *galère*, which has since been so ridiculously tossed, and is now sinking'.[122] Politics seemed now to be characterised by factious conflicts to which England's military peril gave a wider significance and a vivid emphasis. 'Our country is in danger of ruin', wrote Mrs Montagu, 'and little factions tear it to pieces.'[123] The clash of Whig and Tory faded into insignificance by comparison with these bitter rivalries, and the existence of the Tories as a parliamentary unit was temporarily forgotten as observers remarked that 'there appear to be three distinct parties'[124] – those of Fox, Pitt and Newcastle. 'Party' seemed the appropriate word to describe these squadrons, and was so used when men spoke of the Whigs.[125] It was in the interests of none of the major contenders, however, to admit the validity of this analysis. Pitt, 'keeping himself retired and secluded from all access, affected to attract no dependents, to form no party'.[126] Newcastle merely sought to recapture the Whig leadership; Fox sought to impute to Pitt a party allegiance in the form of a Tory alliance which would make Pitt's leadership of the Old Corps impossible. The Tories, equally with Pitt, had a tactical incentive not to engage in such recriminations, for it was soon clear that they would bring about the fall of the ministry. But, in so doing, their reticence harmonised with Pitt's evasiveness as to the party base of his ministry. To this, again, the Old Corps' emphasis on the reprehensibly factious nature of the conflict contributed. The silence of Newcastle's and Pitt's camps meant that, for the first time, an alliance between opposition Whigs and Tories could credibly be represented as having a *Tory* (instead of, as was obvious in the 1730s and 1740s, a *Whig*) connotation. But it was credible exactly because that identification had no tactical, predictive value: it was not tested by political reality, and vanished when the ministry fell. Though presumably the Tories did not object to Fox's attempts to represent the Pitt–Devonshire administration as a Tory *party* ministry, the outcome meant that their name had been taken in vain, devalued by failure as well as confused by misuse.

On the part of Pitt's enemies, it was charged against his ministry that it was 'an administration supported by Tories, Jacobites and Cocoa-Tree Cabals'; that he 'depends for his chief support on an unnatural division' between the King and the Prince of Wales.[127] The second was obviously true; and though the association of the Tories with past Jacobite intrigues was no longer the public preoccupation it once had been, it was soon obviously true also that the Tory party was the major bloc in the Commons which Pitt could count on. His apologists in the press were therefore forced to argue both that Toryism was now virtually harmless – 'we are inclined to think, that the word *Jacobite* is *vox et praeterea nihil*. The name survives after the party is extinct'[128] – and also, not quite consistently, that

we find that the great man has had no further commerce with these same Cocoa Tree Tories, than what ceremony absolutely required...we think with our good friend the TEST, that a coalition of parties is at this time highly expedient. Therefore, if the minister *should* ever be catched drinking a dish of chocolate with a Tory, we shall not entertain the least suspicion of his measures on that account.[129]

The stresses induced by these strategies meant that not only the factions' tactical conduct but also their principles of coherence were at issue in the coming months. Newcastle's departure raised in a pressing form the question whether the Old Corps was essentially a Whig party with personal loyalties linked to its ideological traditions, or a Treasury party.

There appeared to be some truth in both: Newcastle was particularly pleased when Hume Campbell assured him that 'now the time was come for you [Lord Marchmont] and me to show we were his friends and not friends to his power...He said he hoped his friends would stick together and not let him be ill used.'[130] To that end he began to consider an appropriate leader of the Old Corps in the House, in the absence of Fox and Sir George Lyttelton.[131] But Rigby predicted that a minister in command of 'the plenitude of power', the Treasury and the Exchequer together, would reveal of the mercenary rank and file of the Old Corps that 'it was the Treasury for the time being and not Pelham was their deity'.[132] Just as, therefore, Pitt was to seek to avoid a vote which would reveal the numerical weakness of his following, so Newcastle had a disincentive to divide the backbenchers of his own party along a line marked out by the different emphases of self-interest. Threats of divisions in the House were to come not from their camp but from Fox's.

Newcastle, however, not Devonshire, enjoyed the King's public favour, and after his formal resignation Hume Campbell reported the ex-minister 'in high spirits and very merry'; when Newcastle

dined at the public dinner given by Serjeant Murray he called for his cloak, going away, and said aloud, 'It is, thank God, the only cloak I desire or want'; which pleased much and his refusing either office, pension or anything else takes wonderfully with our sovereign the mob who say, 'By G–d, he must be an honest man to do so and is ill used.'[133]

His demands for reward were not unprecedentedly light. He simply did not ask anything for himself: 'I would ask nothing that would not leave us *free* hereafter'. But he was aware of the profits of previous First Ministers, and anxious to use what he saw as probably his last chance to serve his family.[134] This provoked little comment, and his integrity was apparently established. The places he received were, indeed, proof of the King's affection and approval – of which Newcastle openly boasted. With Holdernesse remaining in the ministry, Newcastle had (as he thought) a representative in the Closet. Soon Newcastle was urging him to intervene to protect Tom Pelham in his seat at the Board of Trade,[135] and Holdernesse at once began to provide Newcastle with confidential information (in so far as he was trusted with it) about the ministry's workings. Through him Newcastle learned of the final allocation of offices, including the removal of Dr Simpson to make way for Dr Hay as King's Advocate General, a post probably incompatible with Hay's seat at the Admiralty.[136] Holdernesse was, however, unable to prevent such moves. 'The want of a proper person capable of interposing in the Closet begins to be manifest', wrote Hardwicke; 'but we must not be ministers behind the curtain. The new gentlemen begin to ascribe the disagreeableness of their reception to that cause.'[137] But, whether from Newcastle's greater tact or the new ministers' other worries, that argument was thereafter little heard. Newcastle's standing, too, was not covert but public and ostentatious. 'The Duke of Newcastle', wrote Holdernesse, 'is great in his retreat and does himself great honour by the manner in which he bears what his enemies only call a disgrace.'[138] He continued to hold his levées, which were reported to be as crowded as before; levées at Court were thinly attended, even by the new ministers themselves.[139] The foreign ambassadors still called on him each Wednesday,[140] and via Holdernesse he received summaries or copies of incoming diplomatic dispatches.[141] Inferences were drawn, too, from the precarious position of the new ministry:

most people fear its stability and apprehend very much from the parliamentary interest of N[ewcast]le whose resignation was too heroic not to leave room to believe he foresaw the short duration of his disgrace. The King is still much their friend and while the new [First] Lord of the Admiralty kissed his hand he held it out behind his back and, as they add, very near his a–se, talking all the while to Lord Anson of naval affairs.[142]

FOX'S RELATIONS WITH DEVONSHIRE

In the weeks before Parliament met on 2 December, Fox's relations with Devonshire were under great strain. Despite their popularity without doors, many of the new ministers were in difficulties over their re-election, and Fox sought to increase their problems. 'The new ministers are so little provided with interest in boroughs', wrote Walpole, 'that it is almost an administration out of parliament.'[143] Newcastle declined to return Pitt for his pocket borough of Aldborough, and Lord Brooke reportedly refused to bring him in for Warwick.[144] Eventually Lord Lyttelton, 'who has engaged with the Duke of Bedford for one and one at Okehampton, named Pitt to his Grace as the man to be chose in his room'[145] – presumably to Bedford's surprise, though he did not contest the return. Charles Townshend's prospects at Yarmouth were uncertain, and Potter was devising stratagems for the electors of Aylesbury.[146] Fox set up the young Lord Powerscourt to contest Dr Hay's seat at Stockbridge; boasted to Devonshire of certain success;[147] and asked him to back Lord Conyngham at Sandwich against Claudius Amyand, whom Pitt had removed from an Under-Secretaryship of State to the Board of Customs.[148] Fox retracted a suggestion that Sloper, who had vacated his seat on appointment to the Board of Trade, might stand down at Great Bedwyn in order to provide a seat for Charles Townshend: 'I can, if you will, make Sloper stay (if the Trade is kept open for him) till after the enquiry and then give his seat to Townshend.' But Fox made explicit his reluctance to sacrifice 'a sure friend for a certain enemy. And where your Grace does bring in any of the new ministers' friends I should hope you would exact a promise of neutrality in all questions of enquiry.'[149] Townshend had to be accommodated in the

Saltash seat vacated by Lord Duncannon; he in turn was elected at Harwich in place of John Phillipson, who died on 27 November. The most insoluble problem was that of Dr Hay, for whom no other seat was in sight.[150] Bedford disapproved of Fox's stand as in danger of forcing Pitt to a reconciliation with Newcastle rather than (as he claimed was otherwise obvious) Fox, and as a move which could be used to discredit Fox with the King.[151] Yet despite Fox's, Rigby's and Gower's continuing attempts to persuade Bedford to accept Ireland,[152] Fox persisted. The new ministry interpreted it, as it was, as 'an act of open hostility and vow revenge'.[153]

Augustus Hervey received the impression, on 18 November, that Fox was anxious to discover weak points in Byng's defence.[154] Dr Hay had been retained as Byng's counsel throughout the summer,[155] and was resented by Fox as 'a worthless friend of Legge's'.[156] But, beyond the obvious fact that Fox 'is now very skilfully availing himself of his adversary's errors',[157] the strategy of Fox's opposition to Hay is open to interpretation. It may be that he was exerting pressure on Devonshire in claiming that he thought it likely '(let me do what I will, because of Leicester House)' that Pitt would be induced to join Newcastle; that Fox could do nothing about this, and so refused to 'act a contemptible part for fear others should'.[158] But to Bedford, whom he had left at Woburn on 18th[159] and who now stood far more securely in Fox's confidence than Devonshire, the emphasis was different:

The proscription of me, my lord, proceeds from Leicester House, and yet I am of your Grace's opinion, that sooner or later they are likely to agree with me if I keep the honour and strength that your Grace and other friends have given me; and I do assure your Grace that I shall not fly off so as to lose sight of, much less prevent, such an agreement. I have given your Grace my word that, whenever H.R. Highness, your Grace, and the Duke of Marlborough, or any two of you, tell me that it is in your opinions for the good of the public, there is nobody I will not shake hands with, there are no terms I will not submit to. But your Grace and I differ a little about the manner of bringing to agreement such insolent men as these are. I offered to join them cordially as Paymaster without being of the Cabinet Council. This brought no agreement, but induced that (may I not say insolent?) proposal that G. Grenville should be Paymaster and I Treasurer of the Navy. They are now angry that I oppose Dr Hay; but though they knew the interest [at Stockbridge] was in me, they would not apply to me, but expected that I should, unasked, choose him, for fear of disobliging them. As to representations of me to his Majesty, the King knows and is mightily pleased that I oppose Dr Hay...I own I see danger of their joining the Duke of Newcastle; but I think your Grace's taking Ireland, and my showing strength in the House of Commons (for personal complaisance does harm and spoils them) may effectually prevent it.[160]

Unable openly to oppose Pitt in the House, Fox had nevertheless to find ways of causing trouble sufficient to give his friends a sense of cohesion and common purpose, and Pitt an incentive to buy him off. One such way was electoral disruption. Stockbridge he presented therefore as a point of honour in his contest with Pitt. Anything else could be given up – Sloper's seat surrendered to Charles Townshend or even Dr Hay – the point was that 'Mr Pitt should have thought himself obliged to me. He cannot think me obliged to him. And therefore he builds upon my fear of him, of which I have none, and if his understanding were not blinded by his self-conceit he would know I have not.'[161] Such efforts were successful. The number of Fox's friends remaining in office and even promoted was remarked on; and 'Mr Fox's friends think he is out of employment but not out of power, or, at least, will not be so long'; had Pitt really intended (on his own account or that of Leicester House) to destroy Fox politically, speculated Lord Lyttelton, he would surely have united with Newcastle.[162] Fox remained committed to supporting the ministry's public measures in Parliament, and offset by hopes that Bedford would accept Ireland his reiterated claims that the interest at Stockbridge was his;[163] but other hostilities against the new ministers' re-election he was now recommended to drop.[164]

Fox's second line of attack was the publication of *The Test*, a weekly journal written by Philip Francis and immediately recognised as Fox's mouthpiece. It first appeared on 6 November, and at the outset may have expressed a desire by Fox to dissociate himself from the late ministry in order to keep open the door to a Pitt alliance: the first copy, thought Newcastle, 'proves that Mr Fox makes a merit, of his having differed with his colleagues, and been *no part* of the administration since 1748, till he came to be Secretary of State'.[165]

PITT'S POSITION, AND THE PARLIAMENTARY SESSION BEFORE CHRISTMAS

In retrospect it may seem obvious that Pitt's long-term problem was to engineer a train of events which could lead to an alliance with Newcastle (within which his own position would be assured and not subject to continual erosion) without at the same time rehabilitating Fox politically and making him a contender in such an arrangement. Despite the fact that Fox's position was initially a strong one in these respects, it is not evident that Pitt took any counter measures. Thanks to Pitt's reticence and the consequent lack of detailed evidence, it is possible to establish very little about the tactical perceptions and intentions of the new ministers until they began again to make contact with Newcastle in March and April 1757. Until then, it seems likely that Pitt showed a positive poverty of resource. Holdernesse realised early that 'Our alliance with [the King of Prussia] must and will be supported by all sides.'[166] With experience of the new ministers, that conviction grew: 'by what I can pick up, our foreign system, so far as we may be said to have any, will be pursued, and even perhaps carried farther than it has been, since the unthinking multitude drove us into an American and maritime war, without regard to the continent...'[167] By 26 November, he wrote of Pitt: 'I think his opinions upon foreign affairs *now he is in place* are exactly the same with mine; however different they were some time ago *tempora mutantur et nos* etc.'[168] This realisation lay behind the complacency with which Newcastle's inner circle regarded Pitt's accession: what, to the public, was a cataclysm in government, was, to informed Whigs, defused by the wordly realisation that opposition 'only desired to create as much confusion as might be necessary to bring themselves into power; which being obtained, they were ready to talk a different language, to say that the object was changed, and to pursue the same political system which had ruined the former administration'.[169]

Immobilised with gout at Hayes since about 1 November, Pitt claimed, when it was convenient, to be unable to make informed judgements on fine points of manoeuvre.[170] Many of the detailed arrangements were undertaken by Temple. Pitt, however, drew up the draft of the King's Speech and sent it to Devonshire for consideration, adding his hope that Legge would approve; 'I have drawn it captivating to the people, but with all regard to the King's dignity, and have avoided any word offensive or hostile to those who no longer serve His Majesty.'[171] Devonshire raised no objection.[172] Legge, however, had to be dissuaded from his ambition, as Chancellor of the Exchequer, to write the circular letters inviting MPs to town and to chair the meeting at the Cockpit. Temple used George Grenville as an emissary; he met Legge on 18th, and found him at once waive his claims to both tasks. Grenville hoped the letters could be sent to Hayes to be signed in time to be posted on 20 November.[173] Legge's opinion, he added, was to deal with the speech and the Address on the first day, 'and not to adjourn the Report of the former, for though many of us will be out of Parliament, yet Mr Potter and the two Townshends will both be there the first day of the sessions, and there is no prospect, he believes, of any opposition to it, and the sending the Speech abroad [i.e. without doors] for ten days may be liable to some inconveniences'.[174]

Before Pitt's return to town, which was then planned for about 25th, Devonshire laid the draft speech before George II. It was not approved,[175] though Newcastle suspected from Holdernesse's information that the King had allowed something to remain that he should have removed.[176] Pitt delayed his response until his promised arrival in town on 27th, and in anticipation of a visit from Devonshire warned him that 'A few lines, and that is all, may be parted with.'[177] The text may also have been discussed at a Cabinet meeting at Pitt's town house on his arrival on 30th, the day before the Cockpit meeting.[178] Parliament was to meet on 2 December, but to adjourn for ten days for re-elections; Pitt was expected to take the Seals on 4th. Presumably the Cabinet on 30th approved a revised version of the Speech;[179] and attention shifted to the draft Address from each House in reply, which were also then considered. Temple, however, was absent with a cold, and Pitt probably absent also. It was only the next day that Pitt heard of a move, inspired he thought by Cumberland, to insert in the Lords' Address a passage thanking the King for the Hanoverians' presence in England. Taking such a step as one hostile to his ministry, Pitt threatened Devonshire that he would oppose any such measure in the Commons, and suggested that Temple would do the same in the Lords; Devonshire replied 'that it is against his opinion and that of the Cabinet'. Hurriedly, Pitt arranged to see Bute that evening, surrendering to Legge at the last moment the conduct of the Cockpit meeting (it was given out that he was too ill to attend).[180] Temple discovered this addition from Pitt the following day, and, aware that the Cabinet had unanimously disapproved the night before, wrote to Devonshire threatening to oppose it on 2 December.[181] Gilbert Elliot was told of this privately by George Grenville at the Cockpit meeting on the evening of 1st and asked by him to tell Bute, whom Pitt had presumably not told.[182]

Devonshire waited till the next day to reply to Temple;[183] he wrote in anodyne terms to suggest the little objection there might be to thanking the King for complying with Parliament's request in summoning the Hanoverians at all, and the danger that this point might cause the destruction of 'a system that I flattered myself might be a means of preserving this country'. Yet he failed to disguise his misgivings at sending back the troops at all at a time of almost equal military danger; Holdernesse's intelligence was that the addition to the motion 'was made at Devonshire House' to meet the King's wishes, and that it probably did not go far enough to do so.[184] Faced with the need to retain a basic minimum of royal favour as the condition for Pitt's accepting the Seals at all, Devonshire was unable to meet Temple's demand, and on 2 December Temple left his sickbed to speak against the Lords' Address: an unprecedented move for a Cabinet Councillor, 'unless he was understood to be just going out'. Why, asked Lord Lyttelton, did Temple choose to show his weakness in the ministry? 'What surprised everybody still more was, that, in the House of Commons, Mr Pitt had declared the same day, that the bringing the Hanoverians into England "was not a Court measure but the measure of Parliament".' Lyttelton could not discover, therefore, whether Temple had acted with Pitt's approval, though he heard that Pitt had spoken to Devonshire against the addition.[185] Only Stanhope, however, supported Temple; Bedford spoke against, and the Address passed *nem. con.* Everyone, it seemed, was anxious to support public measures and produce a quiet session.

Devonshire meanwhile had been delicately edging Pitt towards accepting the Seals. This he was due to do on 3 December; but that morning a rumour circulated of a motion to re-commit the Commons' Address and add an acknowledgement similar to that in the Lords'. Pitt left

Court to let it be known in the House that he would refuse the Seals if such a motion was passed; and it was dropped.[186] Devonshire called on Pitt that night to promise him, from the King, a more favourable reception in the Closet. Devonshire protested that he believed 'the thought of being thanked arose in the King: I said [wrote Pitt] wherever it had arisen I was informed that *Mr Fox* in *concert with Lord Egmont* wished to throw the House into confusion upon it.[187] His Grace hoped and believed that intelligence was not founded; that the *Duke of Bedford* had contributed also to stop the progress of the mischief in the House, as soon as the Duke of Devonshire had told him the consequence, which they all agreed would be fatal to the King's affairs.' The King consented, too, to Admiral Forbes' incorporation on the Admiralty Board *vice* John Pitt. 'In short that I was to understand the storms of the Closet would subside.'[188] Pitt duly accepted the Seals on 4th, the last of the new ministers, except Potter, to do so.

The attendance at the Cockpit meeting had been 'very full',[189] but witnessed 'an appearance of irresolution among the new ministers',[190] in part probably at Legge's last-minute employment, in part at the last-minute substitution of Edwin Sandys for Lord Granby to second the Commons' Address, 'an immense fall by way of anticlimax'. But it is by no means clear that the Tories attended: it seems likely that they did not, for James Grenville was to show a copy of the Speech and Address to Sir John Philipps the next morning.[191] The first day's proceedings left very different impressions on different MPs. Nathaniel Ryder thought the Speech 'extremely stiff and without much meaning';[192] Gilbert Elliot was more enthusiastic about George Townshend's moving the Address, 'his speech high upon the necessity of enquiry, seconded by Mr Sandys. Beckford your friend very severe upon the last ministers which occasioned some altercation; Mr Pitt stated his general plan.'[193] It did not provoke marked opposition; yet one MP noticed 'the same appearance of distraction' in the Commons as at the Cockpit,[194] and Lord Lyttelton wrote of the King's Speech: 'It is in a high style, *ad populum*, seems to promise great things. But there is certainly enough of Germany in it; and it by no means agrees with the public declarations made by Lord Temple of no *foreign subsidies*; much less with the language talked the last year.'[195] Temple's demonstration, and the emphasis in the Speech on a militia, may both have had in them something of the nature of a diversion. Pitt did not draw attention to these elements. His speech, thought Lyttelton, was 'moderate and discreet... In short, he spoke like a minister; and unsaid almost all he had said in opposition.' Henry Digby thought Pitt's 'a very artful, able speech'; he

represented the state of affairs abroad and at home as bad as possible, told us that he was afraid we should be beat next summer, talked of making great efforts this year, and when you had done all you could for yourselves, then you must

see how far you could afford to act upon the continent, that you must go as
far as the interest[s] of this country were combined with those of the powers on
the continent, for combined they were.[196]

Barrington also wrote, when his judgement had been confirmed by
events:

The measures as declared and explained by Mr Pitt the first day of the session
differ in nothing from those of the last administration. Every effort in America
consistent with our safety at home, every effort at sea, and whatever this country
can do besides, given to the support of our allies on the continent. I am told
the Admiralty changes nothing in what they find to have been Lord Anson's
plan.[197]

Fox had suggested that a figure of the standing of Lord Granby or
Lord George Sackville should protest against the departure of the
Hanoverians;[198] yet the latter stopped short of open opposition. 'Lord
G. Sackville said, when he knew how Mr Pitt would fill up the gap which
would be made by the Hanoverians being sent back, *effectually* and
immediately, he would then say what he thought of the sending them
back at this juncture of time.'[199] 'He said Mr Pitt's speech had pleased
him, that he was glad to find that he saw the weakness of this country,
and was not an adventurer in administration.'[200] Granby spoke also, but
was occupied in the defence of Newcastle against Beckford's abuse.

Yet this careful tacking evidently did not arouse the suspicions of
the Tories. It was only in late November that their adherence to a Pitt
ministry began to be canvassed, and even then with scepticism. 'I am
sure that last year', wrote John Campbell about the new ministers, 'they
had but few friends in the House of Commons. They cannot depend
upon the Tories, or with them make a sufficient number to carry on
business.' There was much talk of a dissolution of Parliament and an
uncorrupt election;[201] yet

if in this ferment a greater number of Tories should get in, what would be the
better for that? They will never be real friends to any administration under this
Establishment; and I conceive His Grandeur [Pitt] is particularly odious to
them. If they should help to lift him up for a short time, I am persuaded it
would be with no other view, than to let him fall *graviore casu*.[202]

Walpole thought the Tories' 'partiality was not cordial, but founded on
their hatred to Fox, and probably from secret intimations that the
[Dowager] Princess [of Wales], who meant to adopt them, was inclined
to Pitt, and abhorred Fox for his conexion with the Duke of Cumberland'.[203]

On the first day of the sessions, however, Beckford 'praised Fox and
[Pitt], and assured [Pitt] in the name of all the Tories, but without any
authority from them, of his and their most cordial support'.[204] The
possibility was much stronger than Campbell realised of recruiting a party
which was less and less able to sustain organised resentments, and

increasingly eager to endorse any effort at national regeneration.[205]
Within days Hardwicke was writing that, despite the insufficiency of that
party alone, and the problems of their co-operation with Devonshire,
'By everything which one hears, and the declarations of some considerable Tories, the present scheme is to unite with the Tories.'[206] That
intention obviously succeeded. Sir Richard Lyttelton wrote optimisti-
cally:

The Tories are determined to attend, one and all, and support Mr Pitt and his
friends as the only men capable to rescue the kingdom from approaching
destruction and the only men they think honest enough to endeavour to do it
in preference to all other considerations, nor have they themselves any other
motives for the support they give us, or have hinted at any terms for themselves of any kind whatever, and are all of them as desirous as if they had
places to make free with the purse of the public, confident as they are that the
money, though some of it should go into Germany will even there be employed
to British purposes only.[207]

Evidently, there had been a deliberate act of assent by Tory leaders;
yet the only evidence for it is indirect. A group of twelve leading Tories
signed a circular dated 4 December calling others of their party to town
for 13th, the day the enquiry was expected to begin. Its wording, that
'there is *now* a prospect that Government will support constitutional
measures',[208] suggests that its despatch depended on the impression made
in the first day's debate. Pitt was fortunate, however, in having to deal
with a party which was bound by its prior rhetoric to be able to co-
operate with him only on the terms that there be no terms: a predicament which was soon common knowledge. The Secretary at War wrote:

The Tories will support the new administration as a body, and I verily believe
without having made *any* conditions. Mr Pitt told them he desired their
countenance no longer than they approved his conduct. I do not hear that
there is among them or any other set of men any design to act with violence
against the late administration.[209]

Fox had been hampered since October by the behaviour of his chief
patrons: Argyll failed to respond to his frenzied summonses to town
until all was lost,[210] and Bedford continued to refuse to participate in
the new ministry as Lord Lieutenant of Ireland. Fox's prospects, moreover, were widely thought to have been worsened by the first day's events.
Beckford's attempt to be offensive about the late ministers while distinguishing Fox from them was not well received by the House, while
Granby's and Sir Thomas Robinson's defence of Newcastle was greeted
warmly.[211] Meanwhile, Fox had lost the final round in his contest with
Devonshire over the distribution of minor places. That of Surveyor
General of Woods and Forests had been thought of for John Pitt by
William Pitt even before the death of Phillipson, its holder,[212] and
positively asked for after it took place.[213] Fox then asked it for W. G.

Hamilton,[214] as he thought Devonshire had previously promised.[215] Pitt was willing for Hamilton to be otherwise provided for, but insisted on the Woods for John Pitt. Fox took the name of Argyll in vain,[216] railed against Devonshire's 'knowing and owning himself to have been made the instrument of my enemies to deceive me', and recapitulated Devonshire's role in the negotiations of October–November, on which he blamed his own failure to achieve sole power.[217] But Devonshire refused to intervene; John Pitt kissed hands for the place. Fox's malice focussed itself on Devonshire: 'I hate him more than I do or I think ever did any man.'[218] At once it was rumoured that Fox went out of town for five or six weeks, 'giving up the House of Commons'[219] – an intention which Fox essentially confirmed: his absence 'shall be determined by the occasion there may be for my appearance in the House of Commons', he told Walpole. 'Indeed I foresee none, and rather think my situation when I am there will be awkward...But no design is more changeable than this.'[220] Barrington advised that Fox's resolution would collapse, that he would return for the vote on the army;[221] and Newcastle realised that Fox could not, by his mere absence, dissociate himself from the enquiry.[222] Newcastle was right: only a little persuasion by his friends made Fox promise to return by 13th, convinced that 'my absence would be misinterpreted'.[223]

It was quickly suspected that Newcastle's attitude towards the new ministers was not only complacent but conciliatory. Walpole thought Newcastle was 'already hanging out the white flag to Pitt',[224] and though it is not clear what public gestures this involved, Hardwicke asked Charles Yorke to call on Pitt on 28th to make a delicate reconnaissance of Pitt's willingness to approach them.[225] Struck by the apparent impracticability of a ministry based on Tory support, Hardwicke again suggested a meeting a week later.[226] Whatever the outcome, Hardwicke was encouraged to pay Pitt a formal visit on 6 December.[227] Their common persecution in *The Test* led the conversation to its promoter. Hardwicke 'guardedly' revealed his and Newcastle's dissociation 'from all tenders made from *that quarter*', and ignorance of the insertions in the Lords' and Commons' Addresses, which Pitt insisted were at Fox's instigation. Hardwicke warned Pitt of the precariousness of his base, but protested his and Newcastle's desire both to support the King's government and 'to keep this constitution upon its true and *legal balance*' – that is, to resist Cumberland and Fox. Pitt echoed this aim: he would leave office, he implied, rather than owe it to Fox's support; but he left unmentioned the alternative of a deal with Newcastle. Hardwicke then began to lead Pitt towards asking for such an arrangement. Only 'violence in pushing *enquiries* and *censures*', Hardwicke said, would lead them to join Fox, though an enquiry itself was not feared. The merits of their case would convince even Pitt; but 'any kind of violence would create and cement factions in the Parliament, and intrigues in the Court, and he had foresight enough to see how that would probably end': a royal manoeuvre, Hardwicke implied, to dismiss him. Pitt had anticipated this. His moderation over the enquiry had already been made clear in the House, and he explained it as something other than a 'censure'. Nevertheless, he could not stop it, 'after what he himself had formerly declared'. Trouble must also be expected over the Maidstone affair; and though Pitt would not initiate it, someone else was sure to do so, and he then 'could not help going along with it to a certain degree'. Hardwicke treated this as far more serious than Pitt wished to represent it;

but I soon thought I perceived that he had taken some sort of engagements upon this head with the Tories. For he soon passed over to talk of the *Country Gentlemen*; how well disposed they were to support Government, how generous and candid their behaviour had been to him; and what assurances they had given him. I told him I should much rejoice to see any number of gentlemen come into the support of the King's measures; but surely it could not be quite so generous, as to be without any *conditions*; and he might lose more on the one hand, than he gained on the other. He said – no conditions at all; quite free and disinterested; merely to keep the ship from sinking. I smiled and asked how long do you compute it will last upon that foot? He smiled too and said he would not pretend to foretell; but surely this session. From all his discourse upon this head I perceived that this dependence might make him imagine that he need not go very fast towards a coalition, either with us or any other set; for he said he must look about him a little etc., but adhered to his aversion to a *certain corner* of the Court. I laughed, and told him that when he came to converse with those country gentlemen, he would not find that our side of the late administration was the object of their *greatest enmity*.

Plainly, Pitt's euphemisms about country gentlemen pointed to an alliance with the Tory party which rendered him safe vis-à-vis Fox and disinclined him as yet to any closer links with Newcastle. Hardwicke and Newcastle therefore sat back to await developments, speculating in delight at the problems which would beset Pitt from the increasing certainty that 'the *Tories* in a body, are to support the new administration...what will the Whig Duke of Devonshire say to it, the Whig Mr Pitt say for it, or Mr Legge, who Mr Pitt told me, was *the child of the Whigs*. But above all, what will this good Whig House of Commons say to it?'[228] Newcastle was conscious of the irony of a situation in which he had so recently been branded with a Tory label for tactical purposes: 'It is a shame for the *Duke of Devonshire*, and the Whigs, to give into such schemes, especially after the false and infamous reproach that they so lately cast upon others (here, I mean myself).'[229] Yet provided there were no dissolution, Newcastle could draw comfort from several considerations. He considered Barrington's news of General Blakeney's evidence, which would tell heavily against Byng at his trial, went far to justify the late ministers.[230] Though the report did not reach Newcastle, Fox heard that Pitt had been asked privately when the enquiry would begin, and had answered that he did not know.[231] Bedford's final acceptance of the Lord Lieutenancy of Ireland[232] had to be set against the prospects for the conduct of business.

The political battles which seemed to impend in October were suddenly put into cold storage by Pitt's personal complacency over the enquiry; by his sudden relapse, or sham relapse, of gout, which confined him to bed after his interview with Hardwicke;[233] and by the increasing commitment of the ministry to the Prussian alliance and its military consequences. Holdernesse reported that Frederick had become 'the idol of the people of all ranks'.[234] Pitt, he added, 'sees the necessity of the closest union with the King of Prussia, and of forming an army, in conjunction with him, for the defence of Westphalia'.[235] Apart from the imminent return of the Hessian and Hanoverian troops (though they too were destined to join the army of observation), Newcastle was for the moment aware that Pitt's plans coincided with his own intentions.[236] The chief possible reasons for Pitt's quick removal thus evaporated; and Newcastle's motives for supporting him in office until after the enquiry became less mixed. It seemed almost too much to hope that Pitt could commit himself to such an immense expenditure, after his past rhetoric; and Newcastle expected him to resort to rhetorical stratagems, relying on the absence of opposition from the Old Corps. Newcastle had always believed, and continued to believe, that 'if the war is to be carried on with any probability of success, it can only be done by great expenses on the continent; and immense ones in North America; and both Indies. And those who are to undertake it, are not to be envied.' Newcastle was therefore content to leave it for the moment in other hands; he agreed with Hardwicke that Pitt's Tory and popular links would disincline him to approach the Old Corps; on the contrary, he would involve Bedford, Devonshire, the King and Cumberland in 'his Tory scheme' by 'engaging in their military, extensive, continent and American schemes'. Newcastle therefore feared Pitt's position to be stronger than Hardwicke supposed:

The Duke of Devonshire will colour the joining the Tories (for I take that to be a certain fact) with the necessity of getting *everybody* to support the King in this time of danger; the uncertainty, what part *we* would act; the difference between Fox and Pitt, etc. And if I was to give my opinion, what would be the result of all these absurd, inconsistent measures, it should be, that the Duke of Devonshire and the Duke of Bedford, would persuade Mr Pitt of the necessity of silencing Mr Fox, by giving him a high lucrative office, with a peerage perhaps, for himself or his wife, and Fox would take it *thankfully*.

What Newcastle did not realise, however, was that Fox had been silenced already by the consequences of Devonshire's 'betrayal' of him on 2–3 November, by the remaining possibility of a bid for primacy when and if Pitt's ministry collapsed, and by his common implication in the late ministry's record. Of the enquiry, Newcastle perceptively wrote:

I believe they don't propose or expect much from it. They will keep it as a sort of rod over us, and a temptation for the Tories. The attack upon my lord Holdernesse, I agree with your lordship, is promised the Tories; but that will depend upon Mr Pitt's desiring or not, to get rid of my lord Holdernesse from being Secretary of State.

Thus no advances were for the moment to be made to Pitt, thought Newcastle; and none were to be expected from him.[237] Although Holdernesse's latest information called Pitt's commitment to Old Corps points into question, Newcastle continued to think Pitt's attitude would be dictated by the purely tactical problem of how far he would be able to carry with him the Tories and 'what he wrongly calls the People'. It was on this question that Newcastle's attention now focussed, and Pitt's insistence to Holdernesse on publicly condemning the latter's action in the Maidstone affair only confirmed, to Newcastle, its forming part of a deal with the Tories.[238] Nowhere did Newcastle suggest that Pitt was greatly influenced in his actions by the need to square Devonshire, and Hardwicke suggested they were less cordial than even Newcastle had supposed.[239] Devonshire's anger with Fox persisted: he 'says my friendship was not like his, but continues only whilst he can be *useful* to me'.[240] The tactical situation was therefore, for the moment, unusually simple, and the division of forces in the Commons was widely remarked on as being clear-cut. On 13 December Barrington moved, and Legge seconded, a Bill for quartering the Hessian troops until their departure. Legge explained that they were to go as soon as transports could be provided. Sir Cordell Firebrace said he hoped it applied only to troops then in England, not to any that might subsequently arrive; Fox disagreed, 'ruffled the new ministry not a little',[241] and 'declared that the measure of sending away the foreign troops was not resolved upon while he had any share in the administration'.[242] The Act, he argued, should be perpetual.[243] Grenville replied, trying to represent Fox as disapproving of a 'national defence' and relying solely on foreign troops – which, he suggested, could not be relied on to fight if the French landed. Rashly, he challenged any military man to say that they could. Conway and Lord George Sackville both did so, and the House stoutly approved them.[244] Fox, Conway and Lord George Sackville spoke off the question, against the ministry sending away the troops at all, out of 'false notions of popularity',[245] unless they could show that enough would remain for home defence and to send a contingent to North America; Sackville pointed out the irrelevance of any limitation of time in the Bill, since the consent of Parliament was necessary before foreign troops could be brought into the country. 'Lord Egmont, with a sneer, signified his wish, that no question might be put, because he was unwilling that it should go against the administration by a great majority.'[246] There was no division; nor was a motion ever made for the Hessians to remain. Fox, recorded Walpole, had pressed Lord George Sackville to make such a motion in the knowledge that 'the new ministers would have been beaten before they could bring on any of their popular questions'. Sackville, claimed Walpole, had demanded as a prior condition that Bedford, the new Lord Lieutenant of Ireland, would justify the Irish policy of Sackville's father by leaving the Primate one of the Lords Justices on his, Bedford's, departure. Bedford refused, unwilling to take such an unpopular step at the outset of his government: 'The Duke's own plan was to steer impartially between the two factions; at least for his first session';

From that time, Fox had either not fixed what should be the Duke of Bedford's plan, or had been so occupied with his own situation and animosities, as not sufficiently to attend to Ireland. Rigby, devoted to Fox, and thinking himself sure of the Primate whenever he should please to want him, or concluding him totally fallen, and that his own best art of pleasing Fox would be to fling himself into the opposite faction, headed by Lord Kildare, who had married the sister of Lady Caroline Fox; for these, or some of these reasons, he had not had the precaution to model his master [Bedford] to the Primate's views; who, finding himself rejected, or entertained so as to be rejected afterwards, instantly negotiated with Pitt, and worked his friend Lord George to list under the same colours: and other reasons concurred to facilitate that connexion.[247]

One observer recorded that, on 13 December, the House's approval was loud and general for Conway and Sackville but faint for Grenville and 'seemed to come chiefly from the Tories';[248] Dupplin agreed that 'Legge and Grenville addressed themselves to the Tories and that the Tories gave them their approbation',[249] but Fox was far more emphatic in his interpretation. 'The Tories and nobody else, applauded Legge and Grenville. The whole House, except the Tories, approved of me, Lord George Sackville, and Mr Conway.'[250] Had there been a division on the Bill or on the Address, 'the ministers and Tories would have been on one side and the whole House besides upon the other. It was as much marked yesterday as a division could have marked it...',[251] and Dupplin, too, was led to expect that a division would soon be provoked on the question of the troops' departure.[252]

Fox was anxious to stress publicly what Newcastle only remarked on privately: the shocking and incongruous fact, now demonstrated openly, that 'that leader of the Whig party, Legge; and that advocate for the purity of Whiggism, Pitt' were actually in alliance with the Tories.[253] Here Fox adhered to a traditional tactic: in attempting to smear a small group of Whigs with charges of Toryism, he sought to hamper them in the purely internal contest for supremacy within the Old Corps. Fox had seen a copy of the Tory circular, and interpreted their behaviour in the House as conformity to the exact terms of an arrangement.[254] This may have been true: Pitt, explaining the Bill to George Grenville, had added: 'I understand you will find the country gentlemen quite for it ...You might depend that I should not have given into this matter, if

I had not seen the ground clear.'[255] Secondly, Fox claimed that he *now* believed Pitt's ministry would not survive, though 'what it will break into I do not know. If I were forced to guess, I should think into some sort of understanding between Pitt and the Lord Chancellor and Duke of Newcastle and maybe the Tories, in hopes of places to some of them, and to exclude the Duke [of Cumberland] and me.'[256] Fox's links with Devonshire therefore became a matter of more pressing importance, and a reconciliation between them soon followed. Unity was necessary to pass the supplies and deal with the enquiry; then the system would break down, with one of three results. 'A junction between Pitt and the Duke of Newcastle, to which the Tories may probably accede; a junction between Pitt and me; or an impracticability [in the King] which may make them quit and so begins another confusion. Of those three I think the first the likeliest; the second the unlikeliest.'[257] The second, after all, was the system Fox had just destroyed; his conduct could only now be defended on the grounds of that system's impracticability, and his rancour against Newcastle only indulged by its continued rejection. Though Pitt remained confined with gout, it was understood to be a move directed against him personally that Fox then sharply raised the temperature of political exchange.[258]

This he was able to do since the enquiry had been, for the moment, rearranged to follow the vote of supply. It was generally expected among Old Corps backbenchers that an immediate vote would be provoked,[259] and Hume Campbell learnt on 14th

from one of F[ox]'s people that the new folks had determined as a measure to resign if they lost a question in our House and F[ox] is resolved to make them do it upon the foreign troops to be brought on when the land forces are to be voted, if not as soon as the estimates come in. By what I could pick up it will be an address to the King to keep them there. If this succeeds the new folks throw up and things are brought to a crisis sooner than perhaps the Duke of Newcastle wishes. You see this is a back game of F[ox] to recover what he played ill before...[260]

Hardwicke, in touch with the ministry through Charles Yorke, advised: 'I own I think that a division should on all accounts be avoided, for though it will not be right for us to divide from the body of the Whigs, yet I think success upon such a division will be doing the business of other people, and not our own.'[261]

The news that Fox would oppose the Bill for quartering foreign troops quickly spread.[262] It provoked deep alarm among the new ministers' supporters — Lord Egremont, for example, whose covert approval for the new administration it revealed. Granville, who had recently been overbearing towards Holdernesse and heaping loyal flattery on Pitt,[263] sensed the prospects of a change, 'seemed indecisive', and refused to advise a follower how to vote.[264] Northey could guarantee the Tory vote behind the ministry on the issue,[265] but after the scene on 13th, speculation continued to reverberate on 'how far the most powerful party in both Houses, that of the Whigs, will suffer a M[inister] to be born upon the shoulders of the T[orie]s'; success in the pursuit of popular measures would allow the ministry to 'fix, in a great measure, in their favour, the spirit of popularity, almost ever fluctuating, but ever powerful, in this country'; otherwise, the Whig party would 'tear it to pieces'.[266] Plainly, politicians did not suppose that the ministry had yet succeeded in deploying its 'popularity' to political advantage: 'popularity' it may have had, but that would not shield it from the tactical vicissitudes of its minority position, its composition, and its standing in the Closet; 'popularity' was universally admitted to be important, just because no contemporary knew, as no modern historian has succeeded in explaining, how popularity might override a course of events laid down, by such considerations, in the infinite variety of high political manoeuvre. Thus Barrington recorded that the ministry had 'no support but a little popularity which must be short lived; for all ministers must do some right things, than which nothing is more displeasing to the multitude. Besides, the national expectation is raised very high, and the first bad success will enrage the people beyond measure'.[267] Then, too, although a hostile outcry had an obvious direction, techniques did not exist in the mid eighteenth century objectively to monitor that much more diffuse phenomenon, 'popularity', in the nation at large. Politicians' estimates of their own popularity, in so far as they thought this might matter, were in large part reflections of the state of their own morale. Newcastle's, in mid-December, was high.[268] From within the ministry he had been assured: 'I am told that the temper of mankind is softening towards you every day, and that your not disturbing the new administration or their measures is very much approved in the City. Some of your best friends have said in my hearing that if you remain quiet two months everybody must turn their eyes towards you.'[269]

In such a situation the detailed conduct of Commons business was of the first importance; but the evidence establishes little more. Temple apparently relied heavily on George Grenville as the Ministry's Commons spokesman, 'the acting Minister', in the absence of Pitt.[270] It was Grenville whom Pitt approached to insist that the Bill for quartering the Hessians should be confined to the current case only and the general principle of quartering foreign troops be postponed for consideration as a clause in the Mutiny Bill.[271] The Hessian Bill therefore passed in Committee and was reported on 15th without significant debate.[272] Fox's failure to intervene is remarkable. There is no evidence that he was dissuaded from speaking by any of Newcastle's friends, and his intentions cannot be clearly known. In the light of Fox's reconciliation with Devonshire the following morning, it seems possible that he deferred action which he thought certain to bring down Pitt at once and likely to unite Pitt with Newcastle, in the confident expectation that the ministry would fall after the enquiry. For whatever reason, the Commons continued quiet. The land tax at 4s. was voted on 17th with 'no material debate',[273] and the enquiry seemed certain now to begin after Christmas.[274]

Pitt continued to protest at what he considered the impossible expense of the King's German plans. Pitt had agreed to 'a sum, larger by one third than I proposed', only to meet a demand for a subsidy to the Landgrave of Hesse in addition. As if in threat, Pitt had the vote of the estimates of the land forces postponed.[275] Fox had been uncertain what to do,[276] admitting only to a growing conviction that he could not join with Pitt.[277] Pitt also was using a similar expectation as leverage to restrict the estimate for Hessian troops to two months only, telling Barrington (who believed him)

that things must very soon come to an explanation; that Mr Fox had no more friends or followers in Parliament than himself, he thought not to so many; that he was ready to poll the House of Commons as well as the nation against the said Mr Fox; that he conceived the King intended that he (Mr Pitt) should at present have the conduct of his affairs in the House of Commons; and that if factious oppositions were encouraged against what had been determined by the Duke of Devonshire and himself with the King's approbation, he knew what remained for him; to which he added that from what he saw of the difficulties attending his situation even assisted by every support, he thought the day of his retirement would be the happiest day of his life...[278]

Both Fox's and Newcastle's camps thus had an interest in avoiding a decisive vote. As Barrington wrote, 'no day passes in Parliament without immediate danger of a declared majority in the two Houses against the new ministry; an event which I use my best endeavours to prevent, because I dread the consequences of it'.[279] Pitt, too, sought to avoid a vote by his personal absence,[280] since his presence would have provoked his rival; by avoiding all contentious business, or allowing George Townshend to promote it independently; and by making what remained an issue of confidence. Thus Glover described with disillusion the items of parliamentary business that session as 'all within the old narrow circle, trite, trifling and iniquitous',[281] and Henry Digby noticed that the Tories did not look 'extremely zealous just now'.[282] It was not least the fact that nothing of importance had yet been done which preserved Barrington's conviction that no terms had been made with the Tories and that they supported disinterestedly: 'a disposition very unusual in this country, which cannot long subsist'.[283]

That Fox's bluff was called was apparent when the army was voted in Committee, in Pitt's absence, on 22 December. Lord George Sackville explained in detail the allocation of forces and argued that foreign troops could not be spared: before the Hessians left, the House should formally consider their going. Fox, in effect accepting the postponement of a decisive vote, agreed. Legge and Grenville demurred. The troops' departure would be public knowledge: it needed not and would not be reported to the House. If a motion disapproving their departure were made, the onus of opposition would be on others; the ministers would not table a motion which must be a vote of confidence. Fox suggested that, if so, the King should be persuaded to keep some of the Hanoverians;

but he would not move that or any other question that should be thought hostile, that he was for unanimity at present because he thought it for the service of the public, that though he was out of employment, he was not in opposition, that if that was his case, he might do as others had done before him, not object to measures which he did not approve of beforehand, in order to find fault with them afterwards.[284]

Fox 'wished somebody would move' for a call of the House after the recess to consider the matter; and after the Committee was over, a call was ordered for 20 January — 'very late indeed, were any enquiries probable' remarked Walpole. Though the House was adjourned until 6 January, no business was to be expected until 20th.[285]

On 23rd the report was made from the Committee, and approved in a thin House. Egmont, dissatisfied with the previous day's events, demanded a formal notification before the Hessians left; 'that he had not pushed it to a question last night out of tenderness to the Administration whose weakness he would not expose by beating them, as he should have done, by two to one'. Legge and George Grenville again replied, the latter implying that the ministry would resign if beaten on the point. Charles Townshend, 'after a great many fine words about public good, and hoping this national question would not be made an engine for party', disagreed with them, but made clear his unwillingness to quit. The debate ended with attacks by Tories — Northey, Prowse, Velters Cornewall – on Barrington's contemptuous remarks on 22nd about Addresses and Instructions, which he had classed with current pamphlets and newspapers for the 'impudence and insolence of the clamour contained in them'. But again there was no division, as there had been none all session. Fox was known to have left the House until 20 January, and the session ended inconclusively.[286] The crucial vote was thus expected, not on the enquiry, but on a division over the departure of the Hessians on or after 20 January, and on the day Parliament reassembled it was claimed in Fox's camp that the public were eager for the Hessians to remain.[287] George Townshend was reported absent in Norfolk the whole of the session until Christmas,[288] and his Militia Bill was not given its first reading until 26 January.[289]

Fox continued, to some, to profess that his position remained unchanged: the ministry would fall, but he would not alter his situation in the outcome.[290] Inferring from the latest arguments of the *Test*, Newcastle's diagnosis was different. A violent attack on himself and Hardwicke was 'I dare say occasioned by our not having given in (as I expected) to such an immediate attack upon the new ministry, as would have forced them out immediately, and fling everything into the hands of the Protector of the Test'.[291] Plainly, if this was a Fox tactic, his quitting also was with a design 'to fling the whole load of the miscarriage upon us'. The *Con-Test* had also joined in denigrating the late ministry, and the *Test* and *Con-Test* were now much more hostile to it, thought Newcastle, than to each other.[292] A Pitt–Fox reconciliation was thus far more likely than Pitt's joining Newcastle.[293] It is not clear that this was the intention of either journal. Fox was certainly anxious to gather support around him in the Commons and on 24 December seems to have made a bid for Hume Campbell's allegiance. Fox had, he claimed, 'assured the King that when the opportunity was proper there should not be wanting expedients and courage to rid him of the present people and carry on his affairs'.[294] Fox refused to be more specific, but diverted all his resentment against Hardwicke, 'who governed me in everything, that I was called *First Minister*, but in reality it was the *Chancellor*'.[295] Fox therefore felt free to acknowledge Newcastle's superior interest in Parliament and 'seemed to think intimations of amity should come to him'.[296] But without a major re-alignment it was clear to Barrington that if the ministry fell no other combination was possible and chaos would ensue.[297] It began, instead, to be suggested that the ministry would be reconstructed and strengthened by the recruitment of new allies,[298] and John Roberts suggested, after a conversation with Devonshire, that the ministry was anxious to have terms offered by Newcastle. The *Con-Test*, argued Roberts, bore this out: though censuring the late administration, its *personal* hostility was reserved for Fox.[299] Yet, to the contrary effect, Sir Thomas Robinson brought news that the King had spoken to Münchausen with impatience of Newcastle's backwardness: it had left him in an invidious position, for he 'at that moment did not know what was the plan of his ministers, nor the least state of his present affairs'. What was most remarkable was that Münchausen had named Fox as the possible reinforcement; 'so that what was only guessed at before', added Robinson, 'proves now to be plainly the King's meaning'. But if, as he urged on Münchausen, Fox were responsible for the *Test*, plainly no reconciliation was possible with Newcastle. If Pitt's ministry gave up, he reported Andrew Stone, another must be arranged ready to take its place, or 'the whole would fall at once into a total anarchy, and that the gates of the King's palace and the two Houses of Parliament would be besieged by mobs, clamouring for some government or other'.[300]

THE SITUATION AFTER CHRISTMAS

All action over the Hessians, the Militia Bill and the enquiry would therefore come on after Christmas. Pitt, meanwhile, was still engaged in the search for tactical expedients. To avoid foreign mercenaries appearing before Parliament on the British estimates, he proposed to Devonshire that the Hessians be paid for out of a block grant to the King. On 28th, Holdernesse protested against this in the Closet as irregular, and as an evasion of treaty obligations: arguments which persuaded the King to abandon the idea.[301] But, via Münchausen, Michel then gave his backing to the arrangement, saying (presumably by authority) that 'if the King would give Mr Pitt his confidence, and accept the sum offered viz. £300,000 he (Pitt) would never abandon his Majesty's interest in Germany, and that in that case the King should see what *he Mr Pitt would do*': an offer which, Münchausen reported, '*softened* his Majesty towards Mr Pitt'. Münchausen's aim was a Pitt–Newcastle reconciliation; but Newcastle did not believe the King would agree to the arrangement on the pay of the Hessians. Pitt's reported confidence therefore seemed misplaced. Egmont's hostility to the ministers aligned him behind Fox, and Sir George Lee might be expected to follow him; Devonshire showed no sign of wishing for an alliance with Newcastle, and that option seemed not in question. Through Granville, Newcastle learnt of Pitt's condemnation of Fox's opposition as one based on Cumberland; 'that Mr Pitt may have the Duke of Newcastle whenever *he* pleases' (a boast which Newcastle scorned); that Pitt mocked 'the *First Minister* that ever quitted with a majority in Parliament of 150'. This merely proved that the initiative remained with Newcastle, not Pitt. Hardwicke thought Granville responsible for the boast that Pitt might enlist Newcastle, and that Granville sought to frighten 'his friend' Fox to join Pitt.

Newcastle's confidence was confirmed by what he heard of Fox's attitude. If Newcastle's intentions were to let the ministers do as they pleased, Stone reported, Fox had said he had better not attend Parliament. Plainly, Fox resented not being allowed to use the Old Corps majority against Pitt before Christmas; but he now outlined to Stone a plan for them to be held in the House by Fox, Lord George Sackville and Sir Thomas Robinson: a combination, he suggested, equal in debate and superior in numbers. But Newcastle did not believe that Fox's ambitions stopped short at a subordinate role within an Old Corps ministry. Hardwicke agreed: the conversation with Stone showed that Fox 'wishes our friends should join with him in the House of Commons more than we should join with him in the Court'. The crucial role, Newcastle realised, was the King's. His plan was probably 'first, to try to go on with these gentlemen, if they will come up to his terms; then, if that is not practicable, to presume upon my not being disposed to join with Mr Fox, and perhaps to make one more slight attempt for that purpose, and then to fling all into Mr Fox'. Newcastle therefore took a different view to Hume Campbell of the latter's meeting. Fox, Newcastle noticed, had then been highly critical of Newcastle himself and of Hardwicke, especially over the affair of Bute's office: the ministers should have insisted on the Prince of Wales's removal to St James's:

Mr H. Campbell talked very properly to him, that my friends thought he [Fox] had brought about the change in the Administration by his resignation, and consequently many of them were more inclined to my joining with Mr Pitt than with him. Mr Fox did not let drop one word of joining *with us*, but said, the Duke of Newcastle had the *Closet* (I suppose when I was in) and undoubtedly *the House of Commons*.

Mr Fox told Mr H. Campbell, 'That he had told the King, or conveyed to the King, that whenever it was proper, to drive out those gentlemen, there should neither be wanting expedients nor courage to support his affairs.' This is a plain declaration, that Mr Fox will undertake the administration, and I think the King will give it him. He will probably bring in my lord Egmont, Mr Dodington, and if possible Charles Townshend. The Duke of Devonshire he may be sure of, the Duke of Bedford he has, the Duke of Cumberland will be at the head of the whole, and if Leicester House will not compound by means of the Duke of Argyll, they may endeavour to force them.

Newcastle thought it significant that Fox had not mentioned Argyll to him. Hardwicke was less sure; what Fox said 'he had conveyed' to the King might be merely what he said when he resigned, not a subsequent *démarche*, though in either case he had plainly made a bid for Hume Campbell, or at least to dispose him against the ministers.

Granby, Newcastle's chief reliance in the Commons, wanted the enquiry brought on as soon as possible, believing no advance would come from Pitt sooner. Newcastle agreed:

I don't know that at present we have anything to do, but to await events, and to take care that our friends in the House of Commons should not be surprised. I dare say we shall hear no more from His Majesty about *Mr Fox*, and if it was not for *the Duke*, I should not think it impossible, but that the thing would rub on with this ministry. In which he will certainly *at present* be encouraged by my Lord President, (who says) that *these gentlemen* will not lose their places, if they can keep them, and that may make them more desirous of coming up to the King's terms.

Hardwicke encouraged Newcastle's resentment of Fox and pointed to insults similar to those in the *Test* being put forward in the *Monitor*:

The political view of all this is plain. They cannot help seeing that we have some credit in our country. They have also seen the King's *apparent* regard for us, and dread his inclination to take us again; of which the language has been too open. This event *The Test* and his patron dread, as much as the others, unless it be under him as supreme: and therefore, in order to shut the door, all the villainous arts of defamation are to be tried, and the mob is to be halloo'd upon us. But I suppose we are not to be cudgelled into an alliance.

It could not be expected, wrote Hardwicke, that the King would soon dismiss his ministers: appearances at Court were against it. Probably he would wait until supplies had been voted; then, 'throw all in to Mr Fox...whether we join with him or not'. To ally with him, therefore, would be both pointless and dangerous. But Pitt had recently talked to Charles Yorke in anodyne general terms, 'professing great moderation; wishing the enquiry was over; but (which was remarkable) reviving nothing about the Hanoverian soldier; and I find from other quarters, that stock is much fallen'. Pitt even renounced the idea of a dissolution of Parliament. Furthermore, Hardwicke considered 'the measure of the ministers relating to the enquiry, I mean the warmth, or moderation of it, is in suspense till the event of the trials is seen'. Hardwicke therefore agreed with Newcastle's intention to do nothing, attend to the cohesion of his Commons following, and wait for a future crisis.[302] Stone told Newcastle that Mansfield thought alike. Newcastle believed the crisis would come at the call; and that it would then be necessary to demonstrate the power of the Old Corps, though not in order 'to come back to Court'. That would have meant storming the Closet after abandoning it. Newcastle replied reassuringly, full of outrage at the attack on Hardwicke in the *Monitor*; that, the *Test*, and Fox's interview with Hume Campbell he agreed were part of the same political gambit: an attempt to induce Newcastle to take what would prove to be the nominal leadership of a ministry otherwise staffed by Foxites. Newcastle would not, he professed, accept unless Hardwicke secured whatever office he chose, and the whole Royal Family supported the ministry. This last condition was a topical one: Sir Edmund Thomas (Clerk of the Household to the Princess Dowager of Wales) believed 'that Leicester House was not averse to the D[uke] of N[ewcastle]';[303] Newcastle himself knew via Holdernesse that Bute had been with Lady Yarmouth on behalf of Leicester House, 'making strong professions', and there had been some exchange of messages through Devonshire not satisfactory to the junior Court. Bute also visited Lord George Sackville with compliments from the Prince of Wales: 'Lord George answered (as I hear) upon the whole very prudently, conjured the Prince not to think of taking the command from *the Duke* [of Cumberland], which the other said, was not intended, but only, *that regal power should not be exercised*. My friend tells me, that Lord George is not, and will not be attached to or connected with *the Duke*'. Yet the tide of royal favour, Newcastle saw, was plainly running in Fox's and Cumberland's direction. George II had begun his conversation with Holdernesse with the warning: 'If the Duke of Newcastle thinks of coming in again, he must join with Mr Fox'. What was most remarkable, Newcastle told Hardwicke, was that

the King is constantly flinging in something in favour of Mr Fox to Lord Holdernesse. How all this will end, nobody can tell. But I can assure your lordship that I will not be *cudgelled* into an alliance with anybody, and particularly not with Mr Fox. I see no openings on the side of Mr Pitt; and if there were, his measures must alter much, before we can join in earnest with him.[304]

Newcastle, therefore, though he appreciated the strength of a Fox–Cumberland ministry, minimised the likelihood of its being launched. Each of the contenders thus supposed his own prospects vis-à-vis the others to be better than they were. Newcastle continued not to take seriously the prospect of a Fox ministry through the agency of Devonshire (as in November 1756) or of Cumberland (as in April 1757). Fox failed effectively to act against a possible Newcastle–Pitt alliance, directing his attacks at Pitt himself. Pitt, in spurning Fox, failed to bring himself or his followers to within range of a feasible alliance with Newcastle, and was overtaken by events.

THE PARLIAMENTARY SESSION, UNTIL 2 MARCH 1757

Measures, for the moment, came once again under close scrutiny when Parliament met on 7 January. At once it was reported that 'Many constitutional points insisted on by the Tories are to be given up such as triennial Parliaments, Militia Bill etc. which was what Pitt promised the Tories should pass which on his dropping I conclude they will drop him'.[305] Only in its particulars was this exaggerated; Charles Lyttelton similarly doubted whether the Tories 'will long remain in this complying temper'.[306] Pitt saw the King for three-quarters of an hour on 10 January, 'as it is reported, to expostulate and desire to know if H.M. intended to support and to have the administration continue';[307] whatever the answer, Pitt at once had a 'relapse' of 'gout'. This posed problems, for it had to be put about both that he was in danger of death[308] and that he was able to conduct the administration of the war.[309] The Commons, where he did not set foot, remained meanwhile thinly attended,[310] and as devoid of private business as of public.[311]

It was the Townshends who met a group of Tories on 14 January to concert the enquiry. George Townshend assumed responsibility; announced 'that Mr Pitt and the administration would support and assist with papers, etc. but [Pitt] desired to be excused appearing at this meeting for fear of offence somewhere [i.e. in the Closet] but heartily desired an enquiry'; and invited suggestions on procedure. Sir John Philipps spoke for a Committee of the whole House; Charles Townshend for dividing the business and considering American policy in a select committee. Newdigate noted the conclusions: 'Resolved to leave it to the gentlemen in administration to consider what expedient. Question for the Maidstone l[ette]r left to some lawyers to consider.'[312] Whether this last was a ministerial delaying tactic is not apparent. Yet evidently the Tories looked on the ministry as more closely involved in the enquiry than it was willing to admit; and, the same day, George Townshend tried unsuccessfully to call on Pitt. As has been argued

above, Pitt's desire to avoid personal responsibility for the enquiry was
of long standing, and he had a continuing reason to avoid links with
the Tories as such. Yet George Townshend wrote to him the following
day that he would 'put off till the last moment the great national business that lies at our door sooner than proceed in it without your
advice'.[313] Halifax, and doubtless others, expected a motion for the
enquiry to be made on 21st;[314] but on 20th, in a full House, the call
was unanimously postponed to 1 February,[315] and the enquiry also 'laid
aside', as Rigby wrote; 'and I have heard today, the language of the
Tories is to drop all thoughts of it, lest it should hamper their new
friends the new administration, in difficulties that might force them to
quit. This is being steady to them indeed, but what is to become of
their addresses and instructions, and above all their popularity under
this acquiescence, I cannot guess.' Hume Campbell confirmed that 'the
intention of enquiry greatly slackened, that it would be confined to the
Admiralty; and that the enquirers thought, they should do, as much as
they could, if they could fix a real charge on the Admiralty'.[316]

Once this prevarication became known, the ministers were vulnerable
to the charge that they dared not begin the enquiry because, having
examined the evidence, they had found that it exonerated their pre-
decessors in office. Instead, they had 'contented themselves with keeping
this enquiry hanging as it were over their [the old ministers'] heads, to
keep them still under disadvantageous imputations, which they know
will vanish as soon as brought to trial', and to the same end had 'inter-
posed to screen' the Admiral who, personally, was responsible for
Minorca's fall.[317] Despite the delays and evasions, however, the Tories
were hardly likely to lay aside their determination to pursue the enquiry;
it was merely postponed, presumably to be the political follow-up to
Byng's generally-anticipated acquittal.[318] Meanwhile the Commons proceeded quietly with the Mutiny Bill, and with the introduction of a
Militia Bill. Cumberland and the King came to a decision on the
regiments to be sent to America,[319] seemingly without Devonshire's
objection; their plan was finally accepted at a meeting at Pitt's house
on 26th.[320] Northey and George Townshend called for papers from the
Ordnance[321] and, on 24 January, attacked Marlborough over the
Ordnance Estimate for his unusually large daily pay during the recent
invasion scare; Marlborough, to avoid difficulty, later repaid part of
it. Beckford made an ill-prepared attack on Newcastle for encouraging
Sussex smuggling and was worsted by Hume Campbell, Legge and Sir
George Lee, who spoke in Newcastle's defence.[322] On 25th, 'the quarrell
was upon some words to be inserted on the Mutiny Bill to enable the
King to quarter foreign troops *without consent of Parliament*, which
were the litigated words, and no determination taken upon it. Sir
Thomas Robinson observed yesterday that the floor of the House was
covered with gunpowder; to which Mr Charles Townshend only added,

and he believed covered with thatch: I yet don't believe', wrote Rigby, 'the torch will be brought'.[323] In a presumably very thin House, the Old Corps found themselves momentarily in a minority, and 'were obliged to make a shift to adjourn'.[324] On 27th, Henley and Hume Campbell were to meet the Speaker to try to discover a form of words for the Mutiny Bill acceptable to both sides; 'If not, Lord Register [Hume Campbell] thinks it would be better to leave out the whole for if you are to have consent of Parliament before the troops can be quartered you may as well have it at the time, and then the provision is unnecessary. But whether Mr Fox as he started this matter at the beginning of the session will insist upon something being done, and be glad of an opportunity to decide upon the question,' wrote Dupplin, 'I cannot yet learn'.[325] Meanwhile, the Militia Bill was introduced by George Townshend on 26th; it gave an opportunity for much detailed debate on the merits of the scheme and for inconsequential disagreements without leading inevitably to a decisive division. The discussion on 26th revolved around the exposition of two alternative schemes, Townshend's and Conway's; but Newcastle and Hardwicke had not decided which to support, and Hume Campbell accordingly chose not to intervene in the debate. In it, Fox supported Conway's scheme (against Charles Townshend, Lord George Sackville, George Grenville, Legge and Lord Strange) and proposed that the House should choose between the two schemes by a vote in Committee on the first amendment to Townshend's bill.[326]

The result of the conference with the Speaker on 27th is not directly known. But that day in the House, 'Lord Barrington, who moved the clause to the Mutiny Bill, gave it up. This was a fresh victory obtained by the administration against F–x who truckled under'.[327] Possibly Fox was reserving his effort for the Militia Bill, in which Conway's plan came quickly to be identified as Cumberland's, with Fox's open backing.[328] Thus it was that, in this period of postponement and indecision before the result of Byng's court martial was known, the crisis over the Hessians, which had threatened in December, dissolved. Rigby had expected the sentence on 24th,[329] but it was not pronounced until 27th: death, under the 12th Article of War, the interpretation and severity of which then provoked fierce controversy. News of the outcome at once electrified a stagnant political situation; Byng's fate obscured all other issues. It was a damaging blow to the new ministry in several ways. It provided, *ipso facto*, a vindication of the late ministers' conduct of the war. Pitt's eminence rested temporarily on his ability to seem about to 'perform wonders',[330] but in the current disastrous state of the war these wonders would have to be items of domestic legislation. Yet almost all of the other points in a traditional Patriot platform – an effective Militia, a Place Bill, triennial Parliaments – seemed sure to be rejected summarily in the Commons. The enquiry was the only item which the

Old Corps was compelled to welcome, endorse, and see through to its conclusion; it occupied the place of business which would otherwise entail the ministry's certain defeat. It was therefore eventually compelled to attempt to challenge, interpret and overset Byng's sentence: yet to do so would undermine their position in the Closet and the City (as well as damage their popularity with the mob – though there is no evidence that this ever formed part of Pitt's calculations), and their initial reaction was to seek to avoid such a move. But it was at once reported that George II was 'horrid angry' and resented personally any challenge to the Court Martial's decision; from the outset, he was determined to confirm it.[331] Chesterfield had predicted that the ministry's only hope of survival was if Pitt 'had credit enough in the City, to hinder the advancing of the money to any administration but his own; and I have met with some people who think that he has'.[332] Now, this also became problematic.

The enquiry, postponed first in hope of Byng's acquittal, was delayed further while his sentence was disputed[333] and then again by the evident impossibility of an outcome favourable to Pitt. Temple immediately laid the sentence before the King, with the Court Martial's letter to the Admiralty recommending mercy. George II at once ordered a warrant for Byng's execution; but all the Lords of the Admiralty in town (Temple, Forbes, Hunter, Hay and Elliot) refused to sign it until the opinion of the judges had been taken about the legality of the sentence.[334] Reactions to this move at large were various. Lord Lyttelton was dismissive about what the Court Martial claimed were mitigating circumstances,[335] but initially the contrary view was taken by, for example, Admiral West,[336] Henley, Charles Yorke, Westmorland, Stanhope, Sir Francis Dashwood, Waller, Egmont, Sir George Lee, Sir John Cust, Dodington,[337] Gilbert Elliot,[338] Bedford, and even Cumberland.[339] Newcastle deliberately refused to commit himself.[340] The judges' decision was known on 15 February: unanimously, they pronounced the sentence legal. The King insisted on the law taking its course; 'which order I received', wrote Temple, 'with great submission duty and deference'.[341] As long before as 19 November, Augustus Hervey had noticed that Temple appeared eager to condemn the previous Admiralty Board's conduct towards Byng rather than to alleviate his plight.[342] The order for Byng's execution on 28 February was then signed by Temple, Elliot and Hay, Admiral Forbes alone refusing. 'The new ministers would fain save him', wrote John Campbell, 'if they could lay the burthen upon others or get the House of Commons to take the unpopularity on themselves but the ministers seem willing rather to let him die than hazard themselves by saving him'.[343] Waldegrave agreed: Pitt and Temple wanted to save Byng 'partly to please Leicester House, and partly because making him less criminal, would throw greater blame on the late administration. But, to avoid the odium of protecting a man who had been hanged in effigy in every town in England, they wanted the King to pardon him without their seeming to interfere'.[344] Newcastle thought the ministry 'much at a loss what to do upon the sentence of the Court Martial'.[345]

The ministry had in the meantime attended instead to the relationship between the Militia Bill and the enquiry. The Budget (except the guinea lottery) had been delayed.[346] Possibly the ministry sought to preserve that vital item as a security and a lever while more contestable business was in passage, or perhaps it was deferred until Pitt's anticipated early return to the House after his recovery.[347] Townshend was expected to move for the enquiry early in the week beginning Monday, 7 February, but Hardwicke and others expected him to do so only if Pitt could attend.[348] Rigby added

I hear he is today so well as to propose going to Court tomorrow, that journey has hitherto been attended with such bad consequences as to confine him for a considerable time after it. Whether there is anything in the air of that place foreign to his constitution, or he meets with anything hard of digestion that affects his stomach, or what it is I don't know, but he has certainly been very restless after every visit he has paid his new old master.[349]

But Pitt remained at home until he took his seat, appearing in the Commons for the first time after his re-election only on 17 February.

Once the judges' decision was known, there was no more room for evasion; but until then, reasons were found for delay. Through Devonshire, Pitt protested at 'the unexampled injury done Sir Richard Lyttelton' by the King's refusal to promote him major-general over the heads of eight other colonels.[350] On 1 February, Newdigate recorded: 'Walked to Mr Townshend's, met many of the same gentlemen as before. Mr Townshend said he had a commission from Mr Pitt to say that he would support the enquiry in the House. Desired questions might be settled by the gentlemen. A good deal of conversation and that matter but not the questions were settled.'[351] Glover suggests that Townshend was assisted in the detailed business of the enquiry only by himself and the aged Edmund Waller, neither of whom then had a seat.[352] Certainly their unpreparedness contrasts with the elaborate precautions of Newcastle and Hardwicke, who employed a lawyer, P. C. Webb, to arrange evidence on the ministry's strategy and draw up a brief.[353]

For long it had been uncertain at exactly whom or what the investigation would be levelled: Holdernesse's Maidstone intervention, Anson and naval strategy, or the ministry's record as a whole?[354] Intentions seemed equally confused when, on 7th, Charles Townshend began the enquiry with an attack on the terms of a Treasury contract held by Alderman Baker for victualling troops in North America. Fox defended him and dwelt on the unreasonable and premature violence of Charles

Townshend's abuse, but 'with great decency towards the present administration, showed no more inclination towards the last than led to an exculpation of measures he was himself joined in with them'.[355] Townshend moved for papers relating to the contract; Dupplin and Nugent joined him, and moved for more, leading Rigby to think that 'they had wherewith to clear themselves'. This involved yet further delay: one observer suggested 'the great debate' would come on the following week, 14–18 February. Newcastle was markedly confident of the outcome of an enquiry which had begun with two such wild and unsubstantiated attacks on him as Charles Townshend's and Beckford's on Sussex smuggling.[356] The former's was 'imagined only to be a beginning to some greater attack; and as Mr Pitt is expected every day at the House; 'tis imagined business will come on'.[357] The following day, 8th, George Townshend moved in contrastingly moderate language for papers relating to Minorca. Fox moved to enlarge it to cover also intelligence of the French plans for the invasion of England; what Newcastle wrote of as 'our amendment' passed *nem. con.*, and he did not echo Rigby's scepticism about Fox's intentions on either day. The Commons was remarkably tranquil; Newcastle wrote: 'I don't think we have much reason to apprehend the consequences of these enquiries. I hear George Selwyn says, I should send them a *card – to thank them for their obliging enquiries*'.[358] Rigby puzzled over Pitt's non-appearance, though he was reported to be well in his house: 'If so, that is a mystery I am not able to unravel'.[359] Walpole suggested an answer: 'it is plain George Townshend and the Tories are unwilling to push researches that must necessarily reunite Newcastle and Fox'[360] (as indeed the enquiry had shown signs of doing) and that George Townshend's motion 'seemed affectedly limited' to Minorca rather than risk such a reunion by an attack on obvious abuses in America.[361] The following day the Commons returned to the Militia Bill, which occasioned no conflicts. Due to come on again in Committee on 15th, George Townshend warned that it would be attacked 'under a pretence of substituting another plan [Conway's] they have not prepared and never mean'.[362] Townshend failed in his appeal, and on 15th it was postponed, ostensibly because of Pitt's illness.[363]

The same day, the judges' ratification of Byng's sentence was known. On 16th, Temple, Hay, Hunter and Elliot signed the warrant for his execution; Admirals Forbes and West refused to do so, and resigned their seats on the Admiralty Board.[364] On Thursday 17th, Pitt attended the House for the first time since 3 December. He 'brought a message from the King to desire supplies for keeping an army of observation to perform his engagement with the King of Prussia and for the protection of his electoral dominions'.[365] Hardwicke was astonished and delighted: ''Tis a strong continent measure – drawn by Mr Pitt himself!'[366] There was little discussion of it on 17th, since it was referred to the Committee of Supply on the following day; John Campbell deferred doubts about the consistency of Pitt and Legge until he heard the outcome of that day's debate.[367] Attention focussed on 17th on Byng's sentence; the Admiralty formally notified the House that the warrant for his execution had been signed, and the Speaker read a long list of MPs who had been expelled before suffering serious punishments. His implication was obviously that that should be the present course. Lord Strange opposed such a move. Sir Francis Dashwood moved that the Court Martial's sentence and the letter to the Admiralty be laid before the House; Fox opposed this as implying that the Commons should revise the sentence and override the Court Martial, a dangerous precedent. Pitt answered him, speaking

rather in favour of Sir J [sc. F] Dashwood's motion and of Admiral Byng. He seemed however to think that it was premature and it was at last agreed that the communication from the Admiralty should remain in the Journals of the House, but that no notice should be taken of it with a view to the expulsion of Mr Byng or otherwise at present; and if at all, as late as might be before the day appointed for his execution.[368]

Dashwood's initiative was then frustrated by a motion by Fox for the orders of the day.[369]

It may be that Pitt sought a clear field for the following day's business; but probably he was aware of the continuing value of postponing any championship of Byng for as long as possible. Another clash between Pitt and Fox was occasioned by dissenters' petitions against exercising the militia on Sundays; Fox 'seemed rather to have the advantage',[370] but the militia too was postponed.[371] On 18th, the Committee of Supply sat to consider the King's message. According to Glover, 'the country' had not been consulted; Pitt 'ran the hazard of being deserted by all the country gentlemen, hitherto his warmest friends, and to whom he had made some court'.[372] Pitt spoke ably in outlining his foreign policy: £200,000 to be paid to the King of Prussia,

but in lieu thereof we are to stop the payment of £100,000 which we were to have paid to the Empress of Russia if she had acted conformably to treaties. We are also to take 12,000 Hessians into our pay for the summer instead of the 8,000 which we are bound to by treaty; and this is the whole and only expense that we are to be at for foreign affairs. In return for this the King engages to furnish 36,000 of his electoral troops to act with the Hessians and his Majesty and the King of Prussia are also to augment the number to 60,000 men, which are to form an army of observation in Westphalia and act against the French in case they attempt to invade the Empire; and instead of paying the Hanoverians as we did through all the last war, His Majesty engages to pay all the present 36,000 himself.[373]

Pitt declared

that if any gentleman had a mind to attack his consistency he hoped that he would take another day and not enter into personal altercations upon that great national question. That he did not insist upon being literally and nominally consistent as long as he thought he was substantially so; that he never was against granting moderate sums of money to the support of a continent war as long as we did not squander it away by millions.[374]

Lord George Sackville seconded, Pitt thought crucially.[375] Sackville's intervention publicly marked his change of allegiance from Fox to Pitt.[376] Fox replied, renouncing personal altercation, declaring

that it was nothing to him who was or who was not consistent as long as he was satisfied that *he was so*; that he always was for measures of this sort – that he only thought we gave with too scanty a hand to be of real service; that this was completing the promise made in the Address last year; that we were then told that would hang like a millstone about the neck of a new minister but he hoped this would hang an ornament on the neck of this new Minister.[377]

Pitt spoke again briefly, adding 'that it was probable that near £300,000 more would be probably wanted for the payment of 12,000 Hessians which we are obliged by treaty to furnish to the kingdom of Hesse',[378] but there was little debate. The mood of the House was wholly for the generous support of the King of Prussia.[379]

Mr Fox tried to hint at some objections, but he was fallen foul of by Mr Vyner among the Tories and by Mr Beckford in the name of the City and the whole vote was universally approved of as being just the happy medium in which we ought to steer, and passed unanimously being the first subsidy vote that ever did pass so through a British House of Commons. All this gives the most sincere joy to all the friends of the new Administration and it is thought that Mr Pitt and his friends are now got completely into the saddle.[380]

Pitt at least thought himself graciously received in the Closet on 19th;[381] Bute, who had been used to despondency for some time, thought the ministry now reaped the benefit of right measures resolutely persisted in, 'let the inconstant gale of popular favour blow which way it will'.[382] Hardwicke had heard that 'the cry was yesterday for want of concert, and for want of instructions to friends how to act';[383] but the chief difficulty is to account for the conduct of the Tories. An answer, possibly exaggerated, is offered by Glover. He claimed that he visited George Townshend on the night of 17th, whom he found deeply dissatisfied at the following day's business. He had not been consulted, but he understood that Pitt was to postpone the militia to make way for the vote of subsidy. Townshend had spoken to Legge and George Grenville, but neither was willing to divert Pitt from his course. 'In fine it was probable', wrote Glover, 'that an opposition would be made by the disgusted country gentlemen'. Glover took the credit for persuading Townshend against this with theatrical entreaties; and claimed that the latter 'mollified Viner, Northey, Sir Charles Mordaunt, and the other country gentlemen', so securing their acquiescence in the House.[384]

But other evidence is lacking to confirm this account, and it seems likely that Townshend's intervention on the morning of 18th would not have held back the Tories had they not been deeply committed to Pitt's ministry and not violently indisposed to a subsidy arrangement which was both inexpensive and palatable in its details. It is, however, likely that what the Tories approved as an economical deal offended the King as 'shabby, shameful', parsimonious and inadequate: so at least was believed in Fox's camp.[385]

The inaction of the Old Corps on 18th was not quite what Newcastle intended. He was concerned about 'the necessity of taking *some* part, or it will soon become impossible to take *any*, but that of absolute *retirement*...I own, it is hard in our circumstance, to give half a million upon *such a message*, without saying half a word. But the difficulty is, what that word should be'. Newcastle was called on by Sir Thomas Robinson and Dupplin, who brought the opinions of others of the Old Corps in the House. 'They will not distinguish', wrote Newcastle, 'between observations of inconsistency, and misrepresentation of the extent of the present plan; and opposition to a *measure*, we profess ourselves *for*. They think personal reflections might hamper us hereafter, and be of no use at present.' John White emphasised the danger: 'anything that may seem to approach to hostility at present' would only draw 'the load of things upon one's shoulders without being ready to receive or bear the weight'. Newcastle was still of opinion that some protest should be made in Parliament, though only if Temple began it, when the Report was received from the Committee on Monday 21st; but his visitors persuaded him otherwise. They similarly persuaded Hardwicke, though without convincing him of anything beyond their 'resolution not to suffer anything to take place in the House about Byng'.[386] On reflection, Hardwicke was more positive in support of this course of action. Since the resolution passed *nem. con.* in the Committee, it would be too late to say anything effective at the Report stage; and what Fox had said made it far more difficult for Newcastle's friends to 'take a personal or provoking part'. Nor should Newcastle intervene in the Lords, lest it seem as if his Commons following declined to support him. Other opportunities of acting in the Commons, suggested Hardwicke, 'must soon arise'.[387] On 21st, accordingly, the Report passed *nem. con.*; the only friction was personal. Sir John Philipps 'said he had been accused of inconsistency and vindicated himself and [the] Cocoa Tree. Sir Thomas Robinson answered, said the creed of those gentlemen was in the preface to Clarendon's *History*, wrote by one Atterbury'.[388] The Commons then returned to the Committee on the Militia. Conway's scheme was considered on 22 February; but, after a long speech in its support, he withdrew it.[389] On 24th, the Committee considered dissenters' petitions against drilling on Sundays, and removed that provision from the Bill.[390] The 'real reason', wrote one

Anglican clergyman, was not collective piety but an attempt to kill the scheme:

The real reason, I hear, is the fear of putting arms into the hands, and skill to use them into the heads, of so many *disaffected* boobys as there are in abundance in the counties of England. If the French invade you, with the Pretender along with him (and they are not such fools as to come *without him*) – who can say *which side* the Lancashire, Cheshire, Staffordshire, Leicestershire, Devon, Hampshire, Suffolk *Militia will take.*[391]

But this was a grass-roots reaction; it is not clear that the Old Corps in the Commons thought in these terms by February 1757.

Byng still had his sympathisers. Augustus Hervey failed, however, to organise a petition to Parliament by the members of the Court Martial, or to persuade Temple to petition the King with Bedford; but he brought Temple to agree to back any attempt to raise the matter in the Commons. Hervey then consulted Dashwood, Cust and Dodington.[392] On 18th, Hardwicke had heard rumours that Byng's affair would be raised in the House on 21st, either by returning to Dashwood's motion or by moving for the sentence 'under pretence of forwarding a motion for an expulsion'. The Old Corps' role, Hardwicke thought, should then be to confine the proceedings to Byng's expulsion only.[393] Ashburnham had heard, more specifically, that there would be an attempt to repeal the 12th Article of War.[394] On 23 February Sir Francis Dashwood duly moved to appoint a day for considering it, 'which he said the Court Martial had mistaken. Sir John Cust seconded, that the Court Martial should be asked whether they meant negligence or error of judgment.'[395] Barrington replied, objected to any interference with the sentence, and moved for the Order of the Day. Dodington spoke sympathetically to Byng, but would not move for the sentence to be laid before the House. Lord Strange was sceptical of the excuses offered for Byng's conduct; John Campbell suggested that if the Admiralty did not intervene, the Admiral's sentence must be justifiable. Beckford simply called it cruel.[396]

Mr Fox spoke and was of opinion that the House of Commons had nothing to do with it. Mr Pitt spoke and agreed that the House of Commons had nothing to do with it and in consequence of what had fallen from some gentlemen in the debate he declared that he thought the present Lords of the Admiralty were the most improper people to advise the King in this case. That for his own part he declared he wished for mercy for he thought more good would accrue to the discipline of the navy and the good of the service than [from] the strictest justice. This very imprudent declaration has lost him the greatest part of his popularity.[397]

Thus Pitt atttempted a nice distinction: supporting Byng both from justice and humanity, but denying that the legislature was capable of interfering with the royal prerogative of mercy.[398] This finesse was not generally appreciated. Symmer wrote that Dashwood's motion had been 'supported strongly by Mr P[itt] and the new M[inistr]y', but that when the Commons' disapproval became apparent, 'and upon Lord B[arringto]n's proposing to put the previous question, Mr P[itt] who saw that it would be lost for Mr Byng by a most extraordinary majority, desired that Sir Fr[ancis] might withdraw his motion'.[399] Dashwood then desired leave to do so. But Fox, to 'fasten difficulty and unpopularity on the new Minister and his friends', challenged the Board of Admiralty to approach the King if they thought the sentence illegal, instead of shifting the odium onto the sovereign. Pitt tried to explain this away, but Fox's point had stuck: the onus was now on the Admiralty.[400] 'After this talk', wrote Harry Digby, 'the orders of the day were read but as in general the House seemed rather disposed to mercy than severity many people thought he would be pardoned.'[401] Hence Pitt's attempt to avoid responsibility for doing so. But his equivocation within doors was received very differently at large. His intervention, wrote Glover, 'at once threw down the image of public adoration, polluted and defaced by the despicable hands which had raised it: Pitt became hateful to the people of Great Britain, like Anson, like Fox, or Byng'.[402] Egmont, Dodington and Lord Strange joined in the debate with dramatic warnings against shedding Byng's innocent blood. Fox had accused Pitt and the Admiralty of saying nothing in Byng's favour to the King, but leaving on the sovereign all the odium of the sentence; that Pitt 'might represent truly to the King that not one man in the House had spoken against mercy'. This successfully provoked Pitt's moral stand; Fox continued to pursue that line, condemning the Court Martial for the severity of their decision even to the Admiral's warmest friends.[403] But in private, Fox held the opposite view: the Commons, he believed, would not pardon Byng.[404]

That opinion was soon challenged. Conway reported that the King had rejected an appeal from Pitt and Temple on 24th;[405] and the following day, frenzied consultations took place between Walpole, Conway, Augustus Hervey, Dashwood, Lord Talbot, Rodney and members of the Court Martial. Dashwood, Walpole and Hervey put pressure on a 'rather irresolute' Keppel and brought him to seem 'rather inclined' to support a move to have the Commons hear the Court's reasons for advocating mercy.[406] Cleveland advised that an Act of Parliament was necessary to release its members from their oath of secrecy.[407] In the House, Dashwood moved for such an Act. 'Sir John Philipps opposed the motion, saying, the cause was not before the House'; George Townshend seconded Dashwood.[408] In Fox's absence,[409] Pitt 'called on some of the members of the Court [Martial], as he saw some there, to speak out. Mr Keppel then got up, and stammered out something of his desires to be released from his oath of secrecy in order to divulge the reasons which had induced him to so strongly recommend Admiral Byng to mercy and saying they had condemned him against their consciences.'[410] Between 400 and 500 MPs were present, wrote one observer, 'and all in favour of the Admiral, except one [Thornhagh], who moved for the Order of the Day's being read, in order to get rid of Byng's affair, but he was so hunted and roasted by the House, that he was glad to withdraw his motion'.[411] Sir George Lee moved that an Address be presented to the King asking for a suspension of the execution until the House had enquired into the sentence; but this was rejected as unconstitutional, a possible breach of prerogative. Pitt, Grenville and Lord George Sackville thought no Bill to release the Court from its oath was necessary, but Pitt, Noel, Sir George Lee, Fazackerley and Grenville recommended that Keppel see the other members of the Court in town that evening to discover whether, consistently with their oath, they could disclose their motives privately to the King. The House was to sit the next day, and, if they insisted, a Bill was to be passed to release them.[412]

The Commons duly met on Saturday, 26 February. That morning the ministers[413] drew up the text of a message from the King announcing the postponement of Byng's execution for a fortnight in order that the members of the Court Martial could declare their reasons. But Pitt and Legge amended Devonshire's draft to make the King's action a response to what had been requested by 'a member of the House of Commons in his place', presumably an attempt to transfer the onus to that body collectively. Robinson, Granville and Gower all expected trouble from such a phrase – the latter probably maliciously. George II was known to be 'quite outrageous'. 'These new men', wrote Robinson, 'lose themselves everywhere.'[414] Pitt's emphasis on an extra-Parliamentary mandate, in fact (as has been shown) a screen for the indefensible and unsustainable party basis of his ministry, now lent itself to another use. Walpole reported George II replying to Pitt, 'Sir, *you* have taught me to look for the sense of my subjects in another place than in the House of Commons.'[415] Nevertheless, the King approved the message, and Pitt went at once to the Commons to deliver it. Fox, who had been warned by Bedford via Rigby what had happened in Cabinet, seized on the offending passage as a gross breach of the privilege of the House. Pitt 'excused it in the same manner as he had argued at the Council, that it was taking the load more off the King by throwing it upon the Commons'; but this only provoked a severe reprimand from the Speaker.[416] Keppel then announced his and his colleagues' opinion that they could not speak without an Act. Potter at once moved for leave to bring in a bill, which was read twice, committed, reported, and ordered to be engrossed on the same day. Fox argued strongly and ably against it, suggesting a second trial if the Court Martial had mistaken the law, and forcing Keppel to name the others of its members who favoured the Bill.[417] Far from it being the whole of the Court of thirteen, as John Campbell had supposed, there were only four besides Keppel.[418] Dodington and Sackville joined in the Bill's support; Lord Strange and Colonel Haldane spoke against it. The third reading was set for Monday 28th. Halifax expected the Commons to agree to it unanimously, but heard to his anger on 26th that it would be opposed in the Lords.[419] Evidence that Newcastle decided to do so is lacking. But on the basis of the events of the 26th, he inferred that, whatever their attitude to Byng, 'The whole House was against Pitt, and indeed their [the ministers'] part in this is abominable.'[420]

Fox spoke against the Bill, but it was not he or Newcastle's managers, rather Velters Cornewall and Sir John Glynne who insisted on a vote on the 3rd reading. The Bill passed by 153 to 23.[421] Plainly, its opponents felt little need to divide against it. By the previous day, 27 February, there had been rumours that Keppel's few supporters 'had recanted, and would not speak out if absolved from their oath'.[422] On the third reading, wrote Campbell,

the House was informed that Commodore Holmes was very easy, and did not desire the Bill, Mr Keppel had mistaken him...Captain Geary we were told was willing to speak if all the rest were obliged to speak but not otherwise. Admiral Norris and Captain Moore had writ a short letter to Mr Keppel which he read to the House desiring him to solicit the Bill; I think I have good reason to believe that those two had gone back, though they at last thought better of it, and stood to what they had first said.[423]

The ministerial attempt to use these men as a stalking horse was breaking down. But the attempt was sufficiently obvious (it was reported that Keppel was spoken of in the City as 'Mr Pitt's poppet'[424]) to suggest to the politically articulate and to the mob alike that the ministers were behind an attempt to screen Byng.[425] 'I cannot think it can be justly said', wrote John Campbell, 'that the old ministers have shown partiality either for or against him, but the partiality of the new ministry in his favour is very visible. Though they would not venture to show their favour to him in an open manly way to save his life.'[426] This impression was reinforced by events in the Lords, where the Bill was read for the first time on 1 March. Mansfield argued eloquently that that House should relieve the King of the burden of responsibility on that issue,[427] and it was decided to examine the members of the Court Martial the following day 'in regard to what they may have to disclose, and if they declare that they have anything of consequence the Bill will pass to absolve them from their oath'.[428]

On 2 March all thirteen members were examined individually in the Lords. Each was asked the same four questions, two by Hardwicke and two by Halifax. 'They all declared, except Moore, Norris and Keppel, they did not want the Bill, and even those three almost denied what Mr Keppel had himself declared in the House of Commons.'[429] Those three said they did not think the sentence unjust, and being asked whether they had anything to reveal which they thought necessary for his Majesty to know or which they thought might incline him to mercy, answered that their continuance under the obligation of the former oath did not permit them to answer that question. Upon this examination, the Bill was given up even by Lord Temple and Lord Halifax, who had been the chief promoters of it, and was unanimously rejected...[430]

Byng's death thereby became certain and his fate ceased to be a political issue.[431] Temple at once tried to back down. Augustus Hervey was shocked to see him, at the end of the Lords' debate, 'congratulating that House that the sentence was proved to be a legal one, and which made most people imagine there was some compromise between the late and present administration to screen those most infamous delinquents, Lord Anson, Mr Fox and [the] Duke of Newcastle'.[432]

There is no evidence of such a compromise. Temple's retreat marked, rather, the suddenly-obvious precariousness of Pitt's position. Byng's affair was 'looked upon in the City as a trial of the strength of the old and new ministry, in which the latter have greatly lost themselves, and exposed their weakness'.[433] 'So now', wrote Harry Digby, Pitt 'has as at first the majority of the House of Commons against him, the King averse to him, and he has not his popularity which was the only thing that raised him and I believe there is no reason to think the Duke of Devonshire and he are at all better together than they were two months ago'.[434] Though external confirmation is lacking, it is important that Fox's camp believed Pitt and Devonshire to be on bad and deteriorating terms, but that Devonshire stood well with the King; that Fox's own conduct was approved in the Closet; and that in a major division 'the numbers would be much as they were the last winter, Pitt having made no way among the members'.[435] Several considerations had hindered him from doing so. Byng's affair had come to seem more a ministerial attempt to screen him than an Old Corps attempt to make him a scapegoat. Waldegrave wrote that the King, 'not choosing to be [the ministers'] dupe, obliged them to pull off the mask; and the sentence against the Admiral was not carried into execution, till, by their behaviour in Parliament, they had given public proof of their partiality'.[436] The issue's prominence bound Fox closely to the old ministers, from whom he gratefully received briefs in preparation for the forthcoming enquiry,[437] and gave him an added disincentive to provoke a major vote. Neither his nor Newcastle's followers were therefore forced, or given a chance, to decide on the ministry's continuance. Then, its Tory associations, on which Old Corps spokesmen are said to have dwelt in the Commons,[438] stood as a warning against transfers of allegiance. And, finally, Pitt's increasingly frequent attendance at the House only provoked personal clashes with Fox in which the latter came off well: 'though Mr. F. does not pretend to be an equal orator, I can venture to say he has shown superior abilities'.[439] The possibility of a Cumberland–Fox ministry grew ever nearer; and Fox's pessimism of early February was left behind. It was noticed that George II 'appears much easier and happier than he has done for some time past'.[440] Holdernesse wrote:

I think we are at the verge of another ministerial revolution; the conduct of my colleagues in the affair of *Byng* has greatly lowered their popularity, and so exasperated the King that I think they cannot long keep in the saddle. This must be followed by a reconciliation between Newcastle and Fox, which the friends of the latter seem earnestly to wish.[441]

GEORGE II'S OVERTURES TO NEWCASTLE AND FOX, MARCH 1757

Holdernesse's intimations were accurate: the King had already launched overtures to Newcastle and Fox. At the end of February Waldegrave had had an audience on a point of personal business. George II spoke of his aversion to Pitt and Temple and asked about Newcastle's position. Waldegrave replied that 'it was very apparent a great majority in both Houses of Parliament still considered him as their chief, and were ready to act under his direction', most of them from a conviction of Newcastle's imminent return to power, though the Duke himself was torn between fear and ambition. The King then commissioned Waldegrave to tell Newcastle of his, George's, wish to dismiss his ministers and to encourage him to take a resolute part. Several conferences followed. Waldegrave soon asked for a written record of their results,[442] and some of this evidence survives. On 1 March, Newcastle wrote to reassure Waldegrave that he had had no negotiations with Pitt, nor would have without the King's consent. The inner structure of a successful scheme, Newcastle suggested, would be the amicable co-operation of himself, Devonshire, Bedford, Marlborough and Gower, with Hardwicke as Lord Chancellor. On the basis of this could rest 'a thorough concert, and good corespondence' between Newcastle, Hardwicke and Fox. Since the latter was to be Paymaster, not a 'responsible office', as many of the 'considerable speakers' in the Commons as possible should be recruited. Newcastle was modestly uncertain whether such a plan would succeed; he offered to try, if the King commanded, but added a warning against changing the current ministers until the enquiry was over and the supplies raised. The King returned this letter via Waldegrave on 2nd, expressing (Waldegrave reported) approval of its terms.[443] Rigby remarked on Newcastle's showing 'a most surprising affection' in asking after Bedford's return to town;[444] but it is unclear whether delay or ambition was Newcastle's final state of mind. In neither case did he anticipate an immediate Foxite bid for power. Evidently, Newcastle was proceeding on a charitable recollection of the events of the previous autumn; Fox's quiescence for most of the winter may well have seemed the effect of a surrender of ambition. But this was far from accurate in March, if it had ever been. However, Waldegrave believed, and reported to the King (probably on 1 or 2 March) that Newcastle's inclination to delay (two months seemed to Newcastle sufficient to dispose of those two issues) was uppermost; 'Pitt and his followers might then be set at defiance, without any considerable danger.' Waldegrave also advised that the dismissal of Pitt should be deferred, but went much further in warning the King of Newcastle's likely irresolution even then:

That he seemed terrified with the danger to which this country was exposed, dreading the consequences of an unsuccessful war; jealous of Fox, and of those who were to be his associates in the new administration; yet not daring to be the only responsible minister, by taking the whole authority into his own hands. Therefore, though it might be his present intention to resume his seat at the head of the Treasury towards the end of the session of parliament, he seemed too irresolute to know his own mind, and consequently was not to be depended on.

Waldegrave thus obtained the King's permission to talk also to Cumberland and Fox, 'that some plan of administration might be formed, in case the Duke of Newcastle should persevere in his present system of irresolution'.[445] This overture he launched without telling Newcastle, whom he had seen before he met Cumberland and Fox on 4th. Fox had previously, he wrote, been 'sent to, to know whether I would not act with the Duke of Newcastle to rescue H.M., and ordered to draw out a scheme of a new administration upon that foot'. This he then proceeded to do, with the aim of avoiding the familiar slide into a subordinate position which he could expect in any ministry which began as one shared between himself and Newcastle.

I propose that the Duke of Newcastle should be Minister for England, the Duke of Bedford for Ireland, the Duke of Argyll for Scotland, professedly and independently. The Duke of Devonshire, who will not remain Minister (if he would, it were best of all) will be Master of the Horse again. I will have some security, either by peerage to Lady Caroline or pension or reversion, against the next reign, and be Paymaster in this. The management of the Members of the House of Commons and the distribution of favours shall be entirely in the Duke of Newcastle, the management of debates in me. I wished Lord George Sackville might be Secretary of State, but he has foolishly gone to Pitt. However I still would offer it, and believe he would accept it. I would have Charles Townshend, who has left his brother and Pitt, Secretary at War. I would have Lord Halifax First Lord of [the] Admiralty, and Lord Egmont or Lord Dupplin First Lord of Trade. I would have Dupplin or Barrington Chancellor of the Exchequer, and what I wish to be done for my friends, I would have done now, having nothing to ask, there may not be a possibility of quarrel. Now H.M. has sent to the Duke of Newcastle; and I am going to Lord Waldegrave to receive a like message, which I understand is this, that H.M. requires us either to meet or to negotiate through Lord Waldegrave, which we like best, to fix a new administration which may take the place of this immediately. I hear H.M. will have Sir T. Robinson Secretary of State again, which is neither here nor there, and Lord Winchelsea at the Admiralty, which, besides that it makes no vacancy at another place, will by no means grace or assist the new scheme. Lord Granville is superannuated, and will continue where he is.[446]

But though the scheme as explained in Fox's memorandum to the King was the same,[447] its ostensible purpose was different. In a long passage of explanation, much stress was laid on the necessity of turning out the ministers at once. This, Fox treated as justification for granting Newcastle the 'plenitude of power', and for his own self-effacement.

I make the Duke of Newcastle Minister for England, because I conceive the K[ing] neither would nor could maintain his authority without him, against the opposition these men would raise. And I suppose him Prime Minister having the sole management of the H. of Commons, (as in the years '54 and '55) because I know him incapable, whatever he might resolve, of acting in partnership with any man. And he who would have a system last, must form it according to what men are, not according to what they ought to be.

Lord G. Sackville would I suppose be content with the place assigned him, without the disposition of preferments and he and I might answer with spirit and superiority for the debates in the House especially if Mr Charles Townshend is [Secretary at War] which would disconcert them not only in Parliament but in their more private Cabals with Lord Bute and Leicester House and the Scotch, excessively. I place myself where I can possibly give no umbrage to the Minister, and have no access to the King, which I know will be more agreeable to him, and I sincerely wish to be most serviceable to him in the way that may be least disagreeable.

Hardwicke was to be omitted: his prevarication and delay would be fatal in wartime, and in a ministry including both Newcastle and Hardwicke, the latter would be '*the* Minister'. But, added Fox, 'if it is thought otherwise, I shall lament it, but as I shall not be of the intimate or indeed the Cabinet Council, not answerable for what is done there, I shall not refuse to act the part I have here assigned to myself'.[448]

Thus the merit of Fox's scheme was that it could be presented in different quarters both as an act of submission to Newcastle and as a trap in which his power would be strictly circumscribed. But the second was the less plausible of the two and the most difficult to translate into reality. Fox wrote to Lords Ilchester and Digby advancing this second interpretation and asking for advice. This he obviously needed. Fox's chief hope was that he might borrow Newcastle's majority, just as Pitt was later to claim to have borrowed it; but it was not clear how the disguise for this, the plan for a tripartite division of power with Newcastle in a semi-figurehead position in England, could be sustained: Fox may have overestimated the political potential of the warm support which Argyll was currently providing him with.[449] Fox's scheme was especially precarious since it envisaged so many of Newcastle's followers in key positions. This however he was forced to concede, aware already that the King had sent to Newcastle. But Newcastle did not know that Fox was being approached, and Fox's being listed for Paymaster in Newcastle's scheme was not based on knowledge of his, Fox's, acceptance. But, on 4th, Fox heard from Waldegrave what passed at his meeting with Newcastle earlier that day: that he, Newcastle, thought of Egmont as Secretary of State; that Hardwicke wanted Anson restored to the Admiralty; and that both wanted a new administration delayed. Though Fox presumably also heard of Newcastle's willingness that Fox be Paymaster, the last of the three conditions, once he realised that it *was* a condition, implied a much weaker position for him than he envisaged or than he had refused in March 1754. But from Mansfield, who called after Fox had seen Waldegrave, Fox heard that Newcastle's friends were trying to persuade him not to undertake the ministry (from an appreciation of Newcastle's personal inability, as Fox reported); Fox therefore supposed he had time to refine his own plans,[450] since, according to Mansfield, Newcastle 'will be afraid to undertake (at least immediately) what he will let no other man undertake with impunity'.[451]

Ilchester replied advising Fox to pursue his power-sharing scheme with Newcastle, aiming at an 'agreeable and not a responsible place', the Paymastership. 'The prospect of affairs in general,' he continued, 'the age of the King, and disposition of Leicester House, make the coming into the administration or having a responsible place extremely unpleasant, so at all events I desire to fortify you in the resolution of having something permanent and valuable that may support and assist you in the next reign, the rage of which may likely be pointed against you.' By this, he meant above all an English peerage for Fox's wife. Nevertheless, Ilchester dwelt on the difficulties in the way of such an arrangement. The immediate replacement of Anson, before the enquiry, would play into the hands of Newcastle. Halifax would be an acceptable First Lord of the Admiralty; but Ilchester thought he detected an objection in Fox to Winchelsea. Lord George Sackville, he suggested, should be offered a Secretaryship of State, though Ilchester had been unaware of his desertion to Pitt. Egmont in that office, however, as 'an able, talking Secretary in the House of Commons', would pose a real threat to Fox's position there. In the face of the problems surrounding such a scheme, therefore,

I think it very possible the Duke of Newcastle may be persuaded not to take the employment you have designed for him. What to do in that case is a hard question, and I am sure such a one as I can't answer. I can think of but two ways, either to go to the head of the Treasury yourself, or to get the Duke of Bedford to be Lord High Treasurer. If you take the Treasury yourself, which is the most agreeable of great employments, you will immediately become the mark of all the violence of opposition and clamour, but what degree of potency or impotency there is now in the opposition you are a judge, not I. If there is a prospect of things going tolerably prosperously, there is no great danger in venturing there, but national calamities, if any such should happen, may create danger.[452]

Unknown to Ilchester, Fox had written to Lord Digby with two schemes: that just outlined, 'supporting in the House of Commons in an unresponsible employment a Ministry in which you shall or at least shall seem to have no other share', and a firm proposal to take the Treasury himself. Digby thought them 'equally creditable'; what was to be avoided was any scheme which would entail Fox's support of a ministry in which Newcastle held real ministerial power. As many of Newcastle's friends as possible might be recruited; even Newcastle himself provided he did not have 'the name of a minister'. No doubts seemed to trouble Digby that the King would not invite Fox to form a ministry with Newcastle in such a position; the problem seemed rather to be the arrangement of offices. If Fox took the Treasury, thought Digby, he should hold the Exchequer also; a Secretaryship of State should go to Lord George Sackville, 'if not absolutely gone or to be regained', or Egmont;[453] John Campbell and Lord Dupplin were to be joint Paymasters; and Halifax or Winchelsea hold the Admiralty. If neither Sackville nor Egmont could be secured, the 'ablest and most tractable' man in the Lords was to be preferred to Sir Thomas Robinson. In the second scheme the Treasury was to be held by a neutral figure – Waldegrave, Egremont, Gower or Powis. John Campbell could be Chancellor of the Exchequer; Fox, Paymaster; and Dupplin be provided for as Treasurer of the Navy. In either scheme it would be ideal if Mansfield could be persuaded to accept the Chancellorship; Argyll, Bedford and Devonshire should also be courted. The real object, Digby realised, was to include everyone except Newcastle and Hardwicke.[454]

This may have been feasible in advance of the enquiry; but its delay both prolonged Pitt's tenure and strengthened the hand of Newcastle in the forthcoming crisis. What Waldegrave complained of as the latter's irresolution[455] reflected a realisation of this truth. On 4 March, before Fox received the advice he had solicited or replied to Waldegrave, the latter called on Newcastle. He brought the King's order, via Cumberland, for Newcastle to see Fox or send him, Waldegrave, as an intermediary; George II expected Newcastle to arrange and report back through Waldegrave on 'the future administration; which the King would have gone about forthwith'. Newcastle refused. Waldegrave carried back to Cumberland Newcastle's disinclination, not to any particular scheme, but to any action at that moment. Waldegrave went on to see Fox. He found him 'quite changed', in favour of immediate action to unseat the ministers, 'when, by their late behaviour, they had lost their popularity'.[456] The same night, Newcastle saw Mansfield, whom Fox had met earlier in the day. Mansfield had made it clear to Fox that he would throw the whole weight of his advice against Newcastle's taking an immediate part; but Fox had not been convinced that this would produce anything more than delay.[457] Newcastle, however, found congenial Mansfield's warnings of the danger I should run, by engaging in an administration, without any one responsible minister, but myself; and without any certainty of real support from my new colleagues, from friendship and affection, at a time, when miscarriages, of all kinds, were to be apprehended; and the most violent opposition, and resentment, from the successor, to be expected – he called it *laying my head down upon a table to be struck at.*

On 5th, Newcastle therefore told Waldegrave of his refusal to undertake a ministry until the enquiry, and asked that Mansfield's advice also should be relayed to the King. Newcastle still had a role for Mansfield as an intermediary with Hardwicke and Fox. Newcastle had heard (through what channel is not known) that Fox had half threatened that if he, Newcastle, refused, Bedford would undertake the ministry with Fox as Paymaster. The danger of a Fox ministry on some foundation other than one provided by himself and Hardwicke placed Newcastle in a dilemma, and a final answer must soon be given to the King.[458] His problem was to keep a potential ministry in being while preventing Fox from stepping into the breach with royal approval. Mansfield's advice was meant to reinforce Newcastle's opinion that to undertake the ministry before the enquiry would be 'certain destruction' to himself or Fox equally. Mansfield was to enforce this lesson on Fox, and to add that 'whatever difficulties I may have, they do not *now* arise from any backwardness in me, to act with him; or any apprehension, that we should not agree, if other points, and difficulties, could be got over'.[459] But to Waldegrave, Newcastle opened his fears: 'He frequently complained that I was continually pressing him to be the minister, offering in the King's name almost his own terms; when at the same time, his Majesty's confidence in the Duke [of Cumberland] and Fox became every day more apparent.' The Earl might reasonably reply that

necessity obliged the King to trust somebody; and that the influence of others would naturally increase or diminish, in proportion as his Grace showed more or less inclination to give his assistance: and as to the other part of his accusation, though I had encouraged his return to his former employment, and had pressed his reconciliation with the Duke [of Cumberland] and Fox, I had never deceived him with false professions of their personal regard and friendship; having strictly confined myself to the single assertion that they would support him to their utmost in his ministerial capacity, because they had rather the King should be in his hands than in the power of Pitt, Lord Bute, and Leicester House.[460]

The logic of the situation plainly pointed to a Fox–Newcastle reconciliation. The Primate inferred from events in the Lords on 2 March that it had come about, and though he quickly corrected his mistake the apprehension was sown in Pitt's camp.[461] What Waldegrave evidently did not tell Newcastle was that the King, unwilling to press Devonshire to continue beyond the end of the session (which was all that he had promised to do) had already suggested that Waldegrave himself take the Treasury.[462] Evidently, the King's impatience might easily override all tactical considerations. Briefly, it seemed as if it would do so. Fox heard on 7th something which led him to expect the most dangerous of his schemes to be forced upon him, that of taking the Treasury himself.[463] What Fox heard is not known. It may have been a rumour that Winchelsea had been appointed First Lord of the Admiralty and that the rest of the ministry were about to resign;[464] or it may have been an anticipation of Newcastle's final answer to the King. On 9 March Waldegrave received a memorandum, to be read by him in the Closet, carefully setting out Newcastle's position: a firm refusal to enter administration 'till the supplies are raised (of which the present ministers have formed the plan); and till the enquiry is disposed of; which the friends of the late administration will accelerate, to the utmost of their power'. Meanwhile, Newcastle promised to consider the composition of a feasible administration and not to stand in the way of any other ministry which the King might choose to launch.[465] It seems likely that this last offer was an empty courtesy, and that Newcastle continued to believe in the futility of any administration begun before the enquiry. Fox's camp continued to believe that Newcastle would 'neither undertake himself nor let anyone else act with impunity', and that he retained the power to ensure the second.[466]

It is not clear, however, that the enquiry was pressed forward with any greater speed for Newcastle's appreciation of the tactical situation. Commons business continued to be characterised by delay and indecision. The main part of the budget was expected on 4 March, but failed to materialise.[467] Pitt again was struck down by 'gout' on 9 March, and confined to his house. The same day, Charles Townshend, 'who affects to stand upon ground of his own',[468] began his own enquiry into Alderman Baker's contract; but further proceedings were postponed until 14th.[469] Meanwhile the Budget was at last opened by Legge on 10th; but consideration of the taxes which the estimates entailed was postponed to 16th.[470] The Militia Bill was expected again but was not brought on.[471] On 14th the examination of the American contract was completed: the Old Corps thought the result an exoneration of Baker, and that Charles Townshend was forced to climb down; Sir Roger Newdigate thought a 'scandalous bargain' had been screened by 'a majority of advocates of the late administration...a specimen of what is to be expected from enquiries in such a House'.[472] West, however, thought it a disinterested justification: 'the greatest day that ever happened to a minister out of place'. The question passed in the Committee and was reported to the House 'without a division and almost without a negative except the two Townshends and Alderman Beckford'. Sir George Lee, Lord Granby, Lord George Sackville and Fox spoke to effect in defence of the late Treasury, Lee being especially glad of a chance to show his attachment to Newcastle; Legge deferred to their combined advocacy. West added his opinion that Charles Townshend might even be prepared 'to be a manager for the late ministry in the next enquiry'.[473]

This encouragement came at a moment of acute anxiety for Newcastle, caught as he imagined himself between the King, Fox and Pitt.[474] It is not known whether, or to what effect, Mansfield intervened with Fox after Newcastle's request on 5 March that he do so. But the evidence suggests that Fox continued his overtures to the men who might compose his ministry. Via Dodington, Halifax was approached with Fox's appreciation of the situation:

That I wish the King would dismiss Pitt, Lord Temple etc., that I think no one of the late Ministers can now succeed them, but that such a ministry should be formed as the late ministers may support, and as the people cannot complain of. That the Secretary of State must be in the House of Commons; that if the Duke of Devonshire will stay there is no place but First Lord of the Admiralty for his lordship [Halifax] who could fill that place, that I should advise you to succeed him [as President of the Board of Trade], and that Oswald should be Secretary of the Admiralty. That the *conciliabulum* should consist of the Dukes of Devonshire and Bedford, the Earl of Halifax, Lord Mansfield, and the two Secretaries. This is my notion, and if everybody will act the part assigned them, I can answer for the success. If because they will not, or for any other reason H.M. is forced to keep those gentlemen two months longer, I shall look upon them as complete conquerors, and Leicester House the Court. I shall not go to it, but I shall struggle no longer against it.

But Fox was aware, as he confided to Dodington, that he spoke 'without such authority as may justify me at all events in what I say to him'.[475] He had no commission from the King or Cumberland, and his offers sounded both hypothetical and tentative. Moreover, if the threat of Leicester House were as serious as he portrayed it in order to put pressure on Halifax to undertake ministerial responsibility, then there could be little excuse for a schism which excluded Newcastle and Hardwicke; and Fox held out no guarantee that Devonshire would accept the key role assigned to him. Fox was surely by now aware of the King's desire to dismiss his ministers as soon as possible; but he was unable even to admit, what Newcastle confidently asserted, that a two-month delay, allowing for the completion of the enquiry, would bring about the ministry's destruction; for in an administration formed after such a delay, Fox's position would be much weaker vis-à-vis Newcastle's.

How far Halifax shared these doubts is unclear; rather than challenge Fox's analysis, he declined giving Dodington an answer, 'as Mr Fox has no positive and precise proposition to make'. The suggestion about the Admiralty would have to be 'further explained, and the concurrence of all the principal parties...proved, before a man of common sense and prudence would be inclined to pledge himself'.[476] But that was not Halifax's intention; for, *en route* to town the following day, he called on Newcastle at Claremont. In confidence, he accurately disclosed the contents of Fox's letter to Dodington of 12 March, with the additional news that Fox 'flings out in conversation, Lord George Sackville [for] Secretary of State'. With Hardwicke's advice and through Waldegrave's mediation, Newcastle had been uneasily preparing two alternative approaches: a scheme of ministry, and a letter to the King refusing to undertake such a scheme. Now both were irrelevant, for Newcastle understood that Halifax was travelling to town with a positive invitation from Fox to take the Admiralty, and must have supposed Fox to have a royal commission to launch a ministry. Dodington, reported Halifax, had said that Newcastle would and must support Fox's scheme; but Halifax thought such an administration impossible if Newcastle's following did not support it. Nor would he, Halifax, accept as 'the only new minister, and the only responsible one, in a very dangerous, and important office'; 'He sees all that join in it proscribed at one Court, and dependent entirely upon —[477] at the other'. Nevertheless, the King's prerogative overrode such tactical considerations, and Newcastle expected that George II would formally ask him to support Fox's scheme.[478] That expectation was quickly reinforced by the King's insistence that Admiral Smith, not Dr Hay, be returned for the Admiralty borough of Rochester in place of Byng. It was soon widely known that Temple had had a heated audience on that subject on the morning of 15 March; 'there are those at St James's', wrote Holdernesse, 'who think my new colleagues will break upon this point and resign. This incident has made it impossible to settle ecclesiastical matters. The King suspends everything till it shall be known what turn this matter will finally take.'[479] Temple himself heard and believed that Newcastle and Fox had settled an alliance, and expected the ministry's immediate dismissal.[480] Walpole recorded that after such clashes with the King,

Lord Temple sent him word by the Duke of Devonshire, that he could not serve him more, though he should not resign till a convenient opportunity; that he would not even have come out of his Majesty's Closet as a minister, if it would not have distressed those with whom he was connected. Pitt himself kept in the outward room, saying, he no longer looked upon himself as a Minister; and attributing this storm solely to Fox, he bade Lord George Sackville, who was feeling about for a reconciliation between him and Newcastle, tell that Duke, that he was not so averse to him as his Grace had been told; let him judge by my actions, added he, if I have been averse to him.[481]

Fox, who had not received royal authorisation to undertake the government, did not share Temple's expectation. The ministers, he knew, did not intend to resign over the Rochester affair, 'so now things tend to delay again'. Halifax, after seeing Newcastle, evidently declined the offer Dodington took him;[482] Fox was despondent, aware that no-one, even Bedford, would be able to change Halifax's mind; 'Pitt etc. have, by their faults and want of judgment, put themselves into our power; it is now our turn by the same means to make them again masters'.[483] On one hand, the bid for Halifax looked destined to fail. On the other, Fox's excuses looked less and less convincing. Henry Digby had been summarising Newcastle's position by claiming that he, Newcastle, had told George II that if he could not enlist Leicester House, he could not carry on the King's business; but Digby had gone on to predict that Newcastle now would join Leicester House. Instead of giving advice or support, Ellis challenged the assumptions on which it was invited. The question was simply whether Fox was resolute enough to take the lead; delay only weakened his position. Ellis refused to believe that Newcastle would join the junior Court; 'that he should leave it dubious in his conversation with the King whether he would support [a Fox ministry] or not I look upon as an artifice to frighten the King into a mean compliance with these people's [Newcastle's and Hardwicke's] proposals and if he were abandoned enough to go into opposition I believe he would be left by some of his friends'. If the King would act resolutely, Fox could expect a Commons majority. Hume Campbell might be recruited, and Oswald won back from Halifax; Fox himself should take the Treasury rather than risk the disloyalty of an associate in that post;

Your actions have agreed with your public and private declarations, you have declined administration and promised to support any His Majesty should appoint. You have left the field open for all manner of negotiation and now when that is at an end and when the late ministers refuse to serve but on such terms as would be dishonourable for the King to submit to and the Duke of Newcastle also refuses to serve on the same pretence – what remains – Is the King to be given up?[484]

But this was the rhetoric of an outsider; Fox's problem was to persuade enough figures of the first rank to speak in such terms as the necessary public dimension of an alliance. The key office was the Admiralty. Halifax, by his abilities and links with the Old Corps, was its ideal incumbent, though Winchelsea could also fill the post. All pressure was still to be put on Halifax to accept; if he refused, he could not expect to be a Secretary of State even if both the Secretaries were taken from the Lords: the King would not allow it, nor did Fox need another potential Secretary.[485]

Ellis, however, was quite wrong in implying that since Newcastle could not openly oppose a Fox–Cumberland ministry, he could do nothing but acquiesce passively in its formation. From Halifax's information Newcastle saw that the key posts, after the Admiralty, were the Secretary-ships of State. The only contenders for them with Commons seats whom Fox might invite were Lord Egmont, Sir Thomas Robinson, and Lord George Sackville. On 14 March Boone called on Egmont, bringing from Newcastle 'some particulars of moment'. Egmont, confined by illness, was unable to call on Newcastle as the latter requested; but he sent an assurance of his support of 'whatever may put the King's affairs upon a more stable, and rational foundation', especially if it involved Newcastle's return 'into a situation more desirable to your friends'.[486] Though not pledging unequivocal loyalty, Egmont was plainly well disposed; and Newcastle promised soon to follow up this opening with a visit.[487] What, if anything, Fox or Newcastle did about Sackville is unknown; but the loyalty of Sir Thomas Robinson to the old regime must have appeared, to Newcastle, beyond question. Sustained by these considerations and Hardwicke's latest advice that Pitt would not resign on the Rochester affair,[488] Newcastle on 16 March sent the King, via Waldegrave, a final refusal of office 'in the present conjuncture'. In what position, asked Newcastle, would he be to defend himself against blame (which must focus on him) for any future misfortune without a 'responsible minister' in the Commons, with 'perhaps few, or none, elsewhere, who would think themselves equally concerned'. 'I hope', he concluded, 'my conduct in having supported your Majesty's measures, during the present session, will be a proof to your Majesty, how much I shall always have the success of your affairs at heart.'[489]

The King's reaction is not known. It is likely but not certain that some more positive request was then made to Fox; and the latter began at once to curry royal favour. On Friday 18 March, in the Committee of Ways and Means, Fox attacked Legge's proposal to abolish the Wine Licence Office. Its object could not, he argued, be a trivial and distant financial saving; 'it must proceed from some other reason;...he imagined his Majesty might be as well served with one Secretary of State and one Commissioner of the Treasury etc. and that all places and offices might be diminished'.[490] Newdigate noted: 'Mr Fox against the principle of lessening places the bulwarks of the Crown'.[491] Secondly, Fox intensified his overtures to one at least of the prospective key figures in his ministerial system. It seems likely that it was Halifax who was interviewed by Dodington on 18th after seeing Fox the previous day. Dodington found 'the gentleman' diffident: willing to support the ministry, if it were the King's command, but only on condition that another unnamed person, almost certainly Newcastle, would concur in the scheme. Dodington was scornful that 'anybody could, really, think a gentleman's [Newcastle's] word could add security and strength to his acting for his own interest and safety who never in his life, kept it, one moment, *when he thought* it came in competition with one or the other'. This, Dodington realised, was a definite 'hitch', and he added the unpromising news that Mansfield 'does not so warmly approve as it were to be wished'.[492] Though Dodington thought what his interviewee had written to Fox that morning could be 'made such an use of, with the King, as to extort a positive declaration of the concurrence in question', it was not clear that this was so. Halifax's conviction that the system would be unstable without the approval and participation of 'the other necessary parties' (especially Newcastle) only intensified with reflection.

So did his disinclination to leave the Board of Trade (which post, he hinted, might be raised in status) for the Admiralty, though Halifax was prepared to waive this preference if the system could be launched. 'But I neither can nor will pledge myself as a material and responsible party in a system not yet fully explained, and which, as far as I am informed of it, seems to want the necessary support.'[493]

This question had not been further explained when, on 19 March, Fox wrote to Waldegrave enclosing his scheme of ministry for submission to the King.[494] It amounted to an offer, he claimed, of 'giving up all views of ambition...for ever'. He added an account of his meetings with three leading figures. Egmont, Fox suggested, retained no standing at Leicester House and would be inclined to a system which would offend the junior Court. His objection was its probable instability, that 'nothing can last without a person in the House of Commons has the management of it, and that person must be me [i.e. Fox]'. Nevertheless, if Egmont came in, he let it be known that 'he should not look so very high as he believed people wrongly imagined of him' — that is, he did not insist on a Secretaryship of State. Fox did not realise that this was probably Egmont's reason for insisting that in that case he, Fox, take the lead in the Commons to shield him. Rather, Fox thought he had persuaded Egmont out of that insistence by emphasising the unpopularity of Cumberland which Egmont had tried so hard to promote. 'He said that was true if I took the whole ministry, but not if it was properly divided with the Duke of Newcastle etc. That your lordship knows is impossible', Fox wrote to Waldegrave; 'I think I left him not desperate'. This was false optimism: Egmont had seen through Fox's excuse, though without realising it to be such. Fox's fiction, a ministry with himself in an anonymous role, was not viable: and so it was to have no opportunity to shed the pretence and emerge as the Fox–Cumberland ministry which, once launched, might indeed be able to sustain itself. The same problem arose with Hume Campbell; 'and indeed all who disapprove of this scheme as not sufficiently stable [are] intent, on my being the Minister in the House of Commons, joined with the Duke of Newcastle'. That, Fox insisted, was impossible. As before, he rested his case on the necessity of turning out Pitt. Egremont had, he thought, strengthened this case, especially from his close links with Lord Granville and George Grenville. Pitt, Egremont had told Fox, was 'a wicked man and means revenge upon the King...a madman ...the nation must suffer in his hands'.

Egremont favoured a united front of men willing to back the King in Pitt's dismissal. It was such a front that Fox's ministerial scheme had to seem to provide. The first step, he suggested, was to have Holdernesse write to dismiss Pitt and Temple. Devonshire, who was until then to be unconsulted, would next be asked by the King to remain at the Treasury for six months, and if necessary given a promise that he might step down to another Cabinet place on a named day in October or November. This, Devonshire could not refuse 'without seeming to have come in, not for the King's sake, but for Mr Pitt's'.

That his Majesty in the next place see and acquaint the Duke of Newcastle and Lord Hardwicke with this arrangement, showing them that their friends are all employed, and that, when they please themselves to appear upon the stage, room may be easily made for them. They will find their honour and advantage in a warm support of this scheme. First, as the enquiry in the House of Commons will be in the hands of friendly ministers; and that Pitt etc. will no longer be looked up to, as persons that can ever have power in this reign. Secondly, because they are not the movers, nor immediately reap any profits from this change, and therefore will not be exposed to the resentment of Leicester House. Thirdly, because it is (as to them) what they like, *delay*, and such a delay as does by no means exclude them; which any delay that leaves Pitt in place would do.[495]

Newcastle, in turn, might be used to put pressure on Halifax to accept. But, unlike Devonshire, the other recruits were to be previously consulted. Whoever Devonshire pleased might be Chancellor of the Exchequer, though – tactfully – Fox did not disclose to the King that he expected Legge to remain. The 'most essential thing with respect to the House of Commons' was what Fox feared the King would most dislike: Lord George Sackville was to have Pitt's Secretaryship of State. Fox also contemplated Egmont and Sir Thomas Robinson for the place, possibly in the Lords; but they were not named in the last draft of the scheme. Fox 'feared his Majesty might look upon it as a choice given of the three, and would immediately choose Sir T. Robinson; whereas if Lord George will take it, nothing can shake us in the House of Commons'. Perhaps as an afterthought, Fox suggested that if the King would let Holdernesse take another post, Halifax or Winchelsea might replace him, and the Cabinet 'would have no-one of the old administration in it, and consequently could not revive any of the old clamour'. But this was not essential. Halifax was, more importantly, destined for the Admiralty and Dodington to succeed him as President of the Board of Trade (if, as Fox hoped, the King could be dissuaded from installing Egmont there). Egmont was listed as Treasurer of the Navy; and the inner Cabinet was to be composed of Bedford, Mansfield, Devonshire, and the two Secretaries. Fox sought the Paymastership (and, he hinted, a peerage) at the end of the session;

and in the mean time would say, that the administration was in the hands of men of quality, fortune and understanding, and that he (Harry Fox) was ready in Parliament, to prevent Will Pitt, from disturbing their operations; that he would support them, not only as he believed they would act well and wisely for this country; but because he is sure they are men who will not see the succession take place before the demise of the Crown and his Majesty, in his lifetime, no longer King.[496]

Waldegrave read Fox's scheme to the King the same day, 19 March. It was not received enthusiastically; George II 'made many objections, saying, that it possibly might be a good scheme for Fox, his friends and relations; but that for his own part, it did not answer his purposes'.[497] To Fox, Waldegrave slightly softened this reaction; the King, he wrote, 'upon the whole did not seem much displeased, though not quite satisfied'. He failed to respond to Fox's melodramatic warning and, instead, made specific criticisms. Rather than dismissing Temple and Pitt himself, George II 'wished the Parliament would save him that trouble. I told him many would be against them when turned out, who would not choose to attack them whilst they continued in his service. Besides ministers being routed by Parliament might be a bad precedent. This last reason seemed to make some impression'. The King insisted on Robinson rather than Egmont or Sackville as Secretary of State; Waldegrave thought he could be dissuaded, but, believing neither Egmont nor Sackville would accept, he did not try. Then, George II voiced objections to the personal favours asked by Fox at the end of his scheme.

He approved the Duke of Newcastle's promising to support in order to engage Lord Halifax, and wished that you and his Grace might have a meeting. He also approved of the several persons to be sounded thinking it dangerous, in the middle of a sessions, to dismiss one administration before another was formed. I take it for granted that when he sees his Royal Highness, he will explain himself still further.[498]

Despite this prospect, Fox had plainly not been given a commission to form a ministry on the basis of his tender; Waldegrave had only persuaded the King on 19th that the major figures named in Fox's list 'might be talked to, and when his Majesty knew their terms, he might then determine whether he would accept their services...the King told me that I might authorise Fox to treat with the several parties...'[499] But this fell short of others' expectations. It soon became known, at least to Granville, that Fox was 'in no esteem at St. James's'.[500] He was still seeing Waldegrave and Cumberland, but on learning of the King's reaction he declined meeting Newcastle and Hardwicke. Fox was evidently still ignorant of the approach that had been made to Newcastle via Waldegrave, and it seems likely that Fox was implying his refusal to take *any* further step until all his demands were met.[501] Although, therefore, Fox expected Newcastle to be asked for a 'positive declaration' about the role he, Newcastle, would take, Fox did not expect him to be more forthcoming; he was aware also that Mansfield would oppose anything 'that may sooner or later make his patron again a Minister'.[502] Charles Jenkinson thought the possibility of a change of ministry had receded.[503] Fox, too, expected the stalemate to continue. It might however be broken if the ministers could be brought to provoke their own dismissal, and this he attempted to achieve. On the night of the 20th,

Rigby told Fox 'of the report that was propagated with so much industry, of Pitt's refusing to carry a message to the House for four thousand British troops to be sent to Westphalia, and that it was your Grace's opinion it should be contradicted in Parliament'.[504] Fox agreed to do so, having heard a rumour that 'Pitt would not carry such a message and is perforce to be turned out'.[505] But Pitt was not in the House, and the next day Rigby wrote that he was 'gone into the country sick, not meaning to come to Parliament before the Easter holidays I believe'.[506] Fox's attack therefore fell on Legge, whom he demanded should contradict the reports. Legge assured the House that the issue had not been discussed in Cabinet and was not intended by the King or his ministers. Fox then announced that he was authorised by Cumberland to say 'that it was the farthest from his thoughts to take so unreasonable or improper a step'.[507] Nevertheless, it was anticipated that he would soon depart to assume command of the Army of Observation in Germany, whether or not it included English troops, and that meanwhile he remained within doors to protect his health.[508]

Attention focused however not on Cumberland but on the long awaited enquiry. For some time the old ministers had let it be known 'that if the promoters of it shall afterwards drop it, as is sometimes the case in enquiries, they themselves will insist upon it and not let it hang over their heads'.[509] Dodington suggested that the ministers procrastinated and that it was Fox who finally brought it forward.[510] Walpole agreed: George Townshend, he wrote, 'to prevent the [seemingly imminent] change [of ministry] by intimidating, called for more papers; but as Fox wished for nothing more than to dispatch the enquiries, after which he would be at liberty to appear again on the scene, he pressed to have them begin...'[511] On 21 and 22 March, the papers which had been moved for on 8 February were delivered to the Commons by the Admiralty and Secretaries' offices; on 22nd, Fox suggested that the enquiry commence on 19 April, after the Easter recess, and a call of the House was fixed for that day.[512] Meanwhile, Fox's scheme was commending itself to Halifax, who was evidently unaware both of Newcastle's refusal of the King's request on 16 March and of the King's virtual refusal of Fox's offer on 19th. Via Rigby, Bedford heard that Halifax began to look more favourably on the prospects of a Fox ministry, 'if people would act their proper parts with spirit': Newcastle could not fail to support it, after the favour he had received from the King, without alienating his 'best friends'.[513] Fox saw Halifax on 23 March, and advanced three new considerations: that Newcastle had declared (when is not clear) that he would not oppose; that Mansfield had declared that Newcastle ought to support; and that Sir Thomas Robinson would be Secretary of State – as Dodington put it, that he 'had accepted the Seals, by the King's command'.[514] Fox may have been repeating or interpreting Newcastle's reply to the King on 16th, or Newcastle may since have been summoned to an audience;[515] how Fox knew Mansfield's opinions, if he did, is unknown. Nor is it clear that Fox could assure Robinson of the Seals. Hardwicke, Newcastle and Robinson were all in busy consultation at this point,[516] but the evidence does not establish to what effect. It is possible that Robinson and Dupplin had been commanded by the King to take parts in a forthcoming Fox ministry;[517] and that Fox had waived his objection to Robinson as Secretary. Whatever the reality, Fox's three points had their effect. But the same night, Halifax checked Fox's third claim and found, on the contrary, that Robinson 'had sent an absolute refusal, (but not disapproving the plan) and added, that he could not, must not, would not accept'.[518] Halifax, meeting Fox again on 24th, found that Fox had gone too far in his expectations of Halifax's support on the basis of these first impressions. Halifax spelt out his position more clearly in a letter on the same day. Newcastle's support, Halifax thought, was essential; his neutrality, he implied, was not enough. Robinson as Secretary of State would give a good prospect of Newcastle's backing, and Halifax's diffidence would then be overborne:

> though I have no favourable opinion of the stability of the system proposed; yet as it is hurtful to me in the highest degree to be considered as the person who obstructs the execution of his Majesty's intentions, by declining the post in question; however disagreeable the post assigned may be, I will consent to undertake it [i.e. the Admiralty] in case Sir Thomas Robinson shall accept the Seals, which may be considered as a pledge of the Duke of Newcastle's concurrence, and in case his Majesty may be pleased to order me to it. But, if others in his Majesty's service decline the principal parts assigned them, as thinking they can serve his Majesty more effectually in their present posts, I hope I shall not be considered as the obstructor of his Majesty's measures by desiring, upon the same principles, to remain where I am.[519]

Halifax, whose betrayal to Newcastle of Fox and Dodington was obviously still unknown to them, was on safe ground, for he knew that Robinson's refusal made his own offer merely hypothetical.[520] Waldegrave summed up the result of the advances the King had authorised on 19th: it was, he wrote,

> just as I had expected. Lord George Sackville, though he had been violent against Pitt at the beginning of the session, was now connected with him, and had entered into engagements with Leicester House, Lord Egmont's object was a peerage; he therefore pleaded bad health, which would not bear the fatigue of the House of Commons. Lord Halifax would not undertake the direction of the Admiralty, unless the Duke of Newcastle would promise to support him, and his Grace had not any inclination to give the least encouragement. Charles Townshend hated Pitt, and disliked his employment, which was almost a sinecure. Yet did not think it advisable to undertake the defence of an old King, or to be connected with unpopular associates. Lord Strange being then

in the country was not applied to: so Dodington was the only person ready to engage, and he was to be Treasurer of the Navy, which had never been esteemed a ministerial employment.[521]

All therefore turned on Newcastle; yet he remained evasive. He could, wrote Walpole, reflecting Fox's frustration, 'be pinned down to no terms: he advanced to Fox, retreated farther from him, would mention no conditions, nor agree to any'.[522] On 25 March he was visited by Walde-grave with a message from the King. George II, he reported, expected Pitt and Temple soon to quit; what, in that case, should the King do? Would Newcastle draw up a plan of administration to cover that contingency, or their dismissal, 'in which I would immediately take a share; or might come in, at some distant time; or which I might think for his Majesty's service, though I should determine, not to take any part in it myself'?[523] The King's request was quickly public.[524] That evening, Newcastle drew up his answer in consultation with Hardwicke, Mansfield and Andrew Stone. Though denying knowledge of the in-tentions of Pitt and his circle, Newcastle expressed his conviction that they would not resign. If they did, those of the ministers who remained in office were to carry on the government alone until the end of the session; at least three of the Treasury Board would stay, which was enough; if too many left the Admiralty, a provisional Board might be appointed without a First Lord. At the end of the session, a more permanent system might be formed – perhaps Newcastle hinted at his own participation in it. But, before then, to dismiss the current ministers might do great harm.[525] Waldegrave read Newcastle's reply to the King on 26 March and returned it via Stone: 'The King read it very atten-tively...H.M. showed no marks of surprise, or anger; said, "The plan was very imperfect; and that he might have hoped for something more satisfactory from your Grace"; (though Lord Waldegrave thinks, that nothing more, than he was charged with, was expected). The King then complained, in general, that "Everybody thought of themselves, and did not enough consider what he was obliged to go through."' But, after asking Mansfield's opinion, George II found it the same as Newcastle's. Waldegrave was then dismissed with no indication that he would be employed in further negotiations. He took Newcastle's paper to Cumber-land, who read it equally without expression or comment. Waldegrave was left convinced that nothing further would then be done.[526] New-castle agreed, and understood that Waldegrave thought 'that we are come off *tolerably well*'.[527]

Fox's plans, however, were for the moment frustrated. A ministry launched fully finished and built around Halifax at the Admiralty was now impossible. But something might yet be put together, piece by piece, in the hiatus which would follow the ministry's fall. From Cumberland, Fox must have known the details of Newcastle's reply, and it was to his patron that Fox's suggestions were then addressed. The appointment of Winchelsea to the Admiralty, he thought, would provoke the ministers to resign;

> If then H.M. should make me Paymaster and should keep the Seals vacant till the enquiry should be finished which would not be three weeks and then give them to some peer, I am strongly of opinion that everything would follow as H.M. may wish. I shall be ready to leave the Pay Office for any other employment whenever H.M. thinks fit. Lord W[aldegrave] approves of this, and thinks that whenever it becomes necessary for me to be Chancellor of the Exchequer to the Duke of Devonshire or any other Lord whom H.M. may put at the head of the Treasury, this system will be stronger than that of Sir Thomas [Robinson] Secretary, Lord Halifax at the head of the Admiralty and I Paymaster...If H.M. thinks it necessary to make a Secretary of State immediately I would propose Lord Waldegrave, Lord Egremont, Lord Gower, or Lord Winchelsea, in that case Lord Sandwich to the Admiralty.[528]

The 'rain of gold boxes' after Pitt's dismissal in the spring of 1757, and the subsequent imperial significance of the victories of 1759, have set the Pitt–Devonshire administration in several false perspectives. It has been seen as a trial run for the wartime coalition, and, equally with that ministry, the nature of its politics has been rather inferred from the course of the war than understood in its own right. Secondly, the Pitt–Devonshire ministry has been presented as an expression of the national will: the appropriate embodiment of patriotic rejection of an incompetence which Newcastle is held to have personified. Yet, as has been shown, there is no evidence that Pitt was sustained by popular support during his administration, or that he used it to attain power.

In retrospect, Pitt's accession to office in the autumn of 1756 has come to seem inevitable and natural. In fact, Fox was very nearly successful in seeking, as Almon put it, to profit from 'the embarrassment of parties'[529] at that point; his attempt to form an administration failed only narrowly. Fox's pretence in disclaiming all views to ministerial power was seen through: it seemed that he could only then succeed if he allied with Pitt. The latter acted from a position of strength, for he successfully contained the dissatisfactions and rival ambitions of his followers. Fox thought he had been commissioned to form a ministry either with or without Pitt; but the first possibility was pre-empted by Devonshire's deal with his rival. That deal was made possible both by Devonshire's acceptability as a figure who could unite the Pittites, and because Pitt quickly and covertly compromised his Patriot principles. Nevertheless, it has been shown that Fox's ruthless ambition wilted when it was within an ace of success, and his relations with Pitt and Devonshire in October and November clearly reveal that none of the parties were marked out for office through being distinguished by principled views.

Reflecting the precariousness of its inception, the Pitt–Devonshire ministry enjoyed an uncertain tenure throughout its course. Its party composition was an enigma: Pitt depended on an Old Corps majority in the Commons not being used against him, but neither he nor Devonshire could be said to control that voting bloc, and their closest links were rather with the Tories. Also enigmatic was the distribution of authority within the ministry, and the relative standing of its two principals. Fox's participation in opposing the re-elections clearly showed that he did not fear a Newcastle–Pitt reconciliation. Yet his attempts to use the Old Corps majority in the House to attack the ministry failed: it obviously remained loyal to its old managers, and Fox's position could clearly only be advanced by behind-the-scenes intrigue.

Newcastle and Hardwicke felt relatively secure in the belief that Pitt's links with the Tories ruled out a reconciliation between him and Fox. The stratagems employed by Pitt after Christmas, particularly his procrastination and evasions over the enquiry and Byng's sentence, have been revealed above. They explain why Newcastle refrained from bringing down the ministry. The initiative, when it came, was the King's. It has been suggested that 'In his haste to get rid of Pitt and his friends George II had hardly given a thought to their successors'.[530] In fact, the most intricate negotiations were pursued, and frustrated, in elaborate preparations for a new administration. Its eventual emergence is the subject of the next chapter.

7

'The Arbiter of England': the Formation of the Newcastle–Pitt Coalition, April–June 1757

... I am convinced that there are two classes of causes, one ostensible and plausible, calculated to meet the publick eye and mind: the other from private and bye motives, which men scarcely dare to own to themselves.

Shelburne, in Fitzmaurice, *Shelburne*, 1, 79

FOX'S SECOND ATTEMPT TO FORM A MINISTRY, 30 MARCH – 7 APRIL 1757

It was anticipated at Court that Cumberland would leave for Germany to take command of the Army of Observation during the week beginning Sunday, 3 April;[1] in the event he left town for Harwich on Friday 8th and sailed on Sunday, 10th. Walpole records, and there seems little reason to doubt, Cumberland's aversion to that unwelcome task while the ministry remained: 'If to be clogged with orders from Pitt, – if to be obliged to communicate with him, and depend on him for supplies, command itself would lose its lustre. Even if successful, the popularity of Pitt would ravish half his laurels; should he miscarry, his misfortunes would all be imputed to himself'. Walpole claimed that it was Fox who 'snatched at this dilemma';[2] but, in his last week in England, Cumberland too was active in assembling an alternative ministry on the lines of Fox's suggestion of 30 March. The key office was again the Admiralty. Cumberland brought Winchelsea to accept it without making conditions for himself, or about the rest of his Board. Holdernesse was on hand to arrange the formalities, so that Winchelsea could kiss hands on Monday, 4 April. Cumberland also persuaded the King reluctantly to agree to Dupplin's immediate removal from the Paymastership, with another office in compensation only later, to make room for Fox. George II, he reported, 'is still fond of the *previous set* though he abominates their leader [Newcastle] and declared he intended he should never come in again'.[3] The composition of the Admiralty was not known until Monday, and was then still uncertain. Even Walpole called it 'a motley Board'.[4] Temple suggested that Sir Francis Dashwood had declined a seat, and that the King had refused to continue Admiral Forbes,[5] Byng's champion. The Commission named Winchelsea, Boscawen, Rowley, Mostyn, Carysfort, Sandys and Elliot.[6] Yet Fox doubted whether the latter, as a friend of Bute's, would stay;[7]

since Elliot was out of town, this could not at once be known. Fox persuaded Argyll to put pressure on him, on his return, to accept;[8] but Elliot nevertheless refused. 'There may possibly [be] an after game arise according [to] various circumstances', suggested Argyll;[9] but none materialised. Hillsborough undertook an urgent mission from Fox to ask Dodington to accept the Treasurership of the Navy, *vice* George Grenville,

without making conditions at present; and commissioned me to repeat to you his assurances of standing by you, *totis viribus*, if during his Majesty's life any attempt should be made to maltreat you; that he will not stay in a quarter of an hour if such an event was to happen; and if you will be so kind to him as to accept of this for the present, he will be ready to assist in bringing about any practicable exchange that you may wish.

But not only did Dodington's acceptance sound like a favour conferred on Fox; Fox could not yet boast of more recruits than Winchelsea, though the scheme was to be launched on the strength of that example alone.[10] There the acceptances stopped, and though other refusals were evidently not widely known at the time, Walpole suggests that Fox 'tried Lord Granville...courted Devonshire...offered the Treasury to Bedford' without success.[11] 'Sir George Lee, who could not give up the hopes of being Prime Minister, though never thought of but when he could not be so, prepared to accept the Chancellorship of the Exchequer';[12] but never did. Devonshire invited Legge to remain at the Exchequer; he refused.[13] A Fox ministry, it was generally expected, would mean Fox Secretary of State, Bedford First Lord of the Treasury, Dodington Chancellor of the Exchequer and Winchelsea First Lord of the Admiralty;[14] but only the last of these materialised.

Newcastle learnt of these rapid moves only just before their culmination. For, though Mansfield was consulted, first via Wilmot, then by Fox in person on the morning of 4th,[15] the initiative was wholly that of Cumberland and Fox. Returning to town on Monday 4th, Newcastle received Hardwicke's letter of the previous night. Hardwicke had been able to discover nothing certain, at Court on 3rd, about the impending change. Via Sir Thomas Robinson, he heard Waldegrave's prediction (though Waldegrave had probably not seen the King since 26 March), that Temple would be dismissed and replaced by Winchelsea, probably on 4th, to provoke the rest of the ministers to resign. Hardwicke doubted it: he could not discover 'anything that has passed with [Winchelsea], though we have of everybody else, that has been applied to'; nor did Waldegrave speak of anyone having been offered a Secretaryship of State. Robinson, echoing Fox's last scheme in which he was to hold a Secretaryship and Halifax the Admiralty, expected that in case of Temple's dismissal he would be approached; but nothing had yet been said to him. 'I think he has a mind to be advised to accept in that shape', added Hardwicke: a disposition he did nothing to encourage. Devonshire, too, told Hardwicke that he did not know whether Temple would be dismissed before Cumberland's departure: 'This might be merely a *defait*, but if it was not, it does not look as if the execution was so near as tomorrow'.

Newcastle soon discovered otherwise. At Claremont on 3rd, he heard that Granville had persuaded Winchelsea to accept the Admiralty.[16] In town on Monday 4th he received also a letter from Mansfield, just visited by Fox with news of that day's dismissal. 'Lord Gr[anvi]lle is in it strong', reported Mansfield. 'I could not fish whether Lord Hyde[17] was to be Secretary of State. Some expressions dropped make me imagine Lord Egremont may be thought of'.[18] Walpole's account reflects Fox's impression that Mansfield was on his side and had 'endeavoured to fix [Newcastle] to Fox'.[19] If Fox did entertain this misconception, it may be that in calling on Mansfield on 4th he was attempting indirectly to persuade Newcastle to take part in the ministry now forming. If so, Devonshire, too, had been keeping up the pressure, talking openly of his refusal to stay beyond his promised term, the end of the session, and hinting to Hardwicke

as if he wished that your Grace would have made a plan for the King; to which I answered that I was convinced you could not possibly do it without *deceiving* yourself, and his Majesty too. He then said something of permitting some of your friends to accept; to which I answered that I was very sure your Grace had never hindered, nor given them the least word or hint of advice not to accept; but left them to their free inclinations.

As with Sir Thomas Robinson, constitutional propriety warned against coercing the King in the manner of 1746 by concerted resignations or refusals to serve. But if Hardwicke were still trying to prevent the King from dismissing his ministry, he was too late; Devonshire even suggested as a pressing and adequate excuse for 'all this precipitation' that the King 'could not bear the sight' of Temple.[20] But the explanation quickly current was a very different one: 'Change of ministry was resolved upon because of D— going to Hanover', discovered Newdigate in the Commons on 5th.[21] The reputedly popular character of the departing ministry contrasted markedly with a regime allegedly launched by the secret influence of Cumberland. An added handicap was Fox's acceptance of the reversion of Dodington's sinecure place of Clerk of the Pells in Ireland for his own life and that of his sons.[22] It was particularly important, therefore, for Fox to emphasise the disinterested nature of his friends' acceptance of office: that since Newcastle's associates had so resolutely refused their assistance, others must aid the King. Fox claimed he took the Paymastership at the King's own suggestion;[23] but most play was made in this respect with Winchelsea, though detestation of the Grenvilles and a successful previous tenure of the Admiralty may have been other inducements to accept.[24] Newcastle heard that Winchelsea had said

'That when those who had for so many years received favours from the King, and had got immense estates for themselves, and their families, would not come to the King's assistance, when his Majesty was in distress; others, when required, must do it.' And, when he was wished joy, he said, he had no joy, but if the King had ordered him to put himself at the head of a Company of Grenadiers, he would have done it.[25]

Of Fox's other possible Secretaries of State besides Winchelsea–Waldegrave, Gower and Egremont – no overture seems to have been made to the first two. Egremont was widely respected as able and disinterested, but his links with George Grenville[26] probably inhibited his participation in a ministry organised to destroy Pitt's. Already, too, Newcastle had interviewed him, on 1 April. Egremont was reported 'resolved not to go into any scheme of government with the Duke of Cumberland and which is in agitation'; though on good terms with Granville, who was active in Fox's support, Egremont refused to be 'transferred' by him.[27] What offers were made him is not known; but presumably he knew of the widespread expectation, which Fox showed on 5th, that he would accept a Secretaryship.[28] It was probably to avoid such a difficulty that he left for Petworth early, before the holidays began, on 7 April.[29] Walpole claims Egremont 'had consented to accept the Seals of Secretary of State, but soon desired to be excused'.[30] If so, it was probably at this point, after 7th, that Waldegrave was commissioned by the King to offer Dupplin the Exchequer and Sir Thomas Robinson, Pitt's Secretaryship of State; both refused.[31] Meanwhile, Holdernesse visited Temple on 5 April to recover the Seals; Pitt was undecided whether to resign or wait to be dismissed, and attended at Court on 5th and 6th to the King's evident embarrassment.[32] The new Admiralty Board kissed hands on 6th;[33] that day, Pitt told Devonshire of his inclination (the result, thought Walpole, of Legge's persuasion)[34] not to resign but to await the King's orders. Devonshire reported this to the King, and Holdernesse was sent to Pitt the same evening for the seals.[35] Legge resigned that day;[36] James Grenville and Potter on 7th; George Grenville, who had to be summoned to town, on 9th.[37]

These checks given to Fox's ministry at its outset posed in an even more acute form the problem of predicting Fox's game: 'nobody knew, with certainty', declared Newcastle, 'what employment the Great Agent in all this revolution would take, whether *accountable*, or *merely a lucrative* one'.[38] On 5 April, while still confident that Egremont would accept a Secretaryship, Fox wrote:

I see nobody that will take the Treasury [and] management of the House of Commons, and fear that I must be Chancellor of the Exchequer to the Duke of Devonshire [immediately], and his successor [as First Lord of the Treasury]. His Grace stays to any time the King pleases short of next sessions, and before its meeting the King has promised to let him go to a place not ministerial. Nothing can I think much hurt us unless the Duke of Newcastle etc. join with

Leicester House and Pitt, I don't think he will, nor am I sure he could carry many with him if he should.[39]

It may have been this expectation that he might be compelled to step forward into a major office which underlay Fox's indecision on 6th. On that day he was due to kiss hands as Paymaster; yet Holdernesse wrote to the King, claiming the support of Devonshire, Bedford, Granville and Winchelsea, to protest that Dupplin and Potter should first be notified by letter. The King returned his protest with the endorsement 'Mr Fox has desired not to come tomorrow but to put it off till the enquiry is over'.[40] In this acquiescence George II was prompted by Cumberland, who wrote the same night to Fox:

I believe it is certain that the Duke of Newcastle does not think of coming in directly and in the manner I thought when I saw you this evening and the King is glad of it as he foresaw many difficulties in it. I flatter myself that I have got some ground towards naming the Secretary tomorrow and I shall follow it up in the best manner I am able before I see you.[41]

It seems probable that Cumberland engineered the ministry's dismissal on the assumption that Newcastle would immediately be forced to take the Treasury; Walpole had supposed before 7th that Dupplin's and Doddington's[42] refusals of the Exchequer would force Fox to take it, but knew by that day that Fox deferred taking anything till the enquiry was over. Fox's refusal to accept office yet could thus be presented either as an admission of failure or as a continued threat imminently to accept the commanding position if Newcastle did not intervene to do so for him. Calcraft had suggested that Fox would only hold the Paymastership, too, 'pro tempore':[43] but not to take any office was the more effective threat. Thus Erskine predicted to George Grenville that 'Mr Fox is to be First Lord of the Treasury and Chancellor of the Exchequer after the session is over'.[44] Calcraft's revised prediction, too, was that the Treasury would be Fox's office when eventually he did come in;[45] 'The Duke of Newcastle and his party have declined accepting places, Mr Fox is to be nothing till after the enquiry, when if the Duke of Newcastle alters his mind and comes in he'll be Paymaster and his Grace Minister, if not Mr Fox must be Minister and at the head of the Treasury'.[46] Equally with Newcastle, however, Fox was unable to accept the ministry before the enquiry: 'the whole tempest would have been directed at his head'.[47] The formation of a Fox ministry was thus a delicate game of bluff; but Newcastle's studied diffidence, and Devonshire's docile willingness to remain at the end of the session with any colleagues, made the Treasury no longer critical. On Legge's resignation, therefore, the Exchequer Seal was on 8th given temporarily to Mansfield,[48] as it had been to Lord Chief Justice Lee in 1754. The rumour of Egremont's Secretaryship meanwhile spread. John Campbell thought on 7th that he would accept,[49] and Horace Walpole announced it as accomplished. Holdernesse heard the rumour on 6th and asked Granville about it 'abruptly and unexpectedly...by the manner of his answer I am convinced it is intended, though I can't yet learn whether Lord Egremont consents or whether the King has been spoke to'.[50] But Walpole's account suggests that Egremont 'had his hopes soon blasted',[51] and he probably interpreted Fox's deferring office as an admission of failure. On 7th he left town to spend Easter at Petworth, leaving 'most people' with the impression that he had refused the Seals; 'many sensible people seem to think the Administration will go no farther than it has gone'.[52] Calcraft now began to speak of Egremont *or* Lord Hyde as possible Secretaries.[53] Only the Admiralty had actually kissed hands; Dodington told Halifax in the Commons on 6th 'that he was to be Treasurer of the Navy, but he believed not immediately'.[54]

Despite the acute tension of the moment, Fox attended the meeting held at Royston's house on the morning of 6 April to co-ordinate preparations for the enquiry: 'in the present awkward state of things', wrote Royston, 'I do not expect that we shall explain our sentiments to each other very freely'.[55] Nor, evidently, did they. 'What will be the state of the House of Commons', commented Hardwicke, 'and how the new provocations will operate, when they meet, is I think very uncertain. Under the present arrangement of persons, I don't think it will animate the enquiry more'.[56] But the late ministry at once saw the prospect of focusing the enquiry on Fox, a target quite lacking Newcastle's massive probity. Walpole records 'a meeting of Pitt's friends and the Tories', probably before Parliament rose, at which 'it was agreed to push the scrutiny into the military part with great vehemence'. Yet Pitt was in a dilemma. At the meeting he 'promised his support, but feared he should not be able to speak five minutes for his cough. He was aware that Newcastle had left too little power to Fox in their joint administration, for it to be possible with any degree of decency to brand the one, and slide over the errors of the other, with whom Pitt wished to unite'.[57]

THE HOLIDAYS: REFLECTIONS ON TACTICS, 7–19 APRIL 1757

At this point the Easter holidays intervened. Parliament rose on 7th; Newcastle went to Claremont that day, not expected to return until Parliament reassembled on 19th. 'Even down to Lord Barrington, all ministers, and under ministers, are gone into the country for the holidays. The minister-makers at Arthur's are gone to Newmarket, and there is such a scarcity of Members that I begin to be afraid of walking the streets lest the press gang for ministers should seize me and force me into office'.[58] Halifax left town the same day; Hardwicke was reported 'gone into the country for a fortnight'.[59] Worse, from Fox's point of view, was Cumberland's departure.

The enforced lull provoked men to reflect on the tactical situation in general terms, and to speculate on their likely fortunes in the coming reshuffle; for it soon became the accepted view not that a Fox ministry was in being but that an attempt had been made to launch one, and had failed. In these days before Parliament reassembled, Fox was reduced almost to silence; his political inactivity reflected an accurate awareness that his future conduct would be decided for him by Newcastle's choice of role. His only analysis was distorted by a justification of his conduct during the past five weeks:

knowing that the Duke of Newcastle would not share power I promised if his Grace would undertake the Government to support it in the House of Commons without grasping at any [? greater] share of it, sacrificing all views of ambition to H.M. service, and acting either in no employment, or in that of Paymaster without having any share in [the] ministry. The Duke of Newcastle and Lord Hardwicke dare not take the power, nor could find in their hearts, to see it in other hands. They therefore proposed delay without letting H.M. know what they would do, at any future time. H.M. then proposed a Ministry to which they might accede whenever they pleased, and only in the mean time required their promise to support it. This they declined too,

thus justifying Fox, so he claimed, in undertaking a ministry which in fact he both had not undertaken and could not undertake before the enquiry. To Sir Jacob Downing he outlined three possible courses of action:

When these enquiries are over which will last till about this day fortnight and end in nothing; if the Duke of Newcastle and Lord Hardwicke will come in as ministers, I do not propose to do more than support him in the House of Commons without being supposed as formerly to have a share in measures and in power, which I am sure they never would allow me. If they will not come in as ministers but will support, I shall then be desired to take a share and only a share in the administration by perhaps being Chancellor of the Exchequer to some great lord who may be H.M.'s Minister for the House of Lords etc. If they should really join with Leicester House, Lord Bute, etc., then more power will be necessary to the man who in the House of Commons is to stem so strong a tide, and I shall be called perhaps to a post of as much trouble and danger as any man was ever placed in.

Why Fox's position in this second case would not be, or soon become, one of sole dominance was never explained, and the strong incentive for a Newcastle–Bute rapprochement thus disguised. Instead, Fox tried to persuade himself of its impossibility by arguing on a level of abstract justification:

Leicester House is in a rage, and call this the Duke's [Cumberland's] scheme, forgetting that without they assume a right of imposing ministers on the King they can have none to complain, that he remove these. They [Leicester House] extol the Duke of Newcastle for declining to serve, and will offer him any terms, but surely he and Lord Hardwicke will not after 30 years of obligation assist the Prince of Wales to depose their old King and master. I can't believe they will and yet there are who fear it, and I wish H.M. himself is not of the number.

Bute's 'inveteracy' against Cumberland, thought Fox, 'is not to be overcome'; 'at the beginning of the session Leicester House was said to have proscribed me, but now they make no secret of it'. From Fox's own account, therefore, Downing might have inferred the futility of the principle Fox claimed animated his advice, 'to reunite the two Courts'. In fact, Fox's only hope of survival lay in the second of his options, a possibility he had already explored with limited success but which still lay open. This prompted him to stress its possible sources of strength: Bedford's support; Devonshire's decision to remain, who would 'raise the money which Legge could not'; and the likely recruitment of Egremont as Secretary of State.[60] Consequently, Fox's efforts before the enquiry began seem to have been concentrated on the financial problems of raising the supplies after the failure of the form of loan chosen by the previous ministry.[61] There lay another problem: one informant wrote to Halifax of the City's resentment at the dismissal of Pitt and Legge: 'the stream is particularly strong, against Mr F–x and his military administration, which they think stands on an unconstitutional bottom...I have talked with several of the moneyed folks, who declare, they will not advance one penny in support of the intended administration, and it is with great difficulty they give credit, to the alteration...'[62]

Direct evidence for Pitt's intentions and appreciation of the situation before the enquiry began is lacking. Glover offers an account, elsewhere unconfirmed, of two visits he claims to have paid Pitt immediately after his dismissal, the last on 9 April. He did so in an attempt to warn Pitt against his obvious course: 'all orders and conditions of men were now united in one cry for a coalition between him and the Duke of Newcastle, whose instability, treachery, timidity and servile devotion to the King, were indisputably known', and which alone had justified Pitt's opposition. Would a union with Newcastle check the threat of Cumberland's military power?

'Do not imagine', replied he, 'that I can be induced to unite with him, unless sure of power; I mean power over public measures; the disposition of offices, except the few efficient ones of administration, the creating Deans, Bishops, and every placeman besides, is quite out of my plan, and which I willingly would relinquish to the Duke of Newcastle.' 'Give me leave', said I, 'to suppose you united in administration with him; then let us consider the part which he (admitting him to be sincere) will have to act. You have no command in either House of Parliament, and have experienced the personal dislike of the King. You must depend altogether on the Duke of Newcastle for a majority in Parliament, and on his fighting your battles in the closet; and, to speak plainly, using his efforts to alienate a father from a favoured son, who is your declared enemy.'

Newcastle would not allow such a coalition to incline to Leicester House; but if essentially associated with St. James's, it would blast Pitt's honour and reputation. Pitt's reply was evidently evasive: 'Let me assure you that I have drawn a line, which I will not pass: so far, perhaps, I may be driven, but beyond it – never'. Glover urged that the Minorca enquiry be used to establish the incompetence of Newcastle's ministry: Pitt 'gave me assurances that he would take his part in that enquiry; but at the same time, I perceived, he did not mean to go any great lengths; that is, would content himself with showing the incapacity, etc., without insisting too earnestly on their punishment or censure'. Finally Glover urged that the test of Newcastle's sincerity, if a coalition was to be formed, would be his willingness to pass the Militia Bill as it stood, rather than (as was rumoured) to reduce the numbers, in the Lords, from 67,000 to 30,000. No reply is recorded; Pitt probably made none. Glover drew two conclusions: 'one in a loose and general sense, that he would not embark in any foreign measures to the prejudice of this country; the other, in a particular sense, that in all events he would ever withhold his consent from the sending of British troops to Germany'.[63] In both he was mistaken; but he plainly did not believe that Pitt would not explore the option he had advised against. Yet Pitt was not at first to do so in person. He was in a dilemma and vulnerable to this sort of accusation from his followers: it may be no coincidence that he then withdrew from circulation with an attack of 'gout' until he appeared in the Commons for the first day of the enquiry, 25 April, with a theatrical and specious show of infirmity which Walpole so effectively ridiculed.[64]

For Newcastle's and Hardwicke's views the evidence is, in contrast, abundant. Partly they were prompted to reflection by the possibilities suggested by an overture from Legge. Consistently with his betrayal of Fox's overture at Claremont on 13 March, Halifax had already urged on Newcastle that his friend Legge was not on good terms with the leading figures at Leicester House. To all appearances this was true. Glover reported that, at one of his visits, Pitt

spoke of Mr Legge with some indifference, and took notice with a tone and aspect of censure, that he had been silent during all the debates on the enquiry: Legge, to my knowledge on that subject, had been very cool and inattentive; and one morning in particular, at Lord Temple's house, he expressed a wish that the enquiry might not be prosecuted, alleging, that while it remained unexplored, the odium would be more permanent on the authors of our disgraces at Minorca, than, if they should be exculpated in the resolutions of the committee, of which he made no doubt, and perhaps stand approved, either through the want of evidence, or by parliamentary partiality.

Then, at the meeting at Townshend's house (? 23 April) 'it was notorious, that Legge took no part, either through indolence, despair of success, or the apprehension of rendering a coalition more difficult'.[65]

On 6 April, Halifax saw Legge again and reported that 'He thinks you [Newcastle], as every man of sense must do, the only person that can give true ease to the King, and a settlement to the concerns of this unhappy country. He wishes to co-operate under you, but his attachment in another place is such as for the present [to] render it impossible'. Legge was willing to see Newcastle provided the meeting could be kept secret; Oswald, he added, a mutual friend, might be used as an intermediary. He and Halifax 'agree in opinion on the present strange state of things, and think that the quarter to which Legge belongs ought to depend on you for the present without further explanation'. 'I think I see the time almost come', concluded Halifax, 'when your Grace (availing yourself, as I am sure you will do, of the imprudence of your enemies) will be able to gain honour to yourself and give such a settlement to the affairs of your country as nobody but a witch could have thought of some months ago'.[66] Thus he left Newcastle with the impression, which it was not clear he was justified in doing, that something much more than Legge's desertion was in prospect. Dodington later suggested that Legge's overture was 'instigated, I suppose, by [Halifax] and Oswald, who hoped to enhance their favour with the Duke of Newcastle while the negotiation with Mr Pitt was open, by their bringing over so considerable a person' and contributed to by 'the low, shuffling disposition of [Legge's] own heart'.[67] But such a fragmentation of Pitt's following was as much in Newcastle's interest as it was in Halifax's. Newcastle at once had Dupplin write to tell Oswald, whom he was due to see at Claremont on 12th, of his interest in Halifax's disclosure.[68] Meanwhile he set out his own views of his position in a mammoth letter to Hardwicke.[69] Newcastle's immediate expectation was that, as Devonshire told him on 7th, Egremont would accept the Secretaryship despite Newcastle's interview with him on 1st.[70] This Newcastle ascribed to Egremont's loyalty to Granville, whose support of the new ministry was patent. So was Bedford's; a new Admiralty was settled; Lord Hyde would have a place; Dodington would succeed George Grenville. It amounted in all to 'the Duke of Cumberland's administration carried on by Mr Fox'. But Fox's post, Newcastle realised, 'will depend upon the farther turn, that this administration will take'. Its future, however, depended primarily on the King; and he seemed to have accepted Fox's criticisms of Newcastle, distinguishing Hardwicke's conduct and allowing it, but not Newcastle's, a limited justification. To Devonshire, whom he met on 7th, Newcastle urged that Hardwicke 'had concurred with me in everything, which I had said upon this subject', and wrote on 8th to cement the essential alliance. He included an anthology of the King's remarks: to Barrington,

That the Duke of Newcastle was ambitious, that he could agree with nobody, that he had drove everybody out of his service, and that if he was now to come in (or force himself in) with Pitt, he would quarrel with him in a month. That the King had offered *me* everything, to make *me Minister*, and to make my own administration. That if, after that, when I would not come in myself, I should not support his administration, he should have great reason to be angry with me. To my lord Holdernesse, his Majesty was still stronger, that the Duke of Newcastle was negotiating with Pitt etc. That he would enter into opposition (his Majesty in almost all his conversations makes the distinction between your lordship, and me) and said particularly to Lord Holdernesse, 'I shall see, which is King of this country, the Duke of Newcastle or myself'. That was strong, indeed! Mr Fox said to my lord Mansfield, that if the Duke of Newcastle would join Mr Pitt and Leicester House to make the King *prisoner*; the King knew the Duke of Newcastle *could do it*; but his Majesty would not believe it of him.

George II did, however, believe, as Newcastle thought, that he was negotiating with Pitt via the Primate, George Stone. Despite this 'virulence and violence', Newcastle was determined not to be 'the dupe, and tool of those, who now possess the King's confidence, but never will have that of the public'. On 6th, Fox had seen Dupplin to explain that he did not wish to take the Paymastership (not, apparently, that he merely wished to delay taking it); that Fox

hoped, the Duke of Newcastle would take the Administration. That he (Fox) would do anything; that if the Duke of Newcastle would come in, he would be Paymaster, Dupplin might be Chancellor of the Exchequer, and that there would then be the most *harmonious* ministry in the House of Commons, that ever was known. But that if the Duke of Newcastle would not come in, he (Fox) must then have a ministerial office, – pointed out *Chancellor of the Exchequer*, and that I take to be the occasion of the present delay...With my friend Hume Campbell, he went farther, and told him that he wished and desired I would take it, that I should have *carte blanche*, and that he would go early yesterday morning [7th] to the Duke of Devonshire, and send him to me with that proposal. But either he was not early enough at Devonshire House, or his Grace did not think proper to make the proposal.

Nevertheless, thought Newcastle, reflection on the inadequacy and unpopularity of their system ('It is called a *Ducal Government*') would bring the new ministers to make a proposal of that kind. But the creation of a stable system, uniting the two courts, was a problem 'much more easy to wish, than to bring about'. It was also attainable only via a rapprochement with Leicester House. Yet the King had forbidden Newcastle to use the obvious channel to its accomplishment. This, too, Devonshire would do nothing to facilitate. Meeting him on 7th, Newcastle

complained, that the King (after I had assured his Majesty upon my honour, that I had no negotiation with Mr Pitt, and particularly not by the channel of the Primate) should still believe I had. His Grace promised very kindly to disabuse the King, that I had not any such negotiation, *nor will have any negotiation with Mr Pitt.* To that I absolutely objected, and said, I would give no such promise, nor enter into any such engagement, for I was determined to be *entirely free.*

Devonshire's plan, he explained, was to leave the Treasury at the end of the session, meanwhile appointing no Chancellor of the Exchequer, merely adding Oswald to the Treasury Board to help with its current business; and that Oswald 'would then be there for me, if I would take the Treasury'. To this suggestion Newcastle evidently made no comment; Devonshire offered Oswald a seat at the Board later that day, but he refused. Newcastle knew that Devonshire had said elsewhere that the King 'had not reason to be offended' at Newcastle's letter of 25 March refusing his support, and, on 7th, Devonshire's disapproval of Newcastle's stand was not emphatic:

His Grace pressed me much to come in. But what was most remarkable, at last, in a most serious, and friendly manner, said, you may be angry with me, but I will tell you my opinion; you should either determine to come in yourself, and for that purpose make such scheme of ministry, as you should like (and here I may be mistaken, but I think, he did not mean to exclude even some of the ministers, who may be displaced, or may now resign). Or, if you won't do that, you ought to support the King's administration. This the King may expect of you, and this *your friends* will expect of you also. I avoided giving any answer to it, by declaring, that I would keep myself absolutely disengaged.

Newcastle gave no reason for his refusal and no date at which he might come to a decision, for he saw a third alternative to Devonshire's choice: to support or supplant Fox. To Hardwicke, Newcastle forwarded Halifax's letter with news of Legge's overture: 'It looks by Mr Legge's offer to see me in private, as if he thought, *something* could be done, and that, without making Mr Pitt the principal figure in it. Which, if so, might render it more palatable at St James's, especially after a certain great person [Cumberland] is gone from thence'. Oswald was due at Claremont on 12th; the *démarche* would then be carried further, despite the risk of infringing the King's prohibition of a negotiation with Pitt. Evidence was building up that this was a real possibility, and entailed in what was to follow. Charles Yorke had been visited by Dr Warburton on 6th with a feeler from Potter, but Warburton interpreted the Solicitor General's answer as a 'put off'. Then,

Lord Temple very sillily, and a *little impudently*, said to Holdernesse, that these alterations would facilitate the only solid system, viz. their connection with us. I hear, Mr Pitt will rather give himself the air, of not being his own master, that he can take no step of himself, with a view (as I suppose) to make me imagine, that the offensive negative, which he put upon me, was the work of others (Leicester House) and not his own.

Finally, Newcastle heard on 8th via Lord Ashburnham[71] that Temple had told Lord Coventry

that the Princess of Wales, Mr Pitt, and himself, were ready to join with me; that there was nothing else for it, and that he (Lord Temple) thought, that this was the time; Lord Dupplin met Mr Legge at the Duke of Devonshire's this morning (8th), who said people must now unite upon principle; that *they* had been teazed to join *these people*, but he had absolutely declared in that House, he would not do it, that he (Legge) had depended upon the honour, integrity, and discernment of Lord Dupplin's friend; that he would not have anything to do with them (viz. Fox and his friends) that till the enquiry was over, there must be management. This sort of discourse adds to the probability of Lord Halifax's intelligence. Nothing more is to be done till after the enquiry.

But Newcastle conceived of circumstances which might accelerate a decision. The City was in 'a most extraordinary ferment...upon the present dispositions at Court': if that disposition spread, the possibility marked out by Leicester House would demand action, for 'our friends in these circumstances will not remain in suspense'. Though Newcastle could conceive of such a situation, it was, and was to remain, hypothetical; but it was a present spur to bring Hardwicke to agreement on a scheme of action. Newcastle posed three questions:

First, what answer to be returned to any proposal that may be made to me from the King by the Duke of Devonshire, or my lord Waldegrave, for coming into the administration after the enquiry, or at the end of the session. For Mr Fox said, the time as well as everything else should be left to me.

Secondly, what encouragement (if any) should be given to Mr Legge?

Thirdly, what part our friends should act in Parliament, in support of, or in opposition to, this new administration? If (as most probably will be the case) they [the Foxites] should be attacked by Mr Pitt, during the remainder of *this* session.

Newcastle was at no loss for an answer, though (as usual) he professed to be so.

As to the first, I do admit no precise answer can be given, till we know in what manner, and terms the proposal will be made. But I suppose it will be, upon the plan of the administration as now made, with the addition of Lord Egremont for Secretary of State, and Mr Fox Paymaster. If that should be the case, I own I see little difference (except as to the time) from what was the question before; nay, in some respects, it may be worse; for the Secretary of State, and the Admiralty, are now determined without us; the Duke of Devonshire told me, he had always wished that Sir T. Robinson had accepted, that I might have had a Secretary of State to my own liking. But, my lord, the true reason, and cause of our refusal must be known, or I cannot be justified in persevering in my refusal; and that is, that an administration, with a Prince of the Blood, Captain General, at the head of it, with Mr Fox the principal or sole agent, or instrument under him, is what your lordship and I cannot concur in, or take a share of, without evident prejudice to the King's service, and the greatest danger, and strongest imputation upon ourselves. For, without so good a reason as this, we cannot be justified in not coming to the King's assistance, when they do pretend to say, that *carte blanche* has been offered us; much less can we be justified in giving any opposition to the King's administration, such as he can make it.

Never since 1754 had Newcastle felt the need to combat Fox's ambitions in these terms; but never before had he been both pressed to resume office and eager to engineer a reconciliation with Leicester House in the face of a significant section of the Old Corps arguably already in possession of the ministry. A justification and a cement for an alliance with Pitt rather than with Fox lay ready to hand in the rhetoric Pitt and his allies had recently employed; opportunistically, Newcastle took advantage of it. Further, it implied an answer to his second question. The overture from Legge

might furnish means, of making such a proposal to the King of an administration, as might carry conviction, and success with it. And if it could be done, without introducing *immediately* into the King's presence, any of those, who have very justly given him offence, that might possibly do; at least I don't see how anybody would dare to oppose it. Mr Fox has his two reversions, and he might have in this scheme *his Paymaster* in possession.

On the third of his questions, Newcastle professed himself still more strongly at a loss. In fact, he had a definite intention: to undermine Fox's ministry by doing nothing to support it. But having justified Pitt, he must justify also bringing down Fox:

I detest in general the thought of opposition. I have detested and blamed it in *others*, and therefore shall most unwillingly come into it *myself*. But, on the other hand, if *we* support these men, and measures, *both* will undoubtedly (for a time at least) succeed. We then involve ourselves, not only in the unpopularity, but even in the inconveniences, and mischiefs that may arise from the present system: and to the public, it is the same, as if we were parties to the administration. For, without *us*, this administration at present cannot go on. And (if that was a consideration) we should make *ourselves* equally obnoxious *in all places*. Might not there be a middle way (though in general I dislike all *metzo terminos*). Might we not keep off from any immediate engagement with either party, and act according to events, and as particular questions arise? This I know will be difficult, and possibly in no shape satisfactory to our friends who from thence may go, part to one side, and part to the other. Though I have mentioned it, I am afraid, this will be found impracticable.[72]

That the ideal solution was impracticable was an even stronger recommendation of the negotiation with Legge; but its impracticability was a tactical assertion, not an empirical fact. Newcastle sent Hardwicke a list of the House of Lords, showing the expected alignment of groups; but there is no evidence that Newcastle made a similar calculation for the Commons, or that his calculations were based on any such accurate expectation about voting patterns. Nor was a careful measuring of forces important. As Halifax pointed out, 'The quantum of the noble Duke's strength, of which he is doubtful, and I think undervalues, is of little consequence, as it is most assuredly such (be it more or less) as gives him a strong turn of the political scale at present.'[73] As before, Newcastle's task was one of subtle negotiation among the leaders to put together a stable system in a period when most elements of political cohesion were under considerable centrifugal force. During Pitt's ministry, events in and outside Parliament had not raised the problems of opposition and responsibility which the manoeuvre of individuals now confronted him with. Once they *were* raised, it was evident that Newcastle's position on the question of opposition was an unusual one: he had the power to bring down the ministry, but was unwilling from prudence and principle to storm the Closet. Pitt had equivocated between Patriot independence and an alternative, Tory, party base; but Newcastle, not Fox, was still assumed to be in command of the Whigs, and to shoulder a large share of responsibility for their collective acts. Secondly, now that men and measures were both unmistakably unpopular, Newcastle stood revealed as responsible for that which he did not intervene to destroy. His theoretical problem was his inability to conceive of destroying a ministry except in terms of coercing the sovereign. His practical problem was to conceal this theoretical one from rival ministers so as to preserve the means of bringing various sorts of pressure to bear on them without the King entering into the calculation.

Yet Fox and Pitt did not work with any *other* professed, formal notions of opposition. If anything, Pitt was even more deferential towards George II, and Fox's links with Cumberland had similar results. Any widening of the bounds of legitimate opposition therefore came (as with most advances in constitutional precedent) indirectly, the outcome of particular tactical conjunctions, crystallised and real before they were rationalised and asserted as principles. But the practices generated by the crises of the previous few years were submerged in the political settlement of June 1757, to be taken up as elements in a new political rhetoric not in the next constitutional phase, but in the next but one: the 1760s. For the moment, however, the clash of ambition between Newcastle, Fox and Pitt made the question of legitimate opposition so overwhelming that party *qua* Whig and Tory ceased to bear on the question, and was never mentioned in this context.

It was primarily Newcastle, however, who worried over these matters. Hardwicke was preoccupied with the practical possibilities which Legge had suggested, for he had spoken also to Anson. Hardwicke was smugly satisfied that his prediction to Pitt of five months before, that he would be unable to sustain a ministry without the support of Hardwicke's allies, had been justified; 'I believe there is some truth in what Mr Legge insinuated to your lordship, that it was principally owing to the visionary notions of Mr Pitt; and I think those visionary notions much consisted

in the support with which he had flattered himself from the Tories...'
Hardwicke therefore encouraged Anson to visit Claremont and set out
Legge's overture in detail.[74] Meanwhile he replied to Newcastle in terms
which did little more than echo Newcastle's analysis. Prompted, too, by
Newcastle's implications of disloyalty, Hardwicke was careful to stress
his solidarity: nothing had passed between him and the King except
via Waldegrave, all of which Newcastle knew; Fox had misreported
him as saying that he, Hardwicke, and his friends 'would support the
King's measures'. On the contrary, Hardwicke dwelt in self-justification
(as he need not have done to persuade Newcastle) on the threat of
Cumberland and Fox. In launching the new ministry, George II

has never adhered to any one idea, that has been either suggested by others,
or conceived by himself, but has been absolutely resigned to one person
[Cumberland]. I have been told that Horace Walpole said publicly the other
day, that the D[uke] of C[umberland] was going to command in Germany;
held England *in commendam*; and left Mr Fox his viceroy to command in
his absence.

Now, there were even signs of Cumberland's not going at all. Moreover,
'when the King talks of having offered to make you "the Minister" and
to make your own administration, it is surprising that he should not feel
that nobody can possibly be *Minister*, at present, but the two persons who
have formed this fine scheme for him'. Fox's offers of *carte blanche*, of
acting under Newcastle, 'deserve no notice': Newcastle should consider
'who invested him with that power; and may not he, that gives it, be
supposed to be able to take it away?' Newcastle was therefore right to
resist Devonshire's suggestion: that would only have encouraged them
in pursuing '*the principle* of this new scheme'.

Yet, inconsistently, Hardwicke tried to encourage Newcastle to pursue
a Leicester House alliance by suggesting that the prospects of a Fox
administration were not good. Why otherwise did Devonshire refuse to
go on? Egremont was unlikely to accept the Secretaryship of State; and
Fox's refusal to take the Paymastership, despite the fact that to do so
would conveniently remove him from the Commons during the enquiry,
conceded a principle: 'Why is that opinion less offensive in him than
in us?' And, as Newcastle rightly saw, Fox sought to avoid ministerial
office by recruiting Newcastle: 'if you come in, Mr Fox is to be delivered
from *responsibility*'.

By those two routes, Anson arrived at an endorsement of Newcastle's
attitude to Legge, who, thought Anson, was now suggesting that he had
more credit at Leicester House than Pitt. Neither Newcastle nor Hardwicke knew enough of that Court to assess such a claim, but Hardwicke
suggested Newcastle's undertaking to the King did not stand in the way
of a meeting with Legge. Devonshire, too, might be expected to be 'a
kind of middle-man'. If, in reply to Newcastle's second question, Devonshire or Waldegrave were to bring a request from the King to support the

present ministry, Hardwicke evasively suggested that no answer could be given until the exact terms were known. The worst request would be to support the system now forming, which, he warned Newcastle, would be an invitation 'to stick yourself into an administration entirely chosen, and made without you'. The excuse for refusing should then be that no stable system was possible 'but such an one, as may, if possible, unite the whole Royal Family, and bring the *succession* to support and give quiet to the *possession*. Everything else will be perpetual contest.' This was not a constitutional principle, though, among the Whigs, Mansfield had repeated the advice often enough for it almost to seem so in his hands; in Hardwicke's, a happy phrase marked rather his long-sought preference for a Pitt alliance.

On Newcastle's third question, Hardwicke could only echo his ally's aversion to opposition: 'For my own part, I am determined not to go into *a formed general opposition.* I have seen so much of them I am convinced they are the most wicked combinations, that men can enter into; – worse, and more corrupt than any administration, that I ever yet saw...' Until the end of the enquiry, and perhaps of the current session, Newcastle and Hardwicke should avoid party arrangements and vote on measures on their merits. 'I am sensible that this is not the political way to keep a party together, but that is not an objection against doing what I think in my own conscience to be right.'[75] In this, Hardwicke may have been wrong; it *was* the familiar way of keeping together a party *qua* Whig and Tory, but not a plan likely to preserve proprietary 'parties'. Newcastle and Hardwicke thus came, in a moment of crisis, increasingly to treat their followers like a proprietary party, descending to the level of Pitt and Fox in order to combat them there, so that, when the coalition combined them again, something of the tradition of leadership of the old Whig party had been lost. In no sense was this deliberate; in at least one sense it was consciously resisted. For Newcastle and Hardwicke to go into 'formed general opposition' to a Fox ministry built on a Whig basis would have been an admission that the Old Corps had been divided and that Fox was in possession of the chief part of it. Whigs might well be inhibited by the assumption that oppositions were not based on party, as were ministries; as party leaders, Newcastle and Hardwicke could not lead their party into opposition without danger of disintegration. Moreover, such a course at that moment would antagonise the King, disinclining him still further to accept Newcastle back even without Pitt in tow; and if Newcastle joined in Pitt's principled rhetoric of opposition, that too would have to be betrayed if Newcastle re-entered office. Yet it was not suggested that Newcastle must not oppose Fox because to do so would align him with the Tories: that party contributed nothing to the speculations of these days.

Newcastle needed none of this advice. He was already aware of the

significance of Legge's intervention: 'Perhaps it opens the most favourable scene, that has yet appeared.'[76] How far it was concerted among
Pitt's friends is not known, but it was probably not coincidence that
Temple entertained the same anticipations: 'Offers without end to the
Duke of Newcastle, who not only stands his ground, but I have now the
utmost reason to think that his union with us is as good as done, in
which case Foxism must go to the devil...'[77] After Newcastle had
arranged to see Legge secretly on 18th, Mansfield advised him, claiming
confidential knowledge: 'Take for granted that the meeting is by Pitt's
direction, and with general privity.'[78]

Yet Temple and Halifax both over-simplified Newcastle's problem.
Halifax, convinced of the impossibility of 'a junction of the other two
parties',[79] thought it chiefly a matter of Newcastle's resolution:

The present attempt towards administration fails in the outset. An attempt
for power in the Leicester House quarter would be equally unacceptable and
absurd, and has already proved so. And possibly your Grace's interest and
connections might not be sufficient to stand alone in administration without
some auxiliary support. But as you are certainly the strongest of the three
parties, I have no idea of your suffering yourself to be ground between the
other two. Undoubtedly my lord you may step towards, and take the lead,
sure of being joined by either (for a time perhaps by both) as things shall turn
out, and as you shall hereafter determine; for neither of them can find safety
or support but by a junction with you...I think it possible that the Leicester
House people may expect immediately to be taken by the hand, and brought
into power with you; but if they do, they expect too much, and misjudge their
own condition and yours. A treaty of alliance might at present be unsafe for
your Grace, and I am clear in opinion that it is unnecessary, for they will be
yours without it. All I could therefore wish is that for your satisfaction it
might be declared by one or two of the principals, that they would acquiesce
under, and rely upon you.[80]

This, presumably, was all Legge had to offer; Newcastle was to be
encouraged to think this sufficient to warrant his undertaking the
government in the hope of future, more specific, commitments. Halifax
was not confident that he could persuade Newcastle,[81] and the latter's
encouraging letter of 9th made Halifax swing to the other extreme of
confident expectation: 'He must take his part – indeed he must; for he
may command everything now, and it may not be the case some time
hence...I now see the path so clearly before us, that I shall be wild
if it be not followed.' 'The game is so plain, and I think so sure, that
it would be madness to mistake it...The part is such that children
might play it.'[82] (Dangerously, Halifax was slipping into a vein of over-
emphatic, egotistic assertion.) And he summarised his advice to Newcastle,
to prepare Oswald for his meeting on 12th.[83] Here Halifax had gone too
far. Newcastle was not at that point being offered the lead, except as
part of a Fox ministry; 'I have thought the whole affair most seriously
over, and have determined in my own mind, that it will be impossible

for me to come in with this administration, without losing my credit, and reputation entirely, and being reduced from the advantageous light in which I stand now, to make a mean, and indeed despicable figure.'[84]

An arrangement with Leicester House would therefore have to be arrived at before Newcastle would stir; and Newcastle used Oswald to arrange a secret and confidential meeting with Legge for the night of 18 April.[85] Oswald, who had already seen Legge and had had several messages from Bute before his visit to Claremont on 12th, 'imagines that Leicester House is so much frightened with the new administration, that they wish to make up with me, *even without insisting upon any immediate terms for their own people*; but in that', wrote Newcastle, 'he is probably mistaken'. It seems likely that Newcastle was right and that Oswald's confidence was the result of Halifax's briefing; Newcastle was careful to explain to Mansfield that he intended to say nothing to Legge to commit himself.[86] Meanwhile, through Stone (who visited Claremont on 12th), Newcastle heard of Mansfield's audience on 8th. George II began by commending Mansfield's conduct, condemning the Pitt ministry as intolerable, and reproaching Newcastle for his refusal to rescue him; then, as Newcastle explained to Hardwicke,

had recourse only, to what his Majesty said, your lordship said to him upon quitting the Seals, which I remember very well, and was not as his Majesty is pleased now to represent it. The King said, that you told him, that you left your son (the Solicitor General) with him, as a pledge of your duty to him; and that you would support *his measures* under any administration. I remember very well, your lordship's words were, *his public* measures, agreeably to the sense, in which I had before talked to the King.

Newcastle was feeling for a distinction between uncontentious administration and party issues; a problem Mansfield tried to avoid by claiming, like him, that Newcastle and Hardwicke were of one mind.

The King then said, 'But why then will not the Duke of Newcastle promise me his support? His fears prevent him from coming in himself, but they need not hinder him from supporting others.' 'The Duke of Newcastle has given his opinion to your Majesty, that those gentlemen should not be removed *at present*; and if he has promised to support their successors, it might have encouraged a measure, which he had thought not for your Majesty's service.' 'But, will he go into opposition?' 'He will never do anything contrary to his duty and zeal for your Majesty's service'. 'But, tell me your opinion, if the Duke of Newcastle should go into *Opposition, would the Whigs of the House of Commons follow him?*' 'Since your Majesty commands me to tell you my opinion, *I think they would*'. That was a strong answer indeed, and must have an effect. His Majesty made no reply.[87]

In return for this act of support Newcastle agreed, at Stone's prompting, to send Mansfield copies of his, Newcastle's correspondence with Hardwicke and Halifax:

it is very material to have my lord Mansfield on our side; for he is now so well with the King and will have access to him, that I may make great use of him. And there is no one point, that Murray has been so strong upon, as my being well with Leicester House, and I think by Legge and Oswald that my lord Bute seems to think that right for *themselves*.[88]

Newcastle was thus encouraged to welcome Hardwicke's endorsement (which he treated as Hardwicke's own suggestion): if another invitation came from the King, Newcastle would insist that 'no solid plan of administration can be made, without an union of the whole Royal Family'. Thanks to Mansfield, the threat of opposition could still be brought to bear on the King without Newcastle formally committing himself to it and attempting to lead the Whigs along that path, and Newcastle's suggested '*metzo termino*' became practicable: to 'keep off from any immediate engagement with either party'. Meanwhile, a scheme acceptable to the King might be drawn up, if it promised to unite the Royal Family, and if 'the persons lately dismissed (and indeed my lord Temple chiefly) are not proposed to be brought into the Closet'. Yet Newcastle added a warning: 'My own opinion is, that it will end, in these gentlemen filling up their administration, and going on for some time. The King's aversion to Leicester House, will make any junction there most difficult, and his present great anger with me, will not be lessened by any advice I may convey upon that head.' Unknown to Newcastle, Fox was soon urging Devonshire, on the strength of the course the enquiry took in the Commons, to remain at the Treasury as the only figure who could unite the contending individuals. But Newcastle knew that the King had asked Mansfield a question about precedent – whether a man holding an office in the Treasury could also have a seat at that Board – which Newcastle took to imply that Waldegrave, a Teller of the Exchequer, was being considered for the place of First Lord of the Treasury. Fox, Newcastle knew, had been commanded to attend the levée on Wednesday 13th, and he had heard that the King wished '*to talk about the House of Commons*'.[89] Mansfield soon offered a prediction that Pitt (as if to counter such a possibility) would compromise the essential point:

I think I know privately from good authority that the enquiry is over. It will not last above one or two days at most. You should therefore be prepared with modest resolutions to vindicate your innocence.

This meeting with Legge, he added, was arranged with Pitt; it would soon be public; and 'the proposition he is to make will be, under plausible sounds, to overturn this [Fox's] system'.[90] Quickly, now, signs began to appear of cracks in Fox's arrangements. The subscription for a loan of £2,500,000 closed on the night of 14th with only £313,000 subscribed. West, too, confirmed Mansfield's intelligence: 'All the opposition, I see, scout the enquiry.'[91] John Roberts reported that Egremont had refused the Secretaryship of State and that rumour now circulated about two unknowns, Lord Hertford and Lord Denbigh.[92] Stone agreed.[93] Such difficulties probably formed the substance of the discussion when Fox saw the King on 13th and Devonshire on 15th, 'relative to the settling his ministry'.[94] During the holidays, the prospects for a Fox ministry had been steadily eroded. Devonshire was probably referring to his meeting on 15th when he later wrote:

I consulted Mr Fox who though he was willing to undertake any part that the King should choose or even think necessary for his service that he should take, yet seemed to think the game if he was to undertake it, though not desperate yet very difficult and thought it very advisable to endeavour if possible to fix upon some plan that would be solid and permanent, that for his part the king had made him and his family easy for their lives, and that therefore he had nothing to do but to serve the King to the utmost of his powers in any shape that his Majesty should choose and was ready to take any part or no part as should be allotted to him and in the conversation he threw out a hint, that he did not see the impossibility of taking all sides, that he for one should have no objection. I told him that I imagined such a scheme was absolutely impracticable first that the King would never hear of it, next that the parties themselves would never be brought together and lastly that I did not imagine he would like it. He answered that he should have no objection,

but Devonshire put the idea aside as impracticable.[95]

Then, rumours flew of the belated resignation of Charles Townshend. Their subject wrote first to reassure Devonshire that he would not do so without that Duke's knowledge;[96] but three days later he did so,[97] trying, wrote Walpole, to avoid 'as much as possible to have it thought that he quitted from attachment to Pitt'.[98] On the contrary, his was a gesture which had its effect *against* Fox, not *for* Pitt, part of the fracturing of Fox's system which took place just before Parliament reassembled on 19th. Calling on Devonshire to explain his action, Charles Townshend spoke of the current situation. The present plan was plainly impossible; but if Newcastle were to return to the Treasury and Pitt to a Secretaryship, why not form a tripartite coalition by including Fox as Paymaster? Devonshire replied that the scheme was 'certainly a very good one, but that I was afraid it was absolutely impracticable'. Nevertheless, he explained the idea to George II when reporting Townshend's resignation. The King

heard it with more patience than I expected. He said he could never bear the thoughts of Lord Temple; as to Pitt he had not so much objection to him, but he thought him too impracticable to act with anybody and asked my opinion. I told HM that I was afraid the scheme was impossible, that if Mr Pitt would consent to act an under part and confine himself to Secretary of State under the Duke of Newcastle and Mr Fox P[ay]m[aste]r etc., I thought it would be the surest means of giving ease to his Majesty and restoring strength and consistency at home, that possibly the plan his Majesty was now going upon might do, I could not pretend to say whether it would or would not, but that it certainly would be attended with great opposition whereas if this took place there could for the present be none, and another good effect that would arise would be the lessening the weight of another place [Leicester House], for to give the Duke of Newcastle his due the paying court there had never been his failing and if he entered into HM's service again, I should think he might be trusted upon that head. The King ordered me to talk to the Duke of Newcastle to see upon what terms he would come in rather inclined that he should join with Mr Fox, but did not seem to object to the other scheme if that could not take place.[99]

THE ENQUIRY, 19 APRIL–3 MAY 1757

There were thus grounds both for Newcastle's caution, based on the possible reinforcement of Fox's system (for he himself had succeeded in regaining stability by such means in previous crises during 1754–6), and for Walpole's estimate of Newcastle's strength: George II, he wrote, 'is willing to wait, in hopes of prevailing on him to resume the Seals – that Duke is the arbiter of England! Both the other parties are trying to unite with him.'[100] Before Newcastle saw Devonshire as the King had commanded, however, he met Legge at Dupplin's on the night of 18 April, Legge using a back door. The only record of what passed is Legge's:

The whole conversation consisted of generals and exhortations on my part to join with us and make a government upon the basis of a thorough harmony between the King and Leicester House – No particulars whatsoever were mentioned as to the arrangement of offices. Strict secrecy enjoined on both sides and the argument used for it on the part of the Duke of Newcastle was the same with that contained in the message by Mr Oswald.

This was the only interview I ever had with the Duke of Newcastle – He afterwards desired another by Lord Halifax to which I gave a flat refusal. He afterwards declared a wish in the presence of Lord Halifax and Mr Oswald to have separated me from my friends but at the same time said he found it was impracticable. To which they both replied that he always would find it so; for though I was well inclined to a general union I certainly never should swerve from my engagements to my friends.[101]

Dodington, whose source was Halifax, later wrote that 'This treaty (if it had taken place) was for Legge to come in without Mr Pitt, if he persisted in his exorbitant demands.'[102] Legge's memorandum was drawn up in June in self-justification after Newcastle had disclosed the fact of the interview on 18 April to Bute; its accuracy is therefore difficult to assess. But it seems fairly probable that, as Martin told Glover, Legge immediately realised his error; that he admitted the interview to Martin, who advised him at once to admit it to Pitt; that Legge would have done so but for his promise of secrecy to Newcastle; and that Legge was left distracted with remorse,[103] unable to manoeuvre.

Nor is there any record of Newcastle's immediately preceding meeting with Hardwicke. Two memoranda[104] which survive in the Newcastle papers probably record his view of the situation before the interview with Legge rather than as a result of it. They include a précis of the advice that had weighed with him. Devonshire he understood to have advised 'That I should form my own administration – That Fox should be anything or nothing.' Then, what Fox had said to Egmont:

That he [Fox] had now got a provision for his family – that *that* was his sole object. He only wanted, now, some lucrative office, to support his present expenses. That he would act, just as much, and as little, as the Duke of Newcastle would have him – that Lord Egmont should tell the Duke of Newcastle so. And, upon his lordship's telling Mr Fox, that *that* would not be sufficient: that there should be a *junction* between the Duke of Newcastle, and Mr Pitt; Mr Fox replied, that, if that was done, the King would never have an uneasy moment – that the difficulty would be, to make Mr Pitt act a reasonable part – That there might be difficulty with the King; but seemed to think *that* the least difficulty of the two.

Newcastle, also, was led to think that, by Newcastle's remarks to Holdernesse, the King

had been informed, that the Duke of Newcastle had been with the Princess of Wales; and had settled with her the administration. My lord Holdernesse assured the King, that *that* was false. His Majesty said, he should not be displeased with the Duke of Newcastle, if, *in these times*, he had gone to talk to the Princess; but for not acquainting him with it.

Newcastle's intentions therefore were,

First. On no account whatever, to come into, to botch up, or promise support to the present [i.e. Fox's] administration, as now formed; or to the principle, on which it is supposed to be formed.

Secondly. On no account whatever, to come into the administration, till there is a thorough good understanding established in the Royal Family; and Leicester House shall support the administration, so to be formed.

Thirdly. Not to enter, on any account, into general opposition; or to attempt, by force, in Parliament, to remove or replace ministers; or in any degree to force the King, contrary to his inclination, to admit any persons into his administration.

Nevertheless, Newcastle was willing to have precise ideas about, and to draw up a list of, the composition of an alternative ministry: Hardwicke, Chancellor; himself at the Treasury; Pitt in a Secretaryship of State, with Halifax's office raised to that status; Anson, apparently, at the Admiralty. Fox was put down for 'some office', not the Paymastership.[105] How tentative these assignments were is not known. They rested, however, on a clean sweep of Fox's system and a reconstruction of the ministry on a Newcastle basis – developments which could only follow a thorough union with Leicester House. This had not yet come about. For the moment, it was contingent on events in the Commons, where the enquiry opened after a call of the House on 19 April.[106] 'It is thought it will not hold for many days', wrote Symmer. 'Upon the issue of that, we have reason to expect the new ministry will be settled. At the same time, I meet with nobody but are of opinion that the late ministry (I mean the Duke of Newcastle's) will be cleared: this will render it less difficult to form a proper arrangement';[107] 'if it should be warm, it will be nothing but the heat of personal altercation; for it is pretty clearly apprehended that the old administration will be laid under no great distress; for this good reason, that both they who are gone out, and they who are come in, court the person who was at the head of the old administration'.[108]

Walpole's description of the enquiry has, unjustifiably, reduced it to ridicule. But his account follows his prediction of its character after only one day's proceedings. The departments involved, he objected, were at liberty to choose the documents presented; the enquiry began before anyone had time to read them; the Commons set the Clerk of the House

to reading such bushels of letters, that the very dates fill three and twenty sheets of paper; he reads as fast as he can, nobody attends, everybody goes away, and tonight they determined that the whole matter should be read through on tomorrow [Thursday 21st] and Friday, that one may have time to digest on Saturday and Sunday [23rd and 24th] what one has scarce heard, cannot remember, nor is worth the while; and then on Monday, without asking any questions, examining any witnesses, authority or authenticity, the Tories are to affirm that the ministers were very negligent, the Whigs that they were wonderfully informed, provident and active, and Mr Pitt and his friends are to affect great zeal for justice, are to avoid provoking the Duke of Newcastle, and are to endeavour to extract from all the nothings they have not heard, something that is to lay all the guilt at Mr Fox's door. Now you know very exactly what the enquiries are.[109]

But other contemporary accounts lack this element of derision. George and Charles Townshend, wrote Walpole, 'pretended to be managers'[110] against Newcastle, but there is no evidence that the 'prosecution' deliberately neglected to maximise the numbers on their side of the question, or that the outcome did not reflect the true opinion of the House. Moreover, Glover described the preparations on Pitt's side as 'tardy and lukewarm', the result of indifference and incompetence. This self-confessed 'neglect',[111] and the element of tactical disingenuousness, coexisted with that of disinterested enquiry. Newcastle and Hardwicke anticipated that the tactic to be employed was that 'the prosecutors of the enquiry intend to move several questions of fact, which shall arise out of the papers, and carry an appearance of fairness and truth upon the face of them, and yet be capable of having consequential resolutions built upon them, if carried'.[112] The parliamentary campaign therefore turned not on a violent, head-on attack on the old ministry but on a subtle interplay of wording and amendment between a small number of professionals who, *pace* Walpole, were both well prepared and in command of their material. Despite the complexity of the evidence, the attendance of back-benchers was not low: the motion on Friday 22 April to go into Committee on Monday 25th rather than Tuesday passed by 122 to 89, but this was exceptional.[113] In the other divisions there voted on 25 April 408 Members; on 2 June 336 and 346; on 3 June 238 and 310.

George Townshend, from the outset, claimed the enquiry would be 'dispassionate'; but attention focused on Pitt. Allegedly ill the previous week, he attended the enquiry from Monday 25th, when 'the great debate came on'. He too professed moderation; he had 'never said there was corruption or bribery but a weak administration of government'.[114] 'Pitt was gentle and civil to politeness', wrote Fox. 'Nobody has been corrupt, or ill-intentioned, during the period in which Minorca was lost. Affairs had not been wisely administered; "had been weakly administered during that period", was his roughest expression.'[115] This caution was amply justified by the crucial trial of strength over a procedural motion on 25 April, which went against him by 267 to 141. 'What is already done is a sufficient indication of what will follow', wrote an observer on 26th. 'People imagine it will be all over today: and then we may have an administration, such as may be firm and permanent.'[116] In the Commons that day, Pitt's caution lapsed:

Pitt, who did by no means intend, when he got up, to say anything like it; protested that if equality was not preserved (of which he judged and very wrongly) by admitting a question Mr Townshend had to propose; he should walk out of the House, others would do so too, he supposed, and leave it to the majority to conclude their enquiry with what questions they should think fit. But what good would it do them with the people? They (the people) would judge, they would be informed, he would take care they should be informed. Every time he spoke of going and leaving the majority to themselves, the Tories called out with the loudest applause. I said Pitt had not intended, could not intend to say what he had said on so trifling a question, I presumed never would considerately say it upon any.

Once Fox took him to task, Pitt 'answered calmly enough...distinguishing away, that is misrepeating what he had said';[117] 'recollecting how much more useful to him the majority might be than the world, he recomposed himself, and was content that the majority should be responsible for whatever defects the public might find in the judgement given by the House'.[118]

To a large extent, Pitt's bluff had been called; the threat of withdrawal from Parliament (and, by implication, his resignation) was one that he was ultimately unwilling to put into effect. On 27th, accordingly, the House of Lords, which was considering the Militia Bill, halved its proposed numbers to little more than 30,000, as the ministry's friends had feared.[119] One observer even expected that the Bill would be rejected outright the following week,[120] though in fact, on 2 May, the Lords as a whole agreed to most of the amendments made in Committee and allowed it to continue its course.[121] This was a major reverse for the Bill's supporters; but, apparently, Pitt made no difficulties and there was no outcry.

The proceedings of the enquiry occupied two weeks from Tuesday 19 April to Tuesday 3 May. A friend of Fox's explained their temper thus:

We are sometimes very cool and good humoured, sometimes fire and tow, then cool again. Sometimes the enquirers want to drop their enquiry as easily as they can, and sometimes seem to intend mischief. But all this is no wonder as they are guided by a man who has not the command of his own passions, or resolutions; whose ambition is boundless and his pride without measure, and is intoxicated with the adulation of his followers, and the applause of corporations, coffee houses, etc.[122]

Nevertheless, Pitt's intransigence had some effect in extracting advantage from the ministers' willingness to compromise. Although the Commons' resolutions as a whole unmistakably cleared Newcastle's ministry, the final motion vindicating its conduct in general terms was dropped, and the last of the ordinary motions to be debated was amended by the omission of a phrase declaring Byng's fleet sufficient for its mission: 'The withdrawing of Mr Pitt etc., it is thought, would be the certain consequence of this resolution, as it stood at first'.[123]

The final divisions were won by the ministry on 2 May (by 209 to 127 and 212 to 134) and 3rd (by 195 to 115 and 147 to 91).[124] Walpole commented severely on the drop in the ministerial majority, 'many absenting themselves, and many of the independent sort voting with the minority...You may judge what Pitt might have done, if he had pleased; when, though he starved his own cause, so slender an advantage was obtained against him'.[125] West, similarly, had repeated without questioning Lord Bateman's prediction 'that Mr Rigby and near 50 others will be against the vote of approbation'[126] – that is, fifty Whigs. Though that final vote was never taken, the numbers in several divisions are consistent with a large bloc of Whigs voting with the Tories. Yet it is remarkable how little the enquiry acted to highlight or accentuate Whig/Tory distinctions: thus Northey and Prowse spoke in support of Townshend on 25 April without arousing comment on their party origin.[127] The Militia Bill, too, was allowed to proceed unostentatiously: despite many major alterations, it was largely accepted when the Lords returned it to the Commons on 9 May. The result of the amendments had been to reduce the size of the new force by half, to distance it from popular control, and to allow it a temporary existence only. The militia, though permitted to come into being, was as little of a Patriot triumph as was the enquiry. But because of the ministry's weakness, the militia was not, in its later stages, treated as an issue divisive in a party sense. Because of the crucial importance of Whig divisions, the proceedings of the enquiry, too, were conducted in a spirit of neutral investigation and administrative critique, not of party rivalry; and because of the Tories' self-identification with Pitt, they lacked the incentive to emphasise an alternative identity. During the winter of 1756–7, it had been possible for Fox and his publicists to represent the opposition Whig–Tory alliance as having a *Tory*, not a *Whig*, connotation; but this accusation had exhausted its impetus and lapsed. Having been tried and found wanting was thus an added barrier to its being taken up again, by whichever side, as an accurate analysis. Instead, a different categorisation seemed inescapable to those who reflected on the current course of events. Newcastle, wrote one commentator,

holds the balance of party in his hands, and can throw weight into either scale to make it preponderate. Of the three parties now in England, any two will be too strong for the third. Two of those cannot join together, but either of the two are willing to join with your old friend.[128]

AFTER THE ENQUIRY: CONTACTS BETWEEN PITT AND NEWCASTLE, AND THE FAILURE OF ATTEMPTS AT COALITION, 21 APRIL–17 MAY 1757

Though the enquiry had not shut the doors on any possible combination, it had done nothing positive to promote any line of advance. In particular, Fox had not been distinguished from Newcastle's ministry and condemned separately. It was therefore possible to hope that Fox might form part of a Newcastle–Pitt alliance. John Campbell wrote, whether with any authority is unknown, to urge Newcastle to return to the Treasury with a reliable Chancellor of the Exchequer, naming Dupplin; Pitt could have a Secretaryship of State, if he would accept on reasonable terms; Fox, if given the Paymastership, would support measures in the Commons 'without being a Minister', 'not to avoid being responsible, but to avoid all appearance of what some are, and many more pretend to be, afraid of'. But his previous status would make it appropriate for him to attend the Cabinet: then, 'according to Mr Pitt's doctrine, he will be as responsible as if he was a minister'. If Pitt should refuse or the King refuse Pitt, a figure agreeable to Newcastle might have his Secretaryship, and a union of the Old Corps, rallying to George II, would carry on his business against 'Mr Pitt and the Common Council', despite a popular clamour which even the best ministers might nowadays provoke. 'Nobody could think such a settlement [presumably the first one] the ministry of the D[uke] of C[umberland]', concluded Campbell, 'and none but Mr Pitt's new friends the Tories could think it reasonable to exclude the ablest Parliament man in the House of Commons...and refuse his assistance in supporting the government, merely because he is honoured with H.R.H. favour'. Fox and Newcastle should therefore meet to discuss such matters face to face.[129] But it is not clear that they did so. Newcastle did however meet Devonshire, at the latter's instigation, some time between Charles Townshend's resignation and 25 April. Devonshire found Newcastle

though desirous of coming in yet afraid to undertake with Pitt and Leicester House against him. I endeavoured to persuade him that their opposition would not be dangerous if he would act with spirited resolution; our conversation ended with desiring him to form some plan and if I thought it practicable I would propose it to the King; after the first division of the enquiry [on 25 April] I talked again with Mr Fox who said that the numbers showed too plainly where people were looking to, and therefore he wished me to endeavour at a reconciliation of all sides.[130]

Fox received the impression that Devonshire positively desired a Pitt–Newcastle reconciliation in which he, Fox, would be Paymaster – 'indeed that would effectually secure parliamentary quiet, and therefore I told the Duke of Devonshire that I would most willingly subscribe to it. But though I can allow it to be desirable, I can hardly think it practicable'.[131]

One observer later wrote:

They who are devoted to the Duke, since and during the enquiry have been busy in propagating the notion that preference, the latter end of last year, was given to Pitt, on account of his engaging [that] the enquiry should not be managed with force and freedom.[132]

But, under the pressure of events, this truth did not work to inhibit any manoeuvres that necessity seemed to demand. Fox seems not to have made that objection. Contacts between Newcastle and Pitt's camp continued, but the evidence for them is fragmentary. On 21 April Lord Granby, currently a prominent speaker among Newcastle's followers in the Commons, was approached there by 'a friend'[133] with confidential news of

the disposition of Mr Pitt and his friends towards the Duke of Newcastle, without whom it was the opinion of Leicester House, and their own, that nothing could be done for the safety of the whole. That for their own parts, they were ready to support and assist his Grace, whether employed or not themselves, that Mr Pitt in particular would either serve, or not, as was most practicable in the present circumstances; and that as for Lord Temple, he declined being employed at all, nor would there be any difficulty with respect to the providing, or not, for the others. This Lord Granby was desired to convey one way or other to his Grace...

It is unlikely, however, that such a profession to support whether employed or not struck Newcastle as other than a formal courtesy. Granby added his own opinion: 'that nothing should or could be done even with these gentlemen, till they were brought to a clear and precise declaration how far they would go in support of his Majesty's interests upon the continent'.[134] But this was an outdated preoccupation. Newcastle, Hardwicke, Pitt, Bute and Fox negotiated throughout these months in a common awareness of the necessary priority of politics over policy; even assertions to the contrary can be located as outbursts of frustration at tactical failure. Aptly, therefore, George Stone, Primate of Ireland, by chance in London, stood forward as a mediator. Walpole suggests he and Lord George Sackville acted with a design to provoke Bedford to resign his Lord Lieutenancy of Ireland, or at least to safeguard the position of the Primate's party in the Dublin Commons, by contriving a Pitt–Newcastle reconciliation to exclude Fox.[135] The Primate's first meeting with Bute came just before 23 April, and his second probably on 25th. It seems likely that it was the Primate whom Sir Harry Erskine met on Bute's behalf to discover Newcastle's professed intention 'to throw himself entirely on Leicester House'. But many informal contacts were being made on the theme of a possible Pitt–Newcastle union; Bute rightly feared that Devonshire was negotiating behind his back; and it is not clear by whom Erskine was convinced that 'it is thought it will be impossible to persuade the public, and the Duke of Newcastle's acquired friends (acquired by power) that a union can be solid or durable if his Grace is not put into the Treasury; and the difficulty of fixing on another will make it expedient to fix on him'.[136] Nevertheless, this point was at once conceded, and Newcastle's tenure of the Treasury in the impending system was never in doubt. Nor was Pitt seemingly anxious at the outset that Legge take the second place at that Board. Dodington records an explanation corroborated by Glover though not by any other source: that Newcastle

chiefly treated with Mr Pitt by the Primate of Ireland, Stone; one day in the beginning of the negotiation, when Lord Bute and Mr Pitt were in conference with the Primate, and insisted upon very extravagant terms, he begged them as a friend, to be a little more moderate, and before they went so far, to consider if they were quite sure of *all* their friends. They were surprised, and said they thought so. He replied that he thought otherwise, and could, if he would (*for he was authorised to do it*)[137] tell them a very different story. Pitt insisted upon knowing it, or would treat no farther. Upon which he told them this private transaction of Legge's with the Duke of Newcastle. This occasioned great coldness to Legge at Leicester House; which, as soon as he perceived it, gave him great uneasiness.

As yet, however, Legge was not told that his allies were aware of his private overture.[138] When, late in June, he found out, he wrote:

I can't help wishing that at the same time when the Primate revealed by authority from the Duke of Newcastle the supposed influence his Grace had over me in consequence of this interview I had been made acquainted with it; because then I had been relieved from that point of honour to the Duke of

Newcastle which though not observed on his Grace's part prevented my relating the whole conversation next day to Mr Pitt or Lord Bute (as Mr Martin can witness) and showing the absurdity and iniquity of this imputation, as well as the little influence it ought to have had upon the Duke of Newcastle's terms.[139]

Bute's proposals, evidently conveyed by the Primate, are recorded in Newcastle's memorandum of 26 April:[140]

This proposal by Lord B[ute]. That the Duke of Newcastle should send by my lord B[ute] a compliment to the Prince of W[ales] upon His Royal Hss. displeasure with him, at what passed last summer. These [illegible] suggested by the Pr[imate] but neither agreed to. That the Duke of Newcastle should have an immediate interview with Lord B[ute] for that purpose. That the Duke of Newcastle should settle a constant correspondence, and comm[unication] with Lord B[ute]. That he should acquaint him, with what shall pass with regard to public affairs, for the information of the P[rince] of W[ales]. That the Duke of Newcastle shall assure Lord B[ute] of his friendship, and support for the continuance of his confidence with the P[rince] of W[ales]. That the P of W shall in return have a confidence, and friendship for the Duke of Newcastle.

What is remarkable is both the apparent irrelevance of the chronology of the enquiry to these initial overtures, and the non-appearance in them of Pitt. It may be that Bute was launching a private overture and that George Grenville shortly did the same via Egmont.[141] It seems more likely that Bute's overture was concerted with Pitt,[142] and that a reconciliation in the Royal Family both was the chief substantive point at issue and provided the formal terms in which a ministerial arrangement could be described to make it seem other than a contest for the spoils of office. The evidence is too fragmentary to be conclusive. Nevertheless, it is clear that Newcastle responded to Devonshire's invitation in the light of what he, Legge, Bute and George Grenville had said, by drawing up two schemes of ministry and by seeking through Stone to win Devonshire's support for his strategy. One of these schemes seems a precaution against the second possibility suggested by Campbell;[143] the other envisages Newcastle's return to the Treasury with Pitt a Secretary of State, and adjusts the other offices accordingly.[144] Stone was probably aware of such calculations when he met Devonshire on 30 April, and put to him a number of possible outcomes. Devonshire assured Stone

that he would use his utmost endeavours with the King to take in Mr Pitt; *and my lord Temple*, into some Cabinet Council place, if they would be reasonable; and also to bring about a good understanding with Leicester House, of which he saw the necessity. His Grace for that purpose advised, that I should gain my Lord Bute, and blamed himself for not having sufficiently attended to that. He directly proposed that I should *now* see his lordship and promised that he would tell the King, that it was his advice.[145]

This was, for Newcastle, the key: permission to negotiate directly had to be given from the King, or a source next to the throne, without

Newcastle explicitly asking for it. At once, he proceeded via the Primate to arrange meetings with Bute on 3 and 6 May.[146] Devonshire gave Stone the impression that a coalition would be possible; that Legge would prefer a peerage to being Chancellor of the Exchequer; and that the King would insist on Fox having 'some *ministerial office* (Paymaster)'. But Devonshire did not appear to be committed to a coalition in principle. If Leicester House were unreasonable, he urged that Newcastle come in without them. Stone emphasised that this was impossible. If Pitt would not come, Devonshire 'would be better able to carry it on'.[147] Newcastle also stressed, to Hardwicke, that if Pitt would not comply he, Newcastle, would not come in: 'For, though it is not proposed that Mr Fox should be Minister in any degree, a great number of his powerful friends will remain in the Cabinet Council, with one more powerful than any of them always at hand, after *his return to England*'. This danger ought to compel the adherence of Leicester House, 'except they should be determined (as they have sometimes been) to destroy their own interest'. But there were signs that they would not. If, therefore,

the King, Leicester House and Mr Pitt should come into *reasonable terms*, I think we shall be obliged to take our part, and return to our employments, having stipulated for such a number of our friends, as may not make us absolutely dependent on either party.

To avoid that dependence, Newcastle evidently saw that the structure of the ministerial system counted for more, now, than numbers in the Commons. He was willing to allow Winchelsea to remain at the Admiralty; the crucial element, as in the past, would be the team of Newcastle at the Treasury and Hardwicke as Lord Chancellor, and Newcastle laboured to persuade his closest ally to resume the Great Seal.[148] Much of the work, he argued, could be devolved on Mansfield, Newcastle himself would in future leave the 'ordinary business' of the Treasury to the Chancellor of the Exchequer.[149]

Newcastle therefore went to his meeting with Bute on 3 May in a mood of high confidence.[150] Devonshire, it seems, told Bute and Pitt nothing, or 'nothing worthy of much notice', of his interview with Stone.[151] But it is not clear that Bute learnt more of a specific nature from Newcastle. The only evidence for their meetings is a memorandum by Newcastle outlining what were presumably to be his opening remarks.[152] They contain the gestures of deference, duty and regard to the Prince of Wales which Bute had asked for,[153] but evidently no assurance of 'a constant correspondence and communication' or about offices. Rather, Newcastle repeated the standard assurance of his taking any or no office as would best contribute to the King's service. He had not, he was to assure Bute, received a royal invitation to form an administration since just before Temple's dismissal; but such a system, to be lasting, could only be based on a union in the Royal Family.

Newcastle was pleased with his two meetings with Bute on a purely personal level, 'and more particularly so, with what related to his court, as far as regarded myself'; but the difficulty was the terms, not the principle, of a union.[154]

Newcastle met Devonshire again, probably on 3 May.[155] Devonshire discovered Newcastle

had been talked to upon Mr Townshend's plan. He protested he had not negotiated with them,[156] did I think it desperate or would I give him leave to sound; I told him it would certainly [be] very difficult if not desperate but however he might I thought sound them and see upon what terms he could agree with them, and if they would be reasonable I would venture to sound the King upon the terms proposed, which as the enquiry is now over he is to do and I am to have an answer from him on Saturday [7 May]. This, Sir, is the situation of affairs at present, how it will end God knows. I am a little doubtful whether your R.H. will approve...my only aim is to [?break] the King out of the hands of Leicester House which if this plan takes place I should hope he would be secure of, and which must I fear unavoidably happen if the Duke of Newcastle and Mr Pitt join in opposition. Whereas [if] the Duke of Newcastle having this other trial of Pitt is unreasonable (which I think most probable) they will quarrel and his Grace will then either come in without him, or not join him in opposition, and consequently give strength to the administration the King shall then form[157]

– by implication, a heavily Foxite one. Plainly, Devonshire had not yet presented the King with a scheme from Newcastle;[158] but popular report, thought Fox, was that 'the Duke of Newcastle is to come in with me', and Granville told him that he would have the Paymaster-ship. Though 'waiting inactive', doing nothing to seize such a role, Fox plainly welcomed it, 'because, to do H.M.'s business as a minister in these times more power is necessary (and to be given in a distinctive manner too) than H.M. will ever give'.[159]

Pitt, for the moment, was of a similar opinion. Glover met him again 'in the two or three days after the 3rd of May', and warned him as before against a coalition with Newcastle. Pitt, he recorded,

Heard me with attention, showed much regard, and some acquiescence, seeming so at least, possibly, at the instant, real and sincere. At length he assured me, that no consideration should induce him to close with the measure, unless the Duke of Newcastle would pledge himself, and his whole party, in the hands of the Prince of Wales. Hence it was evident, that Leicester House was an additional pressure on Mr Pitt.[160]

It was probably shortly after this, and after Newcastle's two meetings with Bute, that Pitt (through the mediation of the Primate and Lord George Sackville) met Hardwicke.

Pitt insisted that Newcastle should not interfere in the House of Commons, nor with the province of Secretary of State; that is, with neither domestic nor foreign affairs, but should confine himself to the Treasury; yet there too Pitt pretended to place George Grenville as Chancellor of the Exchequer, with Potter and James Grenville. Legge, whom he meant to remove, having conceived insuperable aversion to him since harnessed with himself in the trammels of popularity, he named for the head of the Admiralty, with a peerage. For Lord Temple he demanded the Garter and some post in the Cabinet. The terms were lofty; yet considering his interest in the people, and his experience of Newcastle's engrossing chicanery, he was justifiable in endeavouring to clip the wings of so volatile a constitution.[161]

Plainly, these terms were absurdly high. Pitt cannot have intended to destroy all prospects of a union, and may have wished only to halt the negotiation in order to recapture the initiative from Bute. Waldegrave, however, interpreted things literally: Pitt, 'conscious of his strength, would not allow the Duke of Newcastle any real authority: and his Grace could not yet submit to be only a nominal minister'.[162] Newcastle's reaction was a foregone conclusion. By 7th, it was widely known that he 'has declared that he cannot engage to serve the King without Mr Pitt's assistance'. This came as a shock. His refusal amounted, implied Sandwich, to an attempt to storm the Closet; it justified everyone in rallying to a Fox ministry, which Bedford was urging Devonshire should be launched.[163] Devonshire was, meanwhile, informed by Newcastle of 'the behaviour of these gentlemen' via Andrew Stone.[164] Devonshire was gravely concerned; suggested that Newcastle resume his negotiations with Bute, but had to admit that there was nothing new to propose. Rather, Stone thought him more committed than before to Fox having the Pay Office (which, Stone predicted, Pitt would never agree to).

The Duke of Devonshire said a great deal (as your Grace will easily believe) to show the necessity of your undertaking the administration, without the assistance of these gentlemen, and upon the plan formerly proposed: that your Grace would have *carte blanche*; that Mr Fox would be something, or nothing, as you should think proper; that he, and every honest man, would support you; and much more to that effect. To all which I could only say, that I had not yet perceived, that your Grace had altered your opinion, as to the difficulties, that would attend your undertaking such a work.[165]

Devonshire was therefore willing to comply with Newcastle's request, to 'make a proper report to the K but not as if the negotiation was quite over',[166] but chose to defer it in case it prevented the negotiation being renewed. Fox, too, wrote to Devonshire of his expectation that it would be resumed, and hoped to hear of a Pitt–Newcastle reconciliation when he was to call on Devonshire on 10th; 'They little know, nor do I wish they should know, how heartily I desire their success.'[167] Devonshire had already arranged to meet Newcastle on 9th; meanwhile Stone was sent to ask Mansfield's advice on the situation,[168] and the Primate observed that Newcastle's 'time is necessarily and wisely employed in collecting the opinions of your friends'.[169] Chesterfield was the first to contribute: 'you must if you come in at all come in with a strength of your own that may curb the influence of the Duke of Cumberland and his party, and you can only have that strength by bringing the Prince and Princess of Wales along with you. Therefore it is my opinion that you must agree with them upon the best terms you can, but upon any rather than not agree'. Yet reasonable terms were in prospect; and Pitt's latest demands must and would be modified. The moral was: '*voyez venir* a little longer'.[170]

The Primate saw Pitt on 10th, Newcastle and probably also Bute on 11th,[171] and called again on Newcastle on 12th. Later that day he summarised his advice on paper. Newcastle, he suggested, could take one of four courses: first, 'To come in at the head of the administration which Mr Fox has been hitherto unsuccessfully endeavouring to form'. Second, 'To form an administration by yourself apparently exclusive of Mr Fox' and of Pitt. Third, 'To retire from public business absolutely and in reality'. Fourth, 'to form an administration upon any terms that may [be] found practicable with Mr Pitt etc'. The first had been explored and was now out of the question. The second might appear practicable 'by the acquiescence of one party, whose business it would not then be to oppose': but the system could not survive, for its structure would focus all discontent and popular clamour on Newcastle. The third course would have dishonourable consequences, for Newcastle would be blamed for the ensuing political chaos which he might have intervened to prevent. Only the fourth course was safe; and both Newcastle and Pitt declared they desired it. Thus far was platitude. The heart of George Stone's advice was his opinion of the terms, evidently formed during his meetings on 10th and 11th. The only significant difference, he claimed, was in the choice of Chancellor of the Exchequer: Pitt nominating George Grenville; Newcastle, Lord Dupplin. The Primate threw the whole weight of his advice behind the acceptance of Grenville. Newcastle had a right, 'uncontrolled', to choose that officer; but Pitt had a right, before the ministry was formed, to say 'upon what conditions, and in what circumstances' he would accept. Such an arrangement would leave the Pay Office divided between Dupplin and Potter, and release the latter from a re-election which he could scarcely afford; it would also offer an excuse to check the ambitions of any of Newcastle's followers. Grenville's superiority in business was obvious; and if 'it is the intention of these gentlemen to make your Grace uneasy in business, they will find means of doing it, whoever is Chancellor of the Exchequer'.[172]

The same day, Mansfield drew up a lengthy and reasoned memorandum of advice.[173] He too rejected Armagh's first course, to support the ministry which Fox 'has in some degree set on foot'. Newcastle thereby would have more nominal power than in any other system; but it would be eroded, for any attacks on him would increase his dependence on

Fox for the latter's services in the Commons. Moreover, most of the major offices held by MPs had gone to Fox's friends, both 'when he first acceded to the Duke of Newcastle' and latterly, so that an opposition would soon form round Leicester House out of frustration. Yet Mansfield also rejected the Primate's fourth option, for he had a very different idea of Pitt's terms. They were, he supposed, that Pitt should have a Secretaryship of State; 'the disposal of the Admiralty' now and presumably in the future; and the reinstatement of his dismissed followers. Together, these would make Newcastle Pitt's dependant. The first must be agreed to. But Temple would probably not take the Admiralty: that would go to another friend of Pitt's, and Temple would take some other Cabinet place. Pitt's followers would fill the Admiralty Board, and draw from that a claim to further promotion. Many of Pitt's party would have have to be restored, and good prospects offered to the others; this would disappoint Newcastle's followers and might lead them to advance their careers by an attachment to Leicester House.

Mansfield's task was therefore to envisage a Newcastle–Pitt–Fox union which would in fact be dominated by Newcastle. This was ultimately feasible because neither Fox nor Pitt could form a ministry alone, or unite to do so with each other. 'I think it very likely that considering what may be expected in a future reign, and the difficulties of the present times, Mr Fox may before it is very long think of a profitable retreat with peerage, etc.' Evidently Mansfield was unaware of Fox's current desire to do so; it would have been difficult to distinguish what Fox was currently saying from similar professions used to disguise his ambition over the previous few years, and his sincerity is not now, and was not then, a profitable speculation. Pitt behaved as if Fox's ambition were still real, and events were soon to prove his willingness still to take power if it could be won. The reality of Fox's potential power, too, was Newcastle's security in a three-cornered contest. Not only was it a counterweight to Pitt, but it gave point to the party composition of Pitt's following in a way which Newcastle's rivalry did not. The following on which Pitt could rely, Mansfield saw, was small; 'if he admits the Tories into office, he will lose himself entirely with the Whigs: if he excludes them, they will cool very fast towards him, particularly when they consider him acting as a minister; and when they can no longer either oppose or enquire with him'.

I do not suppose that the friends of this Royal Family would let his Majesty be prevailed on in the present circumstances to call a new Parliament, which to answer the views of those who would advise that measure must consist of Tories (*sic*).

Nor was Pitt 'of capacity, and of temper' to preserve his popularity in the vicissitudes of wartime politics.

Newcastle should therefore draw up and submit to George II a definitive system, 'a scheme of general conciliation'; if it met difficulties, he should explain it to his friends at a meeting and retire to the country. Its terms should be: (i) 'The Treasury to be entirely for himself and those he pleases to nominate'. (ii) 'For Mr Pitt the Secretary of State's office with a full and cordial participation of councils'. (iii) 'An office in the Cabinet for Lord Temple'. (iv) 'The Admiralty in the hands of some man of distinguished merit in office (suppose Lord Halifax) who though attached to his Grace, will not appear in the world to owe his preferment merely to that attachment. The inferior Lords to be divided between the friends of both'. (v) 'An office of some dignity and profit for Mr Fox'. (vi) 'The First Lord of Trade or whatever office is vacated by the new First Lord of the Admiralty to a friend of Mr Pitt's'. (vii) 'The defalcation of inferior places to be made chiefly among Mr Fox's friends – this seems unavoidable, but need not be discussed till the other points are previously settled'.

Self interest and altruism both pointed to this scheme; yet miscalculation of the first, and lack of the second, made it probable that it would be rejected. In that case, Mansfield could only outline the advantages which would arise from Newcastle's having proposed it. The odium for the political consequences would fall on others, and Newcastle's friends be bound closer to him by his refusal to give them up. If a Fox ministry survived, Newcastle could give it enough covert support to prevent a halt to public business, and draw credit from the inevitably increasing antagonism between Cumberland's camp and the Prince of Wales's. If, on the other hand, George II were to recall Pitt, he would be in a more precarious position than during the winter, because of 'the expectation of his joining the Duke of Newcastle, as soon as the enquiry was over, and as circumstances [that] made that junction practicable kept the House of Commons in suspense, and alone maintained him in that short administration'.

In either case Newcastle held the balance. Pitt could destroy a ministry; only Newcastle could create one. 'The public exigence of affairs is such, that the different parties in the state must sooner or later be reconciled...In the present factions (as in a state of war) he that holds out longest will have the advantage in the terms of peace.' The problem was to preserve Newcastle's honour, and therefore his ability to offer coherence and leadership to his following.[174] That problem was pressing and immediate, for the expectation of a union of the two courts, or a 'general coalition' of Newcastle, Pitt and Fox, was widespread.[175] 'Things remain just as unsettled as the day Lord Temple was turned out', wrote Calcraft, 'but this next week must 'tis thought determine them'.[176] Moreover, on 6 May the Duke of Grafton died; Devonshire, at Court on Monday 9th, was unexpectedly offered the vacated place of Lord Chamberlain, George II telling him 'that since he could not be prevailed upon to keep his present employment, he hoped always to have him near his person'.[177] He accepted. Though for the present he retained the Treasury also, his imminent departure from it was now certain.

Devonshire met Newcastle on 9th and Fox on the morning of the 10th; the Primate saw Pitt the same day and Newcastle the following morning, 11th; apparently Armagh succeeded in meeting Bute that afternoon, and reported back to Newcastle on the morning of 12th. Newcastle then saw Devonshire at 8 p.m. on 13th and Hardwicke at 9 p.m.[178] What passed in these meetings, beyond what is suggested by Armagh's letter to Newcastle of 12 May, is unknown. Devonshire was of opinion on 13th that Newcastle and Pitt would not agree in their negotiation: Newcastle 'will not hazard himself, unless he can either get Pitt or Leicester House; and they, I am afraid, are not to be separated; if they should agree, and even to the satisfaction of Mr Fox, the terms will be such as I much question whether the King will be brought to comply with'.[179] This opinion was evidently based on the view of Pitt's terms part of which Waldegrave outlined to Rigby on 10 May: a majority of Pitt's own friends at the Treasury Board, including George Grenville as Chancellor of the Exchequer, Potter, and James Grenville.[180] Andrew Stone however thought the demand of the Exchequer 'rather a proof of their thinking themselves in a situation to make what demands they please, than of their not having a real design to conclude'. Nevertheless, he too stressed that a settlement must soon be reached before the outcome of the campaign in Germany dramatically strengthened or weakened the position of Fox and Cumberland.[181]

Suddenly, there was a prospect that Pitt's terms had been significantly moderated. Newcastle thought that in that case, Devonshire and the King would be compliant. Lord Granby had seen George Grenville, probably on 13th or 14th, and discovered that 'he talked only of one difficulty viz. the *Admiralty*, and said not one word of the Chancellor of the Exchequer, which makes Lord Granby, and me, hope they will give it up'. Granby was to see George Grenville again;[182] meanwhile, Newcastle drew up a scheme of ministry consistent with the new prospect.[183] Granby's second interview went well, and Newcastle drew up a memorandum briefing him for a meeting with Pitt.[184] He came, he was to say, as a common friend. Grenville's yielding offered a prospect of a union; but 'Mr G[eorge] G[renville] not being acquainted with the precise terms, which Mr P. would expect for his friends', he came with Newcastle's approval to discover the terms on which an administration might be launched. Pitt was to be told, in confidence, 'that the Duke of Newcastle has received the King's orders to lay before him a plan of administration'; and a scheme for a Pitt–Fox union on reasonable terms, Newcastle suggested, stood a good chance of being accepted. But there was a note of urgency. Pitt 'must be sensible, that, from a change of circumstances, a thing may have been practicable yesterday, that may not possibly be found practicable today, and may be practicable today, and will not be so tomorrow'. Granby's proposed interview probably took place on 17 May. The result was failure. Fox thought Pitt reiterated the terms which Waldegrave had summarised to Rigby on 10th.[185] On 18th

it was published that Mr Pitt's terms were so extravagant that the Duke of Newcastle could not comply with them – and would take the whole himself – perhaps leave some little trifle for Mr Fox...Pitt's demands were, that his Grace should not meddle in the House of Commons, nor in the province of Secretary of State, but stick to the Treasury, and even there to be controlled by a majority of Mr Pitt's friends.[186]

George Grenville, wrote Walpole, 'finding that the coalition was impeded by what was demanded for him, desired to waive the Exchequer. But Pitt, not apt to bend to difficulties, replied to this concession, that it became Mr Grenville to make it, but he himself should not relax'.[187] The uncertainty of the chronology of Pitt's refusal makes it impossible specifically to explain, for it is unclear how it relates to the parliamentary contest occasioned by the King's request for additional supply. Two Addresses were moved in reply. In the Lords, Waldegrave moved for a grant of £1,000,000; Temple argued to reduce it to £300,000 and limit it to 'English purposes', but did not risk a division. Pitt had already sought to add such a condition in the Commons' motion; Devonshire had refused, and asked Newcastle to 'collect your forces'.[188] It seems likely that this impending clash is what the Primate meant in writing to Bute that 'the confusion which he has so much dreaded is just breaking out and now scarcely avoidable'.[189]

NEWCASTLE'S ALTERNATIVE SCHEME (LEE–EGMONT–HALIFAX): 17 MAY–7 JUNE 1757

The prospect was used by Newcastle to good effect, speaking to his friends at large and briefing Egmont, Hume Campbell, Sir George Lee and Sir Thomas Robinson at a preliminary meeting.[190] It was these of his friends and Lincoln, as Fox supposed, who killed an inclination in Newcastle to yield to Pitt's terms. On 18 May, the day of the debate, Newcastle's resulting alternative scheme was made public: 'to make Sir George Lee Chancellor of [the] Exchequer, Lord Egmont or Lord Halifax Secretary of State and the other First Lord of Trade – Dupplin Treasurer of the Chambers and that I should be Paymaster and Dodington Treasurer of the Navy. This would certainly have made him strong enough in the House of Commons', claimed Fox, 'and a man must be as timid as the Duke of Newcastle not to venture on such

ground'.[191] Newcastle's intentions can be reconstructed from four surviving memoranda. They outline his conduct if he were commanded to
undertake the ministry, and to prepare a plan for that purpose. Pitt's
terms, the King was to be told, were excessive; yet if Newcastle were
to come in, it was 'his humble opinion, that, as far as is practicable,
it will be highly necessary to proceed upon the principle, which induced
him to wish that those gentlemen might return to the King's service'.
A reasonable scheme should be drawn up to remove just ground of
complaint at Leicester House and make possible their future return:
Fox should have no share, and the Commons be known to be in the
charge of a Secretary of State and a Chancellor of the Exchequer
there. George III was to insist that all Cabinet Ministers support such
a ministry; but if Newcastle tried such a plan and found it 'impracticable to carry on the King's affairs with success', he must be allowed
to resign. Yet it is doubtful whether the plans Newcastle drew up
would have met these criteria. The only grounds for the support of
Leicester House seem to be the incorporation of Lee and Egmont, and
the retention of Winchelsea as First Lord of the Admiralty. These are
unlikely to have sufficed,[192] and the many alternatives in Newcastle's
lists suggest both the difficulty of accommodating important figures of
the second rank once stop-gap candidates had been given high office,
and the basic inconsequentiality of those rearrangements in a system
which failed to include Pitt and his allies. But this was not then apparent; one aspirant went so far as to apply for Bute's interest to
succeed Sir George Lee in the Princess's household if he should take
the Exchequer.[193]

Negotiations, meanwhile, were barely kept alive. The Primate probably saw Bute on 18 May;[194] Devonshire saw Fox and Newcastle
separately on 19th, and later that day a meeting of Newcastle, Hardwicke, and Pitt took place at the Pay Office.[195] 'Pitt etc. frightened at
the prospect of their situation', wrote Fox, 'have proposed more moderate terms'[196] – a prospect he evidently found alarming.[197] Newcastle,
too, thought *those gentlemen* begin to be more reasonable, both as to
things and persons',[198] but what this moderation entailed is not certain.
Fox supposed himself still to be destined for Paymaster in the new
scheme,[199] but Newcastle was evidently referring to his meeting on
19th when he wrote 'I had pressed them to say, what terms they would
insist upon; and they, like brokers in the Alley, would not name any,
that they might have a chance for getting *more*'.[200] It may therefore
be Newcastle's own scheme, not the record of an arrangement with
Pitt, which is represented by two undated lists.[201] In Newcastle's
scheme, he took the Treasury with Dupplin at the Exchequer and
Nugent, Potter and James Grenville at the Board; Pitt, a Secretaryship
of State; Temple, the Privy Seal; Halifax, the Admiralty; Legge, the
Board of Trade, plus a peerage; George Grenville, the Paymastership.[202]

Fox presumably therefore was under this misapprehension when the debate on the Vote of Credit came on. The House resolved itself into a Committee of Supply on 18 May; on 19th it received the Report from that Committee, when

Pitt dropped several artful sentences, hostile to those that had been or might be ministers, convertible into excuses for himself, if he should again become a minister. He said, he should not oppose the gross sum upon any foot but on the gift being offered without an iota of restriction: that indeed he had predicted his own fate when he acted on the restrictive plan; that he would support who-ever had contributed to set this government going again: that everybody was free to speak his sentiments on this measure, for no man could tell who would be Minister, who would be trusted with this million: that if it was to be confined to Great Britain and America, he would consent to give a million...The King of Prussia with 170,000 men was worth giving one or two hundred thousand pounds to – but don't let a *conciliabulum* of ministers, when they happen to dine together, settle another subsidiary plan, at once minute and extravagant. Were he Minister, he would have deprecated this measure, nay, would have said more against it, than he would say in the House of Commons. He added some hints on his own popularity, and on the independence of the country gentlemen who favoured him. Fox took up some of Pitt's expressions: if a *conciliabulum* might not decide our measures, he hoped at least *one* man should not dictate them. With regard to independence, he supposed every man there was independent – but who were those particularly applauded for their indepen-dence? Were they those, who, two years ago, lay under the irremissible crime of being Tories? or, who this year had the unknown merit of being so?[203]

Plainly, Pitt had sought to preserve a Patriot stance and to avoid re-jecting a continental involvement which had become inevitable. Egmont and Sir George Lee spoke against him, 'both declaring without reserve, that this nation ought to engage on the Continent in operations of the utmost extent'.[204] Gilbert Elliot recognised the source of his friends' difficulties in making terms, 'after the discoveries that have been made: a continent war in its full extent, and further sums for Germany, not-withstanding former stipulations are already avowed'.[205] Glover records that, on 19th,

After the House was up I joined several of Pitt's friends; and having been informed, that all treaty with the Duke of Newcastle had been broken off two or three days before, I gave them my congratulations on the event, and received this reply from Mr George Grenville. 'Have you not observed from what passed today, what rotten ground we must have stood upon? You see, that no coalition could take place without our plunging into every Hanoverian measure'.[206]

Thus Pitt had checked the independent moves of Bute and George Grenville from within his own camp to compromise, while leaving open, from Newcastle's viewpoint, the possibility of a union. But he had done so at the cost of making it far more difficult for himself to take up the option which he had preserved intact. Fox, who was well informed about the Pitt–Newcastle negotiations of 17–20 May, appreciated this. Thus while even his close relatives increasingly thought Fox wished only for the Pay Office,[207] his ambition was re-awakened. If Newcastle's latest compromise terms were rejected, 'I fear I must take a ministry against which Leicester House and Newcastle House will be already joined'.[208]

Newcastle's task was now merely to persuade the King that he had tried and failed to secure an agreement on reasonable terms. To that end he sent Stone, with a copy of his scheme, to see Devonshire. Devonshire could report nothing about the King's disposition, who was preoccupied with foreign affairs at his last audience, and Devonshire made few comments on the terms. His objections were twofold. The King, he thought, would insist on the Pay Office going to Fox rather than to Newcastle's candidate. As to the Admiralty, the alternative office[209] listed for Winchelsea was adequate compensation; but the King was happy with him in the Closet and would not be so with Halifax or Legge. Moreover, Winchelsea's tenure of the Admiralty had been successful, and he was therefore acceptable to the City. Devonshire then asked whether, 'if these gentlemen were growing moderate on any points', they might yield on the Admiralty. Stone evidently made no answer, merely relaying to Newcastle the question. Devonshire did not object to the other arrangements. 'He supposed, that there might be more difficulty, in making this arrangement now, than there would have been a fortnight (or a few days) ago; but did not represent it as impracticable; nor advise, in any way, against the attempting it'. But Devonshire pressed Newcastle to bring the matter to a conclusion quickly, obtaining a precise account of the demands of Leicester House and presenting the King with a plan based on them. Newcastle ought to see the King with such a plan not later than 25th or 26th.

The reason his Grace [Devonshire] alleged for pressing this point so earnestly, is remarkable. The King, he said, would naturally and very reasonably, be impatient; and that, if there should appear any backwardness, or unnecessary delay, on your Grace's part, that might not only (as it certainly would) give the King some uneasiness; but, considering the alteration of circumstances abroad, encourage some persons to undertake more, than they would have ventured to do some time ago.

Stone interpreted it as a reference to Fox. This was the first news Newcastle had that Fox's position in the Closet had been markedly improved by the Prussian victory at Prague on 6 May, news of which arrived on the morning of the debate on 19th. Devonshire, concluded Stone, would prepare the King to receive such a scheme, if he saw him before Newcastle; but it was not certain that Devonshire would mention 'any of the points upon which he apprehends the greatest difficulty' unless Newcastle asked him to.[210] Evidently Stone had acted as if his mission had been part of an attempt to secure the acceptance of an Egmont–Lee scheme, excluding Pitt; but this was not at all what Newcastle had intended. 'I am amazed', he reproved Stone,

you did not tell the Duke of Devonshire that I had tried all I could to get these gentlemen [on 19th] to specify their conditions, which G. Grenville absolutely refused to do [to Granby]. If you can find out by your brother, or any other way, a method of doing it, I am very ready to try it; but I look upon the thing as over. If the King is (as the Duke of Devonshire supposes) absolutely determined to keep my lord Winchelsea at the head of the Admiralty, and to make Mr Fox Paymaster, it is in vain to hope for a junction with these gentlemen. And indeed the resolution previously declared, to make Mr Fox Paymaster in all events,[211] destroys any plan that I could form. For it declares him *the Favourite*, and that will soon make him *the Minister*. And I do suppose the King thinks he may now make what Minister he pleases; and I am sure, I would not prevent him. My great point at present is, to see how I can get out of these disagreeable negotiations.[212]

The condition of accommodating Pitt had been that Newcastle should have the power to check Fox. Now, the balance of forces had shifted: only slightly, but enough to make that impossible. Newcastle was convinced that his closest allies were in favour of Fox having a position which would make a lasting settlement impossible.[213] Bedford and Devonshire could already be counted; now, Newcastle listed 'my lord Hardwicke thinking of nothing but himself, and *Lord Anson*, and Lord Mansfield of himself, and *Mr Fox*'. To Lincoln he wrote:

The unreasonableness, and arrogance of Mr Pitt, joined to the very wrong way of thinking of my best friends will fling everything into Mr Fox; and that at a time, when public events seem so favourable, that in all probability he will carry all before him, and have the merit of that success, which he has no pretension in the world to; and this comes from *despising him* too much, and what is more, those that are much above him. Could I have had the cheerful concurrence of my friends, I would have defied Mr Fox; and Mr Pitt should not have hurt me. But now, I shall be a dupe to *one*, and a sacrifice to *the other*. The King is elated with his success; he detests Mr Pitt (and he has reason to do so) and all that will protect him. He loves Mr Fox for having opposed Pitt: he will make him his Minister, I believe, he will be able to support him, especially if these preposterous events continue; you may as well talk of removing the Duke of Cumberland as my lord Winchelsea; or of preventing the Duke of Devonshire (who has it) from being Chamberlain, as Mr Fox from being Paymaster; and your lordship will see many of your, and my best friends support that measure...The negotiation with Pitt I give over. It is now too late to think of any other terms for Mr Fox than Paymaster; he, and *his*, possess the Closet. I have been *forced* to fling it away; I shall make a most ridiculous figure, for having done so. But however, that is over. I will make one bold push; I will see the King, lay before him the state of his affairs; he will either be angry with me, or laugh at me, and perhaps be glad to send for Mr Fox immediately; and all the King's best friends will rather have Mr Fox than no government, or perhaps than Mr Pitt.[214]

Newcastle was due to give his final answer to the King on 24th, but deferred his audience until, as Fox expected, Friday 27th.[215] The preceding week gave time for an interplay of evasion and ambition of great subtlety. Fox knew of a Pitt–Newcastle meeting and claimed that Leicester House were conscious of their own weakness: they would, he threatened Waldegrave, 'humour the Duke [of Newcastle], if they can vanquish the King. I think as well as hope that can't be, but they [i.e. Pitt] may work out these treaties (if the King don't put an end to them immediately) such difficulties and terms as may prevent his Grace's [Newcastle's] accepting'.[216] Newcastle had been debating whether 'to employ [Waldegrave] again with the King';[217] but Fox evidently sought to leave Waldegrave with the impression both that Newcastle's scheme was a Lee–Egmont one, for the total exclusion of Pitt, and that Newcastle himself was unlikely to accept even on those terms.[218] When Newcastle had his audience, wrote Fox, 'it is thought he will neither take it with Pitt etc. on the terms they will give him; nor take it without them, on any. If so, the worst for me that can happen, will [be], that I must be at the head of the House of Commons with all the force that can be mustered up against me'. But the possibility of Fox's quietly accepting the Paymastership in a Newcastle administration was now very remote.[219] Either Newcastle and Pitt would join in a system designed to destroy Cumberland's power and exclude him entirely, or Fox would have to undertake the administration himself. Accordingly, he elaborated excuses to cover such a step. To Devonshire he ingeniously urged the unusual danger of Pitt's return to power after *moderating* his terms:

I am extremely uneasy for what I hear is the language of Mr Pitt's friends, and must be the consequence of their coming in. 'They think it their duty to come in and they must not be nice about the terms when the object is so great, no less than to protect the succession and save the country from military government'. If then Mr Pitt comes now, my lord, it is on behalf of *Saville* House (as he calls it)[220] and to no other House will any man hereafter look. H.M. turns out Lord Temple and Mr Pitt. Had Mr Pitt come in again bringing with him a reconciliation between the *whole* Royal Family and as one of the *King's* ministers, acting in his proper sphere, and with his proper share in council and in power it had been well. But now, my lord, if he comes, not to the King, but to secure on one hand the Duke of Newcastle's future favour or safety with the Prince; and, on the other, to secure the Prince of Wales against what is scandalously suggested to him against the Duke. We shall be reproached, my lord, by the world, with giving up the King's honour, and by the Duke [of Cumberland] with giving up *his* most totally.

That is, that Newcastle would be the junior partner in a Newcastle–Pitt coalition, and (what he seemingly had no evidence for) that Pitt would bring it about by – paradoxically – lowering his terms. Yet those terms were only between Newcastle and Pitt: if those two men successfully arranged a deal, the previous relations of Pitt's ministers with the King would mean that Leicester House would storm the Closet, and that the leader of the Commons would in future be 'the Minister of Leicester House'. Nor could Fox's friends be expected to remain in ministerial posts. If Newcastle's scheme were to go forward, it should also include Fox, Winchelsea and Devonshire, especially in view of slights cast by Pitt on Devonshire during the debate on 18 May; but this could not happen. 'For God's sake then my dear lord', exhorted Fox,

prevent this plan from being carried into execution, at any rate and at all events...Prevent it, if you can, by making the Duke of Newcastle *cum suis* take it without them. He shall have every support, every guarantee he can desire. If that can't be, prevent it by making the King firmly reject it, forming a ministry, if necessary, without either the Duke of Newcastle or Pitt. Lastly, if there is no other way, prevent it even by keeping things as they are till the Duke can be thoroughly consulted upon it.

Fox was ready with alternatives:

If the King would form a ministry, though not just such a one as could be wished, I will forfeit my head, if in the course of the summer, the Duke of Newcastle does not come in to make it so, though he should at first resolve the contrary. The King of Prussia's victory and the low condition of Mr Pitt etc. here, make all junction with him and his but such as the King shall choose and dictate absolutely unnecessary. I am sure of it.[221]

Fox asked to meet Devonshire on the morning of 23 May; but there is no record of what took place, and it is not known what part Devonshire played in the manoeuvres which preceded his audience on 27th. All that is known is that he gave Fox a brief, illusory, glimpse of safety, telling him on the night of 24th that:

all treaty between Pitt and the Duke of Newcastle was at [an] end. If it should not be renewed, his Grace [Newcastle] goes to the King on Friday [27th] and will there I think consent to be Minister. If he won't I must. But I think his love of power will in spite of his prudent advisers make me Paymaster. I am, whichever of these things happen, much easier than I was, while the alternative was the King's submission to Leicester House, or my being Minister with the Duke of Newcastle joined with them against me.[222]

Meanwhile, Newcastle and Hardwicke remained in contact with Leicester House. Granby saw Pitt, probably on 24th, to put pressure on him over the point of Chancellor of the Exchequer. Newcastle, Granby suggested, was to give a final answer to George II on Friday 27th. This was offset almost at once by Temple's report to Pitt, from Nugent, that the King would insist on Fox as Paymaster.[223] Both Pitt and Newcastle must have seemed to themselves to be caught between irreconcilable conditions. Arranging to see first Hardwicke, then Bute, on the evening of 24th, Pitt wrote: 'I conceive the Duke of Newcastle finds the distress urgent and is playing his last resources.'[224] Newcastle did indeed suppose that Pitt's obduracy over the Exchequer had 'occasioned the delay, which may have ruined the whole' by allowing Fox's position to improve; but he was still concerned to investigate the possibility of 'reasonable conditions' or even a '*temporary* arrangement' with Pitt.[225] But, that evening, Hardwicke made no progress. The Secretaryship of State was conceded; but Pitt made demands[226] about the Admiralty which were likely to arouse the King's objection, and insisted on the Exchequer for George Grenville. Hardwicke objected: 'This is having the whole administration...Mr. P. admits it was having a good deal', and did not seem satisfied with the prospect even on the terms he demanded. Other offices were also in question – Attorney General and Secretary at War – and a place was to be found for George Townshend; but Pitt did not press these points. Hardwicke resisted even his first demand, and pointed out the danger: 'the King must have an administration. Mr Fox will undertake it. The King's old servants will be called upon to support it. The K. is not unpopular. That will operate. People will be very unwilling to leave the King *weak*.'[227] Possibly it was this warning which induced Pitt to ask for a conference, with Bute present, to discuss the point of the Exchequer.[228] Newcastle agreed, and it took place at Lord Royston's on the evening of the following day, 25 May. According to Hillsborough, Molly Pitt told Nedham that evening 'that Mr P. had been obliged by Leicester House to agree with the Duke of Newcastle upon terms he disapproved'.[229] But this is Walpole's version:

Pitt, the more he foresaw incompliance on the Duke's part, knew how much more grace he should wear (if forced to come to public explanation), by stipulating some advantages to his country, asked if they meant to send abroad any part of the new granted million, as Lord Granville and Fox had declared for doing. Newcastle said, he was not bound by their declarations – 'and you, Mr Pitt, you are not bound against sending any of it, are you?' Pitt replied he was; 'and you, my lord, though you are not *bound* to send any more money abroad, are not you inclined to it?' Newcastle would not explain. Lord Hardwicke proposed to waive this point *ad referendum*; knowing how easily they should settle the nation's concerns, if they could agree upon their own. They then passed to the article of Chancellor of the Exchequer. Pitt urged that he had had it before for one of his friends; Newcastle, that it would mark his having no power at the Treasury. Neither would yield. Even on the First Lord of the Admiralty, Newcastle haggled, pretending the King would not be brought to dismiss Lord Winchelsea...Pitt now found his error; by facilitating Newcastle's escape from the enquiries, he remained at the mercy of that Duke, not the Duke at his.[230]

Newcastle believed Pitt had made no single concession; 'rather more demands and recommendations'.[231] The following day, he drew up a list of them.[232] Pitt was to have a Secretaryship; Temple, an unspecified Cabinet place; the Admiralty Board was to be at Pitt's nomination, Legge with a peerage being First Lord; George Grenville, Chancellor of the Exchequer; James Grenville, a seat at the Treasury; Lord George

Sackville, Secretary at War; places for George Townshend and Sir Henry Erskine; Charles Townshend, Treasurer of the Navy; Pratt, Attorney General; Dr Hay, a seat in Parliament.[233] On Granby's copy of the list, Newcastle added:

N.B. Mr Pitt, at the last meeting [i.e. 25 May], declared, that, as his Majesty thought, his honour, and word, were concerned, in giving the Pay Office to Mr Fox; he (Mr Pitt) begged to be excused from saying anything upon it. At the same meeting, Mr Pitt receded from the proposal of Mr. George Grenville, to be Chancellor of the Exchequer.

When publicly known, it was obvious that the terms 'were undoubtedly sufficient to constitute Mr P. the M—r'.[234] Pitt's insistence on them therefore halted negotiations for the moment, though it was not apparent to Newcastle that they could not be continued. Evidently Granby was now briefed in order to spread Newcastle's account of Pitt's unreasonable behaviour. Waldegrave heard that Legge and the Townshends 'are endeavouring to persuade P. to be less unreasonable'.[235] But, on 26th, Newcastle saw George Townshend.[236] Glover wrote:

By his solemn protestations, that no difference had arisen between him and Pitt on the subject of public measures, but merely on the nomination of a Chancellor of the Exchequer, he misled Colonel Townshend and all the country gentlemen into a disapprobation, if not a dislike, of Mr Pitt. I plainly perceived in many of them, that this disgust proceded from some disappointment in the hopes they had conceived of obtaining employments by means of a coalition.[237]

Waldegrave told Fox, who believed him, that, after his meeting with Pitt, Newcastle 'seems still undetermined, but I think he will accept'.[238] Fox thought Newcastle 'if he were left to himself', would comply with Pitt's terms;[239] but probably overestimated Newcastle's susceptibility to pressure from his closest friends (Lincoln, Ashburnham) to submit to Leicester House.[240] Suddenly, as a result of the meeting on 25th, opinion shifted. Holdernesse thought all negotiation with Pitt at an end; that 'as for *Fox* the people in general of all ranks and denominations except a few of his creatures are so averse to him that it is impossible for him to undertake the management of affairs'; and that Newcastle would have to do so.[241] Devonshire told the proposed plan to Fox on the morning of Friday 27th, who shared Devonshire's approval.[242] Fox explained to Cumberland:

I really believe there is now no longer any danger of Mr Pitt and Lord Temple's appearing again upon the scene. There was so much a week ago that I thought it necessary to lay in my protest in the strongest manner against that, which had it been carried into execution must have been most injurious to HM's and YRH's honour, and under this most provoking circumstance, that such submission was so far from being necessary that the business of the House of Commons I can venture to say may be carried on with ease and security without them; with security, and in time with ease, without either the Duke of Newcastle, or [? train]. People are tired of having no administration, and will be the more easy under any. Reflection and the continued insolence of Pitt have already almost extinguished his popularity.[243]

Newcastle met Sir George Lee on 27th and told him 'that all was settled in general with the King, and he was to be Chancellor of the Exchequer', showing him the ministry list he was about to take to Kensington, and obtaining Lee's consent, as Dodington recorded, 'not without difficulty (and other large conditions, he might have added).'[244] Newcastle then carried into the Closet his plan of administration.[245] He admitted himself happy with his reception; the King 'was pleased most earnestly to command me to return to his service...But nothing is yet settled', and Newcastle asked for a few days' delay to consult his friends.[246] He met Sir George Lee after his audience and the latter left for the country believing he was to have the Exchequer.[247] Marlborough, however, received a different impression, telling Hillsborough 'that he understood the Duke of Newcastle had accepted'.[248] Walpole, too, wrongly records that Newcastle 'promised to be sole Minister',[249] and this version of the outcome quickly spread.[250] Devonshire similarly wrote to Cumberland that Newcastle

has in effect agreed to undertake the King's affairs though he has till Tuesday [31st] to give his final answer; and by what I can collect since both from the King and his Grace it is quite settled as to himself though not as to some particular arrangements. Sir G. Lee thought on for Chancellor of the Exchequer, Sir T. Robinson or Lord Egmont for Secretary of State. The latter declines without being made a peer. Mr Fox Paymaster but not to have anything to do with the management of the House of Commons but to give his assistance in supporting the King's measures there. Lord Hardwicke desires to take no employment at present as he will not suffer anybody to be removed or pensioned on his account. If [at] any time President [of the Council] or Privy Seal should be vacant very willing to accept either of them. Insists on some good post for Lord Anson.[251]

Devonshire similarly informed Fox that though Newcastle

did not absolutely accept, he only desired a day or two to consult his friends, yet in effect you may look upon it as determined. I was in the Closet after him and his Majesty confirmed it and bid me tell you that you were to be Paymaster and to support in the House of Commons, but was to be understood not to have the management or to be answerable for it. I told him that I thought it was the light in which you expected it should be and that I was sure you would do everything that was in your power for his service and ease. There passed civilities in the House of Lords between his Grace and the Duke of Bedford and I believe to their mutual satisfaction, which caused some speculation in the opposite party. Lord Temple and Lord G[eorge] S[ackville] were upon the steps of the Throne [in the Lords] with not the most pleasant countenances I ever saw.[252]

On 27 May, Parliament was adjourned until 6 June; Newcastle left for Claremont for a week, and set about sounding his friends. At once he ran into difficulties. Walpole supposed Newcastle faced the prospect of his ministry with naive optimism; in fact, Newcastle's precautions echo Walpole's own pessimism about the results of undertaking on the current plan:

I think the month of October will terminate the fortune of the House of Pelham forever – his supporters are ridiculous; his followers will every day desert to one or other of the two Princes of the Blood, who head the other factions. Two parts in three of the Cabinet, at least half, are attached to Mr Fox; there the Duke will be overborne; in Parliament will be deserted.[253]

Newcastle carefully related small indications of loyalty to the balance of power within the Cabinet. 'The events that have happened since I saw the King', he noted, 'hinder me from making any plan of administration.' Instead, his mind turned to lesser expedients. Halifax was to win the unattached support of Lord Talbot and Sir Francis Dashwood, and Newcastle thought of proposing to Halifax a temporary system, 'by filling up the Treasury only with Mr Oswald, and leaving all the other offices vacant. Or to appoint Sir T. Robinson Secretary of State for the present, without any alteration, or to appoint Lord Halifax Third Secretary for the Indies.'[254] Whether this was feasible is not clear, for another source reported Halifax 'outrageously angry'.[255] The 'events' which had led Newcastle to cool so quickly were set out in a letter to Devonshire. Bedford had been approached, but his ambiguous answer 'did not show much desire' for Newcastle's return. Hardwicke, whom Newcastle saw on the night of 27th, insisted on Anson as Treasurer of the Navy: 'that will create *me* great difficulties, both in the *City*, and *elsewhere*; and I have some reason to think, may renew the enquiry next session, and will necessarily much embarrass at present, our other arrangements'. Then, the King had said something about Lee which gave Newcastle 'very serious reflections'; yet there was no-one else who could take it, and Newcastle had obviously hidden his doubts from Sir George. Nugent was creating problems; and 'I am afraid some of your friends have been *tampering* with Hume Campbell...the most material man we have.'[256] What Newcastle did not disclose to Devonshire was that he thought the latter to be part of 'Mr Fox's supposed intrigue with Lord Egmont, Lord Register and Sir George Lee'.[257] But Newcastle revealed that he would see Hume Campbell and Robinson and asked Devonshire to lay those difficulties before the King.[258] Waldegrave too was approached to persuade George II that Newcastle's excuses were valid, and invited to Claremont on 29 or 30 May: a day before Devonshire was due there,[259] expecting everything to be settled. At large, these problems not being known, the difficulties were thought to be ones which had in fact been solved: Egmont's insistence on a peerage, and Halifax's on the status of Secretary of State.[260] But Devonshire did not share these misconceptions: he, at least, was still committed to Newcastle's system. He agreed to lay the difficulties before the King, but urged that Newcastle had mistaken Bedford, who, to Devonshire, had said 'that for his part he should quite forget any difference that had been formerly between you...'[261] The difficulties among Newcastle's friends, Devonshire told Fox, 'are such as I make no manner of doubt but that he will get over and are entirely relative to his own particular connections'.[262] Fox agreed. Evidently, he knew nothing of the 'intrigue' in which Newcastle suspected him to have suborned Egmont, Hume Campbell and Sir George Lee. Fox was aware that Rigby had asked Bedford's intentions, 'and his answer was – "That he should support the King's measures in whosoever hands his Majesty placed them; and with respect to his Grace [Newcastle], if he carried them on in such a manner that he could approve, he desired all personal animosities might be forgot".'[263] Bedford, Fox thought, 'if not provoked by ill usage, will do as the King would have him. What I mean by ill-usage, is, the Duke of Newcastle's interfering in Irish matters, which Bedford will always suspect to be at the instigation of the Primate, of whom he has now as bad an opinion as your Grace has long known he merited.' Egmont's refusal of the Secretaryship, Fox correctly saw, could not damage Newcastle's system. Exultantly, he wrote to encourage Devonshire before his interview at Claremont on 31st:

H.M. has put my business in the light I wished; I cannot fail in the execution of it; and (if there is not the most shameful want of spirit in others) the pride of Pitt and Temple and G. Sackville is fallen not to rise again in this reign.[264]

To Ellis, he explained the impossibility of an exclusively Foxite ministry: Halifax, Dupplin and 'everybody' had behaved so as to prevent an offer being made: 'But still we turned them out, and I offered myself fairly, and then the King was afraid, and it has ended in a manner undoubtedly better for himself and me, perhaps not better for the nation.' But Fox had not, he claimed, manoeuvred to bring this about, the Paymastership in a Newcastle ministry:

My endeavours, ever since you fetched me from Bath, have been to make it impossible for Pitt to be the tyrant he intended to be, and to prevent his *striding o'er this narrow world like a Colossus*. In which proud design, I verily think, but for me he had succeeded...We are under the direction of the House of Lords 'tis true. I got rid of the Duke of Newcastle that we might not be so; Pitt proved a worse tyrant, and if we could not change him for the best system, we have narrowly escaped being subjected for this and the next reign too, to a governor arbitrary, insolent, contemptible, he deserves in my opinion all these epithets. And surely, Ellis, to have routed him is something, *si non detur ultra*.[265]

And, on the assumption that Pitt *had* been routed, Fox wrote to Waldegrave to insist that (as Devonshire tentatively suggested) he receive the Paymastership at once, from the King's hands and without Newcastle's intervention: 'I will not assist his Grace as 3rd or 4th man in the House of Commons, by any arrangement of his Grace's. It must be by the King's order, and out of obedience to H.M.' Fox proposed an audience on 1 June to make this demand; meanwhile, he refused to meet Newcastle, and Waldegrave was to exert pressure on him to convince him of Fox's fixity of purpose.[266]

Fox's friends shared his euphoria. Calcraft reported Hardwicke talking of Newcastle's firm acceptance 'in great glee', being reportedly destined for the Privy Seal, and added:

The politicians at the Turk's Head and other *Pitt* coffee houses, are vastly down at the Duke of Newcastle's having accepted, and Pitt left out – You are aiming and lye by for a good opportunity to slip in, is their language.[267]

Pitt too was told via the Primate, in general by letter and in detail via Lord George Sackville and Bute, that Newcastle 'has virtually, though not actually, accepted'.[268] Pitt's friends were of the same opinion. Lord Talbot, Dashwood, Legge, George and Charles Townshend, George Grenville, Samuel Martin and Glover dined together at Dashwood's on 27 May[269] and Legge's on 3 June. By the second meeting 'it was universally understood, that every hope of a coalition was utterly annihilated, to the visible mortification', claimed Glover, 'of most in company' – with whom he disagreed, urging 'my entire disapprobation of Pitt's conduct; first, in negotiating at all; lastly, in resting the coalition on a mere personal point', so allowing Newcastle to erode Pitt's Tory following.[270]

It is not clear that Newcastle ever realised this to be possible, and the tactical prospects from his viewpoint were far less promising than the euphoria and despair of Fox's camp or Pitt's might suggest. Hardwicke explained the situation to Charles Yorke on 28 May. The latter wrote of the negotiations:

I doubt much, whether there was a real meaning to agree, unless on the condition of submitting absolutely to P— as the sole minister; and that, *ante diem*. As to the Duke of Newcastle, who has more than once thrown away a very good game, and is endeavouring too late to retrieve it, I think his present ideas are not very promising nor in execution will last. But I suppose, he means by renewing his access to the King, to prepare and strengthen his favour in the Closet, especially *absente Duce Cumbrio*; and to make use of the summer to work at Leicester House, and to see if P. may not be rendered more tractable, before the next session.[271]

Newcastle's calculations, however, seem for the moment to have been short-term. His attention was still focused on negotiations with his friends, in which he enlisted the offices of Devonshire.[272] Halifax, too, agreed to intervene with Talbot, though with little hope of success. Nevertheless, he professed to take a more optimistic view than Newcastle of 'the difficulties brought upon you by false, designing, self-interested friends' after they had first encouraged Newcastle to undertake the ministry. Egmont could be relied on: he had 'no resource, no retreat to Leicester House', and his health prevented him from becoming either a 'dangerous enemy' or an 'efficient friend'. His object was an English peerage, which could soonest be obtained via Newcastle. 'I should think too', added Halifax, 'that the notion of joining Fox must sit very awkwardly upon his lordship's mind, if he remembers his popular harangues against him some time ago as a supporter of, and advocate for military power. But it is now so much the fashion for people to forget one day, what they have said another, that my last observation may scarce deserve notice...' Then, Sir George Lee was in the same position vis-à-vis Leicester House; 'and...I can hardly suppose he flatters himself with hopes of anything from Fox so good as what is offered by you'. But there was another possibility: 'there may however be a cabal formed, and how far that may carry some men even from their own particular interests I will not pretend to say'. Yet if it affected Lee, might not Granby take the Exchequer temporarily? 'It might likewise be the means of bringing in Talbot, Dashwood, the two Townshends and other of his friends'; but Hume Campbell's loyalty would have to be purchased once again.[273] Newcastle did indeed make efforts to secure the loyalty of Granby and of his father the Duke of Rutland, with some indications of success; though the matter of the Exchequer was not evidently raised.[274] On 30 May, Newcastle drew up a list of 'Speakers – Efficient men' in the Commons, assigned to himself, Fox and Pitt; the numbers were decidedly in his favour, 39, 16 and 23 respectively.[275] Evidently, however, it did not persuade him that an unqualified bid for sole power was possible. Newcastle had spoken at length to Hume Campbell on 28th. Their conversation powerfully reinforced what Newcastle already suspected: that Hume Campbell, Sir George Lee and Egmont, especially the first two, 'were not so forward in undertaking the business of the House of Commons, and acting independently of Mr Fox, as their former discourses [as on 20 and 28 May], and declarations had given me reason to expect'.[276] Newcastle claims to have written to Devonshire on 28th, who showed the letter[277] to George II; that Newcastle's difficulties impressed the King, who was persuaded 'to give me what satisfaction he can, upon the subject of Mr Fox'. Thus released from what had seemed a strict condition, Newcastle was persuaded by Rockingham, Coventry and others that the solution was Fox's exclusion, certainly from the Paymastership.

I have also heard by my Lord Granby, from some of Mr Pitt's friends, who are displeased with his unreasonable demands, and I find, that if Mr Fox comes in to be Paymaster, they will all unite with Mr Pitt in a most strong opposition; but if Mr Fox has nothing they seem disposed even to oppose Mr Pitt, if he should enter into general opposition.[278]

When Devonshire arived at Claremont on 31st, Newcastle had ready for him a temporary scheme by which, as he explained, 'we avoid doing anything for Fox at present, and leave things open...all other schemes are liable to immediate danger. This as least postpones, and gives room for events.'[279] A 'perfect system', he argued, was, for the moment, unattainable; and Newcastle would not undertake on that basis. Instead, he suggested that public business should be carried on by filling up the 'efficient offices' only. He was ready to take the Treasury, if Devonshire insisted on leaving it, bringing only Oswald to the Board and leaving the Chancellorship of the Exchequer vacant; Sir Thomas Robinson would take the vacant Secretaryship of State, Halifax's office be raised to that status, and no other vacancy filled.[280] Such a scheme, Newcastle expected, would give time to see whether any of Pitt's friends would come in, whether a lesser office could be found for Fox, whether Newcastle's friends could be persuaded to accept Fox as Paymaster, or 'whether, in case all this fails, it may not be more practicable for me to go out then, than stay out now'.[281] Devonshire later wrote: 'I told him I did not approve of his scheme, that while things were left open it gave room for Cabal and that he would create greater difficulties to himself every day'.[282]

At once, Hardwicke replied to warn Newcastle against undertaking on 'an incomplete broken plan'.[283] Then, he wrote at greater length and with greater deliberation. The basic difficulty, he claimed, was still to find men other than Pitt or Fox to carry on Commons business, Egmont having been out of the question 'for some time'. Hardwicke understood from Newcastle on 27 May that Sir George Lee and Hume Campbell had been 'more sanguine' on that issue, though Hardwicke had doubted whether they would be sufficient against 'Mr Pitt an open enemy, and Mr Fox not a satisfied, and consequently not a zealous, friend'. But now, evidently, they were willing to conduct business there without Fox; and the terms of Newcastle's compromise scheme did nothing to fill up that 'great void'. It promised only instability and intrigues, and should not be ventured upon; filling up the Secretaryship of State would actually provoke Pitt's hostility. 'I always thought that it would become necessary either to make up with Mr Pitt or Mr Fox': if the first refused and the second alternative were not feasible, it would be better for things to remain as they were with Devonshire in the Treasury. But Newcastle would certainly not, as he had suggested, find it easier to leave office in five months than refuse it now.[284]

Yet the option was still left with Newcastle. Devonshire had an audience on 1 June at which he delivered Newcastle's plan and explained his scheme. The King expected to see Newcastle, and bring the plan to a conclusion, on 3rd. George II preferred as many places as possible to be filled up, but left their number and occupants to Newcastle with the exception only of the Pay Office, which he had promised to Fox. Plainly, the King was anxious for Newcastle's return; Devonshire encouraged this, stressing Newcastle's willingness to do so and that he was hindered only by the actions of his friends.[285] Another such hindrance had already been advanced by Fox, who – evidently before Devonshire's audience – wrote to report Waldegrave's support in his insistence on being Paymaster before Parliament rose for the summer; if that were done, Waldegrave 'thinks the scheme if the Duke of Newcastle pleases, very promising; but otherwise if any places are left unfilled which may create hopes from L[eicester] House, and such uncertainty, will encrease dependents upon that Court'.[286] Fox met Devonshire the same morning to stress his point. Devonshire argued that 'this delay did not arise from any jealousy or diffidence as to him'. Fox was not reassured;

he added, my lord, tell the Duke of Newcastle that if I am made Paymaster now I am ready to declare everywhere that I will not only not interfere in the management of the House of Commons but will not suffer myself to be the channel of recommendation even to his Grace but where he authorises me to be so, that I will take the very first opportunity of declaring in the House my purpose of supporting him and that I will do it as cordially and as zealously as if he was my brother.

But, with a note of desperation, he had added his threat of refusal if he did not have the Pay Office before the end of the session. Devonshire advised compliance,[287] but had evidently not – to the King or to Newcastle – endorsed Fox's insistence. Fox wrote to complain before seeing Devonshire, at dinner, for the second time that day. Pride now contributed powerfully to freeze Fox's tactics.[288] To accept the Paymastership from Newcastle would be 'an affront and not a favour'; 'My being in an employment lower than Sir T. Robinson or Sir G. Lee must be my own, it shall be no other man's arrangement'. He would see the King the following day, 2 June, to make his point; if, by 7th, he had not kissed hands

before the others do...I will that day go and thank HM for past favours, and never more be in the way, of favour or affront...As to consequences, when I am in Wiltshire, let Leicester House govern or not, it is of as little consequence to me as to anybody else. It is only beginning the next reign, and my retirement, sooner.[289]

Fox's pressure for an immediate answer was probably justified. Newcastle had hoped to exclude Fox from the Paymastership in a temporary system, but the King's promise that he have that office destroyed the possibility of such a scheme. It is not clear that Fox did see George II on 2 June; but the following day Devonshire wrote on his behalf to urge the King to agree to Fox's demands before his audience, which he supposed to be due that day.[290] Already, Newcastle declared on 2nd, 'The supposed junction has...created such a flame, that I have been given to understand, that I am to expect a more violent opposition against *me*, than ever was against Sir Robert Walpole.' Against that, Newcastle's inner circle would not support him. Ilchester later wondered whether the 'unreasonable rapaciousness' of Sir George Lee and Hume Campbell 'did not prevent the Duke of Newcastle from going on with the plan he had agreed to the 2nd and 3rd of June, which he did not depart from till he found H. Campbell insisted upon being Treasurer of the Navy or Chambers and Sir George that he would not be Chancellor of the Exchequer unless his brother and nephew were brought into Parliament and well placed...'[291] Evidently preparing Devonshire for a firm refusal, Newcastle asked to meet him on the evening of 2 June;[292] meanwhile he wrote to re-open contacts with Bute, inviting him to a meeting at Royston's on the evening of 3rd.[293] Despite the prospect of 'ruin' from a Fox ministry, Newcastle could not escape the obligation to support such a system if the King launched it: Newcastle, his wife wrote, 'is to give it as a reason, that he can't come in, because Mr F. has an employment, but he will support him, when sole minister'.[294] Once securely established, the prospects for a Fox ministry would be good. Yet, as this danger approached, the chances of preventing its launch rose. It seems likely that Leicester House took an independent initiative, and that it was before receiving Newcastle's letter on 2nd that Bute wrote to Chesterfield; that, as Waldegrave put it, 'Bute was despatched to the Earl of Chesterfield to engage him to propose to the Duke of Newcastle that the treaty might again be renewed'.[295]

Meanwhile, Newcastle had seen the King twice, on 3rd and (probably) 2 June. George II was 'very good, and gracious'; but despite his and Devonshire's pressure to undertake the ministry, accepting Fox as Paymaster, Newcastle insisted on a delay until 7th before giving a final answer;[296] as Fox thought, because Hardwicke was not to return to town until 6th.[297] Newcastle prevented Fox kissing hands immediately, having it postponed 'till the rest was settled'; nevertheless, Newcastle was 'pressed most strongly, and had the strongest assurances, that Fox should have nothing to do in the administration, or in the conduct of the House of Commons, and that upon the first appearance of his meddling, "*I* will turn him out," the King said'. This was an added source of difficulty. 'I hope the alteration was not made with that view', wrote Newcastle, 'to make themselves appear more reasonable, and to prevent my engaging elsewhere'.[298]

'Preposterous as this suspense to government was', wrote Walpole, 'it occasioned no disturbance, scarce a murmur. The people, hating Fox, neglected by Pitt, and despising Newcastle, waited with patience to see which of them was to be their master.'[299] After his audience[300] on 3rd, Newcastle received a letter from Chesterfield, who had seen Bute in town that morning. 'The business was to acquaint me', reported Chesterfield, 'that he [Bute] had prevailed with Mr Pitt to yield in the affair of the Chancellor of the Exchequer; which having been the only stumbling-block, and being now removed, he hoped that everything else would go on smoothly.' Chesterfield had urged that Bute and Newcastle should meet, and Bute had been eager to do so. To Newcastle, Chesterfield offered the hope that Leicester House were 'now in a way of being wiser than they have been lately'.[301] It was this which impressed Waldegrave, to whom Newcastle showed the letter shortly afterwards; evidently Newcastle had preserved the appearance of reluctance to accept what – if acknowledged – would be a source of weakness in bargaining: that a secure system demanded a reconciliation in the Royal Family. But it was now evident to Newcastle that although Leicester House was unaware of his doubts, he knew theirs. Nor did he reveal his thinking to Waldegrave, who was provoked (as Newcastle may have intended) to emphasise the overriding urgency of persuading the King to be reconciled to the Princess Dowager.[302] But Newcastle gave Chesterfield every reason to think he would pursue the possibility which now opened up;[303] and that day forwarded the letter to the King in the hope of royal approval of his intention to negotiate.[304] This he obtained, though with warnings to 'consider' the King's promise to Fox and to be cautious of the number of Pitt's friends to be incorporated.[305] 'I wish you may find them more reasonable than I expect it', added George II. 'But I very much doubt by what I know of them, that you will meet any reason with these impracticable people.'[306]

Newcastle was at pains to seem to retain the initiative, and gave Waldegrave the (misleading) impression that the King's permission to negotiate was only obtained, 'most unwillingly', by Chesterfield's entreaty.[307] And Newcastle drew up a careful examination of the points at issue which indicated a continuing interest in a Pitt coalition. Two great obstacles were identified. On the Paymastership, everything was to be done to persuade Pitt not to obstruct the King's promise; but if he insisted, some equivalent employment or a pension – with a peerage – would have to be found for Fox. Secondly, 'The difficulty of removing my lord Winchelsea, and reinstating the other Lords of the Admiralty.' Whatever happened, Temple must have a Cabinet place; but the King 'will certainly not make Mr Legge a peer, and First Lord of the Admiralty. Lord Halifax declines it. What objection can remain to my lord Winchelsea? Or who can succeed him?' If his removal were essential, he might be provided for as Groom of the Stole; but Newcastle evidently hoped it was avoidable, and that the destinations of the other Lords of the Admiralty could be adjusted. West and Elliot must have seats there, but Hunter might be accommodated at the Board of Trade; Forbes would probably 'not be insisted upon', and Hay could be King's Advocate. But if Newcastle's plan were not accepted, he would be 'under two difficulties':

The King will immediately expect, that the Duke of Newcastle should come in, and support his affairs. On the contrary, Lord Bute has already told the Duke of Newcastle, that Mr Pitt will expect, that, if *his* plan is not accepted, the Duke of Newcastle should previously engage, what part he would take; and particularly, that he would not abet, or assist the administration, to be formed by his enemies.[308]

On 4th, Newcastle knew he was due to see the King on the morning of Monday 6th. Meanwhile he arranged to see Bute after the Drawing Room at Savile House on 4 June, the Prince of Wales's birthday;[309] but first, there was an unplanned encounter at the Drawing Room itself. Bute 'said he had *now* done his part, that *those gentlemen* thought they had done so too, and hinted as if they expected, that everything else should be complied with'. Bute also asked for a meeting, in Pitt's presence, with Newcastle and Hardwicke; and Newcastle chose Royston's house on the evening of 6 June. 'My present thought is', wrote Newcastle, 'that I should get the King on Monday to go to the *utmost lengths*, and open it to Mr Pitt *as the King's ultimatum*.' Newcastle's audience of the Prince of Wales on 4th went 'extremely well' in personal terms. But Newcastle reported to Hardwicke that Bute, at their second meeting,

gave me to understand that *these gentlemen* expect that all their other demands should be complied with; and further that they would desire to know, in case this negotiation should fail, what *we* would do, whether we would support, and *abet*, an administration composed of our *enemies*. I told him, that his lordship himself had disclaimed force, that for my part, I would rather never see London more, than do anything contrary to my duty, or *obligations* to the King. I brought in the King's promise to Mr Fox of the Pay Office, as what HM had insisted upon with *me* yesterday. He said that would embarrass us in our other *regulations*, if there was no other objection to it; which he seemed to think there was. He ended with great politeness, and more seeming openness than ever. He lamented much (as he said the Prince of Wales did) your lordship's resolution not to take the Great Seal again. He said (and the Prince of Wales thought the same) that you was the only man proper for it, and talked upon your lordship's subject, as I could, and always do...I think the point now is to engage me to come in, in case this negotiation miscarries.[310]

But Bute refused to enter into details of a possible scheme. That, thought Newcastle, would have to wait until the meeting on 6th, when, it seemed, the task would be Pitt's.[311] Meanwhile, he was hopeful: 'I think I see a prospect of establishing more ease to the King during his reign, and more success to his affairs, both at home and abroad, than I have ever flattered myself with before...if this negotiation should now miscarry, we shall see nothing but confusion.'[312] Accordingly, he drew up on 5th a scheme of ministry to be laid before the King the next day, and, if he approved, proposed to Pitt in the evening. It envisaged 'some expedient' being found for Fox or for Potter, depending on which of them had the Pay Office. If Potter remained, all of Pitt's friends who went out with him could return: Temple to 'some Cabinet Council place'; Legge with an unspecified employment, or a promise of one, and a peerage; George Grenville to the place of Treasurer of the Navy. James Grenville would

have a seat at the Treasury, 'or equivalent'; Sir Richard Lyttelton the
Jewel Office; John Pitt, Surveyor of the Woods; West and Elliot Lords
of the Admiralty; Hunter, a seat at the Admiralty or Board of Trade;
Dr Hay, Advocate General; Charles Townshend, Treasurer of the
Chamber. Pitt himself would be Secretary of State. Thus all the points
he demanded at his last meeting with Newcastle on 25 May were
conceded except George Grenville as Chancellor of the Exchequer,
which Pitt himself had conceded, and the place of Secretary at War for
Lord George Sackville – there, the King would not permit the dismissal
of Barrington.[313]

Probably about this time, too, Newcastle sent Halifax to Legge

to ask if I would be Chancellor of the Exchequer in answer to which I said
that I should do nothing without the concurrence of my friends – that I
should not think of naming any office for myself and that wherever he found
Leicester House there he would find me – But that I would be Chancellor of
the Exchequer rather than the system should fall to pieces provided my friends
approved.[314]

Newcastle's was a plan which, though it commanded his confidence, was
full of promises and conditions. Nevertheless, as it stood, it received the
King's approval on 6th. Newcastle urged:

'That it is impossible for me to serve your Majesty when it either is, or can
be supposed by my friends, to be in conjunction with Fox. I can't come in,
without bringing in my enemy, Mr Pitt. He turned me out. But I can't serve,
without my enemy.'
[George II] 'He will be unreasonable.'
[Newcastle] 'He is, Sir!'
[George II] 'Beat him as low, as I [i.e. you] can.'
[Newcastle] 'If your Majesty won't approve it, I can't come in alone'.[315]

Newcastle later wrote:

I found the King in a very different disposition from what I hoped, and
indeed expected. His Majesty told me, his honour and word were engaged, to
make Mr Fox Paymaster. His honour was engaged, not to remove my lord
Winchelsea; and seemed to think it equally engaged, not to do anything for
my lord Temple.

Newcastle expressed his concern, and complained that he saw no
prospect of succeeding with Bute and Pitt that evening on such terms.

The King pressed me very strongly to come in, without them; which, I told
him, was now impossible. I gave the King my reasons for the junction with
Mr Pitt etc. and for my not coming in, upon the foot he proposed I should
with Mr Fox; and that *that* was impossible. I also told him the great difficulties,
which Mr Fox would meet with. He said, others told him otherwise.[316]

Devonshire had seen Lady Yarmouth[317] and asked her to tell the King
his opinion that Newcastle should be authorised 'to offer Mr Pitt

reasonable terms provided he would promise to come in himself upon the plan proposed in case Mr Pitt and he could not agree'.[318] Fox had been aware, too, that Waldegrave would see the King on 6th 'and prepare him, to what your Grace and I wish, to gain the Duke of Newcastle's acceptance, and with as little delay as may be'.[319] Waldegrave probably met Newcastle at Kensington after the latter's audience that day, and passed on to Fox an account of it which Fox accepted and retailed as accurate: 'HM gave his Grace little encouragement to think that he would come into such terms as Pitt etc. would accept. And his Grace gave the King as little to think that he would come into his service without them.'[320] Whether this is a true account of Newcastle's audience is difficult to judge. It was in Newcastle's interest to exert such pressure on Fox to waive his insistence on the Paymastership, yet Fox was not aware, before Newcastle's audience, that Newcastle's meeting with Bute on 4th was 'with the King's consent', or of the 'difficulties' Waldegrave supposed Newcastle met with in the Closet.[321] When told of these two things by Waldegrave after Court on 6th, Fox seemed more willing to accommodate his claim to the Pay Office.[322] Waldegrave's account to Fox of Newcastle's audience is also suspect in the light of Devonshire's advice to Newcastle that morning. A reconciliation he spoke of as distinctly possible; he added

One piece of advice, which is that whatever you intend to do, at least let Mr Pitt think that you intend to undertake the King's affairs without him, it is I am sure the only way to make him reasonable, and I am confident that the renewal of the negotiation is entirely owing to their apprehensions that you would undertake, and that you would be able to carry on the King's business without them. I know they thought you would not.[323]

Already, perhaps, Fox was preparing the way for a claim that he accepted from necessity, since nobody else would. On 5th, Fox was aware of Newcastle's meeting with Bute the previous evening; the morning before,

after seeing Lord Bute, G. Grenville told a friend of mine that I should kiss hands for the Treasury or for nothing; and that they had rather see me at the head of the Treasury, than P[ay]master supporting the Duke of Newcastle – I believe it. It follows, my dear lord, that I must give no symptom of a reason to the Duke of Newcastle to fly off...From what the Primate and Lord George [Sackville] told me formerly, and what I see now, I believe keeping me out of all employment, by way of triumph over the Duke, is a favourite point, both with them and some of the Duke of Newcastle's better friends. Whilst there is a hope of that therefore, his Grace will be kept upon the *turnstile*.[324]

But, claimed Fox, 'I own I fear they will frighten his Grace out of' accepting a ministry with Fox's support.[325] Devonshire, too, told Fox he thought Newcastle's negotiation would fail.[326] This prediction was soon tested at Newcastle's meeting with Hardwicke, Pitt and Bute on the evening of 6th. Pitt had been given good reason to be compliant towards Newcastle's suggestions. Hardwicke had not been encouraging about the outcome on 5th; and that day, 'Lord Temple's news, from the opera, is that Fox is to kiss hands as First Lord of the Treasury, tomorrow'.[327]

No account of what passed at that meeting certainly survives. It may be that on 6th which Walpole recorded:

Newcastle persisted that the King *would* retain Lord Winchelsea; and to balance the authority that he saw must fall to Pitt, said to him, 'But you will not act with Fox' – Pitt replied, 'My lord, I never said so – but does your Grace say you would? When you have said you will, I will consult my friends.' Newcastle, not the most intelligible even when he was explicit, took care not to be understood sooner than he was determined; and the conversation ended abruptly.[328]

Yet at large it was thought, probably correctly, that a scheme of ministry was agreed between the four men.[329] Walpole wrote that they could not agree on details but that Newcastle went to Kensington on 7th and 'told the King that he could not act without Mr Pitt and a great plan of that connection'.[330] Though some particulars were undetermined, most had been so far decided on as to amount to an obvious departure from the scheme embracing Lee, Egmont and others, 'those gentlemen', as Waldegrave put it, 'who a few days before had entered into engagements with the Duke of Newcastle, and were waiting in their best clothes, in hourly expectation of being sent for to Court, to kiss his Majesty's hand'.[331] Lee was left wholly unconsulted about the change of plan until Newcastle met him by chance on 16 July.[332] And within days of Newcastle's audience on 7 June, Lee resigned as Treasurer of the Household to the Princess of Wales, as Walpole supposed, 'not brooking the influence of Pitt with her, and finding himself a cypher at that Court, since Lord Bute had become more than Minister there'.[333] Lady Anson thought it an error born of confusion: that Lee, 'who some months since would be nothing *without* Mr Pitt, and for some weeks since would be nothing *with* him', mistimed a gesture aimed against his supplanter: 'Something he had heard I suppose, that he did not understand, about resigning, and so made a mistake, and it may happen to be some time before he hears anything of *resuming*'.[334] He never did. From being poised to assume the Exchequer, he sank at once into political obscurity.

In Newcastle's audience, George II

perceived that all his favourite points were entirely given up: Winchelsea was to be displaced, with a total change of the Admiralty: Fox was not to be Paymaster: and Lord Temple, to whom he had given a negative, was to have a Cabinet Council employment.

Ilchester later claimed Newcastle brought 'higher terms which put the King out of humour, and made him break off abruptly. What he was most angry at, was their insisting that Lord George [Sackville] should be Secretary at War, and Pratt Attorney General'.[335]

At once he regretted this scheme, and asked Newcastle 'whether he would not come in without them?'[336] But Newcastle, as Waldegrave claimed, 'notwithstanding his most solemn promises refused to execute the former plan'.[337] Walpole gave a more Foxite version: that Newcastle

declared to the King, that he could not come in, unless Mr Pitt's whole plan was accepted. The King reproached him bitterly with all his shifts and evasions, and falsehoods; and demanded his assistance for Fox, if he would not himself undertake the service. He waived any such promise, and the King dismissed him in wrath.[338]

FOX'S THIRD ATTEMPT TO FORM A MINISTRY, 7–11 JUNE 1757

After seeing Newcastle on 7th, George II sent Devonshire to summon Fox.[339] In the audience which followed, 'His Majesty began by reproaching him very roughly, said he was the author of all this confusion by resigning last October. After he had dwelled a great while upon that topic he commended him for his behaviour this sessions'.[340] The King, recorded Fox,

with such expressions of distress as were very affecting, told me that they had sent him such terms as if he consented to he must be a prisoner and a slave for life, and should be used accordingly, and commanded me to be his Minister in the House of Commons, asking me if I thought I could carry on his affairs there. I answered, that I could by no means promise success, as the Duke of Newcastle...would give the King no assurances of his assistance. I therefore advised H.M. to do anything [else] that he thought would procure him ease. He said his hope of that was over, it could not be worse for him, and I must try. If nothing better could be thought of, I said; and not else; I was ready to do my best.[341]

Harry Digby, who was aware on 7th of Newcastle's audience that day, knew also that Fox was due to see the King on 8th, but that 'there is I think some doubt whether he shall accept directly or advise his Majesty to treat further with Leicester House'.[342] Something of that uncertainty was shared by Newcastle, who was ordered via Devonshire on 7th 'not to give a final answer to Mr Pitt' until the following day.[343] Nor did Newcastle suppose he had received a 'positive answer' in the Closet, merely a check to his proposals; and Bute reassured him that 'your Grace if you think it proper may still have it in your power to remove all difficulties'.[344] Then, that night, Holdernesse reported that Lady Yarmouth was 'alarmed to the greatest degree' with the King's reaction, 'and seems almost certain, that the resolution of today will not be finally adhered to'. Pitt should not, she had urged, be persuaded 'that all was sans retour', and Fox would be unable to form an administration. Much of the blame for persuading the King otherwise, she implied, lay with Granville – who had preceded Newcastle in the

Closet on 7th. Chesterfield now added his advice against Newcastle's undertaking on the scheme proposed with Fox: 'you would in the next session of parliament have been *nobody*, whereas now that next session must necessarily make you whatever you have a mind to be'; Fox would accept, but his system would collapse in the next session. Newcastle should therefore 'keep free of all engagements or verbal declarations whatsoever, and wait in profound silence the events of next session'.[345]

But this might well have seemed an immense and unnecessary concession to Fox. Nor were the resources of Newcastle's friends exhausted. Already on 7th, before meeting Lady Yarmouth, Holdernesse had decided to resign and had told Newcastle of his decision; Newcastle now relayed the information to Hardwicke, who probably passed it to Pitt.[346] As yet, however, it probably went no further. Newcastle was aware that Fox 'has been spoke to', evidently by the King, and was due to give his answer on the morning of 8th.[347] Walpole supposed it was probably at Fox's suggestion that the King sent for Waldegrave into the Closet that morning.[348] Devonshire, Bedford and Grenville had already urged on Waldegrave that morning the need to rally to the King's support in his 'very disagreeable situation'. George II put the same case more strongly, reproaching Newcastle and offering Waldegrave the Treasury. Waldegrave demurred. A 'steady majority in both Houses of Parliament' was essential; but 'a minister must expect few followers, who had never cultivated political friendships, and had always abhorred party violence'. Yet at last he yielded to the King's entreaties. Devonshire was then sent for and ordered to talk to Fox and Waldegrave that evening to draw up a new plan of ministry. Before this took place, Waldegrave explained his audience to Newcastle, who professed to bear no personal resentment. Waldegrave in turn insisted that 'I had accepted an employment not from choice, but because I thought it a duty to obey my sovereign's lawful commands'. Yet he had plainly thought his role a practicable though onerous one, and was disturbed at his meeting that evening to find Fox 'much changed since the morning; more apprehensive of danger, more doubtful of success': some of his Commons followers had shown reluctance to support and Fox had been 'discouraged' by the King's manner that morning:

Indeed, it was very apparent that his Majesty had neither forgot the circumstances of his being made Secretary of State, nor the consequences of his late resignation; and that he made use of him on the present occasion, not from choice, but because he was the only man of abilities who had spirit to answer Pitt in his own language.

Nevertheless, the three men sat down to settle a ministry as far as could be done, for 'we were obliged to take many things for granted, which at best were doubtful; and to rely on many persons who had not as yet entered into any engagements'. Within these limits, the essentials could be set out. Winchelsea already had an Admiralty Board; Walde-grave was First Lord of the Treasury; Fox, Chancellor of the Exchequer; Egremont, Secretary of State. Bedford was rumoured at large to be destined for the latter post; it is not clear that he played any part in these consultations, and the only evidence for his intentions suggests that he insisted on remaining Lord Lieutenant of Ireland; though willing if necessary to return from Dublin at Christmas to support.[349] 'As to the inferior places, there were numbers ready to take them, though not exactly the men we would have chose; and as to other particulars, we were to wait for events, and avail ourselves of such future advantages, as fortune should please to bestow on us'.[350]

Yet Waldegrave's ministry was to enjoy no such advantages. Lady Yarmouth breakfasted with Holdernesse on 8 June and did not leave till 3 p.m.; she left him still determined to resign, and he at once set about removing his and Newcastle's letter-books from the Secretary of State's office.[351] Newcastle seems to have put no pressure on Holdernesse to resign but kept in close and urgent communication with him, stress-ing that if he were to go, he should go as soon as possible.[352] Holder-nesse's mind was made up by a note from Lady Yarmouth that evening: '*Monsieur Fox a entrepris les affaires*'.[353] He determined to tell the King of his decision in person on 9th, saying nothing previously to Devonshire or, evidently, to anyone else.[354] Newcastle meanwhile met Bute on the evening of 8th with news of Fox's impending appointment the following day.[355] Even Conway was pessimistic: Fox, he wrote, 'calculates upon the venality of mankind and the effect of his M[ajesty]'s favour and power; which might be just in most cases, but I think false in this; where the cry of the people, the general turn of the Parliament, and the influence of Leicester House are against him . . '[356] Ellis made the same prediction from d'Abreu's report of Temple's furious threats – that it was 'the greatest piece of temerity and madness that ever man was guilty of'; that it could not last six hours; and that Fox would not, for that reason, actually receive the Exchequer seal. Any delay was crucial, thought Ellis: 'an administration talked of and an ad-ministration in possession are two very different things'. MPs would be intimidated from declaring for the first; but if Fox actually had the Exchequer, 'it would show that the King had decided'.[357] This analysis was quickly confirmed by events in the Commons, which had reassembled on 7 June.

Ellis came with an air of mysterious importance, and desired the House to adjourn to the 13th following. Lord George Sackville and George Townshend opposed this in joke, the latter saying that a Bill of great consequence relating to Milbourn-port was to be considered that day; yet if Ellis would say that a ministry was to be formed during the proposed recess, he would consent to it. Ellis would say nothing; the House divided, Ellis with ten more against fifty-seven; and thus Fox lost a question even before he was a Minister.[358]

Newcastle and Pitt's friends, reported Elliot, had joined against Fox.[359] Yet it was not evident that the latter was despondent about his prospects there, even on the assumption that Newcastle was 'quite gone to Leicester House'.[360] Fox's sister, on 9th, claimed he 'thinks he is pretty sure of a majority in the House of Commons', despite 'the Duke of Newcastle's party, Leicester House, Pitt's and all the Tories sure against him'.[361] Fox's problems were slightly different. First, his careful neutrality had delayed action until Newcastle was irreversibly committed to Pitt and until the only barrier to the success of a Pitt–Newcastle coalition was the intransigence of George II. Second, Fox had not taken both the Exchequer and the Treasury. Elliot reported that Fox had agreed, in the Closet on 8th, to take both offices if Waldegrave would not accept the Treasury;[362] but the King persuaded him to take it. If so, Fox's sister was recording his ex-post-facto justifications in writing that he refused both offices 'for many reasons; one of which is that his Majesty hates to have anything but a Lord in the latter employment, and another reason is that the popular clamour, which is already so violent against Mr Fox, would in all probability run still higher, as this would have the appearance of trying to get everything into his own hands'. But if that had been done, Waldegrave and Egremont could have been Secretaries of State, the second of whom had also agreed to come in.[363] Thirdly, Fox was faced with an escalating series of resignations. Leeds, Rutland, Rockingham, Northumberland, Coventry 'and others' were reported on 9th as either intending or just about to do likewise,[364] and Walpole wrote that 'by tomorrow it will rain resignations at it did in the year '46'.[365] Holdernesse's resignation on 9th was thought to have intervened to prevent Fox's kissing hands,[366] which was itself thought to be the signal for further resignations,[367] and his position at once appeared desperate.

Waldegrave followed Holdernesse into the Closet on the morning of 9th, found the King undismayed at the loss, and explained the terms of the ministerial system he had drawn up with Devonshire and Fox the previous evening. George II ordered them to meet again that night, plus Granville and Winchelsea. They did so. Waldegrave records Fox as still 'anxious and doubtful' but Granville as sanguine that, though recruits were not yet arriving in numbers, they would join in the course of the summer; 'and though of late years ministers did not think themselves safe without a majority in the House of Commons of one hundred and fifty or two hundred, he remembered the time when twenty or thirty were thought more than sufficient'. Winchelsea, too, 'seemed quite easy and determined; and we parted in tolerable good spirits'.

The following morning, 10th, Newcastle summoned Waldegrave to meet him before the latter went to Court. Newcastle 'began by expressing great uneasiness lest the King should suspect him of having been the cause of Holdernesse's resignation; called God to witness that, far

from having given any sort of encouragement, it was quite unknown
to him, till he received a letter from Lord Holdernesse, acquainting
him with his resolution, a very few hours before it was executed'.
Newcastle showed Waldegrave a letter from Holdernesse to prove his
point; complained of being blamed for every resignation or refusal to
serve, and asked Waldegrave to lay Newcastle's case before the King.
In a memorandum read by George II on 10th, Newcastle firmly denied
that any resignations were conducted in concert with him: he had
foreseen them and warned the King, but they arose out of 'the general
opinion, which the Duke of Newcastle has humbly represented to the
King, would prevail upon the present occasion'.[368] Waldegrave replied
that

it was very certain the King did suspect him, as to some particulars, and I
would give one instance. The Earl of Halifax having been offered a very
considerable employment, had declared to several persons that he should have
accepted with the greatest readiness had he been at liberty to follow his own
inclination; but was under a necessity of refusing, because he thought himself
bound in honour not to take any part without the Duke of Newcastle's consent.[369]

That day, Halifax did indeed write to Fox to decline the post which
he and 'three noble lords' (presumably Devonshire, Bedford and Granville) had evidently offered him, though giving no more specific reason
than that he could not 'in the present state of things effectually serve
his Majesty, or prove instrumental to the ease and prosperity of his
government in any such station'.[370]

In their interview, Waldegrave continued by giving other examples
and asking Newcastle 'whether there might not be some foundation
for his Majesty's suspicions'. Waldegrave claims Newcastle replied by
denying the charges in general only,

that it was hard he should be condemned because some gentlemen endeavoured
to clear themselves by loading him: that it was not his fault if many
persons did apply to him; and that he wished with all his heart they would judge
for themselves. That he had given me notice, some days ago, of a man near
the King's person, a favourite, one in whom his Majesty had the greatest confidence, who would soon resign his employment: that I might easily guess he
meant Holdernesse, though he had not named him; and that with a single word,
he could cause so many resignations, as would give the Court a very empty
appearance.

I did not think it necessary to add to his confusion, by comparing his last
words with the solemn declaration which I was to make, in his Grace's name,
concerning Holdernesse's resignation; but contented myself with telling him,
that if it was in his power to deprive the King of his servants, and if he really
intended it, the sooner it was done, the better; that his Majesty might know with
certainty, what he had to expect, and whom he had to depend on.[371]

Waldegrave was probably the source of the gist of Walpole's account
of Newcastle's responsibility: that he

took pains to promote those resignations, and told Lord Northumberland that they caught like wildfire. The latter replied artfully 'I have great obligations to your Grace, but should think I repaid them very ill by resigning, as it would be contributing to make your Grace distress his Majesty.' Indeed, to the King and others, the Duke solemnly foreswore any knowledge of that measure; and while he enjoined or inculcated it to his friends, he prohibited it to Lord Lincoln and the Duke of Leeds, his relations, that he might tell the King that his own family had stood by his Majesty – a silly finesse, and blown up even by himself, he bragging to Lord Waldegrave of the display of his power in that measure, the very instant after he had denied it with oaths.[372]

Holdernesse proved even more eager than Newcastle to avert the implacable royal hostility he had incurred by a resignation which at last proved, though only by destroying, his political weight. His act, Holdernesse pleaded, 'proceeded from no factious motive, nor was it taken in concert with anybody whatsoever, but arose solely from an opinion that I could not, consistently with my duty to your Majesty, or with my own honour, do otherwise'.[373] Only a solid administration could conduct the war and make peace in face of 'popular clamour'. His duty to the King dictated the frustration of Fox's schemes, which would lead to disaster. Moreover, there was his own position:

From the nature of my department, I must have carried into execution the King's orders, upon the most important objects, either of war or peace, and upon the very points where the stress of the future opposition will certainly lie, and that, without seeing sufficient strength in the Minister, efficatiously to support the King's views in Parliament, and without being sure, that even the small assistance he could give me, would be exerted in my favour, if I should be attacked, but must have stood the shield of a minister with whom I have no connection, and be wounded by the shafts that are aimed at another; having broke with my former friends remain unsupported, and even unpitied.[374]

But what Newcastle proved, despite the widely praised example of Winchelsea, was that the penalties of staying out were far less severe than those of resigning, and the novel constitutional tortures on which Holdernesse was fixed by the King's unmitigated resentment were ones which Newcastle never formulated, and escaped.

From his meeting with Newcastle, Waldegrave went to Kensington. The King, he recorded, was 'much dispirited; complaining that Fox did not succeed in his negotiation; that there would be many more resignations; and that almost everybody abandoned him'. Further negotiation, he feared, 'would be to no purpose'. Waldegrave replied that things were not

quite desperate: for, though we might not have sufficient strength to form an administration, we were strong enough to give our opponents some uneasiness; and by a firm and steady behaviour might oblige them to accept of reasonable terms. That it would be bad policy to lay down our arms, and then negotiate; for that in political, as well as military warfare, it was most safe, as well as honourable, to capitulate sword in hand.

This, he thought, encouraged the King.[375]

Meanwhile, Walpole launched an overture of his own: to save Fox from a 'precipice', as he put it, and to save the country from Newcastle,

that disgraceful man...who had so long perplexed all its councils, and been a principal cause of its misfortunes. He [Walpole] sounded Lord George Sackville, and thinking him not ill-disposed to Fox, and by no means amicable to Newcastle, he proposed his plan to the former. It was, that the King should send *carte blanche* to Pitt, to place the Duke of Dorset at the head of the Treasury, with Lord George for Secretary at War, and, by dissolving the Parliament, dissipate at once Newcastle's influence. Fox, who feared a popular election, disapproved the latter part, and did not relish Lord George in the War Office – too sharp-sighted, and who, to the desertion of Fox, had added a refusal of making Calcraft agent to his regiment. However, he permitted Walpole to propose all this to Lord George, adding that he would take Paymaster (which seemed to be his newest wish), under Pitt, or would even act under him without an employment, with the sole privilege reserved of abusing Newcastle as much as he pleased.

Lord George Sackville owned he should have liked the plan, but was now too far engaged. He confessed he had taken his part, as the contest lay between Leicester House and the Duke; and the rather, as he had long observed that the Duke loved none but men totally detached from all other connexions, and had even been less kind to Conway since his marriage;[376] and, as an insurmountable objection, said, that Lord Bute, who was of scrupulous honour, would now reckon their party bound by these resignations. Thus this plan failed, though the King, whose aversion was diverted from Pitt to Newcastle, would have consented to anything, that might make the treacheries of the latter fall on his own head.[377]

But it became clear on 10 June that both Waldegrave's optimism about having an adequate force in being to serve as a bargaining counter, and Walpole's hope that support could be sustained for any scheme other than a Pitt–Newcastle alliance were misplaced. Dodington was the only major Commons figure to assure Fox of support;[378] but his doing so unconditionally was a mark of his weakness. Halifax, Hume Campbell, Oswald and – claimed Ilchester – Sir George Lee[379] had all refused places. The list of resigners talked of continued to grow: Rutland, Leeds, Dorset, Rockingham, Coventry, Buckingham 'and several in the House of Commons';[380] Lincoln;[381] Ashburnham;[382] Hertford;[383] Nugent; Sir Thomas Robinson; and Barrington.[384] They proved, thought Harry Digby, that Newcastle 'had entered into a treaty with Leicester House and Mr Pitt in order to force the King into whatever terms they agreed'.[385] Calcraft wrote:

The Tories have been to Newcastle House,[386] so they, Leicester House, Lord Bute, Pitt, and his Grace's friends – all join to take the Crown before his Majesty's death. The Dukes of Devonshire, Bedford and Argyll, Lords Granville, Winchelsea, Waldegrave and Northumberland are zealous and sanguine to support the King. But what will be done against this torrent of ingratitude and desertion I can't imagine.[387]

Fox continued to cast around in growing desperation. He and Devonshire both wrote to Lord Strange, in the country, to invite him to accept the Duchy of Lancaster. Fox's letter contained deliberate lies: that he had 'this day taken the seals of Chancellor of the Exchequer. Lord Waldegrave is First Lord of the Treasury; Lord President [Granville], the Duke of Bedford, the Duke of Devonshire, Lord Winchelsea, Lord Waldegrave, the two Secretaries, when they shall be appointed, and myself compose the Council'. Even so, Fox had to offer considerable freedom of action: 'I have told HM that if you did come it would be because of his distress, and that you would come with as much freedom of action as you now enjoyed; and that following as your lordship did your own opinion, he might be sure you would frequently differ from his ministers'.[388] But Devonshire gave the game away, disclosing that only Fox and Waldegrave had accepted major office,[389] and Strange's answer was presumably negative. If, therefore, as Ilchester later claimed, Egremont and Gower were to have been Secretaries of State in Fox's scheme, their inclusion must have been a last-minute addition.[390]

Even before Strange's reply arrived, Fox admitted to Devonshire his opinion that his attempted ministry 'will not do', though undecided whether to push forward in a resolute effort. He had still a choice between 'yielding now and staying to be beat': if the first, he 'might save to the King some friends as Lord Granville, the Duke of Bedford, Lord Gower etc. of whom they will not leave him one if they get the better'.[391] The King

may perhaps too now evade the making Lord George Sackville Secretary at War, a new condition and that which H.M. of all others can least digest. Another new condition too is to turn out the Attorney General and make Pratt. All that I can find they gave up is the Chancellor of the Exchequer, and that seems to have been a collusion, for the Duke of Newcastle would have appointed Legge.[392]

Further thought that morning made it clear to him that he had little choice if he were to be offered the Exchequer the following day:

I can no more make it my act to decline the seals against all the lords I saw tonight [i.e. at the meeting on the evening of 9 June], excepting your Grace; than I can take them without letting the King know that I don't answer for the House of Commons, nor can...I did not ask for them, but I will not decline them, though I sincerely wish there was any other hand in the House of Commons to put them into.[393]

Bedford and Granville remained 'sanguine', thought Devonshire; Gower and Winchelsea 'rather so, at least are for trying – The world in general think it cannot do. The King himself is very low, thinks it will not do, and, in that case, is for giving up, that he may not lose all his friends about him'.[394]

These manoeuvres were accorded complete indulgence by the Commons, partly because they seemed imminently about to produce a ministry, partly because they concerned so wholly the King's prerogative, as yet unchallenged in theory, to choose his ministers. Yet even this was not entirely immune from challenge: on 10 June,

after the House of Commons had sat near an hour in silence and suspense, Sir Francis Dashwood mentioned that they had met several days[395] without having any business to do to the great fatigue of the Speaker and the House and moved to adjourn to Monday. Col. Townshend seconded the motion and said he was glad it was moved for no longer time for that in the present dreadful situation of this country without the appearance of a government he hoped the House would that day resume its ancient right (too long disused) of advising the Crown in this dangerous crisis, and that he wished the House would then be full as he should offer some proposal of that kind.[396]

Newcastle met Hardwicke on the evening of 10th and agreed that 'any motion relating to the forming an administration, or the delays in doing it, would be extremely improper, and disrespectful to the King'; and, via Granby, put pressure on his nephew George Townshend and Sir Francis Dashwood not to make such a motion, which, if put, he threatened to oppose.[397]

The House adjourned until Monday, 13th with no such proposal having been made, and there is no evidence that any of the actors in the central drama were led, driven or agitated by the Commons' belated concern. Nor was Newcastle, centrally, vulnerable to criticism; for, as Devonshire admitted, Newcastle had not yet chosen a course of action on which future resignations would turn. *If* he joined Leicester House and Pitt, those resignations would materialise; but Devonshire evidently assumed that Newcastle had until then been able to maintain an independent stance. Nor could Devonshire believe that Newcastle would depart from it: 'I can hardly think after all the obligations he has had to the King that he can go into opposition; and I don't see how he can justify him[self] because he has not resolution to undertake the King's business that therefore he must force the King into hands that are disagreeable to him and that the King perhaps thinks would be dishonourable to him to take'.[398] Moreover, it was thought in Fox's camp that Newcastle dared not launch his last plan of ministry, with Lee as Chancellor of the Exchequer and Robinson Secretary of State, because he was 'frightened by Leicester House' and merely irresolute.[399] Devonshire's insistence on his own departure, therefore, was based until as late as the point of disintegration of Fox's abortive ministry on a conviction that Newcastle's scope for manoeuvre was far narrower than Newcastle, prepared as he was with excuses, supposed it to be. His opinion was significantly revised only at a meeting on the night of 10 June attended also by Bedford, Granville, Winchelsea, Gower, Fox and Waldegrave. The latter recorded Winchelsea and Granville still 'stout and resolute', but Bedford 'greatly beyond them':

He insisted that our administration would be infinitely the strongest that had ever been known in this country: and was almost in a passion against Fox, for having started some difficulties, and for seeming to doubt our success.

That as to replacing Holdernesse, Lord Gower, at present Lord Privy Seal, and fond of ease and pleasure as much as any man, was ready to change for a more laborious employment, and would be Secretary of State, in case we thought it necessary: as to other resigners, he wished their numbers were more considerable, for that every vacancy would either serve an old friend, or gain a new one.

Lord Gower confirmed what the Duke of Bedford had promised for him; spoke with great modesty, but declared he would take the employment without the least hesitation, if we thought him capable, and could not find a more proper person.

As to myself, I plainly perceived by the King's discourse in the morning, and by some private conversation with the Duke of Devonshire and Fox, that our plan would not be carried into execution, and might possibly be given up the day following. However, it seemed mean and pitiful to leave the King in a worse situation than that in which we had found him. I therefore took the spirited side of the question; and told them, that though I had never been ambitious of being a minister, and though our affairs did not appear to me in the most favourable light, the King having thought proper to require my assistance, I had considered the consequences, had given my word, and was ready to perform my part, whenever I was called upon.

The Duke of Bedford was pleased with this declaration; but whispered me at parting, that it would be to no purpose to give ourselves any further trouble; for we could not possibly go on, without a principal actor in the House of Commons, and that Fox had not spirit to undertake it.

In spite of all our difficulties, it was still the opinion without doors, that we were too desperate to desist, and that our plan of administration would be immediately executed.[400]

Until the last moment, however, Devonshire preserved an appearance of resolution. Before Court on Saturday, 11 June, he was called on by Rockingham and left him convinced that 'the new administration are determined to undertake the Government'. Rockingham was confirmed in his reluctant decision to resign.[401] But Mansfield also called on Devonshire on the morning of 11th

to know whether the King expected him to bring the Seals that day to Court. I told him he did, he then begged of me to consider the consequences of such a step, that it was plain to demonstration that Mr Fox could not carry on the King's affairs, that it would be the ruin of the King and the country as well as his own; that it was so evident and he was so thoroughly convinced that in duty to the King he could not avoid telling him his mind, I own I did not dissuade him from it as I was clearly of the same opinion though I had been backward in saying so as I knew I had now and then been looked upon as too cool and rather backward in the cause. I saw Lord Waldegrave and Mr Fox before I went to Court, who were then convinced it would not do, and were determined to give it up. When I got to Kensington I found the King of the same mind so I desired him to speak to Lord Mansfield and to employ him to endeavour to get the best terms that could be attained for the King.⁴⁰²

According to Ilchester, Fox was determined on the morning of 11 June 'to go and tell the King that it was his opinion it would not do, but if the King would have him, he would undertake it and try'. Mansfield spoke to Ilchester that morning; though urging him that Fox faced 'ruin' if he undertook the government against a Commons majority and a popular outcry,⁴⁰³ he presumably heard the same account, and Mansfield went to court that morning to deliver the Exchequer seal imagining that Fox was present to receive it.⁴⁰⁴ Rutland and Rockingham were both in the antechamber waiting to resign. When Mansfield arrived Fox let him know that he was about to be given the Exchequer, but was astonished at Mansfield's answer: that if the King asked his opinion, he would advise that Fox's scheme would not succeed. Fox reportedly replied 'If his M[ajest]y commands me I shall undertake it'.⁴⁰⁵ Newcastle heard what happened in Mansfield's audience when he met him by chance at Hyde Park Corner after Court. Mansfield

honestly represented to the King, the impossibility of this new ministry taking place; that it could not succeed, that he was sure of it and was so positive in his opinion, that he was ready to give it in the presence of any of those who were in the other room (the Duke of Bedford etc.) if His Majesty would please to call them in. This had such an effect upon the King that his Majesty immediately suspended his new ministry, Lord Mansfield took back his seal, and had orders to speak to my lord Hardwicke and me, to renew our conference with my lord Bute and Mr Pitt, which we shall accordingly do on Monday.

'Thus', added Newcastle triumphantly, 'are the mighty men for a third time put *hors de jeu*'.⁴⁰⁶ In late October 1756, early April 1757 and now again in early June, Newcastle had frustrated the most powerful rival system. Now, it seemed, its defeat was final and crushing: far from having, as Bedford claimed, an impregnable base in the House of Lords, it was those peers, especially members of the Royal Household, who had displayed an apparently spontaneous refusal to serve, a barrier which no manoeuvre by Fox, Bedford, Granville or even Devonshire now had any prospect of removing.

THE FINAL NEGOTIATIONS, 11–29 JUNE 1757

Coming out of the Closet, Mansfield prevented the resignation of Rockingham, who in turn halted Rutland.⁴⁰⁷ His commission was to negotiate again, with 'full powers' as Waldegrave supposed, with Newcastle, Hardwicke, Pitt and Bute; subject only to the conditions that Fox be Paymaster and that Temple should not have an office which would bring him often into the Closet.⁴⁰⁸ Bedford, Gower, Devonshire,

Marlborough, Winchelsea and Bridgewater were present at court to witness, as they supposed, Fox's acceptance of the Exchequer Seal. But Mansfield whispered the result to Fox as he came out, passing Fox on his way in. The 'good company attending in the antechamber were amazed', wrote Hardwicke, 'as you may easily imagine the whole Court was'.[409] Fox, called into the Closet immediately after Mansfield,[410] evidently offered to continue if the King commanded it. George II replied:

No, he did not desire his friends should suffer for him: he found he was to be prisoner for the rest of his life: he hoped, whatever he might be made to do, his friends would not impute to him, for he should not be a free agent: he had not thought that he had so many of Newcastle's *footmen* about him: soon, he supposed, he should not be able to make a Page of the Back-stairs. For Hanover, he must give it up, it cost an hundred and twenty thousand pounds a month for forage alone: he found he must lose his Electoral dominions for an English quarrel: while at the same time he lost all authority in England.[411]

'What seems to vex him most', wrote Ilchester of his brother, 'is that in one of his conversations with the King, his Majesty told him that his resignation in October [1756] had lost him the hearts of the Whigs and I am afraid he feels it in some measure true'.[412] Waldegrave, Devonshire and Bedford then had audiences. Waldegrave explained his opinion that his projected ministry would fall when Parliament met in the autumn, for Newcastle possessed 'a considerable majority' in the Commons, and 'the popular cry without doors was violent in favour of Mr Pitt'. Despite Newcastle's and Pitt's hatred of each other, they would prevent anyone else being minister.

That the whole weight of opposition rested on a single point – his Majesty's supposed partiality to his electoral subjects, which would at any time set the nation in a flame; and that being thought an enemy to Hanover was the solid foundation of Pitt's popularity.

That as to Jacobitism, it was indeed at a low ebb: but there was a mutinous spirit in the lower class of people, which might in a moment break out in acts of the greatest violence: whilst others were sullen and discontented, ignorant of the blessings they enjoyed, sensible only that they paid heavy taxes, and quite indifferent who were their governors.

That in times of peace we might have had opportunities of undeceiving the people, of restoring them to their sober senses; or, if our administration had been overturned, his ministers would have been the only sufferers.

But in our present state of confusion, delay was absolute ruin; for that doing nothing was worse than doing wrong.

It was, therefore, my very humble advice, that His Majesty should give way to the necessity of the times; and if he would graciously overlook some past offences, and would gratify Pitt's vanity with a moderate share of that affability and courteousness, which he so liberally bestowed on so many of his servants, I was convinced he would find him no intractable minister.

That I was not ignorant that Pitt could be guilty of the worst of actions, whenever his ambition, his pride, or his resentment were to be gratified; but that he could also be sensible of good treatment; was bold and resolute, above doing things by half; and if he once engaged, would go farther than any man in this country. Nor would his former violence against Hanover be any kind of obstacle, as he had given frequent proofs that he could change sides, whenever he found it necessary, and could deny his own words with an unembarrassed countenance.

That as to the Duke of Newcastle, who lately fancied himself independent, and had given so much uneasiness, he would find himself in his Majesty's power the moment he entered into employment; for, as all the offices of business would be under the direction of his new allies, he could only be considerable by his interest in the Closet; and that his fear and jealousy of Pitt would be better security for his good behaviour, than a thousand promises.

His Majesty heard everything I said with great patience; and answered with some cheerfulness, that according to my description, his situation was not much to be envied; but he could assure me it was infinitely more disagreeable than I represented it. That he believed few princes had been exposed to such treatment; that we were angry because he was partial to his electorate, though he desired nothing more to be done for Hanover than what we were bound in honour and justice to do for any country whatsoever, when it was exposed to danger entirely on our account.

That we were, indeed, a very extraordinary people, continually talking of our constitution, laws, and liberty. That as to our constitution, he allowed it to be a good one, and defied any man to produce a single instance wherein he had exceeded his proper limits. That he never meant to screen or protect any servant who had done amiss; but still he had a right to choose those who were to serve him, though, at present, so far from having an option, he was not even allowed a negative.

That as to our laws, we passed near a hundred every session, which seemed made for no other purpose, but to afford us the pleasure of breaking them: and as to our zeal for liberty, it was in itself highly commendable; but our notions must be somewhat singular, when the chief of the nobility chose rather to be the dependents and followers of a Duke of Newcastle than to be the friends and counsellors of their sovereign.[413]

What passed in the audiences of Devonshire and Bedford is not known; but the latter at once left for Woburn in fury.[414] The Countess of Kildare feared his resigning the Lord Lieutenancy: that would spell ruin for Kildare's party in the Dublin Commons, 'for the Primate is all powerful with those people', Fox's successors;[415] and Bedford himself thought his and Kildare's interests alike threatened by 'the Board of Treasury which is now forming'.[416]

Ilchester wrote despairingly of his brother's situation: 'I look upon this as the very crisis of his life'; if he did not now obtain the Paymastership or a large pension on Ireland until the reversion to Dodington's place matured, 'no future opportunity will offer', and he would be forced to withdraw from London life.[417] 'The short and true account of the present situation is', he confined to Digby, 'that my brother is quite routed and that Pitt and Newcastle are triumphant'. And in a note on 14th, he added that Pitt insisted on the removal of Argyll, Bedford, Marlborough, Granville, and Gower.[418] Harry Digby had similarly heard on 13th that 'Pitt said he should now insist upon turning out the Dukes of Marlborough, Bedford, and Argyll, and that Lord Gower and Lord Granville must not stay, Lord Granby they said was to succeed the Duke of Marlborough, Lord Temple the Duke of Bedford, and Lord Hardwicke was to be Lord President, but I don't believe they are agreed upon anything'.[419]

Fox's position was one of total weakness. Nor were his followers eager in their gestures of solidarity. Even Bedford was soon reported by Rigby: 'his anger does not operate towards thinking of a resignation, and he dropped last night a word that surprised me a little, that if ever Lord Gower was removed, he did not see the necessity of obliging them with the government of Ireland too...'[420] Bedford himself wrote:

Things are now in so bad a situation for H.M. that I think they could not have been worse, had the plan that was concerted, been attempted, and had failed, but as all that is over at present, I think nothing now remains but to make —'s [sic] captivity as easy as possible, and wait for such events to extricate him totally from it, as the bad hearts and heads of some, and the impracticability of others, of those who are now coming into his service, give me reason to expect.[421]

But it had not always been so. Until the moment of Mansfield's audience, Fox had been willing to try to form a government. Now, Fox set about circulating excuses which gave a quite different impression. Newcastle had chosen to oppose his ministry, he claimed to Ellis – 'not measures for none were mentioned; and I am convinced that upon the first day of next sessions, we should have made very little better figure than you did in your division for adjustment'.[422] Soon, too, Mansfield's conversation in the Closet was reported to have been arranged with Fox, unwilling to embark on a scheme which he knew could not succeed;[423] and the Commons majority which defeated Ellis's motion to adjourn on 8th was said to have been (what Newcastle and Hardwicke knew it was not) 'vastly elated and seemed ripe for any kind of violence that could be proposed, and many think', added Harry Digby, 'there would have been something very extraordinary done by this time if Mr Fox had gone on'.[424] But, claimed Fox, he had spared no efforts: on 8th, when he first saw the King,

I instantly published my acceptance, wrote before I dined to the Duke of Argyll to receive Oswald; and from that time till Saturday noon [11th], went about pressing men into the service; without success indeed; but there was no doubt in those who refused my offers of [my] being fixed in the situation that enabled me to make them. I must add, that from Thursday [9th], when the K[ing] was not only firm but cheerful, till Saturday [11th], when I followed Lord Mansfield into the Closet, I did not see or send message to the King; so that he was infected with no fears of mine.

Thus Fox, in retrospect, disguised both the insecure and hypothetical nature of his commission, and his own tactical defeat, in order to lay the blame for the failure of his system on Newcastle and the oligarchical conspiracy he allegedly organised.

Harry Digby thought an acceptance of defeat better than a bid for power which, failing next winter, would have meant the removal from office of all Fox's friends. Yet Digby believed that Fox's enemies could secure that outcome now if they insisted on it. Fox professed himself happy at not being Chancellor of the Exchequer, 'seemed easy', doubted whether he should have anything, but reassured Digby that he thought his, Fox's, friends would be left in place.[425] For the moment, things seemed to depend on Mansfield, for the King did not mention the negotiation to Hardwicke at the drawing-room on 12th. Nor did Hardwicke see a favourable opening: Fox's failure might make Pitt's friends 'more tenacious of their demands', and 'no one concession has yet been specified'.[426] Harry Digby thought Newcastle had dished Fox only at the cost of leaving himself in a worse position. After Newcastle's behaviour the King would incline to Pitt, who could also command Leicester House; so that if they came in together, Pitt, not Newcastle, would be Minister.[427]

On Sunday 12th, 'it was openly reported by Mr Fox's party that he *would* not come in, by the Duke of Newcastle's that he [Newcastle] came in again and that all would be accommodated, and by Mr P—'s that perhaps it might do, but yet was doubtful, without H.M. would submit to give up Mr Fox, and not desire to have him made Paymaster'.[428] But Pitt was not yet in town; and Newcastle was not due to return from Claremont until Monday 13 June,[429] having last seen the King on 7th. That day Mansfield was due to report to George II what terms were obtainable,[430] and the formal position was that the kissing hands of Fox's ministry had merely been delayed until 13th.[431] On that day the Commons, having no business, adjourned without discussion, on Norbone Berkerley's motion, until 16th.[432] On 16th they met and adjourned until 21st.[433] On Sunday 12 June Halifax dined at Claremont and it may have been at this point that Newcastle sent him a second time to see Legge, to ask, as Legge wrote, 'whether in case I were Chancellor of the Exchequer I would be his Chancellor of the Exchequer. To which I answered that I would enter into no such engagement and that I wondered his Grace should begin a plan that was to be founded in harmony by a proposal that must tend to division'.[434] Meanwhile Mansfield, after encountering Newcastle by chance on 11th, had failed to arrange a meeting with Hardwicke until the following morning. Devonshire was at Park Place, Conway's country house, in a party which included Fox; and Mansfield could not meet him until his return on 13th.[435] Devonshire claimed Mansfield told him that Newcastle, Hardwicke, Bute and Pitt 'had met[436] but had come to no resolution, [and did not see that they were authorised by what he had said to them]; upon this we agreed that the King should send them a message, which when I had got his approbation was sent to them that evening'.[437] Newcastle returned to town on 13th and met Hardwicke, afterwards writing to Bute: 'as the orders we received from the King, were brought to us by my lord Mansfield, we are both of opinion that we should see my lord Mansfield to know more particularly, what his Majesty's orders were and what his pleasure now is in order the better to inform your lordship and Mr Pitt of it'.[438] Newcastle then met Mansfield over dinner and heard the message which the latter brought from Devonshire: that the King desired those who met to draw up and submit a plan of ministry able to carry on his affairs, with two conditions: his word was absolutely engaged to give Fox the Pay Office, and Winchelsea should be taken care of. Otherwise, 'the King is disposed to come into such alterations as shall be necessary to fix and adjust a firm and proper ministry'.[439] Newcastle then at once arranged a meeting at Royston's at nine that evening, 13th, with Hardwicke, Pitt and Bute.[440] Walpole had little expectation of the success of any such negotiation, since he wrongly believed the King to have insisted on Winchelsea remaining in his post.[441] What passed at the meeting on 13th is not recorded, except that Newcastle believed that 'the Admiralty is insisted upon' by Pitt. Nevertheless, the behaviour of Mansfield and Bute left him optimistic about the outcome,[442] and Dupplin thinking of himself at the Exchequer if the system came about;[443] since, perhaps, Legge had waived it. But it is not certain that a scheme of ministry was drawn up. On 14th, Mansfield reported to Devonshire that

they had met the night before upon the message but had come to no resolution; as the spirit of indecision seemed still to prevail among them I proposed to the King a second message to say, that he desired they would immediately lay before him such a plan as they could agree upon and as they thought would be able to carry on the King's affairs. This Lord Mansfield delivered to them but told me that he might beg to decline having anything more to do with [them] for that they meaning Mr Pitt were jealous of him as well as of me, and advised that Lord Hardwicke should report the result of their meetings to the King.[444]

Newcastle then took the initiative by replacing Mansfield with Hardwicke as mediator, and wrote on 14th to ask that Devonshire should effect this by sending Hardwicke a royal summons so that he could explain what had occurred at the meetings with Pitt and Bute.[445] As Fox feared, 'Will not my *friend* Lord Hardwicke, report the King as not so much engaged in honour to me, as your Grace and Lord Mansfield may (through partiality to me as he will say) have represented him'.[446] Devonshire agreed, and added in his reply: 'His Majesty this morning desired that I would speak to Lord Mansfield to acquaint

your Grace and the rest of the persons that met last night [13th] that
he hopes they will prepare and lay before him for his consideration
such a plan of ministry as you can all agree on and think will be able
to carry on his affairs'.[447] From a simple request to discover the terms
available, the King had evidently – before receiving them – chosen to
order a scheme to be drawn up on the basis of them.

Mansfield accordingly called on Hardwicke carrying both the command that a plan of ministry be drawn up, and an invitation that
Hardwicke should report progress to the King the next morning,
15th.[448] Late at night on 14th, Hardwicke called on Pitt bringing

the paper produced by Lord Granby, and told me he (Lord Hardwicke) had
orders from the King to attend him this morning. His language concerning
Lord George [Sackville] in the War Office much the same as Lord Granby's.
Admiralty still the King's points, as well as Fox. Lord Anson being totally
dropped, a hardship; and a point of honour to Lord Hardwicke to mention him
to the King.[449]

Evidently a plan of ministry had been drawn up in collaboration with
Granby, then prominent among Newcastle's supporters in the Commons,
and it was probably this document which Hardwicke presented to the
King in a 'very disagreeable' first audience on the morning of 15th.[450]
It was almost certainly prepared in the light of the meeting on 13th,
and presumably embodied the terms necessary to secure the alliance of
Pitt and Bute, including a Secretaryship of State for Pitt, a Cabinet
place for Temple, First Lord of the Admiralty and a peerage for
Legge, and Lord George Sackville as Secretary at War.[451] Fox was
seemingly excluded from the Paymastership, and Waldegrave brought
news to that effect to Bedford and Rigby at Woburn on 15th.[452] Hardwicke wrote to Anson that, in his audience,

I told his Majesty that I could take no part at all, unless some honourable regard
was shown to your lordship, though I could not just then point out the particular
thing; that I had told the gentlemen with whom we had conferred the same
thing and had formerly humbly conveyed it to his Majesty. In his subsequent
discourse the King, in aggravating the inconveniences that would arise from this
new plan, told me with warmth, that resignations had been talked of; that, in
the way we were going there would be resignations enough; that my lord
Winchelsea was in the next room in order to come into his Closet to resign. The
convenience of this struck me, but I reserved myself. Some minutes afterwards
the King read over my list in heat, objected to Mr Legge being made a peer
and First Lord of the Admiralty, was determined not to do two great things
for one man at the same time, and in this he was peremptory. I then threw
your lordship in his way, but that I was far from knowing what the other
persons would say to it. His Majesty answered quick, 'I shall like it extremely.'[453]

Devonshire also recorded what he understood of Hardwicke's audience:

The King in great anger told him that he was their prisoner and must submit
to what terms they would impose upon him. When Lord Hardwicke came out,

he told me that the King had yielded every point except Lord George Sackville, and desired that Legge might not be set at the head of the Admiralty but preferred Lord Anson. I told his lordship that I imagined he must be mistaken and desired that he would stay till I came out. I took the liberty of expostulating with the King and told him that if he did not yield I had reason to think we could obtain those two points and desired that I might have leave to explain those two points, which I did by telling him that though the King had said he was conquered and therefore obliged to submit yet he expected that they should acquiesce on those points, in which he had told them in his message that he thought his honour was engaged and at the same time intimated if they meant to keep any measures with any of us, that they must show some regard to the King's honour. His lordship promised that he would state it in the light I told him and not as he received it from the King. Lord Winchelsea had declared that he could not remain in the Admiralty and gave it up in the most honourable and respectful manner.[454]

Yet Newcastle was far from happy with the prospect. His position in a coalition would be determined to a significant extent by his standing with the King, and this had been seriously undermined. Before Hardwicke's audience, Newcastle wrote to him and to others to protest his innocence: 'I am now to make a considerable part of [the King's] new administration, possibly not greatly supported (at first at least) by my new colleagues, without that great and material support exerted in the manner it has always been formerly, to my ease, comfort, honour and security; and with the frowns of the Closet'.[455] 'My real crime is, not coming in with Mr Fox. You', he wrote to Ashburnham, 'and my other friends, are responsible for that. My next fault is, not coming in without *these gentlemen*; which it was impossible for me to do, when I would not come in with Mr Fox'.[456] But Newcastle had not done a deal with Pitt: 'You know also, how much I have endeavoured jointly with your lordship to bring these gentlemen to more reasonable terms, and that I never have directly nor indirectly entered into any engagements of any kind with them, and am as much at liberty now, as I was the first hour I saw them, to take any part whatever without them'. Nor had Newcastle engineered the resignations: the failure of Fox's scheme was, rather, an independent confirmation of his advice.[457]

How, if at all, the situation was modified by Hardwicke's audience on 15th is not clear, though Hardwicke thought the news of it made Newcastle 'most happy'.[458] That night, the two of them met Pitt and Bute again and persuaded them to accept Anson at the Admiralty,

if the King adheres to it. Mr Legge may be satisfied in another shape. Nothing I think remains that can create difficulty, except that of Lord George Sackville, Secretary at War, which they hitherto insist upon, and I almost despair, after all my pains, of getting them off from it. If his Majesty would graciously be pleased to yield in that point, I have very sanguine hopes of being able to settle that of Mr Fox to satisfaction, which I do most heartily wish.[459]

Dupplin wrote of the meeting:

things passed with regard to the persons negotiating better than at any of the former. In point of business; it was agreed that Lord Anson should be First Lord of the Admiralty; and Mr L[egge] (if he consented) Chancellor of the Exchequer. Expedients and very valuable ones were proposed as equivalent to Mr F[ox] for the Pay Office, particularly by way of Irish pen[sion], though the giving him the Pay Office, if insisted upon, was not absolutely denied. It was insisted that Lord G[eorge] S[ackville] should be Secretary at W[ar].[460]

Newcastle recorded: 'Mr Potter was Mr Pitt's first point, and the only condition was, that he should be fully satisfied, or Mr Pitt would not consent to Mr Fox's being Paymaster'. Newcastle later claimed that he had even been willing to remove Dupplin from his share of the Pay-mastership without compensation in order that Potter should have an office (until Halifax's resignation temporarily inclined Newcastle to move Dupplin to the Board of Trade in his place).[461] Hardwicke wrote that he reported what had passed in the Closet vis-à-vis Anson to the meeting that evening:

I stated it, as it was in reality, as the King's option. My lord Bute and Mr Pitt received it with the greatest politeness. Lord Bute first broke the ice, declared his particular respect for your lordship, and did great justice to your character and merit in your profession, and declared that he knew those to be the senti-ments of the place to which he belonged. Mr Pitt said he only waited to hear what Lord Bute would say, and most readily concurred in the same sentiments. In short it ended so that all the four plenipotentiaries agreed that your lordship should be again at the head of the Admiralty, if the King continued in the same mind, and Mr Legge have his old office of Chancellor of the Exchequer which he had professed to like better than any other place.[462]

Evidently after the meeting on 15th, Hardwicke received a letter from Devonshire, who had just had a note from the King. George II was afraid that, in his agitation, he had not explained himself fully to Hardwicke in the audience that day. The King, wrote Devonshire, 'orders me to insist upon the Pay Office for Mr Fox and to have no Secretary at War imposed upon him, but either to keep the present one [Barrington], or to let him name one of his own liking, and that Lord Anson should be at the head of the Admiralty preferable to Mr Legge'.[463] Hardwicke was happy to send him the good news about the Admiralty, and forwarded Devonshire's letter to Newcastle. The Secretaryship at War, he pointed out, was now the crucial point.[464]

On 16th, Hardwicke saw Devonshire in the morning and then pro-ceeded to an audience. Devonshire wrote:

Lord Hardwicke reported that they agreed to Lord Anson, and Legge to be Chancellor of the Exchequer, that they had in a manner assented to the Pay Office but persevered in the Secretaryship at War for Lord G[eorge] S[ackville] and hinted that if one was granted there would be no difficulty in the other. The King was very tenacious, insisted on Fox and would not hear of the other, desired his lordship to get it off, gave many hard names to Lord George and concluded that if they forced him upon him they should if ever it was in his power repent it, and that he would treat him as he deserved. That he should look on him as a spy and would treat him as such.[465]

Hardwicke then dined at Dupplin's with Newcastle and others.[466] Dupplin recorded that in the audience

things were calm and placid – the expedient as to the Pay Office was rejected – and it was absolutely insisted upon, that Lord G[eorge] S[ackville] should not be S[ecretary] at W[ar], but that either Bar[rington] shall 'remain or I will name his successor'.[467]

Newcastle thought the King 'much softer' than on the previous day. Then, Legge called at Newcastle House, was offered and accepted the Exchequer,[468] and gave Newcastle 'entire satisfaction'. Evidently after Legge, Charles Townshend called; and while he was with Newcastle, Pitt also joined them.

Charles declared to the Duke of Newcastle and Mr Pitt that if Lord George Sackville was not Sec[retary] at W[ar] he would be contented to be Treasurer of the Chambers. But if Lord George Sackville was Secretary at War he would not take that office and would be displeased if he were Treasurer of the Navy – so ended his private story.

Newcastle and Pitt were then alone together.

The first part of the conversation was *ministerial*; the latter part very frank and easy and confidential. He *recommended* an expedient as to the Pay Office; but he told the Duke of Newcastle that as to Lord George Sackville it was a *sine qua non*, that if that was not yielded, he was not his *own master* upon that subject.[469]

Nevertheless, their conversation was long and agreeable, full of civility and professions of desire for union. 'My dearest sees', Newcastle wrote, 'we have brought things very near'.[470]

Yet still Newcastle was not confident of the outcome. Fox was urging on Devonshire that the King insist on keeping his promise about the Pay Office, threaten Hardwicke to speak to Pitt directly, and perhaps actually do so. 'I believe Pitt, if sent to, would give as good as possible'. And Fox added some suggestions about the remaining ministerial re-arrangements:

Make Halifax Secretary of State *vice* Holdernesse. That sacrifice does the K[ing] some honour and makes room. Pension, or promote [the] Duke of Leeds pensioning some Cab[inet] Councillors to get the Cofferer's place. Pension Cholmondeley – this last must be very easy. I see no use in the King's own changing the Secretary at War, unless lord Duncannon will take it.[471]

In making that suggestion, Fox touched – whether knowingly or not is unclear – on an issue which was, for Newcastle, suddenly of major importance. On 16th, Halifax dropped a bombshell, writing to Newcastle: 'Your Grace must think me an idiot, if you imagine me insensible to the treatment I have received', and complaining of 'not having been able to obtain of my friends what I was offered the other day by those I had no reason to rank as such'. Newcastle's schemes had long included the elevation of Halifax's post of President of the Board of Trade to rank as a third Secretaryship of State. Now, that offer had apparently been withdrawn, presumably too by Newcastle and in order not to trespass on the sphere of Pitt's projected department. Furthermore, it was evidently Newcastle who gave Halifax the impression that the Board of Trade was 'to be lopped also of those valuable *agrémens* which your Grace and I', wrote Rigby 'are of opinion should never have been taken from the Secretary of State of the Southern Province'.[472] Thus frustrated, Halifax now resigned the Board of Trade.[473] Newcastle implored him not to act precipitately: 'I wish the thing you wish, as much as you can do, and will do everything in my power to bring it about, except that of breaking this system, which I am sure you would not suffer me to do'. Barrington was sent as Newcastle's emissary to Halifax that afternoon, 16th;[474] but his mission was a failure. Halifax had an audience on 18th to resign: 'a very rash step', wrote Dupplin, 'of which he most certainly will in cooler moments repent'.[475] Halifax, as Dodington was aware and as Harry Digby was now publicly emphasising,[476] had upset the last scheme for a Fox ministry in order to be third Secretary of State, and was confident until now of that promotion.

Lord Halifax tells all his friends of it, goes to Court, talks to Pitt about it as a thing settled; Pitt stared at him, and told him very coolly, and very truly, that he never had heard one word of it: and that he did not conceive that anybody had a right to curtail his office to that degree which was, already, too much entrenched upon, by the Board [of Trade].[477]

But from Rigby's account it is clear that Halifax had his audience *before* his encounter with Pitt, which can therefore only have confirmed and added to his version of Newcastle's conduct: Pitt

told him the Duke of Newcastle had never agitated this matter for him. He did not, indeed, say he should have given way, but assured him it had never come in contest between them. Nay it appears since, the Duke of Newcastle[478] was so well prepared to part with this bosom friend of his, that my lord Hardwicke this very morning has named my lord Dupplin to the King for his successor, and he will have his place.

Halifax's abuse of Newcastle astonished even Rigby. Between 16th and 18th Newcastle had evidently decided to sacrifice an ally whose treachery to Fox, 'having betrayed all Fox's confidence to him for a week together', had left him politically isolated: 'This very person', as Rigby wrote, 'whose first refusal last week to join with our wishes was one of the principal causes of our failing'.[479]

But this was evidently kept secret from Pitt and Bute until 18th. Hardwicke meanwhile arranged a meeting with Newcastle, Bute and Pitt on the evening of 16th at 9.0, calling alone on Bute beforehand at 7.30.[480] Newcastle wrote of the meeting at 9 p.m.:

Mr Pitt still insists upon Lord George Sackville, and will not be satisfied though Lord George himself desire to be excused. Lord Hardwicke goes again to the King this day, Mr Fox's point will be yielded to but the other will certainly be insisted upon by Pitt to the last. What the King will do, I know not, but I believe he will be forced to yield. Which I own I am very sorry for. However, as I am very well with Pitt, I can't have offended the King, *this week*, if I do go in together, which I think we shall. I hope we shall not be on a disagreeable foot. P.S. My dearest must think, that *they* have given up the Admiralty, when Lord Anson is with their consent and desire to be at the head of it, and in effect, we have now the Treasury, and Admiralty, which they had before, and nothing can be such an honourable acquittal of our old Administration, as Mr Pitt's putting Lord Anson at the head of the Admiralty, when he (Pitt) comes in.[481]

But Hardwicke postponed his scheduled audience until 18th to deal with 'certain difficulties, not yet quite removed'.[482] Devonshire, at Kensington when Hardwicke's letter arrived,[483] still believed that 'they will yield to the King'.[484] Far from being willing to betray Leicester House, the chief 'difficulty' was the reconciliation of Legge. Probably to that end, Hardwicke wrote to ask to see Bute urgently on the morning of 17 June.[485] At that meeting, a unique Memorandum found its way into Bute's possession. Undated but in George II's hand, it urged conciliation.[486] What was said at the meeting is not recorded, nor what passed between Legge and Bute when – as seems possible – they met alone in the evening of 17th or early on the morning of 18th.[487] Yet the general problem was tactical. Except for Legge and Halifax, goodwill was not lacking: the only point was to bring Pitt to agreement on the Secretaryship of War, and it was soon public that this issue alone obstructed a settlement.[488]

The four chief protagonists met again on the night of 17th. Newcastle did not find it enjoyable. Pitt 'insists upon all little points, now that he has given up the great points'. But Legge too was present and in much better humour,[489] presumably as a result of Bute's intervention. By 18th, all difficulties on the part of Leicester House and Pitt seemed to have been smoothed away irrespective of Fox's inclusion or the possible purge of his friends. Before leaving for Kensington that morning, Hardwicke had a note from Newcastle: 'in the present state of things, may it not be as well, not to remove Mr Ellis [Joint Vice Treasurer of Ireland], and thereby risk Mr Fox's taking the Pay Office? If you think with me, that part of the paper may be softened, or totally omitted, and then Oswald must remain where he is'[490] at the Board of Trade. Evidently Newcastle still supposed that Fox was to be

otherwise provided for. His mind had changed by the time Hardwicke
carried their jointly agreed scheme of ministry to the King, and that list
placed Fox unambiguously in the Paymastership.[491] Newcastle was aware
that the three stipulations – Anson, Fox and Lord George Sackville –
'will all go as the King wishes'.[492] But Newcastle or Hardwicke must
have met Pitt before Court on 18th, if, as Newcastle later wrote, the
insistence on Sackville 'was not given up till last Saturday morning, one
hour only before this system is finished, as far as is now done'.[493] Once
in the Closet, Hardwicke found the King's mood markedly improved.
He complimented Hardwicke 'for having done so well. And the Duke of
Devonshire told the Duke of Newcastle that it was his original plan.'
On those terms, the ministry was finally settled. Hardwicke explained
that 'they yielded with regard to the Pay Office and Secretary of War,
that Mr Pitt said he must beg Lord George Sackville's pardon for having
proposed him without his knowledge and that his lordship absolutely
declined it'.[494] Hardwicke informally recommended Dupplin to succeed
Halifax if he persisted in his resignation, but the King did not agree to
the removal of Ellis, 'so that the affair of Lord Duncannon and Mr
Potter is still to be considered'.[495] But the major points had been conceded. Above all, though at the price of accepting Pitt's Admiralty
Board, Anson had been restored, 'by the united voice of all parties and
the concurrence of Savile House, though that must not be talked of'.
Hardwicke congratulated himself on the 'honest dexterity' through
which he had brought it about. It was, he told Anson,

the greatest thing for the King's honour, for the credit of his old administration,
and for your own honour. It does, by their own admission, give the lie to all the
calumnies that have been raised. It contradicts all that had been said upon the
enquiry [though we don't openly talk that style yet][496] and confirms the issue
of that enquiry to be a total justification. The King sees it in that light and
therefore is prodigiously pleased with it. This is the true light wherein it is to
be seen, and the unanimity of the Royal Family upon it, is a most happy and
inviting circumstance, and will, I am confident, induce your lordship to overlook all other circumstances which a little time and opportunity will correct.
I have privately laid in with Lord Bute and Mr Pitt that some one of their
people may be changed upon being otherwise provided for, and they have agreed
to the reasonableness of this.

Newcastle had previously promised Stanley a seat at the Admiralty
Board; and Gilbert Elliot, Hardwicke suggested to Anson, 'I dare say,
will in six weeks be as much yours as theirs. Besides, I am told that
Admiral Forbes is likely not to accept, and, if so, it will make room for
Sir Edward Hawke or any other man we shall like.' Anson should not,
therefore, make trouble but accept the terms which had been obtained.[497]
Some of these afterthoughts can be traced on Newcastle's copy of the
ministerial scheme: Dorset might be moved from Master of the Horse to
be Groom of the Stole, freeing the first post for Temple. 'Q[uery] Stanley'

was set down against the Admiralty and Lord Duncannon for the Treasury Board, in whose place is not clear. Then, Ellis could not be removed as Joint Vice Treasurer of Ireland, lest it renew Fox's agitation.[498] Alternatively, Dorset or Rochford (Groom of the Stole) might be pensioned to make way for Temple. In any event, Lord George Sackville got nothing: 'I think', observed Rigby of Dorset, 'his lordship has not made much of his politics this winter.'[499] But whatever the minor arrangements, Newcastle and Hardwicke were delighted at the outcome and wrote to congratulate Bute, who replied in similar platitudes, crediting Hardwicke with the success of the negotiations.[500]

Pitt also had an audience on 18 June; Devonshire wrote:

The conversation was long, the King spoke plainly to him, told him some truths but upon the whole I hear Pitt was not displeased with it, nor on the other side was the King though Mr Pitt did not give such positive assurances upon a certain point as could have been wished. I have told the King that I really believe it depends upon himself for that if the gentleman sees his way in the Closet he will go as far as another.[501]

From the start, Pitt was implicated as an agent in the new scheme. The previous day he had summoned George Townshend; and before his audience on 18th, both brothers called on him. Rigby wrote:

He told them how matters were settled; that he was going to the King; asked George Townshend if he might name him to his Majesty for any employment, and hoped things had his approbation. His answer was, that he would take nothing; that he had a *friend or two* by whom he would make his sentiments known to his Majesty; that he had not been consulted till it was too late; that he had neither approbation nor disapprobation, or anything left but admiration. And then, turning to Charles, the new Secretary said he hoped he might mention him again for Treasurer of the Chambers. He replied, that he already was Treasurer of the Chambers; that he had no thoughts at this time of resigning that employment; but that he should not go to Court on Monday [20th] with the new administration, but retire into Norfolk tomorrow with his brother. George approved of his language, and they left Mr Pitt equally dissatisfied. Lord Anson's promotion it is has made these shuttlecocks play so ill, I am told.[502]

One observer recorded a rumour that Anson's restoration was at Pitt's recommendation but that Pitt denied it, blaming it on the King.[503]

Charles Townshend had declared to Newcastle and Pitt on 16 June that he would be contented with the Treasurership of the Chambers if Lord George Sackville were not Secretary at War, and on 17th he wrote to ask to see Devonshire urgently, probably in order to withdraw or explain away his earlier (inconclusive) resignation of that post.[504] Walpole wrote: 'Lord Anson is made the pretence; Mr Fox is the real sore to George, Lord George Sackville to Charles',[505] but he was wrong, for the Townshends were aware that Sackville was not to be Secretary at War. But they were probably aware also of Halifax's resignation, and are unlikely to have found unwelcome the general assumption that either Charles Townshend or Dupplin would succeed him, the other being accommodated as Treasurer of the Chambers.[506] Already, therefore, Charles Townshend had by implication been refused the Board of Trade. His brother now named other reasons for dissatisfaction, noting on Pitt's letter of invitation: 'N.B. This was the first time for about a fortnight I had heard anything from Mr Pitt'; on the morning of 18th the two brothers 'to our astonishment heard him avow the ridiculous and dishonest arrangement of men which is now to take place – not the least adoption of any public system of measures being declared or even hinted at by him. Upon this occasion I without hesitation declared my resolution to be no part of it – my brother did the same.' Pitt's only excuse was necessity in the face of the King's insistence – for which he blamed Hardwicke and Newcastle.[507] As Elliot put it, 'there appears to have been little option left betwixt absolute anarchy, and the system which is now rather acquiesced with, than approved'.[508] Yet Newcastle used exactly the same plea. Necessity both compelled and justified the union of three warring elements, and the terms on which they were included: 'full restitution' to Pitt and 'all his friends', as he had insisted; no 'considerable removal' of Fox's friends, or he would probably not have accepted. Fox himself wrote: 'I am wonderfully pleased, and except that poor Dodington is dropped and bears it very ill I have nothing to wish.'[509] Newcastle had several meetings with Pitt the same day to hear his refusal to come in unless Dorset were satisfied and Pratt were Attorney General; Temple met Newcastle and evidently stood by Pitt. Newcastle also had an audience: 'The King told me, he would not turn out my lord Rochford, so we have nothing to do but to make the Warden of the Cinque Ports palatable to the Duke of Dorset.' Stone was sent on that mission the following morning.[510] But it seems that Newcastle may at least have solved the minor problems of Cholmondeley (an Irish pension), Offley (an additional £200 p.a.) and Sir Harry Erskine (Surveyor of the King's Roads).[511]

Furthermore, it was by no means obvious that Fox's following rather than Pitt's was to pay the price of the compromise. It was rumoured that Granville would be removed to make room for Hardwicke,[512] but this did not come about. Rigby advised Bedford:

There has been no thoughts of attacking your Grace, or the Duke of Marlborough, or Lord Gower, on the contrary, I am much mistaken if you have not both sides paying court to you. They are as jealous, and at bottom as much at enmity as ever, and will be striving which shall outdo the other in the means of your future friendship, which, as I make no doubt but you will do, if you manage to the best advantage, you will have it in your power to do whatever you shall think proper.[513]

Fox continued to confer with Devonshire about the disposition of minor posts,[514] and Devonshire succeeded in saving Ellis from dismissal. He would not, reported Fox, 'let Duncannon take it, and indeed both Lord Hardwicke and the Duke of Newcastle have behaved handsomely enough, who said that since it was yielded to the King that I should be Paymaster, it was very wrong to put me into *dilemma,* and tell me if I would have it, it must be with my friends disgraced'.[515]

Loose ends still remained. Temple's place, in particular, had not yet been specified. On 19th, Conway heard a rumour that Temple was to be Privy Seal 'in Lord Gower's room who succeeds the Duke of Dorset on his *resignation*'.[516] Yet Newcastle, the same day, thought it no more than probable that Temple would have that office.[517] Gower's destination, thought one observer, depended on whether Dorset or Rutland could be persuaded to accept a pension.[518] Yet George II at the same time closed one option by deciding on his own initiative to give the only vacant Garter to Waldegrave. Then, there were 'difficulties' about Pratt being Attorney General;[519] 'difficulties' about removing Cholmondeley from his place for a pension, and, by 21st, Thomond had not replied.[520] Then, it became public that Legge 'objects to the Exchequer seals if he can't have Oswald in the Treasury with him and objects to remaining in the King's service if Lord Ha[lifax] is out of it. These three have set up a dirty caballing friendship together meeting every Sunday at Bushey in all the various changes of these last two years. And I suppose this is a trial to bring [?Halifax] back again' – which Fox hoped would be unsuccessful.[521] Oswald, it was similarly reported, 'follows Lord Halifax in his resignation, and even refuses a seat at the Treasury Board'.[522] Hardwicke and Newcastle therefore set about conciliating Legge, who was invited to call on Newcastle before a meeting with Bute and Pitt on 20th.[523] But, on 22nd, Newcastle met Legge at Court and found him strongly of opinion that 'this system must be broke'; however, Pitt then had a long conversation with his ally, after which he changed his mind, telling Newcastle that 'This thing must be tried, and we must do our best.' Newcastle asked Legge to call on Hardwicke on the evening of 22nd:

I beg your lordship would know from him from whence his uneasiness arose, what connection he has with Lord Halifax in this last affair, whether he thinks anything amiss of me, and what? And I wish you could get out of him what passed with Mr Pitt, and upon what he seemed to change his opinion, which certainly was from what Pitt said. I do suspect, that Legge is afraid that Pitt and his friends think that he has left them, and also that he has connexions with Lord Halifax, which [?hampers] him with the Chancellor of the Exchequer.[524]

It seems likely that it was at this point that Legge discovered, from whom is unclear,

that in return for thinking of leaving his friends for the Duke of Newcastle [in their interview on 18 April], the Duke of Newcastle had betrayed him to his friends. He would have expostulated with them, but they would not, and negotiation taking place in their favour, they bid him take the Exchequer Seals under the Duke of Newcastle, and enter into no further eclaircissment.[525]

This caused Legge great distress. As his secretary, Samuel Martin, told Glover, Legge's mistake gave his friends

a handle to impute to him the high terms which the Duke demanded for himself; and the gentleman suspected in his own mind, that the step he had made might have conduced in some degree to inspire his Grace with that confidence. From hence he looked upon it to be a point of honour due to his friends, not to disorder their system by withdrawing himself from it; which otherwise he had certainly done for several reasons, some of a private and personal nature.[526]

After sounding Legge on 22 June, Hardwicke was to call that evening on Newcastle to report. At that meeting Newcastle probably also heard more of Hardwicke's interview that day with Sir Robert Henley, whom Newcastle evidently wished removed from the Attorney Generalship without elevating him to Lord Chancellor.[527] Hardwicke had met him that day and found him compliant,[528] and also to the other two possible contenders for the Great Seal.[529] Mansfield however refused that office, despite Fox's pressing him to accept it.[530] What Hardwicke reported of Legge's disposition is not known, though Pitt thought 'He must accept ...I understand that he will accept, but a more miserable being I have not seen.'[531] Halifax and Oswald were meanwhile in busy consultation, the first afraid for Legge that 'I fear he will ruin his character beyond all redemption'.[532] Newcastle, too, seems to have relied on his acceptance. The betrayal of Legge's overture of 18 April was now doubly effective, for it not only compelled Legge to accept the Exchequer in a position of weakness, so guaranteeing Newcastle's control of the Treasury Board; it also isolated Halifax, making his resignation abortive and finally compelling him to withdraw it. Legge took the Seals, as Dodington wrote, 'detested by Mr Pitt and Leicester House; acting under one whom he hates, who hates him, and has betrayed him; breaking faith with Lord Halifax, without whom he engaged not to act, and with Oswald, to whom he had pledged his honour never to come into the Treasury without him – And all this for Quarter Day!'[533] No wonder, as Glover recorded, that by 27 or 28 June Legge had 'the aspect of a man sinking under self-condemnation and despair'.[534]

By 23 June a few more of the final details had been worked out, and a memorandum by Newcastle evidently embodies the terms agreed to by the King. Dorset might be given an additional salary,[535] and Temple could now take the Privy Seal. Gower would be Master of the Horse, Cholmondeley have a pension on Ireland, Potter a share in the Vice Treasurership of Ireland, and Sir Harry Erskine the post of Surveyor of the King's Roads, the salary made up to the value of a seat at the Board of Trade. But Lord Chief Justice Willes, the remaining contender, with Henley, for the Lord Chancellorship, was creating difficulties. He was willing to take it only if given a peerage and either £2000 per annum on the Irish establishment for life, or if he retained in addition the place of Chief Justice for two terms.[536] Rigby reported a meeting at Newcastle House on the morning of 24th 'to dispose of the Great Seal, but they disagreed and nothing was settled about it'.

So inexplicable was the hiatus that a rumour launched by the Duke of Bridgewater on 24th quickly gained credence: 'that Pitt had absolutely refused to go any farther, if Lord Anson is put at the head of the Admiralty, and that he moreover insists upon Lord Holdernesse's dismission, for Lord Halifax to succeed him and then Oswald will go to the Treasury'.[537] Rigby thought the rumour confirmed by some appearances at Court; by intelligence via Sir Robert Wilmot that Legge's wife 'last night wished herself and her friends quiet in the country, and well out of the very bad scrape they had been drawn into'; and by the problems over the Lord Chancellorship. 'I own, from all these circumstances I cannot help thinking it very likely to break all to pieces again.'[538] Fox's sister wrote:

There is a hitch in regard to Lord Anson's being at the head of the Admiralty. The City cry out against it, and Pitt's friends now say he never came into it, though I believe 'tis very certain he did. Another difficulty is about Lord Halifax, who is angry now with his friend the Duke of Newcastle (for whose sake he refused coming in with what was called Mr Fox's administration, when he might have had what he pleased), and who Mr Legge insists upon being satisfied.[539]

Rigby's fears were unjustified. Newcastle and Pitt collaborated to remove the final difficulties rather than exacerbating them, though Pitt's camp 'insist upon having all settled, before anyone kisses hands'.[540] There is evidence[541] to suggest that someone, probably Bute, made a last-minute stand against Anson, but that Pitt supported the appointment. Then, Dorset called on Newcastle on the morning of 24th, and his affair was settled to his 'entire satisfaction'. Pitt found an MP willing to vacate his seat to allow Dr Hay to come in.[542] But the King had objected to the terms of both Willes and Henley, the last remaining candidates for the Great Seal, as extravagant. George II referred the matter to Hardwicke; Newcastle suggested to Pitt that Willes's demands should be agreed to.[543] On 25th, Hardwicke had an audience to press the King to agree to some solution,[544] first calling on Willes to check the terms he insisted on. He found George II 'very grave and thoughtful' as to Cumberland's position. 'From hence I took advantage to say that, though I hoped this would be retrieved, yet the worse face things wore abroad, the more necessary it became for his Majesty to expedite the settlement of an administration at home.' But the King still resisted Willes's terms, and inclined to Henley's. Hardwicke further suggested to Newcastle that – on Dupplin's information – it might be possible to reconcile Halifax with the offer of a seat at the Cabinet.[545] This further possibility was, however, left unmentioned in the long letter

Hardwicke wrote to Pitt to explain the problem of the Great Seal. The King might, he suggested, agree to Henley as Lord Keeper on Monday 27th; if so, the entire ministry might kiss hands on 28th, and Hardwicke exhorted Pitt: 'For God's sake, Sir, accelerate that, and don't let any minutiae stand in the way of so great and necessary a work.'[546] Pitt needed no encouraging. He urged in reply that it be quickly settled for Henley, which he thought Newcastle undecided about, and that 'when it is considered what mutilations and changes, in essentials, the paper of arrangements has undergone, I trust your lordship will be of opinion that it is quite necessary for me to see what little remains of the system proposed, go into execution at *one* and the *same time*'.[547] Newcastle was equally eager: 'I can scarce have any objection to any regulation, that makes an end'; and willing to agree to Henley, whom he considered 'friendly'. Halifax's possible return was still to be arranged before it was revealed. 'I am afraid P[itt] won't like it, but he must consent to it.'[548] But with that issue evidently still unresolved, Henley was agreed to as Lord Keeper by the King on 27th, though he showed his resentment at the high price in 'pensions and places for *these fellows*'.[549] All that remained was to fix the time and place for kissing hands – a choice Bute was happy to leave to Newcastle.[550]

That took place on 29 June. The omens were not wholly favourable. Holdernesse had been further wounded by the King's gift[551] of the Garter to Waldegrave, and was disposed to resign if there were not some relaxation of the King's continuing hostility; Devonshire told George II of this, reminded him that Pitt would in that case insist on transferring to the Northern Department, and thought he had persuaded the King to show his Secretary of State at least outward civility. Devonshire remained aware that Holdernesse 'has undoubtedly lost himself irretrievably'.[552] Yet, eventually, the King's open aversion moderated. Holdernesse remained, though he was even more dependent on Newcastle. Hardwicke, too, retained a Cabinet seat. Then, by 27th, Halifax showed Devonshire 'a great desire to be friends'.[553] No successor kissed hands for his place with the rest of the ministry. Newcastle believed that Halifax 'would come back, if *some people* would give him a bridge',[554] and Dupplin, who would otherwise have replaced Halifax at the Board of Trade, hoped and expected that some expedient would be found.[555] Parliament rose on 4 July with the matter still undecided; only at the end of September was Halifax at last persuaded to withdraw his resignation in return for a seat at the Cabinet (on a personal, not an ex-officio basis),[556] but at that point the only anticipated source of Parliamentary opposition in the next session was removed.

Newcastle summed up the professed rationale of the coalition:

Our chief aim has been, the union of the Royal Family; the preservation of the King's honour, and authority; and the forming such a system of administration, as may carry on the public service, with weight, dignity and success; and at the same time, as far as was possible, by including the principal persons of all connections.[557]

He added: 'I am mightily pleased with Mr Pitt's behaviour in general, and I doubt not but we shall go on well, if we once launch.'[558] Moreover, 'the Closet mends à *coup d'oeuil*, and I am persuaded, when all our affairs are settled, the King will soon be as good to me as ever'.[559] One observer wrote that Newcastle 'has either been overpowered or had more regard for the public than others, for he has done less for his friends than any of them'.[560] But Newcastle did not evidently engage in calculations about the prospective balance of power within the coalition on the basis of counting heads. Instead, he treated the system as a technical arrangement of major offices among leading contenders for power; the skill with which this pattern had been contrived was its guarantee of security. 'I am now embarked by advice of all my friends', he told Chesterfield, 'and they should support me in it.'[561] Then, from Newcastle's side of the Old Corps, and from Fox's, the system was lauded in a fulsome rhetoric which made play, above all, with its disinterested inclusiveness. Mansfield, too, who boasted that he knew 'more of all the springs which have moved upon this occasion, than perhaps anybody', attributed the same impartiality to Devonshire as he himself professed.[562] Devonshire agreed: 'the plan is undoubtedly the best that could be formed, the only difficulty will be to make it hold...the utmost of my wishes are to see an administration settled that will endeavour with firmness and unanimity to extricate this country out of the dangerous situation it is in at present'.[563]

This rhetoric disguised and defended the ministry from another interpretation: that the coalition 'was formed to destroy the Duke of Cumberland and Fox'.[564] That this result had been achieved at the outset through Fox's being placed in the Paymastership was not obvious; and the potential power of such a combination was a matter for future experiment, not present calculation. Cumberland had been eager at a late date for Fox to undertake the ministry,[565] and Chesterfield was struck with the extent of that Duke's power in the Closet which recent events had demonstrated – especially the King's obstinacy over Fox and the refusal of Lord George Sackville. That power, he urged, 'must some way or other be lessened or at least checked', a task in which Leicester House must join.[566] With Klosterzeven, Cumberland's power disappeared so completely, for the moment, that its latent threat at the coalition's outset is too easy to forget. At the time, too, Fox was both glad that his position had not been further eroded, and encouraged by the prospects for its renewal suggested by the substantial revival of royal power:

H.M. as things are now fixed is better off than after he was forced to yield I imagined he would be. He rejects L[ord] G[eorge] S[ackville], he punishes the

Duke of [?Dorset,] he puts Anson in the A[dmiralty] instead of Legge who was proposed for it, and he may with some satisfaction see Hal[ifax] immediately punish himself and foresee that the Duke of Newcastle will not be the happiest man in the world in consequence of his behaviour to him.[567]

The exclusion of their deserter Lord George Sackville was a particular source of satisfaction in Fox's camp.[568] Moreover, Fox was committed to preserve political peace, 'which most people think cannot long be preserved by this system, but I see no improbability of it...I must see these ministers set out before I can give any guess how they will go on but it seems to be the best system for H.M. and for your R.H. case', he wrote to Cumberland, 'that these miserable times can afford'.[569] The system offered the attractive and not contradictory prospects of present stability and future advance. Rigby heard on 24 June that 'the City begins to be clamorous; if Mr Pitt finds he is losing ground everywhere else, and gaining no power at Court in return for it, depend upon it he will stop short, and then nothing so good can happen to us'.[570]

Charles Townshend summed up the settlement:

the Duke of Newcastle cannot I should imagine be jealous of a union which levels others to himself: Mr Fox's friends could not have hoped anything so favourable to him; it is too late for Mr Pitt to repent; and as to the public and the people they have long been set aside in settlements which relate to them.[571]

Almon, in retrospect, explained the settlement of June 1757 as the triumph and restoration of Pitt,[572] and most historians have accepted such a view. Pitt, however, did not. Even to Hardwicke he admitted his 'forebodings of mind' about 'a plan, which every hour is growing more distasteful';[573] and on 28 June: 'I go to this bitter, but necessary cup with a more foreboding mind, even since last night.' The immediate occasion of Pitt's pessimism was Newcastle's treachery in claiming that he, Newcastle, had 'proposed to me in our conferences Lord Halifax's being Secretary of State for America'. Hardwicke backed Newcastle's story; Pitt denied it vehemently, insisting 'that I could not serve the King with honour and safety if no candour and fidelity of repetition were to prevail'.[574] There is no evidence that Pitt's pessimism was based on anything other than a calculation about the internal structure of the coalition. But that, in itself, was sufficient. As Glover, who believed Pitt received his office 'without any reality of power', wrote:

Mr Pitt, at this juncture, appears to have stood almost single, deserted by the country gentlemen, declining in popularity, and disunited with Legge; his only foundation was Leicester House, and his principal hope of a coalition at last rested on the Duke of Newcastle's horror of Fox.[575]

Almon, Pitt's most articulate contemporary apologist, admitted that Newcastle retained great strength in the new ministry and that

therefore this was the best step that could be taken, because it was an healing one, and while it satisfied the heads of the parties themselves, it could not fail of being agreeable to their numerous friends; and it had one advantage above all these, which was, that it entirely quelled the spirit of faction, no one party being able on its single bottom to do anything; and this coalition, so necessary in a government like ours, gave universal satisfaction to all ranks of people.[576]

The last consideration was an afterthought; Almon offered no theory of how popular pressure operated in the formation of the ministry. Nevertheless a popular dimension existed which might also have prompted in Pitt the same fears. Charles Townshend wrote from the country:

The world here speaks out about the sudden union of Mr Pitt with Lord Anson, and my neighbour Mr Cartwright (the representative of Northamptonshire) told me this afternoon, he will go no more to Parliament in this incurable age, but turn planter and husbandman, to divert his mind from the recollection of his own credulity. Indeed the outcry is loud and universal, confined to no rank of men or limits of expression.[577]

Devonshire, too, recorded what he took to be the general opinion that the ministry (which he thought, at the outset, a strong one) could not last:

Lord Anson is said to be the most unpopular point of the whole system and has ruined the popularity of Mr Pitt and his party; if it has it has had a very good effect. The run is said to be very strong against them and I hope it will continue till they are brought down to such a pitch as that they may be no longer formidable. The misfortune is that in this country it is in the power of any set of people to grow popular at the expense of government, and the more violent the opposition is, the more popular they grow.[578]

What was remarkable about the indignation so widely recognised to exist was that it no longer had a means of political articulation, and, therefore, no political impact. Walpole wrote that the City

was indignant at the re-establishment of Lord Anson: but when the chiefs are accorded, the mob of a faction are little regarded. Men could not but smile observing Pitt return to Court, the moment he had been made free of so many cities for quitting it, exactly as he accepted an employment there before old Marlborough was scarce cold, who had left him £10,000 as a reward for his patriotism.[579]

Already the stresses which were to divide Pitt and Leicester House during the course of the coalition were evident. So were lessons about the impact of the alliance on the Tories. Fox wrote on 21st: 'the Townshends and the Tories...are I hear angry with Pitt. They pretend Anson to be their reason but their reasons are of a different and more interested nature'.[580] On 17 June Edward Bayntun Rolt visited Edward Popham, Tory MP for Wiltshire, and found 'that expectation had been given the Tories by Pitt of their sharing the government'.[581] Now, there was plainly no room for the fulfilment of that understanding or expectation, and side by side with the Whig euphoria at achieving a seemingly impossible coalition ran a theme of outrage at what, in another perspective, was Pitt's act of Patriot apostasy. 'The scene closes', wrote Glover, 'with the retreat of Colonel Townshend and the country gentlemen from London, all disgusted, some from generous, most from interested motives'.[582] But that outrage could not be sustained, since on one hand the nature of Pitt's position in the coalition was debatable and would become fully clear only in the flux of future politics, and since, on the other, objections to Pitt now lacked a coherent party base. A ministry resting on a union both of what everyone now attended to, the three factions which alone carried political weight, and of the Royal Family itself, left few items of a Patriot platform which the Tories could distinctively employ. A tendency to approach the ministry of the day therefore reasserted itself. On 23 June, recorded Bayntun Rolt, 'Mr Northey dined with me [and] owned himself inclined to embark with the Court'.[583]

So the disposition of the Tory party had come at last to turn on the outcome of a manoeuvre among the Whigs: whether or not the Townshends could be accommodated in place. But that this was so was a measure of the Tories' irrelevance to the central questions of politics, the occasions on which power was secured. The desperate events of the previous three months made this so plain that it was taken completely for granted. Devonshire had urged that the best plan 'would be to endeavour to reconcile the three contending factions (for I can call them by no other name)';[584] now, he rejoiced that the final outcome mirrored 'the original plan that I first proposed to the Duke of Newcastle, namely, a general comprehensive plan of the three parties' – Newcastle's, Pitt's and Fox's. The failure of Fox's ministry after Newcastle's refusal on 7 June proved 'the little weight the Crown had to resist the struggles for power among the different parties'.[585] Such being the general assumption, the King's rejection of Newcastle's scheme on that day stood little chance of widespread acceptance. 'His plan', wrote one observer, 'reconciled the three contending parties in the House of Commons, promised fair for a reconciliation in the Royal Family and upon all these accounts [was] a most desirable plan'.[586] It was suggested at first in Fox's camp that the King had been coerced by a 'union between Leicester House, Newcastle, Pitt and the Tories';[587] but with Fox's inclusion in the system that language was dropped. The latter term was left out of the equation; and the universal language was of a coalition between three groups[588] for whom the fact of a coalition, a disinterested rallying to the King in a moment of national danger, was their defence against charges of storming the Closet. Moreover, it was correctly suggested when such a settlement was reached not only that it was at that moment all-inclusive but that the party system had been altered to the point where it no longer provided an easy base for political dissent. Lord Lyttelton wished a friend joy 'of the administration being settled at last in a way that takes in all factions and will leave no head to any'.[589] H. S. Conway's analysis echoed the tension of two weeks earlier, writing of

that *folly and faction* you mention, which I do think are now making greater strides towards making *a cypher* of this once important kingdom than almost at any period I remember to have heard or read of; and what's most provoking in the most trifling and contemptible way; we have seen the nation too often involved in faction from the earliest of our history, but then there were commonly the greatest interests concerned, as in the squabbles between the civil and ecclesiastical powers, the King and Barons, York and Lancaster, Popery and Protestantism, liberty and arbitrary power, such were generally the foundations of those great contests that have weakened and at different periods almost ruined this country. The lesser movements of private faction doubtless subsisted; for men were always men; but I believe, to our present shame, they never made so apparently and almost avowedly as now the capital springs and object of all our motions; nor did the haggling and bartering for places of all ranks and magnitudes ever make the foundation of the system that was to prevail, especially in such a manner as scarce leaves room for the Crown to become a party to the *Treaties*.[590]

Conway was quite correct. A conflict of unparalleled bitterness had been conducted in the terms appropriate to it. Only when the temperature cooled did men return to the problems raised by 'issues'. 'Mr P[itt] must seriously think of foreign affairs' wrote Newcastle on 26 June, 'in a different manner, from what he has hitherto done, or the K[ing] of Prussia will make his separate peace; and we shall lose the Electorate this year, and God knows *what* the next'.[591] But Devonshire's impression was that Pitt 'would do what was required of him provided he saw his way in the Closet'[592] – as indeed he did. By June 1758, Pitt was openly identified with the maintenance of British troops in Germany.[593] An equal surprise is reserved for the reader until the end of Waldegrave's *Memoirs*. His political conduct for three months had rested on a general assumption that there was no barrier to his heading a ministry. Yet now, he wrote, he accepted the Garter all the more willingly for a reason

which I had formerly hinted to his Majesty, but had never fully explained. I must irretrievably have lost both his favour and confidence, the moment I became an acting minister. For I had the misfortune to differ from my master in the most tender point, in relation to German politics: and though I might have done more for the support of Hanover than was consistent with the interest of my country, it would have been far short of his Majesty's expectations, short even of that which has lately been complied with by our patriot minister.[594]

The public rhetoric of wartime politics acted from 1756 to subsume party identities under an umbrella of 'patriotism', that concept having been extended beyond its previous bounds, namely those of an opposition Whig ideology. But the 'issues' generated by the war were still related to the commitment of individuals to their principled professions in a way that was undeniably *political*. Hillsborough satirised with great acuteness the relationships that were to characterise the coalition:

if the Revenue is well conducted, it is from the great ability of Mr L[egge]; if ill, the Duke of Newcastle overrules him, and is so ignorant etc. etc. If you have any naval successes, it is owing to the diligence, parts and wisdom of Mr Pitt's friends at that Board; if the reverse, what else could be expected from Lord Anson? If things in general go well, Mr Pitt is all powerful; if ill, the Duke of Newcastle thwarts and opposes him in everything.[595]

The submergence of most aspects of 'party' did not mean the end of politics. It meant, rather, a deep and silent shift in the nature of political conflict which the technical, factious crises of 1754–7 disguised as well as effected. When, after the war, the re-appearance of formal opposition generated another party system, it was a new one; and it was talked about in a new language of politics. Or rather (to historians' and contemporaries' confusion) in an old language, now laid open to misuse by the destruction of Whig and Tory parties which had survived in direct descent from those of the reigns of William III and Anne.

Conclusion

It is usually assumed that Sir Herbert Butterfield and Sir Lewis Namier, from their different positions, destroyed the 'Whig interpretation of history'. In fact, the absence of a new synthesis allowed much of the old edifice to survive, its anomalous nature unrecognised, to provide foundations for new misinterpretation. Some of these new accretions, and some of the old survivals, have been challenged in this book. Its results can most conveniently be summarised from three perspectives, and in so far as they revise accepted views of the position and activities of what have been argued to be the elements of the central triad in government: Court, Ministry and Commons. Each of these three was affected by changes in the others; equally, revisions in the historiography of one have affected the other two also.

The received account of the constitutional position of the monarch in the reign of George II, for example, has been largely derived from, and coloured by, historians' debates on the constitution vis-à-vis the institutions of party and ministry in the 1760s. As Dr Owen has rightly observed,[1] 'Whig' views of George III supposed that his grandfather, by contrast, behaved with Victorian constitutional propriety in deferring to the will of parliamentary majorities and accepting his ministers' advice; 'Tory' views of George III assumed that George II had been reduced to the position of Doge of Venice by the machinations of Whig oligarchs; that George III merely tried to repair this situation.

The account offered here justifies neither view. Rather, it reveals George II acting self-confidently as the effective head of the executive, though often constrained in his freedom of action by his dependence on Whig leaders for a parliamentary majority. Yet they in turn relied on his support, and neither Crown nor ministers enjoyed an easy or automatic pre-eminence. Questions about the position of the Crown have seldom been rigorously posed of the early eighteenth century. If its scope was widened in the 1760s, however, it does not follow that its power was previously small or diminishing. In so far as they bore on the role of the sovereign, there was nothing original in George III's actions, nor in the charges levelled against him for so acting. Both can be paralleled from the previous reign. What was importantly different in the 1760s was not a new, designing monarch, nor the absence of a Prince of Wales (for Prince George was taken up or put down by politicians in the 1750s to suit their convenience) but the absence of a Whig–Tory alignment in the old sense. Publicists of the 60s, in dealing with political events in terms of prerogative, identified a real problem; for the fragmentation of party groups came, from the accession

CONCLUSION

of George III, both to tilt the previous balance of power in favour of the Crown, and to demand of it a more active involvement in events.

Political attention was not focused on the royal prerogative in earlier decades, and the terms in which politics was described were consequently different. What is most at issue, however, is not the scale of popular influence on the actions of the ministry, but how the degree of the ministry's autonomy ought to be integrated into, and ought not to dominate, an overall map of the relationships and priorities between institutions in national government. The constitution lent itself to a description by contemporaries in terms of a tripartite balance not least because there did exist a real independence, and an approximate parity, between several of its central components. Although it is justified to focus on ministerial politics as the sphere from which most initiatives came, it is not suggested that the ministry was the dominant centre of the political world.[2] The Court and the Commons were equally powerful, though that power was exercised differently. The House of Lords as such poses few problems of explanation in this period; and as Fox described it to Lord Hartington, 'The Lords stand between the Crown and the House of Commons, but it is the House of Commons that stands between the Crown and the privileges and liberties of both Peers and Commons: and after we are nothing, you will not long continue what you wish to be.'[3] To a large extent, the ministry rather than the House of Lords was and remained the political arm of the peerage. While this was so, policy emerged in the interaction of these three institutions; but none of them was visibly marked out for future pre-eminence. The balance fluctuated. In the 1760s, it was to be the Crown which was to gain from the problems which arose between the Commons and a succession of administrations, while it was the Commons which came to the fore, as in 1756–7 and 1746, when the King withdrew his support from uncongenial ministers. At the end of the eighteenth century and beginning of the nineteenth, it was the House of Lords which grew in power and the Crown which declined. No Whig perspective predicted these fluctuations.

The terms in which the structural issues of 1750s politics were expressed revealed the priority of the changing balance of these three elements rather than a controversy over the accountability of ministry or MPs to the electorate or a wider public. Two such structural issues in particular have been dealt with: the role of prerogative and the fear of arbitrary power; and the link between the position of the First Minister vis-à-vis the Crown and contemporary doctrines of departmental individualism.

In the British constitution, wrote one commentator, 'Its monarchy hath a strong tendency to tyranny; its nobles to aristocracy, and the representatives of the people to democracy; for the principles of them all are in its original foundation'.[4] Even de Lolme wrote of 'the silent,

449

though continual, efforts of the Executive power to extend itself'.[5] Arbitrary power was an English preoccupation for a century and a half after the Revolution of 1688; those who warned of its dangers were ever ready to see it under the guise of a vigorous use of the royal authority.[6] The just balance between the institutions of government was, it was feared, always liable to alter and one or other to preponderate.[7] George II did not escape such allegations, nor did his Old Corps ministers;[8] and the justice of such charges was the subject of much contemporary dispute. Earl Waldegrave defended George II thus in 1758:

> He has more knowledge of foreign affairs than most of his ministers, and has good general notions of the constitution, strength, and interest of this country: but being past thirty when the Hanover succession took place, and having since experienced the violence of party, the injustice of popular clamour, the corruption of parliaments, and the selfish motives of pretended patriots, it is not surprising that he should have contracted some prejudices in favour of those governments where the royal authority is under less restraint.
>
> Yet prudence has so far prevailed over these prejudices, that they have never influenced his conduct. On the contrary, many laws have been enacted in favour of public liberty; and in the course of a long reign, there has not been a single attempt to extend the prerogative of the Crown beyond its proper limits.[9]

This was undoubtedly an accurate summary of the official royal position, albeit by a sympathiser. George II's temperament may well have induced a yearning for a situation where, as in Hanover, the royal prerogative was a sufficient counter to political dissent. Such characteristics were allegedly shared by others of his family. Walpole thought that both Cumberland and his sister Princess Amelia 'entered more easily into the spirit of prerogative than was decent in a family brought hither for the security of liberty',[10] though Waldegrave again denied that Cumberland entertained 'even the most distant design of a more criminal nature' than the legitimate ambition to be Regent had George II died during his grandson's minority.[11]

Others thought differently. In a debate of 10 December 1742 on hiring Hanoverian troops, the Jacobite Tory Sir John St Aubyn 'declared it to his sentiment that we lived under a Prince who being used to arbitrary power in his dominions abroad, was minded to establish it here: that all his measures were calculated for that end and this of Hanover troops in particular...'[12] But a contrary outlook could seem equally credible. Lord Egmont, perhaps the most able man still in opposition in 1754, whose inclination against the Court kept him until 1762 from accepting often-repeated offers of high office, argued in a private memorandum that the course of early-eighteenth-century legislation had been a steady extension of the 'popular interest'. The Revolution, he added, by setting up a Pretender had weakened the Crown;

county and borough franchises were growing wider, the number of MPs had steadily grown over the past century, and these, together with the great increase in the wealth of 'the Commons', had tilted the balance firmly towards 'the popular power'.[13]

None of this silenced the apprehensions of those who feared the potential of the Crown for a future exercise of strength. Horace Walpole wrote in 1756:

I am sensible, that prerogative and power have been exceedingly fortified of late within the circle of the Palace; and though fluctuating ministries by turns exercise the deposit, yet there it is; and whenever a prince of design and spirit shall sit in the regal chair, he will find a bank, a hoard of power, which he may play off most fatally against this constitution.[14]

Those fears were allegedly justified, first, by the fact that 'in the eighteenth century the powers of the executive were almost entirely derived from the royal prerogative, and only to a comparatively small extent from statutes which gave additional powers to the King or his ministers...'[15] Prerogative was the principal motive power of executive government; hence the Pelhams were unavoidably associated in fears about the conduct of the King. Their dominance over all opposition, wrote Walpole,

drew the attention of the disaffected, who began to see a prospect of the restoration, if not of the Stuarts, at least of absolute power; and this union was not a little cemented by the harmony of hatred, in which both the Pelhams and the Jacobites concurred against the Duke [of Cumberland] and the Duke of Bedford; neither the one nor the other were disposed at this juncture to stem the torrent.[16]

Fox's ambitions within the ministry gave good grounds for apprehensions of the ambitions (whether justified or not is impossible to know)[17] of his royal ally. Those apprehensions could take the form of fears of the army's power on the part even of such an un-melodramatic figure as Henry Pelham: 'Take my word for it, the Army must get some other kind of friends, than those they have at present, or a stroke will come, possibly not in my time, but in the time of those who may want the use of 'em'.[18]

Secondly, fears of arbitrary power could be sustained since the Revolution settlement had supplied a number of specific limits on what the King could *not* do; it left far less certain what he *could* do.[19] An alarm could therefore be entertained, in general terms, of the balance of institutions in the state. Comparisons were drawn with the fate of parliamentary government both in France and in Ireland, where one writer identified Dorset and Sackville, the Lord Lieutenant and his Chief Secretary, as 'those that are against the Commons'.[20] The same observer echoed Walpole in writing later of the English pamphlet press's attention to 'The fears of Old Whigs that we are in danger of falling into

451

very bad hands (in the next reign)'.[21] Ministerial sympathisers, when expressing such fears, transferred them to another reign and (by implication) to another set of ministers. Yet this transposition was not essential: the meaning was clear when Hardwicke and Murray were stigmatised as 'prerogative lawyers', and the future dominance of parliamentary institutions was beyond the conception of men in a Europe where centralising, absolute administrations were everywhere gaining ground.

Thoughtful men in the 1750s, lacking detailed 'inside' information on politics and public affairs, phrased their concern for their country, instead, as anxiety about the balance of the constitution, with 'the prerogative' standing for 'the position of the Crown'. But prerogative mattered also because political debate at a higher level was seldom conducted as a doctrinal clash, a dispute about what the constitution *was*, which if won would have practical consequence. Constitutional histories, or textbooks of constitutional law in the nineteenth-century sense, did not yet exist exactly because 'the constitution', in the eighteenth century, occupied a different place in political discourse. 'Constitutional' tenets were thought of as broad, general ones, concerning such abstractions as the liberty of the individual and the Hanoverian succession. Those tenets did not offer precise guidance in the formulation and evolution of medium term, middle-order political tactics; and it was on this level that the most interesting innovations occurred in the 1750s as tactical forms were evolved in the business of political manoeuvre. It was, moreover, such middle-order tactical lessons which were to a large extent re-learned by the professional politicians in the two decades after 1742, for Walpole's departure faced them with problems concerning the conduct and cohesion of ministries and oppositions, and the relations of each with the Crown, which they slowly and painfully resolved *de novo*; they were seldom inferred from the party practices of the first decade of the century, and references to those practices were rare.

One such problem was directly confronted by Newcastle's administration in 1754–5. Newcastle's behaviour on leaving office in 1756 and the pamphleteers' assumption of some form of accountability may create an impression that responsible government existed, in a form later familiar, at periods of crisis if not at other times. Yet this would be a false impression. The dispute over the conduct of the ministry (the choice of 'departmental individualism' or the dominance of a First Minister) expresses a different alternative: whether the ministry was to be responsible collectively or individually to the King. Such a choice had further consequences. If they were responsible collectively, their degree of practical responsibility would be lessened, for there was no alternative set of ministers in opposition who could replace them *en bloc*, and the ministry's inner cohesion rather than the royal will became the sanction which made an administration 'accountable'. If the ministers were responsible individually, however, the way was open for a considerable increase in the power of both King *and* Commons at the expense of the ministry.

A claim that departmental individualism in fact described the existing situation could therefore mean one of three things. First, an attempt was made by the King to dissolve the power attendant on Newcastle's pre-eminence in the session of 1754–5 and to emphasise that the tenure of his ministerial servants rested, individually, on royal favour and regard – an orthodoxy which still went unchallenged. It was widely held, also, that 'the office of a Prime Minister is inconsistent with the principles of this constitution'.[22] Secondly, therefore, Newcastle could reply to charges from the Commons that he wielded Prime Ministerial power by claiming that his government actually was one of departments. This defence also acted as a way of frustrating the ambitions of some members of the ministry, ambitions which rested on a view of the administration as a hierarchy of power which could be ascended by the capture of a more commanding position within it. Thirdly, and later, Pitt by contrast charged the ministry with being a government of departments in a way which prevented it from carrying on the war with vigour and decision, and allowed each of its members to dissociate himself from responsibility for most of its unsuccessful policies.[23]

Historians have failed to relate such claims in detail to the tactical intentions of those who advanced them. Thus one writer[24] argued that widening Cabinet divisions early in 1756 proved the *truth* of Pitt's attack on the refusal of ministers to accept responsibility, and that 'The fallacy of Newcastle's conception of the role of the first minister was thereby brutally but accurately exposed'. On the contrary, Newcastle's view was not a description of an independently existing reality, but a political tactic, part of the reality itself; and, moreover, a successful tactic for much of 1754–6. The way, too, in which Newcastle successfully resisted George II's attempts to limit the role of his ministers has been explained above. Those royal attitudes had a longer history. Walpole recorded of June 1751 that

When the King delivered the seals to Lord Holdernesse in the presence of the Duke of Newcastle, he charged him to mind only the business of his province; telling him that of late the Secretary's office had been turned into a mere office of faction. The Duke of Newcastle, who understood the reprimand, and Lord Holdernesse, who did not, complained equally of the lecture.[25]

Professor Pares was right in identifying on the part of the sovereign a general 'tendency to separate and confine' his ministers.[26] George II, unlike George III, was faced with a powerful barrier to the implementation of such desires in the resistance of the professional politicians, derived from the coherence of party until the 1750s. The events of that decade show too the way in which a single constitutional doctrine, admitted to be proper in itself, could have unacceptable consequences if pursued, alone, to its logical conclusions. But it is now clear that George II did not entertain, any more than George III, a deeply laid and long concerted plot to undermine the constitution: far more was it the case that their vigorous expression of accepted doctrines provoked the assertion of the contrary arguments.

From the point of view of the House of Commons, a fully specific narrative of 1754–7 has revealed in its necessary detail the crucial part of that tactical process by which the party system of the early eighteenth century disintegrated. In those years, the Tories were drawn into a Whig dogfight and deeply compromised; the Whigs were riven by person-ally-inspired conflicts for power within a ministry which was still formed on the basis of their party unity. The 'intrigues between fac-tions' of the 1750s, far from being trivial manoeuvres, were the very stuff of politics itself.

In Pitt's camp it could be admitted, in the winter of 1756–7, that party labels had meaning and substance only within changing tactical situations: that in times of political commotion 'almost all men of all denominations' concurred 'to affect the names of Whig and Tory, without fixing any certain meaning to the words, only as they may serve to advance any private scheme, or to favour prejudices ignorantly or designedly propagated, and as implicitly received'. The same writer asked in January 1757:

Is it not time to forget all these hell-born feuds and self-destroying animosities which have so long wasted us?...Let us therefore be unanimous; let us be of no party but one: let us not condemn any man for different principles from our own, so long as he continues to serve his country; nor let us any longer be the dupes of factions, the support of ignorant, selfish, and designing men, but concur to obviate all prejudice, and root out the remembrance of former dis-trusts and unnatural animosities...[27]

The Pittite *Con-Test* defended the brief Devonshire–Pitt ministry on exactly the grounds that it offered the prospect of the abolition of 'the odious distinction of Whig and Tory' through 'a coalition of parties', and appealed to an historical precedent: 'We know that they were coalised for some time under the administration of Lord Godolphin and Marlborough';[28] but Pitt and Devonshire were unable in reality to bring about that arrangement of forces, or even to sustain themselves in office by other means. It was the manoeuvres of the spring and summer of 1757, coming after the conflicts of the previous three years, which engineered an actual coalition. As a result, no significant tactical use could be made of the institution of 'party' while it continued, during 1757–62. Its widely-accepted rationale was that it had trans-cended party: thus the Foxite *Test* was quick to claim, as early as 2 July 1757, that

that wished-for time is at length arrived, and a ministry is formed upon the solid basis of an amicable coalition of all parties. The names of Whig and Tory, Pelhamite and Foxite, old ministry and new ministry, man-mountain and gawkee will now, in all probability, sink into silence and oblivion...

Thus Newcastle, too, was told in 1759 of 'the present doctrine of politics that Whigs are no longer Whigs'.[29] But it was the dramatic events of the war, and its astonishing success from 1759, which came from 1757 to preoccupy the public mind. As Chesterfield wrote in 1758: 'Every-thing goes smoothly in Parliament; the King of Prussia has united all our parties in his support; and the Tories have declared that they will give Mr Pitt unlimited credit for this session...'[30] Conway added:

the Parliament seems dead, the City pretty tame at present and all our atten-tion [is] now [drawn] to the prospect of the terms on which our affairs in Germany are to stand and to the operations of the next campaign, in that variety of scenes where we are concerned...[31]

Military victory and domestic political vicissitudes combined to trans-mute the Tory party and the possible basis of its coherence, in its own eyes and those of its opponents. By 1762, Devonshire could describe the Tories as 'these gentlemen, who three or four years ago would have been angry if you had thought them anything but Jacobites'.[32] That option had evaporated: Pitt proudly and with some truth boasted that the Tories had supported the wartime coalition on Whig principles.[33]

When that coalition broke up in the 1760s, its components drifted off in different directions. The Tories who remained were 'dispersed among the political parties by 1766'; 'many joined the following of Bute, Grenville, Bedford, Rockingham or Pitt, and the remainder were gradually absorbed into the ranks of the independent country gentle-men...'[34] Even before that happened, Bamber Gascoigne had remarked in the Commons on factional conflicts within the ministry, which 'though Whig and Tory [were] destroyed, [were] worse because personal parties [had been] substituted in their stead'.[35] This was not at once obvious. Conway drew an apt distinction between appearance and reality:

the outward face of things bears scarce any marks of change. One sees the same people, in the same places, the same system of war and politics outwardly prevails, the same harmony in our councils and the same silence in our Parlia-ment; [yet] parties seem not only to have lost their animosities, but the very line that distinguished them is effaced. The door is equally open to all deno-minations, and they all come in with equal freedom...[36]

As Devonshire urged on Bute, the Tories were conciliated as individuals, not as a party.[37]

Nevertheless, though the coherence of the parties had been damaged beyond repair, contemporaries spoke in the early 1760s of a *revival* of party conflict. Conflict there undoubtedly was; but it was no longer

CONCLUSION

organised around the axis of party in the former sense. When the language of Whig and Tory was revived, it formed a new polemic in which the old senses of the terms were misused or adapted for present advantage. As Bute was told, of Charles Townshend's self-confessed ambitions in the reshuffle which followed Newcastle's resignation: 'This idea that a Tory administration is to be set up against the Whigs, seems to be devised by himself [Charles Townshend] alone; to promote disturbance that he may profit of it'.[38] When politicians in the early years of George III's reign revived the words 'Whig' and 'Tory', they were 'using them no longer, as in 1760, to denote certain groups of men who called themselves Whigs and Tories, but to indicate differences of opinion between people hitherto called Whigs, about the constitutional rights of the Crown and their proper exercise'.[39] By such elisions as these, however, a new and disturbing framework of politics was accommodated and reconciled to the past, sometimes so far as to disguise the very transition itself, rephrasing the problems which resulted from that discontinuity as personal ones concerning the conduct of George III and Lord Bute. As was once wisely pointed out, 'It has been the peculiar characteristic of English constitutional history that fundamental changes have been reflected as little as possible in outward forms'.[40]

The results of this book have been ones obtained through the extension of narrative technique. But those results have not depended on a claim that narrative or any other method is able to uncover motive explanations. The ascription of motive breaks down at short range, when action is seen in its appropriate detail – that is, at the range at which it would be expected to apply. 'Motive' explanations found acceptable by modern academics too often dissolve in the complexities of real tactical situations. This has an important consequence for the relation between 'political' and 'constitutional' history as familiarly conceived. Any sufficiently rigorous narrative reveals how constitutional precedents, far from being the natural expression of principled motivation, seeming almost to have a life of their own on some abstract plane like that once attributed to a received canon of political thought,[41] are secreted in the interstices of political practice. The political history of most of the eighteenth century, hitherto based on an inadequate narrative, has seldom been able to demonstrate or identify that process. As a result, 'constitutional' history as generally written about this period has usually had two relevant characteristics. One has been its helpless dependence on an abstracted, summarised version of the course of high political events, derived from the current secondary sources. Crucial parts of that abridged narrative, implied or explicit, have here been overset by the redating of letters, the revision of published texts, and the recovery and juxtaposition of the full range of available evidence.

Its second characteristic has been its vulnerability to an ideology

456

CONCLUSION

dealing *a priori* with the sources of political change, the relation of constitutional precedent to political action, and the perspective (almost invariably Whig) along which general political arrangements have, as a result of the first two things, been held to be destined to evolve. A contention of this book is the effective bankruptcy of the ideology concerning the nature and evolution of political action which is traditionally entrenched in constitutional history. That ideology is discredited by the reduction of its 'texts' to the contemporary rationalisations of conduct generated as responses to a series of precisely described tactical situations. This, it is argued, is the only sense in which those texts can be given meaning: as a collection of concrete instances. The reassertion of a traditional genre can be made impossible by a fully specific and appropriately detailed account of actions, showing their limited intelligibility in the light of the evidence rather than their complete (but spurious) intelligibility in the light of an anachronistic, arbitrarily adduced ideology. Constitutional ideology, among other things, fails in the face of a demonstration of the uncertainty surrounding human conduct, which a mass of new evidence, deployed above, leaves less numinous but which, unmistakably and irreducibly, survives.

Notes

1. The quotations are all taken from a recent popular author. But the same assertions can also be found, more cogently argued if less neatly expressed, in the work of a wide range of historians. In either case, what unites the exponents of a 'Whig interpretation of history' with their socialist successors is exactly this curiously English refusal to take politics seriously.
2. J. C. D. Clark, 'The Decline of Party, 1740–1760', *EHR*, XCIII (1978) 499–527; idem, 'A General Theory of Party, Opposition and Government, 1688–1832', *HJ*, XXIII (1980) 295–325.
3. *Thoughts on some late Removals in Ireland* (London, ?1754) p.3
4. J. L. de Lolme, *The Constitution of England, or an Account of the English Government* (London, 1775) p.312; cf. pp.60, 274–5, 309.
5. H. T. Dickinson, *Liberty and Property. Political Ideology in Eighteenth Century Britain* (London, 1977) p.1.
6. Ibid.
7. J. D. B. Miller, *The Nature of Politics* (London, 1962) p.14.
8. Dodington, *Diary*, 25 Jan 1753.
9. Miller, op. cit. pp.17, 19.
10. Ibid. p.14.
11. Walpole, *George II*, I, 92; cf. T. W. Perry, *Public Opinion, Propaganda and Politics in Eighteenth Century England. A Study of the Jew Bill of 1753* (Harvard, 1962) pp.18, 36–7.
12. *The Country Gentleman's Advice to his Son* (London, 1755) p.43.
13. Miller, op. cit. p.14.
14. Walpole, *George II*, I, p.xxxiii.
15. Bolingbroke, *Works* (1844 edn) II, 410; quoted in H. T. Dickinson, *Bolingbroke* (London, 1970) p.264.
16. Dickinson, op. cit. p.12.
17. Dodington, *Diary*: Introduction, p.xvi.
18. Walpole, *George II*, III, 26.
19. E. Weston to R. Trevor, 17/28 Sept 1745: HMC 14th Rep. App. IX, p.132. Weston was then Under Secretary of State for the Northern Department.
20. Cf. Dr Dickinson's condemnation of politics after Walpole's fall as 'Factious struggles between "ins" and "outs"...waged more to gain royal favour than on issues of principle or on questions of national interest.' (*Bolingbroke*, p.273).
21. Cf. P. Langford, 'William Pitt and Public Opinion, 1757', *EHR*, LXXXVIII (1973) p.75 ff.
22. Ibid. p.70.
23. For a recognition that the system of 'representation' could be seen as intended to *check* the popular voice rather than to express it, cf. de Lolme, op. cit. pp.176–7.

24. *A Second Letter to the People of England* (London, 1755) p.1; *An Answer to a Pamphlet, called, A Second Letter to the People* (London, 1755) p.3.
25. The most articulate contemporary discussion of the powers of government in terms of a trust is found in the pamphlet controversy surrounding the Irish crisis of 1753–6; cf. especially: *An Answer to Part of a Pamphlet, intitled, The Proceedings of the Honourable House of Commons of Ireland ... Vindicated* (Dublin, 1754); *Considerations on the late Bill for Payment of the Remainder of the National Debt, etc.* (Dublin, 1754); *The Case Fairly Stated* (Dublin, 1754).
26. Cf. P. Campbell, 'An Early Defence of Party', *Political Studies*, III (1955) 166–7.
27. *An Address to the Cocoa Tree from a Whig* (London, 1762) p.5.
28. Quoted by Sir William Holdsworth, 'The House of Lords, 1689–1783', *Law Quarterly Review*, XLV (1929) p.312.
29. A. B. Cooke and J. Vincent, *The Governing Passion. Cabinet Government and Party Politics in Britain 1885–86* (Brighton, 1974) p.4.
30. Ibid. p.5.
31. I. R. Christie, *Myth and Reality in Late Eighteenth Century British Politics and Other Papers* (London, 1970) p.36.
32. Dodington to Fox, 15 Sept 1756: 51429, f.202.
33. *Memoirs of the Life and Correspondence of the Right Hon. Henry Flood MP* (Dublin, 1838) p.37.
34. *The Test*, 12 Feb 1757.
35. *Serious Thoughts concerning the True Interest and Exigencies of the State of Ireland* (Dublin, 1757) pp.30–31.
36. *A New System of Patriot Policy* (London, 1756) p.80.
37. Langford, 'William Pitt and Public Opinion, 1757', *EHR*, LXXXVIII (1973) 75ff.
38. *A Third Letter to the Right Hon.**** (?Dublin, 1755) pp.1–2.
39. *A New System of Patriot Policy* (London, 1756) p.87.
40. *The Principles of Modern Patriots Expos'd...* (London, 1735).
41. Charles to George Townshend, 19 May 1763: microfilm of the Townshend papers at Raynham, Norfolk RO.
42. The debate is surveyed in R. R. Kaufman, 'The Patron-Client Concept and Macro Politics: Prospects and Problems', *Comparative Studies in Society and History* XVI, (1974) 284–308.
43. Maurice Cowling, *The Impact of Hitler* (Cambridge, 1975) p.ix. For an effective criticism of Plumb's assertions on patronage and corruption, cf. J. B. Owen, 'Political Patronage in 18th Century England', in P. Fritz and D. Williams (eds.), *The Triumph of Culture: 18th Century Perspectives* (Toronto, 1972) pp.369–87. But for the survival of the traditional (i.e. liberal, ahistorical) orthodoxy among political scientists, cf. esp. P. G. Richards, *Patronage in British Government* (London, 1963).
44. *The Prosperity of Britain Proved from the Degeneracy of its People...* (London, 1757) p.42.
45. This expectation is explicit in, for example, B. D. Hayes, 'Politics in Norfolk, 1750–1832' (Cambridge Ph.D. thesis, 1958) p.i (yet cf. his qualifications on pp.143–4, 341); and in E. G. Forrester, *Northamptonshire County Elections and Electioneering, 1695–1832* (London, 1941) pp.1, 152; yet cf.

his qualifications: 'What we find in Northamptonshire is not an aristocratic coalition intended to procure the election of nominees as knights of the shire, but, on the contrary, groups of landowners – both peers and commoners – ranged against each other on party lines which are themselves determined by a mixture of national and purely local interests' (p.7) and 'After 1747 the interrelation of county and national politics is somewhat obscure until . . . 1797' (p.12).

46. A. N. Newman, 'Elections in Kent and its Parliamentary Representation, 1715–54' (Oxford D.Phil. thesis, 1957) p.iv; cf. B. Bonsall, *Sir James Lowther and Cumberland and Westmorland Elections 1754–1775* (Manchester, 1960) pp.6–7, 113, 122; M. Cramp, 'The Parliamentary History of Five Sussex Boroughs, Bramber, Midhurst, Lewes, Rye and Winchelsea 1754–1768' (Manchester MA thesis, 1953) p.5; C. Bradley, 'The Parliamentary Representation of the Boroughs of Pontefract, Newark and East Retford 1754 to 1768' (Manchester MA thesis, 1953) p.16; F. C. Price, 'The Parliamentary Elections in York City 1754–1790' (Manchester MA thesis, 1958) pp.21–2, 52, 75, 87; J. M. Fewster, 'The Politics and Administration of the Borough of Morpeth in the later Eighteenth Century' (Durham Ph.D. thesis, 1960) pp.6, 42–3, 544–8.

47. Newman, op. cit. pp.xviii–ix. It has been argued by J. Money, 'Taverns, Coffee Houses and Clubs. . .' *HJ*, xiv (1971) pp.15–47 that the 'two worlds' of politics, that of the establishment and that of the public without doors, were in fact linked by an unsuspected degree of 'popular articulacy' about political issues. This is not equivalent to a demonstration of the relation between the course of events in these two worlds. That could only follow on a fully adequate account of politics at the centre; for the 1750s at least, such an account has not yet appeared.

48. Newman, op. cit. p.5.

49. R. Pares, *King George III and the Politicians* (Oxford, 1953) p.207.

50. Cf. Namier, *England*, pp.82–3.

51. Lord Kenyon, C.J.: R. v Waddington (1800) 1 East. 158.

52. Willes, J.: R. v Shipley (1784) 3 Doug. 177. For eighteenth-century discussions of intentionality cf. G. Jacob, *A Law Grammar* (6th edn London, 1817) pp.24–6, 32, 115; G. Jacob, *A New Law Dictionary* (London, 1729) sub 'Intendment of Law'; anon., *The Grounds and Rudiments of Law and Equity* (London, 1749) pp.5–6, 144, 151–2; W. Blackstone, *Commentaries on the Laws of England* (Oxford, 1765–69) iv, 20–21, 198–9, 201, 227, 232.

53. Namier, *Structure*, p.42.

54. Sir David Lindsay Keir, *The Constitutional History of Modern Britain since 1485* (9th edn, London, 1969) p.289.

55. R. G. Collingwood, *An Autobiography* (Oxford, 1939). 'Truth' then becomes 'something that belonged not to any single proposition, nor even, as the coherence-theorists maintained, to a complex of propositions taken together; but to a complex consisting of questions and answers'.

56. S. Potter, *One-Upmanship* (London, 1952) p.129.

57. C. R. Middleton, 'The Administration of Newcastle and Pitt: the departments of state and the conduct of the war 1754–60 with particular reference to the campaigns in North America' (Exeter Ph.D. thesis, 1969); idem,

'Pitt, Anson and the Admiralty, 1756–1761', *History*, LV (1970), 189–98; idem, 'A Reinforcement for North America, Summer 1757', *BIHR*, XLI (1968), 58–72; W. K. Hackmann, 'William Pitt and the Generals: Three Case Studies in the Seven Years' War', *Albion*, III (1971), 128–37; E. J. S. Fraser, 'The Pitt–Newcastle Coalition and the Conduct of the Seven Years' War, 1757–60', (Oxford D.Phil. thesis, 1976).

58. Hanbury Williams to Fox, 22 Oct 1743: Ilchester, *Fox*, I, 100.
59. Chesterfield to Huntingdon, 26 Mar 1750: Dobrée, V, 1518.
60. Cf. Mann to Walpole, 21 Aug 1750: HW 20, p.171.
61. J. Campbell to Pryse Campbell, 16 Feb 1741/2: Cawdor MSS, 1/128.
62. Devonshire Diary, 5 Nov 1760: Dev 260/282.
63. Lord Tweeddale to Lord Arniston, 16 Mar 1742: Arniston MSS, II, no.128.
64. E.g. A. Mitchell to R. Dundas, 15 Feb 1743/4: Arniston MSS, III, no.91.
65. Dodington, Memorandum [October 1749]: *Diary*, p.16.
66. Archbishop of Canterbury to H, 14 Sept 1752: Yorke, *Hardwicke*, II, 45.
67. No more misleading title could have been chosen for his textbook by Pierre Muret than *La Prépondérance Anglaise (1715–1763)* (Paris, 1937).
68. Lord Orrery to Thomas Carte, 5 Aug 1752: Countess of Cork and Orrery (ed.) *The Orrery Papers* (London, 1903), II, 116.
69. Dr John Brown, *Estimate of the Manners and Principles of the Times* (London, 1757); cf. Leslie Stephen, *History of English Thought in the Eighteenth Century* (London, 1876) ch. x, 67; R. D. Spector, *English Literary Periodicals and the Climate of Opinion during the Seven Years' War* (The Hague, 1966).
70. J. Campbell to Pryse Campbell, 23 Feb 1743/4: Cawdor MSS, 1/128.
71. Walpole to Mann, 17 May 1749: HW 20, p.58.
72. D. Campbell to Charles Erskine, 16 Jan 1754: NLS 5078, f.7.
73. Findlater to Sir Ludovick Grant, 23 July 1756: SRO Seafield MSS, GD 248/182/2. Cf. Fitzmaurice, *Shelburne*, I, 38: 'All Scotland was enthusiastically devoted to the exiled family, with a very few exceptions. In 1756, going through the country as a traveller, I heard many of them, sober as well as drunk, avow it in the most unreserved manner.'
74. *A Letter to Dr King, occasioned by his Late Apology* (London, 1755) p.120.
75. For a full discussion of these transitions, see J. C. D. Clark, 'A General Theory of Party, Opposition and Government, 1688–1832', *HJ*, XXIII (1980).
76. The conventional view has been that 'the parliamentary systems of the 1750s and 1760s are indistinguishable'. J. H. Plumb, *New Light on the Tyrant George III* (Washington, 1978) p.4.
77. Sedgwick, I, 71. The section of this outline dealing with c.1742–7 is largely drawn from the works of Dr J. B. Owen, Mr R. Sedgwick and his co-authors at the History of Parliament Trust, especially Dr Eveline Cruickshanks. My indebtedness to their research is both patent, and gladly acknowledged.
78. Ibid.
79. Eveline Cruickshanks, *Political Untouchables. The Tories and the '45* (London, 1979) pp.31–2.
80. Ibid. p.30.
81. Ibid. pp.32–5.
82. Ibid. p.38 et seq.

83. Sedgwick, I, 54.
84. J. B. Owen, *The Rise of the Pelhams* (London, 1957) pp.193–7.
85. Ibid. pp.202–3.
86. A. S. Foord, *His Majesty's Opposition 1714–1830* (Oxford, 1964) pp.240–1.
87. Among those named to him as expected to support a Stuart restoration once backed by a French invasion (though with what accuracy cannot be known) were the Dukes of Bedford, Beaufort, Somerset and Norfolk, the Earls of Chesterfield, Orrery, Oxford, Westmorland, Lichfield, Shaftesbury, Shrewsbury and Berkshire, Earl Waldegrave, Lords Bathurst and Gower, Sir John Hynde Cotton, Sir Francis Dashwood, Sir James Dashwood, Sir Walter Bagot, Sir Watkin Williams Wynn; Peniston Powney, George Grenville, Robert Nugent, George Lyttelton, Norbone Berkeley, Armine Wodehouse, Thomas Prowse, James Grenville, William Pitt and many other MPs. Cruickshanks, *Political Untouchables*, pp.44–5, 115–38.
88. Ibid. pp.46–7.
89. Ibid. p.71.
90. Sedgwick, I, 74.
91. Owen, *Pelhams*, pp.258–60.
92. Cruickshanks, *Political Untouchables*, p.76.
93. Sedgwick, I, 74.
94. Ibid. I, 75.
95. The 'New Allies' at this point included a galaxy of talent: Gower, Sandwich, Bedford, Chesterfield, Halifax and their families, the Grenvilles, William Pitt, George Lyttelton, Dodington.
96. Sedgwick, I, p.56; Owen, *Pelhams*, p.307.
97. Owen, *Pelhams*, p.309.
98. Ibid. pp.305–6.
99. Estimates of the allegiance of MPs, after the revisions produced by petitions and double returns, suggest the following:

Election	Ministerial Whigs	Opposition Whigs	Tories
1741	288	129	141
1747	351	92	115
1754	368	42	109

Sources: Sedgwick, I, 57, 100–01 and calculation of four vacant seats; Namier and Brooke I, 62, 185. To the 1754 figures, which are Dupplin's estimate, should be added his figure of 26 'Doubtful'. His total is still nine short of the complete House; but the general trends from 1741 to 1754 are still clear.
100. Egmont Diary, Saturday [23 March 1751]: A. N. Newman (ed.), 'Leicester House Politics, 1750–60, from the Papers of John, Second Earl of Egmont', *Camden Miscellany*, XXIII (Camden 4th ser., vol. 7, London, 1969) p.201.
101. Foord, op. cit. p.265.
102. Dodington, *Diary*, 12 Nov 1749.
103. Cf. Walpole to Mann, 3 May 1749: HW 20, p.46.
104. Walpole to Mann, 4 Mar 1749: HW 20, p.30. A. N. Newman disagrees at this point, suggesting ('Leicester House Politics, 1748–1751', *EHR*, LXXVI (1961) 580) that 'By the end of 1750 most of the Tory members had in

practice allied themselves to the prince, and in his manoeuvres in the Commons the prince could usually rely on their support.'

105. Sedgwick, i, 585.
106. Sir Charles Petrie, *The Jacobite Movement. The Last Phase 1716–1807* (London, 1950) pp.140–59; idem, 'The Elibank Plot, 1752–3', *TRHS*, 4th ser. xiv (London, 1931) 175–96.
107. L. Colley, 'The Tory Party 1727–1760' (Cambridge Ph.D. thesis, 1976) p.9.
108. H to Col. Yorke, 2 Apr 1749: Yorke, *Hardwicke*, ii, 84.
109. Dodington, *Diary*, 5 Feb 1750.
110. Pelham to N, 18 May 1750: Ne(c), HPT transcripts.
111. Walpole to Mann, 2 Apr 1750: HW 20, p.133.
112. Pelham to N, 3/14 Aug 1750: Coxe, *Pelham*, ii, 369.
113. Cf. Ralph to Dodington, 23 Aug 1750: HMC *Various*, vi, p.21.
114. Bayntun Rolt Diary, 10 Sept 1750.
115. Egmont Diary, 24 Nov 1750: *Camden Miscellany*, p.194.
116. Newman, 'Leicester House Politics, 1748–1751', p.582.
117. Walpole to Mann, 19 Dec 1750: HW 20, p.207.
118. N to Col. Pelham, 30 Jan 1751: 32724, f.105.
119. Walpole to Mann, 9 Feb 1751: HW 20, p.221.
120. A. Stone to N, 10 Mar 1751: 32724, f.175.
121. Walpole to Mann, 9 Feb 1751: HW 20, p.221.
122. Sir Henry Erskine, a friend of Egmont's, complained to the Commons of irregularities during his court martial in 1742 at the hands of his then commanding officer in Minorca, Lieutenant General Anstruther.
123. Walpole to Mann, 13 Mar 1751: HW 20, p.229.
124. Sedgwick, i, 59.
125. Egmont Diary, 26 Mar 1751: *Camden Miscellany*, pp.204–5.
126. Dodington, *Diary*, 28 Mar 1751.
127. Ibid. 13 May 1751.
128. Fox to Hanbury Williams, 22 March/2 April 1750/51: Coxe, *Pelham*, ii, 164.
129. Bayntun Rolt Diary, 7 Apr 1751.
130. Walpole, *George II*, i, 201–2.
131. Dodington, *Diary*, 21 Mar 1751.
132. Ibid. 22 Mar 1751.
133. Egmont Diary, 4 Apr 1751: *Camden Miscellany*, p.208.
134. Walpole, *George II*, i, 81.
135. Sedgwick, *Bute*, p.xx.
136. Ibid. p.xxi.
137. Walpole, *George II*, i, 105.
138. Ibid. i, pp.122–32.
139. Dodington, *Diary*, 16 May 1751.
140. Walpole, *George II*, i, 145, 156.
141. N to Stone, 26 Dec 1751: 32725, f.558.
142. Walpole, *George II*, i, 228.
143. N to Dorset, 31 Jan 1752: Sackville MSS, Drayton, i, 48.
144. Walpole to Mann, 2 Feb 1752: HW 20, p.299.
145. Cf. J. L. McCracken, 'The Conflict between the Irish Administration and Parliament, 1753–6', *Irish Historical Studies*, iii (1942–3) 159–79.
146. N to Pelham, 31 May/11 June 1752: Coxe, *Pelham*, ii, 425.

147. A. Stone to N, 10 July 1752: 32727, f.226.
148. Walpole to Mann, 9 Feb 1751: HW 20, p.221.
149. N to H, 21 Mar 1752: 32726, f.314.
150. Walpole to Mann, 23 Mar 1752: HW 20, p.309.
151. Sedgwick, *Bute*, pp.xxii–xxix.
152. Ibid. p.xxxiii.
153. Ryder Diary, 9 Aug 1752.
154. Pelham to N, 29 Sept 1752: 32729, f.400.
155. N to Pelham, 28 Sept 1752: 32729, f.368.
156. Pelham to N, 13 Oct 1752: 32730, f.108.
157. Pelham to N, 18 Nov 1752: 32730, f.258.
158. J. Ralph to Dodington, 1 Feb 1753: HMC *Various*, VI, p.23.
159. Dodington, *Diary*, 27 Nov 1752.
160. Sir George Lee to W. Lee, 12 Feb 1753: Lee of Totteridge MSS.
161. Walpole to Mann, 14 Feb 1753: HW 20, p.357.
162. Sedgwick, *Bute*, p.xxxvii.
163. Walpole, *George II*, I, 332.
164. Pitt to Temple, 19 Mar 1753: *Grenville Papers*, I, 101.
165. Chesterfield to Dayrolles, 6 Apr 1753: Dobrée, v, 2014.
166. Walpole, *George II*, I, 349.
167. N to Pelham, 17 July 1753: 32732, f.295.
168. *The Crisis, or An Alarm to Britannia's true Protestant Sons* (London, 1754), pp.2–4.
169. Walpole, *George II*, I, 357–64; T. W. Perry, *Public Opinion, Propaganda and Politics in Eighteenth Century England*, pp.150–59.
170. Not Sir James Dashwood, as stated by Perry; cf. Dodington, *Diary*, 4 Dec 1753.
171. Dodington, *Diary*, 24 Jan 1754.
172. Chesterfield to Dayrolles, 1 Jan 1754: Dobrée, v, 2069.
173. Walpole, *George II*, I, 349–50.
174. H to N, 1 Jan 1754: 32734, f.3.
175. Pelham to N, 7 Jan 1754: 32734, f.21.
176. Dodington, *Diary*, 24 Jan 1754.
177. Walpole to Mann, 28 Jan 1754: HW 20, p.407.
178. Pryse Campbell to Sir Ludovick Grant, 2 Feb 1754: SRO Seafield MSS, GD 248/176/2.
179. Walpole, *George II*, I, 369.
180. Dodington, *Diary*, 7 Mar 1754.
181. Chesterfield to Dayrolles, 16 Nov 1753: Dobrée, v, 2058.

I. THE ACCESSION OF NEWCASTLE

1. Hartington to Devonshire, two o'clock [6 Mar 1754]: Dev 260/115.
2. Walpole to Mann, 7 Mar 1754: HW 20, p.411.
3. Pitt to Sir G. Lyttelton, [7 Mar 1754]: *Grenville Papers*, I, 106, and LWL.
4. Pitt to N, 7 Mar 1754: 32734, f.180.
5. [Sir Dudley] Ryder Diary, 7 Mar 1754: Harrowby MSS; J. F. Pinney to A. Pinney, 7 Mar 1754: Pinney Papers, 58/3/317.
6. H to [? John Roberts], 6 Mar 1754: Ne(C) 1529.

7. Pelham knew that Lee had already spoken of such an ambition: Ryder Diary, 27 Feb 1754.

8. Sir George Colebrooke, *Retrospection: Or Reminiscences Addressed to my Son Henry Thomas Colebrooke, Esq.* (London, 2 vols., privately printed, 1898–9) I, 9. (Lord Holland's partial transcript is 47589; the original MSS is lost.) This was said before Frederick's death; but the fact that both Lee and Egmont considered themselves leading contenders for the succession to Pelham up to 1754, in their capacity as the chief advisers at Leicester House, casts doubt on Mr O. A. Sherrard's theory (*Lord Chatham: a War Minister in the Making* (London, 1952) pp.235–7) that Pitt regarded Pelham's dying before George II as a disaster since he, Pitt, had otherwise expected to step forward as Prince George's First Minister in the new reign. Mr Sherrard's theory rests on speculation about Pitt's motives on the basis of published correspondence known to previous biographers, not on new evidence or a demonstrable argument about the old. Nor, as Mr Sherrard claims, was Pitt faced with the choice of coming in at once, possibly 'losing caste [*sic*] with Leicester House', or allowing Fox or Murray to take office and waiting for the new reign. As is shown here, Pitt had no power to promote or prevent either development, and in 1754 he had no standing at Leicester House to lose. Although Pitt expressed preferences about the outcome of the negotiations, he was entirely dependent on Newcastle.

9. Bayntun Rolt Diary, 10 Sept 1750.

10. Fitzmaurice, *Shelburne*, I, 42.

11. Cathcart to Loudoun, 7 Mar 1754: Loudoun MSS.

12. Cf. *London Evening Post*, 5–7 Mar 1754.

13. *Whitehall Evening Post*, 5–7 Mar 1754.

14. J. F. Pinney to A. Pinney, 7 Mar 1754: Pinney Papers, 58/3/317.

15. Walpole to Mann, 7 Mar 1754: HW 20, p.411.

16. *Whitehall Evening Post*, 5–7 Mar 1754.

17. *Public Advertiser*, 8 Mar 1754.

18. Chesterfield to Stanhope, 8 Mar 1754: Dobrée, v, 2096.

19. W. Lorimer to Sir Ludovick Grant, 9 Mar 1754: SRO Seafield MSS, GD 248/49/1.

20. Lord Ilchester to Lord Digby, 11 Mar 1754: Digby MSS.

21. Walpole to Mann, 7 Mar 1754: HW 20, p.411.

22. E.g. J. L. McKelvey, *George III and Lord Bute. The Leicester House Years* (Durham, N.C., 1973), p.17.

23. Pitt to Sir G. Lyttelton, [7 Mar 1754]: *Grenville Papers*, I, 106, and LWL. Sherrard's suggestion (*Lord Chatham: a War Minister*, pp.238–40) that Pitt wanted to urge, through the Lytteltons, Fox's promotion to a Secretaryship of State is a misinterpretation of his remark. There is no evidence that Pitt wished to see Fox in a dominant position as 'a stop gap until the new reign'. Far from Pitt meaning 'to keep in the lower ranks so long as the old King survived, but in those lower ranks to build up a reputation which should serve him in good stead when the time came' (p.242), Pitt strove successfully in the next two years to storm the Closet; though he used Prince George as an ally, he dropped him during the course of the wartime coalition when the King's death could be expected to be even more imminent.

24. Pitt to Sir G. Lyttelton, loc. cit.
25. Cf. Pitt to N, 4 Apr 1754: 32735, f.26. Murray was Dodington's first choice to replace Pelham: *Diary*, 7 Mar 1754.
26. Pelham to N, 3/14 Aug 1750: Coxe, *Pelham*, II, 369.
27. Walpole, *George II*, I, 380.
28. 'Observations on Mr Pitt's letters of 1754', nd: Lyttelton MSS, II, 255.
29. Chesterfield to Dayrolles, 1 Jan 1754: Dobrée, v, 2069.
30. Walpole, *George II*, I, 379.
31. Cf. Pitt to G. Grenville, 6 Mar 1754: *Grenville Papers*, I, 105, and LWL; Pitt to N, 6 Mar 1754: 32734, f.173. Pitt had been ill for much of the previous year (Walpole, *George II*, I, 364) and had been confined in Bath with gout since January 1754: cf. Pitt to Pelham, 23 Jan 1754: Ne(C) 450; Pitt to Sir G. Lyttelton, 16 Feb 1754: Lyttelton MSS, II, 229.
32. Walpole, *George II*, I, 379.
33. Pitt to N, 7 Mar 1754: 32734, f.180.
34. E.g. Williams, *Pitt*, I, 219; Sedgwick, *Bute*, pp.xlv–xlvi.
35. *An Address to the City of London* (London, 1762), p.18.
36. Pitt to [Sir G. Lyttelton and the Grenvilles] 7 Mar 1754: *Grenville Papers*, I, 106, and LWL; cf. Pitt to Temple, [7 Mar 1754]: ibid. I, 110, and LWL.
37. *Pace* Mr Sherrard (*Lord Chatham: a War Minister*, p.250), Pitt's reply to Newcastle in June 1754, 'Your Grace will be surprised, but I think Mr Fox should have been at the head of the House of Commons' (Walpole, *George II*, I, 392) was not an ingenuous account of what Pitt's motives had been but a tactic, part of this attempt to align himself with Fox.
38. Pitt to Temple, 11 Mar 1754: *Grenville Papers*, I, 112, and LWL. It is not known whether anything of the sort was done.
39. Lyttelton's letter is not extant, but is replied to by Pitt, 10 Mar 1754: Lyttelton MSS, II, 231.
40. Pitt to Sir George Lyttelton, 10 Mar 1754: Lyttelton MSS, II, 231.
41. He added: 'The Duke of Newcastle alone is feeble: this not to Sir George [Lyttelton].' Pitt to Temple, [7 Mar 1754]: *Grenville Papers*, I, 110, and LWL.
42. Walpole to Mann, 7 Mar 1754: HW 20, p.411.
43. Pitt to Temple, 11 Mar 1754: *Grenville Papers*, I, 112, and LWL.
44. Pitt to Sir G. Lyttelton, 10 Mar 1754: Lyttelton MSS, II, 231. The version in Phillimore, *Lyttelton*, II, 449 prints 'but' instead of 'not', so reversing the sense. As a result, all subsequent biographers of Pitt have claimed, and have misinterpreted the rest of the evidence for 1754 to suggest, that Pitt was *threatening* opposition after Pelham's death; he was, in fact, *renouncing* it. No neater verdict could be found on the calibre of the scholarship commonly brought to bear on the political career of the Earl of Chatham.
45. 'P.S.' to the above letter, on a separate sheet: Lyttelton MSS, II, 235. Printed in Phillimore, *Lyttelton*, II, 469, where it is added in error to Pitt to Lyttelton, 20 May 1754.
46. Chesterfield to Dayrolles, 8 Apr 1748: Dobrée, III, 1131.
47. H to Archbishop of Canterbury, 8 p.m. 11 Mar 1754: 35599, f.165.
48. Dodington, *Diary*, 14 Mar 1754.
49. Ibid. 7 Mar 1754.

50. H to N, 1 Jan 1754: 32734, f.3.
51. Pelham to N, 7 Jan 1754: 32734, f.21.
52. Dodington, *Diary*, 24 Jan 1754. Henry Vane, MP, became Lord Barnard on 27 Apr 1753 and Earl of Darlington on 3 Apr 1754.
53. Dodington, *Diary*, 24 Jan 1754.
54. Ibid. 7 Mar 1754.
55. Hartington to Devonshire, two o'clock [6 Mar 1754]: Dev 260/115.
56. Cf. Ryder Diary, 7 Mar 1754.
57. Dodington, *Diary*, 7 Mar 1754.
58. This was the situation as Newcastle understood it on 11th, and as Dupplin recounted it to Sir Dudley Ryder that day: Ryder Diary, 11 Mar 1754.
59. H to Archbishop of Canterbury, 8 p.m. 11 Mar 1754: 35599, f.165. The messages were presumably verbal, delivered via Hartington; no such letters appear to survive.
60. Dodington, *Diary*, 14 Mar 1754.
61. Ryder Diary, 7 Mar 1754.
62. Holdernesse to Dorset, 7 Mar 1754: Sackville MSS, Kent RO, C145/5.
63. Hartington to Devonshire, two o'clock [6 Mar 1754]: Dev 260/115.
64. Ryder Diary, 7 Mar 1754; J. F. Pinney to A. Pinney, 9 Mar 1754: Pinney Papers, 58/3/318.
65. Dodington, *Diary*, 7 Mar 1754. Dodington heard at Lord Barnard's that evening.
66. [Mrs] C. Digby to 'Neddy' [Edward Digby] 11 Mar 1754: Digby MSS.
67. W. Lorimer to Sir Ludovick Grant, 9 Mar 1754: SRO Seafield MSS, GD 248/49/1.
68. A. N. Newman (ed.), 'Leicester House Politics, 1750–60, from the Papers of John, Second Earl of Egmont', *Camden Miscellany*, XXIII (Camden 4th ser., vol. 7, London, 1969) pp.115–16.
69. Dodington, *Diary*: 9 Sept, 7 Oct 1749; 7, 15 Apr 1751.
70. Ibid. 26 Feb 1751.
71. Ibid. 28 Mar 1751.
72. T. Lewis to H. Lewis, 12 Mar 1754: NLW Harpton Court MSS, C/34. On 4 March 1754 the Bishop of Oxford played a part in defeating Bedford's motion in the Lords to postpone the Marriage Act; probably this is referred to (cf. H. Digby to Lord Digby, 5 Mar 1754: Digby MSS). Nevertheless, the Tory Earl of Oxford was known to be well disposed to the ministry; Walpole recorded him being 'courted' by Henry Pelham in 1751 (*George II*, I, 47).
73. Halifax, Memo, 7 Mar 1751: 32737, f.179.
74. Cf. Ryder Diary, 11 Mar 1754.
75. Pitt to Temple, 11 Mar 1754: *Grenville Papers*, I, 112, and LWL.
76. Pitt to [Sir George Lyttelton and the Grenvilles], [7 Mar 1754]: *Grenville Papers*, I, 106, and LWL.
77. Walpole, *George II*, I, 380.
78. Dodington, *Diary*, 7 Mar 1754.
79. Walpole, *George II*, I, 380.
80. Ryder Diary, 9 Mar 1754.
81. Walpole to Mann, 7 Mar 1754: HW 20, p.411.
82. Ryder Diary, 11 Mar 1754.

83. A rumour that Devonshire would be offered the Treasury appeared in the *Whitehall Evening Post*, 9–12 Mar 1754, and the *Public Advertiser*, 11 Mar 1754. Dodington (*Diary*, 7 Mar 1754) also mentioned Carlisle for the post, as had been intended in one scheme of Prince Frederick's opposition (Newman, 'Leicester House Politics, 1750–60', pp.106, 116). Nothing came of the suggestion.
84. Ryder Diary, 11 Mar 1754. Yet Granville probably called on Newcastle on 9th, before Devonshire's arrival (cf. Bayntun Rolt Diary, 9 Mar 1754), and may therefore have made his suggestion before Devonshire's refusal; Dupplin's account of the negotiation to Ryder may have mistaken the chronology.
85. Cf. Chesterfield to Stanhope, 8 Mar 1754: Dobrée, v, 2096.
86. Dodington, *Diary*, 14 Mar 1754.
87. Lord Ilchester to Lord Digby, 18 Mar 1754: Digby MSS.
88. Ryder Diary, 11 Mar 1754.
89. Waldegrave, *Memoirs*, p.18.
90. N to H, 28 Sept 1755: 35415, f.80. Yet cf. p.201, *infra*.
91. Brother-in-law, Fox.
92. [Mrs] C. Digby to 'Neddy', 11 Mar 1754: Digby MSS.
93. Lord Ilchester to Lord Digby, 11 Mar 1754: Digby MSS.
94. Ryder Diary, 11 Mar 1754.
95. Hartington to N, 4 p.m. 11 Mar 1754: 32734, f.218. Hartington proposed to call on Newcastle after 7 p.m. that day.
96. Ryder Diary, 11, 12 Mar 1754. Ryder's interviews on 11th with Dupplin and Newcastle must have taken place after the arrival of Hartington's letter. Walpole mentions (*George II*, I, 380) Hardwicke using Anson to carry a message of reconciliation to Fox, and messages between the King and Fox via Lady Yarmouth; their contents are unknown.
97. Bayntun Rolt Diary, 10 Mar 1754.
98. Cf. Pitt to Sir G. Lyttelton, 10 Mar 1754: Lyttelton MSS, II, 231 and 235.
99. Pitt to Sir G. Lyttelton, March [10, 1754]: Lyttelton MSS, II, 129. Endorsed by Lyttelton 'Ostensible to Lord Hardwicke.'
100. Pitt to Lyttelton, P.S. [10 Mar 1754]: Lyttelton MSS, II, 235.
101. Lyttelton's memorandum, 'Observations on Mr Pitt's letters of 1754', nd: Lyttelton MSS, II, 255.
102. Ibid.
103. Whether before or after Pitt's message had been received is unknown.
104. Treasurer of the Navy.
105. Ryder Diary, 11 Mar 1754.
106. Cf. Hartington to Devonshire, two o'clock [6 Mar 1754]: Dev 260/115.
107. H to Pitt, 2 Apr 1754: 35423, f.172.
108. Ibid.
109. This was untrue. Only the Sunderland–Aislabie and Wilmington–Sandys combinations in recent years conformed to that pattern: cf. infra, pp.64–7.
110. H to Archbishop of Canterbury, 8 p.m. 11 Mar 1754: 35599, f.165.
111. Cf. Lord Cathcart to Lord Loudoun, 12 Mar 1754: Loudoun MSS.
112. Dodington, *Diary*, 14 Mar 1754.
113. Minute, 12 Mar 1754: 35870, f.245.

114. N to H, Tuesday 3 o'clock [12 Mar 1754]: 35414, f.126.
115. Ryder Diary, 14 Mar 1754: cf. Holdernesse to Dorset, 14 Mar 1754: Sackville MSS, C145/6.
116. Bayntun Rolt Diary, 12 Mar 1754.
117. Fox to Lord Digby, 12 Mar 1754: Digby MSS.
118. Herring to H, 12 Mar 1754: 35599, f.171.
119. Minute, 12 Mar 1754: 35870, f.245. Present were: Lord President (Granville); Lord Steward (Marlborough); Lord Chamberlain (Grafton); Devonshire; Argyll; Hartington; Holdernesse; Anson; Hardwicke.
120. Ibid.; Hardwicke's endorsement.
121. Cf. Hanbury Williams to Fox, Tuesday night [12 Mar 1754]: 51393, f.168.
122. Dodington, *Diary*, 14 Mar 1754.
123. Cf. Ryder Diary, 15 Mar 1754.
124. Ibid.
125. H. Digby to Lord Digby, 14 Mar 1754: Digby MSS.
126. Ryder Diary, 16 Mar 1754; cf. Bayntun Rolt Diary, 15 Mar 1754.
127. Ibid. 23 Mar 1754.
128. Fox to Lord Digby, 12 Mar 1754: Digby MSS.
129. No longer extant. Reconstructed in HW 30, p.122 from Walpole's account of it in *George II*, I, 384–5 and ascribed to 12–13 Mar; Fox's answer to it, dated 13 Mar, is HW 30, p.123.
130. Hanbury Williams to Fox, Tuesday night [12 Mar 1754]: 51393, f.168.
131. Lord Ilchester to Lord Digby, 23 Mar 1754: Digby MSS.
132. Hanbury Williams to Fox, loc. cit.
133. Lord Cathcart to Lord Loudoun, 14 Mar 1754: Loudoun MSS.
134. Ryder Diary, 14 Mar 1754.
135. Chesterfield to Stanhope, 15 Mar 1754: Dobrée, I, 2098.
136. Ryder Diary, 15 Mar 1754. Ryder mistakenly places this conversation before 12 Mar; but Newcastle and Fox did not meet before 13th. The correct date, 13th, is confirmed by Dodington, *Diary*, 14 Mar 1754 (though he wrongly ascribed it to the evening of that day) and by Walpole, *George II*, I, 382.
137. Walpole, *George II*, I, 382–4.
138. Cf. note by Royston on N to H, Thursday [24 Oct 1754]: 35414, f.207.
139. Dodington, *Diary*, 14 Mar 1754.
140. H to N, 4 Sept 1755: 32858, f.442.
141. Horatio Walpole, among contemporaries, made this suggestion – but still blamed Fox for falling into it. 'I am persuaded that his not having at Mr Pelham's death immediately what he desired...was in great measure owing to himself...' Horatio Walpole to Hartington, 10 Oct 1754: Dev 180/21.
142. I.e. deluded into unrealities. E. Partridge, *A Dictionary of Historical Slang* (London, 1972).
143. Walpole, *George II*, I, 383.
144. Ryder Diary, 23 Mar 1754.
145. Walpole, *George II*, I, 384.
146. Ibid.
147. [Lord Ilchester to Lord Digby], 21 Mar 1754: Digby MSS.
148. Lord Ilchester to Lord Digby, 18 Mar 1754: Digby MSS.

149. Sir Lionel Pilkington to Viscount Irwin, 12 Mar 1754: HMC *Various*, VIII, p.176.
150. Lord Ilchester to Lord Digby, 18 Mar 1754: Digby MSS.
151. Fox to Walpole, 13 Mar 1754: HW 30, p.123.
152. N to Fox, 14 Mar 1754: 32734, f.245.
153. Fox to N, 14 Mar 1754: 32734, f.243. A copy was sent to Lord Digby by Fox, endorsed 'Lord Hartington saw this letter before it was sent and said there was not a word too much and that he would justify it everywhere.' A second endorsement is not obviously Hartington's words: 'The promises to Mr Fox were unasked and voluntary.' A copy was also sent to Bedford: Bedford MSS, xxx, 12.
154. Ryder Diary, 14 Mar 1754.
155. Bayntun Rolt Diary, 14 Mar 1754.
156. Chesterfield to Stanhope, 15 Mar 1754: Dobrée, v, 2098.
157. Henry Digby to Lord Digby, 14 Mar 1754: Digby MSS. Most of the alterations and their significance are missed in the text printed in HMC 8th Report, p.221. Fox's deletions of Digby's text are here shown thus [ ]; Fox's insertions thus ( ).
158. Fox to Marlborough, 22 Mar 1754: 51386, f.76; cf. Fox to Lord George Lennox, 22 Mar 1754: BL Loan 57/103, vol. 20 (Bathurst MSS).
159. H. Digby to Lord Digby, 14 Mar 1754: Digby MSS.
160. Cf. Chesterfield to Stanhope, loc. cit.; Herring to H, 17 Mar 1754: 35599, f.177.
161. H. Digby to Lord Digby, 14 Mar 1754: Digby MSS; Fox to Richmond, nd: 51424, f.147.
162. Fox to Richmond, loc. cit.
163. Ryder Diary, 15 Mar 1754.
164. Dodington, *Diary*, 7 Mar 1754.
165. [Lord Ilchester to Lord Digby], 23 Mar 1754: Digby MSS.
166. H. Digby to Lord Digby, 14 Mar 1754: Digby MSS.
167. Ryder Diary, 15 Mar 1754.
168. H to Devonshire, 17 Mar 1754: Dev 253/6.
169. Dodington, *Diary*, 15 Mar 1754.
170. Mann to Walpole, 19 Apr 1754: HW 20, p.421.
171. 'No man but a peer can stand in that gap.' Keene to Castres, 23 Dec [1754]: Sir Richard Lodge (ed.), *The Private Correspondence of Sir Benjamin Keene, K.B.* (Cambridge, 1933), p.391.
172. Cf. *Whitehall Evening Post*, 12–14 Mar 1754.
173. Lady Mary Wortley Montagu to Lady Bute, 28 Apr 1754: R. Halsband (ed.), *The Complete Letters of Lady Mary Wortley Montagu* (Oxford, 1967), III, 50.
174. Mann to Walpole, 29 Mar 1754: HW 20, p.419.
175. Walpole, *George II*, I, 379.
176. Cf. Pitt to Temple, [7 Mar 1754]: *Grenville Papers*, I, 110, and LWL; Chesterfield to Stanhope, 15 Mar 1754: Dobrée, v, 2098.
177. [Mrs] C. Digby to 'Neddy', 11 Mar 1754: Digby MSS.
178. Grafton, like Granville, seems to have written very little; and almost none of their papers are now extant. As a result, the political stature of both is easily underestimated.

179. Lord Halifax 1714–15; Earl of Carlisle 1715; R. Walpole 1715–17; J. Stanhope 1717–18; Earl of Sunderland 1718–21; R. Walpole 1721–42; Earl of Wilmington 1742–3; H. Pelham 1743–54.
180. J. C. Sainty, *Office Holders in Modern Britain I. Treasury Officials 1660–1870* (London, 1972), p.26.
181. Foord, *His Majesty's Opposition*, p.275.
182. Sainty, op. cit. p.26.
183. M. A. Thomson, *The Secretaries of State 1681–1782* (Oxford, 1932), pp.1, 161.
184. T. P. Taswell-Langmead, *English Constitutional History* (10th edn, London, 1946), p.678.
185. Dodington, *Diary*, 16 Apr 1751.
186. Except, temporarily, by Walpole in 1723–4 in the absence abroad of Townshend and Carteret.
187. Walpole, *George II*, I, 386.
188. Foord, *His Majesty's Opposition*, p.275.
189. H. Digby to Lord Digby, 14 Mar 1754: Digby MSS.
190. Ryder Diary, 16 Mar 1754.
191. Lord Ilchester to Lord Digby, 18 Mar 1754: Digby MSS.
192. Ryder Diary, 15 Mar 1754.
193. Fox to Hartington, 16 Mar 1754: Dev 330/18; cf. Walpole, *George II*, I, 386–7 for Fox's public version of the audience.
194. Ryder Diary, 16 Mar 1754.
195. Lord Cathcart to Lord Loudoun, 16 Mar 1754: Loudoun MSS.
196. Cf. Ryder Diary, 15 Mar 1754.
197. Legge to Sir John Eardley Wilmot, 26 Mar 1754: Eardley Wilmot MSS.
198. Walpole to Montagu, 19 Mar 1754: HW 9, p.159.
199. C. Townshend to N, 11 Mar 1754: 32734, f.216; Barrington to N, Wednesday afternoon 13 Mar 1754: ibid. f.229; Bath to N, 13 Mar 1754: ibid. f.233.
200. West to N, 13 Mar 1754: ibid. f.237.
201. Memo, 15 Mar 1754: 32995, f.69.
202. Ibid. f.96 et seq.
203. N to H, Tuesday 3 o'clock [12 Mar 1754]: 35414, f.126.
204. Ryder Diary, 10 Mar 1754.
205. Cf. N to Keene, 18 Apr 1754: 32849, f.83; N to Mr Campion, 25 Apr 1754: 32735, f.180.
206. Holdernesse to Albemarle, 21 Mar 1754: Eg 3457, f.307.
207. Herring to H, 12 Mar 1754: 35599, f.173; cf. Lord Berkeley to Bentinck, 12 Mar 1754: Eg 1721, f.332.
208. H to Pitt, 2 Apr 1754: 35423, f.172.
209. Sir Joseph Yorke to Lady Anson, 15 Mar 1754: 35388, f.7.
210. H to Pitt, 2 Apr 1754: loc. cit.
211. Sir Joseph Yorke to Royston, 22 Mar 1754: 35364, f.7; cf. Sir Joseph Yorke to H, 26 Mar 1754: 35356, f.234.
212. Cf. Herring to H, 17 Mar 1754: 35599, f.177.
213. Sir Joseph Yorke (to Royston, loc. cit.) summed him up: '...able to write, and at the same time...dependent enough not to give jealousy'.
214. News of Robinson's impending promotion, and that Fox would remain

Secretary at War, was soon public: cf. *Whitehall Evening Post*, 16–19 Mar 1754.

215. N to H, Tuesday 6 o'clock [19 Mar 1754]: 35414, f.130.
216. N to H, 1 Sept 1754: 35414, f.163.
217. H to N, 3 Sept 1754: 32736, f.413.
218. Lord Barnard, raised a step in the peerage, appeared as Earl of Darlington.
219. H. Digby to Lord Digby, 20 Mar 1754: Digby MSS.
220. Grenville Narrative: *Grenville Papers*, I, 430.
221. *Daily Advertiser*, 9 Apr 1754. This arrangement had been expected when Lee had been rumoured to be about to retire through ill health: *Public Advertiser*, 5 Jan 1754.
222. *London Gazette*, 16–20 Apr 1754.
223. Legge to [Hartington], half past twelve [19 Mar 1754]: Dev 257/19.
224. H to N, at night 19 Mar 1754: 32734, f.281.
225. Lord Ilchester to Lord Digby, 18 Mar 1754: Digby MSS.
226. Sir Joseph Yorke to Royston, 22 Mar 1754: 35364, f.7.
227. Lord Ilchester to Lord Digby, 21 Mar 1754: Digby MSS.
228. Fox to [Lord Digby], 23 Mar 1754: Digby MSS.
229. Lord Ilchester to Lord Digby, 4 May 1754: Digby MSS.
230. Lady Caroline Fox to Countess of Kildare, 6 [July] 1756: *Leinster Corr*, I, 166.
231. Lord Ilchester to Lord Digby, 18 Mar 1754: Digby MSS.
232. Henry Digby to Lord Digby, 19 Mar 1754: Digby MSS.
233. Lord Ilchester to Lord Digby, 21 Mar 1754: Digby MSS; and 1 May 1754: 51340, f.111.
234. [Lord Ilchester to Lord Digby], 21 Mar 1754: Digby MSS.
235. Cf. Pitt to Lyttelton, 20 Mar 1754: Lyttelton MSS, II, 237.
236. Sir George Lyttelton to H, 23 Mar 1754: 35592, f.294.
237. Walpole, *George II*, I, 387.
238. Pitt to N, 24 Mar 1754: 32734, f.322.
239. Devonshire to Fox, 4 Oct 1755: 51381, f.52.
240. Grenville Narrative, *Grenville Papers*, I, 430.
241. Pitt to Temple, 24 Mar 1754: *Grenville Papers*, I, 115, and LWL.
242. Pitt to Sir G. Lyttelton, 24 Mar 1754: Lyttelton MSS, II, 239.
243. Dodington, *Diary*, 9 Mar 1754.
244. Ibid. 21 Mar 1754.
245. Ibid. 27 Mar and 4 June 1754; Dupplin to N, 11 June 1754: 32735, f.423.
246. Sir G. Lyttelton to N, 25 Mar 1754: 32734, f.344.
247. This was true. Lyttelton was delighted, and had chosen his place rather than that of Treasurer of the Navy, which he was also offered. Sir G. Lyttelton to S. Miller [1] Apr 1754: Sanderson Miller MSS, 661.
248. N to Pitt, 2 Apr 1754: PRO 30/8/1, f.58.
249. Charles Yorke showed him Hardwicke's letter to Pitt of 2 Apr and persuaded Lyttelton of the justice of the Chancellor's position. C. Yorke to H, 2 Apr 1754: 35353, f.155.
250. Sir G. Lyttelton: 'Observations': Lyttelton MSS, II, 255.
251. H to Pitt, 2 Apr 1754: 35423, f.172.
252. Cf. Pitt to N, 2 Apr 1754: 32735, f.14. Misdated 'March –' in *Chatham Corr*, I, 85.
253. Cf. Pitt to Sir G. Lyttelton, 4 Apr 1754: Lyttelton MSS, II, 243.

254. Pitt to N, 4 Apr 1754: 32735, f.26. Misdated 5 Apr in *Chatham Corr*, I, 100.
255. Pitt to H, 4 Apr 1754: 35423, f.175. Misdated 6 Apr in *Chatham Corr*, I, 103.
256. Pitt to Sir G. Lyttelton, 4 Apr 1754: Lyttelton MSS, II, 243.
257. Ibid.
258. Pitt to G. Grenville, 6 Apr 1754: *Grenville Papers*, I, 118, and LWL.
259. Pitt to Sir George Lyttelton, 20 May 1754: Lyttelton MSS, II, 245. Mr Sherrard (*Lord Chatham: a War Minister*, p.258), by assuming that Phillimore's attribution of the postscript to this letter was correct [*Lyttelton*, II, 468] gives the false impression that Pitt was once more, by late May, eager for the political battle. He was not.
260. Pitt to N, 20, 22 Apr 1754: 32735, ff.139, 143.
261. N to Rutland, 26 Mar 1754: 32734, f.356. It was public knowledge: cf. *Whitehall Evening Post*, 28–30 Mar 1754; *Public Advertiser*, 30 Mar 1754.
262. Walpole to Mann, 28 Mar 1754: HW 20, p.416.
263. John Calcraft to Sir G. Hanbury Williams, nd: Williams MSS, *penes* W. S. Lewis.
264. Minute, Tuesday night 2 Apr 1754: 32735, f.22.
265. N to H, Saturday morning [30 Mar 1754]: 35414, f.133.
266. Lord Gower to George II, 4 Apr 1754: Eg 3425, f.5.
267. Ryder Diary, 11 Mar 1754.
268. H. Digby to Lord Digby, 20 Mar 1754: Digby MSS.
269. Ryder Diary, 15 Mar 1754.
270. Walpole to Montagu, 19 Mar 1754: HW 9, p.159.
271. W. Lorimer to Sir Ludovick Grant, 23 Mar 1754: SRO Seafield MSS, GD 248/49/1.
272. Lord Cathcart to Lord Loudoun, 26 Mar 1754: Loudoun MSS.
273. Waldegrave, *Memoirs*, pp.18–19.
274. The Board was: Newcastle; Earl of Darlington; Legge; Viscount Dupplin; R. Nugent.
275. H. Digby to Lord Digby, 20 Mar 1754: Digby MSS.
276. Walpole, *George II*, I, 387: 'he preferred his own more profitable place, less obnoxious to danger and envy. The meaness of his appearance, and the quaintness of his dialect, made him as improper for it as unwilling.'
277. The issue was complicated by the fact that although Dupplin sat in the Commons until he succeeded as Earl of Kinnoul in 1758, he was totally loyal to Newcastle.
278. Dodington, *Diary*, 21 Mar 1754.
279. Cf. p.58, supra.
280. Waldegrave, *Memoirs*, p.145–6.
281. Repeated by, for example, Foord, *His Majesty's Opposition*, p.281.
282. Fox to Hartington, 18 Oct 1756: 35594, f.289.
283. Walpole to Mann, 7 Mar 1754: HW 20, p.411.
284. Walpole to Mann, 5 June 1754: HW 20, p.434. Italics added.
285. Pitt, in disclaiming an intention to launch 'a third party, or flying squadron', tacitly admitted that two parties already existed. Pitt to Sir G. Lyttelton, 10 Mar 1754: Lyttelton MSS, II, 231.
286. N to Horatio Walpole, 14 May 1754: 32735, f.268.
287. W. Guthrie to H. Guthrie, 27 Apr 1754: HMC *Laing*, II, 412. There would seem to be no evidence to confirm Beckford's often-quoted remark to

Bedford that 'the eyes of most people are looking toward your Grace as the head of an opposition, founded on true patriot principles...' Beckford to Bedford, 4 June 1754: *Bedford Corr*, II, 150.

288. Here used as euphemisms for 'Whig' and 'Tory'.
289. Hanbury Williams to Fox, Tuesday night [12 Mar 1754]: 51393, f.168.
290. Chesterfield to Stanhope, 15 Mar 1754: Dobrée, v, 2098.
291. Pitt to N, 24 Mar 1754: 32734, f.322.
292. N to Pitt, 2 Apr 1754: PRO 30/8/1, f.58.
293. Dodington, *Diary*, 27 May 1755.
294. Chesterfield to Stanhope, 15 Mar 1754: Dobrée, v, 2098.
295. Chesterfield to Stanhope, 26 Mar 1754: ibid. 2102.
296. W. Lorimer to Sir Ludovick Grant, 23 Mar 1754: SRO Seafield MSS, GD 248/49/1.
297. Walpole to Mann, 24 Apr 1754: HW 20, p.425.
298. Memo, 33034, f.195.
299. 32995, f.213.
300. 33034, f.179.
301. 33034, f.173.
302. 33034, f.183.
303. 33034, f.197.
304. Dodington, *Diary*, 21 Mar 1754.
305. H to N, 26 Mar 1754: 32734, f.359.
306. H to N, 24 Apr 1754: 32735, f.178.
307. Cf. N to Duchess, 12 June 1754: 33075, f.1.
308. N to Duchess, 2 July 1754: 33075, f.4; cf. Namier, *Structure*, p.226.
309. Walpole, *George II*, I, 391.
310. Walpole, *George III*, I, 30.
311. Walpole, *George II*, I, 381.
312. Cf. N to Sir T. Robinson, Friday morning [17 May 1754]: 32735, f.281.
313. Pitt to William Lyttelton, 1 Apr 1754: Lyttelton MSS, II, 241.
314. Legge to Sir John Eardley Wilmot, 26 Mar 1754: Eardley Wilmot MSS; *Read's Weekly Journal*, 13 Apr 1754.
315. Walpole, *George II*, I, 392.
316. Pitt to Sir G. Lyttelton, 24 Mar 1754: Lyttelton MSS, II, 239.
317. Walpole, *George II*, I, 392.
318. Cf. p.69, supra.
319. Walpole, *George II*, I, 392.
320. Dodington, *Diary*, 21 June 1754.
321. Dodington, *Diary*, 10 June 1754.
322. N, Minute, 30 Aug 1754: 35414, f.173. 'N.B. This minute I took in Mr Stone's presence, and read over to him, who said that all that is above passed yesterday with Mr Fox.'
323. Hon. John Yorke to Royston, 20 July 1754: 35374, f.102.
324. Fox to Hartington, 13 July 1754: Dev 330/19.
325. 12 June 1754: 32995, f.264.
326. Dodington, *Diary*, 2 July 1754.
327. Ibid. 18 and 19 July 1754.
328. Pitt to N, 4 Apr 1754: 32735, f.26.
329. N to H, 18 July 1754: 35414, f.143.

330. N to H, 19 July 1754: 35414, f.145.
331. Fox to Hartington, 18 July 1754: Dev 330/20.
332. Hartington to Devonshire, 23 July 1754: Dev 260/116.
333. Fox to Hartington, [20 July 1754]: Dev 330/21.
334. It apparently took place just before 28 July: Fox reported it to Cumberland. Fox to Hartington, 28 July [1754]: Dev 330/22.
335. Cf. H to N, 18 July 1754: 32736, f.47.
336. Cf. N to Duchess, 2 July 1754: 33075, f.4.
337. N to Lincoln, 3 Aug 1754: Ne (c) 3172.
338. Fox to [Hartington] 28 July [1754]: Dev 330/22.
339. Fox to Hartington, 29 Aug 1754: Dev 330/24; Fox to Waldegrave, 29 Aug 1754: 51380, f.2.
340. Stone recounted Fox's version to Newcastle, who took a careful minute of it: supra, pp.82–3.
341. 'Account of a conversation between Messrs. Stone and Fox, August 29 1754', Dev 330/25 (in Fox's hand).
342. N to H, 1 Sept 1754: 35414, f.163.
343. N to H, 1 Sept 1754: 32736, f.388.
344. 35414, f.173; cf. pp.82–3 above.
345. N to H, 1 Sept 1754: 32736, f.388; cf. Fox to [Hartington], 13 Sept 1754: Dev 330/26.
346. Primate to Lord George Sackville, 1, 17, 27 Aug 1754: Sackville MSS, II, 144, 153, 160.
347. Holdernesse to N, 24 Aug 1754: 32736, f.336.
348. N to H, 1 Sept 1754: 35414, f.163.
349. H to N, 3 Sept 1754: 32736, f.413.
350. N to H, 1 Sept 1754: 32736, f.388.
351. Ibid.
352. Cf. Murray to N, 7 Sept 1754: 32736, f.438; N to Murray, 10 Sept 1754: ibid. f.472.
353. 'Points for consideration with my Lord Chancellor', 11 Sept 1754: 32995, f.311.
354. Hartington to Horatio Walpole, 18 Sept 1754: Dev 260/122.
355. N to H, 21 Sept 1754: 32736, f.554.
356. 'Points for consideration...' loc. cit.
357. Hartington to Horatio Walpole, 18 Sept 1754: Dev 260/122.
358. H to N, 22 Sept 1754: 32736, f.559.
359. N to H, 21 Sept 1754: 32736, f.554.
360. N to Murray, 28 Sept 1754: 32736, f.591.
361. N to H, 21 Sept 1754: 32736, f.554.
362. N to Duchess, 26 Sept 1754: 33075, f.16.
363. N to Murray, 28 Sept 1754: 32736, f.591.
364. Ibid.
365. Ibid.
366. H to N, 27 Sept 1754: 32736, f.583.
367. Dodington, Diary, 8 Oct 1754; Newcastle to Charles Townshend, 2 Nov 1754: 32737, f.249. Among the first rank, Holdernesse and Robinson have been underestimated as a result of their avoidance of disruptive intrigue.
368. N to Murray, 28 Sept 1754: 32736, f.591.

369. Pares, *King George III and the Politicians*, pp.175–81; Thomson, *The Secretaries of State 1681–1782*, pp.13–17, 25–8; and *A Constitutional History of England 1642 to 1801* (London, 1938), pp.362, 365–6.
370. Sedgwick, I, 40, 41. The same doctrine is expounded by J. B. Owen, 'George II Reconsidered' in A. Whiteman et al. (eds.), *Statesmen, Scholars and Merchants* (Oxford, 1973), pp. 131–2 and echoed with qualifications by Lord Blake, *The Office of Prime Minister* (Oxford, 1975), pp.5–7, 23–7.
371. N to H, 3 Sept 1755: 35415, f.58.
372. Melville to Addington, 22 Mar 1803: G. Pellew, *The Life and Correspondence of the Right Honble. Henry Addington, First Viscount Sidmouth* (London, 1847) II, 114.
373. Canning to Spencer Perceval, 31 Aug 1809: Spencer Walpole, *The Life of the Rt Hon. Spencer Perceval* (London, 1874) I, 362. Spencer Walpole was sceptical of this assertion on the grounds of Canning's evident willingness to serve under Lord Chatham before the latter's failure in the Walcheren expedition made that impossible.
374. Sedgwick, I, 61. The quotation, H to N, 29 Oct. 1757: 32875, f.316 has been expanded. Cf. Dame Lucy Sutherland, 'The City of London and the Devonshire–Pitt Administration, 1756–7', *Proceedings of the British Academy*, XLVI (1960) p.150.
375. B. Kemp, *King and Commons 1660–1832* (London, 1957) p.127.
376. E.g. Sedgwick, I, 41.
377. Cf. Pares, *King George III and the Politicians*, p.179: 'In the years between Chatham's failure and his son's rise, the Prime Ministership seems to have developed little, if at all.'
378. Cf. Owen, *Pelhams*, p.268.
379. Cf. Thomson, *A Constitutional History of England 1642 to 1801*, p.362.

2. THE DEFEAT OF THE PITT–FOX ALLIANCE

1. As has been widely supposed, e.g. Pares, *King George III and the Politicians*, pp.45–6; Sedgwick, *Bute*, p.xlvi.
2. Marlborough to Fox, nd [? Aug–Sept 1754]: 51386, f.80.
3. N to H, 1 Sept 1754: 35414, f.163. The orders were for moving American troops from the West Indies to the mainland.
4. Cf. N to H, 1 Sept 1754: 32736, f.388; H to N, 3 Sept 1754: 32736, f.413.
5. Cf. N to H, 4 Sept 1754: 32736, f.424; L. H. Gipson, *The British Empire Before the American Revolution* (New York, 1936–70) VI, 20–43.
6. Walpole, *George II*, I, 399–401.
7. Joseph Yorke to H, 24 Sept 1754: 35356, f.253.
8. Cf. S. Martin, Memo: 41355, f.23.
9. Cf. Lord Fane to Bedford, 3 Oct 1754: Bedford MSS, xxx, 94.
10. H to N, 27 Sept 1754: 32736, f.583.
11. 'Points for consideration with my Lord Chancellor', 11 Sept 1754: 32995, f.311.
12. Cf. Hartington to Horatio Walpole, 18 Sept 1754: Dev 260/122.
13. N to H, 21 Sept 1754: 32736, f.554.
14. N to Duchess, 26 Sept 1754: 33075, f.16. Details of the military arrangements are given in T. W. Riker, 'The Politics behind Braddock's Expedi-

tion', *American Historical Review*, XIII (1907-8), 742-52. There is no evidence for Riker's suggestion that Newcastle was unwilling to pursue a vigorous policy and was compelled to do so by domestic opposition.

15. H to N, 27 Sept 1754: 32736, f.583; Robinson to N, 23 Sept 1754: 32736, f.569.

16. Robinson to N, 22 Sept 1754: 32736, f.563.

17. N to Murray, 28 Sept 1754: 32736, f.591.

18. Sir T. Robinson to N, 29 Sept 1754: 32736, f.601; Fox to Sir T. Robinson, 29 Sept 1754: 32736, f.603.

19. Cf. West to N, 30 Sept 1754: 32736, f. 605. For the diplomatic context, cf. T. R. Clayton, 'The Duke of Newcastle, the Earl of Halifax, and the American Origins of the Seven Years' War'. I am grateful to Mr Clayton for allowing me to read this paper before its publication.

20. N to H, 2 Oct 1754: 32737, f.24.

21. H to N, 3 Oct 1754: 32737, f.27.

22. Hillsborough's account, reported in Dodington, *Diary*, 8 Oct 1754.

23. Robinson to N, 7 Oct 1754: 32737, f.61.

24. Murray to N, 6 Oct 1754: 32737, f.45.

25. N to Duchess, 8 Oct 1754: 33075, f.17.

26. Anson to N, 11 Oct 1754: 32737, f.101.

27. Robinson to N, 11 Oct 1754: 32737, f.105.

28. N to H, 12 Oct 1754: 32737, f.200.

29. E.g. N to Newport, 12 Oct 1754: 32737, f.110.

30. N to Primate, 12 Oct 1754: 32737, f.126.

31. Dodington, *Diary*, 8 Oct 1754.

32. Robinson to N, 12 Oct 1754: 32737, f.135.

33. H to N, 26 Sept 1754: 32737, f.197.

34. H to N, 13 Oct 1754: 32737, f.147.

35. Walpole to Mann, 1 Dec 1754: HW 20, p.453; cf. Joseph Yorke to Royston, 10 Dec 1754: 35364, f.23.

36. N to Horatio Walpole, 26 Oct 1754: 32737, f.207.

37. They did so again on 26 October, securing the King's agreement to a revised draft of Fox's orders (Robinson to N, 26 Oct 1754: 32737, f.201). Riker ('The Politics behind Braddock's Expedition', pp.751-2) failed to realise the unimportance of the adoption of Cumberland's strategy, for he saw it as the initial success of a Fox–Pitt alliance which, in December, 'compelled' Newcastle to admit Fox to the Cabinet. The second half of that claim is challenged below.

38. H to N, 13 Oct 1754: 32737, f.147; H to N, 3 Oct 1754: 32737, f.27.

39. Lord Fane to Bedford, 3 Oct 1754: Bedford MSS, xxx, 94.

40. Ryder Diary, 27 Jan 1755.

41. Dodington, *Diary*, 8 Oct 1754.

42. Armagh to N, 19 Oct 1754: 32737, f.177.

43. N to Murray, 28 Sept 1754: 32736, f.591.

44. 'The House of Commons is to be led (as the Duke of Newcastle weakly thought of managing it after his brother's death in 1754) by *sub-ministers*'. Charles Yorke to Sir Joseph Yorke, 7 Sept 1765: 35428, f.73. Quoted in Paul Langford, *The First Rockingham Administration, 1765-1766* (Oxford, 1973) p.26.

45. Fox to Pitt [? 4 Dec 1754]: PRO 30/8/1, f.81.
46. Walpole to Mann, 1 Dec 1754: HW 20, p.453.
47. N to Bentinck, 17 Dec 1754: 32851, f.325.
48. Dodington, *Diary*, 8 Oct 1754.
49. N to Mr Campion, 1 Oct 1754: 32737, f.1.
50. N to H, 2 Nov 1754: 35414, f.215.
51. Cf. *Parl Hist*, xv, 493–504.
52. Fox to George Grenville, Saturday night [16 Nov 1754]: *Grenville Papers*, I, 132, and LWL.
53. Joseph Yorke to N, 18 Oct 1754: 35435, f.43.
54. N to Horatio Walpole, 26 Oct 1754: 32737, f.207; misdated 20 Oct in W. Coxe, *Memoirs of Horatio, Lord Walpole* (London, 1802) p.149.
55. H to N, 17 Oct 1754: 32737 f.156.
56. Gilbert Elliot to his wife, 11 Nov 1754: NLS Minto MSS, 11006, f.96.
57. Horatio Walpole to Hartington, 10 Oct 1754: Dev 180/21; cf. same to same, Monday evening [11 Nov 1754]: Dev 180/22.
58. Gilbert Elliot to Lord Minto, 16 Nov 1754: NLS Minto MSS, 11001, f.10.
59. N to Argyll, 19 Oct 1754: 32737, f.162.
60. Cf. N's letters to his wife: 33074–33075 passim.
61. N to H, 21 Oct 1754: 35414, f.203.
62. N to H, [24 Oct 1754]: 32737, f.191.
63. H to N, 26 Oct 1754: 32737, f.197. Newcastle shared this view: cf. N to Horatio Walpole, 26 Oct 1754: 32737, f.207.
64. N to Dorset, 26 Oct 1754: 32737, f.203; cf. Stone to N, 7 Oct 1754: 32737, f.59 and Fox to Nugent, 5 and 9 Oct 1754: C. Nugent, *Memoir of Robert, Earl Nugent* (London, 1898) p.259.
65. Murray to N, 6 Oct 1754: 32737, f.45. Surviving examples, all dated 17 Oct 1754, are: Legge to T. Hill, Attingham MSS; Legge to Lord Milton, NLS SC 184, f.226; and Legge to Richard Middleton, Chirk MSS, E 189.
66. N to H, 21 Oct 1754: 35414, f.203.
67. Cf. Horace Walpole to Conway, 24 Oct 1754: Toynbee, III, 255. He was not to get it until 1757; but his promotion to the Colonelcy of the 4th Regiment of Horse may indicate his enjoyment of Cumberland's favour: cf. *Public Advertiser*, 27 July 1754.
68. N to H, 21 Oct 1754: 35414, f.203.
69. H to N, 26 Oct 1754: 32737, f.197. His appointment as King's Advocate General in March 1755 was soon followed by his desertion to the opposition on the question of subsidy treaties.
70. N to Murray, 28 Sept 1754: 32736, f.591.
71. N to H, 21 Oct 1754: 35414, f.203.
72. N to H, [24th Oct 1754]: 32737, f.191.
73. H to N, 26 Oct 1754: 32737, f.197.
74. N to H, 28 Oct 1754: 35414, f.210.
75. Horatio Walpole to N, 30 Oct 1754: 32737, f.213.
76. Cf. Joseph Yorke to Royston, 1 Nov 1754: 35374, f.107.
77. H to N, 3 Nov 1754: 32737, f.255.
78. N to Duchess, 5 Nov 1754: 33075, f.20.
79. Newcastle was unabashed: 'with his leave, it [party advantage] is the think-

ing that must, and ever did determine about the persons to be supported, if their cause admitted of it'. N to H, 8 Nov 1754: 35414, f.218.

80. Cf. Legge to H, 7 Nov 1754: 35593, f.44: Legge to N, 8 Nov 1754: 32737, f.324.

81. Cf. H to N, 9 Nov 1754: 32737, f.328; Horatio Walpole to Hartington, Monday evening [11 Nov 1754]: Dev 180/22. It is not clear whether Fox actually attended either.

82. Beaufort to Brudenell Rooke, 20 Oct 1754: Rooke MSS, D 1833 F1.

83. N to H, 8 Nov 1754: 35414 f.218.

84. James Ralph to N, 5 Nov 1754: 32737, f.272.

85. Cf. *Public Advertiser*, 21 Mar 1754.

86. This account is based on Egmont's memorandum, nd but probably c.30 Nov 1754: 47092, f.151.

87. Joseph Yorke to H, 3 Jan 1755: 35356, f.275.

88. Egmont, Memo: 47092, f.151.

89. Egremont was soon reported as being 'embarked wholly with the Duke of Newcastle': Bayntun Rolt Diary, 2 Feb 1755.

90. Egmont, Memo: 47092, f.151.

91. [J. Almon], *A History of the Parliament of Great Britain, from the Death of Queen Anne, to the Death of King George II* (London, 1764) p.321.

92. Owen, *Pelhams*, p.99.

93. Walpole to R. Bentley, 20 Nov 1754: Toynbee, III, 265; *CJ*, XXVII, p.18.

94. N to Horatio Walpole, 26 Oct 1754: 32737, f.207.

95 Sir E. Turner to S. Miller, 19 Nov 1754: Sanderson Miller MSS, 531.

96. 'Observations on Mr Pitt's letters of 1754': Lyttelton MSS, II, 255.

97. Waldegrave, *Memoirs*, p.31.

98. Lord Fane to Bedford, 3 Oct 1754: Bedford MSS, xxx, 94.

99. Note by Royston on N to H, 21 Oct 1754: 35414, f.203.

100. H to N, Friday night [15 Nov 1754]: 32737, f.344. The argument is omitted in Potter's speech in *Parl Hist*, xv, 342.

101. H to N, loc. cit.

102. 41355, f.15. Samuel Martin's memoranda on events in the Commons, 41355, ff.14–28; ff.14–23 are 26 Nov 1754, other entries as dated. It appears from 41355 f.238 that these notes originally covered 1754–5; but they survive in a fragmentary form only until December 1754.

103. Gilbert Elliot to Lord Minto, 16 Nov 1754: NLS Minto MSS, 11001, f.10.

104. N to H, 17 Nov 1754: 35414, f.223.

105. 41355, f.16. The view that the Exchequer was still a junior office largely reflects Legge's initial inexperience. It is therefore a misconception (e.g. Sedgwick in Namier and Brooke, III, 30) that Newcastle's contempt drove Legge into disloyal connections; this reverses the order of events.

106. Robinson to N, 16 Nov 1754: 32737, f.350.

107. Martin, Memo: 41355, f.17.

108. N to Duchess, 17 Nov 1754: 33075, f.21.

109. N to H, 17 Nov 1754: 35414, f.223. The 2nd Earl of Hardwicke forgot Newcastle's confidence of tactical strength in adding a note, much later, to this letter: 'N.B. The House of Commons certainly does not go on well without a minister in it, and a pretty good speaker too. The Duke of G[rafto]n jumbled through two sessions without one; but then there was

more submission in the majority, and less ability in individuals than in 1754, and no stirring faction at court.'

110. H to N, 17 Nov 1754: 32737, f.357.
111. Egmont, Memo: 47092, f.151.
112. Joseph Yorke to N, 26 Nov 1754: 35435 f.53.
113. H. Shiffner to H. F. Luttrell, 19 Nov 1754: Luttrell MSS. Evidently there were two divisions on that day.
114. *CJ*, xxvii, p.24.
115. Horatio Walpole to Hartington, 21 Nov 1754: Dev 180/24. Another account disagrees: 'Fox, the sons of the Chancellor, Pitt, the Grenvilles, for [Sandwich]. Mr Legge, the Duke of Newcastle's personal friends, Hume Campbell and more than half of the Scotch members, divided against him'. G. Elliot to his wife, 21 Nov 1754: NLS 11006, f.100.
116. Fox to Hartington, 26 Nov 1754: Dev 330/27.
117. Newcastle's support for Watson, too, meant that Wilkes at first petitioned against Delaval alone: cf. Thomas Cockburn to Sir John Hall, 6 Oct 1754: SRO Dunglass MSS, GD 206/261/19; Dupplin to Wilkes, 8 Nov 1754: 30867, f.105.
118. J. Almon, *The Correspondence of the late John Wilkes...in which are introduced Memoirs of his Life* (London, 1805) I, 27.
119. *Reminiscences of Charles Butler, Esq.* (London, 1822–7) I, 144.
120. Fox to Hartington, 26 Nov 1754: Dev 330/27; cf. Ellis to Hartington, 26th November 1754: Dev 335/1; Walpole, *George II*, I, 408.
121. Martin, Memo: 41355, f.20. The speech is not in *Parl Hist*.
122. J. Calcraft to Lord Digby, 26 Nov 1754: Digby MSS.
123. Martin, Memo: 41355, f.21.
124. Ibid. f.17. Waldegrave (*Memoirs*, p.31) called Murray 'the ablest man, as well as the ablest debater, in the House of Commons'.
125. Horatio Walpole to Hartington, 26, 30 Nov 1754: Dev 180/26, 180/29.
126. Ryder Diary, 21 Dec 1754. John Sharpe (? 1700–56), M.P. Callington 1754–d., Solicitor to Treasury 1742–d.
127. Ellis to Hartington, 26 Nov 1754: Dev 335/1.
128. Fox to Hartington, 26 Nov 1754: Dev 330/27.
129. Horatio Walpole to Hartington, 26 Nov 1754: Dev 180/26.
130. Martin, Memo: 41355, ff.22, 24.
131. Ibid. f.24.
132. Hartington to Fox, 23 May 1755: 51381, f.11.
133. Horatio Walpole to Hartington, 30 Nov 1754: Dev 180/28.
134. Grenville Narrative: *Grenville Papers*, I, 431.
135. Reading was compromised through Fox's mediation and Fane's consent, inter alia, not to obstruct a petition against the other sitting Member alone: Strode, a Tory (Fox, Memo: c.18 Nov 1754: 51402, f.12). Strode's death forestalled this arrangement. At Berwick, Wilkes dropped his petition in November 1755 after Delaval joined the ministry following Fox's promotion to the Secretaryship.
136. Horatio Walpole to Hartington, 26 Nov 1754: Dev 180/26.
137. Cf. A. L. J. Lincoln and R. L. McEwen (eds.), *Lord Eldon's Anecdote Book* (London, 1960) pp.15–16, 49, 52.
138. Lord Fane to Bedford, 3 Oct 1754: Bedford MSS, xxx, 94.

139. Fox to G. Grenville, Saturday night [16 Nov 1754]: *Grenville Papers*, 1, 132, and LWL.

140. Bedford's reply to Fane of 4 Oct 1754 is apparently not extant.

141. Rigby to Bedford, 12 Oct 1754; Bedford to R. Wilbraham, 18 Nov 1754 and to Earl of Upper Ossory, 19 Nov 1754: Bedford MSS, xxx, 98, 102, 104; Bedford to Hartington, 23 Nov 1754: Dev 286/1; Bedford, Notes, 15, 23 Nov 1754: Bedford MSS, 58; Hartington to Bedford, 27 Nov 1754: Bedford MSS, xxx, 110.

142. There is strong confirmation for such a view: cf. Pitt to Earl Temple, Friday night [1 Nov 1754]: *Grenville Papers*, 1, 129, and LWL.

143. Fox to Hartington, 26 Nov 1754: Dev 330/27. Fox claims Newcastle told Pitt that he, Newcastle, had related part of his last conversation with the Paymaster to George II. If so, *which* conversation is in doubt. It may have been that on 2 October, since Pitt returned to Bath immediately afterwards; possibly Pitt's desire to be Secretary of State, recorded by Dodington (*Diary*, 8 Oct 1754) was spoken of at that meeting. More probably, the interview occurred after Pitt's demand for royal confidence and regard; but what he may have objected to is not apparent.

144. Cf. p.109 above.

145. Fox to Hartington, 26 Nov 1754: Dev 330/27.

146. Walpole to R. Bentley, 13 Dec 1754: Toynbee, iii, 271.

147. Martin, Memo: 41355, f.22.

148. Trentham to Bedford, 28 Nov 1754: Bedford MSS, xxx, 112.

149. Ryder Diary, 27 Nov 1754.

150. Ellis to Hartington, 26 Nov 1754: Dev 335/1. No post is mentioned; but Fox speaks as if Hartington had been specific.

151. Fox to Hartington, 26 Nov 1754: Dev 330/27.

152. Fox to Lady Caroline, Monday morning [2 Dec 1754]: 51415, f.180.

153. Cumberland to Fox, 27 Nov 1754: 51375, f.37.

154. 'I have not said one word that could possibly be misinterpreted.' Fox to Hartington, 28 Nov 1754: Dev 330/28.

155. Fox to Hartington, 26 Nov 1754: Dev 330/27.

156. Fox to Hartington, 28 Nov 1754; Dev 330/28; Walpole, *George II*, 1, 410-12.

157. Newdigate, Memo: Newdigate MSS, CR 136 B 2205; Peregrine Palmer to ? Dr White, 29 Nov 1754: Bodleian MS Top Oxon. c.209, f.25.

158. Fox to Hartington, 28 Nov 1754: Dev 330/28.

159. Martin, Memo: 41335, f.23.

160. Ibid.

161. Pitt to Lady Hester Grenville, Wednesday 23 [Oct 1754], Saturday 26 [Oct 1754]: E. A. Edwards (ed.), *The Love Letters of William Pitt, First Lord Chatham* (London, 1926), 105, 120.

162. Horace Walpole to Mann, 1 Dec 1754: HW 20, p.453. On Murray's Tory origins, cf. N to Stone, 15 Oct 1762 (quoted in Sedgwick, *Bute*, p.xxviii); Newcastle's reliance on the support of the equally suspect Granville was noticed even at the time: Fox to Hartington, 28 Nov 1754: Dev 330/28. But Granville may have been acting a double part, for he had spoken also of the necessity of the ministry's taking in Fox (Fox to Lady Caroline, 17 Dec 1754: 51415, f.191); Murray, who was later to show himself fully

capable of answering Pitt in debate, may have felt it wiser not to make a stiff reply on the subject of Jacobitism alone.

163. Gilbert Elliot, Memo, nd: NLS Minto MSS, 11032, f.1.
164. Fox to Hartington, 28 Nov 1754: Dev 330/28.
165. Horatio Walpole to Hartington, 28 Nov 1754: Dev 180/27.
166. Ryder Diary, 29 Nov 1754.
167. Walpole, *George II*, 1, 418–19.
168. Fox to Hartington, 28 Nov 1754: Dev 330/28.
169. Horatio Walpole to N, 30 Oct 1754: 32737, f.231.
170. Joseph Yorke to Lady Anson, 24 Dec 1754: 35388, f.37.
171. Charles Yorke told Dudley Ryder 'That Legge puts on an air of dissatisfaction in not having power nor confidence enough with the Duke of Newcastle to do his business in the House of Commons where he does not that business that is expected. But I believe the truth is he finds himself unequal to the task of managing the House privately and publicly, and gives himself this sort of air to disguise his own insufficiency. And C. Yorke thinks so.' (Ryder Diary, 29 Nov 1754.)
172. N to H, Thursday morning [28 Nov 1754]: 35414, f.230.
173. Cf. Ryder Diary, 1 Dec 1754.
174. Egmont, Memo: 47092, f.151.
175. The instructions of August 1753 to Sir Danvers Osborne, Governor of New York, were resented as smacking of arbitrary power: cf. *Public Advertiser*, 7 Feb 1754: Sir Lewis Namier and John Brooke, *Charles Townshend* (London, 1964), pp.37–41; Namier, *Crossroads*, p.204; J. A. Henretta, *'Salutary Neglect': colonial administration under the Duke of Newcastle* (Princeton, 1972), pp.343–4.
176. For the Irish crisis cf. Declan O'Donovan, 'The Money Bill Dispute of 1753' in T. Bartlett and D. W. Hayton (eds.), *Penal Era and Golden Age. Essays in Irish History, 1690–1800* (Belfast, 1979), pp. 55–87. Egmont evidently misunderstood the constitutional disputes over the Irish revenue.
177. Egmont, Memo: 47092, f.151.
178. Walpole, *George II*, 1, 417.
179. Waldegrave, *Memoirs*, p.33. Waldegrave was far more Fox's friend than Newcastle's.
180. N, Memo, 30 Nov [1754]: 32995, f.354.
181. N, Memo, Nov [1754]: 32995, f.355.
182. Egmont, Memo: 47092, f.151.
183. Bayntun Rolt Diary, 2 Dec 1754.
184. Duke of Beaufort to Brudenell Rooke, 2 Dec 1754: Rooke MSS, D 1833 F1.
185. Newdigate Diary, 3 Dec 1754: *CJ*, xxvii, p.42. The Whigs thereby reversed normal procedure by forcing the Tory candidates to present their case first.
186. Martin, Memo: 41355, f.28. The fourth person has not been identified. Newdigate's Diary (2 Dec 1754) contains the entry 'Mitre Tavern to meet Sir J. Dashwood etc.', evidently a pre-arranged meeting; but there is no mention of a deputation subsequently calling on Newcastle.
187. H. Shiffner to H. F. Luttrell, 14 Dec 1754: Luttrell MSS.
188. G. Elliot to his wife, [12 Dec 1754]: NLS 11006, f.106.
189. Fox to Lady Caroline, Monday morning [2 Dec 1754]: 51415, f.180. Walpole

(*George II*, 1, 417) misdated the audience 29 November; but it came only after Newcastle's meeting with Egmont.

190. Martin, Memo: 41335, f.25; cf. Bayntun Rolt Diary, 3 Dec 1754.

191. Waldegrave, Memo [c. 2 Dec 1754]: 51380, f.78. Waldegrave was apparently present and gave Fox the memorandum as a record of what was said.

192. Fox to Lady Caroline, [2 Dec 1754]: 51415, f.182.

193. Fox to [Waldegrave], Monday night [? 2 Dec 1754]: 51380, f.3.

194. The terms are recorded in N's memo of 3 Dec 1754: 32995, f.360, the accuracy of which Waldegrave confirmed. According to Walpole (*George II*, 1, 417), the King chose Waldegrave as an intermediary.

195. Fox to Lady Caroline, Tuesday night [? 3 Dec 1754]: 51415, f.184.

196. Waldegrave, *Memoirs*, p.34.

197. Fox to Pitt, nd, PRO 30/8/1, f.81. This account rests on the ascription of the following order and dates to the letters misdated 25 April 1755 in the *Chatham Correspondence:*

Ch Corr		PRO:	
1, 124	Fox to Pitt	30/8/1, f.81	[Weds 4 Dec 1754]
1, 127	Fox to Pitt	ibid., f.84	[Thurs 5 Dec; footnote, 6 Dec]
1, 128	Fox to King	ibid., f.86	[c. 5 Dec (draft)]
1, 129	Fox to Pitt	ibid., f.88	Friday [6 Dec]
1, 130	Pitt to Fox	ibid., f.90	Friday eight o'clock [6 Dec]
1, 131	Fox to Pitt	ibid., f.92	Friday night [6 Dec]

and to one misdated 26 April 1755:

1, 132	Fox to Pitt	ibid., f.94	[12 Dec 1754]

The false dates given to these letters by the editors of the *Chatham Correspondence*, and added in ink to the originals, have led even recent historians (e.g. Foord, *His Majesty's Opposition*, p.283) to conflate these events with Fox's admission to the Regency Council in April 1755. Fox's failure to exercise significant power within the Cabinet in early 1755 is thus disguised, and Newcastle's alleged attempt to govern the Commons illegitimately, through subordinates, is given false credibility.

198. Cf. 'Answer proposed by my Lord Chancellor, and the Duke of Newcastle to be returned by my Lord Waldegrave to Mr Fox' [4 Dec 1754]: 32995, f.362. Waldegrave gave a copy to Fox: 51380, f.48.

199. Fox to Pitt, nd, PRO 30/8/1, f.81.

200. Ibid.; cf. Waldegrave to N, 4 Dec 1754: 32737, f.407.

201. Boutet, despatch, 16 Dec 1754: Archives des affaires étrangères, Quai d'Orsay, Correspondance politique, Angleterre 437, f.412 (HPT transcript).

202. Walpole, *George II*, 1, 418.

203. Fox to Pitt, PRO 30/8/1, f.84.

204. Pitt to Fox, PRO 30/8/1, f.90.

205. G. Elliot to Lord Minto, 7 Dec [1754]: NLS Minto MSS, 11001, f.12; Bayntun Rolt Diary, 4 Dec 1754.

206. Ryder Diary, 11 Dec 1754.

207. Fox to Pitt, PRO 30/8/1, f.88.

208. Fox to George II, 10 Dec 1754: 51375, f.5.

209. Fox to Pitt, PRO 30/8/1, f.92.

210. H, Memo, 10 Dec 1754: 32995, f.366.

211. Granville's name is unexplainedly missing from the final draft: 32995, f.368.

212. Ibid.; words in square brackets added in final draft.
213. Fox to Waldegrave, Monday night [9 Dec 1754]: 51380, f.4.
214. Walpole, *George II*, I, 420.
215. Fox to Lady Caroline, 12 Dec 1754: 51415, f.187.
216. 'Mr Fox's Conversation with Mr West', 11 Dec 1754: 32995, f.370.
217. 51375, f.7. Waldegrave passed it to Fox.
218. H to N, 15 Dec 1754: 32737, f.449.
219. Fox to Pitt, PRO 30/8/1, f.94.
220. Dodington, *Diary*, 3 Sept 1755.
221. Walpole, *George II*, I, 420.
222. H to N, 15 Dec 1754: 32737, f.449.
223. Archbishop of Canterbury to Sir George Lee, 13 Dec 1754: Corpus Christi College, Cambridge MSS, 566.
224. W. Hamilton to Earl of Huntingdon, 13 Dec 1754: HMC *Hastings*, III, 89.
225. Ryder Diary, 11 Dec 1754.
226. Cf. Sir Gorge Lyttelton to [Bedford], 4 Dec 1754: 32737, f.409 (not sent).
227. Martin, Memo: 41355, f.27; Walpole, *George II*, I, 414–416, claims he suggested to Conway Bedford's 'propensity to reconcile himself to the Court' for Conway to consult with Lyttelton; but that Sir George, with tactless enthusiasm which Newcastle reinforced, bungled the mission despite its feasibility.
228. Ryder Diary, 15 Dec 1754. Murray stressed that the initiative was Lyttelton's; Ryder believed it was a 'roundabout' overture from Newcastle.
229. Walpole calls it the Treasurership of the Household, as had been reported in the press (e.g. *Read's Weekly Journal*, 21 Dec 1754), but there are no signs that Newcastle considered him for the place: cf. Memo, 28 Dec 1754: 32737, f.514. Earlier, Egmont had been spoken of as Secretary of State in the place of Robinson, who was said to be about to replace Pitt (*Read's Weekly Journal*, 14 Dec 1754); this is equally unsubstantiated.
230. Walpole, *George II*, I, 418–22. Boutet reported, presumably on Fox's authority, that Townshend would succeed Fox when Fox was removed to the Paymastership. This may have been mere speculation by the latter. Although Newcastle's memorandum of 12 December shows he had Townshend's name in mind in some connection, we do not know in which; the scheme of using Fox to replace Pitt was even then being abandoned. Pitt's removal alone may have been dropped within two days afterwards (cf. Fox to Lady Caroline, 14 Dec 1754: 51415, f.189).
231. Sir James Carnegie to Lord Milton, 12 Dec 1754: NLS Saltoun MSS, SC 183, f.140.
232. Ibid.
233. Horatio Walpole to N, Friday morning [13 Dec 1754]: 32737, f.445.
234. N to H, 21 Dec 1754: 35414, f.232.
235. N to H, 23 Dec [1754]: 35414, f.234.
236. N to Egmont, 24 Dec 1754: 32737, f.477.
237. Egremont wrote to Newcastle (30 Dec 1754: 32737, f. 522): 'I think Lord Egmont's answer to your Grace's letter...leaves you no doubt of his party being taken without reserve to co-operate with your Grace.'
238. Ibid.
239. N to H, 26 Dec 1754: 35414, f.238.

240. N to Holdernesse, 25 July 1755: Eg 3429, f.153. Exactly when he did so, if not on 26 December, is not clear.
241. Walpole to Mann, 21 Aug 1755: HW 20, p.490.
242. Fox to Hartington, 16 July 1755: Dev 330/45.
243. Cf. Robinson to N, 27 July 1755; 32856, f.268.
244. N to H, 31 Dec 1754: 35414, f.251.
245. Horatio Walpole to Hartington, 14 Jan 1755: Dev 180/30.
246. Walpole to R. Bentley, 13 Dec 1754: Toynbee, III, 271.
247. H to N, 15 Dec 1754: 32737, f.449.
248. Bedford to Hanbury Williams, 28 Jan 1755: Bedford MSS, XXXI, 12.
249. Cf. H to N, 15 Dec 1754: 32737, f.449.
250. Fox to Lady Caroline, 17 Dec 1754: 51415, f.191.
251. Chesterfield to Dayrolles, 17 Dec 1754: Dobrée, v, 2126.
252. N, Memo, 20 Dec 1754: 32995, f.377; cf. N to H, 21 Dec 1754: 35414, f.232.
253. Ryder Diary, 16 Feb 1755.
254. Joseph Yorke to Lady Anson, 10 Dec 1754: 35388, f.33; Joseph Yorke to H, 10 Dec 1754: 35356, f.269.
255. Fox to Lady Caroline, 14 Dec 1754: 51415, f.189.
256. H to N, 15 Dec 1754: 32737, f.449.
257. N, Memo, 20 Dec 1754: 32995, f.377.
258. H to N, 15 Dec 1754: 32737, f.449.
259. Bentinck to Keith, 24 Dec 1754: 35478, f.163.
260. Joseph Yorke to Royston, 24 Dec 1754: 35364, f.25.
261. E.g. through Stone: cf. Ryder Diary, 8 Dec 1754.
262. Fox's links with Pitt seem to have survived the disclosure of what was known to, for example, Ryder.
263. H to N, 26 Dec 1754: 32737, f.485.
264. N to Marlborough, 27 Dec 1754: 32737, f.493.
265. N to Egremont, 28 Dec 1754: PRO 30/47/28, no fol.; cf. Memo, 28 Dec 1754: 35414, f.244.
266. N, Memo, 28 Dec 1754: 32737, f.514. Newcastle's complex solution: 'I think the way, that seems the most probable, would be, to get out, by promotion or pension, Ld Chumley or Sir Wm Yonge [Joint Vice Treasurers of Ireland] for Mr Legge. Or to make Mr Legge Comptroller or Master of the Jewel Office, with the peerage and the promise of Sir W Yonge's place. And in that case, to vacate the Parks, and give the other vacant place, to my Ld Egmont.'
267. Ibid.
268. H to N, 29 Dec 1754: 32737, f.516.
269. N to H, 31 Dec 1754: 35414, f.251.
270. N to H, 2 Jan 1755: 32852, f.27.
271. N to Andrew Stone, 2 Jan 1755: 35414, f.259.
272. N to H, 2 Jan 1755: 32852, f.27.
273. H to N, 3 Jan 1755: 32852, f.63. The King particularly resented the possibility, which Granville may disingenuously have suggested to him, that Newcastle (like Sunderland) would insist on being Groom of the Stole himself as a mark of his power as First Minister.
274. Stone to N, 3 Jan 1755: 32852, f.69; H to N, 3 Jan 1755: 32852, f.63.

275. N to Andrew Stone, 2 Jan 1755: 35414, f.259.
276. N to H, 4 Jan 1755: 35414, f.261.
277. After a request by Hardwicke to Cumberland, short-circuiting any influence in Fox's hands. Cf. H to N, 5 Jan 1755: 32852, f.91.
278. Walpole to Mann, 10 Mar 1755: HW 20, p.468.
279. N, Memo, 28 Dec 1754: 32737, f.514.
280. N to H, 4 Jan 1755: 35414, f.261.
281. N to Lady Katherine Pelham, 25 Jan 1755: 32852, f.260.
282. Chesterfield to Dayrolles, 4 Feb 1755: Dobrée, v, 2134.
283. A. Mitchell to Lord Deskfoord, 6 Feb 1755: SRO Seafield MSS, GD 248/562/55.
284. E.g. Gilbert Elliot to his wife, [28 Jan 1755]: NLS Minto MSS, 11006, f.54.
285. W. Guthrie to H. Guthrie, 4 Feb 1755: HMC *Laing*, II, 414.
286. Newdigate Diary, 11 Jan 1755; *CJ*, XXVII, p.72. The Tories won, 46 to 44; they had earlier lost a motion by 57 to 48.
287. Horatio Walpole to Hartington, 14 Jan 1755: Dev 180/30.
288. Newdigate Diary, 5 Feb 1755; J. Dobson to J. Mordaunt, 6 Feb 1755: Mordaunt MSS, CR 1368, v, 10. On 13 Dec, the Tories had failed by only 73 to 118 to prevent a Whig attempt to exclude Edward Le Grand, presumably a Tory, from the Land Tax Commissioners for Whitehall and St. James's. *CJ*, XXVII, 52.
289. Chesterfield to Dayrolles, 4 Feb 1755: Dobrée, v, 2134; Fox to Collinson, 25 Jan 1755: 28727, f.42 (misdated 25 Jan 1756 in Riker, *Fox*, II, 359).
290. *Parl Hist*, xv, 469–512.
291. Ryder Diary, 9 Feb 1755.
292. *CJ*, XXVII, 120.
293. Bedford to Sir C. Hanbury Williams, 28 Jan 1755: Bedford MSS, XXXI, 12.
294. W. Digby to [? Lord Ilchester], 27 Jan 1755: 51341, f.109.
295. G. Elliot to his wife, [28 Jan 1755]: NLS 11006, f.89; H. Gorges to B. Towney, 5 Feb 1755: HMC 10th Rep. App. VI, p.257.
296. *CJ*, XXVII, p.142.
297. Ibid. pp.146–7.
298. Ibid. p.161.
299. Ibid. p.165.
300. Rev. T. Lindsey to E. of Huntingdon, 20 Feb 1755: HMC *Hastings*, III, 93; Ryder Diary, 15 Feb 1755.
301. Chesterfield to Dayrolles, 4 Feb 1755: Dobrée, v, 2134.
302 Joseph Yorke to Royston, 7 Feb [1755]: 35364, f.32.
303. Cf. the division list for 24 Mar 1755, *BIHR*, XLIX (1976) 80–107; Bayntun Rolt Diary, 2 Mar 1755. The only major figures to vote that day were (for Fox): James Grenville, Richard Rigby, Lord Hillsborough and Sir George Lee (who then changed sides); for Newcastle: Lord Dupplin, Lord Egmont, Nugent, Hume Campbell and Lord George Sackville.
304. N to H, Saturday morning [15 Feb 1755]: 32852, f.469.
305. E.g. Newdigate Diary, 24 Feb 1755.
306. Later an adherent of Pitt.
307. Cf. G. Elliot to his wife, [25 Jan 1755]: NLS 11006, f.113.
308. A. Mitchell to Lord Deskfoord, 15 Feb 1755: SRO Seafield MSS, GD 248/562/55.

309. N to H, Saturday morning [15th Feb 1755]: 32852, f.469; General St Clair to his father, Thursday [20 Feb 1755]: NLS Minto MSS, 11005, f.30.

Speakers: For: Robert Dundas; Col. Haldane; Andrew Mitchell; H. S. Conway; Sir John Mordaunt; Sir George Lyttelton; Sir Thomas Clarke.

Against: Gilbert Elliot; Thomas Potter; Hans Stanley; Lord Strange; William Northey; James Oswald.

Scots voting against: James Oswald; William Mure; Sir Harry Erskine; Gilbert Elliot; General St Clair.

310. N to H, Saturday [22 Feb 1755]: 35414, f.263.

311. Possibly over Joseph Yorke's Colonelcy.

312. Gilbert Elliot to his wife, 27 Feb 1755: NLS Minto MSS, 11006, f.102.

313. Walpole, *George II*, II, 6-9; A. Mitchell to Lord Deskfoord, 1 Mar 1755: SRO Seafield MSS, GD 248/562/55.

314. Falmouth to N, [28 Feb 1755]: 32852, f.634. Others, too, saw it as a victory for Fox's and Bedford's party over Newcastle; cf. J. F. Pinney to A. Pinney, 4 Mar 1755: Pinney Papers, 58/3/355.

315. Walpole, *George II*, II, 11.

316. Newdigate Diary, 28 Feb 1755.

317. Walpole, *George II*, II, 12.

318. Guilford to S. Miller, '4 Mar 1754' [sc. 1755]: Sanderson Miller MSS, 754; *LJ*, XXVIII, 352.

319. Boscawen to N, 3 Mar 1755: 32853, f.44.

320. West to N, 1 Mar 1755: 32853, f.9.

321. Walpole, *George II*, II, 16-17.

322. H to N, 23 Nov 1754: 32737, f.385.

323. Fox to Charles Yorke, 13 Mar 1755: 35430, f.183. Burrell had dropped his petition; Oglethorpe had asked for delay, and the House agreed on 21 Jan that his should be heard only after the Mitchell petition had been settled. Now, Fox arranged for the Report from the Committee of Privileges and Elections to be presented in the last week of the sessions. It was: Molyneux and Webb were declared returned by the House on 24 Apr: *CJ*, XXVII, 112, 292-3.

324. Cf. Bedford to Hanbury Williams, 28 Jan 1755: Bedford MSS, XXXI, 12.

325. Newdigate Diary, 19 Feb 1755.

326. *CJ*, XXVII, 205-13.

327. Bedford also spoke against Newcastle over the Sheriff Depute Bill in the Lords on 15 March: cf. Gilbert Elliot to his wife, 15 Mar [1755]: NLS Minto MSS, 11006, f.120.

328. Newdigate Diary, 4 Mar 1755.

329. Walpole, *George II*, II, 12-13, where the meeting is misdated 5 Mar. The presence of Beckford is evidence against the possibility that the meeting was one of pro-Newcastle Tories only, as Walpole suggested was the case of the meeting on 12 March.

330. Newdigate Diary, 4 Mar 1755.

331. Bayntun Rolt Diary, 5 Mar 1755.

332. Walpole, *George II*, II, 13.

333. Newdigate Diary, 7 Mar 1755.

334. Ryder Diary, 7 Mar 1755. It is possible that Ryder referred to the Horn Tavern meeting on 12 or 24 March.

335. Bayntun Rolt Diary, 10 Mar 1755. On 11th, he found Newcastle 'again desirous to know my opinion of the Tories'.

336. Walpole, *George II*, II, 13. Walpole wished to represent Fox's defeat as a disingenuous manoeuvre; it is more likely to have been a simple Tory preference for Newcastle.

337. Newdigate Diary, 12 Mar 1755.

338. Newdigate Diary, 12 Mar 1755; Boscawen to N, [12 Mar 1755]: 32853, f.260. Tories for the sitting Members (i.e. with Fox): Nathaniel Curzon; Charles Barrow; Gabriel Hanger; George Cooke.

Tories for the petitioners (i.e. with Newcastle): Sir William Meredith; Sir Armine Wodehouse; Humphrey Sturt; Richard Grosvenor.

Dr Newman and Mr Brooke (Namier and Brooke, II, 577 and III, 130) misinterpreted Boscawen's letter to Newcastle and erroneously attributed Hanger to Newcastle and Meredith to Fox; Namier (ibid. II, 287) used it correctly to attribute Curzon to Fox. That the latter interpretation is correct is shown by the consistent voting of both groups of MPs in the division of 12 March (the first four for Clive and Stephenson, the last four for Hussey and Luttrell); by Wodehouse's links with George Townshend, who was a teller for the petitioners in the first division of that day; and by Meredith's with Newcastle (cf. p.147 below).

339. J. F. Pinney to A. Pinney, 13 Mar 1755: Pinney Papers, 55/3/356.

340. G. Elliot to his wife, 12 Mar [1755]: NLS 11006, f.82.

341. Boscawen to N, 20 Mar 1755: 32853, f.395.

342. *CJ*, XXVII, p.172.

343. Newdigate Diary, 13 Mar 1755; Sir E. Turner to S. Miller, 18 Mar 1755: Sanderson Miller MSS, 537.

344. Newdigate Diary, 22 Mar 1755; *CJ*, XXVII, 252.

345. West to N, 22 Mar 1755: 32853, f.439.

346. Cf. West to N, 22 Mar 1755: 32853, f.439. There is evidence that Fox was engaging in some horse-trading in pursuit of votes: cf. Fox to Mrs Lowther 21 Mar 1755: HMC 13th Rep. App. VII, p.127.

347. Cf. Charles Compton to Fox, 22 Mar 1755: 51402, f.13. Though a relative of Fox's and an assiduous attender at the House (Namier and Brooke II, 241), Compton could profess not to have seen it in this light. This may have been an excuse. Compton voted on Fox's side in the Committee, but on 22nd wrote that he had 'entered into [a] promise with a set of gentlemen [? at the Horn Tavern on 7th] to act in conformity with the majority at our next meeting'; on 24th he voted for Newcastle's candidates.

348. Cf. Horatio Walpole to Hartington, 21 Nov 1754: Dev 180/24.

349. Newdigate Diary, 24 Mar 1755. The voting on 24 March was as follows (*CJ*, XXVII, 263):
1st motion to agree with the Committee that Clive had been elected:

| Tellers for the Yeas | Mr Yorke
Mr Ellis | } 183 |
| Tellers for the Noes | Mr Townshend
Mr Nugent | } 207 |

2nd motion to agree with the Committee that Stephenson had been elected: negatived without a division.

3rd motion, to declare that Luttrell had been elected:

Tellers for the Yeas — Sir Roger Newdigate / Mr Jeffreys } 201

Tellers for the Noes — Sir John Philipps / Mr Selwyn } 178

4th motion to declare that Hussey had been elected: passed without a division.

350. Lord Digby to Lord Ilchester, Tuesday [25 Mar 1755]: 51340, f.109; Rigby to Bedford, 8 o'clock [24 Mar 1755]: Bedford MSS, xxxi, 321. Hardwicke's list of Tories voting on 24 March is 35877, f.237; Newcastle's is 33002, f.438. Both agree on the seventeen names for the sitting members. Of those against, Hardwicke's list gives a total of 55 (this, not Newcastle's, is referred to in Lord Digby to Lord Ilchester, supra.) Newcastle's omits Richard Lyster; includes the names of Sir Thomas Mostyn, [Hon. Benjamin] Bathurst and Sir Nicholas Bayly not in Hardwicke's and totals 57 names. A third list, probably from the Townshend papers, has been edited by Dr L. J. Colley, 'The Mitchell Election Division, 24 March 1755', *BIHR*, XLIX (1976), 80–107. The votes of Sir George Lee, John Lee and Sir John Philipps, who changed sides, establish all three documents as relating to the first of the two divisions on that day. The close agreement of Newcastle's and Hardwicke's lists suggests that the Townshend list is inaccurate in counting Pytts, Wigley, Grove and Bankes as absent, and Edwin, Ladbroke, Hanger and Ongley as voting for Clive and Stephenson. The latter list, however, confirms the votes of Lyster, Mostyn, Bathurst and Bayly for Newcastle's candidates. Miss Colley was ignorant of Hardwicke's list; the only support for her astonishing claim (loc. cit. p.82) that contemporaries had difficulty in 'defining who exactly was a Tory' is thus her lack of other evidence for the party identity of Henry Bankes, a successful lawyer (that of Pytts, Wigley and Grove not being in doubt); he is, however, recorded as 'Against' in Newcastle's list, 33034, f.183, probably of May or June 1754. Moreover, it was the majority of the Tories who 'went forth', i.e. left the Chamber to be counted, in both the Mitchell divisions – so introducing a greater risk of error in recording their names, especially if George Townshend were trying to do so while acting as teller. Inaccuracies in that list reflect normal technical difficulties, not an ideological confusion. Since the Whigs were, exceptionally, divided over Mitchell, the Townshend list does not (*pace* Miss Colley) elucidate 'the political orientation of the bulk of that Parliament', nor was the issue itself a 'catalyst for the various political groupings that were then in formation'. Tory behaviour over Mitchell was not an example of 'duplicity', as Miss Colley suggests, but a belated adherence to a generalised commitment to Newcastle.

351. Lord Digby to Lord Ilchester, Tuesday [25 Mar 1755]: 51340, f.109.

352. Rigby to Bedford, 8 o'clock [24 Mar 1755]: Bedford MSS, xxxi, 32.

353. Rigby to Bedford, Saturday night [29 Mar 1755]: Bedford MSS, xxxi, 36. The only certain Tory success so far had been at Salisbury, where all three candidates had been returned: two Tories and a Whig. The two Tories were declared elected on 26 Nov 1754.

Carmarthen had been won by a ministerial Whig, Griffith Philipps, against Sir Thomas Stepney, put up by Sir John Philipps; but after the divisions on 5 Feb won by the Tories by 73 to 71 and 73 to 72, the Tory petition disappears; it is not clear when it was dropped.

At Leicester, two Tories had been returned after a hot contest against Robert Mitford, backed by the Whig Duke of Rutland: but there the Tories were to retain their seats. On 10 April Mitford's petition was ordered to be heard at the Bar of the House in six weeks' time, so effectively killing it: *CJ*, XXVII, p.279.

William Shenstone to Richard Graves, 4 Apr 1755: M. Williams (ed), *The Letters of William Shenstone* (Oxford, 1939) p.441.

355. Lord Digby to Ilchester, Tuesday [25 Mar 1755]: 51340, f.109.
356. Walpole, *George II*, II, 14.
357. *London Evening Post*, 15–17 May 1755.
358. Joseph Yorke to Lady Anson, 31 Mar 1755: 35388, f.57.
359. Same to same, 1 Apr 1755: 35388, f.61.
360. Lord Digby to Ilchester, Tuesday [25] Mar [1755]: 51430, f.109.
361. Fox to Horatio Walpole, 9 Sep [1755]: 51428, f.89.
362. Horatio Walpole to Hartington, 23 Nov 1754: Dev 180/25.
363. Henry Pelham (MP for Tiverton) to [? Thomas Pelham], 27 Mar 1755: 32853, f.480; Horatio Walpole to H, 29 Sept 1755: 35593, f.265.
364. Shenstone to Graves, 4 Apr 1755: M. Williams (ed.), *The Letters of William Shenstone*.
365. N to Joseph Yorke, 14 Apr 1755: 32854, f.115.
366. N, Memo, 'Business that must be dispatched at or before the rising of the Session', 26 Mar 1755: 32996, f.59.
367. H, Memo, 27 Mar 1755: 32996, f.63.
368. N, Memo, 26 Mar 1755: 32996, f.59.
369. N to Holdernesse, 11 July 1755: Eg 3429, f.78.
370. H, Memo, 27 Mar 1755: 32996, f.63.
371. Newdigate Diary, 8, 12, 15 Apr 1755.
372. Newdigate Memo, nd: Newdigate MSS B 2528. Other speakers: for Tories: Nicholas Fazackerley, Sir John Philipps, Colonel Townshend, Norbone Berkeley, Sir Cordell Firebrace, Richard Crowle, George Bowes, George Fox Lane, Richard Beckford, Sir Roger Newdigate. For Whigs: Lord Strange, Lord Barrington, Henry Fox, Sir Richard Lloyd, Sir George Lyttelton, Charles Yorke.
373. Ibid. With Barnard spoke William Northey, Thomas Prowse, Sir Francis Dashwood, John Morton and Sir Roger Newdigate; against him, Horatio Walpole, George Grenville, Henry Fox and Welbore Ellis.
374. W. Belchier to R. Clive, 9 Apr 1755: Clive MSS, Box 21.
375. H, Memo, 27 Mar 1755: 32996, f.63.
376. N, Memo, 26 Mar 1755: 32996, f.59.
377. N, Memo, 'The State of the House of Commons', 18 Apr 1755; 32996, f.81.
378. Cf. Pitt's draft letter, probably to the Grenvilles (PRO 30/8/1, f.96, falsely given a date 'April 1755', and a title 'Remarks on his Correspondence with H. Fox' in *Chatham Corr*, I, 134), which apparently refers to this overture through Horatio Walpole.
379. Royston, Memo, 'The Weak Points of Conduct in the Duke of N's Administration since Mr Pelham's death', nd: 35595, f.4.

380. Walpole, *George II*, I, 418.
381. Joseph Yorke to H, 24 Sept 1754: 35356, f.253.
382. Cf. Bolingbroke, *Works* (4 vols, London, 1844) II, 160.

3. THE RECONSTRUCTION OF THE MINISTRY

1. N to H, Saturday morning [12 Apr 1755]: 35414, f.265.
2. Bayntun Rolt Diary, 11 Apr 1755. Newcastle had earlier spoken resentfully of Granville's hostility over the Mitchell petition and present links with Fox: ibid. 9 Apr 1755.
3. N to H, Saturday morning [12 Apr 1755]: 35414, f.265.
4. Bedford had, inter alia, 'said he had taken a great deal of pains to find out whether we had a ministry or a minister, and if the latter who he was...': J. Milbanke to Thomas Pelham, 26 Mar 1755: 33094, f.110.
5. Cf. Ryder Diary, 8 Mar 1755; Bayntun Rolt Diary, 12 Mar, 15 Apr, 26 Apr 1755.
6. Henry Pelham to [? Thomas Pelham], 27 Mar 1755: 32853, f.480.
7. Rigby to Bedford, 29 Mar 1755: Bedford MSS, XXXI, 36.
8. Bayntun Rolt Diary, 12 Mar 1755.
9. Bayntun Rolt Diary, 18 Mar 1755.
10. Bayntun Rolt Diary, 31 Mar 1755.
11. The *London Evening Post* failed to mention Poulett's motion; few pamphleteers took up the issue of the King's journey, and Pitt only did so later when George II returned home with a collection of subsidy treaties (Dodington, *Diary*, 3 Sept 1755).
12. H to N, 12 Apr 1755: 32854, f.99.
13. Andrew Mitchell to Lord Deskfoord, 26 Apr 1755: SRO Seafield MSS, GD 248/562/55; Walpole, *George II*, II, 21.
14. H to N, 12 Apr 1755: 32854, f.99. H recommended that Granville and Holdernesse should also be invited on 12th; it is not clear whether they were.
15. Waldegrave, *Memoirs*, p.30.
16. Dodington, *Diary*, 27 May 1755.
17. What seems to be Walpole's draft is in Coxe, *Lord Walpole*, p.422; Devonshire was evidently sent, in advance and in confidence, a shorter version: Dev 180/31.
18. Horatio Walpole to N, 14 May 1755: 32854, f.121.
19. This is suggested by Walpole to Newcastle, above, which substantially confirms Waldegrave's memo (see below).
20. Coxe, *Lord Walpole*, p.422.
21. There is no evidence of cool relations between the King and Newcastle at this point. The latter, indeed, was hopeful of securing the election of a King of the Romans and was entering into George II's 'German measures'; he had as yet put no pressure on the King for Pitt's inclusion in the Cabinet. The temper of the Court was highly favourable to Newcastle, whose advice was preferred to Cumberland's (N to Duchess, 20 Apr 1755: 33075, f.26). The 'Duke' can only be Cumberland, whose relations with his father were not uniformly cordial. For the King's occasional jealousy of his son's military career, Walpole, *George II*, II, 139–40; cf. Owen, *Pelhams*, p.274.

22. Waldegrave, Memo, nd (but probably shortly after the meeting on 12 Apr): 51380, f.79.
23. Waldegrave, Memo: 51380, f.79.
24. Horatio Walpole to N, 14 Apr 1755: 32854, f.121.
25. Ibid.
26. Ibid.
27. Cf. Halifax to N, 17 Apr 1755: 32854, f.159.
28. Poulett to Fox, 17 Apr 1755: 51428, f.81; Fox to N, Thursday 5 o'clock [17 Apr 1755]: 32854, f.157.
29. Rigby to Bedford, Thursday [17 Apr 1755]: Bedford MSS, xxxi, 42.
30. *Parl Hist*, xv, 520; Newdigate Diary, 24 Apr 1755; A. Mitchell to R. Dundas, 24 Apr 1755: Arniston MSS, v, no. 146. It had been predicted that Vyner would move the motion in the Commons: Ryder Diary, 13 Apr 1755.
31. Walpole to R. Bentley, 6 May 1755: Toynbee, iii, 304.
32. Chesterfield to Dayrolles, 2 May 1755: Dobrée, v, 2142.
33. Joseph Yorke to Lady Anson, 22 Apr 1755: 35388, f.69.
34. Riker, *Fox*, i, 271.
35. Waldegrave, *Memoirs*, pp.45–6.
36. Walpole, *George II*, ii, 38.
37. Waldegrave, *Memoirs*, p.28.
38. N, Memo, 26 Mar 1755: 32996, f.59.
39. H, Memo, 27 Mar 1755: 32996, f.63.
40. Walpole was trying to find an opportunity to see Pitt alone on 8 April and presumably did so soon after. Horatio Walpole to [? Andrew Stone], 8 Apr 1755: 32854, f.72.
41. N, Memo, 'The State of the House of Commons', 18 Apr 1755: 32996, f.81.
42. Walpole (*George II*, ii, 37) was evidently wrong in claiming that it was Pitt who sent Horatio Walpole to Newcastle 'with a peremptory demand of an explicit answer, whether his Grace would make him Secretary of State on the first convenient opportunity; not insisting on any person's being directly removed to favour him'.
43. Pitt's draft letter [? to the Grenvilles], PRO 30/8/1, f.96; nd but probably after Walpole's visit and almost certainly before Pitt's interview with Fox on 9 May.
44. W. Ellis to Fox, 21 May 1755: 51387, f.9.
45. PRO 30/8/1, f.96.
46. Dodington, *Diary*, 16 July 1755. N's anger was known to Fox and Hartington.
47. Bute to G. Elliot, 27 Apr 1755: NLS Minto MSS, 11014, f.5. Sedgwick (*Bute*, p.xlvii) omitted the final phrase in order to suggest that Bute was already in communication with Pitt, and had concluded terms.
48. Sedgwick, *Bute*, xlvii, Pitt may not, as Sedgwick remarks, have explicitly accused Fox of betraying him during either of their interviews; but a correct appreciation of Fox's conduct during the winter of 1754–5 shows how unnecessary such a protest would have been.
49. Memo, nd: NLS Minto MSS, 11032, f.1.
50. Grenville Narrative, *Grenville Papers*, i, 432–3.
51. Ibid.
52. Ilchester, *Fox*, i, 251.

53. Walpole, *George II*, ii, 37.

54. Ibid. ii, 38.

55. Ibid. ii, 39. Walpole's source, he claimed, was Princess Amelia; but he does not record the Pitt–Fox meeting on 9 May and may have misdated Pitt's audience of the Princess of Wales on 5 May.

56. Dodington, *Diary*, 16 July 1755.

57. 'Memorandum of what passed between the Princess, Sir George, Mr Pitt, and Lord Bute, upon the coalition, 1755', nd: W. H. Smyth (ed.), *Aedes Hartwellianae; or, Notices of the Manor and Mansion of Hartwell* (London, 1851) Appendix, p.146. The original is not extant.

58. McKelvey (*George III and Lord Bute*, p.20) was able to claim that an alliance was firmly concluded only by ignoring the context of Lee's memorandum; he was unable to discover the formal terms of the treaty, exactly because there was no treaty. R. R. Sedgwick wrote ('William Pitt and Lord Bute. An Intrigue of 1755–1758', *History Today*, vi (Oct 1956), 647–54) that 'It was further agreed that, in return for leading this opposition, Pitt should become head of the government in the next reign, with Bute as his second in command at the Treasury'. There is no warrant in the evidence for this claim, either in Lee's memo or in Sedgwick's probable source, Gilbert Elliot's undated memo, NLS 11032, f.54, printed in Namier, *England*, p.105. Bute's suggestions to Pitt about future office in the latter source are vague, and occurred some unspecified time after Pitt and Bute 'came first together'. There is no evidence that Bute (as McKelvey suggests) attended the meeting on 6 May. Pitt was making an individual approach to the Princess and was not received as the spokesman of a Pitt–Bute opposition bloc. None such existed. Furthermore, McKelvey's account of the events of the summer, and his argument (op. cit. p.20–21) that terms were concluded in May on Pitt's first approach to Leicester House, rests on his erroneous ascription of the date '11 [May 1755]' to Bute's letter to Pitt, 'PRO 30/8/24, f.10' (*sc.* f.310). But the figure '11' at the foot of the letter refers to the *time*, 11 am; Bute's letter is in answer to Pitt's of 11 Sept 1755 (Sedgwick, 'Pitt', p.111), and is also properly dated 11 Sept 1755. The theory that a Leicester House opposition run by Pitt and Bute was launched in the spring of 1755 is further given substance by Sedgwick's false attribution of the year, 1755, to Pitt's letter to Bute headed 'Hayes. June 2nd' (Sedgwick, 'Pitt', p.109). Pitt did not buy Hayes until April 1756 and was probably elsewhere in June 1755 (cf. W. Pitt to Thomas Pitt, 20 May 1755: *Chatham Corr*, i, 138); the year is probably 1756 or 1757. The situation was in fact fluid until late September 1755, as is demonstrated below: the Princess, Egmont and Lee all sought to avoid constricting commitments, and long avoided one with Pitt as a dangerous liability.

59. Sir G. Lee to Sir W. Lee, 12 June 1755: Hartwell MSS, Bucks RO, D6/11. McKelvey's claim that Bute 'was in considerable favour with Augusta by the summer of 1755' (op. cit. p.18) is not proved by the evidence he cited, Sir G. Lee to [? Bute], [? 28 July 1755]: 5726D, f.198; 5726B, f.55. Lee was merely forwarding news, probably of the capture of Beauséjour, to the Princess.

60. Dodington, *Diary*, 7 May 1755.

61. Ibid. 9 May 1755.

62. Countess of Kildare to Earl of Kildare, 10 May [1755]: *Leinster Corr*, I, 10.
63. Ibid.
64. Countess of Kildare to Earl of Kildare, 12 May [1755]: *Leinster Corr*, I, 13.
65. Fox to Hartington, 13 May 1755: Dev 330/33. Walpole (*George II*, II, 37–8) does not mention the meeting on 9 May.
66. Temple to G. Grenville, 29 May 1755: *Grenville Papers*, II, 135, and LWL.
67. Dodington, *Diary*, 29 May 1755.
68. Fox to Ellis, 2 June 1755: 51387, f.11.
69. Hartington to Fox, 23 May 1755: 51381, f.11; cf. Fox to Hartington, 2 June 1755: Dev 330/37.
70. Fox to Ellis, 2 June 1755: 51387, f.11.
71. George Grenville claims Pitt had two meetings with the Princess (Narrative: *Grenville Papers*, I, 432). The first was on 5 May; Horace Walpole suggests the second took place just before 12th.
72. Fox's failure to use this knowledge to discredit Pitt in Newcastle's eyes seems almost inexplicable unless in deference to Cumberland's advice.
73. Although Lee and Bute agreed that Temple, Egmont and George Grenville should be told of what had passed.
74. Rigby learned on 30 September (Rigby to Earl Gower, 1 Oct 1755: PRO 30/29/1, f.486) and Bedford, therefore, the following day; Newcastle learned on c. 11–12 October.
75. Ellis to Fox, 21 May 1755: 51387, f.9.
76. Dodington, *Diary*, 27 May 1755.
77. Ibid.
78. E. Pyle to S. Kerrich, 25 Sept 1755: Kerrich MSS, XIV. Pyle mentioned subsidy treaties only through Legge's refusal to sign the Hessian warrant, but drew no further inference. It is necessary to emphasise that these were the terms in which the political debate was apprehended in view of the persistent claim that English factions were distinguished by their views on the way in which authority was to be maintained in the American colonies and by the respective attractions of a naval or a continental war; and that in the 1750's 'domestic constitutional issues had slowly ceased to count for much': A. G. Olson, *Anglo-American Politics, 1660–1775. The Relationship between Parties in England and Colonial America* (Oxford, 1973), p.145.
79. Dodington, *Diary*, 3 Sept 1755.
80. Ibid. 27 May 1755.
81. Legge to Hartington, 24 May 1755: Dev 257/20.
82. I.e. Fox or Pitt.
83. Dodington, *Diary*, 22 May 1755. Dodington hoped to persuade Newcastle to accept a 'mixed' system to anticipate and so avert a disruptive sweep of offices on the King's death: an offer to Newcastle of present support and future protection. There is no indication that this suggestion was ever put to Newcastle in the summer of 1755: the Princess anyway thought it unattainable when Dodington explained it: *Diary*, 27 May 1755.
84. H. Pelham to [? T. Pelham], 27 March 1755: 32853, f.480.
85. J. Milbanke to T. Pelham, 26 Mar 1755: 33094, f.110. J. Ralph to N, 16 May 1755: 32855, f.30.
86. H to N, 16 May 1755: 32855, f.24.

87. Hartington to Fox, 23 May 1755: 51381, f.11; Ellis to Fox, 21 May 1755: 51387, f.9.
88. Ellis to Fox, ibid.
89. Cf. N to Hartington, 17 May 1755: Dev 182/40.
90. N's list of the 1754 Parliament: 33034, f.173.
91. Devonshire to Hartington, 22 May 1755: Dev 163/53.
92. Cumberland to Fox, nd [? May 1755]: 51375, f.43.
93. N to H, 19 May 1755: 32855, f.60.
94. Fox to Hartington, 2 June 1755: Dev 330/37. The version printed in Waldegrave, *Memoirs*, p.159 reverses the sense by misreading 'none' as 'some'.
95. J. Cresset to [? A. Stone], 15 May 1755: 32854, f.528.
96. N to H, 7 June 1755: 35414, f.272.
97. N, Memo, 3 June 1755: 32855, f.314.
98. N to Lincoln, 16 June 1755: Ne(c) 3169.
99. Secker to Sir John Cust, 12 June 1755: *Cust Records*, III, 154.
100. Ellis to Hartington, 18 June 1755: Dev 335/2.
101. E.g. Stone to N, 18 May 1755: 32855, f.50.
102. Stone to N, 24 June 1755: 32856, f.165.
103. *Public Advertiser*, 23 July 1754.
104. Stone to N, ibid.
105. Dodington, *Diary*, 29 June 1755.
106. H to N, 27 June 1755: 32856, f.270.
107. N to H, 27 June 1755: 32856, f.272. Considerable popular admiration of Cumberland was in fact demonstrated when the visit took place on 2 July: cf. E. E. Charteris, *William Augustus Duke of Cumberland and the Seven Years' War* (London, 1925), p.166.
108. Dodington, *Diary*, 29 June 1755.
109. N to H, 27 June 1755: 32856, f.272.
110. Legge to Hartington, 29 June 1755: Dev 257/21.
111. Fox to Marlborough, nd: Blenheim Papers, LM 2.
112. N to H, 4 July 1755: 35415, f.1.
113. Egmont to [Nugent], 'Saturday' nd (but probably 28 June 1755): C. Nugent, *Memoir of Robert, Earl Nugent* (London, 1898), p.207.
114. H to N, Saturday night 5 July 1755: 32856, f.484.
115. N to Holdernesse, 2 July 1755: Eg 3429, f.19.
116. N to H, 4 July 1755: 35415, f.1.
117. H to N, Saturday night 5 July 1755: 32856, f.484.
118. Charles Yorke to H, Monday morning 7 July 1755: 35353, f.169.
119. N to Holdernesse, three letters of 11 July 1755: Eg 3429, ff.78, 82, 90.
120. Fox to Hartington, 16 July 1755: Dev 330/45.
121. Holdernesse to N, 20 July 1755: Eg 3429, f.129; N to Holdernesse, 25 July 1755: Eg 3429, f.153.
122. Hartington, for one, imagined they would not succeed: Hartington to Fox, 30 July 1755: 51381, f.31.
123. N to Holdernesse, 25 July 1755: Eg 3429, f.158.
124. N to Holdernesse, 25 July 1755: Eg 3429, f.153.
125. Walpole, *George II*, II, 36. The news of the arrival of the Duchess in Hanover on 6 July was apparently first reported in England in the *Public*

Advertiser of 21st. Newcastle supposed the Princess knew by 13th (N to H, 13 July 1755: 32857, f.82). However, the *Whitehall Evening Post* had reported the rumour of Prince George's marriage with 'a daughter of Prussia' on 3 May, predicted a visit by the *Duke* of Brunswick-Wolfenbüttel in its issue of 22 May, and firmly forecast a marriage with the eldest Princess of Wolfenbüttel on 14 June. There is room for an alternative explanation of events from May to July which would ante-date the reaction of the Princess reported by Walpole. To Newcastle, however, it later appeared that it was the *arrival* of the Duchess which had triggered the Princess's existing fears; and it is here assumed that speculation is a less acceptable guide to the intentions of Leicester House than the tenor of its negotiations with the ministry. In August, Newcastle told Cresset of Holdernesse's instructions (N to H, 22 Aug 1755: 32858, f.241) and evidently allayed fears that a decision was near to being taken (Cresset to Lee, 21 Aug 1755: Hartwell Papers, RA 74195-6).

126. Waldegrave, *Memoirs*, p.41.
127. Dodington, *Diary*, 6 Aug 1755.
128. Fox to Hartington, 16 July 1755: Dev 330/45.
129. Fox to Hartington, ibid.
130. Dodington, *Diary*, 16 July 1755.
131. Much confusion has surrounded this episode. At the Board, Legge kept silent and the absence of his signature was only noticed afterwards (N to Holdernesse, 25 July 1755: Eg 3429, f.143). Later, the story was elaborated to represent Legge as having patriotically resisted repeated importunities and the occasion blurred until it seemed he had refused his signature to the treaty itself (Rigby to Bedford, 21 Aug 1755: Bedford MSS, xxxi, 70; Walpole, *George II*, II, 35; Sir T. Robinson – not the Secretary of State – to Lord Carlisle, 2 Oct 1755: HMC 15th Rep. App. vi, p.209). In fact, the Hessian treaty was read at the Regency on 24 June 'to the entire approbation of every body there ... we recommended it to my Lord Chancellor, to put the Great Seal, this day, to the ratifications' (N to Holdernesse, 24 June 1755: Eg 3428, f.308). Yet so popular did the story become that Fox spread a similar report of his own refusal to sign the order for the ratification of the Hessian treaty. When it became public, Hardwicke protested he did not know what was meant by it: the warrant for the ratification had come over signed by the King and Holdernesse; the Lords Justices simply made a minute recommending Hardwicke to seal it. It must, he thought, mean Fox not signing the warrant Legge omitted to sign for the first payment of levy-money. 'Your Grace knows that often happens with the lords at the lower end of the table. I fancy he will hardly boast of *that* when the King comes over' (H to N, 23 Aug 1755: 32858, f.259).
132. Bedford heard a dramatised version of events at the Board, but only a month later (Rigby to Bedford, 21 Aug 1755: loc. cit.); Dodington himself learned only a week sooner: *Diary*, 18 Aug 1755.
133. N to Holdernesse, 25 July 1755: Eg 3429, f.156; N to Holdernesse, 29 July 1755: Eg 3429, f.165.
134. Walpole, *George II*, II, 36.
135. Dodington, *Diary*, 6 Aug 1755.

136. The first to appear was [J. Shebbeare], *A Letter to the People of England on the Present Situation and Conduct of National Affairs*, published *c.*15 September. On *c.*20 September the second, *A Letter from a Member of Parliament to . . . the Duke of **** upon the present situation of affairs* advocated concentration on a sea war but dismissed the existing subsidy treaties as unimportant.

137. Walpole to Mann, 21 Aug 1755: HW 20, p.490.

138. Cf. H to N, 28 July 1755: 32857, f.396.

139. N to H, 26 July 1755: 32857, f.382.

140. Dodington, *Diary*, 16 July 1755.

141. Sir T. Robinson to N, 27 July 1755: 32856, f.268.

142. Dodington, *Diary*, 21 July 1755.

143. Grenville Narrative: *Grenville Papers*, I, 434; Legge to Bute, 7 Aug 1755: Bute MSS, Mount Stuart no.42.

144. Devonshire to Fox, 4 Oct 1755: Dev 163/89. Horatio Walpole later discovered this: cf. Horatio Walpole to Devonshire (4th Duke), 25 Dec 1755: Dev 180/41.

145. N to Holdernesse, 1 Aug 1755: Eg 3429, f.197.

146. Horatio Walpole to Devonshire, 9 Aug 1755: Dev 180/34.

147. N to H, 3 Aug 1755: 35415, f.25.

148. N to Holdernesse, 25 July 1755: Eg 3429, f.158.

149. Fox to Hartington, 8 Aug 1755: Dev 330/56.

150. N to Hartington, 8 Aug 1755: 32858, f.57.

151. N to Peregrine Fury, 6 Aug 1755: PRO 30/8/51, f.47.

152. Pitt to Bute, two letters, [9th Aug 1755]: Sedgwick, 'Pitt', p.109.

153. Dodington, *Diary*, 2 Sept 1755.

154. Fox to Hartington, 10 Aug 1755: Dev 330/50.

155. H to N, 9 Aug 1755: 32858, f.74.

156. Cf. Pitt's memo of their cost: PRO 30/8/89.

157. H to N, 11 Aug 1755: 32858, f.104.

158. Fox to Hartington, 10 Aug 1755: Dev 330/50.

159. N to Egmont, 13 Aug 1755: 32858, f.130.

160. Egmont to N, 17 Aug 1755: 32858, f.193.

161. Lady Anson to Lady Grey, 22 Aug [1755]: Robinson MSS, Bedford RO, L30/9/3/49.

162. N to H, 12 Aug 1755: 32858, f.114.

163. H to N, 12 Aug 1755: 32858, f.120.

164. Fox to Hartington, 10 Aug 1755: Dev 330/50.

165. Hartington to Fox, 21 Aug 1755: 51381, f.33. He repeated his promise: Fox to Hartington, 29 Aug 1755: Dev 330/54.

166. Possibly on 14 Nov 1754: cf. *Parl Hist*, xv, 365.

167. H to N, 12 Aug 1755: 32858, f.120; N to Holdernesse, 14 Aug 1755: Eg 3429, f.255.

168. Stone to N, Thursday evening [? 21 Aug 1755]: 32858, f.199.

169. Stone to N, Monday morning 18 Aug 1755: 32858, f.197.

170. N to H, 22 Aug 1755: 32858, f.241.

171. Newcastle told Cresset, presumably on 21st: cf. Cresset to Lee, 21 Aug 1755: Hartwell Papers, RA 74195–6.

172. N to H, 22 Aug 1755: 32858, f.241.

173. Legge, at least, was canvassing support from his acquaintances; cf. Legge to J. Oswald, 26 Aug 1755: *Memorials of the Public Life and Character of James Oswald of Dunniker* (Edinburgh, 1825), p.397.

174. H to N, 23 Aug 1755: 32858, f.259.

175. Fox to Hartington, 1 Sept 1755: Dev 330/57.

176. N to H, 22 Aug 1755: 32858, f.241.

177. H to N, 23 Aug 1755: 32858, f.259.

178. N to H, 22 Aug 1755: 32858, f.241.

179. Fox to Hartington, 29 Aug 1755: Dev 330/55.

180. Holdernesse to N, two letters, 20 Aug 1755: 32858, ff.231, 233.

181. N to Holdernesse, 29 Aug 1755: Eg 3429, f.287.

182. N to A. Stone, Tuesday at night [26 Aug 1755]: 32858, f.294.

183. Ibid.

184. N to H, 22 Aug 1755: 35415, f.46. He did so: cf. Cresset to N, 25 Aug 1755: 32858, f.281. On Cresset's continued blandishments, cf. N to Duchess, 26 Aug 1755: 33075, f.35. Cresset, urging on Newcastle the possibility of an accommodation with Pitt, preserved a conspiratorial secret channel through Andrew Stone: cf. the anonymous letter endorsed 'Mr C', i.e. Cresset to Stone, Monday [1 Sept 1755]: 32858, f.394; Cresset to N, Thursday two o'clock [11 Sept 1755]: 32859, f.59.

185. N to Darlington, 26 Aug 1755: 32858, f.297.

186. Fox to Hartington, 1 Sept 1755: Dev 330/57.

187. N to Stone, [26 Aug 1755]: 32858, f.294.

188. Hartington to N, 18 Sept 1755: 32859, f.136.

189. N to Hartington, 30 Aug 1755: 32858, f.349.

190. Egmont to Pitt, 27 Aug 1755: PRO 30/8/31, f.309.

191. Bute to Pitt, Sunday 31 Aug [1755]: PRO 30/8/24, f.325.

192. Egmont to Pitt, 2 Sept 1755: PRO 30/8/31, f.311; Pitt to Bute, [31 Aug 1755]: Sedgwick, 'Pitt', p.110; Legge to Bute, Saturday night 30 Aug [1755]: Bute MSS, Mount Stuart no.83.

193. Walpole, *George II*, II, 39. Walpole places the story out of sequence, claiming it took place 'soon after' the Pitt–Fox interviews of early May.

194. If so, his silence may be related to his own hopes of the post.

195. Fox to Hartington, 1 Sept 1755: Dev 330/57. Legge was probably the source of the claim, almost certainly a distortion, that Hardwicke had lied to Pitt on 8 August in saying that he knew of no treaty but the Hessian.

196. Sources: N to H, 3 Sept 1755: 35415, f.58; H to N, 4 Sept 1755: 32858, f.442; Walpole, *George II*, II, 41.

197. Dodington, *Diary*, 3 Sept 1755.

198. Waldegrave, *Memoirs*, p.45.

199. News of the ambush and rout of General Braddock's troops on the Ohio, the major campaign then on foot in America, arrived on 24 August: Ryder Diary, 25 Aug 1755.

200. Dodington, *Diary*, 3 Sept 1755.

201. N to Lady Katherine Pelham, 26 Sept 1755: 32859, f.219.

202. N to Duchess, nd [but at night, 2 Sept 1755]: 33075, f.145.

203. Probably that contained in Holdernesse to N, 5 Sept 1755: Eg 3429, f.304.

204. N to Duchess, 11 Sept 1755: 33075, f.36.

205. N to H, 6 Sept 1755: 32859, f.5.

206. 'Disposition of Employments in the House of Commons', 5 Sept 1755: 32996, f.221.
207. Bute to Pitt, 11 [am, 11 Sept 1755]: PRO 30/8/24, f.310. Pitt had been especially doubtful of Egmont: Dodington, *Diary*, 3 Sept 1755.
208. N to Duchess, Saturday [? 13 Sept 1755]: 33075, f.39.
209. N to Duchess, 15 Sept 1755: 33075, f.40.
210. 32996, f.221.
211. H to N, 15 Sept 1755: 32859, f.86.
212. Fox to Hartington, 9.30 p.m. 16 Sept 1755: Dev 330/62.
213. E.g. Stone to N, Tuesday morning [16 Sept 1755]: 32859, f.104; N to Duchess, 17 Sept 1755: 33075, f.41.
214. Ibid.
215. Note on N to H, 28 Sept 1755: 35415, f.82.
216. The two latter, part of Newcastle's 'select committee of relations, his principal advisers in affairs of the greatest importance': Waldegrave, *Memoirs*, p.80.
217. N to Duchess, ibid.
218. N to Duchess, 18 Sept 1755: 33075, f.43.
219. N to Waldegrave, Friday 9 o'clock [19 Sept 1755]: 51380, f.52.
220. Walpole, *George II*, II, 41.
221. Fox to Horatio Walpole, 9 Sept [1755]: 51428, f.89.
222. 'Memorandum relating to Mr Fox': 19 Sept 1755: 32996, f.227.
223. Sources: Fox to Ellis, Sunday morning [21 Sept 1755]: 51387, f.15; N to Hartington, 22 Sept 1755: 32859, f.183.
224. 'Mr Fox's proposal to the Duke of Newcastle, made and in general agreed to September 20th 1755': 51379, f.19. N's memo 'Mr Fox's Paper', taken from this, 32995, f.262, includes also the name of William Sloper.
225. N to Oswald, 25 Sept 1755: Oswald MSS, 25; Stone to Fox, 25 Sept 1755: 51379, f.42.
226. Ryder Diary, 25 Sept 1755.
227. Fox to Hartington, 23 Sept 1755: Dev 330/63. Not until the end of September, for example, did such a well-informed source as Sir Robert Wilmot suggest that 'Leicester House is taking some turn that was not expected': Wilmot to Devonshire, 27 Sept 1755: Dev 290/24.
228. Fox to Hartington, 29 Aug 1755: Dev 330/55.
229. Fox to Devonshire, 27 Sept 1755: Dev 330/66.
230. Cf. Cumberland to Fox, Monday [22 Sept 1755]: 51375, f.53.
231. N to Duchess, 23 Sept 1755: 33075, f.44.
232. N to H, 6 July 1755: 32856, f.559.
233. Fox to Devonshire, 27 Sept 1755: Dev 330/66.
234. N to H, 3 Sept 1755: 35415, f.58.
235. Fox to Hartington, 1 Sept 1755: Dev 330/57. Fox imagined he saw a 'glimpse' of this, but only in the improbable event of Newcastle's offering and Pitt's accepting the Exchequer: cf. Fox to Hartington, 29 Aug 1755: Dev 330/55.
236. [J. Almon], *Anecdotes of the Life of the Rt Hon. William Pitt, Earl of Chatham*, III (London, 1797) p.383.
237. Fox to Hartington, 23 Sept 1755: Dev 330/63.
238. Cumberland to Fox, 25 Sept 1755: 51375, f.55.

239. Waldegrave, *Memoirs*, p.45. Yet Foord claims (*His Majesty's Opposition*, p.283) that Newcastle surrendered to Fox the powers claimed by Pitt.
240. N to Sir Thomas Robinson, 5 Oct 1755: 32859, f.386.
241. Cf. Fox to Hartington, 23 Sept 1755: Dev 330/63. The Secretaryship was not, as Walpole supposed (*George II*, II, 43) arranged by Granville.
242. Fox to Hartington, 23 Sept 1755: Dev 330/63.
243. Cf. West to N, 20 Sept 1755: 32859, f.168, reporting City opinion.
244. J. Yorke to Lady Anson, 30 Sept 1755: 35388, f.101.
245. Argyll to Bute, 9 Oct [1755]: Bute MSS, Mount Stuart no.88.
246. E.g. N to Duchess, 1 and 2 Oct 1755: 33075, ff.47, 48.
247. George II, reported in N to H, 4 Oct 1755: 35414, f.90.
248. Waldegrave, *Memoirs*, p.81-2.
249. N to Lady Katherine Pelham, 26 Sept 1755: 32859, f.219.
250. N to H, 18 Oct 1755: 35415, f.108.

4. 'THAT EXPLODED TRICK'

1. Fox to Devonshire, 27 Sept 1755: Dev 330/66.
2. Duncannon to Hartington, 27 Sept 1755: Dev 294/41.
3. Cf. Fox to Devonshire, 27 Sept 1755: Dev 330/66.
4. Fox to Hartington, 16 Sept 1755: Dev 330/62.
5. Devonshire to Fox, 4 Oct 1755: 51381, f.52.
6. Horatio Walpole to Devonshire, 22 Sept 1755: Dev 180/38.
7. Fox apparently gave at least Pitt grounds to hope, that summer, that he would join him against the Hessian treaty; 'certain it is, that hopes were entertained of Fox's concurrence in the plan to overthrow the Duke of Newcastle, and that the opposition was to take its rise from both the foreign treaties': Glover, *Memoirs*, p.67.
8. Horatio Walpole to H, 29 Sept 1755: 35593, f.265.
9. Walpole to J. Chute, 29 Sept 1755: Toynbee, III, 350.
10. Horatio Walpole to Devonshire, 6 Sept 1755: Dev 180/36.
11. N to H, 4 Oct 1755: 35415, f.90.
12. Cf. Fox to Hartington, 11 Sept 1755: Dev 330/60.
13. This rests on the attribution, from internal evidence, of the date 21-22 Sept 1755 to T. Potter to G. Grenville, nd, *Grenville Papers*, I, 137, and WLC.
14. N to H, 4 Oct 1755: 32859, f.357.
15. J. S. Mackenzie to Bute, 5 Oct 1755: Bute MSS, Mount Stuart no.53.
16. Dodington to Halifax, 6 Sept 1755: HMC *Various*, VI, p.30 (Dodington's Diary records nothing of importance between Pitt's account, on 3 Sept, of his interview with Newcastle the previous day, and Dodington's meeting with Halifax on 5 Oct); Hillsborough to Fox, nd (but *c*. Sept 1755): 51386, f.208; Dodington to Fox, 27 Sept 1755: 38091, f.61.
17. Potter to Grenville, loc. cit.
18. The following is drawn from Potter to Temple, 12 o'clock Monday night, nd [but 6 or 13 Oct 1755]: *Grenville Papers*, I, 140, and LWL.
19. Sir T. Robinson (not the Secretary) to Lord Carlisle, 2 Oct 1755: HMC 15th Rep. App. VI, p.209.
20. N to H, 12 Oct 1755: 35415, f.97.
21. Potter to Temple, loc. cit.

22. Sir R. Wilmot to Devonshire, 30 Sept 1755: Dev 290/55.
23. N to Lady Katherine Pelham, 26 Sept 1755: 32859, f.219.
24. Walpole to Mann, 29 Sept 1755: HW 20, p.500.
25. Walpole to J. Chute, 29 Sept 1755: Toynbee, III, 350.
26. Walpole, *George II*, II, 45.
27. This last important point Rigby had evidently not known when he called on Bedford on 28th; he heard of it only on 30 September, and relied on Gower to tell the Duke on the former's impending visit to Woburn (Rigby to Gower, 1 Oct 1755: PRO 30/29/1, f.486). It seems unlikely that Gower had paid the call or passed on the information by the time of Potter's second meeting with Bedford described in Potter to Temple, loc. cit. Bedford may therefore have been subsequently, in late October, even more dubious of Pitt than is there indicated.
28. Rigby to Gower, 1 Oct 1755: PRO 30/29/1, f.486.
29. Rigby to Fox, 10 Oct 1755: 51385, f.87.
30. Ryder Diary, 7 Dec 1755.
31. Rev. T. Lindsey to Earl of Huntingdon, 10 Oct 1755: HMC *Hastings*, III, 104 – predicted Egmont would succeed Pitt; cf. J. Bonnell to T. Hill, 2 Oct 1755: Attingham MSS – recording a rumour at White's 'that Pitt and Grenvilles are to be out, and Legge, and that Lord Egmont is to be Chancellor to the Exchequer. Others say Lord Egmont will not have it but join the dissatisfied against the Ministry.'
32. Part of the text of the letter is omitted in Yorke, *Hardwicke*, II, 249 giving the false impression that the Princess made the remark in September 1755 instead of March 1754.
33. N to H, 28 Sept 1755: 35415, f.80.
34. 'The Scotch are not used to be impenetrable to such motives', he added later (H to N, 13 Oct 1755: 32860, f.30). But it would seem no offer was made: cf. Sedgwick, *Bute*, p.xlv.
35. H to N, 29 Sept 1755: 35415, f.85.
36. Walpole, *George II*, II, 53.
37. [J. Almon], *Anecdotes of the Life of the Right Honourable William Pitt, Earl of Chatham*, 1 (London, 1793) p.275.
38. N to H, 28 Sept 1755: 35415, f.80.
39. H to N, 29 Sept 1755: 35415, f.85.
40. N to Duchess, 1 Oct 1755: 33075, f.47.
41. Sir T. Robinson to Lord Carlisle, 2 Oct 1755: HMC 15th Rep. App. VI, p.209. Stone to N, Thursday morning [2 Oct 1755]: 32859, f.331 contained an assurance that none of the Princess's actions were '*personally* pointed' against Newcastle.
42. Herring to H, 9 Oct 1755: 35599, f.282.
43. Herring to H, 3 Oct 1755: 35599, f.278. Herring reported the opinion of Lord Chief Justice Willes that Lee was 'full in the opposition', but commented: 'I am confident he is misinformed'.
44. N to H, 4 Oct 1755: 35415, f.90.
45. H to N, 6 Oct 1755: 32859, f.398.
46. Sources: N to H, 12 Oct 1755: 35415, f.97; H to N, 13 Oct 1755: 32860, f.30.
47. Cf. N to Duchess, 7 Oct 1755: 33075, f.50. It coincided with a rumour

that Egmont was to succeed Pitt and Darlington have Yonge's place of Vice Treasurer of Ireland (Rev. T. Lindsey to Huntingdon, 10 Oct 1755: HMC *Hastings*, III, 104) though I can find no evidence that this *was* Newcastle's intention. The press was also suggesting that Egmont would succeed Legge: cf. *Read's Weekly Journal*, 4 Oct 1755.

48. Hume Campbell to Marchmont, 15 Oct 1755: HMC *Polwarth*, v, 294.
49. A friend of Fox, a relative of Argyll, and Lord of the Treasury 1746–54; MP for Inverness Burghs, 1754–61.
50. Willes to N, 22 Oct 1755: 32860, f.134.
51. Hume Campbell to Marchmont, 15 Oct 1755: HMC *Polwarth*, v, 294; cf. N to H, 18 Oct 1755: 35415, f.108.
52. E.g. Hume Campbell to Marchmont, 16 Oct 1755: ibid, v, 301. Fox thought in retrospect that when Pitt broke with him in May, 'mine would have been the more natural as well as more reasonable alliance'. Fox to Hartington, 21 Oct 1755: Dev 330/69.
53. N to H, 18 Oct 1755: 35415, f.108. George II was probably ignorant also of the decline in Stone's influence at Leicester House.
54. Waldegrave, *Memoirs*, p.49.
55. N to H, 18 Oct 1755: 35415, f.108.
56. Walpole to Mann, 29 Sept 1755: HW 20, p.500.
57. Namier, 'The Circular Letters' in *Crossroads*, p.46; Legge to Fox, 17 Oct 1755: 51388, f.132.
58. Argyll to Fox, 2 Oct [1755]: 51429, f.9. Lee hoped for Argyll's support, but was frustrated seemingly by Fox's intervention. Marchmont to Lord Milton, 20 Oct 1755: HMC *Polwarth*, v, 304.
59. Devonshire to Fox, 4 Oct 1755: 51381, f.52.
60. Fox to N, 2 Oct 1755: 32859, f.345. Murray, too, later added a hint to Newcastle in the hope of recruiting Dashwood (Murray to N, 5 Oct 1755: 32899, f.390); how far either was authorised to speak for him is open to doubt: cf. B. Kemp, *Sir Francis Dashwood. An Eighteenth Century Independent* (London 1967) pp.44–5.
61. N to H, 4 Oct 1755: 35415, f.90.
62. J. S. Mackenzie to Bute, 5 Oct 1755: Bute MSS, Mount Stuart no. 53.
63. N to George Townshend, 2 Oct 1755: 32859, f.327.
64. Walpole, *George II*, II, 64.
65. James Grenville to Bute, 7 Oct 1755: Bute MSS, Mount Stuart no. 54.
66. This was true: cf. Dodington, *Diary*, 16 July 1755.
67. N to Halifax, 4 Oct 1755: HMC *Various*, VI, p.31.
68. Fox to Halifax, 4 Oct 1755: 38091, f.63.
69. N to H, 4 Oct 1755: 35415, f.90.
70. Sandwich to Fox, 5 Oct [1755]: 51386, f.156.
71. H to N, 6 Oct 1755: 32859, f.398.
72. Dodington, *Diary*, 6, 8 and 10 Oct 1755: Murray to N, 11 Oct 1755: 32860, f.7; N to H, 12 Oct 1755; 35415, f.97. Halifax announced his resolution to James Grenville on 6th: cf. James Grenville to Bute, 7 Oct 1755, loc. cit. Dodington was shown Newcastle's letter to Halifax of 4 October, contrary to Newcastle's express request.
73. Holdernesse to N, 14 Oct 1755: 32860, f.40; cf. Murray to N, 7 Oct 1755: 32859, f.417. Sackville had been promoted Major General on 22 Feb 1755:

A. Valentine, *Lord George Germaine* (Oxford, 1962) p.29. Newcastle now thought of capturing his goodwill by promoting him to the General Staff (N to H, 18 Oct 1755: 35415, f.108; Sackville to N, 10 Nov 1755: 32860, f.434); but this was not done until 1758 (cf. W. K. Hackmann, 'William Pitt and the Generals: Three Case Studies in the Seven Years' War' *Albion*, III (1971), 131). Possibly, in 1755, a sinecure was the price of his support: cf. N, Memo, 16 Nov 1755: 32996, f.287.

74. Fox to Gower, 14 Oct 1755: PRO 30/29/1, f.490.
75. Walpole, *George II*, II, 47.
76. Gower to Bedford, 14 Oct 1755: Bedford MSS, XXXI, 80; Bedford to Gower, 15 Oct 1755: PRO 30/29/1, f.492. Gower wrote that though Newcastle's 'downfall is not immediate, every political step seems to portend it.'
77. Granville to N, 27 Oct 1755: 32860, f.189.
78. John Yorke to Viscount Royston, 28 Oct 1755: 35374, f.125.
79. Walpole, *George II*, II, 47.
80. N to Horatio Walpole, 16 Oct 1755: 32860, f.48.
81. Fox to J. Campbell, 16 Oct 1755: 51406, f.5.
82. Newcastle offered a commission for a friend, although aware that Elliot 'belongs to the Duke of Argyll entirely' (Marchmont to Hume Campbell, 21 Oct 1755: HMC *Polwarth*, V, 305). Hume Campbell was given good reason to believe Newcastle, who 'says the Duke of Argyll is intimately connected with Fox...' (Hume Campbell to Marchmont, 16 Oct 1755: ibid. p.301; Marchmont to Lord Milton, 20 Oct 1755: ibid. p.304).
83. Hume Campbell to Marchmont, 15 Oct 1755: HMC *Polwarth*, V, 294.
84. Probably a Leicester House lawyer friend of Hume Campbell's from his time as Solicitor General to the Prince of Wales.
85. Hume Campbell to Marchmont, 16 Oct 1755: HMC *Polwarth*, V, 301.
86. N to H, 18 Oct 1755: 35415, f.108.
87. Dodington, *Diary*, 10 and 19 Oct 1755.
88. N to H, loc. cit.
89. Egmont to Sir J. Cust, 21 Oct 1755: *Cust Records*, III, 157. Egmont's standing at Leicester House had been based on his denunciations of Cumberland and the danger of military domination: cf. Sedgwick, *Bute*, pp.xx–xxi. But there is no evidence that the King's resentment against Egmont ever stood in the way of Newcastle's negotiations with him.
90. Cf. Walpole to R. Bentley, 19 Oct 1755: Toynbee, III, 354.
91. Fox to Hartington, 21 Oct 1755: Dev 330/69; R. Wilmot to Devonshire, 24 Oct 1755: Dev 290/37.
92. Horatio Walpole to N, 20 Oct 1755: 32860, f.103; cf. Horatio Walpole to Fox, 20 Oct 1755: 51429, f.121.
93. N to Horatio Walpole, 25 Oct 1755: 32860, f.150.
94. N to Hartington, 28 Oct 1755: Dev 182/60.
95. Horatio Walpole to H, 6 Nov 1755: 35593, f.309.
96. N, Memo, 'Business for my Lord Chancellor tomorrow night', 20 Oct 1755: 32996, f.249.
97. Hume Campbell to Marchmont, 23 Oct 1755: HMC *Polwarth*, V, 307.
98. N to H, 31 Oct 1755: 35415, f.115.
99. Hume Campbell to Marchmont, 23 Oct 1755: HMC *Polwarth*, V, 307.

100. Hume Campbell to Marchmont, 15 Oct 1755: HMC *Polwarth*, v, 294.
101. Marchmont to Hume Campbell, 21 Oct 1755: HMC *Polwarth*, v, 305 – an anticipation of the point made by Namier, *England*, p.62.
102. Hume Campbell to Marchmont, 1 Nov 1755: HMC *Polwarth*, v, 309.
103. Hume Campbell to Marchmont, 8 Nov 1755: HMC *Polwarth*, v, 310.
104. N to H, 1 Nov 1755: 32860, f.268.
105. Hume Campbell to Marchmont, 11 Nov 1755: HMC *Polwarth*, v, 312.
106. Sir R. Newdigate: account of the debate of 13 Nov 1755: HPT transcripts.
107. N: 'Thoughts...relating to the Disposition of Employments', 16 Nov 1755: 32996, f.287; N to Hartington, 29 Nov 1755: 32861, f.131.
108. H to N, 5 Dec 1755: 32861, f.200; Hume Campbell to Marchmont, 9 Dec 1755: HMC *Polwarth*, v, 314; Ryder Diary, 2 Dec 1755.
109. Sir George Lyttelton to N, 6 Oct 1755: 32859, f.402.
110. Sir George Lyttelton to H, 29 Sept 1755: Lyttelton MSS, II, 266; N to Sir George Lyttelton, 1 Nov 1755: 32860, f.273.
111. N to Duchess, Wednesday night [12 Nov 1755]: 33075, f.64.
112. Dupplin to N, 19 Nov 1755: 32861, f.29.
113. N to Duchess, 21 Nov 1755: 33075, f.65. Lyttelton wrote: 'I have this satisfaction, and a great one it is, that I find the public in general approves of my promotion.' Sir G. Lyttelton to H. S. Conway, nd: Lyttelton MSS, II, 276.
114. Fox to N, 20 Nov 1755: 32861, f.41.
115. Fox to N, 1 Nov 1755: 32860, f.266.
116. John Yorke to Royston, 1 Nov 1755: 35374, f.129.
117. N to H, 1 Nov 1755: 32860, f.268.
118. Pitt to Bute, Monday [3 Nov 1755]: Sedgwick, 'Pitt' p.112.
119. H to N, 3 Nov 1755: 32860, f.324.
120. Fox to Hartington, 4 Nov 1755: Dev 330/73.
121. Pitt to Bute, Thursday evening [6 Nov 1755]: Sedgwick, 'Pitt', p.112.
122. Fox to N, Friday night [7 Nov 1755]: 32860, f.402.
123. Fox to H, 12 Nov 1755: 32860, f.454; Bedford to Fox, 12 Nov 1755: 51385 f.3; Fox to N, 13 Nov 1755: 32860, f.469. Bedford was anxious that the words of the Address should not commit him on the Treaties, 'in case I should find it inconsistent with my principles to consent to them'.
124. N. to Duchess, 13 Nov 1755: 33075, f.61.
125. Fox to Hartington, 11 Sept 1755: Dev 330/60.
126. Horatio Walpole to H, 22 Sept 1755: 35593, f.260.
127. Horatio Walpole to Devonshire, 22 Sept 1755: Dev 180/38.
128. J. Watkins to N, 26 Sept 1755: 32859, f.226.
129. E.g. J. Cresset to N, 26 Sept 1755: 32859, f.229.
130. Sir R. Wilmot to Devonshire, 27 Sept 1755: Dev 290/24.
131. E.g. Herring to H, 3 Oct 1755: 35599, f.278.
132. H. Walpole to R. Bentley, 19 Oct 1755: Toynbee, III, 354; cf. N to Duchess, 16 Oct 1755: 33075, f.52.
133. Walpole, *George II*, II, 53.
134. Walpole to Mann, 16 Nov 1755: HW 20, p.509.
135. Sir R. Wilmot to Devonshire, 24 Oct 1755: Dev 290/37.
136. Ibid.; cf. Legge to Devonshire, 24 Oct 1755: Dev 257/22.

137. Fox to Hartington, 28 Oct 1755: Dev 330/70; cf. Bayntun Rolt Diary, 28 Oct 1755.
138. Hartington to Devonshire, 8 Nov 1755: Dev 260/181.
139. Ellis to Hartington, 1 Nov 1755: Dev 335/7.
140. Hartington to Devonshire, 8 Nov 1755: Dev 260/181.
141. John Yorke to Royston, 28 Oct 1755: 35374, f.125; cf. N to Holdernesse, 29 Aug 1755; Eg 3429 f.287.
142. Cf. C. W. Eldon, *England's Subsidy Policy towards the Continent during the Seven Years' War* (Philadelphia, 1938).
143. Horatio Walpole to Devonshire, 9 Aug 1755: Dev 180/34. He continued to approve it: only the Russian treaty was in doubt: cf. Horatio Walpole to Fox, 20 Oct 1755: 51429, f.121.
144. Horace Walpole to Mann, 21 Aug 1755: HW 20, p.490; Edward Walpole to Fox, 7 Oct 1755: 51429, f.76.
145. For which see D. B. Horn, 'The Duke of Newcastle and the Origns of the Diplomatic Revolution' in J. H. Elliot and H. G. Koenigsberger (eds.), *The Diversity of History. Essays in Honour of Sir Herbert Butterfield* (London, 1970); R. Browning, 'The Duke of Newcastle and the Imperial Election Plan, 1749–1754', *JBS*, VII (1967), 28–47.
146. Fox to J. Campbell, 16 Oct 1755: 51406, f.5.
147. G. Grenville to Pitt, 26 Aug 1755: PRO 30/8/34, f.13.
148. Grenville Narrative, *Grenville Papers*, I, p.434.
149. Hartington to Devonshire, 21 Oct 1755: Dev 260/177. But Hartington thought the Hessian treaty the most objectionable, and saw strong arguments in favour of the Russian.
150. N to H, 12 Oct 1755: 35415, f.97.
151. Cf. Ryder Diary, 2 Oct 1755.
152. Mr Tod to Lord Milton, 4 Dec [1755]: NLS SC 189, f.178.
153. W. Pitt to S. Miller, 9 Sept 1755: Sanderson Miller MSS, 583.
154. Thomas Prowse to Pitt, 29 Sept 1755: PRO 30/8/53, f.337.
155. Blackstone to Sir R. Newdigate, 30 Nov 1755: Newdigate MSS, B 1492.
156. Ryder Diary, 20 Mar 1755.
157. Bayntun Rolt Diary, 16 Feb 1755.
158. Ellis to Hartington, 1 Nov 1755: Dev 335/7.
159. Pitt to Bute, Monday [3 Nov 1755]: Sedgwick, 'Pitt', p.112.
160. Fox to Hartington, 4 Nov 1755: Dev 330/73.
161. Fox to N, Friday night [7 Nov 1755]: 32860, f.402.
162. Fox to H, 12 Nov 1755: 32860, f.454; N to Duchess, Wednesday night [12 Nov 1755]: 33075, f.64. Newcastle's figure was 289; Fox estimated 287. Fox to Hartington, 12 Nov 1755: Dev 330/74; Gilbert Elliot to Lord Minto, 15 Nov 1755: NLS 11001, f.14.
163. West to N, 13 Nov 1755: 32860, f.471.
164. Cf. Dorset to N, 21 Dec 1753: 32733, f.503.
165. Ryder had heard as late as 3 November that many Scots, under Argyll's influence, would desert Newcastle: Ryder Diary, 3 Nov 1755.
166. Lord John Cavendish left without voting on the Address (his brother Lord George voted with the majority) in deference to Devonshire's feelings, who 'does not approve of the subsidy treaties, but...if they whose conduct he has approved of in this affair have any design to foment divisions in

the Royal Family he thinks them highly to blame, but he is not acquainted with any facts relating to it...': Lord John Cavendish to Hartington, 15 Nov 1755: Dev 428/o.

167. Memo, 27 Sept 1755: 32996, f.237; 'List of Members who voted against the Address', [13 Nov 1755]: 33034, f.208; Sir G. Elliot to Lord Minto, 15 Nov 1755: NLS 11001, f.14.

168. Newdigate to ?————, 15 Nov 1755: HPT transcripts.

169. Ryder Diary, 22 Nov 1755.

170. For speakers on 13th, see J. Campbell Memo, nd: Cawdor MSS, 1/128; West to N, 13 Nov 1755: loc. cit.; Newdigate's account, 15 Nov 1755: loc. cit.; Dupplin to [? Duchess of Newcastle], 14 Nov [1755]: 32860, f.475; Walpole to Conway, 15 Nov 1755: Toynbee, III, 365; Gilbert Elliot to Lord Minto, 15 Nov 1755: NLS 11001, f.14.

For: Lord Hillsborough; Wyndham O'Brien; Philip Stanhope; W. G. Hamilton; Thomas Alston; Welbore Ellis; Lord Barrington; Sir George Lyttelton; Robert Nugent; William Murray; Sir Thomas Robinson; Horatio Walpole; Henry Fox; Lord Egmont '3/4 for'.

Against: George Colebrooke; Samuel Martin; William Northey; Sir Richard Lyttelton; George Grenville; William Beckford; Sir George Lee; Henry Legge; Thomas Potter; Dr Hay; George Townshend; William Pitt; Admiral Vernon; George Dodington '1/2 agst'; Sir Francis Dashwood '1/2 agst'.

171. Grenville Narrative, *Grenville Papers*, I, p.434.

172. Walpole to Mann, 16 Nov 1755: HW 20, p.509.

173. Walpole to H. S. Conway, 15 Nov 1755: Toynbee, III, 365.

174. West to N, loc cit.

175. Ellis to Hartington, 15 Nov 1755: Dev 335/8.

176. Grenville Narrative, *Grenville Papers*, I, p.434.

177. Dupplin to [? Duchess of N], 14 Nov 1755: 32860, f.475.

178. Walpole, *George II*, II, 51.

179. He made the serious mistake of implying the support of Devonshire, who was 'highly offended': he had never authorised 'such a declaration'. Ellis to Hartington, 15 Nov 1755: loc. cit.

180. N to Duchess, 13 Nov 1755: 33075, f.61; Cumberland to Fox, nd [? 14–16 Oct 1755] 51375, f.57.

181. N to Hartington, 15 Nov 1755: 32860, f.480.

182. A writ for re-election could not be moved until Parliament had met. Foord's speculations (*His Majesty's Opposition*, p.285) on Newcastle's intentions which the alleged delay in Fox's appointment reveals are, therefore, invalid.

183. Fox to Ellis, Sunday night [? 23 Nov 1755]: 51387, f.17.

184. Walpole to Conway, 15 Nov 1755: Toynbee, III, 365.

185. H. S. Conway to Fox, 27 Nov 1755: 51381 f.77.

186. E.g. Walpole to Mann, 16 Nov 1755: HW 20, p.509.

187. Hume Campbell to Marchmont, [21 Nov 1755]: HMC *Polwarth*, v, 312.

188. Viscount Stormont to Earl of Huntingdon, 26 Nov 1755: HMC *Hastings*, III, 111.

189. Rigby to Bedford, Wednesday night [26 Nov 1755]: Bedford MSS, XXXI, 102. This was in the Committee of Ways and Means on 26th; there was

no division when its Report was received by the House on 27th: *CJ*, xxvii, 308 and 315.

190. Newdigate Diary, 21 Nov 1755.

191. N to H, 4 Oct 1755: 35415, f.90. An example of the standard circular letter from the previous session is Legge to Lord Milton, 17 Oct 1754: NLS Saltoun MSS, SC 184, f.226. Fox's excuse in the Commons, that the expression was made illegitimate by the copying error of a secretary, is shown to be false by other examples in his own hand of the phrase 'the conduct of the House of Commons': Fox to Gilbert Elliot, 27 Sept 1755: NLS 11014, f.9; Fox to Devonshire, 27 Sept 1755: Dev 330/66 and 51381, f.48. Fox did, however, employ a clerk and examples of the phrase in a clerk's hand occur in Fox to Sir Ludovick Grant, nd: SRO Seafield MSS, GD 248/100/2; Fox to [? Tweeddale], 3 Oct 1755: NLS Yester MSS, 14422, f.138; and probably also in Fox to John Delaval, 30 Sept 1755: HMC 11th Rep. App. vii, p.76 (the original of which is apparently no longer extant). Fox was also capable of using 'the conduct of his affairs in the House of Commons' in letters in his own hand: Fox to Lord George Sackville, 29 Sept 1755: Germaine MSS; Fox to Mrs Lowther, 29 Sept 1755: Lonsdale MSS; and probably Fox to Legge, 2 Oct 1755: 32859, f.323 (a copy in the Newcastle MSS).

192. Temple to Lady Hester Pitt, 20 Nov 1755: *Grenville Papers*, i, 149 and LWL; William and Lady Hester Pitt to Temple, [21 Nov 1755]: ibid. i, 151, and LWL.

193. Ellis to Hartington, 22 Nov 1755: Dev 335/9.

194. West, Memo for Newcastle, nd [21 Nov 1755]: 32861, f.55.

195. Ellis to Hartington, 22 Nov 1755: Dev 335/9.

196. *CJ*, xxvii, p.306.

197. Dupplin to N, Friday 21 Nov [1755]: 32861, f.61.

198. Holdernesse to N, 21 Nov 1755: 32861, f.59.

199. Fox to Hartington, 25 Nov 1755: Dev 330/78; N to Duchess, 25 Nov 1755: 33075, f.66.

200. N to Hartington, 29 Nov 1755: 32861 f.131.

201. *CJ*, xxvii, 325; R. N. Aldworth, Memo, 2 Dec 1755: Aldworth MSS, Berkshire RO: D/EN 034/8.

202. Fox to Devonshire, 8 Dec 1755: Dev 330/86.

203. Horatio Walpole to Devonshire, 25 Dec 1755: Dev 180/41.

204. Chesterfield to S. Dayrolles, 19 Dec 1755: Dobrée, v, 2169.

205. Rev. T. Lindsey to Huntingdon, 24 Dec 1755: HMC *Hastings*, iii, 111.

206. H. Harris to Sir Charles Hanbury Williams, 26 Dec 1755: Lord Ilchester, *Life of Sir Charles Hanbury Williams* (London, 1929) p.323.

207. H to Charles Yorke, 10 Dec 1755: 35353, f.181.

208. Fox to Devonshire, 11 Dec 1755: Dev 330/87.

209. Ellis to Devonshire, 20 Dec 1755: Dev 335/10.

210. R. N. Aldworth's account (Memo, 10 Dec 1755: Aldworth MSS, D/EN 034/9) suggests that Hume Campbell *did* speak in reply to Pitt.

211. Devonshire agreed: Fox's consistent conduct, and his never having been in opposition, conferred a great advantage over Pitt 'and is a weapon that you will always be able to use against him with success.' Devonshire to Fox, 16 Dec 1755: 51381, f.94.

212. Fox to Devonshire, 11 Dec 1755: Dev 330/87.
213. West to N, 10 Dec 1755: 32861, f.271.
214. Stone, Memo for Newcastle, 10 Dec 1755: 32861, f.275; cf. Newdigate Memo, 10 Dec 1755: Newdigate MSS, B 2549/3; Newdigate Diary, 10 Dec 1755. The speakers on 10th were:
    For: Lord Barrington, Sir George Lyttelton, Lord Dupplin, Col Haldane, Lord Hillsborough, Sir George Yonge, Hume Campbell, William Murray, Henry Fox, Robert Nugent, Sir Thomas Robinson, Robert Henley.
    Against: Thomas Potter; Sir Harry Erskine; Samuel Martin; Robert Vyner; George Grenville; William Pitt; Sir George Lee; Henry Legge; Richard Crowle; Dr Hay; Alderman Beckford.
    Sources: West to N, 10 Dec 1755: 32861, f.271; Fox to Devonshire, 11 Dec 1755: Dev 330/87.
215. Ryder Diary, 10 Dec 1775: Harrowby MSS, Doc 21.
216. Walpole to R. Bentley, 17 Dec 1755: Toynbee, III, 375. Glover, an uncritical partisan of Pitt's, represents his rhetoric as even more terrible in its effect, but does so even less credibly: *Memoirs*, p.69.
217. Ryder Diary, 8 Dec 1755.
218. Stone, Memo, 10 Dec 1755: loc. cit.
219. H. Digby to Sir C. Hanbury Williams, 23 Dec 1755: Stowe MSS, 263, f.2.
220. The speakers were:
    For: Lord Barrington; Charles Cocks; Edward Finch; [?John] Delaval; Hume Campbell; Sir George Lyttelton; Charles Yorke; Col Haldane; Sir John Griffin Griffin; Robert Nugent; Sir Thomas Robinson; Lord George Sackville; Lord Granby; Horatio Walpole; Lord Egmont; Henry Fox.
    Against: Lord Pulteney; Sir Richard Lyttelton; Charles Townshend; George Dodington; Sir Francis Dashwood; Henry Legge; George Grenville; Alderman Beckford; George Townshend; Thomas Potter; William Pitt; James Oswald; James Grenville; Sir George Lee.
    Sources: H. Digby to Sir C. Hanbury Williams, 23 Dec 1755: Stowe MSS, 263, f.2; Sir R. Newdigate, report of debate, 12 Dec 1755: Newdigate MSS, B 2549/3 and Diary, 12 Dec 1755; West, memo, Saturday morning [13 Dec 1755]: 32861, f.290.
221. Fox to Devonshire, 13 Dec 1755: Dev 330/88.
222. Charles Yorke to H, 13 Dec 1755: 35353, f.183.
223. The slight fall in numbers was probably the effect of the long sitting.
224. Horatio Walpole to Devonshire, 25 Dec 1755: Dev 180/41.
225. There were two divisions: the Report on the Russian treaty was approved by 263 to 69 when Pitt, Legge and George Townshend accidentally found themselves counted with the majority. A division was therefore forced on the Hessian treaty, giving the result 259 to 72: cf. H. Digby to Sir C. Hanbury Williams, 23 Dec 1755: Stowe MSS, 263, f.2; *CJ*, XXVII, p.339.
226. Lord George Cavendish to Devonshire, 18 Dec 1755: Dev 431/3.
227. H. Digby to Sir C. Hanbury Williams, 23 Dec 1755: Stowe MSS, 263, f.2.
228. Regina Mingotti (1722–1808); at that time the leading operatic soprano in England.
229. Horatio Walpole to Devonshire, 25 Dec 1755: Dev 180/41.
230. Ryder Diary, — Jan 1756: Harrowby MSS, Doc 21.
231. Mann to Walpole, 6 Dec 1755: HW 20, p.513.

232. Waldegrave, *Memoirs*, pp.52-3.
233. Cf. Stone to N, [30 Dec 1755]: 32856, f.407.
234. Ryder Diary, 7 Dec 1755. The Bathursts were a Tory family. But Lord Bathurst was, in 1756, to be chosen as Treasurer in the new household of the Prince of Wales, with Newcastle's approval.
235. Warburton to Charles Yorke, 3 Jan 1756: Eg 1952, f.51. William Warburton (1698-1779), then a Prebend of Durham and one of the King's Chaplains-in-ordinary. He was made Dean of Bristol by Pitt in September 1757.
236. Ryder Diary, — Jan 1756: Harrowby MSS, Doc 21.
237. Horatio Walpole to Devonshire, 25 Dec 1755: Dev 180/41.
238. E.g. Walpole to Montagu, 20 Dec 1755: HW 9, p.180.
239. Joseph Yorke to Royston, 23 Dec 1755: 35364, f.63.
240. On the supposed buying of votes for the Russian treaty, cf. Namier, *Structure*, pp.179-81.
241. N to H, Saturday morning [6 Dec 1755]: 35415, f.122.
242. Cf. Hartington to N, 5 Dec 1755: 32861, f.202.
243. Fox to Ellis, 9 Dec 1755: 51387, f.19.
244. Fox to Ellis, 16 Dec 1755: 51387, f.20.
245. Ellis to Devonshire, 3 Feb 1756: Dev 335/15.
246. N to H, Wednesday [17 Dec 1755]: 35415, f.127. Percy Wyndham O'Brien was Egremont's brother.
247. Murray to N, Tuesday night [16 Dec 1755]: 32861, f.322.
248. Fox to Dashwood, 16 Dec 1755: Dashwood MSS, B 7/1/3ª; Dashwood to Fox, 17 Dec 1755: ibid. B 7/1/3ᶜ Newcastle earlier thought of Dashwood for the Admiralty Board, but this had proved unacceptable to him.
249. At an interview with Newcastle on 16th: cf. Dodington, *Diary*, 16 Dec 1755.
250. Leeds had ambitions for the place of Privy Seal but was satisfied for the present and willing to make James Brudenell, a loyal supporter of the administration, Deputy Cofferer: Leeds to N, 18 Dec 1755: 32861, f.342.
251. H to N, Sunday night [14 Dec 1755]: 32861, f.298.
252. N to H, 14 Dec 1755: 35415, f.124.
253. N to H, 17 Dec 1755: 35415, f.127.
254. N to Fox, Friday morning [12 Dec 1755]: 32861, f.284.
255. Marlborough made no objection and sympathised in this part of the design: Marlborough to N, 12 Dec 1755: 32861, f.286.
256. Fox, Memo, [18 Dec 1755]: 32861, f.336.
257. Walpole to Montagu, 20 Dec 1755: HW 9, p.180.
258. Fox, Memo, [18 Dec 1755]: loc cit.
259. Walpole to Montagu, 20 Dec 1755: HW 9, p.180.
260. Walpole to Mann, 21 Dec 1755: HW 20, p.516.
261. Walpole to R. Bentley, 17 Dec 1755: Toynbee, III, 375. His unpopularity was the result of his involvement in the Murray-Stone scandal of 1753; cf. Riker, *Fox*, I, 380.
262. Sandwich's acceptance followed it: cf. Fox, Memo: [18 Dec 1755] loc. cit.
263. N to H, Thursday 3 o'clock [18 Dec 1755]: 35415, f.129: the scheme is that contained in Newcastle's undated memo, 32996, f.303.
264. Cf. N to H, 20 Dec 1755: 32861, f.355.
265. Cf. Fox to N, 26 Dec 1755: 32861, f.452.

266. Kemp, *Dashwood* pp.43–45; Murray to N, Tuesday night [16 Dec 1755]: 32861, f.322. Fox had tried to persuade him to accept with the news that Dodington would be Treasurer of the Navy, and Furnese have a seat at the Admiralty Board. Fox to Dashwood, 16 Dec 1755: Dashwood MSS, B 7/1/3ᵃ.

267. Walpole to R. Bentley, 17 Dec 1755: Toynbee, III, 375.

268. Walpole to Mann, 21 Dec 1755: HW 20, p.516.

269. E.g. T. Villiers to N, 24 Dec 1755: 32861, f.419.

270. Devonshire to Ellis, 30 Dec 1755: Dev 260/191.

271. Horatio Walpole to Devonshire, 25 Dec 1755: Dev 180/41; Chesterfield to Dayrolles, 19 Dec 1755: Dobrée, v, 2169. H. S. Conway recognised that the Princess was acting only as an 'ally' of opposition, not as a 'principal' in it. H. S. Conway to Sir George Lyttelton, 12 Dec 1755: Lyttelton MSS, II, 274.

272. Fox to Ilchester, 29 Dec 1755: 51420, f.29.

273. Chesterfield to Dayrolles, 19 Dec 1755: Dobrée, v, 2169.

274 To Fox: Lord Gower; Henry Furnese; Lord Bateman; Richard Rigby; W. G. Hamilton; Lord Berkeley of Stratton; Lord Sandwich; Dodington; George Selwyn.

  To Newcastle: O'Brien; John Talbot; Soame Jenyns; Lord Hobart; Lord Sandys; James Brudenell; Lord Gage.

275. Fox to Ilchester, 29 Dec 1755: 51420, f.29.

276. 33034, f.208.

277. Richard Hussey; Sir Richard Lyttelton; Lord Howe; William Lock; W. R. Chetwynd; Dr Hay; John Martin; Edward Walter; James More Molyneux.

278. John Morton; [? George] Colebrooke; Lord Carnarvon; Sir Francis Dashwood.

279. N to Devonshire, 17 Jan 1756: Dev 182/66.

280. Mann to Walpole, 11 Jan 1756: HW 20, p.521.

281. N to Devonshire, 2 Jan 1756: Dev 182/64; Fox to Devonshire, 17 Jan 1756: Dev 330/107; Horatio Walpole to Devonshire, 20 Jan 1756: Dev 180/43.

282. Walpole to H. S. Conway, 22 Jan 1756: Toynbee, III, 385.

283. Legge to Devonshire, 20 Jan 1756: Dev 257/23.

284 Fox to Sir J. Lowther, 18 Jan 1756: Lonsdale MSS. It is possible that Fox could have carried the point but chose to compromise rather than clash with these blocs; cf. Lord George Cavendish to Devonshire, 20 Jan 1756: Dev 431/5.

285. E.g. West to N, 21 Jan 1756: 32862, f.171; cf. Newdigate Diary, 21 Jan 1756.

286. E.g. *Parl Hist*, xv, 623.

287. N to Waldegrave, Saturday morning [17 or 24 Jan 1756]: 51380, f.54; Fox to Devonshire, 15 Jan 1756: Dev 330/103.

288. Horatio Walpole to Devonshire, 20 Jan 1756: Dev 180/43.

289. Fox to Devonshire, 24 Jan 1756: Dev 330/109.

290. Walpole, *George II*, II, 152.

291. Walpole to H. S. Conway, 24 Jan 1756: Toynbee, III, 388. This verdict on Lyttelton is repeated in Namier and Brooke, III, 74–75.

292. N to Sir George Lyttelton, 24 Jan 1756: 32862, f.204; Dupplin to N, 24 Jan 1756: 32862, f.200.

293. Walpole to H. S. Conway, 24 Jan 1756: loc. cit.
294. Dupplin to N, 24 Jan 1756; loc. cit.; West to N, 24 Jan 1756: 32862, f.202.
295. Lord George Cavendish to Devonshire, 27 Jan 1756: Dev 431/6.
296. Horatio Walpole to Devonshire, 27 Jan 1756: Dev 180/44.
297. Fox to Devonshire, 31 Jan 1756: Dev 330/115.
298. Walpole to Mann, 5 Feb 1756: HW 20, p.525.
299. Walpole to Mann, 25 Jan 1756: HW 20, p.522.
300. N to Charles Yorke, 24 Jan 1756: 35429, f.1.
301. Hardwicke agreed, since Dupplin told him that Granville had told Ellis that the motion was not levelled personally against the latter. H to N, 25 Jan 1756: 32862, f.227.
302. Ellis to Devonshire, 27 Jan 1756: Dev 335/14; Fox to Lady Caroline Fox, 5 Feb 1756: 51415, f.219; Horatio Walpole to Devonshire, 27 Jan 1756: Dev 180/44.
303. Fox to Devonshire, 31 Jan 1756: Dev 330/115; cf. Ellis to Devonshire, 3 Feb 1756: Dev 335/15.
304. Horatio Walpole to Devonshire, 27 Jan 1756: Dev 180/44.
305. Ellis to Devonshire, 3 Feb 1756: Dev 335/15.
306. Fox to Devonshire, 31 Jan 1756: Dev 330/115. Walpole agreed that Fox had the better of the exchanges: cf. Walpole to H. S. Conway, 12 Feb 1756: Toynbee, III, 395. From his informants Devonshire heard the same; cf. Devonshire to Fox, 3 Feb [1756]: 51381, f.147.
307. On 10 February, leave to bring in the Bill was given by 165 to 57; on 18th, it was committed by 215 to 63; on 20th the House decided to sit as a Committee of the Whole House by 213 to 82; on 23rd, when the Bill was reported, an amendment was defeated by 177 to 60, a petitioner refused leave to be heard by 158 to 52, and a witness decided not to be called by 151 to 46; and on 26 February the third reading passed by 198 to 64. CJ, xxvii, 443, 458, 463, 466, 481.
308. Gilbert Elliot to Lord Minto, — Feb 1756: NLS 11001, f.18; Horatio Walpole to Devonshire, 28 Feb 1756: Dev 180/45.
309. Walpole to Mann, 23 Feb 1756: HW 20, p.529.
310. Lord Feversham to Edward Weston, 23 Feb 1756: HMC 10th Rep. App. I, p.311; cf. Pitt to G. Grenville, 21 March 1756: Grenville Papers, I, 156 and WLC. Walpole recorded: 'Mr Pitt has got the gout in his oratory, I mean in his head, and does not come out: we are sunk quite into argument'. Walpole to H. S. Conway, 25 March 1756: Toynbee, III, 407.
311. R. M. Aldworth MSS, Berkshire, RO, D/EN 034/11–12.
312. On 16 March, over the Linnen Bill (W. Tod to Lord Milton, 16 March 1756: NLS Saltoun MSS, SC 193, f.140); on 29 March, for the Address for Hanoverian troops, when he lost the division by 259 to 92 (Newdigate Diary, 29 March 1756); on 14 April, against a Bill facilitating the enlistment of indentured servants in America (Beaufort MSS, 704. 1. 15.); on 11 May, for the King's message on the Prussian treaty; no division (Parl Hist, xv, 703); on May 7 and 12 in the Committee of Supply on the Estimates for Hanover Troops, and on 14 May in the Committee of Ways and Means

when he lost by 210 to 55 a division on a grant of £20,000 to satisfy Prussian claims (Aldworth MSS, D/EN 034/12).

313. *A New System of Patriot Policy* (London, 1756) p.15.
314. C. Jenkinson to S. Miller, 6 Mar 1756: Sanderson Miller MSS, 817; Sir G. Lyttelton to N, Monday morning [1 Mar 1756]: 32863, f.150.
315. Walpole to H. S. Conway, 4 March 1756: Toynbee, III, 402.
316. Ellis to Devonshire, 23 March 1756: Dev 335/18. The opposition did not intend to divide at that stage but the Speaker heard for the Noes.
317. West to N, Wednesday 6 o'clock [17 March 1756]: 32863, f.332; cf. Newdigate Diary, 3 Mar 1756.
318. Fox to Devonshire, 18 Mar 1756: Dev 330/128.
319. N to George II, 3 o'clock [19 March 1756]: 32863, f.362.
320. Thomas Coventry, John Olmius, Sir James Creed, Hitch Yonge, Alderman Baker.
321. Fox to Devonshire, 13 Mar 1756: Dev 330/125.
322. W. Tod to Lord Milton, 16 Mar 1756: NLS Salton MSS, SC 193, f.140.
323. Argyll to N, Friday noon 19 Mar [1756]: 32863, f.366.
324. Fox to N, 20 March 1756: 32863, f.396; N to H, 21 March 1756: 35415, f.161.
325. C. Jenkinson to S. Miller, 23 Mar [1756]: Sanderson Miller MSS, 328; West, Memo, [22 Mar 1756]: 35877, f.244. The Bill passed its third reading by 187 to 88 on 29 March.
326. Legge to Devonshire, 25 Mar 1756: Dev 257/24.
327. Walpole, *George II*, I, 410. Independently, his uncle made the same observation: Horatio Walpole to Hartington, 28 Nov 1754: Dev 180/27.
328. J. R. Western, *The English Militia in the Eighteenth Century* (London, 1965) p.117.
329. *The Opposition* (London, 1755) p.13, published c.4 Dec 1755; cf. Chesterfield to Stanhope, 26 March 1754: Dobrée, V, 2102; *The Protester*, 18 Aug 1753; *An Essay on the Times* (London, 1756) p.41.
330. *The Occasional Patriot* (London, 1756) pp.22–3.
331. The news became public in England early in March; cf. *Public Advertiser*, 9 Mar 1756.
332. Devonshire to Ellis, 2 Mar 1756: Dev 260/203.
333. N to Devonshire, 13 Mar 1756: Dev 182/76; J. C. D. Clark, 'Whig Tactics and Parliamentary Precedent: The English Management of Irish Politics, 1754–1756', *HJ*, XXI, (1978) 275–301.

5. THE RESIGNATION OF NEWCASTLE

1. Sedgwick, I, 61.
2. C. S. Emden, *The People and the Constitution* (2nd edn. Oxford, 1956) pp.46–50, 161; cf. L. M. Wiggin, *The Faction of Cousins* (New Haven, 1958) p.182.
3. P. Langford, 'William Pitt and Public Opinion, 1757', *EHR*, LXXXVIII (1973) 56, 58, 66, 70, 71.
4. Dame Lucy Sutherland, 'The City of London and the Devonshire–Pitt Administration, 1756–7', *Proceedings of the British Academy*, XLVI (1960) 150, 155. Dame Lucy adds that the outcry against Newcastle was in-

sufficient to 'make a withdrawal inevitable. His fall was due in fact to a collapse of leadership in the House of Commons brought about by personal weakness and corporate disunity in the face of public clamour.' Unless one were to quarrel with the use of 'inevitable', this qualification seems at odds with Dame Lucy's 'decisive factor'.

5. Emden, op. cit. pp.47-8.
6. Waldegrave, *Memoirs*, pp. 57-8.
7. Ibid. p.61.
8. Egmont to Sir John Cust, 6 Apr 1756: *Cust Records*, III, 158.
9. Walpole to Conway, 16 Apr 1756: Toynbee, III, 412.
10. Horatio Walpole to H, 4 Apr 1756: 35594, f.40.
11. N to Devonshire, 10 Apr 1756: 32864, f.204; cf. West to N, 19 Apr 1756: 32864, f. 345. There is no evidence for the claim in Yorke, *Hardwicke*, II, 262 that the Bill was introduced in an attempt to align the ministers against a popular measure. Although Horatio Walpole suggested to Hardwicke on 4 Apr that its rejection in the Lords would bring this about, there is, equally, no evidence that Newcastle or Hardwicke were concerned at that possibility.
12. Chesterfield to Alderman Faulkner, Monday [Apr 1756]: Dobrée, v, 2184.
13. N to Devonshire, 10 Apr 1756: 32864, f.204; cf. Devonshire to N, 17 Apr 1756: 32864, f.304.
14. There is evidence that the decision not to oppose the Bill in the Commons was taken independently by Sir George Lyttelton, Fox and Hume Campbell in order to pass other business there more smoothly. But although Newcastle complained of this later (Hume Campbell to Marchmont, 13 July 1756: HMC *Polwarth*, v, 320) there is no evidence that he objected at the time; and, in the Lords, he delayed opposing the Bill until its third reading. Fox admitted to refusing to speak against it in the Commons (Fox to Speaker 22 Oct 1756: 51430, f.8), and his friends later claimed that Newcastle had made use of his, Fox's, failure to halt the Bill in that House to 'disgust the King' (Bedford to Fox, 14 Oct 1756: 51385, f.5). But evidence is lacking that Newcastle misrepresented Fox thus; and, given the latter's conduct, he scarcely needed to do so.
15. Lord George Sackville, for example, then and on 7 May; cf. Fox to N, 7 May 1756: 32864, f.478.
16. Horatio Walpole to H, 4 Apr 1756: 35594, f.40.
17. Sir G. Lyttelton to W. Lyttelton, 28 Apr 1756: Lyttelton MSS, II, 282.
18. Horatio Walpole to H, 4 Apr 1756: 35594, f.40.
19. Horatio Walpole to H, 26 Apr 1756: 35594, f.49.
20. Bayntun Rolt Diary, 5 May 1756.
21. Fox to N, 20 Mar 1756: 32863, f.398.
22. *CJ*, XXVII, 539.
23. Ibid., 549. Walpole, *George II*, II, 185 mistakenly gives 29 April.
24. Northey, Sir John Philipps and Prowse were the only Tories listed by Newdigate as speaking: Newdigate MSS, B 2549/11.
25. Sir G. Lyttelton to W. Lyttelton, 28 Apr 1756: Lyttelton MSS, II, 282.
26. Cf. pp.237-40 below.
27. Lord Breadalbane to Charles Erskine, 30 Mar 1756: NLS 5079, f.29.
28. Newdigate Diary, 29 Mar 1756.

29. Newdigate MSS, B 2549/11; *CJ*, xxvii, p.547.
30. Sir G. Lyttelton to W. Lyttelton, loc. cit.
31. H. Grenville to S. Miller, 15 Apr 1756: Sanderson Miller MSS, 380. He spent much time, too, at Hayes, where he was busy improving his new house: O. A. Sherrard, *Lord Chatham: Pitt and the Seven Years War* (London, 1955) p.106.
32. Devonshire to Fox, 1 Apr 1756: 51382, f.38; Robert Ord to Lord Milton, 8 Apr 1756: NLS Saltoun MSS, SC 193, f.12; Walpole, *George II*, ii, 187.
33. Walpole to Conway, 16 Apr 1756: Toynbee, iii, 412; Horatio Walpole to Devonshire, 17 Apr 1756: Dev 180/50; Mrs Grenville to George Grenville, 20 Apr 1756: *Grenville Papers*, i, 156.
34. Gilbert Elliot to Lord Minto, 6 May [1756]: NLS Minto MSS, 11005, f.44.
35. News arrived on 5 May: Dodington, *Diary*, 5 May 1756.
36. Cf. Chesterfield to Huntingdon, 10 May 1756. Dobrée, v, 2185.
37. His sincerity was less than completely convincing: cf. John Yorke to Royston, 13 May 1756: 35374, f.134.
38. Fox to N, 7 May 1756: 32864, f.478; Newdigate Diary, 7 May 1756; Walpole, *George II*, ii, 188, 193.
39. *CJ*, xxvii, 599.
40. West to N, 8 May 1756: 32864, f.498.
41. H to N, 9 May 1756: 32864, f.504.
42. N to H, 8 May 1756: 32864, f.486.
43. Hume Campbell to Marchmont, 3 June 1756: HMC *Polwarth*, v, 317.
44. Cf. Joseph Yorke to Lady Anson, 11 May 1756: 35388, f.159.
45. West to N, 8 May 1756: 32864, f.498.
46. Sources for this debate: John Yorke to Royston, 13 May 1756: 35374, f.134; Walpole, *George II*, ii, 191-6; Dodington, *Diary*, 12 May 1756.
47. Dodington, *Diary*, 21 May 1756. The ministry had also survived a vote on the Plate Tax by a majority of only two when the opposition divided the House on the first reading after Legge had assured Lyttelton that they would not do so. On the second reading the ministry's majority was overwhelming, and Pitt absented himself. Sir G. Lyttelton to W. Lyttelton, 28 Apr 1756: Lyttelton MSS, ii, 282.
48. Cf. C. Jenkinson to S. Miller, 22 May 1756: Sanderson Miller MSS, 813; Lady Grey to Catherine Talbot, 22 May 1756: Bedford RO, L30/9a/7, p.116; the 23 lords are listed: 35877, f.305.
49. Walpole, *George II*, ii, 201-2.
50. Cf. C. Jenkinson to S. Miller, 19 May 1756: Sanderson Miller MSS, 812.
51. Waldegrave, *Memoirs*, p.58.
52. Sir G. Lyttelton to W. Lyttelton, 8 Aug 1756: Lyttelton MSS, ii, 289.
53. Fox to Hanbury Williams, 29 May 1756: Stowe MSS, 263, f.11.
54. C. Jenkinson to S. Miller, 8 May 1756: Sanderson Miller MSS, 819.
55. Fox to N, Friday night [7 May 1756] 32864, f.478.
56. N to Mr Arundel, 30 Oct 1756: 32868, f.480.
57. N to Fox, 8 May 1756: 51379, f.26.
58. N to Rockingham, 3 Aug 1756: 32866, f.349.
59. N to H, 12 June 1756: 32865, f.277.
60. N to H, 14 Oct 1756: 35416, f.100.
61. Walpole, *George II*, ii, 189.

62. N to H, 19 July 1756: 35415, f.231.
63. N to H, 8 May 1756: 32864, f.486.
64. Cf. West to N, 24 July 1756: 32866, f.268; H to N, 26 July 1756: 32866, f.278.
65. Dodington, *Diary*, 6 May 1756.
66. Ibid. 7 May 1756.
67. Minute, 3 Aug 1756: 32997, f.16.
68. N to H, 8 May 1756: 32864, f.486.
69. H to N, 9 May 1756: 32864, f.504.
70. H to N, 29 Aug 1756: 32867, f.143.
71. John Yorke to Royston, 13 May 1756: 35374, f.134.
72. Ryder Diary, 15 May 1756.
73. Dodington, *Diary*, 18 May 1756.
74. Hume Campbell to Marchmont, 30 Oct 1756: HMC *Polwarth*, v, 328.
75. Dodington, *Diary*, 18 May 1756.
76. Cf. Chesterfield to N, 17 May 1756: Dobrée, v, 2187; Waldegrave, *Memoirs*, p.64. Astonishingly, Walpole claims (*George II*, II, 205) that only now was Pitt's dissociation from Fox (presumably of May 1755) explained by the knowledge of Legge's and Pitt's alliance with Bute. But though the chronology is in doubt, this remark points to the equivocal, secret and probably exaggerated nature of the political links between the Princess and Pitt during the previous year.
77. Minute, 4 Apr 1756: 35870, f.259.
78. Cf. West to N, 8 May 1756: 32864, f.498.
79. Chesterfield to Huntingdon, 10 May 1756: Dobrée, v, 2185.
80. Dodington, *Diary*, 18 May 1756.
81. Fox to Waldegrave, 15 May 1756: 51380, f.6.
82. Chesterfield to Huntingdon, 19 May 1756: Dobrée, v, 2190.
83. Fox to Hanbury Williams, 29 May 1756: Stowe MSS, 263, f.11. Newcastle did speak in the Closet about Fox's conduct, as on 8 July when he told the King of 'some little circumstances about Mr Fox as to little employments in the Treasury and House of Commons'; but the violence of George II's antipathy is good evidence that he needed little prompting from Newcastle. N to H, Thursday [8 July 1756]: 35415, f.213.
84. Murray to N, 24 May 1756: 32865, f.104.
85. Cf. Walpole to Mann, 30 May 1756: HW 20, p.557.
86. Fox to Hanbury Williams, 29 May 1756: Stowe MSS, 263, f.11.
87. Walpole, *George II*, II, 224.
88. N to Murray, 30 May 1756: 32865, f.143.
89. Murray to N, 4 June 1756: 32865, f.205.
90. N to Murray, 30 May 1756: 32865, f.143.
91. Walpole, *George II*, II, 207.
92. Ibid. 207-8.
93. Prince George to Bute [? 2 June 1757]: Sedgwick, *Bute*, p.1 (there dated ? 9 June). Waldegrave (*Memoirs*, pp.73-5) claimed he agreed at once to resign, and told the Prince that the King had already agreed to his, Waldegrave's, own request that he should do so. But it seems likely that Waldegrave's account confuses his two interviews on c.30 and 31 May with his two interviews on 5 and 6 June.

94. Cf. Rigby to Bedford, Tuesday evening 1 June [1756]: Bedford MSS, xxxii, 24; *Public Advertiser*, 9 June 1756; *Read's Weekly Journal*, 12 June 1756. Digby's name was mentioned as a Lord of the Bedchamber.
95. Stone to N, Monday morning 31 May [1756]: 32865, f.161; Walpole, *George II*, II, 206-8.
96. Cf. Rigby to Bedford, Wednesday evening [2 June 1756]: Bedford MSS, xxxii, 27.
97. Fox to Devonshire, 3 June 1756: Dev 330/154; Temple to George Grenville, 3 June 1756: *Grenville Papers*, I, 163 and WLC.
98. C. Townshend to Elliot, 3 June [1756]: NLS Minto MSS, 11014, f.11; Hume Campbell to Marchmont, 3 June 1756: HMC *Polwarth*, v, 317; Fox to N, Wednesday night [14] July [1756]: 32866, f.172.
99. E.g. Joseph Yorke to Holdernesse, 4 June 1756: Eg 3447, f.198.
100. G. Grenville to Pitt, 7 June 1756: PRO 30/8/1, f.114; cf. Sir G. Lyttelton to S. Miller, 3 June 1756: Sanderson Miller MSS 650.
101. As is suggested by Wiggin (*The Faction of Cousins*, p.176) who has then to argue, implausibly, that Potter (cf. infra) completely misunderstood the basic element in the outlook of his allies. In fact, his own advice was fully consonant with their gloom.
102. T. Potter to G. Grenville, 11 June 1756: *Grenville Papers*, I, 166, and WLC; Fox to Ellis, 12 June 1756: 51387, f.25.
103. Potter to Pitt, 4 June 1756: PRO 30/8/1, f.112.
104. N to Duchess, 3 June 1756: 33075, f.78.
105. N to H, Friday [4 June 1756]: 35415, f.186.
106. N to H, 12 June 1756: 32865, f.277. Ilchester was granted an earldom without difficulty.
107. Potter to Pitt, 4 June 1756: PRO 30/8/1, f.112.
108. A report that Pitt was to be promoted to a Secretaryship of State, with Newcastle as the other Secretary, appeared in the *Public Advertiser* for 16 March 1756.
109. The often-repeated view that Pitt did so rests on the false attribution of the date '[3 June 1756]' to Bute's letter to Pitt, [6 July 1758], *Chatham Corr*, I, 156, and the editors' annotations. This error is noticed in Sedgwick, 'Pitt', p.156 and McKelvey, *George III and Lord Bute*, p.47. Bute's letters, misdated '[15 July 1756]' and '[20 July 1756]', *Chatham Corr*, I, 169, 170 are properly dated [26 July 1759] and [May 1758]: cf. McKelvey, pp.97, 66. There is no evidence, therefore, for an involvement which 'made the King more than ever reluctant to accept Pitt as Secretary of State' or 'assured the failure of Pitt's first ministry': Sherrard, *Lord Chatham: Pitt and the Seven Years War*, p.125.
110. N to H, Friday [4 June 1756]: 35415, f.186.
111. N to H, Thursday 8 July 1756: 35415, f.213. It was unfair of Royston to suggest, in a note on this letter, that Newcastle provoked Fox.
112. N to H, 12 June 1756: 32865, f.277.
113. Cf. Stone to N, 31 May 1756: 32865, f.161, reporting Waldegrave's judgement.
114. N to H, 12 June 1756: 32865, f.277; Waldegrave, *Memoirs*, p.76.
115. Waldegrave to N, 14 June 1756: 32865, f.302.
116. N to H, 12 June 1756: 32865, f.277.

117. N to H, 25 June 1756: 35415, f.200
118. Francis Cust to Sir John Cust, 26 June 1756: *Cust Records* III, 162. Murray was to continue as Attorney General, with the Duchy of Lancaster and the promise of a peerage. The Chief Baron was to be Lord Chief Justice, Sir Richard Lloyd succeed him and Charles Yorke become Solicitor-General.
119. H to N, 28 June 1756: 32865, f.449.
120. Murray to H, 26 June 1756: 35594, f.85.
121. N to H, 25 June 1756: 35415, f.198.
122. H to N, 28 June 1756: 32865, f.449. Murray did not kiss hands as Lord Chief Justice until 25 October: *Public Advertiser*, 26 Oct 1756.
123. Fox to Ellis, 12 July 1756: 51387, f.33.
124. N to H, 25 June 1756: 35415, f.198.
125. N to H, 27 June 1756: 32865, f.446.
126. Hume Campbell to Marchmont, 21 June 1756: HMC *Polwarth*, v, 318.
127. Minute, 7 July 1756: 33045, f.68.
128. Cf. Chesterfield to Huntingdon, 2 July 1756: Dobrée, v, 2194.
129. N to Stone, Thursday evening [? 8 July 1756]: 51380, f.59.
130. N to H, Thursday [8 July 1756]: 35415, f.213; N to Murray, 9 July 1756: 32866, f.103.
131. Murray to N, 10 July 1756: 32866, f.111.
132. Hume Campbell to Marchmont, 12 July 1756: HMC *Polwarth*, v, 320.
133. Prince of Wales to George II, 12 July 1756: Royal Archives 52955–6 and 32684, f.92.
134. Bute to Gilbert Elliot, 16 Aug 1756: NLS 11014, f.21.
135. Fox to Ellis, 1 July 1756: 51387, f.27.
136. Fox to [? J. Campbell], 15 July 1756: 51406, f.13.
137. N to H, 12 July 1756: 32866, f.141.
138. N to H, Friday [16 July 1756]: 35415, f.225.
139. Holdernesse to H, 19 July 1756: 35594, f.108.
140. N to H, Thursday [8 July 1756]: 35415, f.213; cf. N to Duchess, 15 Aug 1756: 33075, f.94.
141. Minute, 22 July 1756: 32997, f.11.
142. N to H, 12 July 1756: 32866, f.141.
143. H to N, 18 July 1756: 32866, f.206.
144. Hume Campbell to Marchmont, 29 July 1756: HMC *Polwarth*, v, 322; cf. Fox to Devonshire, 31 July 1756: Dev 330/156.
145. West to N, 24 July 1756: 32866, f.268.
146. Fox to Lady Hervey, 24 July 1756: Ilchester, *Fox*, I, 334. Hardwicke agreed: cf. H to N, 26 July 1756: 32866, f.278.
147. Fox to Devonshire, 31 July 1756: Dev 330/156; Fox to Hanbury Williams, 7 Aug 1756: Ilchester, *Fox*, I, 341. This was especially true after Fox had edited Byng's despatch for publication in a way (as Byng's defenders claimed) designed to prejudice the public against the Admiral.
148. N to H, 26 July 1756: 32866, f.275.
149. Ibid.
150. H to N, 26 July 1756: 32866, f.278.
151. Fox to Devonshire, 31 July 1756: Dev 330/156. Devonshire was kept in ignorance of this ambition.
152. Fox to Hanbury Williams, 7 Aug 1756: Ilchester, *Fox*, I, 341.

153. Minute, 3 Aug 1756: 32997, f.16.
154. Walpole, *George II*, II, 250.
155. Rigby to Bedford, 3 Aug 1756: Bedford MSS, XXXII, 47; Fox to Devonshire, 17 Aug 1756: Dev 330/160 (announcing a visit to Woburn).
156. H to Joseph Yorke, 31 Oct 1756: 35357, f.66; Fox to Devonshire, 4 Aug 1756: Dev 330/158.
157. E.g. Dodington to Oswald, Sunday night [10 Oct 1756]: Oswald MSS, no. 45.
158. H. V. Jones to H, 6 Aug 1756: 35415, f.243; N to Duchess, 6 Aug 1756: 33075, f.90.
159. Stone to N, Wednesday morning [11 Aug 1756]: 32866, f.403.
160. Fox to Devonshire, 12 Aug 1756: Dev 330/159.
161. *George II*, II, 221–2.
162. 'Newcastle, by his procrastination and indecision, had lost whatever opportunity he had to secure the support of Leicester House. Had George II been advised earlier that it was absolutely necessary to accept Bute, and had the King done so with good grace, it might have been possible to convince Leicester House of the advantages of co-operating with the ministry'. McKelvey, op. cit. pp.46–7.
163. Waldegrave, *Memoirs*, pp.65–8.
164. N to Holdernesse, 19 Aug 1756: Eg 3430, f.14.
165. H to N, 20 Aug 1756: 32866, f.492.
166. Murray to N, 25 Aug 1756: 32867, f.46.
167. N to Duchess, 23 Aug 1756: 33075, f.97.
168. Nugent to N, 17 & 24 Aug 1756: 32866, f.470; 32867, f.30.
169. H to N, 20 Aug 1756: 32866, f.492.
170. Dr Samuel Squire (1713–66): Newcastle's chaplain from 1748; Whig propagandist; soon to be appointed Clerk of the Closet to the Prince of Wales in the new Establishment.
171. Dr Squire to N, [26 Aug 1756]: 32867, f.78.
172. Cf. Dodington to Fox and to Dupplin, 30 Aug 1756: two letters, 38091, f.67.
173. Dr Squire to N, [26 Aug 1756]: 32867, f.78.
174. 'Business with the Attorney General and Mr Stone', 27 Aug 1756: 32997, f.32. Oswald was aligned with Newcastle rather than Fox, but his loyalty to the ministry had been carefully equivocal in the hope of securing promotion. Stanley, too, had not been wholly reliable; perhaps with the same intention. Namier and Brooke, III, 237, 468.
175. N to H, 28 Aug 1756: 32867, f.111; Martin Narrative, 41356, f.4.
176. Newcastle's secretary, for one, thought the King would agree to whatever was proposed: H. V. Jones to Royston, 8 Sept [1756]: 35425, f.17.
177. N to H, 28 Aug 1756: 32867, f.123.
178. H to N, 29 Aug 1756: 32867, f.143.
179. N to H, 2 Sept 1756: 32867, f.175.
180. Ibid.
181. H to N, 4 Sept 1756: 32867, f.227.
182. N to H, 2 Sept 1756: 32867, f.175.
183. N to H, 4 Sept 1756: 32867, f.229.
184. Fox to Devonshire, 7 Sept 1756: Dev 330/161.
185. Fox to Devonshire, 10 Sept 1756: Dev 330/164.

186. Murray to N, 24 Sept [1756]: 32867, f.425; Rigby to Bedford, 25 Sept 1756: *Bedford Corr*, II, 197.
187. Fox to Devonshire, 10 Sept 1756: Dev 330/164.
188. N to H, 18 and 23 Sept 1756: 32867, f.325; 32867, f.400.
189. N to Murray, 26 Sept 1756: 32867, f.439.
190. N to Duchess, 9 Sept 1756: 33075, f.101.
191. N to H, 18 Sept 1756: 32867, f.325.
192. H to N, 19 Sept 1756: 32867, f.339.
193. J. Calcraft to Loudoun, 10 Sept 1756: Loudoun MSS, Mount Stuart; T. Potter to G. Grenville, 11 Sept [1756]: *Grenville Papers*, I, 172 and WLC.
194. 'Memorandum with Lord Waldegrave', 16 Sept 1756: 32867, f.335.
195. N, Memos, 12 Sept 1756: 32867, ff.286, 290.
196. Cf. 'Memorandum with Lord Waldegrave', loc. cit.
197. H to N, 19 Sept 1756: 32867, f.339.
198. Waldegrave to N, 18 Sept 1756: 32867 f.321. Fox received a copy, with further comments: 51380, f.61.
199. N to H, 23 Sept 1756: 32867, f.400.
200. H, Memo, 27 Sept 1756: 33045, f.78.
201. Cf. Murray to Rockingham, 1 and 4 Oct 1756: WWM, R1–82, R1–83.
202. N to Fox, 5 Oct 1756: 51379, f.32.
203. Walpole to Mann, 19 Sept 1756: HW 21, p.1.
204. Hume Campbell to Marchmont, 25 Sept 1756: HMC *Polwarth*, v, 325.
205. E.g. Ashburnham to N, 24 Sept 1756: 32867, f.413.
206. Rigby to Bedford, 25 Sept 1756: *Bedford Corr*, II, 197.
207. That is, George II's life and George III's. Sir G. Lyttelton to W. Lyttelton, 6 Oct 1756: Lyttelton MSS, II, 298.
208. Symmer to Mitchell, 8 Oct 1756: 6839, f.12. Robert Symmer was Andrew Mitchell's political agent in London.
209. N to Murray, 26 Sept 1756: 32867, f.439.
210. Fox to N, 25 Sept 1756: 32867, f.431.
211. Minute, 28 Sept 1756: 32997, f.44.
212. Barrington to Northumberland, 29 Sept 1756: Northumberland MSS, BL Microfilm M/295.
213. 'Business for my Lord Chancellor', 26 Sept 1756: 32997, f.36.
214. N to H, 5 Oct 1756: 35416, f.69.
215. Fox to Lady Caroline Fox, 5 Oct 1756: 51416, f.1.
216. Fox to N, 6 Oct 1756: 32868, f.102.
217. Ibid.
218. N to Fox, 7 Oct 1756: 51379, f.34.
219. Murray to N, 10 Oct 1756: 32868, f.194.
220. Fox to [? Stone], [7 Oct 1756]: 51379, f.44.
221. H to N, 7 Oct 1756: 32868, f.120.
222. Ibid. and Cresset to N, 7 Oct 1756: 32868, f.131.
223. Newcastle was aware only that the Prince had shown a conspicuous lack of enthusiasm at the choice of Andrew Stone as his secretary.
224. N to H, 10 Oct 1756: 35416, f.76.
225. Murray to N, 10 Oct 1756: 32868, f.194.
226. Newcastle, notably, did not mention Bute, Egmont, Lee, Dodington or Halifax in this list.

227. N to H, 10 Oct 1756: 35416, f.76.
228. H to N, 11 Oct 1756: 32868, f.203.
229. To what extent the party alignments of George III's reign were the result of this decision is a matter for speculation.
230. Murray to N, 11 Oct 1756: 32868, f.207; N to H, 12 Oct 1756: 32868, f.223.
231. N to H, 12 Oct 1756: 32868, f.223.
232. Fox to Devonshire, 11 Oct 1756: Dev 330/165; Fox to Ellis, Tuesday [12 Oct 1756]: 51387, f.49.
233. Devonshire to Fox, Wednesday [13] Oct 1756: 51382, f.71.
234. Fox to Lord Digby, 11 Oct 1756: Digby MSS. This letter was written to be forwarded by Digby to Bedford.
235. Fox to Lord Digby, 11 Oct 1756: 51423, f.74.
236. Lord Digby to Fox, nd [c. 13 Oct 1756]: 51423, f.78.
237. Fox to N, 13 Oct 1756: 32867, f.247.
238. N to H, 12 Oct 1756: 32868, f.223.
239. H to N, 13 Oct 1756: 32868, f.249.
240. Bedford to Fox, 14 Oct 1756 (with P.S. of 16th): 51385, f.5.
241. Rigby to Bedford, 14 Oct 1756: Bedford MSS, xxxii, 73.
242. Fox to H, [18 Oct 1756]: Dev 330/169 (a copy sent to Devonshire). The phrase was softened to 'in hopes of more power' in the copy Hardwicke received, 35594, f.289.
243. Devonshire to Fox, 20 Oct 1756: 51382, f.73.
244. Bedford to Fox, loc. cit.
245. N to H, 13 Oct 1756: 32868, f.251.
246. Fox to George II, 13 Oct 1756: 32868, f.303.
247. N to H, 13 Oct 1756: 32868, f.251.
248. Walpole, *George II*, ii, 252.
249. N to H, 13 Oct 1756: 32868, f.251.
250. Cf. N to Lady Yarmouth, 13 Oct 1756: 32868, f.256.
251. N to H, 13 Oct 1756: 32868, f.251. Hardwicke thought Barrington spoke on his own initiative, using Newcastle's name to give weight to his remark (H to N, 14 Oct 1756: 32868, f.279). As with Sir George Lyttelton's mission to the Duke of Bedford in December 1754, it seems likely that a subordinate mistook Newcastle's thinking aloud for a precise commission.
252. Egmont to Sir John Cust, 4 Nov 1756: *Cust Records*, iii, 159; Walpole, *George II*, ii, 261–2; Waldegrave, *Memoirs*, p.83–4.
253. Glover, *Memoirs*, pp.82–3.
254. N to H, 13 Oct 1756: 32868, f.251.
255. Fox to H, 18 Oct 1756: 35594, f.289.
256. H to N, 14 Oct 1756: 32868, f.279.
257. Walpole, *George II*, ii, 254–5.
258. 'Mems. for the King', 14 Oct 1756: 32868, f.277.
259. Walpole (*George II*, ii, 252) later suggested that Granville 'had too much experience of Newcastle to think it possible for Fox to go on with him, or to expect that Newcastle would let him'.
260. N to H, 14 Oct 1756: 35416, f.100.
261. H to N, 14 Oct 1756: 32868, f.279.
262. Fox to Lord Digby, [? 14th Oct 1756]: Digby MSS; Granville to Stone,

14 Oct 1756: 35416, f.114; Rigby to Bedford, Friday evening [15 Oct 1756]: Bedford MSS, xxxii, 75.

263. Fox to Ilchester, 16 Oct 1756: 51420, f.36.

264. Ilchester to Fox, 18 Oct 1756: 51420, f.38.

265. Fox to Ilchester, 16 Oct 1756: 51420, f.36; Fox to Devonshire, 16 Oct 1756: Dev 330/168.

266. Fox to Ilchester, 16 Oct 1756: 51420, f.36.

267. N to H, 15 Oct 1756: 35416, f.122.

268. R. Rigby to [Trentham], Saturday morning 16 Oct [1756]: PRO 30/29/1, f.494.

269. H to Pitt, 16 Oct 1756: 32868, f.320.

270. H to N, 16 Oct 1756: 32868, f.318.

271. Fox to [Lord Digby], [c. 16 Oct 1756]: Digby MSS.

272. Holdernesse to N, 17 Oct 1756: 32868, ff.338, 340.

273. Digby to Fox, Monday [18 Oct 1756]: 51423, f.85; Ilchester to Fox, 18 Oct 1756: 51420, f.38.

274. Granville to Fox, Monday 7.30 [18 Oct 1756]: 51430, f.4; cf. Walpole, *George II*, ii, 256–7.

275. Fox to Devonshire, 19 Oct 1756: Dev 330/170.

276. Fox to Bedford, 19 Oct 1756: Bedford MSS, xxxii, 77.

277. Fox to H, 18 Oct 1756: 35594, f.289.

278. Cf. Rigby to [Trentham], 19 Oct 1756: PRO 30/29/1, f.496.

279. Cf. Royston to C. Yorke, 19 Oct 1756: 35360, f.256.

280. Pitt to George Grenville, 17 Oct [1756]: *Grenville Papers*, i, 177 and WLC.

281. T. Potter to Pitt, Sunday past 11 [17 Oct 1756]: PRO 30/8/1, f.125.

282. H to N, 19 Oct 1756: 32868, f.380.

283. Sources for the interview: Martin, Memo, 'Administration 1756': 41356, f.4; H to Joseph Yorke, 31 Oct 1756: 35357, f.66.

284. N to H, 20 Oct 1756: 35416, f.127.

285. Martin, Memo, loc. cit.

286. N to Holdernesse, 18 [sc. 19] Oct 1756: Eg 3430, f.34.

287. N to H, 20 Oct 1756: 35416, f.127; H to Royston, 21 Oct 1756: 35351, f.351.

288. H to Joseph Yorke, loc. cit.

289. Cf. Hume Campbell to Marchmont, 21 Oct 1756: HMC *Polwarth*, v, 326; Holdernesse to Mitchell, 26 Oct 1756: 6832, f.96.

290. R. Rigby to [Trentham], 21 Oct 1756: PRO 30/29/1, f.498.

291. N to H, 2 Sept 1756: 32867, f.175.

292. Fox to Lord Digby, 20 Oct 1756: Digby MSS.

293. Fox to Ilchester, 21 Oct 1756: 51420, f.41.

294. Cf. Dodington to Oswald, Wednesday morning [20 Oct 1756]: Oswald MSS, 47; Hillsborough to Fox, nd [? 19 Oct 1756]: 51386, f.206; Fox to Dodington, 19 Oct 1756: HMC *Various*, vi, 36; Halifax to Dodington, 18 Oct 1756: ibid.; Dodington to Oswald, Tuesday [12 Oct 1756]; Sunday [10 October 1756]: Oswald MSS, 45–6.

295. Fox to Devonshire, 21 Oct 1756: Dev 330/171. It seems probable that this is the visit referred to in Grenville's Narrative, p.435.

296. Fox to Ilchester, 21 Oct 1756: 51420, f.41; Fox to Ellis, Tuesday [? 26 Oct 1756]: 51387, f.51.

297. A copy, dated 21 Oct 1756, is 35416, f.129: Devonshire, First Lord of the Treasury; Pitt, Secretary of State; G. Grenville, sole Paymaster; Temple, Lord Lieutenant of Ireland; J. Grenville his Secretary; Legge, Chancellor of the Exchequer; Charles Townshend, Treasurer of the Chambers; Dr Hay a Lord of the Admiralty; Sir T. Robinson, Secretary of State; and offices for George Townshend, Sir H. Erskine, Lord Pomfret, and Sir Richard Lyttelton.

298. H to Royston, 21 Oct 1756: 35351, f.351.

299. Hume Campbell to Marchmont, 21 Oct 1756: HMC *Polwarth*, v, 326.

300. Sir Robert Wilmot to Devonshire, 22 Oct 1756: Dev 290/53.

301. C. Townshend to George Townshend, 30 Oct 1756: Bod Eng hist d 211, f.3.

302. Sir Robert Wilmot to Devonshire, 22 Oct 1756: Dev 290/53.

303. West to N, 23 Oct 1756: 32868, f.390.

304. H, Memo, 24 Oct 1756: 35870, f.263; Martin Narrative, 41356, f.4.

305. Fox to Devonshire, [26 Oct 1756]: Dev 330/172.

306. Fox to Lord Digby, 25 Oct 1756: Digby MSS.

307. Fox claimed, too, that Sir George was simultaneously asking Pitt 'for mercy'; but there is no evidence of secret overtures of this sort.

308. Fox to Devonshire, [26 Oct 1756]: Dev 330/172.

309. Ibid.; N to H, 14 Oct 1756: 35416, f.100; H. Digby to Lord Digby, 28 Oct 1756: Digby MSS.

310. Cf. Rigby to [Trentham], 26 Oct 1756: PRO 30/29/1, f.500.

311. H. Digby to Lord Digby, 26 Oct 1756: Digby MSS.

312. Fox to Granville, 26 Oct 1756: 51430, f.12.

313. H. Digby to Lord Ilchester, 26 Oct 1756: 51341, f.29.

314. Rigby to [Trentham], 26 Oct 1756: PRO 30/29/1, f.500; Sir John Cope to Wilmot, Sunday [24 Oct 1756]: Catton MSS, vol. 23.

315. Fox to Devonshire, [26 Oct 1756]: Dev 330/172; Fox to Charles Hamilton, 26 Oct 1756: 51408, f.102; Fox to Ellis, Tuesday [? 26 Oct 1756]: 51387, f.51.

316. Walpole to Fox, Wednesday night [27 Oct 1756]: HW 30, p.128.

317. H to Joseph Yorke, 31 Oct 1756: 35357, f.66.

318. Lord George Sackville and Sir George Lyttelton were spoken of for the post (Rigby to Trentham, 26 Oct 1756: PRO 30/29/1, f.500).

319. Martin Narrative, 41356, f.4.

320. Cf. J. Calcraft to Lord Charles Hay, 27 Oct 1756: NLS Yester MSS, Box 15, F2(a).

321. N to Devonshire, 26 Oct 1756: Dev 182/81.

322. Wilmot to Devonshire, 26 Oct 1756: Dev 290/54; Hillsborough to G. Grenville, 26 Oct 1756: *Grenville Papers*, I, 178, and WLC.

323. Fox to Charles Hamilton, 26 Oct 1756: 51408, f.102.

324. Horatio Walpole to H, 4 April 1756: 35594, f.40. He received his peerage in June 1756.

325. Gilbert Elliot to G. Grenville, [25 May 1756]: *Grenville Papers*, I, 159, and WLC.

326. Temple to G. Grenville, 3 June 1756: ibid. I, 163; Charles Townshend to Elliot, 3 June [1756]: NLS Minto MSS, 11014, f.11.

327. Emden, *The People and the Constitution*, p.46.

328. Fitzmaurice, *Shelburne*, I, 36.

329. Potter to Pitt, 4 June 1756: PRO 30/8/1, f.112; Pitt to Grenville, 5 June

NOTES TO PP. 277–80

1756: *Grenville Papers*, I, 165, and WLC; Potter to G. Grenville, 11 June 1756: ibid. I, 166, and WLC.

330. Hume Campbell to Marchmont, 21 June 1756: HMC *Polwarth*, v, 318. Parliament had risen on 27 May.

331. Legge to Bute, 15 June 1756: Bute MSS, Mount Stuart, no. 73; Legge to Pitt, 16 June 1756: PRO 30/8/1, f.116.

332. Legge to Pitt, 3 August 1756: PRO 30/8/48, f.84.

333. Dr Squire to N, [26 Aug 1756]: 32867, f.78.

334. Wiggin, *The Faction of Cousins*, pp. 177–8.

335. Cf. N to H, 2 September 1756: 32867, f.175. Calcraft observed: 'Lord Bute remains sole governor at Leicester House, where Legge is next favourite and much better than Pitt.' Calcraft to Loudoun, 10 September 1756: Loudoun MSS, Mount Stuart.

336. Waldegrave, *Memoirs*, p.78.

337. Fox to Lady Caroline Fox, 5 October 1756: 51416, f.1.

338. Pitt to G. Grenville, 17 October [1756]: *Grenville Papers*, I, 177, and WLC; Grenville Narrative: ibid., 436.

339. T. Potter to Pitt, Sunday [17 October 1756]: PRO 30/8/1, f.125.

340. Walpole, *George II*, II, 154.

341. *Public Advertiser*, 1 Oct 1756. A report of Pitt's promotion was also circulating; both were denied, ibid. 9 Oct 1756.

342. Grenville Narrative, *Grenville Papers*, I, pp.436–7.

343. Cf. Legge to Bute, 15 June 1756: Bute MSS, Mount Stuart, no. 73; Legge to Pitt, 16 June 1756: PRO 30/8/1, f.116.

344. Sutherland, 'The City of London', pp.151–2. Dame Lucy continued to argue, however, that the situation was 'radically changed' by the 'misfortunes' which followed the outbreak of war, especially the loss of Minorca.

345. Dodington, *Diary*, 11 Oct 1756.

346. Dupplin to N, 13 Oct 1756: 32868, f.267.

347. Ilchester to Fox, 18 Oct 1756: 51420, f.38.

348. Walpole, *George II*, II, 254–9.

349. C. Townshend to Sir G. Elliot, [2– Oct 1756]: NLS Minto MSS 11014 f.98.

350. Fox to Lord Digby, 25 Oct 1756: Digby MSS.

351. Fox to Devonshire, [26 Oct 1756]: Dev 330/172.

352. N to Fox, 8 May 1756: 51379, f.26.

353. N to Murray, 30 May 1756: 32865, f.143.

354. N to H, 12 June 1756: 32865, f.277.

355. N to H, 27 June 1756: f.446; Hume Campbell to Marchmont, 15 July 1756: HMC *Polwarth*, v, 322.

356. Cf. N to Duchess, 6 15, 23 Aug 1756: 33075, ff.90, 94, 97.

357. A second wave came from the Quarter Sessions in October. For the dates cf. Dame Lucy Sutherland, 'The City of London', pp.153–4.

358. Bute to Elliot, 16 Aug 1756: NLS Minto MSS, 11014, f.21.

359. West to N, 20 Aug 1756: 32866, f.496.

360. Cf. N to Holdernesse, 19 Aug 1756: Eg 3430, f.14.

361. N to George II, Thursday [19 Aug 1756]: Eg 3430, f.16.

362. E. Law to N, 11 April 1756: 32864, f.225.

363. Josiah Tucker to Dr Birch, 25 Aug 1756: 4319, f.257.
364. Cf. Lord Justice Willes to N, 21 Aug 1756: 32867, f.5.
365. George Townshend to the Mayor of Southampton, 6 Aug 1756: 32866, f.376.
366. An example dated 7 Aug 1756 was in SRO Buccleuch MSS, GD 224 296/3 (now WLC, Townshend MSS); cf. Rev. H. Etough to Lord Walpole, 26 Aug 1756: 9201, f.113; H to N, 26 Aug 1756: 32867, f.72. On the involvement of Wilkes in provoking the Grand Jury of Bedfordshire to address, cf. Royston to H, 24 Aug 1756: 35351, f.343.
367. H to N, 20 Aug 1756: 32866, f.492.
368. N to H, 28 Aug 1756: 32867, f.111.
369. N to H, 2 Sept 1756: 32867, f.175.
370. Lord Walpole to Etough, 1 Sept 1756: 4306, f.179; Lord Walpole to Mayor of Norwich, 1 Sept 1756: 32867, f.166; West to N, 14 Aug 1756: 32866, f.448.
371. Cf. Dampier to Nugent, 2 Sept 1756: 32867, f.206.
372. J. Watkins to N, 2 Sept 1756: 32867, f.209.
373. H to N, 4 Sept 1756: 32867, f.227.
374. J. Calcraft to Loudoun, 10 Sept 1756: Loudoun MSS.
375. Grafton to N, Wednesday [13 Oct 1756]: 32868, f.269; Bishop of Gloucester to N, 13 Oct 1756: 32868, f.271.
376. E.g. Bedford to Fox, 14 Oct 1756: 51385, f.5; Digby to Fox, Monday [18 Oct 1756]: 51423, f.85.
377. E.g. Fox to H, 18 Oct 1756: 35594, f.289.
378. H. Digby to Hanbury Williams, 10 Nov. 1756: Stowe MSS, 263, f.4.
379. Cf. N to H, 14, 15 Oct 1756: 35416, ff.100, 122.
380. Sir G. Lyttelton to Mrs Montagu, 23 Oct 1756: M. Wyndham, *Chronicles of the Eighteenth Century* (London, 1924), p.221.
381. Fox to Devonshire, [26 Oct 1756]: Dev 330/172.
382. Rigby to Trentham, 26 Oct 1756: PRO 30/29/1, f.500.
383. Riker, *Fox*, I, 431; II, 8.
384. Ilchester, *Fox*, I, 337.
385. R. Browning, *The Duke of Newcastle* (New Haven, 1975), p.252; Hume Campbell to Marchmont, 28 Oct 1756: HMC *Polwarth*, V, 327.

6. THE PITT–DEVONSHIRE MINISTRY

1. Wilmot to Devonshire, 26 Oct 1756: Dev 290/54.
2. Martin, Narrative: 41356, f.4. Martin was with Legge at The Holte; Fox to [Legge], 28 Oct 1756: 51388, f.134. The evidence here is at odds with Waldegrave's claim (*Memoirs*, p.87) that the King's commission involved a specific exclusion of Pitt and his adherents.
3. H to Joseph Yorke, 31 Oct 1756: 35357, f.66.
4. Grafton to N, 28 Oct 1756: 32868, f.449.
5. Marlborough to Bedford, 26 Oct 1756: Bedford MSS, XXXII, 79.
6. Cf. Hume Campbell to Marchmont, 28 Oct 1756: HMC *Polwarth*, V, 327; Symmer to Mitchell, 29 Oct 1756: 6839, f.16.
7. J. Calcraft to Lord Charles Hay, 27 Oct 1756: NLS Yester MSS, Box 15, F 2(a).

8. Rigby to Fox, 29 Oct 1756: 51385, f.93 (Bedford gave Rigby this advice on the evening of 27th; but he did not pass it on to Fox until 29th).

9. Cf. Dodington to Halifax, 27 Oct 1756: HMC *Various*, vi, 36.

10. Stone to Fox, Wednesday evening [27 Oct 1756]: 51379, f.48; and Thursday morning [28 Oct 1756]: 51379, f.50. The contents of Granville's message, and the nature of the restriction, are unknown.

11. H to N, 28 Oct. 1756: 32868, f.445.

12. Martin, Narrative: 41356, f.4; Walpole, *George II*, ii, 262–3; Glover, *Memoirs*, p.95.

13. H. Digby to Lord Digby, 28 Oct 1756: Digby MSS.

14. Fox to Argyll, 28 Oct 1756: 51340, f.17.

15. Rigby to Trentham, 28 Oct 1756: PRO 30/29/1, f.502.

16. H. Digby to Lord Digby, 28 Oct 1756: Digby MSS.

17. Ibid. and Lady Caroline Fox to Lord Ilchester, 28 Oct 1756: 51420, f.43.

18. Fox to Lord George Sackville, 28 Oct 1756: Germaine MSS, Ann Arbor.

19. T. Potter to Pitt, Sunday [17 Oct 1756]: PRO 30/8/1, f.125.

20. J. Campbell to Fox, 28 Nov. 1756: 51406, f.27.

21. [Fox to Devonshire], [10 Nov 1756]: Dev. 330/179.

22. Pitt to George Grenville, 17 Oct [1756]: *Grenville Papers*, i, 177, and WLC.

23. *Grenville Papers*, i, p.436. Grenville dates the meeting, probably in error, as on 19th; but Pitt met Lady Yarmouth only on 21st. Possibly there were two meetings; but the evidence is inconclusive, and very little survives for Pitt's actions before the formation of his ministry.

24. Cf. Martin, Narrative: 41356, f.4; Hardwicke to Col J. Yorke, 31 Oct 1756: 35357, f.66. Walpole (*George II*, ii, 257) records the offices in Pitt's list of 21st as having been demanded also in the interview of 19th; but this is not established by other evidence.

25. The meeting with Hardwicke must be referred to; Lady Yarmouth is unlikely to have negotiated with Pitt in this way.

26. Glover, *Memoirs*, pp.83–93. Grenville was put down for Treasurer of the Navy *vice* Dodington, George Townshend for Treasurer of the Household *vice* Lord Berkeley of Stratton. In Pitt's list of 21st (35416, f.129) Grenville was destined for the Paymastership, and George Townshend, though listed, not assigned an office (though it is possible he was meant for a place at the Admiralty Board).

27. Wilmot to Devonshire, 21 Oct 1756: Dev 290/52.

28. Wilmot to Devonshire, 22 Oct 1756: Dev 290/53. Legge had presumably received a letter from Pitt while in the country.

29. Wilmot to Devonshire, 26 Oct 1756: Dev 290/54.

30. Fox to Lord Digby, 25 Oct 1756: Digby MSS. Pitt and Bute presumably met at Leicester House on 24th, when the Prince of Wales's new Household was presented.

31. Wilmot to Devonshire, 26 Oct 1756: Dev 290/54.

32. Ibid.

33. Walpole, *George II*, ii, 265. The dates of these transactions are not clear.

34. N to Mr Arundell, 13 Nov 1756: 32869, f.32.

35. This was untrue. The pamphlet press had repeated the wild charges, which Pitt had voiced in the Commons, that Minorca had been sold to the French.

36. Martin, Narrative: 41356, f.4; cf. Waldegrave, *Memoirs*, pp.87–8.
37. H to Col J. Yorke, 31 Oct 1756: 35357, f.66; cf. Mrs Boscawen to Admiral Boscawen, 27 Oct 1756, in C. Aspinall–Oglander, *Admiral's Wife. Being the Life and Letters of the Hon. Mrs Edward Boscawen from 1719 to 1761* (London, 1940) p.220
38. Fox to Lord George Sackville, 30 Oct 1756: Germaine MSS, Ann Arbor.
39. Martin, Narrative: 41356, f.4.
40. Cf. H. Digby to Lord Ilchester, 30 Oct 1756: 51431, f.33.
41. Wilmot to Devonshire, 30 Oct 1756: Dev 290/56; cf. Lord Ducie to Fox, 30 Oct 1756: 51408, f.173.
42. Fox to Bedford, 30 Oct 1756: *Bedford Corr*, II, 205; Fox to Digby, 30 Oct 1756: 51423, f.88; Fox to J. Campbell, 30 Oct 1756: 51406, f.17.
43. Nathaniel Ryder Diary, 2 Nov 1756.
44. Martin, Narrative: 41356, f.4. At this point the Narrative ends.
45. H to Col J. Yorke, 31 Oct 1756: 35357, f.66.
46. Dated 1 Nov: Dev 330/175A.
47. Grenville Narrative, *Grenville Papers*, I, p.437.
48. Fox, Memo, 1 Nov 1756: Dev. 330/175.
49. Grenville Narrative, ibid. pp.437–8.
50. Fox to Devonshire, 1 Nov 1756: Dev. 330/174. It is not certain that Legge is meant; the wording is inconclusive.
51. Sources for the meeting: Bedford to Duchess, 2 Nov 1756: Bedford MSS, XXXII, 87; Fox, Memo 'Concerning the Surveyor of the Woods', nd [but early Dec 1756]: 51382, f.91.
52. Holdernesse to N, [2 Nov 1756]: 32868, f.538; Dupplin to Lincoln, 2 Nov 1756: Ne (C) 3771.
53. Walpole, *George II*, II, 268.
54. Charles Hamilton to [Marlborough], 2 Nov 1756: 51408, f.105; H. Digby to Lord Ilchester, 2 Nov 1756: 51341, f.34. Walpole suggests Granville's house.
55. Bedford to Duchess, 3.30 Tuesday [? 2 Nov 1756]: Bedford MSS, XXXII, 85.
56. Fox to Egremont, 2 Nov 1756: 51430, f.21.
57. H. Digby to Lord Ilchester, 2 Nov 1756: 51431, f.34.
58. Charles Townshend to George Townshend, Friday [? 29 Oct 1756]: 41178, f.97.
59. Pitt to Devonshire, 2 Nov 1756: Dev 463/1.
60. Devonshire's copy, dated by him 3 Dec 1756, is Dev 303/4.
61. Sir Richard Lyttelton to Pitt, Tuesday night 12 o'clock [? 2 Nov 1756]: PRO 30/8/1, f.127.
62. Bedford to Duchess, 2 Nov 1756: Bedford MSS, XXXII, 87.
63. Walpole, *George II*, II, 268–9.
64. E.g. H. Digby to Lord Ilchester, 6 Nov 1756: 51341, f.36; cf. J. Calcraft to Lord Charles Hay, 6 Nov 1756: NLS Yester MSS, Box 15, F 2(a); H. Digby to Sir C. Hanbury Williams, 10 Nov 1756: Stowe MSS, 263, f.4.
65. Ibid. and Fox, Memo, nd: 51382, f.91; H. Digby to Lord Ilchester, 2 Nov 1756: 51431, f.34; Holdernesse to N, Tuesday night [2 Nov 1756]: 32868, f.542.
66. Waldegrave, *Memoirs*, p.86.
67. Legge to Pitt, 3 Nov 1756: PRO 30/8/1, f.129.

68. Sir Richard Lyttelton to Pitt, Tuesday night 12 o'clock [? 2 Nov 1756]: PRO 30/8/1, f.127.
69. Fox to Bedford, 3 Nov 1756: Bedford MSS, xxxii, 89.
70. Fox to Bedford, [4 Nov 1756]: Bedford MSS, xxxii, 93. Whether Devonshire was in a position to make good such an offer is doubtful.
71. Lady Grey to Lady Mary Gregory, 5 Nov 1756: Bedford RO, L30/9a/2, p.148.
72. Fox to Bedford, loc. cit., and Pitt to Devonshire, Wednesday night [3 Nov 1756]: Dev 463/2. Calcraft later claimed (Calcraft to Loudoun, 12 Nov 1756: Loudoun MSS) that Pitt had also demanded the Lord Lieutenancy of Ireland for Temple, and that the King had refused. But there is no other evidence that Pitt had ever intended Temple for any other place than the Admiralty.
73. Grenville Narrative, *Grenville Papers*, I, p. 438.
74. Fox to Lord George Sackville, 4 Nov 1756: Germaine MSS, Ann Arbor.
75. Fox to Bedford, Memo, 3 Nov 1754: Bedford MSS, xxxii, 91. Rodney's idea of persuading Bedford to take the Admiralty (Rodney to his wife, 4 Nov 1756: PRO 30/20/20/2, f.131) was apparently a purely personal initiative, unconcerted with any leading figure; though a rumour circulated, perhaps as a result, that Bedford had refused that office (Hume Campbell to Marchmont, 11 Nov 1756: HMC *Polwarth*, v, 330).
76. Cf. Lord George Sackville to Fox, 5 Nov 1756: 51340, f.25.
77. Fox to Devonshire, [5 Nov 1756]: Dev 330/176.
78. Gower to Bedford, 9 Nov 1756: Bedford MSS, xxxii, 95.
79. Fox to Devonshire, 5 Nov 1756: Dev 330/177.
80. Fox to Devonshire, Tuesday night [9 Nov 1756]: Dev 330/178.
81. Legge to Devonshire, 4 Nov 1756: Dev 257/25.
82. Walpole to Mann, 4 Nov 1756: HW 21, p.10.
83. Fox to Lord Ilchester, 17 Nov 1756: 51420, f.48.
84. Symmer to Mitchell, 9 Nov 1756: 6839, f.20.
85. Legge to Guilford, 9 Nov 1756: Bod MS, North d 7, f.67.
86. Walpole to Montagu, 6 Nov 1756: HW 9, p.202.
87. Legge to Guilford, loc. cit.
88. H. Digby to Lord Ilchester, 9 Nov 1756: 51341, f.39.
89. Calcraft to Loudoun, 12 Nov 1756: Loudoun MSS.
90. Glover, *Memoirs*, pp.99–100.
91. N to H, 2 Nov 1756: 32836, f.540; N to George II, 8 Nov 1756: 32868, f.603.
92. Temple to Pitt, Tuesday night [9 Nov 1756]: PRO 30/8/1, f.133.
93. Temple to Pitt, 12 pm. Thursday [11 Nov 1756]: PRO 30/8/1, f.135.
94. In a letter, Pitt to Temple, probably of 9 November; no longer extant.
95. Waldegrave wrote (*Memoirs*, pp.86–7; cf. Walpole, *George II*, ii, 264) that Pitt was unwilling to give Charles Townshend a post equal to his abilities, that he 'did not choose to advance a young man to a ministerial office, whose abilities were of the same kind, and so nearly equal to his own'. But Waldegrave was unaware of the tactical difficulties presented by the arrangement of ministerial offices.
96. Grenville would have preferred Potter to have Charles Townshend's place (Grenville calls it Treasurer of the Household; *sc.* Treasurer of the

Chamber), Charles Townshend as Treasurer of the Navy, and himself as sole Paymaster *vice* Dupplin and Darlington. Narrative, p.439.

97. It seems probable that Sloper had long been promised this vacancy by the King: cf. Halifax to Guilford, 13 Nov 1756: Bod MSS, North d 7, f.69.

98. Glover, *Memoirs*, pp.100–01.

99. Calcraft to Loudoun, 12 Nov 1756: Loudoun MSS; Hume Campbell to Marchmont, 28 Oct 1756: HMC *Polwarth*, v, 327.

100. Lord Lyttelton to W. Lyttelton, 25 Nov 1756: Lyttelton MSS, II, 313. Sir George Lyttelton was created Baron Lyttelton of Bewdley, 18 Nov 1756.

101. Temple to Pitt, 12 p.m. Thursday [11 Nov 1756]: PRO 30/8/1, f.135.

102. N to Holdernesse, Saturday morning [13 Nov 1756]: Eg 3430, f.36.

103. N to Mr Arundel, 13 Nov 1756: 32869, f.32.

104. Walpole to Montagu, 6 Nov 1756: HW 9, p.202.

105. Cf. N to Col Yorke, 12 Nov 1756: 32869, f.27.

106. N to Mr Arundel, loc. cit.

107. Ibid. and Holdernesse to Mitchell, 3 Nov 1756: 6832, f.98.

108. G. Elliot to Lord Minto, 13 Nov [1756]: NLS 11001, f.26.

109. Glover, *Memoirs*, p.98.

110. Chesterfield to Huntingdon, 18 Nov 1756: Dobrée, v, 2210.

111. Lord Carysfort to Earl Gower, 14 Nov 1756: PRO 30/29/1, f.508.

112. J. Tucker to Birch, 15 Nov 1756: 4319, f.259.

113. W. Beckford to Pitt, 6 Nov 1756: PRO 30/8/1, f.131.

114. [Andrew Fletcher to Lord Milton], 16 Nov 1756: NLS SC 18, f.132.

115. 'Copy [of a] Letter from London', 16 Nov 1756: NLS SC 190, f.108.

116. Lord Lyttelton to W. Lyttelton, 25 Nov 1756: Lyttelton MSS, II, 313.

117. Walpole to Mann, 13 Nov 1756: HW 21, p.17.

118. Cf. Lord Lyttelton to W. Lyttelton, 25 Nov 1756: loc. cit.

119. N to H, 23 Nov 1756: 35416, f.143.

120. Barrington to Mitchell, 28 Dec 1756: 6834, f.5.

121. Calcraft to Hon. Mrs Cornwallis, 24 Oct 1756: 17493, f.13.

122. Chesterfield to Dayrolles, 26 Nov 1756: Dobrée, v, 2212.

123. Mrs Montagu to Mrs Boscawen, 30 Nov 1756: Aspinall-Oglander (ed.), *Admiral's Wife* p.230.

124. Lady Grey to Lady Mary Gregory, 27 Oct 1756: Bedford RO, L30/9a/2, p.145.

125. Cf. Glover, *Memoirs*, p.99; Nathaniel Ryder Diary, 1 Feb 1757; J. Home to Lord Milton, February 1757: NLS SC 196, f.190; Holdernesse to Mitchell, 22 Feb 1757: Eg 3460, f.183; Symmer to Mitchell, 17 Dec 1756: 6839, f.26; Halifax to Oswald, 15 Apr. 1757: Oswald MSS, Chest IV. Chesterfield to Dayrolles, 28 Feb 1757: Dobrée, v, 2220.

126. Walpole, *George II*, II, 316.

127. *The Enquiry is not Begun! When will it?* (London, 1757).

128. *The Con–Test*, 5 Feb 1757.

129. Ibid., 14 Dec 1756.

130. Hume Campbell to Marchmont, 28 Oct 1756: HMC *Polwarth*, v, 327.

131. H to N, 25 Nov 1756: 32869, f.155.

132. Rigby to Fox, 29 Oct 1756: 51385, f.93.

133. Hume Campbell to Marchmont, 11 Nov 1756: HMC *Polwarth*, v, 330.

Newcastle delivered up the seals on 11th, Fox on 13th, Hardwicke on 19th. Pitt accepted the Seals at Court on 4 December; George Grenville kissed hands on 19 November; most of the other new officers on 15 November.

134. N to H, 2 Nov 1756: 32836, f.540. Newcastle, childless, secured a new dukedom entailed to his nephew and heir, Lord Lincoln. Another nephew, John Shelley, received the reversion of the Clerkship of the Pipe; James West, joint Secretary to the Treasury, the reversion of the Auditorship of the Land Revenues for his and his son's life; Thomas Pelham, the reversion of the Surveyor-Generalship of the Customs of London. Hugh Valence Jones, Newcastle's private secretary, got a reversion to the Comptrollership of the Customs. The Irish peerage given to Percy Wyndham O'Brien was at Devonshire's initiative, and the English barony given to Sir George Lyttelton at the King's (Sir George Lyttelton to W. Lyttelton, 25 Nov 1756: Lyttelton MSS, II, 313), allegedly to the new ministers' 'vexation' (Hume Campbell to Marchmont, 13 Nov 1756: HMC *Polwarth*, v, 331).

135. Cf. N to Col Yorke, 12 Nov 1756: 32869, f.27.

136. Holdernesse to N, at night 15 Nov [1756]: 32869, f.64; N to H, 16 Nov 1756: 32869, f.69; N to Holdernesse, 16 Nov 1756: Eg 3430, f.38.

137. H to N, 17 Nov 1756: 32869, f.76.

138. Holdernesse to Mitchell, 26 Nov 1756: 6832, f.102.

139. North to Guildford, 23 Nov 1756: Bod MS, North d 23, f.51; H. V. Jones to N, 21 Nov 1756: 32869, f.106.

140. Cf. the anonymous intelligence 'Letter from London', 23 Nov 1756: NLS SC 190, f.109; Sir George Lyttelton to W. Lyttelton, 25 Nov 1756: Lyttelton MSS, II, 313; Barrington to Mitchell, 28 Dec 1756: 6834, f.5.

141. Cf. N to Holdernesse, 29 Dec 1756: Eg 3430, f.48: 'I had last night the extracts as far as the 21st. I understand some posts are come in since, I wish you would order the copies of the King of Prussia's papers, as by your goodness I have all the former ones.'

142. George Dempster to Sir Adam Ferguson, 26 [Nov] 1756: J. Ferguson (ed.), *Letters of George Dempster to Sir Adam Ferguson 1756–1813* (London 1934) p.10.

143. Walpole to Mann, 29 Nov 1756: HW 21, p.22.

144. Symmer to Mitchell, 17 Dec 1756: 6839, f.26.

145. Fox to J. Campbell, 14 Dec 1756: 51406, f.30.

146. T. Potter to Wilkes, 14 Nov 1756: 30867, f.126.

147. Fox to Devonshire, Saturday [20 Nov 1756]: Dev 330/182; cf. Fox to Bedford, 20 Nov 1756: Bedford MSS, XXXII, 103.

148. Amyand did not contest the seat against Conyngham and never sat in Parliament again.

149. Fox to Devonshire, Sunday night [21 Nov 1756]: Dev 330/184.

150. Fox later claimed Sloper was given his seat at the Board of Trade on condition that he gave his interest at Great Bedwyn to Hay; but the ministers 'forgot to ask the interest of Lord Bruce and Lord Verney, so Hay lost it'. (H. Digby to Lord Digby, 14 Dec 1756: Digby MSS). There was no poll.

151. Bedford to Fox, 22 Nov 1756: Bedford MSS, XXXII, 105.

152. Cf. Fox to Bedford, 20 Nov 1756: Bedford MSS, XXXII, 103; Rigby to Fox, Sunday night [? 21 Nov 1756]: 51385, f.97.

153. Holdernesse to N, 22 Nov 1756: 32869, f.120; Walpole to Montagu, 25 Nov 1756: HW 9, p.203.
154. *Augustus Hervey Journal*, p.231.
155. Lady Grey to Lady Mary Gregory, 18 Nov 1756: Bedford RO, L30/9a/2, p.158.
156. Fox to Devonshire, 24 Nov 1756: Dev 330/185.
157. Lord Lyttelton to W. Lyttelton, 25 Nov 1756: Lyttelton MSS, II, 313.
158. Fox to Devonshire, Friday night [? 26 Nov 1756]: Dev 330/186.
159. Devonshire to Bedford, [18 Nov 1756]: Bedford MSS, XXXII, 99.
160. Fox to Bedford, 23 Nov 1756: Bedford MSS, XXXII, 107.
161. Fox to Devonshire, Friday night [? 26 Nov 1756]: Dev 330/186.
162. Lord Lyttelton to W. Lyttelton, 25 Nov 1756: Lyttelton MSS, II, 313.
163. Fox to Devonshire, 26 Nov 1756 (bis): Dev 330/187, 330/189; Memo, 'Stockbridge': Dev 330/188.
164. Rigby to Fox, Sunday night [28 Nov 1756]: 51385, f.99.
165. N to H, 23 Nov 1756: 35416, f.143.
166. Holdernesse to Mitchell, 3 Nov 1756: 6832, f.98.
167. Holdernesse to Joseph Yorke, 16 Nov 1756: Eg 3448, f.91.
168. Holdernesse to Mitchell, 26 Nov 1756: 6832, f.102.
169. Waldegrave, *Memoirs*, p.62.
170. Pitt to Devonshire, 23 Nov 1756: Dev 463/5. Pitt was about to leave for Hayes on 1 Nov; cf. W. Pitt to J. Pitt, Monday morning [1 Nov 1756]: Georgiana, Lady Chatterton (ed.), *Memorials, Personal and Historical of Admiral Lord Gambier, G.C.B.* (London, 1861), I, 76.
171. Pitt to Devonshire, 15 Nov 1756: Dev 463/3.
172. Pitt to Devonshire, 16 Nov 1756: Dev 463/4.
173. They were. A copy, dated 20 Nov 1756, is 32869, f.104.
174. G. Grenville to Pitt, 18 Nov 1756: PRO 30/8/1, f.140.
175. Holdernesse to N, 22 Nov 1756: 32869, f.120.
176. N to H, 23 Nov 1756: 35416, f.143.
177. Pitt to Devonshire, 23 Nov 1756: Dev 463/5.
178. Holdernesse to N, 29 Nov 1756: 32869, f.187.
179. Elliot noticed when it was read at the Cockpit that the passage 'the dismission of the Electoral troops', which originally followed 'desirous to remove all causes of discontent', had been moved to the end of the speech (G. Elliot to Bute, 9 o'clock [1 Dec 1756]: Bute MSS, Mount Stuart no. 99).
180. Pitt to Bute, [? 1 Dec 1756]: Bute MSS, Mount Stuart, no. 16; H. Digby to Lord Digby, 7 Dec 1756: Digby MSS.
181. Temple to Devonshire, 4 p.m. 1 Dec 1756: Dev 402/1.
182. G. Elliot to Bute, 9 o'clock [1 Dec 1756]: Mount Stuart, no. 99.
183. Devonshire to Temple, 2 Dec 1756: *Grenville Papers*, I, 184, and WLC.
184. Holdernesse to N, Wednesday night [1 Dec 1756]: 32869, f.211; cf. Glover, *Memoirs*, p.102. Gilbert Elliot thought the amendment 'seemed to have found its way into [the Address] after its being first adjusted' (G. Elliot to his wife, 31 Nov [*sic; sc.* 2 Dec 1756]: NLS 11007, f.30).
185. Lord Lyttelton to W. Lyttelton, 4 Dec 1756: Lyttelton MSS, II, f.317.
186. Mrs Grenville to George Grenville, Saturday [4 Dec 1756]: *Grenville Papers*, I, 185; G. Elliot to his wife, 4 Dec [1756]: NLS 11007, f.20. Glover

(*Memoirs*, pp.102–4) suggests the initiative to re-commit the Address was the King's, and that Granville talked him out of the attempt.

187. Fox was generally thought to be responsible: cf. Walpole to Mann, 8 Dec 1756: HW 21, p.30.

188. Pitt to Bute, Saturday morning [4 Dec 1756]: Bute MSS, Mount Stuart, Pitt letters no. 17.

189. G. Elliot to Bute, 9 o'clock [? 1 Dec 1756]: Bute MSS, Mount Stuart, no. 99.

190. Bayntun Rolt Diary, 1 Dec 1756.

191. James Grenville to George Grenville, 2 Dec 1756 [? *sc.* 1 Dec 1756]: *Grenville Papers*, i, 184, and WLC. This letter was probably written just after the Cockpit meeting on 1st. Later, it was through James Grenville that Sir Charles Mordaunt learnt of the postponement of significant Commons business (Newdigate Diary, 22 Dec 1756); but whether James Grenville was a regular channel of communication with the Tories is not known.

192. Nathaniel Ryder Diary, 2 Dec 1756.

193. G. Elliot to his wife, 31 November [*sic. sc.* 2 Dec 1756]: NLS 11007, f.30.

194. Bayntun Rolt Diary, 2 Dec 1756.

195. Lord Lyttelton to W. Lyttelton, 4 Dec 1756: Lyttelton MSS, ii, f.317.

196. H. Digby to Lord Digby, 7 Dec 1756: Digby MSS.

197. Barrington to Mitchell, 28 Dec 1756: 6834, f.5.

198. Fox to Devonshire, 26 Nov 1756: Dev 330/187.

199. Lord Lyttelton to W. Lyttelton, 4 Dec 1756: loc. cit.

200. H. Digby to Lord Digby, 7 Dec 1756: Digby MSS.

201. Such an expectation survived among the Tories, at least at Bristol: cf. J. Tucker to Dr Forster, 22 Dec 1756: 11275, f.173.

202. J. Campbell to Fox, 30 Nov 1756: 51406, f.28.

203. Walpole, *George II*, ii, 276.

204. Lord Lyttelton to W. Lyttelton, 4 Dec 1756: loc. cit.

205. Cf. Earl of Lichfield to Brudenell Rooke, 13 Nov [1756]: Rooke MSS, D 1833 F 1.

206. H to Charles Yorke, 5 Dec 1756: 35353, f.204.

207. Sir Richard Lyttelton to W. Lyttelton, nd [? mid Dec 1756]: Lyttelton MSS, ii, 296.

208. A copy, addressed to Sir Edmund Isham, is Isham MSS, 2918 (italics added). The signatories were: William Northey, Sir Walter Bagot, Sir Robert Burdett, Hon. John Ward, John Walter, Sir Armine Wodehouse, Lord Lichfield, Lord Windsor, Hon. Robert Lee, Sir John Philipps, Sir Charles Mordaunt, Sir Cordell Firebrace.

    The circular was evidently written out earlier, and the date on which Members were asked to attend after the adjournment, 13 December, filled in afterwards. Another version was probably soon in circulation; Fox recorded seeing a copy signed in addition by Charles Amcotts, Lord Talbot 'and another Lord or two' besides Windsor and Lichfield; Prowse's name was again noticeably absent (Fox to J. Campbell, 14 Dec 1756: 51406, f.30).

209. Barrington to N, 7 Dec 1756: 32869, f.266.

210. He arrived c.18 Nov: Hume Campbell to Marchmont, 18 Nov 1756: HMC *Polwarth*, v, 331.

211. H. Digby to Lord Digby, 7 Dec 1756: Digby MSS; N to Col Joseph Yorke, 6 Dec 1756: 32869, f.260.
212. Pitt to Devonshire, 16 Nov 1756: Dev 463/4.
213. Pitt to Devonshire, [28 Nov 1756]: Dev 463/6.
214. Fox to Devonshire, 29 Nov 1756: Dev 330/190.
215. Fox to Devonshire, 30 Nov 1756: Dev 330/191.
216. Devonshire to Fox, 30 Nov 1756: 51382, f.86.
217. Fox to Devonshire, [3 Dec 1756]: Dev 330/192; Fox, draft letter, nd [but c. 5 Dec 1756]: 51382, f.91; Devonshire to Fox, 4 Dec 1756: 51382, f.89.
218. Fox to his wife, Saturday [4 Dec 1756]: 51416, f.5.
219. Walpole to Fox, 4 Dec 1756: HW 30, p.129; Lord Lyttelton to W. Lyttelton, 4 Dec 1756: Lyttelton MSS, II, f.317.
220. Fox to Walpole, 5 Dec 1756: HW 30, p.130.
221. Barrington to N, 7 Dec 1756: 32869, f.266.
222. N to Holdernesse, 10 Dec 1756: Eg 3430, f.42.
223. Fox to Ellis, 11 Dec 1756: 51387, f.57.
224. Walpole to Mann, 29 Nov 1756: HW 21, p.22.
225. H to Charles Yorke, 28 Nov 1756: 35353, f.200.
226. H to Charles Yorke, 5 Dec 1756: 35353, f.204. It is not clear whether the first meeting took place.
227. Source for the meeting: H to N, 6 Dec 1756: 32869, f.253.
228. N to Holdernesse, 10 Dec 1756: Eg 3430, f.42.
229. N to H, 11 Dec 1756: 32869, f.320.
230. N to H, 5 Dec 1756: 32869, f.249.
231. Ellis to Fox, 11 Dec 1756: 51387, f.59.
232. Bedford's appointment was formally made in Council on 15 Dec: *Public Advertiser*, 14–18 Dec 1756.
233. H to N, 7 Dec 1756: 32869, f.264.
234. Holdernesse to Mitchell, 7 Dec 1756: 6832, f.104.
235. Holdernesse to Joseph Yorke, 7 Dec 1756: Eg 3448, f.108.
236. N to Holdernesse, 10 Dec 1756: Eg 3430, f.42.
237. N to H, 11 Dec 1756: 32869, f.320.
238. N to Holdernesse, 12 Dec 1756: Eg 3430, f.46; Holdernesse to N, Sunday noon [12 Dec 1756]: 32869, f.349.
239. H to N, 12 Dec 1756: 32869, f.347.
240. Fox to his wife, Monday [13 Dec 1756]: 51416, f.7.
241. C. Montagu to Earl of Guilford, 18 Dec 1756: Bod MS, North d 7, f.71.
242. H. Digby to Lord Digby, 14 Dec 1756: Digby MSS.
243. Dupplin to N, 13 Dec [1756]: 32869, f.355.
244. Symmer to Mitchell, 17 Dec 1756: 6839, f.26.
245. Fox to J. Campbell, 14 Dec 1756: 51406, f.30.
246. Glover, *Memoirs*, p.110.
247. Walpole, *George II*, II, 314–6.
248. Symmer to Mitchell, 17 Dec 1756: 6839, f.26.
249. Dupplin to N, 13 Dec [1756]: 32869, f.355.
250. Fox to Lord Digby, 14 Dec 1756: Digby MSS.
251. Fox to J. Campbell, 14 Dec 1756: 51406, f.30.
252. Dupplin to N, 13 Dec [1756]: 32869, f.355.
253. Fox to Lord Digby, 14 Dec 1756: Digby MSS.

254. Fox to J. Campbell, 14 Dec 1756: 51406, f.30.
255. Pitt [to G. Grenville] [12 Dec 1756]: *Grenville Papers*, i, 187, and WLC.
256. Fox to his wife, 14 Dec 1756: 51416, f.9. Fox, by force of habit, still referred to Hardwicke as Lord Chancellor.
257. Fox to his wife, 16 Dec 1756: 51416, f.11.
258. Walpole to Mann, 16 Dec 1756: HW 21, p.32.
259. Cf. Nathaniel Ryder Diary, 14 Dec 1756.
260. Hume Campbell to Marchmont, 14 Dec 1756: HMC *Polwarth*, v, 331.
261. II to N, 15 Dec 1756: 32869, f.367.
262. Cf. Newdigate Diary, 15 Dec 1756.
263. H. V. Jones to N, 7 Dec 1756: 32869, f.268.
264. Bayntun Rolt Diary, 15 Dec 1756.
265. Ibid. 20 Dec 1756.
266. Symmer to Mitchell, 17 Dec 1756: 6839, f.26.
267. Barrington to Mitchell, 28 Dec 1756: 6834, f.5.
268. Bayntun Rolt Diary, 17 Dec 1756.
269. Barrington to N, 11 Dec 1756: 32869, f.331.
270. Calcraft to Earl of Loudoun, 7 Jan 1757: 17493, f.25; Temple to G. Grenville, Tuesday [14 Dec 1756]: *Grenville Papers*, i, 187 and WLC.
271. Pitt to George Grenville, 15 Dec [1756]: *Grenville Papers*, i, 188 and WLC.
272. Nathaniel Ryder Diary, 15 Dec 1756.
273. Nathaniel Ryder Diary, 17 Dec 1756.
274. H. S. Conway to Lord Stormont, 18 Dec 1756: Mansfield MSS, B 1383.
275. Pitt to ?, 18 Dec 1756: 53709 F; Pitt to Devonshire, 19 Dec 1756: Dev. 463/7.
276. Fox to [Lord Digby], 18 Dec 1756: Digby MSS.
277. Fox to his wife, 18 Dec 1756: 51416, f.13.
278. Barrington to N, Thursday evening [? 16 Dec 1756]: 32869, f.387.
279. Barrington to Mitchell, 28 Dec 1756: 6834, f.5.
280. Before Christmas, he appeared only twice at Court (1 and 4 December) and twice in the Commons (2 and 3 December).
281. Glover, *Memoirs*, p.104.
282. H. Digby to Lord Digby, 23 Dec 1756: Digby MSS.
283. Barrington to Mitchell, 28 Dec 1756: 6834, f.5.
284. Rigby to Bedford, 6 p.m. Wednesday [22 Dec 1756]: Bedford MSS, XXXII, f.115; H. Digby to Lord Digby, 23 Dec 1756: Digby MSS.
285. Walpole to Mann, 23 Dec 1756: HW 21, p.34. Byng's Court Martial met on 28 December: its verdict could not be expected by 6 January.
286. H. Digby to Lord Digby, 23 Dec 1756: Digby MSS; Nathaniel Ryder Diary, 23 Dec 1756; Rigby to Bedford, Thursday 7 p.m. [23 Dec 1756]: Bedford MSS, XXXII, f.119 (giving John Waldegrave's account of the debate).
287. Calcraft to Earl of Loudoun, 7 Jan 1757: 17493, f.25.
288. Barrington to Mitchell, 28 Dec 1756: 6834, f.5.
289. *CJ*, XXVII, p.667.
290. Fox to Hanbury Williams, 26 Dec 1756: Stowe MSS, 263, f.12.
291. N to J. Roberts, 26 Dec 1756: 32869, f.399.
292. N to Sir Thomas Robinson, 27 Dec 1756: 32869, f.402.
293. N to Duchess, 27 Dec 1756: 33075, f.111.

294. Hume Campbell to Marchmont, 27 Dec 1756: HMC *Polwarth*, v, 332.
295. N to Duchess, 3 Jan 1757: 33075 f.115.
296. Hume Campbell to Marchmont, 27 Dec 1756: HMC *Polwarth*, v, 332.
297. Barrington to Mitchell, 28 Dec 1756: 6834, f.5.
298. Bayntun Rolt Diary, 23 Dec 1756 (reporting Lord Thomond).
299. J. Roberts to N, 28 Dec 1756: 32869, f.406.
300. Sir Thomas Robinson to N, 28 Dec 1756: 32869, f.410.
301. H. V. Jones to N, 30 Dec 1756: 32869, f.424; N to Bentinck, 30 Dec 1756: 35416, f.155.
302. N to H, 4 Jan 1757: 35416, f.162; H to N, 7 Jan 1757: 32870, f.58.
303. Bayntun Rolt Diary, 24 Jan 1757.
304. N to H, 9 Jan 1757: 32870, f.70.
305. Countess of Mansfield to Lord Stormont, 8 Jan 1757: Mansfield MSS, B 1390.
306. Charles Lyttelton to William Lyttelton, 18 Jan [1757]: Lyttelton MSS, II, 321.
307. Fox to wife, 11 Jan 1757: 51416, f.17.
308. Rigby to Bedford, Thursday evening 20 Jan [1757]: Bedford MSS, XXXIII, 35.
309. Symmer to Mitchell, 20 Jan 1757: 6839, f.32.
310. Rigby to Bedford, Tuesday 8 o'clock [18 Jan 1757]: Bedford MSS, XXXIII, 24.
311. Rigby to Bedford, 27 Jan 1757: Bedford MSS, XXXIII, 47.
312. Newdigate Diary, 14 Jan 1757. Present were: Whigs: George and Charles Townshend; Lord Pultney; Edward Vernon; Tories: William Vaughan; Sir John Philipps; Velters Cornewall; Sir Charles Mordaunt; Sir Armine Wodehouse; William Bagot; Nicholas Fazackerley; Gabriel Hanger; John Morton; William Harvey; Hon. John Ward; John Affleck; Robert Vyner [? senior]; [? William] Beckford; William Northey; Sir Roger Newdigate. Again, Prowse is not listed.
313. George Townshend to Pitt, 15 Jan 1757: PRO 30/8/1, f.168.
314. Rigby to Bedford, Tuesday 8 o'clock [18 Jan 1757]: Bedford MSS, XXIII, 24.
315. *CJ*, XXVII, 660. On 1 Feb the Call was again postponed until 15 Feb; on 15 Feb until 8 March; and on 8 Mar until 29 Mar. But on 22 Mar, Fox suggested its postponement until 19 April, and this was agreed to.
316. West to N, 25 Jan 1757: 32870, f.105.
317. *The Enquiry is not Begun!* (London, 1757).
318. Cf. Charles Lyttelton to William Lyttelton, 18 Jan [1757]: Lyttelton MSS, II, 321; Rigby to Bedford, 20 Jan [1757]: Bedford MSS, XXIII, 35. Byng's trial ended on 20 Jan, and the Court Martial delivered its verdict on 27th.
319. Rigby to Bedford, Monday night 8 o'clock [17 Jan 1757]: Bedford MSS, XXXIII, 22.
320. Rigby to Bedford, Wednesday 6 o'clock [26 Jan 1757]: Bedford MSS, XXXIII, 45.
321. Rigby to Bedford, Wednesday 4 p.m. [19 Jan 1757]: Bedford MSS, XXXIII, f.33.
322. Lord Lyttelton to W. Lyttelton, 30 Jan 1757: Lyttelton MSS, II, 323.

323. Rigby to Bedford, Tuesday night [25 Jan 1757]: *Bedford Corr* II, 225; Newdigate Diary, 25 Jan 1757.
324. Hume Campbell to N, 25 Jan 1757; 32870, f.111.
325. Dupplin to N, past 6 o'clock [26 Jan 1757]: 32870, f.115.
326. Ibid.; Newdigate Diary, 26 Jan 1757; Nathaniel Ryder Diary, 26 Jan 1757.
327. Newdigate Diary, 27 Jan 1757.
328. N to H, Thursday night [27 Jan 1757]: 35416, f.176; Nathaniel Ryder Diary, 1 Feb 1757.
329. Rigby to Bedford, 20 Jan [1757]: Bedford MSS, XXXIII, f.35.
330. Kildare to Fox, 2 Dec 1757: 51426, f.88.
331. Münchausen to N, 28 Jan 1757: 32870, f.125.
332. Chesterfield to his son, 12 Jan 1757: Dobrée, v, 2216.
333. Glover (*Memoirs*, p.116) claims George Townshend deliberately postponed it for this reason.
334. Glover, *Memoirs*, p. 119.
335. Lyttelton to Admiral Smith, 31 Jan 1757: Lyttelton MSS, II, 327.
336. Admiral West to Temple, nd: M. Wyndham (ed.), *Chronicles of the Eighteenth Century* (London, 1924) II, 244.
337. Glover, *Memoirs*, p.120.
338. Gilbert Elliot to Lord Minto, [Feb 1757]: NLS 11001, f.30.
339. Rigby to Bedford, 3 Feb 1757: Bedford MSS, XXXIII, 58.
340. N to Rockingham, 8 Feb 1757: WWM, R 1–87.
341. Temple to Bute, 2 o'clock [Feb 1757]; Bute MSS, Mount Stuart, no. 28; Temple to Bute, [15 Feb 1757]: ibid., no. 28a.
342. *Augustus Hervey Journal* p.231.
343. J. Campbell to his wife, 17 Feb 1757: Cawdor MSS, 1/128.
344. Waldegrave, *Memoirs*, p.91.
345. N to Rockingham, 8 Feb 1757: WWM, R1–87.
346. North to Guilford, 1 Feb 1757: Bod MS, North d.23, f.54.
347. Symmer to Mitchell, 1 Feb 1757: 6839, f.36.
348. H to Anson, 2 Feb 1757: 15956, f.31.
349. Rigby to Bedford, 3 Feb 1757: Bedford MSS, XXXIII, 58.
350. Pitt to Bute, Friday [4 Feb 1757]: Bute MSS, Mount Stuart, Pitt Letters no. 20; Pitt to Devonshire, 4 Feb [1757]: Dev 463/10. It is not clear whether Lyttelton's championing Byng's cause began before or after this refusal.
351. Newdigate Diary, 1 Feb 1757.
352. Glover, *Memoirs*, p.107. It is not clear which Waller is meant.
353. H to P.C. Webb, 2 Jan 1757: 35595, f.2; H to Anson, 26 Jan 1757: 15956, f.27. The ministry's defence, 31959, was published in H. W. Richmond (ed.), *Papers Relating to the Loss of Minorca in 1756* (London, 1913). A list of expected Old Corps supporters was drawn up (6 Feb 1757: 32997, f.113) which suggests that 282 votes were relied on as certain and 107 as doubtful.
354. Cf. H. S. Conway to Lord Stormont, 18 Dec 1756: Mansfield MSS, B 1383.
355. Rigby to Bedford, 7 Feb 1757: Bedford MSS, XXXIII, 71.
356. N to Rockingham, 8 Feb 1757: WWM, R1–87.

357. Lewis Watson to Rockingham, 7 Feb 1757: WWM, R1–86.
358. *CJ*, xxvii, 687; Newcastle to Rockingham, 8 Feb 1757: WWM, R1–87; Newdigate Diary, 8 Feb 1757.
359. Rigby to Bedford, 8 Feb 1757: Bedford MSS, xxxiii, f.74.
360. Walpole to Mann, 13 Feb 1757: HW 21, p.54.
361. Walpole, *George II*, ii, 305.
362. G. Townshend to Pitt, 14 Feb [1757]: PRO 30/8/1, f.172.
363. Newdigate Diary, 15 Feb 1757.
364. B. Tunstall, *Admiral Byng and the Loss of Minorca* (London, 1928) p.256.
365. Nathaniel Ryder Diary, 17 Feb 1757.
366. H to Charles Yorke, 17 Feb [1757]: 35353, f.210.
367. J. Campbell to his wife, 17 Feb 1757: Cawdor MSS, 1/128.
368. Nathaniel Ryder Diary, 17 Feb 1757; cf. Newdigate Diary, 17 Feb 1757. Ryder confused Sir Francis with Sir James, who was out of parliament 1754–61.
369. H. Digby to Ilchester, 1 Mar 1757: 51341, f.42.
370. Nathaniel Ryder Diary, 17 Feb 1757.
371. Newdigate Diary, 17 Feb 1757.
372. Glover, *Memoirs*, p.112.
373. Charles Jenkinson to Sanderson Miller, 19 Feb [1757], Sanderson Miller MSS, 821.
374. H. Digby to Lord Ilchester, 1 Mar 1757: 51341, f.42.
375. Pitt to Bute, 19 February [1757]: Bute MSS, Mount Stuart, Pitt Letters no. 21.
376. Walpole, *George II*, ii, 314–17: '...when Bedford proved as untamed as Pitt had been; and when Pitt condescended to make room in his virtue for Hanover, Lord George, (as the Primate with wonderful frankness avowed to Fox), finding that Mr Pitt "would now pursue human measures by human means", made no difficulty of uniting with him. Lord George gave the same account to Fox too. Another reason of mortal complexion had probably some sway with Lord George – of nothing he was so jealous as of Conway. Fox had supported the latter's plan of militia; and the Duke of Richmond, brother of Lady Caroline Fox, was on the point of marrying Lady Mary Bruce, daughter in law of Mr. Conway. If Lord George then looked on the connexion of Fox and Conway as imminent and certain, no wonder he devoted himself to the contrary faction.'
377. H. Digby to Lord Ilchester, 1 Mar 1757: 51341, f.42.
378. Nathaniel Ryder Diary, 18 Feb 1757.
379. Holdernesse to Mitchell, 22 Feb 1757: Eg 3460, f.183.
380. Charles Jenkinson to Sanderson Miller, 19 Feb [1757]: Sanderson Miller MSS, 821; cf. Newdigate Diary, 18 Feb 1757.
381. Pitt to Bute, 19 Feb [1757]: loc. cit.
382. Bute to Pitt, Saturday [? 19 Feb 1757]: PRO 30/8/1, f.174; misdated 2 Mar 1757 in *Chatham Corr*, i, 223.
383. H to N, 19 Feb 1757: 32870, f.194.
384. Glover, *Memoirs*, p.112–15.
385. H. Digby to Lord Ilchester, 1 Mar 1757: 51341, f.42.

386. N to H, 20 Feb 1757: 32870, f.202; Sir Thomas Robinson to N, 19 Feb 1757; ibid. f.196.
387. H to N, 21 Feb 1757: 32870, f.210.
388. Newdigate Diary, 21 Feb 1757.
389. Walpole, *George II*, II, 318; Newdigate Diary, 22 Feb 1757; Western, *English Militia*, pp.136–7.
390. Newdigate Diary, 24 Feb 1757.
391. E. Pyle to S. Kerrich, 22 Feb 1757: Kerrich MSS, vol. 14.
392. *Augustus Hervey Journal*, p.238.
393. H to N, 19 Feb 1757: 32870, f.194.
394. Ashburnham to N, Monday night [21 Feb 1757]: 32870, f.212.
395. Newdigate Diary, 23 Feb 1757.
396. Walpole, *George II*, II, 318–22.
397. H. Digby to Ilchester, 1 Mar 1757: 51341, f.42.
398. Walpole, *George II*, II, 323.
399. Symmer to Mitchell, 4 Mar 1757: 6839, f.40.
400. Walpole, *George II*, II, 323–6.
401. H. Digby to Lord Ilchester, 1 Mar 1757: 51341, f.42.
402. Glover, *Memoirs*, pp.120–1.
403. *Augustus Hervey Journal*, pp.238–9.
404. Fox to Lady Hervey, 23 Feb 1757: Ilchester, *Fox* II, 25; cf. Pitt to Bute, Wednesday night [23 Feb 1757]: Bute MSS, Mount Stuart, Pitt letters no. 22.
405. Cf. Rigby to Bedford, 10.15 Thursday evening [3 Mar 1757]: Bedford MSS, XXXIII, 95: 'Lord Temple pressed him some days ago very strongly for a pardon for Mr Byng, HM persevered, and told his lordship flatly, he thought him guilty of cowardice in the action, and therefore could not break his word they had forced him to give to his people, to pardon no delinquents. His lordship walked up to his nose, and sans autre cérémonie, said, "what shall you think if he dies courageously?" HM stifled his anger, and made him no reply. I think I never heard of such insolence'. Walpole, *George II*, II, 326 supplies the date, 24 Feb.
406. Walpole (*George II*, II, 327) represents Norris, Keppel and Moore as eager for such a step on 25th, and claims that George Grenville refused their entreaties that day to ask the Commons to absolve them from their oath of secrecy. But Walpole claims, perhaps falsely, that he was unaware, when he arrived at the House on 25th, of Keppel's desire to be released, and that he, Walpole, approached first Fox (unsuccessfully) then Sir Francis Dashwood at the last possible moment to speak on Keppel's behalf (Walpole being temporarily without a seat pending re-election). Walpole's story was probably meant to disguise Keppel's unwillingness to speak.
407. *Augustus Hervey Journal*, pp.239–40.
408. Walpole, *George II*, II, 328.
409. H. Digby to Lord Ilchester, 1 Mar 1757: 51341, f.42.
410. *Augustus Hervey Journal*, pp.239–40.
411. E. Owen to E. Weston, 26 Feb 1757: HMC 10th Rep. App. I, p.312.
412. E. Owen to E. Weston, 26 Feb 1757: loc. cit.; Newdigate Diary, 25 Feb 1757.

413. Cf. Council Minute, 26 Feb 1757: PRO 30/8/78, f.18. Those present: Granville, Gower, Bedford, Devonshire, Argyll, Marlborough, Dorset, Rochford, Temple, Pitt, Legge, Sir Thomas Robinson, Holdernesse.
414. Sir Thomas Robinson to N, 10 o'clock [p.m.] 26 Feb 1757: 32870, f.220.
415. Walpole, *George II*, II, 331. Walpole's source is not known; the remark is not recorded elsewhere, even in his letters of this period. It may well be only a fragment of the myth that began to grow up around Pitt only a few years later.
416. Sir T. Robinson to N, 26 Feb 1757: 32870, f.220; West Memo, nd [26 Feb 1757]: 32870, f.218; Walpole, *George II*, II, 332–3.
417. J. S. Mackenzie to Bute, [26 Feb 1757]: Bute MSS, Mount Stuart, no. 16.
418. Norris, Holmes, Moore and Geary. J. Campbell to his wife, 1 Mar 1757: Cawdor MSS, 1/128.
419. Halifax to Dodington, [26 Feb 1757]: HMC *Various*, VI, p.36.
420. N to Duchess, 27 Feb 1757: 33075, f.119.
421. Newdigate Diary, 28 Feb 1757. This was considered an atypical division, most MPs having already left.
422. *Augustus Hervey Journal*, p.241; Walpole, *George II*, II, 342.
423. J. Campbell to his wife, 1 Mar 1757: Cawdor MSS, 1/128.
424. E. Owen to E. Weston, 5 Mar 1757: HMC 10th Rep. App. I, p.312.
425. Cf. C. Jenkinson to Sanderson Miller, 1 M[ar 1757]: Sanderson Miller MSS, 324.
426. J. Campbell to his wife, 1 Mar 1757: Cawdor MSS, 1/128.
427. Ibid.
428. Charles Jenkinson to Sanderson Miller, 1 M[ar 1757]: Sanderson Miller MSS, 324.
429. *Augustus Hervey Journal*, p.241; *Parl Hist*, xv, cols 807–21; *LJ* xxix, 58–64.
430. Nathaniel Ryder Diary, 8 [*sc.* 2] March 1757.
431. An attempt to have the Common Council of the City of London petition the King in Byng's favour failed; and it was not taken up by any politician at Westminster. Cf. H to N, 11 Mar 1757: 32870, f.260; [West to N], 6 o'clock [11 Mar 1757]: 32870, f.254.
432. *Augustus Hervey Journal*, p.241.
433. E. Owen to E. Weston, 5 Mar 1757: loc. cit.
434. H. Digby to Lord Ilchester, 1 Mar 1757: 51341, f.42.
435. Cf. Calcraft to Loudoun, 4 Mar 1757: 17493, f.49.
436. Waldegrave, *Memoirs*, p.91.
437. Fox also sought to keep Ellis and Hamilton, among his friends, fully informed. Cf. Fox to Lord [? Holdernesse], 6 Mar 1757: 51430, f.54.
438. Glover, *Memoirs*, p.115: 'The court members had constantly been lavish of their sneers on Mr Pitt's connection with Tories and Jacobites.' Glover greatly exaggerated.
439. J. Campbell to his wife, 1 Mar 1757: Cawdor MSS, 1/128.
440. Rigby to Bedford, Thursday evening [3 Mar 1757]: Bedford MSS, XXXIII, 95.
441. Holdernesse to Mitchell, 4 Mar 1757: Eg 3460, f.193.
442. Waldegrave, *Memoirs*, pp.94–6, 99.
443. N to Waldegrave, 1 Mar 1757: 32870, f.230.

444. Rigby to Bedford, Ten o'clock Saturday [? 5 Mar 1757]: Bedford MSS, XXXIII, 97.

445. Waldegrave, *Memoirs*, pp.96–8.

446. Fox to Lord Ilchester, 4 Mar 1757: 51420, f.52.

447. Fox, Memo, nd [? c. 4 Mar 1757]: 51430, f.50 (probably meant to be communicated to the King by Waldegrave) lists: 'D of Newcastle Prime Minister of England and First Lord of the Treasury; D of Devonshire Master of the Horse; Ld G. Sackville Secretary of State, *vice* Pitt, which might make the D of Dorset likewise willing to resign Master of the Horse; Charles Townshend Secretary at War; Earl of Halifax First Lord of the Admiralty; Lord Dupplin First Lord of Trade; D of Bedford Minister independent for Ireland; D of Argyll do. for Scotland; H. Fox Paymaster, with a security to his family, of what sort HM may like best, against the anger of next reign; Lord Ilchester Treasurer of the Chambers; some necessary borough favours, which have been promised, to be performed immediately; if Lord Mansfield would consider this as permanent enough to induce him to be Lord Chancellor it would remain firm'.

448. Ibid.

449. Cf. Calcraft to Loudoun, 4 Mar 1757: 17493, f.49.

450. Fox to Ilchester, 4 Mar 1757: 51420, f.52.

451. Fox to Ilchester, 5 Mar 1757: 51420, f.58.

452. Ilchester to Fox, Saturday morning 12 o'clock March [? 5, 1757]: 51420, f.54.

453. Digby apparently assumed that Holdernesse would continue to occupy the other Secretaryship.

454. Lord Digby to Fox, Tuesday [? 8 Mar 1757]: 51423, f.90.

455. Waldegrave, *Memoirs*, pp.98–9.

456. N to H, 5 Mar 1757: 35416, f.178.

457. Fox to Ilchester, 4 Mar 1757: 51420, f.52.

458. N to H, 5 Mar 1757: 35416, f.178.

459. N to Mansfield, 5 Mar 1757: 32870, f.239.

460. Waldegrave, *Memoirs*, pp.101–2.

461. Sir H. Erskine to Bute, 7 Mar [1757]: Bute MSS, Mount Stuart, no. 29; cf. Bayntun Rolt Diary, 10 Mar 1757.

462. Waldegrave, *Memoirs*, p.100.

463. Fox to Ilchester, 7 Mar 1757: 51420, f.61.

464. Cf. C. Talbot to S. Miller, 9 Mar 1757: Sanderson Miller MSS, CR 125B/224.

465. N, Memo, 9 Mar 1757: 32870, f.250.

466. Ilchester to Fox, 7 Mar 1757: 51420, f.59.

467. Rigby to Bedford, Thursday evening [3 Mar 1757]: Bedford MSS, XXXIII, 95.

468. Symmer to Mitchell, 1 Mar 1757: 6839, f.43.

469. Nathaniel Ryder Diary, 9 Mar 1757.

470. Ibid. 10 Mar 1757. On 10th Fox dwelt on Pitt's inconsistency, noticing 'great unanimity this year in the same things which were greatly found fault with the last ... Mr Fox asked whether the giving money to the Continent this year, was the same thing as being against continental measures before ...' 'Mr Pitt said he was one of the present administra-

tion but had no regard for that but for the good of the whole – that a millstone of two pounds might not sink a man though a millstone of four might' (West to N, [? 11 Mar 1757]: 32870, f.256).

471. Bathurst to Rev. J. Perry, 10 Mar 1757: BM loan 57/1.
472. Nathaniel Ryder Diary, 14 Mar 1757; Newdigate Diary, 14 Mar 1757.
473. [West to N], 10 o'clock 14 Mar [1757]: 32870, f.275; Sir G. Lee to N, 11 Mar 1757: 32870, f.262.
474. Cf. N to H, 12 Mar 1757: 32870, f.264.
475. Fox to Dodington, Saturday morning [12 Mar 1757]: 38091, f.72. This is the scheme set out in Fox's memo, nd [? c. 12 Mar 1757]: 51430, f.61, a list of 'an administration which the late Ministers would engage to support, without being of it, as their return to the ministry now would not fail of reviving the old clamour'. John Tucker, Henry Digby and George Onslow were to be given seats at the Board of Trade; Egmont was to be Treasurer of the Navy; Lord Strange, Chancellor of the Duchy of Lancaster; and Lord Edgcumbe have the Jewel Office. Fox would take the Paymastership at the end of the session.
476. Halifax to Dodington, Saturday night [12 Mar 1757]: HMC *Various*, VI, p.38.
477. *Sic.* Cumberland is probably meant.
478. N to H, 12 Mar 1757: 32870, f.264; 13 Mar 1757: 35416, f.180.
479. Holdernesse to N, Tuesday night [15 Mar 1757]: 32870, f.285. The death of Dr Herring, Archbishop of Canterbury, on 13 March entailed a major reshuffle.
480. Temple to Bute, 15 Mar 1757: Bute MSS, Mount Stuart, no. 22.
481. Walpole, *George II*, II, 379. The date of Temple's message is not clear.
482. Halifax to Fox, Wednesday night [? 16 Mar 1757]: 51430, f.71 (the MSS has the suggested date 23 March – but cf. Halifax to Fox, 24 Mar 1757: 51430, f.73).
483. Fox to Dodington, 15 Mar 1757: 38091, f.74.
484. Ellis to Fox, Tuesday [? 15 Mar 1757]: 51387, f.62.
485. Fox to Dodington, 16 Mar 1757: 38091, f.76.
486. Egmont to N, 14 Mar 1757: 32870, f.279.
487. N to Egmont, 16 Mar 1757: 32870, f.295.
488. H to N, Wednesday morning 16 Mar 1757: 32870, f.297.
489. N to the King, 16 Mar 1757: 32870, f.291.
490. R. Watson to Rockingham [18 Mar 1757]: WWM R1-88.
491. Newdigate Diary, 18 Mar 1757; cf. Fox to Devonshire, 15 Mar 1757: Dev 330/195.
492. Dodington to Fox, near 12 at night 18 Mar [1757]: 38091, f.78. Carswell and Dralle, [Dodington, *Diary*, p.357] suggest Sir Thomas Robinson as possible interviewee.
493. Halifax to Fox, 18 Mar 1757: 51430, f.59.
494. Fox to Waldegrave, 19 Mar 1757: 51380, f.7; a draft of the scheme is almost certainly the undated memo, 51430, f.67.
495. Fox, scheme [c. 19 Mar 1757]: 51430, f.67; cf. Waldegrave, *Memoirs*, pp.102-3.
496. 51430, f.67. The lesser terms were: Lord Strange, Chancellor of the Duchy *vice* Lord Edgcumbe, removed to the Jewel Office or some other compensa-

tion. George Grenville's seat at the Treasury was to go to the Earl of Thomond or John Campbell. Hans Stanley, Thomas Whichcot, John Proby
(Baron Carysfort), and William Gerard Hamilton were to come into seats
at the Admiralty; new Lords of Trade were to be John Tucker, Harry
Digby and George Onslow, with George and Charles Townshend 'if
they will come'; for Fox, if his preferred 'mark of favour' [presumably
a pension] were impossible, a reversion for his children or a pension for
a term of years; an English peerage for Lord Shelburne; and an earldom
for Lord Digby.

497. Waldegrave, *Memoirs*, p.103.
498. Waldegrave to Fox, [19 Mar 1757]: 51380, f.9.
499. Waldegrave, *Memoirs*, pp.104–5.
500. Bayntun Rolt Diary, 21 Mar 1757.
501. Fox to Waldegrave, 20 Mar 1757: 51380, f.10.
502. Fox to Dodington, Sunday night [20 Mar 1757]: 38091, f.79.
503. C. Jenkinson to S. Miller, 22 Mar 1757: Sanderson Miller MSS,
327.
504. Rigby to Bedford, 21 Mar 1757: Bedford MSS, xxxiii, 112.
505. Fox to Dodington, Sunday night [20 Mar 1757]: 38091, f.79.
506. Rigby to Bedford, 22 Mar 1757: Bedford MSS, xxxiii, 115.
507. Newdigate Diary, 21 Mar 1757; Rigby to Bedford, 21 Mar 1757: Bedford
MSS, xxxiii, 112.
508. Rigby to Bedford, 22 Mar 1757: Bedford MSS, xxxiii, 115.
509. Lord Breadalbane to Charles Erskine, 15 Mar 1757: NLS 5079, f.121.
510. Dodington, *Diary*, 21 Mar 1757.
511. Walpole, *George II*, ii, 379.
512. *CJ*, xxvii, p.788; West to N, [22 Mar 1757]: 32870, f.309.
513. Rigby to Bedford, 22 Mar 1757: Bedford MSS, xxxiii, 115.
514. Dodington, *Diary*, 21 Mar 1757.
515. The latter possibility is implied in Rigby to Bedford, 22 Mar 1757:
Bedford MSS, xxxiii, 115.
516. Cf. H to N, 22 Mar 1757: 32870, f.319.
517. Sir T. Robinson to N, 22 Mar 1757: 32870, f.321.
518. Dodington, *Diary*, *sub* 21 Mar 1757.
519. Halifax to Fox, 24 Mar 1757: 51430, f.73.
520. Dodington, *Diary*, 24 Mar 1757.
521. Waldegrave, *Memoirs*, pp.105–6.
522. Walpole, *George II*, ii, 377.
523. 'Message by Lord Waldegrave', 25 Mar 1757: 32870, f.335.
524. Cf. Dodington, *Diary*, 26 Mar 1757.
525. N to George II, 25 Mar 1757: 32870, f.341.
526. Stone to N, 26 Mar 1757: 32870, f.343.
527. N to Duchess, 27 Mar 1757: 33075, f.120.
528. Fox to Cumberland, 30 Mar 1757: 51375, f.91.
529. [J. Almon], *A Review of the Reign of George II* (London, 1762) p.170.
530. Williams, *Pitt*, i, 317.

7. 'THE ARBITER OF ENGLAND'

1. H to N, 3 Apr 1757: 32870, f.358.
2. Walpole, *George II*, II, 376-7.
3. Cumberland to Fox, 2 Apr 1757: 51375, f.95.
4. Walpole, *George II*, III, 2.
5. Temple to George Grenville, [4 Apr 1757]: *Grenville Papers*, I, 191, and WLC. Probably in error, Temple included Lord Hyde in his forecast of the Board, though this made his list eight in number – one too many.
6. Cf. Newdigate Diary, 5 Apr 1757; George II to Holdernesse, [received 5 Apr 1757]: Eg 3425, f.38. 'Lord Carysfort is quite new, I suppose he comes from Lord Sandwich and Lord Gower. From what quarter does young Sandys come?' – H to Royston, 7 Apr 1757: 35351, f.366.
7. Fox to Ilchester, 5 Apr 1757: 51420, f.64.
8. Argyll to Fox, 3 Apr 1757: 51430, f.81.
9. Argyll to Fox, Monday morning 11 [? a.m. 4 Apr 1757]: 51430, f.83.
10. Hillsborough to Dodington, [2 Apr 1757]: HMC *Various*, VI, p.39; Fox to Ilchester, 5 Apr 1757: 51420, f.64.
11. Walpole, *George II*, II, 378.
12. Ibid. III, 2.
13. Ibid. III, 1; Legge to Devonshire, 6 Apr 1757: Dev 257/27.
14. Cf. Nathaniel Ryder to Oliver Peard, 5 Apr 1757: Harrowby MSS, Doc 42.
15. Fox to Mansfield, 1 Apr 1757: Catton MSS vol. 25; Mansfield to N, 4 Apr [1757]: 32870, f.362.
16. N to H, 8 Apr 1757: 35416, f.182. Winchelsea had been First Lord of the Admiralty 1742-4 while Granville (then Lord Carteret) had been Secretary of State.
17. Hon. Thomas Villiers (1709-86), MP for Tamworth 1747-56, created Baron Hyde 3 June 1756.
18. Mansfield to N, 4 Apr [1757]: 32870, f.362.
19. Walpole, *George II*, II, 377.
20. H to N, 3 Apr 1757: 32870, f.358.
21. Newdigate Diary, 5 Apr 1757.
22. He also obtained the King's promise of English peerages for Lord Digby and Lord Shelburne, but George II refused a peerage for Fox's wife.
23. Fox to Ilchester, 5 Apr 1757: 51420, f.64.
24. Cf. Walpole, *George II*, III, 2; Waldegrave, *Memoirs*, p.107.
25. N to H, 8 Apr 1757: 35416, f.182.
26. Cf. Temple to G. Grenville, [4 Apr 1757]: *Grenville Papers*, I, 191 and WLC.
27. Bayntun Rolt Diary, 1 Apr 1757.
28. Fox to Ilchester, 5 Apr 1757: 51420, f.64.
29. The House adjourned on 7 Apr and reassembled on 18 Apr.
30. Walpole, *George II*, III, 2. Later, Walpole corrected himself: 'The truth is, they [the Seals] have never been offered to him in form: he has been sounded, and I believe was not averse, but made excuses that were not thought invincible' (Walpole to Mann, 20 Apr 1757: HW 21, p.75).
31. Waldegrave, *Memoirs*, p.108. Waldegrave is vague about chronology at this point. Walpole (*George II*, III, 3) confirms the offer of a Secretary-ship to Robinson.

32. Cf. Newdigate Diary, '7 Apr 1757'. The date of this entry is in doubt.
33. Royston to H, 5 Apr 1757: 35351, f.364.
34. Walpole, *George II*, III, p.1.
35. N to H, 8 Apr 1757: 35416, f.182; Pitt to Bute, Wednesday 4 o'clock [6 Apr 1757]: Pitt MSS, Mount Stuart, no.23.
36. Cf. Legge to Devonshire, 6 Apr 1757: Dev 257/27.
37. G. Grenville to Holdernesse, 9 April 1757: Eg 3438, f.59.
38. Royston to H, 5 Apr 1757: 35351, f.364.
39. Fox to Ilchester, 5 Apr 1757: 51420, f.64.
40. Holdernesse to George II, 6 Apr 1757: Eg 3425, f.44.
41. Cumberland to Fox, Wednesday night [6 Apr 1757]: 51375, f.97.
42. Confirmation is lacking that Dodington ever was offered the Exchequer.
43. Calcraft to Lord Charles Hay, 6 Apr 1757: NLS Yester MSS, Box 15, F2(a).
44. Sir H. Erskine to George Grenville, [8 Apr 1757]: *Grenville Papers*, I, 189 (misdated 1 Apr), and WLC.
45. Calcraft to Lord Charles Hay, 8 Apr 1757: loc. cit.
46. Calcraft to Loudoun, 9 Apr 1757: 17493, f.56.
47. Walpole, *George II*, III, 3.
48. Mansfield to N, 8 Apr 1757: 32870, f.389.
49. J. Campbell to his wife, 7 Apr 1757: Cawdor MSS, 1/128.
50. Holdernesse to N, Wednesday night [6 Apr 1757]: 32870, f.368.
51. Walpole, *George II*, III, 2.
52. Sir H. Erskine to G. Grenville, [8 Apr 1757]: *Grenville Papers*, I, 189 (misdated 1 Apr), and WLC.
53. Calcraft to Loudoun, 9 Apr 1757: 17493, f.56.
54. Halifax to N, 7 Apr 1757: 32870, f.370.
55. Cf. Royston to H, 5 Apr 1757: 35351, f. 364. It was one of a series of such meetings: others were held at Anson's house on 14th, at Cleveland's on 15th, and another on 18th.
56. H to Royston, 7 Apr 1757: 35351, f.366.
57. Walpole, *George II*, III, 3–4.
58. Erskine to George Grenville, [8 Apr 1757]: loc. cit.; cf. Barrington to Sanderson Miller, 7 Apr 1757: Sanderson Miller MSS, C1256/832.
59. Walpole to Mann, 7 Apr 1757: HW 21, p.72.
60. Fox to Sir J. G. Downing, nd [? c.7–8 Apr 1757]: 51403, f.3. Fox's confidence in Egremont's likely acceptance 'this week' dates the letter no later than Sunday, 10 April.
61. Cf. Devonshire to Fox, 15 Apr 1757: 51382, f.102; West to N, 15 Apr 1757: 32870, f.437; Fox to Devonshire, 19 Apr 1757: Dev 330/198; Legge to Devonshire, 24 Apr 1757: Dev 257/28.
62. Mr Abercromby to Halifax, in Halifax to N, 7 Apr 1757: 32870, f.372.
63. Glover, *Memoirs*, pp.125–32. Glover almost certainly overestimated his own importance, and the theatrical rhetoric of his warnings to Pitt as he records them many be discounted. It is far more difficult to allow for any profiting from hindsight over Pitt's role in the enquiry, or later relations with Leicester House.
64. Walpole, *George II*, III, 8.
65. Glover, *Memoirs*, pp.138–40. Glover's account confuses his meetings with

Pitt on 9 April and *c.* 5 May, so that it is not clear whether Pitt had yet been told of Legge's meeting with Newcastle on 18 April. But it seems probable that Glover was recording Pitt's opinions on 9 April.

66. Halifax to N, 7 Apr 1757: 32870, f.370.

67. Dodington, *Diary*, p.364 (undated entry).

68. Dupplin to Oswald, 7 Apr 1757: Oswald MSS, 49.

69. N to H, 8 Apr 1757: 35416, f.182 (the source for the following).

70. It was presumably at that interview that Egremont was shown a letter of Newcastle's to the King, presumably that of 25 March (Bayntun Rolt Diary, 23 Apr 1757).

71. Cf. N to Duchess, 9 Apr 1757: 33075, f.121.

72. N to H, 8 Apr 1757: 35416, f.182.

73. Halifax to Oswald, 15 Apr 1757: Oswald MSS, Chest IV.

74. H to Anson, 9 Apr 1757: 15956, f.32.

75. H to N, 9 Apr 1757: 32870, f.395.

76. N to Halifax, 9 Apr 1757: 32870, f.401.

77. Temple to Mrs Grenville, Friday 12 o'clock [8 Apr 1757]: *Grenville Papers*, I, 192, and WLC.

78. Mansfield to N, 15 Apr 1757: 32870, f.427.

79. Halifax to Oswald, 15 Apr 1757: Oswald MSS, Chest IV.

80. Halifax to N, 10 Apr 1757: 32870, f.405.

81. Halifax to Oswald, 10 Apr 1757: Oswald MSS, 122.

82. Halifax to Oswald, 15 Apr 1757: Oswald MSS, Chest IV.

83. Halifax to Oswald, 10 Apr 1757: Oswald MSS, 121 (this was written after no. 122, above).

84. N to Duchess, 10 Apr 1757: 33075, f.122; cf. N to Duchess, 11 Apr 1757: 33075, f.124.

85. Oswald to N, 13 Apr 1757: 32870, f.413. Newcastle supposed the secrecy was at Legge's request, to conceal his overture from the rest of Pitt's camp. Legge later claimed it was at Newcastle's 'because it would render all endeavours with the King for a general arrangement fruitless, if His Majesty suspected that the Duke of N had seen me'. Legge, Memo, nd: Rylands MSS, 665, no. 18.

86. N to Mansfield, 13 Apr 1757: 32870, f.411.

87. N to H, 15 Apr 1757: 35416, f.198.

88. N to Duchess, 13 Apr 1757: 33075, f.126.

89. N to H, 15 Apr 1757: 35416, f.198; Fox to Devonshire, [28 Apr 1757]: Dev 330/200.

90. Mansfield to N, 15 Apr 1757: 32870, f.427.

91. West to N, 15 Apr 1757: 32870, f.437.

92. Roberts to N, 15 Apr 1757: 32870, f.435.

93. N to Duchess, 16 Apr 1757: 33075, f.130.

94. Devonshire to [? Fox], 15 Apr 1757: 51382, f.102; Fox to Devonshire, 15 Apr 1757: Dev 330/197.

95. Devonshire to Cumberland, [5 May 1757]: Dev 260/223.

96. Charles Townshend to Devonshire, 19 Apr 1757: Dev 514/0.

97. Charles Townshend to Devonshire, 22 Apr [1757]: Dev 514/1.

98. Walpole, *George II*, III, 2.

99. Devonshire to Cumberland, [5 May 1757]: Dev 260/223.

100. Walpole to Mann, 20 Apr 1757: HW 21, p.75. The expression 'the arbiter of England' is repeated: Walpole, *George II*, III, 7; but, in retrospect, Walpole added ridicule and scorn to his admission of Newcastle's power.
101. Legge, Memo, nd: Rylands MSS, 668, no.18.
102. Dodington, *Diary*, pp.364–5 (undated entry).
103. Glover, *Memoirs*, pp.146–7.
104. Both dated 19 April: 32997, ff.133, 135.
105. 32997, f.133. Sir George Lee, 'or Col. Lee', and Legge were put down as possible Chancellors of the Exchequer, the latter marked 'or a peer, with an employment'. Temple was to have an unspecified Cabinet place; George Grenville to be Treasurer of the Navy; Potter and Elliot to share the Paymastership; James Grenville and Sir Richard Lyttelton 'must wait'. Of Newcastle's friends, the Marquess of Granby was to have the Stag Hounds; Treasury seats for Lord Thomond, Lord Marchmont, and James Oswald; Admiralty: Stanley and Campbell of Calder; Board of Trade: Lord North, John Frederick, Lord Abergavenny, Edward Eliot, Lord Darlington; Garter: Lords Rockingham and Egremont. Board of Green Cloth: Humphrey Morice, Col Lee; Peerages: Lord Egmont, [? Hon. Lewis] Watson, Sir John Rushout, Lord Chetwynd, Lord Downe, Lord Shelburne, Lord Digby, [? George Venables] Vernon.
106. Newdigate Diary, 19 Apr 1757.
107. Symmer to Mitchell, 19 Apr 1757: 6839, f.51.
108. Symmer to Mitchell, 22 Apr 1757: 6839, f.53.
109. Walpole to Mann, 20 Apr 1757: HW 21, p.75.
110. Walpole, *George II*, III, 7.
111. Glover, *Memoirs*, pp.132–4. Only George Grenville was commended – he alone 'seemed to have taken some pains'.
112. H to Anson, 22 Apr 1757: 15956, f.34.
113. J. West, Memo, 22 Apr 1757: 35877, f.357.
114. On 25 April: J. S. Mackenzie MSS, Mount Stuart: notebook of proceedings in the enquiry. Pitt's words are confirmed by West's memo, 25 Apr 1757: 35877, f.359. Symmer to Mitchell, 26 Apr 1757: 6839, f.55.
115. Fox to Devonshire, Tuesday morning [26 Apr 1757]: Dev 330/201.
116. Symmer to Mitchell, 26 Apr 1757: loc. cit.
117. Fox to Devonshire, Tuesday 12 p.m. [26 Apr 1757]: Dev 330/199.
118. Walpole, *George II*, III, 9.
119. Western, *English Militia*, pp.137–40; Walpole, *George II*, III, 11.
120. [Andrew Fletcher to Lord Milton], 28 Apr 1757: NLS SC 19, f.102.
121. *LJ*, XXIX, 134.
122. J. Campbell to his wife, 30 Apr 1757: Cawdor MSS, 1/128.
123. Memo, 27 Apr 1757: 32997, f.144.
124. Newdigate diary, 2 and 3 May 1757; West to N, Tuesday morning ¼ past 1 [3 May 1757]: 32871, f.13.
125. Walpole to Mann, 5 May 1757: HW 21, p.85.
126. West, Memo, Tuesday 7.30 p.m. [? 26 Apr 1757]: 35877, f.361.
127. West, Memo, 25 Apr 1757: 35877, f.359.
128. Symmer to Mitchell, 22 Apr 1757: 6839, f.53.
129. J. Campbell to [? one of Newcastle's secretaries or close friends], nd [? late April, 1757]: 32870, f.467. The dating of this letter is highly conjectural.

130. Devonshire to Cumberland, [5 May 1757]: Dev 260/223.
131. Fox to Cumberland, 6 May 1757: 51375 f.103.
132. Etough to Birch, 1 June 1757: 4306, f.165.
133. Possibly one of the Townshends – cf. n. 141.
134. Sir T. Robinson to N, 22 Apr 1757: 32870, f.443.
135. Walpole, *George II*, III, 14.
136. Sir H. Erskine to Bute, 23 Apr 1757: Bute MSS, Mount Stuart, no.40.
137. There is no other evidence that Newcastle *did* authorise the Primate to make such a disclosure. But since Newcastle would have been the Primate's source, the information was presumably conveyed on the assumption that it would be made use of.
138. Dodington, *Diary*, p.365 (undated entry); cf. Glover, *Memoirs*, p.147.
139. Legge, Mcmo, nd [? late June 1757]: Rylands MSS, 668 no. 18.
140. N, Memo, 'The Pr[imate]', 26 Apr 1757: 32997, f.138. Parts of the text are omitted in McKelvey, *George III and Lord Bute*, pp.56–7.
141. Egmont to N, [29 Apr 1757]: 32870, f.459. Newcastle saw Granby on 30 April and discovered he thought he could win over the two Townshends. N to H, 1 May 1757: 32871, f.1.
142. Cf. Pitt to Bute, Tuesday night [? 3 May 1757]: Pitt MSS, Mount Stuart, no.25.
143. The major offices remained as they were; three men were added to the Cabinet: Sir George Lee as Chancellor of the Exchequer, Halifax raised to 'Secretary of State to the Indies' and Mansfield as Lord Chief Justice. Peerages were assigned to Egmont, Lewis Watson, Legge, Sir Thomas Robinson and Sir John Rushout. The chief of the 'Persons who must be considered upon forming an administration' were Anson, Egmont, Sir George Lee and Halifax. No Paymaster was listed; but the final item is 'Q. Mr Fox some office': N, Memo, 29 Apr 1757: 32997, f.146.
144. N, Memo, 30 Apr 1757: 32997, f.148. Temple is listed as Lord Privy Seal, Gower in turn displacing Dorset (Master of the Horse), and Dorset or Devonshire displacing Rochford (Groom of the Stole). Halifax's station is again raised in rank; Lee or Legge are envisaged at the Exchequer, and Mansfield to join the Cabinet. Winchelsea was to remain at the Admiralty, but with a Board of Newcastle loyalists; James Grenville was 'to wait' rather than take a seat at the Treasury Board, and Fox 'to wait', leaving Dupplin and Potter as Paymasters. George Grenville was to be Treasurer of the Navy. Egmont, and possibly Legge 'with the promise of some employment', and others, were to have peerages.
145. N to H, 1 May 1757: 32871, f.1.
146. Waldegrave, *Memoirs*, p.109; cf. Primate to Bute, 30 Apr 1757: Bute MSS, Mount Stuart, no. 41; Primate to Bute, Wednesday night 4 May [1757]: ibid no. 43; Primate to N, Monday [2 May 1757]: 32871, f.11; Primate to N, Wednesday morning [4 May 1757]: 32871, f.15.
147. This is the scheme envisaged in Newcastle's Memo, 32997, f.146.
148. This is the scheme of 32997, f.148.
149. N to H, 1 May 1757: 32871, f.1.
150. Cf. N to the Duchess, 1 May 1757: 33075, f.131.
151. Pitt to Bute, Tuesday night [? 3 May 1757]: Pitt MSS, Mount Stuart, no. 25.

152. 'Paper of Heads', nd: 32997, f.140.

153. Cf. n. 141.

154. N to Chesterfield, 7 May 1757: 32871, f.39.

155. From Devonshire's account its date is doubtful, though probably after Stone's meeting with him on 30 April. Devonshire claimed it took place after the enquiry, which ended on 3rd, yet he was due to leave for Newmarket on 4th and did not return till 6th (cf. N to Devonshire, 6 May 1757: 32871, f.27).

156. It is not clear whether Newcastle was lying; he would not have been if his meeting with Devonshire took place on 3rd before his meeting with Bute.

157. Devonshire to Cumberland, [5 May 1757]: Dev 260/223.

158. Of which the memoranda already noted, 32997, ff.146, 148 may have been drafts.

159. Fox to Cumberland, 6 May 1757: 51375, f.103.

160. Glover, *Memoirs*, p.138.

161. Walpole, *George II*, III, 14–15. Pitt's suggestion of a peerage for Legge may have been a tactic to exclude him from effective power after the discovery of his interview with Newcastle.

162. Waldegrave, *Memoirs* p.109; cf. N to Chesterfield, 7 May 1757: 32871, f.39.

163. Sandwich to Cumberland, 7 May 1757: Sandwich MSS, Mapperton: F41/7.

164. Hardwicke was evidently told of Newcastle's dealings with Bute, but it is not certain that he was also told of Newcastle's interview with Pitt.

165. Stone to N, 7 May 1757: 32871, f.35.

166. N to Duchess, 8 May 1757: 33075, f.133.

167. Fox to Devonshire, 8 May 1757: Dev 330/203.

168. Stone to N, 7 May 1757: 32871, f.35.

169. Primate to N, 12 May 1757: 32871, f.61.

170. Chesterfield to N, Saturday [7 May 1757]: Dobrée, v, 2225.

171. Primate to Bute, Wednesday 2 o'clock 11 May [1757]: Bute MSS, Mount Stuart, no.45.

172 Primate to N, 12 May 1757: 32871, f.61.

173. Mansfield, Memo, 12 May 1757: 32871, f.57.

174. Ibid.

175. Cf. J. Watkins to N, 10 May 1757: 32871, f.53; Breadalbane to Charles Erskine, 12 May 1757: NLS 5079, f.154; H. Taylor to Sir Jeffrey Amherst, 10 May 1757: Amherst MSS, c 2/6; [? Andrew Fletcher] to Charles Erskine, 3 May 1757: NLS 5079, f.132; Countess of Mansfield to Lord Stormont, 13 May 1757: Mansfield MSS, B 1390.

176. J. Calcraft to Lord Charles Hay, 14 May 1757: 17493, f.65.

177. Rigby to Fox, Tuesday 10 o'clock [10 May 1757]: 51385, f.107; Walpole, *George II*, III, 15. Devonshire received the insignia of office on 16 May.

178. N to Devonshire, [13 May 1757]: Dev 182/84; Primate to Bute, Wednesday 2 o'clock 11 May [1757]: Bute MSS, Mount Stuart, no 45; Primate to N, 12 May 1757: 32871, f.61; Fox to Devonshire, 8 May 1757: Dev 330/203; Stone to N, 7 May 1757: 32871, f.35.

179. Devonshire to Cumberland, 13 May 1757: Dev 260/224.
180. Rigby to Fox, Tuesday 10 o'clock [10 May 1757]: 51385, f.107.
181. A. Stone to N, 14 May 1757: 32871, f.89.
182. N to the Duchess, 15 May 1757: 33075, f.135.
183. N, Memo, 15 May 1757: 32997, f.152. Newcastle is First Lord of the Treasury with Sir George Lee Chancellor of the Exchequer, and Nugent. Lord Thomond shares the Pay Office, presumably with Dupplin; the Admiralty is Lord Halifax, Boscawen, West, Mostyn ['Q. Admiral Forbes'], Stanley, [Elliot?] and Oswald. Legge, with a peerage, heads the Board of Trade with Stone, Rigby, Soame Jenyns, W. G. Hamilton, Thomas Pelham and Hunter. Lord Gower is Lord Privy Seal; Winchelsea (removed from the Admiralty) Groom of the Stole; and, for Fox, an Irish pension. Pitt's Secretaryship of State is presumably assured.
184. N, 'Memds Ld G[ranby]', nd [? c.15 May 1757]: 32870, f.470. The dating is tentative.
185. Fox to Cumberland, 20 May 1757: 51375, f.107.
186. Walpole to Mann, 19 May 1757: HW 21, p.91.
187. Walpole, *George II*, III, 15-16.
188. Devonshire to N, 16 May 1757: 32871, f.97.
189. Primate to Bute, Wednesday morning 9 o'clock 17 May [sc. 18 May 1757]: Bute MSS, Mount Stuart, no.48.
190. N to Devonshire, Friday morning [? 13 May 1757]: Dev 182/85.
191. Fox to Cumberland, 20 May 1757: 51375, f.107.
192. 'Considerations for the Duke of Newcastle's Conduct', 18 May 1757: 32997, f.156; Plans of administration, ibid. ff.158, 162, 164 (f.158 dated 18 May 1757). The order of the last three, in ascending order of neatness, each incorporating the revisions of the last, is f.158, f.164, f.162. The list 32997, f.199 is seemingly a fair copy of f.164.

These lists contain between them a number of alternatives, thus:
Treasury: Newcastle; Sir G. Lee Chancellor of Exchequer; Nugent, Duncannon, Oswald.
Admiralty: Winchelsea, Boscawen, Mostyn; Rowley or Hawke; Lord Carysfort; Sandys; Stanley.
Board of Trade: Halifax; Stone; Thomas Pelham; Rigby; Soame Jenyns; W. G. Hamilton; Lord Middleton; Edward Eliot or Lord North.
Lord Privy Seal: Hardwicke or Gower.
Master of the Horse: Gower or Dorset.
Groom of the Stole: Rochford or Dorset.
Lord Chamberlain: Devonshire.
Secretary of State, South: Egmont or Sir T. Robinson.
Treasurer of the Navy: Anson, Fox, Charles Townshend, Lord Barrington, Dodington.
Paymasters: Dupplin and Darlington, jointly.
Secretary at War: Charles Townshend or Lord George Sackville.
Treasurer of the Chamber: Charles or George Townshend.
Possible peers include Egmont, Sir Thomas Robinson and Fox; or a peerage for Lady Caroline and a pension for Fox himself.
Garters: Rockingham, Waldegrave, Egremont.
The list 32997, f.168 appears to be part of the same scheme.

193. Lord Chandos to Bute, 19 May 1757: Bute MSS, Mount Stuart, no. 50.
194. Primate to Bute, Wednesday morning 9 o'clock 17 May [*sc.* 18 May 1757]: Bute MSS, Mount Stuart, no. 48.
195. N to Devonshire, Thursday at night [19 May 1757]: Dev 182/86; Fox to Devonshire, 19 May 1757: Dev 330/205; Hume Campbell to Marchmont, 19 May 1757: HMC *Polwarth*, v, 332.
196. Fox to Cumberland, 20 May 1757: 51375, f.107.
197. Hume Campbell to Marchmont, 19 May 1757; HMC *Polwarth*, v, 332.
198. N to Devonshire, Thursday at night [19 May 1757]: Dev 182/86.
199. Fox to Cumberland, 20 May 1757: 51375, f.107.
200. N to Lincoln, 21 May 1757: 32871, f.113.
201. 32997, ff.166, 169. The latter is probably a working list with deletions and alterations. Whether *Newcastle* disclosed his terms to *Pitt* is unclear.
202. Other offices:
     Admiralty: Oswald, Stanley, Boscawen, West, Forbes, Eliot; Secretary at War: Lord George Sackville; Treasurer of the Navy: Lord Barrington; Lord Chamberlain: Devonshire; Treasurer of the Chamber: Charles Townshend; Peerage: Egmont.
203. Walpole, *George II*, III, 16–19; cf. J. S. Mackenzie, Memo, 18 May 1757: Mackenzie MSS, Mount Stuart.
204. Glover, *Memoirs*, p.143.
205. G. Elliot to Minto, 19 May [1757]: NLS 11001, f.84.
206. Glover, *Memoirs*, p.143.
207. Cf. Countess to Earl of Kildare, Thursday 19 [May 1757]: *Leinster Corr*, I, 34.
208. Fox to Cumberland, 20 May 1757: 51375, f.107.
209. Which office this was is not clear.
210. Stone to N, 21 May [1757]: Ne(c) 3636.
211. It is not clear that Newcastle previously knew of this declaration, or when.
212. N to Stone, 22 May 1757: 32871, f.120.
213. Cf. N to Duchess, 22 May 1757: 33075, f.136.
214. N to Lincoln, 21 May 1757: 32871, f.113.
215. Fox to his wife, 24 May 1757: 51416, f.31; Walpole, *George II*, III, 21.
216. Fox to Waldegrave, Monday morning [? 23 May 1757]: 51380, f.11.
217. N to Duchess, 22 May 1757: 33075, f.136.
218. Cf. Waldegrave, *Memoirs*, p.109.
219. Fox to his wife, 24 May 1757: 51416, f.31.
220. The actual residence of the Prince of Wales. It adjoined Leicester House, occupied by his mother and his court.
221. Fox to Devonshire, [22 May 1757]: Dev 330/206.
222. Fox to his wife, 25 May 1757: 51416, f.33.
223. Pitt to Bute, Tuesday past 3 [? 24 May 1757]: Pitt MSS, Mount Stuart, no.27.
224. Pitt to Bute, Tuesday 11 o'clock [? 24 May 1757]: Pitt MSS, Mount Stuart, no.26; Pitt to Bute, at dinner [? 24 May 1757]: loc. cit. no.28.
225. N to H, Tuesday morning [24 May 1757]: 35416, f.210.
226. What his demands were is not certain.
227. Memo, 'The Conference between Ld H and Mr P', 25 May 1757: 32997, f.173.
228. H to N, Tuesday night [24 May 1757]: 32871, f.128.

229. Hillsborough to Fox, Saturday night [28 May 1757]: 51386, f.212. Robert Nedham married Catherine, one of Pitt's sisters; 'Molly' Pitt is presumably Mary, Pitt's youngest sister.
230. Walpole, *George II*, III, 21–2. His source was probably Devonshire, who presumably heard an account of it from Newcastle when they met in the Lords on 27th; cf. N to Devonshire, 26 May 1757: Dev 182/87.
231. Ibid.
232. N, Memo, 26 May 1757: 32997, f.177. A similar list, with additions, 32997, f.179, is marked 'copy given to Ld Granby'.
233. Walpole later listed the terms (to Mann, 1 June 1757; HW 21, p.92): 'a full restoration of [Pitt's] friends, with the Admiralty and a peerage for Mr Legge, the blue ribband and I believe Ireland for Lord Temple, and Mr Grenville for Chancellor of the Exchequer, with stipulations that no more money should be sent this year to Germany'.
234. Cf. Symmer to Mitchell, 3 June 1757: 6839, f.61.
235. Waldegrave to Fox, Thursday 5 o'clock [26 May 1757]: 51380, f.13.
236. Hillsborough to Fox, Saturday night [28 May 1757]: 51386, f.212.
237. Glover, *Memoirs*, pp.144–5.
238. Waldegrave to Fox, Thursday 5 o'clock [26 May 1757]: 51380, f.13; Fox to his wife, Thursday evening [26 May 1757]: 51416, f.35.
239. Fox to Richmond, 27 May 1757: BM loan 57/103, vol.20.
240. Cf. Fox to his wife, 24 May 1757: 51416, f.31.
241. Holdernesse to Mitchell, 27 May 1757: 6832, f.152.
242. Devonshire to Cumberland, 27 May 1757: Dev 260/225.
243. Fox to Cumberland, 27 May 1757: 51375, f.113.
244. Dodington, *Diary*, p.364 (undated entry).
245. N, Memo, 27 May 1757: 32997, f.195. A copy is in Hardwicke's papers, 35416, f.212. Another list, 32997, f.193, is a rough draft of 32997, f.197; 32997, f.195, is a fair copy of 32997, f.197.
    The chief provisions are: Treasury: Newcastle, Sir George Lee Chancellor of the Exchequer, Nugent, Duncannon, Oswald. Admiralty: Winchelsea, Rowley, Boscawen, Mostyn, Carysfort, Sandys, Stanley. Board of Trade: Halifax (as Secretary of State), Stone, T. Pelham, Rigby, Soame Jenyns, Hamilton, Middleton, Edward Eliot. Secretary of State: Northern, Holdernesse; Southern, Sir T. Robinson. Paymaster: Fox. Treasurer of the Navy: Anson. Peerages: Fox, Watson, Egmont, Legge, Shelburne, Rushout, Chetwynd, Vernon, Verney.
    A similar list, dated 26 May, 32997, f.191, lists Egmont *or* Robinson for the Secretaryship of State and only Watson and Egmont for peerages. Walpole wrote (*George II*, III, 23) that Dorset was to be removed as Master of the Horse and Gower replace him '(for Lord George Sackville had been designed for Pitt's Secretary at War)', and that Hardwicke was to succeed Gower as Lord Privy Seal. But none of those changes is in Newcastle's lists, 32997, ff.191, 193, 195, 197.
246. N to Mitchell, 27 May 1757: 32871, f.145; Waldegrave, *Memoirs*, pp.109–10.
247. Dodington, *Diary*, p.364 (undated entry).
248. Hillsborough to Fox, Saturday night [28 May 1757]: 51386, f.212.
249. Walpole, *George II*, III, 22.

250. Cf. Fox to Waldegrave, Friday [27 May 1757]: 51380, f.15; Sandwich to Cumberland, 27 May 1757: Sandwich MSS, Mapperton, F 41/8.
251. Devonshire to Cumberland, 27 May 1757: Dev 260/225.
252. Devonshire to Fox, 28 May 1757: 51382, f.107.
253. Walpole to Mann, 1 June 1757: HW 21, p.92.
254. N, Memo, 'Considerations upon the present situation', 28 May 1757: 32997, f.201.
255. Hillsborough to Fox, Saturday night [28 May 1757]: 51386, f.212.
256. N to Devonshire, 28 May 1757: Dev 182/88. Walpole records (*George II*, III, 23) that Hume Campbell had asked for the Treasurership of the Navy in addition to his place of Lord Register; 'When he found another designation of that office [to Anson], he demanded that Lord Edgcumbe should be removed, and the Duchy of Lancaster given to himself for life...'
257. N, Memo, 28 May 1757: 32997, f.201.
258. N to Devonshire, 28 May 1757: Dev 182/88.
259. N to Waldegrave, Saturday morning [28 May 1757]: 32871, f.153.
260. Cf. Ellis to Fox, 28 May 1757: 51387, f.66.
261. Devonshire to N, 28 May 1757: 32871, f.157.
262. Devonshire to Fox, 28 May 1757: 51382, f.107.
263. Rigby to Fox, 28 May 1757: 51385, f.109.
264. Fox to Devonshire, Sunday night [29 May 1757]: Dev 330/207; cf. E. Montagu to [Charles] Lyttelton, 28 May [1757]: Lyttelton MSS, II, 330.
265. Fox to Ellis, 30 May 1757: 51387, f.68.
266. Fox to Waldegrave [31 May 1757]: 51380, f.16.
267. Calcraft to Fox, 28 May 1757: 51398, f.22.
268. Primate to Pitt, 6 a.m. Saturday 29 May [sc. 28 May 1757]: PRO 30/8/1, f.180. Armagh then set out on his return journey to Dublin.
269. Calcraft to Fox, 28 May 1757: 51398, f.22.
270. Glover, *Memoirs*, p.144.
271. C. Yorke to Royston, 1 June 1757: 35360, f.262.
272. N to Devonshire, 29 May 1757: Dev 182/89.
273. Halifax to N, Monday evening 30 May 1757: 32871, f.170.
274. N to Devonshire, 29 May 1757: Dev 182/89; Granby to N, [30 May 1757]: 32871, f.176.
275. N, Memo, 30 May 1757: 32997, f.203.
For Newcastle: Alderman Baker; Sir John Barnard; Lord Barrington; Admiral Boscawen; Hume Campbell; Anthony Champion; Charles Cocks; George Colebrooke; [Thomas] Coventry; Sir Ellis Cunliffe; Sir John Cust; John Delaval; Robert Dundas; Lord Dupplin; Lord Egmont; Edward Eliot; Rose Fuller; Lord Granby; George Haldane; Nicholas Hardinge; Sir Edward Hawke; Richard Hussey; Sir George Lee; Sir Richard Lloyd; Robert Nugent; James Oswald; Thomas Pelham; Charles Pole; Sir Thomas Robinson; Lord Royston; Sir John Rushout; Hans Stanley; John Thornhagh; [? Hon. Thomas] Townshend [(1701-80)]; Hon. Thomas Walpole; James West; John White; Andrew Wilkinson; Charles Yorke [=39; added by Newcastle before the addition of Cunliffe to give 38].
For Fox: George Amyand; John Campbell [MP Inverness Burghs]; Henry Seymour Conway; George Dodington; Edward Finch; Henry Fox;

'Q. John Gore'; Sir John Griffin; William Gerard Hamilton; Sir Robert Henley; Sir John Mordaunt; Savage Mostyn; Richard Rigby; Lord Shelburne; Lord Powerscourt; Lord Strange [=16].

For Pitt: [William] Bagot; [William] Beckford; George Cooke; Lord Downe; 'Q Sir Francis Dashwood'; Sir Harry Erskine; Nicholas Fazackerley; Sir Cordell Firebrace; George Grenville; James Grenville; Henry Bilson Legge; Sir Richard Lyttelton; Samuel Martin; Sir John Philipps; William Pitt; Thomas Potter; Thomas Prowse; Lord Pulteney; Lord George Sackville; George Townshend; Charles Townshend; Robert Vyner [MP Lincolnshire]; Robert Vyner [MP Okehampton] [=23].

276. N to H, 1 June 1757: 35416, f.216.
277. This cannot be N to Devonshire, 28 Apr 1757: Dev 182/82; it seems to be lost.
278. N to H, 1 June 1757: 35416, f.216.
279. N to Duchess, [? 31 May 1757]: 33075, f.140.
280. N Memo, 'Paper for the Duke of Devonshire' [31 May 1757]: Dev 182/90.
281. N to H, 1 June 1757: 35416, f.216.
282. Devonshire to Cumberland, 4 June 1757: Dev 260/228.
283. H to N, 3/4 past five 1 June 1757: 32871, f.189.
284. H to N, Wednesday night 1 June 1757: 32871, f.191.
285. Devonshire to N, Wednesday night 1 June 1757: 32871, f.195.
286. Fox to Devonshire, 1 June 1757: Dev 330/208.
287. Devonshire to N, Wednesday night 1 June 1757: 32871, f.195.
288. His sister, the Countess of Kildare, thought the time of his kissing hands an insufficient reason for upsetting the system: Countess of Kildare to Earl, 2 June [1757]: *Leinster Corr*, I, 39.
289. Fox to Devonshire, 1 June 1757: Dev 330/209.
290. Devonshire to George II, Friday morning 3 June 1757: Dev 260/227.
291. Lord Ilchester to Lord Digby, Monday 3 o'clock [13 June 1757]: Digby MSS.
292. N to Devonshire, 2 June 1757: Dev 182/91.
293. N to Bute, 2 June 1757: Bute MSS, Mount Stuart, no.57.
294. Duchess of N to Lincoln, 3 June 1757: Ne(c) 3159.
295. Waldegrave, *Memoirs*, p.110.
296. N to Chesterfield, 3 June 1757: 32871, f.201; Devonshire to N, 3 June 1757: Dev 260/227.
297. Fox to Dodington, Friday night [3 June 1757]: 38091, f.83.
298. N to H, [4 June 1757]: 35416, f.220.
299. Walpole, *George II*, III, 24.
300. N to Devonshire, 5 June 1757: Dev 182/93.
301. Chesterfield to N, 3 June 1757: 32871, f.199.
302. Waldegrave, *Memoirs*, pp.111–12.
303. N to Chesterfield, 3 June 1757: 32871, f.201.
304. N to Devonshire, Friday at night [3 June 1757]: Dev 182/92; N to George II, 4 June 1757: 32864, f.98.
305. George II to N, 4 June [1757]: 32864, f.100.
306. George II to N, [4 June 1757]: 35416, f.230 (copy).
307. Waldegrave, *Memoirs*, p.112.
308. N, Memo, 4 June 1757: 32997, f.211.

309. N to Bute, 4 June 1757: Bute MSS, Mount Stuart, no.77.
310. N to H, 4 June 1757: 35416, f.220.
311. Bute to N, Sunday night late [5 June 1757]: 32871, f.222.
312. N to Devonshire, 5 June 1757: Dev 182/93.
313. N, Memo, 5 June 1757: 32997, f.214. On Pratt as Attorney General Newcastle had 'no objection to any regulation, that may bring that about'. George Townshend was put down for a Treasury seat at once if possible. And of Sir Harry Erskine: 'some employment to be made vacant for him'.
314. Legge, Memo [? 17–23 June 1757]: Rylands MSS, 668, no.18.
315. N, Memo, 6 June 1757: 32871, f.224.
316. N to Chesterfield, 8 June 1757: 32871, f.240.
317. And, presumably, the King on 4 June: cf. Lady Yarmouth to Devonshire, Samedi matin [4 June 1757]: Dev 523/0.
318. Devonshire to Fox, 6 June 1757: 51382, f.109.
319. Fox to Devonshire [5 June 1757]: Dev 330/210.
320. Fox to Devonshire, 5 p.m. 6 June 1757: Dev 330/211; Fox to Dodington [6 June 1757]: 38091, f.85.
321. Not until 6th was Fox given a full account – cf. Devonshire to Fox, 6 June 1757: 51382, f.109.
322. Waldegrave to N, Monday night [6 June 1757]: 32871, f.228.
323. Devonshire to N, Monday morning 6 June 1757: 32871, f.226.
324. Fox to [? Waldegrave], Sunday 5 o'clock [5 June 1757]: 51380, f.18.
325. Fox to Devonshire, [5 June 1757]: Dev 330/210.
326. Devonshire to Fox, 6 June 1757: 51382, f.109.
327. Pitt to Bute, past 11 o'clock [5 June 1757]: Pitt MSS, Mount Stuart, no.29 (misdated in Sedgwick, 'Pitt', p.123 '[6 June 1757]').
328. Walpole, *George II*, III, 25. Walpole claims the exchange took place in the drawing room at Leicester House and implies that it was on 4 June. But Newcastle's accounts of that day mention exchanges with Bute only, and it seems unlikely that Pitt was present. Walpole's version probably conflates the two encounters, though it is possible that the passage refers to 4 June alone.
329. Cf. Elliot to Minto, 9 [June 1757]: NLS 11001, f.42.
330. Walpole to Mann, 9 June 1757: HW 21, p.97.
331. Waldegrave, *Memoirs*, p.113.
332. Dodington, *Diary*, p.364 (undated entry).
333. Walpole, *George II*, III, 28.
334. Lady Anson to Lord Anson, Sunday night 12 June [1757]: Anson MSS, D615/P(s)1/1.
335. Lord Ilchester to Lord Digby, Monday 3 o'clock [13 June 1757]: Digby MSS. It is not clear that Ilchester was correct at this point.
336. Devonshire to Cumberland, 10 June 1757: Dev 260/229.
337. Waldegrave, *Memoirs*, p.113.
338. Walpole, *George II*, III, 25. Newcastle evidently told Bute the King's answer that evening; cf. N to Holdernesse, near 5 o'clock [? 7 June 1757]: Eg 3430, f.59.
339. Devonshire to Cumberland, 10 June 1757: Dev 260/229.
340. Lord Ilchester to Lord Digby, Monday 3 o'clock [13 June 1757]: Digby MSS.

341. Fox to [Lord Strange], 10 June 1757: 51430, f.94; cf. Fox to Cumberland, 10 June 1757: 51375, f.116.

342. H. Digby to Lord Digby, 7 June 1757: Digby MSS.

343. N to Chesterfield, 8 June 1757: 32871, f.240.

344. N to Bute, 7 June 1757: Bute MSS, Mount Stuart, no.58; Bute to N, 7 June 1757: 32871, f.238.

345. Chesterfield to N, 8 June 1757: 32871, f.244.

346. Holdernesse to N, Tuesday night [7 June 1757]: 35416, f.232. Newcastle forwarded Holdernesse's letter to Hardwicke. The letter which Hardwicke probably wrote to Pitt on that day is no longer extant. Newcastle probably tried to see Holdernesse on the afternoon of 7th, but, failing, met him the following day. Meanwhile he sent not an exhortation to resign but only the news that 'Fox kisses hands tomorrow for Chancellor of the Exchequer, and *probably*, but not *certainly* Lord Waldegrave for head of the Treasury.' (N to Holdernesse, near 5 o'clock [? 7 June 1757]: Eg 3430, f.59).

347. N to Chesterfield, 8 June 1757: 32871, f.240.

348. Walpole, *George II*, III, 26.

349. Countess of Kildare to Earl of Kildare, Thursday 9 [June 1757]: *Leinster Corr*, I, 43.

350. Waldegrave, *Memoirs*, pp.115–20; Mrs Delaney to Mrs Dewes, 9 June 1757: Lady Llanover (ed.), *The Autobiography and Correspondence of Mary Granville, Mrs Delaney* (London, 1861) III, 459.

351. Holdernesse to N, Wednesday [8 June 1757]: 32871, f.246.

352. N to Holdernesse, Wednesday at night 8 June 1757: 32871, f.242.

353. Holdernesse to N, Wednesday night [8 June 1757]: 32871, f.248.

354. Holdernesse to N, Wednesday night [8 June 1757]: 32871, f.250.

355. N to Bute, 8 June 1757: Bute MSS, Mount Stuart, no.60.

356. Conway to Devonshire, Wednesday morning [8 June 1757]: Dev 416/42.

357. Ellis to Fox, 1/2 past 3 [? 8 June 1757]: 51387, f.70. D'Abreu was the Spanish Minister in London.

358. Walpole, *George II*, III, 26–7.

359. Elliot to Minto, 9 [June 1757]: NLS 11001, f.42.

360. Cf. H. Digby to Lord Digby, 9 June 1757: Digby MSS.

361. Countess of Kildare to Earl of Kildare, Thursday 9 [June 1757]: *Leinster Corr*, I, 43.

362. Elliot to Minto, 9 [June 1757]: NLS 11001, f.42.

363. Countess of Kildare to Earl of Kildare, Thursday 9 [June 1757]: loc. cit.

364. H. Digby to Lord Digby, 9 June 1757: Digby MSS.

365. Walpole to Mann, 9 June 1757: HW 21, p.97.

366. Elliot to Minto, 9 [June 1757]: NLS 11001, f.42.

367. Walpole, *George II*, III, 27.

368. N, Memo, 11 [*sc.* 10] June 1757: 32871, f.272.

369. Waldegrave, *Memoirs*, pp.121–3.

370. Halifax to Fox, 10 June 1757: 51430, f.92.

371. Waldegrave, *Memoirs*, pp.124–5.

372. Walpole, *George II*, III, 27–8.

373. Holdernesse to George II, 11 June 1757: Eg 3425, f.46.

374. Holdernesse to Lady Yarmouth, 11 June 1757: Eg 3425, f.48.

375. Waldegrave, *Memoirs*, pp.125–6.

376. In 1747 to the daughter of the future 4th Duke of Argyll.
377. Walpole, *George II*, III, 28–9.
378. Dodington to Fox, Friday morning past 8 o'clock [? 10 June 1757]: 38091, f.86.
379. Ilchester to Lord Digby, Monday 3 o'clock [13 June 1757]: Digby MSS.
380. Devonshire to Cumberland, 10 June 1757: Dev 260/229.
381. Symmer to Mitchell, 10 June 1757: 6839, f.63.
382. F. Frankland to [? T. Pelham], 11 June 1757: 33098, f.71.
383. Lady Sophia Egerton to Bentinck, 10 June 1757: Eg 1719, f.18.
384. Ilchester claimed Rutland was there 'at the particular desire and instigation of Lord Granby' (Ilchester to Lord Digby, loc. cit.).
385. H. Digby to Lord Digby, 11 June 1757: Digby MSS.
386. This claim probably originated with Fox (cf. Fox to Cumberland, 10 June 1757: 51375, f.116); but other evidence to confirm it is lacking.
387. Calcraft to Loudoun, 10 June 1757: 17493, f.69.
388. Fox to [Lord Strange], 10 June 1757: 51430, f.94.
389. Devonshire to Strange, 10 June 1757: Dev 260/230.
390. Lord Ilchester to Lord Digby, Monday 3 o'clock [13 June 1757]: Digby MSS.
391. 'He might perhaps fight off G. Sackville now', he added: Fox to Devonshire, Friday morning [10 June 1757]: Dev 330/213.
392. Fox to Cumberland, 10 June 1757: 51375, f.116.
393. Fox to Devonshire, Friday morning [10 June 1757]: Dev 330/214.
394. Devonshire to Cumberland, 10 June 1757: Dev 260/229.
395. Since 7 June.
396. West to N, 10 June 1757: 32871, f.266.
397. N to Granby, Saturday morning [11 June 1757]: 32871, f.282.
398. Devonshire to Strange, 10 June 1757: Dev 260/230.
399. Calcraft to Loudoun, 10 June 1757: 17493, f.69.
400. Waldegrave, *Memoirs*, pp.126–8.
401. Rockingham to N, Saturday morning 11 o'clock [11 June 1757]: 32871, f.278.
402. Devonshire to Cumberland, 12 June 1757: Dev 260/234.
403. H. Digby to Lord Digby, 11 June 1757: Digby MSS. The order of the various meetings that morning is not clear.
404. Mansfield to H, 7 o'clock Saturday [11 June 1757]: 35595, f.39.
405. Lady Anson to Lord Anson, Sunday night 12 June [1757]: Anson MSS, D 615/P(s)/1/1.
406. N to Holdernesse, Saturday night [11 June 1757]: Eg 3430, f.61; cf. N to Bute, 3.30 p.m. 11 June 1757: Bute MSS, Mount Stuart, no.62.
407. Mansfield to N, 7 o'clock Saturday [11 June 1757]: 35595, f.39.
408. Waldegrave, *Memoirs*, p.129.
409. H to Royston 12 June 1757: 35351, f.372; Lady Anson to Lord Anson, Sunday night 12 June [1757]: Anson MSS, D 615/P(s)/1/1.
410. Barrington to Newcastle, Saturday 7 o'clock [11 June 1757]: 32871, f.274.
411. Walpole, *George II*, III, 30. It is not clear whether Walpole is conflating what the King said to Fox and to Waldegrave; yet cf. H. Digby to Lord Digby, 11 June 1757: Digby MSS.
412. Lord Ilchester to Lord Digby, Monday 3 o'clock [13 June 1757]: Digby MSS.

413. Waldegrave, *Memoirs*, pp.129–32. Conversations in the Closet are usually so briefly reported that this is given *in extenso*. It should be noticed that the King's attitudes are still those of a man self-consciously a foreigner.
414. Lady Anson to Lord Anson, Sunday night 12 June [1757]: Anson MSS, D615P(s)/11.
415. Countess to Earl of Kildare, 14 June [1757]: *Leinster Corr*, I, 47.
416. Bedford to Kildare, 16 June 1757: Bedford MSS, xxxiv, 23.
417. Ilchester to Devonshire, 12 June 1757: Dev 524/0.
418. Lord Ilchester to Lord Digby, Monday 3 o'clock [13 June 1757]: Digby MSS.
419. H. Digby to Lord Digby, 14 June 1757: Digby MSS.
420. Rigby to Fox, 16 June 1757: 51385, f.111.
421. Bedford to Fox, 16 June 1757: 51385, f.17.
422. Fox to Ellis, 12 June 1757: 51387, f.72.
423. G. Elliot to Minto, 14 June [1757]: NLS 11001, f.36.
424. H. Digby to Lord Digby, 14 June 1757: Digby MSS.
425. H. Digby to Lord Digby, 11 June 1757: Digby MSS.
426. H to Royston, 12 June 1757: 35351, f.372.
427. H. Digby to Hanbury Williams, 12 June 1757: Stowe MSS, 263, f.13.
428. Lady Sophia Egerton to Bentinck, 14 June 1757: Eg 1719, f.20.
429. H to Royston, 12 June 1757: 35351, f.372.
430. Fox to Ellis, 12 June 1757: 51387, f.72.
431. Cf. Lady Anson to Lord Anson, 11 June [1757]: Anson MSS, Staffordshire RO.
432. Rigby to Bedford, 13 June 1757: Bedford MSS, xxxiv, 19.
433. F. Frankland to T. Pelham, 16 June 1757: 33094, f.156.
434. Legge, Memo [? 17–23 June 1757]: Rylands MSS, 668, no.18.
435. Mansfield to Devonshire, Sunday noon [12 June 1757]: Dev 525/0; Countess to Earl of Kildare, Sunday 12 June [1757]: *Leinster Corr*, I, 45.
436. A meeting evidently took place on 11th, 12th or 13th for which no evidence survives.
437. Devonshire to Cumberland, 17 June 1757: Dev 260/234 (draft). The passage in brackets was evidently deleted from the text sent.
438. N to Bute, Monday 1/2 past 3 [13 June 1757]: Bute MSS, Mount Stuart, no.201.
439. Devonshire, Memo [13 June 1757]: Dev 260/232; Dupplin to [? Duchess of N], 13 June 1757: 32871, f.298.
440. N to Bute, Monday 1/2 an hour past four [? 13 June 1757]: Bute MSS, Mount Stuart, no.203; Bute to N, Monday [13 June 1757]: 32871, f.294; Bute to N, Monday [13 June 1757]: 32871, f.296.
441. Walpole to Mann, 14 June 1757: HW 21, p.99.
442. N to the Duchess, Tuesday [? 14 June 1757]: 33075, f.150.
443. Dupplin to [? Duchess of N], 14 June 1757: 32871, f.308.
444. Devonshire to Cumberland, 17 June 1757: Dev 260/234.
445. N to Devonshire, Tuesday 5 o'clock [14 June 1757]: Dev 182/94. It seems several meetings of these four took place at this time which passed unrecorded.
446. Fox to Devonshire, 15 June 1757: Dev 330/215.
447. Devonshire to N, Tuesday evening [14 June 1757]: 32871, f.300.

448. Devonshire to H, 14 June 1757: Dev 260/233; Devonshire to Mansfield, 14 June 1757: Mansfield MSS, B 1359.
449. Pitt to Bute, Wednesday 10 o'clock [15 June 1757]: Pitt MSS, Mount Stuart, no.30.
450. H to N, Wednesday 3 o'clock [15 June 1757]: 32871, f.309.
451. Hardwicke's scheme, dated 15 June 1757, is 35870, f.268. Other provisions: Admiralty Board: Legge, Boscawen, West, Forbes, Hunter, Elliot [Stanley deleted], Hay (with a seat in Parliament). Treasury Board: Newcastle, First Lord; Dupplin, Chancellor of the Exchequer; Nugent; James Grenville or Lord Duncannon; Oswald. Treasurer of the Navy: George Grenville. One Vice Treasurer of Ireland *vice* Ellis: James Grenville or Lord Duncannon. Joint Paymaster: Potter. Jewel Office: Sir R. Lyttelton. Surveyor of Woods: John Pitt. Board of Trade: S. Martin. Attorney General: Pratt. Treasurer of the Chamber: Charles Townshend. Employments: George Townshend; Sir Harry Erskine.
452. Rigby to Fox, 16 June 1757: 51385, f.111.
453. H to Anson, Saturday night 11 o'clock 18 June 1757: 15956, f.36.
454. Devonshire to Cumberland, 17 June 1757: Dev 260/234.
455. N to H, Wednesday morning [? 15 June 1757]: 35416, f.236; cf. N to Münchausen, 16 June 1757: 32871, f.319.
456. N to Ashburnham, 15 June 1757: 32871, f.313.
457. N to H, Wednesday morning [? 15 June 1757]: 35416, f.236.
458. H to Anson, 18 June 1757: 15956, f.36.
459. H to Devonshire, Wednesday 12 at night 15 June 1757: Dev 253/11.
460. Lord Dupplin to Lord Lincoln, 16 June 1757: Ne(c) 3667.
461. N to Lord Darlington, 21 June 1757: 32871, f.364.
462. H to Anson, 18 June 1757: 15956, f.36.
463. Devonshire to H, Wednesday evening 9 o'clock [15 June 1757]: 35595, f.43.
464. H to N, 12 p.m. Wednesday night [15 June 1757]: 32871, f.311.
465. Devonshire to Cumberland, 17 June 1757: Dev 260/234.
466. F. Frankland to T. Pelham, 16 June 1757: 33094, f.156.
467. Lord Dupplin to Lord Lincoln, 16 June 1757: Ne(c) 3667.
468. Cf. Legge to Bute, 17 June [1757]: Bute MSS, Mount Stuart, no.68. Legge was wrong in claiming he met Newcastle 'the day before yesterday', i.e. on 15th.
469. Lord Dupplin to Lord Lincoln, 16 June 1757: Ne(c) 3667.
470. N to Duchess, Thursday [? 16 June 1757]: 33075, f.147.
471. Fox to Devonshire, [16 June 1757]: Dev 330/216.
472. Rigby to Bedford, 18 June 1757: Bedford MSS, xxxiv, 25.
473. Halifax to N, 16 June 1757: 32871, f.323.
474. N to Halifax, Thursday 3 o'clock [16 June 1757]: 32871, f.321.
475. Dupplin to [? Duchess of N], 5.30 p.m. 18 June [1757]: 32871, f.335.
476. Bayntun Rolt Diary, 19 June 1757.
477. Dodington, *Diary, sub.*, 6 Apr 1757 (a later addition); cf. A. H. Basye, *The Lords Commissioners of Trade and Plantations, commonly known as the Board of Trade, 1747-1782* (New Haven, 1925), pp.82-3; Fox's Memoir, in Countess of Ilchester and Lord Stavordale (eds.), *The Life and Letters of Lady Sarah Lennox* (London, 1901), i, 36.
478. Misprinted 'Devonshire' in *Bedford Corr*, ii, 249.

479. Rigby to Bedford, 18 June 1757: Bedford MSS, xxxiv, 25.
480. H to Bute, 16 June 1757: Bute MSS, Mount Stuart, no.65; H to Pitt, 16 June 1757: PRO 30/8/1, f.182; Pitt to H, 16 June 1757: 35423, f.183.
481. N to Duchess, Friday [17 June 1757]: 33075, f.148.
482. H to George II, 12.30 17 June 1757: 35595, f.46.
483. Devonshire to H, 17 June 1757: 35595, f.48.
484. Devonshire to Cumberland, 17 June 1757: Dev 260/234. The only provisions of the scheme Devonshire singled out for mention were: Temple, Lord Privy Seal vice Gower; Gower, Master of the Horse vice Dorset; Dorset, a pension.
485. H to Bute, Friday morning 9 o'clock 17 June [1757]: Bute MSS, Mount Stuart, no.66.
486. Bute MSS, Mount Stuart, no.67: 'Use him gentle and kindly. Try to gain him, which you may do. He is disposed to be gained by you. He is jealous, that Pitt is disposed to him; or intends to rule him with a high hand. That prepossession is the predominant passion at present; and all difficulties or reserves are to be put to that account. As soon as that is removed, other things may be made practicable in the course of future meetings.'
487. Legge to Bute, 17 June [1757]: Bute MSS, Mount Stuart, no.68.
488. Cf. Lady Anson to Lord Anson, 17 June 1757: Anson MSS, Staffordshire RO.
489. N to the Duchess, [? 18 June 1757]: 33075, f.149.
490. N to H [18 June 1757]: 35416, f.238.
491. 'Paper carried this day to the King by my lord Hardwicke', 18 June 1757: 32997, f.183.
    Its provisions: Pitt, Secretary of State; Temple, a Cabinet place; Admiralty: Anson, Boscawen, West, Forbes, Hunter, Elliot, Hay (plus a seat in Parliament). Treasury: Newcastle, First Lord; Legge, Chancellor of the Exchequer; Nugent, James Grenville, Oswald. Paymaster: Fox. Treasurer of the Navy: George Grenville. Vice Treasurer of Ireland: 1/3 to Lord Duncannon vice Cholmondeley (Irish pension), 1/3 to Potter vice Ellis. Jewel Office: Sir R. Lyttelton. Seat at Board of Trade: Martin. Attorney-General: Pratt, 'on a proper promotion of Henley, in consequence of the disposition of [the] Great Seal'. Treasurer of the Chamber: Charles Townshend. Treasurer of the Household: Lord Thomond. Master of the Stag Hounds: Lord Bateman. Pension: Tennison. Employments (unspecified): George Townshend and Sir H. Erskine.
492. N to Duchess, [? 18 June 1757]: 33075, f.149.
493. N to Lord Darlington, 21 June 1757: 32871, f.364.
494. Devonshire to Cumberland, 21 June 1757: Dev 260/236.
495. Dupplin to Duchess of N, 5.30 p.m. 18 June [1757]: 32871, f.335.
496. These words are present in the draft, but deleted in the final version.
497. H to Anson, 18 June 1757: 15956, f.49.
498. N, Memo, 18 June 1757: 32997, f.218.
499. Rigby to Bedford, 18 June 1757: Bedford MSS, xxxiv, 25.
500. H to Bute, Saturday night 18 June 1757: Bute MSS, Mount Stuart, no.72; N to Bute, 18 June 1757: ibid. no.74; Bute to Newcastle, 18 June 1757: ibid. no.69; Bute to H, 20 June 1757: 35423, f.235.
501. Devonshire to Cumberland, 21 June 1757: Dev 260/236.

502. Rigby to Bedford, 18 June 1757: Bedford MSS, xxxiv, 25; cf. Walpole to Fox, 18 June 175: HW 30, p.134. Devonshire was then approached to prevent Townshend's name appearing with the new ministry in the *Gazette*: Charles Townshend to Devonshire, Saturday noon [18 June 1757]: Dev 514/3.

503. Lady Sophia Egerton to Bentinck, 20 June 1757: Eg 1719, f.24.

504. Charles Townshend to Devonshire, Friday 5 p.m. [17 June 1757]: Dev 514/2.

505. Walpole to Mann, 20 June 1757: HW 21, p.103.

506. Cf. Symmer to Mitchell, 21 June 1757: 6839, f.67.

507. Pitt to George Townshend, Friday 7 o'clock [17 June 1757] (and endorsement): HMC *Townshend*, p.393 [misdated by Townshend Friday 18 June 1757].

508. Gilbert Elliot to Minto, 18 June [1757]: NLS 11001, f.38.

509. Fox to Ellis, 21 June 1757: 51387, f.78.

510. N to H, Wednesday 1/2 past 6 [? 22 June 1757]: 35416, f.234.

511. N, Memo, 22 June 1757: 32871, f.371.

512. Cf. Lady Sophia Egerton to Bentinck, 17 June 1757: Eg 1719, f.22.

513. Rigby to Bedford, 18 June 1757: Bedford MSS, xxxiv, 25.

514. Fox to Devonshire, 18 June 1757: Dev 330/217.

515. Fox to Ellis, 21 June 1757: 51387, f.78.

516. H. S. Conway to Devonshire, 19 June 1757: Dev 416/44.

517. N to the Speaker, 19 June 1757: 32871, f.340.

518. Symmer to Mitchell, 21 June 1757: 6839, f.67.

519. N to Duchess, 22 June 1757: 33075 f.152.

520. N to Devonshire, Tuesday morning [21 June 1757]: Dev 182/95.

521. Fox to Cumberland, 21 June 1757: 51375, f.118.

522. Symmer to Mitchell, 21 June 1757: 6839, f.67.

523. H to N, 3.45 p.m. 20 June 1757: 32871, f.346.

524. Ibid.

525. Dodington, *Diary*, p.365 (undated entry).

526. Glover, *Memoirs*, pp.148–9.

527. N to H, Wednesday 1/2 past 6 [? 22 June 1757]: 35416, f.234.

528. H to N, 11.45 22 June 1757: 32871, f.373.

529. H to Pitt, 11.30 [a.m.] 22 June 1757: PRO 30/8/1, f.184.

530. Fox to Mansfield, 23 June 1757: 51430, f.103.

531. Pitt to Bute, Wednesday 4 o'clock [22 June 1757]: Pitt MSS, Mount Stuart, no. 32.

532. Halifax to Oswald, past 12, 23 June 1757: Oswald MSS, 120.

533. Dodington, *Diary*, p.365 (undated entry).

534. Glover, *Memoirs*, p.145.

535. An additional £2000 per annum as Warden of the Cinque Ports.

536. N, Memo for George II, 23 June 1757: 32871, f.379.

537. Rigby to Fox, Friday night 24 June [1757]: 51385, f.113.

538. Rigby to Bedford, Arthur's 4 o'clock [24 June 1757]: Bedford MSS, xxxiv, 31.

539. Countess to Earl of Kildare, 24 June 1757: *Leicester Corr*, i, 53.

540. N to Devonshire, Friday morning [24 June 1757]: Dev 182/96.

541. H to Anson, Thursday night 23 June 1757: 15956, f.38.

542. Pitt to N, 26 June 1757: 32871, f.405.
543. Stone to N, Friday morning [24 June 1757]: 32871, f.385; N to Pitt, 24 June 1757: 32871, f.383. Dorset was confirmed for life as Warden of the Cinque Ports.
544. N to Rockingham, 25 June 1757: WWM, R1–90.
545. H to N, Saturday night 25 June 1757: 32871, f.389. News arrived on the evening of 24th of the Prussian defeat at Kolin on 17 June.
546. H to Pitt, Saturday night 25 June 1757: PRO 30/8/1, f.186.
547. Pitt to H, 26 June 1757: 35423, f.188.
548. N to H, 26 June 1757: 32871, f.407.
549. N to the Duchess, Monday [27 June 1757]: 33075, f.155.
550. N to Bute, Monday 4 o'clock [27 June 1757]: Bute MSS, Mount Stuart, no. 87; Bute to N, 27 June [1757]: 32871 f.413.
551. Devonshire was ordered to notify Waldegrave of it on 21 June: cf. Devonshire to Cumberland, 21 June 1757: Dev 260/236.
552. Devonshire to Cumberland, 28 June 1757: Dev 260/239.
553. Devonshire to N, [28 June 1757]: 32871, f.421.
554. N to Duchess, 28 June 1757: 33075, f.157.
555. Lord Dupplin to R. Dundas, 30 June 1757: Arniston MSS, VI, no. 28A.
556. Cf. Basye, Board of Trade, pp.97–100.
557. N to the Speaker, 19 June 1757: 32871, f.340.
558. N to Rockingham, 25 June 1757: WWM, R1–90.
559. N to Ashburnham, 25 June 1757: 32871, f.397.
560. F. Frankland to T. Pelham, 21 June 1757: 33098, f.75.
561. N to Chesterfield, 29 June 1757: 32871, f.444.
562. Mansfield to Devonshire, 20 June 1757: Dev 525/1.
563. Devonshire to Mansfield, 20 June 1757: Mansfield MSS, Bundle 1359.
564. Glover, Memoirs, p.153.
565. Cumberland to Devonshire, 20 June 1757: Dev 332/5.
566. Chesterfield to N, 21 June 1757: 32871, f.367.
567. Fox to Cumberland, 21 June 1757: 51375, f.118.
568. Cf. Hillsborough to Fox, 23 June 1757: 51386, f.215.
569. Fox to Cumberland, 21 June 1757: 51375, f.118.
570. Rigby to Fox, Friday night 24 June [1757]: 51385, f.113.
571. Charles Townshend to his mother, 23 June 1757: Townshend MSS, Raynham, microfilm in Norfolk RO.
572. [J. Almon], A Review of the Reign of George II (London, 1762) p.179.
573. Pitt to H, 26 June 1757: 35423, f.188.
574. Pitt to Bute, Tuesday 11 o'clock [28 June 1757]: Pitt MSS, Mount Stuart, no. 33; cf. Bute to Pitt, Tuesday night [28 June 1757]: PRO 30/8/24, f.295.
575. Glover, Memoirs, p.150.
576. Almon, op. cit. p.179. Italics added.
577. Charles Townshend to his mother, 23 June 1757: loc. cit.
578. Devonshire to Cumberland, 28 June 1757: Dev 260/239.
579. Walpole, George II, III, 34. Sarah, Duchess of Marlborough, left Pitt £10,000 at her death in 1744.
580. Fox to Cumberland, 21 June 1757: 51375, f.118.
581. Bayntun Rolt Diary, 17 June 1757.

582. Glover, *Memoirs*, p.151.
583. Bayntun Rolt Diary, 23 June 1757.
584. Devonshire to Lord Strange, 10 June 1757: Dev 260/230.
585. Devonshire to Lord Strange, 23 June 1757: Dev 260/237.
586. F. Frankland to Thomas Pelham, 11 June 1757: 33098, f.71.
587. H. Digby to Hanbury Williams, 12 June 1757: Stowe MSS, 263, f.13.
588. Walpole to Montagu, 18 June [1757]: HW 9, p.212.
589. Lord Lyttelton to Sanderson Miller, 21 June 1757: Sanderson Miller MSS, 647.
590. H. S. Conway to Lord Stormont, 5 June 1757: Mansfield MSS, Bundle 1383.
591. N to H, 26 June 1757: 32871, f.407.
592. Devonshire to Cumberland, 28 June 1757: Dev 260/239.
593. Cf. Sherrard, *Lord Chatham. Pitt and the Seven Years' War*, p.274.
594. Waldegrave, *Memoirs*, pp.137–8. The exact date on which this was written is unknown. He died in 1763.
595. Hillsborough to Fox, 23 June 1757: 51386, f.215. Similar arguments are advanced and substantiated in E. J. S. Fraser, 'The Pitt–Newcastle Coalition and the Conduct of the Seven Years' War 1757–1760' (Oxford D. Phil. thesis, 1976). Dr Fraser's work is essential reading for an understanding of politics and strategy in those years.

CONCLUSION

1. J. B. Owen, 'George II Reconsidered' in A. Whiteman et al. (eds.) *Statesmen, Scholars and Merchants* (Oxford, 1973) 116–17.
2. It is therefore introducing an anachronism to suggest (R. Browning, *The Duke of Newcastle*, (New Haven, 1975) p.137) that Newcastle's freedom of action was circumscribed by three concentric rings of authority: parliament; the electorate; and the outermost ring, public opinion. Emden (*The People and the Constitution*, p.161) appears to hold the similar view that parliamentary majorities were about defending ministers from 'the people'.
3. Fox to Hartington, 28 Nov 1754: Dev 330/28.
4. *The Constitution. With an Address to a Great Man* (London, 1757).
5. J. L. de Lolme, *The Constitution of England, or an Account of the English Government* (London, 1775) p.91.
6. Cf. J. T. Boulton, *Arbitrary Power: an Eighteenth Century Obsession* (Manchester, 1967); de Lolme, op. cit. Book I, Chapter VII.
7. Cf. *A Second Letter to the People of England* (London, 1755) p.1.
8. E.g. in *The Monitor*, 9 Aug 1755; *A Second Address to the Livery etc.* (London, 1754).
9. Waldegrave, *Memoirs*, p.5.
10. Walpole, *George II*, I, 403.
11. Waldegrave, *Memoirs*, p.24; Sedgwick, *Bute*, pp.xlviii–xlix.
12. Thomas Carte to the Pretender, 4 March 1743; quoted in Sedgwick, I, 72.
13. Memo headed 'Popular Bills', 47090, f.116. Historians have argued (e.g. Plumb, *Growth of Political Stability*) that the franchise was progressively restricted in the early eighteenth century as part of an attempt to curb

the popular interest. It seems odd that Egmont was not aware of such an attempt. If the observations of a shrinking electorate are accurate, it may be that the process was an unconscious reaction to the advance, often remarked on, of the popular interest. Cf. I. R. Christie, 'Economical Reform and "the Influence of the Crown", 1780': *Myth and Reality*, p.301.

14. Walpole, *George II*, I, 376. From the manuscript of the *Memoirs*, it appears that this passage was written between December 1755 and August 1758, and probably at the end of 1755 or early in 1756: *ex inf.* Mr John Brooke.

15. Holdsworth, *A History of English Law*, x, 339; cf. de Lolme op. cit. Book I Chapter VII. Namier (*England*, p.4) was wrong in thinking prerogative a word which had outlasted an idea, or an idea which had outlasted a reality.

16. Walpole, *George II*, I, 239–240.

17. Cumberland's papers in the Royal Archives at Windsor have been 'weeded' and are now almost wholly devoid of political material.

18. Henry Pelham to N, 17 Aug 1752: 32729, f.113.

19. Cf. Pares, *King George III and the Politicians*, pp.33–4.

20. E. Pyle to S. Kerrich, 12 Jan 1754: Kerrich MSS, vol. 14.

21. E. Pyle to S. Kerrich, 11 Jan 1755: Kerrich MSS, vol. 14.

22. *Political Disquisitions. Proper for Public Consideration in the Present State of Affairs. In a Letter to a Noble Duke* (London, 1763) p.2.

23. It is now evident that this was no more than a rhetorical device on Pitt's part. In the wartime coalition, he interfered with the business of the departments far less than Newcastle had done; cf. Middleton, 'Pitt, Anson and the Admiralty'.

24. Browning, *Newcastle*, p.234; cf. Pares, op. cit. p.177.

25. Walpole, *George II*, I, 198–9; cf. Sedgwick, *Bute*, p.xvii for George II's intentions on his accession.

26. Pares, *King George III and the Politicians*, p.149.

27. *The Protest* (London 1757) pp.28, 40.

28. *The Con-Test*, 14 Dec 1756.

29. Quoted in McKelvey, *George III and Lord Bute*, p.108.

30. Chesterfield to Stanhope, 8 Jan 1758: Dobrée, v, 2284.

31. Conway to Lord Stormont, 10 Feb 1758: Mansfield MSS, B 1383.

32. Devonshire Diary, 5 Apr 1762: Dev 260/370.

33. Ibid. 14 Nov 1762: Dev 260/394.

34. Langford, *Rockingham Administration* p.172; Namier and Brooke I, 188.

35. Devonshire Diary, 11 Dec 1761: Dev 260/357.

36. Conway to Lord Stormont, 29 Jan 1761: Mansfield MSS, B 1383.

37. Devonshire Diary, 11 July 1761, 5 Apr 1762: Dev 260/322, 260/370.

38. H. Erskine to Bute, 19 May 1762: Bute MSS, Cardiff 2/181.

39. R. Pares, 'George III and the Politicians', *TRHS* 5th ser., I (1951), 127.

40. Thomson, *A Constitutional History of England 1642 to 1801*, p.311.

41. This sort of attempt to establish general constitutional stances by selective quotation, divorced from a precise political location, is still often adopted: cf. M. Peters, 'The "Monitor" on the constitution, 1755–1765: new light on the ideological origins of English radicalism', *EHR*, LXXXVI (1971), 706–27.

Bibliography

The place of publication is London unless otherwise stated.

MANUSCRIPTS

Some of the collections in the British Library, particularly the Holland House Papers and the Egmont Papers, are still in the course of rearrangement; the volume and folio numbers given in the references must in some cases be taken as provisional.

Several different numbering sequences are in use at Mount Stuart. The letters in Sedgwick, 'Pitt' are here cited as 'Pitt MSS, Mount Stuart'.

The papers of the Lee family, once at Hartwell, were sold in 1938 and widely dispersed. Not all the documents published by Smyth in *Aedes Hartwellianae* can now be traced, though some may be in the still unsorted papers of Sir William Lee in Yale University Library.

The Lyttelton MSS from Hagley were consulted in 1977 in their current locations, the Birmingham Reference Library and the Worcestershire Record Office. They have since been recalled by the present Viscount Cobham; part of the collection was sold at Sotheby's on 12 December 1978. The original references have, however, been retained in the notes.

Antony, Cornwall
    Buller MSS
Badminton, Gloucestershire
    Beaufort MSS
Bedford Estates Office, London
    Bedford MSS (from Woburn)
Bedford Record Office, Bedford
    Lady Lucas' Collection (from Wrest)
Berkshire Record Office, Reading
    Braybrooke MSS (R. A. Neville)
Birmingham Reference Library
    Lyttelton MSS (from Hagley)
Bodleian Library, Oxford
    Dashwood MSS: MS DD Dashwood (Bucks) B 6–11, H1, I2
    Fox MSS: Eng lett d 85; Eng lett c 144
    Grenville MSS: Eng lett d 109
    Minorca MSS: Eng hist c 231
    North MSS: North Adds c 4, c 5; North d 4–8, 23
    Townshend MSS: Eng hist d 211
    Tucker MSS: MS Don c 103, 104, 111, 112; MS Don b 19
    Dr White's MSS: MS Top Oxon c 209
    Wilkes MSS: Eng lett c 57

BIBLIOGRAPHY

Bristol University Library
    Microfilm of the Bayntun Rolt Diaries
    Pinney MSS
British Museum (British Library)
    Anson Papers: 15955–15957
    Bathurst Papers: BM Loan 57: 1, 103
    Bentinck Papers: Egerton MSS 1718, 1719, 1721, 1722, 1729, 1732–1735, 1743, 1744, 1748, 1749, 1755.
    Birch Collection: 4300–4323, 4164, 4207, 4107, 4223
    Blenheim Papers: LM2, LM3
    Bute Papers: 36796, 36797
    Calcraft Papers: 17493
    Chatham Papers: 43771 (Calcraft Correspondence), 53709F
    Chesterfield Papers: Microfilm M/723
    Colebrooke Memoir (transcript): 47589
    Collinson Papers: 28726, 28727, 28558 I
    Colman Papers (Pulteney): 18915
    Coxe Papers: 9131, 9132, 9147, 9200, 9201, 9193–9197
    Dashwood Papers: Egerton MSS 2136
    Dayrolles Papers: 15874, 15875, 15881, 15882, 15888
    Dodington Papers: 38091, 50850A
    Dropmore Papers: 59484, 59485
    Egmont Papers: 47012A, 47014B, 47015A, 47072, 47073, 47090, 47091–47098, 47136–47139
    Forster Papers: 11275
    Gore & Hale Papers: 46912
    Grenville Papers: 42083–42088, 57804–57812, 57814–57816, 57820, 57832, 57834
    Halifax Papers: Egerton MSS 929
    Hanbury Williams Papers: Stowe MSS 253, 263
    Hardwicke Papers: 35349, 35351, 35356, 35357, 35359, 35360, 35363, 35364, 35373, 35374, 35376, 35385, 35388, 35414–35417, 35423–35425, 35429, 35430, 35432, 35433, 35435–35437, 35448, 35449, 35592–35595, 35599, 35600, 35604, 35606, 35631, 35633, 35634, 35635, 35640, 35692, 35870, 35877, 35879, 35881, 35895, 36069, 36085, 35353
    Holdernesse Papers (Leeds Collection): Egerton MSS 3425–3438, 3440–3442, 3444–3449, 3454–3460, 3462–3471, 3478–3482, 3484, 3485
    Holland House Papers (Fox): 51337, 51340, 51341, 51344–51346, 51348, 51349, 51352, 51357, 51375–51388, 51392, 51393, 51396, 51398, 51399, 51402, 51403–51413, 51415, 51416, 51420, 51422–51426, 51428–51430, 51439, 51447
    Keene Papers: 43431–43440, 43443
    Keith Papers: 35477–35481, 35486, 35490, 35491, 35492
    Leeds Papers: 28051
    Ligonier Papers: 57318
    Liverpool Papers: 38197, 38331, 38332
    Mackintosh Collections: 34523
    Martin Papers: 41346, 41349, 41354–41356
    Miscellaneous Collections: 6911, 11394, 5726D, 5726B

BIBLIOGRAPHY

Mitchell Papers: 6804–6806, 6811–6814, 6823, 6824, 6831–6834, 6835, 6836, 6839, 6840, 6856, 6857, 6860, 6861, 6865, 6867, 6870, 6871, 58283–58287, 58290–58293

Newcastle Papers: 32724–32737, 32848–32873, 32684, 32874–32876, 32991B, 32992, 32995–32997, 33002, 33034, 33038, 33039, 33043, 33045, 33053, 33055, 33058, 33060, 33062, 33066, 33067, 33075, 33080, 33087, 33094, 33098.

Northumberland Papers: Microfilm M/295

Phelps Papers: Stowe MSS 256

St Albans Tavern Club Minutes: Microfilm M/602

Titley Papers: Egerton MSS 2694/2695

Townshend Papers: 41178, Microfilm M/730, 38497

Tyrawley Papers: 23634, 23638

Warburton Papers: Egerton MSS 1952, 1954, 1955, 1959

West Papers: 34728, 34729, 34732–34737

Wilkes Papers: 30867, 30875–30877

William Wynne Papers: 41843

Buckinghamshire Record Office, Aylesbury
Hartwell MSS

Cambridge University Library
Parliamentary diary of Edward Harley, later 3rd Earl of Oxford, 1734–51: Add. 6851
Division List of the Mitchell Election Petition, 24 March 1755: Add. 6575

Cambridgeshire Record Office, Cambridge
Cotton of Madingley Papers

Cardiff Central Library
Bute MSS

Carmarthenshire Record Office, Carmarthen
Cawdor MSS

Chatsworth House, Derbyshire
Devonshire MSS

William L. Clements Library, Ann Arbor, Michigan
Grenville Papers
Germaine Papers (from Drayton House)

Cornwall Record Office, Truro
Buller MSS
Johnstone MSS
Enys MSS

Corpus Christi College, Cambridge
Kerrich MSS (MSS. 584–611)
Sir George Lee–Herring Correspondence (MSS. 566)

Cumberland Record Office, Carlisle
Lonsdale MSS

Derby Central Library
Catton Collection (Sir Robert Wilmot)

Dorsetshire Record Office, Dorchester
Calcraft MSS (lately at Rempstone)

Drayton House, Northants
Sackville MSS

Essex Record Office, Chelmsford
    Braybrooke MSS
Gloucestershire Record Office, Gloucester
    Badminton MSS
    Rooke MSS
Hertfordshire Record Office, Hertford
    Lee of Totteride MSS
History of Parliament Trust transcripts (minor collections)
    Amyand MSS
    Bond MSS
    Eliot MSS
    Rose Fuller MSS
    Kemys Tynte MSS
    Money–Kyrle MSS
    West MSS (Alscot)
    Wortley MSS
    Camelford Memoir (photocopy)
Hockworthy House, Somerset
    Oswald MSS
House of Lords Record Office (Historical Collections):
    13   House of Commons speeches, 1755
    18   Sir George Lee papers
    88–93 Onslow papers
India Office Library, London
    Clive MSS
Kent Archives Office, Maidstone
    Amherst MSS
    Dorset (Sackville) MSS
    Fane MSS
    Pratt MSS
Leeds City Library
    Newby Hall MSS (Sir Thomas Robinson)
The Lewis Walpole Library, Farmington, Connecticut
    Grenville Papers
Mapperton House, Dorset
    Sandwich MSS (lately Hinchinbrooke)
Mount Stuart, Isle of Bute
    Bute MSS
    Pitt MSS
    Loudoun MSS
    James Stuart MacKenzie MSS
National Library of Scotland, Edinburgh
    Fletcher of Saltoun MSS
    Yester MSS (Marquess of Tweeddale)
    Minto MSS
    Mure of Caldwell MSS
    Erskine Murray MSS
    Halkett MSS
    Balhaldie MSS

BIBLIOGRAPHY

National Library of Wales, Aberystwyth
    Chirk Castle MSS
    Harpton Court MSS
    Philipps MSS – Add MSS 1089B
    Picton Castle MSS (Sir John Philipps)
    Powis Castle MSS
    Puleston MSS
    Stackpole Letter Book – Add MSS 1352B
    Wynnstay MSS
National Maritime Museum, Greenwich
    Hawke MSS
    Campbell MSS
Norfolk Record Office, Norwich
    Bradfer Lawrence Collection (Townshend MSS)
    Ketton Cremer MSS
    Suffield MSS
    Townshend MSS
    Microfilm of the Charles Townshend MSS at Raynham
Northamptonshire Record Office, Northampton
    Cartwright of Aynho MSS
    Isham MSS
Northumberland Record Office, Newcastle
    Allgood MSS
    Delaval MSS
    Delaval (Hastings) MSS
    Craster MSS
    Blackett (Matfen) MSS
    Naylor Commonplace Book
Nottingham University Library
    Newcastle (Clumber) MSS
Petworth, Sussex
    Wyndham MSS
Public Record Office
    Chatham Papers: PRO 30/8/ : 1, 5–8, 10, 11, 17–21, 24–27, 30–40, 45–57, 60–62, 64, 66, 68–71, 74–78, 82–85, 88, 89, 91, 92, 94, 95, 98–100
    Granville Papers: PRO 30/29/ :1(1–13); 1(14–18); 2
    Egremont Papers: PRO 30/47/ :28, 29
    Neville & Aldworth Papers: PRO 30/50/ : 59, 60
    Powis Papers: PRO 30/53/8
    Shaftesbury Papers: PRO 30/24/28
    Rodney Papers: PRO 30/20/: 13, 15, 20, 24–26
    Hoare (Pitt) Papers: PRO 30/70/: 1, 3, 8
Royal Archives, Windsor Castle
    Cumberland MSS
    Hartwell MSS (Sir George Lee)
    George III MSS (as Prince of Wales)
    George II MSS
    Letters from Frederick Prince of Wales

BIBLIOGRAPHY

Royal Institution of Cornwall, Truro
    Enys Autograph Collection
    Polwhele MSS
John Rylands Library, Manchester
    Legge MSS (MSS 668)
    Namier MSS (MSS 669)
    Bromley-Davenport MSS
Salop Record Office, Shrewsbury
    Attingham MSS
Sandon Hall, Staffordshire
    Harrowby MSS, including the diaries of Sir Dudley Ryder and Nathaniel
      Ryder
Scone Palace, Perth
    Mansfield MSS
Scottish Record Office, Edinburgh
    Seafield MSS
    Hall of Dunglass MSS
    Buccleuch MSS (Dalkeith)
    Buccleuch MSS (Bowhill) – microfilm
    Dundas of Arniston MSS – microfilm
    Loudoun Letterbook – microfilm
Sheffield City Library
    Wentworth Woodhouse Muniments (Rockingham)
Sherborne Castle, Dorset
    Digby MSS
Somerset Record Office, Taunton
    Kemys Tynte MSS
    Luttrell MSS
Staffordshire Record Office/William Salt Library, Stafford
    Anson MSS
    Bagot MSS
    Dartmouth MSS
    Leveson–Gower MSS
East Suffolk Record Office, Bury St Edmunds
    Grafton MSS
West Sussex Record Office, Chichester
    Goodwood MSS: Richmond Papers; Gordon Papers; Laing Papers
Warwickshire Record Office, Warwick
    Newdigate MSS
    Mordaunt MSS
    Sanderson Miller MSS
Worcestershire Record Office, Worcester
    Lechmere MSS
    Lyttelton MSS
Yale University Library
    Townshend MSS
    Bagot MSS
    Sir John Eardley Wilmot MSS

BIBLIOGRAPHY

PERIODICALS

The Protester (2 June–10 Nov 1753)
The Whitehall Evening Post
The Public Advertiser
The Daily Advertiser
The London Gazette
Read's Weekly Journal
The London Evening Post
The London Chronicle
The World
The Monitor (9 Aug 1755–)
The Test (6 Nov 1756–9 July 1757)
The Con–Test (23 Nov 1756–6 Aug 1757)

PAMPHLETS, BROADSIDES, BALLADS AND OTHER CONTEMPORARY WORKS

The place of publication is London unless otherwise stated, though pamphlets published in Dublin were often re-published in London and vice versa.

Items are arranged within years in alphabetical order of title, and the location of one copy of each item has been recorded.

From advertisements of new publications in the daily press, and in the monthly catalogues of the *London Magazine*, it is clear that many pamphlets appeared of which no copy has survived. It has proved impossible to trace 126 such titles from 1753–7 which would otherwise have appeared below.

Also omitted from the following list are a great number of sermons and pamphlets of a religious and moralising nature for those years.

1753

An Address to the Freeholders of the County of Oxford, on the subject of the present Election (BL: 1093 e 37(1)).

A Second Address to the Freeholders of the County of Oxford, in vindication of a former address against the writer of a Letter to the Printer, with a letter to the freeholders of Oxfordshire etc. (BL: 1093 e 37(2)).

An Address to the Friends of Great Britain (BL: T816(3)).

The Advantages of the Revolution Illustrated. By G— B— Esq. (BL: 8132 c 7).

Advice from Horace to Lady S[u]s[a]n [Keck]. [? London ? 1753] (BL: 840 k 6(2)).

Answer to the Appendix of a Pamphlet, entitled, Reflexions on Naturalisation, Corporations and Companies, etc. By Jonas Hanway. (BL: 111 e 18(2)).

An Answer to a late Pamphlet intituled, 'A Free and Candid Inquiry, Addressed to the Representatives etc. of this Kingdom' (Dublin) (BL: 8145 e 83).

Answer to a Pamphlet entitled, 'Considerations on the Bill to Permit Persons Professing the Jewish Religion to be Naturalised' [by William Romaine] (BL: 1093 e 30).

BIBLIOGRAPHY

An Apology for the Naturalisation of the Jews...By a True Believer (CUL: 8.22.23³).

The Ballance; or the merits of Whig and Tory, exactly weighed and fairly determined (BL: 8133 cc 12).

The Bill, Permitting the Jews to be Naturalised by Parliament having been misrepresented...[By P. C. Webb] (BL: 213 i 2 (46)).

The Case and Appeal of James Ashley...Addressed to the Public in General (BL: 6495 b 2).

The Case of Henry Simons, a Polish Jew Merchant; and his Appeal to the Public thereon (BL: 1418 g 33).

The Christian's New Warning Piece: or a full and true account of the Circumcision of Sir E[dward] T[urner] Bart., as it was perform'd at the Bear-Inn in the City of Oxford (BL: G 3640 (2)).

Considerations on the Bill to Permit Persons Professing the Jewish Religion to be Naturalised by Parliament [by Philo-Patriae, pseud.] (BL: T 816 (1)).

A Copy of what Dr Archibald Cameron Intended to have delivered to the Sheriff of Middlesex (BL: C115 i 3 (104)).

The Counterpoise: being Thoughts on a Militia and a Standing Army. By W[illiam] T[hornton] 1st edn 1752 (2nd edn: BL: 8122 f.57).

The Court and Country Interest United; or, Proposals for a Free and Impartial Election (CUL: X. 25. 22).

Court and no Country. A seri-tragi-comi-farcical entertainment (CUL: Hib. 7.750.2²⁵) ['London';? sc. Dublin].

Dedication on Dedication: or, a Second Edition of a Dedication to his Grace the D[uke] of D[orset] (BL: 8145 e 83).

Dissertations on the Ancient History of Ireland, etc. [*By Charles O'Conor*] (BL: 809 i 12).

The Dublin Spy (BL: PP 3587) (no. 1, 22 Aug 1753, to no. xlv, 8 Mar 1754).

The Duke of Newcastle's Letter by His Majesty's order, to Monsieur Michell (BL: 593 d 21 (7)).

An Earnest and Serious Address to the Freeholders and Electors of Great Britain (BL: 1093 e 31).

An Edict to his Grace the D[uke of] D[orset] ... (BL: 1890 ce 5 (225)).

The Election Magazine, or the Oxfordshire Register (Oxford) (BL: 809 e 35).

Esther's Suit to King Ahasuerus in behalf of the Jews. In a letter to a Member of Parliament (BL: T 2231 (22)).

*The False Accusers: or, Who drank the P****'s health? A sermon lately preached in a chapel near St James's...* (BL: 1490 dd 53).

A Fragment of the History of Patrick [? By Dr Allen] (BL: 900 g 32 (2)).

A Free and Candid Inquiry humbly addressed to the Representatives of the several Counties and Boroughs in this Kingdom [By John Brett] (Dublin) (BL: 8145 aaa 57).

Free Will to Freeholders. By C[harle]s L[ucas]s (BL: 8146 f 43).

Further Considerations on the Act to Permit Persons Professing the Jewish Religion to be Naturalised by Parliament [By Philo–Patriae, pseud.] (BL: T 816 (2)).

The Groans of Great Britain: with a table of the contests. Inscribed to all true Britons, by an Englishman (BL: 1093 e 32).

The Groans of Ireland [By Philo–Patriae, pseud.] (BL: 8142 aa 15).

BIBLIOGRAPHY

The Harlequins. A Comedy (BL: 8145 e 83).

Hibernia Pacata: or, a Narrative of the Affairs of Ireland...(Dublin) (BL: 8145 e 83).

His Grace Lionel, Duke of Dorset...his Speech to both Houses of Parliament, at Dublin: on Thursday, the ninth day of October, 1753 (Dublin) (BL: 1890 e 5 (115)).

The History of the Dublin Election with a Sketch of the Present State of Parties in the Kingdom of Ireland. By a Briton (CUL: Hib 7. 753. 7). [Election of 1749].

The Impartial Observer: Being a Modest Reply to what has been lately published relating to the intended Naturalisation of the Jews (BL: T 816(5)).

Insula Sacra et Libera. A List of the Members of the Hon. House of Commons of Ireland who voted for and against the altered Money-Bill, which was rejected on Monday the 17th Day of December, 1753 (CUL: Hib. 00. 753.1).

A Letter from a Free Citizen of Dublin to a Freeholder in the County of Armagh (Dublin) (CUL: Hib. 7. 750. 1²⁴).

A Second Letter from a Free Citizen of Dublin, to a Freeholder in the County of Armagh (Dublin) (CUL: Hib. 7. 750.1²⁵).

A Letter from George the First in Aungier-street, to William the Third on College Green (Dublin) (CUL: Hib. 7. 750. 1²¹).

A Letter from Sir R[ichar]d C[o]x, to a Certain Great Man and his Son. On the Present State of Affairs in Ireland (Dublin) (CUL: Hib. 7. 750. 2²) [i.e. to Dorset and Sackville].

A Letter from the D[uke] of D[orset] to the L[or]d C[hance]ll[o]r of Ireland (BL: 8145 bb 18).

A Letter from the Earl of H—r—ss, to the L[ord] C[hancello]r of Ireland (BL: E 2092 (2)).

A Letter of Advice from an Old Party Writer to a Novice in the Trade, containing some friendly criticisms on the History of Roger, and a Dedication on a Dedication, with several curious instructions in the Art of Political Lying [Dublin] (BL: E 2092).

A Letter to a Friend Concerning Naturalisation...By Josiah Tucker (BL: T 1627(6)).

A Second Letter to a Friend Concerning Naturalisations. By Josiah Tucker (BL: 522 g 4(3)).

A Letter to a Member of Parliament, concerning the Money Bill (Dublin) (BL: 8145 bb 76).

A Letter to a Member of the H[ous]e of C[ommon]s of I[relan]d, on the Present Crisis of Affairs in the Kingdom (BL: 8145 e 83).

A Letter to a Person of Distinction in Town, from a Gentleman in the Country. Containing some remarks on a late pamphlet, intitled, 'A Free and Candid Inquiry' etc (Dublin) (BL: 8145 e 83).

A Second Letter to a Person of Distinction in Town, from a Gentleman in the Country. Containing...some remarks on a late pamphlet, entitled, 'Political Pastime; or, Faction Displayed' (Dublin) (BL: 8145 e 83).

A Letter to the Printer; with a letter to the Freeholders of Oxfordshire. Containing, some few candid remarks on a new pamphlet, intitled, An Address to the Freeholders of the County of Oxford. By 'D.G.' (Oxford) (BL: 1609/947).

A Letter to the Public on the Act for Naturalising the Jews. By 'A.Z.' (BL: T 2231(24)).

A Letter to the Revd. Thomas Fothergill . . . By 'C.P.' (BL: 731 k 11(4)).

Letters Admonitory and Argumentative, from J. H[anwa]y, Merchant, to J. S—r, Merchant, in Reply to Particular Passages, and the General Argument, of a Pamphlet, entitled, Further Considerations on the Bill, etc. (CUL: 8.22.23).

The Life of Dr Archibald Cameron... (CUL: Syn. 7. 75. 35⁶).

A List of Members of the Hon. House of Commons of I[relan]d, who voted on the Question previous to the Expulsion of Arthur Jones Nevill Esq... (CUL: Hib. 7. 756. 1¹⁷).

A Memorial by the E[ar]l of K[i]ld[ar]e to His M[a]j[est]y... (BL: 115 h 20).

The Memorial of J[ames] F[itzgerald], E[arl] of K[ildare]...in behalf of the subjects of I[relan]d (BL: 8132 bb 32 (14)).

A Memorial Presented to his M[a]j[e]s[t]y, by the Right Honourable the Earl of K[il]d[ar]e... (BL: E 2092).

Notes and Observations on the Fundamental Laws of England. By G. Horseman (CUL: Syn. 7. 75. 24²).

Old Interest: a farce of three and forty acts, as it is perform'd with great disaffection at the Th[eatr]e in O[x]f[or]d...Being a true specimen of Old Interest Religion, Old Interest Politicks, Reasoning and Manners, and a full answer to an anonymous pamphlet entitled The circumcision of Sir E. T. etc. By George Greenwood (BL: 162 h 3).

The Other Side of the Question. Being a Collection of what hath yet appeared in defence of the late Act in favour of the Jews [? By R. Flexman] (CUL: Yorke c. 227³).

The Oxfordshire Contest: or the whole controversy between the old and new interest, etc. (BL: G 3633).

Patrick's Purgatory: or, a Fragment shall be Saved (Dublin) (BL: 900 g 32).

The Patriot (Dublin) (BL: 900 g 32).

Political Pastime; or, Faction Displayed. In a Letter to the Author of the Candid Inquiry (Dublin) [? by John Brett] (BL: 8145 bb 96).

A Proposal Humbly Offered to the Legislature of this Kingdom, for the Reestablishment of Christianity [By 'Timothy Telltruth', pseud.] (BL: T 816 (6)).

Queries Relative to the Present Chrisis of Affairs, Humbly Addressed to all true Patriots (BL: E 2092).

The Question, whether a Jew, born within the British Dominions, was, before the making of the late Act of Parliament, a Person capable, by law, to purchase and hold lands to him, and his heirs, fairly stated and considered [? By P. C. Webb] (BL: 1093 e 35).

Reflections of *******. Being a series of political maxims, etc. [? By L. A. de la Beaumelle] (BL: 1489 r 81).

Reflections upon Naturalisation, Corporations, and Companies (BL: 111 e 18 (1)).

A Review of the Proposed Naturalisation of the Jews... By J[onas] H[anway] (BL: T 815 (4)).

Mr Robert S[cot]t's Speech before the H[onourabl]e H[ous]e of C[ommon]s of I[relan]d... (BL: 1890 e 5 (125)).

BIBLIOGRAPHY

The R[o]y[a]l Mistake, or A Catechism for the I[ri]sh Parliament (CUL: Hib. 7. 753. 20).

Seasonable Advice to the Freeholders of the County of Armagh [?Dublin] (CUL: Hib. 7. 753. 21).

Seasonable Thoughts relating to our Civil and Ecclesiastical Constitution [By C. O'Conor] (Dublin) (CUL: Hib. 7. 753. 22).

A Sermon Preached at the Parish Church of St. George, Hanover Square, Sunday, October 28, 1753: on occasion of the clamours against the Act for naturalising the Jews. By the Rev. Mr Winstanley (BL: T 816(4)).

A Short Account of His Majesty's Hereditary Revenue and Private Estate in the Kingdom of Ireland [By Gorges Edmund Howard] (Dublin) (CUL: Hib. 7. 753. 23).

Short Observations upon a Letter lately published, from Somebody to Somebody (Dublin) (BL: 900 g 32 (3)).

Some Queries, Relative to the Jews; Occasioned by a late Sermon: with some other Papers, occasioned by the Queries (BL: T 815 (7)).

Some Remarks on the Late Lord Bolingbroke's famous Letter to Sir William Wyndham, in a course of Letters from a Gentleman in Town to his Friend in the Country. By 'Philalethes', pseud. (CUL: 7540. c. 90).

By Special Command. For the benefit of Ireland, For near two Years in Rehearsal, and will be performed at the Great Booth in College Green... the 7th of October, 1753, a Tragi-comical farcical Entertainment, not acted these three Years, called...Court and Country [? Dublin] (CUL: Hib. 1. 679. 1[75]).

The Spirit of Nations. Translated from the French (BL: 7005 df 14).

The Spirit of Party...Being an introduction to the history of the knight of the Bridge, etc. [By Henry Brooke] (Dublin) (BL: 8145 bb 117).

The True Life of Betty Ireland (Dublin) (BL: 8145 e 83).

A Tryal between Patrick and Roger, with a fragment of the history of Patrick (BL: 900 g 30 (10)).

A Vindication of L[ord] K[ildare]'s Memorial, etc. (Dublin) (BL: 8132 bb 32 (15)).

Vindiciae Judaeorum: or, a Letter in Answer to Certain Questions [By 'Rabbi Manasseh ben Israel', pseud.] (BL: T 816 (8)).

1754

An Account of the Life, Character and Parliamentary Conduct of the Right Hon. Henry Boyle, Esq...to which is added a general answer to a pamphlet entitled Moderation Recommended to Friends of Ireland etc. [By 'Philo Patriae', pseud.] (Dublin) (BL: 10816 b 2).

An Account of the Revenue and National Debt of Ireland. With some observations on the late Bill for paying off the national debt (BL: 1508/797).

An Address from the Free Electors of the Pro[vi]nce of Ul[st]er to Anthony Malone, Esq; The Right Honourable Thomas Carter, etc. and Bellngham [sic] Boyle, Esqrs. Wherein their... Corruption in P[arliamen]t ... are duly considered...[? Dublin] (CUL: Hib. 7. 750. 3⁹).

An Address from the Independent Electors of the County of Westmeath, to Anthony Malone, Esq...[? Dublin] (CUL: Hib. 7. 754. 75).

573

BIBLIOGRAPHY

An Address from the Independent Electors of the...Town of Inniskillen... (Belfast) (BL: 8145 e 83).

An Address from the Independent Freeholders of the P[ro]v[in]ce of M[u]ns[te]r to Sir R[ichard] C[ox] Baronet [Dublin] (BL: E 2092 (14)).

An Address from the Ladies of the Provinces of Munster and Leinster to their Graces the Duke and Duchess of D[orse]t...and Caiaphas, the High Priest ... (BL: 8146 f 33).

An Address to Friends and Foes (Dublin) (BL: 8145 e 83).

An Address to the Inhabitants of Ireland By C. L[uca]s (Dublin) (BL: 8145 bb 71).

An Address to the Livery of the City of London on the approaching election for representatives to serve in parliament. By 'Sir Andrew Freeport', pseud. (BL: 816 m 9 (48)).

A Second Address to the Livery, etc. (BL: 816 m 9 (48)).

An Answer to a Letter, published in the Gazette, relating to the Money Bill [Dublin] (CUL: Hib. 1. 679. 1[84]).

An Answer to Part of a Pamphlet, intitled, the Proceedings of the Honourable House of Commons of Ireland, in Rejecting the Altered Money Bill, on December 17 1753, Vindicated etc. [By David Bindon] (Dublin) (BL: E 2092).

The Authentic History of Doctor Hellebore [? i.e. Charles Lucas] (BL: PP 3726 d).

The Cabinet: Containing, A Collection of curious Papers, relative to the present political Contests in Ireland... (BL: 8145 e 83).

A Candid Enquiry why the Natives of Ireland, which are in London, are More Addicted to Vice than the People of Any Other Nation; even to the Dread and Terror of the Inhabitants of this Metropolis (CUL: Hib. 5. 754. 2).

The Case Fairly Stated, or an inquiry how far the clause lately rejected by the honourable House of Commons, would, if passed, have affected the liberties of the people of Ireland [By John Leland] (BL: E 2092 (15)).

Common Sense; in a letter to a friend (Dublin) (BL: 8145 e 83).

The Conduct of — Coll. Considered (BL: 8364 de 3).

Considerations on the late Bill for payment of the remainder of the National Debt, etc. [By Christopher Robinson] (BL: 8145 bb 50).

A Cottager's Remarks on the Farmer's Spirit of Party [By Charles O'Conor] (Dublin) (BL: 900 g 32 (3)).

The C[ourtie]rs Apology to the Freeholders of this Kingdom for their conduct this S[es]s[io]n of P[a]rl[iame]nt; containing some pieces of interesting humour, necessary to be made known to the free and independent electors of I[relan]d. To which is added, a bill of C[our]t mortality, etc. [? Dublin] (BL: E 2092 (5)).

The Cow of Haslemere: or, the Conjuror's Scrutiny at Oxford (BL: 1346 m 4).

The Crisis, or an Alarm to Britainnia's true Protestant Sons (BL: 8133 c 11).

A Defence of the Case Fairly Stated, against a late pamphlet intitled, Truth against Craft, or Sophistry and Falsehood detected. By the Author of the Case Fairly Stated [i.e. John Leland] (Dublin) (BL: 8145 aaa 16).

A Defence of the Rector and Fellows of Exeter College (BL: 731 k 11 (7)).

A Dialogue between Dick—and Tom—, Esqrs.; Relating to the Present Divisions in I[relan]d (Dublin) (CUL: Hib. 7. 754. 13).

BIBLIOGRAPHY

ΔΙΑΣΠΟΡΑ. *Some Reflections upon the Question relating to the Naturalisation of Jews, considered as a Point of Religion. In a Letter from a Gentleman in the Country, to his friend in Town* (BL: T 815 (5)).

The Doctrine of Passive Obedience and Non-Resistance Considered. With some observations on the necessity and advantages of the Revolution in the year 1688. By [Robert] Wallace (Edinburgh) (BL: 1093 e 44).

An Epistle from Th[oma]s Sh[erida]n, Esq; to the Universal Advertiser (Dublin) (CUL: Hib. 7. 750. 2²).

An Essay on Lying. Inscribed to all True Lovers of their Country (Dublin) (CUL: Hib. 7. 750. 29⁵).

An Essay on the Liberty of the Press chiefly as it respects personal slander [? By the Bishop of Norwich] (CUL: Syn. 7. 75. 19⁵).

The Fable of Jotham: to the Borough-Hunters [by Richard Owen Cambridge] (BL: 11630 g 19 (3)).

The Fatal Consequences of Bribery, exemplified in Judas. By William Reeves (BL: 695 g 11 (1)).

Fifty Queries concerning the present Oxfordshire contest (BL: 1093 e 46).

The Finishing Stoke. Being a Short Supplement to the Queries to the People of Ireland (Dublin) (CUL: Hib. 7. 754. 69).

The Free Citizens' Address to Sir Samuel Cooke, Bart... (BL: E 2092).

A Full Account of the present Dispute in Ireland, between the prerogatives of the Crown, and the Rights of the People: together with Reflections on the Present political Contest in that Kingdom (Dublin) (CUL: Hib. 7. 754. 16).

The History of an Old Lady and her Family (BL: 1416 K 57).

The History of our National Debts and Taxes, from the Year MDCLXXXVIII to the Year MDCCLI [By G. Gordon] (CUL: Ddd. 25. 120).

The History of the Ministerial Conduct of the Chief Governors of Ireland... from...1688, to the never-to-be-forgotten 17th of December, 1753. With a general Review, of the most remarkable Proceedings in Parliament during that Period...To which is prefix'd, An Introductory Survey of the English Ministry... (CUL: Hib. 5. 754. 11).

The History of the Several Oppositions which have been made in England, from the restoration of King Charles the Second both against the Court and the ministrial influence. Representing the many noble attempts made, by British Patriots, for the Establishment of British Liberty. By Sir Myles Stanhope. (CUL: Acton d. 25. 132).

The Honest Man's Apology to his Country for his Conduct. Humbly submitted ...with his Reasons for...accepting a Place from the Crown (Dublin) (CUL: Hib. 7. 754. 19).

An Humble Address to the Worthy Patriots of Ireland on the happy and providential events, which have crowned thier labours in defence of their country [? Dublin] (BL: 8145 e 83).

An Inquiry into the Origin and Consequences of the Public Dept. By a Person of Distinction (Bod: G. Pamph. 1922 (9)).

The Irish Intelligencer (Bod: G. Pamph. 1921 (16)).

Joshua Pym to Dionysius the Areopagite [i.e. Sir Richard Cox] (Dublin) (CUL: Hib. 7. 754. 46).

Kiss a Patriot's A—se. Or, Letters between A[rthu]r R[och]f[or]t Esq. and E[dmun]d P[er]y Esq. etc. (Dublin) (BL: 1414 b 30).

BIBLIOGRAPHY

A Letter from a Merchant in Newry, to A Merchant in Dublin [? Dublin] (CUL: Hib. 1. 679. 85).

A Letter from Dionysius to the Renowned Triumvirate [By David Bindon] (BL: 8145 e 83) [Dionysius=Sir R. Cox].

A Letter from a Gentleman at Cork, to his friend in Dublin. Concerning the Loan Bill, rejected on the 17th Dec. 1753. By 'J.B.' (Dublin) (BL: 8145 bb 1).

A Letter from a P[ri]me S[er]j[ean]t to a H[ig]h P[ries]t, Concerning the Present Posture of Affairs...(Dublin) (CUL: Hib. 7. 754. 30).

A Letter from His G[race] the L[ord] P[rimate] of all I[reland], to the Chevalier de St. George...[? Dublin] (BL: 8145 e 83).

A Letter from a M[ember] of the H[ouse] of C[ommons] to a Gentleman in the North of Ireland (Dublin) (BL: E 2092).

A letter to the Author of the Ode on Mr Pelham's Death...(BL: 1087 c 27 (4)).

A Letter to the Author of the Queries to the People of Ireland [? Dublin] (BL: 8145 e 83).

A Letter to the Freeholders of the County of Norfolk...[By Charles Townshend] (BL: 8138 df 19 (6)).

A Letter to the Public on the Present Posture of Affairs...(Dublin) [By Gorges Edmund Howard] (Dublin) (BL: 8145 bb 48 (1)).

A Second Letter to the Public, on the Present Posture of Affairs...(Dublin) (BL: 8145 bb 48 (2)).

A Third Letter to the Public, on the Present Posture of Affairs...By 'Philo Hibernicus' [i.e. G. E. Howard] (Dublin) (BL: 8145 bb 48 (3)).

A Letter to the Right Honourable James, Earl of Kildare on the present posture of affairs...[By Councillor Madden] (Dublin) (BL: 8145 bb 98).

A Letter to the Rt. Hon. the Lord—. Occasioned by a pamphlet just published, entitled 'Thoughts on the Affairs of Ireland'...By 'M. B. Drapier' (BL: 8145 c. 14).

A Letter to the Tradesmen, Farmers, and the Rest of the Good People of Ireland. By 'L. B. Haberdasher' [i.e. Rev. John Gast] (Dublin) (CUL: Hib. 7. 750. 1⁹).

A Second Letter to the Tradesmen, Farmers and the Rest of the Good People of Ireland. By 'L. B. Haberdasher' [i.e. Rev. John Gast] (Dublin) (BL: E 2092).

Life, Character and Parliamentary Conduct of the Right Honourable Henry Boyle, Esq. (BL: 10816 b 2).

Memoirs of the late Ignoble and Dishonourable R******t S***t, unworthy Representative of the Borough of N[ewr]y (Downpatrick) (CUL: Hib. 1. 679. 86).

Moderation Recommended to the Friends of Ireland, whether of the Court, or Country Party [By 'Hibernicus', pseud] (Dublin) (BL: 8145 bb 36).

The Modern Querists Examined, or a Word of Advice to the Scriblers on both sides of the present Importnat [sic], and interesting Question (CUL: Hib. 7. 750. 3⁵).

A New Ballad. To be sung by the C.....t Party on the Seventeenth Day of December 1754 [? Dublin 1754] (CUL: Hib. 1. 679. 87).

A New Year's Gift, for the New Interest Freeholders; or, a Short Catechism, whereby the Voters of the New Interest may be readily instructed to give

BIBLIOGRAPHY

a full and proper account of themselves and their principles (Bod. G. Pamph. 1922 (51)).

An Ode on the Death of Mr Pelham [By David Garrick] (BL: 11630 g 19 (2)).

Old Interest Fury...(BL: 8132 aa 15 (7)).

Oxfordshire in an Uproar; or the Election magazine [? 1754] (BL: 12363 ddd 5).

The Patriot, or the Irish Packet Open'd (BL: PP 3426) A collected reprint of the Dublin periodical, 25 Oct–6 Dec 1753.

Patriot Queries, occasioned by a Late Libel, entitled, 'Queries to the People of Ireland' ... (Dublin) (BL: 8145 e 83).

Political Fire Eating (Dublin) (BL: 1890 e 5 (141)).

The P[rimate] Vindicated, and the affairs of I[relan]d set in a true Light (BL: 8145 e 83).

The Proceeding of the Honourable House of Commons of Ireland, in rejecting the altered money-bill, on December 17, 1753, vindicated by authorities taken from the law and usage of Parliament. Wherein are occasionally exposed the fallacies of two pamphlets, intitled, 'Considerations on the Late Bill, etc.' and 'Observations relative to the late Bill for paying off the residue of the National Debt' [By Sir Richard Cox] (Dublin) (BL: E 2092 (9)).

The Quaker's Answer to the Weaver's Letter (BL: 8145 aa 20).

Queries to the Querist: or, a Series of 141 Queries, In Vindication of the Conduct and Characters of the Patriots of Ireland...traduced in a...Libel lately published by Dr B[re]tt, entitled Queries to the People of Ireland [? Dublin] (BL: 8145 bb 10).

A Question to be considered. Previous to the Rejection of the Bill for paying off the National Debt, upon Account of inserting to the Preamble, His Majesty's previous Consent...(Dublin) (CUL: Hib. 5. 754. 25).

Remarks on a Pamphlet Intitled, Considerations on the Late Bill, for paying the National Debt, etc. (Dublin) (CUL: Hib. 7. 754. 47$^{1-4}$).

Remarks on two Letters signed Theatricus and Hibernicus, and published in the Dublin Journal of the 12th and 23rd of February 1754 [By 'Libertus', pseud.] (Dublin) (BL: 641 d 30 (14)).

A Reply to the Famous Jew Question...*in a Letter to the Gentlemen of Lincoln's Inn* (BL: 514 f 25 (2)).

The Review: Being a short account of the doctrine, arguments, and tendency, of the writings offered to the public, by the C[our]t Advocates, since last September (Dublin) (BL: 8145 e 83).

Ringing of the Bell: or, a Hue and Cry after Raynard the Fox [By 'Roger Spy', pseud.] (Dublin) (BL: 1890 e 5 (144)).

Roger the Hunt's-Man Hue and Cry after an old Runaway Male Pett Fox (BL: 1890 e 5 (145)).

The Secret History of the two last memorable sessions of Parliament (Dublin) (Bod: G. Pamph. 1922 (19)).

Serious Considerations on the Present State of the Affairs of the Northern Colonies. By Archibald Kennedy (BL: 104 i 47).

Mr S[herida]n's Apology to the Town; with the Reasons which unfortunately induced him to his late Misconduct (Dublin) (BL: E 2092).

Some Cautions offered to the Consideration of those who are to choose Members to serve in the ensuing Parliament. [By George Savile, 1st Marquis of Halifax] (CUL: Syn. 5. 69. 10^{16}. 1st edn 1695; here the 1745 edn).

577

BIBLIOGRAPHY

Some Observations Relative to the late Bill for Paying Off the Residue of the National Debt of Ireland...(Dublin) (BL: E 2092).

The State of Ireland, Laid open to the View of His Majesty's Subjects (CUL: Hib. 5. 798. 3⁷).

A Supplement to the Remarks on a Pamphlet intitled, Considerations on the Late Bill for Paying the National Debt, etc. (Dublin) (CUL: Hib. 7. 754. 50).

Terrae Filius; or, the Secret History of the University of Oxford. By N. Amhurst (BL: PP 6019 i a).

Thoughts on some late Removals in Ireland, in a letter to the...*Earl of Kildare* [By 'Hiberno-Britannicus', pseud.] (BL: 8145 c 31).

Thoughts on the Affairs of Ireland: with the Speeches of the Lord Chancellor, Cardinal Wolsey, and Gerald Earl of Kildare (Bod: G. Pamph. 1922 (6)).

To all the Serious, Honest, and Well-meaning People of Ireland, The following Queries are affectionately Addressed...[? Dublin] [? By Dr John Brett] (CUL: Hib. 7. 754. 67).

To His Grace Lionel, Duke of Dorset...*The Humble Petition of Truth, Virtue and Liberty* (Dublin) (CUL: Hib. 7. 747. 28⁷).

Truth against Craft: or, Sophistry and Falsehood detected. In Answer to a Pamphlet intitled, The Case fairly stated: and likewise to The Defence of the Considerations (Dublin) (CUL: Hib. 7. 754. 70).

Tyranny Display'd. In a Letter from a Looker-on...(Dublin) (CUL: Hib. 5. 754. 23).

The Universal Advertiser. Containing A Collection of Essays, Moral, Political and Entertaining: together with Addresses from several Corporate and other Bodies in Ireland, to their Representatives in Parliament, in relation to their Conduct on the 23rd of November and the 17th of December, 1753 (Dublin) [By Sir Richard Cox]. A reprint of the periodical, from 3 Feb 1753 to 6 Aug 1754 (CUL: Hib. 8. 754. 7).

A Vindication of the Conduct of the Late Manager [Thomas Sheridan] of the Theatre Royal Humbly addressed to the Public (Dublin) (CUL: Hib. 7. 754. 55).

A Vindication of Truth against Craft, in Answer to the Defence of the Case Fairly Stated: in a letter to the Author of said Case and Defence (Dublin) (Bod: G. Pamph. 1921 (14)).

The Weaver's Letter to the Tradesmen and Manufacturers of Ireland (Dublin) (CUL: Hib. 7. 754. 71).

1755

An Address to the Revd Dr Huddesford, Vice Chancellor of Oxford...(BL: 731 K 11 (8)).

The Advertiser's Answer to a Quaker's Letter, concerning a coalition (Dublin) (BL: 8145 e 83).

An Answer to a Pamphlet, called, a Second Letter to the People. In which the subsidiary system is fairly stated, and amply considered. (BL: 8026 bb 11).

An Answer to Mr B[laco]w's Apology...(BL: 1414 b 20).

Mr Blacow's Apology: or, a Letter to William King...*containing an account of the treasonable riot at Oxford, on the reputed birthday of Cardinal Stuart, in February 1747.* By Richard Blacow (BL: 731 K 11 (9)).

BIBLIOGRAPHY

A Candidate Author's Letter to the P[rima]te. By B[ernard] C[lar]ke (Dublin) (BL: 8145 e 83).

The Case of the Roman Catholics of Ireland [By Charles O'Conor]. (Dublin) (CUL: Hib. 7. 755. 13).

A Christmas-Box for the Enemies of Roger, and his Country [On the Earl of Shannon] [? Dublin] (CUL: Hib. 1. 679. 1⁹³).

The Conduct of a Certain Member of Parliament, during the Last Session; and the Motives on which he acted; explained. In a letter to a friend [By Henry Sheares] (Dublin) (BL: 8145 e 83).

A Constituent's Answer to the Reflections of a Member of Parliament upon the present state of affairs at home and abroad...(BL: 8133 aaa 34).

The Counterpoise; being thoughts on a Militia and a standing army [? By W. Thornton] (BL: 716 d 14 (3) – 1752 edition).

The Country Gentleman's Advice to his Neighbours. By Edward Weston (BL: 698 e 12 (5)).

The Country Gentleman's Advice to his Son, on his coming of age, in the year 1755, with regard to his political conduct...[? By Abraham Tucker] (BL: 8401 dd 12 (2)).

The Courtier and Patriot...*An Epistle to His Grace the Duke of Newcastle.* (BL: 11630 g 19 (6)).

A Discourse of Government with relation to Militias. By Andrew Fletcher [1st edn 1697] (BL: 1093 d 122).

A Discourse upon Informations and Informers. (Bod: Vet. A.5 e 59 (2)).

Doctor King's Apology...By Dr William King (Oxford) (BL: 731 k 11 (2)).

The Earl Poulett's Motion in the House of Lords on...*April 24th, for an humble address to be presented to His Majesty*...(CUL: Syn. 3. 75. 6).

An Earnest Address to both Houses of Parliament, upon the Present Posture of Affairs (Bod: G. Pamph. 1923 (13)).

An Elegy On the much and unlamented Death of E[ato]n S[tannard] Esq... (Dublin) (CUL: Hib. 1. 679. 89).

His Excellency William Marquis of Hartington Lord Lieutenant...*his Speech to*...*Parliament, at Dublin*...*Seventh Day of October, 1755* [Dublin] (CUL: Hib. 1. 679. 1⁹⁰).

Faction's Overthrow; or, More fair Warning, and Good Advice to the Nobility, Gentry and Commonalty of Ireland, etc. (Dublin) By J[ohn] G[ast] (BL: 8146 b 10).

A Few Thoughts on the Present Posture of Affairs in Ireland (Dublin) (Bod: G. Pamph. 1922 (22)).

A Few Words more of Advice to the Friends of Ireland, on the present crisis (Dublin) (BL: 8145 bb 52).

Free Thoughts and Bold Truths; or, a Politico-Tritical Essay upon the present situation of affairs (BL: 8138 bb 22).

A Genuine Letter from a Freeman of Bandon, to George Faulkiner (Dublin) (BL: 8145 bb 32).

The Haberdasher's Sermon. As it was today preached at the Taylor's Hall, in Back-Lane, the 21st of December, 1754 (Dublin) (BL: 8145 e 83).

Hezekiah Oldbottom to Joshua Pym (Dublin) (BL: 8145 bb 92).

Hezekiah Oldbottom to the Adviser of the People of Ireland [i.e. Sir R. Cox] (Dublin) (BL: 8145 e 83).

579

BIBLIOGRAPHY

An Historical Account of the Rights of Elections of the several Counties, Cities, and Boroughs, of Great Britain...By Thomas Carew (BL: 504 k 16).

The History of Tom Dunderhead [i.e. Newcastle] (BL: 8145 e 83).

Hue and Cry [? Dublin] (BL: 8145 bb 39).

Informations, and other Papers, relating to the Treasonable Verses found at Oxford July 17, 1754 (Oxford) (BL: T 1624 (1)).

The Important Question Concerning Invasions, a Sea War, Raising the Militia, and Paying Subsidies for Foreign Troops (BL: 8133 c 49).

Ireland Disgraced: or the island of saints become an island of sinners, clearly proved in a dialogue between Doctor B[re]tt and Doctor B[row]ne in Dublin [? 1755] (BL: 8145 aaa 13).

Ireland in Tears, or a Letter to St. Andrew's eldest daughter's youngest son. By Sawney M'Cleaver [? pseud.] (Bod: G. Pamph. 1922 (13)).

Irish State Lottery for the year 1755 (Dublin) (CUL: Hib. o. 755. 2).

A Just and True Answer to a scandalous pamphlet, call'd, A genuine letter from a Freeman of Bandon to G[eorge] F[aulkner] (BL: 8145 bb 30).

The Last Blow; or, an unanswerable vindication of the society of Exeter College (BL: 8132 ee 18 (3)).

A Layman's Sermon, Preached at the Patriot Club of the County of Armagh, the 3rd of September 1755 (Dublin) (BL: 8145 b 74).

A Letter Concerning Prerogative, addressed to C—r N—n, Esq. By 'S— X—' (Dublin) (BL: 8145 bb 126).

A Letter from a By-Stander to a Member of Parliament: Wherein is examined what necessity there is for the maintenance of a large regular land force in this island; what proportion the revenues of the Crown have born to those of the people, at different periods from the Restoration to his present Majesty's accession. And whether the weight of power in the regal or popular scale now preponderates [By Corbyn Morris] (CUL: X. 28. 22^1 – 1st edn 1741).

A Letter from a Member of Parliament to...*the Duke of* ***** *upon the present situation of affairs* (BL: 8133 c 43).

A Letter from the Right Honourable **** ****, *to the Reverend Mr G[A]ST* (Dublin) (BL: 8145 e 83).

A Letter to a Friend in the Country, upon the News of the Town [By John Jones] (CUL: Syn. 5. 74. 11^{12}).

A Letter to Dr King, occasioned by his late Apology...(BL: T 1624 (8)).

A Letter to the Author of the Defence of Exeter College, by way of notes upon his pamphlet, interspersed with serious advice (CUL: Acton d. 25. 1037^4).

A Letter to the Freehold Farmers of Ireland. By Thomas Shuttle (Dublin) (CUL: Hib. 7. 750. 1^7).

A Letter to the King of —. *By an Englishman, not a Member of the House of Commons* (Bod: G. Pamph. 1923 (15)).

A Letter to the People of England on the Present Situation and Conduct of National Affairs [By John Shebbeare] (BL: 8132 a 93 (i)).

A Second Letter to the People of England, on Foreign Subsidies, Subsidiary Armies, and their Consequences to this Nation [By John Shebbeare] (BL: 8132 a 93 (2)).

A Letter to the People of Ireland, Relative to our present Feuds and Jealousies (Dublin) (CUL: Hib. 7. 747. 28^{12}).

BIBLIOGRAPHY

A Letter to the Prime Minister (Dublin) (CUL: Hib. 7. 755. 9).

*[A Letter] To the Right Honourable ****** [i.e. the 4th Duke of Devonshire] (BL: 8145 bb 55).

*A Second Letter to the Right Hon ****](BL: 8145 bb 79).

*A Third Letter to the Right Hon ****](BL: 8146 bbb 12).

A Letter to the Right Honourabel the Earl of Chesterfield, upon the present posture of affairs in Ireland, with some remarks on a late anonymous paper, without a title, but in the manner of a Letter, to some Right Honourable By 'A.B.C.' [? Dublin] (BL: 8145 bb 12).

A Letter to William King, LLD, Principal of St Mary Hall in Oxford. Containing a particular account of the treasonable riot at Oxford, in Feb. 1747. By Richard Blacow (CUL: X. 25. 31).

Letters on the English Nation. By Battista Angeloni, pseud. [i.e. John Shebbeare] (BL: 1250 h 28).

Letters to his Grace the Lord Primate of All Ireland. Containing a Vindication of the Doctrine and Character of St Paul, in answer to the objections of the late Lord Bolingbroke. By John Brett (Dublin) (BL: 3265 b 25).

The Libeller Lashed, or Fair Warning to the Nobility and Gentry of Ireland [? Dublin] (BL: 8145 bb 53).

The Man's mistaken, who thinks the taxes so grievous as to render the nation unable to maintain a war (BL: 8132 c 27).

A Merry Song on a Sad Occasion: Address'd to all the true Friends of Ireland [? 1755] (CUL: Hib. 1. 679. 92).

The Misrepresenter Represented. A Comedy, Not performed in this kingdom since the Year, 1715. Dedicated to Ed[mund] Sex[ton] P[er]y... (Dublin) (CUL: Hib. 7. 757. 13³).

The Moderator; being a true picture of popular discontents (Dublin) (BL: 8145 aaa 97).

Modern Observations on Antient History [Four parts] (Dublin) (BL: 8145 e 83 – for 2nd and 3rd; E 2092 for 1st and 4th).

More Seasonable and Friendly Advice to the People of Ireland [Dublin, 1755] (BL: 8006 bb 6).

The Naked Truth. By ——— Oglethorpe (BL: 102 d 3 (1)).

The Opposition (BL: 8133 c 44).

The Patriot Club Song: made a little before the D[uk]e of D[orse]t was turn'd out of the Government of I[relan]d (BL: 1890 e 5(210)).

Policy and Justice: an Essay. Being A Proposal for Augmenting the Power and Wealth of Great Britain, by Uniting Ireland (CUL: Bbb. 25. 43⁵).

Political Arithmetic, or the Old and New Interest numbers (Bod: G. A. Oxon. 4° 31(8)).

To all Prime Ministers, Chief-Governors, Deputies, Justices and Secretaries etc. (Dublin) (BL: 8133 aaa 15).

A Proper Reply to a Pamphlet, entitled, A Defence of the Rector and Fellows of Exeter College, etc. By George Huddesford (Oxford) (BL: 731 k 11(5)).

A Quaker's Letter to that quondam Favourite, the Irish Earl of Bath [i.e. the Earl of Kildare] (Dublin) (BL: 8145 b 97).

A Quaker's Letter, to the Universal Advertiser, concerning the Coalition (Dublin) (CUL: Hib. 7. 750. 3¹¹).

Reflections upon the Present State of Affairs, at home and abroad, particularly with regard to subsidies, and the differences between Great Britain and France (BL: 8133 c 31).

Remarks on the Resignation of a Noble Lord [Poulett] (BL: 10804 i 7 (1)). [? By 2nd Earl of Egmont].

Seasonable Advice to the Friends of Ireland on the present crisis of affairs (Dublin) (BL: 8145 bb 54).

The Sentiments of a Real Patriot, on the Subject of National Grievances (Dublin) (BL: 8145 bb 114).

Some material and very important remarks concerning the present situation of affairs between Great Britain, France and Spain... (BL: 8026 c 34).

Sybilline Leaves, or Anonymous Papers: containing a Letter to the Lord Mayor of London; with a view of inducing that great metropolis to take the lead in addressing His Majesty for his most gracious and auspicious residence in these Kingdoms... (A copy is in PRO 30/24/28, p.405) (BL: E 2213 (2)).

To all Prime-Ministers, Chief-Governors, Deputies, Justices, and Secretaries, that are or may be. By C[hristopher] R[obinso]n, D[avid] B[indo]n, G[orges] E[dmund] H[oward] and [John] B[re]tt (Dublin) (BL: 8133 aaa 15).

To All the Good People of Ireland, friendly and seasonable advice [? Dublin] (BL: 8145 aaa 62).

A Vindication of a Pamphlet, Lately Published, intituled, The Case of the Roman–Catholics of Ireland (Dublin) (CUL: Hib. 7. 755. 16).

A Vindication of the Irish Earl of Bath... [i.e. Kildare] (Dublin) (BL: 8145 c 83).

A Vindication of the Ministerial Conduct of his Grace the Duke of Dorset in Ireland. By a Servant of the Crown in that Kingdom (Bod: G. Pamph. 1922 (26)).

1756

An Abstract from the Monthly Critical Review of the Advertisement prefixed to the History of Valencia. By 'Don Juan Fernandez', pseud. (BL: E 2092).

An Account of what Passed between Mr G. Thompson of York, and Dr J. Burton, of that City, Physician and Man—midwife, at Mr Sheriff Jubb's Entertainment and the Consequences thereon By George Thompson (BL: E 2093 (1)).

An Address to the Electors of England (BL: 8132 c 29).

An Address to the Great. Recommending better ways and means of raising the necessary supplies than lotteries or taxes. With a word or two concerning an invasion (CUL: X. 27. 38³).

An Address to the Public, in Answer to two Pamphlets, inititled, An Appeal to the People of England, and A Letter to a Member of Parliament, relative to the case of A[dmira]l B[yn]g etc. By 'Ante Italianete', pseud. (BL: 1508/638).

Admiral Byng's Answer to the Friendly Advice... (BL: 1881 c 3 (91)).

Admiral Byng's Complaint (BL: C113 hh 3(8)).

Admiral Byng in Horrors at the Appearance of the Unhappy Souls, who was killed in the engagement crying for revenge (BL: T 1070 (1)).

Advice to the Patriot Club, of the County of Antrim. On the Present State of

BIBLIOGRAPHY

Affairs in Ireland, and some Late Changes in the Administration of that Kingdom (Dublin) (BL: 8145 e 83).

Advice to the Speaker Elect, or, a Letter to the Right Honourable John Ponsonby, Esq. (Dublin) (CUL: Hib. 7. 750. 29^{11}).

Another Dissertation on the Mutual Support of Trade and Civil Liberty, addressed to the author of the former [By B. Newton] (BL: T 1559 (3)).

An Answer to a Pamphlet call'd The Conduct of the Ministry Impartially Examined...By the author of the Four Letters to the People of England [i.e. by John Shebbeare] (BL: 8132 a 44).

An Appeal to Reason and Common Sense; or a Free and Candid Disquisition of the Conduct of A— B—, so far as it relates to matters of fact... (Bod: G. Pamph. 1923 (5)).

An Appeal to the Commons and Citizens of London. By Charles Lucas (Bod: G. Pamph. 1923/27).

An Appeal to the People: containing, the genuine and entire letter of Admiral Byng to the Secr[etary] of the Ad[miralt]y... (BL: 228 e 34 (2)).

An Appeal to the Sense of the People on the Present Posture of Affairs. Wherein the nature of the late treaties are enquired into, and the conduct of the M[in]i[str]y with regard to M[i]n[or]ca, A[me]r[i]ca etc. is considered (BL: 8175 bb 6).

An Appeal to the Throne (BL: 8138 bb 37).

The Block and the Yard Arm. A new ballad, on the loss of Minorca, and the danger of our American rights and possessions (BL: 1876 f 1 (155)).

Boh Peep Boh, or A[dmira]l Bing's apology to the Fribbles (BL: c 113 hh 3(7)).

A British Philippic. Inscribed to the Right Honourable the Earl of Granville [By Joseph Read] (BL: 11630 c 8(2)).

Bungiana, or an assemblage of What-d'ye-call-em's... (BL: 1508/186).

Byng Returned; or, the Council of Expedients (BL: C121 g 9(213)).

A Catalogue of the Political Pamphlets, written in Defence of the Principles and Proceedings of the Patriots of Ireland, and, mostly, published During the Administration of His Grace the Duke of Dorset, in the Memorable Years 1751, 2, 3, 4, and 5. [? Dublin, 1756] (CUL: Hib 7. 750. 29^{13}).

The City Bear Baited, or the Old Patriot turned Courtier [? 1756–7] (Bod: B'side Firth b 18 (91)).

A Collection of Several Pamphlets...relative to the case of Admiral Byng (BL: T1053 (8)).

The Conduct of the Ministry Impartially Examined. In a Letter to the Merchants of London [By D. Mallet] (BL: 1093 e 53).

Considerations on the Addresses lately presented to His Majesty, on Occasion of the loss of Minorca (BL: 102 d 10).

Considerations on the Present State of Affairs, with some Reflections on the Dutch Observator (CUL: x. 28. 26^7).

Considerations on Various Grievances in the Practick Part of our Laws (Dublin) (BL: 6146 b 46).

The Converts, a familiar Tale, addressed to Sir G[eorge] L[yttelton], Chan-[cello]r of the Ex[cheque]r (BL: 643 m 16(19)).

The Counterpoise: or, B[yn]g and M[inistry] fairly stated (Dublin) (BL: 1508/631).

The Crisis. (Bod: G. Pamph. 1923 (1)).

BIBLIOGRAPHY

Deliberate Thoughts on the System of our late Treaties with Hesse Cassel and Russia. By Samuel Martin. (BL: 8072 c 19. Mss text is 41355 ff. 29–98).

A Dissertation on the Following Question: in what manner do trade and civil liberty support and assist each other? [By William Weston] (BL: T 1559 (2)).

A Dissertation on the Following Subject: what causes principally contribute to render a nation populous? And what effect has the populousness of a nation on its trade? By J. Bell (Cambridge) (BL: T 1559 (5)).

A Dream (BL: 1881 c 3 (91*)).

A Dutiful Address to the Throne upon the Present State of G[rea]t B[ritai]n (BL: 1476 aa 25).

An Earnest Address to both Houses of Parliament upon the Present Posture of Affairs. By a Gentleman (BL: E 2213(8)).

England's Alarum Bell: or, a Choak Pear for the H[anoveria]ns. A new ballad [? 1756] (BL: 1876 f 1 (157)).

An Essay on the Times. (BL: 102 d 16).

An Essay on Ways and Means for Raising Money for the support of the Present War. By F[rancis] F[auquier] (BL: E 2213 (3).

The Fatal Consequences which may arise from the want of system in the conduct of public affairs (BL: 8133 c 16).

A Few Plain Matters of Fact, Humbly Recommended to the consideration of the Roman–Catholicks of Ireland [By Robert Clayton] (Dublin) (CUL: Hib. 7. 756.8).

A Few Thoughts on the Times. In a Letter from a Free-Citizen of Dublin, to his Friend in the North (Dublin) (BL: 8145 e 83).

The Fifteenth Ode of the First Book of Horace Imitated, and applied to Mr F[ox] on his being appointed S[ecretary] of S[tate], and taking on the conduct of the — —. By 'Q. Horatius Flaccus', pseud. (BL: 11602 i 13 (5)).

The Freeholder's Ditty (BL: 1876 f 1 (158)).

A Full Account of the Siege of Minorca by the French in 1756... (BL: 1323 c 12).

A Full and Particular Answer to all the Calumnies, Misrepresentations, and Falsehoods, contained in a pamphlet, called A Fourth Letter to the People of England (BL: 1093 e 48).

General B[lakene]y's Account to His Majesty Concerning the Loss of Minorca (BL: c 113 hh 3(11)).

German Cruelty, a Fair Warning to the People of Great Britain (BL: T 1113 (4)).

German Politics: Or, the Modern System Examined and Refuted (1st edn 1745) (BL: 8072 c 31).

Great Britain's True System. By Malachy Postlethwayt (BL: 1138 c 6).

The happy Interview or long look'd for, found out at last. A plain narrative... [? By John Lindsay] (BL: 8560 b 30).

His Majesty's most gracious Speech...on Thursday the second day of December. 1756 [spurious: a parody of speech at opening of session] (BL: B.S. 91/66 (67)).

The History of Reynard the Fox, Bruin the Bear, etc. (BL: 12315 bb 28).

Impartial Reflections on the Case of Mr Byng, as stated in an Appeal to the

People etc., and a Letter to a Member of Parliament, etc. (BL: 228 e 34 (7)).

An Impartial View of the conduct of the M[inist]ry in regard to the war in America; the engagements entered into with Russia, Hesse Cassel and Prussia; the cause of throwing out the Militia Bill; and, the affairs of the Mediterranean. In answer to the many invidious attacks of Pamphleteers, etc. (BL: 102 d 21).

The Importance and Necessity of His Majesty's Declaration of War with France, considered and improved, in a sermon preached May 23rd 1756 By Richard Winter (BL: T 1620 (10)).

The Importance of the Island of Minorca and the Harbour of Portmahon, fully and impartially considered...in a letter from a Merchant to a Noble Lord (BL: 8135 aa 29).

The Last Speech, Confession and Dying Words, of B[o]w[e]n S[out]h[wel]l, Representative in Parliament for the B—h of D—n ... (Downpatrick) [1756] (CUL: Hib. 1. 679. 96).

A Late Epistle to Mr C[levelan]d (BL: 1865 c 4 (153)).

Letter from the Side of the Shannon to Roger. Concerning the late Change of Affairs; by a Gentleman Patriot...(Dublin) (CUL: Hib. 7. 747. 28^{14}).

A Letter to a Member of Parliament in the Country, from his friend in London, relative to the case of Admiral Byng (BL: 518 g 19 (6)).

A Letter to the Free Citizen [? Dublin] (BL: 8145 b 75).

A Letter to the Gentlemen of the Common Council. By a Citizen and Watchmaker (BL: 8132 aaa 16 (2)).

*A Letter to the Inhabitants of Great Britain and Ireland...*By S. Hayward (BL: 1102 f 2 (1)).

A Third Letter to the People of England on Liberty, Taxes, and the Application of Public Money [By John Shebbeare] (BL: 8132 a 93 (3)).

A Fourth Letter to the People of England, on the Conduct of the M[iniste]rs in Alliances, fleets and armies etc. [By John Shebbeare] (BL: 8132 a 93 (5)).

A Fourth Letter to the People of England (BL: 8132 a 93 (4)).

A Fifth Letter to the People of England. On M[inisteria]l Influence and Management of National Treasure (CUL: Hib 7 750 2^{13}).

A Sixth and Last Letter; or, Address to the Parliament, as well as to the People of Great Britain; with a retrospection to all that has been offered on the case and cowardice of Admiral Byng... (CUL: Acton d 25 974^{10}).

A Letter to the Public. By R[ichard] F[enwic]k (BL: 8145 b 76).

A Letter to the Right Honourable William Pitt, Esq.; Being an Impartial Vindication of the Conduct of the Ministry...In Answer to the Aspersions cast upon them by Admiral Byng and his Advocates (BL: 228 e 34 (8)).

A Letter to the Right Reverend the Lord Bishop of London. By Edward Weston (BL: T 1620 (3)).

A Letter to the University of Cambridge on a late Resignation. By a Gentleman of Oxford (BL: 731 i 3 (7)).

Charles Lucas's Prophecy, Concerning the Mock-Patriots of Ireland; Humbly addressed to the Free-Citizens of the City of Dublin (BL: 8146 b 4).

Memoirs of the Life and Actions of General Blakeney... (BL: G 14482 (1)).

Memoirs of the Right Honourable Lady Betty Ireland, with a particular account of her eldest son Roger [i.e. H. Boyle] [? 1756] (BL: 8145 b 56).

BIBLIOGRAPHY

The Ministry Changed: or, the clean contrary way. A new song, to an old tune (BL: 1876 f 1 (156)).

A Modest Address to the Commons of Great Britain, and in particular to the free citizens of London; occasioned by the ill success of our present naval war with France, and the want of a Militia Bill (BL: 102 d 12).

A Modest Apology for the Conduct of a Certain Admiral in the Mediterranean, etc. (BL: 1202 g 20).

More Birds for the Tower, or who'll confess first (BL: c 113 hh 3 (6)).

A Narrative of the Dispute in the Corporation of Kinsale (Dublin) (BL: 8145 e 83).

A Narrative of the Proceedings of Admiral B[yn]g, and of his Conduct off Mahon, the 20th of May (BL: T 1054 (8)).

The New Art of War at Sea, etc. By 'Admiral Bung', pseud. (BL: 1852 d i (9)).

A New Speech from the Old Trumpeter of Liberty Hall. By 'Oxoniensis', pseud. (BL: 1093 b 48).

A New System of Patriot Policy... (BL: 1103 d 22).

Observations upon Mr Fauquier's Essay on Ways and Means for raising Money to support the present War without increasing the Public Debts. By J[oseph] M[assie] (BL: 104 c 48).

The Occasional Patriot; or, an enquiry into the present connections of Great Britain with the Continent [By George Lyttelton] (BL: T 1600 (7)).

The Office and Power of a Judge in Ireland... (Dublin) (BL: 8145 e 83).

Party Spirit in time of Public Danger considered; wherein the national debt, the necessity of our connections on the continent, with the nature of our subsidiary forces, and the ancient mercenaries are fully discussed (BL: 8132 aaa 16 (3)).

A Pathetick Address to all true Britons (BL: 11602 i 14 (13)).

A Political Discourse upon the Different Kinds of Militia... By J. Christian (BL: 1103 g 33).

A Political Treatise on the National Humour. In which the character and conduct of a statesman is generally and impartially considered. Addressed to the Rt. Hon. William Pitt, Esq. (BL: 8132 c 69).

The Principles of the Roman Catholics exhibited in some observations on a pamphlet intituled, Plain Matters of Fact, humbly recommended to the consideration of the Roman-Catholics of Ireland [By C. O'Conor] (Dublin) (CUL: Hib. 7 756 14).

The Proceedings at the New Bayley in Weaver's Square... (Dublin) (BL: 8145 e 83).

The Question of Previous Consent discussed. By a Gentleman of the Bar. (Dublin) (CUL: Hib 7 750 3²).

A Ray of Truth darting thro' the thick clouds of falsehood, etc. (BL: 1884 b 25 (44)).

A Real Defence of A[dmira]l B[yng]'s Conduct. By a lover of truth and a friend to society (BL: 1414 d 83 (5)).

Reflections on the Present State of Affairs: in which are introduced, some hints on the Militia Bill (CUL: Ddd. 25 141¹³).

Reflections Physical and Moral, upon the various...phenomena in the air, water, or on earth, which have happened from the earthquake in Lima to the present time [By James Dawkins, MP] (BL: 4015 c 35).

Reflections Previous to the Establishment of a Militia (BL: 1103 g 34 (1)).

A Refutation of all the Malicious Falsehoods and Misrepresentations, against Sir Richard Cox, Bt., and his eldest son Richard Cox, Esq; Contained in a Paper, entitled, 'A Letter to the Public'. By Sir Richard Cox (BL: 1414 e 62 (5)).

Remarks on a late Pamphlet entitled, Advice to the Patriot Club of the County of Antrim, In a Letter from a Member of that Club to his Friend in Dublin (Dublin) (BL: 8145 b 9).

Remarks on the First and Second Chapter of a late Work, intitled 'Modern Observations on Ancient History' (Dublin) (BL: 8145 e 83).

The Resignation: or, the Fox Out of the Pit, and the Geese in, with B[YN]G at the Bottom (BL: 1103 g 63).

The Royal Conference or a Dialogue between their Majesties G[eorg]e the II^d of E[nglan]d and L[oui]s the XV of F[ranc]e (BL: 8132 de 3 (2)).

A Rueful Story, or Britain in Tears, being the conduct of Admiral B[yn]g in the late engagement off Mahone with a French fleet the 20th of May 1756 (BL: T 1070 (1)).

The School-Boy in Politics (BL: 102 d 17).

A Serious Apology and Modest Remarks on the Conduct of a certain Admiral in the Mediterranean, etc. (BL: G 14482 (2)).

A Serious Call to the Corporation of London to Address his M[ajest]y to remove from his councils...weak and wicked M[inister]s (BL: c 113 hh 3 (4)).

A Serious Defence of some late Measures of the Administration; particularly with regard to the introduction and establishment of foreign troops [By John Douglas] (BL: 8132 aa 15 (8)).

Seven Good Reasons for the Changes at Court being the examination of certain Great Men at the Privy Council (Bod: Firth b 18 (101)).

The Sham Fight: or, Political Humbug. A State Farce...As it was acted by some persons of distinction in the M[e]d[iterranea]n, and elsewhere (BL: 1346 f 46).

A Short Address to Persons of all Denominations occasioned by the Alarm of an Intended Invasion. By George Whitefield (BL: T 1620 (4)).

A Short but Full Defence of the Conduct of a certain Great Man [i.e. Earl of Shannon] (Dublin) (CUL: Hib 7 756 18).

A Short State of the Progress of the French Trade and Navigation... By Malachy Postlethwayt (BL: 1093 e 51).

A Solemn Warning: or, Some Account of the Behaviour of B[owen] S[outhwe]ll, Esq.; While under Sentence of Death [? Downpatrick 1756] (CUL: Hib 1 679 97).

Some Friendly and Seasonable Advice to Mr Admiral Byng. By Isaac Barclay (BL: 515 1 6 (31)).

Some Further Particulars in Relation to the Case of Admiral Byng... (BL: 518 g 19 (5)).

Some Reasons for believing sundry letters and papers ascribed in three late publications to Admiral Byng not only spurious, but also an insidious attempt to prejudice the Admiral's character (BL: 228 e 34 (6)).

A Speedy Repentance the most effectual Means to avert God's Judgements. A sermon preached...February 6, 1756...the Day appointed for a General

Fast...On Account of the late...Earthquakes... By Dr Samuel Squire (BL: 225 i 6 (5)).

The State of the Nation Considered, with Respect to a French Invasion. (CUL: Syn. 5 75 20[11]).

The State–Farce: a Lyrick. Written at Claremont, and inscribed to His Grace the Duke of Newcastle (BL: 11602 i 13 (6)).

Oh! Tempora. Oh! Mores (BL: 1865 c 4 (153)).

The Test Pro-Tested Or, the Pudding Sewed. (BL: c 113 hh 3 (10)).

Thoughts on the Duty of a good Citizen, with regard to War and Invasion; in a Letter from a citizen to his Friend [1756] (CUL: X 28 26[12]).

The Touchstone of Patriotism, in a Series of Interesting Queries to the Publick (Dublin) (BL: 8145 b 106).

The Trial of Roger, for the Murder of Lady Betty Ireland... [Roger=Earl of Shannon] (Dublin) (BL: 8145 e 83).

A View of the Manner in which Trade and Civil Liberty support each other. By William Hazeland (BL: T 1559 (1)).

A Vindication of Natural Society: or, a View of the Miseries and Evils arising to Mankind from every species of Artificial Society [By Edmund Burke] (BL: 8005 d 40).

A Vindication of the R[igh]t H[onourabl]e and H[onourabl]e L[or]ds and Gentlemen, who have been...aspersed and...mis-represented, in a late Anonimous work, intitled, The History of Roger (Dublin) (BL: 8145 e 83 (2)).

The Voice of Liberty. An occasional essay. On the behaviour and conduct of the English Nation, in opposition to Min[i]st[eria]l Oppression. (BL: 8132 c 36).

The Voice of the People: or a collection of Addresses to His Majesty, and Instruction to Members of Parliament...upon the unsuccessful management of the present war, and the establishment of a national militia (BL: 8132 c 81).

Will Br[u]ce's Ghost, Which appeared last Night, and held the following Dialogue with a certain Eminent Politician [? 1756]. (BL: 8145 b 17).

The Wonder of Surry! (BL: L 23 c 3 10).

Wonder upon Wonder: or the Cocoa Tree's Answer to the Surrey Oak (BL: 1876 f i (159)).

1757

An Account of the Facts which appeared on the late Enquiry into the Loss of Minorca, from authentic papers. By the Monitor (BL: E 2048 c (6)).

An Address to His Majesty upon the Present Crisis (BL: 102 d 26).

Admiral Byng's Defence, as presented by him, and read in the Court January 18, 1757 (BL: 1132 c 47 (1)).

Admiral's Forbes's Reasons for not signing Admiral Byng's Dead Warrant (BL: 228 e 35 (10)).

An Alarm to the People of England; showing their Rights, Liberties and Properties, to be in the utmost danger from the present destructive, and unconstitutional association, for the preservation of the Game all over England, which is proved to be illegal (CUL: Acton d 25 974[9]).

An Appeal to his Grace the Lord P[rima]te of all I[relan]d; being a short vindication of the political principles of Roman Catholics...By 'A.B.' (Dublin) (BL: 3938 aaa 40).

An Appeal to the Nation: being a full and fair vindication of Mr Mordaunt, and the other gentlemen employed in the conduct of the late secret expedition, in which the circumstances relating to the miscarriages of that affair are set in a just and satisfactory light (BL: 8132 c 62).

An Appeal to the People: Part the Second. On the different deserts and fate of Admiral Byng and his enemies: the changes in the last administration: the year of liberty or thraldom (BL: 228 e 34).

The Art of Governing by Parties [By John Toland] Repr. 1757 (BL: 1609/ 298).

A Candid Examination of the Resolutions and Sentence of the Court Martial on the Trial of Admiral Byng... (BL: 518 g 19 (4)).

The Case of the Hon. Admiral Byng, Ingenuously Represented (BL: 228 e 35 (1)).

Considerations on the Revenues of Ireland... (CUL: Hib 7 757 7).

The Constitution. With an Address to a Great Man. (BL: E 2214 (2)).

The Constitution. With a Letter to the Author. Number II. (BL: E 2214 (5)).

The Constitution. With some Account of a Bill lately rejected by the H[ouse] of L[ords]. Number III. (BL: E 2214 (6)).

Constitutional Maxims, extracted from a discourse on the establishment of a national and constitutional force. By Charles Jenkinson (1794 reprint). (BL: 1389 d 27 (24)).

The Contest in America between Great Britain and France etc. [? By Dr Mitchell] (BL: 1061 h 5).

The Devil, the Dutch, the King of France, robbing poor old England of three millions (BL: 1876 f 1 (161)).

A Discourse on the Establishment of a National and Constitutional Force in England [By Charles Jenkinson] (Bod: Vet. A5e 45 (8), 1794 edn).

A Discourse Relating to the Present Times, addressed to the Serious Consideration of the Public. By Thomas Thompson (BL: 4474 f 93).

An Enquiry Concerning the Nature and End of a National Militia [? By Maurice Morgan] (BL: E 2048 (3)).

An Enquiry into the Causes of our Ill-Success in the Present War (BL: 102 d 30).

The Enquiry is not begun! When will it? (BL: c 113 hh 3 (12)).

An Epistle from Larry Dunn to all his Countrymen, who wish prosperity to Ireland, and freedom to Par[liamen]ts (Dublin) (BL: 8145 aa 3).

An Essay on Political Lying, etc. (BL: E 2048 (3)).

An Essay on the Nature and Use of the Militia...*By a member of Parliament* [By Lord Ongley] (CUL: Hib 8 757 5).

Essential Queries relating to the Condemnation and Execution of Admiral Byng (BL: C 113 hh 3 (19)).

An Estimate of the Manners and Principles of the Times [By Dr John Brown] (BL: 522 g 10).

An Exact Copy of a Remarkable Letter from Admiral Byng to the Right Hon. W[illiam] P[itt] Esq... (BL: T 1688 (5)).

The Father of the City of Eutopia, or the Surest Road to Riches...*By* 'C.C.' (BL: 906 k 7 (3)).

BIBLIOGRAPHY

A Free Enquiry into the Nature and Origins of Evil [By Soame Jenyns] (BL: 8403 bb 25 (1)).

A Friendly Call to the People of the Roman Catholic Religion in Ireland. By John Brett (Dublin) (BL: 4476 aaa 126).

A Full and Particular Account of a . . . dreadful apparition which appeared to a certain Great Man (BL: c 113 hh 3 25).

A Full Answer to an Infamous Libel, intituled, A Letter to the Right Honourable Lord B[lakene]y (BL: 1045 f 6 (4)).

A Further Address to the Public. Containing Genuine Copies of all the Letters which passed between A[dmira]l B[yn]g and the S[ecreta]ry of the A[dmiral]ty. . . (BL: 518 g 19 (10)).

Further Objections to the Establishment of a Constitutional Militia: Being a Reply to the Monitor (BL: 1103 g 34 (3)).

A Guide to the Knowledge of the Rights and Privileges of Englishmen. . . With an exhortation to the. . . electors of Members to serve in Parliament (BL: 1481 d 45).

The Herald, or Patriot–Proclaimer. By Stentor Telltruth (pseud). (BL: PP 5258 b (2)). Collected edn of periodical.

The Independent Freeholder's Letter to the People of England, upon the One Thing Needful at this Final Crisis (BL: 1608/945).

Is Justice Begun? Let it Continue (BL: c 113 hh 3 (15)).

A Key to the Trial of Admiral Byng, or a brief State of Facts relating to the Action in the Mediterranean. . . (BL: C 113 hh 3 (17)).

King Harry Ninth's Speech to both Houses of P[arliamen]t, December the 1st 1757 (BL: 1879 cc 5 (39)).

A Letter from a Citizen in Dublin, to the Earl of — in London (Bod: G. Pamph. 1173 (9)).

A Letter from a Gentleman in the City to a Member of Parliament in the North of Ireland (Dublin) (CUL: Hib 7 749 1⁸).

A Letter from XO HO, a Chinese Philosopher at London, to his friend LIEN CHI at PEKING (CUL: Hib 7 750 2¹¹).

A Letter to a Gentleman in the Country, from his Friend in London: giving an authentic and circumstantial account of the confinement, behaviour and death of Admiral Byng. . . (BL: 518 g 19 (11)).

A Letter to Admiral Smith, late President of the Court Martial for the Trial of the Hon. John Byng, Esq. (BL: E 2048 (5)).

A Letter to his G[rac]e the D[uk]e of B[edfor]d [By E. S. Pery] (BL: 102 d 24).

A Letter to his Grace the D[uke] of N[EWCASTL]E, on The Duty he owes himself, his King, his Country and his God, at this important moment (BL: E 2214 (7)).

A Letter to Lord Robert Bertie, Relating to his Conduct in the Mediterranean, and his Defence of Admiral Byng (BL: 518 g 19 (7)).

[A] Letter to the Lords of the Admiralty [By Mrs Sarah Byng Osborn] Dated February 17, 1757 (BL: 228 e 35 (11)).

A Letter to the People of England, upon the Militia, Continental Connections, Neutralities, and Secret Expeditions [By John Shebbeare] (BL: 1103 g 31).

A Fifth Letter to the People of England, on the subversion of the Constitution: and, the necessity of its being restored [By John Shebbeare] (BL: 8132 a 93 (6)).

BIBLIOGRAPHY

A Sixth Letter to the People of England, on the Progress of National Ruin... [By John Shebbeare] (BL: 8132 a 93 (7)).

A Letter to the Right Honourable H[enry] F[ox] Esq. By 'S— B—' (BL: 8133 c 8).

A Letter to the Right Honourable Lord A[nson] (BL: E 2214 (4)).

A Letter to the Right Honourable the Lord B[lakene]y, being an enquiry into the merit of his defence of Minorca (BL: E 2048 (8)).

A Letter to the Right Honourable the L[or]ds of the A[dmiralt]y [By the Hon. Sarah Osborn] (BL: C 113 hh 3 (14)).

Letters from an Armenian in Ireland to his Friends at Trebisond, etc. [By Francis Andrews and Edmund Pery] (BL: 8145 bb 6).

Maxims Relative to the Present State of Ireland (Dublin) (CUL: Hib 7 757 12).

The Modern Patriot [? 1757] (BL: 012314 f 60 (3)).

A Morning's Thoughts on reading the Test and the Contest [By J. Hanway]. (BL: 1103 d 16).

Northern Revolutions: or, the Principal Causes of the declension and dissolution of several once flourishing Gothic constitutions in Europe. In a series of letters from the Ghost of Trenchard (BL: 2 parts, 8005 e 36 and 102 d 28).

Observations on Some Remarks in the Monthly Review for March 1757, on a pamphlet entitled, The Independent Freeholder's Letter to the People of England... (BL: 8138 aa 23).

Observations on the Conduct of the late Administration; particularly, in regard to our loss of Minorca: and on our foreign transactions, which may have been the fatal cause of it (BL: 102 d 25).

Observations on the Twelfth Article of War... [By D. Mallet] (BL: 228 e 35 (6)).

An Ode on the Expedition. Inscribed to the Right Hon. W[illiam] P[itt], Esquire. (CUL: 7720 b 20⁹).

The Original Paper delivered by Admiral Byng to the Marshal just before his execution (BL: c 113 hh 3 (22)).

Past twelve o'clock, or, Byng's Ghost (BL: 1876 f 1 (165)).

To the People of England. By 'Triton', pseud. (BL: c 113 hh 3 (13)).

The Political Free-thinker; or, a Real Impartial Enquiry, into the Causes of our late Miscarriages, and our Present Melancholy Situation (BL: 1103 g 52).

The Portsmouth Grand Humbug... (BL: c 113 hh 3 (30)).

The Present State of Europe... (5th edn.) (BL: 08026 ee 1).

The Proceedings of the...Lords...upon the Bill, intituled, An Act to release from the obligation of the oath of secrecy, the members of the court martial appointed for the trial of Admiral J. Byng, etc. (BL: C 113 hh 3 (18)).

Proposals for Carrying on the War with Vigour, raising the supplies within the year, and forming a National Militia (BL: 8132 c 71).

The Prosperity of Britain Proved from the Degeneracy of its People (BL: 8409 d 7 (1)).

The Protest (BL: 1509/840).

The Protestant Interest Considered relatively to the operation of the popery acts in Ireland. (CUL: Hib 7 757 22).

BIBLIOGRAPHY

A Protestant's Address to the Protestants of Ireland... (Dublin) (BL: 4165 aaa 8).

Queries Addressed to Captain C[ornwa]ll... (BL: 228 e 35 (12)).

The Real Character of the Age, in a letter to the Rev. Dr Brown, occasioned by his Estimate of the Manners and Principles of the Times. By 'C.L. St.' (BL: 537 e 5 (3)).

The Report of the General Officers, Appointed to enquire into the Conduct of Major General Stuart, *and Colonels* Cornwallis *and Earl of* Effingham, *December 8th, 1756* (BL: 228 e 35 (4)).

A Seasonable Reply to a scurrilous pamphlet, called, An Essay on Political Lying. By a citizen of London (BL: 8132 c 37).

A Serious Address to the Worthy Livery of the City of London (BL: c 113 hh 3 (32)).

Serious Expostulations on Occasion of a late extraordinary Resolution. By a Member of the Common Council (CUL: Ddd. 23 43⁴).

Serious Reflections on the present State of Domestic and Foreign Affairs... Together with Some Critical Remarks on Lotteries... By James Burrow (BL: T 1113 (6)).

Serious Thoughts concerning the True Interest and Exigencies of the State of Ireland. In a letter humbly addressed to his Grace the D[uke] of B[edfor]d (Dublin) (BL: 8145 c 2).

Short but Serious Reasons for a National Militia. By Soame Jenyns (Reprinted in his *Works*).

A Short History of late Administrations, showing their spirit and conduct: from whence it is made evident, that England is to be saved by the virtue of the people only (BL: 8132 d 20).

A Snake in the Grass detected, or, a Key to an Insidious, Seditious Pamphlet, intitled Northern Revolutions...By a Modern Englishman (BL: 8005 e 37).

Some General Thoughts on Government, And particularly on the Present State of Affairs (Bod: G. Pamph. 1924 (13)).

Some Particular Remarks upon the Affair of the Hanoverian Soldier. By Edward Lancer (BL: 518 e 18 (5)).

Some Queries on the Minutes of the Council of War held at Gibraltar the fourth of May last... (BL: 518 g 19 (9)).

The Sorrowful Lamentation and Last Farewell to the World of Admiral Byng (BL: 1876 f 1 (164)).

The Speech of the Hon Admiral Byng, intended to have been spoken on board the Monarque at the time of his execution (BL: c 113 hh 3 (20)).

The Speech of William the Fourth [i.e. William Pitt] (BL: 5805 g 1 (24)).

The State of Minorca, and its lost condition, when A[dmira]l B[yn]g appeared off that Island (BL: 8132 a 7).

A Tract on the National Interest, and Depravity of the Times: in which The Subjects' Claims to certain rights in R[ichmond] P[ark], are fully considered and digested. Being a supplement to German Cruelty (BL: 1103 g 1).

The Trial of the Hon. Admiral Byng... (BL: 228 e 36).

The Trial of the Honourable John Byng... (BL: 515 l 6 (30)).

Two very singular addresses to the People of England... (CUL: Hib. 7. 757. 17).

Vengeance Crying from the Grave, or the Pitt Buried Alive (BL: C113 hh 3 (29)).

BIBLIOGRAPHY

A Word in Time to both Houses of Parliament; recommended to the perusal of each Member before he either speaks or votes, for or against a Militia Bill... (BL: 1103 g 34 (2)).
To the Worthy Merchants and Citizens of London (BL: 515 1 6 (32)).

Other years (pamphlets cited only):

The Principles of Modern Patriots Expos'd (1735).
An Address to the Cocoa Tree from a Whig (1762).
An Address to the City of London (1762).
Political Disquisitions. Proper for Public Consideration in the Present State of Affairs. In a Letter to a Noble Duke (1763).

Undated

An Address from Lilliput, to the P[a]rl[iamen]t of Ireland...also an epistle... to...Henry Boyle... [? Dublin] (Bod: 22956 E. 73 (8)).
A Letter to E[dmun]d S[exto]n P[er]y, Esq. And the rest of the Patriot Members of the Hon. House of Commons; with Observations on Pensioners. By a lover of his Country. By 'Hibernicus', pseud. (Dublin) (Bod: G. Pamph. 1922 (3)).
A Seasonable Address to the Electors of Great Britain. [? 1753 or 1754] (BL: 08139 b 44).

SECONDARY SOURCES

Books

Adams, R. G., *The Papers of Lord George Germaine. A Brief Description of the Stopford–Sackville Papers now in the William L. Clements Library* (Ann Arbor, 1928).
[Almon, J.], *Anecdotes of the Life of the Rt. Hon. William Pitt, Earl of Chatham* (3rd edn, 3 vols, 1793–7).
[Almon, J.], *Biographical, Literary and Political Anecdotes, of Several of the most eminent persons of the present age* (1797).
Almon, J. (ed.), *The Correspondence of the late John Wilkes* (1805).
[Almon, J.], *The Debates and Proceedings of the British House of Commons from 1743 to 1774* (London, 1766–75).
[Almon, J.], *A History of the Parliament of Great Britain, from the Death of Queen Anne, to the Death of King George II* (1764).
[Almon, J.], *A Review of the Reign of George II* (1762).
Anson, Sir W. R., *Autobiography and Political Correspondence of Augustus Henry, Third Duke of Grafton* (1898).
Aspinall-Oglander, C., *Admiral's Wife. Being the Life and Letters of the Hon. Mrs Edward Boscawen from 1719 to 1761* (1940).
Atherton, H. M., *Political Prints in the Age of Hogarth: a study of the ideographic representation of politics* (Oxford, 1974).
Ayling, S., *The Elder Pitt, Earl of Chatham* (1976).
Ayscough, G. E. (ed.), *The Works of George, Lord Lyttelton* (1774).

BIBLIOGRAPHY

Bagot, *Memorials of the Bagot Family, compiled in 1823* (Blithfield, 1824).

Barrington, S., *The Political Life of William Wildman, Viscount Barrington* (1815).

Barrow, Sir John, *The Life of George, Lord Anson* (1839).

Barrow, Sir John, *Some Account of the Public Life, and a Selection from the Unpublished Writings, of the Earl of Macartney* (1807).

Bartlett, T. and Hayton, D. (eds.), *Penal Era and Golden Age: Essays in Irish History, 1690–1800* (Belfast, 1979).

Basye, A. H., *The Lords Commissioners of Trade and Plantations, commonly known as the Board of Trade, 1747–1782* (New Haven, 1925).

Beckett, J. C., *The Anglo-Irish Tradition* (1976).

Beckett, J. C., *Confrontations. Studies in Irish History* (1972).

Beckett, J. C., *The Making of Modern Ireland 1603–1922* (1966).

Beckett, J. C., *Protestant Dissent in Ireland 1687–1780* (1948).

Beer, S. H., *Modern British Politics* (1965).

Bellamy, *An Apology for the Life of George Ann Bellamy, late of Covent-Garden Theatre. Written by herself* (1785).

Birch, A. H., *Representative and Responsible Government* (1964).

Bissett, A., *Memoirs and Papers of Sir Andrew Mitchell* (1850).

Blackstone, W., *Commentaries on the Laws of England* (Oxford, 1765–9).

Blake, Lord, *The Office of Prime Minister* (Oxford, 1975).

Bonsall, B., *Sir James Lowther and Cumberland and Westmorland Elections, 1754–75* (Manchester, 1960).

Boulton, J. T., *The Language of Politics in the Age of Wilkes and Burke* (1963).

[Boulton, W. B.], *The History of White's* (1892) (Vol. 2 reprints the Betting Book).

Brewer, J., *Party Ideology and Popular Politics at the Accession of George III* (Cambridge, 1976).

Brooke, J., *King George III* (1972).

Brown, P., *The Chathamites* (1967).

Brown, P. D., *William Pitt Earl of Chatham. The Great Commoner* (1978).

Browning, R., *The Duke of Newcastle* (New Haven, 1975).

Burke, Edmund, *The Correspondence of Edmund Burke*, ed. T. W. Copeland et al. (Cambridge, 1958–78).

Butler, C., *Reminiscences of Charles Butler, Esq.* (1822–7).

[Butler, Dr John], *Some Account of the Character of the late Rt. Hon. Henry Bilson Legge* (1764).

Butterfield, Sir Herbert, *George III and the Historians* (1957).

Caldwell, *Selections from the Family Papers Preserved at Caldwell* (Glasgow, 1854).

Cannon, J., *Parliamentary Reform 1640–1832* (Cambridge, 1973).

Carlyle, A., *Autobiography of the Rev Dr Alexander Carlyle, Minister of Inveresk* (Edinburgh, 1860).

Carswell, J. P., *The Old Cause* (1954).

Carswell, J. and Dralle, L. A. (eds.), *The Political Journal of George Bubb Dodington* (Oxford, 1965).

Charteris, E. E., *William Augustus Duke of Cumberland, His Early Life and Times (1721–1748)* (1913).

Chatterton, Georgina Lady, *Memorials, Personal and Historical of Admiral Lord Gambier* (1861).

BIBLIOGRAPHY

Christie, I. R., *Myth and Reality in Late Eighteenth Century British Politics and Other Papers* (1970).

Cobbett, W. (ed.), *The Parliamentary History of England, from the earliest period to the year 1803* (1806–20).

Colebrooke, Sir George, *Retrospection: Or Reminiscences Addressed to my Son Henry Thomas Colebrooke Esq.* (London, privately printed, 2 vols. 1898–9).

Cone, C. B., *Edmund Burke and the Nature of Politics* (Lexington, 1957).

Cooke, G. W., *The History of Party; from the Rise of the Whig and Tory Factions, in the Reign of Charles II, to the Passing of the Reform Bill* (1836–7).

Cooke, W., *Memoirs of Samuel Foote, Esq.* (1805).

Corbett, Sir Julian S., *England in the Seven Years' War* (2nd edn, 1918).

Cork and Orrery, Countess of (ed.), *The Orrery Papers* (1903).

Costin, W. C. and Watson, J. S., *The Law and Working of the Constitution: Documents 1660–1914*, I (1952).

Coxe, W., *Memoirs of the Life and Administration of Sir Robert Walpole, Earl of Orford* (1798).

Coxe, W., *Memoirs of the Administration of the Right Honourable Henry Pelham* (1829).

Coxe, W., *Memoirs of Horatio, Lord Walpole* (1802).

Cradock, J., *Literary and Miscellaneous Memoirs* (1828).

[Croker, J. W.] (ed.), *Letters of Mary Lepel, Lady Hervey. With a Memoir, and Illustrative Notes* (1821).

Cruickshanks, Eveline, *Political Untouchables. The Tories and the '45* (1979).

Cumberland, R., *Memoirs of Richard Cumberland. Written by Himself* (1807).

Cust, Sir Lionel, *Records of the Cust Family. Series III* (1927).

Davis, R. M., *The Good Lord Lyttelton* (Bethlehem, USA, 1939).

[Debrett, J.], *The History, Debates and Proceedings of both Houses of Parliament ...1743 to...1774* (1792).

Dickins, L., and Stanton, M., *An Eighteenth Century Correspondence* (1910).

Dickinson, H. T., *Bolingbroke* (1970).

Dobrée, B. (ed.), *The Letters of Philip Dormer Stanhope, 4th Earl of Chesterfield* (1932).

Dobrée, B., *The Theme of Patriotism in the Poetry of the Early Eighteenth Century* (1949).

[Dutens, L.], *Memoirs of a Traveller now in Retirement* (1806).

[Dyce, A.], *Recollections of the Table-Talk of Samuel Rogers* (1856).

Eardley-Wilmot, *The Memoirs of the Life of the Rt. Hon. Sir John Eardley-Wilmot* (1802).

Edwards, E. A. (ed.), *The Love Letters of William Pitt, First Lord Chatham* (1926).

Eldon, C. W., *England's Subsidy Policy towards the Continent during the Seven Years' War* (Philadelphia, 1938).

Elliot, G. F. S., *The Border Elliots and the Family of Minto* (Edinburgh, 1897).

Emden, C. S., *The People and the Constitution* (2nd edn, Oxford, 1956).

Erskine, Hon. D. (ed.), *Augustus Hervey's Journal* (1953).

Erskine May, Sir Thomas, *The Constitutional History of England Since the Accession of George the Third*, ed. F. Holland (1912).

Ewald, A. C., *The Life and Times of Prince Charles Stuart...* (1875).

BIBLIOGRAPHY

Falkiner, C. Litton, *Essays Relating to Ireland* (1909).

Feiling, Sir Keith, *The Second Tory Party 1714–1832* (1938).

Ferguson, J. (ed.), *Letters of George Dempster to Sir Adam Ferguson 1756–1813* (1934).

Fitzgerald, B. (ed.), *Correspondence of Emily, Duchess of Leinster (1731–1814)* (Dublin, 1949–57).

Fitzgerald, B., *Emily Duchess of Leinster* (1949).

Fitzmaurice, Lord E., *Life of William, Earl of Shelburne* (2nd edn, 1912).

Flood, H., *Memoirs of the Life and Correspondence of the Right Hon. Henry Flood M.P.* (Dublin, 1838).

Foord, A. S., *His Majesty's Opposition 1714–1830* (Oxford, 1964).

Forrester, E. G., *Northamptonshire County Elections and Electioneering, 1695–1832* (1941).

Fritz, P., *The English Ministers and Jacobitism between the Rebellions of 1715 and 1745* (Toronto, 1975).

George, M. D., *English Political Caricature to 1792. A Study of Opinion and Propaganda* (Oxford, 1959).

Gibbons, P. A., *Ideas of Political Representations in Parliament 1660–1832* (Oxford, 1914).

Gipson, L. H., *The Great War for the Empire. The Years of Defeat, 1754–1757* (New York, 1968).

[Glover, R.], *Memoirs by a Celebrated Literary and Political Character, from the Resignation of Sir Robert Walpole, in 1742, to the Establishment of Lord Chatham's Second Administration, in 1757; Containing Strictures on Some of the Most Distinguished Men of that Time* (1813).

Green, T. H. and Grose, T. H. (eds.), *David Hume, Essays Moral, Political and Literary* (1875).

Gunn, J. A. W., *Factions no More. Attitudes to Party in Government and Opposition in Eighteenth Century England* (1972).

Guttridge, G. H., *The Early Career of Lord Rockingham, 1730–1765* (Berkeley, 1952).

Halsband, R. (ed.), *The Complete Letters of Lady Mary Wortley Montagu* (Oxford, 1965–7).

Halsband, R., *The Life of Lady Mary Wortley Montagu* (Oxford, 1956).

Hanson, L., *Government and the Press 1695–1763* (Oxford, 1936).

Harcourt, E. W. (ed.), *The Harcourt Papers* (Oxford, [1880–1905]).

[Hardwicke, Philip Yorke, 2nd Earl of], *Walpoliana* (1781).

Hardy, F., *Memoirs of the Political and Private Life of James Caulfield, Earl of Charlemont* (1810).

Harris, G., *The Life of Lord Chancellor Hardwicke* (1847).

Hartshorne, A. (ed.), *Memoirs of a Royal Chaplain, 1729–1763* (1905).

Hayton, D., and Jones, Clyve (eds.), *A Register of Parliamentary Lists 1660–1761* (Leicester, 1979).

Henderson, A., *The Life of William Augustus, Duke of Cumberland* (1766).

Henley, Robert Lord, *A Memoir of the Life of Robert Henley, Earl of Northington...* (1831).

Henretta, J. A., *'Salutary Neglect': colonial administration under the Duke of Newcastle* (Princeton, 1972).

Holdsworth, W. S., *A History of English Law*, x (1938).

BIBLIOGRAPHY

Holliday, J., *The Life of William late Earl of Mansfield* (1797).

Home, Hon. J. A. (ed.), *Lady Louisa Stuart. Selections from her Manuscripts* (Edinburgh, 1899).

Home, Hon. J. A. (ed.), *The Letters and Journals of Lady Mary Coke* (Edinburgh, 1889-96).

Horn, D. B., *Sir Charles Hanbury Williams and European Diplomacy 1747-58* (1930).

Hotblack, K., *Chatham's Colonial Policy* (1917).

Ilchester, Countess of and Stavordale, Lord (eds.), *The Life and Letters of Lady Sarah Lennox* (1901).

Ilchester, Earl of, *Henry Fox, First Lord Holland* (1920).

Ilchester, Earl of (ed.), *Letters to Henry Fox, Lord Holland, with a few addressed to his brother Stephen, Earl of Ilchester* (1915).

Ilchester, Earl of, *The Life of Sir Charles Hanbury Williams* (1929).

James, F. G., *Ireland in the Empire, 1668-1770* (Cambridge, Mass., 1973).

Johnston, E. M., *Great Britain and Ireland, 1760-1800; a Study in Political Administration* (Edinburgh, 1963).

Johnston, E. M., *Ireland in the Eighteenth Century* (Dublin, 1974).

Journals of the House of Commons

Journals of the House of Lords

Judd, G. P., *Horace Walpole's Memoirs* (New York, 1959).

Keir, Sir David Lindsay, *The Constitutional History of Modern Britain since 1485* (9th edn, 1969).

Kelch, R. A., *Newcastle. A Duke without Money: Thomas Pelham-Holles 1693-1768* (1974).

Kemp, B., *Sir Francis Dashwood. An Eighteenth Century Independent* (1967).

Kemp, B., *King and Commons 1660-1832* (1957).

Kiernan, T. J., *History of the Financial Administration of Ireland to 1817* (1930).

King, W., *Political and Literary Anecdotes of his Own Times* (1818).

Lambert, S., *Bills and Acts. Legislative Procedure in Eighteenth Century England* (Cambridge, 1971).

Lang, A., *The Companions of Pickle* (1898).

Lang, A., *Pickle the Spy* (1897).

Lang, A., *Prince Charles Edward* (1900).

Langford, Paul, *The Excise Crisis* (Oxford, 1975).

Langford, Paul, *The First Rockingham Administration 1765-1766* (Oxford, 1973).

Lewis, W. S. (et al., eds.), *The Yale Edition of Horace Walpole's Correspondence* (New Haven, 1937-).

Lincoln, A. L. J. and McEwen, R. L. (eds.), *Lord Eldon's Anecdote Book* (1960).

Llanover, Lady (ed.), *The Autobiography and Correspondence of Mary Granville, Mrs Delaney* (1861-2).

Lodge, Sir Richard (ed.), *The Private Correspondence of Sir Benjamin Keene, K.B.* (Cambridge, 1933).

Lucas, C., *The Political Constitutions of Great Britain and Ireland, Asserted and Vindicated...* (1751).

Luxborough, *Letters written by the late Right Honourable Lady Luxborough to William Shenstone, Esq.* (1775).

McClelland, J. (ed.), *Letters of Sarah Byng Osborn 1721-1773* (Stanford, 1930).

BIBLIOGRAPHY

McCracken, J. L., *The Irish Parliament in the Eighteenth Century* (Dundalk, 1971).

McDowell, R. B., *Irish Public Opinion 1750–1800* (1944).

Mackay, R. F., *Admiral Hawke* (Oxford, 1965).

McKelvey, J. L., *George III and Lord Bute. The Leicester House Years* (Durham, N.C., 1973).

Mackintosh, J. P., *The British Cabinet* (2nd edn, 1968).

Mahoney, T. H. D., *Edmund Burke and Ireland* (Harvard, 1960).

Manners, W. E., *Some Account of the Military, Political and Social Life of the Right Hon. John Manners Marquis of Granby* (1899).

March, Earl of, *A Duke and his Friends. The Life and Letters of the Second Duke of Richmond* (1911).

Maty, M., *Miscellaneous Works of the Late...Earl of Chesterfield...To which are prefixed, Memoirs of his Life...* (1777).

Munter, R., *The History of the Irish Newspaper 1685–1760* (Cambridge, 1967).

Namier, Sir Lewis, *Crossroads of Power* (1962).

Namier, Sir Lewis, *England in the Age of the American Revolution* (2nd edn, 1961).

Namier, Sir Lewis, *The Structure of Politics at the Accession of George III* (2nd edn, 1957).

Namier, Sir Lewis and Brooke, J., *Charles Townshend* (1964).

Namier, Sir Lewis, and Brooke, J. (eds.), *The History of Parliament. The House of Commons 1754–1790* (1964).

Newman, A. N. (ed.), *The Parliamentary Lists of the Early Eighteenth Century. Their Compilation and Use* (Leicester, 1973).

Newton, T., *The Works of the Right Reverend Thomas Newton, DD,...with some account of his life, and anecdotes of several of his friends, written by himself* (1782).

Nugent, C., *Memoir of Robert, Earl Nugent* (1898).

O'Gorman, F., *The Rise of Party in England. The Rockingham Whigs 1760–82* (1975).

Olson, A. G., *Anglo-American Politics, 1660–1775. The Relationship between Parties in England and Colonial America* (Oxford, 1973).

Omond, G. W. T., *The Arniston Memoirs* (Edinburgh, 1887).

Oswald, *Memorials of the Public Life and Character of the Rt. Hon. James Oswald of Dunniker* (Edinburgh, 1825).

Owen, J. B., *The Pattern of Politics in Eighteenth Century England* (1962).

Owen, J. B., *The Rise of the Pelhams* (1957).

Pares, R., *King George III and the Politicians* (Oxford, 1953).

Pargellis, S., *Lord Loudoun in North America* (New Haven, 1933).

Pargellis, S. (ed.), *Military Affairs in North America 1747–1765. Selected Documents from the Cumberland Papers in Windsor Castle* (New York, 1936).

Pellew, G., *The Life and Correspondence of the Right Honble. Henry Addington, First Viscount Sidmouth* (1847).

Perry, T. W., *Public Opinion, Propaganda and Politics in Eighteenth Century England. A Study of the Jew Bill of 1753* (Harvard, 1962).

Phillimore, R. J. (ed.), *Memoirs and Correspondence of George, Lord Lyttelton, from 1734 to 1773* (1845).

BIBLIOGRAPHY

[Pinkerton, J., *Walpoliana* (1799).

[Public Record Office of Northern Ireland], *Eighteenth Century Irish Official Papers in Great Britain I* (Belfast, 1973).

Richmond, H. W. (ed.), *Papers Relating to the Loss of Minorca in 1756* (1913).

Riker, T. W., *Henry Fox, First Lord Holland* (Oxford, 1911).

Robson, R. J., *The Oxfordshire Election of 1754* (Oxford, 1949).

[Rolt, R.], *Historical Memoirs of His Late Royal Highness, William Augustus, Duke of Cumberland...* (1767).

Rose, G. H. (ed.), *A Selection from the Papers of the Earls of Marchmont* (1831).

Rosebery, Lord, *Chatham. His Early Life and Connections* (1910).

Russell, Lord John (ed.), *The Correspondence of John, Fourth Duke of Bedford* (1842–6).

Ruville, A. von, *William Pitt Earl of Chatham* (1907).

Sainty, J. C., *Office Holders in Modern Britain I. Treasury Officials, 1660–1870* (1972).

Samuels, A. P. I., *The Early Life Correspondence and Writings of the Rt. Hon. Edmund Burke LLD* (Cambridge, 1923).

Sedgwick, R. R. (ed.), *Letters from George III to Lord Bute, 1756–1766* (1939).

Sedgwick, R. R. (ed.), *The History of Parliament. The House of Commons 1715–1754* (1970).

Sherrard, O. A., *Lord Chatham: a War Minister in the Making* (1952).

Sherrard, O. A., *Lord Chatham: Pitt and the Seven Years' War* (1955).

Smith, W. J. (ed.), *The Grenville Papers: being the Correspondence of Richard Grenville, Earl Temple, K. G., and the Right Hon. George Grenville, their friends and contemporaries* (1852–3).

Smyth, W. H., *Aedes Hartwellianae; or, Notices of the Manor and Mansion of Hartwell* (1851–64).

Spector, R. D., *English Literary Periodicals and the Climate of Opinion During the Seven Years' War* (The Hague, 1966).

Spinney, D., *Rodney* (1969).

Stephens, F. G., *Catalogue of Prints and Drawings in the British Museum. Division I. Political and Personal Satires* (1877).

Taafe, Nicholas, Viscount, *Observations on Affairs in Ireland, from the Settlement in 1691 to the Present Time* (1766).

Taswell-Langmead, T. P., *English Constitutional History* (10th edn, London, 1946).

Taylor, W. S., and Pringle, J. H. (eds.), *Correspondence of William Pitt, Earl of Chatham* (1838–40).

Thackeray, F., *A History of the Right Honourable William Pitt, Earl of Chatham* (1827).

Thomas, P. D. G., *The House of Commons in the Eighteenth Century* (Oxford, 1971).

Thomson, M. A., *The Secretaries of State 1681–1782* (Oxford, 1932).

Thomson, M. A., *A Constitutional History of England 1642 to 1801* (1938).

Torrens, W. M., *History of Cabinets: from the Union with Scotland to the Acquisition of Canada and Bengal* (1894).

Toynbee, P. (ed.), *The Letters of Horace Walpole* (Oxford, 1903–25).

Toynbee, P. (ed.), *Reminiscences written by Mr Horace Walpole in 1788, for the amusement of Miss Mary and Miss Agnes Berry* (Oxford, 1924).

BIBLIOGRAPHY

Trevelyan, G. M., *The Two-Party System in English Political History* (Oxford, 1926).

Tunstall, W. C. B., *Admiral Byng and the Loss of Minorca* (1928).

Turner, E. R., *The Cabinet Council of England in the Seventeenth and Eighteenth Centuries, 1622–1784* (Baltimore, 1931–2).

Valentine, A., *Lord George Germaine* (Oxford, 1962).

Veitch, G. S., *The Genesis of Parliamentary Reform* (ed. I. R. Christie, 1965).

Waldegrave, James, 2nd Earl, *Memoirs from 1754 to 1758* (1821).

Walpole, Horace, *Memoirs of the Reign of King George the Second*, ed. Lord Holland (1846).

Walpole, Horace, *Memoirs of the Reign of King George the Third*, ed. G. F. R. Barker (1894).

Walpole, Spencer, *The Life of the Rt. Hon. Spencer Perceval* (1874).

Western, J. R., *The English Militia in the Eighteenth Century* (1965).

Weston, C. C., *English Constitutional Theory and the House of Lords 1556–1832* (1965).

Whiteman, A., et al. (eds.), *Statesmen, Scholars and Merchants. Essays in Eighteenth Century History presented to Dame Lucy Sutherland* (Oxford, 1973).

Wiggin, L. M., *The Faction of Cousins. A Political Account of the Grenvilles, 1733–1763* (New Haven, 1958).

Wilkes, J. W., *A Whig in Power. The political career of Henry Pelham* (Evanston, Ill., 1964).

Williams, B., *The Life of William Pitt, Earl of Chatham* (1913).

Williams, E. N., *The Eighteenth Century Constitution 1688–1815* (Cambridge, 1965).

Williams, M. (ed.), *The Letters of William Shenstone* (Oxford, 1939).

Wortley, Hon. Mrs E. Stuart, *A Prime Minister and his Son. From correspondence of 3rd Earl of Bute and of Lt. General the Hon. Sir Charles Stuart, KB* (1925).

Wyndham, M., *Chronicles of the Eighteenth Century. Founded on the correspondence of Sir Thomas Lyttelton and his Family* (1924).

Yorke, P. C., *The Life and Correspondence of Philip Yorke, Earl of Hardwicke, Lord High Chancellor of Great Britain* (Cambridge, 1913).

Articles

Anson, W. R., 'The Development of the Cabinet, 1688–1760', *EHR*, XXIX (1914), 325–7.

Anson, W. R., 'The Cabinet in the Seventeenth and Eighteenth Centuries', *EHR*, XXIX (1914), 56–78.

Barnes, D. G., 'Henry Pelham and the Duke of Newcastle', *JBS*, I (1961–2), 62–77.

Beckett, J. C., 'Anglo–Irish Constitutional Relations in the later Eighteenth Century', *Irish Historical Studies*, XIV (1964–5), 20–38.

Bond, M. F., 'The Manuscripts of Speaker Arthur Onslow', *BIHR*, XLV (1972), 327–32.

Boulton, J. T., 'Arbitrary Power: An Eighteenth-Century Obsession', *Studies in Burke and his Time*, IX (1968), 905–26.

BIBLIOGRAPHY

Brewer, J., 'The Misfortunes of Lord Bute: A Case-Study in Eighteenth-Century Political Argument and Public Opinion', *HJ*, xvi (1973), 3–43.

Brewer, J., 'Party and Double Cabinet: Two Facets of Burke's *Thoughts*', *HJ*, xiv (1971), 479–501.

Brewer, J., 'Rockingham, Burke and Whig Political Argument', *HJ*, xviii (1975), 188–201.

Brooke, J., 'Party in the Eighteenth Century', in A. Natan (ed.), *Silver Renaissance* (1961), pp.20–37.

Brooke, J., 'Horace Walpole and King George III', in Whiteman, *Statesmen, Scholars and Merchants*, pp.263–75.

Browning, R., 'The British Orientation of Austrian Foreign Policy, 1749–1754', *Central European History*, i (1968), 299–323.

Browning, R., 'The Duke of Newcastle and the Financial Management of the Seven Years War in Germany', *Journal of the Society for Army Historical Research*, il (1971), 20–35.

Browning, R., 'The Duke of Newcastle and the Financing of the Seven Years' War', *Journal of Economic History*, xxxi (1971), 344–77.

Browning, R., 'The Duke of Newcastle and the Imperial Election Plan, 1749–1754', *JBS*, vii (1967), 28–47.

Butterfield, Sir Herbert, 'George III and the Constitution', *History*, xliii (1958), 14–33.

Butterfield, Sir Herbert, 'Some Reflections on the Early Years of George III's Reign', *JBS*, iv (1965), 78–101.

Cannon, J. A., 'The Parliamentary Representation of the City of Gloucester (1727–90)', *Transactions of the Bristol and Gloucestershire Archaeological Society*, lxxviii (1959), 137–52.

Christie, I. R., 'Was there a "New Toryism" in the Earlier Part of George III's Reign?', *JBS*, v (1965–6), 60–76.

Clark, D. E., 'News and Opinion concerning America in English Newspapers, 1754–1763', *Pacific Historical Review*, x (1941), 75–82.

Clark, D. M., 'The Office of Secretary to the Treasury in the Eighteenth Century', *American Historical Review*, xlii (1936–7), 22–45.

Clark, J. C. D., 'The Decline of Party, 1740–1760', *EHR*, xciii (1978), 499–527.

Clark, J. C. D., 'Whig Tactics and Parliamentary Precedent: The English Management of Irish Politics, 1754–1756', *HJ*, xxi (1978), 275–301.

Clark, J. C. D., 'A General Theory of Party, Opposition and Government, 1688–1832', *HJ*, xxiii (1980).

Colley, L. J., 'The Mitchell Election Division, 24 March 1755', *BIHR*, xlix (1976), 80–107.

Colley, L. J., 'The Loyal Brotherhood and the Cocoa Tree: The London Organization of the Tory Party, 1727–1760', *HJ*, xx (1977), 77–95.

Cranfield, G. A., 'The "London Evening Post" and the Jew Bill of 1753', *HJ*, viii (1965), 16–30.

[Croker, J. W.], Review of Phillimore, *Memoirs and Correspondence of George Lord Lyttelton*, in *The Quarterly Review*, lxxviii (1846), 216–67.

Falkiner, C. Litton, 'Correspondence of Archbishop Stone and the Duke of Newcastle', *EHR*, xx (1905), 508–42, 735–63.

Fritz, P., 'Archdeacon William Coxe as Political Biographer' in P. Fritz (ed.), *The Triumph of Culture* (Toronto, 1972).

BIBLIOGRAPHY

Fritz, P., 'The Anti-Jacobite Intelligence System of the English Ministers, 1715-45', *HJ*, xvi (1973), 265-89.

Fryer, W. R., 'Namier and the King's Position in English Politics, 1744-84', *The Burke Newsletter*, v (1963), 246-58.

Fryer, W. R., 'King George III: His Political Character and Conduct, 1760-1784. A New Whig Interpretation', *Renaissance and Modern Studies*, vi (1962), 68-101.

Fryer, W. R., 'The Study of British Politics between the Revolution and the Reform Act', *Renaissance and Modern Studies*, i (1959), 91-114.

Gipson, L. H., 'British Diplomacy in the Light of the Anglo-Spanish New World Issues, 1750-1757', *American Historical Review*, li (1945-6), 627-48.

Goldsmith, M. M., 'Faction Detected: Ideological Consequences of Robert Walpole's Decline and Fall', *History*, lxi (1979), 1-19.

Graham, D., 'The Planning of the Beauséjour Operation and the Approaches to War in 1755', *New England Quarterly*, xli (1968), 551-66.

Haas, J. M., 'The Pursuit of Political Success in Eighteenth-Century England: Sandwich, 1740-71', *BIHR*, xlix (1970), 56-77.

Hackmann, W. K., 'William Pitt and the Generals: Three Case Studies in the Seven Years War', *Albion*, iii (1971), 128-37.

Higonnet, P. L-R, 'The Origins of the Seven Years' War', *Journal of Modern History*, xl (1968), 57-90.

Hill, B. W., 'Executive Monarchy and the Challenge of Parties, 1689-1832: Two Concepts of Government and two Historiographical Interpretations', *HJ*, xiii (1970), 379-401.

Holdsworth, W. S., 'The House of Lords, 1689-1783', *Law Quarterly Review*, xlv (1929), 307-42, 432-58.

Horn, D. B., 'The Cabinet Controversy on Subsidy Treaties in Time of Peace', *EHR*, xxxxv (1930), 463-6.

Horn, D. B., 'The Duke of Newcastle and the Origins of the Diplomatic Revolution', in J. H. Elliott and H. G. Koenigsberger (eds.), *The Diversity of History: Essays in Honour of Sir Herbert Butterfield* (1970), 247-68.

Jarrett, D., 'The Myth of "Patriotism" in Eighteenth-Century English Politics', in J. S. Bromley and E. H. Kossmann (eds.), *Britain and the Netherlands*, v (The Hague, 1975), 120-40.

Kaufman, R. R., 'The Patron-Client Concept and Macro-Politics: Prospects and Problems', *Comparative Studies in Society and History*, xvi (1974), 284-308.

Kemp, B., 'Frederick, Prince of Wales', in A. Natan (ed.), *Silver Renaissance* (1961), 38-56.

Kemp, B., 'Patriotism, Pledges and the People', in M. Gilbert (ed.), *A Century of Conflict 1850-1950. Essays for A. J. P. Taylor* (1966), 37-46.

Langford, P., 'William Pitt and Public Opinion, 1757', *EHR*, lxxxviii (1973), 54-80.

McCracken, J. L., 'The Conflict between the Irish Administration and Parliament, 1753-6', *Irish Historical Studies*, iii (1942-3), 159-79.

McCracken, J. L., 'The Irish Viceroyalty, 1760-73', in H. A. Cronne (ed.), *Essays in British and Irish History in Honour of James Eadie Todd* (1949), 152-68.

BIBLIOGRAPHY

McCracken, J. L., 'Irish Parliamentary Elections 1727–1768', *Irish Historical Studies*, v (1946–7), 209–30.

McCracken, J. L., 'From Swift to Grattan' in B. Farrell (ed.), *The Irish Parliamentary Tradition* (Dublin, 1973), pp.139–48.

Malcomson, A. P. W., 'Speaker Pery and the Pery Papers', *North Munster Antiquarian Journal*, xvi (1973–4), 33–60.

Middleton, C. R., 'A Reinforcement for North America, Summer 1757', *BIHR*, xli (1968), 58–72.

Middleton, C. R., 'Pitt, Anson and the Admiralty, 1756–1761', *History*, lv (1970), 189–98.

Money, J., 'The West Midlands, 1760–1793: Politics, Public Opinion and Regional Identity in the English Provinces during the late Eighteenth Century', *Albion*, ii (1970), 73–93.

Newman, A. N. (ed.), 'Leicester House Politics, 1750–60, from the Papers of John, Second Earl of Egmont', *Camden Miscellany*, xxiii, Camden 4th ser., vol.7 (1969).

Newman, A. N., 'Leicester House Politics, 1748–1751', *EHR*, lxxvi (1961), 577–89.

Newman, A. N., 'The Political Patronage of Frederick Lewis, Prince of Wales', *HJ*, i (1958), 68–75.

Olson, A. G., 'The British Government and Colonial Union, 1754', *William and Mary Quarterly*, xvii (1960), 22–34.

Owen, J. B., 'Political Patronage in 18th Century England', in P. Fritz and D. Williams (eds.), *The Triumph of Culture* (Toronto, 1972), 369–87.

Owen, J. B., 'The Survival of Country Attitudes in the Eighteenth Century House of Commons', in J. S. Bromley and E. H. Kossmann (eds.), *Britain and the Netherlands*, iv (The Hague, 1971), 42–69.

Owen, J. B., 'George II Reconsidered', in Whiteman, *Statesmen, Scholars and Merchants*, 113–34.

Pares, R., 'American versus Continental Warfare, 1739–63', *EHR*, li (1936), 429–65.

Pares, R., 'George III and the Politicians', *TRHS*, 5th ser., i (1951), 127–51.

Peters, M., 'The "Monitor" on the constitution, 1755–1765: new light on the ideological origins of English radicalism', *EHR*, lxxxvi (1971), 706–27.

Petrie, Sir Charles, 'The Elibank Plot, 1752–3', *TRHS*, 4th ser., xiv (1931), 175–96.

Ransome, M., 'The Reliability of Contemporary Reporting of the Debates in the House of Commons, 1727–1741', *BIHR*, xix (1942–3), 67–79.

Riker, T.W., 'The Politics behind Braddock's Expedition', *American Historical Review*, xiii (1907–8), 742–52.

Robbins, C., '"Discordant Parties". A Study of the Acceptance of Party by Englishmen', *Political Science Quarterly*, lxxiii (1958), 505–29.

Savelle, M., 'The American Balance of Power and European Diplomacy, 1713–78', in R. B. Morris (ed.), *The Era of the American Revolution* (New York, 1939), 140–69.

Sedgwick, R.R., 'The Inner Cabinet from 1739 to 1741', *EHR*, xxxiv (1919) 290–302.

Sedgwick, R.R. (ed.), 'Letters from William Pitt to Lord Bute, 1755–1758',

BIBLIOGRAPHY

in R. Pares and A. J. P. Taylor (eds.), *Essays Presented to Sir Lewis Namier* (1956), 108–66.

[Sedgwick, R.R.], 'Sir Robert Walpole 1676–1745. The Minister for the House of Commons', *Times Literary Supplement*, 24 March 1945.

Sedgwick R.R., 'William Pitt and Lord Bute. An Intrigue of 1755–1758', *History Today*, VI (October 1956), 647–54.

Skinner, Q., 'The Principles and Practice of Opposition. The Case of Bolingbroke versus Walpole', in N. McKendrick (ed.), *Historical Perspectives* (1974), 93–128.

Sutherland, Dame Lucy, 'The City of London and the Devonshire–Pitt Administration, 1756–7', *Proceedings of the British Academy*, XLVI (1960), 147–87.

Sutherland, Dame Lucy, and Binney, J., 'Henry Fox as Paymaster General of the Forces', *EHR*, LXX (1955), 229–57.

Temperley, H.W.V., 'Inner and Outer Cabinet and Privy Council, 1679–1783', *EHR*, XXVII (1912), 682–99.

Temperley, H.W.V., 'A Note on Inner and Outer Cabinets; their Development and Relations in the Eighteenth Century', *EHR*, XXXI (1916), 291–6.

Turner, E.R., 'The Cabinet in the Eighteenth Century', *EHR*, XXXII (1917), 192–203.

Turner, E.R., and Megaro, G., 'The King's Closet in the Eighteenth Century', *American Historical Review*, XLV (1940), 761–76.

Turner, E.R., 'Committees of the Privy Council, 1688–1760', *EHR*, XXXI (1916), 545–72.

Turner, E.R., 'The Development of the Cabinet, 1688–1760', *American Historical Review*, XVIII (1912–13), 751–68, XIX (1913–14), 27–43.

Vincitorio, G.L., 'Edmund Burke and Charles Lucas', *Publications of the Modern Language Association of America*, LXVIII (1953), 1047–55.

Watson, J.S., 'Arthur Onslow and Party Politics', in H. R. Trevor–Roper (ed.), *Essays in British History presented to Sir Keith Feiling* (1965), 139–71.

Williams, E.T., 'The Cabinet in the Eighteenth Century', *History*, XXII (1937–8), 240–52.

Theses

Blackley, R.A., 'The Political Career of George Montagu Dunk, Second Earl of Halifax, 1748–1771: A Study of an Eighteenth-Century English Minister', (New York Ph.D. thesis, 1968).

Bradley, C., 'The Parliamentary Representation of the Boroughs of Pontefract, Newark and East Retford 1754 to 1768' (Manchester MA thesis, 1953).

Brewer, J., 'Political Argument and Propaganda in England, 1760–1770' (Cambridge Ph.D. thesis, 1973).

Cannon, J.A., 'The Parliamentary Representation of Six Wiltshire Boroughs, 1754–90' (Bristol Ph.D. thesis, 1958).

Cobb, M.B.B., 'The Breakdown of the Anglo–Austrian Alliance, 1748–56' (London MA thesis, 1935).

Colley, L.J., 'The Tory Party 1727–1760', (Cambridge Ph.D. thesis, 1976).

BIBLIOGRAPHY

Cramp, M., 'The Parliamentary History of Five Sussex Boroughs' (Manchester MA thesis, 1953).

Fewster, J.M., 'The Politics and Administration of the Borough of Morpeth in the later Eighteenth Century' (Durham Ph.D. thesis, 1960).

Fraser, E.J.S., 'The Pitt–Newcastle Coalition and the Conduct of the Seven Years' War, 1757–60' (Oxford D.Phil. thesis, 1976).

Fritz, P., 'Jacobitism and the English Government 1717–31' (Cambridge Ph.D. thesis, 1967).

Greiert, S.G., 'The Earl of Halifax and British Colonial Policy 1748–1756', (Duke University Ph.D. thesis, 1976).

Gwyn, J.R.J., 'The Place of Russia in British Foreign Policy 1748–56' (Oxford B.Litt. thesis, 1961).

Haas, J.M., 'The Rise of the Bedfords, 1741–57: a study in the politics of the reign of George II' (Univ. of Illinois Ph.D. thesis, 1960).

Hayes, B.D., 'Politics in Norfolk, 1750–1832', (Cambridge Ph.D. thesis, 1958).

Howard, T.E., 'Toryism from 1745 to 1761' (Liverpool MA thesis, 1939).

Lowe, S., 'Hampshire County Elections and Electioneering, 1734–1830', (Southampton M.Phil. thesis, 1972).

McCracken, J.L., 'The Undertakers in Ireland and their Relations with the Lords Lieutenant, 1724–1771', (Queens' Univ. Belfast MA thesis, 1941).

McKelvey, J.L., 'Lord Bute and George III: The Leicester House Years', (Northwestern Univ. Ph.D. thesis, 1965).

Middleton, C.R., 'The Administration of Newcastle and Pitt: the departments of state and the conduct of the war, 1754–60, with particular reference to the campaigns in North America' (Exeter Ph.D. thesis, 1968).

Money, J., 'Public Opinion in the West Midlands, 1760–1793' (Cambridge Ph.D. thesis, 1967).

Moses, J.H., 'Elections and Electioneering in the Constituencies of Nottinghamshire, 1702–1832' (Nottingham Ph.D. thesis, 1965).

Newman, A.N., 'Elections in Kent and its Parliamentary Representation, 1715–54' (Oxford D.Phil. thesis, 1957).

O'Donovan, D.P., 'The Money Bill Dispute of 1753: a study in Anglo–Irish relations 1750–6' (Ph.D. thesis, University College Dublin, 1977).

Price, F.C., 'The Parliamentary Elections in York City, 1754–1790' (Manchester MA thesis, 1958).

Rogers, N.C.T., 'London Politics from Walpole to Pitt: Patriotism and Independency in an Era of Commercial Imperialism, 1738–63' (Toronto Univ. Ph.D. thesis, 1975).

Scott, L., 'Under Secretaries of State, 1755–1775' (Manchester MA thesis, 1950).

Spendlove, J.M., 'Government and the House of Commons 1747–54' (Oxford B.Litt. thesis, 1956).

Thomas, G.F., 'John 4th Duke of Bedford' (Cardiff MA thesis, 1953).

Thomas, P. D. G., 'The Parliamentary Representation of North Wales 1715–1784' (Cardiff MA thesis, 1953).

Thomson, D., 'The Conception of Political Party in England, in the period 1740 to 1783' (Cambridge Ph.D. thesis, 1938).

BIBLIOGRAPHY

HMC Reports

First Report (1870), Earl of Charlemont.

Second Report (1871), Bedford MSS; Lyttelton MSS; Willes MSS.

Third Report (1872), Chichester MSS; Earl of Seafield MSS; Dundas (Arniston) MSS; Gunning MSS (Titley); Willes MSS; Lansdowne MSS.

Fourth Report (1874), Macaulay (John Wilkes).

Fifth Report (1876), Lansdowne (Shelburne MSS).

Sixth Report (1877), Leconfield MSS (Letters of Earl of Bristol 1756–8 and of W. Pitt from 1757); Lansdowne MSS.

Eighth Report, Part I (1881), Wingfield Digby MSS; Emly MSS (E. S. Pery); O'Conor MSS; Braybrooke MSS.

Eighth Report, Part III (1881), Ashburnham MSS (Sir Charles Hanbury Williams).

Ninth Report, Part II (1884), Elphinstone (George Keith, Earl Marischal).

Tenth Report, App. I (1885), Weston Underwood (Edward Weston).

Tenth Report, App. IV (1885), Westmorland (Apethorpe) MSS, Fane Letters.

Tenth Report, App. VI (1887), Balfour (Townley).

Eleventh Report, App. IV (1887), *Townshend.*

Eleventh Report, App. VII (1888), Leeds (Holdernesse MSS).

Twelfth Report, App. V (1889), *Rutland,* II.

Twelfth Report, App. X (1891), *Charlemont* I.

Thirteenth Report, App. III (1892), *Fortescue,* I.

Thirteenth Report, App. VII (1893), *Lonsdale.*

Fourteenth Report, App. III (1894), Seafield.

Fourteenth Report, App. IX (1895), Onslow MSS.

Fifteenth Report, App. VI (1897), *Carlisle.*

Buccleuch, I (1899).

Various Collections, VI (1909), Eyre Matcham (Dodington).

Sackville, I (1904), Stopford–Sackville MSS.

Bathurst (1923).

Laing, II (1925).

Hastings, III (1934), (Earl of Huntingdon).

Polwarth, V (1961), Hume Campbell MSS.

Unpublished papers

Clayton, T.R., 'The Duke of Newcastle, the Earl of Halifax, and the American Origins of the Seven Years' War'.

Index

There is no index entry for each of the three main figures, Henry Fox, Thomas Pelham-Holles, Duke of Newcastle, and William Pitt, as they are referred to constantly throughout the text.

INDEX

Crowle, Richard, 146, 490 n372, 508 n214
Cumberland, William Augustus, Duke of, 32, 33, 37, 38, 47, 50, 60, 110, 171, 172, 175, 194, 234, 320, 324, 349, 369, 450; Rengency, 35–6, 113, 154–7; 158, 160–1; and George II, 51, 156, 157; and Fox, 58, 59, 62, 71, 120–1, 129, 165, 192–3, 262, 267, 268, 269, 275, 442–3; and Newcastle, 76, 79, 98, 166; American affairs, 100–2, 103, 104, 109 and Fox's ministerial schemes. spring 1757, 336, 354–5, 356, 358
Cust, Sir John, 204, 219, 324, 330, 551 n275

D'Arcy, Sir Conyers, 188
Darlington, Henry Vane. 1st Earl of, 42, 50, 63, 66, 69, 77, 183, 188, 206, 223, 294, 472 n218
Dashwod, Sir Francis, 2nd Bt., 34, 36, 41, 52, 186, 205, 354, 401, 403, 421, 462 n87; 1754–5 sessions, 116, 142, 150; 1755–6 sessions, 215, 222, 223, 224; and Byng affair, 324, 327, 330–1, 537 n406
Dashwod, Sir James, 2nd Bt., 125, 150, 462 n87
Delaval, John, 117, 119, 508 n220, 551 n275
Denbigh, Lord, 374
Devonshire, William Cavendish, 3rd Duke of, 135, 169–70, 176, 179, 205, 214, 217, 469 n119; and succession to Pelham, 53, 65, 69, 72; overture to Fox, June 1754, 82–3, 84–6, 87–8; and the Regency, 154, 155, 156; and subsidy treaties, 178, 185, 186, 196–7, 212, 506 n179
Devonshire, William Cavendish, 4th Duke of (previously Marquis of Hartington), 36, 38, 50, 120–1, 135, 154, 169–70, 214, 283, 288–300, 358, 364–5, 373, 374; and Fox, 52, 54, 58–62, 63, 67, 69, 85–6, 91, 169, 179, 262, 264, 275, 290, 291, 300–1, 311, 313; and administration with Pitt, 1756–7, 233–4, 283, 284–300; 352; Treasury, 1756, 65, 289, 290, 291; 1756–7 sessions, 303–5, 307–8, 318, 340; Byng affair, 332, 334; Fox's ministerial schemes, spring 1757, 336, 342, 346–7, 355, 356, 374; attempts at coalition Apr–May 1757, 381, 382, 383–5, 386, 389–91; Newcastle's alternative scheme May–June 1757,

394–5, 397, 400, 401–2, 404–7; Fox's attempt to form a ministry June 1757, 414, 420, 421–3; negotiations June 1757, leading to coalition, 423–4, 427–8, 437, 442
Digby, Mrs Charlotte, 54
Digby, Henry, 63, 77, 275, 285, 343–4, 540 n475, 541 n496
Digby, Edward, 6th Baron, 147, 148, 241, 245, 246, 259, 261, 270, 337, 338–9, 541 n496, 542 n22
Dodington, George Bubb, 27, 28, 31, 34–5, 36, 142, 203, 215, 240, 358, 391, 419, 462 n95; and succession to Pelham, 45, 51–2, 73, 79, 82, 83–4; reconstruction of ministry, Apr–Oct 1755, 168, 176, 188, 197–8, 205, 206, 207; Treasurership of Navy, 222, 224; and Byng affair, 240, 324, 330, 331, 332–3; Fox's ministerial schemes, spring 1757, 345, 347, 355, 359, 363
Dorset, Lionel Cranfield Sackville, 1st Duke of, 36, 37, 38, 41, 47, 50, 136, 137, 206, 419, 437, 538 n413; negotiations June 1757, leading to coalition, 435, 436, 437, 439, 440, 451
Duncannon, William Ponsonby, Viscount, 293, 301, 432, 436
Dupplin, Thomas Hay, Viscount, 76–7, 93, 113, 294, 326, 357, 358, 391, 473 n277, 486 n303; and succession to Pelham, 45, 50, 68, 83; Treasury Board, 70, 81, 206; 1755–6 sessions, 204, 207, 208, 223; Fox's ministerial schemes, spring 1757, 336, 339, 350, 354; negotiations June 1757, leading to coalition, 428, 433, 435, 441

Edgcumbe, Richard, 1st Baron, 208, 540 n475, 540 n496
Edgecumbe, Hon. Richard, 222, 294
Egmont, John Perceval, 2nd Earl of, 31, 32–4, 36, 40, 41, 174, 233, 265, 324, 331, 337–8, 344–5; and succession to Pelham, 45, 58, 65; 1754–5 sessions, 93, 111–13, 114, 116, 123–6, 131–3, 136, 139, 140, 143, 486 n303; and Leicester House, 107, 171–2, 174, 208, 229, 252; reconstruction of ministry Apr–Oct 1755, 170, 173, 176, 180–3, 188–90, 201, 203–4, 208; Vice-Treasurership of Ireland, 173, 174, 178, 179, 182–3, 223; and subsidy treaties, 197, 215, 219; 1756–7 sessions, 311, 316; Fox's ministerial schemes, spring 1757, 336,

INDEX

INDEX

Cambridge Studies in the History and Theory of Politics

Editors: Maurice Cowling, G. R. Elton, E. Kedourie, J. R. Pole, and Walter Ullmann.

A series in two parts, studies and original texts. The studies are original works on political history and political philosophy while the texts are modern, critical editions of major texts in political thought. The titles include:

The Political Works of James Harrington, edited by J. G. A. Pocock.

Selected Writings of August Cieszkowski, edited and translated with an introductory essay by André Liebich.

De Republica Anglorum by Sir Thomas Smith, edited by Mary Dewar.

Sister Peg: A Pamphlet Hitherto Unknown by David Hume, edited with an introduction and notes by David R. Raynor.

STUDIES

1867: Disraeli, Gladstone and Revolution: The Passing of the Second Reform Bill, by Maurice Cowling.

The Social and Political Thought of Karl Marx, by Shlomo Avineri.

Idealism, Politics and History: Sources of Hegelian Thought, by George Armstrong Kelly.

The Impact of Labour 1920–1924: The Beginnings of Modern British Politics, by Maurice Cowling.

Alienation: Marx's Conception of Man in Capitalist Society, by Bertell Ollman.

The Politics of Reform 1884, by Andrew Jones.

Hegel's Theory of the Modern State, by Shlomo Avineri.

The Social Problem in the Philosophy of Rousseau, by John Charvet.

The Impact of Hitler: British Politics and British Policy 1933–1940, by Maurice Cowling.

Social Science and the Ignoble Savage, by Ronald L. Meek.

The Liberal Mind 1914–1929, by Michael Bentley.

Political Philosophy and Rhetoric: A Study of the Origins of American Party Politics, by John Zvesper.

Revolution Principles: The Politics of Party 1689–1720, by J. P. Kenyon.

John Locke and the Theory of Sovereignty: Mixed Monarchy and the Right of Resistance in the Political Thought of the English Revolution, by Julian H. Franklin.

Adam Smith's Politics: An Essay in Historiographic Revision, by Donald Winch.

Lloyd George's Secretariat, by John Turner.

The Tragedy of Enlightenment: An Essay on the Frankfurt School, by Paul Connerton.

Religion and Public Doctrine in Modern England, by Maurice Cowling.

Bentham and Bureaucracy, by L. J. Hume.

A Critique of Freedom and Equality, by John Charvet.

The Dynamics of Change: The Crisis of the 1750s and English Party Systems, by J. C. D. Clark.

Nationalism, Positivism and Catholicism: The Politics of Charles Maurras and French Catholics, 1890–1914, by Michael Sutton.

Resistance and Compromise: The Political Thought of the Elizabethan Catholics, by P. J. Holmes.